SOCIOLOGY

ACADEMIC REVIEWERS

We would like to express our thanks to the following people, who have reviewed all or various portions of the manuscript.

Richard T. Schaefer
Robert P. Lamm

Bill Bailey
University of Wisconsin-Stout

Randall Beger
Drury College

Jerry G. Bode
Ball State University

Michael E. Brown
The City University of New York

Gary W. Burbridge
Grand Rapids Junior College

H. Paul Chalfant
Texas Tech University

Arlene Kaplan Daniels
Northwestern University

Melissa Deller
University of Maine

Jess G. Enns
Kearney State College

Michael P. Farrell
*The State University
of New York-Buffalo*

Joe R. Feagin
University of Texas-Austin

Jan Fiola
University of Minnesota

Larry H. Frye
St. Petersburg Junior College

Shahin Gerami
Southwest Missouri State University

Davita Silfen Glasberg
University of Connecticut-Storrs

Jane Gray
Capital University

Gary P. Green
University of Georgia

Nancy A. Greenwood
Purdue University

Harlowe Hatle
University of South Dakota

Alan G. Hill
Delta College

William J. Howard
Lincoln Memorial University

Meg Wilkes Karraker
College of Saint Catherine

Cary S. Kart
The University of Toledo

Mark Kassop
Bergen Community College

Michael A. Katovich
Texas Christian University

Harold R. Kerbo
California Polytechnic State University

Charles D. King
Indiana State University

Martha O. Loustaunau
New Mexico State University

Jerome N. McKibben
Indiana University

Joseph Marolla
Virginia Commonwealth University

H. Andrew Michener
University of Wisconsin-Madison

James D. Miley
Kansas State University

Samuel P. Oliner
Humboldt State University

Anthony M. Orum
University of Illinois-Chicago

Hence Parson
Hutchinson Community College

Robert G. Perrin
University of Tennessee-Knoxville

Ollie Pocs
Illinois State University-Normal

Adrian Rapp
North Harris County College

Roland Robertson
University of Pittsburgh

Sally Scot Rogers
Montgomery College

Joseph A. Scimecca
George Mason University

John Skvoretz
University of South Carolina

John R. Stratton
University of Iowa

Sheldon Stryker
Indiana University-Bloomington

Leann M. Tigges
University of Georgia

Michael Wallace
Indiana University-Bloomington

John R. Weeks
San Diego State University

J. D. Wemhaner
Tulsa Junior College-Metro

J. Sherwood Williams
Virginia Commonwealth University

FOURTH
EDITION

SOCIOLOGY

RICHARD T. SCHAEFER
Western Illinois University

ROBERT P. LAMM

McGRAW-HILL, INC.
*New York   St. Louis   San Francisco   Auckland   Bogotá   Caracas
Lisbon   London   Madrid   Mexico   Milan   Montreal   New Delhi
Paris   San Juan   São Paulo   Singapore   Sydney   Tokyo   Toronto*

SOCIOLOGY

Copyright © 1992, 1989, 1986, 1983 by McGraw-Hill,
Inc. All rights reserved. Printed in the United States of
America. Except as permitted under the United States
Copyright Act of 1976, no part of this publication may
be reproduced or distributed in any form or by any
means, or stored in a data base or retrieval system,
without the prior written permission of the publisher.

4 5 6 7 8 9 0 VNH VNH 9 0 9 8 7 6 5 4 3

ISBN 0-07-055235-5

Library of Congress Cataloging-in-Publication Data
Schaefer, Richard T.
    Sociology / Richard T. Schaefer, Robert P. Lamm.—
4th ed.
        p.   cm.
    Includes bibliographical references and indexes.
    ISBN 0-07-055235-5
    1. Sociology.   2. Social problems.   3. United
States—Social policy.   I. Lamm, Robert P.
II. Title.
HM51.S343   1992
301—dc20   91-17787

This book was set in New Baskerville
by York Graphic Services, Inc.
The editors were Phillip A. Butcher,
Rhona Robbin, and Susan Gamer;
the designer was Joan E. O'Connor;
the production supervisor was Janelle S. Travers.
The photo editor was Elyse Rieder;
the permissions editor was Elsa Peterson.
New drawings were done by Fine Line Illustrations, Inc.
Von Hoffmann Press, Inc., was printer and binder.

Cover painting: Maurice Prendergast, *The Mall,
Central Park, 1901,* watercolor, The Olivia Shaler
Swan Memorial Collection, © 1992, The Art
Institute of Chicago.

Acknowledgments appear on pages 694-698, and on this
page by reference.

ABOUT
THE AUTHORS

Richard T. Schaefer, born and raised in Chicago, is Professor of Sociology and Dean of the College of Arts and Sciences at Western Illinois University. He received his B.A. in sociology from Northwestern University and his M.A. and Ph.D. from the University of Chicago. He has taught introductory sociology for 23 years to students in colleges, adult education programs, nursing programs, and a maximum-security prison. He is the author of the well-received *Racial and Ethnic Groups* (Harper Collins, 1990), now in its fourth edition. His articles and book reviews have appeared in many journals, including *American Journal of Sociology, Phylon: Review of Race and Culture, Contemporary Sociology, Sociology and Social Research,* and *Teaching Sociology.*

Robert P. Lamm is a New York-based freelance writer with extensive experience on social science textbooks and supplements. His essays, profiles, reviews, and fiction have appeared in more than 30 periodicals in the United States, Canada, and Great Britain. He received his B.A. in political science from Yale University, also studied at Sarah Lawrence College, and has taught at Yale, Queens College, and the New School for Social Research.

In addition to their collaboration on all four editions of *Sociology* and its supplements, Schaefer and Lamm served as editors of the reader *Introducing Sociology* (McGraw-Hill, 1987).

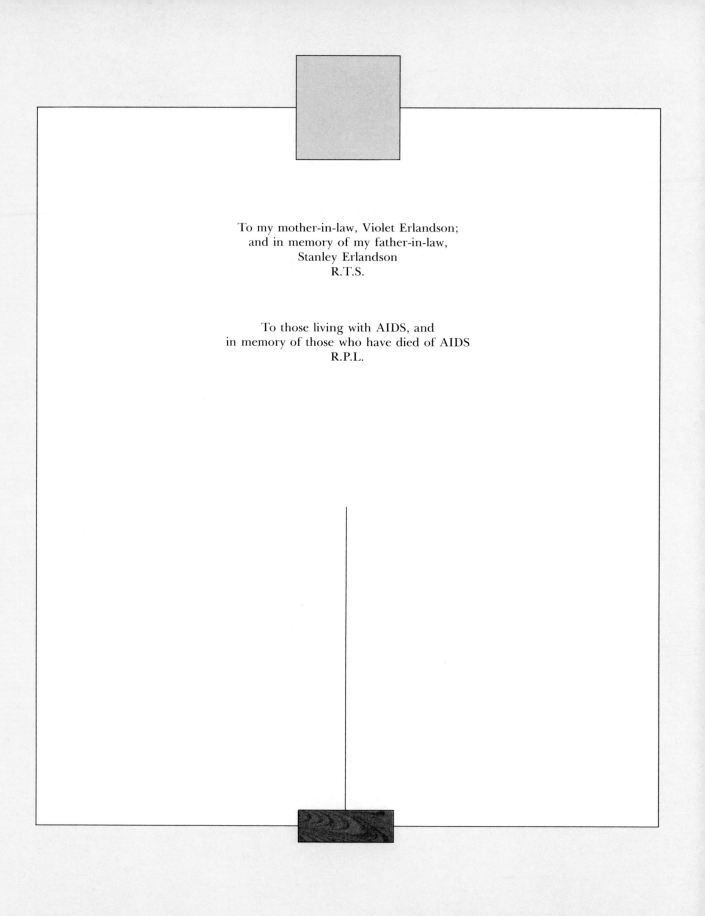

To my mother-in-law, Violet Erlandson;
and in memory of my father-in-law,
Stanley Erlandson
R.T.S.

To those living with AIDS, and
in memory of those who have died of AIDS
R.P.L.

CONTENTS IN BRIEF

CONTENTS

LIST
OF BOXES

BOX

PREFACE

After 23 years of teaching sociology to students in colleges, adult education programs, nursing programs, an overseas program based in London, and even a maximum-security prison, I am firmly convinced that the discipline can play a valuable role in teaching critical thinking skills. Sociology can help students to better understand the workings of their own society and of other cultures. Through the distinctive emphasis on social policy found in this text, students will be shown how the sociological imagination can be useful in examining such public policy issues as bilingualism, the AIDS crisis, capital punishment, the feminization of poverty, censorship of schoolbooks, and affirmative action.

The first three editions of *Sociology* were aimed at instructors seeking a textbook which would be thorough, challenging, and comprehensive—and, at the same time, clear, readable, and lively. In view of the adoption of the text in more than 250 colleges and universities and the enthusiastic response of both instructors and students, I feel that *Sociology* has succeeded in this important goal. At the same time, revising the text provides an opportunity to draw on my own experiences with using it in class, as well as on the suggestions of instructors who have used it and of expert reviewers.

As in the earlier editions, I have taken great care to present the basic concepts and research methods of sociology through the use of understandable definitions and carefully chosen examples. Thus, in Chapter 2, a study of the employment patterns of Black corporate executives is described as a means of introducing the five steps of the scientific method. In Chapter 4, a recent study of college students' interactions after exams is used to explain the concept of impression management. In Chapter 6, I draw on a participant-observation study of Little League baseball teams to illustrate the use of sociograms.

Through their reading of *Sociology*, students will become familiar with the theoretical approaches of functionalism, the conflict perspective, and interactionism. Ideally, they will begin to think like sociologists and will be able to use sociological theories and concepts in evaluating human interactions and institutions. From the first pages of Chapter 1—in which I discuss how a sociologist might view the demographic profile of runners in the New York City Marathon as a reflection of the changing society we live in—the text stresses the distinctive way sociologists examine and question even the most familiar patterns of social behavior.

ORGANIZATION

Sociology is divided into five parts which provide a systematic introduction to the study of human behavior. Part One focuses on sociological theories and research methods. The origins of sociology as a social science are described; and the functionalist, conflict, and interactionist approaches are clearly defined. The challenges and difficulties of sociological research are thoroughly presented; particular attention is given to ethical issues faced by sociologists in conducting research.

In Part Two, students learn how social life is organized. The basic sociological concepts of culture, society, socialization, social interaction, and social structure are defined and explored. The impact of groups and organizations on social behavior is discussed, as are conformity to and deviance from accepted social norms.

Part Three addresses the persistence of social inequality in the United States and other societies. The key sociological concepts of stratification and social mobility are introduced. Separate chapters focus on inequality based on social class, race and ethnicity, gender, and age; and a new chapter (Chapter 9) examines social inequality worldwide.

In Part Four, the critical social institutions of human societies—the family, religion, government, the economy, education, and health care—are analyzed. The discussion of each institution highlights its functions, patterns of organization, and differential treatment of individuals and groups.

Part Five emphasizes change as a characteristic aspect of human societies. Students learn about changes in human communities, the social consequences of population growth, attempts to achieve change through involvement in social movements, and theories of social change.

SPECIAL FEATURES

"Looking Ahead" Questions

Each chapter of *Sociology* begins with "Looking Ahead"—a set of questions designed to interest students in the most important subjects and issues that will be raised.

Chapter Introduction

Following "Looking Ahead," a lively chapter introduction conveys the excitement of sociological inquiry. For example, students begin their work on deviance and social control (Chapter 7) by learning about the ways in which people who decide to be tattooed may be deviating from traditional social norms while at the same time conforming to the views and behavior of significant others. Students begin their work on collective behavior and social change (Chapter 20) by studying the events in late 1989 which culminated in the opening of the Berlin Wall and later the reunification of East and West Germany.

Chapter Overview

Reflecting the positive responses to the format of the first three editions, the introduction is again followed by a chapter overview that describes the content of the chapter in narrative form.

Key Terms

Careful attention has been given to presenting understandable and accurate definitions of each key term. These terms are highlighted in ***bold italics*** when they are first introduced. A list of key terms and definitions in each chapter—with page references—is found at the end of the chapter. In addition, the *glossary* at the end of the book includes the definitions of the textbook's 429 key terms and the page references for each term.

Boxes

The boxes which appeared in earlier editions were praised by both adopters and students because they supplemented the text discussions so closely. The boxed material in this fourth edition is again carefully tied to the basic themes of each chapter. Certain boxes illustrate the application of sociological theories, such as the analysis of functionalist and conflict views of sports in Chapter 1. Others provide detailed analysis of sociological research, such as the examination of role exit in Chapter 5. Still other boxes focus on contemporary issues, such as the pervasive stereotype of Asian Americans as a "model minority" (see Chapter 10).

Illustrations and Tables

Like the boxes, the *photographs, cartoons, figures,* and *tables* are closely linked to the themes of the text, and their captions make the links explicit.

Social Policy Sections

The social policy sections which close virtually all 20 chapters play a critical role in helping students to think like sociologists. These sections focus on current and often controversial issues of public policy such as child care (Chapter 4), the United States policy on immigration and refugees (Chapter 10), abortion (Chapter 11), and disability rights (Chapter 20). In all cases, students are shown the utility of sociological theory and research in understanding and resolving major political issues confronting policymakers and the general public. To help students appreciate the relevance of sociology in studying policy issues, each section begins with a set of questions designed to underscore the connection.

Chapter Summaries

Each chapter includes a brief numbered summary to aid students in reviewing the important themes.

Additional Readings

An annotated list of additional readings concludes each chapter. These works have been selected because of their sociological soundness and their accessibility for introductory students. For the fourth edition, as before, I have included a list of sociological journals and periodicals which focus on the issues discussed in the chapter.

References

Some 2200 books, articles, government documents, scholarly presentations, dissertations, and pamphlets are included in the list of references at the end of the book. These materials have been listed with complete bibliographic information so that they can be retrieved easily by instructors or students. Almost 40 percent of the references have been added especially for the fourth edition.

CHANGES IN THE FOURTH EDITION

Among the most important changes in the fourth edition of *Sociology* are the following.

A New Chapter: "Social Inequality Worldwide" (Chapter 9)

As we head toward the twenty-first century, it is clear that the basic sociological concepts of stratification and social inequality are relevant not only to industrial economies but to developing nations and the emerging global economy. Indeed, the war in the Persian Gulf has reinforced the fact that changes in the economy of the United States are influenced by and influence patterns of inequality beyond our national boundaries. Consequently, it seems important to teach introductory students about worldwide social inequality, including the substantial differences between rich and poor nations, as well as inequality *within* other countries based on gender, race, ethnicity, and class. The major topics examined in this new chapter include:

* Colonialism, neocolonialism, and world systems theory
* Impact of tourism on Bali (Box 9-1)
* Modernization in Kenya (case study)
* Multinational corporations
* Consequences of stratification for developing nations
* Informal economies (Box 9-2)
* Distribution of wealth and income worldwide
* Inequality in Japan (Box 9-3)
* Stratification in Brazil (an extended case study)
* Debt in the Third World (social policy section)

A Stronger Cross-Cultural Focus

In addition to the new chapter on "Social Inequality Worldwide," the fourth edition has new cross-cultural material throughout the text. Among the most important cross-cultural additions are:

* New box on "quality circles" in Japan and the United States (Chapter 6)
* New section on international crime rates (Chapter 7)

- New section on global perspectives on women (Chapter 11)
- New section on aging worldwide (Chapter 12)
- New box on liberation theology (Chapter 14)
- New box on the demography of Islamic nations (Chapter 19)
- New social policy section on the United States' population policy overseas (Chapter 19)

A Stronger Focus on Issues Affecting Women

Earlier editions of *Sociology* have been praised by reviewers and adopters for including material on women in *all* chapters—not only in the chapter on gender stratification. This fourth edition has even more material on women throughout the text. The additions include:

- New material on early women sociologists (Chapter 1)
- New box, "A Feminist View of Public Places" (Chapter 1)
- New social policy section on sexual harassment (Chapter 6)
- New box, "Rape Is a Bias Crime" (Chapter 7)
- New section, "The Status of Brazilian Women" (Chapter 9)
- New box, "Stereotypes of Puerto Rican Women and Men" (Chapter 10)
- New section, "Minority Women: Double Jeopardy" (Chapter 11)
- New social policy section on family leave (Chapter 13)
- New box, "Management Styles of Men and Women" (Chapter 15)
- New box, "Sexism in Medical Research" (Chapter 17)

Combined Chapters

Some of the chapters from the third edition have been combined, for a more concise and logical presentation:

- New chapter on "Government and the Economy" (Chapter 15) reflects a growing recogni-

tion of the interrelationship between a nation's political and economic systems—whether in the United States or in other societies.
- New chapter on "Collective Behavior and Social Change" (Chapter 20) underscores how elements of collective behavior and social movements are major factors in bringing about social change.

New Boxes

The fourth edition has 22 entirely new boxes. As in the third edition, the boxes are divided into four broad categories: "Around the World," "Speaking Out," "Current Research," and "Everyday Behavior." Among the 22 new boxes are:

- Current Research: Useful Statistics (Chapter 2)
- Everyday Behavior: The Eloquence of Sign Language (Chapter 3)
- Current Research: The Process of Role Exit (Chapter 5)
- Everyday Behavior: Self-Help Groups (Chapter 6)
- Speaking Out: Blaming the Victim (Chapter 8)
- Around the World: Inequality in Japan (Chapter 9)
- Speaking Out: Motorists as Welfare Recipients (Chapter 18)
- Around the World: The Demography of Islamic Nations (Chapter 19)

New Social Policy Sections

The fourth edition includes seven entirely new social policy sections:

- Sexual Harassment (Chapter 6)
- Debt in the Third World (Chapter 9)
- Catastrophic Health Care (Chapter 12)
- Family Leave (Chapter 13)
- Inequities in School Financing (Chapter 16)
- Homelessness (Chapter 18)
- United States Population Policy Overseas (Chapter 19)

Other New Sections

Several chapters in the fourth edition also have other new sections:

- Testing for Journal Bias (Chapter 2)
- Culture and Sociological Perspectives (Chapter 3)
- The State as an Agent of Socialization (Chapter 4)
- The Underclass (Chapter 8)
- Gay Relationships (Chapter 13)
- School Choice Programs (Chapter 16)
- Conflict View of Urban Growth (Chapter 18)

Updating

The fourth edition includes the most recent data and research findings. It draws on almost 825 new sources, of which some 470 were published in 1989, 1990, or 1991.

NEW SUPPLEMENTS

Annotated Instructor's Edition

For the fourth edition of *Sociology,* an *Annotated Instructor's Edition* (*AIE*) of the text offers page-by-page annotations to assist instructors in using textbook material. These include several categories: *Classroom Tips* (suggested teaching techniques); *Let's Discuss* (ideas for classroom discussions); *Student Alert* (which anticipate common misconceptions students have); *Policy Pointers* (which show tie-ins between important concepts and social policy applications); *Theory* (examples of the application of the functionalist, conflict, interactionist, and labeling perspectives); *Methods* (examples of the use of experiments, observation research, surveys, and unobtrusive measures); and *Transparencies* (cross-references to overhead transparencies available from McGraw-Hill).

The *Annotated Instructor's Edition* begins with a 152-page *Instructor's Resource Manual.* This manual provides sociology instructors with detailed key points, *additional lecture ideas* (among them alternative social policy issues), *class discussion topics, essay questions, topics for student research* (along with suggested research materials for each topic), and suggested *additional readings* (unlike those in the text itself, these are meant for instructors rather than students). Finally, *media materials* will be suggested for each chapter, including audiotapes, videotapes, and films. I have updated this media list in order to include the latest available sources.

The *Classroom Tips* annotations provided in each chapter of the *Annotated Instructor's Edition* will alert instructors to material in the *Instructor's Resource Manual* (front matter) which is relevant to a particular text discussion, box, or social policy section.

Guide to Critical Thinking

A supplement entitled *Guide to Critical Thinking* is available for the first time to accompany this edition of *Sociology.* Written by Mark Kassop of Bergen Community College in New Jersey, this supplement provides a general introduction to critical thinking and contains critical thinking exercises for each of the text's 20 chapters. These exercises will be useful for instructor's lectures, small group discussions, class debates, homework assignments, or as essay examination questions.

Guide for Non Native Speakers

Another new supplement, *Guide for Non Native Speakers,* is also available to accompany this edition of *Sociology.* Written by Laurie Blass, of San Francisco, who is a specialist on English for non native speakers, this booklet is designed as an additional aid for students for whom English is not their native language. It explains idiomatic expressions, provides assistance in determining the meaning of unfamiliar words, and offers other aids to help students who are non native speakers understand and review text material.

OTHER SUPPLEMENTS

Also accompanying this textbook are the *Students' Guide with Readings*, the *Instructor's Resource Manual*, and two *Test Banks*. I feel it is important for all materials to be developed together, rather than written independently of each other. Consequently, as in previous editions of *Sociology*, these four supplements have been written by the same persons responsible for preparation of this textbook: myself and my coauthor, Robert P. Lamm.

The *Students' Guide with Readings* includes standard features such as detailed *key points*, definitions of *key terms, multiple-choice questions, fill-in questions*, and *true-false questions*. All are keyed to specific pages in the textbook. In addition, the study guide includes a selected *reading* for each chapter, along with *study questions*; and a *"name that sociologist"* section. Perhaps the most distinctive feature is the *social policy exercise*, which is closely tied to the social policy section in the text. Finally, the *"one last look"* section which concludes each chapter of the study guide offers valuable study tips.

As noted above, an *Instructor's Resource Manual* is provided as the front matter for the *Annotated Instructor's Edition*. This *Manual* is available to instructors as a separate supplement. It includes chapter contents, the material in the front matter of the *Annotated Instructor's Edition*, and a list (with page references) of the annotations in the AIE.

The *Test Banks* which accompany *Sociology* can be used with computerized test-generating systems. Each contains about 1500 short-answer questions. Both *multiple-choice questions* and *true-false questions* are included for each chapter; they will be useful in testing students on basic sociological concepts, application of theoretical perspectives, and recall of important factual information. (Multiple-choice questions in the *Test Banks* are labeled "definition," "application," or "information" questions.) Correct answers and page references are provided for all questions.

In addition to the printed format, the *Test Banks* are available in computerized form for use on IBM PCs and compatibles, Apple II and IIc computers, and the Apple Macintosh. Tests can also be prepared by our customized test service. The telephone number for Customized Tests is 800-888-EXAM. McGraw-Hill's local representative can assist professors in obtaining these supplements.

Adopters of *Sociology* can also receive a set of 50 color *overhead transparencies* especially developed for this edition by Richard T. Schaefer. These transparencies include figures and tables drawn from the textbook and from other academic and governmental sources. Cross-references to these transparencies are included in the *Annotated Instructor's Edition* and in the separate *Instructor's Manual*.

Finally, McGraw-Hill also makes available to adopters videos, interactive software, classroom management software, and other materials and services. For more details, contact McGraw-Hill's main office or your local McGraw-Hill representative.

INTRODUCING SOCIOLOGY

Some instructors who use *Sociology* in introductory classes may want to use a sociology reader as a supplement. *Introducing Sociology*, published in 1987 by McGraw-Hill, was edited by Richard T. Schaefer and Robert P. Lamm. It includes 52 selections from sociological journals and popular periodicals which illustrate both the intellectual depth and the diversity of sociology. While providing rigorous coverage, the articles are readable and present basic sociological concepts clearly. The five-part model used in *Introducing Sociology* and the sequence of the 52 articles directly correspond to the organization of this textbook.

SOCIOLOGY UPDATE

Users of the first three editions of *Sociology* responded enthusiastically to a unique supplementary feature: the newsletter *Sociology Update*, written by Richard T. Schaefer and Robert P. Lamm. This newsletter will be continued for the fourth edition and is projected to come out in early January and early September each year. It is intended primarily for instructors but may be photocopied or reproduced for students. It will update tables and figures with the latest data, offer sketches of newly developing policy issues, discuss contemporary research findings in the social sciences, and summarize legislative and judicial decisions that have sociological relevance. All material will be keyed to text pages, thereby aiding instructors in integrating *Update* material into lecture and class discussions.

ACKNOWLEDGMENTS

This edition designates Robert P. Lamm as coauthor. Bob has been an integral part of *Sociology* beginning with the writing of the first edition and was credited as a collaborator in the first three editions of the text. While he continues to serve in the role of professional writer, it seemed to me—10 years after our partnership began—that, in sociological terms, his achieved status should be acknowledged with the title of coauthor. This position best reflects his contributions to and refinement of the contents of *Sociology* to maximize its utility to students and sociologists alike.

Both of us are deeply appreciative of the contributions to this project made by our editors. Phillip Butcher, our sociology editor, has provided insight, constructive criticism, and consistent encouragement. Rhona Robbin, a senior editor at McGraw-Hill, has worked tirelessly as our development editor for more than 11 years. Her thoughtful, sensitive, and respectful guidance has certainly made this a better book. Susan Gamer, our editing supervisor, has helped us to produce a high-quality book and to make many difficult production deadlines.

Additional guidance and support for the fourth edition of *Sociology* were provided by Elyse Rieder, photo editor; Elsa Peterson, permissions editor; William O'Neal, copy editor; Joan O'Connor, designer; and Janelle Travers, production

supervisor. Special thanks go to Peitr Bohen and Jan Gilboy, who worked as editorial assistants on this project. Each handled a variety of administrative tasks cheerfully and reliably.

It is worth noting that *Sociology* has benefited from a continuity of editorial support staff that is unique in the rapidly changing world of college textbook publishing. Rhona Robbin, Sue Gamer, Bill O'Neal, and Joan O'Connor have worked with Bob Lamm and myself on all four editions of the textbook; Phil Butcher and Elsa Peterson have worked on the last three editions. It has greatly helped us to work with a team of talented individuals so familiar with and committed to our book.

I have had the good fortune to be able to introduce students to sociology for many years. These students have been enormously helpful in spurring on my own sociological imagination. In ways I can fully appreciate but cannot fully acknowledge, their questions in class and queries in the hallway have found their way into this textbook.

This edition of *Sociology* continues to reflect many insightful suggestions made by reviewers of the first, second, and third editions. The current edition has benefited from constructive and thorough evaluations provided by 55 sociologists from both two-year and four-year institutions. These academic reviewers are listed on page ii. In addition, my colleagues at Western Illinois University have been most supportive.

The preparation of the manuscript was facilitated by the typing of Janice Wells, Cindy Draughan, and Joyia Greuel.

As is evident from these acknowledgments, the preparation of a textbook is truly a team effort. The most valuable members of this effort continue to be my wife, Sandy; and my son, Peter. They provide the support so necessary in my creative and scholarly activities.

Richard T. Schaefer

PART ONE

THE SOCIOLOGICAL PERSPECTIVE

PART ONE will introduce the fundamental theories and research methods used by sociologists to understand social behavior. Chapter 1 defines the sociological imagination; compares sociology with other social sciences; discusses the origins and founders of sociology; and presents the functionalist, conflict, and interactionist approaches that will be utilized throughout the book. Chapter 2 outlines the basic principles and steps of the scientific method, examines the methods through which sociologists generate data for their research, and explores the ethical issues that sociologists face as they study human behavior. These discussions of sociological theory and research serve as the foundation for our study of the organization of social life (Part Two), social inequality (Part Three), social institutions (Part Four), and social change (Part Five).

THE NATURE OF SOCIOLOGY

> *To attempt to understand human behavior is . . . the most*
> *exciting intellectual challenge in the world.*
> Milton M. Gordon
> The Scope of Sociology, 1988

LOOKING AHEAD

- How does the sociological imagination, as a unique feature of sociology, make sociology different from the other social sciences?
- Why is sociology more than a collection of commonsense observations?
- Why do sociologists regard suicide as a social as well as an individual act?
- How did Émile Durkheim, Max Weber, and Karl Marx contribute to the development of sociological thought?
- How can the sociological perspectives of functionalism and conflict theory be used to better understand the world of sports?
- What career options are available to sociologists?

On an unseasonably warm Sunday in November, more than 25,000 runners jogged across the Verrazano Narrows Bridge to begin the 1990 New York City Marathon. According to estimates, between 1 and 2 million spectators cheered the runners on as they traveled 26 miles 385 yards through all five boroughs of New York City, finishing in Central Park. The male winner, Douglas Wakihuri of Kenya, covered the distance in 2 hours 12 minutes 39 seconds; the female winner, Wanda Panfil of Poland, completed the course in 2 hours 30 minutes 45 seconds.

Typically, at marathons in large cities, huge crowds gather to watch the top runners. In New York, many onlookers hoped to catch a glimpse of crowd favorite Grete Waitz of Norway, who had been the women's winner nine times. For other spectators, however, the crucial goal is to cheer on friends, family members, or coworkers—or simply to shout encouragement and hand cups of water to thousands of strangers struggling to complete this draining race.

Observers view the New York City Marathon in many varied ways. An engineer might wonder about how the stress caused by 25,000 runners would affect the Verrazano Narrows Bridge and other bridges crossed during the race. A sports physician would be worried about how the unusually warm November weather, which reached a high of 73°F on the day of the Marathon, might affect runners. A sports reporter would focus on the victories of Wakihuri and Panfil, neither of whom was favored to win against better-known competitors. A feature writer for a newspaper might focus on Josef Galia, the oldest competitor, at age 92; on Edith Farias, a mother of nine who was running along with six of her seven daughters; on Dave Martin of London, one of more than 8000 runners from 80 foreign countries; or on Zoe Koplowitz, who has multiple sclerosis and runs on two arm supports. Koplowitz, who competes with a long shawl on her back that says "I'm not Grete" (referring to Grete Waitz), finished the 1990 Marathon at 3:55 A.M. after running for 21 hours and 35 minutes (Hanson, 1990).

What if a sociologist joined these spectators? He or she would bring a perspective quite unlike that of the average engineer, sports physician, sports reporter, or feature writer. The sociologist would undoubtedly be interested in the demographic profile of the 25,285 entrants. Data are available that break down these runners by gender, by age, by marital status, by previous racing experience (about 28 percent were first-time marathoners), by state or country of origin (more than 2000 runners came from France), and by occupational background (the entrants included 74 members of the clergy, 183 dentists, 275 homemakers, and 96 musicians). The sociologist would also be interested in the demographic profile of the spectators; the New York City Marathon passes through many diverse neighborhoods, including communities in Brooklyn dominated by Blacks, Italian Americans, Hasidic Jews, Polish Americans, and Hispanics.

The sociologist would not ignore the social meanings underscored by the presence of many women runners, older runners, and runners with disabilities. Until the 1960s, women were routinely excluded from marathons, supposedly unable to tolerate the rigors of such a race; the marathon did not become an Olympic event for women until 1984. Yet the 1990 New York City Marathon had 5249 female entrants—21 percent of the runners. Similarly, until recently, long-distance running was viewed as unhealthy for older persons, but there were 592 runners age 60 or over in the New York Marathon and three runners age 80 or over. For many years, the New York City Marathon banned wheelchair participants and had few disabled runners. By 1990, however, many athletes with disabilities competed in the Marathon, including about 100 members of the Achilles Track Club, most of whom are physically disabled. From a sociological point of view, the increasing representation of women, older people, and people with disabilities in marathon races parallels social changes in American society—as these groups continue to fight against prejudice and discrimination.

For the sociologist, then, the New York City Marathon would be the equivalent of a huge, living laboratory, in which he or she could examine a vast array of issues related to gender, race and ethnicity, social class, age, and disability. Whereas the newspaper feature writer might look for unusual human interest stories, the sociologist would focus on broad social trends evident in who runs in the Marathon, who cheers them on, and what the Marathon tells us about our changing society.

WHAT IS SOCIOLOGY?

As we have seen, the sociologist has a distinctive way of examining human interactions. *Sociology* is the systematic study of social behavior and human groups. It focuses primarily on the influence of social relationships upon people's attitudes and behavior and on how societies are established and change. As a field of study, sociology has an extremely broad scope. Therefore, this textbook deals with families, gangs, business firms, political parties, schools, religions, and labor unions. It is concerned with love, poverty, conformity, discrimination, illness, alienation, overpopulation, and community.

The Sociological Perspective

In American society, newspapers, television, and radio are the usual sources of information about such groups and problems. However, while the basic function of journalists is to report the news, sociologists bring a different type of understanding to such issues. The perspective of sociology involves seeing through the outside appearances of people's actions and organizations (P. Berger, 1963:31–37).

One major goal of this perspective is to identify underlying, recurring patterns of and influences on social behavior. For example, sociologists study the passionate desire of movie or rock music fans to see in person, to talk with, even to grab the clothing of a star. Why do people feel this need so powerfully? To what extent does participation in a crowd of fans allow individuals to act more boldly than they otherwise might? Will people gain greater respect from family members and friends if they have shaken hands with Eddie Murphy and exchanged three sentences of conversation?

The sociological perspective goes beyond identifying patterns of social behavior; it also attempts to provide explanations for such patterns. Here the impact of broad societal forces becomes a central consideration of sociology. Sociologists are not content to look at the individual fan's personality or "unique" reasons for wanting to meet Bruce Springsteen, Madonna, or Michael J. Fox. Rather, they recognize that millions of Americans want to meet celebrities, and they examine the *shared* feelings and behavior of fans within the larger social context of American culture.

The Sociological Imagination

In attempting to understand social behavior, sociologists rely on an unusual type of creative thinking. C. Wright Mills (1959) described such thinking as the ***sociological imagination***—an awareness of the relationship between an individual and the wider society. This awareness allows people (not simply sociologists) to comprehend the links between their immediate, personal social settings and the remote, impersonal social world that surrounds them and helps to shape them.

A key element in the sociological imagination is the ability to view one's own society as an outsider would, rather than from the limited perspective of personal experiences and cultural biases. Thus, instead of simply accepting the fact that movie stars and rock stars are the "royalty" of American society, we could ask, in a more critical sense, why this is the case. Conceivably, an outsider unfamiliar with the United States might wonder why we are not as interested in meeting outstanding scientists, elementary school teachers, or architects.

Sociological imagination can bring new understanding to daily life around us—or even to our view of the past. For example, Claude Fischer (1988:211–233) studied gender differences in telephone use during the half century before World War II and the social meanings of these differences. During the period 1890–1940, telephones became common in middle-class urban homes as well as on many farms.

Fischer (1988:224) observes that, in the period under study, North American women "seemed to have a special affinity for the household telephone and that affinity seemed to involve sociability." He offers a number of possible explanations for this gender difference, among them:

- Women, especially homemakers, were typically more isolated from daily adult contact than men were. Therefore, telephone calls allowed many women to experience some of the social contact that their husbands found in the workplace.

Applying the sociological imagination, Claude Fischer studied gender differences in telephone use during the half-century before World War II. He found that the telephone served as a "technology of sociability" which allowed women to increase their social interactions.

- Women's traditional role as "social managers" for their families led to extensive telephone responsibilities in service to the household, the extended family, the friendship circle, and the community.

Fischer (1988:229) concludes that, like the bicycle and the automobile, the telephone served as a "technology of sociability" that allowed women to increase their social interactions. He adds that "men's jokes about this affinity are, perhaps, at base, simply a defensive acknowledgment of this difference between men and women in personal relations."

In an application of sociological imagination to contemporary behavior, Linda Mooney and Sarah Brabant (1986, 1988) chose to study birthday cards in an effort to measure expressions of love in the United States. They randomly selected 535 birthday cards and coded them in terms of such factors as size, cost, color, stereotyping, tone, and status of the sender and the receiver (e.g., card from daughter to father).

Mooney and Brabant learned that love is rarely stated in explicit terms in birthday cards. Cards with explicit statements of love were more expensive and generally more likely to be sent to women (more specifically, to mothers and sisters). Of all cards sent to mothers, 81 percent contained the word "love," compared with only 44 percent of cards sent to fathers. Similarly, 62 percent of all cards to sisters contained the word "love," while no cards to brothers used the word. These differences suggest that the stereotype of the unemotional male is being reinforced in American birthday cards.

Sociologists put their imagination to work in a variety of areas. Table 1-1 presents a partial list of the specializations within contemporary sociology. Throughout this textbook, the sociological imagination will be used to examine American society (and others) from the viewpoint of respectful but questioning outsiders.

In this chapter, the nature of sociology as a science and its relationship to other social sciences will be explored. The contributions of three pioneering thinkers—Émile Durkheim, Max Weber, and Karl Marx—to the development of sociology will be evaluated. A number of important theoretical perspectives used by sociologists will be discussed. Finally, practical applications of the discipline of sociology for human behavior and organizations will be described.

Sociology and the Social Sciences

In a general sense, sociology can be considered a science. The term *science* refers to the body of knowledge obtained by methods based upon systematic observation. Like other scientific disciplines, sociology engages in organized, systematic

TABLE 1-1 Specializations within Sociology

A PARTIAL LISTING
Methodology and research technology
Sociology: history and theory
Social psychology
Group interactions
Cultural and social structure
Complex organizations
Social change and economic development
Mass phenomena
Communication
Sociology of sport and leisure
Political behavior
Social stratification
Sociology of occupations and professions
Rural sociology and agriculture
Urban sociology
Sociology of the arts
Sociology of education
Sociology of religion
Social control
Sociology of law
Penology and correctional problems
Sociology of science
Demography
The family and socialization
Sociology of sexual behavior
Sociology of health and medicine
Sociology of knowledge
Community development
Policy planning
Radical sociology
Studies in poverty
Studies in violence
Feminist studies
Marxist sociology
Clinical sociology
Sociology of business

SOURCE: Adapted from *Sociological Abstracts*, 1991.

As reflected in this excerpt from the table of contents of Sociological Abstracts—*an online and hardcover database of articles, papers, and books on topics of sociology—the discipline of sociology can be divided into a diverse variety of subfields.*

study of phenomena (in this case, human behavior) in order to enhance understanding. All scientists, whether studying mushrooms or murderers, attempt to collect precise information through methods of study which are as objective as possible. They rely on careful recording of observations and accumulation of data.

Of course, there is a great difference between sociology and physics, between psychology and astronomy. For this reason, the sciences are commonly divided into natural and social sciences. **Natural science** is the study of the physical features of nature and the ways in which they interact and change. Astronomy, biology, chemistry, geology, and physics are all natural sciences. **Social science** is the study of various aspects of human society. The social sciences include sociology, anthropology, economics, history, psychology, and political science.

These academic disciplines have a common focus on the social behavior of people, yet each has a particular orientation in studying such behavior. Anthropologists usually study cultures of the past and preindustrial societies that remain in existence today. They use this knowledge to examine contemporary societies, including even industrial societies. Economists explore the ways in which people produce and exchange goods and services, along with money and other resources. Historians are concerned with the peoples and events of the past and their significance for us today. Political scientists study international relations, the workings of government, and the exercise of power and authority. Psychologists investigate personality and individual behavior. In contrast to other social sciences, sociology emphasizes the influence that society has on people's attitudes and behavior and the ways in which people shape society. Humans are social animals; therefore, sociologists scientifically examine our social relationships with people.

To better illustrate the distinctive perspectives of the social sciences, let us examine sociological and psychological approaches to the issue of gambling. The growing legalization of gambling in the United States has, in effect, increased the number of participants and contributed to a rise in the number of "problem gamblers"—that is,

Viewed from the perspective of psychology, gambling represents an escape into a fantasy world where great fortune can be attained easily. By contrast, in their examination of gambling, sociologists focus on the social networks that develop among many participants.

people who consistently lose more money than they can afford to lose. Gamblers' professed goal is economic gain; yet, because the vast majority end up losing money, their persistence is commonly viewed as "irrational" or even "pathological." Viewed from the perspective of psychology, gambling represents an escape into a fantasy world where great fortune can be attained easily. Eventually, people become so dependent on gambling that the activity fills an emotional need. As a result, they cannot give up gambling without feeling nervous and upset.

By contrast, in their examination of gambling, sociologists focus on the social networks that develop among many participants. Whether they be offtrack bettors, sports bettors, or poker players, gamblers establish friendship groups and work hard to create feelings of conviviality even among casual acquaintances whom they meet through gambling. Consequently, for such persons, gambling is a form of recreation and may even be their primary social activity. This sociological perspective on gambling casts a shadow on recurring efforts to discourage particular individuals from gambling and to discourage the practice in general. Giving up gambling may, in fact, mean forgoing all social interaction that a person has previously found to be meaningful. Alternatively, participation in Gamblers Anonymous—a self-help group for "problem gamblers" modeled on Alcoholics Anonymous—provides a new forum to which ex-gamblers can turn for interaction, understanding, and encouragement. The individual can find social support to replace the friendship groups developed in his or her betting days (Rosecrance, 1986, 1987).

This example shows that by viewing social phenomena from several perspectives, we can enhance our understanding of human behavior. Social science disciplines—in this case study, psychology and sociology—offer distinctive expertise that is valuable in developing a response to those gamblers who wager more money than they can afford to lose.

Sociology and Common Sense

As we have seen, sociology and the other social sciences focus on the study of certain aspects of human behavior. Yet human behavior is something with which we all have experience and about which we have at least a bit of knowledge. Many of us, even without Ph.D. degrees in the social sciences, could make suggestions about how to help "problem gamblers." All of us might well have theories about why movie stars and rock stars are the subjects of so much attention and adulation. Our theories and suggestions come from our experiences and from a cherished source of wisdom—common sense.

In our daily lives, we rely on common sense to get us through many unfamiliar situations. However, this knowledge, while sometimes accurate, is not always reliable, because it rests on commonly held beliefs rather than systematic analysis of facts. It was once considered "common sense" to accept that the earth was flat—a view rightly questioned by Pythagoras and Aristotle. Incorrect commonsense notions are not just a part of the distant past; they remain with us today.

In American society, by common sense we know that, given the unprecedented level of divorces, most first marriages fail to reach their twentieth anniversaries. By common sense we realize that when a racial minority group moves into a previously all-White neighborhood, property values decline. By common sense we know that people panic when faced with natural disasters, such as floods and earthquakes, with the result that all social organization disintegrates.

However, like the view that the earth is flat, these particular commonsense notions are *untrue;* each has failed to be supported by sociological research. Three out of four first marriages in the United States celebrate their twentieth anniversaries, and one out of five reaches the fiftieth! Race has been found to have little relationship to property values; such factors as zoning changes, overcrowding, and age of housing are more significant. Finally, disasters do not generally produce panic. In the aftermath of natural disasters, greater social organization and structure emerge to deal with a community's problems.

Like other social scientists, sociologists do not accept something as a fact because "everyone knows it." Instead, each piece of information must be tested and recorded, then analyzed in relationship to other data. Sociology relies on scientific studies in order to describe and understand a social environment. At times, the findings of sociologists may seem like common sense because they deal with facets of everyday life. Yet it is important to stress that such findings have been *tested* by researchers. Common sense now tells us that the earth is round. But this particular commonsense notion is based on centuries of scientific work upholding the breakthrough made by Pythagoras and Aristotle.

WHAT IS SOCIOLOGICAL THEORY?

Why do people commit suicide? One traditional commonsense answer is that people inherit the desire to kill themselves. Another view is that sunspots drive people to take their own lives. These explanations will not seem especially convincing if you employ the perspective of sociology, but they do represent two beliefs widely held as recently as 1900.

Sociologists are not particularly interested in why any one individual commits suicide; they are more concerned with why *people in general* take their own lives. This leads sociologists to examine the social forces that influence people in deciding whether or not to attempt suicide. In order to undertake such research, sociologists develop theories that offer a general explanation of some type of behavior.

Theories can be regarded as attempts to explain events, forces, materials, ideas, or behavior in a comprehensive manner. Within sociology, a *theory* is a set of statements that seeks to explain problems, actions, or behavior. An effective theory may have both explanatory and predictive power. That is, it can help us to develop a broad and integrated view of the relationships among seemingly isolated phenomena as well as to understand how one type of change in an environment leads to others.

An essential task in building a sociological theory is to examine the relationship between bits of data, gathered through research, that may seem completely unrelated. For example, suppose that you are given data about the number of reported suicides in various European nations in 1869. You are told that there were 5144 reported suicides in France in that year, 1588 in England, and only 462 in Denmark. If you restricted yourself to those data, you might attempt to develop a theory about why there were so many suicides in France and so few in Denmark. However, in researching this very problem, Émile Durkheim looked into suicide data in much greater detail and developed a highly original theory about the relationship between suicide and social factors.

Durkheim was primarily concerned not with the personalities of individual suicide victims, but rather with suicide *rates* and how they varied from country to country. As a result, when he looked at the number of reported suicides in France, England, and Denmark in 1869, he also examined the populations of these nations to determine their rates of suicide. In doing so, he found that whereas England had only 67 reported suicides per million inhabitants, France had 135 per million and Denmark had 277 per million. Thus, in terms of national comparisons, the question then became: "Why did Denmark (rather than France) have a comparatively high rate of reported suicides?"

Durkheim went much deeper into his investigation of suicide rates, and the result was his landmark work *Suicide*, published in 1897. Durkheim refused to automatically accept unproven explanations regarding suicide, including the beliefs that such deaths were caused by cosmic forces or by inherited tendencies. Instead, he focused on such problems as the cohesiveness or lack of cohesiveness of religious and occupational groups.

Durkheim's research suggested that suicide, while a solitary act, is related to group life. Protestants had much higher suicide rates than Catholics did; the unmarried had much higher rates than married people did; soldiers were more likely to take their lives than civilians were. In addition, it appeared that there were higher rates of suicide in times of peace than in times of war and revolution, and in times of economic instability and recession rather than in times of prosperity. Durkheim concluded that the suicide rates of a society reflected the extent to which people were or were not integrated into the group life of the society (see Box 1-1).

Émile Durkheim, like many other social scientists, developed a theory to explain how individual behavior can be understood within a social context. He pointed out the influence of groups and societal forces on what had always been viewed as a highly personal act. Clearly, Durkheim offered a more *scientific* explanation for the causes of suicide than that of sunspots or inherited tendencies. His theory has predictive power, since it suggests that suicide rates will rise or fall in conjunction with certain social and economic changes.

BOX 1-1 • AROUND THE WORLD

FOUR TYPES OF SUICIDE

In his studies of suicide rates in France, England, and Denmark, Émile Durkheim (1951, original edition 1897) divided this disturbing phenomenon into four distinct categories, each of which suggests a particular relationship between the individual and society in terms of group solidarity.

In *altruistic suicide,* a person feels a deep sense of moral obligation and is willing to place the group's welfare above his or her own survival. A spy who is captured and swallows a poison capsule, rather than taking the risk of disclosing secrets, has committed altruistic suicide.

Egoistic suicide is just the opposite. This type of suicide occurs when the individual feels little connection to the larger society and is not affected by social constraints against self-destructive behavior. A lonely person who lives in a skid row hotel room with no friends or family may resort to egoistic suicide.

When a society lacks clear-cut rules of social behavior, *anomic suicide* can result. Such suicides are particularly likely to occur in a time of great social disorder or turmoil, as in the United States shortly after the stock market crash of 1929. People who lost all their savings and were unable to cope with their misfortune turned to anomic suicide.

Sociologists generally focus on these three types because they are the most common, but Durkheim identified a fourth type, fatalistic suicide. Whereas anomic suicide stems from a sense of disorder, *fatalistic suicide* is related to the powerlessness that people feel when their lives are regulated to an intolerable extent. A prisoner who can no longer bear confinement may find a "way out" through fatalistic suicide.

Durkheim's division of suicide into these four categories forms a typology. A *typology* is a classification scheme containing two or more mutually exclusive categories (types); it is used by sociologists to better understand different forms of behavior.

It is important to understand that a theory—even the best of theories—is not a final statement about human behavior. Durkheim's theory of suicide is no exception; sociologists continue to examine factors which contribute to a society's rate of suicide. For example, people across the United States were shocked by the national news reports in 1987 concerning four New Jersey teenagers who together drove into a garage, closed the door, and let carbon monoxide fumes take their lives, thereby engaging in a collective act of suicide. Within little more than a week, 10 more teenagers in four different states killed themselves in garages using carbon monoxide. These suicides were more than a coincidence; sociological research from 1973 through the present documents that the incidence of suicide increases following nationally televised stories about suicide and that teenagers are especially vulnerable to such "copycat" behavior. Studies show that the impact is greatest after the publicized suicide of an entertainer or politician and is somewhat less after the suicide of an artist, criminal, or member of the economic elite (G. Israel and Stack, 1987; D. Phillips and Carstensen, 1986; Stack, 1987; Wasserman, 1984).

ORIGINS OF SOCIOLOGY

People have always been curious about how we get along, what we do, and whom we select as our leaders. Philosophers and religious authorities of ancient and medieval societies made countless observations about human behavior. These observations were not tested or verified scientifically; nevertheless, they often became the foundation for moral codes. Several of the early social philosophers predicted that a systematic study of human behavior would one day emerge. Beginning in the nineteenth century, European theorists made pioneering contributions to the development of a science of human behavior.

Early Thinkers: Comte, Martineau, and Spencer

In France, the nineteenth century was an unsettling time for that nation's intellectuals. The French monarchy had been deposed earlier in the revolution of 1789, and Napoleon had subsequently been defeated in his effort to conquer Europe. Amidst this chaos, philosophers considered how society might be improved. Auguste Comte (1798–1857), credited with being the most influential of these philosophers of the early 1800s, believed that a theoretical science of society and systematic investigation of behavior were needed to improve society.

Comte coined the term *sociology* to apply to the science of human behavior and insisted that sociology could make a critical contribution to a new and improved human community. Writing in the 1800s, Comte feared that France's stability had been permanently impaired by the excesses of the French Revolution. Yet he hoped that the study of social behavior in a systematic way would eventually lead to more rational human interactions. In Comte's hierarchy of sciences, sociology was at the top. He called it the "queen" and its practitioners "scientist-priests." This French theorist did not simply give sociology its name; he also presented a rather ambitious challenge to the fledgling discipline.

Scholars were able to learn of Comte's works largely through translations by the English sociologist Harriet Martineau (1802–1876). But Martineau was a path breaker in her own right as a sociologist; she offered insightful observations of the customs and social practices of both her native Britain and the United States. Martineau's book *Society in America* (1962, original edition 1837) examines religion, politics, child rearing, and immigration in the young nation. Martineau gives special attention to status distinctions and to such factors as gender and race.

Another important contributor to the discipline of sociology was Herbert Spencer (1820–1903). Writing from the vantage point of relatively pros-

(The Bettmann Archive)

Harriet Martineau (1802–1876), an English scholar, was an early pioneer of sociology who studied social behavior both in her native country and in the United States.

perous Victorian England, Spencer did not feel compelled to correct or improve society; instead, he hoped to describe it better. Spencer was familiar with Comte's work but seemed more influenced by Charles Darwin's study *On the Origin of Species.* Drawing on Darwin's insights, Spencer used the concept of evolution of animals to explain how societies change over time. Similarly, he adapted Darwin's evolutionary view of the "survival of the fittest" by arguing that it is "natural" that some people are rich while others are poor.

Spencer's approach to societal change was extremely popular in his own lifetime. Indeed, he dominated scholarly thinking more than Comte did. Unlike Comte, Spencer suggested that societies are bound to change; therefore, one need not be highly critical of present social arrangements or work actively for social change. This viewpoint appealed to many influential people in Great Britain and the United States who had a vested interest in the status quo and were suspicious of social thinkers who endorsed change. We will consider Spencer's views on society and social change in more detail in Chapter 20.

Émile Durkheim

Émile Durkheim's important theoretical work on suicide was but one of his many pioneering contributions to sociology. The son of a rabbi, Durkheim (1858–1917) was educated in both France and Germany. He established an impressive academic reputation and was appointed as one of the first professors of sociology in France. Few sociologists have had such a dramatic impact on as many different areas within the discipline.

Above all, Durkheim will be remembered for his insistence that behavior cannot be fully understood in individualistic terms, that it must be understood within a larger social context. As one example of this emphasis, Durkheim (1947, original edition 1912) developed a fundamental thesis to help understand all forms of society through intensive study of the Arunta, an Australian tribe. He focused on the functions that religion performed for the Arunta and underscored the role that group life plays in defining that which we consider religious. Durkheim concluded that, like other forms of group behavior, religion reinforces a group's solidarity.

Another of Durkheim's main interests was the consequences of work in modern societies. In his view, the growing division of labor found in industrial societies as workers became much more specialized in their tasks led to what he called *anomie*. **Anomie** refers to a loss of direction that is felt in a society when social control of individual behavior has become ineffective. The state of anomie occurs when people have lost their sense of purpose or direction, often during a time of profound social change (as we saw in the discussion of anomic suicide in Box 1-1). In a period of anomie, people are so confused and unable to cope with the new social environment that they may resort to taking their own lives.

As will be seen in the examination of work and the economy in Chapter 15, Durkheim was concerned about the dangers that such alienation, loneliness, and isolation might pose for modern industrial societies. He shared Comte's belief that sociology should provide direction for social change. As a result, he advocated the creation of new social groups—between the individual's family and the state—which would ideally provide a sense of belonging for members of huge, impersonal societies.

Max Weber

Another important theorist who contributed to the scientific study of society was Max Weber (pronounced "VAY-ber"). Born in Germany in 1864, Weber took his early academic training in legal and economic history, but he gradually developed an interest in sociology. Eventually, he became a professor at various German universities. Weber told his students that they should employ *Verstehen,* the German word for "understanding" or "insight," in their intellectual work. He pointed out that much of our social behavior cannot be analyzed by the kinds of objective criteria we use to measure weight or temperature. To fully comprehend behavior, we must learn the subjective meanings people attach to their actions—how they themselves view and explain their behavior.

For example, suppose that sociologists were studying the social ranking of individuals within an electricians' union. Weber would expect researchers to employ *Verstehen* in order to determine the significance of the union's social hierarchy for its members. Sociologists would seek to learn how these electricians relate to union members of higher or lower status; they might examine the effects of seniority on standing within the union. While investigating these questions, researchers would take into account people's emotions, thoughts, beliefs, and attitudes (L. Coser, 1977:130).

We also owe credit to Weber for a key conceptual tool: the ideal type. An *ideal type* is a construct, a model that serves as a measuring rod against which actual cases can be evaluated. In his own works, Weber identified various characteristics of bureaucracy as an ideal type (these will be discussed in detail in Chapter 6). In presenting

FIGURE 1-1 The Early Social Thinkers

	Émile Durkheim 1858–1917	Max Weber 1864–1920	Karl Marx 1818–1883
Academic training	Philosophy	Law, economics, history, philosophy	Philosophy, law
Key works	1893 - *The Division of Labor in Society* 1897 - *Suicide: A Study in Sociology* 1912 - *Elementary Forms of Religious Life*	1904-1905 — *The Protestant Ethic and the Spirit of Capitalism* 1922 — *Wirtschaft and Gesellschaft*	1848 — *The Communist Manifesto* 1867 — *Das Kapital*

SOURCES: Left, Bibliothèque Nationale, Paris; middle, Culver Pictures; right, Culver Pictures.

Many of today's sociological studies draw on the work of these three nineteenth-century thinkers.

this model of bureaucracy, Weber was not describing any particular business, nor was he using the term *ideal* in a way that suggested a positive evaluation. Instead, his purpose was to provide a useful standard for measuring how bureaucratic an actual organization is (Gerth and Mills, 1958:219). Later in this textbook, the concept of ideal type will be used to study the family, religion, authority, and economic systems and to analyze bureaucracy.

Although their professional careers came at the same time, Émile Durkheim and Max Weber never met and probably were unaware of each other's existence, let alone ideas. This was certainly not true of the work of Karl Marx. Durkheim's thinking about anomie was related to Marx's writings, while Weber's concern for a value-free, objective sociology (which will be explored in Chapter 2) was a direct response to Marx's deeply held convictions. Thus, it is no surprise that Karl Marx is viewed as a major figure in the development of several social sciences, among them sociology. (See Figure 1-1.)

Karl Marx

Karl Marx (1818–1883) shared with Durkheim and Weber a dual interest in abstract philosophical issues and in the concrete reality of everyday life. Unlike the others, Marx was so critical of existing institutions that a conventional academic career was impossible, and although he was born and educated in Germany, most of his life was spent in exile.

Marx's personal life was a difficult struggle. When a paper that he had written was suppressed, he fled his native land and went to France. In Paris, he met Friedrich Engels (1820–1895), with whom he formed a lifelong friendship. They lived during a time in which European and North American economic life was increasingly being dominated by the factory rather than the farm.

In 1847, Marx and Engels attended secret meetings in London of an illegal coalition of labor unions, the Communist League. The following year, they finished preparing a platform called *The Communist Manifesto,* in which they argued that the masses of people who have no resources other than their labor (whom they referred to as the *proletariat*) should unite to fight for the overthrow of capitalist societies. In the words of Marx and Engels:

> The history of all hitherto existing society is the history of class struggles. . . . The proletarians have nothing to lose but their chains. They have a world to win. WORKING MEN OF ALL COUNTRIES UNITE! (Feuer, 1959:7, 41).

After completing *The Communist Manifesto,* Marx returned to Germany, only to be expelled. He then moved to England, where he continued to write books and essays. Marx's life there was one of extreme poverty. He pawned most of his possessions, and several of his children died of malnutrition and disease. Marx clearly was an outsider in British society, a fact which may well have affected his view of western cultures (R. Collins and Makowsky, 1978:40).

Marx's thinking was strongly influenced by the work of a German philosopher, Georg Hegel. Hegel saw history as a **dialectical process**—a series of clashes between conflicting ideas and forces. At the end of each clash, a new and improved set of ideas was expected to emerge. In Hegel's view, conflict was an essential element in progress. Conflict led to progress; progress came only through conflict.

In applying Hegel's theories, Marx focused on conflict between social classes, as represented by industrial workers and the owners of factories and businesses. Under Marx's analysis, society was fundamentally divided between classes who clash in pursuit of their own class interests. He argued that history could be understood in dialectical terms as a record of the inevitable conflicts between economic groups. This view forms the basis for the contemporary sociological perspective of conflict theory, which will be examined later in the chapter.

When Marx examined the industrial societies of his time, such as Germany, England, and the United States, he saw the factory as the center of conflict between the exploiters (the owners of the means of production) and the exploited (the workers). Marx viewed these relationships in systematic terms; that is, he believed that an entire system of economic, social, and political relationships had been established to maintain the power and dominance of the owners over the workers. Consequently, Marx and Engels argued that the working class needed to overthrow the existing class system.

Marx's writings inspired those who were subsequently to lead communist revolutions in Russia, China, Cuba, Vietnam, and elsewhere. Even apart from the political revolutions that his work helped to foster, Marx's influence on contemporary thinking has been dramatic. Although he certainly did not view himself as a sociologist, Marx nevertheless made a critical contribution to the development of sociology and other social sciences. Partly, this reflected Marx's emphasis on carefully researching the actual, measurable conditions of people's lives, a practice which foreshadowed the scientific nature of today's social sciences.

In addition, Marx placed great value on the *group* identifications and associations that influenced an individual's place in society. As we have seen, this area of study is the major focus of contemporary sociology. Throughout this textbook, we will consider how membership in a particular gender classification, age group, racial group, or economic class affects a person's attitudes and behavior. In an important sense, this way of understanding society can be traced back to the pioneering work of Karl Marx. (See Figure 1-2 on page 16.)

Twentieth-Century Sociology

Sociology, as we know it in the 1990s, draws upon the firm foundation developed by Émile Durkheim, Max Weber, and Karl Marx. However, the discipline has certainly not remained stagnant over the last century. Sociologists have gained new insights which have helped them to better understand the workings of society.

FIGURE 1-2 Prominent Contributors to Sociological Thought

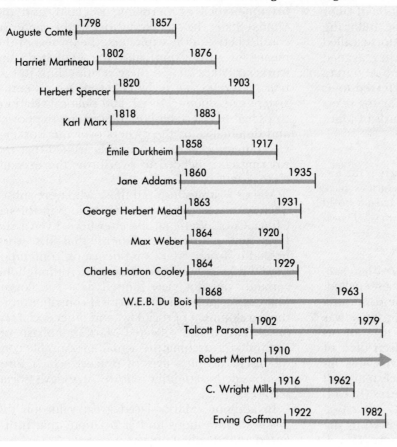

The "time lines" shown here give an idea of relative chronology.

Charles Horton Cooley (1864–1929) was typical of the sociologists who became prominent in the early 1900s. Born in Ann Arbor, Michigan, Cooley received his graduate training in economics but later became a sociology professor at the University of Michigan. Like other early sociologists, he became interested in this "new" discipline while pursuing a related area of study.

Cooley shared the desire of Durkheim, Weber, and Marx to learn more about society. But to do so effectively, Cooley preferred to use the sociological perspective to look first at smaller units—intimate, face-to-face groups such as families, gangs, and friendship networks. He saw these groups as the seedbeds of society in the sense that they shape people's ideals, beliefs, values, and

social nature. Cooley's work brought new understanding to groups of relatively small size.

Many of the leading American sociologists of the early 1900s saw themselves as social reformers dedicated to systematically studying and then improving a corrupt society. They were genuinely concerned about the lives of immigrants in the nation's growing cities, whether these immigrants came from Europe or from the American south. Early female sociologists, in particular, were often active in poor urban areas as leaders of community centers known as *settlement houses*. For example, Jane Addams (1860–1935), a member of and speaker before the American Sociological Society, cofounded the famous Chicago settlement, Hull-House. Addams and other pioneering female sociologists commonly combined intellectual inquiry, social service work, and political activism—all with the goal of assisting the underprivileged and creating a more egalitarian society (Deegan, 1988).

By the middle of the twentieth century, however, the focus of the discipline had shifted. Sociologists restricted themselves to theorizing and gathering information, while the aim of transforming society was left to social workers and others. This shift away from social reform was accompanied by a growing commitment to scientific methods of research and to value-free interpretation of data.

Sociologist Robert Merton (1968:39–72) made an important contribution to the discipline by successfully combining theory and research. Born in 1910 of Slavic immigrant parents in Philadelphia, Merton subsequently won a scholarship to Temple University. He continued his studies at Harvard, where he acquired his lifelong interest in sociology. Merton's teaching career has been based at Columbia University.

Merton has produced a theory that is one of the most frequently cited explanations of deviant behavior. He noted different ways in which people attempt to achieve success in life. In his view, some may not share the socially agreed-upon goal of accumulating material goods or the accepted means of achieving this goal. For example, in Merton's classification scheme, "innovators" are people who accept the goal of pursuing material wealth but use illegal means to do so, including robbery, burglary, and extortion. Merton's explanation of crime is based on individual behavior—influenced by society's approved goals and means—yet it has wider applications. It helps to account for the high crime rates among the nation's poor, who may see no hope of advancing themselves through traditional roads to success. Merton's theory will be discussed in greater detail in Chapter 7.

Merton also emphasized that sociology should strive to bring together the "macro" and "micro" approaches to the study of society. *Macrosociology* concentrates on large-scale phenomena or entire civilizations. Thus, Émile Durkheim's cross-cultural study of suicide is an example of macrosociology. More recently, macrosociologists have examined social control and crime in the Soviet Union (see Chapter 7), the stereotype of Asian Americans as a "model minority" (see Chapter 10), and the population patterns of Islamic countries (see Chapter 19). By contrast, *microsociology* stresses study of small groups and often uses experimental studies in laboratories. Microsociologists have studied the cliques evident among Little League baseball players (see Chapter 6), the social networks of elderly Americans (see Chapter 12), and the differing management styles of women and men (see Chapter 15).

Sociologists find it useful to employ both these approaches. In fact, we can learn a great deal by using macrosociological and microsociological analysis to study the same problem. For example, we might try to understand criminal behavior at the macro level by analyzing crime rates in vari-

(Smithsonian Institution)

Jane Addams (1860–1935), an early pioneer both in the discipline of sociology and in the settlement house movement, was honored on a postage stamp in 1940.

A macrosociological examination of music would seek to identify cross-cultural differences in styles of music, types of instruments, types of interactions among musicians and with dancers, and so forth; and it would assess the sociological significance of these differences. Pictured are Taiko drummers in Japan; Djerma tribesmen from the Niger Republic of Africa, playing string instruments known as molos; *and musicians playing wooden pipe flutes at the Brissaud-Figaro Carnaval in Bolivia.*

ous countries and at the micro level by examining the social forces that influence individuals to become criminals or delinquents.

Contemporary sociology reflects the diverse contributions of earlier theorists. As sociologists approach such topics as divorce, drug addiction, and religious cults, they can draw upon the theo-retical insights of the discipline's pioneers. A careful reader can hear Comte, Durkheim, Weber, Marx, Cooley, Addams, and many others speaking through the pages of current research. In describing the work of today's sociologists, it is helpful to examine a number of influential theoretical approaches.

PERSPECTIVES OF SOCIOLOGY

Sociologists view society in different ways. Some see the world basically as a stable and ongoing entity. They are impressed with the endurance of the family, organized religion, and other social institutions. Some sociologists see society as composed of many groups in conflict, competing for scarce resources. To other sociologists, the most fascinating aspects of the social world are the everyday, routine interactions among individuals that we sometimes take for granted.

These differing perspectives of society are all ways of examining the same phenomena. Sociological imagination may employ any of a number of theoretical approaches in order to study human behavior. From these approaches, sociologists develop theories to explain specific types of behavior. The three perspectives that are most widely used by sociologists will provide an introductory look at the discipline. These are the functionalist, conflict, and interactionist perspectives.

Functionalist Perspective

In the view of functionalists, society is like a living organism in which each part of the organism contributes to its survival. Therefore, the *functionalist perspective* emphasizes the way that parts of a society are structured to maintain its stability. Émile Durkheim's analysis of religion represented a critical contribution to the development of functionalism. As noted earlier, Durkheim focused on the role of religion in reinforcing feelings of solidarity and unity within group life.

The work of Durkheim, Max Weber, and other European sociologists greatly influenced Talcott Parsons (1902–1979), a Harvard University sociologist. Unlike most of his American contemporaries, Parsons was anxious to study in Europe; he went first to the London School of Economics and then to the University of Heidelberg. While at Heidelberg, he attended a regular Sunday morning salon at which Weber's ideas were discussed by scholars.

For over four decades, Parsons dominated American sociology with his advocacy of functionalism. He saw any society as a vast network of connected parts, each of which contributes to the maintenance of the system as a whole. Under the functionalist approach, if an aspect of social life does not contribute to society's stability or survival—if it does not serve some identifiable useful function or promote value consensus among members of a society—it will not be passed on from one generation to the next.

As an example of the functionalist perspective, let us examine prostitution. Why is it that a practice so widely condemned continues to display such persistence and vitality? Functionalists suggest that prostitution satisfies needs of patrons that may not be readily met through more socially acceptable forms such as courtship or marriage. The "buyer" receives sex without any responsibility for procreation or sentimental attachment; at the same time, the "seller" gains a livelihood through this exchange.

Through such an examination, we can conclude that prostitution does perform certain functions that society seems to need. However, this is not to suggest that prostitution is a desirable or legitimate form of social behavior. Functionalists do not make such judgments and do not wish to condone the abuses or crimes that prostitutes and their clients may commit. Rather, advocates of the functionalist perspective hope to explain how an aspect of society that is so frequently attacked can nevertheless manage to survive (K. Davis, 1937).

Manifest and Latent Functions A university catalog typically presents various stated functions of the institution. It may inform us, for example, that the university intends to "offer each student a broad education in classical and contemporary thought, in the humanities, in the sciences, and in the arts." However, it would be quite a surprise if we came across a catalog which declared: "This university was founded in 1895 to keep people between the ages of 18 and 22 out of the job market, thus reducing unemployment." No college catalog will declare that this is the purpose of the university. Yet societal institutions serve many functions, some of them quite subtle. The university, in fact, *does* delay people's entry into the job market.

In order to better examine the functions of institutions, Robert Merton (1968:115–120) made an important distinction between manifest and latent functions. ***Manifest functions*** of institutions are open, stated, conscious functions. They involve the intended, recognized consequences of an aspect of society, such as the university's role in certifying academic competence and excellence. By contrast, ***latent functions*** are unconscious or convert functions and may reflect hidden purposes of an institution. One latent function of universities is to serve as a meeting ground for people seeking marital partners. Latent functions of institutions are sometimes unintended and may even go unrecognized.

Dysfunctions Functionalists acknowledge that not all parts of a society contribute to its stability all the time. A ***dysfunction*** refers to an element or a process of society that may actually disrupt a social system or lead to a decrease in stability.

Many dysfunctional behavior patterns, such as homicide, are widely regarded as undesirable. Yet dysfunctions should not automatically be interpreted as negative. The evaluation of a dysfunction depends on one's own values, or, as the saying goes, on "where you sit." For example, South Africa's wide-ranging system of racial segregation, known as *apartheid,* has been functional for the nation's Whites by raising them to a superior social and economic position. But it has been dysfunctional for Blacks, Asians, and people with mixed-race backgrounds—all of whom have been denied basic rights and have been relegated to second-class status.

Conflict Perspective

In contrast to functionalists' emphasis on stability and consensus, conflict sociologists see the social world in continual struggle. The ***conflict perspective*** assumes that social behavior is best understood in terms of conflict or tension among competing groups. Such conflict need not be violent; it can take the form of labor negotiations, party politics, competition among religious groups for members, or disputes over cuts in the federal budget.

As we saw earlier, Karl Marx viewed struggle between social classes as inevitable, given the exploitation of workers under capitalism. Expanding on Marx's work, sociologists and other social scientists have come to see conflict not merely as a class phenomenon but as a part of everyday life in all societies. Thus, in studying any culture, organization, or social group, sociologists want to know who benefits, who suffers, and who dominates at the expense of others. They are concerned with the conflicts between women and men, parents and children, cities and suburbs, and Whites and Blacks, to name only a few. In studying such questions, conflict theorists are interested in how society's institutions—including the family, government, religion, education, and the media—may help to maintain the privileges of some groups and keep others in a subservient position.

Although contemporary conflict theory was clearly inspired by Karl Marx's analysis, there are important differences between Marxist theories and the conflict perspective. Whereas Marx foretold of an end to conflict through the emergence of a classless communist society, current conflict theorists view conflict as unavoidable. They are less likely to anticipate, much less predict, that the social tensions arising from inequality will be entirely resolved. Moreover, while Marx viewed a total restructuring of society as fundamentally necessary to resolve social problems, contemporary conflict theorists believe that poverty, racism, sexism, inadequate housing, and other problems can be understood and attacked somewhat independently (Agger, 1989).

Like functionalists, conflict sociologists tend to use the macro-level approach. Obviously, though, there is a striking difference between these two sociological perspectives (see Box 1-2). Conflict theorists are primarily concerned with the kinds of changes that conflict can bring about, whereas

BOX 1-2 • EVERDAY BEHAVIOR

FUNCTIONALIST AND CONFLICT VIEWS OF SPORTS

We generally think of the functionalist and conflict perspectives of sociology as being applied to "serious" subjects such as the family, health care, and criminal behavior. Yet even sports can be analyzed using these theoretical approaches.

FUNCTIONALIST VIEW

In examining any aspect of society, including sports, functionalists emphasize the contribution it makes to overall social stability. Functionalists regard sports as a quasi-religious institution which uses ritual and ceremony to reinforce the common values of a society:

- Sports provide learning experiences that socialize young people into such values as competition and patriotism. Athletes became role models and are treated with awe and respect.
- Sports contribute to the adaptive needs of the social system by helping to maintain people's physical well-being.
- Sports serve as a safety valve for both participants and spectators, who are allowed to shed tension and aggressive energy in a socially acceptable way.
- Sports "bring together" members of a community or even a nation and promote an overall feeling of unity and social solidarity.

(UPI/Bettmann Newsphotos)

Functionalist theorists suggest that sports bring together members of a community or even a nation and promote an overall feeling of social solidarity. By contrast, conflict theorists assert that despite the pioneering efforts of such athletes as baseball star Jackie Robinson (shown here) and tennis champion Billie Jean King, Blacks and women continue to face discrimination in the world of sports.

CONFLICT VIEW

Conflict theorists argue that the social order is based on coercion and exploitation. They emphasize that sports reflect and even exacerbate many of the divisions of society, including those based on gender, race, ethnicity, and social class:

- Sports are a form of big business in which profits are more important than the health and safety of the workers (athletes).

- Sports perpetuate the false idea that success can be achieved simply through hard work, while failure should be blamed on the individual alone (rather than on injustices in the larger social system). Sports serve as an "opiate" which encourages people to seek a "fix" or temporary "high" rather than focus on personal problems and social issues.
- Sports maintain the subordinate role of Blacks and Hispanics, who toil as athletes but are largely barred from supervisory positions as coaches, managers, and general managers.
- Sports relegate women to a secondary role as spectators and sexual "prizes" and tend to equate masculinity with brute strength, insensitivity, and domination.

Clearly, there is more to sports than exercise or recreation. From the functionalist perspective, sports reinforce societal traditions, consensus on values, and stability. By contrast, conflict theorists view sports as merely another reflection of the political and social struggles within a society.

SOURCES: Edwards, 1973:84–130; Eitzen, 1984a, 1984b; Eitzen and Sage, 1978: 10–15; Hasbrook, 1986; Messner, 1989; Schneider and Eitzen, 1986.

functionalists look for stability and consensus. The conflict model is viewed as more "radical" and "activist" because of its emphasis on social change and redistribution of resources. On the other hand, the functionalist perspective, because of its focus on the stability of society, is generally seen as more "conservative" (Dahrendorf, 1958).

Throughout most of the 1900s, American sociology was more influenced by the functionalist perspective. However, the conflict approach has become increasingly persuasive since the late 1960s. The widespread social unrest resulting from civil rights battles, urban riots, bitter divisions over the war in Vietnam, the rise of the feminist and gay liberation movements, and the Watergate scandal offered support for the conflict perspective's view that our social world is characterized by continual struggle among competing groups. Currently, conflict theory is accepted within the discipline of sociology as one valid way to gain insight into a society.

One important contribution of conflict theory is that it has encouraged sociologists to view society through the eyes of those segments of the population that rarely influence decision making. Early Black sociologists such as W. E. B. Du Bois (1868–1963) provided research that they hoped would assist the struggle for a racially egalitarian society. Du Bois had little patience for theorists such as Herbert Spencer who seemed content with the status quo. He advocated basic research on the lives of Blacks that would separate opinion from fact. Sociology, Du Bois contended, had to draw on scientific principles to study social problems such as those experienced by Black Americans (Staples, 1976).

Similarly, feminist scholarship in sociology has helped to enhance our understanding of social behavior. A family's social standing is no longer viewed as defined solely by the husband's position and income. Feminist scholars have not only challenged stereotyping of women; they have also argued for a gender-balanced study of society in which women's experiences and contributions are as visible as those of men (Brewer, 1989; Chafetz, 1988; P. Collins, 1986; Fish, 1983).

(UPI/Bettmann Newsphotos)

Sociologist W.E.B. Du Bois (1868–1963), the first Black person to receive a doctorate from Harvard University, later helped organize the National Association for the Advancement of Colored People (NAACP).

Interactionist Perspective

The functionalist and conflict perspectives both analyze society at the macro level. These approaches attempt to explain societywide patterns of behavior. However, many contemporary sociologists are more interested in understanding society as a whole through an examination of social interactions at the micro level—small groups, two friends casually talking with one another, a family, and so forth. The *interactionist perspective* generalizes about fundamental or everyday forms of social interaction. From these generalizations, interactionists seek to explain both macro- and micro-level behavior. Interactionism is a sociological framework for viewing human beings as living in a world of meaningful objects. These "ob-

Interactionists recognize that symbols, as in these photographs, can carry very different meanings in different social contexts.

jects" may include material things, actions, other people, relationships, and even symbols (Henslin, 1972:95).

Focusing on the micro level permits interactionist researchers to better understand the larger society. For example, interactionists have studied the sometimes less-than-honest bargaining practices of automobile dealers and condominium salespeople. The researchers conclude that broad social and economic pressures on dealers and salespeople (such as the limited profit margins of car dealers) force some to employ dubious selling techniques (Farberman, 1975; Katovich and Diamond, 1986).

George Herbert Mead (1863–1931) is widely regarded as the founder of the interactionist perspective. Mead taught at the University of Chicago from 1893 until his death in 1931. Mead's sociological analysis, like that of Charles Horton Cooley, often focused on human interactions within one-to-one situations and small groups. Mead was interested in observing the most minute forms of communication—smiles, frowns, nodding of one's head—and in understanding how such individual behavior was influenced by the larger context of a group or society. However, despite his innovative views, Mead only occasionally wrote articles, and never a book. Most of his insights have been passed along to us through edited volumes of his lectures which his students published after his death.

Interactionists see symbols as an especially important part of human communication. In fact, the interactionist perspective is sometimes referred to as the *symbolic interactionist perspective.* Such researchers note that both a clenched fist and a salute have social meanings which are shared and understood by members of a society. In the United States, a salute symbolizes respect, while a clenched fist signifies defiance. However, in another culture different gestures might be used to convey a feeling of respect or defiance.

Let us examine how various societies portray suicide without the use of words. Americans point a finger at the head (shooting); urban Japanese bring a fist against the stomach (stabbing); and the South Fore of Papua, New Guinea, clench a hand at the throat (hanging). These types of symbolic interaction are classified as forms of **nonverbal communication,** which can include many other gestures, facial expressions, and postures.

Interactionists realize the importance of nonverbal communication as a form of human behavior. Indeed, in certain situations, observing nonverbal communication can be even more illuminating than listening to verbal exchanges. Social psychologists Dane Archer and Robin Akert (1977) studied how well students could determine which of two men had won a one-on-one basketball game they had just played. Some students were shown a videotape (without sound) of the men's interaction after the game; others were given a script of the postgame conversation. Neither the videotape nor the script provided explicit evidence of who won. The researchers found that subjects who saw the videotape were 60 percent more accurate in picking the winner. From an interactionist perspective, words alone are not enough to interpret human behavior; nonverbal cues are indispensable for a full understanding.

Since Mead's teachings have become well known, sociologists have expressed greater interest in the interactionist perspective. Many have moved away from what may have been an excessive preoccupation with the macro level of social behavior and have redirected their attention toward behavior which occurs in small groups. Erving Goffman (1922–1982) made a distinctive contribution by popularizing a particular type of interactionist method known as the **dramaturgical approach.** The dramaturgist compares everyday life to the setting of the theater and stage. Just as actors present certain images, all of us seek to present particular features of our personalities while we hide other qualities. Thus, in a class, we may feel the need to project a serious image; at a party, it may seem important to look like a relaxed and entertaining person. In Box 1-3, Goffman's work on public places is reviewed to see how accurately it speaks to the experiences of women.

One of the most recently developed interactionist approaches is **ethnomethodology,** which focuses on how people view, describe, and explain shared meanings underlying everyday social life and social routines. Harold Garfinkel (1967), who developed the ethnomethodological approach, had his students engage in experiments to see how breaking the unspoken rules of daily life can create confusion. For example, students were asked to address their parents as "Mr. _____" or "Mrs. _____," which so disrupted family interactions that most students had to end the experiment after only a few minutes. Garfinkel asked other students to respond to the casual question "How are you?" with detailed accounts of their physical and mental health, their remaining homework, and even their sex lives. By disturbing social routines, ethnomethodologists can reveal and observe the underlying rules of everyday life.

Ethnomethodological studies have shown that when people have no comparable previous experience to draw on in a decision-making situation, they will become extremely suggestible. For example, one recent study found that jurors are particularly likely to respond to the perceived opinions of the trial judge, rather than to the arguments offered by the opposing lawyers. Instead of trying to make a decision based on the merits of the case, jurors attempt to arrive at a verdict that they believe will meet with the judge's approval (Blanck et al., 1985; Frank, 1991; Garfinkel, 1967:104–115).

The Sociological Approach

Which perspective should a sociologist use in studying human behavior? The functionalist? The conflict? The interactionist? Sociology makes use of all three (see Table 1-2 on page 26), since each offers unique insights into the same problem. Thus, in studying the continued high levels of unemployment in the United States, the functionalist might wish to study how unemployment reduces the demand for goods but increases the need for public services, thereby leading to new jobs in the government sector. The interactionist might encourage us to focus on the impact of

BOX 1-3 • EVERYDAY BEHAVIOR

A FEMINIST VIEW OF PUBLIC PLACES

Feminist sociology is often associated with the conflict perspective because that perspective emphasizes the struggle among competing groups in a society. However, sociologist Carol Brooks Gardner (1989), a symbolic interactionist interested in gender issues, has offered a feminist critique of the influential work on the sociology of public places developed by her dissertation adviser, Erving Goffman (1963b, 1971).

In Gardner's view, the classical sociological examinations of public places present public streets, parks, and roadways as innocuous settings in which strangers either leave each other alone or interact politely. Consequently, Goffman's studies of routine interactions in public places (such as "helping" encounters when a person is lost and asks for directions) underestimate the difficulties commonly experienced by subordinate groups. In Gardner's view (1989:45): "Rarely does Goffman emphasize the habitual disproportionate fear that women can come to feel in public toward men, much less the routine trepidation that ethnic and racial minorities and the disabled can experience." For example, women are well-aware that the ostensibly innocuous helping encounter with a man in a public place can too easily lead to undesired sexual queries or advances. If a man asks for directions or for a match, a woman may have reason to fear that he has a hidden agenda that has sparked the conversation.

As part of her dissertation research, Gardner observed gender behavior in public places in Santa Fe, New Mexico, over an 18-month period; she also conducted 35 in-depth interviews with women and men from Santa Fe about their experiences in public places. In comparing her findings with those of Goffman, she places particular emphasis on the impact of street remarks on women.

Whereas Goffman suggests that street remarks occur rarely—and that they generally hold no unpleasant or threatening implications—Gardner counters (1989:49) that "for young women especially, . . . appearing in public places carries with it the constant possibility of evaluation, compliments that are not really so complimentary after all, and harsh or vulgar insults if the woman is found wanting." She adds that street remarks are occasionally followed by tweaks, pinches, or even blows, which unmask the latent hostility of many male-to-female street remarks.

Gardner acknowledges the pioneering contribution of Erving Goffman to the study of public places, calling his work "original" and "conceptually rich." But she suggests that Goffman's view of interactions in public places gives insufficient attention to the impact of gender. For Gardner, many women have a well-founded fear of the sexual harassment, assault, and rape that can occur in public places. She concludes that "public places are arenas for the enactment of inequality in everyday life for women and for many others" (Gardner, 1989:56; see also Gardner, 1990).

---

unemployment on family life, as manifested in divorce, domestic violence, and dependence on drugs and alcohol. Researchers with a conflict perspective might draw our attention to the uneven distribution of unemployment within the labor force and how it is particularly likely to affect women and racial and ethnic minorities— those groups least likely to influence decision making about economic and social policy.

No one of these approaches to the issues related to unemployment is "correct." Within this textbook, it is assumed that we can gain the broadest understanding of our society by drawing upon all three perspectives in the study of human behavior and institutions. These perspectives overlap as their interests coincide but can diverge according to the dictates of each approach and of the issue being studied.

TABLE 1-2 Comparing Major Theoretical Approaches

	FUNCTIONALIST	CONFLICT	INTERACTIONIST
VIEW OF SOCIETY	Stable, well-integrated	Characterized by tension and struggle between groups	Active in influencing and affecting everyday social interaction
LEVEL OF ANALYSIS EMPHASIZED	Macro	Macro	Micro analysis as a way of understanding the larger macro phenomena
VIEW OF SOCIAL CHANGE	Predictable, reinforcing	Permanent; may have positive consequences	Reflected in people's social positions and their communications with others
VIEW OF THE SOCIAL ORDER	Maintained through consensus and cooperation	Maintained through force and coercion	Maintained by shared understanding of everyday behavior
PROPONENTS	Émile Durkheim Talcott Parsons Robert Merton	Karl Marx W. E. B. Du Bois C. Wright Mills	George Herbert Mead Charles Horton Cooley Erving Goffman

This table shows how the three theoretical approaches can be compared along several important dimensions.

APPLIED AND CLINICAL SOCIOLOGY

As noted before in this chapter, early sociologists were quite concerned with social reform. They wanted their theories and findings to be relevant to policymakers and to people's lives in general. Today, *applied sociology* is the use of the discipline of sociology with the specific intent of yielding practical applications for human behavior and organizations.

Often, the goal of such work is to assist in resolving a social problem. For example, in the last 25 years, six American presidents have established commissions to delve into major societal concerns facing our nation. Sociologists have been called upon to apply their expertise to studying such issues as violence, pornography, crime, immigration, and population. In Europe, both academic and governmental research departments are offering increasing financial support for applied studies.

Another example of applied sociology is the growing local community research movement. One institution which has pioneered in this effort is the Center for the Study of Local Issues, a research unit of Anne Arundel Community College, located in Arnold, Maryland. The center encourages students and faculty to apply social scientific research methods in studying community issues such as employment opportunities for persons with disabilities and patterns of armed robberies. Similarly, in an effort to improve services, the Social Science Center for Community Education, Research, and Service of the University of Wisconsin–Stout has studied the effectiveness of state-funded programs designed to prevent child abuse and the attitudes of college students toward local retail stores and other community resources (Pamperin et al., 1985; see also P. Rossi, 1987).

The growing popularity of applied sociology has led to the rise of the specialty of clinical sociology. Louis Wirth (1931) wrote about clinical soci-

BOX 1-4 • CURRENT RESEARCH

CAREERS IN SOCIOLOGY

The primary source of employment for sociologists is higher education. About 75 percent of recent Ph.D. recipients in sociology sought employment in two-year community colleges, liberal arts colleges, and universities. These sociologists will teach not only majors committed to the discipline but also students hoping to become doctors, nurses, lawyers, police officers, and so forth (B. Huber, 1985).

For sociology students interested in academic careers, the road to a Ph.D. degree (or doctorate) can be long and difficult. This degree symbolizes competence in original research; each candidate must prepare a book-length study known as a *dissertation*. Typically, a graduate student in sociology will engage in 4 to 6 years of intensive work, including the time required to complete the dissertation. Yet this effort is no guarantee of a job as a sociology professor. Over the next decade, the demand for teachers is expected to decline, since there will be fewer students of college age. Consequently, anyone who launches an academic career must be prepared for considerable uncertainty and competition in the college job market (American Sociological Association, 1977:10–11; B. Huber, 1985).

Of course, not all people working as sociologists teach or hold doctoral degrees. Government is the second-largest source of employment for people in this discipline. The Census Bureau relies on people with sociological train-

Where Sociology Graduates Find Employment

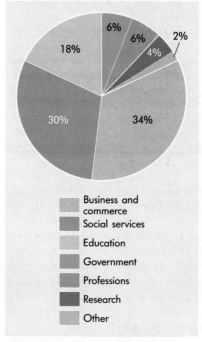

- Business and commerce
- Social services
- Education
- Government
- Professions
- Research
- Other

SOURCE: Watts and Ellis, 1989:301.

Graduates with baccalaureate degrees in sociology find employment in a number of areas, but particularly in business and commerce, social services, and education.

ing to interpret data in a way that is useful for other government agencies and the general public. Virtually every agency depends on survey research—a field in which sociology students can specialize—in order to assess everything from community needs to the morale of the agency's own workers. In addition, people with sociological training can put their

academic knowledge to effective use in probation and parole, health sciences, community development, and recreational services. Some people working in government or private industry have a master's degree (an M.A. or M.S.) in sociology; others have a bachelor's degree (a B.A. or B.S.).

The figure (left) summarizes sources of employment for those with B.A. or B.S. degrees in sociology. Like other liberal arts graduates, sociology majors can generally offer their employers essential job-related skills. Alumni find that their refinement in such areas as oral and written communication, interpersonal skills, problem solving, and critical thinking gives them an advantage over graduates who have pursued more technical degrees (Benner and Hitchcock, 1986).

Reflecting the utility of applied and clinical sociology, the figure shows that the areas of human services, business, and government offer important career opportunities for sociology graduates. Undergraduates are commonly advised to enroll in sociology courses and specialties (refer back to Table 1-1) best-suited for their career interests. For example, students hoping to become health planners would take a class in medical sociology; students seeking employment as social science research assistants would refine their skills in statistics and methods. Internships, such as

(Continues)

BOX 1-4 • CURRENT RESEARCH

CAREERS IN SOCIOLOGY (Continued)

placements at city planning agencies and survey research organizations, offer sociology undergraduates an important opportunity to prepare for careers. Studies show that students who choose an internship placement have less trouble finding jobs, obtain better jobs, and enjoy greater job satisfaction than students without internship

placements (Salem and Grabarek, 1986).

Finally, underscoring the renewed interest in applied sociology, it is clear that an increasing number of sociologists with graduate degrees are being hired by business firms, industry, hospitals, and nonprofit organizations. Indeed, studies show that many soci-

ology graduates are making career changes from social services areas to business and commerce. As an undergraduate major, sociology is excellent preparation for employment in many parts of the business world (B. Huber, 1985, 1987; Watts and Ellis, 1989; Wilkinson, 1980).

---

ology almost 60 years ago, but the term itself has become popular only in recent years. *Clinical sociology* employs a variety of techniques to facilitate change and is similar in certain respects to applied sociology. However, while applied sociology may be evaluative, clinical sociology is dedicated to altering social relationships (as in family therapy) or to restructuring social institutions (as in the reorganization of a medical center).

The Sociological Practice Association was founded in 1978 to promote the application of sociological knowledge to intervention for individual and social change. This professional group has developed a procedure for certifying clinical sociologists—much as physical therapists or psychologists are certified. As another indication of the rise of clinical sociology, as of 1989 the American Sociological Association began publishing a new journal of clinical sociology, *Sociological Practice Review.*

Applied sociologists generally leave it to others to act on their evaluations. By contrast, clinical sociologists bear direct responsibility for implementation and view those with whom they work as their clients. This specialty has become increasingly attractive to sociology graduate students because it offers an opportunity to apply intellectual learning in a practical way. Moreover, shrinking prospects for academic employment have made such alternative career routes appealing (H.

Freeman et al., 1983; H. Freeman and Rossi, 1984; B. Huber, 1985:35–38, 1987; R. Straus, 1985:18).

Applied and clinical sociology can be contrasted with *basic* (or *pure*) *sociology,* which has the objective of gaining a more profound knowledge of the fundamental aspects of social phenomena. This type of research does not necessarily hope to generate specific applications, although such ideas may result once findings are analyzed. When Durkheim studied suicide rates, he was not primarily interested in discovering a way to eliminate suicide. In this sense, his research was an example of basic rather than applied sociology.

Beginning with Chapter 3 of this textbook, which focuses on culture, each chapter will conclude with an example of sociology applied to an area of contemporary social policy. In some cases, a specific issue facing Congress will be examined; in others, there will be a more decentralized issue facing city councils or school boards. For example, government funding of day care centers will be discussed in Chapter 4, Socialization; the AIDS crisis in Chapter 5, Social Interaction and Social Structure; catastrophic health care in Chapter 12, Stratification by Age; and censorship of schoolbooks in Chapter 14, Religion. These social policy sections will demonstrate how fundamental sociological concepts can help us to understand current public policy debates.

In addition, sociology has been used to evaluate the success of programs or the impact of changes brought about by policymakers. Chapter 2, Methods of Sociological Research, will focus on a study of how the corporate response to Blacks' demands for civil rights affected top-ranking African American executives. Chapter 7, Deviance and Social Control, will consider research evaluating the impact of capital punishment on crime rates. Chapter 13, The Family, will discuss an important study of the effects of California's "no-fault" divorce law on women's and men's standards of living. These discussions, along with the social policy sections of the text, will underscore the many practical applications of sociological theory and research.

Sociologists expect the next quarter of a century to be perhaps the most exciting and critical period in the history of the discipline. This is because of a growing recognition—both in the United States and around the world—that current social problems *must* be addressed before their magnitude simply overwhelms human societies. If such predictions prove to be accurate, we can expect sociologists to play an increasing role in the government sector by researching and developing public policy alternatives. Therefore, it seems appropriate for this textbook to include a unique focus on the connection between the work of sociologists and the difficult questions confronting policymakers and the American people.

SUMMARY

Sociology is the systematic study of social behavior and human groups. In this chapter, we examine the nature of sociological theory, the founders of the discipline, theoretical perspectives of contemporary sociology, and the application of sociology to current issues of public policy.

1 An important element in the *sociological imagination* is the ability to view our own society as an outsider might, rather than from the perspective of our limited experiences and cultural biases.

2 In contrast to other *social sciences,* sociology emphasizes the influence that groups can have on people's behavior and attitudes.

3 Sociologists employ *theories* to examine the relationships between observations or between data that may seem completely unrelated.

4 In his pioneering work *Suicide,* published in 1897, Émile Durkheim focused on social factors that contributed to the rates of suicide found among various groups and nations.

5 Max Weber told his students that they should employ *Verstehen,* the German word for "understanding" or "insight," in their intellectual work. In employing *Verstehen,* sociologists consider the thoughts and feelings of those people under study.

6 Karl Marx argued that history could be understood in dialectical terms as a record of the inevitable conflict between the owners of the means of production and the masses of people who have no resources other than their labor (the proletariat).

7 *Macrosociology* concentrates on large-scale phenomena or entire civilizations, whereas *microsociology* stresses study of small groups.

8 In contrast to the emphasis on stability which characterizes the *functionalist perspective* of sociology, the *conflict perspective* assumes that social behavior is best understood in terms of conflict or tension between competing groups.

9 Within the discipline of sociology, the *interactionist perspective* is primarily concerned with fundamental or everyday forms of interaction, including symbols and other types of *nonverbal communication.*

10 *Applied sociology*—the use of the discipline with the specific intent of yielding practical applications for human behavior and organizations—can be contrasted with *basic sociology,* the objective of which is to gain a more profound knowledge of the fundamental aspects of social phenomena.

11 Sociologists expect the next quarter of a century to be perhaps the most exciting and critical period in the history of the discipline because of a growing recognition that social problems *must* be addressed in the near future.

KEY TERMS

Altruistic suicide In Durkheim's view, a suicide that results when the individual places the group's welfare above his or her own survival. (page 11)

Anomic suicide In Durkheim's view, a suicide that results from a society's lack of clear-cut rules of social behavior. (11)

Anomie Durkheim's term for the loss of direction felt in a society when social control of individual behavior has become ineffective. (13)

Applied sociology The use of the discipline of sociology with the specific intent of yielding practical applications for human behavior and organizations. (26)

Basic sociology Sociological inquiry conducted with the objective of gaining a more profound knowledge of the fundamental aspects of social phenomena. Also known as *pure sociology.* (28)

Clinical sociology The use of the discipline of sociology with the specific intent of altering social relationships and facilitating change. (28)

Conflict perspective A sociological approach which assumes that social behavior is best understood in terms of conflict or tension among competing groups. (20)

Dialectical process A series of clashes between conflicting ideas and forces. (15)

Dramaturgical approach A view of social interaction, popularized by Erving Goffman, under which people are examined as if they were theatrical performers. (24)

Dysfunction An element or a process of society that may disrupt a social system or lead to a decrease in stability. (20)

Egoistic suicide In Durkheim's view, a suicide that occurs when an individual feels little connection to the larger society and an absence of social constraints against self-destructive behavior. (11)

Ethnomethodology A sociological approach which focuses on how people view, describe, and explain shared meanings underlying everyday social life and social routines. (24)

Fatalistic suicide In Durkheim's view, a suicide that occurs when the individual feels powerless owing to intolerable amounts of regulation. (11)

Functionalist perspective A sociological approach which emphasizes the way that parts of a society are structured to maintain its stability. (19)

Ideal type A construct or model that serves as a measuring rod against which actual cases can be evaluated. (13)

Interactionist perspective A sociological approach which generalizes about fundamental or everyday forms of social interaction. (22)

Latent functions Unconscious, covert, or unintended functions; hidden purposes. (20)

Macrosociology Sociological investigation which concentrates on large-scale phenomena or entire civilizations. (17)

Manifest functions Open, stated, and conscious functions. (20)

Microsociology Sociological investigation which stresses study of small groups and often uses laboratory experimental studies. (17)

Natural science The study of the physical features of nature and the ways in which they interact and change. (8)

Nonverbal communication The sending of messages through the use of posture, facial expressions, and gestures. (24)

Science The body of knowledge obtained by methods based upon systematic observation. (7)

Social science The study of various aspects of human society. (8)

Sociological imagination An awareness of the relationship between an individual and the wider society. (6)

Sociology The systematic study of social behavior and human groups. (5)

Theory In sociology, a set of statements that seeks to explain problems, actions, or behavior. (10)

Typology A classification scheme containing two or more mutually exclusive categories (types) which is used by sociologists to better understand different forms of behavior. (11)

Verstehen The German word for "understanding" or "insight"; used by Max Weber to stress the need for sociologists to take into account people's emotions, thoughts, beliefs, and attitudes. (13)

ADDITIONAL READINGS

Berger, Peter L. *Invitation to Sociology: A Humanistic Perspective.* New York: Anchor, 1963. Berger takes a thoughtful and whimsical look at the discipline ("There are very few jokes about sociologists"). He argues that sociology has a special responsibility because it focuses so often on human ideals and passions.

Chafetz, Janet Saltzman. *Feminist Sociology: An Overview of Contemporary Theories.* Itasca, Ill.: Peacock, 1988. An overview of the major feminist theories in sociology or theories useful to sociologists that have emerged in the last 2 decades, including Marxist-feminist theories, feminist neo-Freudian theories, and everyday life approaches.

Collins, Randall. *Sociological Insight: An Introduction to Non-Obvious Sociology.* New York: Oxford University

Press, 1982. A concise book that offers striking and "nonobvious" insights regarding religion, power, crime, love, and reason.

Huber, Bettina J. *Employment Patterns in Sociology: Recent Trends and Future Prospects.* Washington, D.C.: American Sociological Association, 1985. A factual and frank appraisal of employment opportunities; available from the ASA at 1722 N St., NW, Washington, D.C. 20036.

Kohn, Melvin L. (ed.). *Cross-National Research in Sociology.* Newbury Park, Calif.: Sage, 1989. This anthology includes 17 essays which present comparative and historical sociological research.

Lee, Alfred McClung. *Sociology for Whom?* New York: Oxford University Press, 1978. Lee, a former president of the American Sociological Association, argues that sociologists are responsible and accountable to the highest scientific and ethical ideals. In his view, sociologists must not compromise these ideals in an effort to serve the interests of administrators, business leaders, publishers, or the political establishment.

Schaefer, Richard T., and Robert P. Lamm (eds.). *Introducing Sociology.* New York: McGraw-Hill, 1987. A collection of 52 thought-provoking articles illustrating the sociological imagination.

Sills, David L. (ed.). *International Encyclopedia of the Social Sciences.* New York: Macmillan, 1968. This authoritative, 17-volume encyclopedia presents articles on most topics of interest to social scientists. The authors of individual articles are often well-respected experts on particular specialties.

Smelser, Neil J. (ed.). *Handbook of Sociology.* Newbury Park, Calif.: Sage, 1988. This collection examines the state of the discipline and focuses on such areas as sociological theory, social inequality, institutions, and social change.

Straus, Roger (ed.). *Using Sociology.* Bayside, N.Y.: General Hall, 1985. Straus offers an illuminating view of clinical and applied sociology.

Journals

Journals and periodicals are an important resource for reviewing the latest sociological research. The major sociological journals that cover all areas of the discipline are the *American Journal of Sociology* (founded in 1895), *American Sociological Review* (1936), *Canadian Review of Sociology and Anthropology* (1984), *Social Forces* (1922), *Social Problems* (1951), *Society* (1963), *Sociological Quarterly* (1960), and *Sociological Review* (1908).

METHODS OF SOCIOLOGICAL RESEARCH

> *The great tragedy of science—the slaying of a beautiful hypothesis by an ugly fact.*
> Thomas H. Huxley
> *Biogenesis and Abiogenesis, 1870*

LOOKING AHEAD

- How do sociologists use the scientific method?
- How can researchers study the impact of Black demands for equal rights on corporate hiring and promotion policies?
- Why does the conclusion of a sociological study invariably point the way to new research?
- What are the practical and ethical challenges faced by sociologists who wish to conduct participant-observation research?
- How can sociologists use unobtrusive measures to study social phenomena indirectly?
- Why is it valuable for sociologists to have a code of ethics?

How do sociologists study human behavior and institutions? Is it accurate to consider sociology a science? What ethical standards guide sociologists in conducting research? As a way of beginning our examination of the principles and methods of sociological research, let us look briefly at an interesting study of the behavior of police officers.

Drawing upon the conflict perspective, which emphasizes that social institutions maintain the privileges of some groups while keeping others in a subservient position, Frances K. Heussenstamm (1971) decided to examine unequal treatment of citizens by law enforcement officers. She wondered if police would be more likely to issue traffic tickets to cars driven by political radicals. As a result, she had her students at California State College at Los Angeles affix the orange-and-black stickers of the Black Panther party to their automobiles. At the time that this research was conducted, the Panthers, a Black radical organization, had been involved in many angry (and some violent) confrontations with California police officers.

All the student drivers selected by Heussenstamm had exemplary driving records. None had received a summons for a moving violation in the previous year. As part of the experiment, students promised to carefully abide by all traffic regulations. Yet, within two hours of affixing the Black Panther stickers, a student received a traffic ticket for an "incorrect lane change." By the fourth day of the study, one student had dropped out of the project after receiving three citations. In 17 days, the 15 student drivers received 33 tickets.

Many questions may come to mind as you consider this example of sociological research. Why did Heussenstamm use bumper stickers in investigating unequal treatment by police officers? Would the college students have received a rash of tickets if they had placed bumper stickers saying "America: Love It or Leave It" on their cars? Would police officers in other localities and states have given as many (or more) citations to Heussenstamm's students?

Effective sociological research can be quite thought-provoking. It may interest us in many new questions about social interactions that require further study. On the other hand, effective research is not always dramatic. In some cases, rather than raising additional questions, a study will confirm previous beliefs and findings.

This chapter, building on what was considered in Chapter 1, will examine sociology as a social science. The basic principles and stages of the scientific method will be described. A number of techniques commonly used in sociological research, such as experiments, participant observations, and surveys, will be presented. Particular attention will be given to the practical and ethical challenges that sociologists face in studying human behavior and to the debate raised by Max Weber's call for "value neutrality" in social science research.

These themes form the core of Chapter 2, and they will also be reflected throughout this textbook. Whatever the area of sociological inquiry—whether culture or organizational behavior, the economy or education—and whatever the perspective of the sociologist—whether functionalist, conflict, interactionist, or any other—there is one crucial requirement. Within the discipline of sociology, all branches of specialization and all theoretical approaches depend on imaginative, responsible research which meets the highest scientific and ethical standards.

Frances K. Heussenstamm had college students place stickers for a Black radical organization on their cars. The drivers, all of whom had exemplary records, quickly accumulated many traffic tickets.

(©1971 by Transaction, Inc.)

WHAT IS THE SCIENTIFIC METHOD?

Like the typical woman or man on the street, the sociologist is interested in the central questions of our time. Is the family falling apart? Why is there so much crime in the United States? How do Americans feel about the increasing federal deficit? Such issues concern most people, whether or not they have academic training. However, unlike the typical citizen, the sociologist has a commitment to the use of the scientific method in studying society. The *scientific method* is a systematic, organized series of steps that ensures maximum objectivity and consistency in researching a problem.

Many of us will never actually conduct scientific research. Nonetheless, it is important that we understand the scientific method, for it plays a major role in the workings of our society. Americans are constantly being bombarded with "facts" or "data." A television news report informs us that

"one in every two American marriages now ends in divorce," yet Chapter 13 will show that this assertion is based on misleading statistics. Almost daily, advertisers cite supposedly scientific studies to prove that their products are superior. Such claims may be accurate or exaggerated. We can make better evaluations of such information—and will not be fooled so easily—if we are familiar with the standards of scientific research. As this chapter will indicate, the scientific method is quite stringent and demands that researchers adhere as strictly as possible to its basic principles.

A key element in the scientific method is planning. When sociologists wish to learn more about human behavior, they do not simply walk out the door or pick up the telephone, and begin asking questions. The scientific method demands precise preparation in developing useful research. If investigators are not careful, research data that they collect may prove to be unacceptable for purposes of sociological study.

BOX 2-1 • CURRENT RESEARCH

USEFUL STATISTICS

I n their effort to better understand social behavior, sociologists rely heavily on numbers and statistics. How large is the typical household today compared with the typical household of 1970? If a community were to introduce drug education into its elementary schools, what would be the cost per pupil? What proportion of Baptists compared with Roman Catholics contribute to their local churches? Such questions, and many others, are most easily answered in numerical terms that summarize the actions or attitudes of many persons.

The most common summary measures used by sociologists are percentages, means, modes, and medians. A **percentage** shows the portion of 100. Use of percentages allows us to compare groups of different sizes. For example, if we were comparing contributors to a town's Baptist and Roman Catholic churches, the absolute numbers of contributors from each group could be misleading if there were many more Baptists than Catholics living in the town. However, through use of percentages, we could obtain a more meaningful comparison, showing the proportion of persons in each group who contribute to churches.

The **mean,** or *average*, is a number calculated by adding a series of values and then dividing by the number of values. For example, to find the mean of the numbers 5, 19, and 27, we add them together (for a total of 51), divide by the number of values (3), and discover that the mean is 17.

The **mode** is the single most common value in a series of scores. Suppose we were looking at the following scores on a 10-point quiz:

10	7
10	7
9	7
9	6
8	5
8	

The mode—the most frequent score on the quiz—is 7. While the mode is easier to identify than other summary measures, it tells sociologists little about all the other values. Hence, you will find much less use of mode in this book than of mean and median.

The **median** is the midpoint or number which divides a series of values into two groups of equal numbers of values. For the quiz discussed above, the median, or central value, is 8. The mean, or average, would be 86 (the sum of all scores) divided by 11 (the total number of scores), or 7.8.

In the United States, the median family income for the year 1989 was $34,213; this indicates that half of all households had incomes above $34,213 while half had lower incomes (Bureau of the Census, 1990b:15). In many respects, the median is the most characteristic value. While it may not reflect the full range of scores, it does approximate the typical value in a set of scores and is not affected by extreme scores.

Some of these statistics may seem confusing at first. But think how difficult it is to study an endless list of numbers to identify a pattern or central tendency. Percentages, means, modes, and medians are essential time-savers in sociological research and analysis.

There are five basic steps in the scientific method that sociologists and other researchers follow. These are (1) defining the problem, (2) reviewing the literature, (3) formulating the hypothesis, (4) selecting the research design and then collecting and analyzing data, and (5) developing the conclusion. An actual example will illustrate the workings of the scientific method.

By 1985, one-fourth of Black families earned more than the median income of Whites (see Box 2-1 for an explanation of the concept of *median income*). At least 25 percent of African Americans are now members of the middle class (Schaefer, 1990:259). Yet has the relative success of certain Blacks included entry into and acceptance among the nation's corporate elite? How might sociologists use the scientific method to study Blacks' status as corporate executives? How might they move from a broad question (Have Black executives been accepted within corporate America?) to a researchable problem?

A sociologist's approach to a research problem is often influenced by his or her theoretical orientation. Thus, functionalists would view Blacks in management positions as a reflection of business firms' need to attract Black customers or clients to maintain stability and prosperity. Conflict theorists would raise the issue of tokenism, questioning whether a small number of African Americans were being placed in highly visible positions to provide the *appearance* of change—while the rest of corporate management remained White. Interactionists would focus on the nature of social relations between the few Black executives and their many White counterparts.

Defining the Problem

The first step in any sociological research project is to state as clearly as possible what you hope to investigate. Drawing on the conflict perspective, sociologist Sharon Collins (1983) had initially relied on census data to study the employment patterns of more affluent Blacks. Collins then wondered: "Did the progress of these individuals represent a genuine restructuring of society that allowed for the entry of Blacks into top executive positions in White-owned corporations?" Or, instead, was it a token response to civil rights pressures? Were African American executives being placed primarily in highly visible personnel and public relations posts that had little likelihood of leading to key policymaking positions in the corporate world?

Early in their research, sociologists face the task of developing an operational definition of each concept being studied. An *operational definition* is an explanation of an abstract concept that is specific enough to allow a researcher to measure the concept. For example, a sociologist interested in status might use membership in exclusive social clubs or professional organizations as an operational definition of high status. A sociologist who intended to examine prejudice might rely on responses to a series of questions concerning willingness to hire or work alongside members of racial and ethnic minority groups.

(Catherine Ursillo/Photo Researchers)

Drawing on the conflict perspective, sociologist Sharon Collins wondered if Black executives were being placed primarily in highly visible personnel and public relations posts that had little likelihood of leading to key policymaking positions in the corporate world.

Whenever researchers wish to study an abstract concept—such as intelligence, sexuality, prejudice, love, or liberalism—they must develop workable and valid operational definitions. Even when studying a particular group of people, it is necessary to decide how the group will be distinguished. Thus, in her study of Blacks in corporate management positions, Sharon Collins (1989:318) needed to develop an operational definition of "top executives." She classified private-sector positions as being "high-level" if a person's major job responsibilities involved planning or implementation of company policy decisions. Collins operationalized this conception by examining job titles; subjects were considered "top executives" if they held titles such as president, chief executive officer, director, vice president, and department manager.

Reviewing the Literature

By conducting a review of the literature—the relevant scholarly studies and information—researchers refine the problem under study, clarify possible techniques to be used in collecting data, and eliminate or reduce the number of avoidable mistakes they make. Thus, in addition to drawing on her earlier research, which relied on census data, Sharon Collins reviewed descriptive studies of college-educated African Americans and gave special attention to studies of African American business executives and professionals. Until rather recently, most Blacks who have achieved great success have done so in professions such as law and medicine or in the government sector. The corporate world has not been so open to Black executives, a fact that underscores the importance of studies such as Collins's.

Formulating the Hypothesis

After reviewing earlier research concerning Black executives and drawing upon the contributions of sociological theorists, the researcher may develop an intuitive guess about the relationship between Black demands for equal rights and corporate hiring and promotion policies. Such a speculative statement about the relationship between two or more factors is called a *hypothesis.*

A hypothesis essentially tells us what we are looking for in our research. In order to be meaningful, a hypothesis must be testable; that is, it must be capable of being evaluated. The statement "God exists" may or may not be true; it clearly cannot be scientifically confirmed. A research hypothesis must also be reasonably specific. "Young people have more fun" and "Florida is nicer than California" are statements that lack the kind of precision that sociologists need in order to collect suitable data.

As part of a study of African Americans in executive positions, one hypothesis might be: "In response to Black demands for equal rights, corporate hiring and promotion policies placed Black executives primarily in highly visible personnel and public relations posts." In formulating a hypothesis, we do not imply that it is correct. We merely suggest that it is worthy of study, that the hypothesis should be scientifically tested and confirmed, refuted, or revised, depending on the outcome of the study (G. Bogue, 1981:11).

A hypothesis usually states how one aspect of human behavior influences or affects another. These aspects or factors are called *variables.* A *variable* is a measurable trait or characteristic that is subject to change under different conditions. Income, religion, occupation, and gender can all be variables in a study. In the hypothesis presented above, there are two variables: "Black demands for equal rights" and "corporate hiring and promotion policies."

In developing hypotheses, sociologists attempt to explain or account for the relationship between two or more variables. If one variable is hypothesized to cause or influence another one, social scientists call the first variable the *independent variable.* The second is termed the *dependent variable* because it is believed to be influenced by the independent variable. In her study of Black executives, Collins was interested in the effect that a particular variable (Black demands for equal rights) might have on corporate hiring and promotion policies. As the causal or influencing characteristic, Black demands for equal rights is the independent variable. The variable that Collins was trying to explain, corporate hiring and promotion policies, is the dependent variable.

According to the hypothesis, Black demands for equal rights have a direct influence on corporate hiring and promotion policies. As shown in Figure 2-1, *causal logic* involves the relationship between a condition or variable and a particular consequence, with one event leading to the other. Under causal logic, the display of Black Panther bumper stickers on one's car may be directly related to or produce a greater likelihood of receiving a traffic ticket. Similarly, the time students spend reviewing material for a quiz may be directly related to or produce a greater likelihood of getting a high score on the quiz.

A *correlation* exists when a change in one variable coincides with a change in the other. Correlations are an indication that causality *may* be present; they do not necessarily indicate causation. For example, data indicate that working mothers are more likely to have delinquent children than are mothers who do not work outside the home. This correlation is actually caused by a third variable: family income. Lower-class households are more likely to have a full-time working mother; at the same time, delinquency rates are higher in this class than in other economic levels. Consequently, while having a mother who works out-

FIGURE 2-1 Causal Logic

Independent variable x	→	Dependent variable y
Black demands for equal rights	→	Corporate hiring and employment policies
Degree of integration into society	→	Likelihood of suicide
Display of Black Panther bumper stickers	→	Likelihood of receiving traffic tickets from police
Parents' church attendance	→	Children's church attendance
Time spend preparing for quiz	→	Performance on quiz
Parents' income	→	Likelihood of children's enrolling in college

An independent variable is hypothesized to cause or influence another variable (a dependent variable). Causal logic involves the effect of an independent variable (often designated by the symbol x) on a dependent variable (generally designated as y) where x leads to y. For example, parents who attend church regularly (x) are more likely to have children who are regular churchgoers (y). Notice that the first three pairs of variables are taken from studies already described in this textbook.

side the home is correlated with delinquency, it does not *cause* delinquency. Sociologists seek to identify the causal link between variables; this causal link is generally advanced by researchers in their hypotheses.

Collecting and Analyzing Data

In order to test a hypothesis and determine if it is supported or refuted, researchers need to collect information. To do so, they must employ one of the research designs described later in the chapter. The research design guides them in collecting and analyzing data.

Selecting the Sample In most studies, social scientists must carefully select what is known as a *sample*. A ***representative sample*** is a selection from a larger population that is statistically found to be typical of that population. There are many kinds of samples, of which the random sample is frequently used by social scientists. For a ***random sample***, every member of an entire population being studied has the same chance of being selected.

By using specialized sampling techniques, sociologists do not need to question everyone in a population. Thus, if researchers wanted to examine the opinions of persons listed in a city directory (a book that, unlike the telephone directory, lists all households), they might call every tenth or

fiftieth or hundredth name listed. This would constitute a random sample.

If Sharon Collins had decided to conduct a survey of Blacks serving as top executives in corporations across the United States, she would have faced the problem of how to develop an appropriate sample of Black executives. Such a sample would have been essential, since the difficulty of questioning *all* Black executives would have been prohibitive. However, Collins chose instead to focus on a smaller target population: African Americans serving as top executives in White-owned corporations in the Chicago area. Still, she had to find a way of identifying her subjects, for there was no readily available list of Black executives in the region.

Collins (1989:318–319) studied corporate listings and identified 52 of the largest firms in Chicago. She then asked people familiar with the city's corporate community to name African American executives in these firms. Collins spoke to informants in these companies to see which Black managers served as top executives, and also asked participants in her study to refer her to other important Black managers. She found that almost one-third of the 52 firms lacked even one Black employee who met her operational definition of "top executive." Nevertheless, Collins identified 87 Blacks who qualified as top executives. Between May 1986 and January 1987 she was able to interview 76 of these men and women.

Generally, researchers are unable to interview as high a proportion of a target population as Collins did.

Creating Scales and Indices It is relatively simple to measure certain characteristics statistically, such as level of education, income, and size of a community. However, it is far more difficult to measure attitudes and beliefs such as patriotism, respect, and tolerance. Sociologists create scales in order to assess aspects of social behavior that require judgments or subjective evaluations. The *scale* and *index* are indicators of attitudes, behavior, and characteristics of people or organizations.

A scale or index typically uses a series of questions to measure attitudes, knowledge of facts, events, objects, or behavior. For example, sociologists might want to learn not only whether respondents favor a constitutional amendment allowing prayer in public schools but also how knowledgeable they are about different alternatives such as a "silent time" for prayer or a daily ecumenical statement read by a teacher. In this type of situation, sociologists can develop a scale to measure citizens' awareness of the debate over school prayer. Throughout this textbook, we will consider how social scientists have developed scales to measure even such elusive concepts as love (see Chapter 13).

Ensuring Validity and Reliability The scientific method requires that research results be both valid and reliable. *Validity* refers to the degree to which a measure or scale truly reflects the phenomenon under study. A valid measure of workers' productivity would accurately indicate how much they had produced over a specified period of time. Similarly, in the study of Black executives, Collins used generally accepted business standards to identify major corporations.

Reliability refers to the extent to which a measure provides consistent results. A reliable measure of workers' productivity would lead to the same results even when used by different researchers. The Chicago study provides detailed information concerning the research methods that Collins used, thereby allowing other social scientists to test the conclusions in other locales.

Developing the Conclusion

Scientific studies, including those conducted by sociologists, do not aim to answer all the questions that can be raised about a particular subject. Therefore, the conclusion of a research study represents both an end and a beginning. It terminates a specific phase of the investigation, but it should also generate ideas for future study (see Figure 2-2). This is true of the research on Black executives conducted by Sharon Collins, which raised important questions both about job segregation in corporations and about the way in which certain employment gains by Blacks might lessen the pressure for further initiatives to assist minorities.

FIGURE 2-2 The Scientific Method

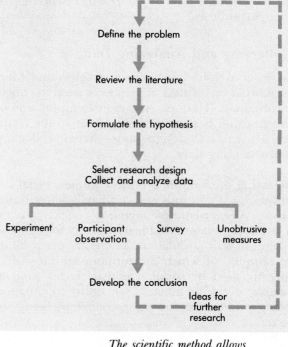

The scientific method allows sociologists to objectively and logically evaluate the facts collected. This can lead to further ideas for sociological research.

Confirming Hypotheses Sociological studies do not always generate data that confirm the original hypothesis. In many instances, a hypothesis is refuted, and researchers must reformulate their conclusions. Unexpected results may also lead sociologists to reexamine their methodology and make changes in the research design. In the study discussed above, however, the data confirmed the hypothesis: in response to Black demands for equal rights, corporate hiring and promotion policies in the Chicago area had indeed placed Black executives primarily in highly visible personnel and public relations posts.

Collins found that 66 percent of the African American executives she interviewed had been tracked into corporate jobs focusing on the handling of "Black problems" or on dealings with a specifically Black consumer market. The vast majority of these executives held jobs involved with affirmative action and urban affairs. In discussing the limitations on Black managers, one executive, who had a master's degree and 4 years of experience in engineering when he was shifted to an affirmative action post, observed:

> When they would send me to some of those conferences about affirmative action . . . you'd walk in and there would be a room full of blacks. . . . It was a terrible misuse at that time of some black talent . . . (Collins, 1989:329).

Controlling for Other Factors The characteristics of Black executives are considered additional variables used in the study, and they are known as *control variables.* A **control variable** is a factor held constant to test the relative impact of the independent variable. Earlier, we noted that family income has an important influence on the relationship between mothers working outside the home and the likelihood that their children will come to be viewed as delinquents. If researchers had not introduced the control variable of "family income," they might have reached a misleading conclusion concerning the effects of mothers' working outside the home.

By use of a control variable, the "time at which Black executives entered the labor force," Collins found support for the view that corporate hiring

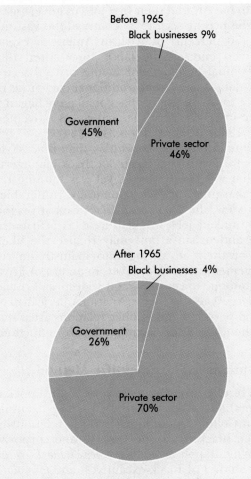

FIGURE 2-3   Initial Employment of Black Executives

SOURCE: Based on S. Collins, 1989:320.

Before 1965, Black executives in the Chicago area were about equally likely to have found their first jobs in government or in the private sector. However, executives who entered the labor force after 1965 overwhelmingly began their careers in the corporate world.

and promotion policies were significantly influenced by Blacks' demands for equal rights. As Figure 2-3 illustrates, respondents who entered the labor force before 1965 (the high point of the Black civil rights movement) were about equally likely to have found their first jobs in government or in the private sector. By contrast, the vast majority (70 percent) of African American executives who entered the labor force after 1965 found initial employment in the private sector. These data suggest that traditional corporate resistance to the hiring of Black managers began to decline in response to the civil rights movement of the 1960s (Collins, 1989:319–324).

Collins (1989:317) concludes that Blacks' demands for civil rights created a Black managerial elite that was highly visible, yet was "administratively marginal" and "economically vulnerable." In her view, the tracking of Black executives into racially linked jobs in such areas as affirmative action and urban affairs may reduce the likelihood of their advancing into mainstream top management posts. Moreover, in an era of growing economic uncertainty and widespread corporate mergers and takeovers, African American managers in personnel and public relations areas may find themselves the victims of staff reductions.

In Summary: The Scientific Method

Let us briefly summarize the process of the scientific method through a review of the example. Sharon Collins *defined a problem* (the relationship between Black civil rights protests and corporate employment policies). She *reviewed the literature* (other studies of Black executives) and *formulated a hypothesis* ("In response to Black demands for equal rights, corporate hiring and promotion policies placed Black executives primarily in highly visible personnel and public relations posts"). Collins identified a target population of Black executives in Chicago firms and then *collected and analyzed the data*. Finally, she *developed the conclusion:* Black activism did influence corporate decision making and lead to the creation of a highly visible (and yet economically vulnerable) Black managerial elite. Thus, through the systematic, organized application of the scientific method, this researcher studied a contemporary social issue and generated meaningful findings of interest to sociologists, civil rights leaders, business executives, and government policymakers.

RESEARCH DESIGNS FOR COLLECTING DATA

An important aspect of sociological research is deciding how data should be collected. A **research design** is a detailed plan or method for obtaining data scientifically. Selection of a research design is a critical step for sociologists and requires creativity and ingenuity. This choice will directly influence both the cost of the project and the amount of time needed to collect the results of the research.

Sociologists regularly use experiments, participant observations, surveys, and unobtrusive techniques to generate data for their research. In her study of Black executives, Sharon Collins relied on interviews, which are a common form of survey research.

Experiments

When sociologists want to study a possible cause-and-effect relationship, they may conduct experiments. An **experiment** is an artificially created situation which allows the researcher to manipulate variables and introduce control variables.

In the classic method of conducting an experiment, two groups of people are selected and compared for similar characteristics such as age or education. The subjects are then assigned by researchers to one of two groups—the experimental or control group. The **experimental group** is exposed to an independent variable; the **control group** is not. Thus, if scientists were testing a new type of antibiotic drug, they would administer injections of that drug to an experimental group but not to a control group.

In response to rising concern about how to deal with the increased incidence of family violence, sociologists Lawrence Sherman and Richard Berk (1984) developed an experiment with the Minneapolis police department to evaluate the desirability of three different responses by the police. Officers called to the scene of a misdemeanor domestic assault were randomly instructed to take one of the following actions: (1) arrest the alleged offender, (2) make the alleged offender leave the residence, thereby separating him or her from the person who had been attacked or threatened, or

(3) offer some form of advice, counseling, or mediation. The researchers took a number of precautions and verified that the police actually handled cases in a way called for by their experimental design. This sociological experiment did not have a control group, since the purpose was to determine which of the three alternative procedures would be most effective in deterring future domestic violence.

Sherman and Berk used two methods to establish which of the three responses by the police was most effective. They checked police records for 6 months to see if a suspect's name appeared again in a case of domestic violence and also interviewed the original victims by telephone over a 6-month period to learn if there had been a repeat incident involving the same alleged offender.

The clearest finding of this experimental study was that suspects who were arrested in domestic violence cases were less likely to be involved in such violence at a later date than suspects who were merely separated from the residence or offered counseling and mediation. Suspects who had been arrested and temporarily jailed (usually for less than a week) were less likely to appear on police records over the next 6 months; when interviewed, the victims of their original violence reported a lower incidence of repeat offenses. Overall, jailing of a suspect was associated with half as many follow-up cases of domestic violence as the other types of response were. Although there is need for further study of this subject, the use of an experiment led to dramatic results with practical applications.

Clearly, it is impossible for sociologists to observe the behavior of *all* police officers handling cases of domestic violence. Yet such experiments can still be valuable, because they place "commonsense" generalizations in a more proper context. Conducting sociological research is more difficult, and therefore more costly, in the field than in a laboratory setting (often on a college campus). Consequently, researchers sometimes must rely on samples composed entirely of college students. Such participants may or may not be representative of the larger American public. There is an additional problem in using a laboratory setting: the responses of subjects in such settings may be different from their responses in less-structured, real-life situations.

Participant Observation

Participant observation is a research technique in which an investigator collects information through direct participation in and observation of a group, tribe, or community under study. This method allows sociologists to examine certain behaviors and communities that could not be investigated through other research techniques. In some cases, the sociologist actually "joins" a group for a period of time to get an accurate sense of how it operates.

During the late 1930s, in a classic example of participant observation, William F. Whyte moved into a low-income Italian neighborhood in Boston. For nearly 4 years, he was a member of the social circle of "corner boys" that he describes in *Street Corner Society*. Whyte revealed his identity to these men and joined in their conversations, bowling, and other leisure-time activities. His goal was to gain greater insight into the community that these men had established. As Whyte (1981:303) listened to Doc, the leader of the group, he "learned the answers to questions I would not even have had the sense to ask if I had been getting my information solely on an interviewing basis." Whyte's work was especially valuable, since, at the time, the academic world had little direct knowledge of the poor and tended to rely for information on the records of social service agencies, hospitals, and courts.

The initial challenge that Whyte faced—and that each participant observer must encounter—was to gain acceptance into an unfamiliar group. It is no simple matter for a college-trained sociologist to win the trust of a religious cult, a youth gang, a poor Appalachian community, or a circle of skid row residents. It requires a great deal of patience and an accepting, nonthreatening type of person. Interestingly, the gender of the participant observer can be a factor in the success of a research project. Sociologist Terry Mizrahi (1986:185) notes that female sociologists studying predominantly male environments can find it difficult to develop the cooperation and trust necessary for effective observation. In her view, more

BOX 2-2 • EVERYDAY BEHAVIOR

HOSPITAL TREATMENT OF "DYING" PATIENTS

David Sudnow spent 9 months in participant-observation research at County Hospital, a large urban facility. In the following selections, Sudnow (1967:101, 104) recalls how patients with the same medical condition received different treatment:

Two persons in "similar" physical condition may be differentially designated dead or not. For example, a young child was brought into the ER [emergency room] with no registering heart beat, respirations, or pulse—the standard "signs of death"—and was, through a rather dramatic stimulation procedure involving the coordinated work of a large team of doctors and nurses, revived for a period of eleven hours. On the same evening, shortly after the child's arrival, an elderly person who presented the same physical signs . . . "arrived" in the ER and was almost immediately pronounced dead, with no attempts at stimulation instituted.

A nurse remarked, later in the evening: "They (the doctors) would never have done that to the old lady (i.e., attempt heart stimulation) even though I've seen it work on them too." During the period when emergency resuscitation equipment was being readied for the child, an intern instituted mouth-to-mouth resuscitation. This same intern was shortly relieved by oxygen machinery, and when the woman "arrived," he was the one that pronounced her dead. He reported shortly afterwards that he could never bring himself to put his mouth to "an old lady's like that."

A few important conclusions can be drawn from Sudnow's research:

1 We must remember that this is an example of an *institution* in operation. It is not so much a matter of one intern's behaving irresponsibly as it is the functioning of a group process which may encourage others to act similarly.

2 Even if we find the intern's behavior distressing, we cannot forget that such behavior *is* part of our society and therefore deserves serious study. Sudnow *observed* hospital practices; this does not mean that he *condoned* these practices.

3 Sudnow's findings underscore the value of effective participant-observation research. If he had visited the hospital once or twice to conduct interviews, he might never have learned about the double standard concerning resuscitation. Since he was at the hospital for 9 months, the nurse and intern became more comfortable with him and ultimately disclosed some revealing information.

attention must be given to the impact of gender on the data-gathering process itself.

Participant observers immediately face another question which has both practical and ethical implications: to whom (if anyone) should they reveal the ultimate purpose of their observations? In our society, many people resent the feeling of being "studied." Thus, if a group *sees* the researcher as an "outsider" and an observer—rather than as a member of the group—its members may feel uneasy and hide many thoughts and emotions. On the other hand, if the researcher disguises his or her identity or purpose, then the group has added a participant (and observer) who is being somewhat dishonest. This may well distort the group process. Moreover, it is not easy to maintain this type of masquerade for weeks or months while attempting to get to know strangers.

Participant observation is, in addition, a most time-consuming method of research. Systematic and thorough observations are essential; the sociologist cannot simply "drop by" the bowling alley or street corner every few weeks. Instead, the researcher may have to wait patiently for a particularly noteworthy or dramatic event. And in some instances, the deeper meanings of a seemingly trivial interaction may become clear to the observer only after months of study. Finally, for this method to be effective, the sociologist must keep detailed records of events and behaviors, even when "nothing" seems to be happening.

Observation research poses other complex challenges for the investigator. Sociologists must be able to fully understand what they are observing. In a sense, then, researchers such as William F. Whyte or David Sudnow (see Box 2-2) must learn to see the world as the group sees it in order to fully comprehend the events taking place around them. This raises a delicate question regarding the effect of the group on the observer—and the observer on the group. The sociologist must retain a certain level of detachment from the group under study, even as he or she tries to understand how members feel. If the research is to be successful, the observer cannot allow the close associations or even friendships that inevitably develop to influence the conclusions of the study. Anson Shupe and David Bromley (1980), two sociologists who have used participant observation, have likened this challenge to that of "walking a tightrope." Despite working so hard to gain acceptance from the group being studied, the participant observer *must* maintain some degree of detachment.

In using participant-observation studies, sociologists are well-aware that the presence of such an observer may affect the behavior of the people being studied. The recognition of this phenomenon grew out of research conducted during the 1920s and 1930s at the Hawthorne plant of the Western Electric Company. A group of researchers headed by Elton Mayo set out to determine how the productivity of workers at this plant could be improved. Investigators examined the impact of variations in the intensity of light and variations in working hours on productivity. To their surprise, they found that *all* steps they took seemed to increase productivity. Even measures that seemed likely to have the opposite effect, such as reducing the amount of lighting in the plant, led to higher productivity.

Why did the plant's employees work harder even under less favorable conditions? Their behavior apparently was influenced by the greater attention being paid to workers in the course of the research. Since that time, sociologists have used the term **Hawthorne effect** when subjects of research perform in a manner different from their typical behavior because they realize that they are under observation.

In addition to its use in basic research, participant observation may also be used to improve the policies and structures of organizations. William F. Whyte (1989), the researcher in the study of Boston corner boys described above, endorses the use of participant observation as a type of applied

(Courtesy of AT&T)

In using participant-observation studies, sociologists are well aware that the presence of an observer may affect the behavior of the people being studied. Recognition of this phenomenon grew out of research conducted during the 1920s and 1930s at the Hawthorne plant of the Western Electric Company.

sociology. Whyte notes that when Norway's shipping industry was faced with severe cutbacks, a team of researchers worked aboard a merchant ship as part of an effort to improve the social organization and efficiency of Norway's fleet. Similarly, when faced with growing competition in the photocopying industry, Xerox Corporation employed a research team to propose cost cutting measures to managers and union leaders. In each case, the methodology of participant observation proved useful in solving practical problems.

Surveys

Almost all of us have responded to surveys of one kind or another. We may have been asked what kind of detergent we use, which presidential candidate we intend to vote for, or what our favorite television program is. A *survey* is a study, generally in the form of an interview or questionnaire, which provides sociologists with information concerning how people think and act. Among our nation's best-known surveys of opinion are the Gallup poll and the Harris poll. As anyone who watches the news during presidential campaigns knows, these polls have become an important part of political life.

When you think of surveys, you may remember many "person on the street" interviews on local television news shows. While such interviews can be highly entertaining, they are not necessarily an accurate indication of public opinion. First, they reflect the opinions of only those people who appear at a certain location. Thus, such samples can be biased in favor of commuters, middle-class shoppers, or factory workers, depending on which street or area the newspeople select. Second, television interviews tend to attract outgoing people who are willing to appear on the air, while they frighten away others who may feel intimidated by a camera. A survey must be based on precise, representative sampling if it is to genuinely reflect a broad range of the population.

In preparing to conduct a survey, sociologists must exercise great care in the wording of questions (see Table 2-1). An effective survey question must be simple and clear enough for people to understand it. It must also be specific enough so that there are no problems in interpreting the results. Even questions that are less structured (What do you think of programming on educational television?) must be carefully phrased in order to solicit the type of information desired. Surveys can be indispensable sources of information, but only if the sampling is done properly and the questions are worded accurately (Ferber et al., 1980).

There are two main forms of surveys: the *interview* and the *questionnaire.* Each of these forms of survey research has its own advantages. An interviewer can obtain a high response rate because people find it more difficult to turn down a personal request for an interview than to throw away a written questionnaire. In addition, a skillful in-

Doonesbury

BY GARRY TRUDEAU

TABLE 2-1 Asking the Correct Question

POOR QUESTION	PROBLEM	BETTER QUESTION
Do you favor urban homesteading?	People may not understand the question.	Do you favor a government program which encourages families to improve inner-city housing?
Did your mother ever work?	Misleading	Did your mother ever work for pay outside the home?
Should it be possible for a woman to obtain a legal abortion?	Too general	Should it be possible for a woman to obtain a legal abortion if there is a strong chance of serious defect in her baby? If she became pregnant as a result of rape?
Do you favor making it legal for 18-year-olds to drink liquor and smoke marijuana?	Double-barreled (two questions in one)	Do you favor making it legal for 18-year-olds to drink liquor? Do you favor making it legal for 18-year-olds to smoke marijuana?
Don't you think that the press is biased and that we should distrust whatever it says?	Biased question; leads people toward a particular response	Would you say that you have a great deal of confidence, some confidence, or very little confidence in the press?

Sociologists try to phrase questions carefully so that there will be no misunderstanding on the part of the respondents. If a question is improperly worded (or biased), the results are useless for the researchers.

terviewer can go beyond written questions and "probe" for a subject's underlying feelings and reasons. On the other hand, questionnaires have the advantage of being cheaper, especially when large samples are used. Also, since the questions are written, the researcher knows that there is some guarantee of consistency, whereas five interviewers can ask the same question in five different ways.

As was discussed with regard to participant observation, the gender (or race) of the researcher can have an impact on survey data. In 1990, the Eagleton Institute of Politics at Rutgers University confirmed that women were more likely to take strong "pro-choice" positions when questioned by a woman about the issue of abortion. For example, 84 percent of women interviewed by another woman agreed that the decision to

have an abortion is a private matter that should be left to the woman to decide without government intervention. By contrast, only 64 percent of women interviewed by a man took the same position. Men's responses seemed unaffected by the gender of the researcher. Similarly, people's responses to questions about housing discrimination may be influenced by the racial and ethnic background of the interviewer. The findings of the Eagleton Institute study underscore the careful attention that sociologists must give to all elements of the research design (Morin, 1990).

Unobtrusive Measures

Social scientists from the University of Arizona studied people's spending and eating habits by examining household garbage left out on the street (Rathje, 1974; Zorn, 1988). Sociologists Joan Luxenburg and Lloyd Klein (1984) monitored citizens' band radio broadcasts near a truck stop in Oklahoma to learn about a relatively new form of soliciting for prostitution. These are two unconventional examples of the use of unobtrusive measures in social scientific research.

Unobtrusive measures include a variety of research techniques that have no impact on who or what is being studied. These are designed as *nonreactive*, since people's behavior is not influenced. As an example, Émile Durkheim's statistical analysis of suicide neither increased nor decreased human self-destruction. Whereas subjects of an experiment are often aware that they are being watched—an awareness that can influence their behavior—this is not the case when unobtrusive measures are used. Consequently, sociologists can avoid the Hawthorne effect by employing unobtrusive methods (Van Maanen, 1982; Webb et al., 1981; see also B. Berg, 1989).

One basic technique of unobtrusive measurement is the use of statistics, as in Durkheim's work. Crime statistics, census data, budgets of public agencies, and other archival data are all readily available to sociologists and other social scientists. Much of this information can be obtained at relatively low cost. For example, political scientist Gary Orfield (1987) was able to obtain computer tapes of enrollments by race for 36,000 schools from the U.S. Department of Education; these tapes helped him to conduct a major study of segregation of public schools in the 1980s.

There is one inherent problem, however, in relying on data collected by someone else: the researcher may not find exactly what is needed. Social scientists studying family violence can use statistics from police and social service agencies on *reported* cases of spouse abuse and child abuse. Yet such government bodies have no precise data on *all* cases of abuse.

Many social scientists find it useful to study cultural, economic, and political documents, includ-

(Wm. Roger Morgan)

Sociologist Carol Auster did a content analysis of Girl Scout handbooks from 1913 to 1984. She found dramatic changes over time in the organization's view of proper roles and career aspirations for women. For example, a "laundress" merit badge from 1917 had given way to an aerospace badge by 1980.

ing newspapers, periodicals, radio and television tapes, scripts, diaries, songs, folklore, and legal papers, to name a few examples. In examining these sources, researchers employ a technique known as **content analysis,** which is the systematic coding and objective recording of data, guided by some rationale.

Suppose you were interested in studying the treatment of women in American society. In pursuing this topic, sociologist Carol Auster (1985) did a content analysis of Girl Scout handbooks from 1913 to 1984. She found dramatic changes over time in the organization's view of proper roles and career aspirations for women. For example, a "laundress" merit badge of 1917 had given way to an aerospace badge by 1980. Early advice such as "None of us like women who ape men" had been replaced by guidelines reflecting less traditional and stereotypical views of men and women. Conflict theorists have often found such research techniques useful in detecting how the media portray women in a negative manner.

In another example of content analysis, the *Chicago Reporter* analyzed 82 comic strips published in May 1989 in the city's two largest newspapers and found that more than 95 percent of human comic strip characters were White, while more than half of the few Black characters appeared in a single comic strip, "Curtis." National studies have found a similar underrepresentation of minority characters, even in areas with large Black, Hispanic, or Asian populations. Noting that comic strips serve as an influential source of values for young children, sociologist Dan Krause observes that the absence of minority characters essentially tells children that "being a minority is not good, not desirable, . . . that the important people are white" (Cruz, 1989:3).

Content analysis is typically viewed as useful in studying print media such as newspapers, magazines, and books. But this technique of unobtrusive measurement can also be used to study the content of movies, television programs, and videos. For example, sociologists Richard Baxter, Cynthia De Riemer, Ann Landini, Larry Leslie, and Michael Singletary (1985) conducted a content analysis of 62 Music Television videos in 23 content categories. Frequent occurrences were found in the categories of visual abstraction, sex, dance,

violence, and crime. The researchers (1985:339) conclude that "music video sexual content may have a decidedly adolescent orientation, suited to its audience; fantasy exceeds experience and sexual expression centers primarily on attracting the opposite sex" (see also Denisoff, 1988).

Unobtrusive measures have also proved to be valuable as a supplement to other research methods. For example, one investigator wished to examine the relationship between reported and actual beer consumption. He obtained a "front door" measure of consumption by asking residents of houses how much beer they drank each week. At the same time, a "backdoor" measure was developed by counting the number of beer cans in their garbage. This backdoor measure produced a considerably higher estimate of beer consumption (Rathje and Hughes, 1975; Webb et al., 1981:17–18).

It is important to realize that research designs need not be viewed as mutually exclusive. As was illustrated in the previous example, two or more methods used together may be especially informative. Moreover, researchers do not need to devise a totally new research design in all cases. The term **replication** refers to the repetition of a given

(Chuck Fishman/Woodfin Camp & Associates)

Content analysis can be employed in studying movies, television programs, or videos. For example, sociologists Richard Baxter, Cynthia De Riemer, Ann Landini, Larry Leslie, and Michael Singletary conducted a content analysis of 62 Music Television videos and found frequent occurrences in the categories of visual abstraction, sex, dance, violence, and crime.

BOX 2-3 • CURRENT RESEARCH

UNDERSTANDING TABLES AND GRAPHS

Tables allow social scientists to summarize data and make it easier for them to develop conclusions. A *cross-tabulation* is a type of table that illustrates the relationship between two or more characteristics.

During 1989, the Gallup organization polled 1227 Americans, ages 18 and over, regarding the issue of whether gay relationships should be legal. Each was interviewed and asked: "Do you think homosexual relations between consenting adults should or should not be legal?" There is no way that, without some type of summary, analysts in the Gallup organization could examine hundreds of individual responses and reach firm conclusions. However, through use of the cross-tabulation presented in the accompanying table, we can quickly see that younger people are more tolerant of gay relationships than are older Americans.

Graphs, like tables, can be quite useful for sociologists. The accompanying illustration shows a type of pictorial graph that often appears in newspapers and maga-zines. It documents that in 1989 the state of New Jersey spent about three times as much per student on elementary and secondary education as Utah did. However, this graph relies on a visual misrepresentation. Through use of two dimensions—length and width—the graph inflates the size of the expenditure level for New Jersey. Although it should appear about three times as large as the Utah level, the New Jersey money bag actually appears about nine times as large. Thus, the graph misleads readers about the comparative spending levels of the two states.

This example underscores the fact that tables and graphs can be easily misunderstood and can even be deceptive. If you are reading a table, be sure to study carefully the title, the labels for variables, and any footnotes. If you are examining a pictorial graph, check to see if the visual representations seem to reflect accurately the statistics being illustrated (L. Fitzgerald and Cox, 1984; Huff, 1954:69; Lewandowsky and Spence, 1990).

Direct Expenditures per Student for Elementary and Secondary Education, 1989

SOURCE: Bureau of the Census, 1990a:144.

Pictorial graphs, such as the one shown above, can be misleading. The money bag for New Jersey is about three times as high as that for Utah, reflecting the fact that New Jersey spent about three times as much state funding on direct expenditures for elementary and secondary education. However, the money bag for New Jersey occupies about 9 times the area on the page. This gives readers a false impression of the two states' comparative levels of funding for education.

Survey question (below): "Do you think homosexual relations between consenting adults should or should not be legal?"

Attitudes on Legalizing Gay Relationships

RESPONDENT	FAVOR LEGALITY, PERCENT	OPPOSE LEGALITY, PERCENT	NO OPINION, PERCENT
18–29 years	61	31	8
30–49 years	53	33	14
50 years and older	32	43	25
$n = 1227$			

SOURCE: Colasanto, 1989a:13.

investigation in substantially the same way it was originally conducted, either by the original scientist or by other scientists.

Howard Bahr, Theodore Caplow, and Bruce Chadwick (1983) replicated the famous Middletown studies conducted by Robert Lynd and Helen Lynd (1929, 1937). Lynd and Lynd's remarkably productive research had examined the effects of industrialization on the small midwestern city of "Middletown"—actually, Muncie, Indiana. More recently, the National Institute of Justice has funded its Spouse Assault Replication Program. The goal of this priority project is to replicate in five cities the Minneapolis experiment discussed earlier in the chapter, which showed that arresting suspects in domestic violence cases was the most effective means of reducing repeat offenses. Broadly, replication can be considered essential to the scientific method as a means of verifying and confirming earlier findings (Garner and Visher, 1988; see also Ferraro, 1989).

ETHICS OF RESEARCH

A biochemist cannot inject a serum into a human being unless it has been thoroughly tested. To do so would be both unethical and illegal. Sociologists must also abide by certain specific standards in conducting research—a **code of ethics.** The professional society of the discipline, the American Sociological Association (ASA), first published the *Code of Ethics* in 1971 (most recently revised in 1989), which put forth the following basic principles:

1 Maintain objectivity and integrity in research.
2 Respect the subject's right to privacy and dignity.
3 Protect subjects from personal harm.
4 Preserve confidentiality.
5 Acknowledge research collaboration and assistance.
6 Disclose all sources of financial support.

In addition, in 1982 the Sociological Practice Association (SPA) introduced ethical standards for sociological practitioners in their clinical work with clients. Both the ASA and the SPA have emphasized that members have a responsibility to monitor not only their own behavior but also that of other sociologists.

On the surface, the basic principles of the ASA's *Code of Ethics* probably seem quite clear-cut. It may be difficult to imagine how they could lead to any disagreement or controversy. However, many delicate ethical questions cannot be resolved simply by reading the six points above. For example, should a sociologist engaged in participant-observation research *always* protect the confidentiality of subjects? What if the subjects are members of a religious cult allegedly engaged in unethical and possibly illegal activities? In Box 2-4 (page 52), we consider this sensitive issue by examining the views of a sociologist who studied a highly controversial religious group (see also S. Heller, 1987; Shupe and Bromley, 1980).

In an important 1984 decision, a federal district court judge held that the research notes of a social scientist should be recognized as confidential and protected under the law. Mario Brajuha, a graduate student in sociology, was working as a waiter and interviewing coworkers for a study of restaurants in the United States. After a suspicious fire took place, he agreed to testify before a grand jury but refused to provide them with his notes, insisting that he must maintain his promise of confidentiality to his interview subjects. Agreeing with Brajuha's position, Judge Jack B. Weinstein ruled: "Serious scholars are entitled to the same protection as journalists. Affording social scientists protected freedom is essential if we are to understand how our own and other societies operate" (COSSA, 1984:3).

The judge's ruling was subsequently overturned by the U.S. Court of Appeals, which held that the case needed to be retried. Eventually, the prosecutors agreed to drop the case against Brajuha if he submitted that portion of his research which he judged not to be confidential. While this case did not fully resolve a scholar's right to maintain control over research notes—or even clarify who is considered to be a researcher or a serious scholar by a court of law—there is reason to be pleased that there was some recognition of the privileged relationship between researchers and their subjects (Brajuha and Hallowell, 1986).

BOX 2-4 • SPEAKING OUT

PRESERVING CONFIDENTIALITY—ONE SOCIOLOGIST'S VIEW

In his book Doomsday Cult, *sociologist John Lofland (1977:xi) analyzes the "first five years in America (1959–1964) of an obscure end-of-the-world religion that went on to become nationally and internationally famous in the 1970s." He explains that this cult, which he refers to as the "Divine Precepts," or "DPs," is led by a Korean man who arrived in the United States in 1971. Lofland adds that, by the 1970s, the DPs had become widely viewed as a "powerful and nefarious social force that had to be countered."*

Many readers of Doomsday Cult *suspected that the DPs were, in fact, Reverend Sun Myung Moon's Unification church (see Chapter 14). However, after years of observation research, Lofland refused to break his initial promise of anonymity and reveal the real names of the DPs and their leader. At the end of the book, Lofland (1977:345–346) explains why he maintained this position:*

. . . First, I continue to have a personal and private obligation to the members with whom I spent many months. I am determined that they will not suffer infamy on my account, despite the fact that some have achieved infamy by their own actions. Second, I am a sociologist rather than an investigative journalist . . . , muckraker or other moralist. . . .

Sociologists must agree to protect the people they study in ex-

(Lyn H. Lofland)

John Lofland.

change for permission to be privy to the secrets of social organization and social life. I made such an agreement with the group reported in this book, and although the fame of the group now makes it difficult to continue this protection, I must try. Anything less endangers the future of sociology itself, threatening to bring it into even more disrepute by giving credence to the charge that sociologists are merely one more breed of muckraker, whistle-blower, undercover agent, police spy, or worse. . . .

The position I offer above is not, of course, absolute. . . . There are a few circumstances in which I would not grant or continue the protections of anonymity. A prime one is if I believed that the DPs seriously threatened the pluralism of American society,

that they had any serious chance of taking over the United States government, I would try to stop them, and use personally identified information on members to do so. That is, a pluralistic and more or less free society is one indispensable condition of practicing sociology itself. I would not stand by and allow them to destroy my discipline (which they would do if they could) and the society that makes that discipline possible. In my judgment, they do not now nor are they ever likely to pose such a threat.

There is an interesting postscript to this story. Despite Lofland's firm efforts to protect the anonymity of the DPs and their leader, it was commonly assumed—and even flatly asserted in print by other scholars—that the DPs were indeed Moon's Unification church. By the early 1980s, Lofland (1985:120–121) finally concluded that "the 'secret' had become absurdly obvious, so obvious that continuing the 'cover' seemed pointless." Consequently, in 1983, he asked the president of the American branch of the Unification church to release him from his 1962 agreement with church officials. This request was granted, but it was agreed that only the organization and its founder would be named by Lofland. He continues to protect the identities of the cult members whom he met during his years of observation research.

Case Studies of Ethical Controversies

Most sociological research uses *people* as sources of information—as respondents to survey questions, participants in experiments, or subjects of observation. In all cases, sociologists need to be certain that they are not invading the privacy of their subjects. Generally, this is handled by assuring those involved of anonymity and by guaranteeing that personal information disclosed will remain confidential. In his study on death in a hospital, Sudnow did not reveal the city in which the institution is found, let alone the institution's identity or the names of medical personnel. However, a study by Humphreys raised important questions about the extent to which sociologists could threaten people's right to privacy.

Tearoom Trade   Sociologist Laud Humphreys (1970a, 1970b, 1975) published a pioneering and controversial study of homosexual behavior in which he described the casual homosexual encounters between males meeting in public restrooms in parks. Such restrooms are sometimes called *tearooms* by homosexual men. As one consequence of this provocative research, the chancellor of the university where Humphreys was employed terminated his research grant and teaching contract.

In order to study the lifestyle of homosexual males in tearooms, Humphreys acted as a participant observer by serving as a "lookout," warning patrons when police or other strangers approached. While he was primarily interested in the behavior of these men, Humphreys also wanted to learn more about who they were and why they took such risks. Yet how could he obtain such information? Secrecy and silence were the norms of this sexual environment. Most of the men under study were unaware of Humphreys's identity and would not have consented to standard sociological interviews.

As a result, Humphreys decided on a research technique that some social scientists later saw as a violation of professional ethics. He recorded the license plate numbers of tearoom patrons, waited a year, changed his appearance, and then interviewed them in their homes. The interviews were conducted as part of a larger survey, but they did

provide information that Humphreys felt was necessary for his work. While Humphreys's subjects consented to be interviewed, their agreement fell short of *informed* consent, since they were unaware of the true purpose of the study.

Although the researcher recognized each of the men interviewed from his observations in the restrooms, there was no indication that they recognized him. Humphreys learned that most of his subjects were in their middle thirties and married. They had an average of two children and tended to have at least some years of college education. Family members appeared to be unaware of the men's visits to park restrooms for casual homosexual encounters.

Even before the public outcry over his research began, Humphreys (1970b:167–173, 1975:175–232) was aware of the ethical questions that his study would raise. He exerted great care in maintaining the confidentiality of his subjects. Their real identities were recorded only on a master list kept in a safe-deposit box. The list was destroyed by Humphreys after the research was conducted.

For social scientists, the ethical problem in this research was not Humphreys's choice of subject matter, but rather the deception involved. Patrons of the tearoom were not aware of Humphreys's purposes and were further misled about the real reasons for the household interviews. However, in the researcher's judgment, the value of his study justified the questionable means involved. Humphreys believed that, without the follow-up interviews, we would know little about the kinds of men who engage in tearoom sex and would be left with false stereotypes.

In addition, Humphreys believed that by describing such sexual interactions accurately, he would be able to dispel the myth that child molestation is a frequent practice in restrooms. One unintended consequence of the research was that it has been increasingly cited by attorneys seeking acquittal for clients arrested in public bathrooms. These lawyers have used the study to establish that such behavior is not unusual and typically involves consenting adults (J. Gray, 1991).

Do these gains in our knowledge and understanding offset Humphreys's actions in encroaching on people's private lives and deceiving them during interviews? Essentially, in reflecting on the study, we are left with a conflict between the right to know and the right to privacy. There is no easy resolution of this clash of principles. Yet we can certainly ask that sociologists be fully aware of the ethical implications of any such research techniques (I. Horowitz and Rainwater, 1970; Von Hoffman, 1970).

Tragic Accident or Suicide? A similar ethical issue—with the right to know posed against the right to privacy—became apparent in research on automobile accidents in which fatalities occur. Sociologist William Zellner (1978) wished to learn if fatal car crashes are sometimes suicides that have been disguised as accidents in order to protect family and friends (and perhaps to collect otherwise unredeemable insurance premiums). These acts of "autocide" are by nature covert, even more so than the sexual behavior of Humphreys's subjects.

In his efforts to assess the frequency of such suicides, Zellner sought to interview the friends, coworkers, and family members of the deceased. He hoped to obtain information that would allow him to ascertain whether the deaths were accidental or purposeful. Persons approached for interviews were told that Zellner's goal was to contribute to a reduction of future accidents. For this reason (as they were falsely informed), Zellner wished to learn about the emotional characteristics of accident victims. No mention was made of the interviewer's suspicions of autocide, out of fear that potential respondents would refuse to meet with him.

Zellner eventually concluded that at least 12 percent of all fatal single-occupant crashes are suicides. This information could be valuable for society, particularly since some of the probable suicides actually killed or critically injured innocent bystanders in the process of taking their own lives. Yet the ethical questions still must be faced. Was Zellner's research unethical because he misrepresented the motives of his study and failed to obtain subjects' informed consent? Or was his deception justified by the social value of his findings?

As in the study of tearoom trade, the answers are not immediately apparent. Like Humphreys, Zellner appeared to have admirable motives and took great care in protecting confidentiality. Names of suspected suicides were not revealed to insurance companies, though Zellner did recommend that the insurance industry drop double indemnity (payment of twice the person's life insurance premium in the event of accidental death) in the future.

Zellner's study raised an additional ethical issue: the possibility of harm to those who were

(UPI/Bettmann Newsphotos)

Are some people who die in single-occupant automobile crashes actually suicides? One sociological study of possible "autocides," which raised interesting ethical questions concerning the right to know and the right to privacy, concluded that at least 12 percent of such accident victims have in fact committed suicide.

interviewed. Subjects were asked if the deceased had "talked about suicide" and if they had spoken of how "bad or useless" they were. Could these questions have led people to guess the true intentions of the researcher? Perhaps, but according to Zellner, none of the informants voiced such suspicions. More seriously, might the study have caused the bereaved to *suspect* suicide—when before the survey they had accepted the deaths as accidental? Again, we have no evidence to suggest this, but we cannot be sure.

Given our uncertainty about this last question, was the research justified? Was Zellner taking too large a risk in asking the friends and families of the deceased victims if they had spoken of suicide before their death? Does the right to know outweigh the right to privacy in this type of situation? And who has the right to make such a judgment? In practice, as in Zellner's study, it is the *researcher*, not the subjects of inquiry, who makes the critical ethical decisions. Therefore, sociologists and other investigators bear the responsibility for establishing clear and sensitive boundaries for ethical scientific investigation.

Testing for Journal Bias As in the case studies described above, the issues of deception and informed consent were central to the controversy sparked by a study of possible bias in social work journals. In 1987, William M. Epstein (1989, 1990), a social worker and consultant on social policy, submitted a fictitious article to 146 professional journals. The article pretended to analyze the value of a "social work intervention" in which an asthmatic child was temporarily separated from the child's parents in an effort to remove the symptoms of the illness (which are often psychosomatic). In half the articles submitted, the purported findings endorsed the effectiveness of the social worker's intervention and the removal of the child; in the other half, the intervention was found to be ineffective.

Among 33 social work journals that reviewed a version of Epstein's fictitious article, the positive version was accepted or possibly accepted by 8 journals and was rejected by 9. By contrast, the negative version of the article (which found intervention to be ineffective) was accepted or possibly accepted by 4 journals and was rejected by 12.

Although he recognizes that these findings are not statistically significant, Epstein argues that the findings suggest a bias among social work journals: articles are more likely to receive positive reviews if they indicate that social work intervention is effective.

John Schuerman, editor of the *Social Service Review*, discovered Epstein's deception and filed a formal complaint against him with the National Association of Social Workers (NASW). In his opinion: "The principle behind the informed-consent rule is that individuals who are the subjects of research should participate knowingly and be given the opportunity to decide if they want to participate." But Epstein counters that it would be impossible to conduct an effective test of journal bias without employing some degree of deception. If editors were informed that their decisions were to be studied, it might influence their acceptance or rejection of articles (Goleman, 1988a:C9, 1988b; Schuerman, 1989; see also Goduka, 1990).

In early 1989, the executive committee of the board of directors of the NASW overturned a hearing committee's recommendations that a letter of censure be sent to Epstein and that he be suspended from association activities for a year if he failed to write a letter to the journals expressing his regret. In the view of the executive committee, the deception involved in Epstein's experiment did not constitute a breach of the NASW's code of ethics (Coughlin, 1989:A40).

Although this ruling is final, it will not end the controversy over Epstein's study. John Schuerman called the decision "extremely unfortunate," noting that the ruling places no limits on the use of deceptive research practices. William Epstein, while saying he was "heartened" by the decision, nevertheless criticized the NASW for failing to rebuke the complainants for violating the spirit of free inquiry and expression (Coughlin, 1989:A41; see also W. Epstein, 1989, 1990).

Did the value of Epstein's findings regarding journal bias justify his use of deceptive methodology? Does the principle of "informed consent" take on a different meaning when social scientists themselves are subjects of research? When balancing the right to know against the right to privacy—as we have in discussing the studies by

Humphreys and Zellner—should the right to privacy of influential journal editors be given less weight than the privacy rights of "ordinary citizens"? These sensitive questions were raised by William Epstein's controversial test of journal bias.

Neutrality and Politics in Research

The ethical considerations of sociologists lie not only in the methods used, but in the way that results are interpreted. Max Weber (1949:1–49, original edition 1904) recognized that sociologists would be influenced by their own personal values in selecting questions for research. In his view, that was perfectly acceptable, but under no conditions could a researcher allow his or her personal feelings to influence the interpretation of data. In Weber's phrase, sociologists must practice *value neutrality* in their research.

As part of this neutrality, investigators have an ethical obligation to accept research findings even when the data run counter to their own personal views, to theoretically based explanations, or to widely accepted beliefs. Durkheim countered popular conceptions when he reported that social (rather than supernatural) forces were an important factor in suicide. Similarly, Humphreys challenged traditional American suspicions when he found that users of tearooms were not preying on heterosexual adolescents or younger boys. In the case of Epstein's study, the ostensibly objective decision making of professional journals was called into question.

Some sociologists believe that it is impossible for scholars to prevent their personal values from influencing their work. As a result, Weber's call for a value-free sociology has been criticized on the grounds that it leads the public to accept sociological conclusions without exploring the biases of the researchers. Furthermore, Alvin Gouldner (1970:439–440), among others, has suggested that sociologists may use objectivity as a sacred justification for remaining uncritical of existing institutions and centers of power. These arguments are attacks not so much on Weber himself as on how his goals have been incorrectly interpreted. As we have seen, Weber was quite clear that sociologists may bring values to their subject matter. In his view, however, they must not confuse their own values with the social reality under study (Bendix, 1968:495).

Peter Rossi (1987:73) admits that "in my professional work as a sociologist, my liberal inclinations have led me to undertake applied social research in the hope that . . . my research might

(Larry Downing/Woodfin Camp & Associates)

Sociologist Peter Rossi was attacked by the Chicago Coalition for the Homeless for hampering its efforts at social reform because his carefully researched estimate of the city's homeless population was far below that offered (with little firm documentation) by the coalition.

contribute to the general liberal aim of social reform. . . ." Yet, in line with Weber's view of value neutrality, Rossi's commitment to rigorous research methods and objective interpretation of data has sometimes led him to controversial findings not necessarily supportive of his own liberal values. For example, when Rossi and a team of researchers carefully attempted to measure the extent of homelessness in Chicago in the mid-1980s, they arrived at estimates of the city's homeless population far below those offered (with little firm documentation) by the Chicago Coalition for the Homeless. As a result, Rossi was bitterly attacked by coalition members for hampering social reform efforts by minimizing the extent of homelessness. Having been through similar controversies before, Rossi (1987:79) concludes that "in the short term, good social research will often be greeted as a betrayal of one or another side to a particular controversy." But he insists that such applied research is exciting to do and can make important long-term contributions to our understanding of social problems.

The issue of value neutrality becomes especially delicate when one considers the relationship of sociology to government. Max Weber urged that sociology remain an autonomous discipline and not become unduly influenced by any one segment of society. According to his ideal of value neutrality, sociologists must remain free to reveal information that is embarrassing to government or, for that matter, supportive of existing institutions (L. Coser, 1977:219–222; Gouldner, 1962). Thus, researchers investigating a prison riot must be ready to examine objectively not only the behavior of inmates but also the conduct of prison officials before and during the outbreak. This may be more difficult if sociologists fear that findings critical of governmental institutions will jeopardize their chances of obtaining federal support for new research projects.

In the United States, the federal government has become the major source of funding for both basic and applied sociological research. This relationship between sociology and government became a matter of public controversy in the early 1980s. In a move viewed by many social scientists as politically motivated, federal agencies sharply reduced yearly increases in support for research in sociology, psychology, and other social sciences. For example, National Science Foundation funding for the social sciences from 1980 to 1990 remained unchanged in constant dollars. Applied sociology continues to receive better treatment than basic sociology; programs related to social impact on the environment, drug abuse, and AIDS have been especially favored (COSSA, 1990a).

Although the American Sociological Association's *Code of Ethics* expects sociologists to disclose all funding sources, the code does not address the issue of whether sociologists who accept funding from a particular agency may also accept their perspective on what needs to be studied. Lewis Coser (1956:27) has argued that as American sociologists have increasingly turned from basic sociological research to applied research for government agencies and the private sector, "they have relinquished to a large extent the freedom to choose their own problems, substituting the problems of their clients for those which might have interested them on purely theoretical grounds." Viewed in this light, the importance of government funding for sociological studies raises troubling questions for those who cherish Weber's ideal of value neutrality in research.

In order to write a research report, students must follow procedures similar to those used by sociologists in conducting original research. Once a topic has been selected, you must define the problems that you wish to study. A review of the literature will generally require library research.

Where can you find information? The following steps will be helpful:

1 Check this textbook and other textbooks that you own. Do not forget to begin with the materials closest at hand.

2 Use the card catalog at the library. This alphabetical index contains information on all books available in a particular library. Consult all subject headings relevant to the topic. The two-volume Library of Congress list of subject headings may be helpful in this process.

3 Locate useful articles that have appeared in periodicals. Three research guides found in most libraries will be especially valuable. The *Reader's Guide to Periodical Literature* indexes many popular magazines, including *Newsweek, Ebony,* and the *New Republic.* The *Social Sciences Index* lists articles in professional journals such as the *American Sociological Review,* the *American Journal of Sociology,* and *Social Problems.* A third index, entitled *Sociological Abstracts,* lists articles from appropriate journals and also provides brief summaries.

4 Investigate doing online searches. Many libraries can conduct computerized searches of indexes using "keywords" that you select. For example, you could examine abstracts of all sociological articles on "nursing homes" published in the last 5 years.

5 Consult the *Encyclopedia of the Social Sciences,* which concentrates on material of interest to social scientists. Each article includes references for further information.

6 Examine government documents. The United States government, states and cities, and the United Nations publish information on virtually every subject of interest to social science researchers. Many university libraries have access to a wide range of government reports. Consult the librarian for assistance in locating such materials.

7 Use newspapers. Major newspaper publish indexes annually or even weekly that are useful in locating information about specific events or issues.

8 Ask people, organizations, and agencies concerned with the topic for information and assistance. Be as specific as possible in making requests.

9 If you run into difficulties, consult the instructor, teaching assistant, or librarian.

Once all research has been completed, the task of writing the report can begin. Here are a few tips:

- Be sure the topic you have chosen is not too broad. You must be able to cover it adequately in a reasonable amount of time and a reasonable number of pages.

- Develop an outline for your report. Be sure that you have an introduction and a conclusion that relate to each other—and that the discussion proceeds logically throughout the paper. Use headings within the paper if they will improve clarity and organization.

- Do not leave all the writing until the last minute. It is best to write a rough draft, let it sit for a few days, and then take a fresh look before beginning revisions.

- If possible, read your paper *aloud.* Doing so may be helpful in locating sections or phrases that do not make sense.

Remember that all information which you have obtained from other sources *must* be cited. If an author's exact words are used, it is essential that they be placed in quotation marks. Even if you reword someone else's ideas, you must indicate the source of these ideas.

Some professors may require that students use footnotes in research reports. Others will allow students to employ the form of referencing used in this textbook, which follows the format of the American Sociological Association. If you see "(Merton, 1968:27)" listed after a statement or paragraph, it means that the material has been adapted from page 27 of a work published by Merton in 1968 and listed in the reference section at the back of this textbook.

SUMMARY

Sociologists are committed to the use of the scientific method in their research efforts. In this chapter, we examine the basic principles of the scientific method and study various techniques used by sociologists in conducting research.

1 There are five basic steps in the *scientific method:* defining the problem, reviewing the literature, formulating the hypothesis, selecting the research design and then collecting and analyzing data, and developing the conclusion.

2 The most common summary measures used by sociologists are *percentages, means, modes,* and *medians.*

3 Whenever researchers wish to study abstract concepts, such as intelligence or prejudice, they must develop workable *operational definitions.*

4 A *hypothesis* usually states a possible relationship between two or more variables.

5 By using specialized sampling techniques, sociologists avoid the necessity of testing everyone in a population.

6 According to the scientific method, research results must possess both *validity* and *reliability.*

7 The conclusion of a research study should ideally generate ideas for future investigation.

8 When sociologists wish to study a cause-and-effect relationship, they may conduct an *experiment.*

9 In the classic method of conducting an experiment, an *experimental group* is exposed to an *independent variable* while a *control group* is not.

10 *Participant observation* allows sociologists to study certain behaviors and communities that cannot be investigated through other research methods.

11 The two principal forms of *survey* research are the *interview* and the *questionnaire.*

12 *Unobtrusive measures* are research techniques that have no impact on what is being studied.

13 In examining cultural, economic, and political documents (such as newspapers, songs, and folklore), researchers use a technique called *content analysis.*

14 The *Code of Ethics* of the American Sociological Association includes among its basic principles objectivity and integrity in research, respect for the subject's right to privacy, and preservation of confidentiality.

15 Max Weber urged sociologists to practice *value neutrality* in their research by ensuring that their personal feelings do not influence the interpretation of data.

KEY TERMS

Causal logic   The relationship between a condition or variable and a particular consequence, with one event leading to the other. (page 38)

Code of ethics   The standards of acceptable behavior developed by and for members of a profession. (51)

Content analysis   The systematic coding and objective recording of data, guided by some rationale. (48)

Control group   Subjects in an experiment who are not introduced to the independent variable by the researcher. (42)

Control variable   A factor held constant to test the relative impact of an independent variable. (41)

Correlation   A relationship between two variables whereby a change in one coincides with a change in the other. (38)

Cross-tabulation   A table that shows the relationship between two or more variables. (50)

Dependent variable   The variable in a causal relationship which is subject to the influence of another variable. (38)

Experiment   An artificially created situation which allows the researcher to manipulate variables and introduce control variables. (42)

Experimental group   Subjects in an experiment who are exposed to an independent variable introduced by a researcher. (42)

Hawthorne effect   The unintended influence that observers or experiments can have on their subjects. (45)

Hypothesis   A speculative statement about the relationship between two or more variables. (38)

Independent variable   The variable in a causal relationship which, when altered, causes or influences a change in a second variable. (38)

Index   An indicator of attitudes, behavior, or characteristics of people or organizations. (40)

Interview   A face-to-face or telephone questioning of a respondent to obtain desired information. (46)

Mean   The number calculated by adding a series of values and then dividing by the number of values. (36)

Median   The midpoint or number which divides a series of values into two groups of equal numbers of values. (36)

Mode   The single most common value in a series of scores. (36)

Operational definition   An explanation of an abstract concept that is specific enough to allow a researcher to measure the concept. (37)

Participant observation A research technique in which an investigator collects information through direct involvement with and observation of a group, tribe, or community. (43)

Percentage The portion of one hundred. (36)

Questionnaire A printed research instrument employed to obtain desired information from a respondent. (46)

Random sample A sample for which every member of the entire population has the same chance of being selected. (39)

Reliability The extent to which a measure provides consistent results. (40)

Replication The repetition of a given investigation in substantially the same way as it was originally conducted, either by the original scientist or by other scientists. (49)

Representative sample A selection from a larger population that is statistically found to be typical of that population. (39)

Research design A detailed plan or method for obtaining data scientifically. (42)

Scale An indicator of attitudes, behavior, or characteristics of people or organizations. (40)

Scientific method A systematic, organized series of steps that ensures maximum objectivity and consistency in researching a problem. (35)

Survey A study, generally in the form of interviews or questionnaires, which provides sociologists and other researchers with information concerning how people think and act. (46)

Unobtrusive measures Research techniques in which the method of study has no influence on the subjects under investigation. (48)

Validity The degree to which a scale or measure truly reflects the phenomenon under study. (40)

Value neutrality Max Weber's term for objectivity of sociologists in the interpretation of data. (56)

Variable A measurable trait or characteristic that is subject to change under different conditions. (38)

ADDITIONAL READINGS

Bok, Sissela. *Lying: Moral Choice in Public and Private Life*. New York: Pantheon, 1978. The author, a philosopher who teaches medical ethics at Harvard University, addresses the use of lying and deception in both public and private life. This book includes chapters on excuses, lies in a crisis, deceptive social science research, and lies to the sick and dying.

Cuba, Lee J. *A Short Guide to Writing about Social Science*. Glenview, Ill.: Scott, Foresman, 1988. A concise (165-page) but thorough summary of the types of social science literature, with suggestions on writing a research paper and organizing an oral presentation.

Denisoff, R. Serge. *Inside MTV*. Rutgers, N.J.: Transaction, 1988. Known for his studies of popular culture, Denisoff employs the sociological perspective to examine a profitable 24-hour cable outlet.

Golden, M. Patricia (ed.). *The Research Experience*. Itasca, Ill.: Peacock, 1976. Golden presents a number of classical sociological studies, along with the researchers' insights regarding the problems they encountered.

Harding, Sue (ed.). *Feminism and Methodology*. Bloomington: Indiana University Press, 1987. A collection of essays which examine the ways in which conventional social scientific research fails to consider gender and to draw upon the feminist perspective.

Huff, Darrell. *How to Lie with Statistics*. New York: Norton, 1954. "Figures don't lie, but liars do figure" is an adage that points to the way that statistics can be abused. Huff offers guidance to the reader unsophisticated in statistics as to how to better understand numbers, graphs, and tables.

Miller, Delbert C. *Handbook of Research Design and Social Measurement* (4th ed.). New York: Longman, 1983. A veritable encyclopedia of scales, indices, and measures used in sociological studies. Also includes guides to library research, writing of reports, and grant funding.

Simon, Julian, and Paul Burstein. *Basic Research Methods in Social Sciences* (3d ed.). New York: Random House, 1985. This authoritative book, frequently used in sociology methods courses, examines the reasons for conducting research and discusses data analysis.

Webb, Eugene J., Donald T. Campbell, Richard D. Schwartz, Lee Sechrest, and Janet Below Grove. *Nonreactive Measures in the Social Sciences* (2d ed.). Boston: Houghton Mifflin, 1981. The authors identify unobtrusive methods of obtaining social science data other than questionnaires or interviews.

Journals

Among the journals that focus on methods of sociological and other social scientific research are the following: *Irb: A Review of Human Subjects Research* (founded in 1979), *Qualitative Sociology* (1977), *Social Science Research* (1972), and *Sociological Methods and Research* (1972).

PART TWO

ORGANIZING
SOCIAL
LIFE

SOCIOLOGIST Peter Berger (1963:18–19) once observed that "the sociologist is a person intensively, endlessly, shamelessly interested" in the doings of people. In Part Two, we begin our study of the organization of social life within human communities and societies.

Chapter 3 examines the basic element of any society: its culture. It considers the development of culture, cultural universals, and variations among cultures. Chapter 4 presents the lifelong socialization process through which we acquire culture and are introduced to social structure. Chapter 5 examines social interaction and the major aspects of social structure: statuses, roles, groups, and institutions. Chapter 6 focuses on the impact of groups and organizations on social behavior. Chapter 7 examines attempts to enforce acceptance of social norms, as well as behavior that violates norms.

3

CULTURE

> *. . . The first wisdom of sociology is this—things are not what they seem. . . . Social reality turns out to have many layers of meaning. The discovery of each new layer changes the perception of the whole.*
> Peter L. Berger
> *Invitation to Sociology*, 1963

LOOKING AHEAD

- How do aspects of a culture develop? How do they spread from one society to another?
- Why is language viewed by sociologists as the foundation of every culture?
- In what ways are norms and sanctions used to reward and penalize behavior?
- Why are test pilots, computer hackers, teenagers, and Appalachians all considered examples of subcultures?
- What is "culture shock"?
- Should English be the sole language of instruction in American schools and universities? Or should bilingualism be an important aspect of American educational policy?

Many presidents of the United States have offended residents of foreign nations by unwittingly violating local customs during trips abroad. During a visit to the People's Republic of China in 1984, President Ronald Reagan insulted a shopkeeper by telling the man to "keep the change" after Reagan paid for a small souvenir. In China, tips are given only to low-status servants, never to respected shopkeepers. One of the most serious presidential blunders was committed by the late Lyndon Johnson while in Thailand in the mid-1960s. During a televised meeting with the royal family, Johnson hitched one foot over his thigh and therefore pointed his shoe directly at the king, clearly unaware that this is viewed as an obscene gesture in many Third World countries. To make matters even worse, at the end of his visit President Johnson gave Thailand's queen a big hug. According to Thai traditions, no one *ever* touches the queen in public (Bulle, 1987a:1).

In an effort to help its employees conducting business abroad to avoid the kinds of misunderstandings described above, the Parker Pen Company has compiled a list of customs, etiquette, rules, gift-giving practices, language idioms, hand gestures, and nonverbal communication patterns from around the world in its book *Do's and Taboos around the World* (Axtell, 1990). This guide to international behavior is intended to assist business people in dealing with unfamiliar cultural and religious practices. The gestures of diverse cultures are so varied that the guidebook even provides an international dictionary of gestures involving the face, hands, and arms. In Peru, raising an eyebrow symbolizes "money" or "pay me"; in Tonga, it means "yes" or "I agree." In most European and Latin American countries, a circular motion of a finger around an ear means "crazy"; in the Netherlands, it means that someone has a telephone call. The "OK" sign of the United States is widely accepted, yet in Brazil it has an obscene meaning and in southern France it represents "zero" or "worthless."

Many presidents of the United States have offended people in foreign nations by unwittingly violating local customs during trips abroad. During a visit to the People's Republic of China in 1984, President Ronald Reagan insulted a shopkeeper by asking the man to "keep the change" after Reagan had paid for a small souvenir.

Different forms of hospitality and gift giving throughout the world are also noted in the guidebook. Although the giving of flowers is welcomed in Europe, one must pay special attention not to offer chrysanthemums in Belgium or Luxembourg—they are viewed as reminders of death! In Hungary, the flowers should be wrapped; in Yugoslavia, they should be an odd number, but never 13. These differences in customs and behavior occur because people live in many unique cultures.

CULTURE AND SOCIETY

Culture is the totality of learned, socially transmitted behavior. It includes the ideas, values, and customs (as well as the sailboats, comic books, and birth control devices) of groups of people. Therefore, patriotic attachment to the American flag is an aspect of culture, as is the Thais' tradition that no one be allowed to touch the queen in public.

Sometimes people refer to a particular person as "very cultured" or to a city as having "lots of culture." That use of the term *culture* is different from our use in this textbook. In sociological terms, *culture* does not refer solely to the fine arts

and refined intellectual taste. It consists of *all* objects and ideas within a society, including ice-cream cones, rock music, and slang words. Sociologists consider both a portrait by Rembrandt and a portrait by a billboard painter to be aspects of a culture. A tribe that cultivates soil by hand has just as much of a culture as a people that relies on diesel-operated machinery. Thus, each people has a distinctive culture with its own characteristic ways of gathering and preparing food, constructing homes, structuring the family, and promoting standards of right and wrong.

Sharing a similar culture helps to define the group to which we belong. A fairly large number of people are said to constitute a *society* when they live in the same territory, are relatively independent of people outside their area, and participate in a common culture. The city of Los Angeles is more populous than many nations of the world, yet sociologists do not consider it a society in its own right. Rather, it is seen as part of—and dependent upon—the larger American society.

A society is the largest form of human group. It consists of people who share a common heritage, which sociologists refer to as a *culture*. Members of the society learn this culture and transmit it from one generation to the next. They even preserve

CHAPTER 3 • CULTURE

their distinctive culture through literature, art, video recordings, and other means of expression. If it were not for the social transmission of culture, each generation would have to reinvent television, not to mention the wheel.

The sharing of a common culture also simplifies many day-to-day interactions. For example, if you plan to go to an American movie theater, you know that you will not need to bring along a chair. When you are part of a society, there are many small (as well as more important) cultural patterns that you take for granted. Just as you assume that theaters will provide seats for the audience, you also assume that physicians will not disclose confidential information, that banks will protect the money you deposit, and that parents will be careful when crossing the street with young children. All these assumptions reflect the basic values, beliefs, and customs of American culture.

Members of a society generally share a common language, and this fact also facilitates day-to-day exchanges with others. Language is a critical element of culture that sets humans apart from other species. When you ask a hardware store clerk for a flashlight, you do not need to draw a picture of the instrument. You share the same cultural term for a small, battery-operated, portable light. However, if you were in England and needed this item, you would have to ask for an "electric torch." Of course, even within the same society, a term can have a number of different meanings. In the United States, *grass* signifies both a plant eaten by grazing animals and an intoxicating drug.

The study of culture is an important part of contemporary sociological work. This chapter will examine the development of culture from its roots in the prehistoric human experience. The major aspects of culture—including language, norms, sanctions, and values—will be defined and explored. The discussion focuses both on general cultural practices found in all societies and on the wide variations that can distinguish one society from another. We will contrast the ways in which functionalist and conflict theorists view culture. The social policy section will look at conflicts in cultural values which underlie current debates over the use of bilingual, bicultural educational programs in American schools.

DEVELOPMENT OF CULTURE

Through advances in culture, human beings have come a long way from our prehistoric heritage. In the 1990s, we can send astronauts to the moon, split the atom, and prolong lives through heart transplants. The human species has produced such achievements as the ragtime compositions of Scott Joplin, the paintings of Van Gogh, the poetry of Emily Dickinson, and the novels of Dostoevsky. We can even analyze our innermost feelings through the insights of Sigmund Freud and other pioneers of psychology. In all these ways, we are remarkably different from other species of the animal kingdom.

The process of expanding culture has already been under way for thousands of years and will continue in the future. The first archeological evidence of humanlike primates places our ancestors back many millions of years. Some 2.5 million years ago people used tools and had containers for storage. From 35,000 years ago we have evidence of paintings, jewelry, and statues. By that time, elaborate ceremonies had already been developed for marriages, births, and deaths (Haviland, 1985).

Tracing the development of culture is not easy. Archeologists cannot "dig up" weddings, laws, or government, but they are able to locate items that point to the emergence of cultural traditions. Our early ancestors, the *hominids,* were primates that had characteristics of human beings. These curious and communicative creatures made important advances in the use of tools. Recent studies of chimpanzees in the wild have revealed that they frequently use sticks and other natural objects in ways learned from other members of the group. However, unlike chimpanzees, the hominids gradually made tools from increasingly durable materials. As a result, the items could be reused and refined into more effective implements.

Cultural Universals

Like the hominids, human beings have made dramatic cultural advances. Despite their differences, all societies have attempted to meet basic human needs by developing aspects of shared, learned behavior known as *cultural universals.*

Bodily adornment is a cultural universal. Shown here are the headgear worn by an Indian man, an Indonesian woman, and a Bolivian man.

Cultural universals, such as language, are general practices found in every culture. Anthropologist George Murdock (1945:124) compiled a list of such universals. The examples identified by Murdock include the following:

Athletic sports	Gift giving
Attempts to influence weather	Hairstyles
	Housing
Bodily adornment	Language
Calendar	Laws
Cooking	Marriage
Courtship	Medicine
Dancing	Music
Decorative art	Myths
Dream interpretation	Numerals
	Personal names
Family	Property rights
Folklore	Religion
Food habits	Sexual restrictions
Food taboos	Surgery
Funeral ceremonies	Toolmaking
Games	Trade
Gestures	Visiting

Many cultural universals are, in fact, adaptations to meet essential human needs, such as people's need for food, shelter, and clothing. Yet although the cultural practices listed by Murdock may be universal, the manner in which they are expressed will vary from culture to culture. For example, one society may attempt to influence its weather by seeding clouds with dry ice particles to bring about rain. Another culture may offer sacrifices to the gods in order to end a long period of drought.

While all cultures share certain general practices—such as cooking, gift giving, and dancing—the expression of any cultural universal in a society may change dramatically over time. Thus, the most popular styles of dancing in the United States during the 1990s are sure to be different from the styles that were dominant in the 1950s or the 1970s. Each generation, and each year, most human cultures change and expand through the processes of innovation and diffusion.

Innovation

The process of introducing an idea or object that is new to culture is known as **innovation.** There are two forms of innovation: discovery and invention. A **discovery** involves making known or sharing the existence of an aspect of reality. The finding of the DNA molecule and the identification of a new moon of Saturn are both acts of discovery. A significant factor in the process of discovery is the sharing of newfound knowledge with others. By contrast, an **invention** results when existing cultural items are combined into a form that did not exist before. The bow and arrow, the automobile, and the television are all examples of inventions, as are Protestantism and democracy.

Diffusion

One does not have to sample gourmet food to eat "foreign" foods. Breakfast cereal comes originally from Germany, candy from the Netherlands, chewing gum from Mexico, and the potato chip from the America of the Indians. Americans have also "exported" our foods to other lands. Residents of many nations enjoy pizza, which was popularized in the United States. However, in Japan they add squid, in Australia it is eaten with pineapple, and in England people like kernels of corn with the cheese.

Just as a culture does not always discover or invent its foods, it may also adopt ideas, technology, and customs from other cultures. Sociologists use the term **diffusion** to refer to the process by which a cultural item is spread from group to group or society to society. Diffusion can occur through a variety of means, among them exploration, military conquest, missionary work, the influence of the mass media, and tourism.

Early in human history, culture changed rather slowly through discovery. As the number of discoveries in a culture increased, inventions became possible. The more inventions there were, the more rapidly further inventions could be created. In addition, as diverse cultures came into contact with one another, they could each take advantage of the other's innovations. Thus, when Americans read a newspaper, we look at characters invented by the ancient Semites, printed by a process invented in Germany, on a material invented in China (Linton, 1936:326–327).

Diffusion may take place over extremely long distances. The use of smoking tobacco began when Indian tribes in the Caribbean invented the habit of smoking the tobacco plant, where it grew wild. Over a period of hundreds of years, tobacco was acquired and cultivated by one neighboring tribe after another. Through diffusion, this practice traveled through Central America and across the North American continent (Kroeber, 1923: 211–214).

Even within a society, diffusion occurs as innovations—discoveries and inventions—gain wider acceptance. For example, the practice of "rap" was evident among certain inner-city Blacks long before most Americans were aware of this form of singing. A 1985 music video by the Chicago Bears football team helped to popularize rap; partly as a result, rap singing groups like Run-D.M.C. became known outside central cities.

While these examples show that diffusion is common within the United States and from culture to culture, it must be emphasized that diffusion of cultural traits does not occur automatically. Groups and societies resist ideas which seem too foreign as well as those which are perceived as threatening to their own beliefs and values. Each culture tends to be somewhat selective in what it absorbs from competing cultures. Europe accepted silk, the magnetic compass, chess, and gunpowder from the Chinese but rejected the teachings of Confucius as an ideology. Many Americans have accepted the idea of *acupuncture,* the Chinese practice of puncturing the body with needles to cure disease or relieve pain, but few have committed themselves to the philosophy behind acupuncture, which involves the idea that the human body contains equal but opposite forces called *yin* and *yang.*

Sociologist William F. Ogburn (1922:202–203) made a useful distinction between elements of material and nonmaterial culture. **Material culture** refers to the physical or technological aspects of our daily lives, including food items, houses, factories, and raw materials. **Nonmaterial culture** refers to ways of using material objects and to cus-

(Both, Louise Gubb/J.B. Pictures)

The use of slogans on T shirts to make political statements originated in the United States during the 1960s. By the late 1980s, this practice had spread across the world through the process of diffusion. However, in 1987 the South African government banned such messages, most of which registered opposition to enforced segregation (apartheid). The government's order was met with public ridicule and was soon rescinded, but many schools in South Africa continue to forbid "unacceptable" slogans.

toms, beliefs, philosophies, governments, and patterns of communication. Generally, the non-material culture is more resistant to change than the material culture is. Therefore, as we have seen, foreign ideas are viewed as more threatening to a culture than foreign products are. This is true both for Americans and for other people of the world. We are more willing to use technological innovations that make our lives easier than we are ideologies that change our way of seeing the world.

Just as American society has selectively absorbed certain practices and beliefs from China and other nonwestern cultures, so too have these cultures been on the receiving end of cultural diffusion. While Japan has only 800,000 practicing Christians in its population of 120 million persons, *Kurisumasu* (the Japanese term for "Christmas") is nevertheless a major holiday. Although *Kurisumasu* is not a religious observance, it is a highly commercial occasion, reflecting obvious American influences. The Japanese are encouraged to buy gifts as they pass through stores filled with tinseled Christmas trees and the sweet sound of Bing Crosby singing "White Christmas" (R. Yates, 1985). In Box 3-1 (page 72), we examine another example of diffusion from the United States to Japan: the sport of baseball.

BOX 3-1 • AROUND THE WORLD

BASEBALL IN JAPAN

Baseball began in Japan in 1873 when a visiting professor from the United States, Horace Wilson, taught his students at Kaisei School (now the University of Tokyo) how to play the game. The popularity of the sport skyrocketed in 1896 after newspaper events reported an unprecedented event: the First Higher School in Tokyo defeated a team of Americans living in Yokohama by a score of 29-4. In the view of one Japanese historian: "Foreigners could not hope to understand the emotional aspect of this victory, but it helped Japan, struggling toward modernization after centuries of isolation, overcome a tremendous inferiority complex it felt toward the West" (Whiting, 1986:109–110).

Another visit by Americans—a 1934 tour by Babe Ruth and other baseball stars—led to the formation of professional baseball leagues in Japan. Today, baseball (or, as the Japanese call it, *bēsuboru*) is the country's dominant spectator sport. Surveys indicate that one out of every two Japanese is a baseball fan, including the prime minister and the emperor. Each year, professional baseball attracts 12 million spectators and huge television audiences. Japan's oldest and most successful team, the Tokyo Yomiuri Giants, draws standing-room-only crowds throughout its 130-game season.

Japanese baseball represents an excellent example of cultural diffusion. While the structure of the game is similar to that of American baseball, the climate and texture of Japanese baseball have been deeply influenced by Japanese cultural values, such as self-discipline, self-sacrifice, politeness, and respect for authority. Great emphasis is placed on *wa,* or "team harmony"; the Japanese are fond of the saying "The nail that sticks up will be hammered down." Consequently, any behavior viewed as overly individualistic or egotistical—violations of training rules, temper tantrums, moodiness, complaints to the media, attacks on umpires, salary disputes—is strongly discouraged. Team aspects of the game are valued highly: the home-run hitter is expected to make sacrifice bunts, the star pitcher to work as both a starter and a reliever.

One of Japan's most famous baseball players, Hiromitsu Ochiai, stands out as an exception to the collective orientation of Japanese baseball. Ochiai—who led his league in home runs, runs batted in, and batting average in both 1985 and 1986—is the highest-paid player in the history of Japanese baseball. Yet he is disliked by many Japanese, who refer to him scornfully as a *goketsu,* or "individual hero." Ochiai has skipped practices, has "held out" for what is seen as an outrageously high salary, and has brashly predicted that he will lead the league in home runs and batting average.

Unlike previous stars such as the great Sadaharu Oh (who hit 868 home runs in his career), Ochiai does not fit the expected Japanese mold of the polite, deferential "team man."

Japan's emphasis on team harmony, however, has not led to full acceptance of foreign players. Two foreign athletes (known as *gaijin*) are allowed on each professional team. Some, notably Oklahoman Randy Bass and former American major leaguer Leron Lee, have had highly successful careers in Japan. Yet almost all *gaijin* complain that they are treated as nothing more than outsiders. "You're an outcast, period," noted Warren Cromartie. "You go 0-5 and it's Yankee go home. You go 5-5 and nobody pays attention to you" (Whiting, 1986:118).

In 1986, the executive committee of Japanese baseball voted unanimously to phase out all *gaijin* eventually, arguing that they are overpaid and unproductive— and that Japanese baseball should be played only by Japanese. However, in 1987, former Atlanta Braves star Bob Horner signed with a Japanese team and enjoyed spectacular success and great popularity. Nevertheless, the future of *gaijin* in Japanese baseball remains uncertain.

SOURCES: M. Shapiro, 1986, 1987; Snyder and Spreitzer, 1983; Whiting, 1986.

ELEMENTS OF CULTURE

The uniqueness of each culture becomes evident when people from many societies come together. From 1975 to 1988, the number of foreign students attending American colleges more than doubled. These visitors to the United States noticed how different their cultural practices were from ours. Asian students had to learn that a request from an instructor to arrange a conference is not necessarily a sign of disgrace. American teachers had to learn that if a foreign student avoids direct eye contact with them, it probably reflects shyness, not disrespect.

Upon returning to their home countries, foreign students may have to adjust again—this time to their native culture. Thus, a 17-year-old woman from Tokyo, studying at a private school in Massachusetts, noted that she missed her mother, her friends, and Japanese food and customs. Yet she added that she had become careless about important Japanese traditions: "Now I often forget to bow when I meet people over there. I find myself saying 'Hi' to older people, which is considered rude" (Brooks, 1981).

Each culture considers its own distinctive ways of handling basic societal tasks as "natural." But, in fact, methods of education, marital ceremonies, religious doctrines, and other aspects of culture are learned and transmitted through human interactions within specific societies. Lifelong residents of Naples will consider it natural to speak Italian, whereas lifelong residents of Buenos Aires will feel the same way about Spanish. Clearly, the citizens of each country have been shaped by the culture in which they live.

Language

Language tells us a great deal about a culture. In the old west, words such as *gelding, stallion, mare, piebald,* and *sorrel* were all used to describe one animal—the horse. Even if we knew little of this period of American history, we could conclude from the list of terms that horses were quite important in this culture. As a result, they received an unusual degree of linguistic attention.

In contemporary American culture, the terms *convertible, dune buggy, van, four-wheel drive, sedan,*

(Stephen Shames/Visions)

The Samal people of the southern Philippines—for whom fish are a main source of both food and income—have terms in their language for more than 70 types of fishing and more than 250 different kinds of fish.

and *station wagon* are all employed to describe the same mechanical form of transportation. Perhaps the car is as important to us as the horse was to the residents of the old west. Similarly, the Samal people of the southern Philippines—for whom fish are a main source of both food and income—have terms for more than 70 types of fishing and for more than 250 different kinds of fish. The Slave Indians of northern Canada, who live in a rather frigid climate, have 14 terms to describe ice, including 8 for different kinds of "solid ice" and others for "seamed ice," "cracked ice," and "floating ice." Clearly, the priorities of a culture are reflected in its language (Basso, 1972:35; Berremen et al., 1971:409–410; Carroll, 1956; Howard, 1989:78).

BOX 3-2 • EVERYDAY BEHAVIOR

THE ELOQUENCE OF SIGN LANGUAGE

Most of us, when we think of *language*, focus on verbal speech. However, many forms of nonverbal communication are properly viewed as language, among them the sign languages used by deaf and hearing people. In the following passage, excerpted from Joanne Greenberg's (1970) novel, *In This Sign*, the author describes how eloquent and moving sign language can be.

Margaret, a hearing child of deaf parents, has become engaged to William Anglin, a hearing child of hearing parents. A family get-together is planned at the home of Margaret's parents, Abel and Janice. The evening proceeds with polite tension until the father of the bride decides to offer a toast:

. . . Janice, her eyes lowered, her mouth crimped defensively, came in with a tray and began to clear the dishes from the table. Out of habit, Mrs. Anglin and her daughter gathered themselves to rise, but Janice shook her head at them, hard, and they subsided into their places. Margaret saw and tried to catch her mother's eye. The Anglins were looking a little terrified. Abel had not sat down and now he was signaling to Margaret. She read his meaning and the knot of anxiety tightened down again. "My father wants to make a toast. . . ."

All the faces turned at once, the expressions suddenly keen and alert. There was a minute of waiting and then he began to speak to them, his Sign slow, balanced and precise. Margaret watched in amazement, translating automatically but unable to convey the difference between the butchered and debased Sign that was his ordinary speech and this haunting and evocative flow of language. The Signs were formal and complete, and they had a grace and subtlety that she had never seen even in the minister's hands; there was also a rhythm, a long, slow measuring made not in beats but in turnings, small lifts and lowerings of the hand in the way that the Deaf Signed songs or poetry. For whom was this being made, all this secret eloquence if not for her alone?

"My father wishes to say—he says—he has heard that on important holidays it is correct for a man to say over his drink what he wishes for the people who are close to him—who are in his thoughts. He says he wants—to—observe all the things that are necessary and correct." She found that her face was contorted with the effort of trying to bring to them the cadence of his words and their quality of yearning. "When Hearing have a child and she grows to be a woman and is married, father—mother—the parents cry at the wedding because she is leaving them and they know they will be lonely for her. When Deaf have such a child, a Hearing child, she grows up in the Hearing world, and when she is married, mother and father do not cry. When the Hearing child leaves the house of the Deaf, their mouths also are taken away from them and their ears are taken away and the child also, whom they love. For this, tears are not enough. . . ."

. . . When Margaret had stumbled in translating his Signs, everyone laughed aloud and when they were quiet again, they found themselves looking not at a deaf man and his interpreter but at a father and daughter.

"My father wants to say now that he hopes for everyone here to have everything for a good life always: food and their family and work to do and peace and also he wishes these things to William."

Abel raised his glass and drank, and everyone murmured something and drank also. They had been moved by Abel's words and by the poetry and beauty of his Signs and they wanted to show him that they were comfortable now in his presence. . . .

Language as the Foundation of Culture Language is the foundation of every culture, though particular languages differ in striking ways. ***Language*** is an abstract system of word meanings and symbols for all aspects of culture. Language includes speech, written characters, numerals, symbols, and gestures of nonverbal communication. As is discussed in Box 3-2, the sign languages used by deaf people and others are an especially vivid example of communication without typical verbal speech.

Language, of course, is not an exclusively human attribute. Even though they are incapable of human speech, primates such as chimpanzees have been able to use symbols to communicate. However, even at their most advanced level, animals operate with essentially a fixed set of signs with fixed meanings. By contrast, humans can manipulate symbols in order to express abstract concepts and rules and to expand human cultures.

In contrast to some other elements of culture, language permeates all parts of society. Certain cultural skills, such as cooking or carpentry, can be learned without the use of language through the process of imitation. However, it is impossible to transmit complex legal and religious systems to the next generation by watching to see how they are performed. You could bang a gavel as a judge does, but you would never be able to understand legal reasoning without language. Therefore, people invariably depend upon language for the use and transmission of the rest of a culture.

While language is a cultural universal, differences in the use of language are evident around the world. This is the case even when two countries use the same spoken language. For example, an English-speaking American visiting London may be puzzled the first time an English friend says she will "ring you up"; she means she will call you on the telephone. Similarly, as we saw at the beginning of the chapter, the meanings of nonverbal gestures vary from one culture to another. Whereas residents of the United States commonly use and attach positive meanings to the "thumbs up" gesture, this gesture has only vulgar connotations in Greece (Ekman et al., 1984).

Sapir-Whorf Hypothesis Language does more than simply describe reality; it also serves to *shape* the reality of a culture. For example, Americans cannot easily make the verbal distinctions about ice that are possible in the Slave Indian culture. As a result, we may be somewhat less likely to notice such differences.

The role of language in interpreting the world for us has been advanced in the ***Sapir-Whorf hypothesis,*** which is named for two linguists. According to Sapir and Whorf, since people can conceptualize the world only through language, language precedes thought. Thus, the word symbols and grammar of a language organize the world for us. The Sapir-Whorf hypothesis also holds that language is not a "given." Rather, it is culturally determined and leads to different interpretations of reality by focusing our attention on certain phenomena.

This hypothesis is considered so important that it has been reprinted by the State Department in its training programs to sensitize foreign service officers to the subtle uses of language. However, many social scientists challenge the Sapir-Whorf hypothesis and argue that language does not determine human thought and behavior patterns. As a result, the hypothesis has been moderated somewhat to suggest that language may *influence* (rather than determine) behavior and interpretations of society reality (Carroll, 1953:46; Kay and Kempton, 1984; Martyna, 1983:34; Sapir, 1929).

Berlin and Kay (1969:14–110) have noted that humans possess the physical ability to make millions of color distinctions, yet languages differ in the number of colors that are recognized. The English language distinguishes between yellow and orange, but some other languages do not. In the Dugum Dani language of New Guinea's West Highlands, there are only two basic color terms—*modla* for "white" and *mili* for "black." By contrast, there are 11 basic terms in English. Russian and Hungarian, though, have 12 color terms. Russians have terms for light blue and dark blue, while Hungarians have terms for two different shades of red. Thus, in a literal sense, language may color how we see the world.

Gender-related language can reflect—although in itself it will not determine—the traditional acceptance of men and women in certain occupations. Each time we use a term like *mailman, policeman,* or *fireman,* we are implying (especially to young children) that these occupations can be filled only by males. Yet it is fact that many women work as *letter carriers, police officers,* and *firefighters*—a fact that is being increasingly recognized and legitimized through the use of such nonsexist language (Martyna, 1983).

Just as language may encourage gender-related stereotypes, it can also transmit stereotypes related to race. Dictionaries published in the United States list, among the meanings of the adjective *black: dismal, gloomy* or *forbidding, destitute of moral light or goodness, atrocious, evil, threatening, clouded with anger.* Dictionaries also list *pure* and *innocent* among the meanings of the adjective *white.* Through such patterns of language, our culture reinforces positive associations with the term (and skin color) *white* and a negative association with *black.* Therefore, it is not surprising that a list which prevents people from working in a profession is called a *blacklist,* while a lie that we think of as somewhat acceptable is called a *white lie.*

Language is of interest to all three sociological perspectives. Functionalists emphasize the important role of language in unifying members of a society. By contrast, conflict theorists focus on the use of language to perpetuate divisions between groups and societies—as in the subtle and not-so-subtle sexism and racism expressed in communication. Interactionists study how people rely upon shared definitions of phrases and expressions in both formal speech and everyday conversation.

Language can shape how we see, taste, smell, feel, and hear. It also influences the way we think about the people, ideas, and objects around us. A culture's most important norms, values, and sanctions are communicated to people through language. It is for these reasons that the introduction of new languages into a society is such a sensitive issue in many parts of the world.

While the United States remains resistant to official use of languages other than English—as we will see later in this chapter, in the social policy section on bilingualism—other societies experience the pervasiveness of the English language. The domination of other languages by English stems from such factors as the demands of world trade, where English is used to negotiate many international business deals. In addition, English pervades rock music throughout the world. The leading Spanish punk rock group Asfalto, the popular Swedish quartet Abba, and the renowned Polish rock singer Michael Lyszynski all record in English (McCrum et al., 1986:13).

This does not mean that English is being enthusiastically welcomed in all countries. In 1990, several of India's largest states took strong stands against the use of English, which increasingly has served as a common link in a multilingual nation. The states of Uttar Pradesh and Madhya Pradesh ordered that all official government work be conducted in Hindi—the dominant language of northern India—and that letters not be answered if written to government offices in English. Critics of the anti-English campaign fear that the Hindi majority intends to force its language on Bengalis and other minorities (Crossette, 1990).

Norms

All societies have ways of encouraging and enforcing what they view as appropriate behavior while discouraging and punishing what they consider to be improper conduct. "Put on some clean clothes for dinner" and "Thou shalt not kill" are examples of norms found in American culture, just as respect for older people is a norm of Japanese culture. ***Norms*** are established standards of behavior maintained by a society.

In order for a norm to become significant, it must be widely shared and understood. For example, when Americans go to the movies, we typically expect that people will be quiet while the film is showing. Because of this norm, an usher can tell a member of the audience to stop talking so loudly. Of course, the application of this norm can vary, depending on the particular film and type of audience. People attending a serious artistic or political film will be more likely to insist on the norm of silence than those attending a slapstick comedy or horror movie.

(Fred Ward/Black Star)

According to the informal norms of American culture, people may greet each other with a handshake or, in some cases, with a hug or a kiss. However, in the mountainous Asian kingdom of Bhutan, residents greet each other by extending their tongues and hands.

Types of Norms Sociologists distinguish between norms in two ways. First, norms are classified as either formal or informal. *Formal norms* have generally been written down and involve strict rules for punishment of violators. In American society, we often formalize norms into laws, which must be very precise in defining proper and improper behavior. In a political sense, *law* is the "body of rules, made by government for society, interpreted by the courts, and backed by the power of the state" (Cummings and Wise, 1989:550). Laws are an example of formal norms, although not the only type. The requirements for a college major and the rules of a card game are also considered formal norms.

By contrast, *informal norms* are generally understood but are not precisely recorded. Standards of proper dress are a common example of informal norms. Our society has no specific punishment or sanction for a person who comes to school or to college dressed quite differently from everyone else. Making fun of nonconforming students for their unusual choice of clothing is the most likely response (E. Gross and Stone, 1964; Stone, 1977).

Norms are also classified by their relative importance to society. When classified in this way, they are known as *mores* and *folkways.*

Mores (pronounced "MOR-ays") are norms deemed highly necessary to the welfare of a society, often because they embody the most cherished principles of a people. Each society demands obedience to its mores; violation can lead to severe penalties. Thus, American society has strong mores against murder, treason, and child abuse that have been institutionalized into formal norms. *Folkways* are norms governing everyday behavior whose violation raises comparatively little concern. For example, walking up a "down" escalator in a department store challenges our standards of appropriate behavior, but it will not result in a fine or a jail sentence. Society is more likely to formalize mores than it is folkways. Nevertheless, folkways play an important role in shaping the daily behavior of members of a culture.

Like mores, folkways represent culturally learned patterns of behavior and can vary from one society to another. Even folkways concerning time are not universally shared. As an example,

BOX 3-3 • AROUND THE WORLD

NORM VIOLATION AMONG INDIAN THUGS

Sociologist Leon Fannin (1989) describes a secret group known as *Thugs* (pronounced "tugs") operating as professional criminals in India from the twelfth century until the 1840s. Typically working in all-male gangs of about 20 members, the Thugs would insinuate themselves into a group of travelers by pretending to be honest merchants anxious to join forces for protection on the roads. After entertaining their gullible victims with songs and jokes during an evening meal, the Thugs would strangle the entire group, bury their bodies in camouflaged graves, and abscond with their valuables. It has been estimated that Thugs killed as many as 40,000 travelers per year.

Even after committing acts of violence, Thugs felt no guilt, shame, or remorse, nor did they view themselves as criminals. As followers of the goddess Kali, a goddess of death and destruction,

members of the group felt morally and divinely justified in their conduct. Fannin (1989:37) writes that the Thugs believed they had been "selected by destiny to be the honorable and duty-bound practitioners of Kali's dictates to kill as many non-Thugs as possible and . . . keep the material possessions of these victims."

An elaborate system of norms, values, beliefs, and symbols guided the Thugs in their criminal activities. Among their fundamental norms and beliefs were the following:

- Kali had selected certain individuals (the Thugs) to carry out the necessary work of killing.
- If members obeyed Kali's commands and participated in her purification rites, they would be absolved of their violent acts.
- A person who had undergone the sacred rite of purification would remain a Thug for life.

- Killing had to be done by strangulation with a blessed cloth (*rumal*); grave digging, with a blessed pickax (*kussee*).
- Thugs were forbidden to kill women, children, holy men, or members of certain outcaste groups. (This norm was often violated, because it was dangerous to allow potential witnesses to survive.)
- Kali would provide omens of both good fortune (the braying of an ass from the left side) and bad fortune (wolves crossing the road from the left to the right side) to guide the Thugs in their search for victims.

Fannin (1989:35) concludes that "these beliefs allowed Thugs to kill prolifically without mercy or remorse, to take pride in their skill at . . . killing and hiding bodies, and to keep their victims' valuables as just recompense."

---

some cultures do not share the western concern with keeping appointments precisely. King Hassan II of Morocco is notorious for arriving late at meetings. In 1980, when Britain's Queen Elizabeth II paid a call, the king kept her waiting for 15 minutes. The queen was not amused, but the Moroccans could not understand why she and the British public were so upset. "The king could never have kept the queen or anybody else waiting," a Moroccan later remarked, "because the king cannot be late" (Levine, 1987:33).

In many societies around the world, folkways exist to reinforce patterns of male dominance. Men's hierarchical position above women within

the traditional Buddhist areas of southeast Asia is revealed in various folkways. In the sleeping cars of trains, women do not sleep in upper berths above men. In hospitals in which men are housed on the first floor, women patients will not be placed on the second floor. Even on clotheslines, folkways dictate male dominance: women's attire is hung lower than that of men (Bulle, 1987b:4).

Acceptance of Norms Norms, whether mores or folkways, are not followed in all situations. In some cases, people evade a norm because they know it is weakly enforced. It is illegal in many states for teenagers to drink alcoholic beverages, yet drinking by minors is common throughout the nation. In fact, teenage alcoholism is one of our country's serious social problems.

In some instances, behavior that appears to violate society's norms may actually represent adherence to the norms of one's particular group. Teenage drinkers often break the laws of a state government in order to conform to the standards of a peer group. Similarly, as is seen in Box 3-3, a secret religious-criminal group in India known as the *Thugs* murdered and robbed travelers as a way of life. Members closely followed the norms of the religion—which dictated even how victims were to be killed—and believed that their behavior was commanded and approved by their sacred goddess, Kali.

Norms are also violated in some instances because one norm conflicts with another. For example, suppose that you live in an apartment building and one night hear the screams of the woman next door, who is being beaten by her husband. If you decide to intervene by ringing their doorbell or calling the police, you are *violating* the norm of "minding your own business" while, at the same time, *following* the norm of assisting a victim of violence.

Even when norms do not conflict, there are always exceptions to any norm. The same action, under different circumstances, can cause one to be viewed either as a hero or as a villain. Eavesdropping on telephone conversations is normally considered illegal and abhorrent. However, it can be done with a court order to obtain valid evidence for a criminal trial. A government agent who uses such methods to convict an organized crime baron may be praised. In our culture, even killing another human being is tolerated as a form of self-defense and is actually rewarded in warfare.

Some social norms are so widely accepted that they rarely need to be verbalized. They are implicitly taught by a society to its members, and there may be very little need to enforce them. An example of such a norm is the prohibition against cannibalism. It is unlikely that you can recall anyone telling you not to eat human flesh. Nevertheless, as members of American society, we almost never consider doing so.

Acceptance of norms is subject to change, as the political, economic, and social conditions of a culture are transformed. For example, under traditional norms in the United States, a woman was expected to marry, rear children, and remain at home if her husband could support the family without her assistance. However, these norms have been changing in recent decades, in part as a result of the contemporary feminist movement (see Chapter 11). As support for traditional norms weakens, people will feel free to violate them more frequently and openly and will be less likely to receive serious negative sanctions for doing so.

Sanctions

What happens when people violate a widely shared and understood norm? Suppose that a football coach sends a twelfth player into the field. Imagine a college graduate showing up in cutoffs for a job interview at a large bank. Or consider a driver who neglects to put any money in a parking meter. In each of these situations, the person will receive sanctions if his or her behavior is detected.

Sanctions are penalties and rewards for conduct concerning a social norm. Note that the concept of *reward* is included in this definition. Conformity to a norm can lead to positive sanctions such as a pay raise, a medal, a word of gratitude, or a pat on the back. Negative sanctions include fines, threats, imprisonment, and even stares of contempt.

In Table 3-1 (on page 80), the relationship between norms and sanctions is summarized. As you can see in this table, the sanctions that are associated with formal norms (those written down and codified) tend to be formalized as well. If a coach sends too many players onto the field, the team will be penalized 15 yards. The college graduate who comes to the bank interview in cutoff blue jeans will probably be treated with contempt by bank officials and will almost certainly lose any chance of getting the job. The driver who fails to put money in the parking meter will be given a ticket and expected to pay a fine.

TABLE 3-1   Norms and Sanctions

| NORMS | SANCTIONS | |
	POSITIVE	NEGATIVE
Formal	Salary bonus	Fine
	Testimonial dinner	Jail sentence
	Medal	Expulsion
	Diploma	Execution
Informal	Smile	Frown
	Compliment	Humiliation
	Cheers	Ostracism

Sanctions serve to reinforce both formal and informal social norms.

Implicit in the application of sanctions is the *detection* of norm violation or obedience. A person cannot be penalized or rewarded unless someone with the power to provide sanctions is aware of the person's actions. Therefore, if none of the officials in the football game realizes that there is an extra player on the field, there will be no penalty. If the police do not see the car which is illegally parked, there will be no fine or ticket. Furthermore, there can be *improper* application of sanc-

tions in certain situations. The referee may make an error in counting the number of football players and levy an undeserved penalty on one team for "too many players on the field."

The entire fabric of norms and sanctions in a culture reflects that culture's values and priorities. The most cherished values will be most heavily sanctioned; matters regarded as less critical, on the other hand, will carry light and informal sanctions.

Values

Each individual develops his or her own personal goals and ambitions, yet culture provides a general set of objectives for members. *Values* are these collective conceptions of what is considered good, desirable, and proper—or bad, undesirable, and improper—in a culture. They indicate what people in a given culture prefer as well as what they find important and morally right (or wrong). Values may be specific, such as honoring one's parents and owning a home, or they may be more general, such as health, love, and democracy.

Values influence people's behavior and serve as criteria for evaluating the actions of others. There

(Rob Nelson/Picture Group)

Sanctions are penalties or rewards for conduct concerning a social norm. A traffic ticket is an example of a negative sanction.

is often a direct relationship between the values, norms, and sanctions of a culture. For example, if a culture highly values the institution of marriage, it may have norms (and strict sanctions) which prohibit the act of adultery. If a culture views private property as a basic value, it will probably have laws against theft and vandalism.

The values of a culture may change, but most remain relatively stable during any one person's lifetime. Socially shared, intensely felt values are a fundamental part of our lives in the United States.

Obviously, not all the 250 million Americans agree on one set of goals. However, sociologist Robin Williams (1970:452–500) attempted to offer a list of basic values in the United States. His list included achievement, efficiency, material comfort, nationalism, equality, and the supremacy of science and reason over faith. Any such effort to describe our nation's values should be properly viewed as but a starting point in defining the American character. Nevertheless, a review of 27 different attempts to describe the "American value system," including the work of anthropologist Margaret Mead and sociologist Talcott Parsons, revealed an overall similarity to the values identified by Williams (Devine, 1972:185).

One commonly cited barometer of American values is the annual survey of the attitudes of entering first-year college students; this survey focuses on an array of issues, beliefs, and life goals. For example, the 7 million respondents to this questionnaire are asked if various values are personally important to them. Over the last 25 years, the value of "being very well-off financially" has shown the strongest gain in popularity; the proportion of first-year college students who endorse this value as "essential" or "very important" rose from 40 percent in 1967 to 74 percent in 1990 (see Figure 3-1 on page 82). By contrast, the value that has shown the most striking decline in endorsement by students is "developing a meaningful life." While this value was the most popular in the 1967 survey, endorsed by more than 80 percent of respondents, it had fallen to seventh place on the list by 1990 and was endorsed by only 43 percent of students entering college (Astin et al., 1987:23, 1990:56).

Nationalism and patriotism have always been important values in the United States. Consequently, a furor erupted in 1989 when artist Dread Scott Tyler placed an American flag on the floor as part of an art exhibit and let it be known that the public could walk on the flag if they wished. Politicians and outraged veterans' organizations protested this controversial work when it was presented at the School of the Art Institute of Chicago. Other artists counterdemonstrated in support of Tyler's right to free expression—which they viewed as a basic American value.

During the 1980s, there was growing support for values having to do with money, power, and status. At the same time, there was a decline in support for certain values having to do with social awareness and altruism, such as "helping others." However, by 1990 there was evidence that college students were once again turning toward social concerns. According to a nationwide survey, 41 percent of first-year students stated that "influ-

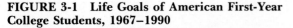

FIGURE 3-1 Life Goals of American First-Year College Students, 1967–1990

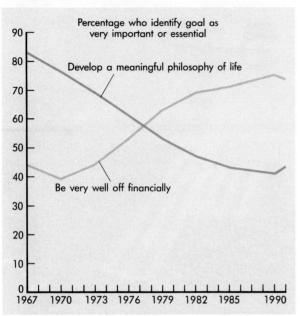

SOURCE: UCLA Higher Education Research Institute, as reported in Astin et al., 1987:23, 97; 1990:56.

Over the last 25 years, entering first-year college students in the United States have become more concerned with becoming "very well-off financially" and less concerned with developing "a meaningful philosophy of life."

encing social values" was a "very important goal." This was the highest score this value had registered over the 25-year history of the poll, exceeding even the 34 percent score in 1969 and 1970. Clearly, like other aspects of culture, such as language and norms, a nation's values are not necessarily fixed (Astin et al., 1990:56; Wiener, 1990).

It is important to emphasize that value systems can be quite different from that of our own culture. In Papua, New Guinea, much of what Americans would consider private property is shared. Different persons may actually hold different rights on the same land. There is no "owner" in our terms; one person may hold cere-monial rights, another fishing rights, another hunting rights, another dwelling rights, and so forth. In 1983, young men in one Papuan village were killed after developing export businesses for their own personal profit. These men were viewed as being too individualistic and as no longer contributing to the common good. This rather extreme example reminds us that what is valued in one society—"being very well-off financially"—may lead to a death sentence in a different culture (Ellis and Ellis, 1989).

CULTURAL INTEGRATION

As we have seen, the values and norms of every culture sometimes conflict with each other. *Cultural integration* refers to the bringing together of conflicting cultural elements, resulting in a harmonious and cohesive whole. In a well-integrated culture, various norms, values, and customs will support one another and fit together well.

Traditionally, the Lapp people of Finland used the dogsled as a basic vehicle for transportation as well as a means of hunting and herding deer. However, in the early 1960s, snowmobiles became integrated into Lapp culture and, to some extent, reshaped the culture. These machines were not useful in hunting, since they made too much noise and frightened away deer. Nevertheless, the dogsled quickly became a thing of the past. Lapps used their new snowmobiles to haul goods and to escort tourists through the country-side.

This change in one element of material culture—the introduction of new technology—has had far-reaching consequences on both material and nonmaterial culture. The Lapps have quickly become much more dependent on their neighbors and the outside world. Whereas herding was traditionally a solitary occupation, a Lapp will now drive across the country with a second snow-mobiler, who can drive him or her back to warmth and safety if the first snowmobile breaks down. New lines of work have emerged because of the need for fuel, for spare parts, and for mechanical servicing. In addition, the ease of travel afforded by the snowmobile has created a much wider network of friendships and family relationships among the Lapps. People can now visit each other much more frequently—despite the long, cold, snowy winters.

While the Lapps have successfully integrated the snowmobile into the rest of their culture, it has nevertheless transformed their culture in certain ways. Social rank has become more important among the Lapps than it was in the days when almost everyone owned reindeer herds of approximately equal size. The need for money to buy and maintain snowmobiles has caused some poor families to lose most of their herds and turn to government assistance. At the same time, those with greater wealth or mechanical ability have been able to keep their machines operating efficiently and to substantially enlarge their herds. Thus, while the coming of the snowmobile has brought Lapps together and into the larger social world, it has simultaneously created new social boundaries within the Lapp culture (Pelto, 1973).

Even relatively minor aspects of a culture can play a role in cultural integration. Children's games and nursery rhymes undoubtedly reinforce the norms and values of a culture, often ending with rather explicit "lessons" about appropriate and inappropriate behavior. Similarly, ceremonies such as weddings, funerals, and confirmations prepare participants for new social roles and reduce the shock of change which might threaten social continuity. Sociologists agree that no culture can be logically divided into separate parts for analysis and be truly understood. Every aspect of culture is intertwined with others and contributes to the culture as a whole (Arensberg and Neihoff, 1964:50–51).

Cultural integration is not always the result of agreement by all members of a culture. Often this process is enforced from the top; less powerful members of society have little choice but to accept the dictates and values of those in control. Conflict theorists emphasize that while cultural integration may exist in certain societies, the norms and values perpetuated are those favorable to the elites and the powerful (see also M. Archer, 1988).

CULTURAL VARIATION

Each culture has a unique character. Cultures adapt to meet specific sets of circumstances, such as climate, level of technology, population, and geography. This adaptation is evident in differences in all elements of culture, including norms, sanctions, values, and language. Thus, despite the presence of cultural universals such as courtship and religion, there is still great diversity among the world's many cultures. Moreover, even within a single nation, certain segments of the populace will develop cultural patterns which differ from those of the dominant society.

Aspects of Cultural Variation

Subcultures Older people living in housing for the elderly, workers in an offshore oil rig, rodeo cowboys, circus performers, and the Thugs of India (refer back to Box 3-3)—all are examples of what sociologists refer to as *subcultures*. A *subculture* is a segment of society which shares a distinctive pattern of mores, folkways, and values which differ from the pattern of the larger society. In a sense, a subculture can be thought of as a culture existing within a larger, dominant culture. The existence of many subcultures is characteristic of complex societies such as the United States. Conflict theorists argue that subcultures often emerge because the dominant society has unsuccessfully attempted to suppress a practice regarded as improper, such as use of illegal drugs.

Members of a subculture participate in the dominant culture, while at the same time engaging in unique and distinctive forms of behavior. Frequently, a subculture will develop an *argot,* or specialized language, which distinguishes it from the wider society. Thus, the phrase "Smokey in a plain wrapper" has special meaning for truck drivers and others who listen to citizens' band radios (CBs). It indicates that a patrol officer is ahead on the road in an unmarked car. The phrase "bear in the woods giving out green stamps" means that the officer is giving out tickets, while "taking pictures" means that police are using a radar gun to monitor driving speeds.

Circus performers are an example of what sociologists refer to as a subculture.

Just as truck drivers have an unusual language for describing highway police, a subculture of law enforcement officers may create its own colorful argot. For example, New York City's transit police use the term *lushworker* to refer to a person who robs drunks or sleeping passengers on subways. The *flop squad* consists of decoy officers who pretend to be asleep in order to attract and then apprehend lushworkers (Theroux, 1982:74).

Argot allows "insiders," the members of the subculture, to understand words with special meanings. It also establishes patterns of communication which cannot be understood by "outsiders." Sociologists associated with the interactionist perspective emphasize that language and symbols offer a powerful way for a subculture to maintain its identity. The particular argot of a given subculture, therefore, provides a feeling of cohesion for members and contributes to the development of a group identity (Halliday, 1978).

There are a number of ways that subcultures develop. Often a subculture emerges because a segment of society faces problems or even privileges unique to its position. Subcultures may be based on common age (teenagers or old people), region (Appalachians), ethnic heritage (Cuban Americans), or beliefs (a militant political group).

Occupations may also form subcultures. In his book *The Right Stuff,* subsequently made into a Hollywood film, Tom Wolfe examined the reclusive fraternity of test pilots who paved the way for American exploration of space. According to Wolfe, members of this subculture shared distinctive norms and values governing their behavior in the air and on the ground. They were expected to pass continual tests of their flying skills, courage, and "righteous quality" in order to prove that they were the "elected and anointed ones who had *the right stuff*" (T. Wolfe, 1980:19).

Certain subcultures, such as that of computer "hackers," develop because of a shared interest or hobby. In still other subcultures, such as that of prison inmates, members have been excluded from normal society and are forced to develop alternative ways of living. Generally, members of a subculture are viewed as outsiders or deviants, though individuals may move from the subculture to the larger culture and back again.

Countercultures Some subcultures conspicuously challenge the central norms and values of the prevailing culture. A *counterculture* is a subculture that rejects societal norms and values and seeks alternative lifestyles (J. Yinger, 1960).

Countercultures are typically popular among the young, who have the least investment in the existing culture. In most cases, a person who is 20 years old can adjust to new cultural standards more easily than someone who has spent 60 years following the patterns of the dominant culture.

By the end of the 1960s, some writers claimed that an extensive counterculture had emerged in the United States, composed of young people who repudiated the technological orientation of our culture. This counterculture was viewed as including primarily political radicals and "hippies" who had "dropped out" of mainstream social institutions. These Americans rejected the pressure to accumulate more and more cars, larger and larger homes, and an endless array of material goods. Instead, they expressed a desire to live in a culture based on more humanistic values, such as sharing, love, and coexistence with the environment. As a political force, the counterculture opposed American involvement in the war in Vietnam and encouraged draft resistance (Flacks, 1971; Roszak, 1969).

One of the newest countercultures of the United States and other western societies consists of "survivalists." Since they frequently live in rural areas—such as the hills of Scotland or desolate stretches of Arizona—it is easy for such persons to escape our attention. Survivalists argue that the solution to humanity's problems lies in living in harmony with nature rather than exploiting it. Many survivalists see nuclear war as inevitable and view solar panels, windmills, greenhouse domes, and compost heaps as their "weapons" in the struggle for continued existence. Others, afraid of being overrun by city dwellers after a nuclear attack, have created armed camps to defend themselves against such refugees. For most survivalists, the ultimate goal is a life free of frustrations and tensions (Coates, 1987; R. Peterson, 1984; P. Rivers, 1976, 1977).

Culture Shock   While visiting his company's automobile factory in Illinois, a Japanese executive is disturbed by his first drive around town. He sees dozens of homemade signs proclaiming "Garage Sale" and cannot understand why residents are selling their garages. The Japanese executive worries that there has been a severe decline in the automobile market. An American tourist arrives in Seoul, Korea, and decides he would like some local meat for dinner. But he is stunned to learn that the specialty in Seoul—recommended in part because it is believed to improve sex—is dog meat. Both the Japanese executive and the American tourist may feel strangely disoriented, uncertain, out of place, even fearful. These are all indications that they may be experiencing *culture shock* (Jolidon, 1988; W. Smith, 1989:5).

All of us, to some extent, take for granted the cultural practices of our society. As a result, it can be surprising and disturbing to realize that other cultures do not follow the American way of life. In fact, customs that seem strange to us are considered normal and proper in other cultures, which may see *our* mores and folkways as odd.

In some parts of Asia, an American tourist who is dining out may learn that dog meat is a specialty and, consequently, may experience culture shock.

Interestingly, members of certain cultures might experience culture shock simply by seeing people kiss. In many parts of the world, kissing is completely absent. Until recently, the Japanese viewed kissing as acceptable only between mother and child. Japanese poets wrote for centuries about the allure of the back of the neck, but were silent about the mouth. In fact, the Japanese had no word for kissing until they borrowed from English to create the term *kissu*. Similarly, until the arrival of westerners (and their motion pictures), kissing was unknown among the Balinese of Oceania, the Lepcha of Eurasia, and the Thonga of Africa. Among these peoples, the mouth-to-mouth kiss was considered dangerous, unhealthy, or disgusting. When the Thonga first saw Europeans kissing, they laughed and remarked: "Look at them! They eat each other's saliva and dirt!" (Ford and Beach, 1951; Tiefer, 1978).

Culture shock over conflicting value systems is not limited to contacts between traditional and modern societies. We can experience culture shock in our own society. A conservative, church-going older person might feel bewildered or horrified at a punk rock concert. Similarly, given traditional notions about gender roles in our culture, many men might be shocked by a women's martial arts class with a female instructor.

People experience anxiety when they leave a familiar culture for an "alien" environment. When you are in a new and puzzling society, you can never be sure how others will react to your actions. Even the simplest gesture—offering to light a cigarette for someone else or leaving a tip in a restaurant—may be misunderstood and viewed as an insult. It is genuinely shocking to lose one's cultural bearings, though such an experience can educate us by clarifying our unquestioned cultural assumptions.

Attitudes toward Cultural Variation

Ethnocentrism Many everyday statements reflect our attitude that our culture is best. We use terms such as *undeveloped, backward,* and *primitive* to refer to other societies. What "we" believe is a religion; what "they" believe is superstition and mythology (Spradley and McCurdy, 1980:28).

It is very tempting to evaluate the practices of other cultures on the basis of our own perspectives. Sociologist William Graham Sumner (1906:13–15) coined the term ***ethnocentrism*** to refer to the tendency to assume that one's culture and way of life are superior to all others. The ethnocentric person sees his or her own group as the center or defining point of culture and views all other cultures as deviations from what is "normal." As one manifestation of ethnocentrism, map exercises reveal that students in many nations draw maps in which their homelands are in the center of the world (see Figure 3-2).

The conflict approach to social behavior points out that the ethnocentric value judgments serve to devalue groups and contribute to denial of equal opportunities. As an example, anthropologist Clyde Kluckhohn (1949:19–20) tells of a teacher just completing her first year in an Indian school after many successful years in the Chicago school system. When asked how her Navaho students compared in intelligence with Chicago students, she replied that sometimes the Indians seemed just as bright, but at other times they acted like "dumb animals." What had provoked this harsh value judgment? A few nights earlier, at a high school dance, the teacher had led a Navaho youth—one of her prize students—over to a young Navaho woman and told him to dance with her. The two students both stood there with their heads down and refused to dance or to speak.

Kluckhohn asked the teacher if the two young people were members of the same clan, and she replied: "What difference would that make?" When he countered, "How would you feel about getting into bed with your brother?" the teacher left in a huff. However, Kluckhohn points out that for the Indians, the type of bodily contact involved in American social dancing has a directly sexual connotation. Moreover, the incest taboos prohibiting sexual contact between members of a clan are as severe as those between biological brothers and sisters. Viewed from a conflict perspective, the teacher's negative and prejudicial comment concerning her Navaho students resulted from her ethnocentrism—specifically, her failure to understand or respect the norms and values of an unfamiliar culture.

FIGURE 3-2 Mental Maps of the World

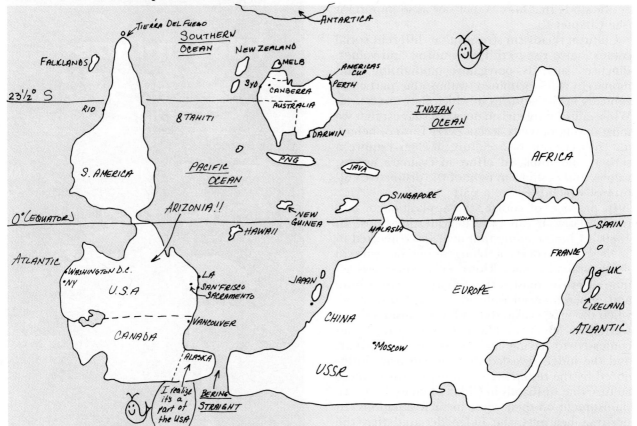

SOURCE: Saarinen, 1988:124.

How do we view the world? Do we see our own homeland in the center? In a map exercise, a student in the People's Republic of China saw China as central, while (as shown in this figure) an Australian student put Australia at the top.

Functionalists note that ethnocentrism serves to maintain a sense of solidarity by promoting group pride. Yet this type of social stability is established at the expense of other peoples. Denigrating other nations and cultures can enhance our own patriotic feelings and belief that our way of life is superior. Of course, ethnocentrism is hardly limited to citizens of the United States. Visitors from many African cultures are surprised at the disrespect that American children show their parents. People from India may be repelled by our practice of living in the same household with dogs and cats. Many Islamic fundamentalists in the Arab world and Asia view American culture as corrupt, decadent, and doomed to destruction. All these people may feel comforted by membership in cultures that, in their view, are superior to ours.

Cultural Relativism It is not necessary to view all cultural variations with an assumption that one's own culture is more humane, more "civilized," and more advanced than others. While ethnocentrism evaluates foreign cultures using the familiar culture of the observer as a standard of correct behavior, *cultural relativism* views people's behavior from the perspective of their own culture. It places a priority on *understanding* other cultures, rather than dismissing them as "strange" or "exotic." Unlike ethnocentrism, cultural relativism employs the kind of value neutrality in scientific study that Max Weber saw as so important (see Chapter 2).

Cultural relativism stresses that different social contexts give rise to different norms and values. Practices such as polygamy, bullfighting, and monarchy are examined within the particular contexts of the cultures in which they are found. While cultural relativism does not suggest that we must unquestionably accept every form of behavior characteristic of a culture, it does require a serious and unbiased effort to evaluate norms, values, and customs in light of the distinctive culture of which they are a part.

In practice, of course, the application of cultural relativism can raise delicate questions. In 1989, a Chinese immigrant man was convicted in a New York court of bludgeoning his wife to death with a hammer. However, the man was acquitted of the most serious charges against him, and was sentenced only to 5 years' probation, when the judge ruled that cultural considerations warranted leniency. The deceased woman had confessed to having had an extramarital affair, and the judge revealed that he had been influenced by the testimony of an expert on Chinese culture that husbands in China often exact severe punishment on their wives in such situations. In posttrial hearings, the judge declared that the defendant "took all his Chinese culture with him to the United States" and therefore was not fully responsible for his violent conduct. In response to this ruling, Brooklyn district attorney Elizabeth Holtzman angrily insisted: "There should be one standard of justice, not one that depends on the cultural background of the defendant. . . . Anyone who comes to this country must be prepared to live by and obey the laws of this country" (Rosario and Marcano, 1989:2).

The variations in cultural norms around the world are readily apparent in standards regarding sexual relations before marriage. An exhaustive study of 150 societies revealed that premarital sex was fully approved of in 65 societies, conditionally approved of in 43, mildly disapproved of in 6 (including the United States), and forbidden in 44. Although American sexual norms are changing, many cultures might nevertheless find our public discouragement of premarital sexual relations

Because people in the United States often assume that foreign products are superior to our own, some companies have created products that *sound* European like Häagen-Dazs ice cream (manufactured in Teaneck, New Jersey). This is an example of xenocentrism.

difficult to understand. Similarly, *we* may be perplexed by the 65 societies which fully approve of such behavior or by the 44 societies which forbid it. What is the "right" answer? What is "proper" sexual conduct? In this case and others, it depends on the norms and values that each individual or culture accepts as valid (G. Leslie and Korman, 1989; Murdock, 1949; Richards, 1972:26).

There is an interesting extension of cultural relativism, referred to as *xenocentrism*. **Xeno-centrism** is the belief that the products, styles, or ideas of one's society are inferior to those that originate elsewhere (W. Wilson et al., 1976). In a sense, it is a reverse ethnocentrism. For example, people in the United States often assume that French fashions or Japanese electronic devices are superior to our own. Are they, or are people unduly charmed by the lure goods from exotic places? Such fascination with British china or Danish glassware can be damaging to competitors in the United States. Some companies have responded by creating products that *sound* European like Häagen-Dazs ice cream (made in Teaneck, New Jersey) or Nike shoes (produced in Beaverton, Oregon). Conflict theorists are most likely to be troubled by the economic impact of xenocentrism in the developing world. Consumers in developing nations frequently turn their backs on locally produced goods and instead purchase items imported from Europe or North America.

CULTURE AND SOCIOLOGICAL PERSPECTIVES

As is readily apparent, sociologists regard culture as a highly significant concept, since it embraces all learned and shared behavior. Nevertheless, there are important differences in the ways in which functionalist and conflict theorists view culture. We have seen that functionalists emphasize the role of language in unifying members of a society while conflict theorists focus on the use of language to perpetuate divisions between groups and societies. Similarly, functionalists stress that cultural integration reflects agreement among members of a society; conflict theorists counter that the norms and values perpetuated are those favorable to the elites and the powerful.

Both sociological perspectives agree that culture and society are in harmony with each other, but for different reasons. Functionalists maintain that stability requires a consensus and the support of society's members; consequently, there are strong central values and common norms. This view of culture became popular in sociology be-ginning in the 1950s, having been borrowed from British anthropologists who saw cultural traits as all working toward stabilizing a culture. As we learned in Chapter 1, the functionalist view of culture can be used to explain why widely condemned social practices such as prostitution continue to survive. From a functionalist perspective, a cultural trait or practice will persist if it performs functions that society seems to need or contributes to overall social stability and consensus.

Conflict theorists concur with functionalists that a common culture may exist, but they argue that it serves to maintain the privileges of some groups while keeping others in a subservient position. A culture, therefore, may offer "reasons" (justifications) for unequal social arrangements. As noted in Chapter 1, Karl Marx identified values in the culture of capitalist societies that justified the exploitation of the working class. Today, a society's culture may seek to explain why Protestants enjoy greater privileges than Catholics (Northern Ireland), why the separate economic development of Blacks is behind that of Whites (South Africa), or why women can be expected to earn less than men (the United States and elsewhere).

The term **dominant ideology** is used to describe a set of cultural beliefs and practices that help to maintain powerful social, economic, and political interests. This concept was first used by Hungarian Marxist Georg Lukacs (1923) and Italian Marxist Antonio Gramsci (1929), but it did not gain an audience in the United States until the early 1970s. In Karl Marx's view, a capitalist society has a dominant ideology which serves the interests of the ruling class. Marx and Engels wrote in 1845:

> The ideas of the ruling class are in every age the ruling ideas; i.e. the class which is the dominant *material* force of society is at the same time its dominant *intellectual* force (Bottomore, 1983:431).

From a conflict perspective, the social significance of the dominant ideology is that a society's most powerful groups and institutions not only control wealth and property; even more important, they control the means of producing beliefs about reality through religion, education, and the media. For example, if all of a society's most important institutions tell women that they should be subservient to men, this dominant ideology will help to control women and keep them in a subordinate position (Abercrombie et al., 1980, 1990; R. Robertson, 1988).

Functionalist and conflict theorists agree, again for different reasons, that variation exists within a culture. Functionalists view subcultures as variations of particular social environments and as evidence that differences can exist within a common culture. However, conflict theorists suggest that variation often reflects the inequality of social arrangements within a society. Consequently, from a conflict perspective, the challenge to dominant social norms by Black civil rights activists, the feminist movement, and the disability rights movement can be seen as a reflection of inequality based on race, gender, and disability status.

A growing number of social scientists believe that a "core culture" cannot be easily identified in the United States. The lack of consensus on national values, the diffusion of cultural traits, the diversity of our many subcultures, and the changing views of young people (refer back to Figure 3-1) all are cited in support of this viewpoint. Yet there is no way of denying that certain expressions of values have greater influence than others even in so complex a society as the United States (Abercrombie et al., 1980, 1990; M. Archer, 1988; Wuthnow and Witten, 1988:52–53).

We see, then, that neither the functionalist nor the conflict perspective can be used exclusively to explain all aspects of a culture. For example, the custom of tossing rice at a bride and groom can be traced back to the wish to have children and to the view of rice as a symbol of fertility, rather than to the powerlessness of the proletariat. Nevertheless, there are cultural practices in our society and others that benefit some to the detriment of many. They may indeed promote social stability and consensus—but at whose expense?

SOCIAL POLICY AND CULTURE

BILINGUALISM

- Should American society consider the norms and values of racial and ethnic subcultures to be as legitimate as those of the dominant culture?

- Should we place greater emphasis on respect for cultural diversity or on promotion of shared cultural standards?

- Is it essential that English be the sole language of instruction in American schools and universities?

- If a community with a large Spanish-speaking minority prints legal documents only in English, is it being ethnocentric and discriminatory?

The questions posed above are part of the passionate debate currently under way in the United States concerning the issue of bilingual, bicultural education. *Bilingualism* is the use of two or more languages in places of work or in educational facilities and the treatment of each language as equally legitimate. Thus, a program of bilingual education may instruct children in their native language (such as Span-

ish) while gradually introducing them to the language of the host society (English). If it is also bicultural, it will teach children about the mores and folkways of both the dominant culture and the subculture.

In the past, American society demanded conformity to a single cultural tradition in terms of language. In a sense, this demand coincided with the functionalist view that language serves to unify members of a society. Immigrant children from Europe and Asia—including young Italians, Jews, Poles, Chinese, and Japanese—were expected to learn English once they entered American schools. In some cases, immigrant children were actually forbidden to speak their native languages on school grounds. There was little respect granted to immigrants' cultural traditions; a young person would often be teased about his or her "funny" name, accent, or style of dress.

In recent decades, this pattern of forced obedience to our dominant culture has been challenged. Beginning in the 1960s, active movements for Black pride and ethnic pride insisted that the traditions of *all* ra-

PART TWO • ORGANIZING SOCIAL LIFE

cial and ethnic subcultures should be seen as legitimate and important. Partly as a result, society began to view bilingualism as an asset. In an educational sense, also, bilingualism seemed one way of assisting millions of people in the United States who do not speak English as their first language, but who might want to *learn* English in order to function more effectively within American society.

Bilingualism has been a particularly sensitive issue for millions of immigrants from Spanish-speaking nations. The difficulties of Hispanic schoolchildren are only worsened by the fact that many teachers reject the philosophy of bilingualism and biculturalism and make their feelings known to students. This can certainly make the Hispanic child feel unwelcome in an American classroom. Furthermore, even teachers who support bilingual goals may be ill-prepared to conduct classes in two languages. Those from English-speaking backgrounds may be uncomfortable teaching in Spanish, and vice versa (Arias, 1986; Commission on Civil Rights, 1974, 1975).

The Teaching English as a Second Language (TESL) program has been the cornerstone of funding for bilingual education, but it is limited in approach. For example, TESL tends to emphasize bilingual, but not bicultural, education. As a result, the program can unintentionally contribute to ethnocentric attitudes, especially if it seems to imply that a minority subculture is not really worthy of study. As conflict theorists are quick to note, it is the interests of the less powerful—in this case, millions of non-English-speaking children—that are least likely to be recognized and respected. An alternative to the TESL approach, viewed with much less favor by advocates of bilingualism, is **English immersion,** under which students are taught primarily in English and their native languages are used only when they do not understand their lessons. In actuality, such instruction usually becomes an English-only "crash program" (Hechinger, 1987).

Research studies evaluating bilingual programs among Navaho-speaking children in Arizona, Chinese-speaking children in New York City, French-speaking children in Louisiana and Minnesota, and Spanish-speaking children in several states have all demonstrated that a quality bilingual program can be effective in improving both general learning skills and performance in reading and speaking English. But some educational researchers seem to agree that studies on bilingual education have been methodologically unsound and thus remain inconclusive (Hakuta and Garcia, 1989; Imhoff, 1990; Willig, 1985).

By 1990, 18 states had declared English to be their official language. Many Hispanic leaders saw these measures as veiled racism.

American policymakers have been rather ambivalent in dealing with the issue of bilingualism. In 1965, the Elementary and Secondary Education Act (ESEA) provided for bilingual, bicultural education. Then, in the 1970s, the federal government took an active role in offering local communities direction as to the proper form for bilingual programs. However, more recently, federal policy has been less supportive of bilingualism. Local schools have been forced to provide an increased share of funding for their bilingual programs. Beginning in 1985, the federal government allowed its funding for bilingual education to be used for alternative types of programs, among them English immersion of Spanish-speaking children in English language programs. Moreover, a 1988 law stipulates that no student can continue in a federally funded transitional bilingual program for more than 3 years unless special requirements are fulfilled.

Bilingualism has also become an increasingly controversial political issue. In 1984, Californians passed by almost a 3-1 margin a statewide referendum supporting repeal of a federal requirement that ballots be printed in foreign languages as well as English. In addition, a proposed constitutional amendment was introduced in the Senate in the mid-1980s to designate English as the "official language of the nation."

A major force behind the proposed constitutional amendment and other efforts to restrict bilingualism is U.S. English, a nationwide organization which by 1990 was estimated to have 350,000 members. Its adherents echo the view of Idaho senator Steve Symms that "many Americans now feel like strangers in their own neighborhoods, aliens in their own country." They agree with former Colorado governor Richard Lamm that the English language is the "social glue" that keeps the country together. By contrast, Hispanic leaders see the U.S. English campaign as a veiled expression of racism. "I wonder whether the movement has as part of its agenda whitening the complexion of the country," asks Joe Trevino, head of the League of United Latin American Citizens. "They say bilingualism threatens national unity," says political columnist Miguel Perez (1986:47, 1989) of U.S. English, "but their racism is a much bigger threat to a Constitution that stands for liberty" (Bauman, 1985:A3; Bland and DeQuinne, 1987; Donahue, 1985; J. Ridgeway, 1986:33).

Despite such challenges, U.S. English seems to be making headway in its efforts to oppose bilingualism. By 1990, 18 states had officially declared English to be their official language. Yet, beyond the symbolic statement being made, the actual impact of these measures is unclear. Indeed, a federal judge ruled in 1990 that Arizona's constitutional amendment making English the language "of all government functions and actions" violates federally protected free speech rights, since it could inhibit legislators from talking to their constituents in other languages (Barringer, 1990; S. Johnson, 1990).

As will be seen when race and ethnicity are considered in Chapter 10, many Americans from minority groups wish to participate freely in the dominant culture *and* to preserve the languages and customs of their native cultures. In a survey of Hispanic Americans, 94 percent felt that they should pass on to their children a sense of belonging to the Hispanic religious and national tradition. For most of the Hispanics questioned, bilingualism was an ideal personal goal (Rangel, 1984).

In theory, it should be possible for people to participate in the dominant culture of the United States while maintaining their distinctive languages and traditions. However, as is evident in the continuing resistance to bilingualism, the ideal of cultural diversity is far from universally accepted in our society. There is still hostility to minorities viewed as "different" and to their attachment to "foreign" languages and customs.

SUMMARY

Culture is the totality of learned, socially transmitted behavior. This chapter examines the basic elements which make up a culture, social practices which are common to all cultures, and variations which distinguish one culture from another.

1 If it were not for the social transmission of culture, each generation would have to reinvent television, not to mention the wheel.

2 The process of expanding human culture has already been under way for thousands of years and will continue in the future.

3 Anthropologist George Murdock compiled a list of general practices found in every culture, including courtship, family, games, language, medicine, religion, and sexual restrictions.

4 Societies resist ideas which seem too foreign as well as those which are perceived as threatening to their own values and beliefs.

5 *Language* includes speech, written characters, numerals, symbols, and gestures and other forms of nonverbal communication.

6 Sociologists distinguish between *norms* in two ways. They are classified as either *formal* or *informal* norms and as *mores* or *folkways*.

7 Some social norms are so widely accepted that they rarely need to be verbalized.

8 The most cherished *values* of a culture will receive the heaviest *sanctions*, whereas matters regarded as less critical will carry light and informal sanctions.

9 Sociologist Robin Williams has offered a list of basic American values, including achievement, efficiency, material comfort, nationalism, equality, and the supremacy of science and reason over faith.

10 In a well-integrated culture, various elements of culture will support one another and fit together well.

11 Generally, members of *subcultures* are viewed as outsiders or deviants.

12 All of us, to some extent or other, take for granted the cultural practices of our society.

13 *Ethnocentric* people see their own culture as superior and view all other cultures as deviations from what is "normal."

14 *Cultural relativism* places priority on understanding other cultures rather than dismissing them as "strange" or "exotic."

15 From a conflict perspective, the social significance of the concept of the *dominant ideology* is that a society's most powerful groups and institutions control the means of producing beliefs about reality through religion, education, and the media.

16 *Bilingualism* has been a sensitive issue for millions of immigrants from Spanish-speaking nations.

KEY TERMS

Argot Specialized language used by members of a group or subculture. (page 83)

Bilingualism The use of two or more languages in workplaces or educational facilities and the treatment of each language as equally legitimate. (90)

Counterculture A subculture that rejects societal norms and values and seeks an alternative lifestyle. (84)

Cultural integration The bringing together of conflicting cultural elements, resulting in a harmonious and cohesive whole. (82)

Cultural relativism The viewing of people's behavior from the perspective of their own culture. (87)

Cultural universals General practices found in every culture. (69)

Culture The totality of learned, socially transmitted behavior. (67)

Culture shock The feeling of surprise and disorientation that is experienced when people witness cultural practices different from their own. (85)

Diffusion The process by which a cultural item is spread from group to group or society to society. (70)

Discovery The process of making known or sharing the existence of an aspect of reality. (70)

Dominant ideology A set of cultural beliefs and practices that help to maintain powerful social, economic, and political interests. (89)

English immersion An approach to bilingual education under which students are taught primarily in English and their native languages are used only when they do not understand their lessons. (91)

Ethnocentrism The tendency to assume that one's culture and way of life are superior to all others. (86)

Folkways Norms governing everyday social behavior whose violation raises comparatively little concern. (77)

Formal norms Norms which have generally been written down and which involve strict rules for punishment of violators. (77)

Hominids Primates that had characteristics of human beings. (60)

Informal norms Norms which are generally understood but which are not precisely recorded. (77)

Innovation The process of introducing new elements into a culture through discovery or invention. (70)

Invention The combination of existing cultural items into a form that did not previously exist. (70)

Language An abstract system of word meanings and symbols for all aspects of culture. It also includes gestures and other nonverbal communication. (74)

Law In a political sense, the body of rules made by government for society, interpreted by the courts, and backed by the power of the state. (77)

Material culture The physical or technological aspects of our daily lives. (70)

Mores Norms deemed highly necessary to the welfare of a society. (77)

Nonmaterial culture Cultural adjustments to material conditions, such as customs, beliefs, patterns of communication, and ways of using material objects. (70)

Norms Established standards of behavior maintained by a society. (76)

Sanctions Penalties and rewards for conduct concerning a social norm. (79)

Sapir-Whorf hypothesis A hypothesis concerning the role of language in shaping cultures. It holds that language is culturally determined and serves to influence our mode of thought. (74)

Society A fairly large number of people who live in the same territory, are relatively independent of people outside it, and participate in a common culture. (67)

Subculture A segment of society which shares a distinctive pattern of mores, folkways, and values which differ from the pattern of the larger society. (83)

Values Collective conceptions of what is considered good, desirable, and proper—or bad, undesirable, and improper—in a culture. (80)

Xenocentrism The belief that the products, styles, or ideas of one's society are inferior to those that originate elsewhere. (89)

ADDITIONAL READINGS

Abercrombie, Nicholas, Stephen Hill, and Bryan S. Turner. *The Dominant Ideology Thesis*. London: Allen and Unwin, 1980. A critique of the view that common cultures emerge as ideological systems.

Archer, Margaret. *Culture and Agency: The Place of Culture in Social Theory*. Cambridge, Eng.: Cambridge University Press, 1988. A sophisticated analysis of the concept of cultural integration which concludes that this concept has limited utility and tends to obscure the nature of cultural systems.

Arens, W., and Susan P. Montague (eds.). *The American Dimension: Cultural Myths and Social Realities*. Port Washington, N.Y.: Alfred, 1976. This collection of essays highlights aspects of American culture which are usually ignored by social scientists. Football games, television soap operas, astrology, and coffee-drinking rituals are among the topics studied.

Arias, M. Beatriz (ed.). "The Education of Hispanic Americans: A Challenge for the Future," special issue of the *American Journal of Education*, **95**(November 1986). This collection of 10 articles looks at bilingual programs in the larger social context of the education of Hispanic Americans.

Bellah, Robert N., Richard Madsden, Anne Swidler, William M. Sullivan, and Steven M. Tipton. *Habits of the Heart: Individualism and Commitment in American Life*. Berkeley,: University of California Press, 1985. Several social scientists team up to summarize the contemporary philosophy of Americans as reflected in such values as individuals and commitment.

Hall, Edward T. *The Silent Language*. New York: Doubleday, 1959. This introduction to communication without words points to ways that people from different cultures can misunderstand one another if they are not familiar with each other's customs.

Harris, Marvin. *Cows, Pigs, Wars and Witches: The Riddles of Culture*. New York: Random House, 1974. Using an entertaining style, anthropologist Harris describes cultural practices quite different from our own, such as the belief in witches, cargo cults, and the potlatch ceremony.

Imhoff, Gary (ed.). *Learning in Two Languages*. New Brunswick, N.J.: Transaction, 1990. This collection of essays brings together the research findings of those who advocate and those who are critical of bilingual education.

Lakoff, Robin. *Language and Women's Place*. New York: Octagon, 1976. Lakoff documents the power of language to reinforce the subordinate status of women.

Lavender, Abraham D. *Ethnic Women and Feminist Values: Toward a "New" Value System*. Lanham, Md.: University Press of America, 1986. A clinical sociologist looks at the distinctive set of values articulated by the feminist movement and at the particular relevance of these values for women from ethnic minorities.

Rokeach, Milton, *The Nature of Human Values*. New York: Free Press, 1973. Reporting on research from sociology, anthropology, political science, psychology, philosophy, and history, Rokeach examines the nature and measurement of values.

Yinger, J. Milton. *Countercultures*. New York: Free Press, 1982. The definitive sociological study of this form of subculture.

Journals

Among the journals that focus on issues of culture and language are *American Anthropologist* (founded in 1888), *Ethnology* (1962), *International Journal of the Sociology of Language* (1974), and *Theory, Culture, and Society* (1982).

4

SOCIALIZATION

4

SOCIALIZATION

> *Children have more need of models than of critics.*
> Joseph Joubert
> *Pensées, 1774*

LOOKING AHEAD

- What would happen if a child was reared in total isolation from other people?
- Will identical twins show similarities in personality traits, behavior, and intelligence if reared apart?
- How do we come to develop self-identity?
- What stages of socialization do we pass through during the life cycle?
- How do the family, the school, the peer group, the mass media, the workplace, and the state contribute to the socialization process?
- What are the social implications of placing young children in child care centers?

Oscar Stohr and Jack Yufe are identical twins who were separated as babies after their parents' divorce. Oscar was reared as a strict Catholic by his maternal grandmother in the Sudetenland of Czechoslovakia. As a member of the Hitler youth movement in Nazi Germany, he learned to hate Jews. By contrast, his brother Jack was reared in Trinidad by the twins' Jewish father. Jack joined an Israeli kibbutz at age 17 and later served in the Israeli army. During World War II, he felt loyal to the British, reflecting his years in Trinidad, and hated the Nazis.

The brothers met briefly in 1954, but Jack was warned by a translator not to tell Oscar that he was Jewish. In 1979, at age 47, the twins were reunited by social scientists interested in studying the degree to which environmental forces shape human behavior. Since Oscar and Jack were born with the same genes, any later differences in personality must result from their dissimilar upbringing.

Researchers found that, while physically alike, the twins differ in many important respects. Jack is a workaholic; Oscar enjoys leisure-time activities. Whereas Oscar is a traditionalist who is domineering toward women, Jack is a political liberal who is much more accepting of feminism. Finally, Jack is extremely proud of being Jewish, while Oscar never mentions his Jewish heritage (Holden, 1987c).

What accounts for such substantial differences between identical twins reared apart? As was seen in Chapter 3, each culture has a unique character which shapes the values and behavior of its members. *Socialization* is the process whereby people learn the attitudes, values, and actions appropriate to individuals as members of a particular culture. For example, Eskimos learn to enjoy eating the raw intestines of birds and fish, while Chinese people eat carp's head and the tripe (stomach tissue) of pigs. Unlike these peoples, Americans have not been socialized to appreciate such foods.

Socialization occurs through human interactions. We will, of course, learn a great deal from those people most important in our lives—immediate family members, best friends, and teachers. But we also learn from people we see on the street, on television, and in films and magazines. From a microsociological perspective, socialization helps us to discover how to behave "properly" and what to expect from others if we follow (or challenge) society's norms and values. From a macrosociological perspective, socialization provides for the passing on of a culture and thereby for the long-term continuance of a society.

Socialization affects the overall cultural practices of a society, and it also shapes our self-images. For example, in the United States, a person who is viewed as "too heavy" or "too short" does not conform to the ideal cultural standard. If he or she is therefore judged unattractive, the evaluation can significantly influence the person's self-esteem. In this sense, socialization experiences can have an impact on the shaping of people's personalities. In everyday speech, the term *personality* is used to refer to a person's typical patterns of attitudes, needs, characteristics, and behavior.

This chapter will examine the role of socialization in human development. It will begin by analyzing the debate concerning the interaction of heredity and environmental factors. Particular attention will be given to how people develop perceptions, feelings, and beliefs about themselves. The chapter will explore the lifelong nature of the socialization process, as well as important agents of socialization, among them the family, schools, and the media. Finally, the social policy section will focus on group child care for young children as a socialization experience.

THE ROLE OF SOCIALIZATION

Researchers have traditionally clashed over the relative importance of biological inheritance and environmental factors in human development. This conflict has been called the *nature versus nurture* (or *heredity versus environment*) debate. Today, most social scientists have moved beyond this debate, acknowledging instead the *interaction* of these variables in shaping human development. However, we can better appreciate how hereditary and environmental factors interact and influence the socialization process if we first examine situations in which one factor operates almost entirely without the other (Homans, 1979).

Environment: The Impact of Isolation

For the first 6 years of her life, Isabelle lived in almost total seclusion in a darkened room. She had little contact with other people with the exception of her mother, who could neither speak nor hear. Isabelle's mother's parents had been so deeply ashamed of Isabelle's illegitimate birth that they kept her hidden away from the world. Ohio authorities finally discovered the child in 1938 when Isabelle's mother escaped from her parents' home, taking her daughter with her.

When she was discovered, despite being more than 6 years old, Isabelle could not speak. Her only communications with her mother had been by simple gestures. Verbally, Isabelle could merely make various croaking sounds. Marie Mason (1942:299), a speech specialist who worked closely with the child, observed that Isabelle

> . . . was apparently unaware of relationships of any kind. When presented with a ball, she held it in the palm of her hand, then reached out and stroked my face with it. Such behavior is comparable to that of a child of six months. She made no attempt to squeeze it, throw it, or bounce it.

Isabelle had been largely deprived of the typical interactions and socialization experiences of childhood. Since she had actually seen few people, she initially showed a strong fear of strangers and reacted almost like a wild animal when confronted with an unfamiliar person. As she became accustomed to seeing certain individuals, her reaction changed to one of extreme apathy. At first, it was believed that Isabelle was deaf, but she soon began to react to nearby sounds. On tests of maturity, she scored at the level of an infant rather than a 6-year-old.

Specialists developed a systematic training program to help Isabelle adapt to human relationships and socialization. After a few days of training, she made her first attempt to verbalize. Although she started slowly, Isabelle quickly passed through 6 years of development. In a little over 2 months, she was speaking in complete sentences. Nine months later, she could identify both words and sentences. Before Isabelle reached the age of 9, she was ready to attend school with other children. By her fourteenth year, she was in sixth grade, doing well in school, and was emotionally well-adjusted. Yet, without an opportunity to experience socialization in her first 6 years, Isabelle had been hardly human in the social sense when she was first discovered (K. Davis, 1940, 1947: 435–437).

Isabelle's experience is important because there are relatively few cases of children deliberately raised in isolation. Her inability to communicate at the time of her discovery—despite her physical and cognitive potential to learn—and her remarkable progress over the next few years underscore the impact of socialization on human development.

Unfortunately, in other cases in which children have been locked away or severely neglected, they have not fared so well as Isabelle. In many instances, the consequences of social isolation have proved to be much more damaging. For example, in 1970 a 13-year-old Californian named Genie was discovered in a room where she had been confined since the age of 20 months. During her years of isolation, no family member had spoken to her, nor could she hear anything other than swearing. Since there was no television or radio in her home, she had never listened to the sounds of normal human speech. It took extensive therapy to socialize Genie and develop her language abilities (Curtiss, 1977:274, 1981, 1982, 1985:108–109; Pines, 1981; see Figure 4-1).

The case studies of Isabelle and Genie document the adverse impact of extreme deprivation. Increasingly, researchers are emphasizing the importance of early socialization experiences for humans who grow up in more normal environments. It is now recognized that it is not enough to care for an infant's physical needs; parents must also concern themselves with children's social development. If children are discouraged from having friends, they will be deprived of social interactions with peers that are critical in their emotional growth.

Studies of animals raised in isolation also support the importance of socialization on development. Harry Harlow (1971), a researcher at the primate laboratory of the University of Wisconsin, conducted tests with rhesus monkeys that had been raised away from their mothers and away from contact with other monkeys. As was the case with Isabelle, the rhesus monkeys raised in isolation were found to be fearful and easily frightened. They did not mate, and the females who were artificially inseminated became abusive mothers. Apparently, isolation had had a damaging effect on the monkeys.

A creative aspect of Harlow's experimentation was his use of "artificial mothers." In one such experiment, Harlow presented monkeys raised in isolation with two substitute mothers—one cloth-covered replica and one covered with wire which had the ability to offer milk. Monkey after monkey went to the wire mother for the life-giving milk, yet spent much more time clinging to the more motherlike cloth model. In this study, artificial mothers who provided a comforting physical

FIGURE 4-1   Genie's Sketches

SOURCE: Curtiss, 1977:274.

This sketch was made in 1975 by Genie—a girl who had been isolated for most of her first 14 years until she was discovered by authorities in 1970. In her drawing, her linguist friend (on the left) plays the piano while Genie listens. Genie was 18 when she drew this picture.

(Harry F. Harlow Primate Laboratory/University of Wisconsin)

Rhesus monkeys display a need for social interaction when they cling to warm, terry cloth "substitute mothers." The monkey here is reaching for milk on a "mother" made of bare wire while remaining on the cloth "mother."

sensation (conveyed by the terry cloth) were more highly valued that those that provided food. As a result, the infant monkeys developed greater social attachments from their need for warmth, comfort, and intimacy than from their need for milk.

Harlow found that the ill effects of being raised in isolation were often irreversible. However, we need to be cautious about drawing parallels between animal and human behavior. Human parents are not covered with cloth (or fur); they use more behavioral means of showing affection for their offspring. Nonetheless, Harlow's research suggests that the harmful consequences of isolation can apply to other primates besides humans (R. W. Brown, 1965:39).

The Influence of Heredity

The isolation studies discussed above may seem to suggest that inheritance can be dismissed as a factor in the social development of humans and animals. However, the interplay between hereditary and environmental factors is evident in two fascinating studies that began to produce results in

1987—one involving pairs of twins reared apart and the second examining the inheritability of a form of mental illness.

Inheritability and Traits of Twins The case of Oscar Stohr and Jack Yufe, discussed at the beginning of the chapter, is a dramatic example of two genetically identical people who nevertheless developed quite different personalities and political values—presumably because of their differing socialization experiences. By contrast, another pair of identical twins reared apart, Jim Springer and Jim Lewis, both chain-smoke the same brand of cigarettes, chew their fingernails, drive the same model blue Chevrolet, and have owned dogs named Toy.

Researchers at the Minnesota Center for Twin and Adoption Research are studying pairs of identical twins reared apart to determine what similarities, if any, they show in personality traits, behavior, and intelligence. Thus far, the preliminary results from the available twin studies indicate that both genetic factors and socialization experiences are influential in human development. Certain characteristics, such as twins' tem-

"Separated at birth, the Mallifert twins meet accidentally."

peraments, voice patterns, and nervous habits, appear to be strikingly similar even in twins reared apart, thereby suggesting that these qualities may be linked to hereditary causes. However, there are far greater differences between identical twins reared apart in terms of attitudes, values, types of mates chosen, and even drinking habits. In examining clusters of personality traits among such twins, the Minnesota studies have found marked similarities in their tendency toward leadership or dominance, but significant differences in their need for intimacy, comfort, and assistance.

Researchers have also been impressed with the similar scores of twin pairs on intelligence tests. Most of the identical twins register scores even closer than those that would be expected if the same person took a test twice. At the same time, however, identical twins brought up in dramatically different social environments score quite differently on intelligence tests—a finding that supports the impact of socialization on human devel-

opment (Holden, 1987b; Plomin, 1989, 1990; Tellegen et al., 1988).

Inheritability and Mental Illness Lancaster County, Pennsylvania, is hardly a likely site for scientific breakthroughs. Often the destination of tourists, this area is best known for its Amish communities—whose distinctive subculture was popularized in a 1985 Hollywood film, *Witness*. For 10 years, a team of psychiatrists and biologists (Egeland et al., 1987) studied the occurrence of manic-depressive behavior in three generations of Amish families. Victims of *manic depression* (or bipolar affective disorders) shift between the extreme emotional states of euphoria and depression. In studying this illness, scientists found that the Amish served as an excellent sample. Their communities keep accurate genealogical records; moreover, many environmental factors which contribute to manic depression, such as alcoholism, drug abuse, unemployment, and divorce, are extremely rare within the Amish subculture.

The findings of the Pennsylvania study suggest a hereditary basis for manic-depressive behavior, which is apparently linked to genes in the specific region of a chromosome. The researchers emphasize that this genetic characteristic neither guarantees nor precludes manic depression; they can report only that people with the characteristic show a *predisposition* to manic-depressive behavior. Note that this degree of specificity was not present in the twin studies discussed earlier. There was no suggestion, for example, that a single gene could be linked to timidity (Goleman, 1986; Wallis, 1987; Woller, 1987).

In reviewing the studies of twin pairs and the Amish, one should proceed with some degree of caution. Janice Egeland, head researcher for the Amish study, notes an encouraging aspect of findings which point to the importance of heredity in human development. "Too often," she argues, "personal embarrassment and social stigma are associated with an illness whose cause is beyond the control of the individual." By contrast, psychologist Leon Kamin fears that overgeneralizing from the Minnesota twin results—and granting too much importance to the impact of heredity—may be used to blame the poor and downtrodden for their unfortunate condition. As

the debate over nature versus nurture continues, we can certainly anticipate numerous replications of these fascinating investigations to clarify the interplay between hereditary and environmental factors in human development (Leo, 1987; Plomin, 1989; Wallis, 1987:67).

Sociobiology

As part of the continuing debate on the relative influences of heredity and the environment, there has been renewed interest in sociobiology in recent years. *Sociobiology* is the systematic study of the biological bases of social behavior. Sociobiologists basically apply naturalist Charles Darwin's principles of natural selection to the study of social behavior. They assume that particular forms of behavior become genetically linked to a species if they contribute to its fitness to survive (van den Berghe, 1978:20). In its extreme form, sociobiology resembles biological determinism by suggesting that all behavior is totally the result of genetic or biological factors and that social interactions play no role in shaping people's conduct.

Sociobiology does not seek to describe individual behavior on the level of "Why is Fred more aggressive than Jim?" Rather, sociobiologists focus on how human nature is affected by the

(David Strickler/Picture Cube)

Psychologists and biologists studied three generations of Amish families in Pennsylvania to determine whether a predisposition toward manic-depressive behavior had been inherited.

genetic composition of a group of people who share certain characteristics (such as men or women, or members of isolated tribal bands). In general, sociobiologists have stressed the basic genetic heritage that is shared by all humans and have shown little interest in speculating about alleged differences between racial groups or nationalities.

The current debate on sociobiology focuses on the work of Edward O. Wilson (1975, 1977, 1978), a zoologist at Harvard University. He contends that heredity may underlie many forms of social behavior, including cannibalism among bees and warfare among humans. Wilson does not deny the importance of socialization among human beings and therefore is not an extreme biological determinist. He does, however, go further than most social scientists by emphasizing the influence of heredity on behavior.

Many social scientists have strongly attacked the main tenets of sociobiology as expressed by Wilson and other theorists (C. Campbell, 1986; Kitcher, 1985). Some researchers insist that intellectual interest in sociobiology will only deflect serious study of the more significant factor influencing human behavior—socialization. Yet Lois Wladis Hoffman (1985), in her presidential address to the Society for the Psychological Study of Social Issues, argued that sociobiology poses a valuable challenge to social scientists to better document their own research. Interactionists, for example, could show how social behavior is not programmed by human biology, but instead adjusts continually to the attitudes and responses of others.

The conflict perspective shares with sociobiology a recognition that human beings do not like to be dominated, yet there the similarity ends. Conflict theorists (like functionalists and interactionists) believe that social reality is defined by people's behavior rather than by their genetic structure. Consequently, conflict theorists fear that the sociobiological approach could be used as an argument against efforts to assist disadvantaged people, such as schoolchildren who are not competing successfully (Caplan, 1978; M. Harris, 1980:514).

In the view of feminist Arleen Rogan (1978:85), sociobiology "opens the door to justifying the oppression of one group by another on the basis of biological inferiority." This warning is not without foundation. Already in Singapore, a bustling westernized country in southeast Asia, parents with less than a college education are rewarded if they agree to be sterilized after the birth of their first or second child. At the same time, parents with degrees are given incentives to have more children. Prime Minister Lee Kuan Yew promoted this policy by declaring that gradual genetic deterioration will cause Singapore's national "levels of competence" to decline (Wellborn, 1987:62).

Wilson has argued that there should be parallel studies of human behavior with a focus on both genetic and social causes. Certainly most social scientists would agree with the sociobiologists' contention that there is a biological basis for social behavior. But there is less support for the more extreme positions taken by certain advocates of sociobiology (Gove, 1987).

THE SELF AND SOCIALIZATION

We all have various perceptions, feelings, and beliefs about who we are and what we are like. How do we come to develop these? Do they change as we age? We were not born with these understandings. Building on the work of George Herbert Mead (1964b), sociobiologists recognize that we create our own designation: the self. The *self* represents the sum total of people's conscious perception of their own identity as distinct from others. It is not a static phenomenon, but continues to develop and change throughout our lives.

Sociologists and psychologists alike have expressed interest in how the individual develops and modifies a sense of self because of social interaction. The work of sociologists Charles Horton Cooley and George Herbert Mead, pioneers of the interactionist approach, has been especially useful in furthering our understanding of these important issues (Gecas, 1982).

Sociological Approaches to the Self

Cooley: Looking-Glass Self In the early 1900s, Charles Horton Cooley advanced the belief that we learn who we are by interacting with others. Our view of ourselves, then, comes not only from direct contemplation of our personal qualities, but also from our impressions of how others perceive us. Cooley used the phrase **looking-glass self** to emphasize that the self is the product of our social interactions with other people.

The process of developing a self-identity or self-concept has three phases. First, we imagine how we appear to others—to relatives, friends, even strangers on the street. Then we imagine how others perceive us (attractive, intelligent, shy or strange). Finally, we develop some sort of feeling about ourselves, such as respect or shame, as a result of these impressions (Cooley, 1902: 152).

A critical but subtle aspect of Cooley's looking-glass self is that the self results from an individual's "imagination" of how others view him or her. As a result, we can develop self-identities based on incorrect perceptions of how others see us. A student may react strongly to a teacher's criticism and decide (wrongly) that the instructor views the student as stupid. This can easily be converted into a negative self-identity through the following process: (1) the teacher criticized me, (2) the teacher must think that I'm stupid, (3) I *am* stupid. Yet self-identities are also subject to change. If the student above received an "A" at the end of the course, he or she might no longer feel stupid.

Mead: Stages of the Self George Herbert Mead (1930:706) acknowledged to Charles Horton Cooley that he was "profoundly indebted" to Cooley's "insight and constructive thought." We are in turn indebted to Mead for continuing Cooley's exploration of interactionist theory and for his contributions to sociological understanding of the self. Mead (1934, 1964a) developed a useful model of the process by which the self emerges, defined by three distinct stages.

During the *preparatory stage,* children merely imitate the people around them, especially family members with whom they continually interact. Thus, a small child will bang on a piece of wood while a parent is engaged in carpentry work or will try to throw a ball if an older sibling is doing so nearby.

As they grow older, children grow more adept at using symbols to communicate with others. **Symbols** are the gestures, objects, and language which form the basis of human communication. By interacting with relatives and friends, as well as by watching cartoons on television and looking at picture books, children begin to understand the use of symbols. Like spoken languages, symbols vary from culture to culture and even between subcultures. "Thumbs up" is not always a positive gesture; nodding the head up and down does *not* always mean "yes." As part of the socialization process, children learn the symbols of their particular culture (Ekman et al., 1984).

Mead was among the first to analyze the relationship of symbols to socialization. As children develop skill in communicating through symbols, they gradually become more aware of social relationships. As a result, during the *play stage,* the child becomes able to imitate the actions of others, including adults. Just as an actor "becomes" a character, a child becomes a doctor, parent, superhero, or ship captain.

Mead noted that an important aspect of the play stage is role taking. **Role taking** is the process of mentally assuming the perspective of another, thereby enabling one to respond from that imagined viewpoint. For example, a young child will gradually learn when it is best to ask a parent for favors. If the parent usually comes home from work in a bad mood, the child will wait until after dinner when the parent is more relaxed and approachable. Although for children role taking may involve conforming to the behavior of others, for adolescents and adults role taking is more selective and creative (R. Turner, 1962).

In Mead's third stage, the *game stage,* the child of about 8 or 9 years old begins to consider several tasks and relationships simultaneously. At this point in development, children grasp not only their own social positions, but also those of others around them. Consider a girl or boy of this age who is part of a scout troop out on a weekend hike in the mountains. The child must understand what he or she is expected to do, but also must recognize the responsibilities of other scouts (as well as the leaders). This is the final stage of development under Mead's model; the child can now respond to numerous members of the social environment.

Mead uses the term **generalized others** to refer to the child's awareness of the attitudes, viewpoints, and expectations of society as a whole. Simply put, this concept suggests that when an individual acts, he or she takes into account an entire group of people. For example, a child who reaches this level of development will not act courteously merely to please a particular parent. Rather, the child comes to understand that courtesy is a widespread social value endorsed by parents, teachers, and religious leaders.

At this developmental stage, children can take a more sophisticated view of people and the social environment. They now understand what specific occupations and social positions are and no longer equate Mr. Williams only with the role of "librarian" or Ms. Franks only with "principal." It has become clear to the child that Mr. Williams can be a librarian, a parent, and a marathon runner at the same time and that Ms. Franks is but one of many principals in our society. Thus, the child has reached a new level of sophistication in his or her observations of individuals and institutions.

Mead is best known for this theory of the self. According to Mead (1964b), the self begins as a privileged, central position in a person's world. Young children picture themselves as the focus of everything around them and find it difficult to consider the perspectives of others. For example, when shown a mountain scene and asked to describe what an observer on the opposite side of the mountain sees (such as a lake or hikers), young children nevertheless describe only objects visible from their own vantage point. This childhood tendency to place ourselves at the center of events never entirely disappears. When an instructor is ready to return term papers or examinations and mentions that certain students did exceptionally well, we often assume that we fall into that select group (Fenigstein, 1984).

As people mature, the self changes and begins to reflect greater concern about the reaction of others. Parents, friends, coworkers, coaches, and teachers are often among those who play a major role in shaping a person's self. Mead used the term **significant others** to refer to those individuals who are most important in the development of the self (Schlenker, 1985:12–13).

(Courtesy American Sociological Association)

Erving Goffman (1922–1982) made a distinctive contribution to sociology by popularizing a particular type of interactionist method known as the dramaturgical approach.

Goffman: Impression Management As was seen in Chapter 1, the interactionist approach, which owes a great deal to both Cooley and Mead, emphasizes the micro (or small-scale) level of analysis. Thus, this sociological perspective is especially suited to an examination of how the self develops. Erving Goffman, a recent sociologist associated with the interactionist perspective, suggested that many of our daily activities involve attempts to convey impressions of who we are.

Early in life, the individual learns to slant his or her presentation of the self in order to create distinctive appearances and to satisfy particular audiences. Goffman (1959) refers to this altering of the presentation of the self as **impression management.** Box 4-1 provides an everyday example of this concept by describing how students engage in impression management after examination grades have been awarded.

In examining such everyday social interactions, Goffman makes so many explicit parallels to the theater that his view has been termed the **dramaturgical approach.** According to this perspective, people can be seen as resembling performers in action. For example, clerks may try to appear busier than they actually are if a supervisor happens to be watching them. Waiters and waitresses may "not see" a customer who wants more coffee if they are on a break.

Face-work is another aspect of the self to which Goffman (1959) has drawn attention. Maintaining the proper image can be essential to continued social interaction; face-saving behavior must be initiated if the self suffers because of embarrassment or some form of rejection. Thus, in re-

BOX 4-1 • EVERYDAY BEHAVIOR

IMPRESSION MANAGEMENT BY STUDENTS AFTER EXAMS

Sociologists Daniel Albas and Cheryl Albas (1988) drew upon Erving Goffman's concept of impression management to examine the strategies that college students employ to create desired appearances after grades have been awarded and examination papers returned. Albas and Albas divide these encounters into three categories: those between students who have all received high grades (Ace-Ace encounters); those between students who have received high grades and those who have received low or even failing grades (Ace-Bomber encounters); and those between students who have all received low grades (Bomber-Bomber encounters).

Ace-Ace encounters occur in a rather open atmosphere because there is comfort in sharing one's high mark with another high achiever. It is even acceptable to violate the norm of modesty and brag when among other Aces, since, as one student admitted, "It's much easier to admit a high mark to someone who has done better than you, or at least as well." Aces casually share not only their grades but also their study tactics; the Ace who has scored highest wins the informal competition for best study tactics.

Ace-Bomber encounters are often sensitive. Bombers generally attempt to avoid such exchanges because "you . . . emerge looking like the dumb one" or "feel like you are lazy or unreliable." When forced into interactions with Aces, Bombers work to appear gracious and congratulatory. For their part, Aces offer sympathy and support for the dissatisfied Bombers and even rationalize their own "lucky" high scores. To help Bombers save face, Aces may emphasize the difficulty and unfairness of the exam, or they may minimize its importance by saying that "it's worth only 10 percent of the total grade."

Bomber-Bomber encounters tend to be closed, reflecting the group effort to wall off the feared disdain of others. Yet, within the safety of these encounters, Bombers openly share their disappointment and engage in expressions of mutual self-pity that they themselves call "pity parties." Face-saving excuses are developed for the Bombers' poor performances, such as: "I wasn't feeling well all week," "I had four exams and two papers due that week," and "I didn't realize there would be so many questions on the lecture material." If the grade distribution in a class included particularly low scores, Bombers may engage in scapegoating the professor, who will be attacked as a sadist who enjoys flunking students, a slave driver who demands too much work, or simply an incompetent.

As is evident from these descriptions, students' impression-management strategies are constrained by society's informal norms regarding modesty and consideration for less successful peers. In classroom settings, as in the workplace and in other types of human interactions, efforts at impression management are most intense when status differentials are most pronounced—as in encounters between the high-scoring Aces and the low-scoring Bombers.

---

sponse to a rejection at a singles' bar, a person may engage in face-work by saying, "I really wasn't feeling well anyway" or "There isn't an interesting person in this entire crowd."

Don't people see through these conscious efforts at impression management? Don't people sometimes blunder in their performances? The answer to both questions is "yes." Yet Goffman points out that in our social encounters we tend to ignore both apparent stage management and mistakes in management. Therefore, the sound of a stomach rumbling in a quiet room is almost always ignored, and we tolerate clumsy and offensive statements from those who we know "mean well." Goffman (1967) has used the term *studied nonobservance* to refer to polite behavior which is intended to allow saving face.

Goffman's approach is generally regarded as an insightful perspective on everyday life, but it is not without its critics. Writing from a conflict perspective, sociologist Alvin Gouldner (1970) sees Goffman's work as implicitly reaffirming the status quo, including social class inequalities. Using Gouldner's critique, one might ask if women and minorities are expected to deceive both themselves and others while paying homage to those in power. Moreover, as discussed in Box 1-3 (refer back to page 25), sociologist Carol Brooks Gardner (1989) has suggested that Goffman's view of interactions in public places gives insufficient attention to women's well-founded fear of the sexual harassment, assault, and rape that can occur there. In considering impression management and the other concepts developed by Goffman, sociologists must remember that by *describing* social reality one is not necessarily endorsing its harsh impact on many individuals and groups (S. Williams, 1986:357–358).

Goffman's work represents a logical progression of the sociological efforts begun by Cooley and Mead on how personality is acquired through socialization and how we manage the presentation of our self to others. Cooley stressed the process by which we come to create a self; Mead focused on how the self develops as we learn to interact with others; Goffman emphasized the ways in which we consciously create images of ourselves for others.

Psychological Approaches to the Self

Psychologists have shared the interest of Cooley, Mead, and other sociologists in the development of the self. Early work in psychology, such as that of Sigmund Freud (1856–1939), stressed the role of inborn drives—among them the drive for sexual gratification—in channeling human behavior. Other psychologists, such as Jean Piaget and Lawrence Kohlberg, have emphasized the stages through which human beings progress as the self develops. (Kohlberg's six-stage model of moral development is discussed in Box 4-2.)

Like Charles Horton Cooley and George Herbert Mead, Freud believed that the self is a social product. But unlike Cooley and Mead, he suggested that the self has components that are always fighting with each other. According to Freud, people are in constant conflict between their natural impulsive instincts and societal con-

straints. Part of us seeks limitless pleasure, while another part seeks out rational behavior. By interacting with others, we learn the expectations of society and then select behavior most appropriate to our own culture. (Of course, as Freud was well-aware, we sometimes distort reality and behave irrationally.)

Research on newborn babies by the Swiss child psychologist Jean Piaget (1896–1980) has underscored the importance of social interactions in developing a sense of self. Piaget found that newborns have no self in the sense of a looking-glass image. Ironically, though, they are quite self-centered; they demand that all attention be directed toward them. Newborns have not yet separated themselves from the universe of which they are a part. For these babies, the phrase "you and me" has no meaning; they understand only "me." However, as they mature, children are gradually socialized into social relationships even within their rather self-centered world.

In his well-known *cognitive theory of development,* Piaget (1954) identifies four stages in the development of children's thought processes. In the first, or *sensorimotor,* stage, young children use their senses to make discoveries. For example, through touching they discover that their hands are actually a part of themselves. During the second, or *preoperational,* stage, children begin to use words and symbols to distinguish objects and ideas. The milestone in the third, or *concrete operational,* stage is that children engage in abstract thinking. They learn that if a formless lump of clay is shaped into a snake, it is still the same clay. Finally, in the fourth, or *formal operational,* stage, adolescents are capable of sophisticated abstract thought and can deal with ideas and values in a logical manner.

Piaget has suggested that moral development becomes an important part of socialization as children become able to think more abstractly. When children learn the rules of a game such as checkers or jacks, they are learning to obey societal norms. Those under 8 years old display a rather basic level of morality: rules are rules, and there is no concept of "extenuating circumstances." However, as they mature, children become capable of greater autonomy and begin to experience moral dilemmas as to what constitutes proper behavior.

BOX 4-2 • AROUND THE WORLD

WOULD YOU STEAL?

A woman was near death from a special type of cancer. One drug that might have saved her life was available only from a druggist who was charging 10 times what it had cost him to make the drug. The woman's husband, Heinz, could offer only half the druggist's fee; the druggist refused to sell Heinz the drug at a lower price and would not let him pay the balance later. Desperate to save his wife, Heinz broke into the drugstore and stole the drug.

Did Heinz act properly in stealing the drug, when it was the only way to save the life of his dying wife? This hypothetical dilemma has been used by researchers in at least 27 countries in an effort to test psychologist Lawrence Kohlberg's six-stage model of moral development. Kohlberg (1963, 1981) argued that we all pass through a series of predictable stages in our moral reasoning. In stage 1, we focus on obedience and punishment; in stage 2, we concentrate on "making a good deal." Stage 3 reasoning emphasizes the need to conform to the expectations of those who are close to us, such as family members; stage 4 reasoning stresses rather predictable obedience to laws, which tend to be obeyed simply because they *are* laws. People who reach stage 5 have a deeper respect for law because it reflects societal consensus on formal norms. In stage 6, people's moral reasoning focuses exclusively on universal moral principles, which in certain instances may supersede the law (as when a crime is necessary to save a dying spouse).

In reviewing the many studies of moral reasoning inspired by Kohlberg's model, psychologist John Snarey (1985, 1987) found that certain patterns of reasoning are evident in rather diverse cultures. Some subjects were presented with culturally adapted versions of Heinz's dilemma: for example, food was substituted for the drug in the story. Nevertheless, respondents in various societies exhibited stage 2 reasoning by focusing on the self-interest of the husband. A Kalskagammuit Eskimo argued that the husband should steal the food because "otherwise nobody will cut fish for him"; a Chinese man in Taiwan endorsed stealing the food because "if she dies, he'll have to pay for the funeral, and that costs a lot." While arriving at a different conclusion, a midwestern American used stage 2 reasoning similar to that of the Eskimo and the Chinese man. He suggested that Heinz should not steal the drug because "he can get married again, and he could collect money for her death from the insurance company and get away on top."

Interestingly, certain societies favor a type of moral reasoning that downplays individual self-interest in favor of a more communal orientation. Members of an Israeli *kibbutz*, a collective economic and social enterprise (see Chapter 13), stated that "Moshe" had every right to steal the drug because the allocation of this valuable resource should be the responsibility of the community. In their view, such resources should be used to promote the ideals of collective equality and happiness rather than individual profit. Similarly, the village leaders of Papua, New Guinea, considered the community responsible for creating Heinz's dilemma, and for resolving it. "If nobody helped him [save his dying wife], and so he stole [to save her], I would say we had caused that problem," suggested one village leader. Using Kohlberg's model, there is no clear method of scoring answers that focus on collective (rather than individual) moral responsibility (Tietjen and Walker, 1984).

Snarey's review of the literature reveals that Kohlberg's six stages of moral reasoning do not emerge identically in the value systems of all cultures. Instead, the differing values of particular cultures influence how members perceive moral choices. Although the order of Kohlberg's stages is generally the same, there is variability both in the rate of people's movement from stage to stage and in their eventual end point of development. On the whole, older subjects in diverse cultures score higher than younger ones on the Kohlberg rankings, thereby underscoring the progressive development of moral reasoning as a person matures.

It is important to note that "Heinz's dilemma" is framed in

(Continued)

BOX 4-2 • AROUND THE WORLD

WOULD YOU STEAL? (Continued)

the above examples as if the respondent is a man faced with a moral decision. Indeed, in most samples used in studying moral development, only men have been used as respondents. Psychologist Carol Gilligan (1982) has criticized Kohlberg's work for failing to pay heed to women's moral perspectives. In her view, while American society expects men to value their independent judgment and self-interest, women are expected to be more concerned with the well-being of others. Gilligan emphasizes that the crucial moral issue for women—how can they be responsible both to themselves and to others?—is nowhere included in Kohlberg's model. Yet most studies to date have found only limited gender differences in moral reasoning (Snarey, 1985: 218–219; L. J. Walker, 1984).

According to both Jean Piaget and Lawrence Kohlberg (see Box 4-2), children give increasing attention to how people think and why they act in a particular way. As a result, children learn to evaluate the intentions behind norms and the consequences of norms in a much more sophisticated manner.

SOCIALIZATION AND THE LIFE CYCLE

Stages of Socialization

The socialization process continues throughout all stages of the human life cycle. In cultures less complex than our own, stages of development are marked by specific ceremonies. Many societies have definite *rites of passage* that dramatize and validate changes in a person's status. For example, a young Aboriginal woman in Australia will be honored at a ceremony at the time of her first menstruation. During these festivities, her first, unborn daughter is betrothed to a grown man. Hence the expression is heard that "there is no such thing as an unmarried woman" (Goodale, 1971). For the Aborigines, there is a sharp dividing line between childhood and the responsibilities of adult life.

This is not the case within American culture, but several psychologists and sociologists have nonetheless assigned particular labels to various periods of socialization. In examining the socialization process in the United States, it is important to understand that we do not necessarily move from one stage to another in the clear-cut way that we are promoted from one grade in school to another. This may lead to some ambiguity and confusion as we develop our selves: At a certain age and level of maturity, are we children or adolescents? At another, are we adolescents or adults? As is evident in Table 4-1, there is increasing disagreement among middle-aged, middle-class Americans about the appropriate age for certain life events.

American society does bear some resemblance to simpler societies such as that of the Aborigines in that we have events marking the assumption of new roles and statuses. The wedding represents a rite of passage for Americans; yet, there is no one ceremony that clearly marks the shift from childhood to adulthood. Instead, we go through a prolonged period of transition known as *adolescence*.

This transition varies depending on certain social factors, especially social class. A person from a poor background may not have any alternatives but to work full time at a rather early age. Because of the need to contribute to the family income or to become financially self-supporting, such a young person may not have the luxury of delaying entry into the labor force by continuing his or her education.

Even after the attainment of adulthood, a person will pass through a series of developmental stages. On the basis of research involving American males, psychologist Daniel Levinson (1978) identified three major transitional periods that

TABLE 4-1 Appropriate Age for Major Life Events

ACTIVITY OR EVENT	APPROPRIATE AGE RANGE	1960 STUDY % WHO AGREE		1979 STUDY % WHO AGREE	
		MEN	WOMEN	MEN	WOMEN
Best age for a man to marry	20–25	80	90	42	42
Best age for a woman to marry	19–24	85	90	44	36
When most people should become grandparents	45–50	84	79	64	57
Best age for most people to finish school and go to work	20–22	86	82	36	38
When most men should be settled on a career	24–26	74	64	24	26
When most men hold their top jobs	45–50	71	58	38	31
When most people should be ready to retire	60–65	83	86	66	41
When a man has the most responsibilities	35–50	79	75	49	50
When a man accomplishes the most	40–50	82	71	46	41
Prime of life for a man	35–50	86	80	59	66
When a woman has the most responsibilities	25–40	93	91	59	53
When a woman accomplishes the most	30–45	94	92	57	48

SOURCE: Passuth et al., 1984.

In two surveys conducted in 1960 and 1979, middle-class, middle-aged Americans were asked the same questions regarding the appropriate age for various events and achievements of adult life. As the data show, age continued to be viewed as a constraint on the timing of events, although there was less agreement on appropriate ages for events in 1979 than there had been in 1960.

occur during men's lifetimes (see Figure 4-2 on page 112). One of these begins at about age 40. American men often experience a stressful period of self-evaluation, commonly known as the **midlife crisis,** in which they realize that they have not achieved basic goals and ambitions and have little time left to do so. Thus, Levinson (1978:199) found that 80 percent of men surveyed experi-

enced tumultuous midlife conflicts within the self and with the external world.

Levinson's formulation was developed to describe the life cycle of *men* in the United States. While his conclusions are relevant for some women—especially those who follow the traditional career patterns of men—they do not necessarily reflect the typical life cycle for women. A

FIGURE 4-2 Developmental Periods in Men's Lifetimes

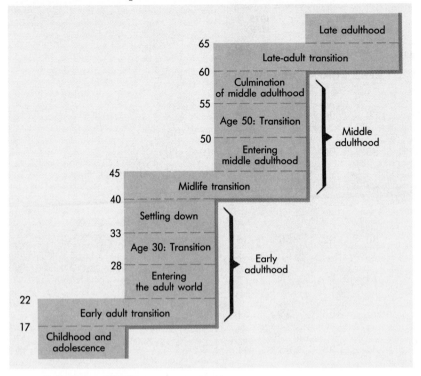

On the basis of his studies of American males, psychologist Daniel Levinson identified three major transitional periods that occur during a man's lifetime: early-adult transition, midlife transition, and late-adult transition.

SOURCE: D. Levinson, 1978:57.

key aspect of Levinson's work is the notion that, as youths, men have a dream of what the adult world is like—a vision that creates excitement and a sense of possibility. Yet, until recently, most women were socialized into visions of the future centering on marriage and children rather than achievements in the paid labor force. Moreover, most women carry the role of "mother" throughout their lives; this role has traditionally been viewed as more time-consuming and more important than the role of "father" is for men. While such patterns are changing, as we will see in Chapters 11 and 13, expectations at different stages of socialization are not yet the same for men and women (Baruch et al., 1983; see also P. Brown, 1987).

Some researchers maintain that the midlife crisis is clearly evident in *both* sexes. In her books *Passages* and *Pathfinders,* Gail Sheehy (1976, 1981:63) found that American women experience fear and confusion in their midlife years as they encounter gaps between their youthful illusions and their day-to-day lives. Sheehy's studies suggest that midlife turmoil may begin somewhat earlier for women than for men, often at about age 35. An important factor in the midlife crises of American women is the fact that they typically outlive male contemporaries, including their husbands. Consequently, as she reaches midlife, a woman faces a future in which she may eventually live alone and may become dependent on her children (Baruch et al., 1983:238–241; Rosenfeld and Stark, 1987:64, 66).

Is the phenomenon of the midlife crisis unique to the United States? In some cultures, people are given specific goals during childhood which they are able to achieve early in life. However, in our society people have unusual flexibility in selecting objectives and aspirations. This has an unintended consequence: it leaves a great deal of room for indecision or even failure.

The final period of transition identified by Levinson is the *late-adult transition*, which occurs between 60 and 65 years of age. At this time, many Americans begin restricting their occupational duties and preparing for retirement. However, it is important to note that the nation's attitudes toward aging have undergone a dramatic change in recent decades. No longer is it widely accepted that older people should simply sit around passively, waiting to die. Instead, there has been an increase in programs to socialize the elderly for meaningful pursuits and continued living. Chapter 12 will analyze in more detail socialization for later years and various theories about aging.

Anticipatory Socialization and Resocialization

The development of a social self is literally a life-long transformation which begins in the crib and continues as one prepares for death. Two types of socialization occur at many points throughout the life cycle: anticipatory socialization and resocialization.

Preparation for many aspects of adult life begins with anticipatory socialization during childhood and adolescence and continues throughout our lives as we prepare for new responsibilities. *Anticipatory socialization* refers to the processes of socialization in which a person "rehearses" for future positions, occupations, and social relationships. A culture can function more efficiently and smoothly if members become acquainted with the norms, values, and behavior associated with a social position before actually assuming that status. In Box 4-3 (page 114), we can see how a young "snaker" (handler of snakes) in India gradually moves into this occupational position.

Occasionally, as we assume new social and occupational positions, we find it necessary to unlearn our previous orientation. *Resocialization* refers to the process of discarding former behavior patterns and accepting new ones as part of a transition in one's life. Such resocialization occurs throughout the human life cycle. It is required, for example, when a young American father becomes absorbed in caring for his infant daughter or son. The father may have been socialized since his childhood to view tasks such as changing diapers, offering midnight feedings with a bottle, and taking the child to the pediatrician as "wom-en's work." Suddenly, he finds himself a parent within a culture that is expecting fathers to become more involved in day-to-day child-rearing duties. This man not only needs to learn new skills but also must set aside his previous attitudes and behavior patterns regarding child rearing.

Viewers of television's *L.A. Law* have watched the resocialization of a mentally disabled character, Benny Stulwicz. When Benny was introduced, he was almost totally dependent on his aging mother. However, after her death, Benny was gradually resocialized into a much different life—working at the law firm as an office aide, living in his own apartment, and forming friendships and romances.

Resocialization in Total Institutions

In certain situations, people are voluntarily (or sometimes involuntarily) resocialized within a highly controlled social environment. Resocialization is particularly effective when it occurs within a total institution. Erving Goffman (1961) coined the term *total institutions* to refer to institutions, such as prisons, the military, mental hospitals, and convents, which regulate all aspects of a person's life under a single authority. The total institution is generally cut off from the rest of society and therefore provides for all the needs of its members. Quite literally, the crew of a merchant vessel at sea becomes part of a total institution. So elaborate are its requirements, so all-encompassing are its activities, that a total institution often represents a miniature society.

Goffman (1961) has identified four common traits of total institutions. First, all aspects of life are conducted in the same place and are under the control of a single authority. Second, any activities within the institution are conducted in the company of others in the same circumstances—for example, novices in a convent or army recruits. Third, the authorities devise rules and schedule activities without consulting participants. Finally, all aspects of life within a total institution are designed to fulfill the purpose of the organization. Thus, all activities in a monastery are centered on prayer and communion with God (Davies, 1989; P. Rose et al., 1979:321–322).

Individuality is often lost within total institu-

BOX 4-3 • AROUND THE WORLD

SNAKERS ARE MADE, NOT BORN

Choto Nath has lived in Bhopura, India, all his life. Now 30 years old, he is a "snaker" like his father, his grandfather, and his male ancestors dating back as far as anyone can recall. This is a matter of intense pride for Choto Nath and his family. Snakers—a term they prefer to "snake charmers"—are regarded as professionals within Indian culture. Their work is seen as involving not only skill but also proper living, spiritual feeling, and respect for tradition. By following in the footsteps of his forefathers, Choto Nath believes he is living out the destiny of who he is meant to be.

Yet even the son of a snaker cannot be expected to develop an immediate love of snakes. At first, children are forbidden to go anywhere near the mysterious covered baskets where the cobras and other snakes sleep. Only when a boy becomes 5 or 6 years old is he allowed to touch the snakes he has observed all his life. At this point, he begins the process of anticipatory socialization for the profession he accepts as his destiny.

When Choto Nath first draped a yellow rat snake around his 5-year-old son, Dari, the boy was clearly unhappy. He had been bitten three times when younger and was a bit shaken by these experiences. Nevertheless, Choto Nath was confident that, in time, Dari would become comfortable with his work as a snaker.

Choto Nath will have much to teach Dari. His son must learn how to catch snakes and must become familiar with the habits of each species. Of course, he must also learn to play the flute in the familiar lilting fashion of snakers. The swaying of the flute back and forth attracts the cobras' attention, but the music itself is aimed at spectators, since snakes have no equivalent of ears and cannot hear the sounds of the flute. Therefore, Dari's anticipatory socialization involves not only the handling of snakes, but also the handling of crowds that he hopes to attract (Skafte, 1979).

(Mary Ellen Mark)

The process of anticipatory socialization begins at an early age for the sons of snakers.

tions. For example, upon entering prison to begin "doing time," a person may experience the humiliation of a *degradation ceremony* as he or she is stripped of clothing, jewelry, and other personal possessions (H. Garfinkel, 1956). Even the person's self is taken away to some extent; the prison inmate loses his or her name and becomes known to authorities as No. 72716. From this point on, daily routines are scheduled with little or no room for personal initiative. The institution is experienced as an overbearing social environment; the individual becomes secondary and rather invisible.

Goffman's concept of a total institution alerts us to the negative aspects of depriving people of contact with the larger society. The power of such institutions in shaping people's behavior was disturbingly illustrated in a famous experiment by Philip Zimbardo (1972, 1974; C. Haney et al., 1973). He and a team of social psychologists carefully screened more than 70 college students for participation in a simulated prison. By a flip of a coin, half were arbitrarily designated as prisoners, the others as guards. The guards were allowed to make up their own rules for maintaining law, order, and respect.

After only six days of operation, Zimbardo and

his colleagues were forced to end the experiment because the student guards had begun to take pleasure in cruel treatment of prisoners. About a third were tyrannical in their arbitrary use of power, while the remaining guards did not agree with this tough approach. At the same time, the prisoners meekly accepted their confinement and mistreatment. More recently, sociologist Ivan Fahs conducted several replications of Zimbardo's model prison experiment over a 4-year period; he came to the same disturbing findings (E. Greene, 1987a).

AGENTS OF SOCIALIZATION

As we have seen, the culture of the United States is defined by rather gradual movements from one stage of socialization to the next. The lifelong socialization process involves many different social forces which influence our lives and alter our self-images. The family is the most important agent of socialization in the United States, especially for children. Five other agents of socialization will be given particular attention in this chapter: the school, the peer group, the mass media, the workplace, and the state. The role of religion in social-

(Topham/The Image Works)

A total institution regulates all aspects of a person's life. A monastery is an example of a total institution; all activities are centered on prayer and communion with God.

izing young people into society's norms and values will be explored in Chapter 14.

Family

The family is the institution most closely associated with the process of socialization. Obviously, one of its primary functions is the care and rearing of children. We experience socialization first as babies and infants living in families; it is here that we develop an initial sense of self. Most parents seek to help their children become competent adolescents and self-sufficient adults, which means socializing them into the norms and values of both the family and the larger society. In this process, adults themselves experience socialization as they adjust to becoming spouses, parents, and in-laws (Gecas, 1981).

The lifelong process of learning begins shortly after birth. Since newborns can hear, see, smell, taste, and feel heat, cold, and pain, they orient themselves to the surrounding world. Human beings, especially family members, constitute an important part of the social environment of the newborn. People minister to the baby's needs by feeding, cleansing, and carrying the baby.

The family of a newborn and other caretakers are not concerned with teaching social skills per se. Nevertheless, babies are hardly asocial. An infant enters an organized society, becomes part of a generation, and typically enters into a family. Depending on how they are treated, infants can develop strong social attachments and dependency on others.

Most infants go through a relatively formal period of socialization generally called *habit training.* Schedules are imposed for eating and sleeping, the termination of breast or bottle feeding, and the acceptance of new foods. In these and other ways, infants can be viewed as objects of socialization, yet they also function as socializers. Even as the behavior of a baby is being modified by interactions with people and the environment, the baby is causing others to change their behavior patterns. He or she converts adults into mothers and fathers, who, in turn, assist the baby in progressing into childhood (Rheingold, 1969).

As both Charles Horton Cooley and George Herbert Mead noted, the development of the self

(Rob Nelson/Picture Group)

Under traditional gender-role socialization in the United States, "toughness" has been seen as masculine—and desirable only in males—while "tenderness" has been viewed as feminine.

is a critical aspect of the early years of one's life. In the United States, such social development includes exposure to cultural assumptions regarding sex differences. The term **gender roles** refers to expectations regarding the proper behavior, attitudes, and activities of males and females. For example, "toughness" has been traditionally seen as masculine—and desirable only in men—while "tenderness" has been viewed as feminine. As we will see in Chapter 11, other cultures do not necessarily assign these qualities to each gender in the way that American culture does.

As the primary agents of childhood socialization, parents play a critical role in guiding children into those gender roles deemed appropriate in a society. Other adults, older siblings, the mass media, and religious and educational institutions also have noticeable impact on a child's socialization into feminine and masculine norms. A culture may require that one sex or the other take primary responsibility for socialization of children, economic support of the family, or religious or intellectual leadership.

Psychologist Shirley Weitz (1977:60–110) has suggested that differential treatment of children by adults is an influential aspect of gender-role socialization. Let us consider a hypothetical example of differential treatment of children which begins in the family. Ron and Louise are twins who both show an unusual interest in science at an early age. For his birthdays, Ron is given chemistry sets, telescopes, microscopes, and the like; however, despite asking for similar gifts, Louise is given miniature dollhouses, beautiful dresses, and dancing lessons.

When the twins are in junior high school, teachers take note of Ron's love for science. They encourage him to do special projects, to help with their laboratory work, and to join the science club. Louise is given no such encouragement; in fact, one teacher considers her fascination with astronomy "strange" for a girl. By the twins' high school years, Ron is known as a "science whiz." The guidance counselor suggests that he attend a college with a strong science program in order to achieve his goal of becoming a biologist. Louise has realized that she would like to become an astronomer, but the counselor and her parents pressure her into preparing for a career as an early childhood teacher—a career which they see as more suitable for a woman.

During their college years, Ron and Louise might develop self-images as "scientist" and "teacher," respectively. On the other hand, Louise might get to college, switch her major, and become an astronomer despite everyone's opposition. Neither of these young people is a passive actor who will inevitably follow the traditional gender roles of American society. Yet it can be extremely difficult to pursue a career, or any other type of life choice, if one's parents, teachers, and the society as a whole seem to be telling you that you are unmasculine or unfeminine for doing so. Without question, differential socialization has a powerful impact on the development of American females and males.

Like other elements of culture, socialization patterns are not fixed. There has, for example, been a sustained challenge to traditional American gender-role socialization in the last 20 years, owing in good part to the efforts of the feminist movement (see Chapter 11). Nevertheless, despite such changes, children growing up in the 1990s are hardly free of traditional gender roles. As Letty Cottin Pogrebin (1981:380), a founder and editor of *Ms.* magazine, wondered, how many parents would move a 6-year-old girl's toy chest into the room of their 6-year-old boy with confidence that he would enjoy its contents?

Interactionists remind us that socialization concerning not only masculinity and femininity, but also marriage and parenthood, begins in childhood as a part of family life. Children observe their parents as they express affection, deal with finances, quarrel, complain about in-laws, and so forth. This represents an informal process of anticipatory socialization. The child develops a tentative model of what being married and being a parent are like. We will explore socialization for marriage and parenthood more fully in Chapter 13.

As noted earlier, children function within the family as agents of socialization themselves. The term *reverse socialization* refers to the process whereby people normally being socialized are at the same time socializing their socializers. For example, young people may affect the way their parents (and other adults) dress, eat, and even think. Sociologist John Peters (1985) studied reverse socialization by surveying the parents of his college students in Canada. Peters found that these parents had been influenced by their children in such areas as sports, politics, clothing, physical appearance, and sexuality (see also Thorne, 1987:95). Anthropologist Margaret Mead (1970:65–91) has suggested that reverse socialization is greatest in societies undergoing rapid social change; in such societies, the young socialize the old to new customs and values.

School

Like the family, schools have an explicit mandate to socialize Americans—and especially children—into the norms and values of our culture. As con-

(Paula M. Lerner/Picture Cube)

In the United States and other cultures, schools serve socialization functions. During the 1980s, Japanese parents and educators were distressed to realize that children were gradually losing the knack of eating with chopsticks. Schools were chosen as the proper institution to remedy this situation.

flict theorists Samuel Bowles and Herbert Gintis (1976) have observed, American schools foster competition through built-in systems of reward and punishment, such as grades and evaluations by teachers. Consequently, a child who is working intently to learn a new skill can nevertheless come to feel stupid and unsuccessful. However, as the self matures, children become capable of increasingly realistic assessments of their intellectual, physical, and social abilities.

Functionalists point out that, as agents of socialization, schools fulfill the function of teaching recruits the values and customs of the larger society. Conflict theorists concur with this observation, but add that schools can reinforce the divisive aspects of society, especially those of social class. For example, American higher education is quite costly despite the existence of financial aid programs. Students from affluent backgrounds thus have an advantage in gaining access to universities and professional training. At the same time, less affluent young people may never receive the preparation that would qualify them for our society's best-paying and most prestigious jobs. The contrast between the functionalist and conflict views of education will be discussed in more detail in Chapter 16.

In teaching students the values and customs of the larger society, American schools have traditionally socialized children into conventional gender roles. Professors of education Myra Sadker and David Sadker (1985:54) note that "although many believe that classroom sexism disappeared in the early '70s, it hasn't." They headed a 3-year study in which field researchers observed students in more than 100 fourth-, sixth-, and eighth-grade classes in four states and the District of Columbia. The researchers found that teachers commonly engage in differential treatment of students based on gender. Teachers praise boys more than girls and offer boys more academic assistance. In addition, they reward boys for assertiveness (for example, calling out answers without raising their hands) while reprimanding girls for similar behavior.

In other cultures as well, schools serve socialization functions. During the 1980s, for example, Japanese parents and educators were distressed to realize that children were gradually losing the knack of eating with chopsticks. Having been seduced by spoons and cheeseburgers, some children could not use *hashi* (chopsticks) at all. Consequently, schools were chosen as the proper institution to remedy this situation. Whereas only 10 percent of school lunch programs provided chopsticks in 1975, this figure had risen to 69 percent in 1983 and to 90 percent by the end of the decade (Hiatt, 1988).

Peer Group

As a child grows older, the family becomes somewhat less important in his or her social development. Instead, peer groups increasingly assume the role of George Herbert Mead's significant others. Within the peer group, young people associate with others who are approximately their own age and who often enjoy a similar social status. For example, in her study of sixth-, seventh-, and eighth-grade girls, sociologist Donna Eder (1985) observed that, at any time, most girls interact primarily with members of a single peer group. While each group's composition may change over the 3-year period, it is generally a select few peers who are important to girls during this developmental period.

Peer groups, such as friendship cliques, youth gangs, and special-interest clubs, frequently assist adolescents in gaining some degree of independence from parents and other authority figures. As we will study in more detail in Chapter 7, conforming to peers' behavior is an example of the socialization process at work. If all of one's friends have successfully battled for the right to stay out until midnight on a Saturday night, it may seem essential to fight for the same privilege. Peer groups also provide for anticipatory socialization into new roles that the young person will later assume.

Teenagers imitate their friends in part because the peer group maintains a meaningful system of rewards and punishments. The group may encourage a young person to follow pursuits that society considers admirable, as in a school club engaged in volunteer work in hospitals and nursing homes. On the other hand, the group may encourage someone to violate the culture's norms and values by driving recklessly, shoplifting, engaging in acts of vandalism, and the like.

Peer groups serve a valuable function by assisting the transition to adult responsibilities. At home, parents tend to dominate; at school, the teenager must contend with teachers and administrators. But, within the peer group, each member can assert himself or herself in a way that may not be possible elsewhere. Nevertheless, almost all adolescents in our culture remain economically dependent on their parents, and most are emotionally dependent as well.

Mass Media

In the last 75 years, such technological innovations as radio, motion pictures, recorded music, and television have become important agents of socialization. Television, in particular, is a critical force in the socialization of American children. Many parents in essence allow the television set to become a child's favorite "playmate"; consequently, children in our society typically watch over 3 hours of television per day. Remarkably, between the ages of 6 and 18, the average young person spends more time watching the "tube" (15,000 to 16,000 hours) than working in school (13,000 hours). Apart from sleeping, watching television is the most time-consuming activity of young Americans.

Relative to other agents of socialization discussed earlier—such as family members, peers, and schools—television has certain distinctive characteristics. It permits imitation and role playing but does not encourage more complex forms of learning. Watching television is, above all, a passive experience; one sits back and waits to be entertained. Psychologist Urie Bronfenbrenner (1970), among others, has expressed concern about the "insidious influence" of television in encouraging children to forsake human interaction for passive viewing.

Critics of television are further alarmed by the programming that children view as they sit for hours in front of a television set. It is generally agreed that children (as well as adults) are exposed to a great deal of violence on television. On Saturday morning cartoon programs, a violent act is presented every 2 minutes. By the time of high school graduation, a young person has witnessed some 18,000 fictional murders on television. Can watching so much violence have a numbing effect on one's sensibilities and moral values? Experiments document that children do tend to become more aggressive and hyperactive after viewing a violent sequence on television. Unfortunately, such studies measure only brief exposure; there

Not only is television an important agent of socialization in the United States; it is even proving to have a significant influence in Samoa, where much of the programming is American.

are no conclusive data on the impact of television violence after weeks, months, and literally years of viewing.

Like other agents of socialization, television has traditionally portrayed and promoted conventional gender roles. A content analysis of child characters on prime-time television revealed that boys are shown as significantly more active, aggressive, and rational than girls. The two sexes are also shown as differing substantially in the types of activities in which they participate. Young girls on prime-time television talk on the telephone, read, and help with housework, whereas boys play sports, go on excursions, and get into mischief. In terms of socialization, television's portrayal of child characters is especially significant, since these characters may be the most meaningful for younger viewers (Peirce, 1989).

Even critics of the medium generally concede that television is not always a negative socializing influence. Creative programming such as *Sesame Street* can assist children in developing basic skills essential for schooling. In addition, television programs and even commercials expose young people to lifestyles and cultures of which they are unaware. This entails not only children in the United States learning about life in "faraway lands," but also inner-city children learning about the lives of farm children and vice versa.

Not only does television educate viewers about members of other cultures and subcultures, it may even influence changes in self-identity. Researchers have long documented the strong differences between Puerto Ricans, Chicanos (Mexican Americans), Cuban Americans, and other Hispanic peoples. Yet the emergence of two nationwide Spanish-language television networks, Univision and Telemundo—watched in 1989 by three-fourths of all Hispanics—has blurred these distinctions somewhat and strengthened the common identity of these minorities as Hispanics. While minimizing certain subcultural differences, television appears to be having a unifying influence on the nation's growing Hispanic population (Mydans, 1989).

Television is unquestionably a powerful agent of socialization in the United States. Indeed, television seems to effectively socialize us to watch television: only 5 percent of adults watch less than 30 minutes per day! In view of the power of television, parents may need to monitor this aspect of a child's environment just as carefully as they evaluate teachers, playmates, and baby-sitters (Huesmann and Malamuth, 1986; Meyrowitz, 1985; R. Roberts, 1987).

While we have focused on criticisms of television as an agent of socialization, it is important to note that similar concerns have been raised regarding the content of popular music (especially rock music and "rap"), music videos, and motion pictures. These forms of entertainment, like television, serve as powerful agents of socialization for many young people in the United States and elsewhere. There has been continuing controversy about the content of music, music videos, and films—sometimes leading to celebrated court battles—as certain parents' organizations and religious groups challenge the intrusion of these media into the lives of children and adolescents. These controversies have often raised the danger of censorship, which will be examined more fully in the social policy section of Chapter 14.

Workplace

A fundamental aspect of human socialization involves learning to behave appropriately within an occupation. In the United States, working full time serves to confirm adult status; it is an indication to all that one has passed out of adolescence. In a sense, socialization into an occupation can represent both a harsh reality ("I have to work in order to buy food and pay the rent") and the realization of an ambition ("I've always wanted to be an airline pilot") (W. Moore, 1968:862).

Occupational socialization cannot be separated from the socialization experiences that occur during childhood and adolescence. We are most fully exposed to occupational roles through observing the work of our parents, of people whom we meet while they are performing their duties (doctors or firefighters, for example), and of people portrayed in the media (presidents, professional athletes, and so forth). These observations, along with the subtle messages we receive within a culture, help to shape—and often limit—the type of work we may consider.

Wilbert Moore (1968:871–880) has divided occupational socialization into four phases. The first phase is *career choice,* which involves selection of academic or vocational training appropriate

for the desired job. If one hopes to become a physician, one must take certain courses, such as biology and chemistry, which are required of applicants to medical school. If one's goal is to become a violin maker, it will be useful to work as an apprentice for an expert practicing that craft.

The next phase identified by Moore is *anticipatory socialization,* which may last only a few months or extend for a period of years. Some American children "inherit" their occupations because their parents run farms or "ma and pa" stores. In Box 4-3, we saw an example of occupational inheritance in the case of Dari, the son of Choto Nath, a snaker. In a sense, these young people are experiencing anticipatory socialization throughout childhood and adolescence as they observe their parents at work. In addition, certain individuals *decide* on occupational goals at relatively early ages and never waver from their choices. A young woman or man may resolve to become a dancer at the age of 11 or 12; the entire adolescent period may focus on training for that future.

The third phase of occupational socialization—*conditioning and commitment*—occurs while one actually occupies the work-related role. *Conditioning* consists of reluctantly adjusting to the more unpleasant aspects of one's job. Most people find that the novelty of a new daily schedule quickly wears off and then realize that parts of the work experience are rather tedious. Moore uses the term *commitment* to refer to the enthusiastic acceptance of pleasurable duties that comes as the recruit identifies the positive tasks of an occupation.

In Moore's view, if a job proves to be satisfactory, the person will enter a fourth stage of socialization, which he calls *continuous commitment.* At this point, the job becomes an indistinguishable part of the person's self-identity. Violation of proper conduct becomes unthinkable. A person may choose to join professional associations, unions, or other groups which represent his or her occupation in the larger society.

Occupational socialization can be most intense immediately after one makes the transition from school to the job, but it continues through one's work history. Technological advances may alter the requirements of the position and necessitate some degree of resocialization. Thus, after years of working at typewriters, secretaries may find themselves adjusting to sophisticated word-processing equipment. In addition, many Americans change occupations, employers, or places of work during their adult years. Therefore, occupational socialization continues throughout a person's years in the labor market (Mortimer and Simmons, 1978:440–441; see also Becker et al., 1961; Ritzer, 1977).

The State

Social scientists have increasingly recognized the importance of the state as an agent of socialization because of its growing impact on the life cycle. Traditionally, family members have served as the primary caregivers in our culture, but in the twentieth century the family's protective function has steadily been transferred to outside agencies such as hospitals, mental health clinics, and insurance companies (Ogburn and Tibbits, 1934:661–778). Many of these agencies are run by the government; the rest are licensed and regulated by governmental bodies. In the social policy section of this chapter, we will see that the state is under pressure to become a provider of child care, which would give it a new and direct role in the socialization of infants and young children.

In the past, the life cycle was influenced most significantly by heads of households and by local groups such as religious organizations. However, in the 1990s the individual as a citizen and an economic actor is influenced by national interests. For example, labor unions and political parties serve as intermediaries between the individual and the state.

The state has had a noteworthy impact on the life cycle by reinstituting the rites of passage that had disappeared in agricultural societies and in periods of early industrialization. For example, government regulations stipulate the ages at which a person may drive a car, drink alcohol, vote in elections, marry without parental permission, work overtime, and retire. These regulations do not constitute strict rites of passage: most 21-year-olds do not vote and most people choose their age of retirement without reference to government dictates. Still, by regulating the life cycle to some degree, the state shapes the socialization process by influencing our views of appropriate behavior at particular ages (Mayer and Schoepflin, 1989).

SOCIAL POLICY AND SOCIALIZATION

THE NEED FOR CHILD CARE

- Is it desirable to expose young children to the socializing influence of day care?
- In the view of conflict theorists, why does child care receive little government support?
- Should the costs of day care programs be paid by government, by the private sector, or entirely by parents?

The rise in single-parent families, increased job opportunities for women, and the need for additional family income have all propelled an increasing number of mothers of young children into the paid labor force of the United States (see Chapter 11). The majority of all mothers with children under the age of 6 are now found in the paid labor force, and the number either working or looking for a job is expected to reach 70 percent by the year 2000. Who, then, will take care of the children of these women during work hours? For two-thirds of all 3-to-5-year-olds for whom national data is now available, the solution has become group child care programs. Day care centers have become the functional equivalent of the nuclear family, performing some of the nurturing and socialization functions previously handled only by family members (Holmes, 1990b).

The first day care centers in the United States were established by wealthy women in the 1850s. These centers cared for unwed mothers and their offspring. Conflict sociologists have noted that day care centers traditionally served as socializing agents which taught middle-class values to needy children. These children

DOONESBURY BY GARRY TRUDEAU

were introduced to books and encouraged to broaden their experiences. However, the idea that middle-class mothers might enter the labor force by choice and place their children in day care centers has met with resistance. Reflecting the entrenched view of women (but not men) as caretakers for children, American society has expected middle-class mothers to focus on their children's needs rather than their own career aspirations.

Studies indicate that children placed in high-quality child care centers are not adversely affected by such experiences; in fact, good day care benefits children. The value of preschool programs was documented in a comparison of full-time Milwaukee preschoolers with a "non-nursery" group. Those children attending the preschool program from ages 3 months to 6 years showed significantly greater language development and greater gains on achievement tests than children in the non-nursery control group did. In addition, research conducted in the last few years indicates that children in day care or preschool programs are more self-sufficient. They react well to separation from their parents and tend to have more stimulating interactions when together. Finally, it appears from recent studies that children may be better off in centers with well-trained caregivers than cared for full time by those mothers who are depressed and frustrated because they wish to work outside the home (G. Collins,

1984:11; Galinsky, 1986; Garber and Herber, 1977; Shell, 1988).

Even if policymakers decide that publicly funded child care is desirable, they must determine the degree to which taxpayers should subsidize it. A number of European nations, including the Netherlands, Sweden, and the Soviet Union, provide preschool care at minimal or no cost. France has a comprehensive system of child care services which are largely financed by tax revenues, including free full-day preschool programs, subsidized day care centers, and licensed care in private homes for infants and toddlers. However, providing first-rate child care in the United States is anything but cheap, with a cost of $4000 a child per year not unusual in urban areas. Thus, a nationally financed system of child care could lead to staggering costs (Lawson, 1989).

Feminists echo the concern of conflict theorists that high-quality child care receives little governmental support because it is regarded as "merely a way to let women work." Nearly all child care workers (94 percent) are women; many find themselves in low-status, minimum wage jobs. The average salary of child care workers in the United States is only about $9000, and there are few fringe benefits. A child care teacher with a college degree earns only 45 percent as much as a similarly educated woman working in other occupations and only 27 percent as much as a similarly educated man. Although parents may complain of child care costs, the staff are, in effect, subsidizing children's care by working for low wages. Not surprisingly, there is a high turnover among child care teachers. In 1988, 41 percent of these teachers left their jobs—a dramatic rise from the rate in preceding years (Hellmich, 1990; Reardon, 1989).

Thus far, few local communities have passed ordinances to encourage child care. However, the city of San Francisco has required developers of new downtown office projects to provide either space or financial support for child care facilities. Developers have the option of including space that can be used rent-free by a nonprofit day care program (including programs sponsored by employers). If they do not exercise this option, developers must contribute $1 per square foot of office space to a special city fund. San Francisco officials endorse such measures because they believe that lack of adequate day car hurts both employers and employees (S. Porter, 1985:52).

What about the private sector? Companies are increasingly recognizing that child care can be good for business, since many employees view it as an important fringe benefit. Between 1984 and 1987, there was an increase of 50 percent in the number of companies that offer subsidized child care, financial assistance for child care, or child referral services. Still, even with this increase, as of 1988, only 2 percent of the nation's larger employers sponsored their own day care centers; only 11 percent offered any services to assist employees in arranging for child care. Moreover, many of these existing programs are too expensive for companies' lower-level employees (Auerbach, 1988; F. Chapman, 1987; McNulty, 1988).

Many policymakers believe that parents—rather than government or the private sector—should be solely responsible for the costs of day care programs. Yet child care is often relied upon because a parent is attempting to increase family income. Unless fees are kept to a minimum, the expenses of day care will wipe out the additional wages earned. Viewed from a conflict perspective, child care costs are an especially serious burden for lower-class families, who already find it hard to take advantage of limited job opportunities.

The difficulty of finding affordable child care has particularly serious implications for mothers who work (or wish to work) outside the home. A survey by the Census Bureau, released in 1983, revealed that

over 200,000 unemployed women had turned down firm job offers in a 4-week period because of problems in arranging child care for children under 5 years old. Another 1.7 million women had decided not to seek employment because of the unavailability of affordable child care. Even if they enter the paid labor force, mothers may find their work performance and opportunities for advancement hindered by child care difficulties. In this regard, a 1987 survey by *Fortune* magazine found that problems with child care—specifically, difficulties in finding child care, dissatisfaction with current child care arrangements, and the frequency with which such arrangements break down—were the most significant predictors of absenteeism and unproductive time at work. Since child care is commonly viewed as a woman's responsibility, working mothers (rather than working fathers) are especially likely to bear the burden of these problems (Auerbach, 1987; Galinsky and Hughes, 1987; O'Connell and Rogers, 1983:16,19).

In a report issued in late 1988, the Child Care Action Campaign—a national coalition of leaders from government, the media, corporations, labor unions, religious groups, and women's groups—asserted that lack of adequate day care is weakening the economy of the United States. The report concludes that child care can expand the nation's labor pool, that early education can improve students' educational performance, that child care enables families to be financially self-sufficient, and that child care improves corporate productivity. In the view of the Child Care Action Campaign: "All sectors of our economy must make a significant investment in child care" (Reisman et al., 1988:10).

Public support for child care has risen markedly in the last 2 decades. In 1987, national surveys showed that 80 percent of adults favored the establishment of more day care services for children (compared with only 56 percent in 1970). In a 1989 survey, two-thirds of parents with children under 14 years of age agreed that government has an obligation to provide child care assistance, and 57 percent of these parents stated that employers have a similar responsibility. But, to date, most government officials and leaders of private enterprise continue to give low priority to the issue of child care. This is ironic given the importance of early childhood socialization to the intellectual and social development of future generations of Americans (Morin, 1989; S. Rebell, 1987).

In 1987, the Act for Better Child Care (known as the *ABC bill*) was introduced in Congress to make child care more affordable for low-income families and to increase the accessibility of high-quality child care for *all* families. The ABC bill continued to be a focal point of discussion for policymakers and finally was approved in greatly modified form in 1990 as the Child Care Act. Consisting of two parts, this act provided for both grants and tax credits to support child care. A total of $2.5 billion was authorized for grants to the states over the years 1991–1993, with most of this funding intended to assist low-income families in obtaining child care services. The new tax credits would allow parents to deduct out-of-pocket child care expenses from their income taxes. While this legislation provides much less financial support for child care than had been proposed years earlier, it nevertheless establishes a precedent for direct federal subsidies through the states for child care programs.

Intense debate continues over the appropriate federal role in child care, focusing on such issues as the possible costs of federal support, the degree to which the federal government should regulate child care centers, and the constitutional question raised by the financing of centers in religious facilities (which account for about one-third of all day care centers). The debate over these issues has thus far hindered enactment of a more comprehensive child care measure by the federal government (Holmes, 1990a; Rovner, 1990).

SUMMARY

Socialization is the process whereby people learn the attitudes, values, and actions appropriate to individuals as members of a particular culture. This chapter examines the role of socialization in human development; the way in which people develop perceptions, feelings, and beliefs about themselves; and the lifelong nature of the socialization process.

1 Socialization affects the overall cultural practices of a society, and it also shapes the images that we hold of ourselves.

2 It is an oversimplification to draw a sharp line between the physical and social aspects of human development.

3 In the early 1900s, Charles Horton Cooley advanced the belief that we learn who we are by interacting with others.

4 George Herbert Mead is best known for his theory of the *self*. He proposed that as people mature, their selves begin to reflect their concern about reactions from others.

5 Erving Goffman has shown that many of our daily activities involve attempts to convey distinct impressions of who we are.

6 On the basis of research involving American men, psychologist Daniel J. Levinson identified three major transitional periods which occur primarily after adolescence: the early-adult transition, the midlife transition, and the late-adult transition.

7 While Levinson's conclusions are relevant for some women, expectations at different stages of socialization are not necessarily the same for men and women.

8 The family is the most important agent of socialization in the United States, especially for children.

9 As the primary agents of socialization, parents play a critical role in guiding children into those *gender roles* deemed appropriate in a society.

10 Like the family, schools have an explicit mandate to socialize Americans—and especially children—into the norms and values of our culture.

11 Peer groups frequently assist adolescents in gaining some degree of independence from parents and other authority figures.

12 Television has been criticized as an agent of socialization because it encourages children to forsake human interaction for passive viewing.

13 We are most fully exposed to occupational roles through observing the work of our parents, of people whom we meet while they are performing their duties, and of people portrayed in the media.

14 By regulating the life cycle, the state shapes the socialization process by influencing our views of appropriate behavior at particular ages.

15 As more and more mothers of young children have entered the labor market of the United States, the demand for child care has increased dramatically.

KEY TERMS

Anticipatory socialization Processes of socialization in which a person "rehearses" for future positions, occupations, and social relationships. (page 113)

Cognitive theory of development Jean Piaget's theory explaining how children's thought progresses through four stages. (108)

Degradation ceremony An aspect of the socialization process within total institutions, in which people are subjected to humiliating rituals. (115)

Dramaturgical approach A view of social interaction, popularized by Erving Goffman, under which people are examined as if they were theatrical performers. (106)

Face-work A term used by Erving Goffman to refer to people's efforts to maintain the proper image and avoid embarrassment in public. (106)

Gender roles Expectations regarding the proper behavior, attitudes, and activities of males and females. (116)

Generalized others A term used by George Herbert Mead to refer to the child's awareness of the attitudes, viewpoints, and expectations of society as a whole. (106)

Impression management A term used by Erving Goffman to refer to the altering of the presentation of the self in order to create distinctive appearances and satisfy particular audiences. (106)

Looking-glass self A phrase used by Charles Horton Cooley to emphasize that the self is the product of our social interactions with others. (105)

Midlife crisis A stressful period of self-evaluation, often occurring between the ages of 35 and 50, in which a person realizes that he or she has not achieved certain personal goals and aspirations and that time is running out. (111)

Personality In everyday speech, a person's typical patterns of attitudes, needs, characteristics, and behavior. (99)

Resocialization The process of discarding former behavior patterns and accepting new ones as part of a transition in one's life. (113)

Reverse socialization The process whereby people normally being socialized are at the same time socializing their socializers. (117)

Rites of passage Rituals marking the symbolic transition from one social position to another. (110)

Role taking The process of mentally assuming the perspective of another, thereby enabling one to respond from that imagined viewpoint. (105)

Self According to George Herbert Mead, the sum total of people's conscious perception of their identity as distinct from others. (104)

Significant others A term used by George Herbert Mead to refer to those individuals who are most important in the development of the self, such as parents, friends, and teachers. (106)

Socialization The process whereby people learn the attitudes, values, and actions appropriate to individuals as members of a particular culture. (98)

Sociobiology The systematic study of the biological bases of social behavior. (103)

Studied nonobservance A term used by Erving Goffman to refer to polite behavior intended to allow saving face. (107)

Symbols The gestures, objects, and language which form the basis of human communication. (105)

Total institutions A term coined by Erving Goffman to refer to institutions which regulate all aspects of a person's life under a single authority, such as prisons, the military, mental hospitals, and convents. (113)

ADDITIONAL READINGS

Bronfenbrenner, Urie. *Two Worlds of Childhood: U.S. and U.S.S.R.* New York: Russell Sage, 1970. The noted psychologist offers insight into the coming of age in these societies and focuses particularly on the role of preschool programs.

Elkin, Frederick, and Gerald Handel. *The Child and Society: The Process of Socialization* (5th ed.). New York: Random House, 1989. This book reviews the social science literature on socialization, examines agents of socialization, and gives special emphasis to gender-role socialization.

Goffman, Erving. *The Presentation of Self in Everyday Life.* New York: Doubleday, 1959. Goffman demonstrates his interactionist theory that the self is managed in everyday situations in much the same way that a theatrical performer carries out a stage role.

Harlow, Harry F. *Learning to Love.* New York: Ballantine, 1971. This heavily illustrated book describes the landmark studies of behavior conducted at the Primate Research Center at the University of Wisconsin.

Hendry, Joy. *Becoming Japanese: The World of the Pre-School Child.* Honolulu: University of Hawaii Press, 1986. Illustrated with photographs, Hendry's book looks at child rearing by Japanese mothers and other caregivers, including teachers at kindergartens and day nurseries.

Kitcher, Philip. *Vaulting Ambition: Sociobiology and the Quest for Human Nature.* Cambridge, Mass.: M.I.T. Press, 1985. A presentation of sociobiology with a detailed critique of its tenets.

Levinson, Daniel. *The Seasons of a Man's Life.* New York: Knopf, 1978. This well-received book outlines the stages of life for men in the United States.

Lott, Bernice. *Women's Lives: Themes and Variations in Gender Learning.* Monterey, Calif.: Brooks/Cole, 1987. An overview of the socialization experiences of women in the United States.

Rose, Peter I. (ed.). *Socialization and the Life Cycle.* New York: St. Martin's, 1979. A variety of articles examine the process of socialization from birth to death and bereavement.

Schlenker, Barry R. (ed.). *The Self and Social Life.* New York: McGraw-Hill, 1985. Social scientists, primarily psychologists, examine the concept of the self as an explanation of behavior.

Sheehy, Gail. *Passages: Predictable Crises of Adult Life.* New York: Dutton, 1976. A best-seller when it appeared, this book presents Sheehy's "sexual diamond" concept. In her view, a man and a woman feel the closest bonds to each other at the age of 18 and in later life but are farthest apart in their late thirties and forties.

Tobin, Joseph J., David Y. H. Wu, and Dana H. Davidson. *Preschool in Three Cultures: Japan, China, and the United States.* New Haven, Conn.: Yale University Press, 1989. A comparative look at formal early childhood education in three nations, drawing upon the views of parents, teachers, and administrators.

Journals

Among the journals that deal with socialization issues are *Adolescence* (founded in 1966), *Journal of Personality and Social Psychology* (1965), and *Young Children* (1945).

5

SOCIAL INTERACTION AND SOCIAL STRUCTURE

All the world's a stage,
And all the men and women
merely players:
They have their exits and
their entrances;
And one man in his time plays
many parts. . . .
William Shakespeare
As You Like It, 1599–1600

LOOKING AHEAD

- How do we redefine reality through social interaction?
- How do sociologists use the term *status?*
- Why are social roles a significant component of social structure?
- How is "networking" helpful in finding employment?
- How do the family, religion, and government contribute to a society's survival?
- How do social interactions in a preindustrial village differ from those in a modern urban center?
- How has the social structure of the United States been affected by the spread of AIDS?

In American society, men and women perform a wide variety of jobs, not all of which are legal. The illegal occupation of burglary is by necessity a social enterprise. Successful burglars rarely work alone; a minimum of three people is typically required for this physically demanding, time-consuming labor. Their work is always performed under the threat of potential discovery, injury, or arrest.

Sociologist Neal Shover (1971, 1973) studied the lives of past and present burglars in order to better understand the social world in which these skilled criminals interact. Shover identifies two levels of social organization in the world of burglary. He uses the term *internal social organization* to refer to the division of labor among burglary "crews." For example, one team member may serve as a "scout" (who excels at locating potentially valuable "scores"), another as a "mechanic" (skilled at opening safes), and a third as a "point man" (who serves as a lookout). Burglars' *external social organization* includes connections with tipsters on the lookout for potential victims, "fences," bail bondsmen, and even "fixes" (dishonest police officers).

Not all burglars are regarded with equal respect by their peers. A "good" thief is viewed as someone who is (1) technically competent, (2) known for personal integrity, (3) a specialist in burglary, and (4) relatively successful at crime. Success is measured both by the value of goods stolen and by how little time, if any, is spent in jail. One man interviewed by Shover had lived off his burglary work for 20 years without ever being jailed—thereby marking him as a very skilled thief in the opinion of his peers. Only about one out of nine thieves achieve the select status of "good burglar" (Bennett and Wright, 1984; D. Walsh, 1986).

Life among burglars is obviously quite different from life in a large corporation, yet the behavior of individuals in each of these worlds is characterized by predictable patterns of social interaction. Sociologists use the term *social interaction* to refer to the ways in which people respond to one another. These interactions need not be face to face; friends talking over the telephone and coworkers communicating over a computer are engaged in social interaction. *Social structure* refers to the way in which a society is organized into predictable relationships.

These concepts are central to sociological study; they focus on how different aspects of behavior are related to one another. In culture are found the elements of a society, while social structure constrains the ways and processes by which these elements are organized. For example, purchasing professional services is an aspect of culture, yet the social structure defines how these services may be acquired. "Good" burglars have identified bail bondsmen or attorneys who will accept property—some of which is certain to be stolen—as compensation for their services, thereby creating a structure by organizing the elements of this interaction (Shover, 1973:510).

Sociologists observe patterns of behavior closely in order to understand and accurately describe the social interactions of a community or society and the social structure of which this behavior is a part. Thus, in examining the social world of burglars, Shover (1973:499–500) studied 34 available autobiographies of professional thieves and 12 journalistic accounts of burglars, conducted interviews with 47 incarcerated burglars, administered questionnaires to 88 burglars confined in prisons, and conducted other interviews with burglars and fences. Using such research methods—as well as any others that may prove useful for a particular study—sociologists can detect systematic patterns of social structure even in communities and subcultures that seem chaotic or aimless to the untrained passerby.

This chapter begins by considering how social interaction shapes the way we view the world around us. Interactions involve negotiation, which results in ever-changing forms of social organization. The chapter will focus on the four basic elements of social structure: statuses, social roles, groups, and institutions. Since much of our behavior occurs in groups, the vital part that groups play in a society's social structure will be emphasized. Social institutions such as the family, religion, and government are a fundamental aspect of social structure. The chapter will contrast the functionalist, conflict, and interactionist approaches to the study of social institutions. It will also examine the typologies developed by sociologists Émile Durkheim and Ferdinand Tönnies for comparing modern societies with simpler forms of social structure. The social policy section will consider the AIDS crisis and its implications for the social institutions of the United States.

SOCIAL INTERACTION AND REALITY

According to sociologist Herbert Blumer (1969a:79), the distinctive characteristic of social interaction among people is that "human beings interpret or 'define' each other's actions instead of merely reacting to each other's actions." In other words, our response to someone's behavior is based on the *meaning* we attach to his or her actions. Reality is shaped by our perceptions, evaluations, and definitions. These meanings reflect the norms and values of the dominant culture and our socialization experiences within that culture.

Defining and Reconstructing Reality

How do we define our social reality? As an example, let us examine how abortion clinics attempt to present themselves to their clients. Two different sociologists examined abortion clinics: one in the 1960s, when abortion was illegal, the other in the late 1970s after the Supreme Court's landmark 1973 decision assuring a right to abortion under most circumstances (see Chapter 11). Before abortion was legal, clinics attempted to reassure women by emphasizing medical professionalism and creating an intentionally sterile atmosphere—much like that of a doctor's office or a hospital. However, by the late 1970s, clinics had begun to deemphasize this clinical focus and instead to stress that they were offering "personalized," nontraditional care. Attention turned to relaxing the client, offering her emotional support, and

An important aspect of social change involves redefining or reconstructing social reality. Members of the environmental group Greenpeace hope to alter social reality by ending people's acceptance of a world with nuclear weapons. In this 1989 protest, Greenpeace sent a "peace fleet" (one sloop and five dinghies) to New York harbor to join a flotilla of military ships and dramatize Greenpeace's opposition to the nuclear threat.

encouraging discussion of any doubts or fears. In each time period, abortion clinics attempted to project and define a particular social reality that would help women to feel more comfortable in seeking out their services (Ball, 1967; Charon, 1985:184; P. M. Hall, 1987:6–7; M. Zimmerman, 1981:151).

The ability to define social reality clearly reflects a group's power within a society. Indeed, one of the most crucial aspects of the relationship between dominant and subordinate groups is the ability of the dominant or majority group to define a society's values. American sociologist William I. Thomas (1923:41–44), an early critic of theories of racial and gender differences, saw that the "definition of the situation" could mold the thinking and personality of the individual. Writing from an interactionist perspective, Thomas observed that people respond not only to the objective features of a person or situation but also to the meaning that the person or situation has for them.

As we have seen throughout the last 30 years—first in the civil rights movement of the 1960s and since then among such groups as women, the elderly, gays and lesbians, and people with disabilities—an important aspect of the process of social

change involves redefining or reconstructing social reality. Members of subordinate groups begin to challenge traditional definitions and instead perceive and experience reality in a new way. For example, the Black activist Malcolm X (1925–1965), an eloquent and controversial advocate of Black power and Black pride in the early 1960s, recalled that his feelings and perspective changed dramatically while in eighth grade. His English teacher advised him that his goal of becoming a lawyer was "no realistic goal for a nigger" and encouraged him instead to become a carpenter. In Malcolm X's (1964:37) words:

It was then that I began to change—inside. I drew away from white people. I came to class, and I answered when called upon. It became a physical strain simply to sit in Mr. Ostrowski's class. Where "nigger" had slipped off my back before, wherever I heard it now, I stopped and looked at whoever said it. And they looked surprised that I did.

Viewed from a sociological perspective, Malcolm X was redefining social reality by looking much more critically at the racist thinking and terminology that restricted him and other African Americans (Charon, 1985:4).

Negotiated Order

As we have seen, people can reconstruct social reality through a process of internal change as they take a different view of everyday behavior. Yet people also reshape reality by negotiating changes in patterns of social interaction. The term **negotiation** refers to the attempt to reach agreement with others concerning some objective. Negotiation does not involve coercion; it goes by many names, including *bargaining, compromising, trading off, mediating, exchanging, "wheeling and dealing,"* and *collusion* (A. Strauss, 1977:2; see also G. Fine, 1984).

Negotiation occurs on many levels. We may negotiate with others regarding time ("When should we arrive?"), space ("Can we have a meeting at your house?"), or even assignment of places while waiting for concert tickets. Burglars commonly bargain with tipsters about how much the tipsters should be paid for the information that they provide—usually a flat 10 percent of the gross proceeds of a "score" (Shover, 1973).

In traditional societies, impending marriages often lead to negotiations between the families of the husband and wife. For example, anthropologist Ray Abrahams (1968) has described how the Labwor people of Africa arrange for an amount of property to go to the bride's family at the time of marriage. In the view of the Labwor, such bargaining over an exchange of cows and sheep culminates not only in a marriage but, more important, in the linking of two clans or families.

While such family-to-family bargaining is common in traditional cultures, negotiation can take much more elaborate forms in modern industrial societies. Consider the tax laws of the United States. From a sociological perspective, such laws are formal norms (reflected in federal and state codes) that constitute the framework in which negotiations take place concerning legitimate tax deductions. If audited, taxpayers will mediate with agents of the Internal Revenue Service. Changes in the taxpayers' individual situations will occur through such negotiations. On a broader level, however, the entire tax code undergoes revision through negotiated outcomes involving many competing interests, including big business, foreign nations, and political action committees (see Chapter 15). The tax structure of the United States can hardly be viewed as fixed; rather, it reflects the sum of negotiations for change at any time (Maines, 1977:242–244, 1982; J. Thomas, 1984).

It is important to understand that negotiations are not merely an aspect of social interaction; they underlie much of our social behavior. Most elements of social structure are not static and are therefore subject to change through bargaining and exchanging. For this reason, sociologists use the term *negotiated order* to underscore the fact that negotiations always take place within social settings. **Negotiated order** refers to a social structure that derives its existence from the social interactions through which people define and redefine its character.

We can add negotiation to our list of cultural universals (see Chapter 3) because all societies provide guidelines or norms in which negotiations take place. Not all behavior involves negotiated order; after all, there are social orders involving manipulation and coercion. Nevertheless, the recurring role of negotiation in social interaction and social structure will be apparent as we examine statuses, social roles, groups, and institutions (Strauss, 1977:234–236, 262).

ELEMENTS OF SOCIAL STRUCTURE

Predictable social relationships can be examined in terms of four elements: statuses, social roles, groups, and social institutions. These elements make up social structure just as a foundation, walls, ceilings, and furnishings make up a building's structure. We know that furnishings can vary widely from those of an office building to the elaborate furnishings of a palace. Similarly, the elements of a society's social structure can vary dramatically.

Statuses

When we speak of a person's "status" in casual conversation, the term usually conveys connotations of influence, wealth, and fame. However,

FIGURE 5-1 Social Statuses

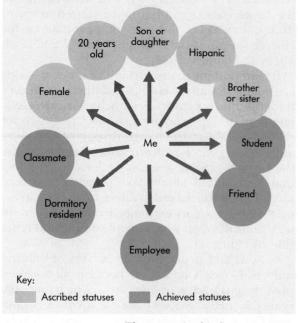

The person in this figure—"me"—occupies many positions in society, each of which involves distinct statuses. The gold circles indicate ascribed statuses; the brown circles represent achieved statuses.

sociologists use *status* to refer to any of the full range of socially defined positions within a large group or society—from the lowest to the highest position. Within American society, a person can occupy the status of president of the United States, fruit picker, son or daughter, violinist, teenager, resident of Minneapolis, dental technician, or neighbor. Clearly, a person holds more than one status simultaneously. For example, Alina is an economist, an author, a sister, a resident of Connecticut, and a Puerto Rican at the same time.

Ascribed and Achieved Status Some of the statuses we hold are viewed by sociologists as *ascribed,* while others are categorized as *achieved* (see Figure 5-1). An *ascribed status* is "assigned" to a person by society without regard for the person's

unique talents or characteristics. Generally, this assignment takes place at birth; thus, a person's racial background, gender, and age are all considered ascribed statuses. These characteristics are biological in origin but are significant mainly because of the social meanings that they have in our culture. Conflict theorists are especially interested in ascribed statuses, since these statuses often confer privileges or reflect a person's membership in a subordinate group. The social meanings of race and ethnicity, gender, and age will be analyzed more fully in Chapters 10, 11, and 12, respectively.

In most cases, there is little that people can do to change an ascribed status. We must adapt to any constraints that such statuses hold for us—although we can attempt to change the way in which society views an ascribed status. As an example, the Gray Panthers hope to restructure social reality by modifying society's negative and confining stereotypes regarding older people (see Chapter 12). If they are successful, the ascribed status of "senior citizen" will not be as difficult for millions of older Americans.

It is important to emphasize that an ascribed status does not necessarily have the same social meaning in every society. In a cross-cultural study, sociologist Gary Huang (1988) confirmed the long-held view that respect for the elderly is an important cultural norm in China. In many cases, the prefix "old" will be used respectfully: calling someone "old teacher" or "old person" has a similar meaning to calling an American judge "your honor." Huang points out that positive age-seniority distinctions in language are absent in the United States; consequently, the term "old man" is viewed as more of an insult than a celebration of seniority and wisdom.

Unlike ascribed statuses, an **achieved status** is attained by a person largely through his or her own effort. Both "bank president" and "burglar" are achieved statuses, as are "lawyer," "pianist," "advertising executive," and "social worker." One must do something to acquire an achieved status—go to school, learn a skill, establish a friendship, or invent a new product.

Master Status Each person holds many different statuses; some may connote higher social positions and some, lower positions. How is one's overall position viewed by others in light of these conflicting statuses? Sociologist Everett Hughes (1945) observed that societies deal with such inconsistencies by agreeing that certain statuses are more important than others. A *master status* is a status that dominates others and thereby determines a person's general position within society. For example, even though he owns a restaurant in San Francisco, Joe Dimaggio's status as a great baseball star far outweighs his status as an entrepreneur. Conversely, as we will see in Chapter 20, many Americans with disabilities find that their status as "disabled" is given undue weight and overshadows their actual ability to perform successfully in meaningful employment.

Race and gender are given such importance in our society that they often dominate one's life. Indeed, such ascribed statuses influence achieved status. As we have seen, Malcolm X found that his position as a Black man (ascribed status) was an obstacle to his dream of becoming a lawyer (achieved status). In the United States, ascribed statuses of race and gender can function as master statuses that have an important impact on one's potential to achieve a desired professional and social status.

Social Roles

What Are Social Roles?   Throughout our lives, we are acquiring what sociologists call *social roles*. A *social role* is a set of expectations for people who occupy a given social position or status. Thus, in the United States, we expect that cab drivers will know how to get around a city, that secretaries will be reliable in handling phone messages, and that police officers will take action if they see a citizen being threatened. With each distinctive social status—whether ascribed or achieved—come particular role expectations. However, actual performance varies from individual to individual. One secretary may assume extensive administrative responsibilities, while another may focus on clerical duties.

The roles we assume are usually defined in the context of social roles performed by others. Thus, we can play the roles associated with being a daughter or son because someone else fulfills the roles associated with the social position of father or mother. In order to perform the roles that accompany the status of employer, a person must have one or more employees. Such social roles are known as *complementary roles,* since they require that the behavior of two or more people interact in specific ways.

As part of his examination of the social organization of burglary, Neal Shover (1973:509) studied "fences" (people who knowingly buy stolen merchandise). A person can perform the role of fence only if someone else fulfills the complementary role of thief and sells merchandise to the fence. Interestingly, Shover found that fences usually have legitimate occupational roles in the business world. Almost half are owners of stores or taverns, while others are television repairers, insurance brokers, and auctioneers. Holding a respectable job is advantageous for fences because it allows them to earn cash to purchase stolen goods, provides business contacts useful in disposing of illicit merchandise, and helps them mask their criminal activities.

Roles are a significant component of social structure. Viewed from a functionalist perspective, roles contribute to a society's stability by enabling members to anticipate the behavior of others and to pattern their own actions accordingly. Yet social roles can also be dysfunctional by restricting people's relationships with each other. If we view a person *only* as a "police officer" or a "supervisor," it will be difficult to relate to this person as a friend or neighbor. The demands and restrictions of certain roles contribute to the process of disengagement known as *role exit* (see Box 5-1 on page 136).

In the quotation at the beginning of the chapter, Shakespeare uses the theater as an analogy for the world as a whole and for the human experience. Actors obviously take on roles, but so do the rest of us. We learn how to fulfill a social role by observing the behavior and interactions of others.

Role Ambiguity and Role Strain   Stage performers sometimes find it difficult to play a particular part. Should a hero be portrayed without faults and shortcomings? Should the more sympathetic qualities of a villain be emphasized? In a similar

BOX 5-1 • CURRENT RESEARCH

THE PROCESS OF ROLE EXIT

Often when we think of assuming a social role, we focus on the preparation and anticipatory socialization that a person undergoes in becoming ready for that role. This is true if a person is about to become an attorney, a chef, a spouse, or a parent. Yet, until recently, social scientists have given less attention to the adjustments involved in *leaving* social roles.

Sociologist Helen Rose Fuchs Ebaugh (1988) developed the term *role exit* to describe the process of disengagement from a role that is central to one's self-identity and reestablishment of an identity in a new role. Drawing on interviews with 185 persons—among them ex-convicts, divorced men and women, recovering alcoholics, ex-nuns, former doctors, retirees, and transsexuals—Ebaugh studied the process of voluntarily exiting from significant social roles.

Ebaugh's interest in role exit grew out of her own background as an ex-nun. She recalls: "I grew up in a small Catholic, German community in Olfen, Texas, where at 18 women had the choice of getting married or joining the convent. The nuns were unwitting feminists back then in that they were the only educated role models we had." She spent 11 years as Sister Helen Rose, but while working on her doctorate at Columbia University, she began questioning her religious life and realized she felt a strong desire to be married and have children (Bartlett, 1988:C1).

Ebaugh has offered a four-stage model of role exit. The first stage begins with doubt—as the person experiences frustration, burnout, or simply unhappiness with an accustomed status and the roles associated with this social position. This doubt leads to what Ebaugh calls *unconscious cueing,* which was evident in the convent in the hairstyles of nuns. In Ebaugh's view, those nuns who let their hair grow longer and turned to fashionable hairstyles were in the initial stage of role exit.

The second stage involves a search for alternatives. A person unhappy with his or her career may take a leave of absence; an unhappily married couple may begin what they see as a temporary separation. Then comes the third stage of role exit: the action stage or departure. Ebaugh found that the vast majority of her respondents identified a clear turning point which made them feel it was essential to take final action and leave their jobs, end their marriages, or engage in other types of role exit. However, 20 percent of respondents saw their role exits as a gradual, evolutionary process that had no single turning point.

The last stage of role exit involves the creation of a new identity. Ebaugh points out: "It is important to maintain contact with some people in the old role, to keep some bridges. . . . It's also important to be able to talk to someone about who one used to be." Consequently, while she is now a sociologist, wife, and mother of two children, Ebaugh has not blocked out her memories of her years in the convent. In fact, in 1988 she attended what would have been her twenty-fifth anniversary as a nun, had she remained in her religious order. "It was a wonderful kind of closure for me," says Ebaugh (Bartlett, 1988:C1).

---

way, as we take on social roles in our day-to-day lives, we may feel uncertain about what is expected of us. *Role ambiguity* refers to unclear expectations associated with particular social positions.

Being someone's friend is one of our society's most loosely defined statuses and thus generates a great deal of role ambiguity. To what extent should you speak up if a close friend seems to be making a disastrous mistake—marrying the "wrong person" or making a dubious career choice? Should you cancel your plans for the weekend if a friend is very depressed and needs company badly? What if you want to see a friend about once a month, but that friend insists on getting together at least once a week?

There are no simple answers to these questions. In good part, this is because there are many varying expectations regarding friendship in our society. It not only has different meanings for each individual but also can have different meanings for the same person within a number of relationships. Thus, in one friendship you are willing to invest a great deal of time, and feel a commitment to "be there" when the friend feels troubled. In another friendship, you prefer to see the person occasionally and avoid any emotional responsibilities.

In some cases, role ambiguity leads to *role strain*—difficulties that result from the differing demands and expectations associated with the same social position. For example, a college professor is expected to teach lecture classes and seminars and to be available for students who need assistance. Yet administrators also insist that professors publish original research, participate on faculty committees, and prepare formal evaluations of students. It may be hard to juggle these duties. Many social positions, like that of professor, present a person with a bewildering and sometimes draining assortment of responsibilities, obligations, and expectations. Professors may seek to negotiate with department heads and deans to resolve these complexities, but some degree of role strain is likely to remain.

Sociologists such as Stephen Marks (1977) have begun to question the assumption that multiple social roles lead to strain. For example, Lewis Coser and Rose Coser (1974) observed that the multiple roles associated with being a mother and working outside the home do not inevitably lead to role strain. In their view, the woman who carries out these multiple roles may feel more fulfilled and happy than if she has to choose between family life and a career. Sociologist Judith Gerson (1985) tested this proposition through a survey comparing female college students, ages 30 to 50, who had one or more children under 19 years of age with mothers of comparable ages who worked as full-time homemakers. While the college students surveyed reported significantly more strain stemming from their multiple roles, they also reported receiving greater gratification in their daily lives than the full-time homemakers did. For this sample of female college students with children, multiple roles had both positive and negative consequences.

(Mark Greenberg/Visions)

It has often been suggested that the multiple roles associated with being a mother and working outside the home lead to role strain. However, sociological research suggests that multiple roles may have positive as well as negative consequences for women.

Role Conflict Imagine the delicate situation of a woman who has worked for a decade on an assembly line in an electrical plant and has recently been named supervisor of the unit she worked in. How is this woman expected to relate to her longtime friends and coworkers? Should she still go out to lunch with them, as she has done almost daily for years? How should she deal with the workers' resentment of an arrogant supervisor who is now her equal and colleague? Is it her responsibility to recommend the firing of an old friend who cannot keep up with the work demands of the assembly line?

Role conflict occurs when incompatible expectations arise from two or more social positions held by the same person. Fulfillment of the roles associated with one status may directly violate the roles linked to a second status. In the example above, the newly promoted supervisor will experience a serious conflict between certain social and occupational roles. As a friend, she should try to protect her former coworker; as a supervisor, she should report an unsatisfactory employee.

Role conflicts call for important ethical choices. In the example just given, the new supervisor has to make a difficult decision about how much allegiance she owes her friend. American culture tells us that success is more important than friendship. If our friends are holding us back, we should leave them and pursue our ambitions. Yet, at the same time, we are told that abandoning our friends is contemptible. The supervisor must decide whether she will risk her promotion out of concern for her friend.

During the Second World War, Christians living in Nazi Germany had to choose between trying to protect Jewish friends and associates and turning them in to the authorities. Remember that the Third Reich had defined Jews as enemies of the state. Protecting such people was considered treason and was dangerous for the person who offered protection. On the other hand, the policies of the Nazi regime, notably its bitter and irrational hatred of Jews, violated humanitarian values. If German Christians did not act to assist Jewish friends—and instead decided to turn them in—the Jews were likely to be murdered. Clearly, if they wished to fulfill the social roles of friendship or being "good neighbors," non-Jews in Germany would be expected to assist innocent victims of the Nazi terror.

Sociologists are particularly interested in how a society and culture inform the individual about conflicting ethical choices. Hitler's Third Reich devised propaganda campaigns to discredit and slander Jews and to encourage citizens to support the regime's persecution of Jews. Despite such propaganda, some individuals resolved their role conflict by making brave and dangerous choices: they opposed the Nazis openly or helped to protect and hide Jews. However, most German Christians supported the nation's leaders and their attacks on European Jews. In the process, these non-Jews turned their backs on the roles associated with being friends and good neighbors (see also Oliner and Oliner, 1989).

People in certain professions seem particularly susceptible to role conflict. For example, journalists commonly experience role conflict during disasters, crimes, and other distressing situations.

Professional photographer Sarah Leen experienced role conflict as she stopped to change a lens and take this picture of the mugging of an intoxicated man in Los Angeles. At the same moment, Leen felt fear for her own safety and wondered whether she should attempt to stop the crime. Note that other bystanders seem oblivious of the entire event.

Female athletes—such as tennis stars Zina Garrison, Chris Evert, and Martina Navratilova—often experience role conflict because of traditionally incongruent identities: being a woman and being an athlete. To resolve such role conflict, female athletes may engage in impression management by presenting a conventionally feminine image, with notable adornment and makeup, when they are not competing in sports.

Sydney Schanberg, a columnist and editor at *New York Newsday* whose experiences as a foreign correspondent in Cambodia formed the basis for the Hollywood film *The Killing Fields*, suggests that there is an "ethical paradox" inherent in being a human being and a "professional observer" at the same time. He notes:

> You run to the scene, and some people are dead or wounded. You scribble notes and snap pictures and at some point you try to decide what you must do. Do you minister to the wounded? Do you give blood? You're required to go back and write a story. Your function is to tell people where you were today, to communicate a scene to them. That is your unspoken oath. But how do you do that and stay human? (J. Gross, 1985:H2, H19).

In some instances, changing gender roles have contributed to role conflict. Sociologist Tracey Watson (1987) studied the ways in which female athletes in college sports programs resolve the conflicts raised by two traditionally incongruent identities: being a woman and being an athlete. On the basketball court, the identity of "athlete" is clearly dominant for these college students. According to an unwritten norm, no makeup is worn during games, much less jewelry; knee pads and Ace bandages are the more likely attire. By contrast, when dressing for a dinner honoring college athletes, these women present a conventional feminine image with notable adornment and makeup.

Clearly, these women resorted to impression management (described by Erving Goffman in Chapter 4) to resolve the role conflicts of women athletes. Nevertheless, as Tracey Watson observed, the general college population took little notice of such impression management and instead stereotyped these athletes as decidedly unfeminine. This stereotyping serves as a reminder that while there has been a significant change in gender roles in the United States—as is evident in the dramatic increase in girls' and women's participation in sports—traditional assumptions about femininity and masculinity remain an influential part of our culture.

Groups

In sociological terms, a ***group*** is any number of people with similar norms, values, and expectations who regularly and consciously interact. The members of a women's college basketball team, of a hospital's business office, or of a symphony orchestra constitute a group. However, the entire

(Jeff Lowenthal/Woodfin Camp & Associates)

(John Running/Stock, Boston)

(Seth Resnick/Stock, Boston)

In American society, groups take all forms. Shown are members of a Black fraternity at the University of Illinois, Shriners in North Dakota, and a choir at Tufts University.

staff of a large hospital would not be considered a group, since the staff members rarely interact with one another at one time. Perhaps the only point at which they all come together is the annual winter party.

Every society is composed of many groups in which daily social interaction takes place. We seek out groups to establish friendships, to accomplish certain goals, and to fulfill social roles that we have acquired. The various types of groups in which people interact will be explored in detail in Chapter 6, where sociological investigations of group behavior will also be examined.

Groups play a vital part in a society's social

BOX 5-2 • EVERYDAY BEHAVIOR

IT'S A SMALL WORLD

How often do you find yourself meeting a person for the first time and unexpectedly discovering that you know someone in common—perhaps even someone who lives far away from either of you? Your response to this discovery will probably be "It's a small world!" or "What a coincidence!" Yet social networking in industrial societies makes such discoveries more than coincidental. According to social scientific research, members of industrial societies typically have 500 to 2500 acquaintances whom they know on a first-name basis. Given these wide circles of contact, it is far from shocking that one of person A's 500 to 2500 acquaintances will also be known to person B.

Social psychologist Stanley Milgram (1967) conducted a study that dramatized the power of networking. A sample of persons in two midwestern cities, labeled as "starters," were given booklets to be channeled toward a person on the east coast—labeled as a "target"—who had been randomly chosen by the researchers. Starters were given the name of the target and certain information about him or her. They were asked to function according to the following guidelines:

1 If the starter did not personally know the target, the starter should mail the folder to an acquaintance (known on a first-name basis) who was more likely to know the target.

2 The acquaintance, in turn, should be asked to advance the booklet further toward the target in the same manner.

3 Starters should make every effort to transmit the booklet to the target using as few intermediaries as possible. Consequently, if the target was a stockbroker, the starter might send it to an acquaintance who worked in a financial institution.

Although some chains were never completed, many were indeed successful. Of the successful ones, none required more than 10 intermediate acquaintances, some took only 2, and the median was 5 intermediaries. The first successful chain (and one of the shortest) took only 4 days. A wheat farmer had as his target the wife of a divinity school student in Cambridge, Massachusetts. The farmer passed the booklet to an Episcopalian minister in his home town, who sent it to a minister who taught at the Episcopalian seminary in Cambridge, who then gave it to the target when he saw her on the street.

Milgram views a median figure of five intermediaries as impressive—especially given the geographical distance between starters and targets. He concludes: "While many studies in social science show how the individual is alienated and cut off from the rest of society, this study demonstrates that, in some sense, we are all bound together in a tightly knit social fabric" (1967:67).

structure. Much of our social interaction takes place within groups and is influenced by the norms and sanctions established by groups. Being a teenager or a retired person takes on special meanings as individuals interact within groups designed for people with that particular status. The expectations associated with many social roles, including those accompanying the statuses of brother, sister, and student, become most clearly defined in the context of a group.

Groups do not merely serve to define other elements of the social structure, such as roles and statuses; they also are an intermediate link between the individual and the larger society. For example, members of occupational or social groups may be acquaintances rather than close friends; consequently, they are likely to connect other members to people in different social circles. This connection is known as a *social network*—that is, a series of social relationships that link a person directly to others and therefore indirectly to still more people. The breadth of such social networks is illustrated in Box 5-2.

Involvement in social networks—commonly known as *networking*—provides a vital social resource in such tasks as finding employment. For example, while looking for a job 1 year after finishing school, Albert Einstein was successful only when the father of a classmate put him in touch with his future employer. These kinds of contacts, even weak and distant contacts, can be crucial in establishing social networks and facilitating transmission of information. According to one 1989 survey, 70 percent of respondents learned about employment opportunities through personal contacts and social networks, while only 14 percent did so through advertisements. Yet, as conflict theorists have emphasized, networking is not so easy for some individuals or groups as for others. In comparison with women, men tend to have longer job histories, a fact which leads to larger networks which can be used in locating employment opportunities. Men are better able to utilize what is literally an "old boy network" (K. Carter, 1989; Fischer, 1977:19; McPherson and Smith-Lovin, 1982, 1986).

Sociologist Melvin Oliver (1988) used the concept of *social network* to better understand life in African American urban neighborhoods, which are often stigmatized as chaotic. Oliver interviewed Black adults in three areas of metropolitan Los Angeles to study their friendship and kinfolk ties. Respondents were *not* found to be socially isolated; they generally had little difficulty identifying members of their social networks. On average, Black residents of these neighborhoods had six to seven persons tied to them through social interactions such as the giving and receiving of emotional and material support.

Of special interest in Oliver's findings was the high "density" of respondents' social networks—the extent to which members of a person's network knew one another. Oliver learned that in the typical social network of these Black residents of Los Angeles, 80 percent of the members were acquainted. While such a high density might be expected in a small town or among students at a liberal arts college, it has not generally been expected of urban African American communities. Oliver's data contradict the stereotype of such neighborhoods as being "disorganized" or even "pathological." Instead, a picture unfolds of an elaborate organization of personal social networks that tie people together within and outside the Black community in bonds of concern and support.

Social Institutions

The mass media, the government, the economy, the family, and the health care system are all examples of social institutions found in American society. **Social institutions** are organized patterns of beliefs and behavior centered on basic social needs. Institutions are organized in response to particular needs, such as replacing personnel (the family) and preserving order (the government).

By studying social institutions, sociologists gain insight into the structure of a society. For example, the institution of religion adapts to the segment of society that it serves. Church work has a very different meaning for ministers who serve a skid row area, a naval base, and a suburban middle-class community. Religious leaders assigned to a skid row mission will focus on tending to the ill and providing food and shelter. By contrast, clergy in affluent suburbs will be occupied with counseling those considering marriage and divorce, arranging youth activities, and overseeing cultural events.

Functionalist View One way to understand social institutions is to see how they fulfill essential functions. Anthropologist David F. Aberle and his colleagues (1950) and sociologists Raymond Mack and Calvin Bradford (1979:12–22) have identified five major tasks, or functional prerequisites, that a society or relatively permanent group must accomplish if it is to survive (see Table 5-1).

1 *Replacing personnel.* Any society or group must replace personnel when they die, leave, or become incapacitated. This is accomplished through immigration, annexation of neighboring groups of people, acquisition of slaves, or normal sexual reproduction of members. The Shakers, a religious sect found in the United States, are a conspicuous example of a group that failed to replace personnel. The Shakers' religious doctrines forbade any physical contact between the sexes; therefore, the group's survival depended on recruiting new members. At first, the Shakers proved quite effective in attracting members; however, their recruitment subsequently declined dramatically. Despite this fact, the Shakers maintained their commitment to celibacy, and their numbers have eventually dwindled to only a few members today (Riddle, 1988).

2 *Teaching new recruits.* No group can survive if many of its members reject the established behavior and responsibilities of the group. As a result, finding or producing new members is not sufficient. The group must encourage recruits to learn and accept its values and customs. This learning can take place formally within schools (where learning is a manifest function) or informally through interaction and negotiation in peer groups (where instruction is a latent function).

3 *Producing and distributing goods and services.* Any relatively permanent group or society must provide and distribute desired goods and services for its members. Each society establishes a set of rules for the allocation of financial and other resources. The group must satisfy the needs of most members at least to some extent, or it will risk the possibility of discontent and, ultimately, disorder.

(Dan Gair/The New York Times)

The Shaker community of New Gloucester, Maine—the last active village of Shakers in the United States—had nine members as of late 1988. Although many observers had predicted that the Shakers' rule of celibacy would doom them to extinction, three younger members joined the Maine community between 1974 and 1988. Shown spinning wool is recruit Meg Haskell, who joined the Shakers in 1984 at age 24.

TABLE 5-1 Functions and Institutions

FUNCTIONAL PREREQUISITE	SOCIAL INSTITUTIONS
Replacing personnel	Family Government (immigration)
Teaching new recruits	Family (basic skills) Economy (occupations) Education (schools) Religion (sacred teachings)
Producing and distributing goods and services	Family (food preparation) Economy Government (regulations regarding commerce) Health care system
Preserving order	Family (child rearing, regulation of sexuality) Government Religion (morals)
Providing and maintaining a sense of purpose	Government (patriotism) Religion

Social institutions are organized patterns of beliefs and behavior which perform functions necessary for a society's survival.

4 *Preserving order.* The native people of Tasmania, a large island just south of Australia, are now extinct. During the 1800s, they were destroyed by the hunting parties of European conquerors, who looked upon the Tasmanians as half-human. This annihilation underscores a critical function of every group or society—preserving order and protecting itself from attack. When faced with the more-developed European technology of warfare, the Tasmanians were unable to defend themselves and an entire people was wiped out.

5 *Providing and maintaining a sense of purpose.* People must feel motivated to continue as members of a society in order to fulfill the previous four requirements. The behavior of American prisoners of war (POWs) while in confinement during the war in Vietnam is a testament to the importance of maintaining a sense of purpose. While in prison camps, some of these men mentally made elaborate plans for marriage, family, children, reunions, and new careers. A few even built houses in their minds—right down to the last doorknob or water faucet. By holding on to a sense of purpose—their intense desire to return to American society and live normal lives—the POWs refused to allow the agony of confinement to destroy their mental health.

Many aspects of a society can assist people in developing and maintaining a sense of purpose. For some people, religious values or personal moral codes are most crucial; for others, national or tribal identities are especially meaningful. Whatever these differences, in any society there remains one common and critical reality. If an individual does not have a sense of purpose, he or she has little reason to contribute to a society's survival.

This list of functional prerequisites does not specify how a society will perform each task. For example, one society may protect itself from external attack by maintaining a frightening arsenal of weaponry, while another may make determined efforts to remain neutral in world politics and to promote cooperative relationships with its neighbors. No matter what its particular strategy, any society or relatively permanent group must attempt to satisfy all these functional prerequisites for survival. If it fails on even one condition, as the Tasmanians did, the society runs the risk of extinction.

Conflict View Conflict theorists do not concur with the functionalist approach to social institutions. While both perspectives agree that institutions are organized to meet basic social needs, conflict theorists object to the implication inherent in the functionalist view that the outcome is necessarily efficient and desirable. Conflict theorists concede the presence of a negotiated order, but they add that many segments of American society—among them the homeless, the disabled, and people with AIDS—are not in a position to negotiate effectively, because they lack sufficient power and resources.

From a conflict perspective, the present organization of social institutions is no accident. Major institutions, such as education, help to maintain the privileges of the most powerful individuals and groups within a society, while contributing to the powerlessness of others. As one example, public schools are financed largely through property taxes. This allows more affluent areas to provide their children with better-equipped schools and better-paid teachers than low-income areas can afford (see Chapter 16). Children from prosperous communities will therefore be better prepared to compete academically than children from impoverished communities. The structure of the American educational system permits and even promotes such unequal treatment of schoolchildren.

Conflict theorists argue that social institutions such as education have an inherently conservative nature. Without question, it has been difficult to implement educational reforms that promote equal opportunity—whether in the area of bilingual education (see Chapter 3), school desegregation (see Chapter 10), or mainstreaming of the handicapped (see Chapter 16). From a functionalist perspective, social change can be dysfunctional, since it often leads to instability. However, from a conflict view, why should we preserve the existing social structure if it is unfair and discriminatory?

Sociologist D. Stanley Eitzen notes a basic paradox of all institutions: they are absolutely necessary, yet they are a source of social problems. He adds that it has become fashionable to attack social institutions, such as the family and the government, in recent years. In Eitzen's view, we should not forget that people depend on institutions for "stability and guarantees against chaos" (1978:545). We must recognize that social institutions are essential yet must not regard permanence as a justification for inequality and injustice.

Interactionist View Social institutions affect our daily lives. Whether we are driving down the street or standing in a long shopping line, our everyday behavior is governed by social institutions. For example, in her fascinating account of behavior within large organizations, *Men and Women of the Corporation*, sociologist Rosabeth

Moss Kanter (1977:34–36) describes lunchtime behavior that comes to be routine. If a visitor comes for lunch, a trip to a posh restaurant is typical. At such lunches, a drink is quite common. At one time, people drank martinis, but more recently wine has become customary. Yet, while social drinking is encouraged, heavy drinking can destroy a person's career.

Interactionist theorists emphasize that our social behavior is conditioned by the roles and statuses which we accept, the groups to which we belong, and the institutions within which we function. For example, the social roles associated with being a judge occur within the larger context of the criminal justice system. The status of "judge" stands in relation to other statuses, such as attorney, plaintiff, defendant, and witness, as well as to the social institution of government. While the symbolic aspects of courts and jails, for example, are awesome, the judicial system derives continued significance from the roles people carry out in social interactions (P. Berger and Luckmann, 1966:74–76).

Viewed from an interactionist perspective, roles, statuses, groups, and institutions are influenced by the overall social structure. In Chapter 1, the terms *microsociology* and *macrosociology* were introduced to distinguish levels of sociological analysis. **Microsociology** stresses study of small groups, as in the case of the business luncheons described above. **Macrosociology,** by contrast, concentrates on large-scale phenomena or entire civilizations. In the next section, a macro approach will be used to examine how the social structure of a society changes with the passage of time. Interactionists often merge the micro and macro approaches rather effectively by examining everyday social interaction to see how the larger social structure either encourages or inhibits such behavior (Maines, 1982).

SOCIAL STRUCTURE AND MODERN SOCIETY

A common feature of modern societies when contrasted with earlier social arrangements is the greater complexity of contemporary life. Sociologists Émile Durkheim and Ferdinand Tönnies offered typologies for contrasting modern societies with simpler forms of social structure.

Durkheim's Mechanical and Organic Solidarity

In his *Division of Labor* (1933, original edition 1893), Durkheim argued that social structure depends on the level of division of labor in a society—in other words, on the manner in which tasks are performed. Thus, a task such as providing food can be carried out almost totally by one individual or can be divided among many people. The latter pattern typically occurs in modern societies; cultivation, processing, distribution, and retailing of a single food item are performed by literally hundreds of people.

In societies in which there is minimal division of labor, a collective consciousness develops with an emphasis on group solidarity. Durkheim termed this **mechanical solidarity,** implying that all individuals perform the same tasks. No one needs to ask, "What do your parents do?" since all are engaged in similar work. Each person prepares food, hunts, makes clothing, builds homes, and so forth. People have few options regarding what to do with their lives, so there is little concern for individual needs. Instead, the group will is the dominating force in society. Both social interaction and negotiation are based on close, intimate, face-to-face social contacts. Since there is little specialization, there are few social roles.

As societies become more advanced technologically, greater division of labor takes place. The person who cuts down timber is not the same person who puts up your roof. With increasing specialization, many different tasks must be performed by different individuals—even in manufacturing one item such as a radio or stove. In general, social interactions become less personal than in societies characterized by mechanical solidarity. We begin relating to others on the basis of their social positions ("butcher," "nurse") rather than their distinctive human qualities. Statuses and social roles are in perpetual flux as the overall social structure of the society continues to change.

In Durkheim's terms, **organic solidarity** involves a collective consciousness resting on the need a society's members have for one another. Once society becomes more complex and there is greater division of labor, no individual can go it alone. Dependence on others becomes essential for group survival. Durkheim chose the term *organic solidarity,* since, in his view, individuals become interdependent in much the same way as organs of the human body.

Tönnies's *Gemeinschaft* and *Gesellschaft*

Sociologist Ferdinand Tönnies (1855–1936) was appalled by the rise of an industrial city in his native Germany during the late 1800s. In his view, this marked a dramatic change from the ideal type of a close-knit community, which Tönnies (1988, original edition 1887) termed *Gemeinschaft,* to that of an impersonal mass society known as *Gesellschaft.*

The **Gemeinschaft** ("guh-MINE-shoft") community is typical of rural life. It is a small community in which people have similar backgrounds and life experiences. Virtually everyone knows one another, and social interactions (including negotiations) are intimate and familiar, almost as one might find among kinfolk. There is a commitment to the larger social group and a sense of togetherness among community members. Therefore, in dealing with people, one relates to them not merely as "clerk" or "manager" but, rather, in a more personal way. With this more personal interaction comes less privacy: we know more about everyone.

Social control in the *Gemeinschaft* community is maintained through informal means such as moral persuasion, gossip, and even gestures. These techniques work effectively because people are genuinely concerned about how others feel toward them. Social change is relatively limited in the *Gemeinschaft;* the lives of members of one generation may be quite similar to those of their grandparents.

By contrast, the **Gesellschaft** ("guh-ZELL-shoft") is an ideal type characteristic of modern urban life. Most people are strangers and perceive little sense of commonality with other community residents. Relationships are governed by social roles which grow out of immediate tasks, such as purchasing a product or arranging a business meeting. Self-interests dominate, and there is gen-

"I'd like to think of you as a person, David, but it's my job to think of you as personnel."

In a Gesellschaft, *people are likely to relate to one another in terms of their roles rather than their individual backgrounds.*

TABLE 5-2 Comparison of *Gemeinschaft* and *Gesellschaft*

GEMEINSCHAFT	GESELLSCHAFT
Rural life typifies this form.	Urban life typifies this form.
People share a feeling of community which results from their similar backgrounds and life experiences.	People perceive little sense of commonality. Their differences in background appear more striking than their similarities.
Social interactions, including negotiations, are intimate and familiar.	Social interactions, including negotiations, are more likely to be task-specific.
There is a spirit of cooperation and unity of will.	Self-interests dominate.
Tasks and personal relationships cannot be separated.	The task being performed is paramount, relationships are subordinate.
There is little emphasis on individual privacy.	Privacy is valued.
Informal social control predominates.	Formal social control is evident.
There is less tolerance of deviance.	There is greater tolerance of deviance.
Emphasis is on ascribed statuses.	There is more emphasis on achieved statuses.
Social change is relatively limited.	Social change is very evident—even within a generation.

Writing in 1887, Ferdinand Tönnies described two contrasting types of social structure: Gemeinschaft *and* Gesellschaft.

erally little consensus concerning values nor commitment to the group. As a result, social control must rely on more formal techniques, such as laws and legally defined punishments. Social change is an important aspect of life in the *Gesellschaft;* it can be strikingly evident even within a single generation.

Table 5-2 summarizes the differences between the *Gemeinschaft* and the *Gesellschaft* as described by Tönnies. Sociologists have used these terms to compare social structures stressing close relationships with those that emphasize less personal ties. It is easy to view *Gemeinschaft* with nostalgia as a far better way of life than the "rat race" of contemporary existence. However, with the more intimate relationships of the *Gemeinschaft* comes a price. The prejudice and discrimination found within *Gemeinschaft* can be quite confining; more emphasis is placed on such ascribed statuses as family background than on people's unique talents and achievements. In addition, *Gemeinschaft* tends to be distrustful of the individual who seeks to be creative or just to be different.

The work of Émile Durkheim and Ferdinand Tönnies shows that a major focus of sociology has been to identify changes in social structure and the consequences for human behavior. At the macro level, they both offer descriptions of societies shifting to more advanced forms of technology. In addition, they identify the impact of these societywide changes at the micro level in terms of the nature of social interactions between people. Durkheim emphasizes the degree to which people carry out the same tasks. Tönnies directs our attention to whether people look out for their own interests or for the well-being of the larger group. Nevertheless, there is a great deal of similarity between the typologies of these European sociologists. They agree that as social structure becomes more complex, people's relationships tend to become more impersonal, transient, and fragmented.

- How has AIDS affected the normal functioning of social institutions in the United States?
- Why is there such a strong stigma attached to infection with the HIV virus and to AIDS?
- How might sociologists influence research on AIDS and AIDS-related issues?

In his novel *The Plague*, Albert Camus (1948) wrote: "There have been as many plagues as wars in history, yet always plagues and wars take people equally by surprise." Regarded by many as the distinctive plague of the modern era, AIDS certainly caught major social institutions—particularly the government, the health care system, and the economy—by surprise.

AIDS is the acronym for *acquired immune deficiency syndrome*. Rather than being a distinct disease, AIDS is actually a predisposition to disease caused by a virus (known as *HIV*) that destroys the body's immune system, thereby leaving the carrier vulnerable to infections such as pneumonia that those with healthy immune systems can generally resist. Contracting the HIV virus can have three outcomes:

- About half those infected show no clinical evidence of AIDS, although they can nevertheless pass on the virus to others.
- Approximately 20 to 30 percent of persons with the HIV virus develop AIDS-related complex (ARC) and experience fever, weight loss, fatigue, and lymph node enlargement. A significant number of these persons will later develop AIDS itself.
- Between 5 and 20 percent of those with the HIV virus develop full-blown AIDS, as defined by the Centers for Disease Control. About 85 percent of persons in this group will die within 5 years of diagnosis. Those who remain alive and active and have had AIDS for at least 3 years are classified as "long-term survivors" (Callen, 1988; Gavzer, 1988, 1990).

AIDS is not transmitted through routine, nonintimate contact in the home or the workplace. Transmission from one person to another appears to require either intimate sexual contact or exchange of blood or body fluids (whether from contaminated hypodermic nee-dles or syringes, transfusions of infected blood, or transmission from an infected mother to her child before or during birth).

As of early 1991, the death toll from AIDS in the United States was more than 100,000; and 1 million Americans were carrying the HIV virus. It is projected that by the end of 1993, the nation's death toll from AIDS may reach as high as 315,000. Among those who have died are well-known figures in the worlds of politics, the arts, entertainment, business, and sports. As has been well publicized, the high-risk groups most in danger of contracting AIDS are homosexual and bisexual men (who account for about 60 percent of all cases in the United States), intravenous (IV) drug users (who account for about 30 percent of all cases), and their sexual partners. Recently, there has been increasing evidence that AIDS is a particular danger for the urban poor, in good part because of transmission via IV drug use. Whereas Blacks and Hispanics represent about 20 percent of the nation's population, they constitute 40 percent of all adult Americans with AIDS. Moreover, 76 percent of infants with AIDS are non-White (L. Altman, 1989; *New York Times*, 1991b).

The staggering rise of AIDS cases has affected American society in a profound way. Harvey Fineberg (1988:128), dean of the Harvard School of Public Health, has observed: "Its reach extends to every social institution, from families, schools, and communities to businesses, courts of law, the military and Federal, state, and local governments." The strain on the nation's health care system has been increasingly evident, as hospitals are becoming overwhelmed by the demands of caring for AIDS patients and the desperate need for more beds to meet the rising AIDS caseload.

On the micro level of social interaction, it has been widely forecast that AIDS will lead to a more conservative sexual climate—among both homosexuals and heterosexuals—in which people will be much more cautious about involvement with new partners. Yet surveys taken in 1987, after a New York City advertising campaign for AIDS prevention, showed that the reported numbers and frequency of sexual contacts in the preceding month had not changed. More than 60 percent of respondents stated that they had failed to use condoms more than "some of the time" (Fineberg, 1988:130; see also D. Altman, 1986:167–173).

While some Americans may refuse to change their sexual behavior, there is little doubt that AIDS has created a climate of fear in the United States and elsewhere. The media have reported numerous stories of people acting out of terror of AIDS. In New Jersey, a 9-year-old boy whose sister had an AIDS-related complex went to school one day, only to discover that more than half the 200 students had been kept home simply because he would be there (Engel and Sawyer, 1985:32).

People with AIDS or infected with the HIV virus have faced a powerful dual stigma. Not only are they associated with a lethal and contagious disease; they have a disease which is disproportionately evident in already stigmatized groups, such as gay males and drug users. This linkage with stigmatized groups delayed recognition of the severity of the AIDS epidemic; the media took little interest in the disease until it seemed to be spreading beyond the gay community. Viewed from a conflict perspective, policymakers have been slow to respond to the AIDS crisis because those in high-risk groups—gay men and IV drug users—are comparatively powerless. As one health care consultant pointedly asked: "Who speaks for the drug abuser in our society? Who's in favor of them?" (J. Gross, 1987:A16; Herek and Glunt, 1988; Shilts, 1987).

Polling data show how the stigma associated with high-risk groups affects people's feelings about AIDS. According to a national survey in 1988, 75 percent of respondents had "a lot" or "some" sympathy for people with AIDS, while 19 percent had "not much" or "no" sympathy. Yet only 36 percent of those questioned indicated that they had a lot of sympathy or some sympathy for "people who get AIDS from homosexual activity," while only 26 percent felt this way about "people who get AIDS from sharing needles while using illegal drugs." The discrepancy in these data reflect a tendency to blame members of high-risk groups for contracting AIDS. Indeed, those who got AIDS without engaging in homosexual behavior or drug use, such as teenage hemophiliacs, are often spoken of as "innocent victims"—with the implication that others with AIDS are "blamable victims" (Herek and Glunt, 1988:888; Kagay, 1988:A12).

In this climate of fear and blame, there has been increasing harassment of homosexual males. Gay

(Alan Reininger/Contact Press Images)

Beginning with a small group of volunteers in San Francisco in 1987, the Names Project has encouraged thousands of people to create quilts commemorating those who have died of AIDS. Shown is a display of quilts in Washington, D.C.

rights leaders believe that the concept of homosexuals as "disease carriers" has contributed to violent incidents directed at people known or suspected to be gay. "What AIDS has done," argues Kevin Berrill of the National Lesbian and Gay Task Force, "is simply give bigots and bashers the justification to attack gays" (D. Altman, 1986:58–70; D. Johnson, 1987:A12).

Fears about AIDS have led to growing discrimination within major social institutions of the United States. For example, people with AIDS have faced discrimination in employment, housing, and insurance. Moreover, it has become increasingly difficult to obtain individual health insurance—or maintain a group policy—for those in creative fields. Actors, musicians, dancers, designers, and painters are suspect in the eyes of insurers because it is believed they are disproportionately likely to be gay and illness-prone. In New York City, a growing number of insurance companies are refusing to offer any new health coverage to people in the arts or to arts groups (Minkowitz, 1989).

Social interaction in the workplace has undoubtedly been affected both by the danger and by the reality of AIDS. According to a 1988 survey, one in five employers in the United States had at least one employee with AIDS. Wells Fargo and Company allows employees with AIDS to continue on the job unless they have other communicable diseases. The company conducts briefing sessions in which coworkers are educated about AIDS and are reassured about their safety. Yet role conflict can arise as an employee is torn between loyalty to an infected friend or coworker and fear of contracting the disease and transmitting it to loved ones (Backer, 1988).

As reports of AIDS cases have increased, there has been growing controversy concerning possible AIDS testing by employers and the government. In 1985, a commercial test for antibodies for HIV became available. Advocates for testing argue that it will allow faster medical treatment for those carrying the HIV virus. This may be especially important, since 90 percent of the persons with the virus are unaware that they have it. Moreover, in countering the argument that testing will lead to infringement on people's rights, noted civil libertarian Nat Hentoff (1987:37) argues that failure to test leads to denial of rights—and potentially to the death—of those who contract AIDS from infected sexual partners.

Opponents of AIDS testing question the scientific usefulness of such tests, especially since they cannot reveal either who is or who will become sick. Many critics of mandatory testing, including former U.S. Surgeon General C. Everett Koop, fear that such measures would drive underground precisely those people (such as IV drug users) who are most likely to test positive. Perhaps most important, opponents of testing fear that any tests for the AIDS virus—except those that are entirely voluntary and anonymous—will lead to discrimination if a person tests positive (or even if he or she is known to have taken such a test). In a major shift in mid-1989, Gay Men's Health Crisis (GMHC), New York City's largest private organization providing AIDS services, endorsed widespread *voluntary* testing for the HIV virus (S. Katz, 1990; Lambert, 1989; J. Ridgeway, 1987).

Any such dramatic crisis is likely to bring about certain transformations in a society's social structure. From a functionalist perspective, if established social institutions cannot meet a crucial need, new institutions are likely to emerge to fulfill that function. In the case of AIDS, self-help groups—especially in the gay communities of major cities—have been established to care for the sick, educate the healthy, and lobby for more responsive public policies. By 1990, Gay Men's Health Crisis had a paid staff of 140 and more than 1600 volunteers typically working in a "buddy system" with those afflicted with AIDS. GMHC counsels about one-third of all New Yorkers with AIDS; as many as 20 percent of the patients it services are heterosexuals. The group operates a telephone hotline, sends advocates to hospitals to insist on better care for patients, and runs legal and financial clinics as well as therapy and support groups for people with AIDS and their loved ones (D. Altman, 1986:84–87; J. Gross, 1987: A16).

GMHC and other groups concerned with AIDS argue that the proper societal response to this deadly disease includes testing of new drugs to combat AIDS, massive public education campaigns regarding the need for "safer sex," wide distribution and proper use of condoms, and effective counseling and support services for those with AIDS, AIDS-related complex, or the HIV virus. AIDS activist organizations bitterly charge that there has been grossly inadequate governmental funding for AIDS-related research and public health efforts. Especially visible and outspoken in this effort is the AIDS Coalition to Unleash Power (ACT-UP), which has conducted controversial protests, sit-ins, and "zaps" in the halls of government, at scientific conferences concerned with AIDS, at New York City's St. Patrick's Cathedral, and at Wall Street. ACT-UP has popularized the slogan it views as the crucial message of the AIDS crisis: "Silence = Death" (France, 1988; J. Gamson, 1989; Shilts, 1989).

How can sociologists use their expertise to assist in responding to the AIDS crisis? In a 1989 address before the American Sociological Association, Canadian sociologist Barry Adam (1991) expressed concern that research on AIDS has been largely conducted by biomedical scientists. Adam argued that sociologists can make an important contribution to AIDS-related research; he outlined four directions for such sociological research:

• How is information about AIDS produced and distributed? Is the distribution of information about how to have "safe sex" being limited or even censored?

AIDS activist organizations bitterly charge that public health efforts and government funding for AIDS-related research have been grossly inadequate. Especially visible and outspoken in this effort is the AIDS Coalition to Unleash Power (ACT-UP), shown here in a protest in San Francisco.

- How does an AIDS "folklore" emerge, and how does it become integrated into a community? Why do certain communities and certain individuals resist or ignore scientific information about the dangers of AIDS?

- How are medical and social services made available to people with AIDS? Why are these services often denied to the poorest patients?

- How is **homophobia** (fear of and prejudice against homosexuality) related to fears concerning AIDS? In what ways does homophobia correlate with other forms of bias?

SUMMARY

Social interaction refers to the ways in which people respond to one another. *Social structure* refers to the way in which a society is organized into predictable relationships. This chapter examines these concepts, which are central to sociological study.

1 Our response to people's behavior is based on the *meaning* we attach to their actions.

2 The ability to define social reality clearly reflects a group's power within a society.

3 People can reshape social reality by negotiating changes in patterns of social interaction.

4 An *ascribed status* is generally assigned to a person at birth, whereas an *achieved status* is attained largely through one's own effort.

5 In the United States, ascribed statuses of race and gender can function as *master statuses* that have an important impact on one's potential to achieve a desired professional and social status.

6 With each distinctive status—whether ascribed or achieved—come particular *social roles*.

7 Roles enable us to anticipate the behavior of others and to pattern our own actions accordingly.

8 Much of our patterned behavior takes place within *groups* and is influenced by the norms and sanctions established by groups.

9 The mass media, the government, the economy, the family, and the health care system are all examples of *social institutions* found in American society.

10 One way to understand social institutions is to see how they fulfill essential functions, such as replacing personnel, training new recruits, and preserving order.

11 The conflict perspective argues that social institutions help to maintain the privileges of the powerful while contributing to the powerlessness of others.

12 Interactionist theorists emphasize that our social

behavior is conditioned by the roles and statuses that we accept, the groups to which we belong, and the institutions within which we function.

13 Émile Durkheim argued that social structure depends on the division of labor in a society.

14 Ferdinand Tönnies distinguished the close-knit community of *Gemeinschaft* from the impersonal mass society known as *Gesellschaft.*

15 The AIDS crisis has affected every social institution in the United States, including the family, the schools, the health care system, the economy, and government.

KEY TERMS

Achieved status A social position attained by a person largely through his or her own effort. (page 134)

Ascribed status A social position "assigned" to a person by society without regard for the person's unique talents or characteristics. (134)

Complementary roles Social roles which require that the behavior of two or more people interact in specific ways. (135)

Gemeinschaft A term used by Ferdinand Tönnies to describe close-knit communities, often found in rural areas, in which strong personal bonds unite members. (146)

Gesellschaft A term used by Ferdinand Tönnies to describe communities, often urban, that are large and impersonal, with little commitment to the group or consensus on values. (146)

Group Any number of people with similar norms, values, and expectations, who regularly and consciously interact. (139)

Homophobia Fear of and prejudice against homosexuality. (151)

Macrosociology Sociological investigation which concentrates on large-scale phenomena or entire civilizations. (145)

Master status A status that dominates others and thereby determines a person's general position within society. (135)

Mechanical solidarity A term used by Émile Durkheim to describe a society in which people generally all perform the same tasks and in which relationships are close and intimate. (145)

Microsociology Sociological investigation which stresses study of small groups and often uses laboratory experimental studies. (145)

Negotiated order A social structure that derives its existence from the social interactions through which people define and redefine its character. (133)

Negotiation The attempt to reach agreement with others concerning some objective. (133)

Organic solidarity A term used by Émile Durkheim to describe a society in which members are mutually dependent and in which a complex division of labor exists. (145)

Role ambiguity Unclear expectations associated with particular social positions. (136)

Role conflict Difficulties that occur when incompatible expectations arise from two or more social positions held by the same person. (137)

Role exit The process of disengagement from a role that is central to one's self-identity, and reestablishment of an identity in a new role. (136)

Role strain Difficulties that result from the differing demands and expectations associated with the same social position. (137)

Social institutions Organized patterns of beliefs and behavior centered on basic social needs. (142)

Social interaction The ways in which people respond to one another. (131)

Social network A series of social relationships that link a person directly to others and therefore indirectly to still more people. (141)

Social role A set of expectations of people who occupy a given social position or status. (135)

Social structure The way in which a society is organized into predictable relationships. (131)

Status A term used by sociologists to refer to any of the full range of socially defined positions within a large group or society. (134)

ADDITIONAL READINGS

Altman, Dennis. *AIDS in the Mind of America: The Social, Political, and Psychological Impact of a New Epidemic.* Garden City, N.Y.: Anchor, 1986. A political scientist examines the impact of AIDS on attitudes toward sex, disease, death, medicine, and politics.

Blumer, Herbert. *Symbolic Interactionism: Perspective and Method.* Englewood Cliffs, N.J.: Prentice-Hall, 1969. A collection of articles previously published by the well-regarded advocate of the interactionist approach.

Charon, Joel M. *Symbolic Interactionism: An Introduction, an Interpretation, and Integration* (2d ed.). Englewood

Cliffs, N.J.: Prentice-Hall, 1985. A concise introduction to the interactionist perspective and its importance to sociology.

Deegan, Mary Jo, and Michael Hill (eds.). *Women and Symbolic Interaction.* Winchester, Mass.: Allen and Unwin, 1987. A varied and useful collection of writings drawing on the interactionist perspective to examine the role of gender in everyday life.

Ebaugh, Helen Rose Fuchs. *Becoming an Ex: The Process of Role Exit.* Chicago: University of Chicago Press, 1988. As described in Box 5-1, sociologist Ebaugh examines the process of disengaging from a significant social role and establishing a new identity.

Kephart, William M., and William M. Zellner. *Extraordinary Groups: An Examination of Unconventional Life-Styles* (4th ed.). New York: St. Martin's, 1991. Among the groups described in this very readable book are the Amish, the Oneida community, the Shakers, the Mormons, Hasidic Jews, Jehovah's Witnesses, and the Romani (commonly known as *Gypsies*).

Rollins, Judith. *Between Women: Domestics and Their Employers.* Philadelphia: Temple University Press, 1985. Drawing on participant observations, Rollins looks at the status of domestic workers and their relations with their employers.

Shilts, Randy. *And the Band Played On: Politics, People, and the AIDS Epidemic.* New York: St. Martin's, 1987. Shilts, a reporter for the *San Francisco Chronicle,* has been assigned to cover AIDS on a full-time basis since 1982. He offers a devastating critique of the nation's political, medical, and media establishments for allowing the AIDS epidemic to reach grave proportions before taking it seriously.

Skolnick, Jerome H., and Elliot Currie (eds.). *Crisis in American Institutions* (7th ed.). Glenview, Ill.: Scott, Foresman, 1988. A collection of readings focused on the problems facing social institutions in the United States.

Spradley, James P. *You Owe Yourself a Drunk: An Ethnography of Urban Nomads.* Boston: Little, Brown, 1970. An insightful review of the social structure of skid row by a cultural anthropologist.

Strauss, Anselm. *Negotiations: Varieties, Contexts, Processes, and Social Order.* San Francisco: Jossey-Bass, 1977. The primary sociological treatment of negotiation in the context of social interaction.

Journals

Among the journals that focus on issues of social interaction and social structure are *Journal of Contemporary Ethnography* (formerly *Urban Life,* founded 1971) and *Symbolic Interaction* (1977). Several relevant publications have devoted special issues to the behavioral implications of AIDS, including *American Psychologist* (September 1988), *Scientific American* (October 1988), and *Social Problems* (October 1989).

6

GROUPS AND ORGANIZATIONS

> *Americans of all ages, all stations in life, and all types of disposition*
> *are forever forming associations. . . . In every case, at the head*
> *of any new undertaking, where in France you would find the*
> *government . . . in the United States you are sure to find an association.*
> Alexis de Tocqueville
> Democracy in America, 1835

LOOKING AHEAD

- How do sociologists distinguish between various types of groups?
- How do sociologists study interactions within small groups?
- What are some of the positive and negative consequences of bureaucracy?
- How have Japanese management techniques been adapted by corporations based in the United States?
- Why do so many Americans join voluntary associations?
- How common is sexual harassment within organizations in the United States?

Many of us know or have been visited by someone employed by a direct-selling organization (DSO) such as Amway, Tupperware, Shaklee, or Mary Kay Cosmetics. These salespeople often go door to door or arrange house parties in an attempt to reach potential customers. Involvement in DSO work is an intense experience; the gatherings of DSO employees have been compared to religious revival meetings. After conducting a study of 42 DSOs, sociologist Nicole Woolsey Biggart (1989) characterized DSOs as "charismatic" because of the awe they arouse in employees.

The strong personal appeal of DSO founders accounts in good part for the intense and passion-ate tone of gatherings. DSO employees speak of their companies' founders in terms not usually applied to corporate chief executive officers (CEOs):

> [Shaklee was] a remarkable man. He was far ahead of his time. He developed Vita-Line minerals, the first product, a year before the word "vitamin" was even coined. He's [had] a special place in my heart (Biggart, 1989:142).

> Even watching [Mary Kay] on TV is real hard for me. I just get this knot in my stomach whenever I see her or listen to her talk or anything (Biggart, 1989:143).

These founders are successful in promoting organizational ideologies that are missionary in character. DSO employees genuinely believe that their clients will be better people and enjoy happier lives by using DSO products.

In most DSOs, the sales force is overwhelmingly female, and many of these salespeople are homemakers. Sociologist Paul DiMaggio points out that DSOs provide these homemakers with income, enhance their marital power, and offer a sense of community. Nevertheless, DiMaggio (1990:210) concludes that DSOs are "prefeminist" because their ideologies are supportive of male dominance: "women should view selling as not quite a job, seek husbands' permission to enroll, place family before career, or, when firms recruit spouses as teams, take backstage roles."

Americans are joiners, whether they join direct-selling organizations, chamber music groups, street gangs, athletic teams, religious institutions, or professional organizations. Many of us ask, "When is the next meeting?" almost as often as we ask, "What should we have for dinner?" As was pointed out in the earlier chapters, social interaction is necessary for the transmission of culture and the survival of a society. Our lives are filled with relatively random and inconsequential interactions, such as conversations with cashiers in stores and supermarkets. However, many social interactions are planned or anticipated. We relate to certain people because we like them, they have something to offer us, they are working to accomplish a goal we share, or we have no other choice.

This chapter will consider the impact of groups and organizations on social interaction. It will begin by noting the distinctions between various types of groups. Particular attention will be given to small groups and to the analysis of interactionist theorists regarding the dynamics of small groups. How and why formal organizations came into existence will be examined, and Max Weber's model of the modern bureaucracy will be described. The tendency of Americans to join voluntary associations, as noted by Alexis de Tocqueville, will be discussed. The social policy section will focus on the issue of sexual harassment, which has become a major concern of both governmental and private-sector organizations.

UNDERSTANDING GROUPS

In everyday speech, people use the term *group* to describe any collection of individuals, whether three strangers sharing an elevator or hundreds at a meeting of the Tupperware sales force. However, as we noted in Chapter 5, in sociological terms a **group** is any number of people with similar norms, values, and expectations who regularly and consciously interact. College sororities and fraternities, dance companies, tenants' associations, and chess clubs are all considered examples of groups. It is important to emphasize that members of a group share some sense of belonging. This characteristic distinguishes groups from mere *aggregates* of people, such as passengers who happen to be together on an airplane flight, or from *categories* who share a common feature (such as being retired) but otherwise do not act together.

A college debating society is typical of groups

(Spencer Grant/Stock, Boston)

In sociological terms, a group *is any number of people with similar norms, values, and expectations who regularly and consciously interact. These firefighters would be considered a group.*

found in the United States. It has agreed-upon values and social norms. All members want to improve their public speaking skills and believe that informed debate on issues of public policy is an essential aspect of democracy. In addition, like many groups, the society has both a formal and an informal structure. It has monthly meetings, run by elected officers, in a student union building. At the same time, unofficial leadership roles are held by the club's most experienced debaters, who often coach new members regarding debating strategies and techniques.

Types of Groups

The study of groups has become an important part of sociological investigation because they play such a key role in the transmission of culture. Sociologists have made a number of useful distinctions between types of groups (see Table 6-1).

Primary and Secondary Groups A 1979 Hollywood film, *The Warriors*, begins with an outdoor meeting of delegates of numerous New York City street gangs in a playground. Each gang has sent nine members to this unusual convocation. Dressed in colorful garb, these gangs represent various neighborhoods and racial and ethnic

TABLE 6-1 Comparison of Primary and Secondary Groups

PRIMARY GROUP	SECONDARY GROUP
Generally small	Usually large
Relatively long period of interaction	Short duration, temporary
Intimate, face-to-face association	Little social intimacy or mutual understanding
Some emotional depth in relationships	Relationships generally superficial
Cooperative, friendly	More formal and impersonal

In distinguishing between types of groups, sociologists have noted the differences between primary and secondary groups.

groups within New York. There are White gangs, Black gangs, Hispanic gangs, and Asian gangs—all assembled in an explosive mix.

This scene from *The Warriors* can be used to illustrate an important distinction made by sociologist Charles Horton Cooley in categorizing groups. Cooley (1902:23–57) coined the term *primary group* to refer to a small group characterized by intimate, face-to-face association and cooperation. The members of the street gang known as the *Warriors* constitute a primary group. So do members of a family living in the same household as well as "sisters" in a college sorority. Primary groups play a pivotal role both in the socialization process (see Chapter 4) and in the development of roles and statuses (see Chapter 5).

When we find ourselves identifying closely with a group, it is probably a primary group. However, Americans participate in many groups which are not characterized by close bonds of friendship, such as large college classes and business associations. The term *secondary group* refers to a formal, impersonal group in which there is little social intimacy or mutual understanding (see Table 6-1). If the diverse gangs portrayed in *The Warriors* had successfully established a city-wide gang organization, it would have been a secondary, rather than primary, group. The distinction between these types of groups is not always clearcut. Some fraternities or social clubs become so large and impersonal that they no longer function as primary groups.

In-Groups and Out-Groups A group can hold special meaning for members because of its relationship to other groups. People sometimes feel antagonistic to or threatened by another group, especially if the group is perceived as being different culturally or racially. Sociologists identify these "we" and "they" feelings by using two terms first employed by William Graham Sumner (1906:12–13): *in-group* and *out-group*.

An *in-group* can be defined as any group or category to which people feel they belong. Simply put, it comprises everyone who is regarded as "we" or "us." The in-group may be as narrow as one's family or as broad as an entire society. The very existence of an in-group implies that there is an out-group viewed as "they" or "them." More formally, an **out-group** is a group or category to which people feel they do not belong.

Americans tend to see the world in terms of in-groups and out-groups, a perception often fostered by the very groups to which we belong. "*Our* generation does not have those sexual hangups." "*We* Christians go to church every week." "*We* have to support *our* troops in the Persian Gulf." Although not explicit, each of these declarations suggests who the in-groups and out-groups are.

One typical consequence of in-group membership is a feeling of distinctiveness and superiority among members, who see themselves as better than people in the out-group. This sense of superiority can be enhanced by a double standard maintained by members of the in-group. Proper behavior for the in-group is simultaneously viewed as unacceptable behavior for the out-group. Sociologist Robert Merton (1968:480–488) describes this process as the conversion of "in-group virtues" into "out-group vices."

The attitudes of certain Christians toward Jews illustrate such a double standard. If Christians take their faith seriously, it is seen as "commendable"; if Jews do the same, it is a sign of "backwardness" and a refusal to enter the twentieth century. If Christians prefer other Christians as friends, it is "understandable"; if Jews prefer other Jews as friends, they are attacked for being "clannish." This view of "us and them" can be destructive, as conflict theorists have suggested. At the same time, it promotes in-group solidarity and a sense of belonging (Karlins et al., 1969).

Reference Groups Both in-groups and primary groups can dramatically influence the way an individual thinks and behaves. Sociologists use the term *reference group* when speaking of any group that individuals use as a standard for evaluating themselves and their own behavior. For example, a high school student who aspires to join a social circle of punk rock devotees will pattern his or her behavior after that of the group. The student will begin dressing like these peers, listening to the same record albums, and hanging out at the same stores and clubs.

Reference groups have two basic purposes. They serve a normative function by setting and

(Drawing by Weber; © 1979 The New Yorker Magazine, Inc.)

"*So long, Bill. This is my club. You can't come in.*"

enforcing standards of conduct and belief. Thus, the high school student who wants the approval of the punk rock crowd will have to follow the group's dictates to at least some extent. He or she will be expected to cut classes along with group members and to rebel against parental curfews. Reference groups also perform a comparison function by serving as a standard against which people can measure themselves and others. A law student will evaluate himself or herself against a reference group composed of lawyers, law professors, and judges (M. Deutsch and Krauss, 1965: 191; H. Kelley, 1952; Merton and Kitt, 1950).

The term *reference group* was coined by Herbert Hyman (1942) in a study of social class. Hyman found that what people thought of as their status could not be predicted solely from such factors as income or level of education. To a certain extent, an individual's self-evaluation of status depended on the groups used as a framework for judgment.

In many cases, people model their behavior after groups to which they do not belong. For example, a college student majoring in finance may read the *Wall Street Journal,* study the annual reports of corporations, and listen to midday stock market news on the radio. The student is engaging in the process of anticipatory socialization (see Chapter 4) by using financial experts as a reference group to which he or she aspires.

It is important to recognize that individuals are often influenced by two or more reference groups at the same time. One's family members, neighbors, and coworkers shape different aspects of a person's self-evaluation. In addition, certain reference group attachments change during the life cycle. A corporate executive who quits the rat race at age 45 to become a social worker will find new reference groups to use as standards for evaluation. We shift reference groups as we take on different statuses during our lives.

Studying Small Groups

In an unusual example of small-group research, social scientists have examined the communications processes and social interactions between members of airline flight crews. One study conducted for the federal government found that 70 percent of all civil-aviation incidents during a 5-year period were attributable to human error, primarily where information was improperly transmitted from one crew member to another or was not transmitted at all. According to psychologist Robert Helmrich, a substantial number of airline accidents arise from the flight crews' failure to work well as a team. Yet close cooperation is difficult to achieve in large airlines because pilots and copilots frequently fly with crew members whom they have never met before (Burrows, 1982).

Studying small groups is an important aspect of sociological research. The term *small group* is used to refer to a group small enough for all members to interact simultaneously, that is, to talk with one another or at least be acquainted. Certain primary groups, such as families, may also be classified as small groups. However, many small groups differ from primary groups in that they do not necessarily offer the intimate personal relationships characteristic of primary groups. For example, a manufacturer may bring together its seven-member regional sales staff twice a year for an intensive sales conference. The salespersons, who live in different cities and rarely see one another, constitute a small secondary group but not a primary group.

We may think of small groups as being informal and unpatterned; yet, interactionist researchers have revealed that there are distinct and predictable processes at work in the functioning of small groups. As sociologist Cecilia Ridgeway (1987) has shown, even nonverbal behavior plays a role in a person's dominance or influence in a group. People who employ direct eye contact and an upright, forward-leaning posture are able to be more persuasive without speaking louder or seeming threatening. Moreover, like formal organizations—which will be examined later in the chapter—small groups have a definite structure (Back, 1981; Nixon, 1979).

Methods of Small-Group Research How do sociologists study interactions within small groups? In a sense, they must develop useful instruments for such investigations, just as natural scientists rely on microscopes and telescopes. Few methods of studying groups are so clearly defined or widely utilized as *interaction process analysis (IPA),* developed by Robert F. Bales (1950a, 1950b, 1968, 1970).

IPA is a technique for classifying every gesture, remark, and statement that occurs within a group in order to analyze the group's structure and processes. The results of this coding permit observers to draw conclusions about how a group establishes norms, confers leadership on members, performs ceremonial tasks, and solves problems. While many coding systems have been developed for small-group research since IPA was first introduced, the general categories in most of these coding systems are similar to those used by Bales in IPA (Trujillo, 1986).

Another technique used in the study of small-group dynamics is the sociogram. A *sociogram* is a depiction of preferred associations among group members. It helps social scientists understand either group dynamics or individual behavior within a small-group setting. A sociogram is constructed by symbolically indicating each group member and his or her preferences according to some stated criterion. For example, in Box 6-1 (pages 162–163), we look at sociograms developed from a participant-observation study of boys who play on Little League baseball teams.

Sociograms were used during World War II to determine the most effective composition for naval air squadrons. Currently, they are routinely used to pictorially illustrate and help establish productive work crews on a job. As these examples (and the study of interactions in airline flight crews) illustrate, small-group research can have practical value (Jenkins, 1948; Palazzolo, 1981: 178–182; see also Moreno, 1953, on the origins of sociograms).

Size of a Group It is not exactly clear at what point a collection of people becomes too large to be called a *small group.* If there are more than 20 members, it is difficult for individuals to interact regularly in a direct and intimate manner. Even within a range of 2 to 20 persons, group size can substantially alter the quality of social relationships. For example, as the number of group participants increases, the most active communicators become even more active relative to others. Therefore, a person who dominates a group of 3 or 4 members will be relatively more dominant in a 15-person group (Bales and Strodtbeck, 1951; Hare, 1976:275–276; Slater, 1958).

Group size also has noticeable social implications for members who do not assume leadership roles. In a larger group, each member has less time to speak, more points of view to absorb, and a more elaborate structure within which to function. At the same time, an individual has greater freedom to ignore certain members or viewpoints than he or she would in a smaller group. Clearly, it is harder to disregard someone in a 4-person work force than in an office with 30 employees or a high school band with 50 members.

German sociologist Georg Simmel (1858–1918) is credited as the first sociologist to emphasize the importance of interaction processes within groups. Reflecting on group size, Simmel (1950:87, original edition 1917) suggested that smaller groups have distinctive qualities and patterns of interaction which inevitably disappear as they expand in size. Larger groups, in Simmel's view, develop particular forms of interaction which are unnec-

(Bildarchiv Preussicher Kulturbesitz)

German sociologist Georg Simmel (1858–1918) pioneered in the study of small-group behavior and developed approaches to the formation of coalitions which are still used today.

essary in small groups. Subsequent research has clarified the social significance of group size on behavior.

The simplest of all social groups or relationships is the ***dyad,*** or two-member group. The conventional marital relationship between a wife and a husband is an example of a dyad, as is a business partnership or a singing team. In a dyad, one is able to achieve a special level of intimacy that cannot be duplicated in larger groups. However, as Simmel (1950) noted, a dyad, unlike any other group, can be destroyed by the loss of a single member. Therefore, the thought of termination hangs over a dyadic relationship perhaps more than over any other type.

Obviously, the introduction of one additional person to a dyad dramatically transforms the character of the small group. The dyad now becomes a three-member group, or ***triad.*** The new member has at least three basic ways of interacting with and influencing the dynamics of the

Friendship Choices at Sharpstone Auto (End of Season)

Friendship Choices at Transatlantic Industries (End of Season)

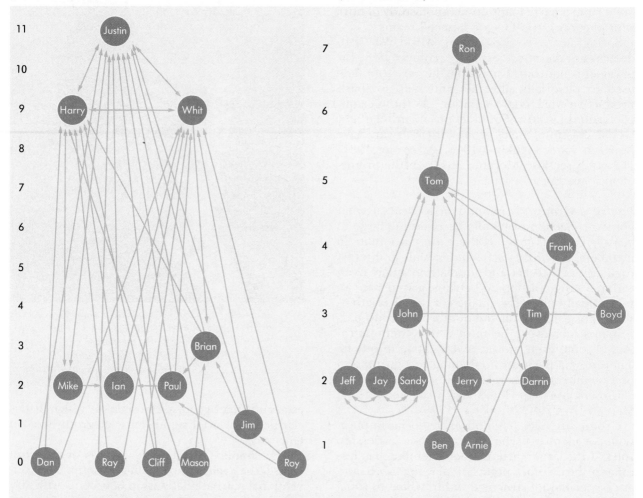

SOURCE: G. Fine, 1987:144.

This sociogram shows that—as discussed in Box 6-1 on the opposite page—the Sharpstone Auto team was dominated by a popular elite clique consisting of Justin, Harry, and Whit.

SOURCE: G. Fine, 1987:141.

This sociogram shows that friendship choices of the Transatlantic Industries team were rather diverse; no elite clique was dominant in terms of popularity.

BOX 6-1 • CURRENT RESEARCH

SOCIOGRAMS OF LITTLE LEAGUE BASEBALL TEAMS

Little League baseball, with its 15,000 chartered leagues, is the best-known and most successful youth sports program in the United States. Sociologist Gary Alan Fine (1987) conducted a participant-observation study of Little League players in the suburbs of Providence, Rhode Island. The two teams Fine observed most closely—Sharpstone Auto and Transatlantic Industries—were outstanding teams who battled it out for first place.

Fine used sociograms to study the friendship patterns of the 9- to 11-year-old boys on these two teams. At the end of the season, players were asked to name their three best friends among their teammates. The vertical numbers on the left of each sociogram indicate the number of friendship choices each boy received out of a maximum of 12.

The differences in the friendship patterns of the teams are clearly evident in the sociograms

(opposite page). Justin, Harry, and Whit constitute an elite clique which dominates the Sharpstone Auto team; each received at least nine friendship choices. Moreover, through his conversations with players, Fine learned that Justin was named as the team leader by everyone on Sharpstone Auto. Neither Justin nor Whit was characterized as "bossy," while only one player felt that way about Harry. Consequently, Sharpstone Auto's social structure was unambiguous and accepted, with the clique of Justin, Harry, and Whit in leadership roles.

By contrast, Transatlantic Industries does not have an elite clique. The most popular player, Ron, received only 7 out of 12 possible friendship choices, while only one other player received as many as 5. Fine found that when he asked Transatlantic players to name the team leader, Ron received the fourth-highest number of selections. Although no group

of players served as the team's dominant core, Fine observed that the Transatlantic team was not racked by dissension.

Fine studied these Little League teams because he was interested in this subculture of preadolescent boys. In particular, Fine wondered how the norms and values of this subculture were transmitted and maintained, since the members of the subculture are constantly changing as boys become too old for the Little League. Fine observed that coaches and older boys serve as significant others who socialize younger boys into Little League norms and values. In addition, team members are not only part of social networks within their teams (as shown in the sociograms); they also have friendship and kin ties with boys from other communities. Through these networks, Little Leaguers learn the distinctive norms, values, and argot of this unique subculture.

---

group. The new person may play a *unifying* role within a triad. When a married couple has its first child, the baby may serve to bind the group closer together. A newcomer may also play a *mediating* role within a three-person group. If two roommates in an apartment are perpetually sniping at each other, the third may attempt to remain on good terms with each and arrange compromise solutions to problems. Finally, a member of a triad can choose to employ a *divide-and-rule* strategy. This is the case, for example, with a coach who hopes to gain greater control over two assistants by making them rivals (Nixon, 1979:9–13).

Coalitions As groups become the size of triads or larger, coalitions can be expected to develop. A *coalition* is a temporary or permanent alliance toward a common goal. For example, in late 1989, a coalition of Democrats and moderate Republicans in the House of Representatives passed (by a narrow 216-206 vote) a controversial measure allowing the federal government to pay for abortions for poor women whose pregnancies result from rape or incest. (The debate over abortion is examined in Chapter 11.)

How do coalitions work within a small group? Imagine that Elena Rivera, Frank DiStefano, and

Alex Smith are all hoping to become editor-in-chief of their college newspaper. The editor-in-chief is selected by a majority vote of the 15 outgoing editors. A few days before the election, it appears that Rivera is a strong favorite. She is estimated to have seven supporters, while DiStefano has five, and Smith only three.

DiStefano and Smith have the option of forming a coalition to stop Rivera. For example, Smith could drop out of the contest and urge his supporters to vote for DiStefano. In return, DiStefano might promise to appoint Smith as his assistant or to some other prestigious job. Such a coalition might be particularly likely if these two candidates have some personal or ideological bond or some common reason for wanting to keep Rivera from becoming editor-in-chief.

On the other hand, a different type of coalition could be developed. In order to assure her victory, Rivera could try to make a deal with Smith. If she receives the support of his three backers, her election would be assured. Thus, in any political, organizational, or small-group setting, there are numerous ways in which coalitions can be created. Repeated experiments by social scientists confirm the complex nature of coalition formation (Caplow, 1956, 1959, 1969; W. Gamson, 1961a, 1961b; M. Shaw, 1981:107–114).

Physical Environment Small groups do not function in isolation. They meet and interact within physical environments which have implications for group dynamics. Rooms, chairs (as opposed to benches), and even the shape of a table can influence a group's performance and exchanges in important ways. For example, if a group is seated at a rectangular table and is allowed to discuss a topic freely, members across the table from each other will direct comments to one another more than they will to those on either side. Use of IPA procedure has confirmed this research finding (Hearn, 1957; Steinzor, 1950; Strodtbeck and Hook, 1961).

Seating arrangements can also influence leadership status. One controlled experiment involved five-person groups seated at a rectangular table, with three members on one side of the table and two on the other. Since interactions are more likely to occur across the table, researchers expected that more leaders would emerge from the two-person side. This was because participants on the two-person side would have easy access to three group members across the table; those on the three-person side would have easy access to only two group members. The data later confirmed these predictions: 70 percent of the leaders emerged from the two-seat side, even though

(Michal Heron/Woodfin Camp & Associates)

Researchers have learned that rooms, chairs (as opposed to benches), and even the shape of a table can influence a group's performance and exchanges in important ways.

it accounted for only 40 percent of the participants. Thus, physical environment can have a clear impact on the dynamics of small groups (Howells and Becker, 1962; M. Shaw, 1981).

The effects of group size, coalition, and physical environment on group dynamics are but three of the many aspects of the small group which have been studied by sociologists. Another area, conformity and deviance, is given particular attention in Chapter 7. Of course, while it is clear that small-group encounters have a considerable influence on our lives, we are also deeply affected by much larger groupings of people.

UNDERSTANDING ORGANIZATIONS

Formal Organizations and Bureaucracies

One poignant message of recent decades has been the power and pervasiveness of large organizations. Statements such as "You can't fight city hall" have underscored the frustrations and despair of the lonely individual in opposing the towering structures of government or big business. In a mock commercial, the telephone operator Ernestine—a character created by the comedian Lily Tomlin—proclaims: "We don't care; we don't have to. We're the phone company!"

Our lives are increasingly dominated by large secondary groups which take the form of formal organizations designed for a specific purpose. A *formal organization* is a special-purpose group designed and structured in the interests of maximum efficiency. Organizations vary in their size, specificity of goals, and degree of efficiency, but are structured in such a way as to facilitate the management of large-scale operations. They also have a bureaucratic form of organization, which will be described later in the chapter. The United States Postal Service, the Boston Pops orchestra, and the college you attend are all examples of formal organizations.

In our society, formal organizations fulfill an enormous variety of personal and societal needs and shape the lives of every American. In fact, formal organizations have become such a domi-nant force that we must create organizations to supervise other organizations, such as the Securities and Exchange Commission (SEC) and other federal regulatory agencies. It sounds much more exciting to say that we live in the "space age" than that we live in the "age of formal organizations"; however, the latter is probably a more accurate description of the 1990s (Azumi and Hage, 1972:1; Etzioni, 1964:1–2).

Development of Formal Organizations How and why have formal organizations come into existence? The first large-scale formal organizations seem to have emerged as central governments became more complex. Under one theory, formal organizations became inevitable in societies which had state-controlled irrigation networks, such as Egypt, Mesopotamia, India, China, and Peru under the Incas. Centralized decisions had to be made about water distribution, and networks for carrying out such policies had to be established.

The growth of formal organizations has been closely tied to the emergence of industrial societies. Earlier societies had not developed large-scale organizations to their fullest extent because their technology was relatively underdeveloped. Consequently, there was no need to accumulate profits to invest in machinery. As mechanical innovations evolved, more sophisticated management emerged to maximize production in order to serve new markets brought about by improved transportation networks and increased consumer demand (Barnouw, 1978:200–201; Braverman, 1974; Jacoby, 1973:9–19).

To see how a formal organization can develop, let us consider the example of a carpenter in colonial New England, whom we call James Wooley. Wooley began his adult life as a self-employed artisan who personally performed all the tasks of his trade. He cut the lumber, sawed it, made furniture, and sold his products himself. Generally, he worked alone in the building that served as his shop, store, and home.

As his village and business grew, Wooley concluded that he had more customers than he could personally serve. At first, he hired a single assistant. A few years later, as he was able to respond

TABLE 6-2 Bureaucratic "Doublespeak"

BUREAUCRACY	EVENT	DOUBLESPEAK
U.S. Army	Accidental explosion of a Pershing missile, killing three servicemen.	An "unplanned rapid ignition of solid fuel."
IBM	Recall of computers to fix defective hard-disk drives.	"Pro-active action."
Eastern Airlines	Discovery of holes in two airplanes during inspection.	Found "surface irregularities."
Chrysler Corporation	Layoff of more than 5000 workers in a Wisconsin auto plant.	The company "initiated a career alternative enhancement program."
Pacific Gas and Electric	Monthly billing to customers	Bills now called "Energy Documents."
Hospital in Philadelphia	Death of a patient as a result of medical malpractice.	A "diagnostic misadventure of a high magnitude."

SOURCES: Hechinger, 1986:C12, National Council of Teachers of English, 1988, 1989a, 1989b.

The Quarterly Review of Doublespeak, a publication of the National Council of Teachers of English, regularly fights language pollution by publishing examples of bureaucratic "doublespeak" designed to mislead people and manipulate social reality.

to demand in neighboring areas, he began to employ a small group of workers. Each of them specialized in a specific aspect of furniture making and took advantage of new tools and innovative carpentry techniques. One worker cut the wood, one made bedposts, one was in charge of staining, and another ran the store. Before long, a carpenter had become the manager of a small furniture factory (Stark et al., 1973:145).

Wooley discovered that by coordinating the work of several assistants efficiently, he could produce furniture more quickly and with less expense. However, this conversion from a one-person operation to a small assembly line illustrates more than simply a change in production techniques. It reflects the emergence of a dramatically different form of organization, known as *bureaucracy*, that has special significance for people's interactions and their relationship to work. A **bureaucracy** is a component of formal organization in which rules and hierarchical ranking are used to achieve efficiency.

Characteristics of a Bureaucracy When we think of the term *bureaucracy*, a variety of images—mostly unpleasant—come to mind. Rows of desks staffed by seemingly faceless people, endless lines and forms, impossibly complex language (see Table 6-2), and frustrating encounters with red

tape—all these have combined to make *bureaucracy* a dirty word and an easy target in political campaigns. As a result, few Americans want to identify their occupation as "bureaucrat" despite the fact that all of us perform various bureaucratic tasks. Elements of bureaucracy are found in almost every occupation in an industrial society such as the United States.

In order to develop a more useful and objective definition of bureaucracy, we must turn to the writings of Max Weber (1947:333–340, original edition 1922). This pioneer of sociology, who was introduced in Chapter 1, first directed researchers to the significance of bureaucratic structure. In an important sociological advance, Weber emphasized the basic similarity of structure and process found in the otherwise dissimilar enterprises of religion, government, education, and business.

Weber viewed bureaucracy as a form of organization quite different from the family-run busi-

TABLE 6-3 Characteristics of a Bureaucracy

CHARACTERISTIC	POSITIVE CONSEQUENCE	NEGATIVE CONSEQUENCE	
		FOR THE INDIVIDUAL	FOR THE ORGANIZATION
Division of labor	Produces efficiency in large-scale corporation	Produces trained incapacity	Produces narrow perspective
Hierarchy of authority	Clarifies who is in command	Deprives employees of a voice in decision making	Permits concealment of mistakes
Rules and regulations	Let workers know what is expected of them	Stifles initiative and imagination	Lead to goal displacement
Impersonality	Reduces bias	Contributes to feelings of alienation	Discourages loyalty to company
Employment based on technical qualifications	Discourages favoritism and reduces petty rivalries	Discourages ambition to improve oneself elsewhere	Allows Peter principle to operate

Max Weber introduced the concept of bureaucracy but tended to emphasize its positive aspects. More recently, social scientists have described the negative consequences (or dysfunctions) of bureaucracy both for the individual within the organization and for the bureaucracy itself.

ness. He developed an ideal type of bureaucracy, which reflects the most characteristic aspects of all human organizations. Since perfect bureaucracies are never achieved, no actual organization will correspond exactly to Weber's ideal type (Blau and Meyer, 1987:19–22). Nevertheless, Weber argued that every bureaucracy—whether its purpose is to run a day care center, corporation, or army—will have five basic characteristics. These characteristics, as well as *dysfunctions* (or potential negative consequences) of bureaucracy, are discussed below and summarized in Table 6-3.

1 Division of labor Specialized experts are employed in each position to perform specific tasks. Thus, the president of the United States need not be a good typist. A lawyer need not be able to complete an income tax form. By working at a specific task, people are more likely to become highly skilled and carry out a job with maximum efficiency. This emphasis on specialization is so basic a part of our lives that we may not realize that it is a fairly recent development in western culture.

Analysis of division of labor by interactionist researchers has led to scrutiny of how various employees at a workplace interact with one another. For example, after a cardiac patient is brought into a surgical recovery room, nurses and technicians independently make 10 or 20 connec-

tions between the patient and various monitoring devices. Later procedures, by contrast, are more likely to involve the cooperative efforts of two or more workers. Through these tasks, medical personnel gain proficiency in delicate and essential procedures (Strauss, 1985:2).

Although division of labor has certainly been beneficial in the performance of many complex bureaucracies, in some cases it can lead to *trained incapacity;* that is, workers become so specialized that they develop blind spots and fail to notice obvious problems. Even worse, they may not *care* about what is happening next to them on the assembly line. Some observers believe that, through such developments, Americans have become much less productive on the job.

Although trained incapacity has negative implications for the smooth running of organizations, it is especially disastrous for the person who loses a job during layoff. An unemployed worker may have spent years becoming proficient at highly technical work and yet may be totally unsuited for

FIGURE 6-1   Organization Chart of a Government Agency

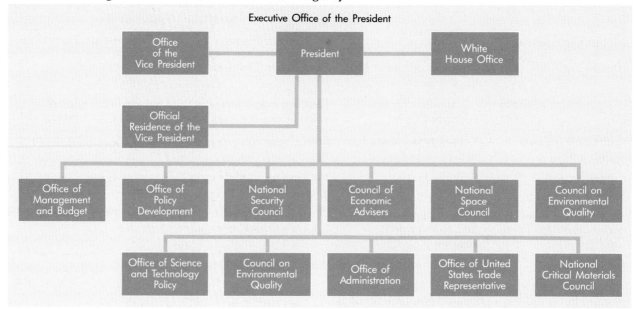

SOURCE: Office of the Federal Register, 1989:86.

The formal structure of a government office is fairly easy to ascertain. Equally important, but less apparent, is the informal chain of command.

other positions, even those which are directly related to his or her former job. As an example, an automotive machinist who pushes buttons on an automobile assembly line in Michigan will lack the proper training and skill to work as an oil industry machinist in Texas (Wallis, 1981).

In some instances, the division of labor (as reflected in the fragmentation of job titles) may actually contribute to sex discrimination by creating unnecessary and inappropriate distinctions between female and male employees. In a study of 368 businesses in California, sociologists James Baron and William Bielby (1986) found that proliferation of job titles tended to increase as men and women reached parity in their level of employment. Apparently, separate job titles—ostensibly designed to reflect a division of labor—were actually being used to preserve traditional occupational segregation by gender.

2 Hierarchy of authority Bureaucracies follow the principle of hierarchy; that is, each position is under the supervision of a higher authority (see Figure 6-1). A professional baseball team is run by an owner, who hires a general manager, who in turn hires a manager. Beneath the manager come the coaches and last the players. In the Roman Catholic church, the pope is the supreme authority; under him are cardinals, bishops, and so forth. Even large medical group practices have boards of directors, executive committees, and administrators (Kralewski et al., 1985).

Recent research suggests that bureaucracies may be a positive environment for women at the lower but not the upper echelons of the hierarchy. Political scientist Kathy Ferguson (1983, 1984) observes that many traits traditionally associated with the feminine gender role—such as valuing warm, supportive, cooperative relationships—are conducive to participation in a bureaucratic organization. However, upwardly mobile women may find their career progress hindered because they function more as facilitators than as innovators, and then are not viewed as aggressive enough to serve in higher management posts. Consequently, although traditional feminine values may be functional for women in the lower levels of bureaucratic structure, they appear to become dysfunctional as women aspire to greater power and prestige.

3 Written rules and regulations Wouldn't it be nice if a bank teller cashed your check for $100 and deliberately handed you six $20 bills, saying: "You have such a friendly smile; here's an extra $20"? It would certainly be a pleasant surprise, but it would also be "against the rules."

Rules and regulations, as we all know, are an important characteristic of bureaucracies. Ideally, through such procedures, a bureaucracy ensures uniform performance of every task. This prohibits us from receiving an extra $20 at the bank, but it also guarantees us that we will receive essentially the same treatment as other customers. If the bank provides them with special services, such as monthly statements or investment advice, it will also provide us with those services.

Through written rules and regulations, bureaucracies generally offer employees clear standards as to what is considered an adequate (or exceptional) performance. In addition, procedures provide a valuable sense of continuity in a bureaucracy. Individual workers will come and go, but the structure and past records give the organization a life of its own that outlives the services of any one bureaucrat. Thus, if you are brought in to work as the new manager of a bookstore, you do not have to start from scratch. Instead, you can study the store's records and accounting books to learn about the payroll, financial dealings with distributors, discount policies on "sale" books, and other procedures.

Of course, rules and regulations can overshadow the larger goals of an organization and become dysfunctional. If blindly applied, they will no longer serve as a means to achieving an objective but instead will become important (and perhaps too important) in their own right. This would certainly be the case if a hospital emergency room physician failed to treat a seriously injured person because he or she had no valid proof of United States citizenship. Robert Merton (1968:254–256) has used the term **goal displacement** to refer to overzealous conformity to official regulations.

The people of Peru became so annoyed by endless governmental rules that they established the Union of Formals and Informals, which is campaigning for across-the-board deregulation. Several bills have been presented to Peru's Congress to "debureaucratize" the state apparatus. Similarly, when Soviet leader Mikhail Gorbachev launched his program of **perestroika** (the restructuring of society) in 1987, he aimed particularly at the government bureaucracy. Integral to *perestroika* was the removal of several layers of officials controlled by Moscow. Ironically, this change proved somewhat dysfunctional from the perspective of the central government, since it allowed ethnic republics more leeway to express their demands for autonomy (Gregory, 1988; Riding, 1988; Schaefer, 1990:495–496).

It is widely believed that the rules and regulations of bureaucracy tend to suppress or destroy the individuality of employees. However, studies conducted by Melvin Kohn (1978) suggest that bureaucracies often encourage intellectual flexibility, tolerance for nonconformity, and willingness to accept change. The complexity and diversified responsibilities of most bureaucratic jobs appear to play an important role in promoting flexibility and openness to change.

4 Impersonality Max Weber wrote that in a bureaucracy, work is carried out *sine ira et studio*, "without hatred or passion." Bureaucratic norms dictate that officials perform their duties without the personal consideration of people as individuals. This is intended to guarantee equal treatment for each person; however, it also contributes to the often cold and uncaring feeling associated with modern organizations.

We typically think of big government and big business when we think of impersonal bureaucracies. Interestingly, during the most turbulent years of the 1960s, student activists bitterly protested the bureaucratic nature of the American university. One of the symbols of the free speech movement at the University of California at Berkeley was an IBM computer card which stated: "Student at U.C.: Do not bend, fold, or mutilate." In the view of dissidents, the university had become one more giant, faceless, unfeeling bureaucracy which cared little for the uniqueness of the individual (P. Jacobs and Landau, 1966:216–219).

5 Employment based on technical qualifications Within a bureaucracy, hiring is based on technical qualifications rather than on favoritism, and performance is measured against specific standards. This is designed to protect bureaucrats against arbitrary dismissal and to provide a measure of security. Promotions are dictated by written personnel policies, and people often have a right to appeal if they believe that particular rules have been violated. Such procedures encourage loyalty to the organization.

In this sense, the "impersonal" bureaucracy can be an improvement over nonbureaucratic organizations. A federal bureaucrat in a civil service position, for example, has ideally been selected on the basis of merit, not because he or she did favors for a political machine. Above all, the bureaucracy is expected to value technical and professional competence, which is essential in the day-to-day functioning of a complex, industrial society such as the United States.

Unfortunately, personnel decisions within a bureaucracy do not always follow this ideal pattern. Dysfunctions within bureaucracy have become well publicized, particularly because of the work of Laurence J. Peter. According to the *Peter principle,* every employee within a hierarchy tends to rise to his or her level of incompetence (Peter and Hull, 1969:25). This hypothesis, which has not been directly or systematically tested, reflects a possible dysfunctional outcome of structuring advancement on the basis of merit. Talented persons receive promotion after promotion until, sadly, they finally achieve positions that they cannot handle (Blau and Meyer, 1987:21; Chinoy, 1954:40–41).

Bureaucratization as a Process As stated earlier, Weber's characteristics of bureaucracy should be seen as describing an ideal type rather than as offering a precise definition of an actual bureaucracy. Sociologist Alvin Gouldner (1950:53–54) notes that not every formal organization will possess all of Weber's characteristics. In fact, there can be wide variation among actual bureaucratic organizations.

Stanley Udy (1959) compared the structure of formal organizations in 150 nonindustrial societies. Like their counterparts in modern industrial nations, these organizations possessed many of—but not necessarily all—the bureaucratic characteristics identified by Weber. Similarly, Richard Hall (1963) tested Weber's ideal type against 10 formal organizations within the United States, including a hotel and a stock brokerage firm. His findings concurred with those of Udy: bureaucracy must be viewed as a matter of degree, that is, as more, or less, bureaucratic. Therefore, in describing organizations, we need to apply the Weberian model carefully, with the understanding that an organization can be more or less rule-oriented, more or less hierarchical, and so forth.

Sociologists have used the term *bureaucratization* to refer to the process by which a group, organization, or social movement becomes increasingly bureaucratic. Earlier in the chapter, we saw the beginnings of this process as carpenter James Wooley became the manager of a small furniture factory in colonial America. Wooley's factory, even early in its operation, took on at least two of Weber's characteristics of bureaucracy: division of labor and hierarchical authority. If the factory continued to grow—and Wooley took on more and more employees—his organization would undoubtedly become more impersonal and he would probably develop more rules and regulations to ensure efficiency.

Normally, we think of bureaucratization in terms of large organizations. In a typical citizen's nightmare, one may have to speak to 10 or 12 individuals in a corporation or government agency to find out which official has jurisdiction over a particular problem. Callers can get transferred from one department to another until they finally hang up in disgust. Interestingly, though, bureaucratization also takes place within small-group settings. Children organizing a school club may elect as many officers as there are club members and may develop various rules for meetings.

As we have seen, bureaucratization is not a finite process, nor does it inevitably lead to a specific structure. For example, sociologists have recognized that organizations may take quite different forms in different cultures. In Box 6-2, we examine the way in which business firms in the United States have adapted Japanese management techniques.

In addition to varying from society to society,

BOX 6-2 • AROUND THE WORLD

QUALITY CIRCLES IN JAPAN AND THE UNITED STATES

As Japanese firms competed increasingly with United States–based corporations in the global marketplace, business leaders and social scientists in this country began to study the management techniques popular in Japan. Of particular interest were *quality circles*—small groups of about 10 to 15 workers that meet periodically with one or two managers to develop ideas for improving productivity and working conditions.

Quality circles are intended to encourage employees in Japanese corporations to share in the responsibilities of their superiors and thereby to identify with the fortunes of the corporation. Ideally, drawing on the collectivist orientation of Japanese culture, the company itself will take on greater meaning for the individual than his or her occupation has. Thus, a Japanese who is meeting someone for the first time will not say, "I am Myeko Sasaki," but rather, "I am Myeko Sasaki of the Yamaha Steel Company." However, Japanese quality circles are institutionalized and therefore not voluntary. There is substantial evidence to suggest that employees' participation in decision making is rather limited; quality circles may serve simply to ratify managerial values and predetermined outcomes (Ferris and Wagner, 1985).

By 1980, 500 firms in the United States had begun experimenting with quality circles. However, employee's participation in these experimental groups has

(Yasuhiko Ishii/Photo Researchers)

A management technique popular in Japan is the quality circle—a small group of about 10 to 15 workers who meet periodically with one or two managers to develop ideas for improving productivity and working conditions.

generally been voluntary. One study compared the attitudes and performance of six quality circles in an American manufacturing firm with a matched group of noninvolved workers. The researchers found that participation in quality circles had a favorable influence on employee's attitudes toward decision making, on their sense of pride in their work, and on group communication. Productivity among members of quality circles rose by 23 percent during the period of study, compared with only a 2 percent productivity rise in the control group. Moreover, there was a 27 percent decline in absenteeism among those employees participating in quality circles (Ferris and Wagner, 1985; Marks et al., 1986).

While these data are impressive, not all quality circles in the United States have been so successful, and many have been relatively

short lived. Sociologist Rosabeth Moss Kanter (1982) adds the caution that workers may view quality circles as an inauthentic, token reform that has no genuine impact on working conditions. Nevertheless, at least in some organizational settings, quality circles have provided opportunities for employees' personal growth, achievement, and recognition. These employees may be especially committed to the solutions they generate in quality circles (K. Davis and Newstrom, 1989:244–245).

bureaucratization also serves as an independent (or causal) variable affecting social change. Conflict theorists have argued that bureaucratic organizations tend to inhibit change because of their emphasis on regulations and security for office-holders. As one example, some public assistance (or welfare) caseworkers are so preoccupied with the required forms for clients that they forget to see whether people's basic needs are being satisfied. Paper becomes more meaningful than people; numbers take precedence over needs.

Oligarchy: Rule by a Few The bureaucratizing influence on social movements has also been a concern of conflict theorists. German sociologist Robert Michels (1915), in studying socialist parties and labor unions in Europe before World War I, found that such organizations were becoming increasingly bureaucratic. The emerging leaders of these organizations—even some of the most radical—had a vested interest in clinging to power. If they lost their leadership posts, they would have to return to full-time work as manual laborers.

Similarly, a team of sociologists studied bureaucratization in "crisis centers." These organizations, born in the counterculture of the 1960s (see Chapter 3), were established to offer counseling and support to persons experiencing divorce, death of a family member, drug and alcohol problems, and other types of emotional crisis. Despite their initial commitment to less bureaucratic, nonhierarchical structures, crisis centers increasingly turned to written job descriptions, organization charts, and written policies regarding treatment of cases and clients (Senter et al., 1983; for a different view, see Rothschild-Whitt, 1979).

Through his research, Michels originated the idea of the *iron law of oligarchy,* under which even a democratic organization will develop into a bureaucracy ruled by a few (the oligarchy). Why do oligarchies emerge? People who achieve leadership roles usually have the skills, knowledge, or charismatic appeal (as Weber noted) to direct, if not control, others. Michels argues that the rank and file of a movement or organization look to leaders for direction and thereby reinforce the process of rule by a few. In addition, members of an oligarchy are strongly motivated to maintain their leadership roles, privileges, and power.

Michels's insights continue to be relevant in the 1990s. Contemporary labor unions in the United States and western Europe bear little resemblance to those organized after spontaneous activity by exploited workers. Conflict theorists have expressed concern about the longevity of union leaders, who are not always responsive to the needs and demands of membership. As Michels noted in his iron law of oligarchy, leaders may become more concerned with maintaining their own positions and power.

At least one recent study, however, raises questions about Michels's views. On the basis of her research on organizations active in the "pro-choice" social movement, which endorses the right to legal abortions, sociologist Suzanne Staggenborg (1988) disputes the assertion that formal organizations with professional leaders inevitably become conservative and oligarchical. Indeed, she notes that many formal organizations in the pro-choice movement appear to be more democratic than informal groups; the routinized procedures that they follow make it more difficult for leaders to achieve excessive power.

It should be added that bureaucracies are not always a conservative force within a society. Political scientist Gregory Kasza (1987) studied military regimes in Japan (in the period 1937–1945), Peru (1968–1975), and Egypt (1952–1970). He found that the civilian bureaucracies serving these military governments actually *promoted* radical policies. For example, Egyptian bureaucrats introduced sweeping land reforms that redistributed 20 percent of all land suitable for cultivation to the country's peasants. In criticizing previous work on bureaucratic conservatism, Kasza emphasizes that different types of regimes may encourage radical, liberal, or conservative bureaucratic policies.

While the "iron law" may sometimes help us to understand the concentration of formal authority within organizations, sociologists recognize that there are a number of checks on leadership. Groups often compete for power within a formal organization, as in an automotive corporation in which divisions manufacturing heavy machinery and passenger cars compete against each other for limited research and development funds. Moreover, informal channels of communication and control can undercut the power of top officials of an organization. This is bureaucracy's "other face."

Bureaucracy's Other Face How does bureaucratization affect the average individual who works in an organization? The early theorists of formal organizations tended to neglect this question. Max Weber, for example, focused on management personnel within bureaucracies, but he had little to say about workers in industry or clerks in government agencies.

According to the ***classical theory*** of formal organizations, also known as the ***scientific management approach,*** workers are motivated almost entirely by economic rewards. This theory stresses that productivity is limited only by the physical constraints of workers. Therefore, workers are treated as a resource, much like the machines that have begun to replace them in the twentieth century. Management attempts to achieve maximum work efficiency through scientific planning, established performance standards, and careful supervision of workers and production. Planning under the scientific management approach involves time and motion studies but not studies of workers' attitudes or feelings of job satisfaction.

It was not until workers organized unions—and forced management to recognize that they were not objects—that theorists of formal organizations began to revise the classical approach. Along with management and administrators, social scientists became aware that informal groups of workers have an important impact on organizations (Perrow, 1986:79–118). One result was an alternative way of considering bureaucratic dynamics, the ***human relations approach,*** which emphasizes the role of people, communication, and participation within a bureaucracy. This type of analysis reflects the interest of interactionist theorists in small-group behavior. Unlike planning under the scientific management approach, planning based on the human relations perspective focuses on workers' feelings, frustrations, and emotional need for job satisfaction.

The gradual move away from a sole focus on physical aspects of getting the job done—and toward the concerns and needs of workers—led advocates of the human relations approach to stress the less formal aspects of bureaucratic structure. Informal structures and social networks within organizations develop partly as a result of people's ability to create more direct forms of communication than the formal structures mandate. Charles Page (1946) has used the term *bureaucracy's other face* to refer to the unofficial activities and interactions which are such a basic part of daily organizational life. Two studies—one of a factory, the other of a law enforcement agency—illustrate the value of the human relations approach.

In Chapter 2, we looked at the Hawthorne studies, which alerted sociologists to the fact that research subjects may alter their behavior to match the experimenter's expectations. This methodological finding notwithstanding, the major focus of the Hawthorne studies was the role of social factors in workers' productivity. As one aspect of the research, an investigation was made of the switchboard-bank wiring room, where 14 men were making parts of switches for telephone equipment. These men were found to be producing far below their physical capabilities. This was especially surprising because they would earn more money if they produced more parts.

Why was there such an unexpected restriction of output? According to the classical theory, productivity should be maximized, since workers had been given a financial incentive. However, in practice the men were carefully subverting this scheme to boost productivity. They feared that if they produced switch parts at a faster rate, their pay rate might be reduced or some might lose their jobs.

As a result, this group of workers established their own (unofficial) norm for a proper day's work. They created informal rules, sanctions, and argot terms to enforce this standard. Workers who produced "too much" were called "speed kings" and "rate busters," while those judged to be "too slow" were "chiselers." Individuals who violated this agreement were "binged" (slugged on the shoulder) by coworkers. Yet management was unaware of such practices and had actually come to believe that the men were working as hard as they could (Etzioni, 1964:33–34; Roethlisberger and Dickson, 1939).

In another study of interactions within bureaucracy, Peter Blau (1963) observed agents working in a federal law enforcement agency. Their work involved auditing books and records and also interviewing employees and employers. If agents encountered a problem or procedure that they could not handle, they were required to consult their superior (a staff attorney) rather than ask each other. However, many were reluctant to follow this established policy for fear that it would adversely affect their job ratings. Therefore, they usually sought guidance from other agents—even though this clearly violated the official rules.

How does one get advice without asking for it? To put it another way, how does one officially respect a policy while in fact subverting it? Typically, when faced with this problem, an agent would describe an "interesting case" to colleagues, slowly allowing them to interrupt. Listeners would remind the agent of new data that might be helpful or suggest other ways of approaching the problem. Yet, of course, the agent had never asked—at least directly—for assistance. These maneuvers permitted law enforcement agents to maintain face, in Goffman's terms (see Chapter 4), with both their coworkers and their superiors.

Both the Hawthorne studies and Blau's research testify to the importance of informal structures within formal organizations. Whenever we examine sufficiently small segments of such organizations, we discover patterns of interaction that cannot be accounted for by the official structure. Thus, while a bureaucracy may establish a clear hierarchy and well-defined rules and standards, people can always get around their superiors. Informal understandings among workers can redefine official policies of a bureaucracy.

Interest in sociological investigation of labor-management relations and workplace behavior has led not only to research opportunities but also to employment opportunities for applied sociologists. According to a 1984 report by the American Sociological Association, about 12 percent of all those who held degrees in sociology were working with corporations. Among their job titles were "management consultant," "training and development manager," "systems analyst," and "personnel director" (Huber, 1984a, 1984b).

Voluntary Associations

By 1990, there were more than 22,000 voluntary associations in the United States—an increase of 36 percent over the 1980 figure. *Voluntary associations* are organizations established on the basis of common interest, whose members volunteer or even pay to participate. The Girl Scouts of America, the American Jewish Congress, the Kiwanis Club, and the League of Women Voters are all considered voluntary associations; so, too, are the American Association of Aardvark Aficionados, the Cats on Stamps Study Group, the Mikes of America, the New York Corset Club, and the William Shatner Fellowship. The nation's largest voluntary association, the American Automobile Association, has 29 million members; the smallest, the School Bus Manufacturers Institute, has only five (Gale, 1990).

The categories of "formal organization" and "voluntary association" are not mutually exclusive. Large voluntary associations such as the Lions Club and the Masons have structures similar to those of profit-making corporations. At the same time, certain formal organizations, such as the Young Men's Christian Association (YMCA) and the Peace Corps, have philanthropic and educational goals usually found in voluntary associations. Interestingly, the Democratic party and the United Farm Workers union are considered examples of voluntary associations. In a sense, belonging to a political party or a union can be a condition of employment and not genuinely voluntary; nevertheless, political parties and unions are usually included in discussions of voluntary associations.

Voluntary associations can provide support to people in preindustrial societies. During the post–World War II period, migration from rural areas of Africa to the cities was accompanied by a growth in voluntary associations, including trade unions, occupational societies, and mutual aid organizations developed along old tribal ties. As people moved from the *Gemeinschaft* of the coun-

A unique voluntary association is the Little People of America (LPA), which was established in 1957 to meet the special needs of our nation's "little people." Members of the LPA are shown here at one of the organization's annual conventions. LPA challenges prejudices concerning little people and encourages members to live meaningful lives within the dominant culture.

tryside to the *Gesellschaft* of the city (refer back to Chapter 5), these voluntary associations provided immigrants with substitutes for the extended groups of kinfolk that they had had in their villages (Little, 1988).

Americans often take the existence of voluntary associations for granted without realizing that the principle of freedom of association is not universally honored. In 1989, many students and workers active in China's democracy movement were killed in and near Beijing, in good part because the Chinese government feared the power that

the new voluntary associations might have. The recognized right of people to combine for a common purpose has its roots in the formation of guilds of artisans as early as the tenth century. However, many religious minorities came to the United States largely because their European homelands would not tolerate groups that challenged dominant norms.

As seen in the quotation introducing this chapter, in the 1830s, the French writer Alexis de Tocqueville (1835) noted the tendency of Americans to create voluntary associations. This is still true in the twentieth century, as evidenced by a study that found 87 voluntary associations in a Nebraska town with fewer than 1400 residents (McPherson and Smith-Lovin, 1986:65).

Residents of the United States belong to such associations for a remarkable variety of reasons. Some join to share in activities, such as members of a college debating society or a senior citizens' hiking club. For others, voluntary associations serve as a potent political force, and they may join national lobbying groups such as the American Civil Liberties Union, or the National Right to Life Committee. Finally, many Americans join "self-help groups" to deal with personal problems that they cannot handle alone (see Box 6-3 on page 176). Clearly, there is no typical voluntary association; the size and complexity of such groups vary dramatically.

Membership in voluntary associations is not random. The most consistent predictor of participation is socioeconomic status—that is, a person's income, education, and occupation. Americans of higher socioeconomic status are more likely to belong to and participate actively in such organizations. Partly, this reflects the cost of group memberships, which may exclude people with limited income from joining (Sills, 1968a:365–366; J. Williams et al., 1973).

Reflecting the occupational patterns of the larger society, voluntary associations in the United States are largely segregated by gender. Half of them are exclusively female, and one-fifth are all-male. The exclusively male associations tend to be larger and more heterogeneous in terms of background of members. As noted in Chapter 5, membership in all-male associations holds more promise for making desirable busi-

BOX 6-3 • EVERYDAY BEHAVIOR

SELF-HELP GROUPS

Overeaters Anonymous, Women Who Love Too Much, Compulsive Shoppers, Children of Aging Parents, Fundamentalists Anonymous, Incest Survivors—these are but six of thousands of self-help groups in which about 15 million Americans participate. A *self-help group* is a mutual aid group "in which people who face a common concern or condition come together voluntarily for emotional support and practical assistance." These groups, known for their near-religious fervor, generally meet without any professional supervision, instead assisting members through peer support (P. Brown, 1988:1).

The nation's oldest and best-known self-help group, Alcoholics Anonymous (AA), was established in 1935 by heavy drinkers who felt that sharing feelings and experiences with other alcoholics was an essential part of recovery. Currently, AA has a worldwide membership of about 1.7 million. Its famous Twelve Step program for recovery emphasizes acceptance of one's addiction, the need for honesty and support, and the acknowledgment of a "higher power" in the universe.

In its early years in the United States, AA was almost exclusively White, male, middle-aged, and middle-class. However, the AA of the 1990s is increasingly multiracial, multiethnic, and diverse in terms of members' social class backgrounds. Women represent perhaps half of all members in large cities, and AA has become much more accepting of openly gay members than it was in the past. Although it maintains a national headquarters, AA is remarkably decentralized and basically consists of rather autonomous local groups. The AA model of group process includes few rules, little hierarchy except for nominal group leaders, and a common purpose of recovery which overcomes any traditional division of labor (Leehrsen, 1990; N. Robertson, 1988).

Sociologist Norman Denzin (1987, 1990) has drawn upon the interactionist approach in his examination of the "self story telling" that takes place in AA and other self-help groups. Denzin suggests that a person who becomes active in AA is socialized into the group's norms, values, and distinctive argot; as a result, the individual learns to view and express his or her life story in a manner structured by the group. As an example, Denzin (1987: 145) quotes a man who had been in AA for 2 years:

Never thought I'd make it. Remember when I first came here. Couldn't talk. Scared to death. Alone. Not that way today. I can talk. I got the Steps. I got the Program. I got my meetings to go to. I got my *Big Book*. Found my story in there. Talk to my mom now. Got my old job back. You people gave me back my life. Thanks.

The success of AA in assisting many recovering alcoholics has unquestionably contributed to the

(AP/Wide World Photos)

The nation's oldest and best-known self-help group, Alcoholics Anonymous (AA), was established in 1935 by heavy drinkers who felt that sharing feelings and experiences with other alcoholics was an essential part of recovery. Its famous Twelve Step program for recovery emphasizes acceptance of one's addiction, the need for honesty and support, and acknowledgment of a "higher power" in the universe.

increase in self-help groups, many of which have borrowed from AA's model. In the last decade, the number of self-help organizations in the United States has more than quadrupled. Alfred Katz, an expert on public health and social welfare, points out that the dramatic rise in these mutual aid efforts reflects a profound dissatisfaction with existing medical and counseling services. "People are dissatisfied with impersonality and bureaucratic runarounds," notes Katz. "They do not want to be dependent on outside professionals. They want to have more of a say" (P. Brown, 1988:7; Leehrsen, 1990).

ness contacts than membership in all-female groups (McPherson and Smith-Lovin, 1986). Although participation varies across the American population, most people belong to at least one voluntary association (see Figure 6-2), while about one-quarter maintain three or more memberships.

Sociologists have applied functionalist analysis to the study of voluntary associations. David Sills (1968a:373–376) has identified several key functions that these groups serve within American society. First, they mediate between individuals and government. Professional associations such as the American Medical Association mediate between their members and government in such matters as licensing and legislation. Second, voluntary associations give people training in organizational skills that is invaluable for future officeholders—and for better performance within most jobs. Third, organizations such as the National Association for the Advancement of Colored People (NAACP), the National Women's Political Caucus, and the American Association of Retired Persons (AARP) help to bring traditionally disadvantaged and underrepresented groups into the political mainstream. Finally, voluntary associations assist in governing. During the influx of Indochinese and Cuban refugees in the late 1970s and early 1980s, religious and charitable groups became deeply involved in helping the federal government resettle refugees.

The importance of voluntary associations—and especially of their unpaid workers (or volunteers)—is increasingly being recognized. Traditionally, unpaid work has been devalued in the United States, even though the skill levels, experience, and training demands are often comparable with those of wage labor. Viewed from a conflict perspective, the critical difference has been that a substantial amount of volunteer work is performed by women. Feminists and conflict theorists agree that, like the unpaid child care and household labor of homemakers, the effort of volunteers has been too often ignored by scholars—and awarded too little respect by the larger society—because it is viewed as "women's work." Failure to recognize women's volunteerism thereby obscures a critical contribution women

FIGURE 6-2   Membership in Voluntary Associations, 1990

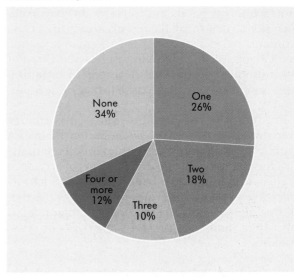

SOURCE: NORC, 1990:369.

Most Americans belong to at least one voluntary association; almost one-fourth maintain three or more memberships.

make to a society's social structure (A. Daniels, 1987, 1988).

Curiously, although membership in voluntary associations in the United States is high, people tend to add and drop affiliations rather quickly. This reflects the fact that a decision to enter a voluntary association typically involves only limited personal objectives (Babchuk and Booth, 1969). As de Tocqueville wrote, Americans are "forever forming associations."

Organizational Change

Just as individuals and relationships change, so too do organizations, both formal and voluntary. The most obvious changes often involve personnel: a new president of the United States is elected, an executive is fired, a star athlete retires. However, sociologists are most interested in how the organization itself changes.

These changes often relate to other social institutions, particularly the government. Its regulatory statutes, licensing procedures, tax laws, and contracting for goods and services directly influence the structure of formal organizations. Government policies relating to affirmative action (see Chapter 15) or disability rights (see Chapter 20) influence the internal decisions of organizations and may even require the hiring of new personnel.

In addition, an organization's goals may change over time along with its leaders and structure. A church starts a basketball league; an oil company purchases a movie studio; a chewing tobacco firm begins to manufacture ballpoint pens. Such actions take place when an organization decides that its traditional goals are no longer adequate. It must then modify its previous objectives or cease to exist.

Goal Multiplication   If an organization concludes that its goals must change, it will typically establish additional goals or expand upon its traditional objectives. For example, in the 1970s many colleges began continuing education programs to meet the needs of potential students holding full-time jobs and wishing to take classes at night. In the 1980s, the Elderhostel movement opened college campuses to older Americans, who could live and learn along with much younger college students.

Goal multiplication takes place when an organization expands its purposes. Generally, this is the result of changing social or economic conditions which threaten the organization's survival. The YMCA has practiced such goal multiplication. Reflecting its name, the Young Men's Christian Association had a strong evangelistic focus during its beginnings in the United States in the 1850s. Bible study and tent revival meetings were provided by the early YMCAs. However, in the early 1900s, the YMCA began to diversify its appeal. It attempted to interest members by offering gymnasium facilities and residence quarters. Gradually, Lutherans, Roman Catholics, Jews, and the "unchurched" were accepted and even recruited as members.

The most recent phase of goal multiplication at the YMCA began in the 1960s. In larger urban areas, the organization became involved in providing employment training and juvenile delinquency programs. As a result, the YMCA received substantial funding from the federal government. This was a dramatic change for an organization whose income had previously come solely from membership fees and charitable contributions.

In the 1980s, the YMCA continued to serve the

(Robert C.V. Lieberman/YMCA of Greater New York)

The Young Men's Christian Association (YMCA) has experienced goal multiplication in recent decades. Its range of activities currently includes social services programs for the disabled, day care centers, fitness classes for office workers, residence dormitories for college students and single adults, and senior citizens' facilities.

poor, as evidenced by the building of a new facility in 1984 in the Watts section of Los Angeles—the first major private construction in the area since the riots of 1965. Yet the organization also maintains a lucrative branch in Beverly Hills and has expanded rapidly to serve middle-class residents of cities and suburbs. The YMCA's impressive range of activities currently includes social service programs for the disabled, day care centers, fitness classes for office workers, residence dormitories for college students and single adults, "learning for living" classes for adults, and senior citizens' facilities (Schmidt, 1990).

These transitions in the YMCA were not always smooth. At times, major contributors and board members withdrew support because of opposition to organizational changes; they preferred the YMCA to remain as it had been. However, the YMCA has survived and grown by expanding its goals from evangelism to general community service (Etzioni, 1964:13; Zald, 1970).

Goal Succession Unlike goal multiplication, *goal succession* occurs when a group or organization has either realized or been denied its goal. It must then identify an entirely new objective that can justify its existence. Cases of goal succession are rare because most organizations never fully achieve their goals. If they do, as in the case of a committee supporting a victorious candidate for public office, they usually dissolve.

Sociologist Peter Blau (1964:241–246), who coined the term *succession of goals*, noted that organizations do not necessarily behave in a rigid manner when their goals are achieved or become irrelevant. Rather, they may shift toward new objectives. A case in point is the Foundation for Infantile Paralysis, popularly known for its annual March of Dimes campaign. For some time, the foundation's major goals were to support medical research on polio and to provide assistance for victims of the disease. However, in 1955 the Salk vaccine was found to be an effective protection against paralytic polio. This left the foundation, so to speak, "unemployed." A vast network of committed staff members and volunteers was suddenly left without a rationale for existence. The group might have disbanded, but instead it selected a new goal—combating arthritis and birth defects—and took on a new name. Like many bureaucracies, it simply refused to die (Etzioni, 1964:13; Sills, 1957:253–271).

SOCIAL POLICY AND ORGANIZATIONS

SEXUAL HARASSMENT

- How common is sexual harassment in the United States?
- Viewed from a conflict perspective, how do the data on sexual harassment reflect inequities based on gender and race?
- In what ways do organizational structures encourage or permit sexual harassment?

A woman who had poured her life into an advertising career that she loved was introduced to her new department head. He made sexual propositions to her, implying that going to bed with him would help her "get to the top." She tried to refuse politely, but his lewd remarks and pointed staring continued over the following months. As she kept on resisting, he also began to find fault with her work. She finally complained to his superior. One week later, she was fired . . . (Lindsey, 1977:47).

Whether they hold managerial or clerical positions, whether they work in a voluntary association or a Fortune 500 corporation, women report being victimized by sexual harassment. *Sexual harassment* has been defined as the "unwanted imposition of sexual requirements in a relationship of unequal power" (MacKinnon, 1979:1). The most blatant example in the office or factory is the boss who tells a subordinate: "Put out or get out." But, under evolving legal standards, *sexual harassment* is recognized as any unwanted and unwelcome sexual advances that interfere with a person's ability to perform a job and enjoy the benefits of a job. These unwelcome ad-

Catherine Broderick (left), pictured with one of her attorneys, brought a sexual harassment complaint against the Washington office of the Securities and Exchange Commission and won the case. Broderick, a lawyer, had refused her supervisor's advances and then had been repeatedly denied promotion.

vances may take the form of subtle pressures regarding sexual activity, inappropriate sexual language, inappropriate touching, attempted kissing or fondling, demands for sexual favors, or sexual assault.

In the 1986 case of *Meritor Savings Bank v. Vinson,* the Supreme Court unanimously held that sexual harassment by a supervisor violates federal law against sex discrimination in the workplace, as outlined in the 1964 Civil Rights Act. If sufficiently severe, sexual harassment constitutes a violation of the law even if the unwelcome sexual demands are not linked to concrete employment benefits such as a raise or a promotion. The justices ruled that the existence of a hostile or abusive work environment—in which a woman feels degraded as the result of unwelcome flirtation or obscene joking—may in itself constitute illegal sex discrimination. In early 1991, a federal judge ruled that the public display of photographs of nude and partly nude women at a workplace constitutes sexual harassment (T. Lewin, 1991; Withers and Benaroya, 1989:6–7).

Women of all ages and racial and ethnic groups— and men as well—have been the victims of sexual harassment. Attorney and political scientist Catharine MacKinnon (1979), the author of an important examination of sexual harassment of working women, has observed that such harassment may occur as a single encounter or as a repeated pattern of behavior. While estimates and definitions vary, a 1988 study of federal employees revealed that 42 percent of all women and 14 percent of all men working for the federal govern-

ment stated they had been sexually harassed within the preceding 2 years. Although the federal bureaucracy had issued regulations prohibiting such harassment during the 1980s, the results of this survey showed there had been no decline in harassment since a similar survey taken 7 years earlier (Havemann, 1988).

Sexual harassment has been commonly reported not only in the federal workplace and in private-sector organizations, but also in institutions of higher learning. According to a study conducted in the period 1982–1985, more than half of female students at the nation's colleges and universities experience some form of sexual harassment, ranging from verbal abuse to unwanted sexual contact or rape. More than 20 percent of women students are sexually propositioned or harassed by their professors (Brodkey and Fine, 1988; L. Fitzgerald et al., 1988).

Whether it occurs in the federal bureaucracy, in the corporate world, or in universities, sexual harassment generally occurs in organizations in which the hierarchy of authority finds White males at the top. One survey in the private sector found that Black women were three times more likely than White women to experience sexual harassment. From a conflict perspective, it is not surprising that women, and especially women of color, are most likely to become the victims of sexual harassment; these groups are typically an organization's most vulnerable employees in terms of job security (J. Jones, 1988).

While it is agreed that sexual harassment is widespread in the United States, it is nevertheless clear that most victims do not report these abuses to proper authorities. In 1985, the most recent year for which data are available, the Equal Employment Opportunity Commission (EEOC) received only 436 official complaints of sexual harassment from the federal government's 2.1 million workers. In the federal survey discussed above, only 5 percent of those who had been harassed stated that they had filed complaints (Havemann, 1988; see also Bozzi, 1989).

"It takes a lot of self-confidence to fight," suggests Catherine Broderick, a lawyer for the Securities and Exchange Commission (SEC) who won a sexual harassment complaint against the agency's Washington office. Broderick had refused her supervisor's advances and then had been repeatedly denied promotions. After a 9-year legal battle, Broderick was victorious in court and won a promotion and years of back pay. Still, her experience is a reminder that pursuing justice against those guilty of sexual harassment can be costly and draining (Saltzman, 1988:56–57).

Even if a victim does have the will to fight, the process of making a sexual harassment complaint in the courts or in most bureaucracies is slow and burdensome. (The responses to the federal survey indicate that it took an average of 482 days to dispose of a sexual harassment complaint.) In many instances, written procedures for complaints lead to goal displacement by those in positions of power; there is more concern for following the regulations than for dealing with and preventing harassment. Part of the problem is that many organizations do not have personnel who are adequately trained to deal with such complaints. This responsibility is often handed to a personnel officer whose only background for the task is a 2-day seminar on sexual harassment.

Many bureaucracies have traditionally given little attention to the pervasive sexual harassment in their midst; the emotional costs of this discrimination suffered by (largely female) employees have not been a major concern. However, more regulations prohibiting sexual harassment have been issued as managers and executives have been forced to confront the costs of sexual harassment *for the organization*. In the 2-year period from 1985 to 1987, job turnover, absenteeism, and lost productivity resulting from sexual harassment cost federal agencies more than $267 million. Such cost estimates have contributed to a growing climate of concern both in government and in the private sector (J. Jones, 1988).

Claudia Withers and Anne Benaroya (1989) of the Women's Legal Defense Fund note that while legal remedies for sexual harassment are available, the enforcement of such legal rights is difficult and expensive for employees. In their view, the main responsibility for preventing and dealing with sexual harassment falls on employers:

> When an employer receives a complaint or otherwise learns of sexual harassment in the workplace, it must investigate promptly and thoroughly. The employer must take immediate and appropriate corrective action by doing whatever is necessary to end the harassment, make the victim whole by restoring her loss, and prevent the misconduct from reoccurring. . . . An effective preventive program should include an explicit policy against sexual harassment that is clearly and regularly communicated to employees, as well as effectively implemented (Withers and Benaroya, 1989:22–23).

SUMMARY

Interaction among human beings is necessary to the transmission of culture and the survival of every society. This chapter examines the impact of small groups and of large, formal organizations on social behavior.

1 When we find ourselves identifying closely with a group, it is probably a *primary group.*

2 Americans tend to see the world in terms of *in-groups* and *out-groups,* a perception often fostered by the very groups to which we belong.

3 *Reference groups* set and enforce standards of conduct and perform a comparison function for people's evaluations of themselves and others.

4 Interactionist researchers have revealed that there are distinct and predictable processes at work in the functioning of *small groups.*

5 Unlike any other group, a *dyad* can be destroyed by the loss of a single member.

6 One poignant and recurring message of recent decades has been the power and pervasiveness of large organizations.

7 Max Weber argued that, in its ideal form, every *bureaucracy* will share these five basic characteristics: division of labor, hierarchical authority, written rules and regulations, impersonality, and employment based on technical qualifications.

8 Bureaucracy can be understood as a process and as a matter of degree; thus, an organization is more or less bureaucratic than other organizations.

9 The informal structure of an organization can undermine and redefine official bureaucratic policies.

10 Americans belong to *voluntary associations* for a variety of purposes—for example, to share in joint activities or to get help with personal problems.

11 Change is an important element in organizational life. An organization may need to change its goals if its original objectives are fully realized or are no longer adequate.

12 Sexual harassment has been commonly reported not only in the federal workplace and in private-sector organizations, but also in institutions of higher learning.

KEY TERMS

Bureaucracy A component of formal organization in which rules and hierarchical ranking are used to achieve efficiency. (page 166)

Bureaucratization The process by which a group, organization, or social movement becomes increasingly bureaucratic. (170)

Classical theory An approach to the study of formal organizations which views workers as being motivated almost entirely by economic rewards. (173)

Coalition A temporary or permanent alliance toward a common goal. (163)

Dyad A two-member group. (161)

Dysfunction An element or process of society that may disrupt a social system or lead to a decrease in stability. (167)

Formal organization A special-purpose group designed and structured in the interests of maximum efficiency. (165)

Goal displacement Overzealous conformity to official regulations within a bureaucracy. (169)

Goal multiplication The process through which an organization expands its purposes. (178)

Goal succession The process through which an organization identifies an entirely new objective because its traditional goals have been either realized or denied. (179)

Group Any number of people with similar norms, values, and expectations who regularly and consciously interact. (157)

Human relations approach An approach to the study of formal organizations which emphasizes the role of people, communication, and participation within a bureaucracy and tends to focus on the informal structure of the organization. (173)

In-group Any group or category to which people feel they belong. (158)

Interaction process analysis (IPA) A technique developed by Robert F. Bales for analyzing a group's structure and processes. (160)

Iron law of oligarchy A principle of organizational life developed by Robert Michels under which even democratic organizations will become bureaucracies ruled by a few individuals. (172)

Out-group A group or category to which people feel they do not belong. (159)

Perestroika Soviet leader Mikhail Gorbachev's plan to restructure Soviet society. (169)

Peter principle A principle of organizational life, originated by Laurence J. Peter, according to which each individual within a hierarchy tends to rise to his or her level of incompetence. (170)

Primary group A small group characterized by intimate, face-to-face association and cooperation. (158)

Quality circles Small groups of about 10 to 15 workers that meet periodically with one or two managers to develop ideas for improving productivity and working conditions. (171)

Reference group A term used by Herbert Hyman when speaking of any group that individuals use as a standard in evaluating themselves and their own behavior. (159)

Scientific management approach Another name for the *classical theory* of formal organizations. (173)

Secondary group A formal, impersonal group in which there is little social intimacy or mutual understanding. (158)

Self-help group A mutual aid group in which people who face a common concern or condition come together voluntarily for emotional support and practical assistance. (176)

Sexual harassment The unwanted imposition of sexual requirements in a relationship of unequal power. (179)

Small group A group small enough for all members to interact simultaneously, that is, to talk with one another or at least be acquainted. (160)

Sociogram A depiction of preferred associations among group members. (160)

Trained incapacity The tendency of workers in a bureaucracy to become so specialized that they develop blind spots and cannot notice obvious problems. (167)

Triad   A three-member group. (161)

Voluntary associations   Organizations established on the basis of common interest whose members volunteer or even pay to participate. (174)

ADDITIONAL READINGS

Biggart, Nicole Woolsey. *Charismatic Capitalism: Direct Selling Organizations in America.* Chicago: University of Chicago Press, 1989. Biggart details the social and cultural factors that have given rise to direct-selling organizations (DSOs) and explores the dynamics of organizational life in these groups.

Daniels, Arlene Kaplan. *Invisible Careers.* Chicago: University of Chicago Press, 1988. A critical look at how work is viewed in the United States, noting the widespread failure to include the unpaid labor disproportionately performed by women.

Ferguson, Kathy E. *The Feminist Case against Bureaucracy.* Philadelphia: Temple University Press, 1984. Ferguson draws on a broad range of social science literature to document how women are at a comparative disadvantage in contemporary bureaucracies.

Fine, Gary Alan. *With the Boys: Little League Baseball and Preadolescent Culture.* Chicago: University of Chicago Press, 1987. Fine examines preadolescent boys in the United States through a participant-observation study of Little League baseball.

Fisher, B. Aubrey, and Donald G. Ellis. *Small Group Decision Making: Communication, and the Group Process* (3d ed.). New York: McGraw-Hill, 1990. Communication specialist Donald G. Ellis has revised the examination of group structure, decision making, and conflict resolution by renowned authority B. Aubrey Fisher.

Jacoby, Henry. *The Bureaucratization of the World.* Berkeley: University of California Press, 1973. Jacoby, a German sociologist, offers a historical perspective on bureaucracies and focuses on the impact of bureaucratization on democratic ideals.

Janis, Irving. *Victims of Groupthink.* Boston: Houghton Mifflin, 1967. A presentation concerning the power that small-group dynamics has over decision making.

Kaminer, Wendy. *Women Volunteering: The Pleasure, Pain, and Politics of Unpaid Work from 1830 to the Present.* Garden City, N.Y.: Anchor, 1984. A historical examination of the prominent role women have played within voluntary associations.

Matyko, Alexander J. *The Self-Defeating Organization: A Critique of Bureaucracy.* New York: Praeger, 1986. Matyko argues that traditional, hierarchical organizations face a crisis because people are less willing to accept such authoritarian arrangements.

Westrum, Ron, and Khalil Samaha. *Complex Organizations: Growth, Struggle, and Change.* Englewood Cliffs, N.J.: Prentice-Hall, 1984. A concise treatment of formal organizations.

Zald, Mayer N. *Organizational Change: The Political Economy of the YMCA.* Chicago: University of Chicago Press, 1970. This sociological study traces the YMCA's transformation from an evangelistic association to a service organization heavily dependent on federal funding.

Journals

Among the journals that focus on the study of groups and organizations are *Administration and Society* (founded in 1969), *Administrative Science Quarterly* (1956), *Clinical Sociology Review* (1981), *Quarterly Review of Doublespeak* (1974), *Small Group Research* (formerly *Small Group Behavior*, 1970), and *Social Psychology Review* (1948).

DEVIANCE AND SOCIAL CONTROL

> *When is conduct a crime, and when is a crime not a crime? When Somebody*
> *Up There—a monarch, a dictator, a Pope, a legislator—so decrees.*
> Jessica Mitford
> Kind and Usual Punishment, 1971

LOOKING AHEAD

- How does a society bring about acceptance of social norms?
- How does obedience differ from conformity?
- How do sociologists view the creation of laws?
- Can we learn deviant behavior from others?
- Why is certain behavior evaluated as "deviant" while other behavior is not?
- Should gambling, prostitution, public drunkenness, and use of marijuana be viewed as "victimless crimes"?
- What are the distinctive features of violent crime in the Soviet Union?
- Is the death penalty appropriate in American society?

Why would a person permanently alter his or her appearance—and challenge traditional social norms—by deciding to be tattooed? Sociologist Clinton Sanders (1989) studied this unconventional behavior by engaging in participant observation. Sanders not only chose to be tattooed himself; he worked for a time as an assistant to a tattooist, stretched the skin of those being tattooed, and calmed the anxieties of men and women receiving their first tattoos.

Sanders found that while those electing to be tattooed were deviating from broad social norms, they were at the same time conforming to the views and behavior of significant others, among them family members and close friends who had already been tattooed. One subject noted: "My father got one when he was in the war and I al-ways wanted one, too" (Sanders, 1989:42). For some people getting their first tattoo, the event is viewed as a rite of passage in which they exercise control over their own bodies and decide how they will look. Their tattoos not only allow them to participate in an unconventional subculture which flaunts authority; the tattoos also allow immediate bonding with strangers whose values are obviously compatible. Veterans, members of motorcycle gangs, and others can identify like-minded people based on the kind of tattoos they display.

Of course, men and women with easily visible tattoos often face disapproval and even hostility from people committed to traditional norms regarding appearance. For women in particular, having a tattoo may be regarded as a departure from conventional gender roles. One woman interviewed by Sanders (1989:55) recalls:

> My father's reaction was just one of disgust because women who get tattoos to him are . . . I don't know . . . they just aren't nice girls. They aren't the type of girl he wants his daughter to be. He let me know that. He let me have it right between the eyes. He said, "Do you know what kind of girls get tattoos?" and just walked out of the room.

Given the possibility of such rejections, it would be reasonable to expect that many people who get tattoos later regret their decision. Yet Sanders found that 66 percent of his subjects had no regrets at all about being tattooed. Moreover, most of those who *did* regret their decision were unhappy because of the poor technical quality of the tattoos they purchased.

People maintain distinctive standards regarding the proper appearance of physicians, military officers, members of the clergy, and even sociologists. (Many colleagues and students would at least be surprised to meet a sociologist with visible tattoos.) As we will see in this chapter, conformity, obedience, and deviance can be understood only within a given social context. If people disrobe publicly, they are violating widely held social norms. However, if the same people disrobe within a "naturist" (or nudist) camp, they are obeying the rules and conforming to the behavior of peers. Clearly, then, what is deviant in one setting may be normal in another.

Conformity and deviance are two responses to real or imagined pressures from others. Americans are socialized to have mixed feelings about both conforming and nonconforming behavior. The term *conformity* can conjure up images of mindless imitation of one's peer group—whether a circle of teenagers wearing punk rock garb or a group of business people dressed in similar gray suits. Yet the same term can also suggest that an individual is cooperative or a "team player." What about those who do not conform? They may be respected as individualists, leaders, or creative thinkers who break new ground. Or they may be labeled as "troublemakers" and "weirdos" (Aronson, 1972:14–15).

This chapter will examine the relationship between conformity, deviance, and social control. It begins by distinguishing between conformity and obedience and then looks at two famous experiments regarding conforming behavior and obedience to authority. The informal and formal mechanisms used by societies to encourage conformity and discourage deviance are analyzed. Particular attention is given to the legal order and how it reflects underlying social values.

The second part of the chapter focuses on theoretical explanations for deviance, including the functionalist approaches employed by Émile Durkheim and Robert Merton, the interactionist-based differential association theory of Edwin Sutherland, and labeling theory, which draws upon both the interactionist and the conflict perspectives.

The third part of the chapter focuses on crime. As a form of deviance subject to official, written norms, crime has been a special concern of policy-makers and the public in general. Various types of crime found in the United States, and the ways in which crime is measured, are surveyed.

The social policy section at the end of the chapter considers a controversy highly influenced by people's perceptions of crime: the debate over capital punishment.

SOCIAL CONTROL

As was seen in Chapter 3, every culture, subculture, and group has distinctive norms governing what it deems appropriate behavior. Laws, dress codes, bylaws of organizations, course requirements, and rules of sports and games all express social norms. Functionalists contend that people must respect such norms if any group or society is to survive. In their view, societies literally could not function if massive numbers of people defied standards of appropriate conduct. By contrast, conflict theorists are concerned that "successful functioning" of a society will consistently benefit the powerful and work to the disadvantage of other groups. They point out, for example, that widespread resistance to social norms was necessary in order to overturn the institution of slavery in the United States.

How does a society bring about acceptance of basic norms? The term **social control** refers to the "techniques and strategies for regulating human behavior in any society" (R. Roberts, 1991:274). Social control occurs on all levels of society. In the family, we are socialized to obey our parents simply because they are our parents. In peer groups, we are introduced to informal norms such as dress codes that govern the behavior of members. In bureaucratic organizations, workers must cope with a formal system of rules and regulations. Finally, the government of every society legislates and enforces social norms—including norms regarding "proper" and "improper" expressions of sexual intimacy.

Most of us respect and accept basic social norms and assume that others will do the same. Even without thinking, we obey the instructions of police officers, follow the day-to-day rules at our jobs, and move to the rear of elevators when peo-

Human behavior is regulated in a society through techniques and strategies of social control.

ple enter. Such behavior reflects an effective process of socialization to the dominant standards of a culture. At the same time, we are well-aware that individuals, groups, and institutions *expect* us to act "properly." If we fail to do so, we may face punishment through informal **sanctions** such as fear and ridicule, or formal sanctions such as jail sentences or fines (see Chapter 3).

Conformity and Obedience

Techniques for social control can be viewed on both the group level and the societal level. People whom we regard as our peers or as our equals influence us to act in particular ways; the same is

true of people who hold authority over us or occupy positions which we view with some awe. Stanley Milgram (1975:113–115) made a useful distinction between these two important levels of social control.

Milgram defined **conformity** as going along with one's peers—individuals of a person's own status, who have no special right to direct that person's behavior. By contrast, **obedience** is defined as compliance with higher authorities in a hierarchical structure. Thus, a recruit entering military service will typically *conform* to the habits and language of other recruits and will *obey* the orders of superior officers.

Asch's Study of Conformity How many of us will "stick to our convictions" regardless of the feelings of others? Social psychologist Solomon Asch (1952:452–483) was interested in the effects of group pressure on people's opinions and tested this question in an experimental setting on a college campus. The results of his investigation indicate that the pressure to conform in group situations can have a powerful impact on social behavior.

Asch brought groups of seven to nine male college students into a classroom and asked them to look at two white cards similar to those shown in Figure 7-1. All students were asked to state publicly which line on the right-hand card most closely corresponded to line A on the left-hand card. However, in each group of students, all but one were actually in league with the researchers and had been coached in advance to select wrong answers to some of the choices. Moreover, the uncoached students—the people who were the real targets of the study—were placed near the end of each group.

On a designated trial, the students coached by Asch all gave the *same* incorrect answer. Remarkably, many uncoached students ignored the evidence of their own senses and conformed to the behavior of the (deliberately incorrect) majority. Of Asch's 123 students put to this test, more than one-third followed the lead of the group and chose the wrong answer even without any explicit pressures to conform.

In this situation—unlike many real-life situations that we face—no money, grade, or friendship was at stake. In fact, the students who had been coached by Asch did not impose any informal sanctions (such as scowls and laughs) on the subjects who maintained their correct observations. Conformity occurred in this case not because external pressures were imposed, but because students had internalized a desire to go along with the group (Aronson, 1972:19).

Milgram's Study of Obedience If ordered to do so, would you comply with an experimenter's instruction to give people increasingly painful electric shocks? Most people would say no; yet, the research of social psychologist Stanley Milgram (1963, 1975; Allen, 1978:34–63) suggests that most of us will obey such orders. In Milgram's words (1975:xi): "Behavior that is unthinkable in an individual . . . acting on his own may be executed without hesitation when carried out under orders."

Milgram placed advertisements in New Haven, Connecticut, newspapers to recruit subjects for what was announced as a learning experiment at Yale University. Participants included postal clerks, engineers, high school teachers, and laborers. They were told that the purpose of the research was to investigate the effects of punishment on learning. The experimenter, dressed in a gray technician's coat, explained that in each testing, one subject would be randomly selected as the "learner" while the other would function as the "teacher." However, this lottery was rigged so that the "real" subject would always be the teacher while an associate of Milgram's served as the learner.

At this point, the learner's hand was strapped to an electric apparatus. The teacher was taken to an electronic "shock generator" with 30 lever switches. Each switch was labeled with graduated voltage designations from 15 to 450 volts. Before beginning the experiment, subjects were given sample shocks of 45 volts, which convinced them of the authenticity of the experiment.

The teacher was instructed by the experimenter to apply shocks of increasing voltage each time the learner gave an incorrect answer on a memory test (recalling paired words such as *blue sky* and *wild duck*). Teachers were told that "although the shocks can be extremely painful, they

FIGURE 7-1   Asch's Comparison Lines

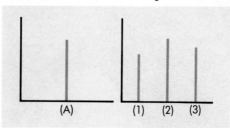

SOURCE: Asch, 1952.

In Solomon Asch's experiments on group pressure, students were told to look at two white cards, similar to those in the figure, and to select the line on the right-hand card which most closely corresponded to line A on the left-hand card. Over one-third of the true subjects accepted incorrect judgments made by a majority of confederates who had been coached by Asch to give deliberately wrong answers.

cause no permanent tissue damage." In reality, the learner did not receive actual shocks; however, subjects in the role of teacher believed that the procedure was genuine.

The learner deliberately gave incorrect answers and acted out a prearranged script. For example, at 150 volts, the learner would cry out, "Experimenter, get me out of here! I won't be in the experiment any more!" At 270 volts, the learner would scream in agony. When the shock level reached 350 volts, the learner would fall silent. If the teacher wanted to stop the experiment, the experimenter would insist that the teacher continue, using such statements as "The experiment requires that you continue" and "You have no other choice; you *must* go on" (Milgram, 1975: 19–23).

The results of this unusual experiment stunned and dismayed Milgram (1975:31) and other social scientists. A sample of psychiatrists had predicted that virtually all subjects would refuse to shock innocent victims. In their view, only a "pathological fringe" of less than 2 percent would continue administering shocks up to the maximum level. Yet almost *two-thirds* of participants fell into the category of "obedient subjects." As Milgram

In one of Stanley Milgram's experiments concerning obedience to authority, a supposed "victim" received an electric shock when his hand rested on a shock plate. At the 150-volt level, the "victim" demanded to be released and refused to place his hand on the shock plate. The experimenter then ordered the actual subject to force the "victim's" hand onto the plate (as shown in the photo). While 40 percent of the true subjects immediately ended compliance at this point, 30 percent did force the "victim's" hand onto the shock plate, even through the 450-volt level, despite his pretended agony.

(1975:5) observed: "Despite the fact that many subjects . . . protest to the experimenter, a substantial proportion continue to the last shock on the generator."

Why did these subjects obey? Why were they willing to inflict seemingly painful shocks on innocent victims who had never done them any harm? There is no evidence to suggest that these subjects were unusually sadistic; few seemed to enjoy administering the shocks. Instead, in Milgram's view, the key to obedience was the experimenter's social role as a "scientist" and "seeker of knowledge."

Milgram pointed out that in the modern indus-trial world we are accustomed to submitting to impersonal authority figures whose status is indicated by a title (professor, lieutenant, doctor) or by a uniform (the technician's coat). The authority is viewed as larger and more important than the individual; consequently, the obedient individual shifts responsibility for his or her behavior to the authority figure. Milgram's subjects frequently stated: "If it were up to me, I would not have administered shocks." They saw themselves as merely doing their duty (Milgram, 1975:xii, 7–8, 137, 144–146).

Viewed from an interactionist perspective, one important aspect of Milgram's findings is the fact that subjects in follow-up studies were less likely to inflict the supposed shocks as they were moved physically closer to their victims. Moreover, interactionists emphasize that teachers assumed responsibility for punishment by *incrementally* administering additional dosages of 15 volts. In effect, the experimenter negotiated with the teacher (see Chapter 5) and convinced the teacher to continue inflicting higher levels of punishment. It is doubtful that anywhere near the two-thirds rate of obedience would have been reached had the experimenter told the teachers to administer 450 volts immediately to the learners (Allen, 1978:42–43; Katovich, 1987).

One haunting memory for the reader of Milgram's *Obedience to Authority* is his discussion of a 43-year-old water inspector who "shocked" the learner up to a maximum of 450 volts—even though he suspected that the learner might have died in the process. After the experiment was over, the water inspector told his wife: "I think I did a good job." She asked, "Suppose the man was dead?" He replied, "So he's dead. I did my job!" (Milgram, 1975:88; see also Gibson and Haritos-Fatouros, 1986:50–58).

Informal and Formal Social Control

The sanctions used to encourage conformity and obedience—and to discourage violation of social norms—are carried out through informal and formal social control. *Informal social control,* as the term implies, is used by people casually. Norms are enforced through the use of the informal sanctions described in Chapter 3. Examples of informal social control include smiles, laughter, raising of an eyebrow, and ridicule.

Techniques of informal control are typically employed within primary groups such as families. Individuals learn such techniques early in their childhood socialization to cultural norms. Since these mechanisms of social control are not formalized, there can be great variation in their use even within the same society. For example, imagine that a teenager is seated on a crowded bus in a seat reserved for elderly and handicapped people. A rather frail-looking elderly man gets on the bus and has nowhere to sit, yet the teenager does not move. One nearby passenger may scowl at the teenager, another may stare until the teenager becomes uncomfortable, while a third may verbalize the control mechanism by telling the teenager to get up.

In some cases, informal methods of social control are not adequate in enforcing conforming or obedient behavior. In the example above, the teenager might look away from the scowling and staring passengers and might tell the third person, "Mind your own business!" At this point, passengers might enlist the aid of the bus driver—whose occupational role carries with it a certain authority—in an attempt to force the teenager to give up the seat. *Formal social control* is carried out by authorized agents, such as police officers, physicians, school administrators, employers, military officers, and managers of movie theaters. As we have seen, it can serve as a last resort when socialization and informal sanctions do not bring about desired behavior.

It is important to emphasize that formal social control is not always carried out only by government officials in response to violations of the law. Certain subcultures within a society exercise formal social control to maintain adherence to their distinctive social norms. For example, if a member of the Old Order Amish religious minority (refer back to Chapter 4) violates the community's standards, he or she will initially be verbally chastised by a member (informal social control). However, if an Amish person commits an especially serious transgression or repeatedly violates accepted norms, the community may invoke its most severe means of formal social control, known as *Meidung*, or "shunning." Within the close-knit Amish community, a formal decision to shun a member amounts to "social death": the person is totally ignored, even by family members. Generally, the shunned member chooses to leave the community rather than endure this painful technique of formal social control (Kephart and Zellner, 1991).

Law and Society

Some norms are considered so important by a society that they are formalized into laws controlling people's behavior. In a political sense, *law* is the "body of rules made by government for society, interpreted by the courts, and backed by the power of the state" (Cummings and Wise, 1989:550). Some laws, such as the prohibition against murder, are directed at all members of society. Others, such as fishing and hunting regulations, are aimed primarily at particular categories of people. Still others govern the behavior of social institutions (corporation law and laws regarding the taxing of nonprofit enterprises). Despite such differences, all these types of laws are considered examples of formal social norms (Chambliss and Seidman, 1971:8).

Sociologists have become increasingly interested in the creation of laws as a social process. Laws are created in response to perceived needs for formal social control. Sociologists have sought to explain how and why such perceptions are manifested. In their view, law is not merely a static body of rules handed down from generation to generation. Rather, it reflects continually changing standards of what is right and wrong, of how violations are to be determined, and of what sanctions are to be applied (Schur, 1968:39–43).

Sociologists representing varying theoretical perspectives agree that the legal order reflects underlying social values. Therefore, the creation of criminal law can be a most controversial matter. Should it be against the law to employ illegal immigrants in a factory (see Chapter 10), to have an abortion (see Chapter 11), or to smoke on an airplane (see Chapter 17)? Such issues have been bitterly debated because they require a choice among competing values. Not surprisingly, laws that are unpopular—such as the prohibition of the manufacture and sale of intoxicating liquors

Viewed from a broad cross-cultural perspective, the creation of criminal law reflects societal values which may differ from one society to another. Along the Khyber Pass in Pakistan, men openly and legally sell opium balls and hashish. By contrast, the sale of refrigerators is illegal because they have been imported secretly to avoid customs duties.

under the Eighteenth Amendment in 1919 and the establishment of a national 55 mile per hour speed limit on highways in 1973—become difficult to enforce owing to lack of consensus supporting the norms.

It is important to underscore the fact that socialization is the primary source of conforming and obedient behavior, including obedience to law. Generally, it is not external pressure from a peer group or authority figure that makes us go along with social norms. Rather, we have internalized such norms as valid and desirable and are committed to observing them. In a profound sense, we *want* to see ourselves (and to be seen) as loyal, cooperative, responsible, and respectful of others.

In American society, and in other societies around the world, individuals are socialized both to want to belong and to fear being viewed as different or deviant.

DEVIANCE

What Is Deviance?

For sociologists, the term *deviance* does not mean perversion or depravity. **Deviance** is behavior that violates the standards of conduct or expectations of a group or society (Wickman, 1991:85). In American society, alcoholics, people with tattoos, compulsive gamblers, and the mentally ill would all be classified as deviants. Being late for class is categorized as a deviant act; the same is true of dressing too casually for a formal wedding. On the basis of the sociological definition, we are all deviant from time to time. Each of us violates common social norms in certain situations.

Deviance involves the violation of group norms which may or may not be formalized into law. It is a comprehensive concept that includes not only criminal behavior but also many actions not subject to prosecution. The public official who takes a bribe has defied social norms, but so has the high school student who refuses to sit in an assigned seat or cuts class. Of course, deviation from norms is not always negative, let alone criminal. A member of an exclusive social club who speaks out against its traditional policy of excluding women, Blacks, and Jews from admittance is deviating from the club's norms. So is a police officer who "blows the whistle" on corruption or brutality within the department.

As we noted earlier, deviance can be understood only within its social context. A nude photograph of a woman or man may be perfectly appropriate in an art museum but would be regarded as out of place in an elementary school classroom. A pharmacist is expected to sell prescription drugs only to people who have explicit instructions from medical authorities. If the pharmacist sells the same drugs to a narcotics dealer, he or she has committed deviant (and criminal) behavior.

Standards of deviance vary from one group (or

TABLE 7-1 Untimely Acts

Ringing a doorbell at 2 A.M.
Working on New Year's eve
Having sex on a first date
Playing a stereo loudly in early morning hours
Having an alcoholic drink with breakfast
An instructor's ending a college class after 15 minutes
Getting married after having been engaged for only a few days
Taking 5 years or more to complete high school

SOURCE: Reese and Katovich, 1989.

Society may regard certain acts as deviant simply because of the time element involved.

subculture) to another. In the United States, it is generally considered acceptable to sing along at a folk or rock concert, but not at the opera. Just as deviance is defined by the social situation, so too is it relative to time. For instance, having an alcoholic drink at 6:00 P.M. is a common practice in our society, but engaging in the same behavior upon arising at 8:00 A.M. is viewed as a deviant act and as symptomatic of a drinking problem. In Table 7-1, we offer additional examples of untimely acts that are regarded as deviant in the United States.

Deviance, then, is a highly relative matter. Americans may consider it strange for a person to fight a bull in an arena, before an audience of screaming fans. Yet we are not nearly so shocked by the practice of two humans' fighting *each other* with boxing gloves in front of a similar audience.

Explaining Deviance

Why do people violate social norms? We have seen that deviant acts are subject to both informal and formal sanctions of social control. The nonconforming or disobedient person may face disapproval, loss of friends, fines, or even imprisonment. Why, then, does deviance occur?

Early explanations for deviance identified supernatural causes or genetic factors (such as "bad

(Helmut Gritscher/Peter Arnold)

(AP/Wide World Photos)

Americans consider bullfighting "strange," yet boxing remains a popular sport in the United States.

blood" or evolutionary throwbacks to primitive ancestors). By the 1800s, there were substantial research efforts to identify biological factors that lead to deviance and especially to criminal activity. While such research has been discredited in the twentieth century, contemporary studies, primarily by biochemists, have sought to isolate genetic factors leading to a likelihood of certain personality traits. Although criminality (much less deviance) is hardly a personality characteristic, researchers have focused on traits that might lead to crime, such as aggression. Of course, aggression can also lead to success in the corporate world, professional sports, or other areas of life.

The contemporary study of possible biological roots of criminality is but one aspect of the larger sociobiology debate discussed in Chapter 4. In general, sociologists reject any emphasis on genetic roots of crime and deviance. The limitations of current knowledge are so significant, the likelihood of reinforcing racist and sexist assumptions so clear, and the implications for rehabilitation of criminals so disturbing, that sociologists have largely drawn upon other approaches to explain deviance (Sagarin and Sanchez, 1988).

Functionalist Perspective According to functionalists, deviance is a normal part of human existence, with positive (as well as negative) consequences for social stability. Deviance helps to define the limits of proper behavior. Children who see one parent scold the other for belching at the dinner table learn about approved conduct. The same is true of the driver who receives a speeding ticket, the department store cashier who is fired for yelling at a customer, and the college student who is penalized for handing in papers weeks overdue.

Durkheim's legacy Émile Durkheim (1964:67, original edition 1895) focused his sociological investigations mainly on criminal acts, yet his conclusions have implications for all types of deviant behavior. In Durkheim's view, the punishments established within a culture (including what we have identified as formal and informal mechanisms of social control) help to define acceptable behavior and thus contribute to stability. If improper acts were not committed and then sanctioned, people might extend their standards as to what constitutes appropriate conduct.

Kai Erikson (1966) illustrated this boundary-maintenance function of deviance in his study of the Puritans of seventeenth-century New England. By today's standards, the Puritans placed tremendous emphasis upon conventional morals. Their persecution of Quakers and execution of women as witches represented continuing attempts to define and redefine the boundaries of their community. In effect, changing social norms created "crime waves," as people whose behavior was previously acceptable suddenly faced punishment for being deviant (Abrahamson, 1978:78–79; N. Davis, 1975:85–87).

Unexpectedly, boundary maintenance re-emerged in the same area some 300 years later. The town of Salem, Massachusetts, draws (and profits from) 1 million visitors per year who come to see the sites of the witch trials and executions. At the urging of descendants of 20 innocent victims who had been executed, a statue was designed to commemorate the slain women. However, protests blocked the public installation of the statue, owing to concern that such a prominent memorial to the *victims* would dampen tourists' interest in witch lore (Driscoll, 1988).

Durkheim (1951, original edition 1897) also introduced the term **anomie** in sociological literature to describe a loss of direction felt in a society when social control of individual behavior has become ineffective. As was noted in Chapter 1, anomie is a state of normlessness which typically occurs during a period of profound social change and disorder, such as a time of economic collapse. People become more aggressive or depressed, and this results in higher rates of violent crime or suicide (refer back to the discussion of Durkheim's four types of suicide in Box 1-1, page 11). Since there is much less agreement on what constitutes proper behavior during times of revolution, sudden prosperity, or economic depression, conformity and obedience become less significant as social forces. It also becomes much more difficult to state exactly what constitutes deviance.

Subsequent theorists have expanded on Durkheim's insights regarding anomie and deviance. For example, after examining juvenile delinquency in a sample of 4000 California youngsters, sociologist Travis Hirschi (1969) concluded that people become free to commit acts regarded as improper, and develop feelings of normlessness, when their ties to conventional society are broken. Later research has confirmed that young

people with fewer ties to society commit more acts of misbehavior (Empey, 1978; D. Gibbons, 1981:140–143).

In Hirschi's view, the process of "bonding" represents a major aspect of social control. The term **bond** refers to the ties of an individual to society and, in particular, to standards of proper behavior. Attachment to family, commitment to societal beliefs and moral standards, and involvement in socially acceptable groups all strengthen the bonds between the individual and society. Of course, if normal societal bonds are disrupted on a massive scale, as is the case during a period of anomie, we can expect a dramatic rise in behavior which violates social norms.

(The Bettmann Archive)

On the basis of his study of the Puritans of seventeenth-century New England, sociologist Kai Erikson suggested that the Puritans' persecution of Quakers and execution of women as witches represented continuing attempts to define and redefine the boundaries of their community.

Merton's theory of deviance A mugger and a secretary do not seem at first to have a great deal in common. Yet, in fact, each is "working" to obtain money which can then be exchanged for desired goods. As this example illustrates, behavior that violates accepted norms (such as mugging) may be performed with the same basic objectives in mind as those of people who pursue more conventional lifestyles.

Using the above analysis, sociologist Robert Merton of Columbia University (1968:185–214) adapted Durkheim's notion of anomie to explain why people accept or reject the goals of a society, the socially approved means to fulfill their aspirations, or both. Merton maintained that one important cultural goal of American society is success, measured largely in terms of money. In addition to providing this goal for Americans, our society offers specific instructions on how to pursue success—go to school, work hard, do not quit, take advantage of opportunities, and so forth.

What happens to individuals in a society with a heavy emphasis on wealth as a basic symbol of success? Merton reasoned that people adapt in certain ways, either by conforming to or by deviating from such cultural expectations. Consequently, he developed the *anomie theory of deviance,* which posits five basic forms of adaptation (see Table 7-2).

Conformity to social norms, the most common adaptation in Merton's typology, is the opposite of deviance. It involves acceptance of both the overall societal goal ("become affluent") and the approved means ("work hard"). In Merton's view, there must be some consensus regarding accepted cultural goals and legitimate means for attaining them. Without such consensus, societies could exist only as collectives of people—rather than as unified cultures—and might function in continual chaos.

Of course, in a society such as that of the United States, conformity is not universal. For example, the means for realizing objectives are not equally distributed. People in the lower social classes often identify with the same goals as those of more powerful and affluent citizens yet lack equal access to quality education and training for skilled work. Even within a society, institutionalized means for realizing objectives vary. For in-

TABLE 7-2   Modes of Individual Adaptation

MODE	INSTITUTIONALIZED MEANS (HARD WORK)	SOCIETAL GOAL (ACQUISITION) OF WEALTH)
Nondeviant		
Conformity	+	+
Deviant		
Innovation	−	+
Ritualism	+	−
Retreatism	−	−
Rebellion	±	±

NOTE: + indicates acceptance; − indicates rejection; ± indicates replacement with new means and goals.

Robert Merton's typology (1968:194) shows that, in many cases, those whose form of adaptation is deviant still accept either the work ethic or the desire for material wealth widely valued by "conformists."

stance, it is legal to gain money through roulette or poker in Nevada, but not in neighboring California.

The other four types of behavior represented in Table 7-2 all involve some departure from conformity. The "innovator" accepts the goals of a society but pursues them with means regarded as improper. For example, Harry King—a professional thief who specialized in safecracking for 40 years—gave a lecture to a sociology class and was asked if he had minded spending time in prison. King responded:

I didn't exactly like it. But it was one of the necessary things about the life I had chosen. Do you like to come here and teach this class? I bet if the students had their wishes they'd be somewhere else, maybe out stealing, instead of sitting in this dumpy room. But they do it because it gets them something they want. The same with me. If I had to go to prison from time to time, well, that was the price you pay (Chambliss, 1972:x).

Harry King saw his criminal lifestyle as an adaptation to the American goal of material success or "getting something you want." According to Merton's anomie theory of deviance, if a society largely denies people the opportunity to achieve success through socially approved avenues, some individuals (like King) will turn to illegitimate paths of upward mobility.

In Merton's typology, the "ritualist" has abandoned the goal of material success and become compulsively committed to the institutional means. Therefore, work becomes a way of life rather than a means to the goal of success. In discussing goal displacement within bureaucracy in Chapter 6, we noted that officials can blindly apply rules and regulations without remembering the larger goals of an organization. Certainly this would be true of a welfare caseworker who refuses to assist a homeless family because their last apartment was in another district. People who overzealously and rigidly enforce bureaucratic regulations can be classified as "ritualists."

The "retreatist," as described by Merton, has basically withdrawn (or "retreated") from both the goals and the means of a society. In the United States, while drug addicts and residents of skid row are typically portrayed as retreatists, there is growing concern about adolescents addicted to alcohol who become retreatists at an early age.

The final adaptation identified by Merton reflects people's attempts to create a new social structure. The "rebel" is assumed to have a sense of alienation from dominant means and goals and to be seeking a dramatically different social order. Members of a revolutionary political organization, such as the Irish Republican Army (IRA) or the Puerto Rican nationalist group Fuerzas Armadas de Liberación Nacional (FALN), can be categorized as rebels according to Merton's model.

Merton has stressed that he was not attempting to describe five types of individuals. Rather, he offered a typology to explain the actions that people *usually* take. Thus, leaders of organized crime syndicates will be categorized as innovators, since they do not pursue success through socially approved means. Yet they may also attend church and send their children to medical school. Conversely, "respectable" people may occasionally cheat on their taxes or violate traffic laws. According to Merton, the same person will move back and forth from one mode of adaptation to another, depending on the demands of a particular situation.

Despite its popularity, Merton's theory of deviance has had relatively few applications. Little effort has been made to determine how comprehensive the five modes of adaptation are—in other words, to what extent all acts of deviance can be accounted for by innovation, ritualism, retreatism, and rebellion. Moreover, while Merton's theory is useful in examining certain types of behavior, such as illegal gambling by disadvantaged people functioning as innovators, his formulation fails to explain key differences in rates. Why, for example, do some disadvantaged groups have lower rates of reported crime than others? Why is criminal behavior not viewed as a viable alternative by many people faced with adversity? Such questions are not easily answered by Merton's theory of deviance (Cloward, 1959; Hartjen, 1978).

Nevertheless, Merton has made a key contribution to sociological understanding of deviance by pointing out that deviants (such as innovators and ritualists) share a great deal with "normal," conforming persons. The convicted felon may hold many of the same aspirations that people with no criminal background have. Therefore, deviance can be understood as socially created behavior, rather than as the result of momentary pathological impulses.

Interactionist Perspective: Cultural Transmission The functionalist approaches to deviance explain why rule violation continues to exist in societies despite pressures to conform and obey. However, functionalists do not indicate how a given person comes to commit a deviant act. The theory of cultural transmission draws upon the interactionist perspective to offer just such an explanation.

There is no natural, innate manner in which people interact with one another. Rather, humans *learn* how to behave in social situations—whether properly or improperly. These simple ideas are not disputed today, but this was not the case when sociologist Edwin Sutherland (1883–1950) advanced the argument that an individual undergoes the same basic socialization process whether learning conforming or deviant acts.

Sutherland's ideas have been the dominating force in criminology. He drew upon the *cultural transmission* school, which emphasizes that criminal behavior is learned through interactions with others. Such learning includes not only techniques of lawbreaking (for example, how to break into a car quickly and quietly) but also the motives, drives, and rationalizations of criminals. The cultural transmission approach can also be used to explain the behavior of people who engage in habitual—and ultimately life-threatening—use of alcohol or drugs.

Sutherland maintained that through interactions with a primary group and significant others, people acquire definitions of behavior that are deemed proper and improper. He used the term *differential association* to describe the process through which exposure to attitudes favorable to criminal acts leads to violation of rules. Recent research suggests that this view of differential association can be applied to such noncriminal deviant acts as sitting down during the singing of the National Anthem or lying to a spouse or friend (E. Jackson et al., 1986).

To what extent will a given person engage in activity regarded as proper or improper? For each individual, it will depend on the frequency, duration, and importance of two types of social interaction experiences—those which endorse deviant behavior and those which promote acceptance of social norms. Deviant behavior, including criminal activity, is selected by those who acquire more sentiments in favor of violation of norms. People are more likely to engage in norm-defying behavior if they are part of a group or subculture that stresses deviant values.

Sutherland offers the example of a boy who is sociable, outgoing, and athletic and who lives in an area with a high rate of delinquency. The youth is very likely to come into contact with peers who commit acts of vandalism, fail to attend school, and so forth, and may, thus, adopt such behavior. However, an introverted boy living in the same neighborhood may stay away from his peers and avoid delinquency. In another community, an outgoing and athletic boy may join a Little League baseball team or a scout troop because of his interactions with peers. Thus, Sutherland views learning improper behavior as the result of

the types of groups to which one belongs and the kinds of friendships one has with others (Sutherland and Cressey, 1978:82).

As another example, differential association theory can be applied to a star high school football player who accepts a bribe from a college recruiter in exchange for a commitment to attend the recruiter's school. Such football stars are typically surrounded by other players, family members, coaches, and recruiters who stress the paramount goals of success in "big-time" football and the money and fame that such success can bring. Consequently, these athletes may be exposed to many people who favor norm-defying behavior and relatively few who oppose the deviant act of accepting a recruiter's bribe.

According to its critics, however, the cultural transmission approach fails to explain the deviant behavior of the first-time impulsive shoplifter or the impoverished person who steals out of necessity. While not a precise statement of the process through which one becomes a criminal, differential association does direct our attention to the paramount role of social interaction in increasing a person's motivation to engage in deviant behavior (Cressey, 1960:53–54; E. Jackson et al., 1986; Sutherland and Cressey, 1978:80–82).

The cultural transmission approach deals not only with the process by which criminal techniques are learned, but also with the content that is actually passed on from one person to another. This content includes methods of committing a crime as well as ways of justifying criminal behavior. The concept of "techniques of neutralization," as described in Box 7-1, illustrates how criminal and other norm-defying sentiments are defined by the deviant person to justify his or her conduct.

Labeling Theory The Saints and Roughnecks were two groups of high school males who were constantly occupied with drinking, wild driving, truancy, petty theft, and vandalism. There the similarity ended. None of the Saints was ever arrested, but every Roughneck was continually in trouble with police and townspeople. Why the disparity in their treatment? On the basis of his participant-observation research in their high school, William Chambliss (1973) concluded that

BOX 7-1 • CURRENT RESEARCH

NEUTRALIZATION OF DEVIANCE AND FEMALE BODYBUILDERS

When we have been observed in an action that others regard as improper, a common response is, "But I didn't do anything wrong." Gresham Sykes and David Matza (1957) clarified the various explanations for wrongdoing that we use in such situations by offering a five-part model of justifications of deviant behavior which they call *techniques of neutralization:*

1 *Denying responsibility.* We argue that larger forces—such as poverty, poor academic preparation, or the bad example of others—drove us to the misdeed.
2 *Denying the injury.* Crimes such as vandalism or obstruction of traffic near a college campus are called *pranks* or *mischief.* Such terminology suggests that these actions are not serious violations.
3 *Blaming the victim.* We admit that we hurt someone else but maintain that the victim "had it coming" or provoked the incident.
4 *Condemning the authorities.* Lawbreakers often insist that police or government leaders are the true guilty parties. The alleged stupidity, brutality, and corruption of authority figures are used to justify deviant or criminal behavior.
5 *Appealing to higher principles or authorities.* People rationalize illegal actions by asserting that they are adhering to standards more important than the law—whether the unwritten criminal code of "never squeal on a friend" or moral and religious beliefs said to justify acts of civil disobedience.

(Alon Reininger/Contact Press Images)

Sensitive to the criticism that women bodybuilders are not "feminine," some participants in the sport "bask in the reflected glory" of a few— such as Rachel McLish—who have been glamorized in the media.

By using these five techniques of neutralization, people who break the law are able to defend their conduct. But how useful is this model in understanding justifications of *noncriminal* deviance? Sociologists Robert Duff and Lawrence Hong (1986, 1988) applied neutralization theory in studying impression management among participants in a relatively new sport: women's bodybuilding. Female bodybuilders are sometimes treated favorably in the media, but they have also been socially stigmatized—partly because of allegations that they use

steroids, but primarily because they represent a blatant departure from traditional gender-role expectations for women.

Drawing upon the results of a mail survey by the International Federation of Bodybuilders, Duff and Hong suggest that female bodybuilders respond to negative feedback from the public and the media by use of three more neutralization techniques:

1 *Claiming benefits.* Women defend their participation in the sport of bodybuilding by claiming that they have developed healthy, strong, and attractive bodies and improved mental health. Such "claims of benefit" have been employed by people engaged in other roles and activities viewed as deviant (N. Friedman, 1974; L. Hong and R. Duff, 1977).
2 *Blasting.* "Blasting" is an attack on critics in order to enhance one's own status (Richardson and Caildini, 1988). Female bodybuilders typically "blast" their critics by portraying them as ignorant, jealous, unhealthy, fat, and lazy.
3 *Basking in reflected glory.* Out of sensitivity to the criticism that women bodybuilders are not "feminine," some participants in the sport "bask in the reflected glory" of a few less muscular, more lithe and slender bodybuilders who have been glamorized in the media. A favorite idol of those engaged in this neutralization technique is Rachel McLish. One

(Continued)

BOX 7-1 • CURRENT RESEARCH

NEUTRALIZATION OF DEVIANCE AND FEMALE BODYBUILDERS (Continued)

female bodybuilder exclaims: "Rachel McLish! She has proven that women can be both beautiful, graceful, and powerful! Without losing their femininity!"

Duff and Hong suggest that both women's and men's bodybuilding may be viewed as a form of "positive deviance" whereby the approved societal emphasis on health and fitness is carried to an extreme. Apparently, in comparison with the neutralization of "negative deviance" (such as crime), neutralization of positive deviance requires fewer techniques and allows for greater reliance on direct and aggressive strategies of justification for one's behavior.

---

social class standing played an important role in the varying fortunes of the two groups.

The Saints effectively produced a facade of respectability. They came from "good families," were active in school organizations, expressed the intention of attending college, and received good grades. Their delinquent acts were generally viewed as a few isolated cases of "sowing wild oats." By contrast, the Roughnecks had no such aura of respectability. They drove around town in beaten-up cars, were generally unsuccessful in school, and were viewed with suspicion no matter what they did.

The Roughnecks were labeled as "troublemakers," whereas the Saints were seen merely as "fun-loving kids." Both groups were gangs of delinquents, yet only one came to be treated that way. More recently, Chambliss's observations concerning juveniles have been confirmed in research using self-reports of delinquents and police records in Seattle, Washington. Sociologist Robert Sampson (1986) found that juveniles from the lower classes who came into contact with the Seattle police because of delinquent behavior were more likely to be arrested and then indicted than were their middle-class counterparts engaged in similar activities.

Such discrepancies can be understood by use of an approach to deviance known as *labeling theory.* Unlike Sutherland's work, labeling theory does not focus on why some individuals come to commit deviant acts. Instead, it attempts to explain why certain people (such as the Roughnecks) are *viewed* as deviants, delinquents, "bad kids," "losers," and criminals, while others whose behavior is similar (such as the Saints) are not seen in such harsh terms.

Reflecting the contribution of interactionist theorists, labeling theory emphasizes how a person comes to be labeled as deviant or to accept that label. Sociologist Howard Becker (1963:9, 1964), who popularized this approach, summed it up with the statement: "Deviant behavior is behavior that people so label." Labeling theory is also called the *societal-reaction approach,* reminding us that it is the *response* to an act and not the behavior that determines deviance. For example, studies have shown that some school personnel and therapists expand educational programs designed for learning-disabled students to include those with behavioral problems. Consequently, a "trouble-maker" can be improperly labeled as learning-disabled, and vice versa (Osborne et al., 1985).

Labeling theory can also help us to understand that while some Americans routinely and often cruelly label severely disabled persons as "vegetables" (see Chapter 20), there are many nondisabled people who do not stigmatize, stereotype, or reject those with severe and obvious disabilities. Robert Bogdan and Steven Taylor (1989) conducted observation studies over a 20-year period at settings in the community that support people with severe disabilities. The researchers supplemented their observations by interviewing agency administrators and caregivers. Bogdan and Taylor found that many family members, friends, and helpers of the disabled are caring and accepting of people with severe disabilities. These nondisabled people assume that the severely disabled have rational thought processes, see individuality in them, view them as reciprocating, and define them as actors in a social environment. Rather than adhering to negative labeling based on obvious "deviant" behavior, the nondisabled accept the severely disabled as valued and loved human beings.

Traditionally, research on deviance has focused on those individuals who violate social norms. In contrast, labeling theory focuses on police, probation officers, psychiatrists, judges, teachers, employers, school officials, and other regulators of social control. These agents, it is argued, play a significant role in creating the deviant identity by designating certain persons (and not others) as "deviant." An important aspect of labeling theory is the recognition that some individuals or groups have the power to *define* labels and apply them to others. This view recalls the conflict perspective's emphasis on the social significance of power.

The labeling approach does not fully explain why certain people accept a label and others are able to reject its application. In fact, this perspective may exaggerate the ease with which our self-images can be altered by societal judgments. Labeling theorists do suggest, however, that differential power is important in determining a person's ability to resist an undesirable label. Competing approaches (including those of both Merton and Sutherland) fail to explain why some deviants continue to be viewed as conformists rather than as violators of rules. According to Howard Becker (1973:179–180), labeling theory was not conceived as the *sole* explanation for deviance; its proponents merely hoped to focus more attention on the undeniably important actions of those people officially in charge of defining deviance (N. Davis, 1975:172; compare with Cullen and Cullen, 1978:36–37).

Conflict Theory Why is certain behavior evaluated as deviant while other behavior is not? According to conflict theorists, it is because people with power protect their own interests and define deviance to suit their own needs. For decades, laws against rape reflected the overwhelmingly male composition of state legislatures. As one consequence, the legal definition of rape pertained only to sexual relations between unmar-

ried persons. It was legally acceptable for a husband to have forcible sexual intercourse with his wife—without her consent and against her will. However, repeated protests by feminist organizations finally led to changes in the criminal law. By 1987, husbands in 25 states could be prosecuted for rape of their wives. In this instance, the rise of the women's liberation movement (see Chapter 11) led to important changes in societal notions of criminality—as it has in educating judges, legislators, and police officers to view wife-battering and other forms of domestic violence as serious crimes (Barden, 1987; MacKinnon, 1983; Schur, 1983:145–156; Toufexis, 1989).

Sociologist Richard Quinney (1974, 1979, 1980) is a leading exponent of the view that the criminal justice system serves the interests of the powerful. Crime, according to Quinney (1970:15–23), is a definition of human conduct created by authorized agents of social control—such as legislators and law enforcement officials—in a politically organized society. He and other conflict theorists argue that lawmaking is often an attempt by the powerful to coerce others into their own morality.

This helps to explain why our society has laws against gambling, drug usage, and prostitution which are violated on a massive scale (we will examine these "victimless crimes" later in the chapter). According to the conflict school, criminal law does not represent a consistent application of societal values, but instead reflects competing values and interests. Thus, marijuana is outlawed in the United States because it is alleged to be harmful to users, yet cigarettes and alcohol are sold legally almost everywhere.

The conflict perspective reminds us that while the basic purpose of law may be to maintain stability and order, this can actually mean perpetuating inequality. For example, researchers have found that African Americans and Hispanics receive stiffer prison sentences and serve longer terms than Whites convicted of similar felonies. A 2-year study prepared for the National Institute of Corrections of the Department of Justice focused on three states which account for 22 percent of American inmates: California, Michigan, and Texas. Minorities were found to be less likely to make bail than Whites and more likely to use court-appointed lawyers.

Should it be against the law to sell or use marijuana? In the 1930s, the Federal Bureau of Narcotics launched a campaign to have marijuana viewed as a dangerous drug rather than as a pleasure-inducing substance. From a conflict perspective, lawmaking is often an attempt by the powerful to coerce others into their own brand of morality. Marijuana is outlawed because it is alleged to be harmful to users, yet cigarettes and alcohol are sold legally almost everywhere.

While no racial differences were found in the types of prison programs to which inmates were assigned, the study documented significant differences in length of sentences:

• In California, sentences for Hispanics are about 6½ months longer than those of Whites. Sentences for Blacks are almost 1½ months longer than those of Whites.

• In Texas, sentences for Hispanics are more than 2 months longer than those of Whites. Sentences for Blacks are 3½ months longer than those of Whites.

• In Michigan, sentences for Blacks are more than 7 months longer than those of Whites (Petersilia, 1983).

Differential sentencing is not totally the responsibility of judges; it may also reflect probation officers' and prosecutors' recommendations and preferences for differential justice (Hagan and Palloni, 1986:439; see also Bishop and Frazier, 1988; Hagan, 1987).

Efforts can be made to reduce bias in sentencing. The state of California has instituted a Determinate Sentencing Act which establishes specific prison terms that judges can impose for certain crimes. An analysis of the practices used in the sentencing of 15,000 offenders under this law showed that once researchers controlled for such factors as weapons use and prior convictions, the race of the offender did not prove to be a factor in sentencing (Klein et al., 1988).

On the whole, however, conflict theorists contend that the criminal justice system of the United States treats suspects and offenders differently, on the basis of racial, ethnic, and social class backgrounds. In commenting on the exercise of discretion in the courts (see Table 7-3), Justice Lois Forer (1984:9) of Philadelphia suggests that there are:

. . . two separate and unequal systems of justice: one for the rich in which the courts take limitless time to examine, ponder, consider, and deliberate over hundreds of thousands of bits of evidence, . . . and hear elaborate, endless appeals; the other for the poor, in which hasty guilty pleas and brief hearings are the rule and appeals are the exception.

While the racial, ethnic, or social class background of criminal suspects and offenders may lead to differential justice, the background of crime *victims* can achieve the same result. A study by the *Chicago Sun-Times* of 400 randomly selected crimes (including rapes, stabbings, and shootings) found that crimes against members of minority groups are more likely to be "downgraded" from felonies to minor offenses, thereby reducing the seriousness of the offense and the potential jail sentence. All the downgraded crimes studied involved a victim from a minority group; in most cases, both the victim and the assailant were Black or Hispanic and lived in a low-income neighborhood. One researcher, reflecting on the social hierarchies of the United States, has suggested that this pattern of differential justice was "victim discounting"—that is, "if the victim is worth less, the crime is worth less" (T. Gibbons, 1985:1, 18).

Quinney (1974) argues that, through such differential applications of social control, the criminal justice system helps to keep the poor and oppressed in their deprived position. In his view, disadvantaged individuals and groups who represent a threat to those with power become the primary targets of criminal law. Yet the real criminals in poor neighborhoods are not the people arrested for vandalism and theft, but rather absentee landlords and exploitative store owners. Even if we do not accept this challenging argument, we cannot ignore the role of the powerful in creating a social structure that perpetuates suffering (Currie, 1986:152–160; Reiman, 1984; Vold, 1979:301–305; for a similar conflict approach to crime, see Turk, 1969).

The perspective advanced by labeling and conflict theorists forms quite a contrast to the functionalist approach to deviance. Functionalists view standards of deviant behavior as merely reflecting cultural norms, whereas conflict and labeling theorists point out that the most powerful

TABLE 7-3   Discretion within the Criminal Justice System

CRIMINAL JUSTICE OFFICIALS	DISCRETIONARY POWERS
Police	Enforce specific laws Investigate specific crimes Search people, vicinities, buildings Arrest or detain people
Prosecutors	File charges or petitions for judicial decision Seek indictments Drop cases Reduce charges Recommend sentences
Judges or magistrates	Set bail or conditions for release Accept pleas Determine delinquency Dismiss charges Impose sentences Revoke probation
Probation officers	File presentence reports Recommend sentences
Correctional officials	Assign people to type of correctional facility Award privileges Punish for disciplinary infractions
Parole authorities	Determine date and conditions of parole Revoke parole

SOURCE: Adapted from Department of Justice, 1988:59.

Conflict theorist Richard Quinney contends that social control is applied differentially to suspects because of their social class backgrounds. In a 1988 report by the Bureau of Justice Statistics, discretionary practices were outlined at various levels of the criminal justice system.

groups in a society can *shape* laws and standards and determine who is (or is not) prosecuted as a criminal. Thus, the label "deviant" is rarely applied to the corporate executive whose decisions lead to large-scale environmental pollution. In the opinion of conflict theorists, agents of social control and powerful groups can generally impose their own self-serving definitions of deviance on the general public.

CRIME

Crime is a violation of criminal law for which formal penalties are applied by some governmental authority. It represents some type of deviation from formal social norms administered by the state. Crimes are divided by law into various categories, depending on the severity of the offense, the age of the offender, the potential punishment that can be levied, and the court which holds jurisdiction over the case.

The term *index crimes* refers to the eight types of crime that are reported annually by the Federal Bureau of Investigation (FBI) in its *Uniform Crime Reports*. This category of criminal behavior generally consists of those serious offenses that people think of when they express concern about the nation's crime problem. Index crimes include murder, rape, robbery, and assault—all of which are violent crimes committed against people—as well as the property crimes of burglary, theft, motor vehicle theft, and arson.

In the United States, many index crimes involve the use of firearms. According to the FBI, in the year 1989, 22 percent of all reported assaults, 33 percent of reported robberies, and 62 percent of reported murders involved the use of a firearm. More than 11,000 Americans died in 1989 through homicides committed with a firearm. Since 1963, guns have killed more than 400,000 Americans, a figure which exceeds the number of our troops who died in World War II. While the general public has consistently favored gun control legislation in recent decades, the nation's major anti–gun control lobby, the National Rifle Association (NRA), has wielded impressive power in blocking or diluting such measures (Department of Justice, 1990a:11, 20, 23).

Types of Crime

Rather than relying solely on legal categories, sociologists classify crimes in terms of how they are committed and how the offenses are viewed by society. In this section, we will examine four types of crime as differentiated by sociologists: professional crime, organized crime, white-collar crime, and "victimless crimes."

Professional Crime Although the adage "crime doesn't pay" is familiar, many people do make a career of illegal activities. A *professional criminal* is a person who pursues crime as a day-to-day occupation, developing skilled techniques and enjoying a certain degree of status among other criminals. Some professional criminals specialize in burglary (see Chapter 5), safecracking, hijacking of cargo, pickpocketing, and shoplifting. Such persons can reduce the likelihood of arrest, conviction, and imprisonment through their skill. As a result, they may have long careers in their chosen "professions."

Edwin Sutherland (1937) offered pioneering insights regarding professional criminals by publishing an annotated account written by a professional thief. Unlike the person who engages in crime only once or twice, professional thieves make a business of stealing. These professional criminals devote their entire working time to planning and executing crimes and sometimes travel across the nation to pursue their "professional duties." Like persons in regular occupations, professional thieves consult with their colleagues concerning the demands of work, thus becoming part of a subculture of similarly occupied individuals. They exchange information on possible places to burglarize, on outlets for unloading stolen goods, and on ways of securing bail bonds if arrested.

Learning technical skills is an important aspect of working as a professional criminal. Sociologist Peter Letkemann (1973:117–136) makes a distinction between two types of criminal skills: those which are extensions of the legitimate social order but are sharpened and refined (such as the ability to detect when homeowners are away) and those skills not easily available to the average citizen (such as opening a safe). The latter are learned in

(N. Tully/Sygma)

Shown is John Gotti, reputed to be the leader of organized crime activities in New York City. Organized crime is a secret, conspiratorial activity that generally evades law enforcement.

the manner suggested by Sutherland in his cultural transmission approach. It is a norm among professional criminals that the chief areas for the exchange of criminal skills are the streets and prisons. Although such skills are not *systematically* taught in either place, they are nonetheless communicated effectively (Chambliss and Seidman, 1971:487; McCaghy, 1980:180–192).

Organized Crime   The term *organized crime* has many meanings, as is evident from a 1978 government report that uses three pages to describe the term. For our purposes, we will consider *organized crime* to be the work of a group that regulates relations between various criminal enterprises involved in smuggling and sale of drugs, prostitution, gambling, and other activities. Organized crime dominates the world of illegal business just as large corporations dominate the conventional business world. It allocates territory, sets prices for illegal goods and services, and acts as an arbitrator in internal disputes (Blakey et al., 1978:107–109).

Organized crime is a secret, conspiratorial activity that generally evades law enforcement. Although precise information is lacking, a presiden-tial commission estimated that organized crime operates in 80 percent of all cities with more than 1 million residents (President's Commission on Law Enforcement and Administration of Justice, 1967:191). Organized crime takes over legitimate businesses, gains influence over labor unions, corrupts public officials, intimidates witnesses in criminal trials, and even "taxes" merchants in exchange for "protection" (National Advisory Commission in Criminal Justice, 1976).

Through its success, organized crime has served as a means of mobility for groups of Americans struggling to escape poverty. Daniel Bell (1953:127–150) used the term *ethnic succession* to describe the process during which leadership of organized crime, held by Irish Americans in the early part of the twentieth century, was transferred in the 1920s to Jewish Americans. In the early 1930s, Jewish crime leaders were in turn replaced by Italian Americans. More recently, ethnic succession has become more complex, reflecting the diversity of the nation's latest immigrants. Colombian, Mexican, Pakistani, and Nigerian immigrants are among those who have begun to play a significant role in organized crime activities.

"HERE WE ARE, CONWAY — THE FINANCIAL DISTRICT. KEEP YOUR EYES OPEN FOR ANY SHADY DEALS AND VIOLATIONS OF THE SECURITIES BUSINESS."

White-collar crime has become a widespread and disturbing reality in the nation's top corporate and financial circles.

White-Collar Crime Edwin Sutherland, who popularized the differential association theory discussed earlier, noted that certain crimes are committed by affluent, "respectable" people in the course of their daily business activities. Sutherland (1949, 1983) likened these crimes to organized crime because they are often perpetrated through the role's of one's occupation (Hagan and Parker, 1985). In his 1939 presidential address to the American Sociological Society, Sutherland (1940) referred to such offenses as **white-collar crimes.** More recently, the term *white-collar crime* has been broadened to include offenses by businesses and corporations as well as by individuals. A wide variety of offenses are now classified as white-collar crimes, such as income tax evasion, stock manipulation, consumer fraud, bribery and

extraction of "kickbacks," embezzlement, and misrepresentation in advertising (Braithwaite, 1985; J. W. Coleman, 1987; Edelhertz, 1983; McCaghy, 1980:242–244; see also Hirschi and Gottfredson, 1987).

A new type of white-collar crime has emerged since Sutherland first wrote on this topic: computer crime. The use of such "high technology" allows one to carry out embezzlement or electronic fraud without leaving a trace, or to gain access to a company's inventory without leaving one's home. An adept programmer can gain access to a firm's computer by telephone and then copy valuable files. It is virtually impossible to track such persons unless they are foolish enough to call from the same phone each time. According to a 1990 estimate, the cost of computer crimes in the United States has reached $3 to $5 billion annually (Conly and McEwen, 1990:2).

White-collar crime has become a widespread and disturbing reality in American society. In a survey of business practices in the period 1975–1984, sociologist Amitai Etzioni (1990) found that 62 percent of *Fortune's* 500 largest industrial corporations were involved in one or more illegal incidents, such as price-fixing, overcharging, fraud, and falsification of tax records. Indeed, the top 100 corporations were guilty of more such crimes than all the other firms combined. Since Etzioni's study was limited to those white-collar crimes *detected* by the government, his findings must be regarded as an underestimate of the prevalence of white-collar crime in the corporate world (Department of Justice, 1987; Reiman, 1984).

In addition to the financial costs of this form of crime, which run into billions of dollars per year, white-collar crime has distinctive social costs, including a decline in the quality of life and a weakening of the social order (Conklin, 1981:50). If those at the top of the nation's economic and social structure feel free to violate the law, less privileged citizens can certainly be expected to follow suit. Ralph Nader (1985:F3), director of the Corporate Accountability Research Group, suggests that "by almost any measure, crime in the suites takes far more money and produces far more casualties and diseases than crime in the streets— bad as that situation is."

Given the economic and social costs of white-collar crime, one might expect this problem to be taken quite seriously by the criminal justice system of the United States. Yet white-collar offenders are more likely to receive fines than prison sentences. In federal courts—where most white-collar cases are considered—probation is granted to 40 percent of those who have violated antitrust laws, 61 percent of those convicted of fraud, and 70 percent of convicted embezzlers (Gest, 1985). In Etzioni's study (1985, 1990), he found that in 43 percent of the incidents either no penalty was imposed or the company was required merely to cease engaging in the illegal practice and to return any funds gained through illegal means (for a different view, see Manson, 1986).

Moreover, conviction for such illegal acts does not generally harm a person's reputation and career aspirations nearly so much as conviction for an index crime would. Apparently, the label "white-collar criminal" does not carry the stigma of the label "felon convicted of a violent crime." In the view of conflict theorists, such differential labeling and treatment are not surprising. The conflict perspective argues that the criminal justice system largely disregards the white-collar crimes of the affluent, while focusing on index crimes often committed by the poor. Thus, if an offender holds a position of status and influence, his or her crime is treated as less serious and the sanction is much more lenient (Katznelson and Kesselman, 1979:352–355; Maguire, 1988).

In one example of differential justice, the Department of Justice agreed to a 1985 plea-bargaining agreement with E. F. Hutton and Company. The firm pleaded guilty to 2000 counts of defrauding American banks of hundreds of millions of dollars through a check manipulation scheme. Hutton agreed to pay a record $2 million fine, to pay the government an additional $750,000 for the costs of the investigation, and to make restitution to the injured parties. In return, the Justice Department agreed not to prosecute any of the E. F. Hutton officials responsible for these white-collar crimes. This aspect of the agreement outraged many legislators, political columnists, and consumer-protection activists (Nader, 1985; Safire, 1985).

More recently, John M. Poindexter, who had served as national security adviser under President Ronald Reagan, was sentenced to 6 months in prison—and was given no fine—for his conviction on five felony counts in the Iran-Contra affair. Poindexter had faced a maximum penalty of 25 years in prison and fines as high as $1.25 million for conspiring to mislead Congress, obstructing congressional inquiries, and making false statements to lawmakers. Former Marine lieutenant colonel Oliver L. North was convicted of three felonies: obstruction of Congress, destruction of National Security Council documents, and acceptance of an illegal gift. He was not sentenced to any jail time, but instead to 2 years of probation, 1200 hours of community service, and a fine of $150,000. North's felony convictions were subsequently "vacated" by an appeals court (Johnston, 1990:A1, A16).

Not all white-collar criminals receive light sentences for serious crimes. For example, after a celebrated 1989 trial on 24 counts of fraud, televangelist Jim Bakker was sentenced to 45 years in prison and a $500,000 fine. On the whole, however, criminal penalties in cases of white-collar crime can be regarded simply as the "price of doing business," since two-thirds of all such corporate fines are less than $10,000 (Etzioni, 1990).

Victimless Crimes   In white-collar or index crimes, people's economic or personal well-being is endangered against their will (or without their direct knowledge). By contrast, sociologists use the term *victimless crimes* to describe the willing exchange among adults of widely desired, but illegal, goods and services (Schur, 1965:169, 1985). Despite the social costs to families and friends of persons engaged in such behavior, many Americans continue to view gambling, prostitution, public drunkenness, and use of marijuana as victimless crimes in which there is no "victim" other than the offender. As a result, there has been pressure from some groups to decriminalize various activities which fall into the category of victimless crimes.

Supporters of decriminalization are troubled by the attempt to legislate a moral code of behavior for adults. In their view, it is impossible to prevent prostitution, gambling, and other victimless crimes. The already overburdened criminal justice system should instead devote its resources to "street crimes" and other offenses which have obvious victims. However, opponents of decriminalization insist that such offenses do indeed bring harm to innocent victims. For example, a person with a drinking problem can become abusive to a spouse or children; a compulsive gambler or drug user may steal in order to pursue this obsession. Therefore, according to critics of decriminalization, society must not give tacit approval to conduct which has such harmful consequences (National Advisory Commission on Criminal Justice, 1976:216–248; Schur, 1968, 1985).

The controversy over decriminalization reminds us of the important insights of labeling and conflict theories presented earlier. Underlying this debate are two interesting questions: Who has the power to define gambling, prostitution, and public drunkenness as "crimes"? And who has the power to label such behaviors as "victimless"? It is generally the state legislatures and, in some cases, the police and the courts.

Again, we can see that criminal law is not simply a universal standard of behavior agreed upon by all members of society. Rather, it reflects the struggle among competing individuals and groups to gain governmental support for their particular moral and social values. For example, such organizations as Mothers Against Drunk Driving (MADD) and Students Against Drunk Driving (SADD) have had success in recent years in shifting public attitudes toward drunkenness. Rather than being viewed as a "victimless crime," drunkenness is increasingly being associated with the potential dangers of driving while under the influence of alcohol. As a result, the mass media are giving greater (and more critical) attention to people guilty of drunk driving, while many states have instituted more severe fines and jail terms for a wide variety of alcohol-related offenses.

Crime Statistics

Crime statistics are among the least reliable social data. However, since they deal with an issue of grave concern to the American public, they are frequently cited as if they are quite accurate. Such statistics do serve as an indicator of police activity, as well as an approximate indication of the level of certain crimes. Yet it would be a mistake to interpret these data as an exact representation of the incidence of crime.

International Crime Rates Given the difficulties of developing reliable crime data in the United States, it is still more difficult to make useful cross-national comparisons. Nevertheless, with some care, we can offer preliminary conclusions about how crime rates differ around the world.

During the 1980s, violent crimes were far more common in the United States than in western Europe. Murders, rapes, and robberies were reported to police at rates four to nine times higher in the United States. Rates for other violent crimes were also higher in this country than in western Europe, but the difference in rates of property crimes was not so great. For example, in 1984, the most recent year for which comparative data are available, the burglary rate in the United States was about 20 percent higher than that of western Europe, while rates of auto theft and larceny in the United States were twice as high.

Rates of violent crime in the United States were also higher than in Canada, Australia, and New Zealand, while rates of burglary and automobile theft were comparable in these four countries. As discussed in Box 7-2, the homicide rate of the United States is fairly similar to that of the Soviet Union, but the rate of reported rape in the United States is more than five times as high as in the Soviet Union. A 1990 report by the National Center for Health Statistics compared homicide rates for young males in the United States with rates in 21 other countries. The homicide rate for young males in the United States was four times higher than that of any other nation studied, and was at least 20 times as high as the homicide rate for young males in such diverse nations as France, Poland, and Japan (Clines, 1989; Fingerhut and Kleinman, 1990).

Why are rates of violent crime so much higher in the United States? While there is no simple answer to this question, sociologist Elliot Currie (1985) has suggested that our society places greater emphasis on individual economic achievement than do other societies. At the same time, may observers have noted that the culture of the

BOX 7-2 • AROUND THE WORLD

SOCIAL CONTROL AND CRIME, SOVIET STYLE

Soviet justice has traditionally been viewed with great skepticism in the west. It was long assumed that legal procedures were a clever fiction designed to mask the arbitrary rule of the Communist party. Human rights activists knew that they could not expect Soviet courts to provide them with fundamental legal rights.

In the area of civil law, however, Soviet justice does assist citizens in settling personal and family problems. According to a study by Ger Van den Berg (1985), approximately 80 percent of the cases that appear before Soviet courts are civil cases. Family matters, primarily divorce cases, account for 60 percent of all civil cases, while labor and housing disputes account for another 15 percent. Whereas in western countries civil cases focus primarily on economic issues, in the Soviet Union they generally concern matters of individual rights.

Soviet legal services are easily affordable and are accessible to the vast majority of the population. Free or inexpensive legal assistance is provided by the *advokatura* (the Soviet bar), the *yuriskonsul't* (a legal adviser at a workplace), trade union organizations, and local units of city government. In civil cases (and in nonpolitical criminal cases), the lawyer-client relationship is respected, and trials are conducted in public.

American sociologist Louise Shelley (1985:70) observes: "While the civil system [of the So-

viet Union] is fair and accessible, the criminal justice system is harsh and often arbitrary." Criminal deviance is viewed as an unacceptable assault on the "socialist order" as well as on crime victims. Soviet policy regarding social control essentially dictates that no individual who commits a crime can be allowed to escape punishment. Criminal cases are rarely discharged or overturned because of violations of criminal procedure. Instead, police, prosecutors, and judges—all traditionally subject to the control of the Communist party—have been expected to produce arrests and convictions.

Since Soviet crime data were not published until recently, it has been difficult to assess the frequency of crime, or patterns of crime, within the nation. However, police and court statistics have been made available to selected Soviet researchers. According to Shelley (1980, 1987), the distinctive features of Soviet violent crime are that (1) it is more often committed in groups than is true in other countries at similar levels of development, (2) rape is relatively rare, although it is underreported because women are reluctant to admit that they have been brutalized, (3) the Soviet Union has a high homicide rate, which is now comparable with the American figure, (4) juveniles are responsible for a disproportionate share of violent crime, (5) there is a higher correlation between alcohol use and violent crime than in most nations for which data are

available, and (6) the Soviet Union has an unusual geography of crime, owing to patterns of directed internal migration which shift the highest degree of criminality from the nation's largest cities to medium-sized cities.

In terms of white-collar crime, the Soviet Union suffers from pervasive corruption: a substantial "underground economy" provides citizens with illegal and unreported personal gain and is supported by bribery of Communist party and legal officials.

The late Soviet leader Yuri Andropov began a "cleanup campaign" against such corruption; the campaign has been continued by current leader Mikhail Gorbachev, who is the first lawyer ever to be appointed as general secretary of the Communist party. In mid-1987, Soviet newspapers announced tougher penalties, including fines and jail terms, for persons found guilty of bribery or of involvement in the "gray market." But, with millions of Soviet citizens believed to be engaged in such activities, this underground economy will be hard to eradicate.

The Gorbachev era has included other efforts to reform the criminal justice system. At the 1988 Soviet party conference, Communist party leaders proposed to redirect the legal system so that it ceased to be an "organ of coercion" and instead became an institution of protection. In early 1989, Major General Anatoly

(Continued)

BOX 7-2 • AROUND THE WORLD

SOCIAL CONTROL AND CRIME, SOVIET STYLE (Continued)

Smirnov of the Interior Ministry provided the first disclosure of detailed crime statistics by Soviet authorities in 56 years. Smirnov reported that per capita crime in the nation had risen by about 18 percent in 1988. The government newspaper *Izvestia* subsequently revealed that over the period 1987–1988, murders rose by 14 percent, rapes by more than 5 percent, assault and battery by more than 31 percent, and violent robberies by almost 43 percent. The disclosure of crime data was a dramatic breakthrough for Soviet authorities—especially since these data demonstrated that the country was experiencing a serious crime wave. Still, as of 1990, the promised overhaul of the legal system remained under discussion.

SOURCES: Barringer, 1986:L21; Cullen and Cullen, 1977; Fein, 1989:A9; Kudryautsev, 1990; Lazarev, 1989:57; Shelley, 1980:111–122, 1985:69–73; Solomon, 1987a, 1987b; Thornburgh, 1990; Van den Berg, 1985.

United States has long tolerated, if not condoned, many forms of violence. When coupled with sharp disparities between poor and affluent citizens, significant unemployment, and substantial alcohol and drug abuse, these factors combine to produce a climate conducive to crime. Finally, the comparatively easy availability of firearms in the United States makes crime relatively more lethal than in other countries (Fingerhut and Kleinman, 1990).

Trends in crime also vary from one nation to another. In the period 1980–1984, the rate of crimes reported to the police in the United States fell for each offense studied, with the exception of rape. The decreases in crime ranged from 12 percent for auto theft to 24 percent for burglary. By contrast, the average crime rates in western Europe, Canada, Australia, and New Zealand increased for all crimes except murder—for which there were insufficient data to make reliable comparisons (Department of Justice, 1989a:16).

Use and Meaning of Crime Statistics Typically, the crime data used in the United States are based on the index crimes described earlier. The crime index, published annually by the FBI as part of the *Uniform Crime Reports,* includes statistics on murder, rape, robbery, assault, burglary, larceny-theft, motor vehicle theft, and arson (see Table 7-4). Obviously many serious offenses, such as those referred to as *white-collar crimes,* are not included in this index (although they are recorded elsewhere). In addition, the crime index is disproportionately devoted to property crimes, whereas most citizens are more worried about violent crimes against people. Thus, a significant decrease in the number of rapes and robberies could be overshadowed by a slightly larger increase in the number of automobiles stolen, thereby leading to the mistaken impression that *personal* safety is more at risk than before.

The most serious limitation of such official crime statistics is that they include only those crimes actually *reported* to law enforcement agencies. As is clear in Figure 7-2, many crimes are not reported, including about half of all assaults and robberies. In these instances, victims typically feel that the experience has been too personal to reveal to police officers and other strangers or that the crime is "not important enough."

Use of official police statistics clearly presents major methodological problems for sociologists and other researchers in understanding crime. Partly because of the deficiencies of police data, the *National Crime Survey* was introduced in 1972 as a means of learning how much crime actually takes place in the United States. The Bureau of Justice Statistics, in compiling this report, seeks information from law enforcement agencies but also interviews members of 100,000 households annually and asks if they have been victims of a specific set of crimes during the preceding year.

TABLE 7-4 National Crime Rates and Percent Change

CRIME INDEX OFFENSES IN 1989	NUMBER REPORTED	RATE PER 100,000 INHABITANTS	PERCENT CHANGE IN RATE	
			SINCE 1985	SINCE 1980
Violent crime				
Murder	21,500	9	+10	−15
Forcible rape	94,500	38	+3	+4
Robbery	578,330	233	+12	−7
Aggravated assault	951,710	383	+27	+28
Total	1,646,040	663	+19	+11
Property crime				
Burglary	3,168,200	1,276	−1	−4
Larceny-theft	7,872,400	3,171	+9	+0.1
Motor vehicle theft	1,564,800	631	+37	+26
Total	12,605,400	5,078	+9	−5
Total index crime	14,251,440	5,741	+10	−4

NOTE: Arson was designated an index offense beginning in 1979; data on arson are still incomplete as of 1989.
SOURCE: Department of Justice, 1990a:48.

FIGURE 7-2 Percent of Crime Reported to the Police, 1988

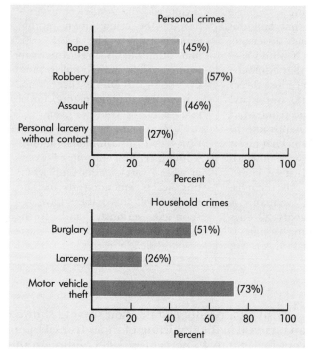

SOURCE: Department of Justice, 1990b:80.

Above: *The crime index, published annually by the FBI, is the major source of information on crime in the United States (although victimization surveys are increasingly being used).*

In general, ***victimization surveys*** question ordinary people, not police officers, to learn how much crime occurs.

The FBI has noted that forcible rape is one of the nation's most underreported crimes, primarily owing to the victims' feelings of fear, embarrassment, or both. Using victimization surveys, we can better assess the underreporting of rape. As noted earlier, the feminist movement has spoken out strongly regarding the way in which rape reflects men's hatred of women (see Box 7-3 on page 212).

Left: *A large proportion of serious crimes go unreported. Only about one-half of rapes, robberies, and assaults are reported to the police. Larceny—theft without the use of force—is reported even less frequently; the reason primarily given by victims is that they do not consider it important enough.*

BOX 7-3 • SPEAKING OUT

RAPE IS A BIAS CRIME

In 1990, President George Bush signed into law the federal Hate Crime Statistics Act, which directs the Department of Justice to gather data on crimes motivated by the victim's race, religion, ethnicity, or sexual orientation. However, gender is not included on the list of categories to be analyzed. Ann Pellegrini (1990:E13), a doctoral candidate in philosophy and religion at Harvard University, is critical of the new law's failure to monitor hate crimes against women, among them rape:

Ann Pellegrini.

. . . Opponents of collecting statistics on hate crimes against women argued that it would only repeat other documentation of crimes against women. The number of male-female rapes committed annually is already tabulated, as is the number of women murdered by their male partners.

But when rapes *are* reported and counted, at no point is the phenomenon of rape interpreted as a hate crime against a gender category of people. Similarly, the frequency with which men murder female partners is nowhere documented as such. And although the vast majority of people killed by serial murderers are women and although serial murderers are, without exception, men, nowhere are statistics compiled that enumerate the victims by sex.

Women make up about 52 percent of the U.S. population. Counting hate crimes against them would reveal that half the population is, as a class, at serious risk of a hate crime. It would also mean recognizing that violence against women is the most direct expression of cultural misogyny. Is it possible to see and name what is always there? Is it possible to isolate from the system what just *is* the system? The answer on both counts ought to be: Just say know.

Know that every 18 seconds, nationwide, some woman is beaten. Know that every 22 days in Massachusetts some woman is murdered by her male lover. Yet in reporting on Charles Stuart, accused of murdering his wife in Boston and manipulating racist sentiments to escape blame, few if any in the media talked about the frequency of such hate crimes in the state. Of the 5000 women murdered annually in the U.S., about one-third are killed by their male lovers.

Similarly, in all the public uproar and media hoopla over the Central Park jogger rape, much attention was focused on the racial configuration of the attack: black teenagers, white victim. There was also speculation about class warfare: poor urban kids, yuppie investment banker.

What virtually went without saying was the gender configuration of the crime: men raping, women raped. The F.B.I. estimates that one in three American women will at some point in their lives be raped. One in three is not a measure of abnormality, but a marker of the commonplace. . . .

Currently, the Hate Crimes Statistics Act discriminates against women; it says nothing of women's lives—and deaths. Only when this act is amended to include women will this nation have responded seriously and forthrightly to prejudice in all its various and deadly forms.

Growing attention has been given to this offense in the media—with recent focus on date and acquaintance rape (see Chapter 13)—and law enforcement agencies have sensitized their officers to the plight of victims.

Partly as a result, victimization surveys showed an increase in the reporting of rapes from 41 percent in 1980 to 45 percent in 1988 (although the figure had reached as high as 61 percent in 1985). Thus, victimization data document the fact that while many rapes are still not reported, the proportion of rapes that *are* reported is somewhat higher than it was in the past. Moreover, victimization data reveal that virtually no rape victim fails to report this crime because she feels she does not have evidence. The most common reason, offered by 20 percent of those who fail to report rapes, is that the victim fears further reprisal from the offender (Department of Justice, 1990b:80, 89).

Victimization data are also useful in developing a more accurate cross-cultural picture of the frequency of crime. According to a 1984 international Gallup poll conducted in 19 nations, the United States ranked sixth in terms of frequency of crime, with 12 percent of adults reporting that they had had money or property stolen during the previous year. Five nations had higher proportions of crime victims: Colombia, (33 percent), Brazil (21 percent), the Netherlands (14 percent), Canada (13 percent), and the United Kingdom (13 percent). By contrast, in Belgium, South Korea, and Japan, 5 percent or less of adults reported that they had had money or property stolen in the last year (John, 1985).

Unfortunately, like other crime data, victimization surveys have particular limitations. They require first that victims understand what has happened to them and also that victims disclose such information to interviewers. Fraud, income tax evasion, and blackmail are examples of crimes that are unlikely to be reported in victimization studies. Nevertheless, virtually all households have been willing to cooperate with investigators for the *National Crime Survey* (see Skogan, 1981, for a detailed analysis of victimization surveys).

Who Commits Index Crimes? Is the United States currently experiencing a crime wave, or has there actually been an increase in law-abiding behavior? As reported in the FBI's crime index, crime rates rose steadily during the last half of the 1980s (see Table 7-4). These increases may reflect a gradual tendency of the public to report a higher proportion of crimes to the police. At the same time, observers believe that the increases in crime in the late 1980s would have been even higher but for a decline in the number of males in the high-crime age group of 14 to 24 years.

Even with its weaknesses, the *Uniform Crime Reports* offers useful insights into the profile of people convicted of index crimes. Sociologists are especially interested in how factors of gender, age, race, and social class shape the profile of lawbreakers.

By gender Most index crimes are committed by males. This is hardly surprising, since our society's gender roles have traditionally given distinct encouragement to boys to become "masculine"—meaning, among other things, physically strong, aggressive, and "tough." Over 87 percent of all people arrested for murder, rape, robbery, and assault in 1989 were male. Among crimes tabulated nationally, females account for the majority of those arrested only in the cases of prostitution and running away from home. However, arrests of females are growing at a somewhat faster rate than arrests of males, and so familiar patterns may be changing somewhat. In 1989, of those arrested, 21 percent were female, compared with only 13 percent in 1965 (Department of Justice, 1990a:177).

By age Index crimes are predominantly an activity of the young. This reflects in part the strenuous nature of many index crimes, but it also stems from the visibility of juveniles, which makes them more subject to supervision and apprehension and, thus, more likely to be included in statistics on criminal activity. About 41 percent of those arrested for index crimes in the United States are under 25 years of age. Young persons are less heavily represented among white-collar criminals, since it generally requires time and skill to achieve the status of a white-collar position (Department of Justice, 1990a:182–183).

By race and class According to the *Uniform Crime Reports*, Blacks account for 31 percent of all arrests even though they represent only about 12 percent of the American population. This higher arrest rate is not surprising for a group that is disproportionately poor—and therefore much less able to afford private attorneys who might be able to prevent formal arrests from taking place. Even more significantly, the high arrest rate of African Americans reflects the *Uniform Crime Re-*

ports' focus on index crimes (mainly property crimes), which are the crimes most often committed by low-income people (Department of Justice, 1990a:190).

In contrast to certain popular misconceptions about crime, minorities and the poor are especially likely to become the *victims* of serious crimes. According to victimization surveys, Black and Hispanic households are more likely to be touched by crime than are White households;

members of families earning less than $7500 per year are more likely to become victims of rape, robbery, or assault than are more affluent persons. Perhaps the most telling statistics are lifetime victimization rates. The likelihood that a Black male in the United States will be a homicide victim during his life is 1 out of 30. For Black females, it is 1 out of 132; for White males, 1 out of 179; and for White females, 1 out of 495 (Department of Justice, 1989a:13, 1990b).

SOCIAL POLICY AND CRIMINAL JUSTICE
DEBATE OVER THE DEATH PENALTY

- Has social science research demonstrated that the death penalty has a deterrent effect on those who might commit capital crimes?
- To what extent is race a factor in the imposition of the death penalty?
- How do conflict theorists view the application of the death penalty in the United States?

Historically, execution has served as a significant form of punishment for deviance from social norms and criminal behavior. For centuries, the death penalty was used in North America for murder, alleged witchcraft, and a few other crimes. Little thought was given to its justification; capital punishment was assumed to be morally and religiously justified. In 1834, Pennsylvania became the first American state to end its use of executions. Currently, 36 states, the military, and federal statutes provide for execution for selected crimes.

The debate over the death penalty has traditionally focused on its appropriateness as a form of punishment and its value in deterring criminals. Viewed from the functionalist perspective of Émile Durkheim, sanctioning of deviant acts helps to reinforce the standards of proper behavior within a society. In this light, supporters of capital punishment insist that fear of execution will prevent at least some criminals from committing serious offenses. Moreover, in their view, the death penalty is justified even if it does not serve as a deterrent, because such criminals deserve to die for their crimes.

By contrast, opponents of capital punishment have

long attacked it as "legalized murder." In early 1987, Amnesty International, an international human rights organization, announced that it was launching a worldwide campaign against the use of capital punishment in the United States. Franca Sciuto, head of the organization's executive committee, declared: "There is no place in civilized society for the gas chamber, the gallows, or the electric chair" (*New York Times*, 1987a:A17).

Opponents of the death penalty point out that a 1985 report identified 343 Americans wrongly convicted of offenses punishable by death since 1900, 25 of whom were actually executed. For example, in 1979 a Black man was sentenced to death for the murder of a 4-year-old White girl. He received a stay only days before his scheduled execution when the victim's mother implicated another person; the man's conviction was subsequently overturned. Critics argue that the possibility of error in the criminal justice system in itself makes capital punishment morally offensive. They also insist that the death penalty violates the Eighth Amendment's prohibition against "cruel and unusual punishment." Thus far, they have failed to persuade the Supreme Court that their constitutional argument is valid (*Harper's*, 1984; Margolick, 1985).

In 1972, the Supreme Court decided a landmark case involving capital punishment, *Furman v. Georgia*. In a split 5-4 decision, the Court ruled that capital punishment per se was not a violation of the Constitution. Nevertheless, the majority held that the imposition of the death penalty for the three defendants in the case was unconstitutional because aggravating or mitigat-

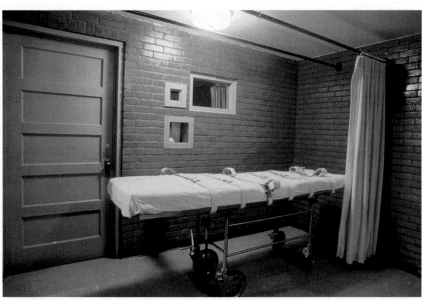

(Sygma)

Methods of capital punishment used in the United States include lethal injection (shown here), electrocution, the gas chamber, hanging, and the firing squad.

ing factors were not considered. Before handing down the death penalty, lower courts must consider the circumstances of the crime and the character and previous record of the defendant. In 1976, in the case of *Gregg v. Georgia*, the court held that executions can be appropriate so long as they do not involve needless pain or suffering and are not grossly out of proportion to the severity of the crime.

These rulings were especially significant, since no executions had taken place since 1967. In part, this reflected a lull in the criminal justice system as officials waited to see how the Supreme Court would assess the constitutionality of the death penalty (S. Reid, 1981:53–65). In the aftermath of the Court's decisions, one execution took place amidst national publicity in 1977 and another in 1979. Executions became somewhat more common in the 1980s; in 1989, there were 16. Moreover, there were more inmates on "death row" in 1990 than at any other time in American history (see Figure 7-3 on page 216).

Will execution of these criminals actually deter other people from committing capital crimes? This issue is difficult to resolve, since the alternative punishment is usually a very long confinement in prison—hardly an incentive for a would-be felon. Most of those executed have been found guilty of murder; however, only a minority of murders (perhaps 20 percent) are found to be premeditated acts. Thus, it is unlikely that capital punishment would deter most killers, since they rarely

weigh the consequences of their actions. Yet it is possible that other criminals could be dissuaded from violent conduct because of their fear of the death penalty. Social science research in this area has been inconclusive; some studies even suggest that an execution may have a "brutalizing" effect on the public and may be associated with an *increase* in the rate of homicide. Moreover, in some countries, among them Canada, the murder rate has fallen after abolition of the death penalty (Bonn, 1984:78–81; *Crime and Delinquency*, 1980; Forst, 1983).

In recent years, the issue of differential justice has become a more important aspect of the debate over capital punishment. Conflict theorists have argued that the poor and non-White are particularly vulnerable to this form of sanctioning. Almost all death row inmates are indigent; many have had poor representation at their trials by court-appointed attorneys. "In one capital case I handled on appeal," recalls Stephen Bright of the Southern Prisoners' Defense Committee in Atlanta, "I went to the trial attorney, and he could not produce one piece of paper from the case. Not even a copy of the indictment to show he had represented the guy." After conviction, indigent inmates on death row typically cannot afford to pay for lawyers to handle their time-consuming appeals. Many state and local governments have failed to provide adequate funding for the defense of indigents charged with or convicted of capital crimes. Skilled private attorneys tend to

FIGURE 7-3 Inmates on Death Row, 1989

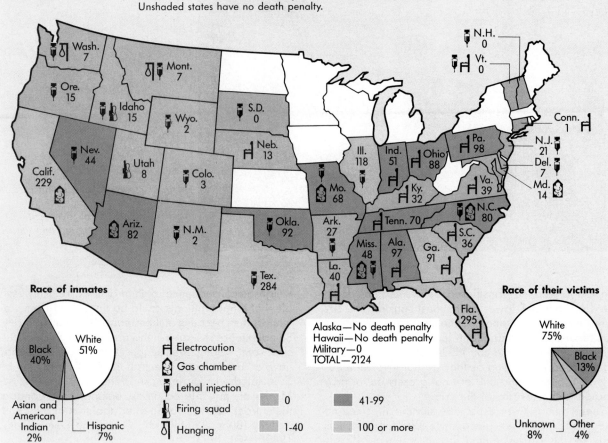

Distribution of 2124 inmates by state as of January 1989
Unshaded states have no death penalty.

Wash. 7

Mont. 7

Ore. 15

Idaho 15

Wyo. 2

S.D. 0

Neb. 13

Ill. 118

Ind. 51

Ohio 88

Pa. 98

N.H. 0

Vt. 0

Conn. 1

N.J. 21

Del. 7

Md. 14

Nev. 44

Utah 8

Colo. 3

Mo. 68

Ky. 32

Va. 39

N.C. 80

Calif. 229

Ariz. 82

N.M. 2

Okla. 92

Ark. 27

Tenn. 70

S.C. 36

Tex. 284

Miss. 48

Ala. 97

Ga. 91

La. 40

Fla. 295

Race of inmates

Black 40%
White 51%
Asian and American Indian 2%
Hispanic 7%

Electrocution
Gas chamber
Lethal injection
Firing squad
Hanging

0
1-40
41-99
100 or more

Alaska—No death penalty
Hawaii—No death penalty
Military—0
TOTAL—2124

Race of their victims

White 75%
Black 13%
Unknown 8%
Other 4%

source: Department of Justice, 1989b.

More Americans face the death penalty today than at any other time in the nation's history.

avoid this low-paying, emotionally draining work (Blodgett, 1987; Hengstler, 1987:58).

Race, as well, appears to be a factor in the imposition of the death penalty. Beginning with the pathbreaking research of sociologist Harold Garfinkel (1949), empirical evidence indicates that the key factor is not so much the race or class background of the killer as the race of the victim. In this regard, sociologist Elizabeth Lynch Murphy examined the first 4 years of administration of the death penalty after it was reinstituted in the United States in 1977. She found that state attorneys were twice as likely to seek the death penalty when a Black was convicted of killing a White as when a Black killed a Black or a White killed a White (McManus, 1985:47).

Although some 60 percent of all homicide victims in the United States are African American, 75 percent of the inmates currently on death row were convicted of killing Whites. Viewed from a conflict perspective, such data suggest that, in applying the death penalty, the American judicial system treats Black lives as cheaper than White lives. Prosecutors are less likely to argue for a death sentence—and juries and judges less likely to impose it—when the murder victim is Black.

Statistically based arguments against the death penalty suffered a grave blow as a result of the 1987 Supreme Court ruling in the case of *McCleskey v. Kemp.*

In an appeal of a murder conviction, the defense presented data showing that the murderer of a White person in Georgia was 11 times more likely to receive a death sentence than the murderer of a Black person. However, in a 5-4 decision that provoked bitter dissents, the Court held that such "apparent disparities" in sentencing do not in themselves constitute unlawful racial discrimination. Instead, the defendant in any such criminal case "must prove that the decision makers in *his* case acted with a discriminatory purpose." The ruling in *McCleskey v. Kemp* removed one of the last major hurdles restricting application of capital punishment in the United States. In a stinging critique, Benjamin Hooks, executive director of the National Association for the Advancement of Colored People (NAACP), accused the justices of giving a "green light" for "an even broader imposition of the death penalty on black victims" (Baldus et al., 1986; Elsasser, 1987:8; Radelet, 1989; S. Taylor, 1987a:B13).

Like the Supreme Court majority, federal legislators have been unwilling to use social science research to invalidate discriminatory application of the death penalty. The Racial Justice Act, proposed by Senator Edward Kennedy of Massachusetts, would prohibit the imposition of any federal or state death sentence if it furthered a "racially discriminatory pattern." In introducing this bill, Kennedy cited studies demonstrating racial disparities in the sentencing and imposition of the death penalty since the Supreme Court's 1972 ruling in *Furman v. Georgia*. The Racial Justice Act was included in the Omnibus Crime Act of 1990 but was deleted from the larger anticrime package during Senate debate (COSSA, 1990b).

The issue of cost has also been raised in the debate over the death penalty. If convicted murderers are not sentenced to death, they are generally given lengthy prison terms or even life imprisonment. Is it fair, some Americans ask, that taxpayers be asked to subsidize the care of these offenders for decades? But criminals in the United States are not executed immediately after sentencing. Instead, 33 of the 36 states with capital punishment offer automatic provisions for appeals from death row residents. There are almost always extended judicial proceedings, as well as petitions to state governors to commute sentences to life imprisonment. Typically, judicial review occurs at 11 different levels. According to a 1989 estimate, a single death sentence can cost as much as $3 million in court, prison, and legal costs—a sum that in some states equals that of imprisoning an offender for 280 years. With these expenses in mind, the alleged financial savings from the death penalty disappear (A. Malcolm, 1989).

The controversy over capital punishment has persisted for centuries and remains a subject of heated debate in American political life. A 1990 national survey reported that 72 percent of those questioned favor capital punishment for certain crimes. Yet the issues raised by the death penalty continue to haunt not only inmates facing execution but also legislators, judges, and private citizens concerned about the equitable application of social controls (Dionne, 1990).

SUMMARY

Conformity and deviance are two ways in which people respond to real pressures or to imagined pressures from others. In this chapter, we examine the relationships between conformity, deviance, and mechanisms of social control.

1 A society uses *social control* to bring about acceptance of basic norms.

2 Stanley Milgram defined *conformity* as going along with one's peers, whereas *obedience* is defined as compliance with higher authorities in a hierarchical structure.

3 Examples of *informal social control* include smiles, laughter, raising of an eyebrow, and ridicule.

4 Some norms are considered so important that they are formalized into *laws* controlling people's behavior.

5 Socialization is the primary source for effecting conforming and obedient behavior, including obedience to law.

6 Standards of *deviance* vary from group to group and also vary over time.

7 For functionalist theorists, deviance helps to define the limits of proper behavior.

8 The theory of *differential association* holds that deviance results from exposure to attitudes favorable to criminal acts.

9 An important aspect of *labeling theory* is the recognition that some people are *viewed* as deviant while others engaged in the same behavior are not.

10 The conflict perspective views laws and punishments as reflecting the interests of the powerful.

11 *Crime* represents a deviation from formal social norms administered by the state.

12 The category of *index crimes* includes murder, rape, assault, and other serious offenses that people think of when they express concern about crime.

13 *White-collar crimes* have serious economic and social costs for American society.

14 Crime statistics are among the least reliable social data, partly because so many crimes are not reported.

15 The debate over the death penalty in the United States has centered on such issues as cruelty of punishment and differential justice.

KEY TERMS

Anomie Durkheim's term for the loss of direction felt in a society when social control of individual behavior has become ineffective. (page 195)

Anomie theory of deviance A theory developed by Robert Merton which explains deviance as an adaptation either of socially prescribed goals or of the norms governing their attainment. (196)

Bond A term used by Travis Hirschi to refer to the ties of an individual to society and, in particular, to standards of proper behavior. (195)

Conformity Going along with one's peers, individuals of a person's own status, who have no special right to direct that person's behavior. (188)

Crime A violation of criminal law for which formal penalties are applied by some governmental authority. (204)

Cultural transmission A school of criminology which argues that criminal behavior is learned through social interactions. (198)

Deviance Behavior that violates the standards of conduct or expectations of a group or society. (193)

Differential association A theory of deviance proposed by Edwin Sutherland which holds that violation of rules results from exposure to attitudes favorable to criminal acts. (198)

Formal social control Social control carried out by authorized agents, such as police officers, judges, school administrators, and employers. (191)

Index crimes The eight types of crime reported annually by the FBI in the *Uniform Crime Reports*. These are murder, rape, robbery, assault, burglary, theft, motor vehicle theft, and arson. (204)

Informal social control Social control carried out by people casually through such means as laughter, smiles, and ridicule. (190)

Labeling theory An approach to deviance popularized by Howard S. Becker which attempts to explain why certain people are *viewed* as deviants while others engaging in the same behavior are not. (200)

Law In a political sense, the body of rules made by government for society, interpreted by the courts, and backed by the power of the state. (191)

Obedience Compliance with higher authorities in a hierarchical structure. (188)

Organized crime The work of a group that regulates relations between various criminal enterprises involved in smuggling and sale of drugs, prostitution, gambling, and other activities. (205)

Professional criminal A person who pursues crime as a day-to-day occupation, developing skilled techniques and enjoying a certain degree of status among other criminals. (204)

Sanctions Penalties and rewards for conduct concerning a social norm. (188)

Social control The techniques and strategies for regulating human behavior in any society. (187)

Societal-reaction approach Another name for *labeling theory*. (200)

Techniques of neutralization Justifications for deviant behavior. (199)

Victimization surveys Questionnaires or interviews used to determine whether people have been victims of crime. (211)

Victimless crimes A term used by sociologists to describe the willing exchange among adults of widely desired, but illegal, goods and services. (207)

White-collar crimes Crimes committed by affluent individuals or corporations in the course of their daily business activities. (206)

ADDITIONAL READINGS

Becker, Howard S. (ed.). *The Other Side: Perspectives on Deviance.* New York: Free Press, 1964. A collection of articles on labeling theory that first appeared in the journal *Social Problems.*

Brownmiller, Susan. *Against Our Will: Men, Women, and Rape.* New York: Simon and Schuster, 1975. An important study of the crime of rape, by a contemporary feminist writer.

Cullen, Francis T., William J. Maakestad, and Gray Cavender. *Corporate Crime under Attack.* Cincinnati:

Anderson, 1987. Building on Edwin Sutherland's insights on white-collar crime, these researchers describe the Ford Pinto case as a grievous example of corporate crime.

Erikson, Kai. *Wayward Puritans: A Study in the Sociology of Deviance*. New York: Wiley, 1966. An insightful attempt to extend the functionalist approach to historical materials (in this case, to the Puritan settlers of seventeenth-century Massachusetts).

Gaylord, Mark S., and John F. Galliher. *The Criminology of Edwin Sutherland*. Rutgers, N.J.: Transaction 1987. An intellectual biography of Sutherland which places the development of differential association theory into its social context.

Hills, Stuart L. (ed.). *Corporate Violence: Injury and Death for Profit*. Totowa, N.J.: Rowman and Littlefield, 1987. An anthology covering such examples of white-collar crime as workplace crimes, environmental pollution, and victimization of the consumer.

King, Harry. *Box Man: A Professional Thief's Journal*. New York: Harper and Row, 1972. A fascinating autobiography with an introduction and commentary by sociologist William Chambliss.

Reiman, Jeffrey H. *The Rich Get Richer and the Poor Get Prison* (2nd ed.). New York: Wiley, 1984. A comprehensive look at the criminal justice system from the conflict perspective, with a special focus on white-collar crime.

Sanders, Clinton R. *Customizing the Body: The Art and Culture of Tattooing*. Philadelphia: Temple University Press, 1989. Sanders offers a brief history of the practice of tattooing and discusses his participant observation of those who work as tattooists.

Schur, Edwin M. *Labeling Women Deviant: Gender, Stigma, and Social Control*. Philadelphia: Temple University Press, 1983. An examination of the criminal justice system in its broadest context as it applies to women. Includes coverage of sexual harassment, rape, family violence, and mental illness.

Silberman, Charles E. *Criminal Violence, Criminal Justice*. New York: Random House, 1978. A readable and critical account of crime and our society's mechanisms for dealing with it.

Wilson, James Q., and Richard J. Hernstein. *Crime and Human Nature*. New York: Simon and Schuster, 1986. A challenging, controversial approach to crime that examines the relationship of law-abiding behavior to intelligence, personality, and even body type.

Journals

Among the journals which focus on issues of deviance, crime, and social control are *Crime and Delinquency* (founded in 1955), *Criminology* (1961), and *Law and Society Review* (1966).

PART THREE

SOCIAL INEQUALITY

PART THREE focuses on the structure and processes of social inequality. Chapter 8 examines the important sociological concepts of stratification and social mobility, as well as inequality based on social class, with special emphasis on the United States. In Chapter 9, we consider stratification and mobility abroad and give particular attention to the inequality evident in the world's developing nations. Chapter 10 deals with inequality based on racial and ethnic background and focuses on prejudice and discrimination against minority groups. Chapter 11 discusses inequality based on gender and the position of women as an oppressed majority. In Chapter 12, sociological analysis of the aging process is presented, and inequality based on age is examined.

221

8

STRATIFICATION AND SOCIAL MOBILITY

*All animals are equal. But some
animals are more equal than others.*
George Orwell
Animal Farm, *1945*

LOOKING AHEAD

- How are societies organized to deny privileges to some members while extending them to others?
- How did Karl Marx and Max Weber contribute to our understanding of social class?
- Can life be organized without structured inequality?
- How do sociologists measure social class?
- How is the ideology of "blaming the victim" used to minimize the problems of poverty in the United States?
- How likely are people in the United States either to move into or to rise out of poverty?
- Why do women and their children constitute an increasing proportion of our nation's poor?

Residents of the United States like to think of our country as a land of opportunity and equality. We are certainly aware that the United States is an affluent land in which we enjoy luxuries not common in the world's developing nations. Yet a shocking study released in 1990 by a prestigious medical journal reveals that a man in Harlem, a predominantly Black neighborhood in New York City, is less likely to live to the age of 65 than is a man in Bangladesh, one of the poorest nations of the world. Whereas 55 percent of men in Bangladesh will reach age 65, the same will be true for only 40 percent of men in Harlem.

According to this study, based on data from the period 1979–1981, the factors contributing to

Harlem's high mortality rate, in order, were cardiovascular disease, cirrhosis, homicide, tumors, and drug dependency. However, as the researchers note, the problem of mortality among 25- to 44-year-olds in Harlem has become even more severe since 1980, with acquired immune deficiency syndrome (AIDS) now established as the most common cause of death in this age group in Harlem. The researchers add that Harlem's high mortality rate is not unique; they have identified 53 other health areas, predominantly inner-city neighborhoods with high Black or Hispanic populations, that have age-adjusted mortality rates approximately twice the national average for Whites (McCord and Freeman, 1990).

Ever since people began to speculate about the nature of human society, their attention has been drawn to the differences that can be readily observed between individuals and groups within any society. The term ***social inequality*** describes a condition in which members of a society have different amounts of wealth, prestige, or power. All societies are characterized by some degree of social inequality.

When a system of social inequality is based on a hierarchy of groups, sociologists refer to it as ***stratification:*** a structured ranking of entire groups of people that perpetuates unequal economic rewards and power in a society. These unequal rewards are evident not only in the distribution of wealth and income, but even in the distressing mortality rates of impoverished communities such as Harlem. Stratification involves the ways in which social inequalities are passed on from one generation to the next, thereby produc-

According to a study released in 1990 by a prestigious medical journal, a man in Harlem, a predominantly Black neighborhood in New York City, is less likely to live to the age of 65 than a man in Bangladesh, one of the poorest nations in the world.

(Jacques Chenet/Woodfin Camp & Associates)

ing groups of people arranged in rank order from low to high.

Stratification is one of the most important and complex subjects of sociological investigation because of its pervasive influence on human interactions and institutions. Social inequality is an inevitable result of stratification in that certain groups of people stand higher in social rankings, control scarce resources, wield power, and receive special treatment. As we will see in this chapter, the consequences of stratification are evident in the unequal distribution of wealth and income within industrial societies. The term *income* refers to salaries and wages. By contrast, *wealth* is an inclusive term encompassing all of a person's material assets, including land and other types of property.

Of course, each of us wants a "fair share" of society's rewards, and we often come into conflict over how these rewards should be divided. Family members argue over who should be given money to buy new clothing or take a vacation; nations go to war over precious resources such as oil or minerals. As a result, sociologists have directed their attention to the implications of stratification in ranking members of a society.

This chapter will focus on the unequal distribution of socially valued rewards within human societies. It begins with an examination of four general systems of stratification. Particular attention will be given to Karl Marx's theories of class and to Max Weber's analysis of the components of stratification. In addition, functionalist and conflict theorists' explanations for the existence of stratification will be considered and contrasted, and a synthesis of these views offered by sociologist Gerhard Lenski will be presented.

The second part of the chapter will explain how sociologists measure social class. The consequences of stratification in terms of poverty, health, educational opportunities, and other aspects of life will be discussed. In the third part of the chapter, the movement of individuals up and down the social hierarchies of the United States will be examined. Finally, in the social policy section, we will consider government efforts to assist women living in poverty.

UNDERSTANDING STRATIFICATION

Systems of Stratification

This section will examine four general systems of stratification—systems of slavery, castes, estates, and social classes. These should be viewed as ideal types useful for purposes of analysis. Any stratification system may include elements of more than one type. For example, the American south of the eighteenth century had both social classes dividing Whites and institutionalized enslavement of Blacks.

Slavery The most extreme form of legalized social inequality for individuals or groups is *slavery.* The distinguishing characteristic of this system of stratification is that slaves are owned by other people. They are legally treated as property, just as if these human beings were equivalent to household pets or appliances.

Slavery has varied in the way it has been practiced. In ancient Greece, the main source of slaves consisted of captives of war and piracy. Although slave status could be inherited by succeeding generations, it was not necessarily permanent. A person's status might change depending on which city-state happened to triumph in a military conflict. In effect, all citizens had the potential of becoming slaves or of being granted freedom, depending on the circumstances of history. By contrast, in the United States and Latin America, racial and legal barriers were established to prevent the freeing of slaves.

Whenever and wherever it has existed, slavery has required extensive coercion in order to maintain the privileges and rewards of slave owners. For example, it is estimated that as many as 9000 Blacks were involved in an 1822 slave revolt in Charleston, South Carolina, led by a carpenter and former slave named Denmark Vesey. Imagine the resources that must have been needed to crush such a massive rebellion. This is but one reflection of the commitment to social control required to keep people trapped in lives of involuntary servitude (Franklin and Moss, 1988; Schaefer, 1990).

Castes *Castes* are hereditary systems of rank, usually religiously dictated, that are relatively fixed and immobile. The caste system is generally associated with the Hindu religious faith in India, Sri Lanka (Ceylon), and Pakistan. There are four major castes in India, called *varnas.* A fifth category of outcastes, referred to as *untouchables,* is considered to be so lowly and unclean as to have no place within this system of stratification. Caste membership is established at birth, since children automatically assume the same position as their parents. Each caste is quite sharply defined, and members are expected to marry within the same caste.

Caste membership generally determines one's occupation or role as a religious functionary. An

(Courtesy of the New-York Historical Society, New York City)

As this picture shows, Blacks were bought and sold at auctions during the long period in which slavery was permitted in the United States. Whenever and wherever slavery has existed, extensive coercion has been needed to maintain the privileges and rewards of slave owners.

example of an occupational caste is that of snake handlers (refer back to Box 4-3 on page 114). The caste system promotes a remarkable degree of differentiation. Thus, the single caste of chauffeurs has been split into two separate subcastes: drivers of luxury cars have a higher status than drivers of economy cars.

In recent decades, industrialization and urbanization have taken their toll on India's rigid caste system. Many villagers have moved to urban areas where their low-caste status is unknown. Schools, hospitals, factories, and public transportation facilitate contacts among different castes that were previously avoided at all costs. In addition, there have been governmental efforts to reform the caste system. India's 1950 constitution abolished discrimination against untouchables, who traditionally had been excluded from temples, schools, and most forms of employment. Yet, despite certain changes, the caste system remains the most important system of stratification in India (Anant, 1978; Glen and Johnson, 1978).

Sociologists have also used the term *caste* to describe stratification systems that emphasize racial distinctions. The type of differential treatment given to White, "Colored," Asian, and Black people in the Republic of South Africa, and to a lesser extent to racial groups in the United States (see Chapter 10), brings to mind certain aspects of India's caste system.

(Drawing by Sempé; © 1984 The New Yorker Magazine, Inc.)

"Their intentions are, in fact, quite simple. They say they would like to be here inside and for us to be outside."

Estates   A third type of stratification system, called *estates,* was associated with feudal societies during the Middle Ages. The **estate system,** or feudalism, required peasants to work land leased to them by nobles in exchange for military protection and other services. The basis for the system was the nobles' ownership of land, which was critical to their superior and privileged status. As in systems based on slavery and caste, inheritance of one's position largely defined the estate system. The nobles inherited their titles and property, whereas the peasants were born into a subservient position within an agrarian society.

As the estate system developed, it became more differentiated. Nobles began to achieve varying degrees of authority. By the twelfth century, a priesthood emerged in most of Europe, as did classes of merchants and artisans. For the first time, there were groups of people whose wealth did not depend on land ownership or agriculture. This economic change had profound social consequences as the estate system ended and a class system of stratification came into existence.

Social Classes   A *class system* is a social ranking based primarily on economic position in which achieved characteristics can influence mobility. In contrast to slavery, caste, and estate systems, the boundaries between classes are less precisely defined, and there is much greater movement from one stratum, or level, of society to another. Yet class systems maintain stable stratification hierarchies and patterns of class divisions. Consequently, like the other systems of stratification described thus far, class systems are marked by unequal distribution of wealth and power.

Income inequality is also a basic characteristic of a class system. In 1989, the median family income in the United States was $34,213. In other words, half of all families had higher incomes in that year and half had lower incomes. Yet this fact may not fully convey the income disparities in our society. In 1987, about 36,000 tax returns reported incomes in excess of $1 million. At the same time, some 6 million households reported incomes under $5000 (Bureau of the Census, 1990a:320, 1990b:35).

There are many ways in which sociologists conceptualize social class; a common method is to look at class in terms of income differences. Table 8-1 offers a picture of the relative number of Americans earning various incomes. However, such data do not provide a complete picture of class; among other limitations, they fail to consider sources of wealth apart from income.

Sociologist Daniel Rossides (1990:404–416) has conceptualized the class system of the United States using a five-class model. While the lines separating social classes in his model are not so sharp as the divisions between castes, he shows that members of the five classes differ significantly in ways other than their levels of income.

About 1 to 3 percent of Americans are categorized by Rossides as upper-class, a group limited to the very wealthy. These people form intimate associations with one another in exclusive clubs and social circles. By contrast, the lower class, consisting of approximately 20 percent of Americans, is disproportionately populated by Blacks, Hispanics, single mothers with dependent children, and people who cannot find regular work. This class lacks both wealth and income and is too weak politically to exercise significant power.

Both of these classes, at opposite ends of the nation's social hierarchy, reflect the importance of **ascribed status,** which is a social position "assigned" to a person without regard for the person's unique characteristics or talents. The nation's most affluent families generally inherit wealth and status, while many members of racial and ethnic minorities inherit disadvantaged status. Age and gender, as well, are ascribed statuses that influence a person's wealth and status. While privilege and deprivation are not guaranteed in the United States, those born into extreme wealth or poverty will often remain in the same class position they inherited from their parents.

Between the upper and lower classes in Rossides's model are the upper middle class, the lower middle class, and the working class (see Box 8-1). The upper middle class, numbering about 10 percent of the population, is composed of professionals such as doctors, lawyers, and architects. They participate extensively in politics and exercise leadership roles in the types of voluntary associations described in Chapter 6. The lower middle class, which accounts for approximately 30 percent of the American population, includes less affluent professionals (such as elementary school teachers and nurses), owners of small businesses, and a sizable number of clerical workers. While not all members of this varied class hold college degrees, they share the goal of sending their children to institutions of higher education.

Rossides describes the working class—about 40 percent of the population—as people holding regular manual or blue-collar jobs. Certain members of this class, such as electricians, may have higher incomes than people in the lower middle class. Yet, even if they have achieved some degree of economic security, they tend to identify with manual workers and their long history of involvement in the American labor movement.

Class is seen by sociologists as a key determi-

TABLE 8-1   Family Income in the United States, 1989

INCOME LEVEL	PERCENT DISTRIBUTION
$75,000 and over	11.3
$50,000 to $74,999	17.7
$35,000 to $49,999	19.8
$25,000 to $34,999	16.4
$15,000 to $24,999	16.7
$10,000 to $14,999	8.1
$5000 to $9999	6.3
Under $5000	3.6

SOURCE: Bureau of the Census, 1990b:35.

In 1989, half of all American families earned more than $34,213 in income; half of all families earned less than that amount.

BOX 8-1 • CURRENT RESEARCH

IS THE MIDDLE CLASS DISAPPEARING?

The belief that the poor can rise to middle-class status has long been central to the image of the United States as a "land of opportunity." However, according to Lester C. Thurow, noted professor of economics and management at the Massachusetts Institute of Technology, the American middle class is actually disappearing. Using a widely accepted definition of a middle-class household as one with an income between 75 percent and 125 percent of the nation's median household income, the range of American middle-class incomes in 1989 was $21,680 to $36,133. On the basis of this standard, about 23 percent of American households were classified as middle class in 1989, as compared with 28 percent in 1967.

Closer analysis by Thurow indicates that, of those who relinquished their middle-class standing, about half rose to a higher ranking in the American class system, while half dropped to a lower position. Consequently, in Thurow's view, the United States is slowly moving toward a "bipolar income distribution." In simpler terms, a broadly based middle class is being replaced by a growing population of rich and poor Americans. Economist Ravi Batra (1987:F2) observes that the "United States is fast becoming a nation of two classes, with the haves growing richer, the have-

nots growing poorer, and the middle class slowly sinking into oblivion."

Thurow and a number of other scholars have identified a number of factors which contribute to the decrease in the proportion of households categorized as middle class:

• *Unemployment.* The economy of the United States has experienced serious rates of unemployment since the late 1970s. When a prime wage earner loses his or her job, a household may suddenly fall from middle-class to lower-class status. Foreign competition has been especially damaging for those heavy industries, such as steel and automobile manufacturing, which employ a substantial number of skilled and blue-collar workers. When such industries shrink, the American middle class shrinks along with them.

• *New growth industries and nonunion workplaces.* Through the efforts of strong labor unions, workers in traditional heavy industries have generally achieved middle-class incomes. By contrast, new "high tech" industries such as microelectronics remain largely unorganized by unions, and these workers fall into the category of low-wage assemblers. Still another growth area in the economy, fast-food restaurants, has added employment

opportunities, but again at the low end of the wage scale.

• *The rise in single-mother households.* The United States has witnessed a staggering rise in the divorce rate. In 1965, there were 479,000 divorces; by 1989, there were almost 1.2 million. This increase in the divorce rate has contributed to an equally dramatic rise in the proportion of households headed by single mothers (see Chapter 13). While most divorced and separated women retain custody of their children, few are able to command incomes as high as those earned by their husbands. As a result, many households headed by single mothers lose the middle-class status that they had enjoyed before the divorce.

• *The rise in two-income households.* The discussion above has focused on factors which have led Americans to fall below their previous middle-class standing. However, the increase in households with dual wage earners—which will be discussed in more detail in Chapters 11 and 13—has had the opposite effect. With the benefit of a second income, many of these households have been able to leave the middle class and achieve even higher incomes and status.

SOURCES: Batra, 1987:F2; Bluestone and Harrison, 1987:F3; Bureau of the Census, 1990b:23; National Center for Health Statistics, 1990:4; Thurow, 1984:F3.

nant of people's values, attitudes, and behavior. For example, studies have found that working-class young people are likely to engage in sexual intercourse before the age of 17, whereas middle-class young people typically wait until 19 and become intimate with fewer partners before marriage. Theorists suggest that the less successful, less satisfying nature of life in the lower classes encourages people to seek emotional fulfillment through sexual relationships. At the same time, the values of middle- and upper-class families discourage early sexual behavior (B. Miller and Moore, 1990:1030; Weinberg and Williams, 1980).

Yet another example of how class influences behavior is seen in research on social participation. Sociological studies consistently find that the number of memberships in voluntary associations increases as a person ascends the occupational hierarchy. Members of upper-class households belong to five times as many organizations as members of lower-class families. Moreover, when an organization includes people from mixed class backgrounds, those from higher social classes are more likely to serve as leaders (Gilbert and Kahl, 1987:142–143).

Social class is one of the independent or explanatory variables most frequently used by social sci-entists. The chapters to follow will analyze the relationships between social class and divorce patterns (Chapter 13), religious behavior (Chapter 14), formal schooling (Chapter 16), and residence and housing (Chapter 18), as well as other relationships in which social class is a variable.

Perspectives on Stratification

As sociologists have examined the subject of stratification and attempted to describe and explain social inequality, they have engaged in heated debates and reached varying conclusions. No theorist stressed the significance of class for society—and for social change—more strongly than Karl Marx. Marx viewed class differentiation as the crucial determinant of social, economic, and political inequality. By contrast, Max Weber questioned Marx's emphasis on the overriding importance of the economic sector and argued that stratification should be viewed as a multidimensional phenomenon.

Karl Marx's View of Class Differentiation   Sociologist Leonard Beeghley (1978:1) aptly noted that "Karl Marx was both a revolutionary and a social scientist." Marx was concerned with stratification in all types of human societies, beginning

(The Bettmann Archive)

In his analysis of capitalism, Karl Marx argued that the bourgeoisie owns the means of production, such as factories and machinery; and that while attempting to maximize profit, the bourgeoisie exploits workers, who must exchange their labor for subsistence wages.

with primitive agricultural tribes and continuing into feudalism. But his main focus was on the effects of class on all aspects of nineteenth-century Europe. Marx focused on the plight of the working class and felt it imperative to strive for changes in the class structure of society.

In Marx's view, social relations during any period of history depend on who controls the primary mode of economic production. His analysis centered on how the relationships between various groups were shaped by differential access to scarce resources. Thus, under the estate system, most production was agricultural, and the land was owned by the nobility. Peasants had little choice but to work according to terms dictated by those who owned land.

Using this type of analysis, Marx examined social relations within *capitalism*—an economic system in which the means of production are largely in private hands and the main incentive for economic activity is the accumulation of profits (Rosenberg, 1991). Marx focused on the two classes that began to emerge as the estate system declined—the bourgeoisie and the proletariat. The *bourgeoisie,* or capitalist class, owns the means of production, such as factories and machinery, while the *proletariat* is the working class. In capitalist societies, the bourgeois maximize profit in competition with other firms. In the process, they exploit workers, who must exchange their labor for subsistence wages.

According to Marx, exploitation of the proletariat will inevitably lead to the destruction of the capitalist system. But, for this to occur, the working class must first develop *class consciousness*—a subjective awareness held by members of a class regarding their common vested interests and the need for collective political action to bring about social change. Workers must often overcome what Marx termed *false consciousness,* or an attitude held by members of a class that does not accurately reflect its objective position. A worker with false consciousness may feel that he or she is being treated fairly by the bourgeoisie or may adopt an individualistic viewpoint toward capitalist exploitation ("*I* am being exploited by *my* boss"). By contrast, the class-conscious worker realizes that *all* workers are being exploited by the

bourgeoisie and have a common stake in revolution (Vanneman and Cannon, 1987).

For Karl Marx, the development of class consciousness is part of a collective process whereby the proletariat comes to identify the bourgeoisie as the source of its oppression. Through the guidance of revolutionary leaders, the working class will become committed to class struggle. Ultimately, the proletariat will overthrow the rule of the bourgeoisie and the government (which Marx saw as representing the interests of capitalists) and will eliminate private ownership of the means of production. In his rather utopian view, classes and oppression will cease to exist in the postrevolutionary workers' state.

Where Marxist revolutions have taken place, as in the Soviet Union, the People's Republic of China, and Cuba, it has been primarily large landowners and feudalistic ruling elites—rather than industrial capitalists—who have been overthrown. Indeed, some Marxist-based regimes, as in eastern Europe, have given way to western-style democracies. Contemporary Marxist theorists such as Paul Baran (1960:5–9) contend that the absence of revolutionary class struggle in developed nations such as the United States, Great Britain, and West Germany results from exploitation of less developed nations. These theorists argue that the poor nations of the world have been kept poor so that western capitalists can amass large profits, "buy off" the industrial proletariat within their borders (through comfortable salaries and benefits), and prevent workers from rebelling.

Many of Marx's predictions regarding the future of capitalism have not been borne out. Marx failed to anticipate the emergence of labor unions, whose power in collective bargaining weakens the stranglehold that capitalists maintain over workers. Moreover, as contemporary conflict theorists note, he did not foresee the extent to which the political liberties present in western democracies and the relative prosperity achieved by the working and middle classes could contribute to what he called *false consciousness.* Many people have come to view themselves as individuals striving for improvement within "free" societies with substantial mobility—rather than as members of

In Max Weber's analysis, status *is a cultural dimension that involves ranking groups in terms of the degree of prestige they possess. Justices of the United States Supreme Court, shown here, are unquestionably a high-status group in our society.*

social classes facing a collective fate. Despite these limitations, the Marxist approach to the study of class is useful in stressing the importance of stratification as a determinant of social behavior and the fundamental separation in many societies between two distinct groups, the rich and the poor.

Max Weber's View of Stratification   Unlike Karl Marx, Max Weber insisted that no single characteristic (such as class) totally defines a person's position within the stratification system. Instead, writing in 1916, he identified three analytically distinct components of stratification: class, status, and power (Gerth and Mills, 1958).

Weber used the term *class* to refer to people who have a similar level of wealth and income. For example, certain workers in the United States provide the sole financial support for their families through jobs which pay the federal minimum wage. According to Weber's definition, these wage earners constitute a class, because they have the same economic position and fate. In this conception, Weber agreed with Marx regarding the importance of the economic dimension of stratification. Yet Weber argued that the actions of individuals and groups could not be understood solely in economic terms.

Weber used the term *status group* to refer to people who have the same prestige or lifestyle, independent of their class positions. In his analysis, status is a cultural dimension that involves the

ranking of groups in terms of the degree of prestige they possess. An individual gains status through membership in a desirable group, such as the medical profession. Weber further suggested that status is subjectively determined by people's lifestlyes and therefore can diverge from economic class standing. A successful pickpocket may be in the same income class as a college professor. Yet the thief is widely regarded as a member of a low-status group, while the professor holds high status in our culture.

Status considerations influence our routine, everyday behavior more than we realize. In a revealing experiment, researchers had a 31-year-old man walk across the street while the nearby traffic signal flashed "Wait!" In one situation the man wore soiled clothes to simulate a low-status person, while in another he wore a neat, stylish suit. Unsuspecting pedestrians were much more likely to imitate the well-dressed man—by crossing the street against the signal—than they were the man in dirty clothing. Apparently, even the outward trappings associated with high status are enough to influence people's behavior (Lefkowitz et al., 1955).

For Weber, the third major component of stratification, power, reflects a political dimension. *Power* is the ability to exercise one's will over others. In the United States, power stems from membership in particularly influential groups, such as corporate boards of trustees, government bodies, and interest groups. As we will explore more fully in Chapter 15, conflict theorists generally agree that two major sources of power—big business and government—are closely interrelated. For example, sociologist Peter Freitag (1975) found that over three-fourths of all cabinet members of the United States in the period 1897–1973 had served as either an officer or a lawyer for a large corporation.

In Weber's view, then, each of us has not one rank in society but three. A person's position in a stratification system reflects some combination of his or her class, status, and power. Each factor influences the other two, and in fact the rankings on these three dimensions tend to coincide. Thus, John F. Kennedy came from an extremely wealthy family, attended exclusive preparatory schools, graduated from Harvard University, and went on to become president of the United States. Like Kennedy, many Americans from affluent backgrounds achieve impressive status and power.

At the same time, these dimensions of stratification may operate somewhat independently in determining a person's position. A widely published poet may achieve high status while earning a relatively modest income. Successful professional athletes have little power, but enjoy a relatively high position in terms of class and status. In order to understand the workings of a culture more fully, sociologists must carefully evaluate the ways in which it distributes its most valued rewards, including wealth and income status, and power (Duberman, 1976:35–40; Gerth and Mills, 1958: 180–195).

Is Stratification Universal?

Is it necessary that some members of society receive greater rewards than others? Can social life be organized without structured inequality? Do people need to feel socially and economically superior to others? These questions have been debated by social theorists (and by the "average" woman and man) for centuries.

Such issues of stratification have also been of deep concern to political activists. Utopian socialists, religious minorities, and members of recent countercultures have all attempted to establish communities which, to some extent or other, would abolish inequality in social relationships. Some of these experiments, including the Israeli kibbutz and the communes of the 1960s, will be described in Chapter 13.

Social scientific research has revealed that inequality exists in all societies—even the simplest of cultures. For example, when anthropologist Gunnar Landtman (1968, original edition 1938) studied the Kiwai Papuans of New Guinea, he initially noticed little differentiation among them. Every man in the village performed the same work and lived in similar housing. However, upon closer inspection, Landtman observed that certain Papuans—the men who were warriors, harpooners, and sorcerers—were described as "a little more high" than others. By contrast, villagers who were female, unemployed, or unmarried were considered "down a little bit" and were barred from owning land.

Stratification is universal in that all societies maintain some form of differentiation among members. Depending on its values, a society may assign people to distinctive ranks based on their religious knowledge, skill in hunting, beauty, trading expertise, or ability to provide health care. But why has such inequality developed in human societies? How much differentiation among people, if any, is actually essential?

Functionalist and conflict sociologists offer contrasting explanations for the existence and necessity of social stratification. Functionalists maintain that a differential system of rewards and punishments is necessary for the efficient operation of society. Conflict theorists argue that competition for scarce resources results in significant political, economic, and social inequality.

The Functionalist Answer Would people go to school for many years to become physicians if they could make as much money and gain as much respect working as street cleaners? Functionalists reply in the negative, which is partly why they believe that a stratified society is universal.

In the view of Kingsley Davis and Wilbert Moore (1945), society must distribute its members among a variety of social positions. It must not only make sure that these positions are filled but also see that they are staffed by people with the appropriate talents and abilities. Thus, rewards, including money and prestige, are based on the importance of a position and the relative scarcity of qualified personnel. Yet this assessment often devalues work performed by certain segments of society, such as women's work as homemakers or in occupations traditionally filled by women.

Davis and Moore argue that stratification is universal and that social inequality is necessary so that people will be motivated to fill functionally important positions. One critique of this functionalist explanation of stratification holds that unequal rewards are not the only means of encouraging people to fill critical positions and occupations. Personal pleasure, intrinsic satisfaction, and value orientations motivate people to enter particular careers. Functionalists agree but note that society must use *some* type of rewards to motivate people to enter unpleasant or dangerous jobs, as well as jobs that require a long training period. However, this response does not justify stratification systems such as slave or caste societies in which status is largely inherited. Similarly, it is difficult to explain the high salaries our society offers to professional athletes or entertainers on the basis of importance of these jobs to the survival of society (R. Collins, 1975; Kerbo, 1991:129–134; Tumin, 1953, 1985:16–17).

Even if stratification is inevitable, the functionalist explanation for differential rewards does not explain the wide disparity between the rich and the poor. Critics of the functionalist approach point out that the richest 10 percent of households account for 21 percent of the nation's income in Sweden, 25 percent in the United States, and 32 percent in Switzerland. In their view, the level of income inequality found in contemporary industrial societies cannot be defended—even though these societies have a legitimate need to fill certain key occupations (World Bank, 1990:237).

The Conflict Response As was noted in Chapter 1, the intellectual tradition at the heart of conflict theory begins principally with the writings of Karl Marx. Marx viewed history as a continuous struggle between the oppressors and the oppressed which would ultimately culminate in an egalitarian, classless society. In terms of stratification, he argued that the dominant class under capitalism—the bourgeoisie—manipulated the economic and political systems in order to maintain control over the exploited proletariat. Marx did not believe that stratification was inevitable, but he did see inequality and oppression as inherent in capitalism (E. Wright et al., 1982).

Contemporary conflict theorists believe that human beings are prone to conflict over such scarce resources as wealth, status, and power. However, where Marx focused primarily on class conflict, more recent theorists have extended this analysis to include conflicts based on gender, race, age, and other dimensions. Sociologist Ralf Dahrendorf, formerly president of the respected London School of Economics and now at Oxford University, is one of the most influential contributors to the conflict approach.

Dahrendorf (1959) has argued that while Marx's analysis of capitalist society was basically correct, it must be modified if it is to be applied to *modern* capitalist societies. For Dahrendorf, social classes are groups of people who share common interests resulting from authority relationships. In identifying the most powerful groups in society, he includes not only the bourgeoisie—the owners of the means of production—but also the managers of industry, legislators, the judiciary, heads of the government bureaucracy, and others. In one respect, Dahrendorf has merged Marx's emphasis on class conflict with Weber's recognition that power is an important element of stratification (Cuff and Payne, 1979:81–84).

Conflict theorists, including Dahrendorf, contend that the powerful of today, like the bourgeois of Marx's time, want society to run smoothly so that they can enjoy their privileged positions. The status quo is satisfactory to those with wealth, status, and power; thus, they have a clear interest in preventing, minimizing, or at least controlling societal conflict.

The powerful, such as leaders of government, use limited social reforms to buy off the oppressed and reduce the danger of challenges to their dominance. For example, minimum wage laws and unemployment compensation unquestionably give some valuable assistance to needy Americans. Yet these reforms also have the effect

TABLE 8-2 Perspectives on Stratification Compared

QUESTION	FUNCTIONALIST VIEW	CONFLICT VIEW	LENSKI'S VIEW
Is stratification universal?	Yes.	Yes.	Yes.
Is stratification necessary?	Some level of stratification is necessary in order to ensure that key social positions are filled. But slavery and caste systems are unnecessary.	Stratification is not necessary. In fact, it is a major source of societal tension and conflict.	Although stratification has been present in all societies, its nature and extent vary enormously depending on level of economic development.
What is the basis for stratification?	Societal-held values.	Ruling class values.	Both societal-held and ruling class values.
Will there be changes over time in a society's level of stratification?	Degree of stratification may change gradually.	Degree of stratification must be reduced so that society will become more equitable.	There will be evolutionary changes in degree of stratification.

of pacifying those who might otherwise become disgruntled and rebellious. Of course, in the view of conflict theorists, such maneuvers can never eliminate conflict, since workers will continue to demand equality and the powerful will not give up their control of society.

Conflict theorists see stratification as a major source of societal tension and conflict. They do not agree with Davis and Moore that stratification is functional for a society or that it serves as a source of stability. Rather, conflict sociologists argue that stratification will inevitably lead to instability and to social change (R. Collins, 1975:62; L. Coser, 1977:580–581).

Lenski's Approach: A Synthesis Sociologist Gerhard Lenski, Jr. (1966; Lenski et al., 1991) has offered a view of stratification which synthesizes certain elements of the functionalist and conflict approaches (see Table 8-2). Lenski believes that each of these perspectives is valid under certain conditions and that different stages of technological development lead to different systems of stratification.

Lenski describes the process of change in economic systems as their level of technology becomes more complex, beginning with hunting and gathering and culminating eventually with

The view of stratification offered by sociologist Gerhard Lenski, Jr., synthesizes certain elements of the functionalist and conflict approaches.

industrial society (see Chapter 15). In subsistence-based, hunting-and-gathering societies, people are focused on survival. While inequality and differentiation are evident, a stratification system based on social class does not emerge, because there is no real wealth to be claimed.

Essentially, Lenski agrees with functionalists that the key resources of a society are allocated as rewards for persons who occupy important roles. However, as a society advances in terms of technology, it becomes capable of producing a considerable surplus of goods—more than enough to attract members to valued occupations. Consequently, a definite and rigid social class system develops with, for example, a ruling class, a merchant class, and a peasant class. Surplus resources are disproportionately distributed to those individuals and classes with the greatest status, influence, and power.

Such unequal allocation of resources leads to the societal tension and conflict discussed by Marx and by Dahrendorf and other contemporary conflict theorists. Yet, in Lenski's view, inequality does not necessarily increase with industrialization. In order to minimize strikes, slowdowns, and industrial sabotage, the elites share a portion of the economic surplus with the lower classes. At the same time, the elites are able to maintain their power and privilege.

We now return to the question posed earlier—"Is stratification universal?"—and consider the sociological response. Some form of differentiation is found in every culture, including the advanced industrial societies of our time. As Lenski has argued, the allocation of surplus goods and services—controlled by those with wealth, status, and power—reinforces the social inequality which accompanies stratification systems. While this reward system may once have served the overall purposes of society, as functionalists contend, the same cannot be said for present disparities separating the "haves" of current societies from the "have-nots."

Later in this chapter, we will observe the ways in which people's very health and well-being are influenced by their positions in the stratification system. Whatever their theoretical differences, sociologists agree that social class is an extremely important variable in stratification.

STRATIFICATION BY SOCIAL CLASS

Measuring Social Class

In everyday life, people in the United States are continually judging relative amounts of wealth and income by assessing the cars people drive, the neighborhoods in which they live, the clothing they wear, and so forth. Yet it is not so easy to locate an individual within our social hierarchies as it would be in caste or estate systems of stratification, where placement is determined by religious dogma or legal documents. In order to determine someone's class position, sociologists generally rely on the objective method.

The *objective method* of measuring social class views class largely as a statistical category. Individuals are assigned to social classes on the basis of criteria such as occupation, education, income, and residence. The key to the objective method is

that the *researcher* makes a determination about an individual's class position.

The first step in using this method is to decide what indicators or causal factors will be measured objectively, whether wealth, income, education, or occupation. The prestige ranking of occupations has proved to be a useful indicator in determining a person's class position. The term **prestige** refers to the respect and admiration with which an occupation is regarded by society. "My daughter, the physicist" has a very different connotation from "my daughter, the waitress." Prestige is independent of the particular individual who occupies a job, a characteristic which distinguishes it from esteem. **Esteem** refers to the reputation that a specific person has within an occupation. Therefore, one can say that the position of president of the United States has high prestige, even though it has been occupied by people with varying degrees of esteem.

Table 8-3 illustrates the results of an effort to assign prestige to a number of well-known occupations. In a series of national surveys from 1972 to 1990, sociologists drawing upon earlier survey responses assigned prestige rankings to about 500 occupations, ranging from physician to judge to shoeshiner. The highest possible score in terms of prestige was 90, while the lowest was 10. As the data indicate, physician, lawyer, and airline pilot were among the most highly regarded occupations. Sociologists have used such data to assign prestige rankings to virtually all jobs and have found a stability in rankings from 1925 through 1990 (Hodge and Rossi, 1964; Nakao and Treas, 1990; NORC, 1990).

Sociologists have become increasingly aware that studies of social class tend to neglect the occupations and incomes of women as determinants of social rank. In an exhaustive study of 589 occupations, sociologists Mary Powers and Joan Holmberg (1978) examined the impact of women's participation in the paid labor force on occupational status. Since women tend to dominate the relatively low-paying occupations, such as bookkeepers and secretaries, their participation in the work force leads to a general upgrading of the status of most male-dominated occupations.

The objective method of measuring social class has traditionally focused on the occupation and

TABLE 8-3 Prestige Ranking of Occupations

OCCUPATION	SCORE	OCCUPATION	SCORE
Physician	82	Bank teller	50
College teacher	78	Electrician	49
Lawyer	76	Police officer	48
Dentist	74	Insurance agent	47
Bank officer	72	Secretary	46
Airline pilot	70	Air traffic controller	43
Clergy	69	Mail carrier	42
Sociologist	66	Owner of a farm	41
Secondary school teacher	63	Restaurant manager	39
Registered nurse	62	Automobile mechanic	37
Pharmacist	61	Baker	34
Elementary school teacher	60	Salesclerk	29
Accountant	56	Gas station attendant	22
Painter	56	Waiter and waitress	20
Librarian	55	Laundry operator	18
Actor	55	Garbage collector	17
Funeral director	52	Janitor	16
Athlete	51	Usher	15
Reporter	51	Shoeshiner	12

SOURCE: NORC, 1990.

In a series of national surveys conducted between 1972 and 1990, occupations were ranked in terms of prestige. The highest possible score was 90, the lowest 10. Some of the results are presented above.

education of the husband in measuring the class position of two-income families. With more than half of all married women now working outside the home (see Chapter 11), this represents a serious omission. Furthermore, how is class or status to be judged in dual-career families—by the occupation regarded as having greater prestige, the average, or some other combination of the two occupations?

Research in the area of women and social class is just beginning, because until recently few sociologists had raised such methodological questions. One study found that over the last 20 years married men have typically used their own occupations to define their class positions—whether or not their wives worked outside the home. By contrast, there has been a noticeable change in how married women define their class positions. Whereas in the 1970s married women tended to attach more weight to their husbands' occupations than to their own in defining their class positions, by the 1980s they began to attach equal weight to their own occupations and those of their husbands (N. Davis and Robinson, 1988).

Advances in statistical methods and computer technology have also multiplied the factors used to define class under the objective method. No longer are sociologists limited to annual income and education in evaluating a person's class position. Today, studies are published which use as criteria the value of homes, sources of income, assets, years in present occupations, neighborhoods, and considerations regarding dual careers. While the addition of these variables will not necessarily lead to a different picture of class differentiation in the United States, it does allow sociologists to measure class in a more complex and multidimensional way.

Whatever the technique used to measure class, the sociologist is interested in real and often dramatic differences in power, privilege, and opportunity in a society. The study of stratification is a study of inequality. Nowhere is this more evident than in the distribution of wealth and income.

"And just why do we always call my income the second income?"

Studies of social class tend to ignore the occupations and incomes of wives and focus on the incomes of husbands in determining social rank or measuring the class position of two-income families.

Consequences of Social Class in the United States

Wealth and Income The period beginning in the late 1940s and lasting through the early 1960s was a remarkable time in the history of the United States: income increased in all groups in the nation's population. While social and economic inequality had not been eliminated, virtually all Americans earned more than they had before. Unfortunately, the widespread expectation that earning power would continue to rise has proved to be untrue. Over the period 1967–1989, the median family income in the United States, after controlling for inflation, rose by only 0.6 to 1.4 percent per year, depending on which consumer price index one uses (Bureau of the Census, 1990b:13–15).

By all measures, income in the United States is distributed unevenly. Nobel prize–winning economist Paul Samuelson has described the situation in the following words: "If we made an income pyramid out of a child's blocks, with each layer portraying $500 of income, the peak would be far higher than Mount Everest, but most people would be within a few feet of the ground" (Samuelson and Nordhaus, 1989:644).

Samuelson's analogy is certainly supported by recent data on incomes. In 1989, the top fifth (or 20 percent) of the nation—earning $45,224 or more—accounted for almost 47 percent of total wages and salaries. By contrast, the bottom fifth of the population—earning $11,417 or less—accounted for less than 4 percent of income (Bureau of the Census, 1990c:5, 17).

As Figure 8-1 shows, there has been modest redistribution of income in the United States over the past 60 years. From 1929 through 1969, the government's economic and tax policies seemed to shift income shares somewhat to the poor. However, in the last 20 years—especially during the 1980s—federal budgetary policies favored the affluent. Moreover, while the salaries of highly skilled workers and professionals have continued to rise, the wages of less skilled workers have decreased when controlled for inflation.

As a result, the income gap between the richest and poorest groups of Americans has increased over the last 2 decades. According to data gathered for the House Ways and Means Committee, from 1979 to 1987 the personal income of the richest one-fifth of the population rose by 15.6 percent, while the personal income of the poorest one-fifth declined by 9.8 percent (Cutler, 1989; Kerbo, 1991:32–35; F. Levy, 1987; Reich, 1990; Tolchin, 1989).

As concentrated as income is in the United States, wealth is much more unevenly distributed. As Figure 8-2 (page 240) shows, in 1983 the richest fifth of the population held almost 80 percent of the wealth. A study by the Bureau of the Census (1986b:10) found that more than 1.6 million American households had assets over $500,000, while 9.6 million households were in debt (had a negative net worth).

Moreover, according to a study by the Federal Reserve Board, the distribution of wealth in the United States is becoming increasingly uneven. In 1963, the richest 0.5 percent of the population held 26 percent of the national wealth, while the poorest 90 percent of households held 34 percent. By 1983, while the richest 0.5 percent of households (approximately 420,000 households) still held 26 percent of the total wealth of the United States, the share held by the poorest 90 percent of households had fallen to 28 percent. With these measures of wealth and income in mind, it seems clear that our society is becoming more sharply divided into "haves" and "have-nots" (Kerbo, 1991:40–44, 57; Wines, 1986:3).

Poverty What are the consequences of this uneven distribution of wealth and income? Approximately one out of every nine Americans lives below the poverty line established by the federal government. Yet the category of the "poor" defies any simple definition—and counters common stereotypes about low-income persons. For example, many Americans believe that the vast majority of the poor are able to work but will not. Yet, as of 1989, only about 60 percent of poor persons do not work, primarily because they are ill or disabled, are maintaining a home, or are retired.

From 1929 to 1969, there was some redistribution of income in the United States to the less affluent. But over the last 20 years this trend has reversed, with the distribution of income shifting in favor of the most affluent.

FIGURE 8-1 Distribution of Income in the United States, 1929, 1969, and 1989

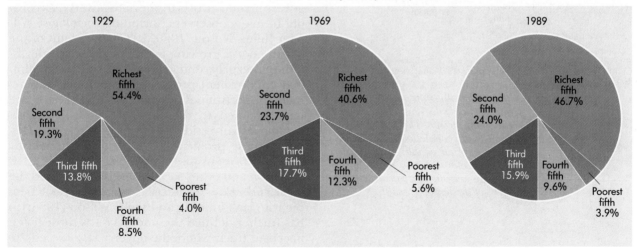

NOTE: 1929 data for the bottom two-fifths are an estimate by the authors based on data from Bureau of the Census, 1975a.
SOURCES: Bureau of the Census, 1975a:301; 1975c:384; 1990c:5.

FIGURE 8-2 Comparison of Distribution of Income and Wealth

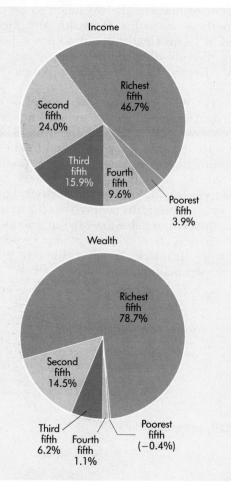

Income

Richest fifth 46.7%

Second fifth 24.0%

Third fifth 15.9%

Fourth fifth 9.6%

Poorest fifth 3.9%

Wealth

Richest fifth 78.7%

Second fifth 14.5%

Third fifth 6.2%

Fourth fifth 1.1%

Poorest fifth (−0.4%)

SOURCES: Income data are for 1989 and are from Bureau of the Census, 1990c:5. Data on wealth are for 1983 and are from Kerbo, 1991:40; and J. Smith, 1986.

As these data illustrate, wealth in the United States is distributed much less evenly than income. The richest 20 percent of the population hold close to 80 percent of all wealth. By contrast, the poorest fifth are, as a group, in debt to an amount equivalent to −0.4 percent of the nation's wealth.

Fully 40 percent of the poor do work outside the home, although only a small portion (9 percent of all low-income adults) work full-time throughout the year (Bureau of the Census, 1990b:65).

A sizable number of the poor live in poverty areas known as *urban slums,* but a majority of low-income Americans live outside these poverty areas. Included among the poor of the United States are elderly citizens, children living in single-parent families with their mothers, and over 10,000 men in military service who cannot adequately support their large families. Table 8-4 provides additional statistical information regarding low-income Americans.

Since World War II, an increasing proportion of the nation's poor have been women—many of whom are divorced or never-married mothers. Currently, two out of three adults classified as "poor" by the federal government are women. In 1959, female-headed households accounted for 26 percent of the nation's poor; by 1989, that figure had risen to 52 percent (Bureau of the Census, 1990b). We will examine this alarming trend, known as the *feminization of poverty,* in the social policy section later in this chapter.

The underclass   In 1989, 44 percent of poor Americans were living in central cities. These urban residents have the greatest visibility among low-income Americans and are the focus of most governmental efforts to alleviate poverty. According to many observers, including sociologist William Julius Wilson (1980, 1987), the plight of the urban poor is growing worse, owing to the devastating interplay of inadequate education and limited employment prospects. Traditional employment opportunities in the industrial sector are largely closed to the unskilled poor. For low-income urban residents who are Black and Hispanic, these problems have been heightened by past and present discrimination.

Wilson and other social scientists have used the term ***underclass*** to describe long-term poor people who lack training and skills. Wilson (1988:15) has further defined the underclass as those living in census tracts where the poverty rate exceeds 40 percent. Consequently, the underclass can be viewed as both a social and a statistical phenomenon. Members of the underclass live in a neigh-

TABLE 8-4   Who Are the Poor in the United States?

GROUP	PERCENT OF THE POPULATION OF THE UNITED STATES	PERCENT OF THE POOR OF THE UNITED STATES
Under 15 years old	22	35
15 to 65 years old	66	54
Over 65 years old	12	11
2-member families	42	33
3- to 4-member families	45	43
Families with 5 or more members	13	24
Whites	84	66
Blacks	12	30
Hispanics	8	17
People in families with male heads of households	84	48
People in families with female heads of households	16	52

In 1989, the poverty level for a family of four was $12,675.

NOTE: Percentages in the racial and ethnic category exceed 100 percent, since Hispanic people can be either Black or White.
SOURCE: Adapted from Bureau of the Census, 1990b:7, 56–59, 67.

borhood adapting to social isolation and limited economic opportunities in which the basic elements of community life—stores, schools, religious institutions, and recreational facilities—are difficult if not impossible to maintain.

Conflict theorists, among others, have expressed alarm at the portion of the nation's population living in this lower rung of the stratification hierarchy and at society's reluctance to address the lack of economic opportunities for these Americans. While the underclass is not composed exclusively of subordinate racial and ethnic minorities, it is disproportionately concentrated among urban Blacks and Hispanics. In 1980, only 7 percent of all poor Whites lived in the extreme poverty areas of the nation's five largest cities, compared with 32 percent of all poor Hispanics and 39 percent of all poor Blacks. According to national estimates, the underclass constitutes only about 2 million of the nation's 32 million poor. Yet the underclass produces a disproportion-

ate share of social problems (Wilkerson, 1987; W. Wilson, 1988).

As part of a national survey of race relations commissioned by the NAACP Legal Defense and Educational Fund (1989), researchers conducted face-to-face interviews in mid-1988 with 347 chronically poor African Americans in eight cities. Among the findings were the following:

• Women constitute 78 percent of the Black underclass.
• The median income of chronically poor Black households over the last 5 years has been $4900.
• At least 61 percent of those surveyed had not held a job in the last 2 years.
• Some 44 percent of those surveyed had either never held a job or never received any training for work.

At the same time, members of the African American underclass share many of the most basic goals and aspirations of our society. For example, 55 percent of respondents state that they hope their children will go to college.

Poverty is not new. Yet the concept of the underclass describes a chilling development: individuals and families, whether employed or not, who are beyond the reach of any safety net provided by existing social programs. In addition, membership in the underclass is not an intermittent condition but a long-term attribute. The underclass is understandably alienated from the larger society and engages sporadically in illegal behavior. Of course, these illegal acts hardly encourage society to genuinely address the long-term problems of the underclass.

Studying poverty The efforts of sociologists and other social scientists to better understand poverty are complicated by the difficulty of developing a satisfactory operational definition of poverty. This problem is evident even in government programs which conceive of poverty in either absolute or relative terms. *Absolute poverty* refers to a minimum level of subsistence below which families should not be expected to exist. This standard theoretically remains unchanged from year to year. Policies concerning minimum wages, housing standards, or school lunch programs for the poor imply a need to bring citizens up to some predetermined level of existence.

By contrast *relative poverty* is a floating standard of deprivation by which people at the bottom of a society, whatever their lifestyles, are judged to be disadvantaged in comparison with the nation as a whole. Most of our country's current social programs view poverty in relative terms. Therefore, even if the poor of the 1990s are better off in absolute terms than the poor of the 1930s or 1960s, they are still seen as deserving special assistance from government.

One commonly used measure of relative poverty is the federal government's *poverty line,* which serves as an official definition of which Americans are poor. In 1989, for example, any family of four with a combined income of $12,675 or less fell below the poverty line. This definition determines which individuals and families will be eligible for certain governmental benefits.

By 1990, there was growing debate over the validity of the poverty line as a measure of poverty and a standard for allocating government benefits. Some critics charge that the poverty line is too low; they note that the federal government continues to use 20-year-old nutritional standards in assessing people's level of poverty. If the poverty line is too low, then government data will

(Owen Franken/Stock, Boston)

A substantial number of Americans, including this rural Kentucky family, hover at or near the poverty level.

underestimate the extent of poverty in the United States, while many deserving poor citizens will fail to receive benefits. Yet other observers dispute this view and argue that the poverty line may actually overestimate the number of low-income Americans because it fails to consider nonmonetary benefits such as the food stamps that some poor people receive from the government (DeParle, 1990).

Our view of poverty in the United States has been greatly refined by the publication of sociologist Greg Duncan's book *Years of Poverty, Years of Plenty* (1984, 1987), based on a 15-year study of family income dynamics by the University of Michigan's Institute for Social Research. Duncan's analysis reveals that the "poor" are not a static social class. Instead, the composition of the poor continually changes, with some families moving above the poverty level after a year or two while others slip below the level.

According to data from the institute's study, only 2 percent of Americans remain persistently poor—a finding which casts doubt on the image of the poor as a permanent underclass trapped in poverty. However, a more recent study by the Bureau of the Census (1990d) showed that 82 percent of persons living below the poverty line in 1986 had been poor throughout the previous year. Blacks and Hispanics were found to be more likely than Whites to remain in poverty.

Why does such pervasive poverty continue within a nation of vast wealth? Herbert Gans (1971:21–23) has applied functionalist analysis to the existence of poverty and has identified various social, economic, and political functions that the poor perform for society. Among these are the following:

- The presence of poor people means that society's "dirty work"—physically dirty or dangerous, dead-end and underpaid, undignified and menial jobs—will be performed at low cost.
- Poverty creates jobs for occupations and professions which "service" the poor. It creates both legal employment (public health experts, welfare caseworkers) and illegal jobs (drug dealers, numbers "runners").
- The identification and punishment of the poor as deviants uphold the legitimacy of conventional social norms regarding hard work, thrift, and honesty (see Chapter 7).
- The poor serve as a measuring rod for status comparisons. Within a relatively hierarchical society, they guarantee the higher status of more affluent Americans. Indeed, as is described in Box 8-2 (page 244), the affluent may justify inequality (and gain a measure of satisfaction) by "blaming the victims" of poverty for their disadvantaged conditions.
- Because of their lack of political power, the poor often absorb the costs of social change. Under the policy of deinstitutionalization, released mental patients have been "dumped" primarily into low-income communities and neighborhoods. Urban renewal projects to restore central cities have typically pushed out the poor in the name of "progress."

Consequently, in Gans's view, poverty and the poor actually satisfy positive functions for many nonpoor groups in American society.

Unemployment   As we have seen in our discussion of poverty, a substantial portion of poor people experience intermittent or long-term unemployment. As sociological research points out, unemployment affects the entire society and has far-reaching consequences on both the macro and the micro levels. On the societal, or macro, level, unemployment leads to a reduced demand for goods and services. Sales by retail firms and other businesses are affected adversely, and this can lead to further layoffs. Wage earners must contribute to unemployment insurance and welfare programs that assist those without jobs.

From the micro level, the unemployed person and his or her family must adjust to a loss of spending power. Both marital happiness and family cohesion can be adversely affected. In addition, there is an accompanying loss of self-image and social status, since our society and others view unemployment as a kind of failure. According to one estimate, a 1.4 percent increase in the unemployment rate of the United States is associated with a 5.7 percent increase in suicide, a 4.7 percent increase in admissions to state mental hospitals, and an 8.0 percent increase in homicides (Tipps and Gordon, 1983).

BOX 8-2 • SPEAKING OUT

BLAMING THE VICTIM

Psychologist William Ryan struck a vulnerable chord in 1971 when he coined the phrase "blaming the victim" to describe how some people essentially justify inequality by finding defects in the victims rather than examining the social and economic factors that contribute to poverty, racism, and other national problems. In the following selection, Ryan (1976:3–8) explains the generic process of "blaming the victim" and notes that this process is aimed not only at disadvantaged people in the United States but also at residents of the world's less developed nations:

(Courtesy William Ryan, photo by Carillo)

William Ryan.

. . . Consider some victims. One is the miseducated child in the slum school. He is blamed for his own miseducation. He is said to contain within himself the causes of his inability to read and write well. The shorthand phrase is "cultural deprivation," which, to those in the know, conveys what they allege to be inside information: that the poor child carries a scanty pack of intellectual baggage as he enters school. He doesn't know about books and magazines, they say. . . . They say if he talks at all . . . he certainly doesn't talk correctly. . . . In a word, he is "disadvantaged" and "socially deprived," they say, and this, of course, accounts for his failure (*his* failure, they say) to learn much in school. . . .

What is the culturally deprived child *doing* in the school? What is wrong with the victim? In pursuing this logic, no one remembers to ask questions about the collapsing buildings and torn textbooks; the frightened, insensitive teachers; the six additional desks in the room; the blustering, frightened principals; the relentless segregation; the callous administrator; the irrelevant curriculum; the bigoted or cowardly members of the school board; the insulting history book; the stingy taxpayers; the fairy-tale readers; or the self-serving faculty of the local teachers' college. We are encouraged to confine our attention to the child and to dwell on all his alleged defects. Cultural deprivation becomes an omnibus explanation for the educational disaster area known as the inner-city school.

This is Blaming the Victim. . . .

The generic process of Blaming the Victim is applied to almost every American problem. The miserable health care of the poor is explained away on the grounds that the victim has poor motivation and lacks health information. The problems of slum housing are traced to the characteristics of tenants who are labeled as "Southern rural migrants" not yet "acculturated" to life in the big city. . . . It would be possible for me to venture into other areas—one finds a perfect example in literature about the underdeveloped countries of the Third World, in which the lack of prosperity and technological progress is attributed to some aspect of the national character of the people, such as lack of "achievement motivation." . . .

Blaming the Victim is, of course, quite different from old-fashioned conservative ideologies. . . . The new ideology attributes defect and inadequacy to the malignant nature of poverty, injustice, slum life, and racial difficulties. The stigma that marks the victim and accounts for his victimization is an acquired stigma, a stigma of social, rather than genetic, origin. But the stigma, the defect, the fatal difference . . . is still located *within* the victim, inside his skin. . . . It is a brilliant ideology for justifying a perverse form of social action designed to change, not society, as one might expect, but rather society's victim.

The unemployment rate of the United States is traditionally represented as a percentage, such as about 5 to 6 percent in 1990. Such statistics can minimize the problem; it is more striking to realize that in 1990, over 7 million Americans were unemployed at any one time. But even this latter figure may disguise the severity of unemployment. The federal government's Bureau of Labor Statistics regards as unemployed only those people *actively* seeking employment. Thus, in order to be counted as unemployed, a person must not hold a full-time job, must be registered with a government unemployment agency, and must be engaged in writing job applications and seeking interviews. Quite simply, the official unemployment rate leaves out millions of Americans who are effectively unemployed but have given up and are not seeking work.

The burden of unemployment in the United States is unevenly distributed throughout the nation's labor force. Women are about 20 percent more likely than men to be unemployed and are less likely to be rehired following layoffs. Racial minorities and teenagers have unemployment rates twice that of adult White males. The unemployment rate for Black teenagers in urban areas is about 43 percent, well above the rate for the nation as a whole during the Depression of the 1930s, which was 25 percent. Again, such statistics do not include those who have dropped out of the system—who are not at school, not at work, and not looking for a job. If we add discouraged job seekers to the official statistics, the rate of unemployment and underemployment for Black teenagers in central-city areas climbs to 90 percent (Gordus and Yamakawa, 1988; Swinton, 1987).

Stratification and Life Chances Poverty and unemployment unquestionably have a marked influence on people's lives. Max Weber saw class as closely related to people's **life chances**—that is, their opportunities to provide themselves with material goods, positive living conditions, and favorable life experiences (Gerth and Mills, 1958:181).

Life chances are reflected in such measures as housing, education, and health. Occupying a higher position in a society will improve one's life chances and bring greater access to social rewards. By contrast, people in the lower social classes are forced to devote a larger proportion of their limited resources to the necessities of life. Sociologist Paul Blumberg (1980:181) observed that those in the lowest tenth of the United States in income spend over 40 percent of their daily income for food, compared with only 11 percent for the highest tenth.

The affluent and powerful not only have more material possessions than others; they also benefit in many nonmaterial ways. For example, as is shown in Figure 8-3 (page 246), children from higher-income families (the richest quartile) are much more likely to attend college than are children in less affluent families. In 1989, 78 percent of all high school graduates ages 18 to 24 from families in the richest quartile (that is, families earning $58,100 and over) were enrolled in or had attended college. For families in the poorest quartile (earning less than $20,000), the comparable figure was 45 percent. This gap in educational opportunity has remained significant and fairly constant over the last 20 years (Mortenson and Wu, 1990:42 and table 19).

As is true of educational opportunities, a person's health is affected in important ways by his or her class position (see Chapter 17). The chances of a child's dying during the first year of life are approximately 70 percent higher in poor families than for the middle class. This higher infant mortality rate results in part from the inadequate nutrition received by low-income expectant mothers. Even when they survive infancy, the poor are more likely than the affluent to suffer from serious, chronic illnesses such as arthritis, bronchitis, diabetes, and heart disease. In addition, the poor are less likely to be protected from the high costs of illness by private health insurance. They may be employed in jobs in which health insurance is not a fringe benefit; may not be employed full time and, thus, may be ineligible for employee health benefits; or may simply be unable to afford the premiums. Moreover, the occupations of the American lower classes tend to be more dangerous than those of more affluent citizens (J. Erickson and Bjerkedal, 1982; R. Kessler et al., 1989; Paneth, 1982; Szymanski, 1983:301–314).

Like disease, crime can be particularly devastat-

FIGURE 8-3 College Participation Rates by Family Income, 1970 to 1989

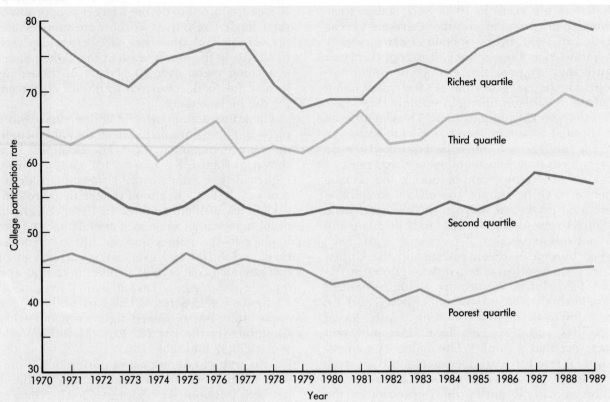

SOURCE: Mortenson and Wu, 1990:42 and table 19.

This figure shows college participation rates of high school graduates over the last 20 years. Despite the existence of financial aid programs to assist the college-bound from lower-income backgrounds, a poor young person in the United States continues to be much less likely to go to college than a more affluent one. In 1989, 78 percent of all high school graduates in the richest quartile in terms of family income (families earning $58,100 and over) were enrolled in or had attended college. For families in the poorest quartile (earning less than $20,000), only 45 percent of high school graduates were enrolled in or had attended college in 1989.

ing when it affects the poor. Lower-income Americans, who can hardly afford to lose any of their limited funds, are more likely to be robbed as well as to be assaulted or raped than are more affluent citizens (Langan and Innes, 1985). Furthermore, if accused of a crime, a person with low income and status is likely to be represented by an overworked public defender. Whether innocent or guilty, such a person may sit in jail for months because of an inability to raise the money for bail.

Even in the armed forces, social class standing in civilian life can be crucial to determining a person's fortunes. Members of lower classes were more likely to be drafted when the military draft was in operation. Once in the service, people from low- and moderate-income backgrounds are more likely to die in combat. Research indicates that during the wars in Korea and Vietnam (see Figure 8-4), soldiers from the lower social classes suffered a higher casualty rate than the more affluent, who tended to be among the ranks of officers (F. Peterson, 1987; J. Willis, 1975; Zeitlin et al., 1973:328).

Two other studies document the impact of class, status, and power on the likelihood that a young man would end up fighting in Vietnam. A Harvard University undergraduate from the class of 1970 surveyed his 1200 classmates and found that only 56 had entered the U.S. military and only 2 had served in Vietnam. Another report revealed that of the 234 sons of United States senators or members of the House of Representatives who reached draft age during the war in Vietnam, more than half (118) received draft deferments. Only 19 of these young men engaged in combat in Vietnam; only one was wounded (Baskir and Strauss, 1978:9; MacPherson, 1984:141).

Differences in life chances based on race and ethnicity were evident in 1991 during the war in the Persian Gulf. Only two members of Congress (one of whom was Hispanic) had children serving in Operation Desert Storm. Although Blacks and Hispanics together constitute only 20 percent of all young adults in the United States, about 36 percent of the nation's military personnel in the Gulf were Black or Hispanic. In some respects, these data reflect the irony that the all-volunteer armed forces offer more career options for many minority citizens than are available to them in civilian life (Howlett and Keen, 1991).

In these and many other areas of life, stratification is important. This is true not only in the United States but around the world. For example, despite reforms in Sweden aimed at opening educational opportunities to all classes, the gap between working-class and upper-class young people remains. Swedish educator Allan Svensson has reported 1982 data showing that the chances of a Swede's becoming a doctor, dentist, or lawyer are nearly 50 times greater if he or she comes from the upper class rather than from the lower class. Similarly, in the Soviet Union, children from a peasant background are one-fifth as likely to go to college as are children from well-educated families (Ryd, 1982; Shipler, 1983:197).

Wealth, status, and power may not ensure happiness, but they certainly provide additional ways

FIGURE 8-4 Occupations and Poverty Status of Fathers of Servicemen Killed in the War in Vietnam

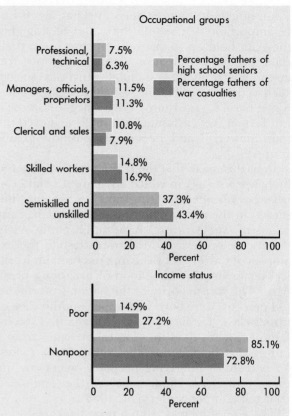

SOURCE: Data from Zeitlin et al., 1973:328.

These graphs contrast the occupations and incomes of fathers of servicemen from Wisconsin killed in Vietnam with fathers of Wisconsin high school seniors. It appears that sons of poor and working-class fathers were disproportionately likely to die in combat. For example, whereas not quite 15 percent of the fathers of high school seniors were poor, more than 27 percent of the fathers of war casualties were poor.

of coping with one's problems and disappointments. For this reason, the opportunity for advancement is of special significance to those who are on the bottom of society looking up. These people want the rewards and privileges that are granted to high-ranking members of a culture.

SOCIAL MOBILITY

It is clear that stratification matters, that class position quietly influences one's life chances. It can be important that people have the feeling that they can hold on to or even improve upon their class position. But how significant—how frequent, how dramatic—is mobility in a class society such as the United States? Ronald Reagan's father was a barber, and Jimmy Carter began as a peanut farmer, yet each man eventually achieved the most powerful and prestigious position in our country.

Does this mean that the United States is a genuinely open society in which any parent's child can become president? Thus far, no woman has served in the nation's highest office, nor has any man who was African American, Hispanic, Asian American, or Jewish. Moreover, despite the examples of Carter and Reagan, class remains a critical factor in one's likelihood of becoming president. The vast majority of the nation's presidents (82 percent) were born into upper-middle-class or upper-class families. Even Abraham Lincoln, famous for his days in a log cabin, came from a family that belonged to the community's richest 15 percent of taxpaying property owners by the time young Abraham reached the age of 5 (Baltzell and Schneiderman, 1988).

The rise of a child from a poor background to the presidency—or to some other position of great prestige, power, or financial reward—is an example of social mobility. The term *social mobility* refers to movement of individuals or groups from one position of a society's stratification system to another.

Open versus Closed Class Systems

Sociologists use the terms *open class system* and *closed class system* to distinguish between two ideal types of class system in terms of social mobility. An *open system* implies that the position of each individual is influenced by the person's achieved status. *Achieved status,* as we saw in Chapter 5, is a social position attained by a person largely through his or her own effort. In an open class system, competition among members of society is encouraged. The United States is moving toward this ideal type as it attempts to reduce barriers to mobility faced by women, racial and ethnic minorities, and people born in lower social classes.

At the other extreme of the social mobility system is the *closed system,* in which there is little or no possibility of individual mobility. The slavery and caste systems of stratification, and to a lesser extent the estate system, are examples of closed systems. In such societies, social placement is based on ascribed characteristics, such as race or family background, which cannot easily be changed. As noted earlier, *ascribed status* is a social position "assigned" to a person by society without regard for the person's unique characteristics or talents.

As with other ideal types, the extremes of open and closed systems do not actually exist as pure forms. For example, in caste societies mobility is occasionally possible through **hypergamy**—a woman's marriage to a man of a higher caste. In the relatively open class system of the United States, children from affluent families retain many privileges and advantages. Therefore, any class system should properly be regarded as open or closed in varying degrees.

Types of Social Mobility

Following the lead of Pitirim Sorokin (1959, original edition 1927), contemporary sociologists distinguish between horizontal and vertical social mobility. *Horizontal mobility* refers to the movement of a person from one social position to another of the same rank. If we use the prestige rankings presented earlier in Table 8-3, an athlete who becomes a reporter would be experiencing horizontal mobility. Each occupation has the same prestige ranking: 51 on a scale ranging from a low of 10 to a high of 90. If the reporter later left a Los Angeles newspaper for a similar job at a newspaper in Chicago, he or she would once again experience horizontal mobility.

Most sociological analysis, however, focuses on vertical rather than horizontal mobility. *Vertical mobility* refers to the movement of a person from one social position to another of a different rank. An athlete who becomes a lawyer (prestige ranking of 76) would experience vertical mobility. So,

BOX 8-3 • EVERYDAY BEHAVIOR

"YOU CAN'T TAKE DORCHESTER OUT OF THE BOY"

Sociologist David Karp (1986) recalls growing up in Dorchester, a lower-middle-class neighborhood of Boston. Throughout his school years, he heard the saying "You can take the boy out of Dorchester, but you can't take Dorchester out of the boy." In effect, such a proposition (or a revised proposition applicable to both men and women) suggests that coming of age in a less-than-affluent community is a master status—a significant ascribed status that follows people throughout their lives (see Chapter 5). Karp observes that an important and typically neglected aspect of social mobility is the process whereby the individual subjectively experiences his or her new status.

In studying mobility, Karp conducted 100 in-depth interviews with professionals in their fifties who reflected on their career paths. One-fourth of these professionals explicitly noted that they had risen from lower-class or working-class origins, thereby experiencing upward intergenerational mobility. In moving into social networks largely populated by professionals from middle-class

backgrounds, many of these men and women felt an initial bewilderment. "My feeling was that these people were onto something better than what I knew," admits a male psychologist. "I was scared about what they would think of me." A female public relations director for a hospital adds that she consciously sought to overcome her working-class origins: "I felt coming from my background a great need to prove myself" (Karp, 1986:24–25).

However successful these professionals are today, Karp's interview subjects are periodically reminded of their lower-class or working-class roots. While they may have escaped Dorchester and similar neighborhoods, it is not so easy to escape the prejudices within their current social networks concerning lower-class and working-class people. An innocent (or not-so-innocent) remark by a friend or coworker may underscore the glaring contrast between the childhoods of those who grew up in affluence and those from communities like Dorchester. As one result, the upwardly mobile professionals who spoke with Karp may never feel fully at home

in their new and more luxurious surroundings. For example, the public relations director quoted above feels uncomfortable calling upon affluent people and asking them to make substantial financial contributions to her hospital.

Moreover, because they have experienced some degree of upward mobility, such professionals seem to accept barriers to future advancement. They admit to holding their positions with a good deal of discomfort and insecurity. As one economist told Karp, "I'm probably better than I give myself credit for. . . . I tend to be hard on myself" (Karp, 1986:31). Many of these men and women had not expected to get as far as they did, given their modest origins, and some appear to limit their further achievements owing to a continuing sense of self-doubt.

Clearly, upward intergenerational mobility requires certain sensitive adjustments to one's new social environment. As Karp's interviews illustrate, people's class of origin (such as "Dorchester") can influence their feelings and self-images throughout their lives (see also Aversa, 1987).

too, would an athlete who becomes a sales clerk (prestige ranking of 29). Thus, vertical mobility can involve moving upward or downward in a society's stratification system (C. Heller, 1969: 309–310).

One way of examining vertical social mobility is to contrast intergenerational and intragenerational mobility. *Intergenerational mobility* involves changes in the social position of children relative

to their parents. Thus, a plumber whose father was a physician provides an example of downward intergenerational mobility. A film star whose parents were both factory workers illustrates upward intergenerational mobility. The impact of such mobility on the individual cannot be understated. In Box 8-3, we view upward intergenerational mobility from an interactionist perspective.

Intragenerational mobility involves changes in a person's social position within his or her adult life. A woman who enters the paid labor force as a teacher's aide and eventually becomes superintendent of the school district has experienced upward intragenerational mobility. A man who becomes a taxicab driver after his accounting firm goes bankrupt has undergone downward intragenerational mobility.

Another type of vertical mobility is *structural* or *stratum mobility.* These terms refer to the vertical movement of a specific group, class, or occupation relative to others in the stratification system. For example, historical circumstances or changes in the labor market may lead to the rise or decline of an occupational group within the social hierarchy. Military officers and strategists are likely to be regarded highly in times of war or foreign policy crises. As our information retrieval systems rely increasingly on machines, computer technicians are receiving respect previously reserved for lawyers and scientists. An influx of immigrants may also alter class alignments—especially if the new arrivals are disproportionately highly skilled or unskilled.

Efforts at structural mobility may be consciously undertaken by the groups themselves. Thus, in an effort to generate more dignified and prestigious images of their work, garbage collectors have begun to call themselves "sanitation engineers" and maids have selected the label "household technicians."

Even in the rigid caste systems of India, one low-status group, the subcaste of "toddy tappers," attempted to improve itself through structural mobility. Toddy tappers, also known as *Nadars,* had the historic task of climbing palmyra palm trees to collect the sap, known as *toddy.* Often these persons would become deformed or physically disabled after a lifetime of climbing; some even fell to their deaths. However, during the 1700s, the Nadars became dissatisfied with their oppressive work and low status and organized a movement to raise their collective status within the caste system. Gradually, more and more Nadars refused to tap the palms, and some began to learn mercantile skills. Members of the caste became vegetarians—a practice associated with higher castes. There was strong resistance to the Nadars' effort to improve their social standing, including riots protesting their actions at the end of the nineteenth century. Today, Nadars in rural areas still work as toddy tappers, but those in cities are more prosperous and are viewed as higher in rank. While the Nadars have not fully succeeded in achieving upward structural mobility, they have gained a deeper sense of self-respect and have widened their options within a generally restrictive caste system (Hardgrave, 1969; Spradley and McCurdy, 1980:161–166).

Social Mobility in the United States

The belief in upward mobility is an important aspect of American society. Does this mean that the United States is indeed the land of opportunity? Not if the phrase "land of opportunity" implies that such ascriptive characteristics as race, gender, and family background have ceased to be significant in determining one's future prospects.

Two sociological studies conducted a decade apart offer insight into the degree of mobility in the American occupational structure. The highly regarded work of Peter Blau and Otis Duncan (1967) was followed by the research of David Featherman and Robert Hauser (1978), two of Duncan's students, who replicated the earlier study. Taken together, these investigations led to several noteworthy conclusions. First, occupational mobility (which can be intergenerational or intragenerational) has been common among males. Approximately 60 to 70 percent of sons are employed in different and higher-ranked occupations than their fathers.

Second, although there is a great deal of mobility in American society, much of it covers a very "short distance." By this, researchers mean that people who reach an occupational level different from that of their parents usually advance or fall back only one or two out of a possible eight occupational levels. Thus, the child of a laborer may become an artisan or a technician, but he or she is less likely to become a manager or professional. The odds against reaching the top, then, are extremely high unless one begins from a relatively privileged position.

Third, as the later study by Featherman and Hauser (1978:381–384) documents, occupational mobility among African Americans remains sharply limited by racial discrimination (see Chapter 10). Even when the researchers compared Black and White males who had similar levels of schooling, parental background, and early career experience, the achievement levels of Blacks were less than those of Whites. The researchers have also noted that Blacks are more likely than Whites to be downwardly mobile and less likely to be upwardly mobile. Featherman and Hauser offer evidence that there is a modest decline in the significance of race; yet, their conclusions must be regarded with some caution, since they did not consider households with no adult male present or individuals who were not counted in the labor force (Gintis, 1980).

A final conclusion of both studies is that education plays a critical role in social mobility. The impact of formal schooling on adult status is even greater than that of family background (although, as we saw in our discussion of stratification and life chances, family background influences the likelihood that one will receive a higher education). Furthermore, education represents an important way of effecting intergenerational mobility. Three-fourths of college-educated men achieved some upward mobility, compared with only 12 percent of those who received no schooling (see also J. Davis, 1982).

It should be noted, however, that the impact of education on mobility has diminished somewhat in the last decade. While completing a college education remains essential for occupational success, an undergraduate degree—a B.A. or B.S.—serves less as a guarantee of upward mobility than it did in the past—simply because more and more entrants into the job market now hold such a degree. Moreover, intergenerational mobility is declining, since there is no longer such a stark difference between generations. Whereas in earlier decades many high school-educated parents successfully sent their children to college, today's college students are increasingly likely to have college-educated parents (Hout, 1988).

Many Americans continue to believe that anyone with ability can get ahead and that anyone who cannot make it is personally responsible for his or her failures. Yet, as the research of Blau and Duncan, as well as that of Featherman and

Hauser, suggests, social mobility in our culture is restricted in important ways. Disadvantaged individuals simply do not have an equal chance of becoming heart surgeons, distinguished novelists, or members of the United States Senate. In fact, as Christopher Jencks (1979) and his associates have indicated in their book *Who Gets Ahead?* family background remains a crucial factor in one's movement within this country's stratification system. Children from families in the top 20 percent in terms of income will, as adults, have incomes of 150 to 186 percent of the national average. By contrast, children from the bottom 20 percent will earn only 56 to 67 percent of the national average during their adult years. Once again, stratification makes a difference.

Thus far, although we have given some consideration to the impact of race on mobility, we have primarily dealt with social mobility as a monolithic phenomenon. However, gender, like race, is an important factor in one's mobility. Earlier we noted that studies of class have only recently given serious consideration to the occupations and incomes of women as determinants of social rank. Studies of mobility, even more than those of class, have traditionally ignored the significance of gender, but some research findings are now available which explore the relationship between gender and mobility.

As we will discuss in more detail in Chapter 11, women's employment opportunities are much more limited than men's. According to recent research, women are more likely than men to withdraw entirely from the paid labor force when faced with downward mobility because of a substantial gap between their employment skills and the jobs being offered them. This withdrawal violates an assumption common to traditional mobility studies: that most people will aspire to upward mobility and seek to make the most of their opportunities.

In contrast to men, women have a rather large range of clerical occupations open to them. Yet many of these positions have modest salary ranges and limited prospects for advancement, thereby severely restricting the possibility of upward mobility. Moreover, self-employment as shopkeepers, entrepreneurs, independent professionals, and the like—an important road to upward mobility for men—has often been closed to women. Although sons commonly follow in the footsteps of their fathers, women are unlikely to move into these areas even when their fathers held such positions. Consequently, gender remains an important factor in shaping social mobility within American society. Moreover, as we will discuss in the social policy section, women are especially likely to be trapped in poverty and unable to rise out of their low-income status (Hout, 1988; Kerbo, 1991:360–362).

THE FEMINIZATION OF POVERTY

- How do sociologists view the life chances of low-income single mothers and their children?
- According to conflict theorists, why are women more likely than men to fall below the poverty line?
- To what extent has the feminization of poverty become a cause for concern around the world?

Since World War II, a disturbing trend has been evident in the United States: the *feminization of poverty*. This term is used by social scientists to refer to the increasing proportion of the nation's poor who are female. As noted earlier, in 1959 female-headed households accounted for 26 percent of the nation's poor; by 1989, that figure (as seen in Table 8-4) had risen to 52 percent (Bureau of the Census, 1990b:56).

About half of American women in poverty are in "transition," coping with an economic crisis caused by the departure, disability, or death of a husband. The other half tend to be economically dependent either on the welfare system or on friends or relatives living nearby. The study of poverty by Greg Duncan (1984:79–82) discussed earlier pointed to women's role among welfare recipients. Female heads of households were overrepresented (67 percent) among persistent welfare recipients and constituted an even larger share (78 percent) of those recipients continually dependent on welfare sources for more than half of all income.

A key factor in the feminization of poverty has been the increase in families with women as single heads (see Chapter 13). In the period 1970–1988, the number of such families living in poverty—whether headed by divorced or never-married mothers—rose by 86 percent. By contrast, there was a 2 percent decrease during the same period for other types of families living below the poverty line. In 1988, among single mothers with children under the age of 18, the poverty rate was 38 percent for Whites, 56 percent for Blacks, and 59 percent for Hispanics (Bureau of the Census, 1989a:58, 62–65).

According to economist Isabel Sawhill of the Urban Institute, the feminization of poverty accounts for virtually all the 53 percent increase in the nation's poverty rolls since 1970. Consequently, the President's National Advisory Council on Economic Opportunity has warned that if this trend were to continue, the "poverty population would be composed solely of women and their children before the year 2000" (Rodgers, 1987:7). Not surprisingly, the life chances of these low-income families are far from ideal. Children whose mothers live in poverty run an increased risk of birth defects and malnutrition. They are more likely to fare poorly in elementary school and to drop out of high school than are children from other types of families. Low-income single mothers suffer higher levels of stress than other Americans and are much less likely to receive adequate medical care.

It must be emphasized that poor women share many social characteristics with poor men: low educational attainment, lack of market-relevant job skills, and residence in economically deteriorating areas. However, in the view of conflict theorists, the higher rates of poverty among women can be traced to three distinct causes. Because of the difficulty in finding affordable child care (see Chapter 4), sex discrimination on the job (see Chapter 11), and sexual harassment (see Chapter 6), women are at a clear disadvantage in the labor market in terms of both horizontal and vertical social mobility. As one reflection of this problem, the median income of a full-time, year-round, female worker was only $18,769 in 1989, compared with $27,331 for a comparable male worker (Bureau of the Census, 1990b:53).

The burden of supporting a family is especially difficult for single mothers not only because of low salaries but also because of inadequate child support. According to studies by the Bureau of the Census (1990e), the average payment for child support in 1987 was a mere $2710 per year, or about $52 per week. This level of support is clearly insufficient for rearing a child in the 1990s. Moreover, of the 5.6 million American women scheduled to receive child support payments from their former husbands in 1987, only 51 percent actually received all the money they were scheduled to get, while 25 percent received some of the money due and 24 percent did not receive any of the scheduled payments. In light of these data, federal and state officials have intensified efforts to track down delinquent parents and ensure payment of child support. Policymakers acknowledge that such enforcement efforts have led to substantial reductions in welfare expenditures (Hinds, 1989).

Welfare payments to single mothers remain far from adequate. About 4 million women receive Aid to Families with Dependent Children (AFDC) benefits for themselves and their 7 million dependent children. However, in 1988, the average monthly AFDC payment for a family was only $379. In the view of the Children's Defense Fund, AFDC benefits in most states are "intolerably low, failing to provide even a minimum level of decency" (Bureau of the Census, 1990a:367; Ehrenreich and Stallard, 1982:219–220).

As concern has increased about the feminization of poverty, members of the Congressional Caucus on Women's Issues have developed a remedial legislative package known as the *Economic Equity Act*. By the late 1980s, the bills in this package covered both work and family issues affecting women and their children. The work sections of the package would require pay equity for jobs of comparable skill, equal access to commercial credit, health and pension benefits for temporary and part-time workers, and other measures of economic security. The family sections address a wide range of issues, including the need for high-quality, affordable child care services (see Chapter 4) and for stronger enforcement of child support laws (L. Williams, 1987:B9).

While conflict theory would seem to embrace the view of women as overwhelmingly victimized by poverty, not all sociologists concur. Martha Gimenez (1990) argues that the feminization of poverty view ignores the fact that not all women are at risk; she emphasizes that poverty is a class issue, not a gender issue. With this in mind, too strong a focus on women—or, for that matter, on racial or ethnic minorities—may

By 1989, female-headed households accounted for 52 percent of the low-income population of the United States, reflecting what has been called the feminization of poverty.

serve to obscure relevant societal forces that affect *all* poor people. Consequently, from Gimenez's perspective, while certain measures (such as child support enforcement) carry special significance for low-income women, the true remedy for the nation's poverty will require a more significant restructuring and redistribution of wealth and income.

While American policymakers attempt to address the problem of the feminization of poverty, this distressing phenomenon has become evident around the world. During the last decade, female-headed families have become an increasing proportion of Canada's low-income population. This trend is also noticeable throughout Europe, in developing countries, and even in three widely differing nations whose legislation on behalf of women is the most advanced in the

CHAPTER 8 • STRATIFICATION AND SOCIAL MOBILITY

world: Israel, Sweden, and the Soviet Union. In these countries, national health care programs, housing subsidies, and other forms of government assistance cushion the impact of poverty somewhat, yet the feminization of poverty advances nevertheless (Abowitz, 1986; Rodgers, 1987:95–111; H. Scott, 1985).

SUMMARY

Stratification is structured ranking of entire groups of people that perpetuates unequal economic rewards and power in a society. In this chapter, we examine four general systems of stratification, various components of stratification, the explanations offered by functionalist and conflict sociologists for the existence of social inequality, and the relationship between stratification and social mobility.

1 All cultures are characterized by some degree of ***social inequality.***

2 The most extreme form of legalized social inequality for individuals or groups is ***slavery.***

3 In contrast to other systems of stratification, the boundaries between social classes are less precisely defined.

4 Karl Marx viewed class differentiation as the crucial determinant of social, economic, and political inequality.

5 Max Weber identified three analytically distinct components of stratification: class, status, and power.

6 Functionalists argue that stratification is necessary so that people will be motivated to fill society's important positions; conflict theorists see stratification as a major source of societal tension and conflict.

7 The category of the "poor" defies any simple definition and counters common stereotypes about low-income people.

8 The affluent and powerful not only have more material possessions than others; they also benefit in terms of educational opportunities, health, and even casualty rates while in the armed forces.

9 ***Social mobility*** is more likely to be found in an ***open system*** that emphasizes ***achieved status*** than in a ***closed system*** that focuses on ascribed characteristics.

10 Despite prevailing beliefs about the possibilities of upward mobility in the United States, our society places significant restrictions on the mobility of individuals and groups.

11 A key factor in the feminization of poverty has been the dramatic increase in single-mother households.

KEY TERMS

Absolute poverty A standard of poverty based on a minimum level of subsistence below which families should not be expected to exist. (page 242)

Achieved status A social position attained by a person largely through his or her own effort. (248)

Ascribed status A social position "assigned" to a person by society without regard for the person's unique talents or characteristics. (228)

Bourgeoisie Karl Marx's term for the capitalist class, comprising the owners of the means of production. (231)

Capitalism An economic system in which the means of production are largely in private hands, and the main incentive for economic activity is the accumulation of profits. (231)

Castes Hereditary systems of rank, usually religiously dictated, that are relatively fixed and immobile. (226)

Class A term used by Max Weber to refer to people who have a similar level of wealth and income. (232)

Class consciousness In Karl Marx's view, a subjective awareness held by members of a class regarding their common vested interests and need for collective political action to bring about social change. (231)

Class system A social ranking based primarily on economic position in which achieved characteristics can influence mobility. (227)

Closed system A social system in which there is little or no possibility of individual mobility. (248)

Estate system A system of stratification under which peasants were required to work land leased to them by nobles in exchange for military protection and other services. Also known as *feudalism.* (227)

Esteem The reputation that a particular individual has within an occupation. (236)

False consciousness A term used by Karl Marx to describe an attitude held by members of a class that does not accurately reflect its objective position. (231)

Horizontal mobility The movement of an individual from one social position to another of the same rank. (248)

Hypergamy A woman's marriage to a man of a higher caste. (248)

Income Salaries and wages. (225)

Intergenerational mobility Changes in the social position of children relative to their parents. (249)

Intragenerational mobility Changes in a person's social position within his or her adult life. (250)

Life chances Max Weber's term for people's opportunities to provide themselves with material goods, positive living conditions, and favorable life experiences. (245)

Objective method A technique for measuring social class that assigns individuals to classes on the basis of criteria such as occupation, education, income, and place of residence. (236)

Open system A social system in which the position of each individual is influenced by his or her achieved status. (248)

Power The ability to exercise one's will over others. (232)

Prestige The respect and admiration with which an occupation is regarded by society. (236)

Proletariat Karl Marx's term for the working class in a capitalist society. (231)

Relative poverty A floating standard of deprivation by which people at the bottom of a society, whatever their lifestyles, are judged to be disadvantaged in comparison with the nation as a whole. (242)

Slavery A system of enforced servitude in which people are legally owned by others and in which enslaved status is transferred from parents to children. (226)

Social inequality A condition in which members of a society have different amounts of wealth, prestige, or power. (224)

Social mobility Movement of individuals or groups from one position of a society's stratification system to another. (248)

Status group A term used by Max Weber to refer to people who have the same prestige or lifestyle, independent of their class positions. (232)

Stratification A structured ranking of entire groups of people that perpetuates unequal economic rewards and power in a society. (224)

Stratum mobility Another name for *structural mobility*. (250)

Structural mobility The vertical movement of a specific group, class, or occupation relative to others in the stratification system. (250)

Underclass Long-term poor people who lack training and skills. (240)

Vertical mobility The movement of a person from one social position to another of a different rank. (248)

Wealth An inclusive term encompassing all of a person's material assets, including land and other types of property. (225)

ADDITIONAL READINGS

Dahrendorf, Ralf. *Reflections on the Revolution in Europe.* New York: Random House, 1990. A noted sociologist views recent events in this region as a vote for an open society over a closed society, but warns that the continuing challenge will be to sustain economic growth.

Ehrenreich, Barbara. *Fear of Falling: The Inner Life of the Middle Class.* New York: Pantheon, 1989. This journalistic but well-documented volume looks at the nature of classes in the United States.

Levy, Frank. *Dollars and Dreams: The Changing American Income Distribution.* New York: Russell Sage, 1987. A detailed examination of the changes over time in the nation's income distribution.

Rodgers, Harrell R., Jr. *Poor Women, Poor Families.* Armonk, N.Y.: Sharpe, 1987. This book analyzes data on the changing profile of low-income families over the last 30 years and provides a clear view of poverty among women.

Vanneman, Reeve, and Lynn Weber Cannon. *The American Perception of Class.* Philadelphia: Temple University Press, 1987. Two sociologists argue that class consciousness does exist in the United States, especially among the working class.

Voydanoff, Patricia, and Linda C. Majka (eds.). *Families and Economic Distress.* Newbury Park, Calif.: Sage, 1988. Published in cooperation with the National Council on Family Relations, this volume documents the effects of unemployment and economic dislocation on the family.

Wilson, William Julius (ed.). *The Ghetto Underclass: Social Science Perspectives.* Newbury Park, Calif.: Sage, 1989. This book examines the use of the term *underclass* by social scientists and the applicability of this concept to the poor of the United States.

Journals

Among the journals focusing on issues of stratification, social class, and social mobility are *American Journal of Economics and Sociology* (founded in 1941), *Humanity and Society* (1977), and *Review of Black Political Economy* (1970). See also the *Current Population Reports* series published by the Bureau of the Census.

9

SOCIAL INEQUALITY WORLDWIDE

For any state, however small, is in fact divided into two, one the state of the poor, the other of the rich; these are at war with one another.

Plato
The Republic, ca. 290 B.C.

LOOKING AHEAD

- How has the process of diffusion contributed to the emergence of a world marketplace?
- What are the four cultural phases evident in societies undergoing modernization?
- What impact do multinational corporations have on the world's developing nations?
- Which nations have the highest and lowest levels of income inequality?
- How does immigration influence social mobility?
- How has the legacy of slavery shaped race relations in Brazil?
- Why is there such international concern over growing debt in the Third World?

Alan Durning (1990:22), a global environmental researcher, notes that in the world's industrial nations, the twentieth century is often viewed as an "era of economic miracles." Yet Durning pointedly adds that the "poor tell a different tale."

As one example, a young Guatemalan Indian woman describes the misery and powerlessness of life on the coffee plantations where her family and thousands of other Indians have worked as migrant workers:

> Two of my brothers died in the plantation. The first, he was the eldest, was called Felipe. . . . They'd sprayed the coffee with pesticide by plane while we were working, as they usually did, and my brother

couldn't stand the fumes and died. . . . The second one, his name was Nicolás, . . . died when I was eight. . . . He was two then. When my little brother started crying, crying, crying, my mother didn't know what to do. . . . He lasted fifteen days. . . . (Durning, 1990:30).

Durning points out that while the world has 157 billionaires and perhaps as many as 2 million millionaires, some 100 million people live on city streets, in garbage dumps, and under bridges. He emphasizes that the concerns of the rich differ radically from those of the poor:

> Americans spend $5 billion each year on special diets to lower their calorie consumption, while the world's poorest 400 million people are so undernourished they are likely to suffer stunted growth, mental retardation, or even death. As water from a single spring in France is bottled and shipped to the prosperous around the world, 1.9 billion people drink and bathe in water contaminated with deadly parasites and pathogens. More than half of humanity lacks sanitary toilets. In 1988 the world's nations devoted $1 trillion—$200 for each person on the planet—to the means of warfare, but failed to scrape together the $5 per child it would have cost to eradicate the diseases that killed 14 million that year (Durning, 1990:22).

As Durning reminds us, worldwide stratification is evident in the gap between those enjoying lavish wealth and those suffering from overwhelming poverty. This chapter will focus on stratification around the world, beginning with an examination of who controls the world marketplace. The impact of colonialism and neocolonialism on social inequality will be studied, as will world systems theory and the immense power of multinational corporations. After this macro-level examination of the disparity between rich and poor countries, we will focus on stratification *within* the nations of the world through discussions of the distribution of wealth and income, comparative perspectives on prestige, and comparative social mobility. To better understand inequality in another country, we will present a case study of stratification in Brazil. Finally, in the social policy section, we will address the crisis of skyrocketing Third World debt and its contribution to social inequality and world poverty.

STRATIFICATION IN THE WORLD SYSTEM: A GLOBAL PERSPECTIVE

As we saw in Chapter 3, the term *diffusion* refers to the process by which a cultural item is spread from group to group or society to society. Diffusion has been escalating in recent decades because of improved worldwide transportation and communication. In a very real sense, the world is not so large as it once was: one can travel from New York to Tokyo, or reach someone a continent away by telephone or FAX machine, much more quickly than has ever been possible. One result is that the world can now be conceived of as a single marketplace.

There is even evidence of a certain commonality in buyers' preferences around the world. The manufactured goods that appear in the stalls and markets of Accra, Ghana, are no longer markedly different from goods available in Djakarta, Indonesia. The plastic pail has replaced the gourd, the earthen pot, and the banana leaf. Electric batteries have taken over many of the functions of kerosene, wood, and vegetable oil (R. Vernon, 1977:4).

While the marketplace is gradually being unified in terms of space and tastes, the profits of business are not equally shared. There remains a substantial disparity between the world's "have" and "have-not" nations. For example, in 1990 the average value of goods and services produced per citizen (per capita gross national product) in the United States, Canada, Switzerland, and Norway was more than $16,760. By contrast, the figure was $400 in several poorer countries. The 140 developing nations accounted for 75 percent of the world's population but possessed only 20 percent of all wealth (Haub et al., 1990; Strasser et al., 1981). These contrasts are vividly illustrated in Figure 9-1 (page 260). Two forces discussed below are particularly responsible for the domination of the world marketplace by a few nations: the legacy of colonialism and the advent of multinational corporations.

Colonialism, Neocolonialism, and World Systems Theory

Colonialism is the maintenance of political, social, economic, and cultural domination over a people by a foreign power for an extended period of time (W. Bell, 1981b). In simple terms, it is rule by outsiders. The long reign of the British Empire over much of North America, parts of Africa, and India is an example of colonial domination. The same can be said of French rule over Algeria, Tunisia, and other parts of north Africa.

Relations between the colonial nation and the colonized people are similar to those between the dominant capitalist class and the proletariat as described by Karl Marx. In the words of political philosopher Albert Memmi (1967:8), who grew up in Tunisia under French colonial rule:

> [The colonizer] finds himself on one side of a scale, the other side of which bears the colonial man. If his living standards are high, it is because those of the colonized are low; if he can benefit from plentiful and undemanding labor and servants, it is because the colonized can be exploited at will. . . ; if he can easily obtain administrative positions, it is because they are reserved for him and the colonized are excluded from them; the more freely he breathes, the more the colonized are choked.

By the 1980s, colonialism had largely become a phenomenon of the past; most of the world's nations that were colonies before World War I had achieved political independence and established their own governments. However, for many of

FIGURE 9-1 Worldwide Gross National Product per Capita

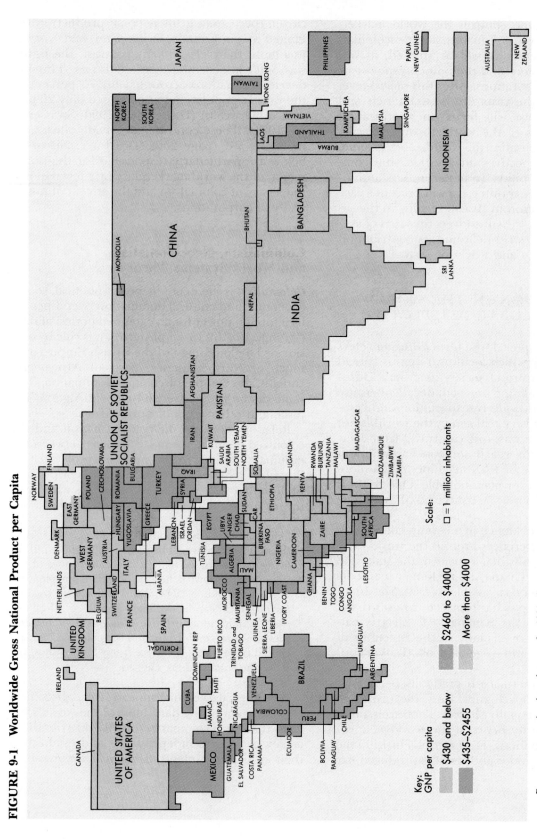

NOTE: Data on gross national product are for 1988, the most recent year for which such comparative data are available.
SOURCES: Crow and Thomas, 1983:14; Haub et al., 1990.

This stylized map reflects the different sizes in population of the world's nations. The color for each country shows the gross national product (the total value of goods and services produced by the nation in a given year) per capita. As the map shows, some of the world's most populous nations—such as the People's Republic of China, India, Indonesia, Bangladesh, and Pakistan—are among the countries with the lowest standard of living as measured by per capita gross national product.

these countries, the transition to genuine self-rule was not yet complete. Colonial domination had established patterns of economic exploitation that continued even after nationhood was achieved—in part because former colonies were unable to develop their own industry and technology. Their dependence on more industrialized nations, including their former colonial masters, for managerial and technical expertise, investment capital, and manufactured goods kept former colonies in a subservient position. Such continuing dependence and foreign domination is known as *neocolonialism.*

The economic and political consequences of colonialism and neocolonialism are quite evident. Drawing on the conflict perspective, sociologist Immanuel Wallerstein (1974, 1979) views the global economic system as divided between nations who control wealth and those from whom capital is taken. Neocolonialism is one means by which industrialized societies accumulate even more capital. Wallerstein has advanced a *world systems theory* of unequal economic and political relationships in which certain industrialized nations (among them, the United States, Japan, and Germany) and their multinational corporations are in a dominant position at the *core* of the system. Found at the *semiperiphery* of the system are countries with marginal economic status, such as Israel, Ireland, and South Korea. Wallerstein suggests that the poor developing countries of Asia, Africa, and Latin America are on the *periphery* of the world economic system. Their economies are controlled and exploited by core nations and corporations much as the old colonial empires ruled their colonies (Kerbo, 1991:495–498).

In addition to their political and economic impact, colonialism and neocolonialism have an important cultural component. The colonized people lose their native values and begin to identify with the culture of the colonial power (see Box 9-1 on page 262). The native language of the country is discarded and even hidden as people attempt to emulate the colonizers. Therefore, in the view of opponents of contemporary neocolonialism, every consumer product, film, or television program exported or designed by a colonial nation is an attack on the traditions and cultural autonomy of the dependent people. Even the popularity of *Batman* or *Dallas* may be viewed as a threat to native cultures when such programs dominate their media at the expense of local art forms. In reflecting on the dangers posed by television, Sembene Ousmane, one of Africa's most prominent writers and filmmakers, noted: "[Today] we are more familiar with European fairy tales than with our own traditional stories" (R. Emerson, 1968; T. McPhail, 1981:244–245; Memmi, 1967:105–108; Schramm et al., 1981; *World Development Forum,* 1990:4).

Modernization

For millions of people around the world, the introduction of television into their cultures is but one symbol of a revolutionary transition in day-to-day life. Contemporary sociologists use the term *modernization* to describe the far-reaching process by which a society moves from traditional or less developed institutions to those characteristic of more developed societies.

Wendell Bell (1981a), whose definition of modernization we are using, notes that modern societies tend to be urban, literate, and industrial. They have sophisticated transportation and media systems. Families tend to be organized within the nuclear family unit rather than the extended-family model (see Chapter 13). On the individual level, members of societies which have undergone modernization shift allegiance from such traditional sources of authority as parents and priests to newer authorities such as government officials.

Historian C. E. Black (1966) has identified four cultural phases common to all modernizing societies, which we can apply to a case study of the Republic of Kenya, an African nation of 25 million people (see Figure 9-2 on page 263). Black's first stage involves the introduction of modern ideas and social institutions. Initially, the impact of technological and institutional changes can be quite unsettling. The introduction of improved health measures in Kenya led to a rise in the birthrate, a decline in the death rate, and an overall increase in population growth; yet, at first, there were not adequate food supplies or school facilities to cope with the larger population.

BOX 9-1 • SPEAKING OUT

THE IMPACT OF TOURISM ON BALI

Growing opportunities for leisure have brought increasing numbers of tourists from the United States and other industrialized nations to remote sites in the developing countries. In the following selection, anthropologist Colin Turnbull (1982:26) strongly condemns tourists' insensitive and often ethnocentric behavior when visiting the island of Bali:

To the Balinese, their home is known as Pulau Dewata, or "Island of the Gods." But sometimes it seems that in the last few years the gods of Bali have descended in the form of tourists. With swimsuits and cameras as their sacred symbols, they appear to hold the power of both desecration and consecration.

The Balinese have traditionally considered their island to be safe as well as sacred, but tourism has changed that, too; from tourism and tourists there is little safety. . . . On this small and densely populated island (approaching 3 million people for its 2000 square miles), every village, if not every family, has somehow been affected by the massive influx of tourists, an influx so sudden and rapid, the islanders have had little time to adapt.

It would be easy enough to paint a totally negative picture of the impact of tourism on Bali. The

(UPI/Bettmann Newsphotos)

Colin Turnbull.

once beautiful sandy beach at Kuta, for instance, is now littered with bodies in various states of undress, interspersed with pimps, hawkers, and masseurs who move from body to body, plying their services. When I was there last year the beach was patrolled by two well-dressed prostitutes riding on scooters for ready pickup and delivery. Even the water was not entirely safe; to reach it one ran the risk of being run down by tourist youths racing and trick riding on motorcycles. And once in the water there was the danger of being hit by speedboats, towing large rubber dinghies loaded with shrieking tourists who seemed to have come thousands of miles to do what they could have done at home. . . .

Bali's modernization, urban development, and extraordinary economic growth, with all the corresponding benefits of medical, social, and educational services that had previously not existed, also have their negative aspects. It could be argued that prior to the descent of the tourist gods, for whose benefit the island seems largely to be administered, some of these services were not needed; they are needed now to combat problems brought by tourism itself. The economic benefits touch only a few, and the cost to all is high in terms of damage to the social fabric. How high might be measured by the increase in the rate of teenage suicide. . . .

The effect of tourism is perhaps most insidious and most pervasive in a cultural setting such as Bali. What is a small amount of money for the tourist may be a small fortune to the Balinese. Individual wealth in such measure, together with other material appurtenances of Western civilization brought by tourism, readily lures young men and women, even boys and girls, away from their homes and villages. Too late, they discover they have also been lured away from the security their traditions offered and from the ideals their lives were built around. . . .

Although Kenya is over 85 percent rural, modernization is clearly underway in its cities.

FIGURE 9-2   Stages of Modernization

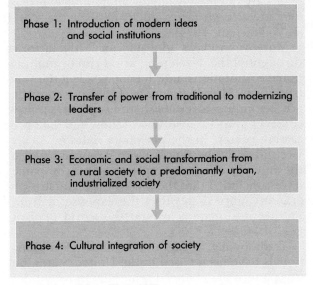

Phase 1: Introduction of modern ideas and social institutions

Phase 2: Transfer of power from traditional to modernizing leaders

Phase 3: Economic and social transformation from a rural society to a predominantly urban, industrialized society

Phase 4: Cultural integration of society

SOURCE: Adapted from Black, 1966.

Historian C. E. Black has identified four cultural phases common to all modernizing societies.

The next stage of modernization is marked by the transfer of power from traditional to modernizing leaders. For Kenya and most other developing nations, colonialism stimulated the initial use of modern technology, but it also delayed the development of new leaders. Kenya remained a British colony until 1962, and its people exercised little authority, as European settlers clung to their privileges and power.

Black's third phase of modernization involves economic and social transformation from a rural, horticultural society to a predominantly urban, industrialized society. Kenya is over 85 percent rural; at least one-third of its labor force is still engaged in subsistence agriculture or bartering of goods. Therefore, the nation has not completed this phase of modernization. Nevertheless, urbanization is clearly under way. Nairobi, the nation's capital and largest city, has grown twice as fast as the country as a whole.

The final stage of Black's model is the cultural integration of society (refer back to Chapter 3), which requires fundamental reorganization of the social structure. Ascribed characteristics such as gender and race become less important in gaining power. In contemporary Kenya, the 2 percent of the population descended from early European and Asian immigrants still play a dominant role in commerce and industry. However, their dominance has decreased somewhat since the nation achieved independence. Among Kenyans who are Black, the Kikuyu people, who account for 20 percent of the nation's population, are influential in the central government and the economy.

Upon independence, Kenyans turned to the charismatic Jomo Kenyatta, longtime organizer against colonial rule, for political leadership. Popularly elected and in office until his death in 1978, Kenyatta maintained a model of *harambee,* a Swahili term which means "let us all pull together." This motto symbolized his effort to bring together Kenyans—rural and urban, Black and White, of various tribes and groups. As one indicator of Kenyatta's effectiveness, presidential succession occurred peacefully following his death.

However, social inequality and ethnic unrest persist in contemporary Kenya. While a small, privileged African elite holds disproportionate wealth and power, the World Bank has estimated per capita annual income at $330. In 1985, the poorest 40 percent of people in Nairobi received only 13 percent of income. According to United Nations studies, about 30 percent of the nation's population is malnourished. The political situation in Kenya has been characterized as a retreat from democracy. Kenya has become a one-party state which no longer uses a secret ballot in elections and which exercises censorship of the press. In early 1991, the editor of the *Nairobi Law Monthly* was arrested for publishing the manifesto of a new political party (Barnet, 1990; Cowell, 1983; Harden, 1987; Perlez, 1991; Segal, 1982; C. Thompson et al., 1982).

From a conflict perspective, modernization in developing countries such as Kenya often perpetuates their dependence on more industrialized nations. For example, Kenya is the second-largest recipient of American assistance in sub-Saharan Africa, owing in good part to Kenya's anticommunist posture and to a 1980 defense agreement that gives the United States access to its airports and seaports. Conflict theorists view such continuing dependence on foreign powers as an example of contemporary neocolonialism.

Sociologist York Bradshaw (1988) has modified Immanuel Wallerstein's world system analysis as it relates to Kenya. After examining changes in the economy and the role of foreign capital since 1963, Bradshaw concluded that while multinational corporations obviously find it profitable to invest in Kenya, they do not completely dominate the nation's economy. These corporations are heavily taxed and are required by law to form joint ventures with local business people. However, as noted earlier, a small, privileged elite benefits from such foreign investment—while most Kenyans gain little from economic development.

Multinational Corporations

A key role in the neocolonialism of the 1990s is played by worldwide corporate giants. The term **multinational corporations** refers to commercial organizations which, while headquartered in one country, own or control other corporations and subsidiaries throughout the world. Such private trade and lending relationships are not new; merchants have conducted business abroad for hundreds of years, trading gems, spices, garments, and other goods. However, today's multinational giants are not merely buying and selling overseas; they are also *producing* goods all over the world (I. Wallerstein, 1974).

Moreover, today's "global factory" (the factories throughout the developing world run by multinational corporations) now has alongside it the "global office." Multinationals based in core countries are beginning to establish reservations services, centers to process insurance claims, and data processing centers in the periphery nations. As service industries become a more important part of the international marketplace, many companies have concluded that the low costs of overseas operations more than offset the expense of transmitting information around the world (J. Burgess, 1989).

Traditionally, a high percentage of multinationals have been based in the United States, but this pattern has changed somewhat in recent decades (see Table 9-1). The size of these global corporations should not be underestimated. For example, Samsung, only the twentieth-largest multinational, had 1989 sales of $35.2 billion—a figure

TABLE 9-1 The 20 Largest Industrial Companies in the World

RANK	COMPANY	HEADQUARTERS	INDUSTRY	SALES IN BILLIONS OF DOLLARS	PROFITS IN MILLIONS OF DOLLARS
1	General Motors	Detroit	Motor vehicles	127.0	4,224
2	Ford Motor	Dearborn, Mich.	Motor vehicles	96.9	3,835
3	Exxon	New York	Petroleum refining	86.7	3,510
4	Royal Dutch/ Shell Group	The Hague/ London	Petroleum refining	85.5	6,482
5	International Business Machines	Armonk, N.Y.	Computers	63.4	3,758
6	Toyota Motor	Toyota City, Japan	Motor vehicles	60.4	2,631
7	General Electric	Fairfield, Conn.	Electronics	55.3	3,939
8	Mobil	New York	Petroleum refining	51.0	1,809
9	Hitachi	Tokyo	Electronics	50.9	1,447
10	British Petroleum	London	Petroleum refining	49.5	3,499
11	IRI	Rome	Metals	49.1	1,778
12	Matsushita Electric Industrial	Osaka, Japan	Electronics	43.1	1,664
13	Daimler-Benz	Stuttgart, Germany	Motor vehicles	40.6	3,585
14	Philip Morris	New York	Food, tobacco	39.1	2,946
15	Fiat	Turin, Italy	Motor vehicles	36.7	2,410
16	Chrysler	Highland Park, Mich.	Motor vehicles	36.2	359
17	Nissan	Tokyo	Motor vehicles	36.1	890
18	Unilever	London/ Rotterdam	Food	35.3	1,730
19	E.I. du Pont de Nemours	Wilmington, Del.	Chemicals	35.2	2,480
20	Samsung	Kyonggi Do, South Korea	Electronics	35.2	515

SOURCE: Pak and Solo, 1990:269.

In 1990, 17 of the world's 50 largest industrial firms ranked by sales had their headquarters in the United States. By contrast, American-based firms had accounted for 42 of the 50 leaders in the year 1960.

which exceeded the final value of goods and services of Nigeria and Sri Lanka combined for the year. Even more striking is the fact that the sales of the top 200 multinational corporations account for almost 30 percent of the gross *world* product (George, 1988:12; World Bank, 1990:182).

Foreign sales represent an important source of profit for multinational corporations. For example, foreign subsidiaries account for about 40 percent of all sales of larger multinationals headquartered in the United States. In general, foreign sales have grown more rapidly than domestic sales for such corporations, a fact which encourages them to expand into other countries (in many cases, the developing nations). The economy of the United States is heavily dependent on foreign commerce, much of which is conducted by multinationals. According to a 1991 report by the Bureau of the Census (1991a), 1 out of 7 manufacturing jobs in the United States had to do with the export of goods to foreign countries (R. Müller and Domike, 1981).

Multinational corporations can have a positive impact on the developing nations of the world. They bring jobs and industry to areas where subsistence agriculture previously served as the only means of survival. Multinationals promote rapid development through diffusion of inventions and innovations from industrial nations. Viewed from a functionalist perspective, the combination of skilled technology and management provided by multinationals and the relatively cheap labor available in developing nations is ideal for a global enterprise. Multinationals can thus take maximum advantage of technology while reducing costs and boosting profits.

The international ties of multinational corporations also facilitate the exchange of ideas and technology around the world. Their worldwide influence contributes to interdependence among nations, which may prevent certain disputes from reaching the point of serious conflict. A country cannot afford to sever diplomatic relations, or engage in warfare, with a nation that is the headquarters for its main business suppliers or is a key outlet for exports.

Conflict theorists challenge this favorable evaluation of the impact of multinational corporations and emphasize that multinationals exploit local workers to maximize profits. They point out that when business firms build plants in places such as South Korea, residents (including those as young as 13 years old) may work 7 days a week, 10 hours a day, for as little as 62 cents an hour. More than 80 percent of the low-skilled assembly jobs in these plants are held by women, many of whom earn only $5 *per day*. These women perform monotonous, painstaking work under stressful and hazardous working conditions. For example, a study in South Korea found that most electronics assembly workers developed severe eye problems after 1 year of employment (Ehrenreich and Fuentes, 1981; Gittelsohn, 1987).

Because there is a pool of cheap labor available in the developing world, multinationals are able to move factories out of countries such as the United States, where organized labor insists on decent wages and humane working conditions, thereby increasing unemployment in core nations. Moreover, in the developing world it is difficult to build strong trade unions in factories run by multinational corporations. The ever-present danger exists that if labor's demands become threatening, the firm will simply move its plant elsewhere. As a result, governments seeking to attract or keep multinationals may develop a "climate for investment" which includes repressive antilabor laws restricting union activity and collective bargaining. Conflict theorists therefore conclude that, on the whole, multinational corporations have a negative social impact on workers in both industrialized and developing nations (Bluestone and Harrison, 1982; Harrison and Bluestone, 1988).

Several sociologists have surveyed the effects of foreign investment and concluded that although it may initially contribute to a host nation's wealth, it eventually increases economic inequality within developing nations. This is true in terms of both income and ownership of land. The upper and middle classes of such countries benefit most from economic expansion, while the lower classes are less likely to benefit. Such disparities result from the peculiarly uneven economic development which results from foreign investment. Multinationals invest in limited areas of an economy and in restricted regions of a nation. Although certain sectors of the host nation's

(Mary Beth Camp/Matrix)

Many American multinational corporations have opened factories in the developing world to take advantage of the pool of cheap labor. In this photograph, workers in the People's Republic of China are making "Big Bird" dolls for Hasbro.

economy expand, such as hotels and expensive restaurants, this very expansion appears to retard growth in agriculture and other economic sectors (Bornschier et al., 1978; Wallerstein, 1979).

Recent studies suggest that multinationals tend to generate income for a developing nation's elite, while at the same time undermining the market for goods produced by the poor. Moreover, multinationals consciously act to prevent reductions in inequality in host countries. For example, foreign corporations oppose increases in minimum wage levels and issue grants to support legislation that would restrict labor union activity. While the relationship between foreign investment and economic inequality needs further research, the best data currently available point directly to the conclusion that multinational corporations intensify inequality in the developing world (Moran, 1978).

Sociologist Dale Wimberley (1990) studied the impact of foreign investment on the infant mortality rates of 63 developing nations, among them Brazil, Egypt, India, and the Philippines. (The *infant mortality rate*—the number of deaths of infants under 1 year of age per 1000 live births in a given year—is widely regarded as an effective measure of general health care in a society.) Wimberley found that a reduction in the infant mor-

tality rate was most likely to occur when there was *less* penetration by multinational corporations into the local economy. How could outside investment be detrimental to a society's level of health? Wimberley concluded that foreign investment promotes low-wage labor and therefore income inequality within developing countries—which, in turn, retards advances in health care (Bornschier and Chase-Dunn, 1985; Bradshaw, 1988).

In many respects, the rise of multinational corporations has become a threat to national sovereignty. The economically poor countries of Asia, Africa, and Latin America rely almost totally upon foreign nations for their advanced technology, a reliance that perpetuates patterns of neocolonialism. Yet this dilemma is not limited to developing countries. Foreign corporations (mostly headquartered in the United States) control 60 percent of Canada's manufacturing, 75 percent of its petroleum and natural gas industry, and 60 percent of its mining and smelting industries (J. W. Coleman and Cressey, 1980:41–42).

One of the most flagrant illustrations of the power of multinationals took place in Chile. In 1970, International Telephone and Telegraph (ITT) attempted to stop a Marxist politician, Salvador Allende, from coming to power—even though he was running for the Chilean presidency in a free and democratic election. After Allende was victorious, ITT and the Central Intelligence Agency (CIA) participated in the overthrow of the legally constituted government. In 1973, Allende and many of his supporters died during a bloody military coup. The elected regime was then replaced by a military dictatorship which was widely denounced for its violations of human rights (A. Sampson, 1973:259–288).

The power of multinational corporations has become almost staggering. At present, managers of Exxon, Fiat, British Petroleum, and similar firms have more power than most sovereign governments to determine where people will live and what work (if any) they will perform. By the year 2000, according to one estimate, a few hundred corporations will account for more than half the value of goods and services produced in the entire world. Clearly, multinational corporations are reshaping economic life and are transforming the societies in which they function (Barnet and Müller, 1974; Michalowski and Kramer, 1987; R. Müller and Domike, 1981; R. Vernon, 1977).

Consequences of Stratification for Developing Nations

As discussed above, colonialism, neocolonialism, and foreign investment by multinationals have often had unfortunate consequences for residents of developing nations. From 1950 to 1980, the gap between the world's rich and poor nations continued to grow, primarily because the rich nations got even richer. As for the decade of the 1980s, it is estimated that more than 40 Third World countries finished the decade poorer in per capita terms than they started it. The world's 14 most-devastated nations—including Zambia, Bolivia, and Nigeria—saw per capita income plummet as dramatically as it did in the United States during the Great Depression of the 1930s. With these trends in mind, researcher Alan Durning (1990:26) observed that the term "developing nation" has become a cruel misnomer; many of the world's less affluent nations are disintegrating rather than developing.

The day-to-day impact of the economic backslide in Africa, Latin America, and parts of Asia during the 1980s has been tragic. Malnutrition has risen in Burma, Burundi, the Gambia, Guinea-Bissau, Jamaica, Niger, Nigeria, Paraguay, the Philippines, Nicaragua, El Salvador, and Peru. According to the World Bank, life expectancy declined in nine African countries over the period 1979–1983. Today, more than 100 million Africans are believed to lack sufficient food to sustain themselves in good health (Durning, 1990:26; World Bank, 1990).

The 1980s were a particularly cruel decade for Latin America. El Salvador, Nicaragua, and Peru, all torn by war, went into economic tailspins. According to Peru's government, one-third of the country's children are malnourished to the extent that they have stunted growth. The per capita income of the average Latin American—only about $3500 in 1980—declined by 9 percent over the next 8 years (Durning, 1990:26–27). Faced with soaring unemployment and desperate poverty, many residents were forced to participate in, and were often exploited within, their countries' underground economies (see Box 9-2, page 270).

It should be noted that there have been hopeful signs in at least some developing nations. According to various estimates, Indonesia has reduced the proportion of its population living in poverty by 25 to 50 percent over the last 2 decades. Thailand has reportedly made a 50 percent reduction since 1960. Although there is controversy concerning data for India and Pakistan, some experts believe that the poverty rates in these Asian neighbors declined by several percentage points during the 1980s (Durning, 1990:27; World Bank, 1990).

What factors have contributed to the recent difficulties of developing nations? Certainly runaway population growth—which will be discussed in detail in Chapter 19—has hurt the standard of living of many Third World peoples. So, too, has the accelerating environmental decline evident in the quality of air, water, and other natural resources. Still another factor has been the developing nations' collective debt of $1.3 trillion.

Today, poor nations are paying rich countries $50 billion each year in debt and interest pay-

(J.Y. Rabeuf/The Image Works)

Shown is a family living in a garbage dump in Guatemala City. The 1980s were a particularly cruel decade for Latin America; many people were faced with soaring unemployment and desperate poverty.

ments beyond what they receive in new loans. If we add to this figure the estimates of capital flight involving wealthy citizens of poor nations, the annual outflow of funds may reach $100 billion. As viewed from a world systems approach, a growing share of the human and natural resources of developing countries is being redistributed to the core industrial nations (Durning, 1990:25–26; Kerbo, 1991:498). We will examine the problem of Third World debt in the social policy section at the end of the chapter.

Unfortunately, the massive exodus of money from poorer regions of the world only intensifies their destruction of natural resources. From a conflict view, less affluent nations are being forced to exploit their mineral deposits, forests, and fisheries in order to meet their debt obligations while offering subsistence labor to local workers. The poor turn to the only means of survival available to them: marginal lands. They plow mountain slopes, burn plots in tropical forests, and overgraze grasslands—often knowing that their actions are destructive to the environment. But they see no alternative in their agonizing fight for simple survival (Durning, 1990:26; Waring, 1988).

(David Austen/Woodfin Camp & Associates)

Workers are shown cutting down a forest in Papua, New Guinea. From a conflict perspective, less affluent nations are being forced to exploit their mineral deposits, forests, and fisheries in order to meet their debt obligations while offering subsistence labor to local workers.

BOX 9-2 • CURRENT RESEARCH

THE INFORMAL ECONOMY

G oods and services do not have to be produced and consumed in officially recognized and registered businesses. Instead, they can be made, sold, and traded by members of informal social networks. Anthropologists studying developing nations and preindustrial societies have long acknowledged such networks, but only recently have these networks been identified as common to all societies (Ferman et al., 1987).

The term *informal economy* refers to transfers of money, goods, or services that are not reported to the government. Participants in this economy avoid taxes, regulations, and minimum wage provisions, as well as certain expenses incurred in bookkeeping and financial reporting. In industrial societies, the informal economy embraces transactions that are individually quite small but which can be quite significant when taken together. One major segment of this economy involves illegal transactions—such as pros-

(Wesley Boxcel/Photo Researchers)

titution, sale of illegal drugs, gambling, and bribery—leading some observers to describe it as an "underground economy." Yet the informal economy also includes unregulated child care services, garage sales, and the unreported income of craftspeople, street ven-

In some cases, a community's informal economy is highly organized. The city of Lima, Peru, has more than 80,000 street vendors—known as ambulantes— *who offer a wide range of consumer goods.*

STRATIFICATION WITHIN NATIONS: A COMPARATIVE PERSPECTIVE

The world marketplace is highly stratified, with affluent, industrialized nations well in control while poorer developing countries face desperate problems. Worldwide stratification is evident not only in the disparity between rich and poor nations (in Wallerstein's terms, between countries at the core and at the periphery of the world economic system) but also *within* nations in the substantial gap between rich and poor citizens.

Stratification in developing nations is closely related to their relatively weak and dependent position in the world economic system. As discussed earlier, local elites work hand in hand with multinational corporations and prosper from such alliances, while the exploitation of industrial and agricultural workers is created and perpetuated by the economic system and prevailing developmental values. Consequently, foreign investment in developing countries tends to increase economic inequality (Bornschier et al., 1978; Kerbo, 1991:507–511).

BOX 9-2 • CURRENT RESEARCH

THE INFORMAL ECONOMY (Continued)

dors, and employees who receive substantial tips. According to estimates, the informal economy may account for as much as 10 to 20 percent of all economic activity in the United States (Fiola, 1990; Hershey, 1988; C. Simon and Witte, 1982; Waring, 1988).

Although these informal economic transactions take place in virtually all societies—both capitalist and socialist—the pattern in developing countries differs somewhat from the informal economy of industrialized nations. In the developing world, government bureaucracies are often unable to respond to increased requests for licenses or services, thereby forcing legitimate entrepreneurs to go "underground." Informal industrial enterprises, such as textile factories and repair shops, tend to be labor-intensive. Underground entrepreneurs cannot rely on advanced machinery, since a firm's assets can be confiscated for failure to operate within the open economy.

In some cases, a community's informal economy is highly organized. The city of Lima, Peru, has more than 80,000 street vendors—known as *ambulantes*—who offer a wide range of consumer goods. Organizations established by the *ambulantes* collect dues from vendors and have used these funds to construct some 270 local markets. In addition, the vendors' organizations assign and enforce property rights to particular locations on Lima's streets.

Viewed from a functionalist perspective, the burdensome bureaucratic regulations of developing societies have contributed to the rise of an efficient informal economy in certain countries. Nevertheless, these regulatory systems are dysfunctional to overall political and economic well-being. Since informal firms typically operate in remote locations to avoid detection, they cannot easily expand even when they become profitable. Given the limited protection for their property and

contractual rights, participants in the informal economy are less likely to save and invest their income.

Informal economies have also been criticized for promoting highly unfair and dangerous working conditions. In his study of the underground economy of Spain, sociologist Louis Lemkow (1987) found that workers' incomes were low, there was little job security, and safety and health standards were rarely enforced. Both the Spanish government and the nation's trade unions seemed to ignore the exploitation of participants in the informal economy. Yet, especially in the developing world, the existence of a substantial underground economy—estimated, for example, to account for about one-third of the gross domestic product of Peru—reflects the absence of an economic system accessible to all residents (de Soto, 1989; Fiola, 1990; Hosier, 1987; Portes et al., 1989; World Bank, 1987:74–75).

Distribution of Wealth and Income

In Chapter 8, we noted that in 1989, the top fifth (or 20 percent) of the United States population—earning $45,224 or more—accounted for almost 47 percent of total wages and salaries in the nation. By contrast, the bottom fifth of the population—earning $11,417 or less—accounted for less than 4 percent of all income (Bureau of the Census, 1990c:5, 17).

As Figure 9-3 (page 272) shows, the degree of income inequality varies markedly around the world. Of the seven nations contrasted, Brazil (which will be studied in detail later in the chapter) had the greatest gap between its most affluent and least affluent residents. The top fifth in Brazil received 63 percent of total wages and salaries, whereas the bottom fifth accounted for only 2 percent of income. This disparity is found in many developing countries, where small elites control a large portion of the nation's income. There are 10 countries around the globe in which the most affluent 10 percent receive at least 40 percent of income, and they are all developing

FIGURE 9-3 Distribution of Income in Seven Nations

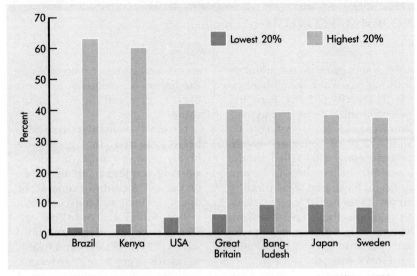

This figure shows the distribution of household income by population fifths in seven countries. Data were collected by the World Bank and by United Nations agencies. As the figure shows, the proportion of income held by the most affluent 20 percent of the population is highest in Brazil (63 percent) and Kenya (60 percent) and lowest in Sweden (37 percent). By comparing the bars for the poorest and richest quintiles (20 percent of the population), we can see that the gap between the highest and lowest quintiles is smallest in Sweden and Japan. Consequently, these two nations have the lowest level of income inequality of the seven countries pictured.

NOTE: Data are considered comparable although based on statistics covering 1972 to 1982.
SOURCE: World Bank, 1989:222–223, 245–246; 1990:236–237.

countries: Brazil (the leader at 46 percent), Kenya, Sri Lanka, Botswana, Guatemala, Mauritius, Mexico, Panama, Turkey, and Zambia.

In examining the world's advanced industrial economies, researchers have found that the lowest degree of income inequality is found in Sweden, Japan, Norway, and Belgium. By contrast, the highest inequality of income is evident in the United States, Canada, Great Britain, France, and Australia (World Bank, 1989:222–223, 245–246; 1990:236–237). Redistributive tax policies have reduced income inequality in many European nations; the factors which contribute to Japan's comparatively low level of income inequality are explored in Box 9-3.

It is difficult to compare the level of inequality in the socialist countries of the Soviet Union, China, or, at least until recently, eastern Europe with that of advanced market economies. Socialist nations have traditionally been reluctant to publish data that might undermine the official claim that social equality prevails within their borders. Yet the limited information available does suggest that stratification persists within these nations, although it is less pronounced than in the United

States. For example, economist Aaron Vinokur reported in 1986 that more than 40 percent of the wealth of the Soviet Union is held by 10 percent of the population. This is not surprising, since wages are not the same for all workers. Industrial engineers earn 50 percent more than white-collar workers, who in turn earn 50 percent more than laborers on Soviet collective farms (Kerbo, 1991:460–493; Szelenyi, 1983; Vinokur and Ofer, 1986:24).

As we saw in Chapter 8, wealth in the United States is much more unevenly distributed than income. The richest fifth of the American population holds almost 80 percent of the nation's wealth (refer back to Figure 8-2 on page 240). This extreme concentration of wealth is evident in most industrial societies. In the United Kingdom, for example, the distribution of wealth is even more lopsided than it is in the United States. In good part, this is because many Americans with rather modest incomes own automobiles and homes, whereas ownership of automobiles or homes is less common among poorer residents of Great Britain (Samuelson and Nordhaus, 1989:646–648).

BOX 9-3 • AROUND THE WORLD

INEQUALITY IN JAPAN

A tourist visiting Japan may at first experience a bit of culture shock after noticing the degree to which everything in Japanese life is ranked: corporations, universities, even educational programs. These rankings are widely reported and accepted. Moreover, day-to-day social interactions are shaped by rankings: Japanese find it difficult to sit, talk, or eat together unless the relative rankings of those present have been established, often through the practice of *meishi* (the exchange of business cards).

This apparent preoccupation with ranking and formality suggests an exceptional degree of stratification. Yet researchers have determined that Japan's level of income inequality is among the lowest of major industrial societies (refer back to Figure 9-3). Whereas the pay gap between Japan's top corporate executives and the nation's lowest paid workers is about 8 to 1, the comparable figure for the United States would be 37 to 1. In addition, the lucrative stock options received by top executives of American corporations are actually prohibited by law in Japan (Abegglen and Stalk, 1985:187, 192; Kerbo, 1991:421–423; Nakane, 1970:30).

This relative level of equality in Japanese society is rather recent; it dates back to post-World War II economic changes, including extensive land reform and the breakup of powerful holding companies. Among the factors

(Yasuo Kobayishi/Newsweek)

contributing to a lower level of inequality in Japan are a booming economy combined with a labor shortage, an educational system that treats students alike regardless of family background at least through their junior high school years, restraints on excessively high incomes, relatively little discrimination against male heads of households, and certain governmental policies that serve to redistribute income (Kerbo, 1991:431–432, 454–457).

Still another factor that works against inequality is that Japan is rather homogeneous—certainly when compared with the United States—in terms of race, ethnicity, nationality, and language. Japan's population, racially and ethnically, is 98 percent Japanese, but there is discrimination against the

Working women in Japan are shown marching in a rally for equal job opportunities. While women constitute nearly 37 percent of Japan's work force, they are generally restricted to subordinate positions.

nation's Chinese and Korean minorities, and the *Buraku* constitute a low-status subculture who encounter extensive prejudice (Kerbo, 1991:448–449, 455).

There has been growing controversy concerning Japan's treatment of its Korean minority. About 675,000 Koreans live in Japan, of whom more than 85 percent were born there. It is not easy for Koreans to obtain Japanese citizenship; without citizenship, they cannot vote, cannot work as teachers or government officials, and must carry alien registration cards at all times (a prac-

(Continued)

BOX 9-3 • AROUND THE WORLD

INEQUALITY IN JAPAN (Continued)

tice that has been likened to the South African requirement that Blacks carry passbooks). Koreans disproportionately work for low wages, without safety standards, and without any real hope of advancement. Moreover, because discrimination is so common, less than 5 percent of Koreans use their own names in business circles; similarly, many young Koreans use Japanese aliases to conceal their heritage in schools. In 1991, after protests by 14,000 Koreans, Japan agreed to end the mandatory fingerprinting of Koreans required under its Alien Registration Law (Makihara, 1990; *New York Times,* 1991a).

Gender discrimination and inequality are deep-rooted. Japanese girls do not receive the same encouragement to achieve in education that boys do. Not surprisingly, therefore, men are much more likely than women to attend four-year universities. The percentage of women enrolled at the nation's highest-ranked universities is less than 10 percent. While women constitute nearly 37 percent of Japan's work force, they are generally restricted to subordinate positions and have difficulty getting even entry-level jobs in Japan's largest corporations. A Labor Ministry study found that in 1987, of the 16.2 million Japa-

nese women who worked outside the home, only 48,600 (0.3 percent) held administrative positions.

In 1985, Japan's parliament—at the time, 97 percent male—passed an Equal Employment bill which encourages employers to end sex discrimination in hiring, assignment, and promotion policies. But feminist organizations remain dissatisfied because the law lacks strong sanctions to prevent continued discrimination against women (Brinton, 1988, 1989; Buckley and Mackie, 1986:182; Chira, 1988; Kerbo, 1991:445–448; Rohlen, 1983).

Prestige

Sociologists have recognized that comparative research is essential in determining whether observed patterns of stratification are unique to a single nation, are restricted to a particular type of society (such as industrial or developing nations), or are applicable to a wide range of societies (Kalleberg, 1988). We have seen that societies as different as Brazil, Bangladesh, the United States, and Japan all share a marked inequality in the distribution of income (refer back to Figure 9-3). But, as we saw in Chapter 8, a person's class position, defined largely in economic terms and reflecting his or her level of wealth and income, is but one component of stratification.

By ranking the prestige of various occupations, sociologists can gain a deeper understanding of another aspect of inequality. How do perceptions in the United States regarding the prestige of occupations compare with those held in other societies? In an effort to study stratification from a

cross-cultural perspective, sociologist Donald Treiman (1977) examined the reputation that certain jobs had in 53 different nations. People were asked to rate occupations, and the results were tabulated along a scale ranging from 0 to 100, with higher scores being more prestigious. As the data presented in Table 9-2 illustrate, Treiman found a high degree of correlation or similarity in all contemporary societies, including both industrialized and nonindustrialized nations.

Treiman's pioneering research inspired subsequent efforts to gather and compare data from many societies using the objective method of measuring stratification differences. In one important study, sociologists Nan Lin and Wen Xie (1988) interviewed a random sample of residents of Beijing, the capital of the People's Republic of China, to study occupational prestige. The researchers recognized the potential bias of sampling those who live in one of China's most cosmopolitan cities. They found that 47 percent of the 1774 respondents questioned were professionals, manag-

TABLE 9-2 Comparative Ranking of Occupations

OCCUPATION	NATION					
	USA	CANADA	NIGERIA	POLAND	THAILAND	USSR
Physician or medical officer	78	83	70	81	73	77
Captain	63	67	66	44	69	60
High school teacher	63	63	58	70	70	57
Bank manager	53	67	58	49	54	NA
Truck driver	32	31	49	44	29	45

NOTE: People in the Soviet Union were not asked to rank bankers; hence, this category is marked "NA" (data not available).
SOURCE: Treiman, 1977:318–405.

The table above presents a sampling of data collected by sociologist Donald Treiman regarding the ranking of various occupations throughout the world. The findings reveal a striking similarity of ratings in the six nations.

ers, or administrators—whereas this was true of only 23 percent of residents of other urban areas. Nevertheless, given the constraints on acquiring social scientific data, this study offers unique insights regarding stratification in the world's most populous nation.

Lin and Xie found that physicians were near the top of the occupational hierarchy in terms of prestige, while police officers were near the middle and garbage collectors were close to the bottom—a finding similar to the results of surveys in the United States (refer back to Table 8-3 on page 237). Interestingly, however, teachers and professors received much lower prestige ratings in China, reflecting the comparatively limited economic rewards they receive relative to other occupations. The Chinese respondents gave a much higher prestige rating to textile workers than did respondents in the United States. In explaining this finding, Lin and Xie point out that textile workers in China fare much better relative to other workers than they do in the United States or Europe.

As one part of their analysis, the researchers compared the prestige rankings of male and female respondents. Although China has officially maintained a national policy of gender equality since 1949, occupational segregation by gender has not been completely eliminated. Partly as a result, the prestige rankings of Chinese men and women seemed to reflect the structure of occupational opportunity. Males, for example, gave higher ratings than females to such occupations as natural scientist, athlete, driver, and mechanic—all of which are more likely to be held by males.

Each gender showed a tendency to rate more highly those occupations most open to it (Lin and Xie, 1988:808–809).

Treiman's cross-cultural research reminds us that prestige distinctions are universal; the study of China by Lin and Xie underscores this finding. Even a society that has experienced revolutionary movements and decades of Communist party rule still exhibits noticeable stratification in rating some occupations as most prestigious and others as less desirable.

Social Mobility

In Chapter 8, we saw that the amount of social movement in a society—both upward and downward—is rather limited in societies characterized by slavery, caste, and estate systems of stratification. For example, a study of agricultural households in central India between 1975 and 1983 found that, on average, 84 percent of those who were poor in any year had been poor in the previous year. Over the 9-year period of study, 44 percent of households had been poor for 6 or more years, and 19 percent were poor in all 9 years (World Bank, 1990:135).

It would be incorrect, however, to assume that the degree of social mobility and the means for obtaining mobility are the same in all class sys-

(Alex Quesada/Matrix)

Nicaraguan immigrants are shown at work in Miami. Sociological research suggests that high rates of immigration contribute to an expansion of job opportunities and therefore facilitate social mobility.

tems. Three sociologists—Andrea Tyree, Moshe Semyonov, and Robert Hodge (1979)—compared social mobility in 24 nations. They found mobility to be highest in Israel, Canada, Australia, and the United States, four nations which share a recent history of having received large numbers of immigrants. High rates of immigration imply rapid population growth and more extensive social change. These factors contribute to an expansion of job opportunities, which in turn facilitates social mobility. Conversely, the researchers (Tyree et al., 1979:417) found that mobility was lowest in nations such as Italy, the Philippines, Brazil, and Colombia, all of which have comparatively low rates of immigration.

More recent studies of intergenerational mobility in industrialized nations have found that (1) there are substantial similarities in the ways that parents' positions in stratification systems are transmitted to their children; (2) as in the United States, mobility opportunities in other nations have been influenced by structural factors, such as labor market changes which lead to the rise or decline of an occupational group within the social hierarchy; (3) immigration continues to be a significant factor shaping a society's level of intergenerational mobility (Grusky and Hauser, 1984;

Haller et al., 1990; Hauser and Grusky, 1988; Kalleberg, 1988:208; Kerbo, 1991:364–366).

Cross-cultural studies suggest that intergenerational mobility has been increasing in recent decades, at least among men. Dutch sociologists Harry Ganzeboom and Ruud Luijkx joined by American sociologist Donald Treiman (1989) examined surveys of mobility in 35 industrial and developing nations; they found that almost all the countries studied had witnessed increased intergenerational mobility between the 1950s and 1980s. In particular, there was a common pattern of movement away from agriculture-based occupations.

How extensive is mobility within socialist countries? Although studies of nations with centrally planned economies, such as Hungary and Poland, reveal little inheritance of wealth, there is no evidence of any substantial level of mobility. It will be interesting to study these countries in the 1990s to see if the growth of privately owned businesses leads to sharp increases in social mobility (Dahrendorf, 1990; Wong, 1990).

Mobility patterns in industrialized countries are usually associated with intergenerational or intragenerational mobility. However, within developing nations, micro-level movement from one occupation to another is often overshadowed by macro-level social and economic changes. For example, there is typically a substantial wage differential between rural and urban areas, which leads to high levels of migration to the cities. Yet the urban industrial sectors of developing countries generally cannot provide sufficient employment for all those seeking work. Consequently, such internal migration contributes to an expansion of the informal economies described earlier in Box 9-2 (Thirlwall, 1989:103).

Only recently have researchers begun to investigate the impact of gender differences on the mobility patterns of developing nations. Many aspects of the development process—especially modernization in rural areas and the rural-to-urban migration described above—may result in the modification or abandonment of traditional cultural practices and even marital systems. The effects on women's social standing and mobility are not necessarily positive. Through development and modernization, women's vital role in food production deteriorates, thereby jeopardizing both their autonomy and their material well-being. The movement of families to the cities weakens women's ties to relatives who can provide food, financial assistance, and social support (Alam, 1985; Boserup, 1977; Tiano, 1987).

One recent effort to investigate gender and mobility took place in Sri Lanka (formerly known as Ceylon). Researchers examined the impact of foreign aid—in the form of plans to improve agricultural production, irrigation, and rural electrification—on the local population. Virtually all the foreign aid programs were more successful in increasing the incomes of men than of women. Where women's incomes did rise, it was usually in such occupations as rubber and tea cultivation, in which women earn almost 40 percent less than their male counterparts. Overall, foreign aid in Sri Lanka had the unintended consequence of increasing income inequality between male and female workers; similar conclusions were reached in studies conducted in India and Malaysia (Stoeckel and Sirisena, 1988).

Our examination of the distribution of wealth and income within various countries, of comparative studies of prestige, and of cross-cultural research on mobility consistently reveals that stratification based on class, gender, and other factors is evident within a wide range of societies. Clearly, a worldwide view of stratification must involve not only the sharp contrast between wealthy and impoverished nations, but also the stratification hierarchies within industrialized societies, developing countries, and even socialist regimes ostensibly committed to abolishing inequality.

STRATIFICATION IN BRAZIL: A CASE STUDY

Thus far in the chapter, our discussion of stratification, inequality, and mobility has examined a wide range of societies—industrialized and developing, capitalist and socialist. In illustrating the dynamics of stratification outside the United States, it will be helpful to study one country in somewhat more detail.

Brazil is an economic giant; it has the world's eighth-largest economy. Brazil's 150 million people constitute a majority of all South Americans. As in the United States, race relations in Brazil reflect the legacy of European colonization and the slave trade. As in many developing countries, women in Brazil are speaking out against their traditional second-class status. Moreover, in recent years, Brazil has been the focus of considerable international attention, both because of the destruction of the Amazon rain forest and the nation's serious debt problems. For these reasons, Brazil seems an ideal choice for such a case study.

The gap between Brazil's richest and poorest citizens is one of the widest in the world—and it has grown since 1960 (refer back to Figure 9-3). The lives of poor people are often bleak, especially when they are confronted with the lavish wealth of the nation's elite. A poster on the waiting room door in the only medical station in Rocinha, the largest slum neighborhood in Rio de Janeiro, warns of an outbreak of leprosy. "Everybody's suffering here," explains a nurse, "but we all have views. We see their mansions, but they don't see us" (Dabrowski et al., 1989:64; C. Wood and de Carvalho, 1988).

In contrast to the upper class in the United States, the Brazilian upper class (the top 1 percent

(H. Collart Odinetz/Sygma)

These Brazilian homes are raised from the ground because of the floods of the Amazon River. The lives of poor people in Brazil are often bleak, especially when they are confronted with the lavish wealth of the nation's elite.

in terms of income) is composed primarily of large landowners and successful immigrant industrialists. Reflecting the continuing impact of colonialism and neocolonialism, less than one in five of Brazil's leading industrialists are children or even grandchildren of Brazilians. The upper middle class, comprising about 2 percent of the population, includes professionals, civil servants, and military officers, while the middle class (about 24 percent of the population) is composed of craftspeople, white-collar workers, government employees, and workers in service occupations. Finally, at the bottom of Brazil's stratification hierarchy are the rural and urban poor, who together constitute an overwhelming majority (73 percent) of the nation's people (Fiechter, 1975:15–17).

Race Relations in Brazil: The Legacy of Slavery

To someone knowledgeable in American racial and ethnic relations, Brazil seems familiar in a number of respects. Like the United States, Brazil was colonized by Europeans (in Brazil's case, the Portuguese) who overwhelmed the native population. Like the United States, Brazil imported Black Africans as slaves to meet the demand for laborers. Even today, Brazil is second to the United States in the number of people of African descent, excluding nations on the African continent.

Brazil depended much more on slave trade than the United States did. Franklin Knight (1974:46) has estimated that some 3.5 million slaves were brought to Brazil from Africa—about eight times the number brought to the United States. At the height of slavery, however, each nation had approximately 4 to 4.5 million slaves. Brazil's reliance on African-born slaves meant that typical Brazilian slaves had closer ties to Africa than did their American counterparts. Revolts and escapes were more common among slaves in Brazil. The most dramatic example was the slave *quilombo* (or hideaway) of Palmores, where 20,000 inhabitants repeatedly fought off Portuguese assaults until 1698 (Degler, 1971:7–8, 47–52).

Today, rather than being classified simply as "Black" or "White" (as is typical in the United States), Brazil's racial groupings constitute a type of **color gradient** on a continuum from light to dark skin color. Consequently, Mulattos (persons of mixed racial ancestry) are viewed as an identifiable social group. According to the 1980 census, Brazil's population was 55 percent *Branco* (White), 38 percent Mulatto, 6 percent *Preto* (Black), and 1 percent other. Over the last 50 years, the proportion of Mulattos has grown, while the proportion of both *Brancos* and *Pretos* has declined (Brazil, 1981; C. Wood and de Carvalho, 1988:135–153).

Historian Carl Degler (1971) has suggested that the key difference in Brazilian and American race relations is Brazil's "Mulatto escape hatch," under which Mulattos are not classified with Blacks. But, while lighter skin color does appear to enhance status in Brazil, the impact of this escape hatch has been exaggerated. Recent income data show that Mulattos earn 42 percent more income than Blacks, but this difference is not especially remarkable, given that Mulattos have more formal schooling. More striking is the finding that Whites earn 98 percent more income than Mulattos. As a result, the most significant distinction appears to be that between Whites and all Brazilian "people of color," rather than between the country's Blacks and Mulattos (Dzidzienyo, 1987; Silva, 1985).

In 1988, Brazil marked as a national holiday the hundredth anniversary of the abolition of slavery, but for 40 to 50 percent of Brazil's people of color there was little rejoicing. Zézé Motta, Brazil's leading Black actress and a longtime campaigner for Black civil rights, observed: "We have gone from the hold of the ship to the basements of society." Of 559 members of the nation's Congress, only 7 were Black. Whites are still seven times more likely to graduate from college, while job advertisements continue to seek individuals of "good appearance" (a euphemism for light skin). Even Black professionals such as physicians, teachers, and engineers earn 20 to 25 percent less than their lighter-skinned counterparts (T. Robinson, 1989; Simons, 1988:1; Webster and Dwyer, 1988).

Continued denial that racial inequality exists in Brazil means that there is little pressure to assist poor Blacks, because their subordinate status is perceived to reflect class, not differential racial treatment. Even more than in the United States, class prejudice reinforces racial prejudice to the point of obscuring it. Lower-class Whites, Mulattos, and Blacks certainly experience limited opportunities because of lifelong poverty. For many Brazilians, nevertheless, skin color represents an added source of prejudice and discrimination (Freyre, 1946, 1959, 1963; Webster and Dwyer, 1988).

The Status of Brazilian Women

The position of women in Brazil is typical of that of women in many developing nations. While Brazil is more industrialized than most developing countries, it still has a labor surplus and high rates of unemployment. These factors contribute to the exclusion of large numbers of women from the Brazilian work force. Consequently, many women in Brazil's cities, especially migrant women, must seek income within the informal

(Owen Franken/Stock, Boston)

Domestic service is still the leading form of employment for Brazilian women.

economy (which accounts for 40 percent of Brazil's gross national product) in such jobs as domestic servants and street vendors. Domestic service is still the leading form of employment for Brazilian women. Factory work is generally reserved for those women who have grown up in cities and have more education than migrants from rural areas (Fiola, 1990: Sarti, 1989:76).

Although women's participation in Brazil's informal economy is accepted, traditional views of women's role in society discourage married women's employment in full-time jobs outside the family. With many children working, a large family means more wage earners—but having a large family reduces women's employment options. Finally, factory owners are reluctant to hire married women because of the maternity benefits to which permanently employed pregnant women are entitled (Patai, 1988; Safa, 1983:96; C. Wood and de Carvalho, 1988:174–175).

In 1932, Brazilian women won the right to vote and became the first women in Latin America to gain suffrage. In recent decades, women have emphasized their identities as mothers and homemakers in protesting shortages in food and other necessities. Moreover, women have taken the lead in demonstrating against human rights violations, including the "disappearances" of loved ones. In many of these protests, women have attacked the violence of their nation's male leaders (Patai, 1988).

Feminist initiatives are evident in contemporary Brazil, but have been met with resistance. Often, in working for social change, women's groups must present issues in a way that will be less threatening to the larger, male-dominated Brazilian society. For example, in order to receive broad public support, feminists defend the need for child care centers as a "workers' issue," a "children's issue," or a "health issue," rather than as a "women's issue" (Alvarez, 1989).

In 1985, the National Council for Women's Rights was established within the Ministry of Justice. This was the first time that the Brazilian government had formally recognized the existence of sexual inequality in the country and had taken steps to guarantee full equality for women. Among the council's goals are the elimination of sexism within the criminal justice system and the reduction of violence against women (Sarti, 1989:88).

As one response to feminist protests regarding violence against women, Brazil has created more than 70 women's police stations run by all-female staffs at which policewomen take all statements and make arrests. These stations are intended to provide a "secure and sympathetic atmosphere" in which women can report crimes such as rape, incest, and battering. If they are injured, they can receive immediate medical treatment at these stations. The first women's police station was opened in São Paulo in 1985; by 1988, such stations were found in 16 of Brazil's 24 states (*World Development Forum*, 1988).

Brazilian feminists won an important victory in 1991, when the nation's Supreme Court ruled that a husband who kills his wife can no longer be acquitted on the grounds of "legitimate defense of honor" because of her alleged adultery. This defense had been used by attorneys to win acquittals for thousands of husbands on trial for killing their wives. Brazilian women had rallied against it throughout the 1980s, using the slogan "Lovers Don't Kill." The Supreme Court majority declared that such killings defend "not honor, but vanity, exaggerated self-importance, and the pride of a lord who sees a woman as his personal property" (Brooke, 1991b:B16).

Brazil's Economy and Environment

By the 1990s, Brazil's economy had reached a state of crisis. The rate of inflation had risen as high as 2700 percent in 1989, meaning that workers could get a raise every week and still not stay ahead of inflation. At the same time, Brazil's foreign debt of $130 billion was the largest of any developing nation. Brazil has found itself unable to pay the principal or interest on its debt since 1989; as a result, the United States Export-Import Bank demoted Brazil to its riskiest loan category.

In response to this crisis, President Fernando Collor de Mello—the country's first directly elected civilian president in 29 years—announced a startling economic plan in early 1990. In an effort to modernize the Brazilian economy and to "liquidate" inflation, the president proposed declaring a moratorium on internal debt, privatizing state-controlled companies, imposing new taxes, loosening foreign exchange controls, establishing a new currency, and streamlining the government bureaucracy. Roberto Mueller, the editor of Brazil's leading economic newspaper, admitted: "I'm stunned. I've never seen anything so gigantic in my life" (Brooke, 1990b:1).

The president's program provoked controversy as soon as it was introduced. While few would argue with the general goal of better integrating Latin America's largest economy into the world economic system, certain aspects of the recovery plan seemed likely to hurt less affluent citizens. Brazil's civil service unions quickly declared that they would oppose the privatization of the 188 state companies. By late 1990, some 250,000 civil servants—mainly from middle-class and working-class backgrounds—had lost their jobs as part of the closing or consolidation of government agencies. Unions have called hundreds of strikes to protest the dismissals of public employees and private-sector workers (Brooke, 1990b, 1990c; Silverstein, 1990).

As of early 1991, there was little evidence that the president's bold economic plan was achieving success. After briefly stabilizing, the inflation rate had again increased to 20 percent per month; at the same time, the real wages of Brazilian workers had declined by 16 percent from their 1989 average. Brazil's trade surplus has eroded, and the nation's overall economic output decreased by 4 percent in 1990—the worst performance in a decade. In a survey conducted in late 1990 by a São Paulo newspaper, only 26 percent of respondents said that their lives had improved since the Collor plan was announced (Brooke, 1990c, 1991a; Silverstein, 1990).

Brazil's severe economic troubles have contributed to environmental destruction in the mineral-rich areas surrounding the Amazon River. This destruction has become a global concern. Each year, some 12,000 square miles of the Amazon rain forest are cleared for crops and livestock through burning—an area larger than Belgium. It is believed that the elimination of the rain forest affects worldwide weather patterns and heightens the gradual warming of the earth in a process known as the *greenhouse effect*. This destruction is additionally unfortunate in that the

(Sygma)

More than 40,000 illegal gold prospectors have been mining in the traditional lands of Brazil's Yanomani Indians. The miners destroy forests and pollute rivers with chemicals used in purifying gold.

Amazon region represents a potential source of important pharmaceutical advances, including drugs that might cure diseases (Linden, 1989).

The burning of the rain forest is not the only aspect of Brazil's environmental troubles. By 1990, environmental activists around the world were expressing concern about the conflict between mining companies and the Yanomani Indians, considered to be the last major isolated Indian tribe in the Americas. More than 40,000 illegal gold prospectors have been mining in the traditional lands of the Yanomani over the last 3 years. The miners are primarily poor Brazilians who move from gold rush to gold rush—all the while destroying forests and polluting rivers with chemicals used in purifying gold. In the view of

Fernando César Mesquita, president of the Brazilian Institute of Environment and Renewable Resources, "the miners leave a trail of devastation wherever they go. They level nature around the mines. They leave the rivers useless" (Brooke, 1990a:3; Schmink and Wood, 1989).

The miners' presence in the Amazon lands has been a disaster not only for the environment, but also for the Yanomani. As a result of their contact with miners, more than half the 9000 Yanomani Indians in northern Brazil have contracted malaria and other deadly diseases. Yet the Yanomani have been largely without medical care since Funai (Brazil's national agency for Indian affairs) closed two health posts in their territory in 1988. In 1990, Indian rights organizations as far away as London launched demonstrations to protest the mistreatment of the Yanomani by the mining companies and the Brazilian government (Brooke, 1990a; Rabben, 1990a).

The conflict over the Yanomani lands is but one of many in Brazil in which multinational mining companies and the government are pitted against Indian tribes and environmentalists. Underlying these disputes is overt racism against Indians, whose concern for their traditional lands is disparaged by land speculators and developers. However, in contrast to the miners in the Yanomani territories, thousands of Indians and other forest residents have learned to conduct extensive activities without devastating the environment (Rabban, 1990a, 1990b).

SOCIAL POLICY AND WORLDWIDE INEQUALITY

DEBT IN THE THIRD WORLD

- In what ways does the problem of Third World debt exacerbate the disparity between the world's rich and poor nations?
- Why were Latin American countries especially likely to fall into debt?
- What steps has the United States government taken to respond to the crisis of Third World debt?

In August 1982, a U.S. Treasury official recalls, the finance minister of Mexico, Jesús Silva Herzog, "showed up on our doorstep and turned his pockets inside out." In a sense, Mexico could not pay its bills to the rest of the world. Mexico was not the first developing country unable to meet the payments on its debt, but it was the first one large enough to threaten the international finance system. By the end of 1982, a dozen nations shared the same problem. But the situation has become much worse since then: as of 1990, total Third World debt had reached $1.3 trillion (Farnsworth, 1990; George, 1988; Lissakers, 1983:160).

Why have these figures caused such alarm? The United States alone has a federal debt in excess of $2 trillion. The crucial difference is that lenders expect the United States to meet its debt-service payments (the interest on loans), whereas many developing nations now find it impossible to fulfill all their obligations. Unlike the personal debts people have with banks, creditors do not really expect international borrowers to repay the loan itself, just so long as they regularly pay off the interest. However, in 1987, Brazil became the first country to suspend interest payments to foreign creditors.

The bitter irony is that the debt payments of developing countries go to the more affluent, industrialized nations of the world. In effect, therefore, the savings of residents of lower-income, periphery countries are used to finance increases in consumption within prosperous core societies. Yet the investment policies of governments and lending institutions fail to genuinely take into account the impact of debt arrangements on poverty, much less the distribution of wealth and income (L. Brown, 1986:6; Pastor, 1986).

Viewed from the perspective of world systems theory, the global debt crisis has only intensified the Third World dependency begun under colonialism, neocolonialism, and multinational investment. International financial institutions are pressuring indebted countries to adopt austerity measures in order to more easily meet their interest payments. Developing nations may be forced to devalue their currencies, freeze workers' wages, increase privatization of industry, and reduce government services and employment. As we saw earlier in our discussion of Brazil, the consequences of such policies often include high inflation, reduced purchasing power, substantial layoffs of government workers, and higher unemployment—all of which are harmful to a nation's overall economic development (Bradshaw and Huang, 1991; George, 1988:77–85; Roddick, 1988:81–104).

World systems theorists add that the policies dictated by international financial institutions are destructive to the quality of life in developing countries. For example, in 1990, as part of an austerity program designed to ease debt repayment, the African nation of Zambia ended governmental subsidies which had reduced citizens' costs in buying food. Once the "free market" determined food prices, these prices increased dramatically, quickly leading to intense antigovernment riots. At least 23 persons died during the unrest, which included an unsuccessful attempt to overthrow Zambia's government. Such an explosive response to austerity measures is not unusual; since 1976, Third World countries have witnessed more than 85 protests directed toward austerity programs intended to facilitate international debt payments (Bradshaw and Huang, 1991; Walton and Ragin, 1988, 1989).

Ironically, developing countries in Africa have largely been spared from the Third World debt crisis, simply because the world banking community has regarded these nations as such a bad credit risk that they have received relatively few loans. But the newly industrializing countries of Latin America presented a more desirable target for investors who had accumulated substantial amounts of capital in the 1970s owing to rising petroleum prices. The Latin American countries received substantial loans, but quickly ran into trouble as interest rates went up and Latin American exports failed to keep pace. Consequently, by 1990, Latin American governments and banks held about two-thirds of the $1.3 trillion Third World debt. As one result of this burdensome debt, per capita output in Latin America declined by 7 percent during the 1980s (Farnsworth, 1990:D1; Thirlwall, 1989:314).

In response to the debt crisis, in 1985 the Reagan administration launched the Baker Plan (named after James Baker, who was then secretary of the treasury). Secretary Baker's plan encouraged additional bank lending to developing countries committed to a serious economic overhaul. Although it gave these nations more time to implement overdue economic reforms,

the Baker Plan nevertheless proved to be a failure because it contributed to further increases in Third World debts.

In 1989, essentially acknowledging the failure of the Baker Plan, the Bush administration announced the Brady Plan (directed by Secretary of the Treasury Nicholas Brady). This initiative permits the forgiving of 20 percent of the existing loans to 39 developing countries—chiefly in Latin America and Africa—but only if these nations introduce tough economic reforms designed to promote market-oriented economies. The Brady Plan came in the aftermath of outspoken public statements by some South American leaders, who decried the northward migration of their countries' capital in a type of financial neocolonialism from which there seemed no escape (Bluestein, 1989; Farnsworth, 1990; Kenen, 1990).

The Baker and Brady plans can be viewed as part of a worldwide strategy to deal with excessive Third World debt that has been developed since 1985 by the International Monetary Fund in cooperation with international bankers. The three critical components of this strategy are (1) expand the exports of developing nations through promotion of sustained economic growth in the industrial sector, (2) reduce the imports of developing countries while, at the same time, cutting their government spending, and (3) resume the lending of investment capital to Third World nations once the situation has stabilized (L. Brown, 1986:7; Selowsky and van der Tak, 1986).

These goals are not easily accomplished; they place extensive responsibility on already debt-ridden countries. Yet, thus far, there has been at least a measure of success. No massive default has occurred; some nations have begun to reduce imports and government spending. Nevertheless, the essential component of the debt-reduction strategy—sustained economic growth—is far from being achieved. In nearly all the heavily indebted Third World countries, average per-person income in real terms (that is, taking inflation into account) has been declining. The economies of these nations have been seriously hurt by decreases in the prices of coffee and sugar and by widely fluctuating oil prices. While these economic changes may benefit residents of affluent core countries, they can be devastating to the poor in developing nations and can even, as in Zambia, lead to violence among citizens (Bradshaw and Huang, 1991; Thirlwall, 1989: 318).

The complexity of the debt crisis defies the usual pro-and-con format of many social policy issues debated in classrooms and legislatures, yet the stakes are very high. In 1983, just weeks after Mexico's debt problems received worldwide attention, Tanzanian cabinet minister Amir Jamal (1983:73, 75–76) noted:

> The least that the industrialized countries ought to do, in the name of human decency, is to ensure that the global institutions under their control assist the poor countries in making adjustments. . . . Economic policies cannot be managed on quicksand. . . . Are the industrialized countries convinced that it is in their interest to push poor countries to the wall?

From time to time, the image of the world as a "global village" has been popular in the media. Certainly, industrialized countries and multinational corporations can move quickly around the globe to find the resources they need. Moreover, for the first time in human history, it is within our technological grasp to substantially reduce, if not eliminate, absolute poverty. Yet the handling of the Third World debt crisis does not suggest that our global village is acting with a sense of mutual responsibility to alleviate the suffering of the world's most impoverished people (Bradshaw and Huang, 1991; Pratt, 1983:55–56).

SUMMARY

Worldwide stratification can be seen both in the gap between rich and poor nations and in the inequality within countries around the world. This chapter examines stratification within the world economic system, modernization, the impact of multinational corporations on developing countries, and the distribution of wealth and income in various nations.

1 While the world has 157 billionaires, some 100 million people are homeless.

2 In 1985, the world's 140 developing countries accounted for 75 percent of the world's population but possessed only 20 percent of all wealth.

3 Former colonized nations are kept in a subservient position, subject to foreign domination, through the process of *neocolonialism.*

4 Drawing on the conflict perspective, sociologist Immanuel Wallerstein views the global economic system as divided between nations who control wealth (*core nations*) and those from whom capital is taken (*periphery nations*).

5 Historian C. E. Black has identified four cultural phases common to all societies undergoing the process of *modernization.*

6 Conflict theorists argue that *multinational corporations* have a negative social impact on workers in both industrialized and developing nations.

7 The day-to-day impact of the economic backslide in Africa, Latin America, and parts of Asia during the 1980s has been tragic.

8 Of the world's advanced industrial economies, Sweden and Japan have the lowest degree of income inequality.

9 Prestige rankings of occupations by residents of Beijing, China, are similar to those in the United States.

10 Social mobility is especially likely to be high in nations which share a recent history of having received large numbers of immigrants.

11 In contrast to the upper class of the United States, the Brazilian upper class is composed primarily of large landowners and successful immigrant industrialists.

12 Brazil's Blacks and Mulattos earn significantly less income than Whites do.

13 Brazil's severe economic troubles have contributed to environmental destruction in the mineral-rich areas surrounding the Amazon River.

14 The problem of Third World debt is especially severe in Latin America.

KEY TERMS

Colonialism The maintenance of political, social, economic, and cultural dominance over a people by a foreign power for an extended period of time. (page 259)

Color gradient The placement of people on a continuum from light to dark skin color rather than in distinct racial groupings by skin color. (278)

Diffusion The process by which a cultural item is spread from group to group or society to society. (259)

Infant mortality rate The number of deaths of infants under 1 year of age per 1000 live births in a given year. (267)

Informal economy Transfers of money, goods, or services that are not reported to the government. (270)

Modernization The far-reaching process by which a

society moves from traditional or less developed institutions to those characteristic of more developed societies. (261)

Multinational corporations Commercial organizations which, while headquartered in one country, own or control other corporations and subsidiaries throughout the world. (264)

Neocolonialism Continuing dependence of former colonies on foreign countries. (261)

World systems theory Immanuel Wallerstein's view of the global economic system as divided between certain industrialized nations who control wealth and developing countries who are controlled and exploited. (261)

ADDITIONAL READINGS

Bornschier, Volker, and Christopher Chase-Dunn. *Transnational Corporations and Underdevelopment*. New York: Praeger, 1985. A detailed analysis of the impact of multinational corporations on developing nations.

Braun, Denny. *The Rich Get Richer*. Chicago: Nelson-Hall, 1991. Sociologist Braun looks at growing inequality within the United States, as well as throughout the world, with a special focus on the rise of multinational corporations.

Brown, Lester. *State of the World*. New York: Norton. Published annually by the Worldwatch Institute, this review examines the major social and environmental issues confronting the world.

Ferman, Louis A., Stuart Henry, and Michele Hoyman (eds.). *The Informal Economy*. Newbury Park, Calif.: Sage, 1987. Published as the September 1987 issue of the *Annals of the American Academy of Political and Social Science,* this volume provides an overview of the informal economy in both industrial and developing nations.

Fontaine, Pierre-Michel (ed.). *Race, Class, and Power in Brazil*. Los Angeles: UCLA Center for Afro-American Studies, 1986. A collection of essays examining the lives of Black Brazilians.

Tinker, Irene (ed.). *Persistent Inequalities: Women and World Development*. New York: Oxford University Press, 1990. Tinker's anthology offers an overview of past and current debates regarding the role of women in world development and the impact of development on women.

Treiman, Donald J. *Occupational Prestige in Comparative Perspective*. New York: Academic Press, 1977. The classic review of studies of prestige in industrialized and developing nations.

Wallerstein, Immanuel. *The Capitalist World Economy*. Cambridge, Eng.: Cambridge University Press, 1979. Economist Wallerstein suggests that the unequal exchange of goods and services between industrialized and developing countries serves to widen the gap between the world's haves and have-nots.

Waring, Marilyn. *If Women Counted: A New Feminist Economics*. San Francisco: Harper and Row, 1988. Waring, a social scientist from New Zealand, considers how women's labor is overlooked in the global economy.

Willis, David K. *Klass: How Russians Really Live*. New York: St. Martin's, 1986. A journalistic account of social class in the Soviet Union, with special emphasis on the country's affluent elite.

The World Bank. *World Development Report*. New York: Oxford University Press. Published annually by the International Bank for Reconstruction and Development (the United Nations agency more commonly referred to as the World Bank), this volume provides a vast array of social and economic indicators regarding world development.

Journals

Among those journals that consider the issues of worldwide stratification and uneven development are the *International Journal of Urban and Regional Research* (founded in 1976), *International Labour Review* (1921), *Journal of Developing Areas* (1965), *Latin American Research Review* (1956), *Review of Income and Wealth* (1954), and *World Development* (1973).

10

RACE AND ETHNICITY

What happens to a dream deferred?
Does it dry up like a raisin in the sun?
Or fester like a sore—And then run?
Does it stink like rotten meat?
Or crust and sugar over—like a syrupy sweet?
Maybe it just sags like a heavy load
Or does it explode?
Langston Hughes
Harlem, 1951

LOOKING AHEAD

- In sociological terms, why are Blacks, American Indians, and Jews considered minority groups?
- Why are stereotypes harmful to members of racial and ethnic minorities?
- How does the Marxist perspective view race relations?
- What types of interracial contact can foster tolerance between dominant and subordinate groups?
- Is it harmful to Asian Americans to view them as a "model minority"?
- What challenges does the United States face from contemporary immigration?

In 1989, David Dinkins became New York City's first African American mayor, after a long political career which began in Harlem. Historically, Harlem has been the intellectual, cultural, and political center of New York's Black community. It has served as a focal point for the hopes, dreams, frustrations, and anger of Black writers, artists, and activists. As Langston Hughes suggests in his poem, many Black Americans have had to put off their dreams, perhaps forever. But what happens to such unfulfilled dreams?

Hughes observes that they may dry up within people's minds, weigh heavily on them, or eat away painfully at them. He ends by warning that the frustrations of Black Americans may ultimately explode.

The portrait of Harlem drawn by Langston Hughes is, in a wider sense, a vision of the neighborhoods of many racial and ethnic minorities of the United States. Similar statements could describe the lives of American Indians on reservations or Chicanos (Mexican Americans) in the inner cities of the southwest. These and other minorities have experienced the often bitter contrast between the American dream of freedom, equality, and success and the grim realities of poverty, prejudice, and discrimination.

The social definitions of race and ethnicity, like that of class, affect people's place and status in society's stratification system. This is true in the United States and around the world. In 1986, West Germany moved to close its doors to refugees from Turkey, Sri Lanka, and other nations. In taking this step, Chancellor Helmut Kohl proclaimed: "We are not a nation of immigration. And we do not want to become one." In 1989, Chinese university students rioted, protesting the presence of African students. As they stormed the African students' residence hall, the Chinese students screamed: "Kill the Black devils." Then in

1990, Japan decided to continue its policy of prohibiting people of Korean ancestry from working as schoolteachers or in any governmental position (M. Beck, 1989; Hiatt, 1990; Markham, 1986:A7).

This chapter will focus primarily on the meaning of race and ethnicity in the United States. It will begin by identifying the basic characteristics of a minority group and distinguishing between racial and ethnic groups; then it will consider the functionalist, conflict, and interactionist perspectives on race and ethnicity. The next sections of the chapter will examine the dynamics of prejudice and discrimination and their impact on intergroup relations. Particular attention will then be given to the experiences of racial and ethnic minorities in the United States. Finally, the social policy section will explore the immigration policy of the United States.

MINORITY, RACIAL, AND ETHNIC GROUPS

Sociologists frequently distinguish between racial and ethnic groups. The term *racial group* is used to describe a group which is set apart from others because of obvious physical differences. Whites, Blacks, and Asian Americans are all considered

racial groups in the United States. Unlike racial groups, an *ethnic group* is set apart from others primarily because of its national origin or distinctive cultural patterns. In the United States, Puerto Ricans, Jews, and Polish Americans are all categorized as ethnic groups.

Minority Groups

A numerical minority is a group that makes up less than half of some larger population. The population of the United States includes thousands of numerical minorities, including television actors, green-eyed people, tax lawyers, and descendants of the Pilgrims who arrived on the *Mayflower*. However, these numerical minorities are not considered to be minorities in the sociological sense; in fact, the number of people in a group does not necessarily determine its status as a social minority (or dominant group). When sociologists define a minority group, they are primarily concerned with the economic and political power, or powerlessness, of that group. A *minority group* is a subordinate group whose members have significantly less control or power over their own lives than the members of a dominant or majority group have over theirs.

Sociologists have identified five basic properties

(AP/Wide World Photos)

Members of a minority group have a strong sense of group solidarity, which develops partly as a result of the prejudice and discrimination they experience. Armenian Americans are shown at a 1988 march to the Soviet mission to the United Nations; their goal was a reunited homeland and an end to ethnic tensions and riots there.

of a minority group—physical or cultural traits, unequal treatment, ascribed status, solidarity, and in-group marriage (M. Harris, 1958:4–11):

1 Members of a minority group share physical or cultural characteristics that distinguish them from the dominant group. Each society has its own arbitrary standard for determining which characteristics are most important in defining dominant and minority groups.

2 Members of a minority experience unequal treatment and have less power over their lives than members of a dominant group have over theirs. For example, the management of an apartment complex may refuse to rent to African Americans, Hispanics, or Jews. Social inequality may be created or maintained by prejudice, discrimination, segregation, or even extermination.

3 Membership in a dominant (or minority) group is not voluntary; people are born into the group. Thus, race and ethnicity are considered *ascribed* statuses (see Chapter 5).

4 Minority group members have a strong sense of group solidarity. William Graham Sumner, writing in 1906, noted that individuals make distinctions between members of their own group (the *in-group*) and everyone else (the *out-group*). In-groups and out-groups were discussed in Chapter 6. When a group is the object of long-term prejudice and discrimination, the feeling of "us versus them" can and often does become extremely intense.

5 Members of a minority generally marry others from the same group. A member of a dominant group is often unwilling to join a supposedly inferior minority by marrying one of its members. In addition, the minority group's sense of solidarity encourages marriages within the group and discourages marriages to outsiders.

Race

As already suggested, the term *racial group* is reserved for those minorities (and the corresponding dominant groups) set apart from others by obvious physical differences. But what is an "obvious" physical difference? Each society determines which differences are important while ignoring other characteristics that could serve as a basis for social differentiation. In the United States, differences in both skin color and hair color are generally quite obvious. Yet Americans learn informally that differences in skin color have a dramatic social and political meaning, while differences in hair color are not nearly so socially significant.

When observing skin color, Americans tend to lump people rather casually into such general categories as "Black," "White," and "Asian." More subtle differences in skin color often go unnoticed. However, this is not the case in other societies. Many nations of Central America and South America have **color gradients** distinguishing people on a continuum from light to dark skin color. African slaves were brought to almost all these countries; these people intermarried, to varying degrees, with each other or with indigenous Indians. Consequently, as noted in Chapter 9, Brazil has approximately 40 racial groupings, while in other countries people may be described as "Mestizo Hondurans," "Mulatto Colombians," or "African Panamanians." Viewed in this light, residents of the United States must recognize that what we see as "obvious" differences are subject to each society's social definitions.

The largest racial minorities in the United States are Blacks (or African Americans), American Indians, Japanese Americans, Chinese Americans, and other Asian peoples. Information about the population and distribution of racial groups in this country is presented in Table 10-1 on the opposite page.

Biological Significance of Race Viewed from a biological perspective, the term *race* would refer to a genetically isolated group with distinctive gene frequencies. It is impossible to scientifically define or identify such a group. Consequently, contrary to popular belief, there are no "pure races." Nor are there physical traits—whether skin color or baldness—that can be used to describe one group to the exclusion of all others. If scientists examine a smear of human blood under a microscope, they cannot tell whether it came from a Chinese or a Navajo, a Hawaiian or an African American.

Migration, exploration, and invasion have further compromised the maintenance of pure races and led to increased racial intermingling. Scientific investigations suggest that the percentage of North American Blacks with White ancestry ranges from 20 percent to as much as 75 percent. Such statistics undermine a fundamental assumption of American life: that we can accurately categorize individuals as "Black" or "White" (Herskovits, 1930:15; D. Roberts, 1975).

Some people would like to find biological explanations which could help us to understand why certain peoples of the world have come to dominate others (refer back to the discussion of sociobiology in Chapter 4). Given the absence of pure racial groups, there can be no satisfactory biological answers for such social and political questions.

Social Significance of Race One of the most crucial aspects of the relationship between dominant and subordinate groups is the ability of the dominant or majority groups to define a society's values. American sociologist William I. Thomas (1923:41–44), an early critic of theories of racial and gender differences, saw that the "definition of the situation" could mold the personality of the individual. To put it another way, Thomas, writing from the interactionist perspective, observed that people respond not only to the objective features of a situation or person but also to the meaning that situation or person has for them. Thus we can create false images or stereotypes that become real in their consequences. *Stereotypes* are unreliable generalizations about all members of a group which do not recognize individual differences within the group.

In the last 25 years, there has been growing awareness of the power of the mass media to introduce stereotypes into everyday life. As one result, stereotyping of racial and ethnic minorities in Hollywood films, on television, and in Broadway shows has come under increasing fire. For example, in 1991, Asian American groups in New York City picketed the opening of the musical *Miss Saigon.* One of their charges was that the show continued the traditional stereotype of Asian women as either prostitutes or exotics. Hispanics note that Hollywood has traditionally presented them as vicious bandits, lazy peasants, or humorous buffoons; the stereotyping of Puerto

TABLE 10-1 Racial and Ethnic Groups in the United States, 1990

CLASSIFICATION	NUMBER IN THOUSANDS	PERCENT OF TOTAL POPULATION
Racial groups		
Whites	199,686	80.3
Blacks	29,986	12.1
American Indians, Eskimos, Aleuts	1,959	0.8
Chinese	1,645	0.7
Filipinos	1,407	0.6
Japanese	848	0.3
Asian Indians	815	0.3
Koreans	799	0.3
Vietnamese	615	0.2
Laotians	149	0.1
Cambodians	147	0.1
Ethnic groups		
White ancestry		
Germans	17,160	7.9
British and Scottish	13,116	6.1
Irish	9,760	4.5
Italians	6,110	2.8
Poles	3,498	1.6
French	3,047	1.4
Jews	5,925	2.6
Hispanics	22,354	9.1
Mexican Americans	13,496	5.4
Puerto Ricans	2,728	1.0
Cubans	1,044	0.4
Other	5,086	2.0
Total (all groups)	248,710	

NOTE: Percentages do not total 100 percent, and subheads do not add up to figures in major heads, since overlap between groups exists (e.g., Polish American Jews). Therefore, numbers and percentages should be considered approximations. Data on White ancestry are for 1979. Data on Jews are for 1980.
SOURCES: Bureau of the Census, 1981a, 1981b:55–56, 1981c:32, 1991b, 1991c; Himmelfarb and Singer, 1981; news release of June 12, 1991, "Census Bureau Releases 1990 Census Counts on Specific Racial Groups"; and authors' estimates.

BOX 10-1 • SPEAKING OUT

STEREOTYPES OF PUERTO RICAN WOMEN AND MEN

Puerto Rican women have typically experienced a kind of "double jeopardy," since they experience inequality based on both ethnicity and gender. In the following selection, Lourdes Miranda King (1974:21–22), the founder of the National Conference of Puerto Rican Women, discusses the stereotypes too often applied to Puertorriquenas (Puerto Rican women), as well as the stereotypes of Puerto Rican men.

The Puerto Rican woman is too often pictured as a passive female bending first to the will of her father, then of her husband—an obscure figure shuffling to the needs of her children and the men in her family.

This image has become an excuse to justify excluding her from full participation in the life of the United States. It reinforces the Anglo American stereotype of the Latin woman as childlike, pampered, and irresponsible.

The view supports the notion that Puerto Rican women deserve their subordinate status. After all, are not many of them employed in service occupations and as unskilled laborers? That must mean

(Courtesy Lourdes Miranda King)

Lourdes Miranda King.

they are suited only for demeaning work and is proof enough that they belong in that category. If one adds the prevalent assumption that Puerto Rican women are all alike the stereotype is complete.

In many ways, the image of the Puerto Rican woman is similar to that of Puerto Rican men. That image is embellished by the perception of Latin men as indolent skirtchasers, in addition to being irresponsible and undependable. They, too, are at the

bottom of the occupational ladder—which serves, in turn, to justify their exclusion and discrimination.

The adoption of the terms *macho* and *machismo* from Spanish to describe the supreme male chauvinist reflects the Latin male stereotype. Is it a coincidence that earlier the English borrowed Don Juan, the stereotype of the great lover?

Surely, other cultures have created words and literary figures to portray the traits of lovers, "banty-roosters," and authoritative males. If such spontaneous labels faithfully reflect life, as has been pointed out, then the selection of words from one culture for the popular language of another must reflect deep-rooted value judgments and cultural assumptions.

Official statistics show the disastrous results brought about by false assumptions. The overall situation of Puerto Ricans in the United States attests to the low esteem in which they are held. By any standards, Puerto Ricans are a severely deprived ethnic group.

Rican women and men is discussed in Box 10-1 above. Similarly, Jack Shaheen (1984:52, 1988), a professor of mass communications, is critical of prime-time television for perpetuating four myths about Arabs: "They are fabulously wealthy; they are barbaric and uncultured; they are sex maniacs with a penchant for white slavery; and they are prone to terrorist acts." While the use of stereotyping can promote in-group solidar-

ity, conflict theorists point out that stereotypes contribute to prejudice and thereby assist the subordination of minority groups (Schaefer, 1990:63–66; see also Gates, 1989).

In certain situations, we may respond to stereotypes and act on them, with the result that false definitions become accurate. This is known as the *self-fulfilling prophecy.* A person or group is described as having particular characteristics and then begins to display the very traits that were said to exist. In assessing the impact of self-fulfilling prophecies, we can refer back to labeling theory (see Chapter 7), which emphasizes how a person comes to be labeled as deviant and even to accept a self-image of deviance.

Self-fulfilling prophecies can be especially devastating for minority groups (see Figure 10-1) Such groups often find that they are allowed to hold only low-paying jobs with little prestige or opportunity for advancement. The rationale of the dominant society is that these members of a minority lack the ability to perform in more important and lucrative positions. Minority group members are then denied the training needed to become scientists, executives, or physicians and are locked into society's inferior jobs. As a result, the false definition has become real: in terms of employment, the minority has become inferior because it was originally defined as inferior and was prevented from achieving equality.

Because of this vicious circle, talented people from minority groups may come to see the worlds of entertainment and professional sports as their only hope for achieving wealth and fame. Thus, it is no accident that successive waves of Irish, Jewish, Italian, Black, and Hispanic performers and athletes have made their mark on American society. Unfortunately, these very successes may con-vince the dominant group that its original stereotypes are valid—that these are the only areas of society in which minorities can excel. Furthermore, athletics and the arts are well known in our society as highly competitive arenas. For every Gloria Estefan, Michael Jordan, Jose Canseco, or Oprah Winfrey who "makes it," many, many more will end up disappointed (Allport, 1979:189–205; Merton, 1968:475–490; Myrdal, 1944:75–78, 1065–1070).

Sociologist Harry Edwards (1984:8–13) agrees that the self-fulfilling prophecy of "innate Black athletic superiority" can have damaging consequences. Edwards points out that although this perception of athletic prowess may cause many Black Americans to be channeled into sports, at best, only about 2500 of them currently make a living in professional sports as players, coaches, trainers, team doctors, and executives. In his view, Blacks should no longer "put playbooks ahead of textbooks," and the Black community should abandon its "blind belief in sport as an extraordinary route to social and economic salvation."

African Americans and other minorities do not always passively accept harmful stereotypes and self-fulfilling prophecies. In the 1960s and 1970s, many subordinate minorities in the United States rejected traditional definitions and replaced them

FIGURE 10-1 Self-Fulfilling Prophecy

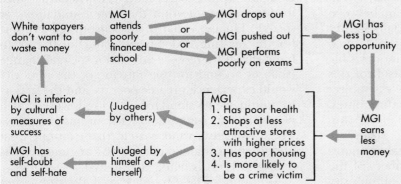

NOTE: MGI stands for "minority group individual." Arrows represent direction of negative cumulative effect.

SOURCE: Schaefer, 1990:24; see also Daniels and Kitano, 1970:21.

The self-validating effects of definitions made by the dominant group are shown in this figure. A minority-group person attends a poorly financed school and is left unequipped to perform jobs which offer high status and high pay. He or she then gets a low-paying job and must settle for a lifestyle far short of society's standards. Since the person shares these standards, he or she may begin to feel self-doubt and self-hatred. This last aspect of the cycle has been called into question in recent research.

with feelings of pride, power, and strength. "Black is beautiful" and "Red power" movements among Blacks and American Indians were efforts to take control of their own lives and self-images. However, although a minority can make a determined effort to redefine a situation and resist stereotypes, the definition that remains most important is the one used by a society's most powerful groups. In this sense, the historic White, Anglo-Saxon, Protestant norms of the United States still shape the definitions and stereotypes of racial and ethnic minorities.

Ethnicity

An ethnic group, unlike a racial group, is set apart from others because of its national origin or distinctive cultural patterns. Among the ethnic groups in the United States are peoples referred to collectively as *Hispanics,* such as Puerto Ricans, Mexican Americans, Cubans, and other Latin Americans (refer back to Table 10-1 on page 291). Other ethnic groups in this country include Jewish, Irish, Polish, Italian, and Norwegian Americans.

The distinction between racial and ethnic minorities is not always clear-cut. Some members of racial minorities, such as Asian Americans, may have significant cultural differences from other groups. At the same time, certain ethnic minorities, such as Hispanics, may have obvious physical differences which set them apart from other Americans.

Despite such problems of categorization, sociologists continue to feel that the distinction between racial groups and ethnic groups is socially significant. In most societies, including the United States, physical differences tend to be more visible than ethnic differences. Partly as a result of this fact, stratification along racial lines is less subject to change than stratification along ethnic lines. Members of an ethnic minority sometimes can, over time, become indistinguishable from the majority—although this process may take generations and may never include all members of the group. By contrast, members of a racial minority find it much more difficult to blend in with the larger society and to gain acceptance from the majority.

STUDYING RACE AND ETHNICITY

Relations among racial and ethnic groups have lent themselves to analysis from the three major perspectives of sociology. Viewing race from the macro level, functionalists observe that racial prejudice and discrimination serve positive functions for dominant groups, whereas conflict theorists see the economic structure as a central factor in the exploitation of minorities. The micro-level analysis of interactionist researchers stresses the manner in which everyday contact between people from different racial and ethnic backgrounds contributes to tolerance or leads to hostility.

Functionalist Perspective

It would seem reasonable to assume that racial bigotry offers no essential benefits for society. Why, then, does it exist? Functionalist theorists, while agreeing that racial hostility is hardly to be admired, point out that it indeed serves positive functions for those practicing discrimination.

Anthropologist Manning Nash (1962) has identified three functions that racially prejudiced beliefs have for the dominant group. First, such views provide a moral justification for maintaining an unequal society that routinely deprives a minority of its rights and privileges. Southern Whites justified slavery by believing that Africans were physically and spiritually subhuman and devoid of souls (Hoebel, 1949:85–86). Second, racist beliefs discourage the subordinate minority from attempting to question its lowly status, since to do so is to question the very foundations of society. Finally, racial myths encourage support for the existing order by introducing the argument that if there were any major societal change (such as an end to discrimination), the minority would experience greater poverty and the majority would see its standard of living lowered. As a result, Nash suggests, racial prejudice grows when a society's value system (for example, that underlying a colonial empire or a regime perpetuating slavery) is being threatened.

Although racial prejudice and discrimination may serve the interests of the powerful, such unequal treatment can also be dysfunctional to a society and even to its dominant group. Sociologist

Arnold Rose (1951:19–24) outlines four dysfunctions associated with racism:

1 A society which practices discrimination fails to use the resources of all individuals. Discrimination limits the search for talent and leadership to the dominant group.
2 Discrimination aggravates social problems such as poverty, delinquency, and crime and places the financial burden to alleviate these problems on the dominant group.
3 Society must invest a good deal of time and money to defend its barriers to full participation of all members.
4 Goodwill and friendly diplomatic relations between nations are often undercut by racial prejudice and discrimination.

Conflict Perspective

Conflict theorists would certainly agree with Arnold Rose that racial prejudice and discrimination have many harmful consequences for society. Sociologists such as Oliver Cox (1948) and Robert Blauner (1972) have used the *exploitation theory* (or Marxist class theory) to explain the basis of racial subordination in the United States. As we saw in Chapter 8, Karl Marx viewed the exploitation of the lower class as a basic part of the capitalist economic system. Under a Marxist approach, racism keeps minorities in low-paying jobs, thereby supplying the capitalist ruling class with a pool of cheap labor. Moreover, by forcing racial minorities to accept low wages, capitalists can restrict the wages of *all* members of the proletariat. Workers from the dominant group who demand higher wages can always be replaced by minorities who have no choice but to accept low-paying jobs (O. Cox, 1976; H. Hunter and Abraham, 1987; C. Johnson, 1939).

This Marxist perspective seems persuasive in a number of instances. Japanese Americans were the object of little prejudice until they began to enter jobs that brought them into competition with Whites. The movement to keep Chinese immigrants out of the United States became most fervent during the latter half of the nineteenth century, when Chinese and Whites fought over dwindling work opportunities. Both the enslavement of Blacks and the removal westward of American Indians were, to a significant extent, economically motivated (McWilliams, 1951:144–150).

However, though some examples support the exploitation theory of race relations, it is too limited to explain prejudice in its many forms. Not all minority groups have been economically exploited to the same extent. In addition, many groups (among them the Quakers and Mormons) have been victimized by prejudice for reasons other than economic ones. Still, as Gordon Allport (1979:210) concludes, the exploitation theory correctly "points a sure finger at one of the factors involved in prejudice, . . . rationalized self-interest of the upper classes."

Interactionist Perspective

A Black woman is transferred from a job on an assembly line to a similar position working next to a White man. At first, he is patronizing, assuming she must be incompetent. She is cold and resentful; even when she needs assistance, she refuses to admit it. After a week, the growing tension between the two leads to a bitter quarrel. Yet, over time, each slowly comes to appreciate the other's strengths and talents. A year after they begin working together, these two workers become respectful friends. This is an example of what interactionists call the *contact hypothesis* in action.

The *contact hypothesis* states that interracial contact of people with equal status in cooperative circumstances will cause them to become less prejudiced and to abandon previous stereotypes. The factors of *equal status* and a *pleasant, noncompetitive atmosphere* must be underscored. In the example above, if the two workers had been competing for one vacancy as a supervisor, the racial hostility between them might have worsened (Allport, 1979:261–282; Schaefer, 1990:81–84).

As African Americans and other minorities slowly gain access to better-paying and more responsible jobs in American society, the contact hypothesis may take on even greater significance. The trend in our society is toward increasing contact between individuals from dominant and subordinate groups. This may be one hope of eliminating—or at least reducing—racial and ethnic stereotyping and prejudice.

PREJUDICE AND DISCRIMINATION

False definitions of individuals and groups are perpetuated by prejudice. *Prejudice* is a negative attitude toward an entire category of people, often an ethnic or racial minority. If you resent your roommate because he or she is sloppy, you are not necessarily guilty of prejudice. However, if you immediately stereotype your roommate on the basis of such characteristics as race, ethnicity, or religion, that is a form of prejudice.

In recent years, college campuses across the United States have been the scene of bias-related incidents. Student-run newspapers and radio stations have ridiculed racial and ethnic minorities; threatening literature has been stuffed under the doors of minority students; graffiti endorsing the views of White supremacist organizations such as the Ku Klux Klan have been scrawled on university walls. In some cases, there have even been violent clashes between groups of White and Black students. These distressing incidents serve as a reminder that prejudice is evident among both educated and uneducated members of our society (Hively, 1990).

Prejudice can result from *ethnocentrism*—the tendency to assume that one's culture and way of life are superior to all others (see Chapter 3). Ethnocentric people judge other cultures by the standards of their own group, which leads quite easily to prejudice against cultures viewed as inferior.

One important and widespread form of prejudice is *racism,* the belief that one race is supreme and all others are innately inferior. When racism prevails in a society, members of subordinate groups generally experience prejudice, discrimination, and exploitation. In 1990, as concern mounted about racist attacks in the United States, Congress passed and President George Bush signed into law the Hate Crimes Statistics Act. This law directs the Department of Justice to gather data on crimes motivated by the victim's race, religion, ethnicity, or sexual orientation (refer back to Box 7-3 on page 212).

Research on prejudice points to two key components: first, personality factors (which tend to be emphasized by psychologists) and, second, structural factors (which have been studied most thoroughly by sociologists).

In recent years, college campuses across the United States have been the scene of bias-related incidents. Dartmouth College students are shown at a 1990 rally against racism and anti-Semitism.

The Authoritarian Personality and Scapegoating

Psychologists have attempted to determine whether certain types of people are more likely to be prejudiced than others. Theodore Adorno and his coworkers developed a model of a prejudiced individual which they call the **authoritarian personality**. The psychologists used a variety of tests and relied on a sample of more than 2000 respondents, ranging from middle-class professionals to inmates of San Quentin state prison.

While serious questions have been raised about their sampling procedures, the study produced some useful results. On the basis of this study, researchers claimed to have isolated the basic characteristics of the authoritarian personality: superstition, toughness, adherence to convention, and obedience to authority. In their view, the authoritarian personality is particularly likely to use minorities as a scapegoat (Adorno et al., 1950; see also Vander Zanden, 1983:131–138).

A **scapegoat** is a person or group that one blames irrationally for one's own problems or difficulties. The authoritarian personality cannot express resentment against those who are in control of either society or that person's immediate environment. Instead, he or she looks for some target for undeserved aggression—commonly Blacks, Jews, or other minorities subject to widespread prejudice. Scapegoating is also used by people who do not display the characteristics of the authoritarian personality, but who nevertheless blame some group for their own failures. A man who is a middle manager in "Silicon Valley" in northern California may irrationally decide that upwardly mobile Asian immigrants are responsible for his inability to win a promotion that he feels he "has coming."

The Structural Component

While personality factors are important contributors to prejudice, structural factors must also be given serious consideration. Societies develop social norms that dictate—for example—not only what foods are desirable (or forbidden), but also which racial and ethnic groups are to be favored (or despised). These norms are often reinforced by the social institutions of a society's social structure, such as government, religion, education, and the economy.

Social psychologist Thomas Pettigrew (1981) collected data that substantiated the importance of such social norms in encouraging or discouraging prejudice. Pettigrew found that Whites in the southern states were more anti-Black than Whites in the northern states and that Whites in the United States were not so prejudiced against Blacks as were Whites in the Republic of South Africa. Pettigrew's research revealed no significant variation between the two societies in terms of the presence of authoritarian individuals. He therefore concluded that structural factors explained differences in the levels of prejudice between these regions.

A more recent study by psychologist J. Louw-Potgieter (1988) supports this view. Typically, personality studies have maintained that White South Africans rear their children in a strict, disciplined, and patriarchal manner. These studies tend to ascribe authoritarianism particularly to the Afrikaners, who are the leaders of government and the architects of rule by the nation's White minority. Yet Louw-Potgieter finds that empirical research does not support these assumptions. Indeed, previous work in South Africa shows evidence in one sample that Black students are more authoritarian than White students (Heaven and Niewoudt, 1981).

Louw-Potgieter points to studies showing intergroup variability in the levels of prejudice that can be explained only by the kinds of structural variables first described by Pettigrew. Consequently, in explaining prejudice in South Africa, both personality and structural factors need to be considered. The structural factors identified by Louw-Potgieter include group membership, group position, peer pressure, ideology, and the media.

The personality and structural approaches to prejudice should not be viewed as mutually exclusive. Social circumstances provide cues for a person's attitudes; personality determines the extent to which people follow social cues and the likelihood that they will encourage others to do the

Discriminatory Behavior

The biased attitudes of the prejudiced person often lead to discriminatory behavior. *Discrimination* is the process of denying opportunities and equal rights to individuals and groups because of prejudice or other arbitrary reasons. Imagine that a White corporate president with a stereotyped view of Asian Americans has an executive position to fill. The most qualified candidate for the job is a Korean American. If the president refuses to hire this candidate and instead selects an inferior White candidate, he or she is engaging in an act of racial discrimination.

Prejudiced *attitudes* should not be equated with discriminatory *behavior*. Although the two are generally related, they are not identical, and either condition can be present without the other. For example, a prejudiced person does not always act on his or her biases. In the situation described above, the White president might choose—despite his or her stereotypes—to hire the Korean American. This would be prejudice without discrimination. On the other hand, a White corporate president with a completely respectful view of Korean Americans might refuse to hire them for executive posts out of fear that biased clients would take their business elsewhere. In this case, the president's action would constitute discrimination without prejudice.

Institutional Discrimination

Discrimination is practiced not only by individuals in one-to-one encounters but also by institutions in their daily operations. Social scientists are particularly concerned with the ways in which structural factors such as employment, housing, health care, and government operations maintain the social significance of race and ethnicity. *Institutional discrimination* refers to the denial of opportunities and equal rights to individuals and groups which results from the normal operations of a society.

Institutional discrimination continuously imposes more hindrances on—and awards fewer benefits to—certain racial and ethnic groups than it does others. In some cases, even ostensibly neutral institutional standards can turn out to have discriminatory effects. For example, in 1966, Chicago's Puerto Rican neighborhood was torn apart by riots. The complaint of police brutality was voiced frequently in the Puerto Rican community. In the aftermath of the riots, the Chicago Police Department admitted that it had no Puerto Rican officers.

Why was this the case? Subsequent investigations revealed that the police maintained a height requirement for officers which kept many otherwise qualified Puerto Ricans from applying. As a group, Puerto Ricans are shorter of stature than Whites or Blacks, and they found this arbitrary requirement impossible to overcome. In effect, through this standard, the Chicago police were saying, "Puerto Ricans need not apply." Later, the height requirement was revised, allowing Puerto Ricans to enter the police force, and there was some improvement in relations between police and community.

The use of height requirements unnecessarily geared to the physical proportions of White males—without regard for the actual requirements needed to perform the job—is but one of many forms of institutional discrimination identified in a report by the U.S. Commission on Civil Rights (1981:9–10). Other forms of institutional discrimination include:

- Rules requiring that only English be spoken at a place of work, even when it is not a business necessity to restrict the use of other languages
- Preferences shown by law and medical schools in the admission of children of wealthy and influential alumni, nearly all of whom are White
- Restrictive employment-leave policies, coupled with prohibitions on part-time work, that make it difficult for the heads of single-parent families (most of whom are women) to obtain and keep jobs.

The social policy section on affirmative action in Chapter 15 will examine legal prohibitions against institutional discrimination.

Discrimination in American society has proved difficult to eradicate. The 1960s saw the passage of many pioneering civil rights laws, including the landmark 1964 Civil Rights Act (which prohibits discrimination in public accommodations and publicly owned facilities on the basis of race, color, creed, national origin, and gender). In two important rulings in 1987, the Supreme Court held that federal prohibitions against racial discrimination protect members of all ethnic minorities—including Hispanics, Jews, and Arab Americans—even though they may be considered to be White. Yet discriminatory practices continue to pervade nearly all areas of life in the United States.

In part, this is because—as Manning Nash's functionalist analysis suggests—various individuals and groups actually *benefit* from racial and ethnic discrimination in terms of money, status, and influence. Discrimination permits members of the majority to enhance their wealth, power, and prestige at the expense of others. Less qualified people are hired and promoted simply because they are members of the dominant group. Such individuals and groups will not surrender these advantages easily.

A member of a racial or ethnic minority in the United States is likely to face various forms of prejudice and discrimination from dominant group members and from important institutions of our society. This is the underlying and painful context of American intergroup relations. Of course, such prejudice and discrimination are hardly unique to the United States. By 1990, as one result of the successful revolts against Communist rule in the Soviet Union and eastern Europe, traditional and long-suppressed ethnic rivalries had once again erupted into open conflict in many areas.

Throughout the region, national, racial, and ethnic minorities have bitterly protested against mistreatment by dominant groups. In the Soviet Union, there has been increasing resistance to the control exercised by the nation's ethnic Russian majority. Growing national assertiveness has been evident in the Ukraine, Estonia, Latvia, and Lithuania; at the same time, there as been conflict between Armenians and Azerbaijanis and rioting in the Central Asian republics. Across eastern Europe, protests have been heard from Hungarians living in Rumania, from Turks living in Bulgaria, from Serbs living in Yugoslavia's Croatian republic, from Albanians living in Yugoslavia's Serbian republic, and from Slovaks living in Czech-dominated Czechoslovakia. Moreover, long-standing prejudices against Jews and Gypsies are being expressed more openly in many of these nations (Bohlen, 1990; Burg, 1989; Schaefer, 1990:492–496).

PATTERNS OF INTERGROUP RELATIONS

The traditional clashes between ethnic groups in the Soviet Union and eastern Europe are but one aspect of intergroup relations. Racial and ethnic groups can relate to one another in a wide variety of desirable and undesirable ways, ranging from friendships and intermarriages that require mutual approval to behaviors imposed on the subordinate group by the dominant group. Undesirable patterns include **genocide**—the deliberate, systematic killing of an entire people or nation.

This term has been used in reference to the killing of 1 million Armenians by Turkey beginning in 1915 (Melson, 1986:64–66). It is most commonly applied to Nazi Germany's extermination of 6 million European Jews, as well as members of other ethnic minorities, during World War II. However, the term *genocide* is also appropriate in describing American policies toward Indians in the nineteenth century. In 1800, the American Indian population of the United States was about 600,000; by 1850, it had been reduced to 250,000 through warfare with the cavalry, disease, and forced relocation to inhospitable environments.

The *expulsion* of a people is another extreme means of acting out racial or ethnic prejudice. In 1979 Vietnam expelled nearly 1 million ethnic Chinese from the country, partly as a result of centuries of hostility between the two Asian neighbors. These "boat people" were abruptly eliminated as a minority within Vietnamese society.

There are four patterns that can be identified which describe typical intergroup relations as they occur in North America and throughout the world: (1) amalgamation, (2) assimilation, (3) segregation, and (4) pluralism. Each pattern defines the dominant group's actions and the minority group's responses. Intergroup relations are rarely restricted to only one of the four patterns, although invariably one does tend to dominate. Therefore, these patterns should be viewed primarily as ideal types.

Amalgamation

Amalgamation describes the end result when a majority group and a minority group combine to form a new group. Through intermarriage over several generations, various groups in the society combine to form a new group. This can be expressed as $A + B + C = D$, where A, B, and C represent different groups present in a society, and D signifies the end result, a unique cultural-racial group unlike any of the initial groups (Newman, 1973).

The belief in the United States as a "melting pot" became very compelling in the first part of the twentieth century, particularly since it suggested that the nation had an almost divine mission to amalgamate various peoples into one American people. However, many Americans were not willing to have American Indians, Jews, African Americans, Asian Americans, and Irish Roman Catholics as a part of the melting pot. Therefore, this pattern does not adequately describe dominant-subordinate relations existing in the United States.

Amalgamation does, however, take place elsewhere. Strange as it may seem, the famous mutiny aboard *HMS Bounty* gave rise to a melting pot. In 1790, the mutineers of the British naval vessel landed on inhabited Pitcairn Island in the south Pacific. They settled on the island along with Polynesians from Tahiti. In an ensuing conflict, all the Polynesian men and most of the Britishers died. Despite these violent beginnings, a fusion later took place, leading to a culture shared by people of mixed blood who "never had to eat the bitter bread of social or economic prejudice" (H. Shapiro, 1936:211).

Assimilation

Many Hindus in India complain about Indian citizens who copy the traditions and customs of the British. In Australia, Aborigines who have become part of the dominant society refuse to acknowledge their darker-skinned grandparents on the street. Within the United States, there are Italian Americans, Polish Americans, Hispanics, and Jews who have changed their ethnic-sounding family names to names typically found among White, Protestant families.

Assimilation is the process by which a person forsakes his or her own cultural tradition to become part of a different culture. Generally, it is practiced by a minority group member who wants to conform to the standards of the dominant group. Assimilation can be described as an ideology in which $A + B + C = A$. The majority A dominates in such a way that members of minorities B and C imitate A and attempt to become indistinguishable from the dominant group (Newman, 1973).

Assimilation can strike at the very roots of a person's identity as he or she seeks to gain full acceptance as an "American." Hence, Nathan Birnbaum changed his name to George Burns, and Joseph Levitch became Jerry Lewis. Despite such efforts, assimilation does not necessarily bring acceptance for the minority group individual. A Chinese American may speak flawless English, go faithfully to a Protestant church, and know the names of all members of the Baseball Hall of Fame. Yet he or she is still *seen* as different and may therefore be rejected as a business associate, a neighbor, or a marriage partner.

Segregation

Segregation refers to the physical separation of two groups of people in terms of residence, workplace, and social functions. Generally, it is imposed by a dominant group on a minority group. However, segregation is rarely complete; intergroup contact inevitably occurs even in the most segregated societies.

The Republic of South Africa severely restricts the movement of Blacks and other non-Whites through a wide-ranging system of segregation

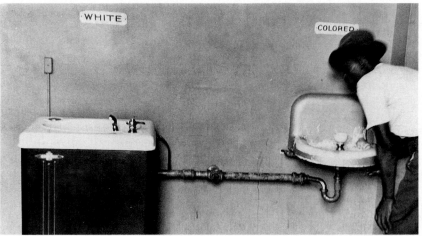

When segregation was common in the American south, "Jim Crow" laws enforced official segregation of the races. In a blatant example of institutional discrimination, photographed by Elliot Erwitt in North Carolina in 1950, Blacks were not allowed to use a water fountain reserved for Whites. Instead, Blacks had to drink out of a nearby sink.

known as **apartheid.** Apartheid involves many forms of segregation, ranging from the creation of homelands where Blacks are assigned to live to maintenance of racially separate facilities (including taxis, park benches, and restrooms) in South African cities. Moreover, Blacks are not allowed to vote in elections for the South African parliament. From a conflict perspective, apartheid can perhaps best be understood as a twentieth-century effort to reestablish the paternalistic form of race relations typified by the master-slave relationship (van den Berghe, 1978:108).

The situation of Blacks under apartheid is often desperate. Despite the affluence of South Africa, resulting from such assets as diamonds and oil, Blacks typically live in extreme poverty. For example, Blacks who work in cities are forced to live in all-Black satellite "townships" from which they travel to work. The townships are effectively shantytowns with few amenities: only occasional paved roads and electric lights on streets, no water or electricity in people's homes. Not surprisingly, the seeds of racial unrest are certainly sown in conditions like these.

Housing practices in the United States have often forced subordinate racial and ethnic groups into certain neighborhoods, usually undesirable ones. In addition, members of a minority group may voluntarily seek to separate themselves from the dominant majority because they fear reprisals. This is not, however, the primary factor contributing to segregation. The central causes of

residential segregation in the United States appear to be the prejudices of Whites and the resulting discriminatory practices in the housing and lending markets. Data consistently show that Blacks, Hispanics, and (to a *somewhat* lesser extent) Asians face segregation in the nation's metropolitan areas. Such housing segregation is evident around the world: studies in Sweden, for example, document that migrants from Chile, Greece, and Turkey are confined to segregated areas of Swedish cities (Andersson-Brolin, 1988; Massey and Denton, 1989a, 1989b).

Even today, Blacks and other minorities are apprehensive about moving into—or even passing through—certain White neighborhoods of the United States. In 1989, four young Black men read an advertisement for a used car and went to Bensonhurst, a predominantly White neighborhood of New York City. Unbeknownst to them, an angry mob of White youths was on the lookout for Blacks whom they believed had been invited to a party by a Bensonhurst woman. The Black visitors to the neighborhood were mistaken for the woman's friends and were attacked by the mob; one young Black man, Yusuf Hawkins, was shot to death.

The Bensonhurst attack reflected an alarming rise in racial violence across the United States. According to the Justice Department's Community Relations Service (1990), the number of reported incidents involving racial harassment and hate groups rose by 19 percent over the period

1987–1989. This increase may represent more frequent reporting of hate crimes, but it may also indicate that there has been a reduction of inhibitions against expressing racial and ethnic intolerance (Goleman, 1990b).

Pluralism

In a pluralistic society, a subordinate group will not have to forsake its lifestyle and traditions. *Pluralism* is based on mutual respect between various groups in a society for one another's cultures. It allows a minority group to express its own culture and still to participate without prejudice in the larger society. Earlier, amalgamation was described as A + B + C = D, and assimilation as A + B + C = A. Using this same approach, we can conceive of pluralism as A + B + C = A + B + C. All the groups are able to coexist in the same society (Newman, 1973).

In the United States, pluralism is more of an ideal than a reality. There are distinct instances of pluralism: the ethnic neighborhoods in major cities, such as Germantown, Little Tokyo, Andersonville (Swedish Americans), and Spanish Harlem. Yet there are also limits to such cultural freedom. In order to survive, a society must promote a certain consensus among its members regarding basic ideals, values, and beliefs. Thus, if a Rumanian migrating to the United States wants to move up the occupational ladder, he or she cannot avoid learning the English language.

Several authors argue persuasively that Switzerland exemplifies a modern pluralistic state. The absence both of a national language and of a dominant religious faith leads to a tolerance for cultural diversity. In addition, various political devices have been adopted to safeguard the interests of ethnic groups in a way that has no parallel in the United States. By contrast, Great Britain has found it difficult to achieve cultural pluralism in a multiracial society. East Indians, Pakistanis, and Blacks from the Caribbean and Africa are experiencing prejudice and discrimination within the dominant White British society. There is increasing pressure to cut off all Asian and Black immigration and to expel those non-Whites currently living in Britain.

RACE AND ETHNICITY IN THE UNITED STATES

Few societies have a more diverse population than the United States does. The American nation is truly a multiracial, multiethnic society. Of course, this has not always been true. The different groups listed in Table 10-1 have come to the United States as a result of immigration, colonialism, and, in the case of Blacks, the institution of slavery.

Racial Groups

The largest racial minorities in the United States include Black Americans, American Indians, Chinese Americans, Japanese Americans, and Indochinese Americans.

Black Americans "I am an invisible man," wrote Black author Ralph Ellison in his novel *Invisible Man* (1952:3). "I am a man of substance, of flesh and bone, fiber and liquids—and I might even be said to possess a mind. I am invisible, understand, simply because people refuse to see me."

Over 3 decades later, many Blacks (or African Americans) still feel invisible. The United States, with over 30 million Blacks, has the second-largest Black population in the world. However, despite their large numbers, African Americans have long been treated as second-class citizens. Currently, by the standards of the federal government, nearly 1 out of every 3 Blacks—as opposed to 1 out of every 10 Whites—are poor (Bureau of the Census, 1990a:12, 251).

Contemporary institutional discrimination and individual prejudice against Black Americans are rooted in the history of slavery in the United States. As many as 15 to 20 million Blacks may have come to this nation in chains. Even in bondage, the Africans were forced to assimilate and were stripped of much of their African tribal heritage. Yet the destruction of African cultures was not complete; some aspects survived in oral literature, religious customs, and music. Black resistance to slavery included many slave revolts, such as those led by Denmark Vesey in South Carolina in 1822 and Nat Turner in Virginia in 1831. Still, most Blacks remained subject to the arbitrary and

During the 1950s and 1960s, Blacks were inspired by the leadership of Dr. Martin Luther King, Jr., who led numerous boycotts and marches on behalf of civil rights. More recently, Blacks have been inspired by Nelson Mandela, leader of the African National Congress. Mandela, who spent almost 28 years in South African prisons, was released in 1990 and toured the United States later that year.

often cruel actions of their White owners (Du Bois, 1909; Herskovits, 1941, 1943).

The end of the Civil War did not bring genuine freedom and equality for Blacks. The "Jim Crow" laws of the south, which were designed to enforce official segregation, were upheld as constitutional by the Supreme Court in 1896. In addition, Blacks faced the danger of lynching campaigns, often led by the Ku Klux Klan, during the late nineteenth and early twentieth centuries. From a conflict perspective, the dominance of Whites was maintained formally through legalized segregation and maintained informally by means of vigilante terror and violence (J. Franklin and Moss, 1988).

A turning point in the struggle for Black equality came in the unanimous Supreme Court decision in the 1954 case of *Brown v. Board of Education of Topeka, Kansas.* The Court outlawed segregation of public school students, ruling that "separate educational facilities are inherently unequal." In the wake of the *Brown* decision, there was a surge of activism on behalf of Black civil rights, including boycotts of segregated bus companies and sit-ins at restaurants and lunch counters which refused to serve Blacks.

During the decade of the 1960s, a vast civil rights movement emerged, with many competing factions and strategies for change. The Southern Christian Leadership Conference (SCLC), founded by Dr. Martin Luther King, Jr., used nonviolent civil disobedience to oppose segregation. The National Association for the Advance-

ment of Colored People (NAACP) favored use of the courts to press for legal equality for African Americans. But many younger Black leaders, most notably Malcolm X, turned toward an ideology of Black power. Proponents of **Black power** rejected the goal of assimilation into White, middle-class society. They defended the beauty and dignity of Black and African cultures and supported the creation of Black-controlled political and economic institutions (Carmichael and Hamilton, 1967).

Although numerous courageous actions have taken place to achieve Black civil rights, Black and White America are still separate, still unequal. From birth to death, Blacks suffer in terms of the life chances described in Chapter 8. Life remains quite difficult for millions of poor Blacks, who must attempt to survive in ghetto areas shattered by high unemployment and abandoned housing. The economic position of Blacks is shown in Table 10-2. As the table illustrates, the median income of Blacks is only 57 percent that of Whites, and the unemployment rate among Blacks is close to 2 and one-half times that of Whites (Bureau of the Census, 1990a).

The economic position of Black women and their children is particularly critical (refer back to the social policy section on the feminization of poverty in Chapter 8). A 1988 survey of Black female heads of households showed that only 34 percent of them worked full time; the poverty rate for Black, single mothers with children is 60 percent. Economist Bernard Anderson of the

TABLE 10-2   Relative Economic Positions of Blacks and Whites, 1988

CHARACTERISTIC	BLACKS	WHITES	RATIO, BLACK TO WHITE
Completed college, persons 25 or over	11.3%	20.9%	.54
Median family money income	$19,329	$33,915	.57
Unemployment rate	11.7%	4.7%	2.49
Persons below the poverty level	31.6%	10.1%	3.33

SOURCE: Bureau of the Census, 1990a:133, 380, 450, 458.

Despite some Black progress in the 1960s and 1970s, there remains a wide gap in the economic positions of Blacks and Whites in the United States. For example, the median income of Blacks is only 57 percent that of Whites, while the Black unemployment rate is almost 2 and one-half times that of Whites. This gap reflects the pervasiveness of institutional discrimination.

Despite advances in the election of Black officials, many Blacks still feel they are outsiders in the political process of the United States.

Rockefeller Foundation observes: "You cannot discuss Black poverty without discussing the dreadful condition of life and opportunity among Black women who are poor and raising children" (Bureau of the Census, 1989a:71; Noble, 1984:E20; Rawlings, 1989:23).

There have been economic gains for *some* Blacks—especially middle-class Blacks—over the last 30 years (refer back to the study of Black executives described in Chapter 2). For example, Department of Labor data show that Blacks in management areas of the labor market increased nationally from 2.4 percent of the total in 1958 to 6.0 percent in 1988. Yet Blacks still represent 4 percent or less of all physicians, engineers, scientists, lawyers, judges, and marketing and financial managers. Moreover, in an especially important area for developing role models, African Americans, Hispanics, and other minorities together account for less than 1 percent of all upper-level managers in the mass media (Bureau of the Census, 1990a:389; J. Nelson, 1987).

In many respects, the civil rights movement of the 1960s left institutionalized discrimination against Blacks untouched. Consequently, in the 1980s, Black leaders worked to mobilize Black political power as a force for social change. Between 1969 and 1986, the number of Black elected officials increased by more than fivefold. By 1989, there were 299 Black mayors in the United States, more than two-thirds of them in cities in the south. Black mayors held office in many of the nation's largest cities, including New York, Philadelphia, Detroit, Atlanta, Los Angeles, and New Orleans (Joint Center for Political Studies, 1989).

Encouraged by the mayoral victories of Andrew Young in Atlanta and Harold Washington in Chicago, the Reverend Jesse Jackson mounted a campaign for the 1984 Democratic nomination for president. Aided by a dramatic turnout of Black voters, Jackson made a strong showing, winning 18 percent of the votes cast in Democratic presidential primaries. Jackson's success inspired more Blacks to run for national offices and statewide offices. He himself ran for president again in 1988 and won about 29 percent of the votes in Democratic primaries, second only to the 43 percent won by Massachusetts governor Michael Dukakis.

American Indians: The Native Americans

There are approximately 2 million Native Americans. These Americans represent a diverse array of cultures, distinguishable by language, family organization, religion, and livelihood.

"I don't think they're interested in colored beads anymore."

Native American activists have bitterly protested the mistreatment of Indians in American society. They have expressed particular contempt for the Bureau of Indian Affairs (BIA).

To the outsiders who came to the United States—European settlers and their descendants—the native people came to be known as "American Indians." By the time that the Bureau of Indian Affairs (BIA) was organized as part of the *War Department* in 1824, Indian-White relations had already included 3 centuries of mutual misunderstanding (P. Berg, 1975). As we saw earlier, many bloody wars took place during the nineteenth century in which a significant part of the nation's Indian population was wiped out. By the end of the nineteenth century, schools for Indians operated by the BIA or church missions prohibited the practice of Indian cultures. Yet such schools did little to make the children effective competitors in White society.

Today, American Indians are an impoverished people; life is difficult, whether they live in cities or on the reservations. For example, the death rate of Navajo babies over 18 weeks old is 2 and one-half times that of the overall population of the United States. In 1987, the National Urban Indian Council estimated that 60 to 80 percent of Native Americans living in cities are unemployed (Giago and Illoway, 1982; D. Martin, 1987:46).

In 1972, a regional director of the Commission on Civil Rights characterized government policy toward Indians as "assimilate—or starve!" Indians who choose to abandon all vestiges of their tribal cultures may escape certain forms of prejudice. Those Indians who remain on the reservation and cherish their cultural heritage will suffer the consequences of their choice (Muskrat, 1972).

Native American activists have bitterly protested the mistreatment of Indians in American society. The latest battleground—not only in the United States, but also in Brazil (refer back to Chapter 9)—has been land and natural resources. Reservations typically contain a wealth of resources. In the past, Indian tribes have lacked the technical knowledge to negotiate beneficial agreement successfully with private corporations; when they had such ability, the federal government often stepped in and made the final agreements more favorable to corporations than to residents of the reservations. More recently, however, a coalition of Indian tribes has had impressive results in its bargaining efforts. An Atlantic Richfield Company (ARCO) offer of $300,000 for an oil pipeline right-of-way on a Navajo reservation was converted through skillful negotiating into a contract that will bring the tribe $78 million over 20 years.

Some critics of these agreements worry that unchecked energy development on Indian lands could disrupt traditional culture and values and cause environmental pollution of the lands. There is even evidence that the federal government has decreased its assistance to Indians, using as its justification this newfound wealth. Regardless, Native Americans seem to have little choice but to develop those mineral resources which they enjoy and to use the increased revenue to diversify tribal economies (Schaefer, 1990:199–200).

Chinese Americans Unlike African slaves and American Indians, the Chinese were initially encouraged to immigrate to the United States. From 1850 to 1880, over 200,000 Chinese immigrated to this country, lured by job opportunities created by the discovery of gold. As employment possibilities decreased and competition for mining grew, the Chinese became the target of a bitter campaign to limit their numbers and restrict their rights. Chinese laborers were exploited, then discarded.

In 1882 Congress enacted the Chinese Exclusion Act, which prevented Chinese immigration and even forbade Chinese in America from sending for their families. As a result, there was a steady decline in the Chinese population until after World War II. More recently, the descendants of the nineteenth-century immigrants have been joined by a new influx from Hong Kong and Taiwan. The groups of immigrants sometimes form sharp contrasts in their degree of assimilation, desire to live in Chinatowns, and feelings about this country's relations with the People's Republic of China (Kwong and Lum, 1988).

There are currently about 1.65 million Chinese Americans in the United States. Unlike African Americans and American Indians, many Chinese Americans have entered lucrative occupations. This has led to the popular concept that the strides made by Chinese Americans (and other Asian Americans) constitute a success story. We examine the consequences of this "model minority" image in Box 10-2 (page 308).

Many Chinese immigrants struggle to survive under living and working conditions that belie the "model minority" stereotype. New York City's Chinatown district is filled with illegal sweatshops in which recent immigrants—many of them Chinese women—work for minimal wages. Even in "legal" factories in the garment industry, hours are long and rewards are limited. A seamstress typically works 11 hours per day, six days a week, and earns about $10,000 a year. Other workers, such as hemmers and cutters, earn only $5000 per year (Lum and Kwong, 1989).

Japanese Americans There are approximately 800,000 Japanese Americans in the United States. As a people, they are relatively recent arrivals to this nation. In 1880 there were only 148 Japanese in the United States, but by 1920 there were over 110,000. The early Japanese immigrants—who are called the *Issei*—were usually males seeking employment opportunities in America. Along with Chinese immigrants, they were seen as a "yellow peril" by many White Americans, and they were subjected to widespread prejudice and discrimination.

(Courtesy, Department of Manuscripts and University Archives, Cornell University Library)

Gene Sogioka's watercolor "The Loneliness of Poston" shows an evacuation camp for Japanese Americans in Poston, Arizona, during World War II. The camp was located on a deserted Indian reservation near the Colorado River. Born in California, Sogioka worked as a background artist for Walt Disney studios and taught art part-time. He was taken to Poston along with his wife Mini and their very young daughter. Sogioka was hired by the wartime Bureau of Sociological Research to document the lives of the confined Japanese Americans through his artwork (Gesensway and Roseman, 1987:166).

BOX 10-2 • CURRENT RESEARCH

ASIAN AMERICANS AND THE "MODEL MINORITY" STEREOTYPE

President Ronald Reagan once called Asian Americans "our exemplars of hope and inspiration." Articles in *Time* and *Newsweek* on this minority have featured headlines such as "A Formula for Success" and "The Drive to Excel." There seems to be no end to the praise for Asian Americans (McLeod, 1986; Ramirez, 1986).

It is commonly believed that Asian Americans constitute a model or ideal minority group, supposedly because, despite past suffering from prejudice and discrimination, they have succeeded economically, socially, and educationally without resorting to political and violent confrontations with Whites. Some observers see the existence of a model minority as a reaffirmation that anyone can get ahead in the United States with talent and hard work.

Indeed, there is an implicit critique of Blacks, Hispanics, and others for failing to succeed as well as the model minority has. Viewed from a conflict perspective, this becomes yet another instance of "blaming the victim" (refer back to Box 8-2 on page 244), for the hidden allegation is that any minorities who have been less successful than Asian Americans are completely responsible for their own failures. Proponents of the model minority view add that because Asian Americans have achieved success, they have ceased to be a disadvantaged minority (Hurh and Kim, 1989).

While Asian Americans have registered many distinctive achievements, the model minority stereotype tends to overstate the group's success. For example, wide publicity was given to 1980 census data showing that the median income of Asian American families was $23,600, while the median income of White families was only $20,800. But these data are misleading. Asian Americans live almost exclusively in urban areas, where incomes are higher. Since 63 percent of Asian families have two or more wage earners (compared with only 55 percent of White families), the individual wages of the typical Asian American worker may be rather low (Hirschman and Wong, 1984:598–600; Oxnam, 1986:89).

The concept of a model minority ignores the diversity among Asian Americans: there are rich and poor Japanese Americans, rich and poor Filipino Americans, and so forth. Moreover, even when certain Asian Americans are clustered at the higher-paying end of the stratification system, there may nevertheless be limits on how far they can advance. A study conducted in 1988 showed that only 8 percent of Asian Americans were classified as "officials" and "managers," compared with 12 percent for all groups (Takaki, 1990).

The dramatic success of Asian Americans in the educational system has undoubtedly fueled the model minority stereotype. In comparison with their numbers in the population of the United States, Asian Americans are over-represented by far as students in the nation's most prestigious public and private universities. Their success can be attributed, in part, to the belief in many Asian cultures in the value of education, family pressures to succeed, and the desire to use academic achievement as a means of escaping discrimination.

By the 1980s, there were growing charges that well-known universities were using unofficial quotas (similar to those historically used against Jewish applicants) to restrict the percentage of Asian American students. In 1989, several selective universities announced plans to substantially revise their admissions policies to correct what was termed "possible unintentional discrimination" against Asian American students.

In 1941, the attack on Pearl Harbor by Japan—by then allied with Hitler's Germany—had severe repercussions for Japanese Americans. The federal government decreed that all Japanese Americans on the west coast must leave their homes and report to "evacuation camps." They became, in effect, scapegoats for the anger that other Americans felt concerning Japan's role in World War II. In an unprecedented application of guilt by virtue of ancestry, 113,000 Japanese Americans were forced to live in hastily built camps by August 1943 (Hosokawa, 1969).

BOX 10-2 • CURRENT RESEARCH

ASIAN AMERICANS AND THE "MODEL MINORITY" STEREOTYPE (Continued)

However, in 1990, the Department of Education charged that the mathematics department of the University of California at Los Angeles (UCLA) had been guilty of racial discrimination in denying admission to five Asian American applicants (Jaschik, 1990).

Even the positive stereotype of Asian American students as "academic stars" can be dysfunctional. Asian Americans who do only modestly well in school may face criticism from parents or teachers for their failure to conform to the "whiz kid" image. In fact, despite the model minority label, the high school dropout rate for Asian Americans is increasing rapidly. California's special program for low-income, academically disadvantaged students has a 30 percent Asian American clientele, and the proportion of Asian students in the program is on the rise (Tachibana, 1990).

Recent immigrants from Asia are especially likely to be victimized by the model minority stereotype. For example, immigrants account for most of the 40 percent of Asian students admitted to the University of California at Berkeley who fail to graduate, yet these students may not be receiving adequate counseling and language assistance. Nadine Tang, a social worker, notes: "There are Asian students who are flunking out, who are on academic probation. You see some Vietnamese boat people who are doing pretty well academically but not emotionally. The pressure on them to succeed is made even greater by the myth that all of them succeed, and that can lead to severe psychological problems" (Bernstein, 1988:16).

Ben Fong-Torres (1986:7) worries that while reports of Asian American successes may inspire pride within this minority, they may also intensify fear and envy in the dominant White majority. Combined with resentment about the growing economic dominance of Japan, such jealousy may contribute not only to racial slurs and biases against Asian Americans but to violent attacks as well. In 1982, two White males began arguing with a Chinese American, Vincent Chin, whom they mistook for being of Japanese descent and blamed for the dire straits of the American automobile industry. The Whites chased Chin into a parking lot and repeatedly beat him with a baseball bat; he died 4 days later. Much to the shock of the local Asian American community, Chin's accused killers were allowed to make a plea-bargaining agreement whereby they were sentenced to only 3 years' probation and fined $3700 each.

Reviewing evidence of attacks on Asian Americans, U.S. Civil Rights Commissioner John Bunzel declared in 1987 that such incidents are "pernicious and disturbing" and are part of a "resurgence of an ugly anti-Asian sentiment in the United States." Partly in response to such hostility, numerous voluntary associations of Asian students have been organized on campuses to bring people together and to combat racism (E. Greene, 1987b; Wickenhaver, 1988).

Viewed from a conflict perspective, the model minority stereotype is likely to provoke further prejudice and discrimination against a racial minority quite easily viewed as "different." Full social acceptance of Asian Americans may be hindered if they are resented for becoming "too successful too fast." Ginger Lew, a Washington attorney and former State Department official, concludes that the "'model minority' myth is just that. It's not true in terms of income or status. Stereotypes, whether positive or negative, are a disservice to the community" (Oxnam, 1986:89, 92; Schaefer, 1990:360–369).

Financially, the Federal Reserve Board placed the losses of evacuation for Japanese Americans at nearly half a billion dollars, or more than $4500 per person. Accounting for inflation, this figure represents a loss of about $27,000 per person today. Moreover, the psychological effect on these citizens—including the humiliation of being labeled as "disloyal"—was immeasurable. Eventually, the American-born Japanese, the *Nisei,* were allowed to enlist in the Army and serve in a segregated combat unit in Europe. Others resettled in the east and midwest to work in factories.

In 1983, the federal Commission on Wartime Relocation and Internment of Civilians recommended government payments to all surviving Japanese Americans held in detention camps during World War II. The commission reported that the detention was motivated by "race prejudice, war hysteria, and a failure of political leadership." It added that "no documented acts of espionage, sabotage, or fifth-column activity were shown to have been committed" by Japanese Americans (Pear, 1983).

In 1988, President Ronald Reagan signed unprecedented legislation, entitled the Civil Liberties Act, in which the United States government apologized for the forced relocation of 120,000 Japanese Americans and established a $1.25 billion trust fund to pay reparations to persons placed in detention camps. Under the new law, the federal government was to issue individual apologies for all violations of Japanese Americans' constitutional rights. Beginning in 1990, awards of $20,000 were to be given to each of the approximately 65,000 surviving Japanese Americans who had been interned by the federal government.

Indochinese Americans The problems of American involvement in Vietnam did not end with the withdrawal of military assistance, or even with the evacuation of all American personnel from South Vietnam. The final tragedy was the reluctant welcome given to the refugees from Vietnam, Cambodia, and Laos by Americans and people of other nations. One week after the evacuation of Vietnam in April 1975, a Gallup poll reported that 52 percent of Americans were against giving any sanctuary to the Asian refugees, 36 percent were in favor, and 12 percent were undecided. The primary objection to Vietnamese immigration was that it would further increase unemployment (Gallup Opinion Index, 1975; Schaefer and Schaefer, 1975).

The initial 135,000 Vietnamese refugees who fled in 1975 were joined by another 800,000 fleeing later fighting that plagued Indochina. The United States eventually accepted about 250,000 Asian refugees for political settlement. Numerous others were stranded in overcrowded refugee camps administered by the United States. Yet, in a sense, those who reached the refugee camps were the lucky ones. It is estimated that 30 to 35 percent of those who left Vietnam in rickety boats did not survive (Haupt, 1979).

Most Indochinese refugees faced problems similar to those experienced by immigrants to this country in the past. Generally, they had to accept jobs which were well below their occupational positions in southeast Asia; with geographical mobility came downward social mobility. One difference in this case was that the voluntary agencies coordinated by the federal government became conspicuously involved in locating homes for the Indochinese refugees. Pressured by many communities who feared being overwhelmed by immigration, these agencies attempted to disperse the refugees throughout the nation.

However, such efforts failed, largely because the Indochinese refugees, like European immigrants before them, sought out their compatriots. As a result, Indochinese communities and neighborhoods have begun to emerge, especially in California, Texas, and New York. In such areas, where Indochinese Americans have been able to reestablish some of the distinctive cultural practices of their homelands, the outlook is for a more pluralistic solution to their adjustment, rather than adjustment involving complete assimilation.

Ethnic Groups

Unlike racial minorities, members of subordinate ethnic groups are generally not hindered from assimilating into the dominant American society by physical differences. However, members of ethnic minority groups still face many forms of prejudice and discrimination. This will be apparent as we examine the situations of the country's largest ethnic groups—Hispanics, Jews, and White ethnics.

Hispanics: Mexican Americans and Puerto Ricans Taken together, the various groups which are included under the general terms *Hispanics* and *Latinos* represent the largest ethnic minority in the United States. It is estimated that there are more than 22 million Hispanics in this country, including 13 million Mexican Americans, over 2 million Puerto Ricans, and smaller

Taken together, the various groups which are included under the general terms Hispanics *and* Latinos *represent the largest ethnic minority in the United States.*

numbers of Cubans and people of Central or South American origin.

The various Hispanic groups share a heritage of Spanish language and culture. Yet people whose first language is Spanish have serious problems with assimilation into American society. An intelligent student for whom English is a second language may be presumed slow or even unruly by English-speaking schoolchildren, and frequently by English-speaking teachers as well. This self-fulfilling prophecy can lead to the immediate labeling of Hispanic children as underachievers, as hampered by learning disabilities, or as suffering from emotional problems—all labels which some of the children may then fulfill. As we saw in the social policy section of Chapter 3, bilingual education has been introduced as a means of easing the educational difficulties experienced by Hispanic children and others whose first language is not English.

The educational difficulties of Hispanic students certainly contribute to the generally low economic status of Hispanics. According to 1988 studies by the Bureau of the Census (1990a:134, 450, 460), only 10 percent of Hispanic adults have completed college, compared with 20 percent for the overall American population. At the

same time, the median family income of Hispanics is only 64 percent that of Whites. In 1988, 5.4 million Hispanics (or 27 percent of all Hispanics in the United States) lived below the poverty line.

Despite common problems, there is considerable diversity among the various Hispanic groups found in the United States. The largest Hispanic population comprises Mexican Americans, who can be further subdivided into those descended from the residents of the territories annexed after the Mexican-American War of 1848 and those who have immigrated from Mexico to the United States. The opportunity for a Mexican to earn in 1 hour what it would take an entire day to earn in Mexico has motivated millions of legal and illegal immigrants to come north. We will examine the controversy concerning illegal immigrants in the social policy section at the end of this chapter.

The second-largest segment of Hispanics in the United States is composed of Puerto Ricans. Since 1917, residents of Puerto Rico have held the status of American citizens. Many have migrated to New York and other eastern cities. Unfortunately, Puerto Ricans experience serious poverty both in the United States and on the island. Those living in the continental United States have barely half the family income of Whites. As a result, a reverse migration began in the 1970s; more Puerto Ricans began leaving for the island than were coming to the mainland.

Both Puerto Ricans and Mexican Americans have made efforts to organize for a better life in the United States. The nation's foremost Mexican American political activist has been Cesar Chavez, the leader of the United Farm Workers (UFW). His union's pioneering efforts to improve wages and working conditions for agricultural workers in California and the southwest—many of whom are Mexican American—have become almost legendary.

The union has faced formidable problems, with membership dwindling from a high of 50,000 to less than 20,000 in 1989. It has taken on as adversaries many elected officials, the owners of grape and lettuce fields, and the powerful Teamsters' union. In addition, the UFW's efforts to improve the lives of migrant workers have been hurt by reduced governmental enforcement of regulatory legislation. The Labor Department, for example, has only two officials to oversee North Carolina's 1000 migrant worker camps. The agenda for the United Farm Workers and its allies remains full (Schaefer, 1990:307–311).

Politically, Puerto Ricans in the United States have not been so successful as Mexican Americans in organizing for their rights. For many mainland Puerto Ricans—as for many residents of the island—the paramount political issue is the destiny of Puerto Rico itself. Should it continue in its present commonwealth status, petition for admission to the United States as the fifty-first state, or attempt to become an independent nation? This question has divided Puerto Rico for decades and remains a central issue in Puerto Rican elections. As of 1991, a referendum was under consideration in which Puerto Ricans could express their preferences regarding the future status of their homeland.

The fastest-growing segment, by far, of the Hispanic community consists of residents from Central or South America. Until recently, this group has not been closely studied; government data have rarely differentiated these peoples by nationality and have instead lumped them together as "other." Yet people from Chile and Costa Rica may have little in common other than their hemisphere of origin and the Spanish language. Moreover, immigrants from Brazil speak Portuguese, those from Surinam speak Dutch, and immigrants from French Guiana speak French. As we will discuss in the social policy section, increasing numbers of Central Americans and South Americans have fled to the United States in recent decades to escape political unrest. Many have had difficulty gaining official status as refugees. The arrival of immigrants and refugees from countries in Central and South America has contributed to changes in the racial and ethnic balance of the population of the United States (see Box 10-3).

Jewish Americans Jews constitute almost 3 percent of the American population. They play a prominent role in the worldwide Jewish community because the United States has the world's largest concentration of Jews. Like the Japanese, many Jewish immigrants came to this country and became white-collar professionals. But again, as in the case of the Japanese, Jewish achievements have come despite prejudice and discrimination.

Anti-Semitism, that is, anti-Jewish prejudice, in the United States has often been vicious, although rarely so widespread and never so formalized as in Europe. In many cases, Jews have been used as scapegoats for other people's failures. This was clearly indicated in a study of World War II veterans by Bettelheim and Janowitz (1964). The researchers found that men who had experienced downward mobility (for example, job failure) were more likely to blame their setbacks on Jewish Americans than on their own shortcomings.

Jews have not achieved equality in American society. Despite high levels of education and professional training, they are still conspicuously absent from the top management of large corporations (except for the few firms founded by Jews). Until the late 1960s, many prestigious universities maintained restrictive quotas that limited Jewish enrollment. Social clubs and fraternal groups frequently limit membership to gentiles (non-Jews), a practice upheld by the Supreme Court in the 1964 case of *Bell v. Maryland.*

One recent study suggests that anti-Semitism in the corporate world may be declining. In 1985 and 1986, sociologist Samuel Klausner (1988) and his colleagues questioned 444 people with Master of Business Administration (M.B.A.) degrees

BOX 10-3 • CURRENT RESEARCH

RACE AND ETHNICITY IN THE YEAR 2080

As we approach the beginning of the twenty-first century, the United States is on the verge of again being transformed racially and ethnically. The birthrate of the resident population is so low that this group is not replacing itself and will actually be reduced in the near future (see Chapter 19). At the same time, the United States is experiencing relatively high rates of immigration. Most immigrants are Hispanics or Asians—a far cry from the overwhelmingly European immigration of the late nineteenth and early twentieth centuries.

What of the future? We can expect that the Black and Hispanic populations of the United States will grow more rapidly than the White and Asian populations, because these groups are comparatively younger and will therefore have higher rates of reproduction.

The anticipated immigration of Hispanics and Asians will also have an impact on the nation's racial and ethnic composition.

The accompanying figure presents two projections of the population of the United States for the year 2080. One assumes an annual legal immigration rate continuing at the current level of 500,000 people per year. The other projection assumes a higher annual immigration rate of 1 million people per year. As these projections illustrate, the Hispanic population of the United States will increase dramatically in the next 100 years. By 2080, Hispanics will outnumber Blacks and could account for more than 23 percent of the nation. Similarly, the proportion of Americans classified as "Asians or other" will rise substantially, perhaps to as much as 12 percent of the population.

Because of these population shifts, the proportion of White, non-Hispanic Americans will decrease significantly. In fact, by the year 2080, the combined Black, Hispanic, and Asian populations may be approximately equal to the number of Whites.

This does not necessarily mean that the White population will lose its historic social dominance, but it certainly suggests that the United States of 2080 will be a vastly different society.

SOURCE: Bouvier and Davis, 1982.

Assuming continuing high rates of immigration over the next 100 years—500,000 or 1 million immigrants per year—the proportion of Americans who are White and non-Hispanic will decrease substantially by the year 2080. By contrast, there will be a striking rise in the proportion of both Hispanics and Asian Americans.

Population of the United States by Race and Ethnicity, 1980 and 2080 (Two Projections)

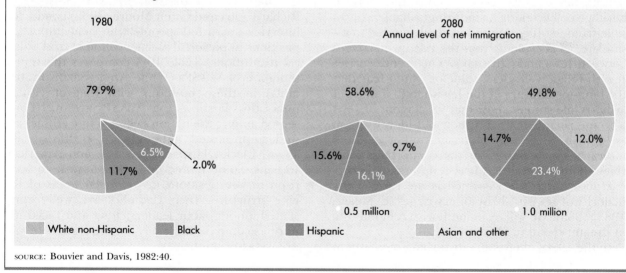

SOURCE: Bouvier and Davis, 1982:40.

In the year 1990, the Anti-Defamation League (ADL) of B'nai Brith reported the highest number of anti-Semitic incidents in the United States in the 12 years that ADL has published its annual audit.

from three business schools. The purpose of the study was to compare the experiences of Jewish and non-Jewish executives who began their careers at the same business schools. Researchers tested seven indicators of discrimination and, in each case, *failed* to find evidence of discrimination against Jewish executives. The same study, however, did detect substantial discrimination against Black and female executives.

As is true for other minorities discussed in this chapter, American Jews face the choice of maintaining ties to their long religious and cultural heritage or becoming as indistinguishable as possible from gentiles. Many Jews have tended to assimilate, as is evident from the rise in marriages between Jews and Christians. This trend worries Jewish religious leaders, some of whom fear that the long-term future of the Jewish faith is in jeopardy. While studies show that 78 percent of Jews who intermarry maintain their self-identification as "Jewish" after their marriages, other research indicates that children in these interfaith marriages do not identify as Jewish if the gentile parent does not convert—which is the case in the majority of Jewish-Christian marriages (E. Mayer, 1983, 1985). We will examine Jewish religious life in greater detail in Chapter 14.

In the 1980s, there were disturbing increases in acts of violence against Jews and Jewish institutions. This same period was marked by a wave of cross burnings and bombings directed at Blacks living in primarily White neighborhoods. These actions seemed to coincide with renewed activity among anti-Semitic White supremacist groups such as the Ku Klux Klan and the Aryan Nation. The Anti-Defamation League of B'nai Brith (1991) reported that in 1990 anti-Semitic incidents reached the highest level they had been since the organization began collecting statistics 12 years earlier. Such threatening behavior only underscores the fears of many Jewish Americans, who find it difficult to forget the Holocaust—the extermination of 6 million European Jews by the Nazi Third Reich during the late 1930s and 1940s.

White Ethnics A significant segment of the American population is made up of White ethnics whose ancestors have come from Europe within the last 100 years. In terms of ancestry, the nation's White ethnic population includes about 17 million German Americans, 10 million Irish Americans, 6 million Italian Americans, and 3.5 million Polish Americans, as well as immigrants from other European nations. Some of these people continue to live in close-knit ethnic neighborhoods, while others have largely assimilated and have left the "old ways" behind (Bureau of the Census, 1982:10).

To what extent are White ethnics found among the nation's top decision makers? Sociologists Richard Alba and Gwen Moore (1982) conducted interviews with 545 people who held important positions in powerful social, economic, and political institutions. Table 10-3 compares the representation of WASPs (White Anglo-Saxon Protestants) in these positions with that of certain minorities. It shows that WASPs are overrepresented among the nation's elite; White ethnics are underrepresented, although not so dramatically as are Blacks, Hispanics, Asians, and American Indians. Some ethnic minorities appear to have risen to key positions in particular areas of the elite structure. Irish Catholics are well represented among labor leaders; Jews and racial minorities compare favorably among leaders of voluntary associations.

TABLE 10-3   Representation of Minorities in the Elite of the United States

	WASPs, %	OTHER WHITE PROTES-TANTS, %	IRISH CATHOLICS, %	OTHER WHITE CATHOLICS, %	JEWS, %	BLACKS, HISPANICS, ASIANS, AMERICAN INDIANS, %
National population Men born before 1932	22.9	22.5	4.2	17.2	2.9	14.4
College-educated men born before 1932	31.0	19.8	6.0	15.5	8.9	5.2
Overall elite	43.0	19.5	8.5	8.7	11.3	3.9
Business	57.3	22.1	5.3	6.1	6.9	0.0
Labor	23.9	15.2	37.0	13.0	4.3	2.2
Political parties	44.0	18.0	14.0	4.0	8.0	4.0
Voluntary associations	32.7	13.5	1.9	7.7	17.3	19.2
Mass media	37.1	11.3	4.8	9.7	25.8	0.0
Congress	53.4	19.0	6.9	8.6	3.4	3.4
Political appointees	39.4	28.8	1.5	13.6	10.6	3.0
Civil servants	35.8	22.6	9.4	9.4	15.1	3.8

SOURCE: Alba and Moore, 1982.

White ethnics and racial minorities have often been antagonistic to one another because of economic competition—an interpretation in line with the conflict approach to sociology. As Blacks, Hispanics, and American Indians emerge from the lower class, they will initially be competing with working-class Whites for jobs, housing, and educational opportunities. In a time of high unemployment and inflation, any such competition can easily generate intense intergroup conflict.

In many respects, the plight of White ethnics raises the same basic issues as that of other subordinate people in the United States. How ethnic can people be—how much can they deviate from an essentially White, Anglo-Saxon, Protestant norm—before society punishes them for a willingness to be different? Our society does seem to reward people for assimilating. Yet, as we have seen, assimilation is no guarantee of equality or freedom from discrimination.

This table shows the representation of WASPs (White Anglo-Saxon Protestants), Irish Catholics, and others among the leaders of powerful social, economic, and political institutions of the United States. The representation of each group within the nation's overall elite and within particular types of positions is compared with the percentage of group members who are men born before 1932 or college-educated men born before 1932. These comparative data are offered because older males and college-educated males have traditionally been the groups from which members of the elite have emerged. As the data show, the proportion of WASPs found in the overall elite (43.0 percent) is far higher than the proportion who are men born before 1932 (22.9 percent) or are college-educated men born before 1932 (31.0 percent).

- Why are immigrants "pulled" and "pushed" to the United States?

- From a conflict perspective, how does the nation's treatment of illegal immigrants reinforce stratification based on class, race, and ethnicity?

- In what way does the debate over immigration and refugee policy reflect the deep value conflicts in the culture of the United States?

The words of poet Emma Lazarus—"Give us your tired, your poor, your huddled masses yearning to breathe free . . ."—are inscribed on the Statue of Liberty, long the symbol of hope for those who wanted to come to the United States. Yet, by the beginning of the twentieth century, this country had begun to turn its back on some of the huddled masses. As early as 1882, people of Chinese descent were prohibited from establishing permanent residence in the United States. Campaigns soon began to limit entry of other peoples regarded as "undesirable."

In the 1920s, the United States instituted an immigration policy that gave preference to people from western Europe, while making it difficult for residents of southern and eastern Europe, Asia, and Africa to enter the country. Then, during the late 1930s and early 1940s, the federal government refused to lift or loosen restrictive immigration quotas in order to allow Jewish refugees to escape the terror of the Nazi regime. In line with this policy, the *S.S. St. Louis,* with more than 900 Jewish refugees on board, was denied permission to land in the United States in 1939. This ship was forced to sail back to Europe, where it is estimated that at least a few hundred of its passengers later died at the hands of the Nazis (Morse, 1967; G. Thomas and Witts, 1974).

As in the past, immigration remains a controversial part of American public life. Perhaps the greatest controversy has resulted from the federal government's apparent inability to control illegal or undocumented immigration. Illegal immigrants are commonly known as *illegal aliens* and are sometimes referred to as *undocumented workers.* They come to the United States in search of higher-paying jobs than are available in their home countries. The immigrants are pulled here by the lure of prosperity and better lives for their chil-

dren, while they are pushed out of their native lands by unemployment and poverty. Despite fears to the contrary, immigrants—whether legal or illegal—have had only a slight impact on the employment prospects of longtime United States citizens. In general, immigrants are employed in jobs that employers find difficult to fill and that many residents do not want (Borjas, 1990).

Nearly 100 countries are represented by those illegal aliens apprehended annually by the Immigration and Naturalization Service (INS). For example, since Ireland's economic difficulties reached severe proportions in 1982, some 150,000 Irish immigrants—most of them illegal aliens—have come to the United States. About 25,000 have settled in Boston, where 40 percent of residents claim Irish ancestry. "It was truly a choice of life on the dole [welfare] or working in America," recalled John, a 31-year-old illegal immigrant from Ireland who asked a reporter not to use his last name (Diesenhouse, 1987:E6).

Throughout the 1980s, there was a growing perception that the United States had lost control of its borders and simply was no longer able to prevent illegal immigrants from entering. With public pressure for immigration control on the rise, Congress ended a decade of debate by approving the Immigration Reform and Control Act of 1986. The act marked a historic change in immigration policy. For the first time, hiring of illegal aliens was outlawed, and employers caught doing so became subject to fines and even prison sentences.

Just as significant a change was the extension of legal status to illegal aliens who had entered the United States before January 1, 1982, and had lived here continuously since then. After 2 years as lawful temporary residents of the United States, these immigrants could apply to become permanent residents eligible for American citizenship in another 5 years. Eventually, 1.7 million persons applied for legalization. About 70 percent were from Mexico; almost 54 percent reside in California (Suro, 1989).

It appears that the 1986 immigration law has had mixed results. According to data compiled by the U.S. Border Patrol, arrests along the Mexican border declined substantially in the first 3 years after the law took effect. However, in the fiscal year ending in September 1990, more than 1 million illegal immigrants were arrested crossing the border, an increase of more than 22 percent over the previous year. By 1990, it was estimated that 1.8 to 3.1 million illegal immigrants continued to live in the United States. Wayne Cornelius, director of the Center for United States–Mexican Studies at the University of California at San Diego, suggests that while employer sanctions may have initially deterred many people from illegally entering the United States, the widespread use of fraudulent documents has eroded the deterrent effect of these sanctions (Espenshade, 1990; Suro, 1990b; see also Davidson, 1990).

Although the Immigration Reform and Control Act prohibited employers from discriminating against legal aliens because they were not American citizens, a 1990 report by the General Accounting Office revealed that the law had produced a "widespread pattern of discrimination" against people who looked or sounded like foreigners. The report estimates that some 890,000 employers initiated one or more discriminatory practices in response to the 1986 immigration law. Although these firms employ nearly 7 million workers, fewer than 1000 complaints of discrimination have been filed with government agencies—in good part because most employees are unaware of the protections included in the Immigration Reform and Control Act (C. Brown, 1990:3).

Critics of the new immigration law emphasize that while it has been extremely beneficial for many immigrants who qualified for amnesty, it has had a devastating impact on those who could not qualify. Many aliens in this situation are being overworked or underpaid by unscrupulous employers, who are well-aware that these workers have few options. Consequently, millions of illegal immigrants continue to live in fear and hiding, subject to even more severe harassment and discrimination than before. From a conflict perspective, these immigrants—primarily poor and Hispanic—are being firmly entrenched at the bottom of the nation's social and economic hierarchies.

Just as the United States has traditionally presented itself as a haven for immigrants, so too has the nation taken pride in its history of welcoming political refugees. Despite periodic public opposition, the United States government is committed to accepting about 130,000 additional refugees per year as part of an agreement to relieve the pressure on international refugee camps. Under the Refugee Act of 1980, aliens may qualify for political asylum in the United States if they have a "well-founded fear of persecution" in

(J.P. Laffont/Sygma)

Throughout the 1980s, there was a growing perception that the United States had lost control of its borders and simply was no longer able to prevent illegal immigrants from entering. In this photograph, Mexicans have climbed over a grill to illegally enter the United States.

their homelands "on account of race, religion, nationality, membership in a particular social group, or political opinion."

Begun in 1982, the **sanctuary movement** of loosely connected organizations offers asylum, often in churches, to those who seek refugee status but are regarded by the Immigration and Naturalization Service as illegal aliens. By giving shelter in homes, offices, or religious institutions to those refused asylum, participants in the sanctuary movement are violating the law and become subject to stiff fines and jail sentences. Nevertheless, movement activists believe that such humanitarian assistance is fully justified. Activists argue that there is a double standard underlying decisions regarding refugee status. In their view, the federal government commonly and unfairly refuses asylum applications from citizens of countries allied with the United States—such as El Salvador, Haiti, and Pakistan—even when these immigrants face grave dangers should they be deported to their homelands.

In mid-1988, when immigration officials began implementing the employer sanctions provisions of the Immigration Reform and Control Act of 1986, some activists in the sanctuary movement began harboring undocumented workers. Catholic clergy have taken the lead in this effort to protect illegal immigrants. By late 1988, three priests in Los Angeles were under criminal investigation by the INS, facing possible felony charges for offering assistance to illegal aliens. Reverend Luis Olivares, one of the priests under investigation, openly defended his actions: "This is an outgrowth of the sanctuary movement. We've expanded it to include the undocumented. It doesn't make any difference to us whether you die by a bullet or by hunger; you're still dead" (Hernández, 1988:17).

Throughout American history, as we have seen, there has been intense debate over the nation's immigration and refugee policies. In a sense, this debate reflects the deep value conflicts in the culture of the United States and parallels the "American dilemma" identified by Swedish social economist Gunnar Myrdal (1944). One strand of American culture—well epitomized by Emma Lazarus's words, "Give us your tired, your poor, your huddled masses yearning to breathe free . . ." has emphasized egalitarian principles and a desire to help people in their time of need. At the same time, however, hostility to potential immigrants and refugees—whether Chinese in the 1880s, European Jews in the 1930s and 1940s, or Mexicans and Salvadorans today—reflects not only racial, ethnic, and religious prejudice, but also a desire to maintain the dominant culture of the in-group by keeping out those viewed as outsiders. The conflict between these cultural values is central to the "American dilemma" of the 1990s.

SUMMARY

The social dimensions of race and ethnicity are important factors in shaping people's lives in the United States and other countries. In this chapter, we examine the meaning of race and ethnicity and study the major racial and ethnic minorities of the United States.

1 A *racial group* is set apart from others by obvious physical differences, whereas an *ethnic group* is set apart primarily because of national origin or distinctive cultural patterns.

2 When sociologists define a *minority group,* they are primarily concerned with the economic and political power, or powerlessness, of the group.

3 In a biological sense, there are no "pure races" and no physical traits that can be used to describe one group to the exclusion of all others.

4 *Prejudice* is a negative attitude toward an entire category of people, often an ethnic or racial minority.

5 Prejudiced attitudes often lead to *discrimination,* but the two are not identical, and each can be present without the other.

6 *Institutional discrimination* results from the normal operations of a society.

7 Four patterns describe typical intergroup relations in North America and elsewhere: *amalgamation, assimilation, segregation,* and *pluralism.*

8 In the United States, the most highly rewarded pattern of intergroup relations is assimilation. Pluralism remains more of an ideal than a reality.

9 Contemporary prejudice and discrimination against Black Americans are rooted in the history of slavery in the United States.

10 Asian Americans are commonly viewed as a "model minority," a stereotype not necessarily beneficial to members of this group.

11 The various groups included under the general term *Hispanics* represent the largest ethnic minority in the United States.

12 Much of the debate in the United States concerning immigration has centered on the federal government's apparent inability to control illegal or undocumented immigration.

KEY TERMS

Amalgamation The process by which a majority group and a minority group combine through intermarriage to form a new group. (page 300)

Anti-Semitism Anti-Jewish prejudice. (312)

Apartheid The policy of the South African government designed to maintain the separation of Blacks,

Coloureds, and Asians from the dominant Whites. (301)

Assimilation   The process by which a person forsakes his or her own cultural tradition to become part of a different culture. (300)

Authoritarian personality   A psychological construct of a personality type likely to be prejudiced and to use others as scapegoats. (297)

Black power   A political philosophy promoted by many younger Blacks in the 1960s which supported the creation of Black-controlled political and economic institutions. (304)

Color gradient   The placement of people on a continuum from light to dark skin color rather than in distinct racial groupings by skin color. (290)

Contact hypothesis   An interactionist perspective which states that interracial contact of people with equal status in noncompetitive circumstances will reduce prejudice. (295)

Discrimination   The process of denying opportunities and equal rights to individuals and groups because of prejudice or for other arbitrary reasons. (298)

Ethnic group   A group which is set apart from others because of its national origin or distinctive cultural patterns. (289)

Ethnocentrism   The tendency to assume that one's own culture and way of life are superior to all others. (296)

Exploitation theory   A Marxist theory which views racial subordination in the United States as a manifestation of the class system inherent in capitalism. (295)

Genocide   The deliberate, systematic killing of an entire people or nation. (299)

Institutional discrimination   The denial of opportunities and equal rights to individuals or groups which results from the normal operations of a society. (298)

Issei   The early Japanese immigrants to the United States. (307)

Minority group   A subordinate group whose members have significantly less control or power over their own lives than the members of a dominant or majority group have over theirs. (289)

Nisei   American-born Japanese who were descendants of the Issei. (309)

Pluralism   Mutual respect between the various groups in a society for one another's cultures, which allows minorities to express their own cultures without experiencing prejudice. (302)

Prejudice   A negative attitude toward an entire category of people, such as a racial or ethnic minority. (296)

Racial group   A group which is set apart from others because of obvious physical differences. (289)

Racism   The belief that one race is supreme and all others are innately inferior. (296)

Sanctuary movement   A movement of loosely connected organizations that offers asylum, often in churches, to those who seek refugee status but are regarded by the Immigration and Naturalization Service as illegal aliens. (317)

Scapegoat   A person or group that one blames irrationally for one's own problems or difficulties. (297)

Segregation   The act of physically separating two groups: often imposed on a minority group by a dominant group. (300)

Self-fulfilling prophecy   The tendency of people to respond to and act on the basis of stereotypes, a predisposition which can lead to validation of false definitions. (292)

Stereotypes   Unreliable generalizations about all members of a group that do not recognize individual differences within the group. (291)

ADDITIONAL READINGS

Alba, Richard D. *Ethnic Identity: The Transformation of White America.* New Haven, Conn.: Yale University Press, 1990. A sociologist looks at the changing patterns of ethnic identity in the United States and focuses on the myths that today's White ethnics hold about their place in American history.

Deloria, Vine, Jr., and Clifford M. Lytle. *American Indians, American Justice.* Austin: University of Texas Press, 1983. Deloria, a longtime Native American activist and founder of the National Congress of American Indians, explores federal Indian law and its implications for land and water rights as well as cultural preservation.

Freeman, James M. *Hearts of Sorrow: Vietnamese American Lives.* Stanford, Calif.: Stanford University Press, 1989. Freeman presents in-depth interviews with 40 men and women who recall their lives in Vietnam, their relocation amidst warfare, and their adjustment to the culture of the United States.

Gesensway, Deborah, and Mindy Roseman. *Beyond Words: Images from America's Concentration Camps.* Ithaca, N.Y.: Cornell University Press, 1987. Through the use of pictures, charcoal drawings, and watercolor prints, we gain insight into the experiences of Japanese Americans confined in evacuation camps during World War II.

Goldscheider, Calvin. *Jewish Continuity and Change: Emerging Patterns in America.* Bloomington: Indiana University Press, 1986. A sociological analysis of Jewish American patterns of behavior and how these have changed since the 1960s.

Hovannisian, Richard G. (ed.). *The Armenian Genocide in Perspective.* New Brunswick, N.J.: Transaction, 1986. A collection of scholarly accounts of the massacre of the Armenian people—an example of genocide which remains largely ignored by governments and forgotten by the world's peoples.

Malcolm X, with Alex Haley. *The Autobiography of Malcolm X.* New York: Grove, 1964. Written just before his assassination, Malcolm's autobiography relates his vivid and controversial history, including his leadership role in and subsequent disenchantment with the Nation of Islam.

Moore, Joan, and Harry Pachon. *Hispanics in the United States.* Englewood Cliffs, N.J.: Prentice-Hall, 1985. A concise sociological examination of Hispanic Americans.

Peters, William. *A Class Divided: Then and Now* (expanded ed.). New Haven, Conn.: Yale University Press, 1987. A description of the well-publicized effort by an elementary school teacher to sensitize children to the impact of prejudice and discrimination by dividing her class into privileged brown-eyed children and inferior blue-eyed children.

Quinley, Harold E., and Charles Y. Glock. *Anti-Semitism in America.* New Brunswick, N.J.: Transaction, 1983. Political scientist Quinley and sociologist Glock explore anti-Semitism in the United States, with special focus on the educational system, the news media, and political institutions.

Schaefer, Richard T. *Racial and Ethnic Groups* (4th ed.). Glenview, Ill.: Scott, Foresman, 1990. Comprehensive in its coverage of race and ethnicity, this text also discusses women as a social minority and minority relations in Great Britain, Northern Ireland, the Soviet Union, Brazil, and South Africa.

Steinberg, Stephen. *The Ethnic Myth: Race, Ethnicity, and Class in America* (new ed.). Boston: Beacon, 1989. The author, a sociologist, asserts that locality, class, and migration—rather than race and ethnicity—are the primary determinants of the economic destiny of the nation's minorities.

Takaki, Ronald. *Strangers from a Different Shore: A History of Asian Americans.* Boston: Little, Brown, 1989. An overview of the historical experiences of diverse groups of Asian Americans.

Wilson, William Julius. *The Declining Significance of Race: Blacks and Changing American Institutions* (2d ed.). Chicago: University of Chicago Press, 1980. While acknowledging the disadvantaged position of Blacks, Wilson argues that class is more important than race in determining Blacks' access to privilege and power.

Journals

Among the journals that focus on issues of race and ethnicity are *Amerasian Journal* (founded in 1971), *The Black Scholar* (1969), *Contemporary Jewry* (1978), *Ethnic and Racial Studies* (1978), *Hispanic Journal of Behavioral Studies* (1979), and *Phylon: Review of Race and Culture* (1940). Local publications produced by racial and ethnic communities are also useful.

STRATIFICATION
BY GENDER

STRATIFICATION BY GENDER

> *I really think that women ought to have representatives, instead of being arbitrarily governed without having any direct share allowed them in the deliberations of government.*
> *Mary Wollstonecraft*
> A Vindication of the Rights of Woman, *1792*

LOOKING AHEAD

- How are girls socialized to be "feminine" and boys to be "masculine"?
- How are gender roles apparent in everyday conversations between men and women?
- Why is it that, despite outnumbering men, women are viewed as a subordinate minority by sociologists?
- How pervasive is sex-typing of jobs? Are there many jobs viewed either as "men's work" or as "women's work"?
- When married women work outside the home, do their husbands assume equal responsibility for housework and child care?
- Why is it said that women from racial and ethnic minorities face a kind of "double jeopardy"?
- How does the world view of feminists involved in defending abortion rights differ from that of antiabortion activists?

To what extent has the United States become more open to women's participation in traditionally male-dominated occupations and activities? One way of answering this question is to examine the world of sports, long known for its exclusion of women. In mid-1989, 12-year-old Victoria Bruckner of San Pedro, California, became the first girl to play for a United States team in the Little League World Series. In a first-round game against Tampa, Florida, Bruckner had a single in two at-bats, walked twice, and scored three times. She played first base and had an outstanding game defensively, throwing out runners at home plate and third base to complete double plays (*New York Post*, 1989).

Victoria Bruckner's breakthrough was not an isolated event; it reflected growing involvement of girls and women in athletic activities of all kinds. A 1988 survey conducted under the direction of the Women's Sports Foundation found strong support for girls' participation in sports. Of more than 1000 mothers and fathers polled in a random national sample, 87 percent stated that sports are as important for girls as for boys. Moreover, of the 513 daughters of these parents surveyed—whose ages ranged from 7 to 18 years old—82 percent reported that they currently participated in sports, while 89 percent indicated that they planned to make sports a part of their adult lives. Reflecting on the survey data, Dorothy Harris, a professor of exercise and sports science, commented: "The word 'tomboy' no longer exists in the athletic dictionary" (Eskenazi, 1988:A29).

But resistance to change remains evident in the world of sports. In 1989, after 6 years of high ratings as an umpire in AAA ball, the top level of baseball's minor leagues, Pam Postema was chosen to umpire in major league spring training games. It seemed possible that she would be named as the first female umpire in the majors when the regular season started. However, pitcher Bob Knepper spoke out against her aspirations, stating: "This is not an occupation women should be in. In God's society, woman was created in a role of submission to the husband. It's not that woman is inferior, but I don't believe women should be in a leadership role." Knepper's remarks caused controversy, and Postema was not selected for promotion to the major leagues. After completing another season in AAA ball, Postema learned that her contract would not be renewed. Openly bitter about the end of her career as an umpire, Postema remarked: "If I'm not good enough to make it as an umpire, there'll never be a woman who can make it" (Vecsey, 1989:S3).

As Pam Postema learned, our society continues to view many forms of work as "women's work" or "men's work," using as a basis sexual stereotypes. A person's gender thus becomes a means for categorizing people and is given a distinct social significance. We saw in Chapter 4 that men have traditionally been designated as the "providers" for the family, while women have been expected to assume almost total responsibility for child care and household duties. Differentiation based on gender is evident in virtually every human society about which we have information.

We saw in Chapters 8, 9, and 10 that most societies establish hierarchies based on social class, race, and ethnicity. This chapter will examine the ways in which societies stratify their members on the basis of gender. It will begin by looking at how various cultures, including our own, assign women and men to particular social roles. Then it will consider sociological explanations for gender stratification. Next, it will focus on the unique situation of women as an oppressed majority within American society. Particular attention will be given to the social, economic, and political aspects of women's subordinate position, and to the consequences of gender stratification for men. The chapter will also examine the emergence of the contemporary feminist movement. Finally, the social policy section will analyze the intense and continuing controversy over abortion.

GENDER IDENTITY AND GENDER ROLES

There are obvious biological differences between the sexes. Most important, women have the capacity to bear children, whereas men do not.

(Mel Evans/NYT Pictures)

Reflecting the changing gender roles of American society, Pam Postema became a baseball umpire and eventually was promoted to the class AAA American Association—a minor league only one step below major-league baseball. However—reflecting resistance to change—Postema was not promoted to the major leagues and eventually was fired despite years of successful work at the AAA level.

These biological differences contribute to the development of **gender identity**, the self-concept of a person as being male or female. Gender identity is one of the first and most far-reaching identities that a human being learns. Typically, a child learns that she is a girl or he is a boy between the ages of 18 months and 3 years (Cahill, 1986).

Many societies have established social distinctions between the sexes which do not inevitably result from biological differences. This largely reflects the impact of conventional gender-role socialization. In Chapter 4, **gender roles** were defined as "expectations regarding the proper behavior, attitudes, and activities of males and females." The application of traditional gender roles lead to many forms of differentiation between women and men. Both sexes are physically capable of learning to cook and type, yet most western societies determine that these tasks should be performed by women. Both men and women are capable of learning to weld and fly airplanes, but these functions are generally assigned to males.

It is important to stress that gender identity and gender roles are distinct concepts. Gender identity is based on a sense of oneself as male or female; gender roles involve socialization into norms regarding masculinity and femininity. Yet being male does not necessarily mean being "masculine" in a traditional sense; being female does not necessarily mean being "feminine." Thus, a woman who enters a historically male occupation such as welding, and who displays such traditionally masculine qualities as physical strength and assertiveness, may have a positive and highly secure gender identity. She may feel quite comfortable about being female—and, in fact, proud to be a woman—without feeling feminine as femininity has conventionally been defined. Similarly, a gentle, sensitive man who rejects the traditional view of masculinity may be quite secure in his gender identity as a man (Bem, 1978:20–21; L. Hoffman, 1977; C. West and Zimmerman, 1987).

Gender Roles in the United States

Gender-Role Socialization All of us can describe the traditional gender-role patterns which have been influential in the socialization of American children. Male babies get blue blankets, while females get pink ones. Boys are expected to play with trucks, blocks, and toy soldiers; girls are given dolls and kitchen goods. Boys must be masculine—active, aggressive, tough, daring, and dominant—whereas girls must be feminine—soft, emotional, sweet, and submissive.

It is *adults,* of course, who play a critical role in guiding children into those gender roles deemed appropriate in a society. Parents are normally the first and most crucial agents of socialization (see

Chapter 4). But other adults, older siblings, the mass media, and religious and educational institutions also exert an important influence on gender-role socialization in the United States.

Psychologist Shirley Weitz (1977:60–110) has pointed to two mechanisms which are primarily responsible for gender-role socialization: differential treatment and identification. In an illuminating study of differential treatment, a baby was sometimes dressed in pink and called "Beth" and at other times dressed in blue and called "Adam." Adults who played with the baby indicated that, without question, they *knew* whether the child was male or female from its behavior. They remarked on how sweet and feminine *she* had been, and on how sturdy and vigorous *he* had been. Clearly, these adults perceived the baby's behavior on the basis of their understanding of its sex. Such gender-related assumptions commonly lead to differential treatment of girls and boys (Will et al., 1976).

The process of identification noted by Weitz is more complex. How does a boy come to develop a masculine self-image whereas a girl develops one that is feminine? In part, they do so by identifying with females and males in their families and neighborhoods and in the media. If a young girl regularly sees female characters on television working as defense attorneys and judges, she may believe that she herself can become a lawyer. And it will not hurt if women that she knows—her mother, sister, parents' friends, or neighbors—are lawyers. By contrast, if this young girl sees women portrayed in the media only as models, nurses, and secretaries, her identification and self-image will be quite different.

The portrayal of women and men on television has tended to reinforce conventional gender roles. A cross-cultural content analysis of television advertising in the United States, Mexico, and Australia found sexual stereotyping common in all three countries. Australia was found to have the lowest level of stereotyping, but even in that country, feminist groups were working to eliminate the "use of the woman's body to sell products" (Courtney and Whipple, 1983:183; Gilly, 1988).

In the United States, women have traditionally been presented on prime-time television as home-

makers, nurses, and household workers—positions which reflect stereotyped notions of women's work. However, by the late 1980s, women had achieved a better image on prime-time programs. A 1987 study found that 75 percent of the women portrayed on these shows were employed outside the home; only about 8 percent were full-time homemakers. Indeed, television seemed to be presenting an overly favorable picture of the types of jobs women hold. In 1987, more than half of women characters on prime-time shows had professional careers, while only 25 percent worked in clerical or service jobs. Researchers noted that the real-life portrait was "almost exactly reversed"; 47 percent of women held clerical or service jobs while only 24 percent worked in professional or managerial jobs (Cabrera, 1989:113; Waters and Huck, 1989:50).

Females have been most severely restricted by traditional American gender roles. Throughout this chapter, we will see how women have been confined to subordinate roles within the political and economic institutions of the United States. Yet it is also true that American gender roles have restricted males.

Men's Gender Role Boys are socialized to think that they should be invulnerable, fearless, decisive, and even emotionless in some situations (Cicone and Ruble, 1978). These are difficult standards to meet; yet, for boys who do not "measure up," life can be trying. This is especially true

for boys who show an interest in activities thought of as feminine (such as cooking) or for those who do not enjoy traditional masculine activities (such as competitive sports). Following are one man's recollections of his childhood, when he disliked sports, dreaded gym classes, and had particular problems with baseball:

> During the game I always played the outfield. Right field. Far right field. And there I would stand in the hot sun wishing I was anyplace else in the world. Every so often a ball looked like it was coming up in my direction and I prayed to God that it wouldn't happen. If it did come, I promised God to be good for the next 37 years if he let me catch it—especially if it was a fly ball (Fager et al., 1971:36).

Boys who do not conform to the designated male gender role, like the right fielder quoted above, face constant criticism and even humiliation both from other children and from adults. It can be agonizing to be treated as a "chicken" or a "sissy"—particularly if such remarks come from one's father or brothers. At the same time, boys who successfully adapt to cultural standards of masculinity may grow up to be inexpressive men who cannot share their feelings with others. They remain forceful and tough—but as a result they are also closed and isolated (Balswick and Peek, 1971).

In the last 20 years, inspired in good part by the contemporary feminist movement (which will be examined later in the chapter), increasing num-

BOX 11-1 • SPEAKING OUT

STATEMENT OF PRINCIPLES BY
THE NATIONAL ORGANIZATION FOR MEN AGAINST SEXISM

In the last 20 years, men in the United States have come together at various times to voice their opposition to traditional gender roles and their support for feminism and gay rights. The National Organization for Men Against Sexism (NOMAS), formerly known as the National Organization for Changing Men, was founded in the mid-1980s and has put forward the following statement of principles:

The National Organization for Men Against Sexism is an activist organization of men and women supporting positive changes for men. NOMAS advocates a perspective that is pro-feminist, gay-affirmative, and committed to justice on a broad range of social issues including race, class, age, religion, and physical abilities. We affirm that working to make this nation's ideals of equality substantive is the finest expression of what it means to be men.

We believe that the new opportunities becoming available to women and men will be beneficial to both. Men can live as happier and more fulfilled human beings by challenging the old-fashioned rules of masculinity that embody the assumption of male superiority.

Traditional masculinity includes many positive characteristics in which we take pride and find strength, but it also contains qualities that have limited and harmed us. We are deeply supportive of men who are struggling with the issues of traditional masculinity. As an organization for changing men, we care about men and are especially concerned with men's problems, as well as the difficult issues in most men's lives.

As an organization for changing men, we strongly support the continuing struggle of women for full equality. We applaud and support the insights and positive social changes that feminism has stimulated for both women and men. We oppose such injustices to women as economic and legal discrimination, rape, domestic violence, sexual harassment, and many others. Women and men can and do work together as allies to change the injustices that have so often made them see one another as enemies.

One of the strongest and deepest anxieties of most American men is their fear of homosexuality. This homophobia contributes directly to the many injustices experienced by gay, lesbian, and bisexual persons, and is a debilitating restriction for heterosexual men. We call for an end to all forms of discrimination based on sexual-affectional orientation, and for the creation of a gay-affirmative society.

We also acknowledge that many people are oppressed today because of their race, class, age, religion, and physical condition. We believe that such injustices are vitally connected to sexism, with its fundamental premise of unequal distribution of power.

Our goal is to change not just ourselves and other men, but also the institutions that create inequality. We welcome any person who agrees in substance with these principles to membership in the National Organization for Men Against Sexism.

---

bers of men in the United States have criticized the restrictive aspects of the traditional male gender role. Some men have taken strong public positions in support of women's struggle for full equality (see Box 11-1). Yet, after comparing responses by high school students to survey questions posed in 1956 and 1982, educators Miriam Lewin and Lilli Tragos (1987) concluded that teenage males of the 1980s still emphasized both gender-role differentiation and the symbols of male dominance more than their female counterparts did. This study, as well as research by Peter Stein (1984), suggests that young women's views of gender-role issues have undergone a significant change in recent decades, while young men's views have been largely unaffected.

Accounts in the mass media commonly indicate that a "new man" emerged in the 1980s. Journalist Anthony Astrachan (1986:402) defines this "new man" as:

. . . one who has abandoned or transcended most traditional male sex roles and the male attempt to monopolize power. He doesn't insist on being the sole or dominant earner of family income and he resists being a slave to his job even though he prizes competence and achievement. He believes that men are just as emotional as women and should learn to express their feelings, and he can talk about his own problems and weaknesses. The new man supports women's quest for independence and equality with more than lip service.

However, after an extensive study of men in the United States, Astrachan estimates that only 5 to 10 percent of men come close to (or are moving toward) this ideal definition. Apparently, then, the traditional male gender role remains well entrenched as an influential element of our culture (see also Kimmel, 1987; Lamm, 1977; Pleck, 1981, 1985).

Cross-Cultural Perspective

To what extent do the actual biological differences between the sexes contribute to the cultural differences associated with gender? This question brings us back to the debate over "nature versus nurture" presented in Chapter 4. In assessing the alleged and real differences between men and women, it is useful to examine cross-cultural data.

The research of anthropologist Margaret Mead points to the importance of cultural conditioning—as opposed to biological factors—in defining the social roles of males and females. In her book *Sex and Temperament,* Mead (1963, original edition 1935; 1973) describes the typical behaviors of members of each sex in three different cultures within New Guinea:

In one [the Arapesh], both men and women act as we expect women to act—in a mild parental responsive way; in the second [the Mundugumor], both act as we expect men to act—in a fierce initiating fashion; and in the third [the Tchambuli], the men act according to our stereotypes for women—are catty, wear curls, and go shopping—while the women are energetic, managerial, unadorned partners (Mead, 1963: preface to 1950 ed.).

As is evident, Mead found two societies (the Arapesh and the Mundugumor) in which there was no dramatic gender-role differentiation between women and men. From the perspective of western society, we might say that these cultures created women and men who are both feminine (the Arapesh) or both masculine (the Mundugumor). In the third culture analyzed by Mead, the Tchambuli, expectations for each sex were almost the reverse of those found in the United States.

Mead (1963:260, original edition 1935) concludes:

The material suggests that . . . many, if not all, of the personality traits which we have called masculine or feminine are as lightly linked to sex as are the clothing, the manners, and the form of headdress that a society at a given period of time assigns to either sex.

If all differences between the sexes were determined by biology, then cross-cultural differences, such as those described by Mead, would not exist. Her findings therefore confirm the influential role of culture and socialization in shaping gender-role differentiation. There appears to be no innate or biological reason to designate completely different gender roles for men and women.

In any society, gender stratification requires not only individual socialization into traditional gender roles within the family, but also the promotion and support of these traditional roles by other social institutions such as religion and education. Moreover, even with all major institutions socializing the young into conventional gender roles, every society has women and men who resist and successfully oppose these stereotypes: strong women who become leaders or professionals, gentle men who care for children, and so forth. With these realities in mind, it seems clear that differences between the sexes are not dictated by biology. Indeed, the maintenance of traditional gender roles requires constant social controls—and these controls are not always effective.

Androgyny

Today, few social roles are completely restricted to either women or men within American society.

(Michal Heron/Woodfin Camp & Associates)

In the view of some theorists, our society is gradually turning away from traditional gender roles toward a concept of androgyny, *under which both females and males are allowed to choose from the full range of human behaviors on the basis of their own unique personalities and circumstances rather than their gender.*

Giving birth is limited to women, but an increasing number of women are voluntarily abstaining from bearing children (see Chapter 13). Those women who do opt for motherhood are often sharing the moment of birth with their husbands, who assist their wives in the delivery room as coaches. Motherhood is not viewed as the only legitimate occupation for adult women, and family specialists no longer counsel against mothers' working outside the home (Bernard, 1974, 1975:15; Maccoby and Jacklin, 1974:348–374; Schaefer, 1990).

In the view of some theorists, our society is gradually turning away from traditional stereotypes toward a concept of androgyny. The term **androgyny** is used to describe a lifestyle in which there is no gender-role differentiation and one can be both "masculine" and "feminine." Both females and males are allowed to choose from the full range of human behaviors on the basis of their own unique personalities and circumstances rather than their gender. Thus, the same person could be aggressive or expressive, rational or emotional, tough or sentimental, depending on the dictates of a particular situation.

Psychologist Sandra Lipsitz Bem has strongly advocated the potential benefits of an androgynous lifestyle. Bem (1978:6) is highly critical of the impact of traditional gender roles in restricting the behavior of both females and males:

> As women, we have become aware of the fact that we are afraid to express our anger, to assert our preferences, to trust our judgment, to take control of situations. As men, we have become aware of the fact that we are afraid to cry, to touch one another, to own up to our fears and weaknesses.

She adds that extreme femininity can lead to dependency and denial of one's own needs, whereas extreme masculinity can lead to arrogance and exploitation of others.

In Bem's view, the androgynous person would combine the best aspects of traditional femininity and masculinity while avoiding the most harmful exaggerations of each. Preliminary research suggests that men and women who are most flexible in terms of gender roles are generally more competent and have a higher sense of self-esteem than those who adhere to more traditional gender-role behavior (Spence and Helmrich, 1978). Bem's own studies (1978:7–19) reveal that, unlike people more oriented to conventional masculinity or femininity, androgynous women and men are high in both independence and nurturance. She concludes, therefore, that widespread acceptance of androgyny would lead to more effective and healthy human functioning.

As research on androgyny has continued, social scientists have questioned the desirability of merging traditional feminine and masculine characteristics. Recent work on androgyny suggests that both women and men can transcend these familiar stereotypes. Thus, the value of the androgynous vision may involve more than simply revising or combining polarized gender roles; androgyny may signal an end to defining social roles in terms of masculinity and femininity (J. Doyle, 1985:357–359; Kimlicka et al., 1983).

EXPLAINING STRATIFICATION BY GENDER

As we will consider further in Chapter 13, cross-cultural studies indicate that societies dominated by men are much more common than those in which women play the decisive role. Sociologists have turned to all the major theoretical perspectives to understand how and why social distinctions between males and females are established. Each approach focuses on culture, rather than biology, as the primary determinant of gender differences. Yet, in other respects, there are wide disagreements between advocates of these sociological perspectives.

The Functionalist View

Within the general framework of their theory, functionalists maintain that gender differentiation has contributed to overall social stability. Sociologists Talcott Parsons and Robert Bales (1955:13–15, 22–26) argue that in order to function most efficiently, the family requires adults who will specialize in particular roles. They view the current arrangement of gender roles as arising out of this earlier need to establish a division of labor between marital partners.

Parsons and Bales contend that women take the expressive, emotionally supportive role and men the instrumental, practical role, with the two complementing each other. *Instrumentality* refers to emphasis on tasks, focus on more distant goals, and a concern for the external relationship between one's family and other social institutions. *Expressiveness* denotes concern for maintenance of harmony and the internal emotional affairs of the family. According to this theory, women's interest in expressive goals frees men for instrumental tasks, and vice versa. Women become "anchored" in the family as wives, mothers, and household managers, whereas men are anchored in the occupational world outside the home. Parsons and Bales do not explicitly endorse traditional gender roles, but they imply that a division of tasks between spouses is functional for the family unit.

Given the typical socialization of women and men in American society, the functionalist view is initially persuasive. However, it would lead us to expect girls and women with no interest in children to become baby-sitters and mothers. Similarly, males with a caring feeling for children might be "programmed" into careers in the business world. Clearly, such differentiation between the sexes can have harmful consequences for the individual who does not fit into prescribed roles, while also depriving society of the contributions of many talented individuals who are confined owing to stereotyping by gender. Even if it were considered ideal for one marital partner to play an instrumental role and the other an expressive role, the functionalist approach does not convincingly explain why men should be categorically assigned to the instrumental role and women to the expressive role.

Viewed from a conflict perspective, this functionalist approach masks underlying power relations between men and women. Parsons and Bales never explicitly present the expressive and instrumental tasks as unequally valued by society, yet this inequality is quite evident. Although social institutions may pay lip service to women's expressive skills, it is men's instrumental skills that are most highly rewarded—whether in terms of money or prestige. Consequently, according to feminists and conflict theorists, any division of labor by gender into instrumental and expressive tasks is far from neutral in its impact on women.

The Conflict Response

Conflict theorists contend that the relationship between females and males has been one of unequal power, with men in a dominant position over women. Men may originally have become powerful in preindustrial times because their size, physical strength, and freedom from childbearing duties allowed them to dominate women physi-

(Billy E. Barnes/Stock, Boston)

Conflict theorists emphasize that men's work is uniformly valued, while women's work (whether unpaid labor in the home or wage labor) is devalued.

cally. In contemporary societies, such considerations are not so important, yet cultural beliefs about the sexes are now long established. Such beliefs support a social structure which places males in controlling positions.

In this sense, traditional gender roles do not simply assign various qualities and behaviors to females and males. Feminist author Letty Cottin Pogrebin (1981:40) suggests that the two crucial messages of gender-role stereotypes are that "boys are better" and "girls are meant to be mothers." In order for a system of male dominance to maintain itself, she argues, children must be socialized to accept traditional gender-role divisions as natural and just. Sociologist Barbara Bovee Polk (1974:418), in describing the "conflicting cultures approach" to gender differences, observes that "masculine values have higher status and constitute the dominant and visible culture of the society. They . . . provide the standard for adulthood and normality." According to this view, women are oppressed because they constitute an alternative subculture which deviates from the prevailing masculine value system.

Thus, conflict theorists see gender differences as a reflection of the subjugation of one group (women) by another group (men). If we use an analogy to Marx's analysis of class conflict (see Chapters 1 and 8), we can say that males are like the bourgeois, or capitalists; they control most of the society's wealth, prestige, and power. Females are like the proletarians, or workers; they can acquire valuable resources only by following the dictates of their "bosses." Men's work is uniformly valued, while women's work (whether unpaid labor in the home or wage labor) is devalued.

Admittedly, the issue of women's economic and social subordination was relatively marginal in Marxist theory, which saw class oppression as paramount. However, the plight of women was not entirely ignored. Friedrich Engels, a close associate of Karl Marx, argued that women's subjugation coincided with the rise of private property during industrialization (Feuer, 1959:393–394). Only when people moved beyond an agrarian economy could males "enjoy" the luxury of leisure and withhold rewards and privileges from women. Women, in effect, became the sexual property of men. As Engels suggested, political and economic power in western industrial societies is concentrated in male hands, and there is significant social differentiation between the sexes.

From a conflict perspective, male dominance of

our society goes far beyond the economic sphere. Throughout this textbook, we have discussed disturbing aspects of men's behavior toward women. The ugly realities of rape (refer back to Box 7-3 on page 212), wife battering (see Chapter 13), sexual harassment within organizations (refer back to Chapter 6), and street harassment (refer back to Box 1-3 on page 25) all illustrate and intensify women's subordinate position. Even if women reach economic parity with men, even if women win equal representation in government, genuine equality between the sexes cannot be achieved if these attacks remain as common as they are today.

Both functionalist and conflict theorists acknowledge that it is not possible to change gender roles drastically without dramatic revisions in a culture's social structure. For functionalists, there is potential for social disorder, or at least unknown social consequences, if all aspects of traditional gender stratification are disturbed. Yet, for conflict theorists, no social structure is ultimately desirable if it is maintained by oppressing a majority of its citizens. These theorists argue that gender stratification may be functional for men—who hold power and privilege—but it is hardly in the interests of women (R. Collins, 1975:228–259; N. Goodman and Marx, 1978:312–315; Polk, 1974; Schmid, 1980).

The Interactionist Approach

Sociologists associated with the interactionist perspective generally agree with conflict theorists that men hold a dominant position over women. For example, recalling the Marxist view that the man is like the bourgeoisie within the home whereas the woman is like the proletariat, Erving Goffman (1977:315) has observed:

> A man may spend his day suffering under those who have power over him . . . and yet on returning home each night regain a sphere in which he dominates. . . . Wherever the male goes, apparently, he can carry a sexual division of labor with him.

While conflict theorists studying gender stratification typically focus on macro-level social forces and institutions, interactionist researchers often examine gender stratification on the micro level of everyday behavior. As an example, studies show that up to 96 percent of all interruptions in cross-sex (male-female) conversations are initiated by men. Men are more likely than women to change topics of conversation, to ignore topics chosen by members of the opposite sex, to minimize the contributions and ideas of members of the opposite sex, and to validate their own contributions. These patterns reflect the conversational (and, in a sense, political) dominance of males. Moreover, even when women occupy a prestigious position, such as that of physician, they are more likely to be interrupted than their male counterparts are (P. Fishman, 1978; A. Kohn, 1988; C. West, 1984; C. West and Zimmerman, 1983; D. Zimmerman and West, 1975).

In certain studies, all participants are advised in advance of the overall finding that males are more likely than females to interrupt during a cross-sex conversation. After learning this information, men reduce the frequency of their interruptions, yet they continue to verbally dominate conversations with women. At the same time, women reduce their already low frequency of interruption and other conversationally dominant behaviors after they are told of the general patterns of male dominance (Orcutt and Harvey, 1985).

These findings regarding cross-sex conversations have been frequently replicated. They have striking implications when one considers the power dynamics underlying likely cross-sex interactions—employer and job seeker, college professor and student, husband and wife, to name only a few. From an interactionist perspective, these simple, day-to-day exchanges are one more battleground in the struggle for sexual equality—as women try to "get a word in edgewise" in the midst of men's interruptions and verbal dominance.

WOMEN: THE OPPRESSED MAJORITY

Many people—both male and female—find it difficult to conceive of women as a subordinate and oppressed group. Yet, when one looks at the political structure of the United States, one has to look hard to find many women. In the 102d Congress, which took office in January 1991, there were only 31 women. They accounted for 29 of the 435 members of the House of Representatives and 2 of the 100 members of the Senate. This merely continued a historical pattern; through the year 1991, less than 130 women had *ever* served in the United States Congress, as compared with well over 11,400 men.

Other statistics reveal a similar picture. In 1991, only 3 of the nation's 50 states had female governors. In October 1981, Justice Sandra Day O'Connor of the Arizona Court of Appeals was sworn in as the nation's first female Supreme Court justice. But no woman has ever served as president of the United States, vice president, speaker of the House of Representatives, or chief justice of the Supreme Court.

This lack of women in decision-making positions is evidence of women's powerlessness in the United States. In Chapter 10, five basic properties which define a minority or subordinate group were identified. If we apply this model to the situation of women in this country, we find that a numerical majority group fits our definition of a subordinate minority (Dworkin, 1982; Hochschild, 1973:118–120):

1 Women obviously share physical and cultural characteristics that distinguish them from the dominant group (men).
2 Women experience unequal treatment. In the year 1988, the median income for year-round, male workers was $27,342; for comparable female workers, it was only $18,545 (Bureau of the Census, 1990a:453). Though they are not segregated from men, women are the victims of prejudice and discrimination in the labor force, in the legal system, and in other areas of society. Moreover, as we saw in Chapter 8, women are increasingly dominating the ranks of the impoverished, leading to what has been called the *feminization of poverty*.
3 Membership in this subordinate group is involuntary.
4 Through the rise of contemporary feminism, women are developing a greater sense of group

solidarity. (The women's movement will be studied later in the chapter.)
5 Women are not forced to marry within the group, yet many women feel that their subordinate status is most irrevocably defined within the institution of marriage (Bernard, 1972).

The most common analogy used for purposes of analysis is that of the positions of women and Blacks. Many scholars (H. Hacker, 1951, 1974; Myrdal, 1944; A. Rich, 1979; Stimpson, 1971) have drawn attention to striking parallels between the two groups, among them the following:

• Both are limited by ascribed characteristics (Black's skin color and women's gender).
• Both were denied suffrage when the Constitution of the United States was first drafted in 1787.
• Both have historically been treated as property within the American legal system (Black slaves as the property of their masters, women as the property of their husbands).
• Women and Blacks, despite intense struggles for equal rights, remain significantly underrepresented in the American political system.
• Both groups are subject to negative and prejudicial stereotypes.
• Both are generally given menial jobs with low pay and few prospects for advancement.
• Women and Blacks have traditionally been ignored in the writing of American history.

Of course, there are also many differences. Perhaps most important, Blacks have faced widespread patterns of segregation, whereas women frequently live in intimate relationships with members of the dominant male sex.

Just as African Americans are victimized by racism, women suffer from the sexism of American society. *Sexism* is the ideology that one sex is superior to the other. The term is generally used to refer to male prejudice and discrimination against women. In Chapter 10 it was noted that Blacks can suffer from both individual acts of racism and institutional discrimination. *Institutional discrimination* was defined as the denial of opportunities and equal rights to individuals or groups which results from the normal operations of a society. In the same sense, women can be said to suffer both from individual acts of sexism (such as sexist remarks and acts of violence) and from institutional sexism.

It is not simply that particular American men are biased in their treatment of women. All the major institutions of our society—including the armed forces, large corporations, the media, the universities, and the medical establishment—are controlled by men. These institutions, in their "normal," day-to-day operations, often discriminate against women and perpetuate sexism. Consequently, if the central office of a nationwide bank sets a policy that single women are a bad risk for loans—regardless of their incomes and investments—the *institution* will discriminate against women in state after state. It will do so even at bank branches in which loan officers hold no personal biases concerning women, but are merely "following orders." We will examine institutional discrimination against women within the educational system in Chapter 16.

Why is there sexism in American society? Why do individual males, and male-dominated institutions, discriminate against women? Barbara Bovee Polk (1974:419) has summarized the "power analysis" of sex differentiation, which holds that it is in men's interest to maintain power and privilege over women:

Power over women in personal relationships gives men what they want, whether that be sex, smiles, chores, admiration, increased leisure, or control itself. Men occupy and actively exclude women from positions of economic and political power in society. These positions give men a heavily disproportionate share of the rewards of society, especially economic rewards.

Yet with the power that comes to men comes responsibility. And with increased responsibility can come increased stress. Men have higher reported rates of certain types of mental illness than women do and greater likelihood of death due to heart attack or strokes (see Chapter 17). The pressure on men to succeed—and then to remain on top in a competitive work world—can be espe-cially intense. This is not to suggest that gender stratification is as damaging to men as it is to women. But it is clear that the power and privilege which men enjoy are no guarantee of mental and physical well-being. Jimmy Carter, shortly after becoming president of the United States, summed up the potential problems of the male role: "If you're a woman doing more than your mother did, you feel successful. If you're a man and you're not president, you feel like a failure" (E. Goodman, 1977; Pogrebin, 1981:63–64).

Thus far, we have focused primarily on the social and political aspect of women's subordinate position in the United States. Before we turn to the economic situation of women within the American work force, we will first look briefly at the situation of women around the world.

The Global Perspective

Women experience second-class status throughout the world. It is estimated that women grow half the world's food, but they rarely own land. They constitute one-third of the world's paid labor force but generally are found in the lowest-paying jobs. Single-parent households headed by women—which appear to be on the increase in many nations—are typically found in the poorest sectors of the population. As was discussed in Chapter 8, the feminization of poverty has become a global social phenomenon.

The Population Crisis Committee (1988), a nonprofit group which promotes international family planning programs, has attempted to assess and compare the status of women in five major areas: health, control over childbearing, education, employment, and legal protection. The purpose of this study was to illustrate the vast differences between the lives of women in the world's richest and poorest countries, and to point out common factors that contribute to maintaining women's second-class status, such as teenage marriage and childbearing, employment discrimination, and lack of access to education.

In general, the richer the country, the greater the measure of women's equality found by researchers. Western industrialized countries tended to rank high: Sweden scored 87 points out

Women have second-class status throughout the world. However, according to a study by the Population Crisis Committee, this inequality is especially evident in African, middle eastern, and south Asian countries.

of a possible 100 for the highest score, while the United States ranked third with 82.5 points. By contrast, African, middle eastern, and south Asian countries clustered at the bottom of the list, with Bangladesh ranking last at 21.5 points. But there were exceptions to these general patterns. Despite its economic prosperity, Saudi Arabia ranked "extremely poor" in terms of women's equality with a score of 29.5. A few low-income nations, among them Sri Lanka and China, ranked fairly well, with scores of 60 and 58.5, respectively. At the same time, Japan and Ireland—the only developed countries that have not attempted to equalize pay scales and benefits for women and men—scored in the "fair" category with 68.5 and 66 points, respectively.

In reviewing the global perspective on women's equality, two conclusions can be offered. First, as anthropologist Laura Nader (1986:383) has observed, even in the relatively more egalitarian nations of the west, women's subordination is "institutionally structured and culturally rationalized, exposing them to conditions of deference, dependency, powerlessness, and poverty." While the situation of women in Sweden and the United States is significantly better than in Saudi Arabia and Bangladesh, women nevertheless remain in a

second-class position in the world's most affluent and developed countries. Second, as was discussed in Chapter 9, there is a link between the wealth of industrialized nations and the poverty of developing countries. Consequently, the affluence of western nations has come, in part, at the expense of women in Third World countries.

Women in the American Work Force

"Does your mother work?" "No, she's just a housewife." This familiar exchange reminds us of women's traditional role in the United States, and it reminds us that women's work has generally been viewed as unimportant. The United States Commission on Civil Rights (1976:1) concluded that the passage in the Declaration of Independence proclaiming that "all men are created equal" has been taken too literally for too long. This is especially true with respect to employment.

A Statistical Overview Women in the United States are increasingly participating in the nation's paid labor force. No longer is the adult woman associated solely with the role of homemaker. Instead, millions of women—married and

FIGURE 11-1 Trends in Women's Participation in the Paid Labor Force, 1890–1988

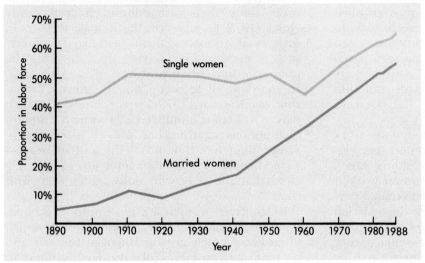

SOURCE: Bureau of the Census, 1975a:132–133; 1990a:334.

In 1988, 65 percent of single women and 57 percent of married women were in the paid labor force of the United States.

TABLE 11-1 Participation in the Labor Force by Marital Status, 1950 and 1988

SEX AND MARITAL STATUS	PERCENT IN LABOR FORCE	
	1950	1988
Total employed		
Women	33.9	60.0
Men	86.8	76.0
Married people with spouse present		
Women	23.8	56.5
Men	91.6	81.5
Married women with spouse present		
No children under 18 years old	30.3	48.9
Children 6–17 years old only	28.3	72.5
Children under 6 years old	11.9	57.1
Women working, with spouse absent[a]		
Children 6–17 years old only	63.6	75.5
Children under 6 years old	41.4	52.6

[a]Includes divorced and separated. 1950 data also include widowed.
SOURCES: Bureau of the Census, 1976:27–32; Department of Labor, 1988; and authors' estimate.

As the table shows, a growing number of women—married and single, with and without children—are participating in the nation's paid labor force.

single, with and without children—are working outside the home. In fact, a greater proportion of women are seeking and obtaining paid employment than ever before in our country's history. In 1988, more than 57 percent of adult American women held jobs outside the home, compared with 43 percent in 1970. A majority of women are now members of the paid labor force, not full-time homemakers (Bureau of the Census, 1990a:380).

The most dramatic rise in the female work force has been among married women (see Figure 11-1 and Table 11-1 on the preceding page). In 1988, 57 percent of married women worked outside the home, compared with less than 5 percent in 1890; and more than half the married women with children under 6 years old were in the labor force. Yet this change in women's work lives is not a recent revolution. Women's participation in the paid labor force has increased steadily throughout the twentieth century.

Unfortunately, women entering the American job market find their options restricted in important ways. Particularly damaging to women workers is occupational segregation, or confinement to sex-typed "women's jobs." For example, in 1988 women accounted for 99 percent of all secretaries, 96 percent of all private household workers, and 95 percent of all registered nurses (Bureau of the Census, 1990a:388–391).

Entering such sex-typed occupations places women in "service" roles which parallel the traditional gender-role standard under which housewives "serve" their husbands and children. Paddy Quick (1972:17) observes that female workers in such occupations perform "wifelike functions" such as ego-building, tidying up, answering the phone, getting coffee, and serving as a sex object. In analyzing these occupational patterns, Catharine MacKinnon (1979:18) concludes: "In such jobs, a woman is employed as a woman." Stereotypic notions regarding her "proper" place in life—rather than her unique talents and interests—shape her role in the labor force just as they dictated that she play with dolls rather than with trucks.

By contrast, women are not found in occupations historically defined as "men's jobs," which often carry much greater financial rewards and prestige than women's jobs do. For example, in 1988 women accounted for approximately 45 percent of the nation's paid labor force. Yet they represented only 7 percent of all engineers, 9 percent of all dentists, 20 percent of all physicians, and 20 percent of all lawyers and judges (Bureau of the Census, 1990a:380, 389). A general picture of women's employment in various occupations appears in Table 11-2.

In 1990, women held less than 1 percent of all senior management positions in the Fortune 500 corporations, and most of these women reported to male chief executives. Women now account for

(Drawing by Shirvanian; © 1983 The New Yorker Magazine, Inc.)

"Honey, I'm home!"

"Honey, I'm home!"

The most dramatic rise in the female work force has been among married women.

TABLE 11-2 Employment of Women in Selected Occupations, 1950 and 1988

	WOMEN AS PERCENT OF ALL WORKERS IN THE OCCUPATION	
OCCUPATION	1950	1988
Professional workers	40	50
Engineers	1	7
Lawyers and judges	4	20
Physicians	7	20
Dentists	n.a.	9
Registered nurses	98	95
College teachers	23	39
Other teachers	75	73
Managers	14	32
Sales workers	35	49
Clerical workers	62	82
Machine operators	34	41
Transport operatives	1	9
Service workers	57	61

NOTE: n.a. = not available.
SOURCES: Bureau of the Census, 1990a:389–391; Department of Labor, 1980:10–11.

Although strides have been made in some areas, many occupations continue to be filled routinely by members of one sex.

more than one-fourth of all students pursuing a master of business administration (M.B.A.) degree. Yet a 1990 survey of graduates of 20 highly ranked business schools revealed that female M.B.A.s earn an average of $54,749 in their first year after graduation—about 12 percent less income than the $61,400 earned by comparable male M.B.A.s (Fierman, 1990a; Roman, 1990).

Key roles in the mass media and the entertainment industry have similarly been regarded as "men's jobs." According to studies released in 1989, women hold only 6 percent of top management jobs in the news media, compared with 25 percent of middle-management jobs and 57 percent of entry-level jobs. The researchers suggest that women face biases in salaries and promotions, and are segregated into "dead-end jobs" with little decision-making authority. Hollywood studios have also been reluctant to place women in positions of authority. In 1990, women directors—who account for 20 percent of the membership of the Directors Guild of America—received assignments for 5 percent of all feature films, less than 3 percent of television movies, and

0 percent of television mini-series (Rasky, 1989a; Rohter, 1991).

How pervasive is sex-typing of occupations? In one study, researchers compiled a "segregation index" to estimate the percentage of women who would have to change their jobs to make the distribution of men and women in each occupation mirror the relative percentage of each sex in the adult working population. This study showed that 58 percent of women workers would need to switch jobs in order to create a labor force without sex segregation (J. Jacobs, 1990; Reskin and Blau, 1990).

The result of the workplace patterns described throughout this section is that women earn much less money than men do in the paid labor force of the United States. In 1988, the median income of full-time female workers was 68 percent that of full-time male workers. Given these data, it is hardly surprising to learn that many women are living in poverty, particularly when they must function as heads of households. In the discussion of poverty in Chapter 8, it was noted that by 1988, female heads of households and their children

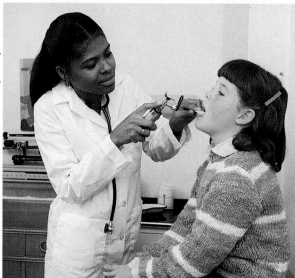

In the last two decades, there has been a striking increase in the proportion of women students in American medical schools.

accounted for 53 percent of the nation's poor. Yet not all women are in equal danger of experiencing poverty. As will be discussed more fully later in the chapter, women who are members of racial and ethnic minorities suffer from the double jeopardy of stratification by race and ethnicity as well as by gender (Bureau of the Census, 1989a:57, 1990a:453).

There are certain encouraging trends in women's employment patterns. Despite traditional gender-role socialization and sexist attitudes that have limited their employment opportunities, women *are* moving into at least some jobs that have generally been held by men. For example, between 1969 and 1986, the proportion of women students in medical schools in the United States rose almost fourfold, from 9.1 percent in 1969 to 33.9 percent in 1986. Nevertheless, even as more women have entered the medical profession, initial indications are that they often enter specialties with relatively lower financial rewards and less prestige than those chosen by men. Many women have opted for pediatrics, whereas surgery remains largely a male field. Moreover,

women doctors may feel constrained by family and child care pressures that do not seem to constrain their male counterparts. A well-established physician on a medical school faculty recalls that she had to adjust her career because of the "double-bind" she faced as a woman and a doctor (Bourne and Wikler, 1978:435; Brozan, 1986; Lorber, 1984; S. Martin et al., 1988).

What can be done to close the gap between the earnings of women and men? In the 1980s, pay equity—also known as *comparable worth*—emerged as a controversial solution in the effort to alleviate the second-class status of women within the paid labor force. ***Pay equity*** calls for equal pay for different types of work judged to be comparable through measurement of such factors as employees' knowledge, skills, effort, responsibility, and working conditions. Pay equity goes beyond the idea of "equal pay for equal work" by encouraging equal pay for different (but comparable) work.

Many public employers, including the states of New York and New Jersey, have developed voluntary plans to put pay equity policies into effect. According to the National Committee on Pay Equity, by 1988 more than 1500 local governments and school districts in 24 states had taken steps to address the issue of pay equity. During the 1980s, more than $450 million was allocated by state and local governments to upgrade employees' pay in such traditional "women's jobs" as clerk, typist, librarian, and nurse—with the goal of bringing their salaries up to the level of those of maintenance workers, gardeners, and other government workers in male-dominated classifications (T. Lewin, 1989:8; Saetre, 1989).

Social Consequences of Women's Employment
There have already been many obvious consequences of women's increasing involvement in the American paid labor force. As was seen in Chapter 4, the need for child care facilities has grown, and there have been pressures for greater public financing of day care. Even the rise of fast-food chains partially reflects the fact that many women are no longer home and cooking during the day.

In theory at least, women should gain in self-esteem and power within the family as they move outside the home and function as productive wage earners. In an ongoing study of women between the ages of 35 and 55, researchers have found that "for employed women, a high-prestige job, rather than a husband, is the best predictor of well-being" (Baruch et al., 1980:199, 1983). Holding this type of position appears to be the factor most influential in a woman's self-esteem. Of course, as we have seen in this chapter, the number of women employed in high-prestige jobs is rather small.

In terms of power dynamics, women clearly gain some degree of power by earning their own incomes. Studies indicate that when a woman provides sole support for her family, employment even in a low-status occupation has a positive effect on her self-esteem (L. Hoffman and Nye, 1975). For married women, such income from employment can be effective security in case of separation or divorce. In the past, many full-time homemakers had little confidence in their ability to make a living. As a result, some remained in unsatisfying marriages, believing that they had no alternative way to survive. This is still the case for a considerable number of women in the United States and around the world.

As women become increasingly involved in employment outside the home, men will have an opportunity to become more involved in the care and socialization of children. In industrial societies, the demands on men as primary wage earners have traditionally contributed to a deemphasis on the social roles of being a father. Freda Rebelsky and Cheryl Hanks (1973) examined interactions between fathers and babies and found that the longest time period any father in the sample devoted to his infant was 10 minutes 26 seconds. The average period of verbal interaction between father and baby was only *38 seconds per day*. More recently, psychologist Wade Mackey (1987) conducted a cross-cultural study of 17 societies—including Morocco, Hong Kong, Ireland, and Mexico—and found that the limited father-child interactions in the United States were typical of all the societies surveyed.

American fathers currently find little time for the basic tasks of child rearing (see Box 11-2, page 342). Some men have reworked their job commitments to maximize the amount of time they can spend with their children. For example, a Connecticut salesperson comes home for lunch so that he can play with his 7-month-old daughter. On weekends, he rises at 6:00 A.M. so that he can spend time alone with her. Yet, although Bell Telephone has offered men the option of 6-month paternity leave since 1969, there have been few takers. It remains difficult for men in two-parent households to deviate from their traditional occupational roles in order to become more involved in child rearing (Langway, 1981).

The division of household and child care duties is far from trivial in defining power relations within the family. Heidi Hartmann (1981:377) argues that "time spent on housework, as well as other indicators of household labor, can be fruitfully used as a measure of power relationships in the home." Hartmann points out that as women spend more hours per week working for wages, the amount of time they devote to housework decreases, yet their overall "workweek" increases. However, men in dual-career marriages do not spend more time on housework chores than husbands of full-time homemakers do.

More recent studies indicate that the gender gap in housework persists. Drawing on data from a 1985 national survey, sociologist John Robinson (1988) reports that while men have increased their share of some household duties—among them, pet care and paying of bills—women in the United States continue to perform 2 hours of housework for each hour done by men. In 1985, not including time spent on child care, women averaged 19.5 hours of housework each week, compared with only 9.8 hours for men. These data represent a partial narrowing of the inequality regarding housework. In 1975, men had averaged 7.0 hours per week on household tasks, compared with 27.0 for women.

Data from a 1989 national survey suggest that men and women hold somewhat differing perceptions of who does the housework. When asked whether housework was shared equally, 59 percent of women but only 45 percent of men responded that the woman in the couple does more housework. Forty-six percent of men but only 35 percent of women stated that housework is shared equally between male and female partners. Overall, the survey underscored the common sex seg-

BOX 11-2 • SPEAKING OUT

A FATHER AND HIS BABY

Letty Cottin Pogrebin, who is an editor of MS. *magazine and the author of various books on nonsexist child rearing, believes that an increasing number of American fathers are taking an active role in rearing children. In the following selection, Pogrebin (1982:44) reflects on the difficulties of integrating family needs and public life:*

While a faculty member was introducing me to a college lecture audience, the hushed auditorium was pierced by a tiny child's high voice imitating a fire-engine siren. There was much rustling as heads turned toward the back where a man was trying to silence a baby of 18 months or so. The baby responded with "wroooeeeee," just as the introducer spoke my name. I sensed the collective embarrassment, watched the father hustle toward the exit, child in arms, nervously patting the child to keep it still.

From the podium, I called after him: "To the father in the back row, please remain with us. If your baby begins squealing during

Letty Cottin Pogrebin.

(Courtesy Letty Cottin Pogrebin, photo by Nadine Markova)

my speech, I will make an extra effort to be heard and the audience will listen a little harder. Although you happen to be a man, you are in the position of millions of women who, because of their sole responsibility for their children, exempt themselves from public events, or are excluded from places of education or entertainment.

"When we assume some of that responsibility," I continued, "we help parents remain in our midst. If we have learned to work, think, and speak, and listen to one another over the sounds of male technology—over the air conditioners, phones, jet planes, stock market tickers, photocopiers, wire service machines, and computers—we can make an accommodation for the human sound of one baby in a college auditorium."

The audience roared their approval. The father stayed in his seat. I delivered my speech and eventually the baby fell asleep.

A few days later, my husband and I attended a concert in Manhattan. When a baby started mewing in the balcony, its father stayed, but its mother carried it from the concert hall.

Perhaps when more fathers are caretakers of children and more mothers are in control of the podium, family needs will be accommodated in public life.

---

regation evident in the performance of household tasks (see Figure 11-2 on the opposite page). For example, 78 percent of women report that they do all or most of their families' meal preparation, and 72 percent say they do all or most of the child care. By contrast, 74 percent of men indicate that they do all or most of the minor home repairs and 63 percent state that they do all or most of the yard work (DeStefano and Colasanto, 1990:28–29, 31).

A study of Canadian married couples by sociol-

ogist Susan Shaw (1988) offers insight into the rather different ways in which men and women view housework. Specifically, men are more likely than women to view these activities as "leisure"—and are less likely to view them as "work." The reason for this gender difference is that these tasks continue to be seen as women's work. Consequently, men perceive themselves as having more freedom of choice in engaging in housework and child care; they are more likely than women to report that cooking, home chores, shopping, and child care are, in fact, leisure. Confirming earlier research, Shaw found that the employment status of women had little effect on this gender difference.

The continuing disparity in household labor has a rather striking meaning in terms of power relationships within the family (a subject which will be examined more fully in Chapter 13). As married women have taken on more and more hours of paid employment, they have been only partially successful in getting their husbands to assume a greater role in needed homemaking duties, including child care. As a result, in Hartmann's view, increasing numbers of wives become subject to a "double burden"—long workweeks both at home and outside the home. In this sense, womens' growing participation in

the paid labor force is hardly bringing them greater freedom or greater power (see also Rexroat and Shehan, 1987).

Sociologist Arlie Hochschild (1989, 1990) has used the phrase "second shift" to describe the double burden—work outside the home followed by child care and housework—that many women face and few men share equitably. On the basis of interviews with and observations of 52 couples over an 8-year period, Hochschild reports that the wives (and not their husbands) drive home from the office while planning domestic schedules and play dates for children—and then begin their second shift. Drawing on national studies, she concludes that women spend 15 fewer hours in leisure activities each week than do their husbands. In a year, these women work an extra

FIGURE 11-2 Division of Household Tasks by Gender

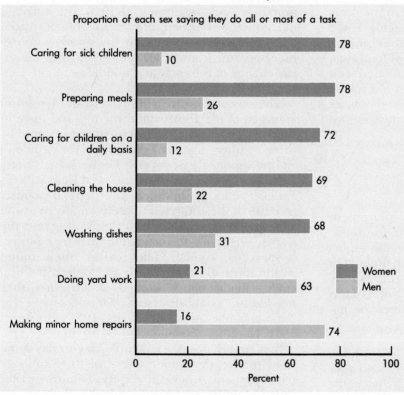

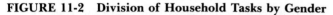

NOTE: Questions regarding child care were asked only of respondents with children living at home.
SOURCE: DeStefano and Colasanto, 1990:31.

In a national survey conducted in 1989, men and women indicated who they felt did all or most of a variety of household tasks. Segregation of housework and child care was evident, and other studies indicate that women spend more than twice as much time on housework as men—even when child care is not included.

month of 24-hour days because of the second shift phenomenon; over a dozen years, they work an extra year of 24-hour days.

Hochschild found that the married couples she studied were fraying at the edges, and so were their careers and their marriages. The women she spoke with hardly resembled the beautiful young businesswomen pictured in magazine advertisements, dressed in power suits but with frilled blouses, holding briefcases in one hand and happy young children in the other. Instead, many of Hochschild's female subjects talked about being overtired and emotionally drained by the demands of their multiple roles. They were much more intensely torn by the conflicting demands of work outside the home and family life than their husbands were. Hochschild (1990:73) concludes that "if we as a culture come to see the urgent need of meeting the new problems posed by the second shift, and if society and government begin to shape new policies that allow working parents more flexibility, then we will be making some progress toward happier times at home and at work." This view is shared by many feminists, who have advocated greater governmental and corporate support for child care (refer back to Chapter 4), more flexible family leave policies (see Chapter 13), and other reforms designed to ease the burden on the nation's families.

Women: Emergence of a Collective Consciousness

Many people believe that the feminist movement is a new and recent development in American history. But, in fact, the fight for women's rights dates back at least as far as colonial times. On March 31, 1776, months before the signing of the Declaration of Independence, Abigail Adams wrote to her husband John Adams, later the nation's second president:

. . . I desire you would remember the Ladies, and be more favourable and generous to them than your ancestors. Do not put such unlimited power in the hands of Husbands. Remember all Men would be tyrants if they could. If particular care and attention is not paid to the Ladies, we are determined to foment a Rebellion, and will not hold ourselves bound

by any Laws in which we have no voice, or representation (A. Rossi, 1973:10–11).

In a formal sense, the American feminist movement was born in upstate New York, in a town called Seneca Falls, in the summer of 1848. On July 19, the first women's rights convention began, attended by Elizabeth Cady Stanton, Lucretia Mott, and other pioneers in the struggle for women's rights. This first wave of *feminists*, as they are currently known, battled ridicule and scorn as they fought for legal and political equality for women. They were not afraid to risk controversy on behalf of their cause; in 1872 Susan B. Anthony was arrested for attempting to vote in that year's presidential election.

Ultimately, the early feminists won many victories, among them the passage and ratification of the Nineteenth Amendment to the Constitution, which granted women the right to vote in national elections beginning in 1920. But suffrage did not lead to other reforms in women's social and economic position, and the women's movement became a much less powerful force for social change in the early and middle twentieth century.

The second wave of American feminism emerged in the 1960s and came into full force in the 1970s. In part, the movement was inspired by three pioneering books arguing for women's rights: Simone de Beauvoir's *The Second Sex*, Betty Friedan's *The Feminine Mystique*, and Kate Millett's *Sexual Politics*. In addition, the general political activism of the 1960s led women—many of whom were working for Black civil rights or against the war in Vietnam—to reexamine their own powerlessness as women. The sexism often found within allegedly progressive and radical political circles made many women decide that they needed to establish their own movement for "women's liberation" (S. Evans, 1980; Firestone, 1970:15–40; J. Freeman, 1973, 1975).

Sometimes, it was very simple, day-to-day situations that made women aware of their subordinate status in American society. Feminist writer Jane O'Reilly (1972:55) described such an occurrence:

In suburban Chicago, the party consisted of three

After many decades of struggle, women gained the right to vote in national elections beginning in 1920. However, women's suffrage did not dramatically change the position of women within American society.

couples. The women were a writer, a doctor, and a teacher. The men were all lawyers. As the last couple arrived, the host said, jovially, "With a room full of lawyers, we ought to have a good evening." Silence. Click! "What are we?" asked the teacher. "Invisible?"

More and more women became aware of sexist attitudes and practices—including attitudes they themselves had accepted through socialization into traditional gender roles—and began to challenge male dominance. A sense of "sisterhood," much like the class consciousness that Marx hoped would emerge in the proletariat (see Chapter 8), became evident. Individual women identified their interests with those of the collectivity *women*. No longer were they "happy" in submissive, subordinate roles ("false consciousness" in Marxist terms).

This new sense of group solidarity and loyalty was fostered within feminist consciousness-raising groups. In these small discussion groups, women shared their personal feelings, experiences, and conflicts. Many discovered that their "individual" problems were shared by other women and often reflected sexist conditioning and powerlessness. Such awareness of common oppression is a precondition for social change. Consciousness does not always lead to efforts to transform social con-

ditions, but it is essential in mobilizing a group for collective action.

Through the strength gained in consciousness raising, the women's movement has undertaken public protests on a wide range of issues. Feminists have endorsed passage of the equal rights amendment, government subsidies for child care (see Chapter 4), greater representation of women in government (see Chapter 15), affirmative action for women and minorities (see Chapter 15), federal legislation outlawing sex discrimination in education (see Chapter 16), and the right to legal abortions (which will be discussed later in this chapter). Feminists have condemned violence against women in the family (see Chapter 13), sexual harassment in organizations (see Chapter 6), forced sterilization of poor and minority women, sexist advertising and pornography, and discrimination against lesbians and gay men.

In an overview of the feminist campaign for social change, Barbara Bovee Polk (1974:422–430) distinguishes a number of basic approaches:

1 Attempts by women to resocialize themselves and overcome traditional gender conditioning
2 Efforts to change day-to-day personal interactions with men and other women and to avoid conventional sexist patterns

3 Use of the media and academic world to combat sexism and resocialize others to more egalitarian values and greater respect for women
4 Challenges to male dominance of social institutions through demonstrations, boycotts, lawsuits, and other tactics
5 Creation of alternative institutions, such as women's self-help medical clinics (see Chapter 17), publishing houses, and communes.

The women's movement has employed all these approaches simultaneously in its efforts to transform American society and promote women's rights.

Feminists have made certain political gains in the last 20 years and have undoubtedly made the nation (and the world) more aware of women's oppressed status. Yet, throughout the 1980s, there appeared to be a conservative backlash against the women's movement—even though 67 percent of women surveyed in 1989 believed that the United States "continues to need a strong women's movement to push for changes that benefit women" (Dionne, 1989). Clearly, the long struggle that had been initiated by Abigail Adams, Susan B. Anthony, and other early women's rights activists is far from won.

Minority Women: Double Jeopardy

We have seen that the historical oppression of women limits them by tradition and law to specific roles. Many women experience differential treatment not only because of gender but because of race and ethnicity as well. These citizens face a "double jeopardy"—that of subordinate status twice defined. A disproportionate share of this low-status group are also impoverished, so that the double jeopardy effectively becomes a triple jeopardy. The litany of social ills continues for many if we consider old age, ill health, disabilities, and the like.

Feminists have addressed themselves to the particular needs of minority women, but overshadowing the oppression of these women because of gender is the subordinate status imposed because of race and ethnicity. The question for African American women, Chicanas (Mexican American women), Asian American women, and others appears to be whether they should unify with their "brothers" against racism or challenge them for their sexism. One answer is that, in a truly just society, both sexism and racism must be eradicated.

The discussion of gender roles among Blacks has always provoked controversy. Advocates of Black nationalism contend that feminism only distracts women from full participation in the Black struggle. The existence of feminist groups among Blacks, in their view, is simply a divide-and-conquer strategy that serves the dominant White society. By contrast, Black feminists such as Florynce Kennedy argue that little is to be gained by adopting or maintaining the gender-role divisions of the dominant society that place women in a subservient position. Historically, Black women have been more likely than White women to suffer from unemployment; Black women clearly stand to gain from increased employment and educational opportunities (Giddings, 1984; Ladner, 1986).

The plight of Chicanas is usually considered part of either the Chicano or the feminist movement, ignoring the distinctive experience of Chicanas. In the past, these women have been excluded from decision making in the two institutions that most directly affect their daily lives: the family and the church. The Chicano family, especially in the lower class, feels the pervasive tradition of male domination. The Roman Catholic church relegates women to supportive roles while reserving the leadership positions for men (Burciaga et al., 1977; Rosaldo, 1985:415).

Activists among minority women do not agree on whether priority should be granted to equalizing the sexes or to eliminating inequality among racial and ethnic groups. Chicana feminist Enriqueta Longauex y Vasquez (1970:384), while acknowledging the importance of the Chicano movement, believes in stressing sexual equality: "When a man can look upon a woman as human, then, and only then, can he feel the true meaning of liberation and equality."

Perhaps it would be most useful to conclude that both components of inequality cannot be ignored. Helen Mayer Hacker (1973:11), who pioneered research on both Blacks and women, stated before the American Sociological Association: "As a partisan observer, it is my fervent hope that in fighting the twin battles of sexism and racism, Black women and Black men will [create] the outlines of the good society for all Americans." Recent history of various movements for equal rights indicates that while disputes over priorities continue, there is widespread recognition that social equality among all people is the ultimate goal (see also Andersen, 1988).

THE BATTLE OVER ABORTION

- Why has the issue of abortion rights been a fundamental concern of the feminist movement?
- What differences are apparent in the social backgrounds of women active in the "pro-choice" and "pro-life" movements?
- From a conflict perspective, how are the factors of race, class, and ethnicity an important part of the abortion controversy?

Few issues seem to stir as much intense conflict as abortion. Until about 20 years ago, it was very difficult for a woman to terminate a pregnancy legally in the United States and most other industrial nations. Beginning in the late 1960s, a few state governments began to reform statutes and make it easier for a woman to obtain a legal abortion. However, with abortion permissible only in a small minority of states, and only under certain conditions, a large number of women continued to have illegal abortions (P. Conover and Gray, 1983).

The fight for the right to safe, inexpensive, and legal abortions was a key priority of the feminist movement of the late 1960s and early 1970s. Feminists argued that the right to abortion was fundamental to women's sexual and reproductive freedom. In their view, women—not legislators or judges—should have an unconditional right to decide whether, and under what circumstances, they would bear children. Feminists further insisted that no law would ever prevent women

Feminists and other "pro-choice" activists argue that the movement opposed to legal abortion is not genuinely "pro-life." These critics charge that "right-to-lifers" care about needy women only while they are pregnant and fail to support government programs to aid women who do choose to bear children.

347

from obtaining abortions. The issue was simply whether these abortions would be performed safely by doctors, or dangerously by "back room" abortionists or by the pregnant women themselves (Petchesky, 1990; E. Willis, 1980).

The critical victory in the struggle for legalized abortion came in the 1973 Supreme Court decision of *Roe v. Wade.* The justices held, by a 7-2 margin, that the "right to privacy . . . founded in the Fourteenth Amendment's concept of personal liberty . . . is broad enough to encompass a woman's decision whether or not to terminate a pregnancy." However, the Court did set certain limits on a woman's right to abortion. During the last 3 months of pregnancy, the fetus was ruled capable of life outside the womb. Therefore, states were granted the right to prohibit all abortions in the third trimester except those needed to preserve the life, physical health, or mental health of the mother. In subsequent decisions in the 1970s, the Supreme Court upheld the right of a woman to terminate pregnancy without the consent of her husband or (in the case of younger, unmarried women) her parents.

The Court's decision in *Roe v. Wade,* while generally applauded by "pro-choice" groups, which support the right to legal abortions, was bitterly condemned by those opposed to abortion. For people who call themselves "pro-life," abortion is a moral and often a religious issue. In their view, human life actually begins at the moment of conception rather than at the moment of a baby's delivery. On the basis of this judgment, the fetus is a human life, not a potential person. Termination of this life, even before it has left the womb, is viewed as essentially an act of murder. Consequently, antiabortion activists were alarmed by the fact that by 1989, over 22 million legal abortions had taken place in the United States in the years since the Supreme Court decision in *Roe v. Wade* (Bureau of the Census, 1990a:71; Luker, 1984:126–157).

Sociologist Kristin Luker (1984:158–191) has offered a detailed study of activists in the pro-choice and pro-life movements (see Table 11-3). Luker interviewed 212 activists in California, overwhelmingly women, who spent at least 5 hours per week working for one of these movements. According to Luker, each group has a "consistent, coherent view of the world." Feminists involved in defending abortion rights typically believe that men and women are essentially similar; they support women's full participation in work outside the home and oppose all forms of sex discrimination. By contrast, most antiabortion activists believe that men and women are fundamentally different. In their view, men are best suited for the public world of work, whereas women are best suited for the demanding and crucial task of rearing children. These activists are troubled by women's growing participation in work outside the home, which they view as destructive to the American family and ultimately to society as a whole.

In the mid-1970s, the antiabortion movement focused not only on legislative initiatives to prevent abortions but also on termination of government funding of abortions. In 1976, Congress passed the Hyde amendment, which prohibited use of Medicaid funds to pay for abortions except when the woman's life was in danger or when she was the victim of rape or incest. The effects of the Hyde amendment were dramatic: federally funded abortions were reduced by 99 percent. Although some states were willing to pay for abortions in the absence of federal funding, the majority were not. Consequently, for 3 million women of childbearing years relying on Medicaid, many of them teenagers, it became more difficult to exercise the right to a legal abortion (Schultz, 1977).

For at least some low-income women, the results of this federal policy have been fatal. In 1977, Rosaura Jimenez of Texas became the first woman known to die of complications following an illegal abortion after implementation of the Hyde amendment. Viewing the issue from a conflict perspective, it was not surprising that the first group to lose access to legal abortions comprised poor women, of whom a significant number are Black and Hispanic.

The battle over government funding for abortions continued throughout the 1980s. In 1984, Congress widened its ban on Medicaid-financed abortions, making an exception only for cases in which a woman's life was endangered. However, in 1989, the ban on federal funding was lifted for women whose pregnancies result from rape or incest. As of 1989, 37 states followed the federal policy by refusing to fund abortions except in the cases noted above (Barringer, 1989; *Washington Post,* 1984).

In recent years, influenced by the votes of conservative justices appointed by Ronald Reagan during his presidency, the Supreme Court has allowed state legislatures to restrict women's ability to obtain abortions. In the key 1989 case of *Webster v. Reproductive Health Services,* the Court upheld, by a 5-4 vote, the state of Missouri's right to prohibit public hospitals from performing abortions and to prohibit public employees from performing or assisting in abortions

TABLE 11-3   Social Backgrounds of Women Active in the Pro-Choice and Pro-Life Movements

PRO-CHOICE WOMEN	PRO-LIFE WOMEN
Only 8 percent did not finish college	30 percent did not finish college
18 percent have some type of postgraduate or professional degree	6 percent have some type of postgraduate or professional degree
94 percent work in the paid labor force	63 percent do not work in the paid labor force
Tend to be employed in major professions, as administrators, as owners of small businesses, or as executives in large businesses	Tend to be full-time homemakers; when active in the paid labor force, tend to be teachers, social workers, and nurses
When married, are typically married to men with good incomes	When married, are typically married to skilled workers or small businessmen with moderate incomes
One in three have an income of $50,000 per year	One in seven has an income of $50,000 per year
One-fourth have incomes of less than $20,000 per year	Almost half (44 percent) have incomes of less than $20,000
23 percent have never married	16 percent have never married
14 percent have been divorced	5 percent have been divorced
Typically have 1–2 children	Typically have 2–3 children; 23 percent have 5 or more children; 16 percent have 7 or more

SOURCE: Adapted from Luker, 1984:194–197.

In her study of pro-choice and pro-life activists in California, sociologist Kristin Luker found that the overwhelming majority of activists in each movement were women. However, there were striking differences in the social background of these women activists.

not necessary to save a pregnant woman's life. While the *Roe v. Wade* decision was not overturned, the Court's majority seemed to invite legislators to enact restrictions that would further narrow the right to legal abortion. Like the Hyde amendment, the Missouri restrictions appeared likely to make access to abortion extremely difficult for low-income women. Then, in two 1990 cases, the Supreme Court upheld state laws that require pregnant teenagers to notify both parents before obtaining an abortion. The Court ruled that such laws were constitutional so long as they included a "judicial bypass" alternative, whereby young women who are pregnant and do not wish to notify their parents can appear before a judge to seek court permission to have an abortion.

The issues of parental notification and parental consent have become an especially sensitive aspect of the abortion debate. The respected Alan Guttmacher Institute estimates that over 1 million American teenagers become pregnant each year and that 42 percent of them decide to have abortions. Pro-life activists argue that the parents of these teenagers should have the right to be notified about—and to permit or prohibit—these abortions. In their view, parental authority deserves full support at a time in which the traditional nuclear family is embattled. However, pro-choice activists counter that many pregnant teenagers come from troubled families where they have been abused. These young women may have good reason to avoid discussing such explosive issues with

(Laura Sikes/Sygma)

In recent years, the militant antiabortion group Operation Rescue has attempted to shut down abortion clinics through picketing and harassment of patients and clinics. In 1989, 11,800 people were arrested for blockading providers of abortions; many were part of actions associated with Operation Rescue (Hancock, 1990).

their parents. Moreover, the option of a judicial bypass may be intimidating for a teenager, and maintaining confidentiality may be impossible if, for instance, the young woman lives in a small town and is known to those who work in or near the courthouse (Salholz, 1990).

In their attack on parental notification and consent requirements, pro-choice activists frequently discuss the death of Becky Bell. In the summer of 1988, this 17-year-old pregnant high school junior went to a Planned Parenthood clinic in Indianapolis to examine her options. She decided to have an abortion but was afraid to hurt her parents with the news that she had become pregnant. Since state law in Indiana required that she seek the consent of one parent, Bell planned to travel to Kentucky for an abortion. But she became desperate, attempted to abort herself, and died. Becky Bell's grieving father has become an outspoken opponent of the parental consent laws that he believes contributed to his daughter's death. "I am not against laws governing abortion," says William Bell. "What I am against is that legislators said my daughter had to come to me. Therefore she was denied the right to make a safe choice" (Salholz, 1990:32).

As of 1990, the American people appeared to support the right to legal abortion in principle, but were ambivalent concerning certain applications of that right. In a national survey, 71 percent of respondents stated that a woman should be allowed to have an abortion if she and her doctor agree to it. However,

when asked if a "woman should be able to get an abortion if she wants one no matter what the reason," only 43 percent of respondents agreed with the statement (*American Enterprise,* 1990).

By 1990, abortion had become a controversial issue in western Europe. As in the United States, many European nations bowed to public opinion and liberalized abortion laws in the 1970s. While Ireland, Belgium, and Malta continue to prohibit abortion, it is legal in other western European countries. Austria, Denmark, Greece, the Netherlands, Norway, and Sweden have abortion laws that allow a woman to have an abortion upon request. Other countries have more restrictive legislation, especially concerning abortions in the later stages of pregnancy. By the late 1980s, inspired by their counterparts in the United States, antiabortion activists had become more outspoken in Great Britain, France, Italy, Spain, and Germany (Simons, 1989).

In both western Europe and the United States, rural women experience difficulty in finding a physician who will perform an abortion. According to a survey by the Alan Guttmacher Institute, the number of abortion providers in rural areas of the United States declined by 19 percent over the period 1985–1988. The inability to find a physician, clinic, or hospital that will perform an abortion forces rural women in this country and Europe to travel long distances to get an abortion. Viewed from a conflict perspective, this is one more financial and emotional burden that falls especially heavily on low-income women (T. Lewin, 1990d).

SUMMARY

Differentiation based on gender is evident in virtually every human society about which we have information. As with race, the biological fact of gender is given a distinct social significance by society.

1 *Gender identity* is one of the first and most far-reaching identities that a human being holds.

2 Parents are normally the first and most crucial agents of socialization; they guide children into *gender roles* deemed appropriate by society.

3 Members of the female sex have been more severely restricted by traditional American gender roles, but these roles have also restricted males.

4 The research of anthropologist Margaret Mead points to the importance of cultural conditioning in defining the social roles of males and females.

5 Functionalists maintain that sex differentiation contributes to overall social stability, whereas conflict theorists contend that the relationship between females and males has been one of unequal power, with men in a dominant position over women.

6 As one example of their micro-level approach to the study of gender stratification, interactionists have analyzed men's verbal dominance over women through conversational interruptions.

7 Although numerically a majority, in many respects women fit the definition of a subordinate minority group within American society.

8 In terms of power dynamics, women clearly gain some additional degree of power by earning their own incomes.

9 As women have taken on more and more hours of paid employment outside the home, they have been largely unable to get their husbands to take a greater role in homemaking duties, including child care.

10 The fight for women's rights in the United States dates back as far as colonial times.

11 A new sense of group solidarity and loyalty among women was fostered in feminist consciousness-raising groups.

12 Minority women experience double jeopardy through differential treatment based not only on gender but also on race and ethnicity.

13 The issue of abortion has bitterly divided the United States and pitted pro-choice activists against pro-life activists.

KEY TERMS

Androgyny A term used to describe a lifestyle in which there is no gender-role differentiation and one can be both "masculine" and "feminine." (page 330)

Expressiveness A term used by Parsons and Bales to refer to concern for maintenance of harmony and the internal emotional affairs of the family. (331)

Gender identity The self-concept of a person as being male or female. (325)

Gender roles Expectations regarding the proper behavior, attitudes, and activities of males and females. (326)

Institutional discrimination The denial of opportunities and of equal rights to individuals or groups which results from the normal operations of a society. (334)

Instrumentality A term used by Parsons and Bales to refer to emphasis on tasks, focus on more distant goals, and a concern for the external relationship between one's family and other social institutions. (331)

Pay equity A policy of equal pay for different types of work judged to be comparable through measurement of such factors as employees' knowledge, skills, effort, responsibility, and working conditions. Also known as *comparable worth*. (340)

Sexism The ideology that one sex is superior to the other. (334)

ADDITIONAL READINGS

England, Paula, and George Farkas. *Households, Employment, and Gender.* New York: Aldine, 1986. The authors integrate the study of the household with research on paid employment.

Epstein, Cynthia Fuchs. *Deceptive Distinctions: Sex, Gender, and the Social Order.* New Haven, Conn.: Yale University Press, 1988. A feminist sociologist surveys social scientific research on gender.

Giddings, Paula. *When and Where I Enter.* New York: Morrow, 1984. Giddings, an editor at Howard University Press, has written a superb historical account of Black women in the United States.

Goldin, Claudia. *Understanding the Gender Gap: An Economic History of American Women.* New York: Oxford University Press, 1990. Goldin presents a historical framework for understanding how women have been assigned to particular occupations with lower pay than those held by men.

Gray, Francine du Plessix. *Soviet Women: Walking the Tightrope.* Garden City, N.Y.: Doubleday, 1990. An examination of the social experiences of women in a country where 92 percent are employed outside the home.

Hess, Beth B., and Myra Marx Ferree (eds.). *Analyzing Gender: A Handbook of Social Science Research.* Newbury Park, Calif.: Sage, 1987. Included in this anthology is treatment of popular culture, female sexuality, family roles, religion, and the women's health movement.

Hochschild, Arlie Russell, with Anne Machung. *The Second Shift: Working Parents and the Revolution at Home.* New York: Viking Penguin, 1989. A critical look at housework in dual-career couples, in which Hochschild observes that women's duties at home constitute a "second shift" after their work in the paid labor force.

Jaggar, Alison M. *Feminist Politics and Human Nature.* Totowa, N.J.: Rowman and Allanheld, 1983. This heavily documented book carefully discusses feminist politics and makes distinctions between liberal, Marxist, radical, and socialist perspectives.

Kimmel, Michael S. (ed.). *Changing Men.* Newbury Park, Calif.: Sage, 1987. This anthology includes 19 articles discussing research on men and masculinity.

Luker, Kristin. *Abortion and the Politics of Motherhood.* Berkeley: University of California Press, 1984. A highly regarded study of pro-choice and pro-life activists.

Richardson, Laurel, and Verta Taylor. *Feminist Frontiers II: Rethinking Sex, Gender, and Society.* New York: Random House, 1989. This revised work summarizes the social perspective on gender in the United States.

Rothenberg, Paula S. *Racism and Sexism: An Integrated Study.* New York: St. Martin's, 1988. A collection of more than 70 articles focusing on the experiences of and difficulties faced by women of color.

Journals

Among the journals that focus on issues of gender stratification are *Gender and Society* (founded in 1987), *Sex Roles* (1975), and *Signs: Journal of Women in Culture and Society* (1975).

STRATIFICATION
BY AGE

12

STRATIFICATION
BY AGE

> *When I get older, losing my hair,*
> *Many years from now . . .*
> *Will you still need me,*
> *Will you still feed me,*
> *When I'm sixty-four?*
> *John Lennon and Paul McCartney*
> *"When I'm Sixty-Four," 1967*

LOOKING AHEAD

- Why are the elderly considered a minority or subordinate group?
- Why does the aging of the world's peoples represent a major success story of the late twentieth century?
- In what ways do functionalists and interactionists take opposing views of the aging process?
- Do Americans tend to accept negative stereotypes of the elderly?
- How common is abuse of the elderly?
- Why are older Americans so concerned about the issue of catastrophic health care?

Is life in one's later years dominated by an inevitable loss of identity, self-esteem, and individuality? Many older people in Sweden, Denmark, and Finland would answer with a resounding "no." These Scandinavian countries have pioneered an approach to aging known as "open old-age care," under which older citizens are encouraged and helped to live their later years in dignity in their own homes. "Home helpers" paid by local governments visit the elderly and perform such chores as housekeeping, cleaning, shopping, and cooking.

Through the aid of home helpers, many older people are able to avoid "warehousing" in nursing homes. Dora Philipson, an 82-year-old widow in a suburb near Copenhagen, Denmark, lives alone in her furnished apartment and plays her piano every day. She relies on home helpers for certain housekeeping duties, but otherwise is able to take care of herself. Philipson is happy living in her familiar apartment complex. "Here, one feels secure," she declares, "yet at the same time you remain an individual. I can live the way I want, and I don't feel lonely, because I know most of my neighbors" (Szulc, 1988:5).

Denmark's Social Affairs Minister, Mimi Stilling Jakobsen, a 39-year-old working mother, has spoken out strongly against the warehousing of the elderly. "Now we see the new generation of retired people," says Jakobsen. "They are different from my grandparents. They want to jog, to travel, to read books, to lead their own lives—so you can't put them in a nursing home with a needle to sew, some small pills to keep them quiet, and some pocket money" (Szulc, 1988:5).

The approach to housing for older people is quite different in the United States. Segregation of the elderly in nursing and retirement homes is but one reminder that age, like race and gender, is an ascribed status that forms the basis for social differentiation. As we will see throughout the chapter, age is another aspect of the multidimensional concept of stratification. Yet even within various age strata, people are further differentiated by gender, class, race, and ethnicity (Quadagno, 1989b).

Although this chapter examines aging around

the world, it will focus primarily on the position of older people within the age-stratification system of the United States. It will examine various theories developed to explain the impact of aging on the individual and society, including disengagement theory and activity theory. Particular attention will be given to the growing proportion of elderly Americans. The effects of prejudice and discrimination on older people and the rise of a growing political consciousness among the elderly will be discussed. The social policy section will explore the issue of catastrophic health care, which has particular relevance for older Americans.

AGING AND SOCIETY

Like other forms of stratification, age stratification varies from culture to culture. One society may treat older people with great reverence, while another sees them as "unproductive" and "difficult." Societies differ, as well, in their commitment to providing social services to assist older citizens. For example, in 1987, Sweden had 1500 home helpers per 100,000 older people in need of such aid; by contrast, the United States had only 66 helpers to serve the same-sized population (Szulc, 1988:7).

The elderly were highly regarded in the culture of traditional China. The period beginning at about age 55 was probably the most secure and comfortable time for men and women. As the closest living contact with people's ancestors, older family members received deference from younger kin and had first claim on all family resources. As China has become more urbanized and less traditional, older people without children have been given special assistance by trade unions and have also been granted limited welfare benefits (Foner, 1984; P. Olson, 1987, 1988).

Not all societies have traditions of caring for the elderly. Among the Fulani of Africa, older men and women move to the edge of the family homestead. Since this is where people are buried, the elderly sleep over their own graves, for they are already viewed as socially dead. Among the Mardudjara, a hunting-and-gathering culture of Australia, disabled older members are given food;

In Scandinavian countries, "home helpers" paid by local governments visit the elderly and perform such chores as housekeeping, cleaning, shopping, and cooking.

however, when frequent travel becomes unavoidable, some are left behind to perish (Stenning, 1958; Tonkinson, 1978:83).

Some 25 societies are known to have practiced **senilicide**—the killing of the aged—because of extreme difficulties in providing basic necessities such as food and shelter. In the past, Eskimo culture encouraged elderly members to leave the settlement and die quietly in the cold. At the opposite extreme are the people of the Andaman Islands off Australia. In their culture, older members hold dominant positions in the social structure. Anthropologists have classified Andaman society as an example of **gerontocracy,** or rule by the elderly. This term is derived from the Greek word *geras,* meaning "old age" (Amoss, 1981; Foner, 1985; Guemple, 1969; Hoebel, 1954:76–79; Radcliffe-Brown, 1922:81).

It is understandable that all societies have some system of age stratification and associate certain social roles with distinct periods in one's life. Some of this age differentiation seems inevitable; it would make little sense to send young children off to war or to expect most older citizens to han-

(Drawing by Ed Fisher; © 1983 The New Yorker Magazine, Inc.)

"That was back then. I now espouse gerontocracy."

dle physically demanding tasks such as loading goods at shipyards. However, as is the case with stratification by gender (see Chapter 11), age stratification in the United States goes far beyond the physical constraints of human beings at different ages (Babbie, 1980:299–300).

"Being old," in particular, is a master status that commonly overshadows all others in the United States. Moreover, this status is generally viewed in negative terms. In one experiment, college students from three states were shown photographs of men who appeared to be 25-, 52-, and 73-years-old and were asked to evaluate these men for a job. Unbeknownst to the students, the photographs were all of the same person, who had used disguise and makeup to alter his appearance. The results of the study revealed significantly more negative evaluations for the (apparently) older job applicant than for the other applicants. The "older" person was viewed as less competent, less intelligent, less reliable, and less attractive (W. Levin, 1988).

We can draw upon the insights of labeling theory (see Chapter 7) in sociological analysis of the consequences of aging. Once people are labeled

"old" in the United States, this designation will have a major impact on how they are perceived and even on how they view themselves. As will be discussed more fully later in the chapter, negative stereotypes of the elderly contribute to their position as a minority group subject to discrimination.

Chapter 10 introduced five basic properties of a minority group. This model may be applied to older Americans in order to clarify the subordinate status of the elderly (M. Harris, 1958:4–11; J. Levin and Levin, 1980):

1 The elderly share physical characteristics that distinguish them from younger people. In addition, their cultural preferences and leisure-time activities are often at variance with those of the rest of society.
2 The elderly experience unequal treatment in employment and may face prejudice and discrimination.
3 Membership in this disadvantaged group is involuntary.
4 Older Americans have a strong sense of group solidarity, as is reflected in the growth of senior citizens' centers, housing projects, and advocacy organizations.
5 Although the elderly may be single, divorced, or widowed, many older couples share their minority status.

In analyzing the elderly as a minority, we find one crucial difference between older people and other subordinate groups such as Blacks and women. All of us who live long enough will eventually assume the ascribed status of being an older person.

AGING WORLDWIDE

In an important sense, the aging of the world's populations (see Figure 12-1) represents a major success story which has unfolded during the later stages of the twentieth century. Through the efforts of both national governments and international agencies, many societies have drastically reduced the incidence of diseases and their rates of death. Consequently, these nations—especially the industrialized countries of Europe and North

FIGURE 12-1 Persons 65 Years and Over as a Percentage of National Populations

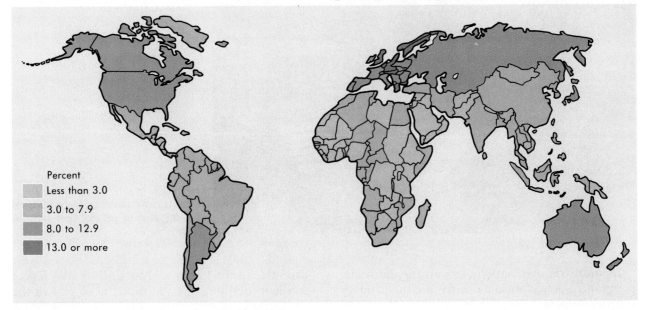

Percent
Less than 3.0
3.0 to 7.9
8.0 to 12.9
13.0 or more

SOURCE: Bureau of the Census, as reported by Kinsella, 1988:1.

America—have increasingly high proportions of older members. This does not mean, however, that such nations have aged gracefully. Belated recognition of the demographic and socioeconomic changes associated with aging has often resulted in suffering (Kinsella, 1988).

When compared with other industrialized nations, Japan has a relatively youthful population; only 10 percent of the nation's people are over 65 years of age. However, Japan's population is aging faster than that of any other country as a result of falling birth- and death rates. Japan has traditionally honored its older citizens and even has a national holiday, Respect for the Aged Day, on September 15. Yet the proportion of elderly people living with adult children has decreased substantially in recent decades. Changing attitudes in Japanese culture seem to include a decline in the belief that children are obligated to support their aging parents. Policymakers are clearly worried that the Japanese government will be expected to fill this vacuum and provide financial and emotional support for the nation's rapidly growing elderly population (L. Martin, 1989).

While the proportion of persons 65 years and over in the world's developing nations is increasing slowly, 23 of those nations have more than 2 million elderly persons, including Brazil, Poland, Vietnam, Rumania, and Turkey.

In most developing countries, aging has not yet emerged as a dominant social phenomenon. Rarely are special resources directed to meet the needs of people over 60, even though they are likely to be in poorer health than their counterparts in industrialized nations. Since many younger adults in developing nations immigrate to the cities, rural areas have higher proportions of older people. Formal social support mechanisms are less likely to exist in rural areas, yet at least family caregivers are present. In the cities, these caregivers enter and remain in the work force, which makes it more difficult for them to care for elderly family members. At the same time, urban housing in developing countries is often poorly suited to traditional extended-family arrangements (Kinsella, 1988; Neysmith and Edwardh, 1984).

Japan has traditionally honored its older citizens and even has a national holiday, Respect for the Aged Day, on September 15.

In industrialized nations, governmental social programs, such as Social Security, are the primary source of income for older citizens. However, given the economic difficulties of developing countries (refer back to Chapter 9), few of these nations are in a position to offer extensive financial support to the elderly. Regionally, South American countries provide the most substantial benefits, often assisting older people in both urban and rural areas. By contrast, such government support is nonexistent in many African states (Heisel, 1985; Kinsella, 1988).

Ironically, modernization in the developing world, while bringing with it many social and economic advances, has at the same time undercut the traditionally high status of the elderly. In many cultures, the earning power of younger adults now exceeds that of older family members. Consequently, the leadership role of the elderly has come into question, just as the notion of retirement has been introduced in the cultures of developing nations (Cowgill, 1986).

Studies in China show that care of the elderly has become a concern of government—especially in urban areas where traditional values have undergone the greatest erosion. The financing of such support programs will remain a long-term problem in China and other developing countries. Nevertheless, cross-cultural research indicates that as the family and agriculture play less of a role in defining the status of the elderly in the developing world, new institutional support mechanisms such as job retraining and adult education may fill this void (Cohn, 1982; P. Olson, 1988; Palmore and Manton, 1974).

EXPLAINING THE AGING PROCESS

Aging is one important aspect of socialization—the lifelong process through which an individual learns the cultural norms and values of a particular society. As we saw in Chapter 4, there are no clear-cut definitions for different periods of the aging cycle in American society. The term **age grades** refers to cultural categories that identify the stages of biological maturation. The ambiguity found in our culture about exactly when these age grades begin and end reflects the ambivalence with which we approach the aging process, especially at its end point. Thus, while *old age* has typically been regarded as beginning at 65, which corresponds to the retirement age for many American workers, this definition of old age is not universally accepted in our society.

The particular problems of the aged have become the focus for a specialized area of research and inquiry, known as *gerontology.* **Gerontology** is the scientific study of the sociological and psychological aspects of aging and the problems of the aged. It originally developed in the 1930s, as an increasing number of social scientists became aware of the plight of the elderly.

Gerontologists rely heavily on sociological principles and theories to explain the impact of aging on the individual and society. They also draw upon the disciplines of psychology, anthropology, physical education, counseling, and medicine in their study of the aging process. Two influential views of aging—disengagement theory and activity theory—can be best understood in terms of the sociological perspectives of functionalism and interactionism, respectively. The conflict perspective can also contribute to our sociological understanding of aging.

Functionalist Approach: Disengagement Theory

Elaine Cumming and William Henry (1961) introduced an explanation of the impact of aging known as *disengagement theory.* This theory, based on a study of elderly people in good health and relatively comfortable economic circumstances, contends that society and the aging individual mutually sever many of their relationships. In keeping with the functionalist perspective, disengagement theory emphasizes that a society's stability is assured when social roles are passed on from one generation to another.

According to this theory, the approach of death forces people to drop most of their social roles—including those of worker, volunteer, spouse, hobby enthusiast, and even reader. These functions are then undertaken by younger members of society. The aging person, it is held, withdraws into an increasing state of inactivity while preparing for death. At the same time, society withdraws from the elderly by segregating them residentially (retirement homes and communities), educationally (programs designed solely for senior citizens), and recreationally (senior citizens' social centers). Implicit in disengagement theory is the view that society should *help* older people to withdraw from their accustomed social roles.

Since it was first outlined 3 decades ago, disengagement theory has generated considerable controversy. Some gerontologists have objected to the implication that older people want to be ignored and "put away"—and even more to the idea that they should be encouraged to withdraw from meaningful social roles. Robert Atchley (1967, 1985:125–204) found that even people retired for more than 20 years had extremely positive attitudes toward the norm of getting intrinsic satisfaction from work. Critics of disengagement theory insist that society forces the elderly into an involuntary and painful withdrawal from the paid labor force and from meaningful social relationships.

Disengagement theory does not consider the possibility that older people may encounter *encouragement* from friends, relatives, or former work associates to remain involved and engaged. Colleagues at work may discourage early retirement, and communities may call on older citizens to continue using their skills as volunteers. Research studies show that older people are as likely to increase their involvement in activities and job-related tasks as they are to decrease involvement. Thus, a retired accountant may offer financial advice to service organizations; a retired teacher may assist refugees in learning English.

Studies of other age groups suggest that disengagement is not exclusively associated with any particular age grade. For example, sociologist Helen Rose Fuchs Ebaugh (1988) uses the concept of disengagement to help describe the larger process of role exit (refer back to Box 5-1 on page 136). In some instances, disengagement from a social role is gradual and minimal, while in others it may be rapid and complete. Currently, sociologists agree with the assumption implicit in disengagement theory that aging should not be viewed simply as a personal process, but rather as a social phenomenon interrelated with the social structure and institutions of any particular society. Nevertheless, most sociologists and gerontologists do not regard disengagement theory as a valid explanation of aging (Riley, 1987).

Interactionist Approach: Activity Theory

Often seen as an opposing approach to disengagement theory, *activity theory* argues that the elderly person who remains active will be best-adjusted. Proponents of this perspective acknowledge that a 70-year-old person may not have the ability or desire to perform various social roles that he or she had at age 40. Yet they contend that old people have essentially the same need for social interaction as middle-aged people.

Activity theorists point out that the activities of one's life are constantly changing. Therefore, the older person—like people at earlier stages of the life cycle—should have the option of replacing earlier activities with new pursuits. Rather than advocating withdrawal of the elderly from society and withdrawal of society from the elderly, activity theorists believe that the elderly should maintain the activities of middle age and "full membership in the social world" (Havighurst, 1961).

The improved health of older Americans—sometimes overlooked by social scientists—has strengthened the arguments of activity theorists. Illness and chronic disease are no longer quite the scourge of the elderly that they once were. The recent emphasis on fitness, the availability of better medical care, greater control of infectious diseases, and the reduction of fatal strokes and heart attacks have combined to mitigate the traumas of growing old. Accumulating medical research also points to the importance of remaining socially involved. Among those who decline in their mental capacities later in life, deterioration is most rapid in old people who withdraw from social relationships and activities.

Research findings have consistently supported the principal arguments of activity theory (see Box 12-1) and have failed to confirm key contentions of disengagement theory. Unfortunately, the substitutions recommended for older people by activity theorists have not been readily available in the United States. The labor force has not traditionally been predisposed to welcome retired workers to new careers, and the economy has not been structured to offer paying positions to older citizens. However, some companies have recently initiated programs to hire retirees for full-time or part-time work. For example, about 130 of the 600 reservationists for the Days Inn motel chain are over 60 years of age. As many firms find a shortage of qualified workers who can fill positions, they are turning to older people who still want to work (T. Lewin, 1990c).

Admittedly, many activities open to the elderly involve unpaid labor—even though younger adults may receive salaries for comparable work. Such unpaid workers include hospital volunteers (versus aides and orderlies), drivers for charities such as the Red Cross (versus chauffeurs), tutors (as opposed to teachers), and craftspeople for charity bazaars (as opposed to carpenters and dressmakers). Robert Butler (1980:9) of the National Institute of Aging recalls a 1929 cartoon that aptly described the activities open to the elderly. It showed an old man sitting outside an antique store. The caption read: "Some antiques have a market value; others haven't."

Disengagement theory suggests that older people find satisfaction in withdrawal from society. Functionally speaking, they conveniently recede into the background and allow the next generation to take over. Proponents of activity theory view such withdrawal as harmful for both the elderly and society and focus on the potential contributions of older Americans to the maintenance of society. In their opinion, aging citizens will feel satisfied only when they can be useful and productive in *society's* terms—primarily by working for wages (Dowd, 1980:6–7; Quadagno, 1980: 70–71).

The Conflict Response

Conflict theorists have criticized both disengagement theory and activity theory for failing to consider the impact of social structure on patterns of aging. Neither approach attempts to question why social interaction "must" change or decrease in old age. In addition, these perspectives often ignore the impact of social class in the lives of the elderly.

The privileged position of the upper class generally leads to better health and vigor and to less likelihood of facing dependency in old age. Affluence cannot forestall aging indefinitely, but it can soften the economic hardships faced in later years. By contrast, working-class jobs often carry greater hazards to health and a greater risk of dis-

BOX 12-1 • CURRENT RESEARCH

OLDER AMERICANS AND SOCIAL NETWORKS

According to sociologist Ethel Shanas (1982), the image of older Americans as isolated from families, friends, and neighbors is a myth. Many, in fact, are deeply involved in rewarding family networks. Sociologist Joan Aldous (1987) has explored the intergenerational relations of couples in their early and mid-sixties. As parents, these men and women are caught up in a web of associations through letters and phone calls as well as family visits and celebrations. They may provide gifts, chauffeur services, and care for their grandchildren; at the same time, their adult children may provide these couples with household help and care during illnesses. Consequently, there appears to be an exchange relationship between elderly couples and their offspring.

What of those older citizens—accounting for about 30 percent of the nation's elderly population—who live alone? A 1984 survey of 42,000 households by the National Center for Health Statistics found that 88 percent of elderly Americans living alone had gotten together with either friends or neighbors during the 2 weeks before the interview. Of those respondents who had children, nearly one-fourth saw a child every day, and one-third spoke with a child over the telephone every day. In line with the arguments of activity theorists, the study concludes that the "preponderance of the evidence is that there is some relationship between social contact and support and mortality." Other studies have suggested that older people who frequently see their friends and relatives are likely to live longer than those who are more isolated (*New York Times*, 1986a:32).

Social networks also play an important role in providing life satisfaction for the elderly. Sociologist Christine Adamski-Mietus (1983) found that participation in ethnic, cultural, and community activities contributed to the life satisfaction of elderly Polish Americans in New Jersey. There was evidence that life satisfaction for these older people increased when they intensified their involvement in "Polonia," the Polish American community. By contrast, life satisfaction declined when circumstances limited people's ability to maintain interaction with others in Polonia. Those found to be most disengaged by Adamski-Mietus were also found to be lowest in terms of life satisfaction.

---

ability; aging will be particularly difficult for those who suffer job-related injuries or illnesses. Working-class people also depend more heavily on Social Security benefits and private pension programs. During inflationary times, their relatively fixed incomes from these sources hardly keep pace with the escalating costs of food, housing, utilities, and other necessities (Atchley, 1985).

Conflict theorists have noted that the transition from agricultural economies to industrialization and capitalism has not always been beneficial for the elderly. As a society's production methods change, the traditionally valued role of older people within the economy tends to erode. Although

pension plans, retirement packages, and insurance benefits may be developed to assist older people, those whose wealth allows them access to investment funds can generate the greatest income for their later years (Dowd, 1980:75; Hendricks, 1982; L. Olson, 1982).

The conflict approach views the treatment of older people in the United States as reflective of the many divisions in our society. From a conflict perspective, the low status of older people is reflected in prejudice and discrimination against them, age segregation, and unfair job practices—none of which are directly addressed by either disengagement or activity theory. All three of these topics will be discussed later in the chapter.

AGE STRATIFICATION IN THE UNITED STATES

The "Graying of America"

As is evident in Figure 12-2 below, an increasing proportion of the population of the United States is composed of older citizens. Men and women aged 65 years and over constituted only 4 percent of the nation's population in the year 1900, but by 1990 this figure had reached 12.6 percent. It is currently projected that by the year 2030, almost 22 percent of Americans will be 65 and older. Moreover, while the proportion of elderly people continues to rise, the "old old" segment of the population (that is, people 85 years old and over) is growing at an ever faster rate. By 2030, the proportion of the population 85 and over will reach 2.7 percent, compared with only 0.2 percent in 1930 (Gelman, 1985:62; Spencer, 1989:8).

It should be noted that the "graying of America" is not a uniform trend. As Figure 12-3 shows, the highest proportion of older Americans is found in Florida, Iowa, Pennsylvania, and states in the midwestern farm belt. In recent years, the growth of the elderly population has been most evident in the west and the southeast owing to in-migration of retirees; this pattern is likely to continue throughout the balance of the twentieth century.

While the United States is noticeably graying, the nation's older citizens are in a sense getting younger, owing to improved health and nutrition. As psychologist Sylvia Mertz told a symposium on aging in 1986, the activities of a contemporary 70-year-old "are equivalent to those of a 50-year-old a decade or two ago" (Horn and Meer, 1987:76). From the perspective of activity theory, this is obviously a welcome change which should be encouraged.

There is significant variation in wealth and poverty among the nation's older people. A key factor in the financial state of the elderly is Social Security. While modest when compared with other nations' pension programs, Social Security nevertheless provides 38 percent of all income received by older people. Currently, about one-eighth of the nation's elderly population is below the poverty line; without Social Security, that figure would rise to half (J. Hess, 1990a:453). At the extremes of poverty are those groups who were more likely to be poor at earlier points in the life cycle: female-headed households and racial and ethnic minorities.

Women account for 60 percent of Americans 65 years old and over. Older women experience a double burden: they are female in a society which favors males and they are elderly in a society which values youth. The social inequities that women experience throughout their lifetimes (see Chapter 11)—whether in terms of wealth, status, or power—only intensify as they age. As a result, in 1987 some 25 percent of elderly women living alone were below the poverty line (Bureau of the Census, 1990a:13, 460; see also Duncan and Smith, 1989; J. Levy, 1988).

FIGURE 12-2 Actual and Projected Growth of the Elderly Population

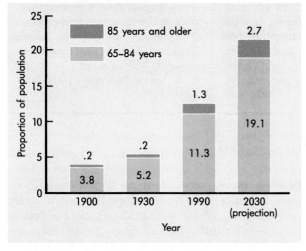

NOTE: 1990 data estimated by the Bureau of the Census, based on 1988 data.
SOURCE: Bureau of the Census data in Gelman, 1985:62 and in Spencer, 1989:8.

An increasing proportion of the population of the United States is aged 65 and over. It is projected that by the year 2030, this group will constitute 21.8 percent of the nation's population. Moreover, projections point to a dramatic rise in the proportion of the "old old" (persons aged 85 and over).

FIGURE 12-3   Persons 65 Years and Over as a Percentage of the Total Population, 1989

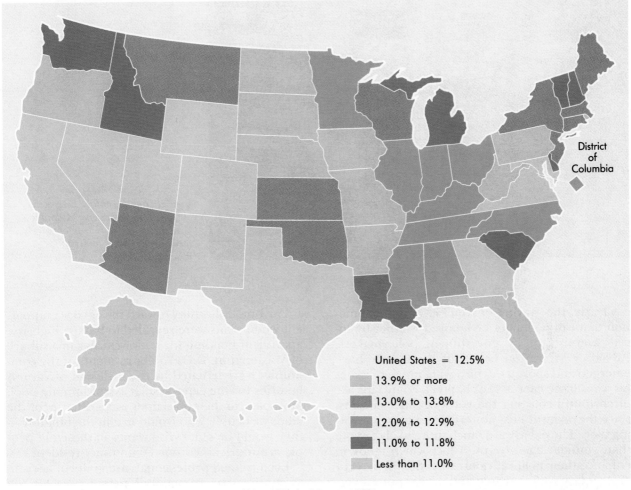

United States = 12.5%

- 13.9% or more
- 13.0% to 13.8%
- 12.0% to 12.9%
- 11.0% to 11.8%
- Less than 11.0%

SOURCE: Bureau of the Census data in American Association of Retired Persons, 1991.

The highest proportion of elderly Americans live in Florida, Iowa, and Pennsylvania.

Viewed from a conflict perspective, it is not surprising that older women experience a double burden; the same is true of elderly members of racial and ethnic minorities. For example, in 1987 the proportion of older Hispanics with incomes below the poverty line (27 percent) was almost three times as large as the proportion of older Whites (10 percent) in this condition. The median household income of older Blacks was about $12,000; for older Hispanics, it was $15,300; for older Whites, it was $21,000. With such data in mind, Lou Glasse, president of the Older Women's League, noted that life is especially difficult for older women from minority groups: "In virtually every aspect of their lives, from income to housing, minority women will be forced to struggle harder to achieve a smaller piece of the pie" (Bureau of the Census, 1990a:446, 460; L. Williams, 1986:A21).

Viewed from a conflict perspective, older women experience a double burden; the same is true of elderly members of racial and ethnic minorities.

Clearly, the graying of America is a phenomenon that can no longer be ignored—either by social scientists or by government policymakers. Advocacy groups on behalf of the elderly have emerged and spoken out on a wide range of issues (as we will see later in the chapter). Politicians are often found courting the votes of older citizens, since they constitute a powerful and growing voting bloc. The elderly are much more likely to vote than younger age groups, a fact which tends to enhance their political clout. In 1988, 69 percent of Americans 65 years old and over reported voting, compared with 57 percent of the total population and only 33 percent of people ages 18 to 20 (Bureau of the Census, 1990a:262).

Ageism

Physician Robert Butler (1975, 1989), the founding director of the National Institute on Aging, coined the term ***ageism*** to refer to prejudice and discrimination against the elderly. Ageism reflects a deep uneasiness among young and middle-aged people about growing old. For many, old age symbolizes disease, disability, and death; seeing the elderly serves as a reminder that *they* may become old and infirm.

For Butler, hostility toward the aged was apparent when plans were revealed to build a high-rise apartment building for senior citizens in a suburb of Washington, D.C. Young residents of the community were irritated by the inclusion of various luxuries for the elderly, such as a swimming pool. Most basic to their objections was a distaste for the kinds of people who would live in the building—they would be old. "Who wants all those old people around?" asked one community resident.

Even trained professionals are guilty of ageism, as in the case of medical personnel who too quickly diagnose patients as senile or view their ailments as imaginary or "nothing but old age." The consequences of ageism among physicians and other health care professionals can be especially serious. For example, a 1987 study revealed that older women with breast cancer frequently receive less medical treatment than they should, because of their age. "The lives of these patients may be needlessly shortened," noted Dr. Sheldon Greenfield. "Our findings indicate that age itself affects the way physicians treat patients with breast cancer and that they provide less than optimal care for older patients, even those who are in apparent excellent health" (Greenfield et al., 1987; *New York Times*, 1987b:A17).

Ageism is but one aspect of age stratification in the United States. Age stratification is also evident in negative stereotypes of the elderly, segregation of older people into retirement communities and special housing projects, competition among different generations in the labor force, and abuse of the elderly within family relationships.

Stereotypes of the Elderly

There is considerable adherence to negative stereotypes of the elderly in the United States. Studies of college undergraduates and graduates report widespread perceptions of older citizens as stubborn, touchy, quarrelsome, bossy, and meddlesome. Even less judgmental feelings about the elderly can reflect a belief in the superiority of the young. A typical comment is: "When an older person is walking very slowly right in front of me, I feel pity" (B. Hess and Markson, 1980:65).

Not surprisingly, the elderly resent such negative and patronizing stereotypes. As Irene Paull, the author of *Everybody's Studying Us,* a biting commentary on mistreatment of older people, pointed out: "Not only is our age not respected. In some mysterious way it is supposed to undermine our faculties and reduce us to the infantile." Yet, in contrast to such stereotypes, studies show that older workers are as productive as younger workers, less accident-prone, and more reliable (Barmash, 1982; Paull and Bülbül, 1976:7).

Content analysis of television programming in the mid-1980s suggests that there has been a substantial increase in representation of elderly characters. Ironically, however, the negative stereotype of older Americans evident in the 1970s was replaced with unrealistic favorable images. For example, 21 percent of older women characters on prime-time shows were owners of their own businesses—three-fourths of which were large corporations—while in reality less than 2 percent of American women of any age are corporate executives. Similarly, one-fourth of all female characters over 50 were millionaires, whereas only 0.2 percent of real-life women over 50 earn as much as $75,000 annually (Kallan, 1986).

Clearly, television has yet to present accurate portrayals of the lives of older Americans. These findings are important, since, as we noted in Chapter 4, television is one of the critical agents of socialization in American society. If television presents a misleading stereotype of the elderly as millionaires, it will undercut awareness of the problems that many older people face and may reduce support for public policies designed to combat ageism and assist the needy elderly.

(Jeffrey Muir Hamilton/Stock, Boston)

In contrast to the stereotype of elderly Americans as frail and inactive, increasing numbers of older persons engage in vigorous physical activity.

Age Segregation

Age segregation is an important feature of the landscape of the United States. This form of segregation, every bit as evident as racial segregation, occurs when people at similar points in the life cycle cluster together. As we have seen, some Americans, like residents of the Washington suburb discussed earlier, prefer that the elderly and their problems be kept away from them—isolated in retirement communities and special housing projects. Neighborhoods have also opposed the conversion of single-family homes into apartments for students or fraternity and sorority houses.

For the older American, age segregation is most obvious in nursing homes. Currently, 5 percent of people over 65 years old live in nursing homes. Entering a nursing home means becoming part of a total institution (see Chapter 4). Activities are determined by the institution and are rarely tailored to the individual preferences of residents. Most of one's personal possessions must be left behind, since available space is limited. Of those who enter such institutions, the majority enter in their late seventies or early eighties, when their health is failing or they lack financial resources needed to live on their own (T. Lewin, 1990a:A22).

Elderly people who are relatively healthy and financially secure have a greater range of housing options. Studies have not firmly established how such people feel about living in residential communities for the retired, condominiums, hotels catering to the aged, and "seniors'" housing projects. Apparently, older people living in planned communities score higher on life satisfaction scales than retirees in age-integrated communities do. However, these findings must be assessed with caution. Residents of retirement communities also tend to have higher incomes than most elderly people and describe themselves as in better health. Older people who are concentrated (or perhaps one might say "trapped") in inner-city neighborhoods tend to be less happy than those living in more affluent and heterogeneous areas (D. Harris and Cole, 1980:168–172; La Gory et al., 1980, 1981, 1985).

At the beginning of the chapter, we discussed

(Nancy Schiff/Black Star)

Shown is the late Representative Claude Pepper of Florida, the chief congressional advocate for the elderly during the 1970s and 1980s. Pepper died in 1989 at the age of 88. He had built a reputation as "Mr. Social Security" through his strong defense of the Social Security and Medicare programs. One of Pepper's last legislative achievements was the passage of a 1986 federal law banning mandatory retirement based on age.

the home helper services which have become commonly available to older people in Sweden, Denmark, and Finland. Efforts are under way in certain parts of the United States to develop innovative programs that will assist elderly men and women who wish to continue living in their homes. Wisconsin's model Community Options Program provides aid to 7700 people who need long-term care, half of them elderly and half younger disabled people. The program helps to provide virtually any service needed to keep a person at home, such as paying a neighbor to cook certain meals or finding a nurse to make home-care visits. These services are offered at no cost to the poor and on a sliding scale to others. Lorraine Barniskis, an official in the state's Division of Community Services, comments: "Our underlying philosophy is that anyone can be served at home." By contrast, Oregon has created a network of foster homes for the elderly whereby couples take in an unrelated older person. The state is encouraging developers to construct "assisted living" apartments at which older residents can live in private quarters while receiving group meals in a dining room, housekeeping services, and nursing care (T. Lewin, 1990a, 1990b:A22; see also S. Hughes, 1988; Jansen, 1987).

Age segregation has at least one distinct advantage for the elderly; it helps them to organize politically and to wield influence within government circles. It is undoubtedly no coincidence that the chief congressional advocate for older citizens in recent decades—the late U.S. representative Claude Pepper of Miami—represented the retirement area of southern Florida. Nevertheless, such patterns of age segregation are hardly likely to promote mutual understanding among Americans of differing age groups.

Competition in the Labor Force

In the United States in the year 1900, fully two-thirds of men aged 65 and over were found in the paid labor force, working either full time or part time. However, by 1988, this was true of less than one out of six (Bureau of the Census, 1990a: 378). Even so, many younger adults continue to view older workers as "job stealers," a biased judgment similar to that directed against illegal immigrants (see Chapter 10). This belief not only intensifies age conflict but also leads to age discrimination.

Although age discrimination (defined as discrimination against people 40 years old and over) has been illegal in the United States since 1968, it still persists within our society. In the words of Claude Pepper:

Age discrimination has oozed into every pore of the workplace. It stalks mature workers and severs them from their livelihoods, often at the peak of their careers. . . . Those who lose their jobs because of age discrimination often never recover from the shock of the experience (Weaver, 1982:A12).

The young, too, feel that they are victimized within the job market because of their age. For example, in the 1980s Congress debated a law setting a lower minimum wage for teenagers in order to encourage increased employment of young people. Canada, the Netherlands, New Zealand, and Sweden all have instituted such sub–minimum wage programs for younger workers. Economists critical of the congressional proposal insisted that it would lead to exploitation of teenagers at low wages; older employees feared that they would lose their jobs to those who could be hired at this lower minimum wage rate.

The Social Security system has also provoked age conflict within the paid labor force of the United States. Younger Americans are increasingly unhappy about paying Social Security taxes, especially since they worry that they themselves will never receive benefits from the fiscally insecure program. Reflecting such concerns, Americans for Generational Equity (AGE) was established in 1984 to represent the interests of "younger and future generations of Americans," which presumably might diverge from the interests of the elderly. Backed by contributions from banks, insurance companies, and corporations offering health care services—all of which are private-sector competitors of Social Security and Medicare—AGE argues that the poor and the young suffer because society misappropriates too much funding for older people (Quadagno, 1989a).

Abuse of the Elderly

Abuse and neglect of elderly Americans within the family have received increasing public attention in recent years. This change reflects both the larger numbers of older people and the establishment of more vocal groups to represent their concerns. It is estimated that between 4 and 10 percent of the elderly have suffered from physical abuse, verbal abuse, or neglect. If these findings are generalized across the nation, it would mean that by 1995, there would be about 1.3 to 3.4 million abused elderly people in the United States (Bureau of the Census, 1990a:16; Gelles and Cornell, 1990:102).

In the past, observers have typically viewed "elder abuse" as the result of stress caused by the demands and dependency of an older person. This conclusion, which found its way into scholarly writing, in effect blames the victim for the abusive behavior of another (refer back to Box 8-2 on page 244). In actuality, as research shows, the typical situation involves abuse of an older person who is *supporting* an abusive dependent child or, to a lesser extent, a physically or mentally disabled spouse. It is the abuser, not the abused person, who is in a dependent position.

Sociologist Karl Pillemer (1985:154) describes the case of an elderly woman whose daughter moved in with her following the daughter's divorce. The daughter would not seek employment or do any housework. Instead, she remained at home most of the time, struck her mother, and threw a pan of scalding water on her. When confronted with such behavior, most abused older people do not move out, because they feel trapped by their sense of family obligation.

In general, as is true of wife beating and child abuse, the number of reported cases of abuse of the elderly is undoubtedly well below actual incidence. As a result of growing public concern, legislation in many states has redefined the concept of "domestic violence" to include abuse of the elderly as well as child abuse and violence between spouses. A more general discussion of violence within the family will be presented in Chapter 13.

Since 1980, bills have been introduced in Congress to establish a national center concerned with abuse of adults, which would assist states in preventing, identifying, and treating instances of abusive behavior. Despite the absence of such a federal law, by 1990 every state but New Jersey had adopted mandatory-reporting laws covering abuse of adults or had passed some type of adult protective-service law. However, state policies vary widely in terms of who should report such abuse, who should respond to such reports, and how much funding is available for support ser-

The Gray Panthers organization, founded in 1971, has about 40,000 dues-paying members dedicated to the fight against ageism.

vices for victims (National Aging Resource Center on Elder Abuse, 1990).

The Elderly: Emergence of a Collective Consciousness

During the 1960s, students at colleges and universities across the country became concerned about "student power" and demanded a role in the governance of educational institutions. In the following decade, the 1970s, many older Americans became aware that they were being treated as second-class citizens. Just as the National Organization for Women (NOW) had been established to bring about equal rights for women, the Gray Panthers organization was founded in 1971 to

BOX 12-2 • SPEAKING OUT

AN OLDER PERSON SPEAKS TO YOUNGER GENERATIONS

Irene Paull, a fiction writer and long-time activist in civil rights, antiwar, and gray power causes, offered the following message to younger Americans (Paull and Bülbül: 1976:79):

We are not a special interest group. We are simply your mothers, fathers, and grandparents. We are not asking you for a handout. We ran the world until you came along. Operated the factories. Tilled the soil. Bore the children. Taught them. Tended the sick. Built freeways and railroads, dug subways. We are simply the generation or two that preceded you. When we are gone you will move up to the vanguard and another generation will wonder what to do with you short of pushing you off a cliff.

Irene Paull.

We are asking you, our children and grandchildren, for nothing that is not due us. At the cost of great sacrifice, and many casualties,

(© 1976 by Bülbül and Irene Paull)

we built the labor unions and the farm unions; won the eight-hour day; eliminated child labor; won Social Security and the concept that health care is a human right, not an act of someone's charity.

Millions of us fought all our lives for a peaceful world. We did not achieve it. Do not indict us for our failure. We leave it to you to wage that struggle not in millions but in tens of millions.

When we ask for a chance to live our old age in comfort, creativity, and usefulness, we ask it not for ourselves only, but for you. We are not a special interest group. We are your parents and grandparents. We are your roots. You are our continuity. What we gain is your inheritance.

---

work for the rights of the elderly. Moreover, as NOW has enlisted the aid of male allies, the Gray Panthers have actively sought and received aid from younger Americans.

In order to combat prejudice and discrimination against older people, the Gray Panthers issue publications and monitor industries particularly important to the elderly, such as health care and housing. For example, the condition of nursing homes in the United States prompted Gray Panther leader Maggie Kuhn to declare: "We throw away people, and before we throw them away, we warehouse them in institutions. We make them vegetables. . . ." Currently, the group has about 40,000 dues-paying members dedicated to the fight against ageism (G. Collins, 1987:C8).

The growing collective consciousness among older Americans also contributed to the establish-

ment of the Older Women's League (OWL) in 1980. OWL focuses on access to health insurance, Social Security benefits, and pension reform. OWL leaders and the group's 20,000 members hope that the organization will serve as a critical link between the feminist movement and activists for "gray power" (Sorrel and Sojourner, 1982: 6–7).

Still another manifestation of the new awareness of older Americans is the formation of organizations for elderly homosexuals. One such group, New York City's Senior Action in a Gay Environment (SAGE) has 3500 members. Like more traditional senior citizens' groups, SAGE sponsors workshops, classes, dances, and food deliveries to the homebound. At the same time, SAGE's activities provide a supportive gay environment where older lesbians and gay men can share their experiences. The vitality of such organizations helps to dispel the stereotype of aging homosexuals as inevitably isolated, lonely, and bitter (Alexander, 1988).

The largest organization representing the nation's elderly is the American Association of Retired Persons (AARP). AARP was founded in 1958 by a retired school principal who was having difficulty getting insurance because of age prejudice. Many of AARP's services involve discounts and insurance for its 31 million members, but the organization also functions as a powerful lobbying group which works for legislation that will benefit the elderly. For example, AARP has backed passage of a uniform mandatory-reporting law for cases of abuse of the elderly, which would be accompanied by enough federal funds to guarantee enforcement and support services.

The potential power of AARP is enormous: it is the second-largest voluntary association in the United States (behind only the Roman Catholic church) and represents one out of every four registered voters in the United States. While criticized for its lack of minority membership (the group is 97 percent White), AARP has endorsed voter registration campaigns, nursing home reforms, and pension reforms (Hornblower, 1988; Ornstein and Schmitt, 1990).

There are several reasons why the influence of older citizens is expected to grow in coming decades. As noted earlier, their numbers are increasing substantially in the United States, and the elderly are more likely to go to the polls than other age groups are. In addition, through the efforts of many senior citizens' groups, including those described above, the elderly have become much more forceful in demanding their rights (see Box 12-2).

SOCIAL POLICY AND STRATIFICATION BY AGE

CATASTROPHIC HEALTH CARE

- Why is chronic illness such a financial catastrophe for many Americans?
- In what ways has the battle over catastrophic health care intensified generational conflict?
- How can health care issues be viewed through the conflict perspective?

Despite general improvements in the quality of life for many older people in the United States, millions still face problems of poor housing, social isolation, physical disabilities, and limited incomes. Existing social welfare legislation for the elderly—including Social Security (begun in 1935) and Medicare (begun in 1965)—brought the federal government new responsibilities in assisting older people. Although these measures represented major changes in the social policy of the United States, they were nevertheless quite conservative because they tied benefits to labor force participation and to the understanding that the individual still bore financial responsibility for numerous necessities (Quadagno, 1984).

In the last 20 years, policymakers have faced still another challenge: the often desperate situation of individuals and families who must bear the cost of long-term care for someone with a chronic condition. Although this problem affects certain younger people, it is especially critical for the elderly. For example, those 65 years old and over have a 44 percent chance of entering a nursing home at some point. Although only 13 percent can expect to spend a year or more in a nursing home, such a prolonged stay can be a financial disaster, since nursing home care costs an average of $30,000 per year (Eckholm, 1990).

Many elderly people are in no position to cope with the costs of long-term care. As of 1988, the average older person was spending $2394 (or 18.1 percent of his or her income) for out-of-pocket health care costs. Given these expenditures, only older people with substantial savings have sufficient protection against the financial strain of long-term illness. The situation is especially difficult because Medicare, which supports elderly and disabled people on Social Security, will cover acute but not chronic illnesses (J. Hess, 1990b:698).

For the elderly, chronic illness, rather than infectious

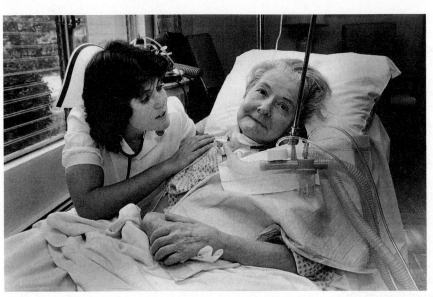

Many elderly people are in no position to cope with the costs of long-term care for a catastrophic illness.

disease, is now the prevalent form of illness. Most chronic-illness management in the United States takes place at home, but state and local governments typically offer only limited financial support and social services for families who choose to care for a chronically ill person at home. By contrast, other countries—among them, Canada, Great Britain, and the Scandinavian nations—offer much more extensive coverage for long-term care. The Netherlands, for example, provides long-term nursing home care for the entire population, with costs paid by the government (Strauss, 1987; Tolchin, 1990b).

In response to the growing crisis over the financial burden of long-term care, the Catastrophic Medicare Act of 1988 was approved. This law was intended to shield older Americans from the staggering costs of chronic illness; it significantly expanded the Medicare program by limiting the amount of funds that Medicare's 33 million beneficiaries must pay for hospitalization and physicians' services. However, in a dramatic and controversial breakthrough, many older people were required to pay additional taxes to pay for this program. Those with a taxable income under $5000 would pay nothing, but those earning over $45,000 would pay $908 annually (Torres-Gil, 1990).

The American Association of Retired Persons (AARP) initially supported the 1988 law. However, as the costs of the measure became clear, members of Congress began to face angry protests from the elderly. Special-interest groups such as the National Committee to Preserve Social Security and Medicare attacked the funding procedures for this program as a form of age discrimination. Why, they asked, should the elderly be expected to carry the costs of this badly needed reform? After all, older people pay school taxes even though few have children in public schools (A. Miller, 1989b; Ornstein and Schmitt, 1990).

At times, the debate over the impact of the Catastrophic Medicare Act became bitter; it certainly inflamed generational conflict. Newspapers and national news magazines chastized the elderly as "greedy geezers" and covered the controversy in an ageist manner, suggesting that older people have poor memories and therefore cannot remember how much better their lives have become. One writer associated with Americans for Generational Equality (AGE) published an "op-ed" column in the *New York Times* entitled "Elderly, Affluent—and Selfish" (M. Greene, 1989; J. Hess, 1990b:702).

As in past decades when Social Security and Medicare were debated and enacted into law, public debate on the issue of catastrophic illness has focused on money: should older Americans pay the cost of governmental coverage for long-term illness? From a conflict perspective, such debate obscures larger questions about health care. The United States remains the only western industrial democracy that does not view health care as a basic right. Under American capitalism, illness may be exploited for profit, and there is neither a national health care system nor national health insurance. Conflict theorists emphasize the need for structural reform of health care so that services can be delivered more equitably among different social classes, age groups, and regions of the country (L. Olson, 1982:149).

After continuing protest by older people, an unusual reversal took place: in mid-1989, the Catastrophic Medicare Act of 1988 was repealed by an overwhelming margin. After the repeal, legislators warned that it could be at least another decade before Congress again considers the difficult issues of long-term care and nursing home coverage. Although public opinion polls continue to show overwhelming support for government protection against the financial nightmare of chronic illness, many legislators doubt that the American public will ever endorse the taxes needed to support such protective legislation (Clift, 1989; Tolchin, 1990a:A20).

In the view of some experts, the least costly way to improve the health of the nation's elderly would be to invest a greater portion of funding in the health of tomorrow's older citizens. In the United States, governmental health care assistance is almost totally directed to the old, the disabled, and the poor. By contrast, other countries—among them, Great Britain, France, and Japan—have national health programs which devote about equal per capita expenditures to children and to the elderly. It is argued that a redistribution of spending would ultimately produce a measurable increase in the health of all people in the United States. Of course, such a long-range effort, even if successful, would not address the immediate problems of those who must pay for catastrophic health care (Makin, 1990:54).

The United States Bipartisan Commission on Comprehensive Health Care—called the "Pepper Commission" to honor Claude Pepper—recommended in 1990 that the nation adopt a $43-billion-a-year plan for long-term care, with the majority of funding used to support home health care. In order to defuse generational conflict, the commission suggested that this program support long-term care for severely disabled and chronically ill people of all ages. About 40 percent of Americans with severe disabilities are under the age of 65 (Tolchin, 1990a:A20).

Will such a plan ever become law? "It will happen by the end of the decade," insists economist Uwe Reinhardt, an expert on health care policy. "But first we will really have some dark days. Our system now is like a sick man who knows he is sick but doesn't want to go to the doctor because he fears what he might find out. We all know that the system is failing. But almost nobody wants to sit down and figure out what we need to make it work" (Spector, 1990:6).

SUMMARY

Age, like gender and race, is an ascribed status that forms the basis for social differentiation. This chapter examines theories regarding the aging process, age stratification in the United States, and the growing political activism of the nation's elderly population.

1 Like other forms of stratification, age stratification varies from culture to culture.

2 "Being old" is a master status that seems to overshadow all others in the United States.

3 The aging of the world's populations represents a major success story which has unfolded during the later stages of the twentieth century.

4 The particular problems of the aged have become the focus for a specialized area of research and inquiry known as *gerontology*.

5 *Disengagement theory* implicitly suggests that society should help older people to withdraw from their accustomed social roles, whereas *activity theory* argues that the elderly person who remains active will be best-adjusted.

6 An increasing proportion of the American population is composed of elderly citizens.

7 There is considerable adherence to negative stereotypes about the aged in the United States.

8 The elderly are especially likely to be victims of age segregation; many live in "seniors'" public housing projects or residential communities for the retired.

9 As is true of wife beating and child abuse, the number of reported cases of abuse of the elderly is undoubtedly well below actual incidence.

10 The American Association of Retired Persons (AARP) works as a powerful lobbying group backing legislation that will benefit senior citizens.

11 The Catastrophic Medicare Act of 1988, intended to shield older Americans from the staggering costs of chronic illness, was repealed in mid-1989 after strong protests from elderly people regarding additional taxes that they would pay.

KEY TERMS

Activity theory An interactionist theory of aging which argues that elderly people who remain active will be best-adjusted. (page 361)

Age grades Cultural categories that identify the stages of biological maturation. (360)

Ageism A term coined by Robert N. Butler to refer to prejudice and discrimination against the elderly. (366)

Disengagement theory A functionalist theory of aging introduced by Cumming and Henry which contends that society and the aging individual mutually sever many of their relationships. (361)

Gerontocracy Rule by the elderly. (357)

Gerontology The scientific study of the sociological and psychological aspects of aging and the problems of the aged. (360)

Senilicide The killing of the aged. (357)

ADDITIONAL READINGS

Atchley, Robert C. *The Social Forces in Later Life: An Introduction to Social Gerontology* (4th ed.). Belmont, Calif.: Wadsworth, 1985. This volume, intended as a textbook for courses on the social aspects of gerontology, provides a basic understanding of aging.

Butler, Robert N. *Why Survive? Being Old in America.* New York: Harper and Row, 1975. The now-classic, Pulitzer prize–winning study that introduced the term *ageism* to our understanding of older people.

Cowgill, Donald O. *Aging around the World.* Belmont, Calif.: Wadsworth, 1986. Known for his theory about the impact of modernization on the status of the elderly, Cowgill examines cultural variation in the treatment of the elderly.

Dychtwald, Ken, with Joe Flower. *Age Wave: The Challenges and Opportunities of an Aging America.* Los Angeles: Tarcher, 1989. Psychologist Dychtwald presents a rapid-paced, journalistic account of aging in the United States. He emphasizes the benefits of an aging nation both for the individual and for the larger society.

Foner, Nancy. *Ages in Conflict.* New York: Columbia University Press, 1984. A systematic review of anthropological studies of age stratification.

Marshall, Victor W. (ed.). *Later Life: The Social Psychology of Aging.* Beverly Hills, Calif.: Sage, 1986. This reader emphasizes the interactionist approach to aging; it includes such topics as construction of self and networking.

Olson, Laura Katz. *The Political Economy of Aging: The State, Private Power, and Social Welfare.* New York: Columbia University Press, 1982. Drawing on the conflict perspective, Olson argues that capitalistic societies are structured to deprive those outside the privileged core (such as older people) of wealth and power.

Palmer, John L., Timothy Smeeding, and Barbara Boyle Torrey (eds.). *The Vulnerable.* Washington, D.C.: Urban Institute, 1988. This study focuses on the changes in well-being among the nation's two largest dependent groups—children and the elderly—and the potential implications for public policies.

Pillemer, Karl A., and Rosalie S. Wolf (eds.). *Elder Abuse: Conflict in the Family.* Dover, Mass.: Auburn House, 1987. The 15 selections in this book explore family conflict as it affects the elderly. Both retirement research and treatment models are presented.

Quadagno, Jill S. (ed.). *Aging, the Individual, and Society: Readings in Social Gerontology.* New York: St. Martin's, 1980. An anthology with selections on theories of aging, stereotyping of the elderly, retirement, and health care.

Soldo, Beth J., and Emily M. Agree. *America's Elderly.* Washington, D.C.: Population Reference Bureau, 1988. This concise (53-page) monograph presents an overview of older Americans with an emphasis on population and other statistical data.

Vail, Elaine. *A Personal Guide to Living with Loss.* New York: Wiley, 1982. A sensitively written book dealing with death. Vail draws on the relevant social scientific and legal materials.

Journals

Among the journals that focus on issues of aging and age stratification are *Aging and Society* (founded in 1981), *The Gerontologist* (1961), *Journal of Gerontology* (1946), and *Youth and Society* (1968). Issues devoted to age and aging appeared in *The Annals* (May 1989), *Daedalus* (Winter 1985), and *Sociological Quarterly* (No. 4, 1988).

PART FOUR

SOCIAL INSTITUTIONS

PART FOUR will consider sociological analysis of major institutions, including the family, religion, government, the economy, education, and health care. As noted earlier in the text, *social institutions* are organized patterns of beliefs and behavior centered on basic social needs.

Chapter 13 focuses on the functions of the family and its importance as a cultural universal. Chapter 14 discusses the dimensions, functions, and organization of religion. Chapter 15 looks at government and the economy, with particular emphasis on types of governments and economic systems. Chapter 16 considers the functions of education, schools as social organizations, and recent trends in education. Chapter 17 analyzes sociological perspectives on health and illness, the health care system of the United States, and mental illness.

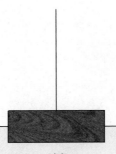

13

THE FAMILY

LOOKING AHEAD

- Are all families necessarily composed of a husband, a wife, and their children?
- What functions does the family perform for society?
- Do married women who work outside the home have greater marital power than full-time homemakers?
- What factors influence our selection of a mate?
- Should gay and unmarried heterosexual couples have the same legal protections and benefits as married couples?
- Why does the United States have such a high rate of teenage pregnancy?
- What can be done to prevent violence between family members?
- What arguments can be offered on behalf of and against family leave legislation?

Consider this scenario—"The original plot goes like this: first comes love. Then comes marriage. Then comes Mary with a baby carriage. But now there's a sequel: John and Mary break up. John moves in with Sally and her two boys. Mary takes the baby Paul. A year later Mary meets Jack, who is divorced with three children. They get married. Paul, barely 2 years old, now has a mother, a father, a stepmother, a stepfather, and five stepbrothers and stepsisters—as well as four sets of grandparents (biological and step) and countless aunts and uncles. And guess what? Mary's pregnant again" (Kantrowitz and Wingert, 1990:24).

In the view of demographers, as many as a third of all children born in the United States in the 1980s may live with a stepparent before they reach the age of 18. According to the Bureau of the Census (1990a), there were more than 7 million American children living in stepfamilies by 1990. These stepfamilies (also known as *blended families* or *reconstituted families*) are one by-product of the high rates of divorce and remarriage in the United States. "Most people have a personal connection with a stepfamily," notes sociologist Frank Furstenberg. "If it's not their parents, it's their child or their grandparents or their husband's parents" (Kantrowitz and Wingert, 1990:24; Spanier and Furstenberg, 1987: 424).

Among other cultures of the world, there are family patterns quite different from those of American stepfamilies. In the Toda culture of southern India, a woman may be simultaneously married to several men. Fatherhood is not always connected with actual biological facts; any husband may establish paternity by presenting a pregnant woman with a toy bow and arrow. The Balinese of Indonesia permit twins to marry each other because they believe that twins have already been intimate in the womb. In the Banaro culture of New Guinea, the husband is forbidden to have intercourse with his wife until she has first borne a child by another man chosen for that purpose. Once the wife has proved that she can bear children, the husband is then allowed to have sexual

(Erika Stone/Photo Researchers)

By 1990, more than 7 million American children were living in stepfamilies.

relations with her (Leslie and Korman, 1989:15, 30, 39).

As these examples illustrate, there are many variations in "the family" from culture to culture. What do *you* consider a family? A 1987 national survey in the United States asked adults if they would regard certain living arrangements as a "true family" (Kalette et al., 1987). The percentages of those responding affirmatively were as follows:

Married couple, at least one child	99%
Married couple, no children	95%
Single parent, living with children	91%
Unmarried couple living together	45%
Homosexual couple rearing children	33%
Two homosexuals living together	20%

Clearly, even within the United States, people cannot agree on a definition of a family. Consequently, when someone speaks of his or her family, we cannot assume that this family resembles ours in form and structure. For some, the family may consist of only a handful of people; for others, it may involve hundreds. For some, the family may represent a hope for the future; for others, it

may seem an outmoded barrier to personal growth.

A *family* can be defined as a set of people related by blood, marriage (or some other agreed-upon relationship), or adoption who share the primary responsibility for reproduction and caring for members of society. In this chapter, we will see that the family is universal—found in every culture—though varied in its organization (Weigart and Thomas, 1971). We will look at the primary functions of the family and the variations in marital patterns and family life in the United States. Particular attention will be given to the increasing number of Americans who are living in dual-career or single-parent families. The social policy section will examine the recent debate over family leave legislation.

THE FAMILY: UNIVERSAL BUT VARIED

The family as a social institution is present in all cultures. Although the organization of the family can vary greatly, there are certain general principles concerning its composition, descent patterns, residence patterns, and authority patterns.

FIGURE 13-1 Types of Households in the United States, 1960, 1980, and 1990

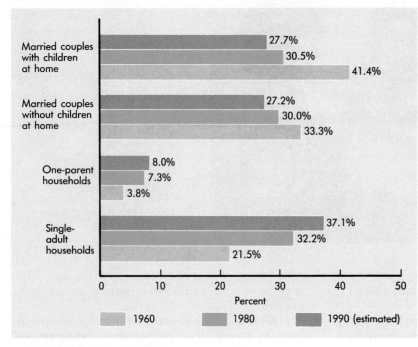

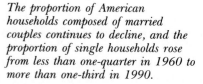

The proportion of American households composed of married couples continues to decline, and the proportion of single households rose from less than one-quarter in 1960 to more than one-third in 1990.

SOURCE: Masnick and Bane, 1980:56.

Composition: What Is the Family?

In American society, the family has traditionally been viewed in very narrow terms—as a married couple and their unmarried children living together. However, this is but one type of family, what sociologists refer to as a ***nuclear family.*** The term *nuclear family* is well-chosen, since this type of family serves as the nucleus, or core, upon which larger family groups are built. As we saw in the survey data presented above, people in the United States see the nuclear family as the preferred family arrangement. Yet, as is shown in Figure 13-1, by 1990 only about one-quarter of American households fit this model. (The term *household* is used by the Bureau of the Census to refer to related or unrelated individuals sharing a residence as well as to people who live alone.)

As Figure 13-1 illustrates, the proportion of households in the United States composed of married couples with children at home has de-creased steadily over the last 30 years. At the same time, there have been substantial increases in the number of single-person and single-parent households. Similar trends are evident in other industrialized nations, including Canada, Great Britain, and Japan (see Figure 13-2).

A family in which relatives in addition to parents and children—such as grandparents, aunts, or uncles—live in the same home is known as an ***extended family.*** While not common, such living arrangements do exist in the United States. The structure of the extended family offers certain advantages over that of the nuclear family. Crises such as death, divorce, and illness involve less strain for family members, since there are more people who can provide assistance and emotional support. In addition, the extended family constitutes a larger economic unit than the nuclear family. If the family is engaged in a common enterprise—for example, running a farm or a small business—the additional family members may represent the difference between prosperity and failure.

In considering these differing family types, we have limited ourselves to the form of marriage characteristic of the United States—monogamy. The term **monogamy** describes a form of marriage in which one woman and one man are married only to each other. Some observers, noting America's high rate of divorce, have suggested that "serial monogamy" is a more accurate description of the form that monogamy takes in the United States. Under **serial monogamy,** a person is allowed to have several spouses in his or her life but can have only one spouse at a time.

Some cultures allow an individual to have several husbands or wives simultaneously. This form of marriage is known as **polygamy.** You may be surprised to learn that most societies throughout the world, past and present, have preferred polygamy, not monogamy. Anthropologist George Murdock (1949, 1957) sampled 565 societies and found that over 80 percent had some type of polygamy as their preferred form.

There are two basic types of polygamy. According to Murdock, the most common—endorsed by the majority of cultures he sampled—was polygyny. **Polygyny** refers to the marriage of a man to more than one woman at the same time. The various wives are often sisters, who are expected to hold similar values and have already had experience sharing a household. In polygynous societies, relatively few men actually have multiple spouses. Most individuals live in typical monogamous families; having multiple wives is viewed as a mark of status.

The other principal variation of polygamy is **polyandry,** under which a woman can have several husbands at the same time. As we saw earlier in the chapter, this was the case in the culture of the Todas of southern India. Yet, despite such examples, polyandry tends to be exceedingly rare. It has been accepted by some extremely poor societies which practice female infanticide (the killing of baby girls) and thus have a relatively small number of women. Like many other societies, polyandrous cultures devalue the social worth of women.

FIGURE 13-2   Married-Couple Households with Children in Industrialized Nations, 1960 and 1990

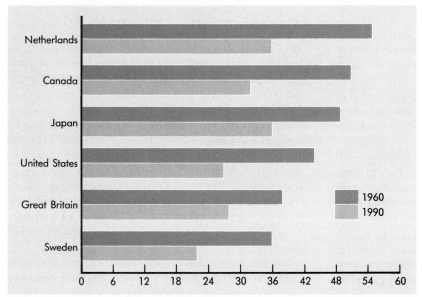

SOURCE: Bureau of Labor Statistics data in Sorrentino, 1990:46–47; and authors' estimates.

As in the United States, the proportion of all households consisting of a married couple with children is declining in many other industrialized nations.

Descent Patterns: To Whom Are We Related?

In the late 1970s, many Americans were deeply moved by Alex Haley's successful quest for his family tree, which was documented in his book *Roots* and later popularized on network television. Beginning with stories passed down by his grandmother, Haley was able to trace his heritage back to Africa—to a man named Kunta Kinte who lived in Gambia, West Africa, and was brought to the United States in chains by slave traders.

Many of us, like Alex Haley, have retraced our roots by listening to elderly family members tell us about their lives—and about the lives of ancestors who died long before we were even born. Yet a person's lineage is more than simply a personal history; it also reflects societal patterns that govern descent. In every culture, children are introduced to relatives to whom they are expected to show an emotional attachment. The state of being related to others is called **kinship.** Kinship is culturally learned and is not totally determined by biological or marital ties. For example, adoption creates a kinship tie which is legally acknowledged and socially accepted.

The family and the kin group are not necessarily the same. While the family is a household unit, kin do not always live together or function as a collective body on a daily basis. Kin groups include aunts, uncles, cousins, in-laws, and so forth. In a society such as the United States, the kinship group may come together only rarely, as for a marriage or funeral. However, kinship ties frequently create obligations and responsibilities. We may feel compelled to assist our kin and feel free to call upon relatives for many types of aid, including loans and baby-sitting.

How are kinship groups identified? The principle of descent assigns people to kinship groups according to their relationship to an individual's mother or father. There are three principal ways of determining descent. In the United States, the system of **bilateral descent** is followed, which means that both sides of a person's family are regarded as equally important. No higher value is given to the brothers of one's father as opposed to the brothers of one's mother.

Most societies—according to Murdock, 64 percent—give preference to one side of the family or the other in tracing descent. **Patrilineal** (from Latin *pater*, "father") **descent** indicates that only the father's relatives are important in terms of property, inheritance, and the establishment of emotional ties. Conversely, in societies which favor **matrilineal** (from Latin *mater*, "mother") **descent,** only the mother's relatives are significant; the relatives of the father are considered unimportant.

Family Residence: Where Do We Live?

In every society, there are social norms concerning the appropriate residence of a newly created family. Under the **neolocal** pattern of residence, which is prevalent in the United States, a married couple is expected to establish a separate household. However, if we take a cross-cultural view, it becomes clear that the American ideal type of neolocal residence is relatively uncommon. In many societies, the bride and groom live either with his parents (the **patrilocal** pattern) or with her parents (the **matrilocal** pattern). In such cultures, it is felt that the new couples need the emotional support and especially the economic support of kinfolk.

Authority Patterns: Who Rules?

Imagine that you have recently married and must begin to make decisions about the future of your new family. You and your spouse face many questions. Where will you live? How will you furnish your place of residence? Who will do the cooking, the shopping, the cleaning? Whose friends will be invited to dinner? Each time a decision must be made, an issue is raised: "Who has the power to make the decision?" In simple terms, who rules the family? From a conflict perspective, these questions must be examined in light of traditional gender stratification (see Chapter 11), under which men have held a dominant position over women.

Societies vary in the way that power within the family is distributed. If a society expects males to dominate in all family decision making, it is termed a **patriarchy.** Frequently, in patriarchal societies, the eldest male wields the greatest power. Women hold low status in such societies and rarely are granted full and equal rights within the legal system. It may be more difficult, for example, for a woman to obtain a divorce than it is for a man. By contrast, in a **matriarchy,** women have greater authority than men. Matriarchies may have emerged among Indian tribal societies and in nations in which men were absent for long periods of time for warfare or food gathering.

Some marital relationships may be neither male-dominated nor female-dominated. The third type of authority pattern, the **egalitarian family,** is one in which spouses are regarded as equals. This does not mean, however, that each decision is shared in such families. Mothers may hold authority in some spheres, fathers in others. In the view of many sociologists, the egalitarian family has begun to replace the patriarchal family as the social norm. A study of Detroit families by Robert Blood, Jr., and Donald Wolfe (1960) supports this contention (see Box 13-1, page 386).

FUNCTIONS OF THE FAMILY

Do we really need the family? A century ago, Friedrich Engels (1884), a colleague of Karl Marx, described the family as the ultimate source of social inequality because of its role in the transfer of power, property, and privilege. More recently, conflict theorists have argued that the American family contributes to societal injustice, denies opportunities to women that are extended to men, and limits freedom in sexual expression and mate selection.

In order to evaluate such issues, it is helpful to use the tools provided by the functionalist perspective, which encourages us to examine the ways in which an institution gratifies the needs of its members and contributes to the stability of society. The family fulfills a number of functions, such as providing religious training, education, and recreational outlets. Yet there are six paramount functions performed by the family; they were first outlined a half-century ago by sociologist William F. Ogburn (Ogburn and Tibbits, 1934):

1 *Reproduction.* For a society to maintain itself, it must replace dying members. In this sense, the family contributes to human survival through its function of reproduction.

2 *Protection.* Unlike the young of animal species, human infants need constant care and economic security. They experience an extremely long period of dependency, which places special demands on elder family members. In all cultures, the family assumes ultimate responsibility for the protection and upbringing of children.

3 *Socialization.* Parents and other kin monitor a child's behavior and transmit the norms, values, and language of a culture to the child (see Chapters 3 and 4). Of course, as conflict theorists point out, the social class of couples and their children significantly influences the socialization experiences to which they are exposed and the protection they receive.

4 *Regulation of sexual behavior.* Sexual norms are subject to change over time (changes in customs for dating) and across cultures (Islamic Saudi Arabia compared with more permissive Denmark). However, whatever the time period or cultural values in a society, standards of sexual behavior are most clearly defined within the family circle. The structure of society influences these standards so that, characteristically in male-dominated societies, formal and informal norms permit men to express and enjoy their sexual desires more freely than women may.

5 *Affection and companionship.* Ideally, the family provides members with warm and intimate relationships and helps them feel satisfied and secure. Of course, a family member may find such rewards outside the family—from peers, in school, at work—and may perceive the home as an unpleasant place. Nevertheless, unlike other institutions, the family is obligated to serve the emotional needs of its members. We *expect* our relatives to understand us, to care for us, and to be there for us when we need them.

6 *Providing of social status.* We inherit a social position because of the "family background" and reputation of our parents and siblings. The family unit presents the newborn child with an ascribed status of race and ethnicity that helps to determine his or her place within a society's stratifica-

BOX 13-1 • CURRENT RESEARCH

MARITAL POWER

Sociologists Robert Blood, Jr., and Donald Wolfe (1960) developed the concept of *marital power* to describe the manner in which decision making is distributed within families. They defined power by examining who makes the final decision in each of eight important areas that, the researchers argue, traditionally have been reserved entirely for the husband or for the wife. These areas include what job the husband should take, what house or apartment to live in, where to go on vacation, and which doctor to use if there is an illness in the family. Using this technique, Blood and Wolfe (1960:22–23) surveyed families in the Detroit area and concluded that the "aggregate balance of power falls slightly in the husband's direction." They added that, in general, it seemed appropriate to "label these as relatively egalitarian couples."

Recent research suggests that money plays a central role in determining marital power. Money has different meanings for members of each sex: for men it typi-

cally represents identity and power; for women, security and autonomy. Apparently, money establishes the balance of power not only for married couples but also for unmarried heterosexual couples who are living together. Married women with paying work outside the home enjoy greater marital power than full-time homemakers do (Blumstein and Schwartz, 1983; Godwin and Scanzoni, 1989; Kaufman, 1985).

Labor not only enhances women's self-esteem but also increases their marital power, because some men have greater respect for women who work at paying jobs. Sociologist Isik Aytac (1987) studied a national sample of households in the United States and found that husbands of women holding management positions share more of the domestic chores than other husbands. In addition, as a wife's proportional contribution to the family income increases, her husband's share of meal preparation increases. Aytac's research supports the contention that the traditional divi-

sion of labor at home can change as women's position in the labor force improves and women gain greater marital power.

Comparative studies have revealed the complexity of marital power issues in other cultures. For example, anthropologists Marida Hollos and Philip Leis (1985) studied family decision making in rural communities in Portugal. It has generally been assumed that men play a dominant role in such families, but the researchers found that outward appearances are far from accurate. Although women allow men to appear outspoken and decisive in public—especially in the presence of strangers—women apparently exercise substantial authority within the family.

Hollos and Leis note that similar patterns are evident in rural Greece, France, and Yugoslavia. In their view, these findings underscore the difficulties faced by researchers in studying marital power—especially when they conduct cross-cultural studies (Kranichfeld, 1987).

---

tion system. Moreover, family resources affect children's ability to pursue certain opportunities such as higher education and specialized lessons.

It is apparent, then, that the family has been assigned at least six vital functions in human societies. However, one might ask if the family can effectively fulfill these weighty responsibilities. To answer this question, we must begin a more detailed examination of marital and family life in the United States of the 1990s.

MARRIAGE AND FAMILY IN THE UNITED STATES

Currently, nearly 95 percent of all Americans in their early fifties are married or have been married in the past. Historically, the most consistent aspect of family life in the United States has been the nation's high rate of marriage. In this part of the chapter, we will examine various aspects of love, marriage, and parenthood in the United States.

Courtship and Mate Selection

In certain traditional cultures, arranged marriages are common, and courtship practices are severely restricted. For example, some Japanese traditionalists favor arranged marriages for their children. A go-between will often take a young man to a public place for a *kagemi* (a hidden look) at a young woman viewed as a likely candidate for marriage. The woman is unaware that she is being evaluated to see if her appearance is acceptable (Hendry, 1981:116–123). Similarly, "secret looks" are common in rural Egypt. A boy from a village observes:

> One favorite place for us to get a glimpse of girls is at the village water source. The girls know that and like to linger there. If we see one we like and think she might be suitable, we ask our parents to try to arrange a marriage, but usually not before we have some sign from the girl that she might be interested (Rugh, 1984:137).

As is true in this Egyptian village, the process of courtship in the United States requires people to rely heavily on intricate games, gestures, and signals. For example, how do you act when you have just met an attractive stranger in a bookstore, in a supermarket, or at a party? Do you come right out and say, "I'd really like to see you again," after just meeting the person? Or do you find elaborate and slightly disguised ways of showing your interest and testing how the other person feels about you?

An important aspect of the courtship process is labeling. Sociologist Robert Lewis (1973) reports that early labeling as a couple by family and friends results in a greater likelihood that the relationship will be maintained over time. By contrast, the absence of such labeling—or a negative reaction from those people termed *significant others* by George Herbert Mead (see Chapter 4)—can result in a weakening of the couple's relationship.

The process of courtship is clearly influenced by the values of the particular society in which we live. But what about our *choices* in mate selection? Why are we drawn to a particular person in the first place? To what extent are such judgments shaped by the society around us?

Marriages that are exogamous with respect to race are increasing but still account for only a small minority of marriages in the United States.

(Willie L. Hill, Jr./Stock, Boston)

Theories of Mate Selection Many societies have explicit or unstated rules which define potential mates as socially acceptable or unacceptable. These norms can be distinguished in terms of endogamy and exogamy. **Endogamy** (from the Greek *endon,* "within") specifies the groups within which a spouse must be found and prohibits marriage with others. For example, in the United States, many people are expected to marry within their own racial, ethnic, or religious group and are prohibited from marrying anyone outside the group. Endogamy is intended to reinforce the cohesiveness of the group by suggesting to the young that they should marry someone "of our own kind."

By contrast, **exogamy** (from the Greek *exō,* "outside") requires mate selection outside certain groups, usually one's own family or certain kinfolk. The *incest taboo,* a social norm common to virtually all societies, prohibits sexual relationships between certain culturally specified relatives. For Americans, this taboo means that we must marry outside the nuclear family. We cannot marry our siblings, and in most states we cannot marry our first cousins.

Endogamous restrictions may be seen as preferences for one group over another. In the United States, such preferences are most obvious in racial barriers. Until the 1960s, some American states outlawed marriages involving interracial couples. This practice was challenged by Richard Loving (a White man) and Mildred Jeter Loving (a part-Black, part-Indian woman), who married in 1958. Eventually, in 1967, the Supreme Court ruled that it was unconstitutional to prohibit marriage solely on the basis of race. The decision struck down statutes in Virginia and 16 other states (Simpson and Yinger, 1985:302–304).

Mate selection has been likened to a filtering process. We select a future spouse by passing him or her through a series of filters. Rules of endogamy and exogamy initially define the field of eligible candidates. Proximity or propinquity—that is, nearness to a person—narrows the field even more. The end result of this filtering process may be marriage or cohabitation outside of marriage (Murstein, 1976:99–105).

The Love Relationship Love and mate selection do not necessarily coincide. For example, feelings of love are not a prerequisite for marriage among the Yaruros of inland Venezuela or in other cultures where there is little freedom for mate selection. As Linton Freeman (1958:27–30) has shown, the Yaruro male of marriageable age does not engage in the kind of dating behavior so typical of American youth. Rather, he knows that, under the traditions of his culture, he must marry one of his mother's brothers' daughters or one of his father's sisters' daughters. The young man's choice is further limited because one of his uncles selects the eligible cousin that he must marry.

Many of the world's cultures give priority in mate selection to factors other than romantic feelings. In some societies, marriages are arranged, often by parents or religious authorities. The newly married couple is expected to develop a feeling of love *after* their legal union is formalized. Economic considerations also play a significant role in mate selection in certain societies.

In the United States, love is important in the courtship process. Neolocal residence places added importance on the affectional bond between husband and wife. The couple is able to develop its own emotional ties, free of the demands of other household members for affection. Sociologist William Goode (1959) observed that spouses in a nuclear family have to rely heavily on each other for the companionship and support that might be provided by other relatives in an extended-family situation.

American parents value love highly as a rationale for marriage, and they encourage love to develop between young people. In addition, the theme of romantic love is reinforced in songs, films, books, magazines, television shows, and even cartoons and comic books. At the same time, our society expects parents and peers to help a person confine his or her search for a mate to "socially acceptable" members of the opposite sex.

Psychologist Zick Rubin (1970) attempted to measure love and determine its effects on people's relationships. He developed a scale of items used to measure love—as well as another scale to measure "liking"—and administered questionnaires to college students. Rubin also arranged for 78 couples to be observed through a one-way mirror while they waited to fill out the questionnaires. Researchers precisely recorded the amount of time that couples spent gazing into one another's eyes. It was learned that couples who score higher on the love scales spent more time gazing at each other than couples with lower scores did.

Rubin wondered if this love would last over time. Consequently, he divided his sample into two groups: those who saw marriage as something meant for those in love ("romantics") and those who saw marriage as highly dependent on economic security ("nonromantics"). Among the romantics, love scores were found to be closely related to later courtship progress. After 6 months, those with high love scores were found to be more intensely involved with each other or engaged. However, there was evidence to suggest that the more in love the nonromantics had been, the more likely they were to have broken up later. One implication of these findings is that passionate romantic love may be dysfunctional for those who place a high value on security.

In the United States, traditional gender-role socialization has made it easier for women to express love and other feelings of social intimacy than it is for men. The qualities identified with intimacy—emotional warmth, expressiveness, vulnerability, and sensitivity—are associated with the female but not the male gender role. Studies show that men are more likely than women to base their perceptions of love and intimacy on sex, on providing practical help, and on simply being in the presence of a loved one. One husband attempted to demonstrate his affection for his wife by washing her car; he was bewildered when she failed to understand the intended message of his assistance (Cancian, 1986; L. Thompson and Walker, 1989:847).

Family Patterns

Cohabitation Saint Paul once wrote: "It is better to marry than to burn." However, as journalist Tom Ferrell (1979) has suggested, more people than ever "prefer combustible to connubial bliss." One of the most dramatic trends of recent years has been the tremendous increase in male-female couples who choose to live together without marrying, thereby engaging in what is commonly called *cohabitation.*

The number of such households in the United States rose sixfold in the 1960s and increased fivefold between 1970 and 1988. The dramatic rise in cohabitation has been linked to greater acceptance of premarital sex and delayed entry into marriage. In 1981, a survey of colleges found that 87 percent—including all the public institutions examined—had no rules prohibiting off-campus cohabitation. According to a 1988 national survey, 11 percent of women who had never married were cohabiting while 44 percent of women who had married in the early 1980s had cohabited at some time (Bumpass and Sweet, 1989; London, 1991; L. Middleton and Roark, 1981).

Increases in unmarried coupling have also been found in France, Sweden, Denmark, and Australia. One report notes that in Sweden it is almost universal for couples to live together before marriage. Demographers in Denmark call the practice of living together *marriage without papers*. In Australia, these couples are known as *de factos* (Blanc, 1984; A. Levinson, 1984).

One of the crucial variables in such living situations is the extent to which they offer the kind of lifelong commitment promised by marriage. For many college students, cohabitation is a logical extension of a highly valued dating relationship. However, this living arrangement is more likely to serve as a final step in the courtship process than as an alternative to marriage. Surveys consistently show that 98 percent of American college students anticipate marrying at some time during adulthood (Peterman et al., 1974).

For some people in the United States, living together may represent a kind of trial marriage that will eventually lead to a traditional marriage with their current partner (or some other person). Margaret Mead (1966) gave the idea of trial marriage her support when she suggested that marriage be contracted in two stages. The *individual marriage* would involve a minimal legal commitment but would become a legally binding *parental marriage* once a child was expected. Mead's formulation has not yet won wide acceptance. However, in many instances, a couple engaged in extended cohabitation comes to view the relationship as a partnership somewhat like marriage—but with unresolved legal implications. In Box 13-2 on page 391, we will discuss legislation intended to offer benefits and protections to couples who have established such domestic partnerships.

It would be incorrect, however, to associate cohabitation only with college campuses, sexual experimentation, or trial marriages. According to a study in Los Angeles, working couples are almost twice as likely to cohabit as college students. At the same time, census data show that 28 percent of unmarried couples have one or more children present in the household. These cohabitants can be regarded as more similar to spouses than to dating partners. Moreover, in contrast to the common perception that people engaged in cohabitation have never married, researchers report that about half of all Americans involved in cohabitation have been previously married. Indeed, cohabitation serves as a temporary or permanent alternative to matrimony for many men and women who have experienced marital disruption. Clearly, cohabitation should not be regarded as a pastime limited to the unmarried and the inexperienced (London, 1991; Spanier, 1983).

Remaining Single Current data indicate that more Americans are postponing entry into first marriages than was true in the past. In 1988, 61 percent of all women 20 to 24 years of age had never married, compared with only 36 percent in 1970. Still, less than 10 percent of women and men are likely to remain single throughout their lives (Bureau of the Census, 1990a:4; Saluter, 1989).

The trend toward maintaining an unmarried lifestyle is related to the growing economic independence of young people. This is especially significant for women. In 1890, women accounted for only one-sixth of the paid labor force; they are now approximately half of it (see Chapter 11). From a financial point of view, it is often no longer necessary for a woman to marry in order to enjoy a satisfying life.

There are many reasons why a person may choose not to marry (see Table 13-1). Singleness is an attractive option for those who do not want to limit their sexual intimacy to one lifetime partner. In addition, some Americans do not want to become highly dependent on any one person—and do not want anyone depending heavily on them. In a society which values individuality and personal self-fulfillment, the single lifestyle can offer certain freedoms that married couples may not enjoy.

Gay Relationships According to estimates, lesbians and gay men together constitute perhaps 10 percent of the nation's population. Their lifestyles vary greatly. Some live alone, others with roommates. Some live in long-term, monogamous relationships with a lover and with children from former marriages (see Box 13-2). Others remain married and have not publicly acknowledged their homosexuality.

TABLE 13-1 Singleness: An Alternative to Marriage

ATTRACTIONS OF BEING SINGLE	ATTRACTIONS OF BEING MARRIED
Career opportunities	Economic security
Sexual availability	Regular sex
Exciting lifestyle	Desire for family
Self-sufficiency	Sustained love
Freedom to change and experiment	Security in personal relationships

SOURCE: Adapted from P. Stein, 1975. Also appears in P. Stein, 1981:18.

More Americans are making a conscious choice to remain single. As the balance sheet above indicates, there are attractions to being single as well as to being married.

(J. Ross Boughman/Visions)

Some lesbian and gay male couples rear the children of one or both partners.

BOX 13-2 • EVERYDAY BEHAVIOR

DOMESTIC PARTNERSHIP LEGISLATION

In their extensively researched study, *American Couples,* sociologists Philip Blumstein and Pepper Schwartz (1983) personally interviewed 400 couples, of whom 180 were homosexual. One of these couples was Henry and Gene, longtime best friends from a small town in Illinois who became lovers and have lived together for 38 years. Henry, 56, is an executive in a department store; Gene, 55, is a free-lance illustrator. Because Henry's family would not accept their relationship, they moved to Chicago to share a home. As Henry recalls: "We were so much in love that nothing, *nothing* would have stopped us. . . . We would have faced any odds, including censorship of the family or whatever else faced us" (Blumstein and Schwartz, 1983:504).

The most troublesome issue for Henry and Gene is not sex, fidelity, or money, but travel. Gene hates taking trips, admits that he is "totally against traveling," and prefers to stay at home. Henry has begged and pleaded to get Gene to take vacations with him, but to no avail. Nevertheless, Blumstein and Schwartz (1983:508) observe that "Henry and Gene have spent their lives together and nothing is going to break them up. . . . Their emotional life is secure and well protected. . . . This is a childhood romance that flowered into adult commitment."

Despite 38 committed years together, Henry and Gene—like millions of other gay and heterosexual couples in the United States—do not enjoy many legal rights and privileges that our society grants to married couples. If Henry's department store offers an excellent health plan, he will not be able to arrange coverage for Gene; if one of these men becomes seriously ill and is confined to a hospital, the other may be denied visiting privileges because he is not "family." With these inequities in mind, certain municipalities have passed legislation or adopted executive orders to provide benefits to "domestic partners."

Under such policies, a *domestic partnership* may be defined as "two unrelated adults who have chosen to share one another's lives in a relationship of mutual caring, who reside together, and agree to be jointly responsible for their dependents, basic living expenses, and other common necessities." In order to qualify as domestic partners in New York City, which has extended bereavement leave to its municipal workers, a couple must have lived together for at least 1 year, must attest that they have a "close and committed personal relationship involving shared responsibilities," and must officially register their partnership with city officials. The most passionate support for domestic partnership legislation has come from gay activist organizations, who emphasize that lesbian and gay male couples are prohibited from marrying— and therefore from gaining traditional partnership benefits—in all 50 states. However, among those whose long-term relationships would qualify them as domestic partners, only about 40 percent are gay; the vast majority are cohabiting heterosexual couples (Dittersdorf, 1990:6; Isaacson, 1989).

In 1984, Berkeley, California, became the first community to enact domestic partnership legislation, under which qualifying couples would receive the same city employment benefits available to married couples. Since then, seven other municipalities— among them Seattle, Los Angeles, and Madison, Wisconsin—have offered health benefits, sick leave, or bereavement leave to domestic partners. Some employers and organizations now provide similar benefits, including the American Psychological Association, Columbia University, and the newspaper *The Village Voice* (Dittersdorf, 1990; Luxenburg and Guild, 1989:16).

While various states and cities are considering domestic partnership legislation, such proposals face strong opposition from conservative religious and political groups. In the view of opponents, support for domestic partnership undermines the historic societal preference for the nuclear family. Advocates of domestic partnership counter that such relationships fulfill the same functions for the individuals involved and for society as the traditional family and should enjoy the same legal protections and benefits. As one measure of the continuing controversy over this issue, a domestic partnership ordinance passed in San Francisco in mid-1989 was narrowly overturned by voters in a referendum later that year.

The contemporary gay liberation movement has given an increasing number of lesbians and gay males the support to proclaim their sexual and affectional preferences. Gay activists were distressed in 1986 when a divided Supreme Court ruled, by a 5-4 vote, that the Constitution does not protect homosexual relations between consenting adults, even within the privacy of their own homes. Nevertheless, as of 1991, the states of Wisconsin, Massachusetts, Connecticut, and Hawaii; the District of Columbia; and more than 65 municipalities had enacted gay civil rights protections (see also Luxenburg and Guild, 1989).

Marriage without Children Childlessness within marriage has generally been viewed as a problem that can be solved through such means as adoption and artificial insemination. Some couples, however, *choose* not to have children and regard themselves as child-free, not childless. They do not believe that having children automatically follows from marriage, nor do they feel that reproduction is the duty of all married couples. In this regard, a 1980 census survey found that 6 percent of married women between the ages of 18 and 34 did not expect to give birth during their lifetimes. Another 11 percent of widowed and divorced women felt the same way. Although child-free couples continue to remain a minority, the number of these couples increased by 75 percent between 1968 and 1985 (D. Bloom and Bennett, 1986:23; Pebley and Bloom, 1982:21).

Economic considerations have contributed to this shift in attitudes; having children has become quite expensive. In 1990, the U.S. Department of Agriculture estimated that the average upper-middle-class family will spend $265,249 to feed, clothe, and shelter a child from birth to age 22. If the child attends college, that amount could double, depending on the college chosen. With such financial pressures in mind, some couples are having fewer children than they otherwise might, and others are weighing the advantages of a child-free marriage (Rock, 1990).

Parenthood and Child Care Caring for children is a universal function of the family, yet societies vary in assigning this function to family members. Among the Nayars of southern India, the biologi-cal role of fathers is acknowledged, but the mother's eldest brother is responsible for her children (Gough, 1974). By contrast, uncles play only a peripheral role in child care in the United States.

Despite such differences, the socialization of children is essential to the maintenance of any culture. Consequently, as we saw in Chapter 4, parenthood is one of American society's most important (and most demanding) social roles. Sociologist Alice Rossi (1968, 1984:5–10) has pointed to four factors related to socialization that complicate the transition to parenthood. First, there is little anticipatory socialization for the social roles of caregiver. Subjects most relevant to successful family life—such as child care and home maintenance—are given little attention in the normal American school curriculum. Second, only limited learning occurs during the period of pregnancy itself. Third, the transition to parenthood is quite abrupt. Unlike adolescence, it is not prolonged; unlike socialization for work, one cannot gradually take on the duties of care-giving. Finally, in Rossi's view, our society lacks clear and helpful guidelines concerning successful parenthood. There is little consensus on how parents can produce happy and well-adjusted offspring—or even on what it means to be "well-adjusted." For these reasons, socialization for parenthood involves difficult challenges for most Americans.

One recent development in family life in the United States has been the extension of parenthood, as adult children continue to (or return to) live at home. Currently, more than half of all children ages 20 to 24 and one out of five of those ages 25 to 34 live with their parents. Some of these adult children are still pursuing an education, but in many instances financial difficulties are at the heart of the living arrangements. While rents and real estate prices skyrocketed in the 1980s, salaries for younger workers did not keep pace and many found themselves unable to afford their own homes. Not surprisingly, the average age of marriage for both men and women rose during the 1980s. Moreover, with half of all marriages now ending in divorce—most commonly in the first 7 years of marriage—divorced sons and daughters are now returning to live with their parents, sometimes with their own children (Bureau of the Census, 1990a:49).

Parenthood is one of the most important social roles. Shown here are an American mother with her children, an Indonesian woman with her son and an older relative, and Japanese parents sitting on a park bench with their children.

Is this living arrangement a positive development for family members? Social scientists have just begun to examine this phenomenon, sometimes called the "boomerang generation" in the popular press. One survey in Virginia seemed to show that neither the parents nor their adult children were happy about continuing to live together. The children often felt resentful and isolated, but the parents also suffered, since learning to live without children in the home can be viewed as an essential stage of adult life and indeed may be a significant turning point for a marriage (*Berkeley Wellness Letter,* 1990:1–2).

Adoption In a legal sense, ***adoption*** is a "process that allows for the transfer of the legal rights, responsibilities, and privileges of parenting from legal parents to new legal parents" (E. Cole, 1985:638). In many cases, these rights are transferred from biological parents (often called *birth parents*) to adoptive parents. Viewed from a functionalist perspective, government has a strong interest in encouraging adoption. Kenneth Watson (1986:5) of the Chicago Child Care Society notes: "Adoption is seen as a neat solution to three of society's vexing problems: unplanned pregnancy outside of marriage, children in need of families to rear them, and infertile couples unable to have children."

Policymakers have both a humanitarian and a financial stake in promoting adoption. In theory, adoption offers a stable family environment for children who otherwise might not receive satisfactory care. Moreover, government data show that unwed mothers who keep their babies tend to be of lower socioeconomic status and often require public assistance to support their children (C. Bachrach, 1986). Consequently, various levels of government may lower their social welfare expenses if children are transferred to economically self-sufficient families. From a conflict perspective, such financial considerations raise the ugly specter of adoption's serving as a means whereby affluent (often infertile) couples are allowed to "buy" the children of the poor.

The largest single category of adoption in the United States is adoption by relatives. In most cases, a stepparent adopts the children of a spouse. There are two legal methods of adopting an unrelated person: adoptions arranged by licensed agencies and private agreements sanctioned by the courts (known as *independent adoptions*). Currently, 45 states allow for both types of adoption, while 5 states permit only those adoptions handled by agencies (E. Cole, 1985:639–640, 662–663; Salvatore, 1986:60).

According to the National Committee for Adoption, an association of private adoption agencies, the number of adoptions between unrelated people in the United States decreased from 82,800 in 1971 to 51,157 in 1986 (the last year for which complete data are available). This change was due largely to a decline in the number of children available for adoption. Key factors contributing to this diminishing pool of children include wider use of contraceptives, a rise in the number of abortions (see Chapter 11), and a lessening of the social stigma faced by single parents who keep their babies (Lawson, 1991:Cl; R. Lindsey, 1987a:30).

According to a recent study by the National Center for Health Statistics, about 200,000 women in the United States sought adoption in 1988. The alleged "parent surplus" often described in the mass media reflects an abundance of childless couples anxious to adopt White, nondisabled babies. Ironically, at the same time that these parents wait for babies, many children and adolescents from minority backgrounds or with disabilities live in group homes or in foster-care situations (M. Harris, 1988; Hilts, 1990d).

Dual-Career Families In the traditional nuclear family, the husband serves as the sole breadwinner, while the wife fills the roles of mother and homemaker. However, an increasing proportion of American couples are rejecting this model for a "dual-career" lifestyle. Currently, the majority of all married couples have two partners active in the paid labor force. In one-fourth of couples, both partners are "permanently committed" to their careers in that they have worked for at least 5 years.

Why has there been such a rise in the number of dual-career couples? A major factor, especially among less affluent families, is economic need. In 1988, the median income for married-couple families with an employed wife was $42,709, com-

An increasing proportion of American couples are rejecting the traditional nuclear family model for a "dual-career" lifestyle.

pared with $27,220 (or 36 percent less) in families in which only the husband was working outside the home. Other factors contributing to the rise of the dual-career model include the nation's declining birthrate (see Chapter 19), the increase in the proportion of women with a college education, the shift in the economy of the United States from manufacturing to service industries, and the impact of the feminist movement in changing women's consciousness (Bureau of the Census, 1990a:451; Spain and Nock, 1984).

In a sense, members of dual-career couples must undergo a process of resocialization (see Chapter 4). A newly married couple may intend to have a "two-career household" and share child care in an egalitarian manner. Their parents, however, may have followed the conventional nuclear family pattern described earlier. Thus, neither of the newlyweds may have had useful role models of a dual-career lifestyle. Each may have to overcome previous socialization into traditional expectations regarding marriage and the "proper" roles of husbands and wives.

How does the dual-career model affect gender roles and marital power? As noted in Box 13-1, married women who work for pay outside the home enjoy greater marital power than full-time homemakers. However, the fact that both spouses

have careers is no guarantee that a marriage will be genuinely egalitarian. As women have taken on increasing hours of paid employment outside the home, they have been largely unable to get their husbands to take a greater role in child care and household duties. For example, a survey of dual-career families in the Canadian city of Edmonton revealed that mothers typically stay home from work to care for sick children. Even though both fathers and mothers stated that such duties should be shared, in practice this important responsibility fell largely upon women, thereby perpetuating an aspect of traditional gender roles. As was discussed in Chapter 11, sociologist Arlie Hochschild (1989, 1990) has used the phrase "second shift" to describe the double burden— work outside the home followed by child care and housework—that many women face and few men share equitably (Northcott, 1983; see also Hertz, 1986).

Single-Parent Families *Single-parent families,* in which there is only one parent present to care for the children, can hardly be viewed as a rarity in the United States. Because of continuing increases in the nation's rates of divorce and unwed motherhood, 42 percent of White children living today and 86 percent of Black children will spend

BOX 13-3 • AROUND THE WORLD

PREGNANCY AMONG TEENAGERS

According to a study released in 1985 and updated in 1989 by the Alan Guttmacher Institute, American teenagers become pregnant, give birth, and have abortions at much higher rates than adolescents in almost any other industrialized nation. And the United States is the only developed country in which pregnancy among teenagers has been on the rise in recent years.

This 2-year study compared teenage pregnancy rates in 37 developed countries. It provided a detailed examination of teenagers' sexual practices, pregnancy rates, and abortion rates, along with public policy, in six of these countries, among them the United States. The other five nations chosen for intensive study included Canada, Great Britain, France, the Netherlands, and Sweden. According to the study, the pregnancy rate for Americans 15 to 19 years old is 96 births per 1000. This compares with 14 per 1000 in the Netherlands, 35 in Sweden, 44 in Canada, and 45 in England. The abortion rate among teenagers for the United States was found to be as high as the combined abortion rates and birthrates for the other nations studied.

Many Americans with traditional attitudes toward sexuality and family life have suspected that the availability of birth control methods and sex education information in the United States and other developed

(Frank Siteman/Stock, Boston)

Currently, the United States has the highest birthrate among teenagers of any industrialized nation.

countries leads to increases in pregnancy among teenagers. However, the data from the Guttmacher Institute's study contradict this view. The researchers point out that the *lowest* rates of pregnancy among teenagers are found in countries with liberal attitudes toward sex, easily accessible birth control services for young people, and comprehensive sex education programs.

According to this study, the level of teenage sexual activity in the United States is approximately the same as in the other nations studied. Why, then, are rates of pregnancy among adolescents so much higher in this country? In comparison with the other five countries studied in detail, the United States has a higher level of religious belief and observance; perhaps as one result, the re-

searchers found a more puritanical view of adolescent sexual activity. In European countries, where a more "matter-of-fact" attitude toward teenage sexuality prevails, governments typically focus on preventing increased pregnancy and childbearing among adolescents rather than on restricting sexual behavior. Contraceptive services are made available to sexually active teenagers at low cost through national health programs.

Jacqueline Darroch Forrest, research director of the Alan Guttmacher Institute, suggests that "teenagers in the United States are less likely to use contraception and among those who do use it, they are less likely to use the pill, which is considered to be the most effective method." The authors of the study observe that a comprehensive sex education program which emphasizes both the sexual and the emotional components of intimate relationships—such as the official curriculum taught in all grades in Sweden—can be a major factor in reducing rates of pregnancy among adolescents. The researchers conclude that the United States should follow the lead of western European countries by making both contraception and sex education more available to teenagers.

SOURCES: Brozan, 1985:A1, C7; Henshaw and Van Vort, 1989; E. Jones et al., 1985, 1986.

a significant portion of their adolescence in one-parent homes (Kotulak, 1986).

Whether judged in economic or emotional terms, the lives of single parents and their children are not inevitably more difficult than life in a traditional nuclear family. It is as inaccurate to assume that a single-parent family is necessarily "deprived" as it is to assume that a two-parent family is always secure and happy. Nevertheless, life in a single-parent family can be extremely stressful. Ronald Haskins, director of the Child Development Institute at the University of North Carolina, observes: "It's a big and risky undertaking when so many parents try to raise so many children alone" (Mann, 1983:62).

There is a clear association between the increase in families headed by single mothers and the feminization of poverty (see Chapter 8). Families headed by divorced or never-married mothers represent the fastest-growing segment of the female poor. The economic problems of single mothers result from such factors as sex discrimination in the paid labor force, the high costs of child care, inadequate welfare benefits, and fathers' failure to pay court-ordered child support.

A family headed by a single mother faces especially difficult problems when the mother is a teenager. Currently, the United States has the highest birthrate for teenagers of any industrialized nation (see Box 13-3). The birthrate among unmarried teenagers in this country doubled between 1960 and 1985. In 1987, there were more than 930,000 births to unwed mothers in the United States; of these, nearly 33 percent were to teenagers. Young single mothers commonly must drop out of school; as a consequence, most have few marketable skills and become dependent on family members or welfare benefits for financial support (Bureau of the Census, 1990a:67).

Why might low-income teenage women wish to have children and face the obvious financial difficulties of motherhood? Viewed from an interactionist perspective, these women tend to have low self-esteem and limited options; a child may provide a sense of motivation and purpose for a teenager whose economic worth in our society is limited at best. Given the barriers that many young women face because of their gender, race, ethnicity, and class, many teenagers may believe that they have little to lose and much to gain by having a child. In a 1988 survey of 13,000 high school sophomores from varied economic backgrounds, one out of four said that they would consider having a child if they became pregnant while unmarried. A follow-up study showed that these respondents were two to three times more likely than their reluctant peers to actually have become mothers (Abrahamse et al., 1988; V. Alexander et al., 1987; Gimenez, 1987; Zelnick and Young, 1982).

Variations in American Family Life

Within the United States, there are many variations in family life associated with distinctions of social class, race, and ethnicity. An examination of such variations will give us a more sophisticated understanding of contemporary family styles in our country.

Social Class Differences Various studies have documented the differences in family organization among social classes in the United States. In the upper class, there is a particular emphasis on lineage and maintenance of family position. One is considered not simply a member of a nuclear family but rather a member of a larger family tradition ("the Rockefellers" or "the Kennedys"). As a result, upper-class families are quite concerned about what they see as "proper training" for children.

Lower-class families do not often have the luxury of worrying about the "family name"; they must first struggle to pay their bills and survive the crises often associated with life in poverty. Such families are more likely to have only one parent in the home, a situation which presents special challenges in terms of child care and financial needs. Children in lower-class families typically assume adult responsibilities—including marriage and parenthood—at an earlier age than children of affluent homes. In part, this is because they may lack the money needed to remain in school.

Social class differences in family life may not be as striking as they once were. In the past, family specialists agreed that there were pronounced contrasts in child-rearing practices. Lower-class families were found to be more authoritarian in rearing children and more inclined to use physical punishment. Middle-class families were more permissive and more restrained in punishing their children. However, these differences may have narrowed as more and more families from all social classes have turned to the same books, magazines, and even television talk shows for advice on rearing children (M. Kohn, 1970; Luster et al., 1989).

Among the poor, adult women often play a significant role in the economic support of the family. Adult males may earn low wages, may be unemployed, or may be absent from the family. In 1989, 32 percent of all families headed by women with no husband present were below the government poverty line. This compared with only 6 percent for all traditional dual-parent families (Bureau of the Census, 1990b:11).

Many racial and ethnic groups appear to have distinctive family characteristics. However, racial and class factors are often closely related. In examining family life among racial and ethnic minorities, we must remember that certain patterns may be the result of class as well as cultural factors.

Racial and Ethnic Differences It is often assumed that racial and ethnic minorities in the United States find it difficult to maintain healthy family lives because of prejudice and discrimination (see Chapter 10). However, the majority of Black families have maintained two-parent family environments.

There are many negative and inaccurate stereotypes in the United States regarding the African American family. It is true that a significantly higher proportion of Black than of White families have no husband present in the home (see Figure 13-3). Yet Black single mothers are often part of stable, functioning kin networks, despite the pressures of sexism and racism. Members of these networks—predominantly female kin such as mothers, grandmothers, and aunts—share goods and services and thereby ease financial strains. In addition to these strong kinship bonds, Black family life has emphasized deep religious commitment and high aspirations for achievement. The strengths of the Black family were evident during

FIGURE 13-3 One-Parent Families among Blacks and Whites, 1970 and 1988

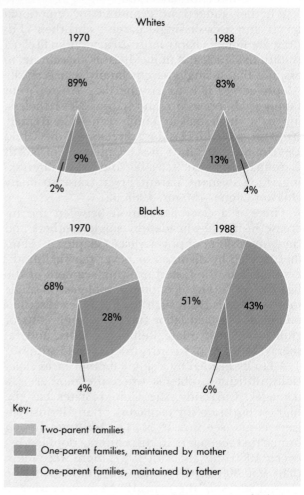

SOURCES: Bureau of the Census, 1990a:38; Department of Labor, 1986.

In 1988, 43 percent of Black families, but only 13 percent of White families, were maintained by the mother with no husband in the home.

slavery, when Blacks demonstrated a remarkable ability to maintain family ties despite the fact that the slave enjoyed no legal protections (Gimenez, 1987; R. Hill, 1972, 1987).

Sociologists have also taken note of differences in family patterns between other racial and ethnic groups. For example, Mexican American men have been described as exhibiting a sense of virility, of personal worth, and of pride in their maleness that is called *machismo.* Mexican Americans are also described as being more familistic than many other subcultures. *Familism* refers to pride in the extended family expressed through the maintenance of close ties and strong obligations to kinfolk outside the immediate family (S. Wallace, 1984).

Research data indicate that machismo and familism are in decline among Mexican Americans. Various factors, including the feminist movement, urbanization, upward mobility, and assimilation make machismo and familism more of a historical footnote with each passing generation. Like earlier immigrants from Europe and Asia, Mexican Americans are likely to gradually adopt the norms of the dominant culture regarding family life (J. Moore and Pachon, 1985:96–98; E. Stevens, 1973).

Violence in the Family

A television reporter wears long-sleeved, high-collared blouses to hide her bruises. Her husband, a businessman, frequently batters her body but never touches her face. The reporter once filed charges against him but later dropped them out of fear that the beating might become public knowledge.

Deidre still has painful flashbacks about her abusive stepfather. The smell of a country barn or the scent of the after-shave he used to wear brings it all back: how he forced her to have sex with him at the family's rural home. Deidre's mother was sick; her stepfather made the child believe that her mother would die if she told her the truth (*Changing Times,* 1981; R. Watson, 1984:32).

Wife battering, child abuse, abuse of the elderly (see Chapter 12), and other forms of domestic violence are an ugly reality of family life in the United States. In a sense, domestic violence begins even before marriage in the form of violent behavior within dating and courtship relationships. According to a 1990 review of recent research, while there has been great variance from survey to survey, as many as 67 percent of high school and college students have reported that they have been the victims of such attacks. As with other forms of abuse, victims of courtship violence are reluctant to tell others about their experiences; if they do, they typically tell their peers rather than their parents or teachers. This lack of early intervention is especially regrettable, since studies of battered women in shelters indicate that 51 percent have been physically abused in

(Rick Friedman/Black Star)

Child abuse and other forms of domestic violence are an ugly reality of American family life. This drawing was made by a sexually abused child.

earlier dating relationships (Gelles and Cornell, 1990:65–66).

Violence during dating resembles other assaults in that it may involve pushing, slapping, punching, hitting with a weapon, and choking. Yet its consequences differ in one important respect: assaults or rapes by strangers leave victims wary of being alone, but rape by an acquaintance often causes the victim to become fearful of trusting someone again or forming close relationships. According to victimization surveys, one-third of victims of reported rapes identify the attacker as an acquaintance or date (Makepeace, 1986).

It is difficult to measure precisely the prevalence of domestic violence, since many Americans are reluctant to call the police or bring charges against family members. With so many cases remaining unreported, researchers find it difficult to determine whether the level of domestic violence in the United States is increasing or decreasing. Studies find that 20 to 40 percent of couples seeking divorce cite "physical abuse" as their major complaint, while married couples who are not contemplating divorce report a similar incidence of violence. Moreover, consistently throughout the 1970s and 1980s, 34 percent of all female murder victims in the United States—more than 2800 a year—were killed by members of their own families. Family violence, of course, is a worldwide problem; it can be especially harsh in societies that devalue particular members of the family circle, such as children born outside of marriage, stepchildren, disabled children, female babies, or wives in general (Gelles and Cornell, 1990:28–31, 67–68; Gelles et al., 1988; T. Randall, 1990b:940; Stocks, 1988).

Wife battering, as in the case of the television reporter described earlier, is all too common. According to a survey published in 1984, one in four wives report that they have been slapped by their husbands. One in 6 have been forced to have sex against their will, one in 10 have been beaten with fists, and one in 18 have been threatened with weapons by their husbands (Andrews, 1984; Ferraro and Johnson, 1983).

Even with regard to child abuse, public concern has been rather recent. In 1976, for example, national surveys revealed that only about 10 percent of Americans viewed child abuse as a serious problem. By 1983, the proportion had increased to 90 percent. With growing public awareness has come a rise in the reporting of such incidents. In 1976, 669,000 cases of child abuse were reported to state and local authorities; by 1987, that figure had increased to about 2.2 million. According to the National Committee for the Prevention of Child Abuse, about 1300 children in the United States died in 1988 alone as a result of abuse or neglect (Gelles and Cornell, 1990:47, 50; Magnuson, 1983).

Viewed from a conflict perspective, domestic violence should be seen in terms of dominance and control. It is one means by which men reinforce their power over women and adults reinforce their power over children. Nevertheless, despite the obvious inequities in domestic violence cases, victims of such assaults are often accused of "asking for" or provoking the abusive behavior. This is a classic example of "blaming the victim" for the misdeeds of others (refer back to Box 8-2 on page 244). In the case of wife beating, for example, feminists and conflict theorists emphasize that blaming the victim is but another reflection of men's power over women (K. Quinn et al., 1984:2; Stets and Pirog-Good, 1987; see also Caputi and Russell, 1990).

Intervention in cases of domestic violence may draw upon an interactionist approach by attempting to bolster the self-esteem of victims. Existing programs dealing with wife beating avoid telling the women what to do; instead, they help them to assess their internal strengths, and they provide information about available resources. Counselors typically believe that the female victim should not blame herself or excuse the offender. When working with men who are batterers, counselors encourage them to accept responsibility for their violent behavior and to learn other, nonabusive ways of communicating their feelings (C. Anderson and Rouse, 1988:139).

The magnitude of the problem is indeed distressing. Some form of violence occurs in 25 percent of all marriages. Of those women needing emergency surgical procedures, at least one in every five—and perhaps as many as one in three—is a victim of domestic violence. Sociologist Murray Straus has estimated that at least 8 million people in the United States are assaulted every year by family members. Straus suggests that people are far too tolerant of domestic violence because there is a common feeling that what goes on behind closed doors in nobody else's business (Kantrowitz, 1988:59; T. Randall, 1990a:939; see also M. Straus and Gelles, 1990).

DIVORCE IN THE UNITED STATES

"Do you promise to love, honor, and cherish . . . until death do you part?" Every year, large numbers of Americans of all social classes and racial and ethnic groups make such legally binding agreements. Yet an increasing number of these promises are apparently not realistic, given our nation's rising divorce rate.

Statistical Trends in Divorce

Just how common is divorce? Surprisingly, this is not a simple question. Divorce statistics are difficult to collect and even more difficult to interpret.

The media frequently report that one out of every two marriages end in divorce. However, this figure is misleading, since it is based on a comparison of all divorces which occur in a single year (regardless of when the couples were married) against the number of new marriages in the same year. As the first column of Table 13-2 indicates, there were 51.3 divorces in 1990 for every 100 new marriages. But that could, in fact, represent 51.3 divorces for every 3000 marriages that occurred in the decades leading up to 1990.

A more accurate perspective on divorce can be obtained if we examine the number of divorces per 1000 married women (see the second column in Table 13-2). In the early 1970s, the divorce rate per 1000 married women exceeded the all-time high set in 1946. Using these statistics, we can see that the number of divorces per 1000 married women has more than doubled over the last 30 years. Nevertheless, about half of couples remain married; about 70 percent of those who obtain a divorce before age 35 later remarry, half of those within 3 years after a first divorce (Bumpass et al., 1990; J. Sweet and Bumpass, 1987).

While the nation's high rate of remarriage is regarded as an endorsement of the institution of marriage, it does lead to the new challenges of a remarriage kin network composed of current and prior marital relationships. This network can be particularly complex if children are involved or if an ex-spouse remarries. As is shown in Figure 13-4 (page 402), by 1989 about 15 percent of children in the United States lived with a parent and a stepparent.

A study published in early 1989 predicts that about two-thirds of all first marriages in the United States are likely to end in separation or divorce. In the view of Teresa Castro Martin and Larry L. Bumpass of the Center for Demography

TABLE 13-2   Divorce Rates in the United States

YEAR	DIVORCES PER 100 MARRIAGES PERFORMED	DIVORCES PER 1000 MARRIED WOMEN, 15 YEARS OLD AND OVER
1920	13.4	8.0
1930	17.0	7.5
1940	16.9	8.7
1946	26.6	17.8
1950	23.1	10.3
1960	25.8	9.2
1970	32.8	14.9
1980	49.7	22.6
1990	51.3	24.2[a]

[a]Data for 1989.
SOURCES: National Center for Health Statistics, 1974, 1990, 1991; authors' estimates.

Divorce rates have fluctuated since World War II, but represent a two- to threefold increase from pre-1940 levels.

FIGURE 13-4 Living Arrangements of Children by Type of Family, 1989

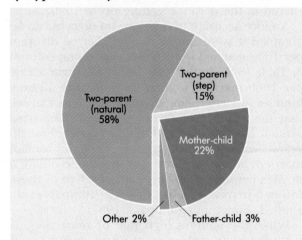

Two-parent (natural) 58%

Two-parent (step) 15%

Mother-child 22%

Other 2%

Father-child 3%

SOURCES: Bureau of the Census, 1989c:16, 1990f:3; and authors' estimates.

As of 1989, less than 60 percent of children under 18 years old in the United States lived in two-parent families with both their biological parents.

and Ecology, University of Wisconsin, the decline in divorces in the United States between 1980 and 1987 does not mean that a long-term return to more stable family life is under way. The researchers (1989:49) conclude that the "diversity in family life created by patterns of divorce and remarriage is likely an intrinsic feature of modern family life rather than a temporary aberration."

The current high divorce rate of the United States is not the result of a sudden explosion; rather, signs of such a tendency can be seen even in early American history. Residents of colonial America could receive divorces more easily than their counterparts anywhere in the western world. The divorce rate in the United States doubled between 1900 and 1920 and rose steadily until 1980, when it began to level off. Furthermore, the country's *teenage* divorce rate is more than twice the overall national average (Bureau of the Census, 1990a:88).

Divorce is a complex and difficult experience for all family members. Anthropologist Paul

Bohannan (1970) has identified six overlapping experiences which arise from divorce and which vary in intensity depending on the couple. The "six stations of divorce," as Bohannan calls them, include:

1 *Emotional divorce*, which represents the problem of the deteriorating marriage
2 *Legal divorce*, based upon the grounds on which the marriage will be dissolved
3 *Economic divorce*, which deals with the division of money and property
4 *Coparental divorce*, which includes decisions regarding child custody and visitation rights
5 *Community divorce*, or the changes in friendships and institutional ties that a divorced person experiences
6 *Psychic divorce*, focused on the person's attempt to regain autonomy and self-esteem.

As Bohannan has observed, the "undivorced" rarely appreciate the difficulties that the divorced person experiences in mastering these stations of divorce (Gerstel, 1987).

An increasing number of families in the United States are coping with the traumas of divorce by experimenting with joint or shared custody arrangements. Joint custody has become popular, since it allows each parent meaningful time with children and promotes an egalitarian sharing of decision-making authority. However, adults unable to live together as husband and wife may find it difficult to cooperate in resolving important issues of parenthood. Three recent studies by psychologist Judith Wallerstein and her colleagues suggest that joint custody arrangements do not benefit all children and, in certain instances, may be harmful for children whose parents have separated or divorced. As of 1986, 30 states allowed joint custody, but only 13 of these states regarded this as the preferred child custody arrangement (Brozan, 1984; Chesler, 1986; Kolata, 1988; Sweeney, 1983; J. Wallerstein and Blakeslee, 1989).

Factors Associated with Divorce

Why does the United States have such a high frequency of divorce? There is no fully satisfactory answer to this question. Table 13-3 indicates factors which are associated with a higher probability of divorce among married couples. In addition to these strains in each individual relationship, however, there are overall social changes which contribute to the nation's rising divorce rate.

Perhaps the most important factor in the increase in divorce throughout the twentieth century has been the greater social acceptance of divorce. In particular, this increased tolerance has resulted from a relaxation of negative attitudes toward divorce among various religious denominations. Although divorce is still seen as unfortunate, it is no longer treated as an unpardonable sin by most religious leaders (Gerstel, 1987; Thornton, 1985).

A few other factors deserve mention. Many states have adopted more liberal divorce laws in the last 2 decades. Divorce has become a more practical option in newly formed families, since they now tend to have fewer children than in the past. A general increase in family incomes, coupled with the availability of free legal aid for some poor people, has meant that more couples can afford the traditionally high legal costs of divorce proceedings. Finally, as society provides greater opportunities for women, more and more wives are becoming less dependent on their husbands—both economically and emotionally. They may then feel more able to leave if the marriage seems hopeless. The most extreme cause of marital breakdown, domestic violence, was discussed earlier in the chapter.

No-Fault Divorce

A major transformation in American family law has taken place in the last 2 decades through the

TABLE 13-3 Likelihood of Divorce

FACTORS ASSOCIATED WITH HIGHER PROBABILITY OF DIVORCE
Marriage at a very young age (15 to 19 years old)
Short acquaintanceship before marriage
Short engagement or no engagement
Parents with unhappy marriages
Disapproval of marriage expressed by kin and friends
General dissimilarity in background
Membership in different religious faiths
Failure to attend religious services
Disagreement of husband and wife on role obligations
Urban background
FACTORS ASSOCIATED WITH LOWER PROBABILITY OF DIVORCE
Marriage at or above the average ages 25 years old for males, 23 years old for females
Acquaintanceship of 2 years or more before marriage
Engagement of 6 months or more
Parents with happy marriage
Approval of marriage expressed by kin and friends
Similarity of background
Membership in same religious faith
Regular attendance at religious services
Agreement of husband and wife on role obligations
Rural background

SOURCES: Adapted from Goode, 1976:537–538; see also Fergusson et al., 1984. Median age of marriage from Bureau of the Census, 1990a:87.

Research has shown that many factors are associated with greater or lesser probability of divorce.

"Congratulations on your divorce!" exclaims this greeting card. The greater acceptance of marital dissolution in American society has led to a new custom—sending cards to people congratulating them on their divorce.

introduction of no-fault divorce laws. **No-fault divorce** is a process whereby divorce is granted without proving one of the parties guilty of marital misconduct (J. Friedman, 1984:166). In 1970, California became the first state to institute a no-fault divorce law. Currently, all states but South Dakota have some type of no-fault provision; at least 18 states have "pure" no-fault divorce laws in which irretrievable marital breakdown is the *only* grounds for dissolving a marriage (Spanier and Anderson, 1979; Weitzman, 1985:41).

No-fault divorce legislation represents a radical departure from traditional fault-based divorce law. Under the adversary system of divorce, courts carefully assess the past behavior of each spouse to determine who is at fault. Ideally, courts will deliver moral justice to the "good spouse" while assigning punishment (often in financial terms) to the "bad spouse." By contrast, no-fault laws ignore the couple's moral history as a basis for divorce awards. Such laws instead attempt to provide an equitable dissolution based upon the needs of the two parties and any dependent children (Weitzman and Dixon, 1983).

Supporters of no-fault divorce argue that by avoiding issues of blame, no-fault proceedings can reduce the hostility of marital dissolution, thereby benefiting the two parties and their children. Unfortunately, the benefits of no-fault laws may be overshadowed by the economic consequences of this practice. Sociologist Lenore Weitzman (1985:339) conducted a 10-year study of the social, economic, and legal consequences of California's no-fault law and found it to be a "financial catastrophe for most women." In the first year after a divorce, a woman's standard of living *decreases* by 73 percent, while her ex-husband's *increases* by 42 percent. These data confirm similar findings in an earlier study of 5000 American families conducted by the University of Michigan's Institute for Social Research (S. Hoffman and Holmes, 1976).

The differential impact of no-fault settlements is a direct result of the way in which American courts divide marital property. Requiring proof of fault had long provided the one protection for economically dependent homemakers and mothers. If a woman had not given her husband grounds for divorce, she could agree to the divorce on the grounds of her husband's behavior— but only if she had been assured of adequate economic support for herself and the couple's children (Weitzman, 1985; see also Arendell, 1986).

This decrease in women's standard of living also results from the fact that women generally assume custodial responsibility of the couple's children, whereas men are largely freed of this economic burden. Child support may be ordered by a court; however, according to Weitzman, it averages less than the costs of day care alone. Moreover, after experiencing a divorce, women are typically much less prepared to be self-supporting than men. While marriage gives men an opportunity to build their careers, it acts as more of a career liability for women.

Advocates of current no-fault divorce laws argue that "equitable distribution" of property has benefited women in states where formerly they were not entitled to any assets held in their husbands' names. In addition, some critics of Weitzman's study argue that she fails to distinguish adequately between settlements negotiated before a divorce trial and settlements that are, in fact, court-ordered.

Weitzman (1985) proposes changes in the divorce process which would preserve the no-fault ethic but eliminate its crippling consequences for women and children. The primary focus of these changes is on fairer standards for property division, alimony, and child support. For example, long-married older homemakers with little or no experience in the paid labor force would be granted a greater share of the marital assets. By contrast, payments to younger women would taper off as they become self-sufficient. Some states are revising their no-fault laws by giving judges more precise guidance in the division of marital property. Yet it remains difficult to accommodate the depressed postdivorce standard of living that many women with custody of their children must face (Lacayo, 1986).

ALTERNATIVE HOUSEHOLD ARRANGEMENTS

Some people are not satisfied with traditional marriage and family arrangements and prefer to live in some form of community with others. In a sense, they wish to create entirely new families, not necessarily including blood relatives or a spouse, with which they will live. Two such experiments in cooperative living are the Israeli kibbutz and the American commune.

The first kibbutzim were founded in 1910, long before the modern state of Israel was established. A **kibbutz** is a group of individuals and families joined together to constitute an economic and social community. Although conscious Marxist thinking is no longer a dominant part of kibbutz life, it was fundamental to the socialist pioneers who founded the kibbutz movement. Most kibbutzim began as collective farming enterprises, growing vegetables and fruits, but many have expanded into industrial production in recent decades.

Kibbutz life in Israel has attracted great interest because it represents an attempt to transform so-cialist ideology into day-to-day living. The kibbutz owns all assets of the community, and individual property ownership is discouraged. All members are involved in governance, which is typically handled in committee work and community meetings. Child care is considered a responsibility of the entire community rather than being totally delegated to the family. On many kibbutzim, children do not live in homes with their parents. Instead, they reside in special "children's houses" (Schlesinger, 1977; Spiro, 1954; Tiger and Shepher, 1975).

Like the kibbutz, the **commune** involves a form of cooperative living. Communes are perhaps the best known and least understood of alternative lifestyles. They are often incorrectly associated with the rebellious 1960s. Few Americans are aware that some of the nation's most influential

The Israeli kibbutz represents one of the world's best-known experiments in collective living. Shown is the nursery school at Kibbutz Eyn Hachoresch.

communes existed in colonial and nineteenth-century America. One such group was the Oneida community of New York State, founded in 1848 by a religious leader named John Noyes. In this community, not only private property but also exclusive sexual relationships were informally outlawed (Kephart and Zellner, 1991).

As of 1990, there were an estimated 3000 communes in the United States. They are found primarily in rural areas of the country, though they are occasionally established in urban centers. Many Americans join such communes in order to escape the sense of alienation and isolation that they encounter in the "straight" (conventional)

world. Often they live in communes for a few months or years and then return to more traditional living arrangements. Some communes have strict moral codes which sharply restrict sexual behavior and prohibit the use of drugs. Others have few rules; each member is free to do whatever he or she pleases within general standards established by the group (B. Berger, 1981; Larrabee, 1990; Zablocki, 1980).

The emergence of alternative lifestyles is no guarantee of basic changes in American family structure. Those people involved in experimental living arrangements still constitute a very small minority of the American people.

SOCIAL POLICY AND THE FAMILY

FAMILY LEAVE

- How do the family leave policies of the United States compare with those of other industrialized nations?
- How have the changes in family life in the United States affected the debate over family leave legislation?
- Why do restrictive family leave policies have a particularly harsh impact on women who work outside the home?

Even in 1990, James Callor remained bitter. Eight years earlier, his 6-year-old daughter Jaymee Ann was dying of cancer. Callor, who worked at a coal mine in Utah, asked for unpaid leave to be with his daughter, but his supervisor refused. Two weeks later, Jaymee Ann died. "I did everything I could for her," says Callor, "but it would have been a lot easier on our family if the company had seen fit to help" (L. Phillips, 1990:4A).

Like James Callor, most male and female employees in the United States are not able to take leave for the birth or adoption of children or for the care of ill family members. According to a 1989 survey by the Bureau of Labor Statistics, 37 percent of workers at companies with 100 or more employees are eligible for unpaid maternity leave, while 17 percent can take unpaid paternity leave, 2 percent can take paid maternity leave, and 1 percent can take paid paternity leave. (These disparities reflect the continuing impact

of traditional gender roles regarding which parent should care for infants.) Parental leaves are even less common in smaller firms; policies allowing leave time for adoption or the care of sick family members are rare in both large and small businesses (S. Holmes, 1990c; Meisenheimer, 1989:20–22).

As of mid-1991, the only federal legislation relevant to parental leave was the Pregnancy Discrimination Act of 1978, which prohibits discrimination in any granting of employment, promotion, job security, seniority rights, or disability benefits at the time of pregnancy or childbirth. The Families and Work Institute reports that, as of 1990, 13 states required parental leave for both mothers and fathers, while another 10 states mandated maternity but not paternity leave. Only 3 states guarantee leave for employees who adopt children, who need to care for a seriously ill family member, or who have a serious health problem themselves (*Congressional Digest*, 1988; Hackett, 1990a; T. Lewin, 1990e).

The United States remains the only industrialized nation which has no mandatory maternity leave. In 75 other countries, women who become pregnant can enjoy a paid maternity leave averaging between 4 and 5 months, with benefits averaging between 60 and 90 percent of the woman's standard wage. Many nations also offer women the option of an unpaid, job-protected leave for at least 1 year. Sweden, which has the most comprehensive parental leave policies in

Many American business firms continue to resist the idea of parental leave.

the world, allows parents to take up to 12 months of leave to care for children. As a means of encouraging more egalitarian family life, Sweden allows this leave time to be divided between a child's parents. While on parental leave, employees are paid from a national insurance fund; the employee receives 90 percent of his or her pay for the first 9 months of leave and a flat rate for the remaining 3 months (*Congressional Digest*, 1988:131; Hopper and Zigler, 1988:325; Meisenheimer, 1989:23).

During the 1980s, there was increasing pressure on policymakers in the United States to follow the lead of other countries and adopt strong family leave legislation. The critical factor contributing to the growing pressure has been the dramatic rise in the number of women, including mothers of young children, in the nation's paid labor force (refer back to Chapter 11). For many two-parent families, it is a financial necessity for both parents to earn income outside the home. If such families have a new baby or a child with a serious illness, a parent who wishes to provide home care may have to forfeit his or her wages and fringe benefits to do so. Medical leave issues are especially important for single-parent families, since the parent (generally a mother) may be the only person able to provide home care for a sick child. From a conflict perspective, the emotional and financial stresses associated with juggling work outside the home and caring for children fall heavily on women—and will continue to do so unless men assume equal responsibility for child care, housework, and other domestic tasks.

By 1990, a broad national coalition had come together to support federal family and medical leave legislation. Among the diverse organizations joined in

this effort were the Service Employees International Union, the National Organization for Women, the U.S. Catholic Conference, the Gray Panthers, and the Nine to Five National Association of Working Women. Proponents of family leave measures argue that they would strengthen family life by allowing parents time with infants or adopted children at crucial points of the life cycle, by giving parents a better opportunity to adjust to their new roles, and by providing job security for employees facing stressful life changes or crises. Supporters of family leave add that such policies would assist business firms by reducing job turnover, especially of female employees who are most likely to suffer from role strain. Given the lack of affordable, quality child care (refer back to Chapter 4), family leave is viewed as essential for both single-parent and dual-career families (*Congressional Digest,* 1988:142; Hopper and Zigler, 1988:333–335; Kantrowitz and Wingert, 1989).

The main opposition to family leave legislation has come from the business community, led by the United States Chamber of Commerce and the National Association of Manufacturers. Business groups insist that government should not intrude into the relationship between employer and employee, especially where benefits are involved. These organizations argue that mandatory family leave will reduce employers' flexibility in developing the best possible benefits packages for different groups of employees. Moreover, opponents of family leave legislation contend that such requirements will be particularly burdensome for small business firms that cannot afford additional benefits and that cannot easily move personnel to fill the slots of others on leave (*Congressional Digest*, 1988:129, 139).

A key disagreement between supporters and critics of family leave legislation has involved the projected costs of such a federal law. The Chamber of Commerce estimated the total cost of a national leave policy to be a staggering $27.2 billion, but a 1989 study by the General Accounting Office of the federal government put the annual cost at only $188 million, or about $5.30 per employee. The dire projections of business lobbyists were further undercut by a survey of 360 companies in Oregon, which has had a family leave law in effect since 1988. Researchers found that 93 percent of employers reported no increased work load for managers, more than 80 percent reported no increase in health insurance payments, and 66 percent reported no increase in administrative costs (Hackett, 1990a; S. Holmes, 1990c; see also Wisendale and Allison, 1989:188).

A federal family bill was first introduced in Congress in 1985 by Representative Patricia Schroeder. After years of debate and many revisions in proposed legislation, Congress passed the Family and Medical Leave Act in mid-1990. This measure required companies to grant workers up to 3 months of unpaid leave for the birth or adoption of children or for the care of sick family members. Employees who took such leaves for up to 3 months could do so without fear of losing their jobs. However, the act applied only to companies with at least 50 employees at a work site; as a result, 90 percent of the nation's business firms and 50 percent of all workers would have been exempt from the law's provisions (S. Holmes, 1990c).

Soon after its passage by the House of Representatives and the Senate, the Family and Medical Leave Act was vetoed by President George Bush. In his veto message, Bush stated that while he encouraged business firms to voluntarily offer family leaves to employees, he strongly objected to any federal requirement that companies do so. Business organizations cheered the president's veto, but Senator Christopher Dodd, the chief sponsor of family leave legislation in the Senate, promised: "George Bush is going to have a family leave bill on his desk every year he's in office" (S. Holmes, 1990d, 1990f:A16).

Despite the veto, the American public continues to voice strong support for family leave legislation. In a survey by Louis Harris Associates in mid-1990, 74 percent of respondents endorsed a law guaranteeing a woman up to 12 weeks of unpaid parental leave, while 24 percent opposed such a law and 2 percent were unsure. It is expected that the fight for family leave policies will shift to state legislatures. As of mid-1990, some 30 states had considered various types of family leave bills in the previous year (S. Holmes, 1990f; T. Lewin, 1990e).

SUMMARY

The *family,* although it has many varying forms, is present in all human cultures. This chapter examines the state of marriage and the family in the United States and considers alternatives to the traditional nuclear family.

1 There are many variations in the family from culture to culture and even within the same culture.

2 The structure of the *extended family* can offer certain advantages over that of the *nuclear family.*

3 Sociologists are not agreed on whether the *egalitarian family* has replaced the *patriarchal family* as the social norm in the United States.

4 Sociologists have identified six basic functions of the family: reproduction, protection, socialization, regulation of sexual behavior, companionship, and the providing of social status.

5 In the United States, love plays a significant role in the courtship process.

6 More and more Americans are choosing to remain single, and increasing numbers of people are living together without marrying.

7 Some married couples are defying traditional social norms by making a conscious decision not to have children.

8 Currently, the majority of all married couples have two partners active in the paid labor force.

9 Within American society, there are considerable variations in family life associated with social class, racial, and ethnic divisions.

10 It is difficult to measure precisely the prevalence of domestic violence, since many Americans are reluctant to call police or bring charges against family members.

11 Among the factors which contribute to the rising divorce rate in the United States are the greater social acceptance of divorce and the liberalization of divorce laws in many states.

12 Policymakers in the United States have considered measures that would require employers to provide their workers with unpaid family and medical leave.

KEY TERMS

Adoption In a legal sense, a process that allows for the transfer of the legal rights, responsibilities, and privileges of parenthood from legal parents to new legal parents. (page 394)

Bilateral descent A kinship system in which both sides of a person's family are regarded as equally important. (384)

Cohabitation The practice of living together as a male-female couple without marrying. (389)

Commune A small, self-supporting community joined voluntarily by people dedicated to cooperative living. (405)

Egalitarian family An authority pattern in which the adult members of the family are regarded as equals. (385)

Endogamy The restriction of mate selection to people within the same group. (387)

Exogamy The requirement that individuals select mates outside certain groups. (387)

Extended family A family in which relatives in addition to parents and children—such as grandparents, aunts, or uncles—live in the same home. (382)

Familism Pride in the extended family expressed through the maintenance of close ties and strong obligations to kinfolk. (399)

Family A set of people related by blood, marriage (or some other agreed-upon relationship), or adoption who share the responsibility for reproducing and caring for members of society. (381)

Incest taboo The prohibition of sexual relationships between certain culturally specified relatives. (388)

Kibbutz A collective society in Israel in which individuals and groups join together in an economic and social community. (405)

Kinship The state of being related to others. (384)

Machismo A sense of virility, personal worth, and pride in one's maleness. (399)

Marital power A term used by Blood and Wolfe to describe the manner in which decision making is distributed within families. (386)

Matriarchy A society in which women dominate in family decision making. (385)

Matrilineal descent A kinship system which favors the relatives of the mother. (384)

Matrilocal A pattern of residence in which a married couple lives with the wife's parents. (384)

Monogamy A form of marriage in which one woman and one man are married only to each other. (383)

Neolocal A pattern of residence in which a married couple establishes a separate residence. (384)

No-fault divorce A process whereby divorce is granted without proving one of the parties guilty of marital misconduct. (404)

Nuclear family A married couple and their unmarried children living together. (382)

Patriarchy A society in which men are expected to dominate family decision making. (385)

Patrilineal descent A kinship system which favors the relatives of the father. (384)

Patrilocal A pattern of residence in which a married couple lives with the husband's parents. (384)

Polyandry A form of polygamy in which a woman can have several husbands at the same time. (383)

Polygamy A form of marriage in which an individual can have several husbands or wives simultaneously. (383)

Polygyny A form of polygamy in which a husband can have several wives at the same time. (383)

Serial monogamy A form of marriage in which a person can have several spouses in his or her lifetime but can have only one spouse at a time. (383)

Single-parent families Families in which there is only one parent present to care for children. (395)

Social institutions Organized patterns of beliefs and behavior centered on basic social needs. (377)

ADDITIONAL READINGS

Blumstein, Philip, and Pepper Schwartz. *American Couples: Money, Work, Sex.* New York: Morrow, 1983. An ambitious examination of couples in the United States: married, cohabiting, lesbian, and gay male.

Cherlin, Andrew (ed.). *The Changing American Family and Public Policy.* Washington, D.C.: Urban Institute Press, 1988. A collection of articles considering the link between public policy and family-related issues in the United States.

Gelles, Richard J., and Claire Pedrick Cornell. *Intimate Violence in Families* (2d ed.). Newbury Park, Calif.: Sage, 1990. An examination of all aspects of domestic violence, including reviews of research on incidence. For a similar analysis, see M. Straus and Gelles, 1990.

Hertz, Rosanna. *More Equal Than Others: Women and Men in Dual-Career Marriages.* Berkeley: University of California Press, 1986. A study of the lives of dual-career corporate couples in 34 different organizations in the Chicago metropolitan area.

Mindel, Charles H., Robert W. Habenstein, and Roosevelt Wright, Jr. (eds.). *Ethnic Families in America: Patterns and Variations* (3d ed.). New York: Elsevier, 1988. A collection of articles on the family lives of various racial and ethnic groups in the United States, including Italian Americans, Greek Americans, and Irish Americans.

Mintz, Steven, and Susan Kellogg. *Domestic Revolutions: A Social History of American Family Life.* New York: Free Press, 1988. A historian and an anthropologist look at changes in family life in the United States over the last 4 centuries; they conclude that this social institution has changed dramatically in its structure, role, and conception.

Oved, Yaacov. *Two Hundred Years of American Communes.* New Brunswick, N.J.: Transaction, 1987. A comprehensive history of religious, secular, and socialist communes in the United States, among them Icaria, Ephrator, Oneida, and the Shaker communities.

Sussman, Marvin B., and Suzanne K. Steinmetz (eds.). *Handbook of Marriage and the Family.* New York: Plenum, 1982. An authoritative compilation of 30 original contributions covering family perspectives, diversity, life cycle processes, and therapy.

Weitzman, Lenore J. *The Divorce Revolution: The Unexpected Social and Economic Consequences for Women and Children in America.* New York: Free Press, 1985. A sociological examination of the impact of no-fault divorce laws on custody arrangements and property settlements.

Journals

Among the journals focusing on the family are *Family Planning Perspectives* (founded in 1969), *Family Relations* (1951), *International Family Planning Perspectives* (1975), *Journal of Family Issues* (1980), and *Journal of Marriage and the Family* (1938).

14

RELIGION

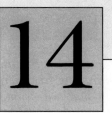

14

RELIGION

> *Congress shall make no law respecting an establishment of religion,*
> *or prohibiting the free exercise thereof.*
> First Amendment
> Constitution of the United States, 1787
>
> *Religion is the sigh of the oppressed creature, the feelings of a*
> *heartless world. . . . It is the opiate of the people.*
> Karl Marx
> Introduction to the Critique of the Hegelian
> Philosophy of Right, 1844

LOOKING AHEAD

- What are the manifest and latent functions of religion?
- Why did Karl Marx view religion as a form of social control within an oppressive society?
- What did Max Weber mean when he referred to the "Protestant ethic"?
- What are the basic forms of religious organization?
- Are women being accepted into the clergy of the United States?
- Why is religious fundamentalism on the rise in the United States and in other countries?
- What efforts are being made by religious groups to censor textbooks and other materials used in American public schools?

When Americans think of religion, a variety of diverse images come to mind. We may picture a solemn church service in a small New England town, a passionate revival meeting in the deep south, or a Hare Krishna group chanting on the streets of San Francisco. If we consider religions around the world, we may imagine Islamic travelers on a pilgrimage to Mecca, Orthodox Jews praying at the Western Wall of Jerusalem, or an African tribe engaged in a ritual celebrating the birth of a child.

In Chapter 3 various **cultural universals** were identified—general practices found in every culture—such as dancing, food preparation, the family, and personal names. Religion is clearly such a cultural universal; religious institutions are evident in all societies. At present, an estimated 4 billion people belong to the world's many religious faiths (see Figure 14-1).

Religion is found throughout the world because it offers answers to such ultimate questions as why we exist, why we succeed or fail, and why we die. It is difficult to determine with certainty when religious behavior began, but anthropological evidence suggests that such behavior was evident at least 100,000 years ago. The remains of early people in Europe reveal ceremonial burials with artifacts placed near the deceased, which implies that they believed in an afterlife. Apparently, the human species has long been preoccupied with spiritual concerns (Elaide, 1978; A. Wallace, 1966:224–227).

In contemporary industrial societies, scientific and technological advances have increasingly affected all aspects of life, including the social institution of religion. The term **secularization** refers to the process through which religion's influence on other social institutions diminishes. When this process occurs, religion will survive in the private sphere of individual and family life; indeed, it may thrive on a personal level. At the same time,

FIGURE 14-1 Proportion of the World Population by Religion

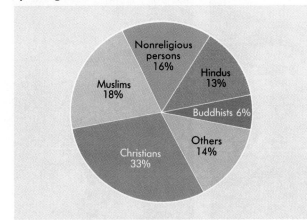

The world's two largest religious faiths are Christianity (accounting for 33 percent of the world population) and Islam (18 percent).

other social institutions—such as the economy, politics, and education—maintain their own sets of norms independent of religious guidance (McNamara, 1984:345–347; Shupe and Bromley, 1985:58).

This chapter will focus on religion as it has emerged in modern industrial societies. It will begin with a brief overview of the approaches that Émile Durkheim first introduced and those that later sociologists have used in studying religion. The basic functions of religion as a source of societal integration and social control and as a means of providing social support will be explored. Particular attention will be given to the insights of Karl Marx and Max Weber regarding the relationship between religion and social change. Three important dimensions of religious behavior—belief, ritual, and experience—will be examined, as will the basic forms of religious organization.

The remainder of the chapter will analyze the increasing influence of religion on contemporary life in the United States. Even within the same society, people turn to a variety of religions for answers to ultimate questions of existence. Therefore, the discussion examines not only the dominant religious beliefs and practices of organized Christian faiths but also the rich spiritual and cultural tradition of American Jews. The revival of a conservative approach to religion, termed *resurgent fundamentalism,* will be studied. Finally, the social policy section of the chapter will examine the controversy over censorship of textbooks and other materials used in public school curricula.

DURKHEIM AND THE SOCIOLOGICAL APPROACH TO RELIGION

The purpose of this chapter is to describe the role of religion from a sociological perspective. Sociologists are interested in the social impact of religion on individuals and institutions. Consequently, if a group believes that it is being directed by a "vision from God," a sociologist will not attempt to prove or disprove this "revelation." Instead, he or she will assess the effects of the religious experience on the group (McGuire, 1981:1–2).

Émile Durkheim was perhaps the first sociologist to recognize the critical importance of religion in human societies. He saw its appeal for the individual, but—more important—he stressed the *social* impact of religion. In Durkheim's view, religion is a collective act and includes many forms of behavior in which people interact with others. As in his work on suicide (see Chapter 1), Durkheim was not so interested in the personalities of religious believers as he was in understanding religious behavior within a social context.

Durkheim initiated sociological analysis of religion by defining **religion** as a "unified system of beliefs and practices relative to sacred things." In his formulation, religion involves a set of beliefs and practices that are uniquely the property of religion—as opposed to other social institutions and ways of thinking. Durkheim (1947:37, original edition 1912) argued that religious faiths distinguish between the everyday world and certain events that transcend the ordinary. He referred to these realms as the *sacred* and the *profane.*

Religion can take many forms. Shown are Hindus bathing in the Ganges River and worshippers at a Jain temple in India, and lamas performing a religious ritual on New Year's Day in Tibet.

The **sacred** encompasses those elements beyond everyday life which inspire awe, respect, and even fear. People become a part of the sacred realm only by completing some ritual, such as prayer or sacrifice. Believers have faith in the sacred; this faith allows them to accept what they cannot understand. By contrast, the **profane** includes the ordinary and commonplace. Interestingly, the same object can be either sacred or profane depending on how it is viewed. A normal dining room table is profane, but it becomes sacred to Christians if it bears the elements of a

カさねガさねの神だのみ。

ご注意ください、傘の置き忘れ。

Émile Durkheim's distinction between the sacred and the profane is evident in this poster distributed by the Tokyo subway system. A sorrowful figure of Jesus urges absent-minded riders not to leave umbrellas in subway cars. While an image of Jesus is sacred for Christians, it is used in a profane manner in Japan—a nation whose dominant faiths are Shintō and Buddhism.

communion. For Confucians and Taoists, incense sticks are not mere decorative items; they are highly valued offerings to the gods in religious ceremonies marking new and full moons.

Following the direction established by Durkheim almost a century ago, contemporary sociologists evaluate religions in two different ways. The norms and values of religious faiths can be studied through examination of their substantive religious beliefs. For example, we can compare the degree to which Christian faiths literally interpret the Bible, or Muslim groups follow the Qur'an (or Koran), the sacred book of Islam. At the same time, religions can be evaluated in terms of the social functions they fulfill, such as providing social support or reinforcing the social norms. By exploring both the beliefs and the functions of religion, we can better understand its impact on the individual, on groups, and on society as a whole.

FUNCTIONS OF RELIGION

Since religion is a cultural universal, it is not surprising that it fulfills several basic functions within human societies. In sociological terms, these include both manifest and latent functions (see Chapter 1). Among the manifest (open and stated) functions of religion are defining the spiritual world and giving meaning to the divine. Because of its beliefs concerning people's relationships to a beyond, religion provides an explanation for events that seem difficult to understand.

By contrast, latent functions of religion are unintended, covert, or hidden. Church services provide a manifest function by offering a forum for religious worship; at the same time, they fulfill a latent function as a meeting ground for unattached members.

In viewing religion as a social institution, sociologists evaluate its impact on human societies. The first two functions of religion that will be discussed in this section—integration and social control—are oriented toward the larger society. Thus, they are best understood from a macro-level viewpoint in terms of the relationship between religion and society as a whole. The third function—providing social support—is more oriented toward the individual and can be understood more effectively from a micro-level viewpoint. The fourth function, promoting social change, is illustrated using Max Weber's macro-level concept of the Protestant ethic.

The Integrative Function of Religion

Émile Durkheim viewed religion as an integrative power in human society—a perspective reflected in functionalist thought today. Durkheim was concerned with a perplexing question: "How can human societies be held together when they are generally composed of individuals and social groups with diverse interests and aspirations?" In his view, religious bonds often transcend these personal and divisive forces. Durkheim acknowledged that religion is not the only integrative force—nationalism or patriotism may serve the same end.

Why should religion provide this "societal glue"? Religion, whether it be Buddhism, Christianity, or Judaism, offers people meaning and purpose for their lives. It gives them certain ultimate values and ends to hold in common. Although subjective and not always fully accepted, these values and ends help a society to function as an integrated social system. For example, the Christian ritual of communion not only celebrates a historical event in the life of Jesus (the last supper) but also represents a participation in the unity (communion) of believers. Similarly, funerals, weddings, bar and bat mitzvahs, and confirmations serve to integrate people into larger communities by providing shared beliefs and values about the ultimate questions of life.

The integrative function of religion is particularly apparent in traditional, preindustrial societies. In these cultures, gathering of crops, exercise of authority by leaders, relationships among kinfolk, and artistic expression are all governed by religious beliefs and rituals. In industrial societies, religion helps to integrate newcomers by providing a source of identity. For example, Italian American immigrants, after settling in their new social environment, came to identify strongly with the Catholic church. Many Italian Catholic congregations in American cities became neighborhood centers that helped members to preserve their ethnic heritage while adjusting to an unfamiliar culture. In a rapidly changing world, religious faith can provide an important sense of belonging. Later in this chapter, we will see that the failure of traditional religions to satisfy people's need for identity has contributed to the rise of religious cults in the United States (Greeley, 1972:108–126; K. Roberts, 1984:57–58).

There is probably no better example of a nationally unifying religious symbol than the Virgin

(Alain Dejean/Sygma)

In recent years, Lebanon has been the scene of bitter clashes between native Christians and Muslims, as well as fighting involving Israelis, Palestinians, and Syrians. The soldier shown in the foreground is a Lebanese Christian who carries the image of a madonna on his rifle.

of Guadalupe of Mexico. According to the accepted account, the Virgin Mary appeared in 1531 to Juan Diego, a Christianized Indian, and commanded him to inform church officials of her desire to see a church built in her honor in Guadalupe. Diego failed at first to gain approval for the new church, but then, on the direction of the Virgin Mary, placed some roses in a cloak and presented this cloak to the archbishop. Astonished, the archbishop opened the cloak to find the Virgin's image stamped on it. The church was subsequently built, and Diego's cloak still hangs on the central altar with the miraculous image.

This story and church are accepted in Mexico as symbols of salvation and success. It gives Indians a unique role in the history of Christianity in Mexico—both in terms of their place in society and in heaven. The account of Diego and his vision is also integrative from a historical perspective, since the site of his vision was a shrine to Tonantzin, a much-loved Aztec goddess of earth and maize. The names of Guadalupe and Tonantzin are still used interchangeably by some Indians living in central Mexico (W. Johnson, 1961:136; Wolf, 1979).

Although the integrative impact of religion has been emphasized here, it should be noted that religion is not the *dominant* force maintaining social cohesion in contemporary industrial societies. People are also bound together by patterns of consumption, laws, nationalistic feelings, and other forces. Moreover, in some instances religious loyalties are dysfunctional; they contribute to tension and even conflict between groups or nations. During the Second World War, the Nazis attempted to exterminate the Jewish people, and approximately 6 million European Jews were killed. In modern times, nations such as Lebanon (Muslims versus Christians), Northern Ireland (Roman Catholics versus Protestants), and India (Hindus versus Muslims and, more recently, Sikhs) have been torn by clashes that are in part based on religion.

Religion and Social Control: The Marxist Critique

As we saw in the quotation beginning the chapter, Karl Marx described religion as an "opiate" particularly harmful to oppressed peoples. In his view, religion often drugged the masses into submission by offering a consolation for their harsh lives on earth: the hope of salvation in an ideal afterlife. For example, during the period of slavery in the American south, White masters forbade Blacks to practice native African religions, while encouraging them to adopt the Christian religion. Through Christianity, slaves were prodded to obey their masters; they were told that obedience would lead to salvation and eternal happiness in the hereafter. Viewed from a conflict perspective, Christianity may have pacified certain slaves and blunted the rage that often fuels rebellion (McGuire, 1981:186; J. Yinger, 1970:598).

Marx acknowledged that religion plays an important role in legitimating the existing social structure. The values of religion, as already noted, reinforce other social institutions and the social order as a whole. From Marx's perspective, religion promoted stability within society and therefore helps to perpetuate patterns of social inequality. In a society with several religious faiths, the dominant religion will represent the ruling economic and political class.

Marx concurred with Durkheim's emphasis on the collective and socially shared nature of religious behavior. At the same time, he was concerned that religion would reinforce social control within an oppressive society. Marx argued that religion's focus on otherworldly concerns diverted attention from earthly problems and from needless suffering created by unequal distribution of valued resources (Harap, 1982).

Religion reinforces the interests of those in power. For example, India's traditional caste system defined the social structure of that society, at least among the Hindu majority (see Chapter 8). The caste system was almost certainly the creation of the priesthood, but it also served the interests of India's political rulers by granting a certain religious legitimacy to social inequality.

Even in societies not as visibly ruled by religious dogma, religion legitimates the political sector. Military chaplains work to maintain the morale of combat troops during warfare; they do not counsel that taking a human life is morally wrong. The Dutch Reformed church in South Africa—the church of most South African governmental leaders—has traditionally insisted that the regime's policy of apartheid reflects God's intention that certain racial groups be kept separate (refer back to Chapter 10). This "legitimating function of religion," as Max Weber called it, may be used to explain, justify, or rationalize the exercise of power. Whether through the divine right of a monarch or the administration of an oath of office on a Bible, religion provides legitimacy for political rulers and leaders (P. Berger, 1973:311; Marty, 1987).

In the view of Karl Marx and later conflict theorists, religion is not necessarily a beneficial or admirable force for social control. For example, contemporary Christianity, like the Hindu faith, reinforces traditional patterns of behavior that call for the subordination of the powerless. Assumptions about gender roles leave women in a subservient position both within Christian churches and at home. In fact, women find it as difficult to achieve leadership positions in many churches as they do in large corporations (see Box 14-3 on page 434). While women play a significant role as volunteers in community churches, men continue to make the major theological and financial judgments for nationwide church organizations. Conflict theorists argue that to whatever extent religion actually does influence social behavior, it reinforces existing patterns of dominance and inequality.

From a Marxist perspective, religion functions as an "agent of de-politicization" (J. Wilson, 1978:355–356). In simpler terms, religion keeps people from seeing their lives and societal conditions in political terms—for example, by obscuring the overriding significance of conflicting economic interests. Marxists suggest that by inducing a "false consciousness" among the disadvantaged (see Chapter 8), religion lessens the possibility of collective political action that can end capitalist oppression and transform society.

It should be noted, however, that religious leaders have sometimes been in the forefront of movements for social change. During the 1960s, Dr. Martin Luther King, Jr., supported by numerous ministers, priests, and rabbis, fought for civil rights for Blacks. In the 1980s, many religious groups spoke out against the involvement of the United States in the arms race. The efforts of religious groups to promote social change extend beyond the United States; in Box 14-1 we focus on religious activism in Latin America.

Religion and Social Support

Most of us find it difficult to accept the stressful events of life—death of a loved one, serious injury, bankruptcy, divorce, and so forth. This is especially true when something "senseless" happens. How can family and friends come to terms

In times of tragedy, religion provides social support and helps people cope with their problems. In this photograph, a woman is comforted at the funeral of a police officer.

(Michael Grecco/Stock, Boston)

with the death of a talented college student, not even 20 years old, from a terminal disease?

Through its emphasis on the divine and supernatural, religion allows us to "do something" about the calamities we face. In some faiths, one can offer sacrifices or pray to a deity with the belief that it will change one's earthly condition. At a more basic level, religion encourages us to view our personal misfortunes as relatively unimportant in the broader perspective of human history—or even as part of an undisclosed divine purpose. Friends and relatives of the deceased college student may see this death as being "God's will" and as having some ultimate benefit that we cannot understand. This perspective may be much more comforting than the terrifying feeling that any of us can die senselessly at any moment—and that there is no divine "answer" as to why one person lives a long and full life whereas another dies tragically at a relatively early age.

As we saw earlier, religion offers consolation to oppressed peoples by giving them hope that they can achieve salvation and eternal happiness in an

BOX 14-1 • AROUND THE WORLD

LIBERATION THEOLOGY

Many religious activists, especially in Latin America, support *liberation theology,* which refers to use of a church in a political effort to eliminate poverty, discrimination, and other forms of injustice evident in secular society. Advocates of this religious movement sometimes display a sympathy for Marxism; many believe that radical liberation, rather than economic development in itself, is the only acceptable solution to the desperation of the masses in impoverished developing countries. Despite resistance from Pope John Paul II and others in the Catholic hierarchy—who insist that clergy should adhere to traditional pastoral duties and keep a distance from radical politics—activists associated with liberation theology believe that organized religion has a moral responsibility to take a strong public stand against the oppression of the poor, racial and ethnic minorities, and women (Berryman, 1987; Boff and Boff, 1984; Leathers, 1984:1161; R. Wright, 1987:B2).

The term *liberation theology* has a recent origin, dating back to the 1973 publication of the English translation of *A Theology of Liberation.* This book was written by a Peruvian priest, Gustavo Gutiérrez, who lived in a slum area of Lima during the early 1960s. After years of exposure to the vast poverty around him, Gutiérrez concluded: "The poverty was a destructive thing, something to be fought against and destroyed. . . . It became crystal clear that in order to serve the poor, one had to move into political action" (R. Brown, 1980:23).

Gutiérrez's discoveries took place during a time of increasing radicalization among Latin American intellectuals and students. An important element in their radicalization was the theory of *dependencia,* developed by Brazilian and Chilean social scientists, which argued that the reason for Latin America's continued underdevelopment was its dependence on industrialized nations (first Spain, then Great Britain, and, most recently, the United States). A related approach shared by most social scientists in Latin America was a Marxist-influenced class analysis that viewed the domination of capitalism and multinational corporations as central to the problems of the hemisphere. As these perspectives became more influential, a social network emerged among politically committed Latin American theologians who shared experiences and insights. One result was a new approach to theology which rejected the models developed in Europe and the United States and instead built on the cultural and religious traditions of Latin America (Sigmund, 1990:32).

In the 1970s, many advocates of liberation theology expressed strong Marxist views and saw revolutionary struggle to overthrow capitalism as essential to ending the suffering of Latin America's poor. More recently, liberation theology seems to have moved away from orthodox Marxism and endorsement of armed struggle. As an example, Gutiérrez (1990: 214, 222) has written that one does not need to accept Marxism as an "all-embracing view of life and thus exclude the Christian faith and its requirements." Gutiérrez adds that the proper concerns of a theology of liberation are not simply the world's "exploited classes," but also "races discriminated against," "despised cultures," and the "condition of women, especially in those sectors of society where women are doubly oppressed and marginalized."

afterlife. Similarly, during times of national tragedy (assassinations, invasions, and natural disasters), people attend religious services as a means of coping with problems that demand political and technological as well as spiritual solutions. On more of a micro level, clergy are often the first source of aid sought out by people faced with a crisis. In a 1990 survey in Texas, respondents were asked to whom they would go first to discuss personal problems. The highest percentage, 41 percent, stated that they would turn to clergy, as contrasted with 29 percent who would choose medical doctors and 21 percent who would go to psychiatrists or psychologists (Chalfant et al., 1990; McGuire, 1981:186; J. Yinger, 1970:598).

Religion and Social Change: The Weberian Thesis

For Karl Marx, the relationship between religion and social change was clear: religion impeded change by encouraging oppressed people to focus on otherworldly concerns rather than on their immediate poverty or exploitation. However, Max Weber (1958a, original edition 1904) was unconvinced by Marx's argument and carefully examined the connection between religious allegiance and capitalist development. His findings appeared in his pioneering work *The Protestant Ethic and the Spirit of Capitalism,* first published in 1904.

Weber noted that in European nations with both Protestant and Catholic citizens, an overwhelming number of business leaders, owners of capital, and skilled workers were Protestant. In his view, this was no mere coincidence. Weber pointed out that the followers of John Calvin (1509-1564), a leader of the Protestant Reformation, emphasized a disciplined work ethic, this-worldly concern, and rational orientation to life that has become known as the **Protestant ethic.** One by-product of the Protestant ethic was a drive to accumulate savings that could be used for future investment. This "spirit of capitalism," to use Weber's phrase, contrasted with the moderate work hours, leisurely work habits, and lack of ambition that he saw as typical of the times (Winter, 1977; J. Yinger, 1974).

What were the Calvinist religious principles that Weber saw as so conducive to capitalism? Calvinism believed in the doctrine of **predestination,** which holds that people either will be among the elect, who are rewarded in heaven, or will be condemned to hell. One's predestined future was not dependent on being righteous or sinful while on earth. Nevertheless, many Calvinists viewed hard work at a vocation as an outward sign of one's inner Christianity and as an indication that one would be rewarded in the afterlife. In addition, hard work served as a means of reducing anxiety over one's possible future in hell. For these rea-

sons, Weber argued, Calvinism and, to a lesser degree, other branches of Protestant religion initiated change in society favorable to capitalistic behavior. Whereas Marx had seen religion as a consequence of the economy, Weber believed that religion helped to shape a new economic system.

Few books in the sociology of religion have aroused as much commentary and criticism as *The Protestant Ethic and the Spirit of Capitalism.* It has been hailed as one of the most important theoretical works in the field and as an excellent example of macro-level analysis. Like Durkheim, Weber demonstrated that religion is not solely a matter of intimate personal beliefs. He stressed that the collective nature of religion has social consequences for society as a whole.

Despite this insight, some casual readers of Weber have found it difficult to accept his ideas. A common but misguided criticism is that Weber naively assigned too much significance to the effects of Calvinism. However, he never argued that the Protestant ethic was *necessary* for the development of capitalism. In Weber's own words (1958a:91, original edition 1904):

> . . . We have no intention whatever of maintaining such a foolish and doctrinaire thesis as that . . . capitalism as an economic system is a creation of the Reformation.

It is clear that capitalism has flourished in Japan without Calvinism (or, for that matter, Christianity). In an interesting application of the Weberian thesis, sociologist Robert Bellah (1957) examined the relationship between Japanese religious faiths and capitalism. Bellah determined that, as was true of Calvinism, these faiths stressed values of hard work and success and thus paved the way for the rise of Japanese capitalism.

Conflict theorists caution that Weber's theory—even if it is accepted—should not be regarded as an analysis of mature capitalism as reflected in the rise of large corporations which transcend national boundaries (see Chapter 9). The primary disagreement between Karl Marx and Max Weber concerned not the origins of capitalism, but rather its future. Unlike Marx, Weber believed that capitalism could endure indefinitely as an economic system. He added, however, that the decline of religion as an overriding force in society opened the way for workers to express their discontent more vocally (R. Colllins, 1980).

We can conclude that, although Weber provides a convincing description of the origins of European capitalism, this economic system has subsequently been adopted by non-Calvinists in many parts of the world. Contemporary studies in the United States show little or no difference in achievement orientation between Roman Catholics and Protestants. Apparently, the "spirit of capitalism" has become a generalized cultural trait rather than a specific religious tenet (Greeley, 1989a).

RELIGIOUS BEHAVIOR

All religions have certain elements in common, yet these elements are expressed in the distinctive manner of each faith. The patterns of religious behavior, like other patterns of social behavior, are of great interest to sociologists, since they underscore the relationship between religion and society.

Dimensions of Religious Behavior

Religious beliefs, religious rituals, and religious experience all help to define what is sacred and to differentiate the sacred from the profane. Let us now examine these three dimensions of religious behavior.

Belief Some Americans believe in life after death, in supreme beings with unlimited powers, or in supernatural forces. *Religious beliefs* are statements to which members of a particular religion adhere. These views vary dramatically from religion to religion.

Religious beliefs can be subdivided into values and cosmology. *Religious values* are shared conceptions of what is good, desirable, and proper that arise out of religious faith. These values govern personal conduct and may have direct impact on other social institutions. For example, religious values regarding marriage will influence patterns of family life in a society—perhaps by discouraging couples from seeking divorce. Even the economy can be reinforced by religious values. The sacred character of the child Jesus for Christians promotes the seasonal exchange of gifts as an expression of caring for others. Retailing establishments encourage this form of interaction, and an entire society (including non-Christians and nonbelievers) is affected by the gift exchange (Young, 1981).

The term *cosmology* refers to a general theory of the universe. The cosmology of a religion explains the ultimate questions; offers a divinity or hierarchy of gods and goddesses; and describes heaven, hell, life, and death. Several North American Indian accounts of creation tell of a succession of animals which dived into a flood of waters. The animals emerged with bits of mud or sand, and from this the earth was formed. Among some Asian and African peoples and some Indian tribes, it is believed that, in antiquity, a spider spun the earth. The same spider laid an egg out of which the first male and female human beings developed (Dundes, 1962).

The account of the creation found in Genesis, the first book of the Old Testament, is also part of a cosmology. Many Americans strongly adhere to the biblical explanation of creation and insist that this view be taught in public schools. These people, known as *creationists,* are worried by the secularization of society and oppose educational curricula which directly or indirectly question biblical scripture.

Ritual *Religious rituals* are practices required or expected of members of a faith. Rituals usually honor the divine power (or powers) worshiped by believers; they also remind adherents of their religious duties and responsibilities. Rituals and beliefs can be interdependent; rituals generally involve the affirmation of beliefs, as in a public or private statement confessing a sin (K. Roberts, 1984:96–107). Like any social institution, religion develops distinctive normative patterns to structure people's behavior. Moreover, there are sanctions attached to religious rituals, whether rewards (pins for excellence at church schools) or penalties (expulsion from a religious institution for violation of norms).

In American society, rituals may be very simple,

(Bob Daemmrich/Stock, Boston)

A Roman Catholic girl is shown participating in a communion service. From an interactionist perspective, religious rituals serve as important face-to-face encounters in which people reinforce their religious beliefs and their commitment to their faith.

Some rituals actually induce an almost trance-like state. The Plains Indians eat or drink peyote, a cactus containing the powerful hallucinogenic drug mescaline (see Box 14-2). Similarly, the ancient Greek followers of the god Pan chewed intoxicating leaves of ivy in order to become more ecstatic during their celebrations. Of course, artificial stimulants are not necessary to achieve a religious "high." Devout believers, such as those who practice the pentecostal Christian ritual of "speaking in tongues," can reach a state of ecstasy simply through spiritual passion.

Sacrifice is a rather widespread ritual. It is generally based on the hope that if a person gives up something of value to honor a supreme being, he or she will receive a divine blessing. A common sacrificial custom within industrial societies is making a contribution to a religious institution, as in the practice of tithing (giving one-tenth of one's income to a church). Other examples of religious sacrifice include fasting on holy days (such as Yom Kippur, the Day of Atonement for Jews) and giving up worldly pleasures (as Christians do for Lent). Yet the most ancient form of sacrifice—still commonly found throughout the world in the 1990s—is the burial of goods with a corpse. Such artifacts as food, clothing, money, and weapons are intended to provide the soul of the deceased with whatever will be needed during an afterlife. In American society, the provision of comfortable coffins for well-dressed corpses and the regular placement of flowers near a grave are forms of sacrifice offered in a similar spirit.

Experience In sociological study of religion, the term *religious experience* refers to the feeling or perception of being in direct contact with the ultimate reality, such as a divine being, or of being overcome with religious emotion. A religious experience may be rather slight, such as the feeling of exaltation a person receives from hearing a choir sing Handel's "Hallelujah Chorus." But many religious experiences are more profound, among them the act of being "born again"—that is, having a turning point in life during which one makes a personal commitment to Jesus.

According to a 1990 national survey, 38 percent of Americans claimed that they had had a born-again Christian experience at some time in

such as saying grace at a meal and observing a moment of silence to commemorate someone's death. Yet certain rituals, such as the process of canonizing a saint, are quite elaborate. Most religious rituals in our culture focus on services conducted at houses of worship. Thus, attendance at a service, silent and spoken reading of prayers, and singing of spiritual hymns and chants are common forms of ritual behavior that generally take place in group settings. From an interactionist perspective, these rituals serve as important face-to-face encounters in which people reinforce their religious beliefs and their commitment to their faith.

BOX 14-2 • EVERYDAY BEHAVIOR

PEYOTE, RELIGION, AND THE LAW

As he carefully beats his drum to create the chant of a Sioux Indian sun dance, Alfred Smith explains why he eats peyote. "I am not a drug dealer or a drug addict," insists Smith. "I am trying to find my way on a spiritual path." Smith's religious ritual involves a cactus indigenous to the Rio Grande Valley. Cactus tops, also known as "peyote buttons," contain the hallucinogen mescaline. Ingestion of this powerful drug is a sacrament for tens of thousands of members of the Native American church (Howlett, 1989:3A).

Peyotism has a long history. A reference to the religious use of peyote in Mexico appears in Spanish historical sources as early as 1560. Peyotism spread from Mexico to the United States and Canada; by the latter part of the nineteenth century, it was well established in this country. Today, Indians from many tribes practice peyotism. Despite the absence of recorded theology and dogma, the practices of Navajo members in Arizona closely resemble those of adherents in California, Montana, Oklahoma, Wisconsin, and Saskatchewan. These men and women accept certain Christian teachings but also believe that peyote embodies the Holy Spirit and that those who partake of peyote will enter into direct contact with God (Deloria and Lytle, 1983:234–235).

Since peyote is a drug which has the same legal classification as cocaine, heroin, and LSD, the practice of peyotism raises serious legal questions. The federal government and 23 states exempt the religious use of peyote from criminal penalties—a policy that defenders view as an application of the First Amendment guarantee of free exercise of religion. But the state of Oregon does not accept peyotism; its refusal to do so became the center of a controversy that made its way to the United States Supreme Court.

Under Oregon law, it is a crime to possess or use peyote. Two members of the Native American church—one of them Alfred Smith—were dismissed from their jobs for use of peyote and then were refused unemployment benefits by the state's employment division. Officials ruled that the men's illegal use of peyote made them ineligible for government benefits.

In 1990, the Supreme Court held, by a 6-3 vote, that prosecuting people who use illegal drugs as part of religious rituals is not a violation of the First Amendment guarantee of religious freedom. Dissenting justices and civil libertarians worried that this ruling inevitably would be used against the rituals of "minor" (but not "major") religions. Indeed, Justice Sandra Day O'Connor called the majority opinion "incompatible with our nation's fundamental commitment to individual religious liberty" (L. Greenhouse, 1990:A10).

---

their lives—a figure which translates into nearly 70 million adults. An earlier survey found that Baptists (61 percent) were the most likely to report such experiences; by contrast, only 18 percent of Catholics and 11 percent of Episcopalians stated that they had been born again. The collective nature of religion, as emphasized by Durkheim, is evident in these statistics. The beliefs and rituals of a particular faith can create an atmosphere either friendly or hostile to this type of religious experience. Thus, a Baptist would be encouraged to come forward and share such experiences with others, whereas an Episcopalian would receive much less support if he or she claimed to have been born again (Gallup Opinion Index, 1978; Princeton Religion Research Center, 1990b).

Organization of Religious Behavior

The collective nature of religion has led to many forms of religious association. In modern societies, religion has become increasingly formalized. Specific structures such as churches and synagogues are constructed for religious worship; individuals are trained for occupational roles within

The Catholic Church in Spain is an example of an ecclesia.

various fields. These developments make it possible to distinguish between the sacred and secular parts of one's life—a distinction that could not be made in earlier societies in which religion was largely a family activity carried out in the home.

Sociologists find it useful to distinguish between four basic forms of organization: the ecclesia, the denomination, the sect, and the cult. As is the case with other typologies used by social scientists, this system of classification can help us to appreciate the variety of organizational forms found among religious faiths. Distinctions are made between these types of organizations on the basis of such factors as size, power, degree of commitment expected from members, and historical ties to other faiths.

Ecclesiae An *ecclesia* (plural, *ecclesiae*) is a religious organization that claims to include most of or all the members of a society and is recognized as the national or official religion. Since virtually everyone belongs to the faith, membership is by birth rather than conscious decision. Examples of ecclesiae include the Lutheran church in Sweden, the Catholic church in Spain, Islam in Saudi Arabia, and Buddhism in Thailand. However, there can be significant differences even within the category of *ecclesia*. In Saudi Arabia's Islamic regime,

leaders of the ecclesia hold vast power over actions of the state. By contrast, the Lutheran church in contemporary Sweden has no such power over the Riksdag (parliament) or the prime minister.

Generally, ecclesiae are conservative in that they do not challenge the leaders or policies of a secular government. In a society with an ecclesia, the political and religious institutions often act in harmony and mutually reinforce each other's power over their relative spheres of influence. Within the modern world, ecclesiae tend to be declining in power.

Denominations A *denomination* is a large, organized religion that is not officially linked with the state or government. Like an ecclesia, it tends to have an explicit set of beliefs, a defined system of authority, and a generally respected position in society (Doress and Porter, 1977). Denominations count among their members large segments of a population. Generally, children accept the denomination of their parents and give little thought to membership in other faiths. Denominations also resemble ecclesiae in that few demands are made on members. However, there is a critical difference between these two forms of religious organization. Although the denomination is considered respectable and is not viewed as a challenge to the secular government, it lacks the official recognition and power held by an ecclesia.

No nation of the world has more denominations than the United States. In good measure, this is a result of our nation's immigrant heritage. Many settlers in the "new world" brought with them the religious commitments native to their homelands. American denominations of Christianity, such as those of the Roman Catholics, Episcopalians, and Lutherans, were the outgrowth of ecclesiae established in Europe. In addition, new Christian denominations emerged in the United States, including the Mormons and Christian Scientists.

Sects In contrast to the denomination is the sect, which Max Weber (1958b:114, original edition 1916) termed a "believer's church," because affiliation is based on conscious acceptance of a specific religious dogma. A *sect* can be defined as a relatively small religious group that has broken away from some other religious organization to renew what it views as the original vision of the faith. Many sects, such as that led by Martin Luther during the Reformation, claim to be the "true church" by seeking to cleanse the estab-

lished faith of what they regard as innovative beliefs and rituals (Stark and Bainbridge, 1985).

Sects are fundamentally at odds with society and do not seek to become established national religions. Unlike ecclesiae, sects require intensive commitments and demonstrations of belief by members. Partly owing to their "outsider" status in society, sects frequently exhibit a higher degree of religious fervor and loyalty than more established religious groups do. Recruitment is focused mainly on adults; as a result, acceptance comes through conversion.

Sects are often short-lived; however, if able to survive, they may become less antagonistic to society and begin to resemble denominations. In a few instances, sects have been able to endure over several generations while remaining fairly separate from society. Sociologist J. Milton Yinger (1970:226–273) uses the term *established sect* to describe a religious group that is the outgrowth of a sect, yet remains isolated from society. The Hutterites, Jehovah's Witnesses, Seventh-Day Adventists, and Amish are contemporary examples of established sects in the United States.

Cults As psychotherapist Irvin Doress and sociologist Jack Nusan Porter (1977:3–4) have sug-

(Alan Carey/The Image Works)

The Hutterites are a contemporary example of an established sect found in the United States. Shown is a Hutterite community in Rifton, New York.

TABLE 14-1 Characteristics of Ecclesiae, Denominations, Sects, and Cults

CHARACTERISTIC	ECCLESIA	DENOMINATION	SECT	CULT
Size	Very large	Large	Small	Small
Wealth	Extensive	Extensive	Limited	Variable
Religious services	Formal, little participation	Formal, little participation	Informal, emotional	Variable
Doctrines	Specific, but interpretation may be tolerated	Specific, but interpretation may be tolerated	Specific, purity of doctrine emphasized	Innovative, pathbreaking
Clergy	Well-trained, full-time	Well-trained, full-time	Trained to some degree	Unspecialized
Membership	By virtue of being a member of society	By acceptance of doctrine	By acceptance of doctrine	By an emotional commitment
Relationship to the state	Recognized, closely aligned	Tolerated	Not encouraged	Ignored

SOURCES: Adapted from G. Vernon, 1962; see also Chalfant et al., 1987:91–92.

gested, the word *cult* has taken on a negative meaning in contemporary American society and is used more as a means of discrediting religious minorities than of categorizing them. They note that some groups, such as the Hare Krishnas, are labeled as "cults" because they seem to come from foreign (often nonwestern) lands and have customs perceived as "strange." This reflects Americans' ethnocentric evaluations of that which differs from the commonplace.

It is difficult to distinguish sects from cults. A **cult** is a generally small, secretive religous group that represents either a new religion or a major innovation of an existing faith. Cults are similar to sects in that they tend to be small and are often viewed as less respectable than more established faiths.

However, unlike sects, cults normally do not result from schisms or breaks with established ecclesiae or denominations. Some cults, such as contemporary American cults focused on UFO sightings or expectations of colonizing outer space, may be totally unrelated to the existing faiths in a culture. Even when a cult does accept certain fundamental tenets of a dominant faith—such as belief in the divinity of Jesus or Muhammad—it will offer new revelations or new insights to justify its claim to be a more advanced

Ecclesiae, denominations, and sects are best viewed as ideal types along a continuum; cults are outside the continuum because they generally define themselves as a new view of life rather than in terms of existing religious faiths.

religion (Doress and Porter, 1977:3, 1981; Stark and Bainbridge,1979, 1985:27).

As is true of sects, cults may undergo transformation over time into other types of religious organizations. An example is the Christian Science church, which began as a cult under the leadership of Mary Baker Eddy. Today, this church exhibits the characteristics of a denomination (Johnstone, 1988:88).

Comparing Forms of Religious Organization
Clearly, it is no simple matter to determine whether a particular religious group falls into the sociological category of ecclesia, denomination, sect, or cult. Yet, as we have seen, these ideal types of religious organizations have somewhat different relationships to society. Ecclesiae are recognized as national churches; denominations, although not officially approved, are generally respected. By contrast, sects as well as cults are much more likely to be at odds with the larger culture.

Ecclesiae, denominations, and sects are best viewed as ideal types along a continuum rather than as mutually exclusive categories. Some of the primary characteristics of these ideal types are summarized in Table 14-1. Since the United States has no ecclesia, sociologists studying this nation's religions have naturally focused on the denomination and the sect. These religious forms have been pictured on either end of a continuum, with denominations accommodating to the secular world and sects making a protest against established religions. Cults have also been included in Table 14-1 but are outside the continuum because they generally define themselves as a new view of life rather than in terms of existing religious faiths (Chalfant et al., 1987:89–99).

RELIGION IN THE UNITED STATES

As mentioned earlier, the United States includes a wide variety of religious denominations. Figure 14-2 (page 430) illustrates the fact that particular Christian faiths dominate certain areas of the country in terms of membership. Of course, for most nations of the world, such a "religious map" would hardly be useful, since one faith accounts for virtually all the religious followers. The diversity of beliefs, rituals, and experiences that characterize religious life in the United States reflects both the nation's immigrant heritage and the First Amendment prohibition against establishment of an ecclesia.

By far the largest single denomination in the United States is Roman Catholicism, yet at least 23 other religious faiths have 1 million or more members (see Table 14-2 on page 432). These particular statistics are conservative, since other faiths are growing in size. For example, there are close to 5 million Muslims in the United States. Protestants collectively accounted for about 56 percent of the nation's adult population in 1990, compared with 28 percent for Roman Catholics and almost 3 percent for Jews (Princeton Religion Research Center, 1990a:29). The United States also includes a smaller number of people who adhere to such eastern faiths as Hinduism, Confucianism, and Taoism. As Figure 14-3 (page 431) reveals, certain faiths, such as Episcopalianism,

Judaism, and Lutheranism, have a higher proportion of affluent members. Adherents of other faiths, including Baptists and evangelicals, are comparatively poor.

Beliefs and Practices

At present, religion continues to be an important influence on American society. According to 1986 surveys, only 4 percent of the adults in the United States can be described as "totally nonreligious." (These people have no religious preference, are not members of a congregation, rarely or never attend religious services, and state that religion is either "not very important" or "not at all important" in their lives.) By contrast, more than 9 in 10 Americans identify a specific religious preference, with a majority claiming to be active members of their congregations. When residents of 11 nations were asked to indicate the importance of God in their lives, Americans registered the third-highest score, slightly behind Mexicans and South Africans and far ahead of Hungarians, Japanese, Danes, and Swedes (Gallup Opinion Index, 1987:14, 18; Princeton Religion Research Center, 1986:5).

Studies suggest, however, that religion is not uniformly on the upswing in the United States. There is a great deal of switching of denominations and, as in the past, considerable interest in new ways of expressing spirituality. It would be incorrect to conclude either that religion is slowly being abandoned or that Americans are turning to religion with the zeal of new converts. The future may well bring periods of religious revivalism but also times of decline in religious fervor (Chalfant et al., 1987:312–315).

One of the most common religious rituals in the Protestant and Catholic faiths is church attendance. The Gallup poll has provided the only regular measurement of such attendance; in 1990, it reported that during an average week, 40 percent of the adults in the United States attended church. As is apparent in Figure 14-4 (page 431), Protestants' attendance has remained relatively constant over the period 1958–1990. By contrast, Catholics' attendance suffered a dramatic decline, beginning in 1964, which began to level off only in the 1970s.

FIGURE 14-2 Predominant Christian Faiths by Counties of the United States

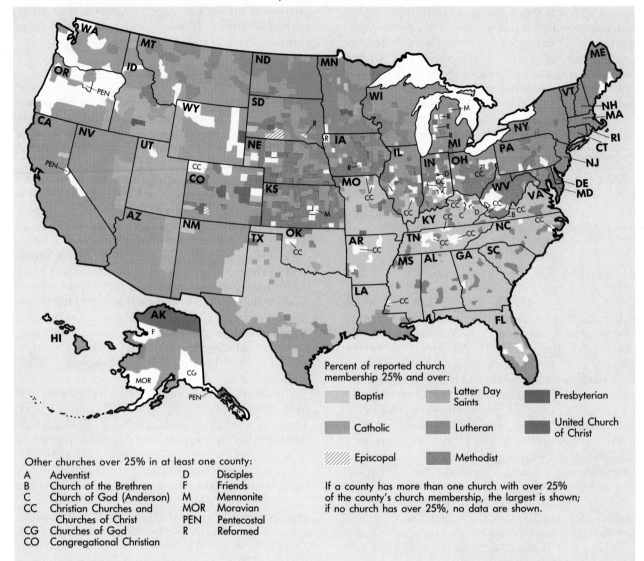

Percent of reported church membership 25% and over:

- Baptist
- Latter Day Saints
- Presbyterian
- Catholic
- Lutheran
- United Church of Christ
- Episcopal
- Methodist

If a county has more than one church with over 25% of the county's church membership, the largest is shown; if no church has over 25%, no data are shown.

Other churches over 25% in at least one county:

A	Adventist	D	Disciples
B	Church of the Brethren	F	Friends
C	Church of God (Anderson)	M	Mennonite
CC	Christian Churches and Churches of Christ	MOR	Moravian
		PEN	Pentecostal
CG	Churches of God	R	Reformed
CO	Congregational Christian		

SOURCE: B. Quinn et al., 1982.

The diversity of Christian religious life in the United States is apparent here. Many different Christian faiths account for 25 percent or more of the church members in a county. Among non-Christian faiths, only Judaism may figure so significantly—in New York County (Manhattan) of New York City and in Dade County, Florida (which includes Miami Beach).

FIGURE 14-3 Income and Denominations

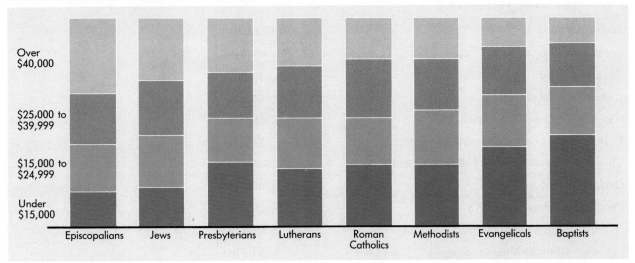

SOURCE: Gallup Opinion Index, 1987:20–27, 29.

The figure above reveals the different income groups that denominations attract. All denominations have both affluent and poor members, yet some have a higher proportion of affluent members (as measured by income) while others are comparatively poor.

FIGURE 14-4 Church Attendance of Protestants and Catholics in a Typical Week, 1958 through 1990

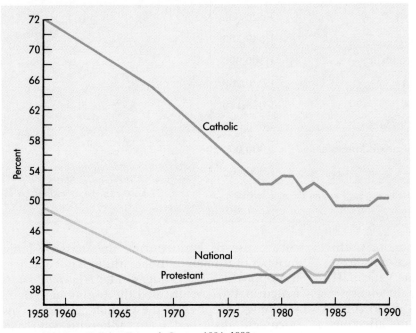

SOURCES: Princeton Religion Research Center, 1984, 1990c.

Church attendance among American Protestants and Catholics began to increase in the late 1970s after two decades of decline.

TABLE 14-2   Religions with at Least 1 Million Members in the United States, 1987–1988

RELIGIOUS BODY	MEMBERSHIP
Roman Catholic church	54,918,949
Southern Baptist Convention	14,812,844
United Methodist church	9,055,575
National Baptist Convention, U.S.A.[a]	5,500,000
Evangelical Lutheran Church in America	5,251,534
Church of Jesus Christ of Latter-Day Saints	4,000,000
Church of God in Christ[a]	3,709,661
Presbyterian church (U.S.A.)	2,929,608
National Baptist Convention of America[a]	2,668,779
Lutheran Church–Missouri Synod	2,604,278
Episcopal church	2,455,422
African Methodist Episcopal church	2,210,000
Assemblies of God	2,147,041
United Synagogue of America	2,000,000
Greek Orthodox church[a]	1,950,000
United Church of Christ	1,644,787
Churches of Christ	1,626,000
American Baptist Churches in the U.S.A.	1,549,563
Union of American Hebrew Congregations	1,300,000
African Methodist Episcopal Zion church	1,220,260
Christian Church (Disciples of Christ)	1,073,119
Christian Churches and Churches of Christ	1,070,616
Union of Orthodox Jewish Congregations of America	1,000,000
Orthodox Church in America[a]	1,000,000

[a]Data are for 1982 or earlier and therefore may not be comparable with the more recent data.
SOURCE: Jacquet, 1990:247–255.

Several hundred religions are practiced in the United States. Of these, 24 have at least 1 million members.

The sharp decline in churchgoing among Catholics has been attributed to the impact of Vatican II and the *Humanae Vitae* encyclical. Vatican II was an ecumenical convention brought together by Pope John XXIII that met from 1962 to 1965. It issued a series of sweeping reforms affecting Catholic rituals, including termination of the exclusive use of Latin during the mass. A large number of Roman Catholics (though not a majority) opposed these changes. The *Humanae Vitae*, issued in 1967, reaffirmed the traditional family planning teachings of the Catholic church. This document disturbed many adherents who had expected—or at least hoped for—a more liberal

(John C. Hillery)

This photograph was not taken in the middle east. Actually, the Islamic center shown is found outside of Toledo, Ohio; you can see a Greyhound bus driving by! The presence of such a center in the midwest underscores the diversity of religious life in the United States.

papal stance on issues of birth control and sexuality (Greeley, 1989b:47–52).

One significant change in religious practices in the United States has been the increase in the number of women in the clergy (see Box 14-3, page 434). Although all the nation's religions pay tribute to saintly and wise women, women have been traditionally represented in religious beliefs and rituals as a weaker sex, less capable than men of handling religious authority. In recent decades, however, there has been increasing resistance to beliefs and practices which relegate women to second-class status within the world of organized religion (Carmody, 1989).

Resurgent Fundamentalism

In the late 1960s, something rather remarkable took place in the world of organized religion. For the first time in the history of the United States, most of the major Christian denominations began to shrink in size. The Presbyterians, Lutherans, Methodists, and Episcopalians all decreased in membership, while Roman Catholics remained stable primarily because of an influx of practicing Catholics from Latin America. However, not all religious faiths were in decline. During this same

period, groups such as the Southern Baptist Convention, the Assemblies of God, the Mormons, the Jehovah's Witnesses, and the Seventh-Day Adventists began overflowing with vitality. These fundamentalist groups share a conservative, "back-to-basics" approach to religion and stress strict interpretation of the Bible. The term ***fundamentalism*** refers to adherence to earlier-accepted religious doctrines and often is accompanied by a literal application of historical beliefs and scriptures to today's world.

This religious revival, called *resurgent fundamentalism* by theologian Martin Marty (1980), has been accompanied by noticeable growth among evangelical and pentacostal faiths. ***Evangelical faiths*** are Christian faiths which place great emphasis on a personal relationship between the individual and God and believe that each adherent must spread the faith and bear personal witness by openly declaring the religion to nonbelievers. ***Pentecostal faiths*** hold many of the same values but also believe in the infusion of the Holy Spirit into services and in such religious experiences as faith healing and "speaking in tongues." Fundamentalists are not necessarily evangelical or pentecostal; they may seek to restore doctrine and literal interpretations within the structure of

BOX 14-3 • EVERYDAY BEHAVIOR

WOMEN IN THE CLERGY

Throughout history and in many diverse cultures, the highest positions of spiritual leadership within organized religion have been reserved for men. Even today, the largest denomination in the United States, Roman Catholicism, does not permit women to be priests. The largest Protestant denomination, the Southern Baptist Convention, has voted against ordaining women (even though some of its autonomous churches have women ministers). Other American faiths that do not allow women clergy include the Lutheran Church—Missouri Synod, the Greek Orthodox Archdiocese of North and South America, the Orthodox Church in America, the Church of God in Christ, the Church of Jesus Christ of Latter-Day Saints, and Orthodox Judaism.

Despite these restrictions, there has been a notable rise in female clergy in the last 15 years. According to the National Council of Churches, by 1985 about 7.5 percent of all clergy in the United States were women. Female enrollment in American seminaries has steadily increased since the early 1970s. For example, in 1973 women accounted for 10 percent of Protestant theological students; by 1986, the proportion of women had risen to 26 percent. Similarly,

(Seth Resnick/Stock, Boston)

There has been a notable rise in the number of female clergy in the United States in the last 15 years.

with Conservative Judaism's joining Reform Judaism and Reconstructionism in ordaining women rabbis, the number of female rabbis in the United States increased to an all-time high of 130 by mid-1986.

Clearly, many branches of Protestantism and Judaism have been convinced that women have the right to be ordained as spiritual leaders. Yet a lingering question remains: once ordained, will these female ministers and rabbis be *accepted* by congregations? Will they advance in their calling as easily as male counterparts, or will they face blatant or subtle discrimination in their efforts to secure desirable posts within their faiths?

It is too early to offer any definitive answers to these questions, but thus far women clergy continue to face lingering sexism after ordination. According to a 1986 random sampling of 800 lay and ordained leaders of the United Church of Christ, women find it difficult to secure jobs in larger, more prestigious congregations. Women ministers in other Protestant faiths, such as the United Methodists and the Presbyterians, have encountered similar problems. Although they may be accepted as junior clergy or as copastors, women may fail to receive senior clergy appointments. In Reform Judaism, a congregation that already has a female cantor is unlikely to accept a woman rabbi.

Women clergy are well-aware that their struggle for equality is far from over. The Reverend Joan Forsberg, an administrator at the Yale Divinity School, tells women graduates that they must view their efforts as part of a larger, long-term process of change. "Even if you don't see change overnight," she notes, "you must remind yourself that you *are* making a difference for future generations."

SOURCES: Brooks, 1987:15; Goldman, 1986; Lehman, 1985; O'Driscoll, 1985; Stump, 1986.

---

established faiths such as Catholicism or Islam (Ammerman, 1987:4–5; H. Cox, 1984; Elder, 1990; J. Hunter, 1983; D. Kelley, 1977; Marty, 1980).

Sociologists Dean Hoge and David A. Roozen (1979) offered statistical support for Marty's conceptualization of resurgent fundamentalism. They found that in recent decades, denominations experiencing the most growth tended to emphasize local evangelism, maintain a lifestyle and morality apart from mainstream culture, and deemphasize social action and religious universalism.

Martin Marty points out that this fundamentalist revival has surprised many observers of American religious life. It had been widely assumed that, in the face of increasing secularization, the only religions likely to survive would be those which were least demanding and most tolerant of differences in religious interpretation. Instead, people seem anxious to return to traditional sources of collective religious feeling that Durkheim viewed as fundamental to religion's role in society.

What has led to this dramatic change in religious life? Sociologist Wade Clark Roof (1976, 1978), in a North Carolina survey, found that religious commitment was strongly associated with local community attachment. Since the evangelical and pentecostal churches are more likely to support local values—as opposed to a world view tolerant of nontraditional lifestyles—it is not surprising that such faiths have grown in popularity. In addition, the intense commitment and proselytizing spirit of members of fundamentalist churches serve as key factors in their success. Dean Kelley (1979), an executive with the National Council of Churches and an authority on religious behavior, points out that "strict" churches which expect members to practice what they preach have proved to be more effective recruiters than more liberal churches have (see also J. Hunter, 1985).

The resurgence of Christian fundamentalism has led to intense debate regarding an otherwise secular area of American life—the school system. In the 1980s, the fundamentalist movement pursued three main goals regarding public schools: pressuring Congress and the courts to permit school prayer, revising school curricula to give the biblical explanation of creation equal weight with scientific theories of evolution, and generally increasing fundamentalist religious content in school textbooks while blocking the study of material viewed as reflecting an antireligious point of view (W. Stevens, 1987b:6). We will discuss the battle over school curricula and textbooks in the social policy section at the end of the chapter.

The United States is not the only country in which fundamentalism has become more popular in recent decades. In a troubled secular and technological age, many people around the world are turning to well-ordered, even authoritarian, explanations of religious matters. Protestant fundamentalism has become a significant force in Northern Ireland, a nation torn by religious strife between Protestants and Catholics. Fundamentalist Ashkenazic Jews have emerged as an increasingly important political bloc within the state of Israel; in Jerusalem, they have clashed with secular Jews over public showings of movies during the Sabbath hours. In Iran and other Islamic nations, there has been a dramatic return to literal interpretation of the sacred book, the Qur'an. Islamic fundamentalists have protested against family planning measures in Egypt, the assessment of interest charges by banks in Pakistan, and secular laws intended to promote a unifying ideology in Indonesia (S. Marshall, 1984).

This renewed interest in fundamentalist faiths reflects the integrative function of religion—as individuals seek to affirm a religious identity in a manner they find difficult within established denominations. While American society remains largely secular, members of religious institutions are choosing faiths that place greater emphasis on strict religious teachings and public declaration of religious experience.

The Electronic Church

An important development in American religious life has been the dramatic rise of religious programming in the media. Many religious groups—but especially fundamentalist Christians—have become dissatisfied with the content of secular television. At the same time, they have realized that the mass media represent an effective means of spreading religious values and conducting fundraising. Technological advances such as UHF-TV, cable television, and satellite transmission have facilitated the rise of the "electronic church."

According to the National Religious Broadcasters (NRB), the industry's trade association, there were 221 television stations in the United States owned by religious organizations in 1987. In 1977, there was only one religious cable service;

After being convicted of fraud and conspiracy for his financial dealings, televangelist Jim Bakker is led away. Bakker was sentenced to 45 years in prison and was fined $500,000. An appeals court later set aside the 45-year term and ordered that Bakker be resentenced.

as of 1987, there were nine, reaching a potential audience of 36 million subscribers. In 1989, about half of American adults watched religious television programs at least occasionally, while 21 percent watched weekly. The most loyal followers of such programming are evangelicals, at least half of whom are weekly viewers. Studies show that the audience for religious programs grew slightly but steadily throughout the 1980s (Beck, 1987; Princeton Religion Research Center, 1989a).

The programming of the electronic church is not solely religious. There is particular focus on issues concerning marriage and the family, death and dying, and education; yet more political topics such as communism and the military are also discussed (Abelman and Nevendorf, 1985). Although many television ministries avoid political positions, others have been quite outspoken. Most noteworthy in this regard is pentecostal minister Pat Robertson, a strong conservative. Robertson founded the Christian Broadcasting Network in 1961, served for many years as host of CBN's syndicated religious talk show *The 700 Club,* and took leave of his television posts in 1986 to seek the Republican nomination for president in 1988.

Television evangelists have used the media to solicit millions of dollars in contributions to support their schools, overseas missionary programs, and media campaigns. In 1987, Ben Armstrong, executive director of the NRB, estimated that the electronic church constituted a $2 billion industry annually (K. Beck, 1987:11). By the mid-1980s, there was growing concern about the solicitation efforts of television evangelists; critics charged that deeply religious viewers with modest incomes were unwittingly supporting the lavish lifestyles of some of these well-publicized ministers. These ethical questions intensified in 1987 when pentecostal minister Jim Bakker—president of the PTL cable network—was forced to resign amidst charges of moral and financial misconduct. In early 1988, not long after the Bakker scandal became public, television evangelist Jimmy Swaggert of the Assembly of God broke with his church rather than accept its sanctions for his involvement with a prostitute.

In light of the trend toward secularization noted earlier in the chapter, it is striking that fundamentalist clergy have come to rely so heavily on modern communications technology. While these religious leaders directly attack many core values of the secular world, they are nevertheless willing to use its artifacts in their spiritual campaigns. Sociologist James Hunter (1985:156) argues that fundamentalists see "technology as either neutral and thus not challenging to their own faith, or positive—as a gift from God to further his work on earth—and, thus, an enhancement to faith."

It is not yet clear what effect the electronic church has had on the overall strength of organized religion in the United States. What is clear, however, is that Americans have become increasingly distrustful of television evangelists—especially since Jim Bakker's resignation as head of the PTL ministry in 1987. In a 1989 survey, large majorities of respondents described televangelists as dishonest (70 percent), insincere (67 percent), lacking a special relationship with God (67 percent), and uncaring (62 percent). Moreover, 79 percent of those questioned stated that television evangelists cannot be trusted with their followers' donations. According to Arbitron ratings of television viewing, the audience for the top 20 syndicated religious programs declined from more than 11 million viewers in 1985 to 7.7 million in 1990 (Princeton Religion Research Center, 1989a; Shipp, 1991).

Jews in the United States

Outside the Christian faith, the largest single religious group in the United States is Jews. As noted earlier, Jews constitute almost 3 percent of the American population. Interestingly, Jews in the United States can be viewed both as an ethnic minority (see Chapter 10) and as a religious denomination. Many people in the United States consider themselves to be culturally Jewish—and are seen by others as Jewish—even though they do not participate in Jewish religious life. Available data suggest that about 60 to 70 percent of American Jews are affiliated with a temple or synagogue, but only 20 to 30 percent attend services more frequently than once a month (Kleinman, 1983).

The diversity of religious faiths in the United States is manifested not only in the variety of denominations, but also in the diversity within the same faith. For example, Judaism can be divided into three major branches or denominations: Orthodox, Conservative, and Reform. No precise data exist on the number of American Jews in each category. However, through data obtained in community studies of Jews in six major metropolitan areas as well as a national survey, it is estimated that Conservative Jews constitute 35 to 55 percent of the American Jewish community, Reform Jews 25 to 34 percent, and Orthodox Jews 13 to 22 percent (Kleinman, 1983; Lazerwitz and Harrison, 1979; Liebman, 1973:61).

The differences in religious beliefs and practices between Orthodox, Conservative, and Reform Jews are based on their relationships to traditional religious codes and rituals. All three faiths embrace a philosophy founded on the Torah, the first five books of the Old Testament. Orthodox Jews are the most strict in following religious law. For example, they observe *kashrut*, a detailed set of religious restrictions governing food preparation and consumption. By contrast, Reform Jews have altered many traditional religious rituals, conduct services largely in English (rather than Hebrew), and have ordained a growing number of women as rabbis. Such practices are unacceptable and disturbing to many Orthodox Jews. Conservative Judaism can be seen as a kind of middle ground between the traditionalism of the Orthodox and the more "modernized" practices of Reform Judaism.

As is true of Protestant denominations, there

(David Austen/Stock, Boston)

Traditionally, the bar mitzvah ceremony—the rite of passage of a 13-year-old into the Jewish community's adult responsibilities—was reserved for males. However, beginning in the 1950s, many Reform and Conservative synagogues in North America have offered similar bar mitzvah ceremonies for young women.

are distinct social class differences between Jewish faiths. Reform Jews have the highest proportion of wealthy and well-educated adherents, whereas Orthodox Jews have the lowest proportion. Once again, Conservative Jews fall in between the other major Jewish denominations in terms of social class. In some cases, poor Jews from immigrant backgrounds strictly follow traditional Jewish law, but their grandchildren move into the middle class and turn to Reform Judaism. This reflects, at least in part, the process of assimilation to the norms of the dominant culture (Goldscheider, 1986; Lazerwitz and Harrison, 1979; Liebman, 1973:84).

Sects and Cults in the United States

Since the arrival of the Puritans in colonial Massachusetts, the United States has been a fertile ground for new faiths. In fact, religious dissent, like political dissent, has been viewed as a basic element in American freedom. However, the feelings of the American people concerning religious sects and cults have been badly shaken by reports of violence, questionable business practices, and undue pressures to hold onto their followers. Indeed, when a 1989 survey asked Americans what groups they did not want as neighbors, members of religious sects and cults scored highest—well ahead of racial and ethnic minorities. Fully 62 percent of respondents did not want sect and cult members as neighbors, as compared with only 5 percent for Jews, 5 percent for Protestants, and 3 percent for Roman Catholics (Princeton Religion Research Center, 1989b).

It has been estimated that as many as 2 to 3 million Americans—primarily between the ages of 18 and 25—belong to religious sects and cults. One study of cults in the United States counted about 600 such groups in 1983. Older cults are generally based on more established forms of Christianity; more recent sects and cults reflect the influence of Hinduism and Buddhism in the United States. The majority of the newer cults are less than 20 years old, and, lacking the dogma, ritual, and validation that come from association with more established religions, many may therefore depend for survival on the emotional appeal of a charismatic leader (R. Lindsey, 1987b).

Why do young Americans join religious cults? Irwin Doress and Jack Nusan Porter (1977) note several reasons that lead people to become members of such religious organizations. Many have come from families beset by problems and conflicts and have had difficulties coping with a world filled with violence, drugs, and sexual permissiveness. For these young people, a cult may offer a new, seemingly secure and appreciative "family" filled with love, caring, and acceptance. The puritanical aspects of cults—the rigid discipline, enforced celibacy, and banning of drugs and alcohol—may represent a welcome change from the responsibilities of adult life in a rapidly changing society.

In addition, cults appeal to the political idealism and spiritual longings of recruits and offer an opportunity to commit their entire lives to the search for a better world. Even the names of cults—the Children of God, the Family, and so forth—may seem attractive to troubled people who feel a deep need to belong to *something* and feel connected to *someone*. Consequently, cults provide the feeling of identity and sense of community that some people find difficult to achieve within more traditional religious groups.

Perhaps no contemporary sect or cult has aroused so much controversy in the United States as has the Unification church (refer back to box 2-4 on page 52). The Unification church was founded in South Korea in the mid-1950s by the Reverend Sun Myung Moon, an ex-Presbyterian evangelist born in Korea in 1920. Moon's theology is a distinctive blend of Buddhism, Taoism, and his own interpretations of the Old and New Testaments. For example, the church teaches that Jesus failed to complete his mission of salvation; people need to be restored to God's divine grace through the advent of a new messiah (Moon himself). Followers call him "Father" or acknowledge him with such grand terms as "Lord of the Second Advent" and "Master of Mankind" (Coughlin, 1983).

Officials of the church claim that it has 45,000 members in the United States, but most outside observers estimate between 5000 and 15,000. The Unification church has come under strong attack for its deceptive methods of luring young people to weekend retreats and for its alleged brainwashing of them once they arrive. However, according to one sociological study, only 10 percent of those who attend the church's 2-day retreats become members for even 1 week, and only 4 percent are still church members 2 years later (Barker, 1986a:339–340, 1986b; Lamm, 1983).

In 1982, Moon was convicted of filing false income tax returns. A variety of national religious groups came to his defense—arguing that the government was improperly intruding into the internal financial operations of the Unification church—but Moon was sentenced to an 18-month prison term. Upon leaving prison in 1985, however, Moon found his religious and financial empire still intact. Individuals and organizations associated with Moon currently control a global web of businesses, including a major daily newspaper in the United States, the *Washington Times* (Osen, 1987; J. Ridgeway, 1988; Rothmyer, 1984).

SOCIAL POLICY AND RELIGION

CENSORSHIP OF SCHOOLBOOKS

- To what extent does the First Amendment protect the sharing of ideas in school classrooms and libraries?
- Do parents have the right, in the name of their religious beliefs, to protect their children from books whose values or language they find objectionable?
- Is judicial "book burning" the wave of the future?

In recent years, governmental and educational policymakers have had to confront these sensitive issues much more frequently in response to efforts to censor school curricula. During recent school years, including 1988–1989, such distinguished works as Alice Walker's Pulitzer prize–winning novel *The Color Purple,* John Steinbeck's *Of Mice and Men,* and Arthur Miller's *Death of a Salesman* were attacked for use of "objectionable language." William Shakespeare's *Macbeth* was criticized for dealing with witchcraft and Satanism, while *Romeo and Juliet* came under fire for allegedly promoting teen suicide and drug abuse. More recently, the popular teen novels of Judy Blume have been targeted because of their references to sexual encounters. Remarkably, in 1990, a California school district locked away 400 copies of "Little Red Riding Hood" in a storage room after an official charged that the children's story condoned the use of alcohol (Eskey, 1990; *New York Times,* 1990d; *Phi Delta Kappan,* 1986).

An increasing proportion of challenges to school textbooks and library materials are being backed by groups with religious associations, such as the National Association of Christian Educators, as well as by national conservative groups such as Concerned Women of America and the Eagle Forum. For many religious fundamentalists concerned about the values taught in public schools, the influence of secular humanism has become a rallying cry. *Secular humanism* can be defined as a set of values and ideas growing out of modern science that disassociates itself from religious teachings. Philosopher Paul Kurtz, an acknowledged secular humanist, sees it as a "method of investigation, basing evidence on hypotheses and reason." Yet opponents of secular humanism use the term broadly and loosely, linking it to immorality, atheism, evolution, socialism, world government, and other ideas or values seen as dangerous or evil (Holden, 1987a:19).

The best-known aspect of the battle against secular humanism in school systems has been the challenge to scientific explanations of evolution. As discussed earlier, people known as *creationists* support a literal interpretation of the book of Genesis regarding the origins of the universe and argue that evolution should not be presented as established scientific fact. Their efforts recall the famous 1925 "monkey trial," in which high school biology teacher John T. Scopes was indicted for violating a Tennessee law making it a crime to teach in public schools "any theory which denies the story of the divine creation of man as taught in the Bible" and which holds instead that "man is descended from a lower order of animals." Despite a stirring defense by noted criminal lawyer Clarence Darrow, Scopes was convicted and fined $100, although a higher court later reversed his conviction on a technicality (S. Taylor, 1987b).

FEIFFER

In the 1968 case of *Epperson v. Arkansas*, the Supreme Court overturned an Arkansas law which barred any teaching of evolution in the state's public schools. This led creationists and other opponents of secular humanism to a new strategy: they endorsed "balanced-treatment legislation" under which school systems would be forced to give the biblical account of creation equal weight in their curricula with scientific theories of evolution. By 1982, 3 states—Arkansas, Louisiana, and Mississippi—had passed such balanced-treatment legislation, and another 18 states were considering various forms of creation science bills (Stuart, 1982; S. Taylor, 1987b).

However, in a key 1982 ruling, a federal district court judge overturned a balanced-treatment law passed in Arkansas. Judge William Ray Overton declared that "creation science . . . has no scientific merit or educational value." He added that the balanced-treatment law was "simply and purely an effort to introduce the Biblical version of creation into the public school curricula" and therefore violated the First Amendment guarantee of separation of church and state. Then, in 1987, the Supreme Court, by a 7-2 vote, held that states may not require the teaching of

creationism alongside evolution in public schools if the primary purpose of such legislation is to promote a religious viewpoint. Writing for the majority, Associate Justice William Brennan argued that a Louisiana balanced-treatment law "actually serves to diminish academic freedom by removing the flexibility to teach evolution without also teaching creation science" (Stuart, 1982:Al; S. Taylor, 1987c:7).

Although fundamentalists suffered a major defeat in the Louisiana case, there are many other battlegrounds in their campaign against secular humanism. In 1983, a group of fundamentalist parents in Tennessee brought suit in federal court, arguing that the school district was exposing their children to secular humanist materials which violated the families' religious beliefs. For example, a selection from *The Diary of Anne Frank* was criticized for implying that all religions are equal; *The Wizard of Oz* was attacked for diminishing the role of God in determining human qualities. In 1986, a federal judge ruled in favor of the parents and allowed them to remove their children from the reading classes. However, his decision was overturned in 1987, as an appeals court ruled that public school students can be required to read and discuss textbooks even though the lessons may offend their religious beliefs (Clendenin, 1986; *New York Times,* 1987c).

In the same year, a federal judge in Alabama ruled that 44 textbooks used in the state's public schools promoted a humanistic "religion" and neglected the role of traditional religion in American history and culture. Deciding in favor of a group of conservative Christian parents, he ordered the textbooks removed from the public schools. But an appeals court did not agree; it found that the books did not promote secular humanism or any antagonism toward God-centered religions (*New York Times,* 1987d; Toner, 1987).

Challenges to textbooks are especially sensitive for publishers because in 22 states—among them Texas, California, North Carolina, and Florida—statewide textbook adoption procedures exist for the selection of elementary and high school texts. If a publisher's junior high school American history textbook or high school chemistry textbook is adopted by an entire state, the publisher will receive substantial revenues. Consequently, larger states with statewide adoption procedures can exert considerable influence on the content of textbooks used in public schools. In 1989, California's state board of education adopted new textbook and teaching guidelines; responding to fundamentalist pressure, the board removed a reference to evolution as "scientific fact." However, the guidelines continue to offer strong support for the teaching of evolution in a state that accounts for 11 percent of all textbook sales in the United States (Willwerth, 1989).

Unfortunately, censorship efforts—even when unsuccessful—may have a chilling effect on school officials and publishers, leading them to remove or fail to use many valuable and rich sources out of fear of controversy. "Such timidity," warns Francis Roberts, a superintendent of schools in New York State, "may be the most serious form of censorship." He adds: "I find that in daily practice, public schools are more apt to be conserving institutions mirroring rather than challenging the values of the local culture." Without a willingness and ability to experiment with new materials, he concludes, teachers will restrict themselves to the safest, least controversial options, thereby justifying the view that "schools are places where the bland lead the bland" (Quade, 1984:32).

For others, of course, the dangers of censorship to freedom of thought and expression are paramount. What kind of society will we have, they wonder, if students are prevented from reading such works as *The Color Purple, The Diary of Anne Frank, Romeo and Juliet,* and even *The Wizard of Oz* and "Little Red Riding Hood"? Anticensorship activists worry that if efforts to restrict school materials are successful, they will contribute to growing censorship outside the educational world. Those who are willing to censor what children read—even if in the name of their religious beliefs and values—may also favor censorship of what *adults* read.

SUMMARY

Religion is found throughout the world because it offers answers to such ultimate questions as why we exist, why we succeed or fail, and why we die. This chapter examines the dimensions and functions of religion, types of religious organizations, and the role of religion in American life.

1 In contemporary industrial societies, scientific and technological advances have increasingly affected all aspects of life, including the social institution of religion.

2 Émile Durkheim stressed the social aspect of religion and attempted to understand individual religious behavior within the context of the larger society.

3 Religion can provide values and ends which help a society to function as an integrated social system.

4 From a Marxist point of view, religion lessens the possibility of collective political action that can end capitalist oppression and transform society.

5 Max Weber argued that Calvinism (and, to a lesser degree, other branches of Protestant religion) produced a type of person more likely to engage in capitalistic behavior.

6 *Religious beliefs, religious rituals,* and *religious experiences* are interrelated and help to reinforce one another.

7 Sociologists have identified four ideal types of religious organization: the *ecclesia,* the *denomination,* the *sect,* and the *cult.*

8 By far the largest single denomination in the United States is Roman Catholicism, although Protestant faiths collectively accounted for about 56 percent of the nation's adult population in 1990.

9 Despite the restrictions that exist against ordaining women in certain faiths, there has been a noticeable rise in female clergy in the United States over the last 15 years.

10 In the late 1960s, while major Christian denominations were beginning to shrink in size, a resurgence of *fundamentalism* began in the United States.

11 An important development in American religious life has been the dramatic rise of religious programming in the media.

12 It has been estimated that as many as 2 to 3 million Americans—primarily between the ages of 18 and 25—belong to religious sects and cults.

13 In recent years, there have been increasing efforts by fundamentalists and others to censor books and other materials used in school curricula.

KEY TERMS

Cosmology A general theory of the universe advanced by a religion. (page 423)

Creationists People who support a literal interpretation of the book of Genesis regarding the origins of the universe and argue that evolution should not be presented as established scientific fact. (423)

Cult A generally small, secretive religious group that represents either a new religion or a major innovation of an existing faith. (428)

Cultural universals General practices found in every culture. (414)

Denomination A large, organized religion not officially linked with the state or government. (426)

Ecclesia A religious organization that claims to include most of or all the members of a society and is recognized as the national or official religion. (426)

Established sect J. Milton Yinger's term for a religious group that is the outgrowth of a sect, yet remains isolated from society. (427)

Evangelical faiths Christian faiths which place great emphasis on a personal relationship between the individual and God and believe that each adherent must spread the faith and bear personal witness by openly declaring the religion to nonbelievers. (433)

Fundamentalism Adherence to earlier-accepted religious doctrines, often accompanied by a literal appli-

cation of historical beliefs and scriptures to today's world. (433)

Liberation theology Use of a church, primarily Roman Catholicism, in a political effort to eliminate poverty, discrimination, and other forms of injustice evident in secular society. (421)

Pentecostal faiths Religious groups similar in many respects to evangelical faiths, which in addition believe in the infusion of the Holy Spirit into services and in religious experiences such as faith healing and "speaking in tongues." (433)

Predestination A Calvinist doctrine which holds that people either will be among the elect, who are rewarded in heaven, or will be condemned to hell and that their futures are not dependent on being righteous or sinful while on earth. (422)

Profane The ordinary and commonplace elements of life, as distinguished from the sacred. (416)

Protestant ethic Max Weber's term for the disciplined work ethic, this-worldly concerns, and rational orientation of life emphasized by John Calvin and his followers. (422)

Religion According to Émile Durkheim, a unified system of beliefs and practices relative to sacred things. (415)

Religious beliefs Statements to which members of a particular religion adhere. (423)

Religious experience The feeling or perception of being in direct contact with the ultimate reality, such as a divine being, or of being overcome with religious emotion. (424)

Religious rituals Practices required or expected of members of a faith. (423)

Sacred Those elements beyond everyday life which inspire awe, respect, and even fear. (416)

Sect A relatively small religious group that has broken away from some other religious organization to renew what it views as the original vision of the faith. (427)

Secularization The process through which religion's influence on other social institutions diminishes. (414)

ADDITIONAL READINGS

Bellah, Robert H., and Frederick E. Greenspan (eds.). *Uncivil Religion: Interreligious Hostility in America.* New York: Crossroads, 1987. This anthology examines conflicts between Protestant and Catholic groups, as well as between established and newer religions.

Carmody, Denise Lardner. *Women and World Religions*

(2d ed.). Englewood Cliffs, N.J.: Prentice-Hall, 1989. A feminist examination of world religions and women's religious experiences.

Chalfant, H. Paul, Robert E. Beckley, and C. Eddie Palmer. *Religion in Contemporary Society* (2d ed.). Palo Alto, Calif.: Mayfield, 1987. The authors draw upon sociological research in order to study the organization, leadership, and current trends of religious life in the United States.

Cox, Harvey. *Religion in the Secular City.* New York: Simon and Schuster, 1984. The author of the important 1965 book *The Secular City,* Cox looks at religion in the 1980s with special focus on resurgent fundamentalism, the role of television, and religion in Latin America.

Demac, Donna A. *Liberty Denied: The Current Rise of Censorship in America.* New Brunswick, N.J.: Rutgers University Press, 1990. An examination of censorship in schools and libraries, use of libel suits to curtail speech, the debate over pornography, and actions of the Bush administration to restrict information.

Greeley, Andrew M. *Religious Change in America.* Cambridge, Mass.: Harvard University Press, 1989. Examines social trends in religious doctrine, church attendance, financial contributions, and social attitudes.

Hammond, Phillip E. (ed.). *The Sacred in a Secular Age.* Berkeley: University of California Press, 1985. An excellent anthology dealing with the sociology of religion.

Hoover, Stewart M. *Mass Media Religion: The Social Sources of the Electronic Church.* Newbury Park, Calif.: Sage, 1988. A sociological examination of religious television.

Lofland, John. *Doomsday Cult* (enlarged ed.). New York: Irvington, 1977. This book is based on the author's 1963 participant observation in a cult later identified as the Unification church. It has been updated, with a new focus on the cult's successes in recruitment and fund-raising during the 1970s.

Princeton Religion Research Center. *Religion in America, 1990 Report.* Princeton, N.J.: Princeton Religion Research Center, 1990. A wide-ranging examination of American attitudes toward religion which is updated annually.

Shupe, Anson, and Jeffrey K. Hadden (eds.). *The Politics of Religion and Social Change.* New York: Paragon House, 1988. This volume considers religion throughout the world and its interplay with politics, focusing on such topics as religion in South Africa, the experiences of Muslims in communist nations, the impact of Zionism on the mideast, and liberation theology.

Sigmund, Paul E. *Liberation Theology at the Crossroads: Democracy or Revolution?* New York: Oxford University Press, 1990. A careful look at liberation theology, with appendixes reprinting some of the writings of Gustavo Gutiérrez.

Stark, Rodney, and William Sims Bainbridge. *The Future of Religion.* Berkeley: University of California Press, 1985. An examination of contemporary religion, from traditional denominations to cults.

Journals

The sociological study of religion is reflected in the *Journal for the Scientific Study of Religion* (founded in 1961), *Review of Religious Research* (1958), *Social Compass* (1954), and *Sociological Analysis* (1940). The monthly newsletter *Emerging Trends,* published by the Princeton Religion Research Center beginning in 1979, provides the latest survey data on religious life.

15

GOVERNMENT AND THE ECONOMY

LOOKING AHEAD

- How do capitalism, socialism, and communism differ as ideal types?
- How are systems of power and authority organized?
- Can Americans be considered apathetic in their political behavior?
- Is the United States run by a small ruling elite?
- How does a profession differ from an occupation?
- Have affirmative action programs gone too far—or not far enough—in an effort to combat discrimination against women and minorities?

By 1990, people across the United States were well-aware of the devastating crisis in the nation's savings and loan industry. The Resolution Trust Corporation, established by the federal government in 1989, had already overseen the closing of 148 savings and loan institutions that had gone bankrupt. It was in the process of attempting to sell 285 more institutions, while still another 400 were expected to come under the control of the corporation. According to estimates, as many as 95 percent of all savings and loan companies were in a precarious financial position (J. Knight, 1990).

As the savings and loan crisis continued, there were varying, but ever-increasing, estimates as to the eventual cost of the government "bailout" of the industry. One such estimate, $370 billion—offered by the General Accounting Office in late 1990—was translated into comparative data by researchers. That same figure would have funded the U.S. Food for Peace program at its 1989 level for 336 years. Similarly, $370 billion would have funded the Drug Enforcement Agency for 647 years; it would have supported the federal government's prenatal care programs for 1771 years (J. Knight and Schmidt, 1990; Maraniss and Atkinson, 1989).

What led to this financial crisis? After achieving record profits in 1978, the savings and loan industry went into a tailspin in the early 1980s. Competition for consumers' savings had intensified after the creation of money market accounts and other high-interest investment opportunities by brokerage houses and mutual funds. At the same time, a 1982 federal law encouraged savings and loan companies to move away from the home mortgage business toward a new emphasis on riskier but potentially more profitable commercial and real estate loans. Finally, as part of a larger effort to streamline the federal bureaucracy and reduce government regulation of business, the Reagan administration cut the number of federal examiners and auditors for the savings and loan industry by 75 percent over the period 1981–1985. By 1983, there were fewer than 800 examiners for the entire United States; because of low pay and high turnover, many of these examiners had been on the job less than 2 years (L. J. Davis, 1990:62; Maraniss and Atkinson, 1989; P. Taylor, 1990).

Consequently, the industry was simultaneously facing greater competition, was shifting toward riskier investments, and was increasingly without government supervision. In this environment, it became easy for unscrupulous owners and officers of savings and loan institutions to make fraudulent loans and exchanges of land—or to pay themselves astronomical salaries supplemented by lavish fringe benefits. Charles H. Keating, Jr., who ran the now infamous Lincoln Savings and Loan, determined that his own services to the institution were worth as much as $3.2 million per year. He hired almost his entire immediate family to work at Lincoln; regulators believe that the Keating family was paid a minimum of $34 million by Lincoln during the 1980s. According to a 1990 estimate, the failure of Lincoln Savings and Loan may cost taxpayers more than $2 billion (L. J. Davis, 1990:58–59).

The savings and loan crisis has clearly shaken the economic system of the United States. The term *economic system* refers to the social institution through which goods and services are produced, distributed, and consumed. As with social institutions such as the family, religion, and government, the economic system shapes other aspects of the social order and is, in turn, influenced by them. Throughout this textbook, we have been reminded of the economy's impact on social behavior—for example, individual and group behavior in factories and offices. We have studied the work of Karl Marx and Friedrich Engels (see Chapters 1 and 8), who emphasized that the economic system of a society can promote social inequality. And we learned (in Chapter 9) that foreign investment in developing countries can intensify inequality among residents.

Like the nation's economic system, the political system of the United States has been shaken by the savings and loan crisis. The term *political system* refers to the social institution which relies on a recognized set of procedures for implementing and achieving the goals of a group. Each society must have a political system in order to maintain recognized procedures for allocating valued resources. Thus, like religion and the family, the economic and political systems are cultural universals; they are social institutions found in every society.

A society's economic system is deeply intertwined with its political system. In the example of the savings and loan crisis, the political system of the United States influenced the economy by encouraging the savings and loan industry to shift to riskier investments. At the same time, policymakers reduced government regulation of the industry by cutting the number of federal examiners and auditors. In the 1990s, the political system will have to face the consequences of the savings and loan crisis, for taxpayers will eventually bear the burden of the bailout of the industry.

Chapter 15 will present sociological analysis of the impact of government and the economy on people's lives. We will begin with macro-level analysis of the variety of economic systems used by preindustrial and industrial societies to handle tasks of production and distribution. Next we will examine the sources of power in a political system and will describe three types of authority identified by Max Weber. In studying government and politics in the United States, we will give particular attention to political socialization, citizens' participation in political life, the changing role of women in politics, and the influence of interest groups on decision making. The question "Who really rules the United States?" will be posed, and the elite and pluralist models of power will be contrasted. Then, using micro-level sociological analysis, we will consider work and the workplace. Finally, the social policy section will focus on the intense debate over affirmative action, which has been endorsed as a remedy for sex and race discrimination on the job.

ECONOMIC SYSTEMS

Preindustrial Societies

The earliest written documents known to exist, clay tablets from about 3000 B.C., were found in 1981 in Iran, Iraq, and Syria. It is fitting commentary on the importance of the economic sector that these tablets record units of land and agricultural products such as grain. Of course, economic life has grown exceedingly complex during the intervening 5000 years. One key factor in this change has been the development of increasingly

Preindustrial economic systems still exist in the 1990s. Shown here are Kenyan women in East Africa carrying wood on their heads.

sophisticated technology for tasks of production and distribution.

The term **technology** refers to the application of knowledge to the making of tools and the utilization of natural resources. The form that a particular economic system takes is not totally defined by the available technology. Nevertheless, the level of technology will limit, for example, the degree to which a society can depend on irrigation or complex machinery.

Sociologists Gerhard Lenski and Jean Lenski developed a classification scheme which categorizes societies on the basis of their economic systems. In their view, the first type of society to emerge is the **hunting-and-gathering society,** in which people rely on whatever foods and fiber are readily available in order to live. The amount of technology in such societies is minimal. People are constantly on the move in search of food, and there is little division of labor into specialized tasks (Lenski et al., 1991).

Hunting-and-gathering societies are composed of small, widely dispersed groups. Each group consists almost entirely of people related to one another. As a result, kinship ties are the source of authority and influence, and the family takes on a particularly important role. Since resources are scarce, there is relatively little inequality in terms of material goods. Social differentiation within the hunting-and-gathering society is based on such ascribed characteristics as gender, age, and family background.

Horticultural societies, in which people plant seeds and crops rather than subsist merely on available foods, emerged perhaps 9000 years ago. In contrast to the hunters and gatherers, members of horticultural societies are much less nomadic. Consequently, they place greater emphasis on the production of tools and household objects. Yet technology within such societies remains rather limited. Cultivation of crops is performed with the aid of digging sticks or hoes.

As farming in horticultural societies gradually becomes more efficient, a social surplus is created. The term **social surplus** refers to the production by a group of people of enough goods to cover their own needs, while at the same time sustaining individuals who are not engaged in agricultural tasks. Through the emergence of a surplus, some individuals in horticultural societies begin to specialize in such tasks as governance, military defense, and leadership of religious observance. As noted in Chapter 8, increasing division of labor can lead to a hierarchical social order and to differential rewards and power. The concept of social surplus and its consequences in terms of stratification will be examined more fully in Chapter 18.

The last stage of preindustrial development in Lenski and Lenski's model is the *agrarian society.* As in horticultural societies, members of agrarian societies are primarily engaged in the production of food. However, because of the introduction of new technological innovations such as the plow, farmers dramatically increase their crop yield. It becomes possible to cultivate the same fields over generations, thereby allowing the emergence of still larger settlements.

The technology of the agrarian society continues to rely on the physical power of humans and animals. Nevertheless, there is more extensive division of labor than in horticultural societies. Individuals focus on specialized tasks, such as repair of fishing nets or work as a blacksmith. As human settlements become more established and stable, political institutions become more elaborate and concepts of property rights take on growing importance. The comparative permanence and greater surpluses of agrarian society make it more feasible to create artifacts such as statues, public monuments, and art objects and to pass them on from one generation to the next.

Industrial Societies

Although the industrial revolution did not topple monarchs, it produced changes as significant as those resulting from political revolutions. The *industrial revolution,* which took place largely in England during the period 1760–1830, was a scientific revolution focused on the application of nonanimal sources of power to labor tasks. It involved changes in the social organization of the workplace, as people left the homestead and began working in central locations such as factories.

As the industrial revolution proceeded, societies relied on new inventions that facilitated agricultural and industrial production and on new sources of energy such as steam. Many societies underwent an irrevocable shift from an agrarian-oriented economy to an industrial base. No longer did an individual or family typically make an entire product. Instead, the division of labor became increasingly complex, especially as manu-

facturing of goods became more common (Lenski et al., 1991).

The process of industrialization had distinctive social consequences. Families and communities could not continue to function as self-sufficient units. Individuals, villages, and regions began to exchange goods and services and become interdependent. As people came to rely on the labor of members of other communities, the family lost its unique position as the source of power and authority. The need for specialized knowledge led to more formalized education, and education emerged as a social institution distinct from the family.

In general terms, an *industrial society* can be defined as a "society that relies chiefly on mechanization for the production of its economic goods and services" (Dushkin, 1991:283–284). There are two basic types of economic systems which distinguish contemporary industrial societies: capitalism and socialism. As described in the following sections, capitalism and socialism serve as ideal types of economic systems. No nation precisely fits either model. Instead, the economy of each industrial state represents a mixture of capitalism and socialism, although one type or the other will generally be more useful in describing a society's economic structure.

Capitalism In the preindustrial societies described earlier, land functioned as the source of virtually all wealth. However, the industrial revolution required that certain individuals and institutions be willing to take substantial risks in order to finance new inventions, machinery, and business enterprises. Consequently, bankers, industrialists, and other holders of large sums of money replaced landowners as the most powerful economic force. These people invested their funds in the hope of realizing even greater profits and thereby became owners of property and business firms.

The transition to private ownership of business was accompanied by the emergence of the capitalist economic system. As we saw in Chapter 8, *capitalism* is an economic system in which the means of production are largely in private hands and the main incentive for economic activity is the accumulation of profits (Rosenberg, 1991). In practice, capitalist systems vary in the degree to which private ownership and economic activity are regulated by government.

During the period immediately following the industrial revolution, the prevailing form of capitalism was what is termed *laissez-faire* ("let them do"). Under the principle of laissez-faire, as expounded and endorsed by British economist Adam Smith (1723–1790), people could compete freely with minimal government intervention in the economy. Business retained the right to regulate itself and essentially operated without fear of government regulation (Smelser, 1963:6–7).

Two centuries later, capitalism has taken on a somewhat different form. Private ownership and maximization of profits remain the most significant characteristics of capitalist economic systems. However, in contrast to the era of laissez-faire, contemporary capitalism features extensive government regulation of economic relations. Without restrictions, business firms can mislead consumers, endanger the safety of their workers, and even defraud the companies' investors—all in the pursuit of greater profits. As a result, the government of a capitalist nation often monitors prices, sets safety standards for industries, passes legislation to protect the rights of consumers, and regulates collective bargaining between labor unions and management. Yet, under capitalism as an ideal type, government rarely takes over ownership of an entire industry.

Contemporary capitalism also differs from laissez-faire in another important respect: the tolerance of monopolistic practices. A *monopoly* exists in a market when it is controlled by a single business firm. Domination of an industry allows the firm to effectively control a commodity so that it can dictate pricing, standards of quality, and availability. Buyers have little choice but to yield to the firm's decision; there is no other place to purchase the product or service. Clearly, monopolistic practices violate the ideal of free competition cherished by Adam Smith and other supporters of laissez-faire capitalism.

As is true in the United States, the government of a capitalist nation can outlaw monopolies through antitrust legislation. Such laws prevent any business from taking over so much of the competition in an industry that it gains control of the market. The federal government allows monopolies to exist only in certain exceptional cases, such as the utility and transportation industries. Even then, regulatory agencies are established to scrutinize these officially approved monopolies and protect the public. Yet, as conflict theorists point out, while *pure* monopolies are not a basic element of the American economy, competition is much more restricted than one might expect in what is called a *free enterprise system*. In numerous industries, a few companies largely dominate the field and exclude new enterprises from entering the marketplace.

An *oligopoly* is a market with relatively few sellers. In the United States, three cereal companies account for 80 percent of the market. Moreover, control of the domestic production of 98 percent of locomotives, 96 percent of automobiles, 88 percent of chewing gum, and 81 percent of cigarettes is held by no more than four firms in each of these respective industries. The nation's economy has remained concentrated in the hands of a small number of companies. In 1988, the 334 largest manufacturers, each with assets of at least $1 billion, accounted for 73 percent of all net profits. These statistics indicate that the principle of free competition has been seriously compromised in contemporary capitalist societies (Bureau of the Census, 1990a:541; Galbraith, 1978: 189–196; Nader et al., 1976:209).

Socialism Socialist theory has its roots in the writings of Karl Marx and Friedrich Engels (see Chapter 1). These European radicals were disturbed by the exploitation of the working class as it emerged during the industrial revolution. In their view, capitalism forced large numbers of people to exchange their labor for wages. As was detailed in Chapter 8, the owners of an industry profit from the labor of their workers, primarily because they pay workers less than the value of the goods produced.

As an ideal type, a socialist economic system represents an attempt to eliminate such economic exploitation. Under *socialism,* the means of production and distribution in a society are collectively rather than privately owned. The basic objective of the economic system is to meet people's needs rather than to maximize profits. Socialists reject the laissez-faire philosophy that free competition benefits the general public. Instead, they believe that basic economic decisions should be made by the central government, which acts as the representative of the people. Therefore, government ownership of all major industries—including steel production, automobile manufacturing, and agriculture—is a major feature of socialism as an ideal type.

In practice, socialist economic systems vary in the extent to which private ownership is tolerated. For example, in Great Britain, a nation with certain aspects of both a socialist and a capitalist economy, passenger airline service is concentrated in the government-owned corporation British Airways. Yet private airline companies are allowed to compete with it.

Socialist societies also differ from capitalist nations in their commitment to social service programs. For example, the United States government provides health care and health insurance for the elderly and destitute through the Medicare and Medicaid programs (see Chapter 17). By contrast, socialist countries typically offer government-financed medical care for *all* citizens. In theory, the wealth of the people as a collectivity is used to provide health care, housing, education, and other key services for each individual and family.

In recent decades, the Soviet Union, the People's Republic of China, Vietnam, Cuba, and the nations of eastern Europe were popularly thought of as examples of communist economic systems. However, this is actually an incorrect usage of a term with sensitive political connotations. As an ideal type, **communism** refers to an economic system under which all property is communally owned and no social distinctions are made on the basis of people's ability to produce. In Marx's view, communist societies will naturally evolve out of the stage of socialism. The socialist state or government of each nation will eventually "wither away," as will all inequality and social class differentiation. Although the leaders of many twentieth-century revolutions—including the Russian Revolution of 1917 and the Chinese Revolution of 1949–1950—have proclaimed the goal of achieving a classless communist society, all nations known as *communist* in the twentieth century have remained far from this ideal.

In the late 1980s, dramatic political and economic changes took place in the Soviet Union and

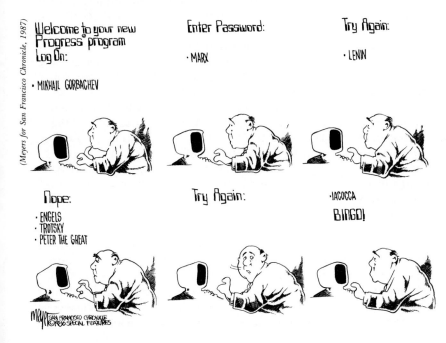

This cartoon draws attention to the mixed economy of the Soviet Union: Soviet leader Mikhail Gorbachev must log into his computerized "Progress" program by using the name of the world-famous American automobile executive Lee Iacocca—rather than Marx, Lenin, or some other cherished socialist hero.

eastern Europe. The year 1989 saw a remarkable transformation of eastern European politics. At the beginning of the year, Hungary was alone in the region in taking initial and hesitant steps toward a competitive political system. By December, however, the political dominance of the Communist party was dissolving not only in Hungary, but also in Poland, East Germany, Czechoslovakia, Bulgaria, and Rumania.

At the same time that Communist party rule was being overthrown, many of these nations—including Hungary, Poland, Czechoslovakia, and East Germany (now part of a newly unified Germany)—were moving away from centrally controlled economies toward western-style market economies, if not full-fledged capitalism. The pace of change was astonishing. Under the leadership of Prime Minister Margaret Thatcher, Great Britain had taken 10 years to privatize less than 10 percent of British industries. Yet, as Hungarian economist Marton Tardos observed: "Here we have to privatize six times as much in three years [as Britain did in a decade]. If we do not privatize a significant amount in three years, we fear the Hungarian economy will collapse" (S. Greenhouse, 1990:E3).

Why have there been such unprecedented political and economic changes in the Soviet Union and eastern Europe? A critical factor was Soviet leader Mikhail Gorbachev's willingness to encourage "pro-reform" elements in his own country and other nations long under the shadow of their powerful neighbors. Other factors which contributed to the startling events in the region were the unpopularity (and eventually the removal) of longtime Communist party leaders; the courage of intellectuals in openly criticizing Communist dominance; the growing involvement of the general population in public protests against Communist rule; the recognition by Communist leaders that their economies were in a precarious state; and the decision of the Soviet leadership not to intervene in eastern Europe, thereby allowing the overthrow of Communist regimes (Schopflin, 1990).

As we have seen, capitalism and socialism serve as ideal types of economic systems. In reality, the economy of each industrial society—including the United States, Great Britain, and the Soviet Union—includes certain elements of both capitalism and socialism. Whatever differences, whether they more closely fit the ideal type of capitalism or socialism, all industrial societies rely chiefly on mechanization in the production of goods and services.

Postindustrial Societies

The significant changes in the occupational structure of industrial societies as their focus shifts from manufacturing to service industries have led social scientists to call technically advanced nations *postindustrial societies*. Sociologist Daniel Bell (1973:20) defines **postindustrial society** as a society whose economic system is based on the production of information rather than of goods. Large numbers of people become involved in occupations devoted to the teaching, generation, or dissemination of ideas (Molitor, 1981).

Taking a functionalist perspective, Bell views this transition from industrial to postindustrial society as a positive development. He sees a general decline in organized working-class groups and a rise in interest groups concerned with such national issues as health, education, and the environment. Bell's outlook is functionalist because he portrays postindustrial society as basically consensual. Organizations and interest groups will engage in an open and competitive process of decision making. The level of conflict between diverse groups will diminish, and there will be much greater social stability.

Conflict theorists take issue with Bell's analysis of postindustrial society. For example, Michael Harrington (1980:125–126), who alerted the nation to the problems of the poor in his book *The Other America,* was critical of the significance Bell attached to the growing class of white-collar workers. Harrington conceded that scientists, engineers, and economists are involved in important political and economic decisions, but he disagreed with Bell's claim that they have a free hand in decision making, independent of the interests of the rich.

Harrington followed in the tradition of Marx by arguing that conflict between social classes will continue in postindustrial society. Similarly,

(Sepp Seitz/Woodfin Camp & Associates)

Sociologist Daniel Bell defines a postindustrial society *as one whose economic system is based on the production of information rather than goods.*

French sociologist Alain Touraine (1971) suggests that the common interests of workers in service industries will provide the basis for a new type of working-class movement. Differing with Bell's vision of postindustrial consensus, Touraine predicts that class-related antagonisms will increase in the future (Montagna, 1977:50–55). Other observers, reflecting a conflict perspective, have noted that the move to a postindustrial society in the United States has led to a loss of manufacturing jobs, a lessening of the role of unions in protecting and avocation the rights of workers, and an increase in the number of unemployed, underemployed, and homeless Americans.

In summary, postindustrial society may differ from industrial society in terms of the labor that people do, but perennial social problems will not disappear. As sociologist Paul Blumberg (1980:217) has suggested, scarcity, poverty, inequality, and unemployment are still with us—despite the birth of a postindustrial world.

POLITICS AND GOVERNMENT

A cultural universal common to all economic systems is the exercise of power and authority. The struggle for power and authority inevitably involves *politics,* which political scientist Harold Lasswell (1936) defined as who gets what, when, and how. In their study of politics and government, sociologists are concerned with social interactions among individuals and groups and their impact on the larger political and economic order.

Power

Power is at the heart of a political system. In Chapter 8, Max Weber's concept of power was examined, and *power* was defined as the ability to exercise one's will over others. To put it another way, if one party in a relationship can control the behavior of the other, that individual or group is exercising power. Power relations can involve large organizations, small groups, or even people in an intimate association. As we saw in Chapter 13, Blood and Wolfe (1960) devised the concept of *marital power* to describe the manner in which decision making is distributed within families (refer back to Box 13-1 on page 386).

There are three basic sources of power within any political system—force, influence, and authority. *Force* is the actual or threatened use of coercion to impose one's will on others. When leaders imprison or even execute political dissi-

BOX 15-1 • AROUND THE WORLD

TERRORIST VIOLENCE

The 1972 murders of Israeli athletes during the Olympic games in Munich; the 1979 seizure of the United States embassy in Iran; the 1991 attempt by the Irish Republican Army (IRA) to assassinate British Prime Minister John Major; numerous attacks on civilians in airports, trains, and city streets—all reflect the growing climate of terrorist violence around the world. *Terrorism* is the use or threat of violence against random or symbolic targets in pursuit of political aims. While terrorism often is related to international political controversies, there is domestic terrorism as well: for example, the bombing of women's health clinics that offer abortions by certain antiabortion activists (Getron, 1989; Gibbs, 1989; M. Wilson and Lynxwiler, 1988).

An essential aspect of contemporary terrorism involves use of the media. Terrorists may wish to keep secret their individual identities, but they want their political messages and goals to receive as much publicity as possible. Drawing upon Erving Goffman's dramaturgical approach, sociologist Alfred McClung Lee (1983) has likened terrorism to the theater, where certain scenes are played out in a predictable fashion. Whether through phone calls to the media, anonymous manifestos, or other means, terrorists typically admit responsibility for and defend their violent acts.

For terrorists, the end justifies the means. The status quo is viewed as oppressive; desperate measures are believed essential to end the suffering of the deprived. Convinced that working through the formal political process will not effect desired political change, terrorists insist that illegal actions—often directed against innocent people—are needed. In a sense, terrorists hope to intimidate society and thereby bring about a new political order (Paul, 1987).

Some political commentators have argued that terrorism defies definition because one person's "terrorist" is another person's "freedom fighter." In this view, we carry our biases into our evaluation of terrorist incidents and criticize only those perpetrated by groups who do not share our political goals (Herman and O'Sullivan, 1990).

Sociologists reject this critique, countering that even in warfare there are accepted rules outlawing the use of certain tactics. For example, civilian noncombatants are supposedly immune from deliberate attack and are not to be taken prisoner. If we are to set objective standards regarding terrorism, then we should condemn *any and all people* who are guilty of certain actions, no matter how understandable or even admirable some of their goals may be (R. Miller, 1988).

dents, they are applying force; so, too, are terrorists when they seize an embassy or assassinate a political leader (see Box 15-1). *Influence,* on the other hand, refers to the exercise of power through a process of persuasion. A citizen may change his or her position regarding a Supreme Court nominee because of a newspaper editorial, the expert testimony of a law school dean before the Senate Judiciary Committee, or a stirring speech at a rally by a political activist. In each case, sociologists would view such efforts to persuade people as examples of influence. The third source of power, *authority*, will be discussed in the next section of this chapter.

Types of Authority

The term *authority* refers to power that has been institutionalized and is recognized by the people over whom it is exercised. Sociologists commonly use the term in connection with those who hold legitimate power through elected or publicly acknowledged positions. It is important to stress that a person's authority is limited by the constraints of a particular social position. Thus, a referee has the authority to decide whether a penalty should be called during a football game but has no authority over the price of tickets to the game.

Max Weber (1947, original edition 1913) devel-

(Marc & Evelyne Bernheim/Woodfin Camp & Associates)

A Yoruba king and elders in Nigeria. The king's young attendants carry his ceremonial swords, symbols of traditional authority.

oped a classification system regarding authority that has become one of the most useful and frequently cited contributions of early sociology. He identified three ideal types of authority: traditional, legal-rational, and charismatic. Weber did not insist that only one type of authority is accepted in a given society or particular organization. Rather, all can be present, but their relative importance will vary. Sociologists have found Weber's typology to be quite valuable in understanding different manifestations of legitimate power within a society.

Traditional Authority In a political system based on *traditional authority,* legitimate power is conferred by custom and accepted practice. The orders of one's superiors are felt to be legitimate because "this is how things have always been done." For example, a king or queen is accepted as ruler of a nation simply by virtue of inheriting the crown. The monarch may be loved or hated,

competent or destructive; in terms of legitimacy, that does not matter. For the traditional leader, authority rests in custom, not in personal characteristics, technical competence, or even written law. Traditional authority is absolute in many instances because the ruler has the ability to determine laws and policies.

Legal-Rational Authority Power made legitimate by law is known as *legal-rational authority.* Leaders derive their legal-rational authority from the written rules and regulations of political systems. For example, the authority of the president of the United States and the Congress is legitimized by the American Constitution. Generally, in societies that are based on legal-rational authority, leaders are conceived of as having specific areas of competence and authority. They are not viewed as having divine inspiration, as are the heads of certain societies with traditional forms of authority.

BOX 15-2 • SPEAKING OUT

MARTIN LUTHER KING ON WAR AND PEACE

One source of charismatic appeal is the eloquence of a political or religious leader. Certainly this was true of Dr. Martin Luther King, Jr., whose famed "I have a dream" speech during the 1963 march on Washington for civil rights inspired many Americans of all races. King was well-aware of the ways in which political decisions on the world scene influenced domestic issues. In the following selection, excerpted from the conclusion of his last book, Where Do We Go from Here: Chaos or Community? *King (1968:181, 185–186, 191) addresses the danger of nuclear weapons and the need to cherish peace:*

. . . A final problem that mankind must solve in order to survive in the world house that we have inherited is finding an alternative to war and human destruction. Recent events have vividly reminded us that nations are not reducing but rather increasing their arsenals of weapons of mass destruction. The best brains in the highly developed nations of the world are devoted to military technology. The proliferation of nuclear weapons has not been halted, in spite of the limited-test-ban treaty [of 1963]. . . .

It is not enough to say, "We must not wage war." It is necessary to love peace and sacrifice for it. We must concentrate not merely on the eradication of war but on the affirmation of peace. A fascinating story about Ulysses and the Sirens is preserved for us in Greek literature. The Sirens had the ability to sing so sweetly

(UPI/Bettmann Newsphotos)

Dr. Martin Luther King, Jr.

that sailors could not resist steering toward their island. Many ships were lured upon the rocks, and men forgot home, duty and honor as they flung themselves into the sea to be embraced by arms that drew them down to death. Ulysses, determined not to succumb to the Sirens, first decided to tie himself tightly to the mast of his boat and his crew stuffed their ears with wax. But finally he and his crew learned a better way to save themselves: They took on board the beautiful singer Orpheus, whose melodies were sweeter than the music of the Sirens. When Orpheus sang, who would bother to listen to the Sirens?

So we must see that peace represents a sweeter music, a cosmic melody that is far superior to the discords of war. Somehow we

must transform the dynamics of the world power struggle from the nuclear arms race, which no one can win, to a creative contest to harness man's genius for the purpose of making peace and prosperity a reality for all the nations of the world. In short, we must shift the arms race into a "peace race." If we have the will and determination to mount such a peace offensive, we will unlock hitherto tightly sealed doors of hope and bring new light into the dark chambers of pessimism. . . .

We are now faced with the fact that tomorrow is today. We are confronted with the fierce urgency of *now.* In this unfolding conundrum of life and history there is such a thing as being too late. Procrastination is still the thief of time. Life often leaves us standing bare, naked and dejected with a lost opportunity. The "tide in the affairs of men" does not remain at the flood; it ebbs. We may cry out desperately for time to pause in her passage, but time is deaf to every plea and rushes on. Over the bleached bones and jumbled residues of numerous civilizations are written the pathetic words: "Too late." There is an invisible book of life that faithfully records our vigilance or our neglect. "The moving finger writes, and having writ moves on. . . ." We still have a choice today: nonviolent coexistence or violent coannihilation. This may well be mankind's last chance to choose between chaos and community.

Charismatic Authority Weber also observed that power can be legitimized by the charisma of an individual. The term *charismatic authority* refers to power made legitimate by a leader's exceptional personal or emotional appeal to his or her followers. Charisma allows a person to lead or inspire without relying on set rules or traditions. Interestingly, charismatic authority is derived more from the beliefs of loyal followers than from the actual qualities of leaders. So long as people *perceive* a leader as possessing qualities that set him or her apart from ordinary citizens, that leader's authority will remain secure and often unquestioned.

Unlike traditional rulers, charismatic leaders often become well known by breaking with established institutions and advocating dramatic changes in the social structure and the economic system. The strong hold that such individuals have over their followers makes it easier to build protest movements which challenge the dominant norms and values of a society. Thus, charismatic leaders such as Jesus, Joan of Arc, Mahatma Gandhi, and Martin Luther King (see Box 15-2) all used their power to press for changes in accepted social behavior. But so did Adolf Hitler, whose charismatic appeal turned people toward violent and destructive ends.

Observing from an interactionist perspective, sociologist Carl Couch (1990) points out that the growth of the electronic media has facilitated the development of charismatic authority. During the 1930s, the heads of state of the United States, Great Britain, and Germany all used radio to issue direct appeals to citizens. In recent decades, television has allowed leaders to "visit" people's homes and communicate with them. In 1950, for example, President Harry Truman announced the outbreak of the Korean war on television. By 1990, Iraq's president, Saddam Hussein, was posing with foreign "guests" (actually, hostages) to convey a particular message to an international audience (see also Wasielewski, 1985).

If charismatic authority is to extend beyond the lifetime of the leader, it must undergo what Weber (1947:363–386, original edition 1913) called the *routinization of charismatic authority*—the process by which the leadership qualities originally associated with an individual are incorpo-

rated into either a traditional or a legal-rational system. Thus, the charismatic authority of Jesus was transferred to the apostle Peter and subsequently to the various prelates (or popes) of the Christian faith. Similarly, the emotional fervor supporting George Washington was routinized into the constitutional system of the United States and the norm of a two-term presidency. Once routinization has taken place, authority evolves into a traditional or legal-rational form.

As was noted earlier, Weber used traditional, legal-rational, and charismatic authority as ideal types. In reality, particular leaders and political systems combine elements of two or more of these forms. Presidents Franklin D. Roosevelt, John F. Kennedy, and Ronald Reagan wielded power largely through the legal-rational basis of their authority. At the same time, they were unusually charismatic leaders who commanded the personal loyalty of large numbers of citizens.

POLITICAL BEHAVIOR IN THE UNITED STATES

As citizens of the United States, we take for granted many aspects of our political system. We are accustomed to living in a nation with a Bill of Rights, two major political parties, voting by secret ballot, an elected president, state and local governments distinct from the national government, and so forth. Yet, of course, each society has its own ways of governing itself and making decisions. Just as we expect Democratic and Republican candidates to compete for public offices, residents of the People's Republic of China and Cuba are accustomed to the domination of the Communist party. In this section, we will examine a number of important aspects of political behavior within the United States.

Political Socialization

In Chapter 5, five functional prerequisites that a society must fulfill in order to survive were identified. Among these was the need to teach recruits to accept the values and customs of the group. In a political sense, this function is crucial; each suc-

(Leif Skoogfors/Woodfin Camp & Associates)

In the United States, children are socialized to view representative democracy as the best form of government and to cherish such values as freedom, equality, and patriotism. One part of this socialization process is teaching children about symbols of the nation's political heritage, such as the Liberty Bell.

ceeding generation must be encouraged to accept a society's basic political values and its particular methods of decision making.

Political socialization is the process by which individuals acquire political attitudes and develop patterns of political behavior. This involves not only learning the prevailing beliefs of a society but also coming to accept the surrounding political system despite its limitations and problems (Marger, 1981:321–323). In the United States, people are socialized to view representative democracy as the best form of government and to

cherish such values as freedom, equality, patriotism, and the right of dissent.

The principal institutions of political socialization are those which also socialize us to other cultural norms—including the family, schools, and the media. Many observers see the family as playing a particularly significant role in the process. "The family incubates political man," observed political scientist Robert Lane (1959:204). In fact, parents pass on their political attitudes and evaluations to their sons and daughters through discussions at the dinner table and also through the example of their political involvement or apathy. Early socialization does not always *determine* a person's political orientation; there are changes over time and between generations. Yet research on political socialization continues to show that parents' views have an important impact on their children's outlook (Jennings and Niemi, 1981:384).

The schools can be influential in political socialization, since they provide young people with information and analysis of the political world. Unlike the family and peer groups, schools are easily susceptible to centralized and uniform control; consequently, totalitarian societies commonly use educational institutions for purposes of indoctrination. Yet, even in democracies, where local schools are not under the pervasive control of the national government, political education will generally reflect the norms and values of the prevailing political order.

In the view of conflict theorists, American students learn much more than factual information about our political and economic way of life. They are socialized to view capitalism and representative democracy as the "normal" and most desirable ways of organizing a nation. At the same time, competing values and forms of government are often presented in a most negative fashion or are ignored. From a conflict perspective this type of political education serves the interests of the powerful and ignores the significance of the social divisions found within the United States (Marger, 1981:324–325).

Like the family and schools, the mass media can have obvious effects on people's thinking and political behavior—this is one reason why the media were included among the agents of socialization discussed in Chapter 4. Beginning with the Kennedy-Nixon presidential debates of 1960, television has given increasing exposure to political candidates. One result has been the rising importance of politicians' "images" as perceived by the American public. Today, many speeches given by our nation's leaders are designed not for immediate listeners but for the larger television audience. Moreover, as the United States heads toward each presidential election, television now plays an important role (formerly the province of political parties and newspapers) in identifying the leading candidates for each party and narrowing the field of contenders (Gans, 1979).

Participation and Apathy

In theory, a representative democracy will function most effectively and fairly if there is an informed and active electorate communicating its views to government leaders. Unfortunately, this is hardly the case in the United States. Virtually all Americans are familiar with the basics of the

TABLE 15-1 Political Party Preferences in the United States, 1990

PARTY IDENTIFICATION	PERCENTAGE OF POPULATION
Strong Democrat	12
Not very strong Democrat	23
Independent, close to Democrat	10
Independent	11
Independent, close to Republican	11
Not very strong Republican	21
Strong Republican	12

SOURCE: NORC, 1990:100.

According to the results of a national survey conducted in 1990, approximately 45 percent of the citizens of the United States identify to some extent with the Democratic party, while about 44 percent identify with the Republican party.

political process, and most tend to identify to some extent with a political party (see Table 15-1), but only a small minority (often members of the higher social classes) actually participate in political organizations on a local or national level. Studies reveal that only 8 percent of Americans belong to a political club or organization. Not more than one in five has *ever* contacted an official of national, state, or local government about a political issue or problem (Orum, 1989:249).

The failure of most Americans to become involved in political parties has serious implications for the functioning of our democracy. Within the political system of the United States, the political party serves as an intermediary between people and government. Through competition in regularly scheduled elections, the two-party system provides for challenges to public policies and for an orderly transfer of power. An individual dissatisfied with the state of the nation or a local community can become involved in the political party process many ways, such as by joining a political club supporting candidates for public office, or working to change the party's position on controversial issues. If, however, people do not take interest in the decisions of major political parties, public officials in a "representative" democracy will be chosen from two unrepresentative lists of candidates.

In the 1980s, it became clear that many people in the United States were turned off by political parties, politicians, and the specter of big government. The most dramatic indication of this growing alienation comes from voting statistics. Voters of all ages and races appear to be less enthusiastic than ever about American elections, even presidential contests. For example, almost 80 percent of eligible voters in the United States went to the polls in the presidential election of 1896. Yet by the 1988 election, turnout had fallen to less than 58 percent of all eligible voters. By contrast, elections in the late 1980s brought out 84 percent or more of the voting-age population in Australia, France, Italy, the Netherlands, New Zealand, and Sweden (Cummings and Wise, 1989:349; Milbrath, 1981; Rodgers and Harrington, 1981:20–28).

Declining political participation allows institu-

TABLE 15-2 Surveys of Voter Participation in the Presidential Elections of 1972 and 1988

	1972 (NIXON-MCGOVERN)		1988 (BUSH-DUKAKIS)	
GROUP	PERCENT REGISTERED	PERCENT WHO VOTED	PERCENT REGISTERED	PERCENT WHO VOTED
Total U.S. population	72.3	63.0	66.6	57.4
Whites	73.4	64.5	67.9	59.1
Blacks	65.5	52.1	64.5	51.5
Hispanics	44.4	37.4	35.5	28.8

SOURCES: Bureau of the Census, 1985:1, 3; 1990a:439.

tions of government to operate with less of a sense of accountability to society. This issue is most serious for the least powerful individuals and groups within the United States. Voter turnout has been particularly low among younger Americans and members of racial and ethnic minorities. In 1988, only 36 percent of eligible voters aged 18 to 20 went to the polls. According to a postelection survey, only 51.5 percent of Black voters and 28.8 percent of Hispanics reported that they had actually voted (see Table 15-2). Moreover, the poor—whose focus understandably is on survival—are traditionally underrepresented among voters as well. The low turnout found among these groups is explained, at least in part, by their common feeling of powerlessness. Yet such voting statistics encourage political power brokers to continue to ignore the interests of the young, the less affluent, and the nation's minorities.

Sociologist Anthony Orum (1989:255–258) notes that people are more likely to participate actively in political life if they have a sense of *political efficacy*—that is, if they feel that they have the ability to influence politicians and the political order. In addition, citizens are more likely to become involved if they trust political leaders or feel that an organized political party represents their interest. Without question, in an age marked by the rise of big government and by revelations of political corruption at the highest levels, many Americans of *all* social groups feel powerless and distrustful. Yet such feelings are especially intense among the young, the poor, and minorities. As a result, many view political participation, including voting, as a waste of time.

According to data obtained in federal postelection surveys, in which voters were questioned 2 weeks after the 1972 and 1988 presidential elections, there was a relatively light turnout among Black and Hispanic voters in both years. The percentage of Blacks who voted in 1988 was close to the 1972 figure, whereas there was a substantial decline in voting among Whites and Hispanics.

Cross-national comparisons, while confirming the relatively low level of voting in the United States, also suggest that Americans are *more* likely than citizens of other nations to be active at the community level, to contact local officials on behalf of themselves or others, and to have worked for a political party. Perhaps this contrast reflects how unusual it is for people to be directly involved in national political decision making in the modern world. Nevertheless, it is possible that if tens of millions of Americans did not stay home on Election Day—and instead became more active in the nation's political life—the outcome of the political process might be somewhat different.

Women in Politics

In 1984, women in the United States achieved an unprecedented political breakthrough when Representative Geraldine Ferraro of New York became the Democratic nominee for vice president of the United States. Never before had a woman received the nomination of a major party for such high office.

Nevertheless, women continue to be dramatically underrepresented in the halls of government. When the 102d Congress took office in January 1991, it included only 29 women (out of 435 members) in the House of Representatives and only 2 women (out of 100 members) in the Senate. While the number of women in state legislatures in 1991 was more than four times larger than it was 20 years ago, only three states had women governors. As of 1990, women held no more than 17 percent of the available positions at any level of public office (Center for the American Woman and Politics, 1990).

Sexism (see Chapter 11) has been the most serious barrier to women interested in holding office. Female candidates have had to overcome the prejudices of both men and women regarding women's fitness for leadership. Not until 1955 did a majority of Americans state that they would vote for a qualified woman for president. Moreover, women often encounter prejudice, discrimination, and abuse after they are elected.

Despite these problems, more women are being elected and more of them are identifying themselves as feminists. The traditional woman in politics was a widow who took office after her husband's death to continue his work and policies. However, women being elected in the 1990s are much more likely to view politics as their own career rather than as an afterthought. These trends are not restricted to the United States; Figure 15-1 (page 462) shows the representation of women in the governments of 10 nations around the world.

A new dimension of women and politics emerged beginning in the 1980s. Surveys detected a growing "gender gap" in the political preferences and activities of males and females. Women were more likely to register as Democrats than as Republicans and were also more critical of the policies of the Reagan administration. According to political analysts, the Democratic party's continued support for the right to choose a legal abortion is attracting women voters. At the same time, virtually all polling data indicate that women are substantially less likely than men to favor large defense budgets and military intervention overseas; these policies have become more closely associated with the Republican party of the 1980s and 1990s than with the Democrats.

Politicians have begun to watch voting trends among women carefully, since women voters can prove decisive in close elections. In the 1990 elections for the House of Representatives, Election Day voter polls showed that women voted for Democratic candidates by a 54 to 46 percent margin, while men split their votes evenly between Republican and Democratic candidates. Similarly, a significant gender gap was evident in the 1988 presidential race. ABC News reported that George Bush was ahead of Michael Dukakis among women by only 50 to 49 percent but gained men's backing by a dramatic 57 to 47 percent margin (Center for the American Woman and Politics, 1989; *New York Times*, 1990e).

DOONESBURY   by Garry Trudeau

FIGURE 15-1 Women in Government around the World

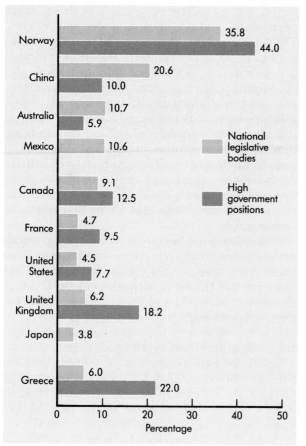

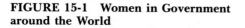

NOTE: Figure for "high government positions" in Mexico and Japan is zero.

SOURCES: Center for the American Woman and Politics, 1987; Inter-Parliamentary Union, 1990.

While women are more likely to hold top political offices in some countries than in others, nowhere do they reach parity with men.

Interest Groups

This discussion of political behavior has focused primarily on individual participation (and non-participation) in decision-making processes of government and on involvement in the nation's political parties. However, there are other important ways that American citizens can play a role in the nation's political arena. Because of common needs or common frustrations, people may band together in social movements such as the civil rights movement of the 1960s or the anti–nuclear power movement of the 1980s (A. Sherman and Kolker, 1987:17). We will consider social movement in more detail in Chapter 20. Americans can also influence the political process through membership in interest groups (some of which, in fact, may be part of larger social movements).

An ***interest group*** is a voluntary association of citizens who attempt to influence public policy. The National Organization for Women (NOW) is considered an interest group; so, too, are the Juvenile Diabetes Foundation and the National Rifle Association (NRA). Such groups are a vital part of the political process of the United States. Many interest groups (often known as *lobbies*) are national in scope and address a wide array of social, economic, and political issues.

Typically, we think of interest groups as being primarily concerned with regulatory legislation. However, as political scientist Barbara Ann Stolz (1984) points out, even the federal criminal code has become a target for interest-group activity. Business organizations have sought to strike the "reckless endangerment" provision that, in effect, makes it a crime for a business to engage knowingly in conduct that will imperil someone's life. These efforts underscore the interrelationship between the nation's political system and economic system. As in this example, interest groups often attempt to spur legislative and political actions that will protect or advance the groups' economic interests.

One way in which interest groups influence the political process is through their political action committees. A ***political action committee*** (or ***PAC***) is a political committee established by an interest group—a national bank, corporation, trade association, or cooperative or membership association—to accept voluntary contributions for candidates or political parties. The first political action committees were established in 1943 by organized labor. According to the Federal Election Commission, by 1976, there were 922 PACs; by 1990, there were more than 4000 (Minzesheimer, 1986).

These political action committees distribute substantial funds to candidates for public office. In the 1990 elections, for example, PACs gave congressional candidates nearly $159 million, of which $109 million was from PACs established by business groups and $37 million from labor PACs. The power of well-heeled PACs representing interest groups threatens the independence of lawmakers and, therefore, the integrity of the democratic process (*USA Today*, 1991).

Interest groups are occasionally referred to as **pressure groups,** implying that they attempt to force their will on a resistant public. In the view of functionalists, such groups play a constructive role in decision making by allowing orderly expression of public opinion and by increasing political participation. They also provide legislators with a useful flow of information.

Conflict theorists stress that although a very few organizations do work on behalf of the poor and disadvantaged, most interest groups in the United States represent affluent White professionals and business leaders. Studies show that Blacks running for public office receive substantially less money from PACs than do White candidates. From a conflict perspective, the overwhelming political clout of these powerful lobbies discourages participation by the individual citizen and raises serious questions about who actually rules a supposedly democratic nation (Wilhite and Theilmann, 1986).

MODELS OF POWER STRUCTURE IN THE UNITED STATES

Who really holds power in the United States? Do "we the people" genuinely run the country through elected representatives? Or is it true that, behind the scenes, a small elite of Americans controls both the government and the economic system? It is difficult to determine the location of power in a society as complex as the United States. In exploring this critical question, social scientists have developed two basic views of our nation's power structure: the elite and the pluralist models.

Elite Model

Karl Marx essentially believed that nineteenth-century representative democracy was a sham. He argued that industrial societies were dominated by relatively small numbers of people who owned factories and controlled natural resources. In Marx's view, government officials and military leaders were essentially servants of the capitalist class and followed their wishes. Therefore, any key decisions made by politicians inevitably reflected the interests of the dominant bourgeoisie. Like others who hold an **elite model** of power relations, Marx thus believed that society is ruled by a small group of individuals who share a common set of political and economic interests.

The Power Elite In his pioneer work, *The Power Elite*, sociologist C. Wright Mills described a small ruling elite of military, industrial, and governmental leaders who controlled the fate of the United States. Power rested in the hands of a few, both inside and outside of government—the **power elite.** In Mills's (1956:3–4) words:

> The power elite is composed of men whose positions enable them to transcend the ordinary environments of ordinary men and women; they are in positions to make decisions having major consequences. . . . They are in command of the major hierarchies and organizations of modern society.

In Mills's model, the power structure of the United States can be illustrated by the use of a pyramid (see Figure 15-2, page 464). At the top are the corporate rich, leaders of the executive branch of government, and heads of the military (whom Mills called the "warlords"). Below this triumvirate are local opinion leaders, members of the legislative branch of government, and leaders of special-interest groups. Mills contended that such individuals and groups would basically follow the wishes of the dominant power elite. At the bottom of society are the unorganized, exploited masses.

This power elite model is, in many respects, similar to the work of Karl Marx. The most striking difference is that Mills felt that the economically powerful coordinate their maneuvers with

FIGURE 15-2 C. Wright Mills's Model of the American Power Structure

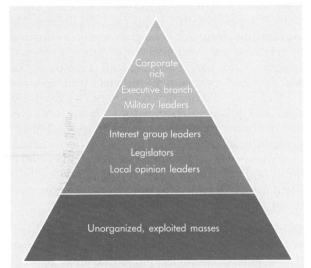

Corporate rich
Executive branch
Military leaders

Interest group leaders
Legislators
Local opinion leaders

Unorganized, exploited masses

SOURCE: Adapted from Kornhauser, 1961:253.

In the view of sociologist C. Wright Mills, power in the United States rested in the hands of big business, the federal government, and the military. All others members of society played a secondary and largely irrelevant role in decision making.

the *military* and *political* establishments in order to serve their mutual interests. Yet, reminiscent of Marx, Mills argued that the corporate rich were perhaps the most powerful element of the power elite (first among "equals"). And, of course, there is a further dramatic parallel between the work of these conflict theorists. The powerless masses at the bottom of Mills's power elite model certainly bring to mind Marx's portrait of the oppressed workers of the world, who have "nothing to lose but their chains."

A fundamental element in Mills's thesis is that the power elite not only has relatively few members but also operates as a self-conscious, cohesive unit. Although not necessarily diabolical or ruthless, the elite comprises similar types of people who regularly interact with one another and have essentially the same political and economic interests. Mills's power elite is not a conspiracy but

rather a community of interest and sentiment among a small number of influential Americans (A. Hacker, 1964).

Admittedly, Mills failed to clarify when the elite acts against protests and when it tolerates them; he also failed to provide detailed case studies which would substantiate the interrelationship among members of the power elite. Nevertheless, his challenging theories forced scholars to look more critically at the "democratic" political system of the United States.

The Ruling Class   Sociologist G. William Domhoff (1967, 1970, 1983) agreed with Mills that the United States is run by a powerful elite. But, rather than fully accepting Mills's power elite model, Domhoff (1983:1) argued that the nation is controlled by a social upper class "that is a ruling class by virtue of its dominant role in the economy and government." This socially cohesive ruling class owns 20 to 25 percent of all privately held wealth and 45 to 50 percent of all privately held common stock.

Unlike Mills, Domhoff (1983:17–55) was quite specific about who belongs to this social upper class. Membership comes through being part of a family recognized in *The Social Register*—the directory of the social elite in many American cities. Attendance at prestigious private schools and membership in exclusive social clubs are further indications that a person comes from America's social upper class. According to Domhoff, members of this class who hold leadership roles within the corporate community join with high-level employees of profit making and nonprofit institutions controlled by the upper class to exercise power.

In Domhoff's view, the ruling class should not be seen in a conspiratorial way, as "sinister men lurking behind the throne." On the contrary they tend to hold public positions of authority. Almost all important appointive government posts—including those of diplomats and cabinet members—are filled by members of the social upper class. Domhoff contends that members of this class dominate powerful corporations, foundations, universities, and the executive branch of government. They control presidential nominations and the political party process through campaign contributions. In addition, the ruling class exerts a significant (though not absolute) influence within Congress and units of state and local government (Domhoff, 1983:116–156; see also Steiber, 1979).

Perhaps the major difference between the elite models of Mills and Domhoff is that Mills insisted on the relative autonomy of the political elite and attached great significance to the independent power of the military. By contrast, Domhoff suggests that high-level government and military leaders serve the interests of the social upper class. Both theorists, in line with a Marxian approach, assume that the rich are interested only in what benefits them financially. Furthermore, as advocates of elite models of power, Mills and Domhoff argue that the masses of American people have no real influence on the decisions of the powerful (Eitzen, 1988:565–573).

Pluralist Model

Several social scientists have questioned the elite models of power relations proposed by Marx, Mills, Domhoff, and other conflict theorists. Quite simply, the critics insist that power in the United States is more widely shared than the elite model indicates. In their view, a pluralist model more accurately describes the American political system. According to the **pluralist model**, "many conflicting groups within the community have access to government officials and compete with one another in an effort to influence policy decisions" (Cummings and Wise, 1989:235).

Veto Groups David Riesman's *The Lonely Crowd* (Riesman et al., 1961) suggested that the American political system could best be understood through examination of the power of veto groups. The term *veto groups* refers to interest groups that have the capacity to prevent the exercise of power by others. Functionally, they serve to increase political participation by preventing the concentration of political power. Examples cited by Riesman include farm groups, labor unions, professional associations, and racial and ethnic groups. Whereas Mills pointed to the dangers of rule by an undemocratic power elite, Riesman

insisted that veto groups could effectively paralyze the nation's political processes by blocking *anyone* from exercising needed leadership functions. In Riesman's words, "The only leaders of national scope left in the United States are those who can placate the veto groups" (Riesman et al., 1961:247). A more detailed contrast between the models of the American power structure proposed by Mills and Riesman can be found in Table 15-3 (page 466).

Dahl's Study of Pluralism Community studies of power have also supported the pluralist model. One of the most famous—an investigation of decision making in New Haven, Connecticut—was reported by Robert Dahl in his book, *Who Governs?* (1961). Dahl found that while the number of people involved in any important decision was rather small, community power was nonetheless diffuse. Few political actors exercised decision-making power on all issues. Therefore, one individual or group might be influential in a battle over urban renewal but at the same time might have little impact over educational policy. Several other studies of local politics, in such communities as Chicago and Oberlin, Ohio, further document that monolithic power structures do not operate on the level of local government.

Just as the elite model has been challenged on political and methodological grounds, the pluralist model has been subjected to serious questioning. Domhoff (1978) reexamined Dahl's study of decision making in New Haven and argued that Dahl and other pluralists had failed to trace how local elites prominent in decision making were part of a larger national ruling class. In addition, studies of community power, such as Dahl's work in New Haven, can examine decision making only on issues which become part of the political agenda. This focus fails to address the possible power of elites to keep certain matters entirely out of the realm of government debate. Conflict theorists contend that these elites will not allow any outcome of the political process which threatens their dominance. They may even be strong enough to block *discussion* of such measures by policymakers (P. Bachrach and Baratz, 1962:947–952; Block, 1977; Kerbo and Della Fave, 1979; A. Sherman and Kolker, 1987:169–170).

TABLE 15-3   Two Portraits of the Power Structure of the United States

ASPECTS	MILLS	RIESMAN
Levels	**a** Unified power elite **b** Diversified and balanced plurality of interest groups **c** Mass of unorganized people who have practically no power over elite	**a** No dominant power elite **b** Diversified and balanced plurality of interest groups **c** Mass of unorganized people who have some power over interest groups
Changes	**a** Increasing concentration of power	**a** Increasing dispersion of power
Operation	**a** One group determines all major policies **b** Manipulation of people at the bottom by group at the top	**a** Policymakers shift with the issue **b** Monopolistic competition among organized groups
Bases	**a** Coincidence of interests among major institutions (economic, military, governmental)	**a** Diversity of interests among major organized groups **b** Sense of weakness and dependence among those in higher as well as lower status
Consequences	**a** Enhancement of interests of corporations, armed forces, and executive branch of government **b** Decline of politics as public debate **c** Decline of responsible and accountable power—loss of democracy	**a** No one group or class is favored significantly over others **b** Decline of politics as duty and self-interest **c** Decline of capacity for effective leadership

SOURCE: Kornhauser, 1961.

Sociologists C. Wright Mills and David Riesman differ as to the degree of consolidation of power in the United States. Mills argues that a power elite of highly concentrated and overlapping bases of power exists, whereas Riesman sees power dispersed among competing groups.

We can end this discussion by reinforcing the one common point of the elite and pluralist perspectives—power in the American political system is unequally distributed. All citizens may be equal in theory, yet those high in the nation's power structure are "more equal."

ASPECTS OF THE ECONOMY

Occupations and Professions

Whatever we call it—*job, work, occupation, gig, stint, position, duty,* or *vocation*—it is what we do for pay. The labor for which we are financially rewarded relates to our social behavior in a number of ways. As we saw in Chapter 4, preparation for work is a critical aspect of the socialization process. In addition, our social identities or what Charles Horton Cooley termed the *looking-glass self,* are influenced by our work. A person who asks, "What do you do?" expects us to indicate our occupation. This underscores the importance of our work in defining who we are for others and, indeed, for ourselves. Of course, work has more than a symbolic significance; our positions in the stratification system are determined in good part by our occupations or those of the primary wage earners in our families.

In the United States and other contemporary societies, the majority of the paid labor force is involved in the service sector of the economy—

providing health care, education, selling of goods, banking, and government. Along with the shift toward service industries, there has been a rise in the number of occupations viewed as professions. There is no single characteristic that defines a profession. In popular usage, the term *profession* is frequently used to convey a positive evaluation of work ("She's a real professional") or to denote full-time paid performance in a vocation (as in "professional golfer").

Sociologists use the term **profession** to describe an occupation requiring extensive knowledge which is governed by a code of ethics. Professionals tend to have a great degree of autonomy; they are not responsible to a supervisor for every action, nor do they have to respond to the customer's wishes. In general, professionals are their own authority in determining what is best for their clients.

It is widely agreed that medicine and law are professions, whereas driving a taxi is an occupation. However, when one considers such jobs as funeral director, firefighter, and pharmacist, it is not clear where "occupations" end and "professions" begin. Moreover, in recent decades, a growing number of occupational groups have claimed and even demanded professional status—often in an attempt to gain greater prestige and financial rewards. In certain instances, existing professions may object to the efforts of a related vocation to achieve designation as a profession. They may fear that a loss in business or clientele will result or that the status of their profession will be downgraded if still more occupations are included. As we will see in Chapter 17, the hostility of the medical profession toward chiropractors is an example of such a conflict between an established profession and an occupation which has aspired to professional status.

In Chapter 6, it was noted that our society is increasingly dominated by large formal organizations with bureaucratic structures. Since autonomy is an important characteristic of professions, there is an inherent conflict in serving as a professional within a bureaucracy, such as being a staff physician in a hospital or a scientist in a corporation. The organization follows the principle of hierarchy and expects loyalty and obedience. Yet professionalism demands the individual re-

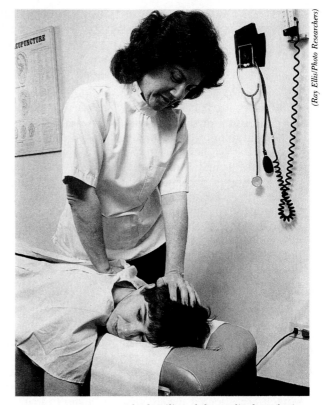

(Ray Ellis/Photo Researchers)

The hostility of the medical profession toward chiropractors is an example of a conflict between an established profession and an occupation aspiring to professional status.

sponsibility of the practitioner. Bureaucracy fosters impersonality, yet professions emphasize close relations with one's professional colleagues. Consequently, working in a large organization represents a kind of trade-off for most professionals. While they resent limitations on their freedom and individual initiative, they appreciate the security that the organization provides (Pavalko, 1971:188–192, 1972:250–293). Box 15-3 (page 468) explores certain differences in the behavior of male and female managers within financial organizations.

Workers and the Workplace

For millions of Americans, work is a central activity of day-to-day life. Work may be satisfying or deadening; the workplace may be relatively dem-

BOX 15-3 • CURRENT RESEARCH

MANAGEMENT STYLES OF MEN AND WOMEN

Are women's work orientations and behaviors essentially the result of their positions in the paid labor force? If so, then we could expect men and women holding the same job to relate to their colleagues in basically the same way. Sociologist Anne Statham (1987) tested this proposition by interviewing 22 female managers and 18 male managers in three types of organizations: a financial institution, a manufacturing firm, and a technical institute.

Men and women managers were found to behave differently—a result which seems related to the differential socialization of each sex. Statham's findings did not support the familiar notion that women are oriented toward people or expressivity while men are oriented toward tasks or instrumentality (refer back to Chapter 11). Instead, her study determined that women are both task-

and person-oriented. Even the person-orientation exhibited by women managers could be seen as contributing to their task accomplishment. By contrast, male managers show little concern about *how* they go about doing their work or even getting tasks accomplished. They profess to know much less than female managers about day-to-day occurrences in their areas of responsibility.

Statham does not argue that either sex's management style is better than the other's. However, she does emphasize that the differences in these approaches may lead to significant misunderstanding between men and women in the workplace. Male managers will typically leave women subordinates to struggle through on their own because they believe this is the "best way to manage." At the same time, male subordinates resent women managers who "stand over their shoulders" because the

men interpret such managerial behavor as a lack of confidence (whereas the female manager believes she is "demonstrating her concern for the employee").

Statham's research underscores the need to reexamine and modify the assessment of managerial behaviors. Her microsociological study, relying on an interactionist perspective, documents that men and women do indeed function differently as managers—and that disharmony may result when these contrasting managerial styles meet in the workplace. But feminist sociologist Cynthia Fuchs Epstein cautions against applying such findings to *all* women in business—although they seem to cast women in a positive light. Epstein argues that even favorable generalizations and stereotypes fail to "capture the rich variation" evident among women (Fierman, 1990:116; see also Rosener, 1990).

ocratic or totally authoritarian. Although the conditions and demands of people's work lives vary, there can be little doubt of the importance of work and workplace interactions in our society and others.

Work and Alienation: Marx's View All the pioneers of sociological thought were concerned that changes in the workplace resulting from the industrial revolution would have a negative impact on workers. Émile Durkheim (1933, original edition 1893) argued that as labor becomes more and more differentiated, individuals experience *anomie,* or a loss of direction. Workers cannot feel

the same fulfillment from performing one specialized task in a factory as they did when they were totally responsible for creating a product. As was noted in Chapter 6, Max Weber suggested that impersonality is a fundamental characteristic of bureaucratic organizations. One result is the cold and uncaring feeling often associated with contemporary bureaucracies. But the most penetrating analysis of the dehumanizing aspects of industrialization was offered by Karl Marx.

Marx believed that as the process of industrialization advanced within capitalist societies, people's lives became increasingly devoid of meaning. While Marx expressed concern about the damaging effects of many social institutions, he focused on what he saw as a person's most important activity: labor. For Marx, the emphasis of the industrial revolution on specialization of factory tasks contributed to a growing sense of alienation among industrial workers (Erikson, 1986).

The term *alienation* refers to the situation of being estranged or disassociated from the surrounding society. The division of labor increased alienation because workers were channeled into monotonous, meaningless repetition of the same tasks. However, in Marx's view, an even deeper cause of alienation is the powerlessness of workers in a capitalist economic system. Workers have no control over their occupational duties, the products of their labor, or the distribution of profits. The very existence of private property within capitalism accelerates and intensifies the alienation of members of the working class, since they are constantly producing property which is owned by others (members of the capitalist class).

The solution to the problem of worker's alienation, according to Marx, is to give workers greater control over the workplace and the products of their labor. Of course, Marx did not focus on limited reforms of factory life within the general framework of capitalist economic systems. Rather, he envisioned a revolutionary overthrow of capitalist oppression and a transition to collective ownership of the means of production (socialism) and eventually to the ideal of communism.

Yet the trend in capitalist societies has been toward concentration of ownership by giant corporations (refer back to Chapter 9). In 1986, 74 percent of the paid labor force of the United States was employed in business firms with more than $25 million in sales. Through mergers and acquisitions, such corporations become even larger, and individual workers find themselves the employees of firms with overwhelming size and power. For example, there were 3487 mergers in 1988 alone, involving $250 billion in business. This was twice the number of mergers that occurred in 1980; the 1988 mergers accounted for three times as much economic activity (Bureau of the Census, 1990a:529, 534).

In the 1980s, the term *burnout* was increasingly being used to describe the stress experienced by a wide variety of workers, including professionals, self-employed persons, and even unpaid volunteers. Whereas Marx had focused on alienation among the proletarians, whom he viewed as powerless to effect change within capitalist institutions, the broader concept of work-related anxiety now covers alienation among more affluent workers with a greater degree of control over their working conditions. From a conflict perspective, we have masked the fact that alienation falls most heavily on the lower and working classes by making it appear to be endemic from the boardroom to the shop floor (G. Walker, 1986).

Workers' Satisfaction Workers' alienation (as measured by their dissatisfaction) is an admittedly elusive concept for researchers, since a worker can be more alienated at one job than at another without necessarily feeling unhappy. Most studies of alienation have focused on how structural changes in the economy serve to increase or decrease workers' satisfaction. In general, people with greater responsibility for a finished product (such as white-collar professionals and managers) experience less of a sense of alienation than those with little responsibility.

For both women and men working in blue-collar jobs, the repetitive nature of work can be particularly unsatisfying. The automobile assembly line is commonly cited as an extreme example of monotonous work. Studs Terkel (1974:159), in his book *Working*, presents an account of such labor, described by a spot-welder:

> I stand in one spot, about two- or three-feet area, all night. The only time a person stops is when the line stops. We do about thirty-two jobs per car, per unit, forty-eight units per hour, eight hours a day. Thirty-two times forty-eight times eight. Figure it out, that's how many times I push that button.

Robert Blauner's (1964) research revealed that printers—who often work in small shops and supervise apprentices—were more satisfied with their work than laborers on automobile assembly lines who performed repetitive tasks. However, in contrast to Terkel's bleak description of work on the assembly line, William Form (1967) found that automobile workers in the United States, Italy, India, and Argentina were fairly satisfied

For both men and women in blue-collar jobs, the repetitive nature of the work can be particularly unsatisfying.

with their work. In part, this may be because monotonous work does not *necessarily* lead to alienation. Sociologist Clark Molstad (1986) found that some workers prefer the safety and security of boring tasks. They wish to avoid jobs with great responsibility and many "hassles."

How do we reconcile these positive reports with the concerns expressed by Durkheim, Weber, and Marx regarding alienation among workers?

A number of general factors can be identified which reduce the level of dissatisfaction of contemporary industrial workers. Higher wages give workers a sense of accomplishment apart from the task before them. A shortened workweek has increased the amount of time that people can devote to recreation and leisure, thereby reducing some of the discontent stemming from the workplace. For example, the average industrial worker spent 60 hours a week on the job in 1880, compared with the 40-hour workweek which began in the 1930s (Bureau of the Census, 1975a). Unions have given many workers an opportunity to exercise some influence in decision making. Finally, numerous studies from an interactionist perspective have shown that positive relationships with coworkers—often including the use of humor—can make a boring job tolerable or even enjoyable (Seckman and Couch, 1989).

Sociologist Donald Roy (1959) examined workers' satisfaction through a 2-month period of participant observation within a small work group of factory machine operatives. Drawing on the interactionist perspective, Roy carefully recorded the social interactions among members of his work group, including many structured "times" and "themes" designed to break up long days of simple, repetitive work. For example, food breaks were ritualized into coffee time, peach time, banana time, fish time, Coke time, and lunch time—each of which occurred daily and involved distinctive responsibilities, jokes, and insults. Roy (1959:166) concludes that his observations "seem to support the generally accepted notion that one key source of job satisfaction lies in the informal interaction shared by members of a work group." The patterned conversation and horseplay of these workers reduced the monotony of their long, repetitive workdays.

Although the factors identified above undoubtedly contribute to workers' job satisfaction, there is an alternative explanation for apparent satisfaction with jobs. Sociologist and conflict theorist George Ritzer (1977:284–288) has suggested that the relatively positive impression many workers present is misleading. In his view, manual workers are actually so deeply alienated that they come to expect little from their jobs. Their satisfaction comes from nonwork tasks, and any job-related gratification results from the receipt of wages. Ritzer's interpretation explains why manual workers—although they are allegedly satisfied with their occupations—would not choose the same line of work if they could begin their lives over.

AFFIRMATIVE ACTION

- How has the Supreme Court ruled regarding the constitutionality of affirmative action programs adopted by local governments and universities?
- How does the American public view preferential treatment for women and members of racial minorities?
- What does sociological research reveal regarding the impact of affirmative action programs?

The term *affirmative action* first appeared in an executive order issued by President John F. Kennedy in 1963. That order called for contractors to "take affirmative action to ensure that applicants are employed, and that employees are treated during employment, without regard to their race, creed, color, or national origin." Four years later, the order was amended to prohibit discrimination on the basis of sex, but affirmative action remained a vague concept. Currently, ***affirmative action*** refers to positive efforts to recruit minority group members or women for jobs, promotions, and educational opportunities.

A variety of court decisions and executive branch statements have outlawed certain forms of job discrimination based on race, sex, or both, including (1) word-of-mouth recruitment among all-White or all-male work forces, (2) recruitment exclusively in schools or colleges that are limited to one sex or are predominantly White, (3) discrimination against married women or forced retirement of pregnant women, (4) advertising in male and female "help wanted" columns when gender is not a legitimate occupational qualification, and (5) job qualifications and tests that are not substantially related to the job. Also, the lack of minority (Black, Asian, American Indian, or Hispanic) or female employees may in itself represent evidence of unlawful exclusion (Commission on Civil Rights, 1981).

In the late 1970s, a number of bitterly debated cases on affirmative action reached the Supreme Court. In 1978, in the *Bakke* case, by a narrow 5-4 vote, the Supreme Court ordered the medical school of the University of California at Davis to admit Allen Bakke, a White engineer who originally had been denied admission. The justices ruled that the school had violated Bakke's constitutional rights by establishing a fixed quota system for minority students. The Court added, however, that it was constitutional for universities to adopt flexible admissions programs that use race as one factor in decision making. The following year, in the *Weber* case, the Supreme Court ruled, by a 5-2 vote, that the United Steelworkers of America did not have to admit a White laboratory technician, Brian Weber, to a training program in Louisiana. The justices held that it was constitutional for the union to run a program for training skilled technicians which, in promoting affirmative action, admitted one Black for every White.

Defenders of affirmative action insist that it is needed to counter continuing discrimination against women and minorities. White males still hold the overwhelming majority of prestigious and high-paying jobs. In fact, despite affirmative action, the gap in earning power between White males and others has remained unchanged over the last 20 years.

As of 1988, the median income for year-round, full-time, White male workers was $28,262 (see Figure 15-3 on page 472). This compared with $20,716 for Black males, $18,833 for White females, and $16,867 for Black females. The differences between Blacks and Whites remain even when researchers control for differences in education. When a family's primary wage earner has obtained a high school diploma, Whites earn $8000 more than Blacks per year. Even when they hold graduate degrees, Blacks earn $6600 less than comparable Whites (Bureau of the Census, 1989d:90, 104–105, 1989e:44–45).

Even if they acknowledge such disparities, the ma-

FIGURE 15-3 Median Income by Race and Gender, 1988

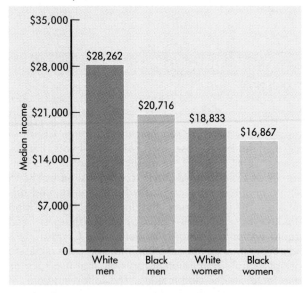

NOTE: Median income is from all sources and is limited to year-round, full-time workers over 15 years of age.
SOURCE: Bureau of the Census, 1989e:44–45.

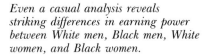

Even a casual analysis reveals striking differences in earning power between White men, Black men, White women, and Black women.

jority of Americans doubt that everything done in the name of affirmative action is desirable. Public opinion appears united against hiring or admissions programs that offer preferential treatment to women and racial minorities. Surveys conducted throughout the 1980s consistently showed that very few Americans favored such preferential efforts. Many respondents insisted that these programs unfairly penalize White males and should properly be viewed as "reverse discrimination" (Colasanto, 1989b; L. Harris, 1987:188–193).

In recent years, the Supreme Court, increasingly dominated by a conservative majority, has issued many critical rulings concerning affirmative action programs. In a key case in early 1989, the Court invalidated, by a 6-3 vote, a Richmond, Virginia, law that had guaranteed 30 percent of public works funds to construction companies owned by minorities. In ruling that the Richmond statute violated the constitutional

right of White contractors to equal protection under the law, the Court held that affirmative action programs are constitutional only when they serve the "compelling state interest" of redressing "identified discrimination" by the government or private parties.

Writing for the majority, Associate Justice Sandra Day O'Connor added that any "rigid numerical quota," no matter how small, is constitutionally suspect. The Court's ruling was a major victory for the Reagan administration, which had consistently urged the justices to adopt a strict standard for evaluating affirmative action claims. In a bitter dissenting opinion, Associate Justice Harry Blackmun observed: "I never thought that I would live to see the day when the city of Richmond, Virginia, the cradle of the Old Confederacy," having voluntarily attempted to "lessen the stark impact of persistent discrimination," would then have its effort ruled unconstitutional by "this Court, the supposed bastion of equality" (L. Greenhouse, 1989:A1, A19).

Has affirmative action actually helped to alleviate employment inequality on the basis of race and gender? Sociologist Dula Espinosa (1987) studied the impact of affirmative action on a California municipal work force whose hiring practices were traced from 1975 through 1985. As a federal contractor, the city was required to comply with federal guidelines regarding employment practices, including making "good faith efforts" to increase employment opportunities for women and minorities. Espinosa found that employment inequality by gender and ethnicity did indeed decrease during the 10-year period studied.

Espinosa adds, however, that most of the reduction in the city's level of employment inequality occurred just after the affirmative action policy was first introduced. In Espinosa's view, once immediate progress can be seen, an organization may then become less inclined to continue to implement an affirmative action policy. Moreover, while high levels of inequality may be relatively easy to address initially, sustaining positive results may take longer because of institutional discrimination. Espinosa concludes that affirmative action was successful to some degree in reducing employment inequality in the city studied, but clearly had its limitations as well.

Sociologists In Soo Son, Suzanne Model, and Gene Fisher (1989) studied income data and occupational mobility among Black male and White male workers in the period 1974–1981 to examine possible class polarization among Blacks. The researchers found that while Black college graduates made substantial gains as a result of affirmative action, less advantaged Blacks apparently did not benefit from it. The researchers (1989:325) conclude that the "racial parity achieved by young college-educated blacks in the 1970s will be maintained only if the government's commitment to affirmative action does not slacken."

By 1990, however, it was clear that the Bush administration was hostile to most affirmative action measures. President Bush vetoed the proposed Civil Rights Act of 1990, which had been widely supported by minority groups and women. This law would have reversed recent Supreme Court rulings that have made it more difficult for workers to win antidiscrimination lawsuits. Although the act explicitly ruled out the use of quotas as a remedy for discrimination, the president and other opponents nevertheless insisted that it would increase the pressure on employers to rely on quotas as a protection against lawsuits. Later in 1990, an official of the Department of Education declared that most college scholarships specifically designated for minority students were illegal. Although the ruling was modified within a week by an embarrassed Bush administration, it demonstrated that the federal government was unlikely to support affirmative action efforts.

SUMMARY

The *economic system* of a society has an important influence on social behavior and on other social institutions. Each society must have a *political system* in order to have recognized procedures for the allocation of valued resources. This chapter examines the economic systems found in preindustrial and *industrial societies,* the dimensions of the American political system, and the social nature of the workplace.

1 Sociologists Gerhard Lenski and Jean Lenski have categorized preindustrial societies as *hunting-and-gathering societies, horticultural societies,* and *agrarian societies.*

2 The scientific revolution known as the *industrial revolution* produced dramatic social and economic changes.

3 Economic systems of *capitalism* vary in the degree to which private ownership and economic activity are regulated by government, but all emphasize the profit motive.

4 The basic objective of *socialism* is to meet people's needs, rather than to maximize profits.

5 In *postindustrial society,* large numbers of people become involved in teaching and disseminating ideas.

6 There are three basic sources of *power* within any political system: *force, influence,* and *authority.*

7 Max Weber provided one of the most useful and frequently cited contributions of early sociology by identifying three ideal types of authority: *traditional, legal-rational,* and *charismatic.*

8 The principal institutions of *political socialization* in the United States are the family, schools, and media.

9 Women are becoming more successful at winning election to public office.

10 An *interest group* is often national in scope and frequently addresses a wide variety of social and political issues.

11 Advocates of the *elite model* of the power structure of the United States see the nation as being ruled by a small group of individuals who share common political and economic interests, whereas advocates of a *pluralist model* believe that power is more widely shared among conflicting groups.

12 In comparison with other occupations, *professions* tend to have a great deal of autonomy.

13 Karl Marx believed that the powerlessness of workers under capitalism was a primary cause of *alienation.*

14 Despite the recent *affirmative action* programs, White males continue to hold the overwhelming majority of prestigious and high-paying jobs in the United States.

KEY TERMS

Affirmative action Positive efforts to recruit minority group members or women for jobs, promotions, and educational opportunities. (page 471)

Agrarian society The most technologically advanced form of preindustrial society. Members are primarily engaged in the production of food but increase their crop yield through such innovations as the plow. (449)

Alienation The situation of being estranged or disassociated from the surrounding society. (469)

Authority Power that has been institutionalized and is recognized by the people over whom it is exercised. (454)

Capitalism An economic system in which the means of production are largely in private hands, and the main incentive for economic activity is the accumulation of profits. (449)

Charismatic authority Max Weber's term for power made legitimate by a leader's exceptional personal or emotional appeal to his or her followers. (457)

Communism As an ideal type, an economic system under which all property is communally owned and no social distinctions are made on the basis of people's ability to produce. (451)

Economic system The social institution through which goods and services are produced, distributed, and consumed. (447)

Elite model A view of society as ruled by a small group of individuals who share a common set of political and economic interests. (463)

Force The actual or threatened use of coercion to impose one's will on others. (453)

Horticultural societies Preindustrial societies in which people plant seeds and crops rather than subsist merely on available foods. (448)

Hunting-and-gathering society A preindustrial society in which people rely on whatever foods and fiber are readily available in order to live. (448)

Industrial revolution A scientific revolution, largely occurring in England between 1760 and 1830, which focused on the application of nonanimal sources of power to labor tasks. (449)

Industrial society A society which relies chiefly on mechanization for the production of its economic goods and services. (449)

Influence The exercise of power through a process of persuasion. (454)

Interest group A voluntary association of citizens who attempt to influence public policy. (462)

Laissez-faire A form of capitalism under which people compete freely, with minimal government intervention in the economy. (450)

Legal-rational authority Max Weber's term for power made legitimate by law. (455)

Marital power A term used by Blood and Wolfe to describe the manner in which decision making is distributed within families. (453)

Monopoly Control of a market by a single business firm. (450)

Oligopoly A market with relatively few sellers. (450)

Pluralist model A view of society in which many conflicting groups within a community have access to governmental officials and compete with one another in an attempt to influence policy decisions. (465)

Political action committee (PAC) A political committee established by an interest group—a national bank, corporation, trade association, or cooperative or membership association—to accept voluntary contributions for candidates or political parties. (462)

Political efficacy The feeling that one has the ability to influence politicians and the political order. (460)

Political socialization The process by which individuals acquire political attitudes and develop patterns of political behavior. (458)

Political system The social institution which relies on a recognized set of procedures for implementing and achieving the goals of a group. (447)

Politics In Harold D. Lasswell's words, "who gets what, when, how." (453)

Postindustrial society As defined by Daniel Bell, a society whose economic system is based on the production of information rather than the production of goods. (452)

Power The ability to exercise one's will over others. (453)

Power elite A term used by C. Wright Mills for a small group of military, industrial, and government leaders who control the fate of the United States. (463)

Pressure groups A term sometimes used to refer to interest groups. (463)

Profession An occupation requiring extensive knowledge and governed by a code of ethics. (467)

Routinization of charismatic authority Max Weber's term for the process by which the leadership qualities originally associated with an individual are incorporated into either a traditional or a legal-rational system of authority. (457)

Socialism An economic system under which the means of production and distribution are collectively owned. (450)

Social surplus The production by a group of people of enough goods to cover their own needs, while at the same time sustaining individuals who are not engaged in agricultural tasks. (448)

Technology The application of knowledge to the making of tools and the utilization of natural resources. (448)

Terrorism The use or threat of violence against random or symbolic targets in pursuit of political aims. (454)

Traditional authority Legitimate power conferred by custom and accepted practice. (455)

Veto groups David Riesman's term for interest groups that have the capacity to prevent the exercise of power by others. (465)

ADDITIONAL READINGS

Bensman, David, and Roberta Lynch. *Rusted Dreams: Hard Times in a Steel Community.* New York: McGraw-Hill, 1987. An analysis of a southeast Chicago neighborhood hit hard by plant closings that threw half the local labor force out of work.

Domhoff, G. William. *Who Rules America Now? A View for the '80s.* Englewood Cliffs, N.J.: Prentice-Hall, 1983. Updating his earlier classic, *Who Rules America?* Domhoff argues that the United States is run by a socially cohesive ruling class which dominates the political process.

Enloe, Cynthia. *Bananas, Beaches, and Bases: Making Feminist Sense of International Politics.* Berkeley: University of California Press, 1990. Enloe studied the lives of women on military bases and diplomatic wives as part of her examination of the male-determined agenda of international politics.

Leff, Walli F., and Marilyn G. Haft. *Time without Work.* Boston: South End, 1984. A collection of personal accounts of people in the United States who are not working.

Luthans, Fred, Richard M. Hodgetts, and Kenneth R. Thompson (eds.). *Social Issues in Business* (5th ed.). New York: Macmillan, 1987. A useful collection of short readings dealing with the social responsibilities of business, including material on consumer activism, ecological issues, and equal rights.

Mills, C. Wright. *The Power Elite.* New York: Oxford University Press, 1956. Mills argues that the United States is ruled by an elite consisting of the "political directorate," "corporate rich," and "warlords."

Orum, Anthony M. *Introduction to Political Sociology: The Social Anatomy of the Body Politic* (3d ed.). Englewood Cliffs, N.J.: Prentice-Hall, 1989. A fine sociological overview of the political system. Orum presents a detailed account of the relevant work of Karl Marx, Max Weber, and Talcott Parsons.

Randall, Vicky. *Women in Politics: An International Perspective* (2d ed.). Chicago: University of Chicago Press, 1987. An examination of women in politics and their relationship to men in both industrialized western nations and developing nations.

Statham, Anne, Eleanor M. Miller, and Hans O. Mauksch (eds.). *The Worth of Women's Work.* Albany: State University of New York Press, 1988. An examination of women's work both inside and outside the home.

Terkel, Studs. *Working.* New York: Random House, 1974. The best-selling author presents the concerns and problems of Americans engaged in a variety of occupations.

Woronoff, Jon. *The Japan Syndrome: Symptoms, Ailments, and Remedies.* New Brunswick, N.J.: Transaction, 1986. A sociological examination of the workplace in contemporary Japan.

Zwerdling, Daniel. *Workplace Democracy.* New York: Harper and Row, 1980. A fascinating account of workers' control and self-management in the United States, Great Britain, Spain, and Yugoslavia.

Journals

Among the journals focusing on issues of government and the economy are the *American Political Science Review* (founded in 1906), *Congressional Digest* (1921), *Congressional Quarterly Weekly Report* (1943), *Industrial and Labor Relations Review* (1947), *Insurgent Sociologist* (1969), *Social Policy* (1970), *Terrorism* (1988), and *Work and Occupations* (1974).

16

EDUCATION

LOOKING AHEAD

- How does education transmit the norms and values of a culture?
- In what ways do schools function as agents of social control?
- Does tracking of students serve to maintain social class differences across generations?
- In what ways is a school like a bureaucracy?
- Why are mentors especially important for Black and female students pursuing careers in the academic world?
- What accounts for the dramatic differences in funding available to various school districts?

Education does not have a single face. In Liverpool, England, children are guided in singing "God Save the Queen." At a Christian school in Virginia, students learn the account of the origin of life found in the first chapter of Genesis. An Amahuaca youth in the Peruvian rain forest learns from his father how to make arrows. In a suburban Chicago high school, each student learns to program a microcomputer. At a state university on the west coast, a woman receives college credits for years of homemaking and parenthood.

Deborah Fallows, an American, lived with her family in Japan and southeast Asia for 4 years. In reflecting on the differences in education in Japan and the United States, Fallows recalls her initial shock and embarrassment when she attended the first two after-school meetings of parents with their children's sixth-grade teacher—

only to discover that the main focus of discussion each time was the impact of having her son Tommy join the class. Eventually, Fallows came to realize that Japanese students acquire a keen sense of how to function as part of a group. Consequently, these Japanese parents had a personal stake in a foreign child's adjustment to his new classmates. "How the group dealt with him," Fallows (1990:25) concludes, "was part of their children's lessons in group behavior."

In a sense, education is an important aspect of *socialization*—the lifelong process of learning the attitudes, values, and behavior appropriate to individuals as members of a particular culture. In their years in Japan, Deborah Fallows' two sons were exposed to the socialization process in that nation's schools—where young girls and boys learn to make group decisions, to value the welfare of the group, and to assess success or failure based on the performance of the group. By contrast, children in American schools are socialized into our culture's emphasis on the importance of the individual.

Socialization may occur in a classroom, but, as we learned in Chapter 4, it may also take place through interactions with parents, friends, and even strangers. Socialization results as well from exposure to books, films, television, and other forms of communication. When such learning is explicit and formalized—when people consciously teach while others adopt the social role of learner—this process is called **education.**

From its inception, the United States has placed great value on developing an educated electorate. In contrast to the European monarchies of the eighteenth and nineteenth centuries, the American representative democracy gave citizens the right to select their nation's leaders. Yet suffrage was initially limited to landowning White males. Since many Americans—including women, Blacks, Indians, and less affluent White males—were excluded from voting, there seemed little need to train them to become part of an "educated electorate." Mass public education did not exist in the nation's early decades; even the sons of White male property owners were generally educated in either private or parochial schools.

Until the 1830s, American education was totally administered by localities, and the quality of education differed dramatically throughout the nation. However, a breakthrough occurred in 1837 when Horace Mann (1796–1859) campaigned for the Massachusetts state board of education. Mann was an eloquent advocate of the "common school," a school designed for average children who could not afford private schools. Under his leadership, school appropriations increased, and the first "normal schools" (state-supported colleges for training teachers) were established. Such reforms widened educational opportunities and helped to provide the nation with a skilled labor force needed in a time of growing industrialization. During the late nine-

teenth and early twentieth centuries, schools also assumed the function of assimilating immigrants into the culture and values of the United States.

In the last 50 years, an increasing proportion of Americans have obtained high school diplomas, college degrees, and advanced professional degrees. As is shown in Figure 16-1, the proportion of people 25 to 29 years of age with a high school diploma has increased from 38 percent in 1940 to 86 percent in 1988. Similarly, the proportion of 25- to 29-year-olds with a college degree has risen from less than 6 percent in 1940 to almost 23 percent in 1988.

Currently, nearly 59 million Americans attend public or private schools—or about 25 percent of the nation's population. As a result, education has become a major industry in the United States. More than 3 million people are employed as teachers, clerical staff, food service workers, grounds keepers, and full-time administrators.

Clearly, education has become a vast and complex social institution throughout the world. It prepares citizens for the various roles demanded by other social institutions, such as the family, government, and the economy. This chapter contrasts the functionalist and conflict analyses of the educational system of the United States. Functionalists stress the importance of education in

FIGURE 16-1 Educational Attainment in the United States, Persons 25 to 29 Years Old, 1940–1988

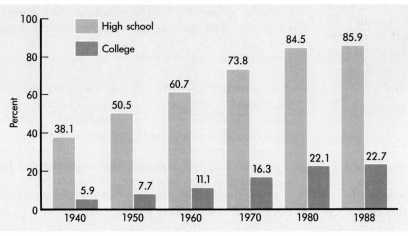

SOURCE: Bureau of the Census, 1990a:134.

Since 1940, the proportion of Americans 25 to 29 years old with a high school diploma has more than doubled; the proportion with a college degree has nearly quadrupled.

Ole the Viking serves as a reminder of the ethnic heritage of Augustana College, in Sioux Falls, South Dakota. This popular statue is often a site for student gatherings and celebrations. The same is true of the UCLA Bruin, a statue of the mascot of the University of California at Los Angeles.

transmitting culture, maintaining social control, and promoting social change. To conflict theorists, however, education preserves social class distinctions instead of promoting equality. Interactionists generally focus on micro-level classroom dynamics, such as how teachers' expectations about students affect the students' actual achievements.

This chapter also analyzes schools as formal organizations. Particular attention is given to the bureaucratization of schools, the role of teachers as employees, and the student subculture. Current trends in education in the United States—minimum-competency testing, school choice programs, mainstreaming of students with disabilities, the impact of Title IX on women's education, and adult education—are discussed. Finally, the social policy section examines the controversy over the inequities in school financing across the United States.

SOCIOLOGICAL PERSPECTIVES ON EDUCATION

Functionalist View

Like other social institutions, education has both manifest (open, stated) and latent (hidden) functions. The most basic *manifest* function of education is the transmission of knowledge. Schools teach students how to read, speak foreign lan-

guages, and repair automobiles. Education has another important manifest function: bestowing status. Owing to widespread criticism of the differential way in which this function is performed, it will be considered later, in the section on the conflict view of education.

In addition to these manifest functions, schools perform a number of *latent* functions. Among these are transmitting culture, promoting social and political integration, maintaining social control, and serving as agents of change.

Transmitting Culture As a social institution, education performs a rather conservative function—transmitting the dominant culture. Through schooling, each generation of young people is exposed to the existing beliefs, norms, and values of our culture. We learn respect for social control and reverence for established institutions, such as religion, the family, and the presidency. Of course, this is true in many other cultures as well. While American schoolchildren are hearing about the greatness of George Washington and Abraham Lincoln, British children are hearing about the greatness of Queen Elizabeth I and Winston Churchill.

The educational system of each society reflects its distinctive culture and the influence of other social institutions, including the government and economy. For example, in the Soviet Union educational curricula for young children reinforce the collective orientation of socialist ideology. In some nursery and elementary schools, a huge stone is placed in the playground. No child alone can move it even a few inches, but the entire class, *working together,* can push the stone a few feet. Through such projects, students are taught the value of cooperating toward a common goal. By contrast, students in the United States might compete in teams to see which could move the stone farthest. Soviet teachers are trained to reward group performance rather than to single out individual students for praise. Slower students are "adopted" by other classmates so that they can fulfill the group's goal, whether it be by completing an algebra problem or drawing a map (Parelius and Parelius, 1978:34–36).

A dispute over Japanese textbooks provides an interesting case study of the transmission of culture through education. In mid-1982, Japanese newspapers reported that high school social studies textbooks dealing with the nation's wartime aggression and atrocities had been "watered down" by Japan's Ministry of Education. For example, where the expansion into Manchuria in the 1930s had previously been termed an "invasion," it was now to be called an "advance." Japanese atrocities in Korea in 1919 and later in Manchuria were rationalized as a "response to local resistance." Critics charged that these changes not only distorted history but might contribute to a revival of Japanese militarism. Despite vehement protests from China and South Korea, the revised language was retained, but teachers were instructed to take these criticisms into account as they prepared their lessons (Seddon, 1987).

As we learned in our discussion of censorship of schoolbooks in Chapter 14, debates over curricula have become common in the United States in the last decade. Such distinguished works of literature as Alice Walker's Pulitzer prize–winning novel *The Color Purple,* John Steinbeck's *Of Mice and Men,* and Arthur Miller's *Death of a Salesman* have been the target of censorship efforts within local school districts.

On the college level, there has been growing controversy over the general education or basic curriculum requirements of colleges and universities. Critics charge that standard academic curricula have failed to represent the important contributions of women and people of color to history, literature, and other fields of study. The underlying question raised by this debate, still to be resolved, is which ideas and values are essential for instruction? What culture should be transmitted by the schools and colleges of the United States?

Promoting Social and Political Integration
Education serves the latent function of promoting social and political integration by transforming a population composed of diverse racial, ethnic, and religious groups into a society whose members share—to some extent at least—a common identity (Touraine, 1974:115). As noted earlier, American schools have historically played an important role in socializing the children of immigrants into the norms, values, and beliefs of the dominant culture. From a functionalist perspective, the common identity and social integration fostered by education contribute to societal stability and consensus.

In the past, the integrative function of education was most obvious through its emphasis on promoting a common language. As was discussed in the social policy section of Chapter 3, immigrant children were expected to learn English. In some instances, they were even forbidden to speak their native languages on school grounds. More recently, bilingualism has been defended both for its educational value and as a means of encouraging cultural diversity. However, in the view of its critics, bilingualism undermines the social and political integration that education has traditionally promoted.

The debate over bilingualism underscores the fact that not everyone may want to be integrated into the dominant culture of the United States. For example, members of Amish communities (refer back to Chapter 4) shun most modern conveniences, such as electricity, automobiles, radio,

Schools do more than teach the "three Rs"—reading, 'riting, and 'rithmetic. They also attempt to control and regulate students' behavior, reflecting the social values of the dominant society.

ing, writing, and mathematics. Schoolchildren are introduced to standards of proper conduct in public life which are quite different from the rules of behavior in their families. Like other social institutions such as the family and religion, education prepares young people to lead productive and orderly lives as adults by introducing them to the norms, values, and sanctions of the larger society.

Through the exercise of social control, students are taught various skills and values which will be essential in their future positions within the labor force. They learn punctuality, discipline, scheduling, and responsible work habits, as well as how to negotiate their way through the complexities of a bureaucratic organization. In effect, then, schools serve as a transitional agent of social control—between parents and employers in the life cycle of most individuals. As a social institution, education reflects the interests of the family and in turn prepares young people for their participation in yet another social institution—the economy. Students are being trained for what is ahead, whether it be the assembly line or the office (Bowles and Gintis, 1976; M. Cole, 1988).

From a functionalist perspective, social control socializes students to the impersonal rules of society. This function is undertaken by schools not only through transmitting the existing culture but also by re-creating within their walls the social control found in other institutions such as government and the economy. A national survey in 1989 asked American adults what qualities were important in the development of a child. Nearly as many responded with "the ability to get along with others" as with the more academically related answer "learning to think for oneself" (Elam and Gallup, 1989).

As will be discussed more fully later in the chapter, schools are highly bureaucratic organizations. Many teachers rely on the rules and regulations of schools in order to maintain order. Unfortunately, the need for control and discipline can take precedence over the learning process. Teachers may focus on obedience to the rules as an end in itself—a shift in priorities which reflects the type of goal displacement that was considered in Chapter 6. If this occurs, students and teachers alike become victims of what Philip Jackson

and television. The Amish maintain their own schools, which end at the eighth grade, and do not want their children socialized into many American norms and values. In some states, Amish parents have been prosecuted for violating compulsory education laws which require education beyond eighth grade. However, in 1972, the Supreme Court upheld a lower court ruling that Wisconsin's compulsory education law violated the First Amendment rights of the Amish to free exercise of religion (Kephart and Zellner, 1991:34).

Maintaining Social Control In performing the manifest function of transmitting knowledge, schools go far beyond teaching such skills as read-

(1968) has termed the *hidden curriculum*—the standards of behavior that are deemed proper by society. According to this subtle "curriculum," children must wait before speaking until the teacher calls on them and must regulate their activities according to the clock or bells. In addition, they are expected to concentrate on their own work rather than assist other students who learn more slowly.

In a classroom overly focused on obedience, value is placed on pleasing the teacher and remaining quiet—rather than on creative thought and academic learning (Leacock, 1969:59–61). If students become accustomed to habitual obedience to authority, the type of distressing behavior which was documented by Stanley Milgram in his classic obedience studies (see Chapter 7) may result.

The social-control function of education is not limited to patterns of rules and behavior. Schools direct and even restrict students' aspirations in a manner that reflects societal values and prejudices. School administrators may allocate substantial educational funds for athletic programs while giving much less support to music, art, and dance. Moreover, as we saw in Chapter 4, teachers and guidance counselors may encourage male students to pursue careers in the sciences but steer equally talented female students into careers as early childhood teachers. Such socialization into traditional gender roles can be viewed as a form of social control.

Education as an Agent of Change   Thus far, this discussion has focused on conservative functions of education—on its role in transmitting the existing culture, promoting social and political integration, and maintaining social control. Yet education can stimulate or bring about desired social change. Sex education classes were introduced in public schools in response to the soaring pregnancy rate among teenagers. Affirmative action in education has been endorsed as a means of countering racial and sexual discrimination (see Chapter 15). Project Head Start—an early childhood program serving 400,000 children annually—has sought to compensate for the disadvantages in school readiness experienced by children from low-income families.

Education also promotes social change by serving as a meeting ground where each society's distinctive beliefs and traditions can be shared. In 1990, there were 387,000 foreign students in the United States, of whom about 85 percent were from developing nations (R. Wilson, 1990). Cross-cultural exchanges between these visitors and citizens of the United States ultimately broaden the perspective of both the hosts and their guests. The same is certainly true when students from the United States attend schools in Europe, Latin America, Africa, or the far east.

Numerous sociological studies have revealed that increased years of formal schooling are associated with openness to new ideas and more liberal social and political viewpoints. Sociologist Robin Williams (R. Williams et al., 1964:374–375) points out that better-educated people tend to have greater access to factual information, a diversity of opinion, and subtle distinctions of analysis. Formal education stresses both the importance of qualifying statements and the need at least to question (rather than simply accept) established "truths" and practices. As we saw in Chapter 2, scientific method relies on *testing* hypotheses and reflects the questioning spirit that characterizes modern education. For these reasons, education can make one less likely to champion outmoded beliefs and prejudices and more likely to promote and accept social change (Schaefer, 1976:127).

Conflict View

Sociologist Christopher Hurn (1985:48–76) has compared the functionalist and conflict views of schooling. According to Hurn, the functionalist perspective portrays the major features of contemporary education in fundamentally benign terms. For example, it argues that schools rationally sort and select students for future high-status positions, thereby meeting society's need for talented and expert personnel. By contrast, the conflict perspective views education as an instrument of elite domination. Schools convince subordinate groups of their inferiority, reinforce existing social class inequality, and discourage alternative and more democratic visions of society.

Conflict theorists take a critical view of the social institution of education. They argue that the educational system socializes students into values dictated by the powerful, that schools stifle individualism and creativity in the name of maintaining order, and that the level of change promoted by education is relatively insignificant. From a conflict perspective, the inhibiting effects of education are particularly apparent in the creation of standards for entry into occupations, the differential way in which status is bestowed, and the existence of a dual system of private and public schools.

Credentialism Today, a college diploma has become virtually a minimum requirement for entry into the paid labor force of the United States, just as a high school diploma was 50 years ago. This change reflects the process of *credentialism*—a term used to describe the increase in the lowest level of education needed to enter a field.

The discussion of the economy in Chapter 15 looked at the growing trend of professionalization of occupations. Credentialism is one symptom of this trend. Employers and occupational associations typically contend that such changes are a logical response to the increasing complexity of many jobs (R. Collins, 1979:5; Dore, 1976:5; Hurn, 1985:95). However, in many cases, employers raise degree requirements for a position simply because all applicants have achieved the existing minimum credential.

Conflict theorists have observed that credentialism may reinforce social inequality. They note that applicants from poor and minority backgrounds are especially likely to suffer from the escalation of qualifications, since they lack the financial resources needed to obtain degree after degree. In addition, upgrading credentials serves the self-interest of the two groups most responsible for this trend. Educational institutions have a vested interest in prolonging the investment of time and money that people make by staying in school. Moreover, as Christopher Hurn (1985:56–57) has suggested, current jobholders have a stake in raising occupational requirements. Credentialism can increase the status of an occupation and is crucial to demands for higher pay. Max Weber anticipated such possibilities as far back as 1916, concluding that the "universal

clamor for the creation of educational certificates in all fields makes for the formation of a privileged stratum in businesses and in offices" (Gerth and Mills, 1958:240–241).

Credentialism is evident not only in the United States and the other industrialized nations but also in the developing countries of the world. In some of these nations, the number of people with credentials far exceeds the available positions. For example, in the early 1970s, the schools of Sri Lanka (Ceylon) were producing 70,000 children per year with the equivalent of a grade school education, 100,000 with high school diplomas, and another 12,000 with higher degrees. These 182,000 new graduates joined unemployed graduates of previous years in competing for roughly 70,000 new jobs (Dore, 1976:4–5).

Bestowal of Status Both functionalist and conflict theorists agree that education performs the important function of bestowing status. As noted earlier, an increasing proportion of Americans are obtaining high school diplomas, college degrees, and advanced professional degrees (refer back to Figure 16-1). From a functionalist perspective, this widening bestowal of status is beneficial not only to particular recipients but to the society as a whole. In our discussion of stratification in Chapter 8, we noted the view of Kingsley Davis and Wilbert Moore (1945) that society must distribute its members among a variety of social positions. Education can contribute to this process by sorting people into appropriate levels and courses of study that will prepare them for appropriate positions within the labor force.

Conflict sociologists are far more critical of the differential way education bestows status; they stress that schools sort pupils according to social class background. Although the educational system helps certain poor children to move into middle-class professional positions, it denies most disadvantaged children the same educational opportunities afforded children of the affluent (see Figure 16-2). In this way, schools tend to preserve social class inequalities in each new generation (Labaree, 1986; Mingle, 1987).

Money contributes to this disparity. In all but a few cases, public schools in the United States have been financed through local property taxes. Since

FIGURE 16-2   Education of Minority Group Students
in the United States

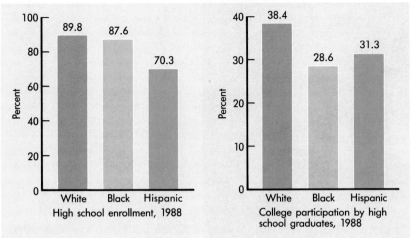

SOURCE: Bureau of the Census, 1990a:150–151.

Although enrollment of racial and ethnic minorities in American colleges increased throughout the 1970s and early 1980s, these groups remain underrepresented at all levels of higher education.

the total value of property tends to be lower in areas with many low-income families, these school districts generally have less money available for education. The inequities in school financing will be discussed more fully in the social policy section at the end of the chapter.

Class differences can also be reinforced within a single school. Working-class children are much more likely to be viewed as destined for subordinate positions and therefore placed in high school vocational or general tracks. The term *tracking* refers to the practice of placing students in specific curriculum groups on the basis of test scores and other criteria. Tracking begins very early in the classroom, often in reading groups during first grade. These tracks can reinforce the disadvantages that children from less affluent families may have if they have not been exposed to reading materials and writing instruments in their homes during early childhood years.

Sociologists Glenna Colclough and E. M. Beck (1986) considered three factors that contribute to the role of education in maintaining social class differences: public versus private schooling, economic disparities between school communities, and tracking of students into curriculum groups. The researchers found that tracking was the most

significant mechanism for sorting and channeling students into desirable or subordinate positions in society. To put it another way, the placement of a student into either a college-bound or a vocational track will have more of an influence on his or her future than sending the student to a private school, a public school, a school in an affluent community, or a school in a low-income neighborhood. Moreover, as noted above, tracking is related to students' social class backgrounds and therefore serves to maintain class inequalities across generations. In addition, tracking contributes significantly to the racial isolation of the classroom, leading to the absence of integrated learning environments even in schools with diverse student populations (Oakes, 1985; Oakes et al., 1990; Vanfossen et al., 1987).

Differential access to higher education and tracking are evident not only in the United States but also in many nations around the world (see Box 16-1 on page 487). Japan's educational system mandates equality in school funding and insists that all schools use the same textbooks. Nevertheless, it is the more affluent Japanese families who can afford to send their children to *juku,* or cram schools. These afternoon schools assist high school students in preparing for examinations

(Bob Daemmrich/The Image Works)

Shown is a high school cosmetology class. Working-class students may be placed in vocational tracks as part of the general practice of tracking.

which determine admission into prestigious colleges (McGrath, 1983:66; Rohlen, 1983; M. White, 1987).

In the view of conflict theorists, the educational inequalities resulting from funding disparities and tracking are designed to meet the needs of modern capitalist societies. Samuel Bowles and Herbert Gintis (1976:131–148) argue that capitalism requires a skilled, disciplined labor force and that the educational system of the United States is structured with that objective in mind. Citing numerous studies, they offer support for what they call the *correspondence principle.*

According to this approach, schools attended by different social classes promote the values expected of individuals in each class and perpetuate social class divisions from one generation to the next. Thus, working-class children, assumed to be destined for subordinate positions, are more likely to be placed in high school vocational and general tracks which emphasize close supervision and compliance with authority. By contrast, young people from more affluent families are largely directed to college preparatory tracks which stress leadership and decision-making skills—corresponding to their likely futures. While the correspondence principle continues to be persuasive, researchers have noted that the

impact of race and gender on students' educational experiences may even overshadow that of class (M. Cole, 1988).

There are, however, interesting exceptions to this pattern. In such cities as New York, Boston, and Chicago, special "magnet" or "option" public high schools have been created to offer enriched programs in specialties such as computer science, health professions, and the performing arts. Through a selective process, public school students—many from working-class backgrounds—can bypass the normal tracking system and benefit from unique curricula with broad career themes (Weiss, 1984).

Private versus Public Schools For every American child who attends a private school, six children go to public schools. It was hardly surprising, then, that a storm of protest followed a study by sociologist James S. Coleman and his associates (J. S. Coleman et al., 1982) which concluded that private high schools provide a better education than public high schools. This project used data from more than 1000 public and private high schools. It was the most extensive examination of nonpublic schools ever conducted in the United States.

Coleman found, even when controlling for

BOX 16-1 • AROUND THE WORLD

INEQUALITY IN EDUCATION

As was discussed in Chapter 8, educational achievements play a critical role in social mobility. Consequently, concern has been expressed that subordinate minorities in the United States—such as Blacks, Hispanics, and American Indians—do not have positive experiences in schools that will assist them in later competition in the job market. This country's minorities, however, are not alone in this experience.

The anthropologist John Ogbu (1978) looked at educational opportunities and achievements in six societies and found group inequality in all of them. In Great Britain, for example, Black West Indian immigrants and their descendants (many of whom are born in Britain) perform poorly in school. By contrast, in New Zealand it is the native Maori people—the original islanders now outnumbered and dominated by White Europeans—who have the greatest difficulty in the educational system. Whites are 350 times more likely than Maori to attend college.

In these societies, race was the critical factor differentiating successful and unsuccessful educational performance. However, in studying other societies, Ogbu found that inequality was evident even when racial distinctions were absent. In India, people from lower-caste backgrounds (refer back to Chapter 8) are physically indistinguishable from other residents. Yet children from the lower castes are much less likely to attend the private schools that launch Indians toward better careers. While lower-caste children account for more than 15 percent of India's population, they constitute only about 5 percent of those attending college.

In studying Japan, Ogbu found that the nation's Buraku minority essentially occupies a lower-caste position. For centuries, the Buraku have been assigned jobs viewed as undesirable in Shinto and Buddhist traditions, such as the slaughter of animals to make leather goods. While the Buraku tend to live in segregated communities in both rural and urban areas, their children often attend school with other Japanese chil-

dren. Yet only 10 percent of Buraku children go on to high school, as compared with 85 percent of Japan's non-Buraku schoolchildren.

Ogbu found certain common themes in all the societies he studied (one of which was the United States). The dominant groups in each society agree on the importance of education and the key role of educational attainment in shaping one's position in adult life. At the same time, however, folk explanations ascribe failure in school to the alleged inferiority of the nation's subordinate minorities. Yet, as Ogbu points out, minority group members have traditionally had good reason to view education as a less than useful investment of time and effort. The societies he studied have only recently begun to reward subordinate minorities equally for equivalent training and ability. Therefore, as prejudice and discrimination against subordinate groups decline, members of such minorities will have more to gain from successful performance in the educational system.

---

such important factors as parents' social class and education, that private school students do better than their public school counterparts on tests of reading and mathematical ability and measures of self-esteem. The gains in test performance from sophomore to senior year are also greater among private school students. The study suggests that private schools have fewer absences, instances of cutting classes, and fights, along with more homework, smaller classes, and greater participation in

athletics. In line with Coleman's findings, more recent research by sociologists Barbara Falsey and Barbara Heyns (1984) indicates that students who graduate from private schools are much more likely to enroll in college than public school graduates are. These differences persist even when ability levels, students' aspirations, and social class backgrounds are controlled.

The study by Coleman of public and private schools has been criticized on various methodo-

(Mike Yamashita/Woodfin Camp & Associates)

From a conflict perspective, private schools can be seen as promoting religious and social class division.

logical grounds. Some researchers have questioned the sampling procedures and tests of ability used by Coleman and his staff. Others have noted that this study made no attempt to examine measures of actual academic achievement, such as class ranking or grade point average. Perhaps most seriously, critics have suggested that Coleman's research may actually be measuring the earlier educational performance of public and private elementary and junior high schools more than that of high schools (Fiske, 1981:1; L. Middleton, 1981; E. West, 1984:16–18).

Viewed from a conflict perspective, private schools can be seen as promoting division along lines of religion and social class. About two-thirds of private school students are in schools affiliated with religious denominations. In addition, although private high schools include students from all income levels, they have a greater proportion from higher social classes than public high schools do. Using a conflict approach, one can argue that Coleman's study may weaken the already negative image of public education and encourage more affluent parents to send their children to private schools. This could accelerate the trend toward a dual school system: public schools for the disadvantaged, private schools for the privileged.

Interactionist View

In George Bernard Shaw's play *Pygmalion*, later adapted into the hit Broadway musical *My Fair Lady*, flower girl Eliza Doolittle is transformed into a "lady" by Professor Henry Higgins. He changes her manner of speech and teaches her the etiquette of "high society."

Is it actually possible to change someone's behavior simply by treating the person differently? Because of their focus on micro-level classroom dynamics, interactionist researchers have been particularly interested in this question. The labeling approach (see Chapter 7) and the concept of the self-fulfilling prophecy (see Chapter 10) suggest that if we treat people in particular ways, they may fulfill our expectations. Children labeled as "troublemakers" come to view themselves as delinquents. A dominant group's stereotyping of racial minorities may limit their opportunities to break away from expected roles.

Can this labeling process operate in the classroom? Howard Becker (1952) studied public schools in low-income and more affluent areas of Chicago. He noticed that administrators expected less of students from poor neighborhoods, and he wondered if this view was being accepted by teachers. Subsequently, in *Pygmalion in the Class-*

room, psychologist Robert Rosenthal and school principal Lenore Jacobson (1968) documented what they referred to as a ***teacher-expectancy effect***—the impact that a teacher's expectations about a student's performance may have on the student's actual achievements.

Between 1965 and 1966, children in a San Francisco elementary school were administered a verbal and reasoning pretest. The researchers then randomly selected 20 percent of the sample and designated them as "spurters"—children of whom teachers could expect superior performance. On a later verbal and reasoning test, the spurters were found to score significantly higher than before. Moreover, teachers evaluated them as more interesting, more curious, and better-adjusted than their classmates. These results were quite striking, since the spurters—unbeknownst to the teachers—had been *arbitrarily* classified in the "superior" group. Apparently, teacher's perceptions that these students were exceptional led to noticeable improvements in performance.

Studies in the United States have revealed that teachers wait longer for an answer from a student believed to be a high achiever and are more likely to give such children a second chance. In one experiment, teachers' expectations were even shown to have an impact on students' athletic achievements. Teachers obtained better athletic performance—as measured in the number of sit-ups or push-ups performed—from those students of whom they expected higher numbers (R. Rosenthal and Babad, 1985).

The teacher-expectancy effect has been confirmed in a rather surprising setting: a training base for the Israeli army. Instructors for a combat command course were purposely given incorrect information about the "command potential" of 105 men about 4 days before the trainees arrived. Once the course began, the trainees who had been labeled "high in potential" did indeed learn more than others. These trainees also developed more favorable attitudes toward the combat command course (Eden and Shani, 1982).

Despite these findings, some researchers continue to question the validity of this "Pygmalion effect." Further research is needed to clarify the relationship between teacher expectations and actual student performance. Yet, drawing on the studies described above, interactionists emphasize that ability may not be so completely predictive of academic success as one might think.

Schools as Formal Organizations

Horace Mann would be amazed at the scale of modern American schools. For example, New York City's school system, the largest in the nation, currently enrolls as many children as there were in the entire country's secondary schools in 1911 (Sizer, 1984:206). In many respects, today's schools, when viewed as an example of a formal organization, are similar to factories, hospitals, and business firms. The parallels between schools and these other organizations will become more apparent as we examine the bureaucratic nature of schools, teaching as an occupational role, and the student subculture.

Bureaucratization of Schools The bureaucratization of American schools has resulted not only from the growing number of students being served by individual schools and school systems but also from the greater degree of specialization required within a technologically complex society. It is simply not possible for a single teacher to transmit culture and skills to children of varying ages who will enter many diverse occupations (Goslin, 1965:132–142).

Chapter 6 examined Max Weber's insights on bureaucracy as an ideal type. Weber noted five basic characteristics of bureaucracy, all of which are evident in the vast majority of schools, whether at the elementary, secondary, or even college level.

1 *Division of labor.* Specialized experts are employed to teach particular age levels of students and specific subjects. Public schools now employ instructors whose sole responsibility is to work with children who have learning disabilities or physical impairments. In a college sociology department, one professor may specialize in sociology of religion, another in marriage and the family, and a third in industrial sociology.
2 *Hierarchy of authority.* Each employee of a school system is responsible to a higher authority. Teachers must report to principals and assistant

principals and may also be supervised by department heads. Principals are answerable to a superintendent of schools, and the superintendent is hired and fired by a board of education. Even the students are hierarchically organized by grade and within clubs and organizations.

3 *Written rules and regulations.* Teachers and administrators must conform to numerous rules and regulations in the performance of their duties. This bureaucratic trait can become dysfunctional; the time invested in completing required forms could instead be spent in preparing lessons or conferring with students.

4 *Impersonality.* As was noted in Chapter 6, the American university has been portrayed as a giant, faceless bureaucracy which cares little for the uniqueness of the individual. As class sizes have increased at schools and universities, it has become more difficult for teachers to give personal attention to each student. In fact, bureaucratic norms may actually encourage teachers to treat all students in the same way despite the fact that students have distinctive personalities and learning needs.

5 *Employment based on technical qualifications.* At least in theory, the hiring of teachers and college professors is based on professional competence and expertise. Promotions are normally dictated by written personnel policies; people who excel may be granted lifelong job security through tenure. Teachers have achieved these protections partly because of the bargaining power of unions (Borman and Spring, 1984; Tyler, 1985).

Functionalists take a generally positive view of the bureaucratization of education. Teachers can master the skills needed to work with a specialized clientele, since they no longer are expected to cover a broad range of instruction. The chain of command within schools is clear; students are presumably treated in an unbiased fashion because of uniformly applied rules. Finally, security of office protects teachers from unjustified dismissal. In general, then, functionalists observe that bureaucratization of education increases the likelihood that students, teachers, and administrators will be dealt with fairly—that is, on the basis of rational and equitable criteria.

By contrast, conflict theorists argue that the trend toward more centralized education has harmful consequences for disadvantaged Americans. The standardization of educational curricula, including textbooks, will generally reflect the values, interests, and lifestyles of the most powerful groups in our society and may ignore those of racial and ethnic minorities. In addition, the disadvantaged, more so than the affluent, will find it difficult to sort through complex educational bureaucracies and to organize effective lobbying groups. Therefore, in the view of conflict theorists, low-income and minority parents will have even less influence over citywide and statewide educational administrators than they have over local school officials (Bowles and Gintis, 1976; M. Katz, 1971).

Teachers: Employees and Instructors Whether they serve as instructors of preschoolers or graduate students, teachers are employees of formal organizations with bureaucratic structures. In Chapter 15, it was noted that there is an inherent conflict in serving as a professional within a bureaucracy. The organization follows the principle of hierarchy and expects adherence to its rules; professionalism demands the individual responsibility of the practitioner. This conflict is very real for teachers, who experience all the positive and negative consequences of working in bureaucracies (refer back to Table 6-3 on page 167).

On a day-to-day level, the occupational status of *teacher* brings with it many perplexing stresses. While teachers' academic assignments have become more specialized as a result of the increasing division of labor within education, the demands on their time remain diverse and contradictory. In analyzing the work of schoolteachers, sociologist C. Wayne Gordon (1955) noted the conflicts inherent in serving as an instructor, a disciplinarian, and an employee of a school district at the same time. For college professors, different types of role strain arise. While formally employed as teachers, they are expected to work on committees and are encouraged to conduct scholarly research. In many colleges and universities, security of position (tenure) is based primarily on the publication of original scholarship. As a result, instructors must fulfill goals that compete for time.

On a day-to-day level, the occupational status "teacher" brings with it many perplexing stresses.

College professors rarely have to occupy themselves with the role of disciplinarian, but this task has become a major focus of schoolteachers' work. Clearly, maintenance of order is essential in establishing an educational environment in which students can actually learn. Yet the nation's schools have been the scene of increasingly violent misbehavior in recent years. An estimated 100,000 pupils in the United States carry guns to school each day (Ostling, 1989).

The costs of combatting violence in the schools can become staggering. For example, after a bullet whistled past a gym teacher in Long Beach, California, the junior high school spent $160,000 to build a 10-foot wall to separate its rear boundary from a nearby housing project which had been the scene of frequent gunfights between gang members. New York City's schools now operate the nation's eleventh-largest security force. Most schools in the city have locked doors, 15 use metal detectors, and 10 allow entry only with computerized identification cards (Ostling, 1989).

Given these difficulties, does teaching remain an attractive profession in the United States? In 1969, when teachers were already having difficulty finding jobs because of growing educational cutbacks, fully 75 percent of parents indicated that they would like their children to become public school teachers. By 1990, that figure had fallen to 51 percent. In the minds of parents, the status of teaching as a career for their children had declined. In 1990, 3.9 percent of first-year male college students and 13.2 percent of first-year female students indicated that they were interested in becoming teachers. While these figures reflect a modest upturn in the appeal of teaching in recent years, they are dramatically lower than the 12.7 percent of first-year male students and 37.5 percent of first-year female students who had such occupational aspirations in 1968 (Astin et al., 1987:46, 70; Astin et al., 1990:17, 33; Elam, 1990:47).

Undoubtedly, students' feelings about the attractiveness of teaching have been influenced by the economics of the profession. In 1988, the average salary for all public elementary and secondary teachers was $28,031. This salary places teachers somewhere near the average of all wage earners in the United States. By contrast, university students in Japan line up for coveted teaching jobs. By law, Japanese teachers are paid 10 percent more than employees in the top-level civil service job, which places them among the top 10 percent of wage earners in the nation (H. Johnson, 1988; Richburg, 1985).

As was noted in Chapter 8, the status of any job

reflects several factors, including the level of education required, financial compensation, and the respect given the occupation within society. Teaching is feeling pressure in all three areas: the amount of formal schooling required for this profession remains high, but the public has begun to call for new competency examinations for teachers; the statistics cited above demonstrate that teachers' salaries are significantly lower than those of many professionals and skilled workers; finally, as we have seen, the prestige of the teaching profession has declined in the last decade. It is not surprising, then, to find that many teachers become disappointed and frustrated and leave the educational world for other careers. Many are simply "burned out" by the severe demands, limited rewards, and general sense of alienation that they experience on the job (see Chapter 15).

Perhaps typical of the burned-out teacher was a 33-year-old Brooklyn woman interviewed by a reporter in 1981. When she arrived at her school in the late 1960s, she asked to work with slow learners. By 1981, although still regarded as a creative teacher, she felt overwhelmed by factors beyond her control—budget cuts, vandalism, overwrought parents, and undisciplined students. She was taking night courses and planning to enter a new line of work. "I used to think that I was the only one who could reach my classes, that I ought to stay against all the odds," she remarked. Then she added, "I feel like I'm the only chump left. I've done my bit for society. Maybe someone else should try now" (Coppola, 1981:81).

In 1987, a Rand Corporation report estimated attrition among teachers in the United States at 9 percent annually. The researchers noted that the "teacher burnout" rate had been as high as 17 percent per year in the 1960s. However, although the current rate is much lower, it has raised even greater concern among educators because the profession is no longer attracting a sufficient number of college graduates. Until 20 years ago, a steady supply of women and minority group members entered teaching. However, as career options have widened for these groups in recent decades (refer back to Chapters 10 and 11), many people have chosen to enter higher-paying occupations, rather than teaching (Grissmer and Kirby, 1987; Solórzano, 1986).

The Student Subculture Earlier, various functions of education, such as transmitting culture, maintaining social control, and promoting social change, were described. An additional latent function which relates directly to student life can be identified: schools provide for students' social and recreational needs. Education helps toddlers and young children develop interpersonal skills that are essential during adolescence and adulthood. During high school and college years, students may meet future husbands and wives and may establish lifelong friendships (J. W. Coleman and Cressey, 1980:96).

When people observe high schools, community colleges, or universities from the outside, students appear to constitute a cohesive, uniform group. However, the student subculture is actually much more complex and diverse. High school cliques and social groups may be established on the basis of race, social class, physical attractiveness, placement in courses, athletic ability, and leadership roles in the school and community. Remarkably, in his study of Elmtown, allowing for the fact that an individual could belong to more than one social group, August Hollingshead (1975:154) found some 259 distinct cliques in a single high school. These cliques, whose average size was five, were centered on the school itself, on recreational activities, and on religious and community groups.

A similar diversity can be found at the college level. Burton Clark and Martin Trow (1966)—and, more recently, Helen Lefkowitz Horowitz (1987)—have identified distinctive subcultures among college students. Looking at their analyses together, we can present four ideal types of subcultures.

The *collegiate* subculture focuses on having fun and socializing. These students define what constitutes a "reasonable" amount of academic work (and what amount of work is "excessive" and leads to being labeled as a "grind"). Members of the collegiate subculture have little commitment to academic pursuits. By contrast, the *academic* subculture identifies with the intellectual concerns of the faculty and values knowledge for its own sake. The *vocational* subculture is primarily interested in career prospects and views college as a means of obtaining degrees which are essential for ad-

Social cliques consisting of athletes are one aspect of the larger student subculture of a high school.

vancement. Finally, the *nonconformist* subculture is hostile to the college environment and seeks out ideas that may or may not relate to studies. Indeed, they may be removed from the dominant college culture but may find outlets through campus publications or issue-oriented groups. Each college student is eventually exposed to these competing subcultures and must determine which (if any) seem most in line with his or her feelings and interests.

The typology used by these researchers reminds us that school is a complex social organization—almost like a community with different neighborhoods. However, it is important to note that these four subcultures are not the only ones evident on college campuses in the United States. For example, one might find subcultures of Vietnam veterans or former full-time homemakers at community colleges and four-year commuter institutions. The striking increase in older college students will be discussed more fully later in the chapter.

Professor of education Donald Smith (1980, 1981) has studied a distinctive collegiate subculture: Black students at predominantly White universities. Smith suggests that Black students associate primarily with other Blacks because they perceive predominantly White campuses as hostile environments. These students must function academically and socially within universities with few Black faculty members or Black administrators, frequent harassment of Blacks by campus police, and little emphasis in the curricula on Black contributions. According to Smith, Black students at primarily White institutions experience isolation, alienation, and loneliness. Even the Black subculture offers inadequate support because of internal conflicts as well as external pressure from university authorities to downplay racial identification and solidarity (see also Feagin, 1989).

EDUCATION IN THE UNITED STATES: CURRENT TRENDS

Most of this chapter has focused on the basic processes and social structure of educational institutions in the United States. This section will examine a number of important educational innovations that have been proposed or implemented within the last 20 years.

It is worth noting that Americans believe that change is needed in the nation's educational system. A 1990 survey revealed that only 18 percent of respondents were prepared to give a grade of "A" to their communities' elementary schools. Only 2 percent were willing to give this top grade to the public schools in the nation as a whole. But such dissatisfaction is hardly unique to the United States. In a comparative analysis of more than 3500 policymakers and organization leaders in the United States, Great Britain, and West Germany, researchers found agreement that each country's educational system was not functioning well and that reforms were essential (Elam, 1990:52; Landsberger et al., 1988).

No matter what the public sentiment, the constraints against change in American education can be formidable. Educators may resist theories or techniques that seem "untested" or "too experimental." Taxpayers are reluctant to spend more money on unproven programs. Nevertheless, our educational system is badly in need of change, and certain proposals to fundamentally reshape this institution have attracted considerable attention.

Minimum-Competency Testing

Over the last 3 decades, standard procedure in American schools was to pass children from one grade to the next on the basis of age rather than actual educational attainment. This practice was called *social promotion;* it stemmed from a belief that the stigma of being left back might cripple motivation and self-esteem and further impede learning. Educators thus recognized the importance of the student subculture in academic success and failure. However, in the 1970s, more and more Americans—both inside and outside the educational world—became upset about the number of students graduating from high school who had never mastered basic skills. As a result, a nationwide movement emerged in support of *minimum-competency tests (MCTs),* which measure the knowledge that a child possesses in such areas as reading, writing, and mathematics.

Currently, school districts in 33 states require that some test be passed before a student can graduate from high school. Those who fail must enter a remedial program to prepare for retesting. However, a minimum-competency test does not grade students or place them at some level or percentile. Instead, it simply indicates whether the student has or has not achieved a minimum level of proficiency in a subject or skill. While the manifest function of the MCT is to certify the learner, the latent effect is to restore the credibility of the high school diploma in the minds of employers.

Minimum-competency testing is not without its critics. The MCT has been attacked on the grounds that it does not genuinely represent students' abilities. In addition, concern has been expressed that teachers may train students to pass the MCT, rather than educate them in a broader manner. Again, the social role of the teacher is made more difficult. Teachers may resent the pressure to focus their educational efforts on MCTs and may feel that they too have "failed" if their students do not pass the tests. Indeed, a 1990 Gallup survey of teachers found that 78 percent believe that the emphasis on standardized tests has increased in the last decade and 73 percent report that they are being pressured to spend more time preparing students for tests (D. Kelly, 1990b).

The debate over minimum-competency testing raises a fundamental question about the functions of education. Communities and policymakers must resolve whether schools should concentrate on the manifest function of teaching skills—by stressing reading, writing, and mathematics—or should take a broader view of education which embraces the arts, the humanities, and the social sciences. A move toward certifying abilities represents a further step toward credentialism. To date, while parents strongly support the general principle of going "back to the basics," they have been reluctant to sacrifice the alleged frills of a more rounded educational approach.

School Choice Programs

In the last 10 years, policymakers in many school districts across the United States have allowed parents to choose where to send their children. Such plans often attempt to stimulate better performances from local schools by mandating that some type of financial reward will follow students as they move to new schools.

The most common of these choice programs is the open enrollment option, under which public school students are free to cross district boundaries and bring with them the per-pupil state funding that they represent. Open enrollment programs have been adopted in four states thus far. Minnesota has the most comprehensive program, but only 0.5 percent of its students participate, and many of these do so for athletic reasons. Even those educators who are most enthusiastic about open enrollment admit that caution must be taken so that disadvantaged students are not turned away when they apply for transfer. As one superintendent in suburban Minneapolis asked, "We'll market our winning hockey teams and merit scholars, but who's going to speak for the risky and the needy?" (C. Leslie, 1988: 78–79).

A variation of the open enrollment plan has been applied within large school districts such as New York City's East Harlem: local administrators are forced to improve their offerings or go out of business if they cannot attract and keep students. Since the program began in 1973, three schools in East Harlem have been compelled to close, reorganize themselves, and then reopen with new and improved "alternative" classes. Thus far, open enrollment in this district appears to be quite a success, and test scores have improved sharply. In 1973, only 15 percent of students read at grade level; today, 64 percent do. The restructured schools have become so lively that they attract children from affluent neighborhoods outside the district.

Open enrollment programs have also been used to bring about desegregation, but with only limited success. Beginning in 1982, schools in predominantly Black areas of St. Louis and in 16 largely White suburbs permitted students to cross boundaries within their combined system. This plan relies heavily on the use of magnet schools; 28 special programs in St. Louis are designed to admit student populations that are 55 percent African American. In 1988, almost 11,000 Black students from the city were voluntarily bused to the plan's suburban schools. Yet only 581 White children from the suburbs transferred to magnet schools in St. Louis, leaving the city's public schools with a student population that is 76 percent Black.

Still another type of choice program uses vouchers or tuition tax credits, which provide for the transfer of public funds to the public or private school of parents' choice. This alternative has been unpopular even among advocates of school choice plans. Generally, critics argue that voucher or tuition tax credit programs involving private schools give these schools an unfair advantage in attracting students and funding. Private schools can exclude prospective students who may be difficult to educate, whereas public schools are obligated to serve any and all students. Currently, no true voucher plan exists, although Minnesota has experimented with the use of tuition tax credits (Bailey, 1990; C. Leslie, 1988).

In 1991, President George Bush offered a strong endorsement for school choice programs. Under a plan proposed by the Bush administration, state and local school districts would be encouraged to revise their regulations so that parents could use their tax dollars to send children to public or private schools. At the same time, the administration is supporting efforts to rewrite federal laws that restrict aid to children in private and parochial schools (Chira, 1991; see also Meier, 1991).

Mainstreaming

Perhaps no area of contemporary education is as widely misunderstood as education for students with disabilities. Disagreement even exists as to who should (and should not) be considered "handicapped," but for the most part educators agree that this category includes those who are mentally retarded, hearing-handicapped (or acoustically disabled), visually impaired, speech-handicapped, emotionally disturbed (or socially maladjusted), learning-disabled, and physically handicapped. Of course, each of these classifications is subject to varying definitions and further subdivisions. In addition, many children are multiply handicapped, experiencing two or more of these conditions.

Current policy regarding American schoolchildren with disabilities was shaped by the passage in

1975 of Public Law 94–142 (Education of All Handicapped Children Act), which took full effect in 1980. With a few exceptions, this law calls for local school districts to provide an individualized education plan (IEP) for every handicapped child. In addition, Public Law 94–142 holds that states wishing to receive federal funds to educate disabled students must place these students within the "least restrictive environment." In other words, children with disabilities must be educated in the atmosphere most similar to a regular classroom that is suitable for them. The practice of promoting maximum integration of handicapped children with nonhandicapped children is known as *mainstreaming*.

By 1991, the federal government had spent more than $16 billion to implement mainstreaming through the provisions of Public Law 94–142. One student in nine in the nation's public schools is now covered by this law. According to the Department of Education, 69 percent of all students with disabilities are participating in regular classes and receiving only support services. Most of the rest are in separate classes in regular school buildings (Gartner and Lipsky, 1987; see also A. Asch, 1989; P. Ferguson and Asch, 1989).

An important goal of mainstreaming is to break down societal prejudices regarding disabled people. Viewed from the perspective of labeling theory (see Chapter 7), mainstreaming is an attempt to remove the stigma attached to children with disabilities. It is hoped that, through day-to-day interactions with handicapped children, non-handicapped peers (as well as parents and teachers) will become more accepting of those with disabilities. Student life will be altered as young people with and without disabilities share classroom experiences. Yet, despite this rather humane objective, mainstreaming has not been received with enthusiasm by teachers or by parents of nondisabled children.

In particular, such parents fear that integration of disabled students into classrooms will make it more difficult for their own children to receive a high-quality education. Actually, mainstreaming does not dictate that *all* handicapped children be placed in regular classrooms. Only those able to function in traditional school settings are affected. But this distinction is sometimes ignored by an apprehensive public. Other difficulties faced by children with disabilities and their parents within the educational system are described in Box 16-2.

An obvious prerequisite for mainstreaming is extensive preparation for classroom teachers. In many states, requirements for teaching certification are gradually being modified to include training for work with disabled students. Yet these changes typically do not affect practicing teachers, who must be offered the needed skills through in-service training programs. As our society takes greater interest in the special educa-

(Richard Hutchings/Photo Researchers)

According to federal legislation which took effect in 1980, children with disabilities must be educated in the atmosphere most similar to a regular classroom that is suitable for them. Shown is a child with Down's syndrome who has been "mainstreamed" into a class of nondisabled students.

BOX 16-2 • SPEAKING OUT

A FATHER'S PERSPECTIVE ON SPECIAL EDUCATION

Many parents of children with disabilities have offered personal narratives as a source of data to assist society in general and the educational system in particular in better supporting such children and their families. In the following selection, Philip M. Ferguson (P. Ferguson and Asch, 1989:120, 122–124), a special education researcher and the father of a disabled son, addresses some of the difficulties in the relations between parents of children with disabilities and special education professionals:

The Education of All Handicapped Children Act (P.L. 94–142) has dramatically affected the lives of parents. Despite a continuing gap between programs promised and programs delivered, the basic procedural guarantees of parent participation and mandated responsibility of the public school system have made a crucial difference in the lives of many families whose needs would probably have been brushed aside a decade earlier. . . .

Despite the improvements in services over the years, several problematic features of parent-professional relationships seem to persist. . . . A "cult of expertise" seems to gather devotees equally from among the ranks of educators, doctors, therapists, and professionals of all levels and degrees. Parent narratives repeatedly describe the power struggles around that most valuable cultural commodity: specialized knowledge.

(Courtesy Philip Ferguson)

Philip Ferguson with his son Ian.

The negative version of this is to devalue the worth of knowledge that parents have about their own children. Concerns are dismissed. Requests are patronized. Reports of home behavior are distrusted. Certainly, this is not true of all parent-professional relationships, but it seems endemic to special education with its historic association with a clinical model that has little room for "amateurs." The positive version of this is to overvalue the knowledge of experts. This leads to educators and others persistently defining problems of children and parents so as to require "specialists" for their comprehension, not to mention their solution. Unfortunately, the benefits of P.L. 94–142 have also brought an increased reliance on brigades of therapists and specialists when often a commitment to the common sense of generic service providers would more than suffice. Parents are taught from the first diagnosis that "more is better" when it comes to the involvement of experts.

In my own experience, I vividly recall a meeting to discuss my son's annual IEP (individualized education program) for the coming school year. When my wife and I entered the room we found ten professionals of various species arrayed around the table, each convinced that his or her information was the most essential to Ian's progress and his parents' edification. By the time introductions had been completed the time allotted for the conference was half gone. My vow then, as yet unfulfilled, was to attend at least one IEP conference for Ian before he left school accompanied by a phalanx of ten or twelve solemn-faced parents. Then, the professionals and parents could trade introductions, shake hands all around, and like some pregame football ritual decide with a coin toss which side would speak first. Of course, I would wear the striped shirt. . . .

Parents and professionals can certainly be powerful allies. Unfortunately, too many professionals—both traditional and progressive—seem to believe that the phrase "parents' rights" means only the right to listen and agree, not to consider and decide.

tional needs of students with disabilities, new teaching credentials will be required and new adult education programs for teachers developed (Gartner and Lipsky, 1987).

The issue of mainstreaming students with disabilities is not merely an educational issue. Public Law 94–142 is viewed by many, including members of a growing movement for disability rights (see Chapter 20), as civil rights legislation designed to end unjust segregation of disabled students. The goal of integrating disabled people into educational and other institutions is a challenge to the American credo of equality and justice for all.

Title IX and Women's Education

The educational system of the United States, like many other social institutions, has long been characterized by discriminatory treatment of women. In 1833 Oberlin College became the first institution of higher learning to admit female students—some 200 years after the first men's college was established. But Oberlin believed that women should aspire to become wives and mothers, not lawyers and intellectuals. Female students washed men's clothing, cared for their rooms, and served them at meals. Women were also forbidden to speak in public. In the 1840s Lucy Stone, then an Oberlin undergraduate and later one of the nation's most outspoken feminist leaders, refused to write an essay for graduation because it could be read only by a male student (Fletcher, 1943; Flexner, 1972:29–30, 342).

In the twentieth century, sexism in education has been manifested in many ways—in textbooks with negative stereotypes of women, counselors' pressure on female students to prepare for "women's work," and unequal funding for women's and men's recreational programs. But perhaps nowhere has educational discrimination been more evident than in employment of teachers. The positions of university professor and college administrator, which hold relatively high status in the United States, have generally been reserved for men. Yet public school teachers, who have much lower status, are largely female. In 1988 women constituted 85 percent of all grade school teachers, but only 39 percent of college faculty posts were held by women. In addition, women are even more severely underrepresented in the highest levels of the academic world. According to federal data for 1987, only 12 percent of all full professors were female, while American colleges had an average of only 1.1 women in senior administrative positions (Bureau of the Census, 1990a:389; Center for Educational Statistics, 1987:158; Rohter, 1987).

Even when they hold the same degrees as men, women academics often receive lower salaries. According to data compiled by the National Research Council, in 1985 the median full-time salary for men with Ph.D. degrees in the humanities was $36,100, as compared with $30,900 for women with the same qualifications. In the sciences and engineering, the gap between men and women with Ph.D.s was still higher. The median salary for men was $46,100; for women, it was $35,600 (Rohter, 1987).

There has, however, been an increase in the proportion of women continuing their schooling (see Figure 16-3). Whereas in the past women

FIGURE 16-3 Proportion of High School Graduates That Enroll in College, by Gender, 1960–1988

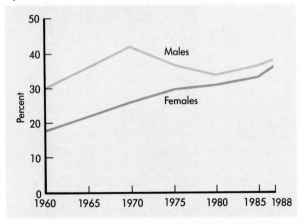

SOURCES: Bureau of the Census, 1987:140, 1990a:151; and authors' estimates.

Enrollment of women in American higher education has continued to grow since 1960. Enrollment of men increased substantially during the war in Vietnam, declined throughout the 1970s, and began to rise again in the 1980s.

were underrepresented in college enrollment, today 54 percent of undergraduate students in the United States are female. Access to graduate education for women has also increased dramatically; for example, the percentage of doctoral degrees awarded to women rose from 14 percent in 1950 to 35 percent in 1987. Professional schools, as well, have become much more open to women. The proportion of women graduates from medical schools has increased from 6 percent in 1960 to 32 percent in 1987. Twenty-four percent of all dental school graduates are now female, compared with less than one percent in 1960. Similarly, 40 percent of all law school graduates are women, compared with less than 3 percent in 1960 (Bureau of the Census, 1990a:153, 161, 163).

Pressure from the feminist movement (see Chapter 11) played a major role in opening the doors of these institutions. In the late 1960s and early 1970s, there was increasing criticism of sex discrimination in higher education. One result was federal action to deal with this problem. In 1972 Congress passed a series of amendments to the Education Act of 1972 which have become collectively known as the *Title IX provisions*. These regulations, which were interpreted through guidelines developed by the Department of Health, Education, and Welfare in 1974 and 1975, were designed to eliminate sexist practices from almost all school systems. As a result of Title IX, schools must make the following changes, where necessary, or risk loss of all federal funding:

1 Schools must end sexist hiring and promotion practices for faculty members (see Box 16-3 on page 500).
2 Schools must eliminate all sex-segregated classes and extracurricular activities. This means an end to all-female home economics and all-male shop classes. (Single-sex gym and hygiene classes are still permitted.)
3 Schools cannot discriminate on the basis of sex in admissions or financial aid. (Single-sex schools and colleges, though, are allowed to continue restricting admission to members of one sex.)
4 Schools cannot inquire if an applicant is married, pregnant, or a parent.
5 Schools must provide more opportunities for women's sports. In many cases, they must spend

(Paula Lerner/Woodfin Camp & Associates)

In recent decades, there has been a dramatic increase in the proportion of medical school graduates who are women.

substantially the same amount on women's athletics as they spend on men's sports. They must also provide comparable coaching, facilities, and housing for male and female athletes. (But they are allowed to spend different amounts for certain types of sports, among them men's football and basketball.)

Title IX is, without question, one of the most controversial steps ever taken by the federal government to promote and ensure equality. Critics believe it goes too far and argue that the federal government should stay out of the educational world. Conflict theorists maintain that such arguments reflect an underlying desire to protect the privileged position of males rather than a genuine concern over federal control. Other critics of Title IX concur with the conflict view but argue that this legislation does not go far enough in equalizing opportunity. Feminists generally hailed the passage of Title IX, although they were somewhat disappointed that sex stereotyping in textbooks and educational curricula was not outlawed and that elementary schools and military academies were exempted (Commission on Civil Rights, 1976:76–82; Schaefer, 1990).

BOX 16-3 • CURRENT RESEARCH

WOMEN, BLACKS, MENTORS, AND HIGHER EDUCATION

Although the number of women serving as faculty members at the nation's most prestigious universities has increased substantially in the last 15 years, the proportion of Black faculty members has remained extremely small or even declined. Many college administrators argue that the primary reason for this disparity is the sizable difference between the numbers of women and Blacks earning Ph.D. degrees. According to data from the National Center for Education Statistics, the proportion of women earning doctorates rose from 23 percent in 1976 to 35 percent in 1987. However, in the same period, there was a slight *decrease* in the proportion of African Americans among those who were enrolled at any level of higher education. With this trend in mind, the Carnegie Corporation's 1990 report on quality education for minorities called for an end to "educational neglect" of such students, pointing out that most minority students remain in schools that are "decidedly unequal" to those attended by Whites (Bureau of the Census, 1990a:152, 161; Quality Education for Minorities Project, 1990).

Sociologist James Blackwell insists that the key problem for Black graduate students is the lack of a "critical mass" of Black faculty members to serve as mentors and role models. In Blackwell's view: "Statistically, the institutions that do the best job of enrolling Blacks in graduate school and producing Black Ph.D.'s are those with the highest number of Black faculty" (Butterfield, 1984:6).

A study of women's difficulties in graduate school by survey researcher Helen Berg and economist Marianne Ferber (1983:629–648) also points to the importance of mentors. Berg and Ferber studied 1816 students admitted to the graduate school of the University of Illinois at Urbana-Champaign between 1968 and 1975, of whom 44 percent were female. They found that men and women fare differently in graduate school; much of the difference can be attributed to female students' relative lack of success in forming close professional relationships with male faculty members.

Why are mentors so important for African American and female graduate students? With the academic world still dominated by White males, critics insist that there is a need for mentors to assist such students in overcoming the "chilly campus climate." Black and female students are often excluded from informal social networks that can influence one's success in graduate school and as a faculty member. Ideally, if there were more Black and female mentors, Black and female graduate students would more easily gain access to such social networks and to the "inside information" they often provide (K. Moore, 1982; Sandler, 1986).

Adult Education

Picture a "college student." Most likely, you will imagine someone under 25 years of age. This reflects the belief that education is something experienced and completed during the first 2 or 3 decades of life and rarely supplemented after that. However, many colleges and universities have witnessed a dramatic increase in the number of older students pursuing 2-year, 4-year, and graduate degrees. These older students are more likely to be female—and are more likely to be Black or Hispanic—than is the typical 19- or 20-year-old college student. Viewed from a conflict perspective, it is not surprising that women and minorities are overrepresented among older students; members of these groups are the most likely to miss out on higher education the first time around (F. Best and Eberhard, 1990).

In 1983, one-third of all students taking credit courses in colleges in the United States were 25 years old or older. However, by the mid-1990s, this figure will rise to 40 percent (see Figure 16-4). Obviously, sociological models of the collegiate subculture will have to be revised significantly in light of such changes. Moreover, as the age of the "typi-

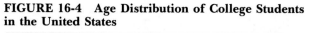

FIGURE 16-4 Age Distribution of College Students in the United States

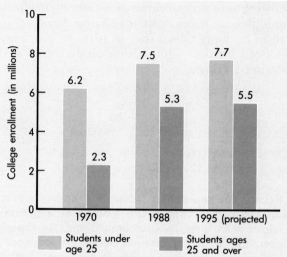

SOURCE: Bureau of the Census, 1990a:151.

By the mid-1990s, older students will account for 40 percent of all students in colleges in the United States.

cal" college student increases, there will be a growing need for on-campus child care (refer back to Chapter 4). This is especially true in community colleges, where the median age of students is already 31.

It should be noted that the nation's colleges *need* older students. Given the expected decrease in population in the age group 18 to 24 years old over the period 1983–1995, institutions of higher learning will have to find new consumers for their services in order to survive financially. This need has led colleges across the United States to develop adult education programs. Currently, about half of all adults take part in some type of adult education.

One aspect of the adult education boom involves the rapidly changing nature of the business world in an age of technological innovation. Business firms have come to accept the view of education as lifelong and may encourage (or require) employees to learn job-related skills. Thus, secretaries are sent to special schools to be trained to use word-processing systems and video display units. Realtors attend classes to learn about alternative forms of financing for home buyers. In

Many colleges and universities in the United States have had a substantial increase in the number of older students pursuing two-year, four-year, and graduate degrees.

occupation after occupation, longtime workers and professionals are going back to school to adapt to the new demands of their jobs.

All the trends discussed in this section will transform the relationship between education and society. For example, the use of minimum-compe-

tency tests ties schooling more closely to society's judgments about which skills must be mastered. Growing reliance on minimum-competency testing is likely to be accompanied by further credentialism in many fields; this, in turn, will increase the need for new adult education programs and retraining efforts.

SOCIAL POLICY AND EDUCATION

INEQUITIES IN SCHOOL FINANCING

- Viewed from a conflict perspective, why is there such concern about inequities in school financing?
- How does the United States compare with other industrialized nations in its per capita spending for education?
- What position has the Supreme Court taken on inequities in school financing?

Russell High School, located in the state of Kentucky, pays its teachers an average of about $27,000 a year; some 70 percent of Russell's graduates go on to college. The school's major equipment need is a trophy case. Just 80 miles away, Kentucky's Prestonsburg High School pays teachers about 21 percent less than Russell does; only half of Prestonsburg's graduates attend college. At Prestonsburg High, equipment needs include textbooks, projectors, and other supplies essential for classroom instruction. What accounts for these substantial differences? In Kentucky, as in many other states, educational quality depends in good part on a community's ability to pump money into its school system. Prestonsburg is in a poorer area than Russell and therefore is able to spend about 13 percent less per pupil (Mayfield, 1989).

In most states, such disparities in school funding have emerged because school financing systems are based largely on local property taxes. Consequently, even if it taxes at a higher rate than a wealthier district does, realistically a poor district cannot raise enough funds through property taxes to spend comparable amounts of money on education. Districts like the region which supports Prestonsburg High School simply do not have sufficiently valuable property to tax (O'Brien, 1990:10).

Boundaries separating richer and poorer school districts typically reflect racial imbalances, especially in states with large metropolitan areas. As experts report, the wealthier districts serve predominantly White school populations, while less affluent districts often serve predominantly Black and Hispanic populations. From a conflict perspective, these disparities in school financing reinforce inequality based on class, race, and ethnicity. Such disparities may diminish the role that education has traditionally played in promoting social mobility in the United States (refer back to Chapter 8) and may therefore contribute to the maintenance of stratification from generation to generation.

Figure 16-5 illustrates the disparities within certain states, as well as between states, in per pupil expenditures. In New York and Texas, wealthier districts outspent poorer ones by almost a nine to one margin during the 1986–1987 school year. Other states, such as Kentucky and Rhode Island, had much smaller disparities, but primarily because even the more affluent districts in these states spent comparatively little on education. Studies conducted since 1987 suggest that the funding inequities between richer and poorer districts have actually widened in recent years. While educational expenses have increased across the nation, less affluent districts have been unable to keep pace (Glaub, 1990).

Some observers view these financing disparities as symptomatic of an even larger problem: the low priority given in the United States to the funding of education. In 1990, the Economic Policy Institute released a study comparing the levels of preschool through secondary school funding in 16 industrialized nations. After adjustments for the size of school populations, the United States was found to rank fourteenth, ahead

FIGURE 16-5 Disparities in per Pupil Expenditures, 1986–1987

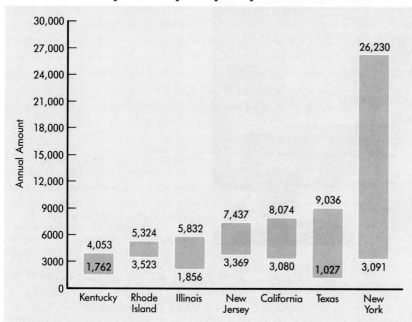

NOTE: The data shown reflect the range in per pupil expenditures for kindergarten through twelfth-grade programs in school districts with enrollments of more than 100 students.
SOURCES: Bureau of the Census data, presented to the House Education and Labor Committee and reported in O'Brien, 1990:10–13.

There are wide disparities across the United States in the level of funds that school districts spend per pupil.

of only Ireland and Australia. If spending for colleges and other postsecondary institutions is included, the United States rises into a three-way tie for second place among these nations. Still, critics of this country's priorities are distressed by the apparent lack of commitment to pre-collegiate education. Referring to the many difficulties of schools in the United States, educational analyst M. Edith Mishel notes: "We don't say money will solve the problem. But we don't think you can solve it without money" (D. Kelly, 1990a:D1; Rasell and Mishel, 1990).

In recent years, there have been an increasing number of legal challenges to the district-by-district school financing inequities within various states. In 10 states, including Kentucky in 1989, state courts have ruled that the funding of school systems violates state constitutions by discriminating against students in poor areas. The latest of these rulings took place in New Jersey, where affluent Princeton's schools have one computer for each eight children while poorer Camden's schools have only one computer for each 58 children (Mayfield, 1989; Hanley, 1990).

In 1990, the New Jersey Supreme Court ruled that the state government must ensure that poorer cities spend as much on education as wealthy suburbs. In a unanimous decision, the court ordered the state legislature to increase funding for less affluent districts so that they could offer all students a "thorough and efficient" education. In the words of Chief Justice Robert Wilentz, students in poorer districts "have already waited too long for a remedy, one that will give them the same level of opportunity, the same chance, as their colleagues who are lucky enough to be born in a richer suburban district." Unlike the rulings in Kentucky and other states, which have established minimum spending levels for all districts while permitting wealthy districts to exceed these levels, the New Jersey decision ordered the state to provide sufficient aid so that poorer districts could keep up with the wealthier ones (Sullivan, 1990:Al, B4).

The resistance to such rulings in New Jersey and other states reflects the tradition of home rule, under which local communities control their own schools. Many towns in the United States, especially wealthy

Because of overcrowding in local schools in Brooklyn, a borough of New York City, a classroom has been set up in a school gymnasium. Across the United States, poor school districts lack the financing available in more affluent areas.

towns, are proud and protective of their schools. Parents and taxpayers in these districts worry that states may equalize school funding by holding all districts to low levels of expenditure. "Why should our kids be held back?" ask citizens in affluent areas. In response, proponents of equalization measures concede that disparities are inevitable, since the cost of living varies widely even within a state and since about 80 percent of a school's budget is spent on personnel. Nevertheless, these advocates argue, while some variation between districts can be expected, the extreme inequities in spending shown in Figure 16-5 are unjust and unacceptable (Hanley, 1990; Suro, 1990a; see also Jansen, 1991).

While challenges to disparities in school funding have multiplied on the local level, there has been much less action within the federal government, owing to reluctance to become involved in a "local matter." One case, however, reached the U.S. Supreme Court in 1973. In a Texas lawsuit, *San Antonio v. Rodriguez*, attorneys for the plaintiffs argued that financing inequities violate students' constitutionally protected right to a high-quality education. Attorneys for the state countered that Texas did indeed provide an adequate minimum education and that any differences in spending between school districts were an unfortunate consequence of the need to preserve local control of schools.

In a 5-4 decision, the Supreme Court rejected the plaintiffs' contention that equal access to education is guaranteed under the Fourteenth Amendment to the Constitution. Moreover, the Court ruled that it is the states' responsibility to address any inequities in school financing. While the *Rodriguez* litigation was unsuccessful, it did prompt the Texas state legislature to reform the way schools are financed. However, state judges ruled that the legislature had not gone far enough in closing the gap between richer and poorer school districts; as a result, Texas officials have been ordered to adopt a wealth-neutral school financing system by 1995 (Natale, 1990; B. Walker, 1990).

In early 1990, concerned by states' failure to correct funding disparities, Representative Augustus Hawkins of California introduced the Fair Chance Act in Congress. This bill would require the secretary of education to annually review each state's funding to see if disparities exist and then compel states to correct any such disparities if they wish to continue receiving federal education funds. While there is a good chance of winning support for an annual review of financing inequities, it will not be easy to persuade legislators and the president to endorse the cutoffs in funding that could result under the Fair Chance Act (O'Brien, 1990).

It will take years to assess the impact of recent court rulings in Kentucky, New Jersey, and other states concerning equalization of school financing. But some educators remain hopeful that their districts will benefit from such rulings. The principal of Kentucky's Prestonsburg High School says that if "[I'm] funded as well as . . . the more affluent high schools, then I know I can compete with them" (Mayfield, 1989:8A).

SUMMARY

Education is a process of learning in which some people consciously and formally teach while others adopt the social role of learner. This chapter examines the functionalist, conflict, and interactionist views of education; assesses schools as an example of formal organizations; and discusses current trends in American education.

1 Transmission of knowledge and bestowal of status are manifest functions of education.

2 As a social institution, education has as its primary purpose a rather conservative function—transmitting the existing culture.

3 Schools perform a latent function as agents of social control by attempting to regulate the behavior of students.

4 Education can be a major force for bringing about or stimulating social change.

5 In the view of conflict theorists, schools "track" pupils according to their social class backgrounds, thus preserving class-related inequalities.

6 Teacher expectations about a student's performance can sometimes have an impact on the student's actual achievements.

7 Today, most schools in the United States are organized in a bureaucratic fashion. Weber's five basic characteristics of bureaucracy are all evident in schools.

8 Many teachers are leaving the educational world and moving into other occupations, owing in part to such factors as inadequate salaries and violence in the schools.

9 A nationwide movement has emerged in support of *minimum-competency tests* of basic skills as a means of assessing students' educational progress.

10 School choice programs often attempt to stimulate better performance from local schools by mandating that some type of financial reward will follow students as they move to new schools.

11 Public policy toward students with disabilities was dramatically reshaped by Public Law 94–142, which calls for local school districts to place these children in the "least restrictive environment."

12 The positions of university professor and college administrator, which hold relatively high status in the United States, have generally been reserved for men.

13 An important trend in contemporary education in the United States involves the development of adult education programs.

14 In most states, disparities in school funding have emerged because school financing systems are based largely on local property taxes.

KEY TERMS

Correspondence principle A term used by Bowles and Gintis to refer to the tendency of schools to promote the values expected of individuals in each social class and to prepare students for the types of jobs typically held by members of their class. (page 486)

Credentialism An increase in the lowest level of education required to enter a field. (484)

Education A formal process of learning in which some people consciously teach while others adopt the social role of learner. (478)

Mainstreaming The practice, mandated by Public Law 94–142, of integrating handicapped children into "regular" classrooms whenever possible by placing each child in the "least restrictive environment." (496)

Minimum-competency tests (MCTs) Tests which measure a child's knowledge of basic skills, such as reading, writing, and mathematics. (494)

Social promotion The practice of passing children from one grade to the next on the basis of age rather than actual educational achievement. (494)

Teacher-expectancy effect The impact that a teacher's expectations about a student's performance may have on the student's actual achievements. (489)

Tracking The practice of placing students in specific curriculum groups on the basis of test scores and other criteria. (485)

ADDITIONAL READINGS

Bowles, Samuel, and Herbert Gintis. *Schooling in Capitalist America: Educational Reforms and the Contradictions of Economic Life* New York: Basic Books, 1976. An insightful critical examination of educational reform from a conflict perspective. See also a collection of reviews of this book in M. Cole, 1988.

Boyer, Ernest L. *High School: A Report on Secondary Education in America.* New York: Harper and Row, 1983. This book results from a Carnegie Foundation effort involving a team of 25 educators studying secondary education.

Crouse, James, and Dale Trusheim. *The Case against the S.A.T.* Chicago: University of Chicago Press, 1988. A critique of the well-known standardized test which outlines the adverse impact it has on poor and minority students and questions whether the S.A.T. genuinely is useful in the college admissions process.

Cusick, Philip A. *Inside High School: The Student's World.* New York: Holt, 1973. What is everyday life like in schools in the United States? Using techniques of participant observation in the tradition of William F. Whyte's *Street Corner Society,* Cusick immersed himself in the daily routine of an urban high school.

Horowitz, Helen Lefkowitz. *Campus Life.* Chicago: University of Chicago Press, 1987. A comprehensive look at undergraduate cultures from the end of the eighteenth century to the present.

Hurn, Christoper J. *The Limits and Possibilities of Schooling* (2d ed.). Boston: Allyn and Bacon, 1985. Hurn provides a useful analysis of controversial methodological issues in education, such as IQ testing, teacher-expectancy effect, and equality of opportunity.

Oakes, Jeannie. *Keeping Track: How High Schools Structure Inequality.* New Haven, Conn.: Yale University Press, 1985. An explanation of how tracking promotes social inequality.

Powell, Arthur G., Eleanor Farrar, and David K. Cohen. *The Shopping Mall High School: Winners and Losers in the Educational Marketplace.* Boston: Houghton Mifflin, 1985. On the basis of their study of 15 secondary schools, the authors argue that the "losers" in the high school marketplace are the majority of students not served by special programs.

Scimecca, Joseph A. *Education and Society.* New York: Holt, 1980. This textbook on the sociology of education emphasizes the conflict perspective.

White, Merry. *The Japanese Educational Challenge: A Commitment to Children.* New York: Free Press, 1987. A look at the strengths and weaknesses of the Japanese educational system, with an emphasis on the early years.

Journals

The sociology of education is reflected in *Educational Record* (founded in 1920), *Education and Urban Society* (1968), the *Harvard Educational Review* (1974), *Journal of Educational Finance* (1975), *Phi Delta Kappan* (1915), and *Sociology of Education* (1927).

17

HEALTH AND MEDICINE

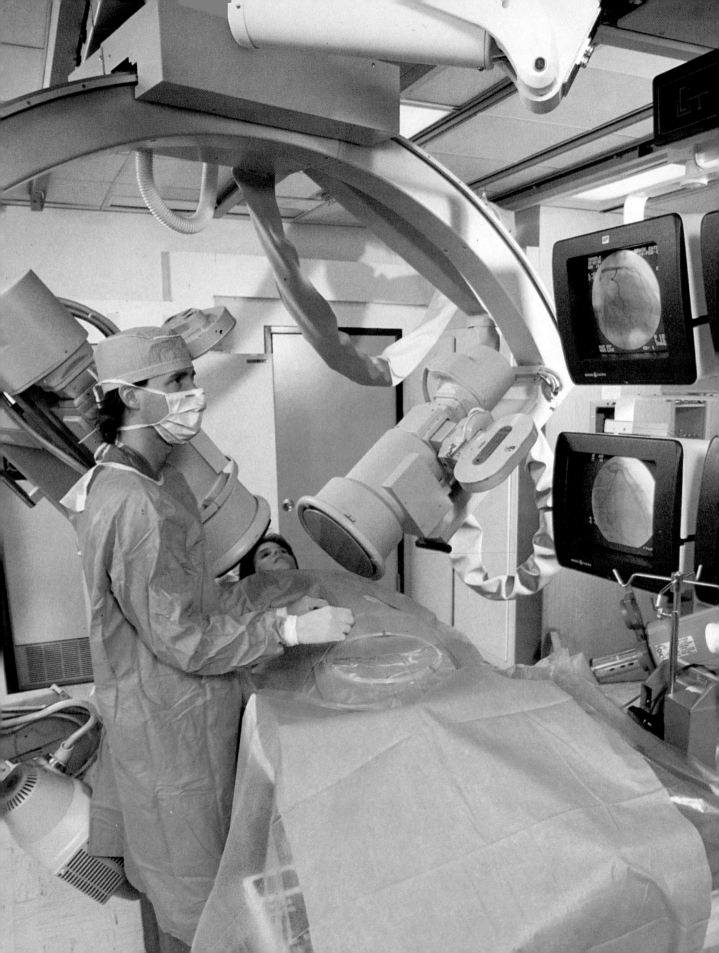

HEALTH AND MEDICINE

LOOKING AHEAD

- In what ways are health and illness socially defined?
- What behavior does American society require of people considered to be "sick"?
- How does medicine function as a mechanism of social control?
- Does gender, race, ethnicity, or social class influence a person's likelihood of experiencing illness, disease, and disability?
- What role has the federal government played in providing and financing health care for United States citizens?
- How do sociologists apply labeling theory to the study of mental illness?
- Why has the regulation of smoking become a concern not only of health care experts but also of policymakers?

There is agreement that the general health of individuals should be viewed as an important factor in assessing a society's quality of life. Yet *health*—like such related terms as *wellness, sickness,* and *disease*—is actually an elusive concept. Although these terms may initially appear to belong in the realm of the physical sciences, their meanings are clearly shaped by social definitions of behavior.

Throughout this book, we have repeatedly seen that the same actions can be defined differently depending on the social actors and the larger social context. For example, dyschromic spirochetosis—a disease characterized by spots of various colors on the skin—is so common in a particular South American Indian tribe that people who do not have it are regarded as abnormal. Indeed, the few single men who do not suffer from this disease are excluded from many of the tribe's social activities because they are viewed as "strange" (Zola, 1983:39).

As a further reflection on the relativistic nature of health, certain ailments are found only in one or a few societies. The term *culture-bound syndrome* refers to a disease or illness that cannot be understood apart from its specific societal context (Cassidy, 1982:326). For example, a hysterical reaction called *pibkoktog* occurs among Eskimo peoples; it is followed by convulsions and ultimately by a form of amnesia (the person cannot recall any of the experience). In a 1982 study conducted in Nigeria, at least half of all students questioned reported suffering from "brain fog," with symptoms including burning or crawling sensations (Landy, 1985; Prince, 1985).

Most research on culture-bound syndromes has traditionally occurred in nonwestern societies. However, in the last 15 years, a culture-bound syndrome quite evident in the United States, anorexia nervosa, has received increasing attention. First described in England in the 1860s, this condition is characterized by an intense fear of becoming obese and a distorted image of one's body. Those suffering from anorexia nervosa (primarily young women in their teenage years or

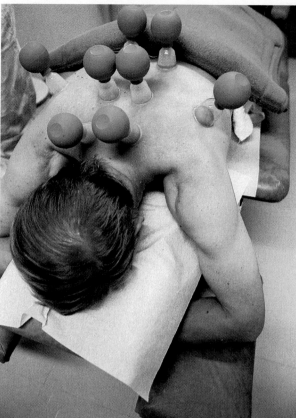

Health care takes many forms around the world. Cupping—a traditional practice used in ancient China, India, Egypt, Greece, and Rome—survives in modern Finland. Physiotherapists use suction cups to draw out blood in order to lower blood pressure, improve circulation, and relieve muscular pain. Acupuncture, which originated in ancient China, has become increasingly popular in the United States. Patients are treated through insertion of needles at various points on the body. Still another form of treatment is mud therapy, which is shown being applied to a man in Heilongjiang Province in China.

twenties) drastically reduce their body weight through self-induced semistarvation and self-induced vomiting. Anorexia nervosa is best understood in the context of western culture, which typically portrays the slim, youthful body as healthy and beautiful, whereas the fat person is viewed as ugly and lacking in self-discipline (Chernin, 1981; R. Hahn, 1985; Prince, 1985; Swartz, 1985).

The existence of culture-bound syndromes such as brain fog and anorexia nervosa underscores the impact of culture on definitions and perceptions of health and illness. Moreover, there are striking cultural differences in the application of health care measures. For example, the rate of surgical removal of the gall bladder is five times higher in Canada than in England or Wales. Even within the United States, there are significant differences, by locality, in physicians' tendency to prescribe medication, to hospitalize patients, and to perform surgery (Mumford, 1983:13). In many instances, social factors contribute to the evaluation of a person as "healthy" or "sick."

How, then, can we define health? We can imagine a continuum with health on one end and death on the other. In the preamble to its 1946 constitution, the World Health Organization defined **health** as a "state of complete physical, mental, and social well-being, and not merely the absence of disease and infirmity" (Leavell and Clark, 1965:14). With this definition in mind, the "healthy" end of our continuum represents an ideal toward which we are oriented rather than a precise condition that we expect to attain. Along the continuum, people define themselves as "healthy" or "sick" on the basis of criteria established by each individual, relatives, friends, coworkers, and medical practitioners. This relativistic approach to health allows us to view it in a social context and to consider how it varies in different situations or cultures (Twaddle, 1974; Wolinsky, 1980:64–98).

In this chapter, we will consider a sociological overview of health, illness, health care, and medicine as a social institution. We will begin by examining how functionalists, conflict theorists, interactionists, and labeling theorists look at health-related issues. Then we will study the distribution of diseases in a society by gender, social class, and race and ethnicity. Particular attention will be given to the evolution of the health care system. Sociologists are interested in the roles that people play within the health care system and the organizations that deal with issues of health and sickness. Therefore, we will analyze the interactions among doctors, nurses, and patients; the role of government in providing health services to the needy; the rise of hospital chains; and alternatives to traditional health care. The chapter continues with an examination of mental illness in which we contrast the medical and labeling approaches to mental disorders. In the social policy section, we will focus on growing restrictions on smoking both by government and in the workplace.

SOCIOLOGICAL PERSPECTIVES ON HEALTH AND ILLNESS

Why is it that we may consider ourselves sick or well when others do not agree? Who controls definitions of health and illness in our society, and for what ends? What are the consequences of viewing oneself (or being viewed) as ill or disabled? Drawing on four sociological perspectives—functionalism, conflict theory, interactionism, and labeling theory—we can gain greater insight into the social context shaping definitions of health and treatment of illness.

Functionalist Approach

Although illness is a phenomenon evident in all societies, functionalists contend that an overly broad definition of illness would impose serious difficulties on the workings of a society. Illness entails at least a temporary disruption in a person's social interactions both at work and at home. Consequently, from a functionalist perspective, "being sick" must be controlled so as to ensure that not too many people are released from their societal responsibilities at any one time.

"Sickness" requires that one take on a social role, even if temporarily. The *sick role* refers to societal expectations about the attitudes and behavior of a person viewed as being ill (S. H. King, 1972). Sociologist Talcott Parsons (1951:428–

479,1972,1975), well known for his contributions to functionalist theory (see Chapter 1), has outlined the behavior required of people considered "sick." They are exempted from their normal, day-to-day responsibilities and generally are not blamed for their condition. Yet they are obligated to try to get well, and this may include seeking competent professional care. Attempting to get well is particularly important in the world's developing countries. In modern automated industrial societies, we can absorb a greater degree of illness or disability, but in horticultural or agrarian societies the issue of workers' availability is a much more critical concern (Mechanic, 1978:84–85; Schwartz, 1987: 23–24).

According to Parsons's theory, physicians function as "gatekeepers" for the sick role, either verifying a patient's condition as "illness" or designating the patient as "recovered." The ill person becomes dependent on the doctor, because the latter can control valued rewards (not only treatment of illness, but also excused absences from work and school). Parsons suggests that the doctor-patient relationship is somewhat like that between parent and child. Like a parent, the physician grants the patient the privilege of returning to society as a full and functioning adult (S. Bloom and Wilson, 1979; Freidson, 1970:206; Parsons and Fox, 1952).

There have been a number of criticisms of the concept of the sick role. In the view of some observers, patients' judgments regarding their own state of health may be related to their gender, age, social class, and ethnic group. The sick role may be more applicable to people experiencing sudden, short-term illnesses than to those with recurring, long-term illnesses. Even simple factors such as whether a person is employed or not seem to affect willingness to assume the sick role.

Sociologist David Mechanic (1962, 1978) finds it more useful to think of a "tendency to adopt the sick role." A person's level of stress may cause him or her to adopt this role, whereas others with the same clinical conditions will not accept it. Mechanic emphasizes that each patient is unique, a fact that Parsons's formulation seems to obscure. Nonetheless, Parsons's model continues to be relied upon for functionalist analysis of the relationship between illness and societal expectations for the sick (Freidson, 1970; Kassebaum and Baumann, 1965).

Conflict Approach

Whereas functionalists seek to explain how health care systems meet the needs of society as well as those of individual patients and medical practitioners, conflict theorists take issue with this view. They express concern that the profession of medicine has assumed a preeminence that extends well beyond whether to excuse a student from school or an employee from work. Sociologist Eliot Freidson (1970:5) has likened the position of medicine today "to that of state religions yesterday—it has an officially approved monopoly of the right to define health and illness and to treat illness." Conflict theorists use the term "medicalization of society" to refer to the growing role of medicine as a major institution of social control (Conrad and Schneider, 1980; McKinlay and McKinlay, 1977; Zola, 1972, 1983).

What is the significance of medicine as a mechanism of social control? In Chapter 7, we learned that social control involves techniques and strategies for regulating behavior in order to enforce the distinctive norms and values of a culture. Typically, we think of informal social control as occurring within families and peer groups, whereas formal social control is carried out by authorized agents such as police officers, judges, school administrators, and employers. However, viewed from a conflict perspective, medicine is not simply a "healing profession"; it is a regulating mechanism as well.

How is such social control manifested? First, medicine has greatly expanded its domain of expertise in recent decades. Society tolerates such expansion of the boundaries of medicine because we hope that these experts can bring new "miracle cures" to complex human problems as they have to the control of certain infectious diseases. Consequently, as the medicalization of society has proceeded in the twentieth century, physicians have become much more involved in examining a wide range of issues, among them sexuality (including homosexuality), old age, anxiety, obesity, child development, alcoholism, and drug addiction. The social significance of medicalization is

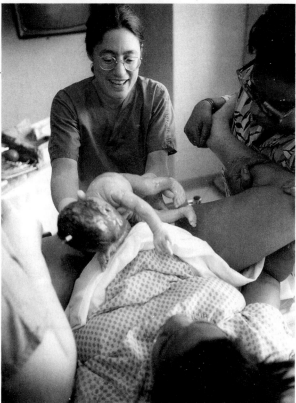
(Stephen Shames/Visions)

Nurse-midwives have sought licensing to achieve professional respectability, but physicians continue to exert power to ensure that midwifery remains a subordinate occupation.

nurse-midwives outside the realm of acceptable medicine. For example, in 1990 a federal appeals court upheld a lower court ruling that the American Medical Association had led a conspiracy to destroy the chiropractic profession by labeling all chiropractors as "unscientific cultists" and depriving them of association with medical doctors and hospitals (*New York Times*, 1990a; Zola, 1972).

Similarly, the medical profession has long opposed midwifery, even when it involves trained nurse-midwives. Despite the fact that midwives first brought professionalism to child delivery, they have been portrayed as having invaded the "legitimate" field of obstetrics. Nurse-midwives have sought licensing as a means of achieving professional respectability, but physicians continue to exert power to ensure that midwifery remains a subordinate occupation. Although there has been a resurgence of interest in midwifery and in the delivery of babies at home (rather than in hospitals), midwives face serious institutional barriers to achieving full professional status within the health care system of the United States (M. Radosh, 1984; P. Radosh, 1986; Zia, 1990).

By working to keep such people from receiving reimbursement as deliverers of health care, medicine creates an artificial scarcity of physicians' skills. Moreover, according to conflict theorists, the professional aura of doctors allows some to assert power and knowledge in ways which may be medically dangerous. Sociologist Marcia Millman (1977) argues, for example, that coronary bypass surgery, a serious and expensive procedure, has proliferated to the point where its benefits are being overstated to some patients.

The medicalization of society is but one concern of conflict theorists as they assess the workings of health care institutions. As we have seen throughout this textbook, when analyzing any issue, conflict theorists wish to know who benefits, who suffers, and who dominates at the expense of others. Viewed from a conflict perspective, there are certainly glaring inequalities in health care delivery. For example, there are 549 people per physician in the United States, while African nations have 20,000 to 70,000 people per physician. Within the United States, as well, there is an unequal distribution of medical services on the basis

that once a problem is viewed using a *medical model*—once medical experts become influential in proposing and assessing relevant public policies—it becomes more difficult for "common people" to join the discussion and to exert influence on decision making. It also becomes more difficult to view these issues as being shaped by social, cultural, or psychological factors, rather than by physical or medical factors (Caplan, 1989; Conrad and Kern, 1986:378; Conrad and Schneider, 1980; Starr, 1982).

Second, medicine serves as an agent of social control by retaining absolute jurisdiction over many health care procedures. It has even attempted to guard its jurisdiction by placing health care professionals such as chiropractors and of both income and geographical location of facilities and personnel (Bureau of the Census, 1986a:822; Navarro, 1976; Waitzkin, 1986, 1989; Waitzkin and Waterman, 1974:15).

Conflict theorists emphasize that such inequities in health care resources have clear life-and-death consequences. For example, in 1990 the *infant mortality rate* (the number of deaths of infants under 1 year of age per 1000 live births in a given year) ranged as high as 154 per 1000 live births in Ethiopia and 122 in Haiti. By contrast, Sweden's infant mortality rate was only 5.8 infant deaths per 1000 live births and Japan's was only 4.8. From a conflict perspective, the dramatic differences in infant mortality rates around the world (see Figure 17-1) reflect, at least in part, unequal distribution of health care resources based on the wealth or poverty of various communities and nations.

In 1990, the United States had a rate of 9.7 infant deaths per 1000 live births (although it is estimated that the rate in some poor, inner-city neighborhoods in this country exceeds 30 deaths per 1000 live births). Yet, despite the wealth of the United States, as least 21 nations have lower infant mortality rates, among them the United Kingdom, Canada, Iceland, and Japan. Conflict theorists point out that, unlike the United States, many of these 21 countries offer some form of government-supported health care for all citizens, which typically leads to greater availability and use of prenatal care than in this country (Haub et al., 1990).

Interactionist Approach

In examining health, illness, and medicine as a social institution, interactionists generally focus on micro-level study of the roles played by health care professionals and patients. They emphasize that the patient should not always be viewed as passive, but instead as an actor who often shows a powerful intent to see the physician (Alonzo, 1989; Zola, 1983:59).

One way in which patients play an active role in health care is by failing to follow a physicians' advice. For example, despite physicians' instructions, nearly half of all patients stop taking medications long before they should. Some take an incorrect dosage on purpose, and others never even fill their prescriptions. Such noncompliance results in part from the prevalence of self-medication: in our society, many people are accustomed to self-diagnosis and self-treatment. Sociologist Irving Kenneth Zola (1983:191–192, 238) found that at least 70 percent of the college students he surveyed had medicated themselves within the preceding 36 hours. Although many of the medicines used were of little consequence, this high rate of self-medication nevertheless demonstrates that many Americans are far from being fully dependent on physicians.

FIGURE 17-1   Infant Mortality Rates, 1988–1989

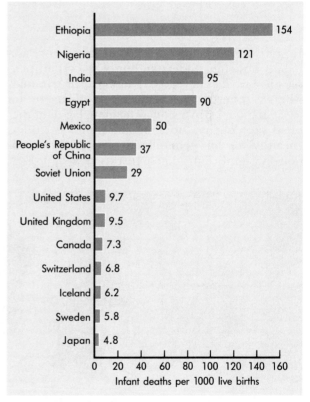

SOURCE: Haub et al., 1990.

Infant mortality rates vary dramatically from nation to nation. The United States has a comparatively low rate, but several other nations have even lower rates.

In their studies of the roles played by physicians and patients, interactionists point out that the same symptoms may be presented differently by different groups of people. In one study, patients were interviewed while waiting to see physicians; the symptoms presented were compared with the eventual diagnosis and an evaluation of the condition's urgency. Researchers found that first-generation Irish American patients had a tendency to understate their symptoms, whereas first-generation Italian American patients were more likely to generalize and overstate their symptoms. Such results remind us that health care interactions occur within a larger social context and are influenced by the norms and values of distinctive subcultures (Zola, 1966; see also Wolinsky, 1980:67–68).

Labeling Approach

In studying deviance, we used labeling theory as a means of better understanding why certain people are *viewed* as deviants, "bad kids," or criminals whereas others whose behavior is similar are not (see Chapter 7). In a similar fashion, labeling theorists suggest that the designation of a person as "healthy" or "ill" generally involves social definition by significant others. Just as police, judges, and other regulators of social control have the power to define certain people as criminals, health care professionals (especially physicians) have the power to define certain people as "sick." Moreover, like labels that suggest nonconformity or criminality, labels associated with illness commonly reshape not only how we are treated by others but also how we see ourselves. In our society, then, there are serious consequences attached to any labels which suggest less than perfect physical or mental health (Becker, 1963; C. Clark, 1983; Schwartz, 1987:82–84).

The power of such a label was poignantly revealed by British sociologist Ann Holohan in describing a vivid personal experience. Holohan visited a physician for treatment of what she believed to be a routine breast infection arising from an earlier injury. However, the physician found a lump, told her that she might have cancer, and recommended that she enter the hospital for a biopsy. Holohan (1977:88) relates the shock she felt as she left the clinic and returned to the "outside world":

It seemed incredible that nothing had changed—the sun was still shining, the road sweeper gathering the leaves. I sat in my car and immense waves of panic engulfed me. I drove blindly home and recall very

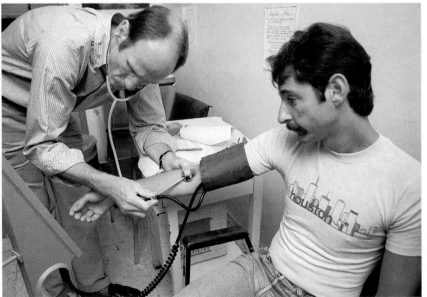

(J. Ross Baughman/Visions)

A physician is shown examining a patient with AIDS. A person who has AIDS must deal not only with the devastating medical consequences of the disease itself but also with the distressing social consequences of a feared label.

little of the actual journey . . . . Yet I was no "sicker" than before my consultation. All that had changed was the possibility of a medical label for my symptom.

Upon returning home, Holohan attempted to deny the seriousness of her illness. She rationalized that since she could still perform household chores, she could not possibly have cancer. Eventually, Holohan did enter the hospital and undergo a biopsy; the results showed that she did not have a malignant tumor.

By the late 1980s, the power of another label—"person with AIDS"—had become quite evident. Once someone is told by a physician that he or she has tested positive for HIV, the virus associated with AIDS, the patient must deal with the possibility that death may not be far away. Immediate and difficult questions must then be faced: should one tell one's family members, one's spouse or lover, one's friends, one's coworkers, one's employer? How will each of them respond? As discussed in the social policy section of Chapter 5, people's intense fear of this deadly disease has led to prejudice and discrimination—even social ostracism—against those who have (or are suspected of having) AIDS. Consequently, a person who has AIDS must deal not only with the devastating medical consequences of the disease, but also with the distressing social consequences associated with this feared label.

Labeling theorists argue that even physical traits can, in a sense, be socially "created" through labels. Typically, blindness is viewed as a clear-cut physical condition. However, on the basis of first-hand observation of programs and organizations in the United States, sociologist Robert Scott (1969) contends that social service agencies actually encourage blind people to become helpless and dependent. Many impaired clients, though "legally blind," are able to read with special lenses. Yet, when they inquire about temporary financial assistance, they are enrolled in long-term training programs. The agencies also encourage blind clients to segregate themselves and to scale down their vocational and social expectations. If clients resist agency typecasting as "blind," they are written off as hopeless and uncooperative. Scott notes that not all agencies encourage dependency

among those with impaired vision, but adds that our society tacitly endorses treatment of such people as helpless. In the social policy section of Chapter 20 (see page 624), we will examine prejudice and discrimination against people with disabilities.

In another application of labeling theory to treatment of the blind, health statistician Marc Berk (1985) examined rates of reported blindness throughout New York State—where all physicians and optometrists are required by law to report the names of blind patients to the state government. Berk found that in counties with a higher proportion of physicians and optometrists, a higher proportion of residents are classified as blind. He found no similar pattern involving the distribution of health care professionals and reported rates of infectious diseases. Berk's research suggests that deviance is indeed in the "eye of the beholder" (or, more accurately, in the "perceptions of the beholder," whether the beholder is sighted or not). The prevalence of a condition such as blindness apparently depends in part on the number of official beholders available to apply this label.

An Overview

As has been noted throughout this book, the four sociological approaches described above should not be regarded as mutually exclusive. In the study of health-related issues, they share certain common themes. First, any person's health or illness is more than an organic condition, since it is subject to the interpretation of others. Owing to the impact of culture, family and friends, and the medical profession, health and illness are no longer purely biological occurrences but are sociological occurrences as well. Second, since members of a society (especially industrial societies) share the same health delivery system, health is a group and societal concern. Although health may be defined as the complete well-being of an individual, it is also the result of his or her social environment. As we will see in the next section, even such factors as a person's gender, social class, race, and ethnicity can influence the likelihood of contracting a particular disease (Cockerham, 1989:171).

SOCIAL EPIDEMIOLOGY AND HEALTH

Social epidemiology is the study of the distribution of disease, impairment, and general health status across a population. In its earliest period, epidemiology concentrated on the scientific study of epidemics, focusing on how they started and spread. Contemporary social epidemiology is much broader in scope and is concerned not only with epidemics but also with nonepidemic diseases, injuries, drug addiction and alcoholism, suicide, and mental illness. Epidemiology draws on the work of a wide variety of scientists and researchers, among them physicians, sociologists, public health officials, biologists, veterinarians, demographers (see Chapter 19), anthropologists, psychologists, and (in studies of air pollution) meteorologists.

In social epidemiology, as well as in studies of population and crime victimization, two concepts are commonly employed: incidence and prevalence. *Incidence* refers to the number of new cases of a specific disorder occurring within a given population during a stated period of time, usually a year. For example, the incidence of AIDS in the United States in 1988 was 30,897 cases. By contrast, *prevalence* refers to the total number of cases of a specific disorder that exist at a given time. The prevalence of AIDS in 1988 was 47,022 cases and had nearly doubled by 1989 (Bureau of the Census, 1990a:117).

When incidence figures are presented as rates, or as the number of reports per 100,000 persons, they are called *morbidity rates*. Sociologists find it useful to consider morbidity rates because they reveal that a specific disease occurs more frequently among one segment of a population compared with another. The term *mortality rate* refers to the incidence of death in a given population. We will examine mortality rates in greater detail when we consider population issues in Chapter 19.

Gender

A large body of research indicates that, in comparison with men, women experience a higher prevalence of many illnesses. There are varia-tions—for example, men are more likely to have parasitic diseases whereas women are more likely to become diabetic—but, as a group, women appear to be in poorer health than men. This seems noteworthy and surprising, especially in view of women's greater longevity rates and lower mortality rates at all ages. Sociologist Lois Verbrugge (1985:162–163) observes:

> In sum, women have more frequent illness and disability, but the problems are typically not serious (life threatening) ones. In contrast, men suffer more from life threatening diseases, and these cause more permanent disability and earlier death for them. One sex is "sicker" in the short run, and the other in the long run.

The apparent inconsistency between the "short-run" ill health of women and their greater longevity deserves an explanation, and researchers have advanced a theory. Women's lower rate of cigarette smoking (which reduces their risk of heart disease, lung cancer, and emphysema), lower consumption of alcohol (which reduces the risk of auto accidents and cirrhosis of the liver), and lower rates of employment in dangerous occupations explain about one-third of their greater longevity than men—despite women's otherwise poorer health record. Moreover, some clinical studies suggest that the genuine differences in morbidity between women and men may be less pronounced than is evident in the data on morbidity. Researchers argue that women are much more likely than men to seek treatment, to be diagnosed as having diseases, and therefore to have their illnesses reflected in data examined by epidemiologists.

From a conflict perspective, women have been particularly vulnerable to the medicalization of society, with everything from birth to beauty treated in an increasingly medical context. Such medicalization may contribute to women's higher morbidity rates as compared with those of men (Conrad and Kern, 1986:25–26; Riessman, 1983; for a different view, see Gove and Hughes, 1979). Ironically, while women have been especially affected by medicalization, medical researchers have often excluded women from clinical studies. The controversy over this issue is discussed in Box 17-1.

BOX 17-1 • CURRENT RESEARCH

SEXISM IN MEDICAL RESEARCH

One study, using 22,071 volunteer subjects, found that taking small doses of aspirin can reduce the risk of a heart attack. These results, reported in 1988, gave physicians in the United States a valuable piece of information. But there was a major problem: not one of the 22,071 subjects was a woman. Consequently, older women—the women most likely to experience heart problems—had no way of knowing if the results of the study would be applicable to them.

This male-only study is not unprecedented. A study designed to learn whether smoking increases the risk of getting cataracts involved 838 male subjects and no women. A research project exploring the links between heart disease and high cholesterol, lack of exercise, and smoking used 12,866 male subjects and, again, no women. Representative Patricia Schroeder, noting the absence of women in many medical studies, concludes: "At this point, doctors just aren't getting the kind of guidance they need when they try to prescribe to women" (Purvis, 1990:59–60).

As of 1987, research on women's health issues funded by the National Institutes of Health (NIH) constituted only 13.5 percent of the NIH budget. With such data in mind, Representative Schroeder and Representative Olympia Snowe, cochairs of the Congressional Caucus on Women's Issues, charge that women's health has been jeopardized by researchers' failure to include women as subjects in studies (Berney, 1990:24).

Female physicians and researchers charge that sexism is at the heart of such research practices. "White men control these things," insists Dr. Kathy Anastos, a New York City internist. "When, for scientific reasons, they have to limit diversity, they choose to study themselves. Then when they get the results, they apply them to everyone. It's very unscientific" (Berney, 1990:27).

Even when women *are* the subjects of medical research, conclusions may be drawn and widely popularized despite fragmentary data. In 1990, the prestigious *New England Journal of Medicine* ran an editorial focusing on the relative inability of the female digestive system to metabolize alcohol as effectively as that of the male. This conclusion was based on a study of only 20 men and 23 women; moreover, 12 of the women were alcoholics, and all 23 had been hospitalized for surgery for gastric dysfunction. In criticizing this editorial, Jeanne Mager Stellman (1990:A23), a professor of clinical public health, and Joan E. Bertin, an executive of the Women's Rights Project of the American Civil Liberties Union, ask: "Where was the usual caution and prudence of the New England Journal in the overextrapolation of data from hospitalized patients to the healthy population, and why was this story front-page news?"

Critics of current medical research practices insist that there is a desperate need for studies with women subjects. Estelle Ramey, a recently retired physiology researcher, points out that researchers have far too little information on the impact of cholesterol and diet on women's health. Ramey adds that the lack of research on women and heart disease is especially shocking, since heart disease is the number one killer of women. There is also a shortage of data on women with AIDS—even though the proportion of AIDS patients who are female has increased. With such issues in mind, the NIH Task Force on Women's Issues submitted a 1990 report recommending expansion of research on women, especially low-income women and women of color (Berney, 1990:26–27; Cotton, 1990a:1050).

Social Class

Social class is clearly associated with differences in morbidity and mortality rates. Although Americans from higher social classes have greater life expectancy than the less affluent, they are more likely to experience peptic ulcers. The lower classes, by contrast, are more likely to suffer from certain forms of cancer, as well as from problems

**FIGURE 17-2   Days of Disability
by Family Income, 1987**

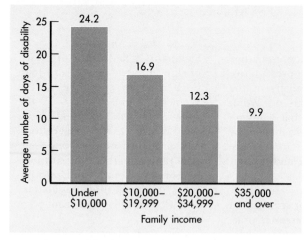

SOURCE: Bureau of the Census, 1990a:115.

*The lower a family's income, the
higher its incidence of disabling
illness, as measured by days of
disability per person.*

related to alcoholism and drug abuse. Studies in the United States and in other countries have consistently shown that people in the lower classes have higher rates of mortality and disability. In general, there appears to be two to three times as much serious illness among low-income Americans as among the nation's population as a whole (Graham and Reeder, 1979:76; see also Lemkow, 1986). As Figure 17-2 indicates, the lower the family income, the higher the incidence of disabling illness which prevents going to work or to school.

Why is class linked to health? Crowded living conditions, substandard housing, poor diet, and stress all contribute to the ill health of many low-income people in the United States. In certain instances, poor education may lead to a lack of awareness of measures necessary to maintaining good health. Yet financial strains are certainly a major factor in the health problems of less affluent Americans. Given the high costs of quality medical care—which we will explore more fully later in the chapter—the poor have significantly less access to health care resources.

In addition, the occupations of people in the lower classes of the United States tend to be more dangerous than those of more affluent citizens. Miners, for example, must face the possibility of injury or death due to explosions and cave-ins; they are also likely to develop respiratory diseases such as black lung. Workers in textile mills may contract a variety of illnesses caused by exposure to toxic substances, including one disease commonly known as *brown lung disease* (R. Hall, 1982). In recent years, the American public has learned of the perils of asbestos poisoning, which is a particular worry for construction workers.

In the view of the Karl Marx and contemporary conflict theorists, capitalist societies such as the United States care more about maximizing profits than they do about the health and safety of industrial workers. As a result, government agencies do not take forceful action to regulate conditions in the workplace, and workers suffer many preventable, job-related injuries and illnesses.

Cross-cultural research suggests that it would be incorrect to assume that the availability of medical care is the critical factor contributing to class differences in mortality. Aaron Antonovsky (1972) examined mortality rates in 30 nations—most of which, unlike the United States, had made dramatic strides in equalizing access to health care. Except in the Netherlands (which, as a nation, has the lowest mortality rates ever recorded), the upper social classes were favored on every measure in the other 29 countries. Apparently, even the more equitable availability of health care does not overcome the impact of poverty and poor nutrition on the health of the lower classes.

According to a 1988 analysis by health specialists in Great Britain, almost 40,000 adult deaths *each year* in that nation can be attributed to class differences. Members of the lower social classes experience higher mortality because of their greater vulnerability to such factors as dangerous jobs and inadequate housing. It is little wonder, then, that the World Health Organization has asked countries to reduce differences in health status due to economic advantages by at least 25 percent by the year 2000 (Scott-Samuel and Blackburn, 1988).

Race and Ethnicity

Health profiles of many racial and ethnic minorities reflect the social inequality evident in the United States. The poor economic and environmental conditions of groups such as Blacks, Hispanics, and American Indians are manifested in high morbidity and mortality rates for these groups. Some afflictions, such as sickle-cell anemia among Blacks, have a clear genetic basis. But, in most instances, environmental factors contribute to differential rates of disease.

Compared with Whites, Hispanics are more likely to live in poverty, to be unemployed, and to have little education. These factors contribute to Hispanics' increased risk of contracting a variety of diseases. For example, Hispanics are four times more likely than Whites to suffer from tuberculosis, are three times more likely to contract diabetes, and are also more likely to have cancer of the stomach, pancreas, and cervix. Hispanic children suffer disproportionately from lead poisoning and measles. Although Hispanics constitute only about 8 percent of the population of the United States, they account for 14 percent of reported cases of AIDS, including nearly 21 percent of AIDS cases among women and 22 percent among children (Council on Scientific Affairs, 1991; Novello et al., 1991).

The morbidity and mortality rates for Blacks are also distressing. Compared with Whites, Blacks have higher death rates from diseases of the heart, pneumonia, diabetes, and cancer. In 1987, the death rate for strokes was twice as high among African Americans as it was among Whites. Such epidemiological findings reflect in part the higher proportion of Blacks found among the nation's lower classes. According to a study released in 1990 by the federal government, White Americans can expect to live 75.6 years. By contrast, life expectancy for Blacks is 69.2 years, while for Black men it is only 64.9 years and has been *decreasing* since the mid-1980s (Hilts, 1990c; *New York Times*, 1990b).

What accounts for these racial differences? According to a national survey conducted in 1986, Blacks of all income levels are substantially worse off than Whites in terms of access to physicians.

The occupations of people in the lower classes of the United States tend to be more dangerous than those of the more affluent.

For example, African Americans had a lower rate of visits to physicians, which is especially disturbing, since rates of serious illness are higher among Blacks than Whites. The survey points to significantly less use of medical care by Blacks, and adds that Blacks are less likely than Whites to have medical insurance. Finally, in comparison with Whites, Blacks were found to be less satisfied with the health care they received from physicians and hospital personnel (Blendon et al., 1989).

A study in Massachusetts found that substantial racial inequalities exist in the provision of cardiac care. In comparison with Blacks, a significantly higher proportion of Whites admitted to Massachusetts hospitals with heart problems undergo cardiac bypass operations and cardiac catheterizations. These racial differences are evident even among patients hospitalized with serious heart problems (Wenneker and Epstein, 1989).

Moreover, drawing upon the conflict perspective, sociologist Howard Waitzkin (1986) suggests that racial tensions contribute to the medical problems of Black Americans. In his view, the stress resulting from racial prejudice and discrimination helps to explain the higher rates of hypertension found among African Americans (and Hispanics) compared with Whites. Hypertension is twice as common in Blacks as in Whites; it is believed to be a critical factor in Blacks' high mortality rates from heart disease, kidney disease, and stroke. Although there is disagreement among medical experts, some argue that the stress resulting from racism and suppressed hostility exacerbates hypertension among Blacks (Goleman, 1990a).

Just how significant is the impact of poorer health on the lives of the nation's less educated people, less affluent classes, and minorities? Drawing upon a variety of research studies, population specialist Evelyn Kitagawa (1972) estimated the "excess mortality rate" to be 20 percent. In other words, 20 percent more people were dying than otherwise might have, because of differentially poor health linked to race and class. Using Kitagawa's model, we can calculate that if every person in the United States were White and had at least 1 year of college education, some 436,000 fewer Americans would have died in 1990 and in each succeeding year (Bureau of the Census; 1990a;15).

HEALTH CARE IN THE UNITED STATES

As all Americans are well-aware, the costs of health care have skyrocketed in recent years. For example, in 1990 total expenditures for health care in the United States reached $660 billion, a 57 percent increase over the 1985 figure (see Figure 17-3). Moreover, it is estimated that by the year 2000, total expenditures for health care will rise to $1.5 to $2 *trillion* (Locin, 1990).

The rising costs of medical care are especially apparent in the event of catastrophic illnesses or confinement in a nursing home (refer back to Chapter 12). Bills of tens of thousands of dollars are not unusual in treatment of cancer, Alzheimer's disease, and other chronic diseases requir-

FIGURE 17-3   Total Health Care Expenditures in the United States, 1965–1990

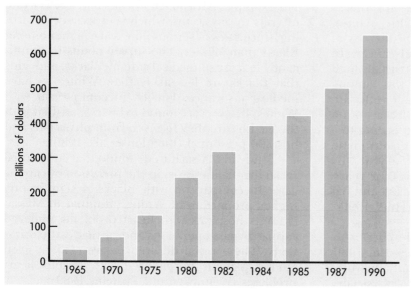

SOURCES: Easterbrook, 1987:40, 42; Locin, 1990; Stacey, 1987.

Expenditures for health care in the United States have continued to rise, reaching an all-time high of $660 billion in 1990.

Advertisements for New York City's Doctors Hospital stress speedy emergency-room service.

ing custodial care; the costs of treating a person with AIDS can range from $60,000 to $140,000. At the same time, some 1.4 million people in the United States currently pay an average of $22,000 per year for nursing home care (Ebron and Weissberg, 1987; O. Friedrich, 1987:38).

The "graying of America" (see Chapter 12) is clearly a factor in rising health care costs. Older Americans typically have longer stays in the hospital than younger patients, and the elderly obviously account for an overwhelming percentage of nursing home expenditures. Insurance coverage and existing federal assistance programs, such as Medicare, provide reimbursement for not quite half of all medical costs. For example, a 70-year-old person who enters the hospital four times for heart problems and surgery can easily spend $6000 that will not be covered by Medicare. Proposals to fill this " medigap," as it has been called, reflect concern about such unknown and potentially staggering costs (Mechanic, 1986; W. Stevens, 1987a).

Meanwhile, as health care has become "big business" in the United States, hospitals are implementing unprecedented marketing campaigns to fill empty beds. According to a marketing research survey, the nation's hospitals spent $1.1 billion on marketing in 1986, of which $500 million was spent on advertising. Advertisements for

hospitals now routinely appear on television and radio, on buses and subways, and on billboards. Hospitals are also offering such amenities as candlelight dinners for new parents, gourmet menus, and stylish furniture for private patients (T. Lewin, 1987:F1, F28).

Clearly, the health care system of the United States has moved far beyond the days when general practitioners living in a neighborhood or community typically made house calls and charged modest fees for their services. How did health care become big business involving nationwide hospital chains and marketing campaigns? How have these changes reshaped typical interactions between doctors, nurses, and patients? How does the nation's health care system compare with those of other western, capitalist nations and of socialist countries? We will address these questions in the next section of the chapter.

A Historical View

According to sociologist Paul Starr (1982), writing in his critically acclaimed book, *The Social Transformation of American Medicine,* the authority of medical professionals rests on a system of standardized educational licensing. The establishment of such a system maintains authority from one generation to the next and transmits authority from the profession as a whole to its individual members. However, health care in the United States has not always followed this model.

The "popular health movement" of the 1830s and 1840s emphasized preventive care and what is termed "self-help." There was strong criticism of "doctoring" as a paid occupation. New medical philosophies or sects established their own medical schools and challenged the authority and methods of more traditional doctors. By the 1840s, most states had repealed medical licensing laws. However, through the leadership of the American Medical Association (AMA), founded in 1848, "regular" doctors attacked lay practitioners, sectarian doctors, and female physicians in general. (For a different view, see Navarro, 1984.)

The emergence of massive, organized philanthropy in the early twentieth century—administered by such organizations as the Rockefeller and Carnegie foundations—had a critical impact in reshaping and centralizing American medicine. Beginning in 1903, extensive foundation support was allocated to create a respectable American medical profession. A researcher employed by the Carnegie Corporation was sent to tour the nation in order to determine which medical schools should receive funding. After the publication of the Flexner report in 1910, numerous medical schools that he found unworthy of financial aid were forced to close. Among them were six of the nation's eight Black medical schools and most of the alternative schools which had been open to female students. In state after state, tough licensing laws were adopted to restrict medical practice to traditional doctors from approved institutions. As one result, babies could no longer be delivered by midwives in most states; the practice of obstetrics was restricted to physicians (Ehrenreich and English, 1973).

Once authority was institutionalized through standardized programs of education and licensing, it was conferred upon all who successfully completed these programs. Recognition became relatively unambiguous. The authority of the physician no longer depended on lay attitudes or the person occupying the sick role; it was increasingly built into the structure of the medical profession and the health care system. As the institutionalization of health care proceeded, the medical profession gained control over both the market for its services and the various organizational hierarchies that govern medical practice, financing, and policymaking. By the 1920s, physicians controlled hospital technology, the division of labor of health personnel and, indirectly, other professional practices such as nursing and pharmacy (R. Coser, 1984).

Physicians, Nurses, and Patients

The preeminence of physicians within the health care system of the United States has traditionally given them a position of dominance in their dealings with both patients and nurses. The functionalist and interactionist perspectives combine to offer a framework for understanding the professional socialization of physicians as it relates to patient care. Functionalists suggest that established physicians and medical school professors serve as mentors or role models who transmit knowledge, skills, and values to the passive learner—the medical student. Interactionists emphasize that students are molded by the medical school environment as they interact with their classmates. Both approaches argue that the typical training of physicians in the United States leads to rather dehumanizing physician-patient encounters. Despite many efforts to formally introduce a humanistic dimension of patient care into medical school curricula, patient overload and cost-containment efforts of hospitals tend to reduce positive relations. Moreover, widespread publicity concerning malpractice suits and high medical costs has further strained the physician-patient dyad (Becker et al., 1961; Merton et al., 1957; Mizrahi, 1986:14).

In an extreme example of such estrangement, physicians will actively attempt to avoid seeing certain patients. In some hospitals, the acronym GROP is used to mean "get rid of patients." As a resident physician at a southern medical school declared:

> Really the only thing that's taught in internship is efficiency and getting things done the quickest way and hopefully the best way possible. But the quickest is more important. . . . How fast you can get the patient out of the hospital (Mizrahi, 1986:50).

In a participant-observation study at a public hospital, sociologist Terry Mizrahi (1986) found that GROP does not work randomly. Physicians are especially likely to attempt to GROP when patients are dirty, uneducated, unable to describe their conditions, argumentative, prone to complain constantly, or neglectful in their own care. Mizrahi found that middle-class patients were uncommon at the public hospital and were unlikely to be GROPed unless they became abusive or needlessly sought treatment. Among the more desirable patients—those least subject to GROP attempts—were people with rarely seen illnesses or conditions that were difficult to diagnose.

These problems in medicine have taken their toll on contemporary physicians. A survey conducted for the American Medical Association in 1989 revealed that 39 percent of doctors either definitely or probably would not go into medicine today if they were in college and knew what they now know about the field. This disenchantment is somewhat similar to the "burnout" experienced by teachers (refer back to Chapter 16), yet it is nevertheless surprising because physicians (unlike schoolteachers) enjoy substantial incomes and high prestige. Despite these benefits, the physicians surveyed report that they are disillusioned by the growing competition for patients, increased government regulation of medicine, and worrisome malpractice litigation (L. Altman and Rosenthal, 1990).

Interactionists have closely examined how compliance and negotiation occur between physician and patient. They concur with Talcott Parsons' view that the relationship is generally asymmetrical, with doctors holding a position of dominance and control of rewards. While the dominant position of doctors is evident in many societies, there are important cross-cultural differences in physician-patient interactions. For example, whereas doctors in the United States typically used to lie to patients rather than reveal a diagnosis of terminal cancer, this is no longer the case. Most patients ask for and expect a truthful diagnosis; most physicians respect this request, even when it means revealing that the patient is likely to die. By contrast, Japanese physicians commonly tell patients that they have pneumonia when they actually have lung cancer, or that they have a benign ulcer

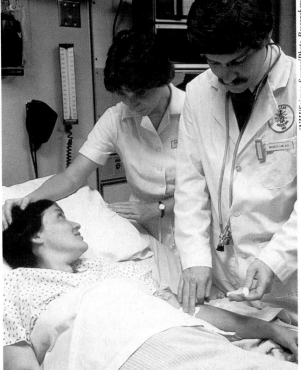

(NIH/Science Source/Photo Researchers)

Like other women in subordinate roles, nurses have been expected to perform their duties without challenging the authority of men.

when they have stomach cancer. Often, however, physicians do not need to lie in these situations, because many Japanese patients will not even ask for a diagnosis (Long and Long, 1982).

Just as physicians in both Japan and the United States have maintained a dominant position in their interactions with patients, doctors have similarly controlled interactions with nurses. Despite their training and professional status, nurses commonly take orders from physicians. Traditionally, the relationship between doctors and nurses has paralleled the male dominance of American society: most physicians have been male, whereas virtually all nurses have been female.

Like other women in subordinate roles, nurses have been expected to perform their duties without challenging the authority of men. Psychiatrist Leonard Stein (1967:699–700) refers to this process as the *doctor-nurse game*. According to the rules of this "game," the nurse must never disagree openly with the physician. When she has recommendations concerning a patient's care, she must communicate them indirectly in a deferential tone. For example, if asked by a hospital's medical resident, "What sleeping medication has been helpful to Mrs. Brown in the past?" (an indirect request for a recommendation), the nurse will respond with a disguised recommendation statement, such as "Pentobarbital mg 100 was quite effective night before last." Her careful response allows the physician to authoritatively restate the same prescription as if it were *his* idea.

Although the doctor-nurse game continues, the rules may be changing. Steven Rank and Cardell Jacobsen (1977) conducted an experiment in which physicians ordered nurses to administer overdoses of the sedative valium to patients. With nursing supervisors present as safeguards to protect patients, 16 of the 18 nurses tested refused to administer the ordered dosage. Given the growing professionalism of nursing and changes in traditional gender roles (see Chapter 11), male dominance in doctor-nurse relationships is likely to be reduced to some extent.

Indeed, by the 1980s nurses in the United States were increasingly speaking out, engaging in political action, walking picket lines, and joining lawsuits—all with the goals of better pay, more respect for their professional expertise, and transformation of the health care system. Margretta Styles, president of the American Nurses Association (ANA), notes: "Nursing is 97 percent female, and the problems we face are typical of those faced in women's professions, especially low pay and low status." Both inside the hospital and in the larger political system, nurses have organized to battle for autonomy, an improved image, and fair compensation for their skill and dedication (Holcomb, 1988:74).

As an increasing number of women continue to enter the medical profession as doctors, both the traditional doctor-nurse game and typical physician-patient relationships may be affected. A 1977 survey by the Department of Health and Human Services revealed that female physicians spend more time with each patient than their male counterparts do. More recent research suggests that women physicians are not as authoritarian as men in doctor-patient encounters and that they find it easier to communicate with dying patients and their families. However, although the new wave of female doctors may favor less hierarchical relationships with patients and nurses than their male counterparts, they will also face more challenges to their authority. Studies show that male patients are more likely to interrupt or question female physicians than they are male doctors (Arond, 1984:27; C. Weisman and Teitelbaum, 1985; C. West, 1984).

The Role of Government

Cindy Martin died in 1990 at age 26, after 4 months of surgery and intensive care at Presbyterian University Hospital in Pittsburgh. In the aftermath of her death, her husband's insurance company received a bill for $1.25 million. While accountants attempted to untangle the costs of seven surgical procedures performed on Cindy Martin—including heart, liver, and kidney transplants—this case underscored troubling issues regarding the high cost of health care. Who should pay for the expensive medical procedures of the 1990s? What role, if any, should government play in providing medical care and health insurance for United States citizens (Freudenheim, 1990)?

During the twentieth century, one European nation after another has adopted government-sponsored national health insurance or created a national health service (see Box 17-2). By contrast, the United States government has been much less active in providing health care for its citizens. Concerned about possible threats to physicians' professional autonomy and their dominant position in the health care system, the American Medical Association has exacerbated fears about the dangers of "socialized medicine." The public has been encouraged to believe that the "sacred doctor-patient relationship" would become much less personal and intimate in any governmental health system. At present, the United States remains the only western industrial democracy that does not treat health care as a basic right. Conflict theorists argue that this difference reflects an underlying and disturbing aspect of

BOX 17-2 • AROUND THE WORLD

HEALTH CARE IN OTHER INDUSTRIALIZED NATIONS

The United States is not alone in facing serious health care challenges; each industrialized society has many similar problems. Although no medical system is without its unique difficulties—and none is completely transferable to the United States—we can nevertheless gain useful insights by examining the health care programs of other countries.

Like the United States, Canada relies on private physicians and hospitals for day-to-day health care. Yet, beginning in the period after World War ll, Canada gradually introduced a national health policy that guaranteed medical care as a right for all citizens. Income taxes are used to finance *public* medical insurance. Medical fees are set by the government, and private health insurance is prohibited.

Sweden goes beyond Canada's health insurance policies by offering a national health system. Medical care is delivered primarily by publicly funded hospitals and clinics; a national health insurance system sets fees for health care services and reimburses providers of health care. Such health care arrangements are costly, yet health care in Sweden consumes no more of the nation's gross national product than it does in the United States. At the same time, Swedish national health insurance is integrated with other governmental benefit programs. For example, a Swedish worker who is ill not only receives health care benefits from the government but is also paid a percentage of his or her salary. If the person is so disabled that he or she cannot work, a governmental pension program goes into operation.

Since 1949, the National Health Service (NHS) has been the principal deliverer of health care in the United Kingdom. The NHS is financed through general taxation—although British citizens pay minor charges for prescriptions, eyeglass frames, and certain dental procedures. Physicians typically are paid salaries by the NHS, yet some see private patients as well. Consequently, a two-tiered system of public and private care remains in effect.

Since instituting the National Health Service, the United Kingdom appears to have achieved a lower rate of infant mortality, a slightly higher rate of life expectancy among males, and a dramatically improved level of eye care. However, the British health care program has proved to be quite costly; by the late 1980s, the NHS was in a state of crisis. As of 1988, over 660,000 people were on waiting lists for elective surgery, while about 30,000 nurses were quitting NHS jobs each year because of low pay. Many British health care workers and public interest groups insist that the National Health Service is being underfunded for its many responsibilities.

What about health care in an industrialized *socialist* society? In the Soviet Union, the government has traditionally assumed responsibility for ownership and operation of all health care facilities. Although private medical practice has never been prohibited, it has been rare for a physician to work outside the official health care system. As the nation moves toward a market economy in the early 1990s, there may be significant changes in health care delivery, but the future remains unclear.

Currently, unlike doctors in other industrialized countries, Soviet physicians are unorganized. Professional associations have no power to influence salaries or health care policies. As one result of this situation, physicians' salaries are in the same range as those of high school teachers. Doctor-patient relationships in the Soviet Union tend to be impersonal, although some patients offer physicians gifts or money to personalize the treatment they receive. An individual patient has little say in who his or her doctor will be, and there are no consumer interest groups to influence health care policies and practices.

Despite their differences, all four countries—Canada, Sweden, Great Britain, and the Soviet Union—view health care as a basic right of all citizens. Canada has instituted a national health insurance program, and the other three nations have established comprehensive national health systems. By contrast, the United States has neither national health insurance nor a national health system. As we seek to improve the delivery of health care services in this country, it may be prudent to consider the broad measures that have been implemented by other industrial societies.

SOURCES: Conrad and Kern, 1986; D'Anastasio, 1987; DeYoung, 1988; Knaus, 1981; Lohr, 1988; Spector, 1989; Twaddle and Hessler, 1987:335–342; Vayda and Deber, 1984.

American capitalism: illness may be exploited for profit (R. Harris, 1966; P. Taylor, 1985:9; Waitzkin and Waterman, 1974:14; Wohl, 1984).

The first significant involvement of the federal government in the financing of health care came with the 1946 Hill-Burton Act, which provided subsidies for building and improving hospitals, especially in rural areas. An even more important change came with the enactment of two wide-ranging government assistance programs: Medicare, essentially a compulsory health insurance plan for the elderly; and Medicaid, a noncontributory federal and state insurance plan for the poor. These programs greatly expanded federal involvement in health care financing for needy Americans. In addition, over 1000 government-subsidized community health centers are located in low-income, medically underserved communities (Blendon, 1986).

Given rates of illness and disability among elderly people, Medicare has had particularly noteworthy impact on the American health care system. Initially, Medicare simply reimbursed health care providers such as physicians and hospitals for the costs of their services. However, as the overall costs of Medicare increased dramatically, the federal government introduced a price-control system in 1983. All illnesses were classified into 468 diagnostic-related groups (DRGs); a reimbursement rate was set for each condition and remains fixed regardless of the individual needs of any patient.

In effect, the federal government told hospitals and doctors that it would no longer be concerned with their costs in treating Medicare patients; it would reimburse them only to a designated level. If a patient is sicker than average (that is, the average set for a particular illness) and requires extra care, the hospital must absorb any expenses beyond its DRG allowance. However, if the patient is less ill than average for an illness, the hospital can essentially make a profit from the fixed level of reimbursement (Downs, 1987; Easterbrook, 1987:49).

The purpose of the DRG system is to lower national health care costs by pressuring hospitals and physicians to avoid unnecessary testing of patients, unnecessarily long hospital stays, and so forth. Indeed, hospitals *are* releasing patients

sooner; the average hospital stay for a Medicare patient declined by 19 percent, from 10.32 days in 1982 to 8.38 days in 1985 (Chapman, 1986:11). Yet, as was noted by Joe Feinglass (1987:28), project director of the Housestaff Cost Awareness Project at Northwestern Hospital in Chicago:

> . . . DRGs create strong incentives for hospitals to transfer or refuse to admit unprofitable patients whose treatment is likely to cost more than the DRG rate. Poor and chronically ill elderly patients, who often have longer lengths of stay and incur higher costs than other patients, are viewed as undesirables by hospital administrators.

Profit-motivated shifting of patients, through either premature discharge or transfer, is a new ethical issue that American hospitals are only beginning to confront (D. Evans, 1985; Veatch, 1986).

The DRG system of reimbursement has contributed to the controversial practice of "dumping," under which patients whose treatment may be unprofitable are transferred by private hospitals to public facilities. Many private hospitals in the United States have begun to conduct routine "wallet biopsies" to investigate the financial status of potential patients; those judged as undesirable are then refused admission or are dumped. Since the introduction of DRGs, some urban public hospitals have reported 400 to 500 percent increases in the number of patients transferred from private hospitals (Feinglass, 1987).

Such dumping can have grave consequences for patients. In 1984, a Harvard Medical School team analyzed records of 458 patients transferred during a 6-month period to a public hospital in Oakland, California. Researchers found that in 7.2 percent of cases, the patients were transferred before being stabilized medically; their care suffered as a result. Viewed from a conflict perspective, such practices are especially likely to hurt those Americans at the bottom of stratification hierarchies based on social class, race and ethnicity, gender, and age (P. Taylor, 1985:9).

People who carry no health insurance are especially likely to experience dumping. According to 1990 estimates, about 28 percent of the nation's population had no health insurance for at least 1 month during a 28-month period of study. The uninsured typically include self-employed people with limited incomes, illegal immigrants, and single and divorced mothers who are the sole providers for their families (refer back to the social policy section on the feminization of poverty in Chapter 8). Blacks and especially Hispanics are less likely than Whites to have private health insurance. A 1989 national survey found that 32 percent of Hispanics, 20 percent of Blacks, and 10 percent of Whites had no health insurance during 1988 (Nelson and Short, 1990; Treviño et al., 1991:235).

Americans without health insurance may be vulnerable to a lower quality of medical care than those who are covered. A team of researchers from Harvard Medical School examined the care received by 37,994 patients with Medicaid, private health insurance, or no insurance to compare the treatment of hospital patients with circulatory disorders or chest pains. Privately insured patients were found to be anywhere from 28 percent to 80 percent more likely to receive various medical and surgical procedures than were those without insurance or with Medicaid. While researchers did not assess the need for such procedures, other studies have shown that Medicaid and uninsured patients typically have greater medical needs than others because they have less access to primary medical care. This study raises serious questions about the quality of care given to patients with heart disease; it suggests that the financial status of the patient plays a significant role in the utilization of medical procedures (Wenneker et al., 1990).

In an especially disturbing development, certain hospitals have refused admission to seriously ill or injured people without private health insurance who cannot make substantial cash deposits. For example, G. A. Lafon, a 56-year-old Texas laborer with no health insurance, suffered serious grease burns on his side and back. Lafon was turned away from emergency rooms in three for-profit hospitals near his home because he could not provide deposits ranging from $500 to $1500. "Kind of makes you feel like a dog," reflected Lafon. Eventually, he received a skin graft and 19 days of hospital care at a county-owned facility. Although a 1986 federal law prohibits most hos-

(Health Care Plan of New Jersey)

In response to the rising costs of medical care and health insurance, many people in the United States have joined health maintenance organizations (HMOs).

pitals from turning away patients who are seeking emergency care, monitoring and enforcement remain weak (Ansell and Schill, 1987; P. Taylor, 1985:8).

As one response to the rising costs of medical care and health insurance, many people in the United States have joined **health maintenance organizations (HMOs)** which provide comprehensive medical services for a preestablished fee. In several respects, the HMO resembles a student health clinic at a residential college; it offers some of the same advantages (guaranteed health care, fixed costs, convenience) and disadvantages (impersonality, occasional long lines, lack of choice of physicians). Encouraged by federal and state policies, membership in HMOs grew by more than 20 percent per year in the early 1980s. By 1988, 10 percent of all employees in the United States were enrolled in some type of health maintenance organization. But the spectacular growth of HMOs has clearly slowed; beginning in 1987, many HMOs lost money and some went out of business. Surviving HMOs have typically responded by raising their fees by 10 to 20 percent, which only adds to the burden on those who find it difficult to pay for either private health insurance or membership in an HMO (Freudenheim, 1988; A. Miller, 1989a:47; *Rand,* 1988).

The Rise of Hospital Chains

During the 1970s, profit-making hospital chains grew at an even faster rate than did the computer industry. By 1985, these chains owned or managed more than 20 percent of the hospitals in the United States. Several chains have become multinational corporations; for example, American Medical International owns or manages facilities in England, Spain, Switzerland, Singapore, France, and Venezuela, as well as in the United States. By the 1980s, many of the largest investor-owned hospitals had begun to sell less profitable facilities, and the consolidation of the hospital industry seemed to have slowed. Nevertheless, the existence of hospital chains represents a new and important development in American health care (Castro, 1984; Goldsmith, 1986; Kinkead, 1980).

Like convenience stores and other consumer-oriented businesses, hospital chains use demographic data for marketing decision making. In order to improve its rate of hospital occupancy, Louisville-based Humana, Inc., a chain which owns or operates 100 hospitals and 200 MedFirst neighborhood facilities, relies heavily on demographic data. Occupancy at Humana's West Hills Medical Center in Canoga Park, California, had leveled off at 45 percent in 1978 when the market research staff began to study the facility. They mapped the locations of competing hospitals, population growth and family income by zip-code area, doctors' locations, and driving distances. This market research helped hospital planners decide what types of medical specializations to offer, which doctors to approach as potential staff members, and which advertising techniques would best attract the general public and medical personnel.

Humana then flooded potential customers of the West Hills Center with Insta-Care cards, advertised that it would waive the $180 deductible fee previously required of Medicare patients, and began a Cradle Club, which offered prenatal classes and store discounts to expectant mothers. Humana also helped West Hills staff physicians find office sites in a nearby town with many young, privately insured families. The chain anticipated that the doctors would later refer these desirable patients to the hospital. Apparently, Humana's overall marketing campaign was successful; in the period 1979–1980, the revenues of West Hills increased by $2.7 million, and its occupancy rate rose 7 percentage points (Adams, 1984; Castro, 1984; Kinkead, 1980).

Like other hospital chains, Humana has come under fire for its dumping, wallet biopsies, and failure to provide indigent care. For example, in 1983, the Kentucky attorney general's office ordered one Humana facility to end its practice of telling parents that they could not take their newborns home until they had paid their bills. But, after they agreed to abandon this policy, hospital officials then required deposits before admission. Pregnant women were asked to pay a deposit of $1200 to gain admission; women who could not produce the deposit were sent to another institution more than 100 miles away. As for care of the indigent, in 1984 the Humana hospital in Memphis provided none, whereas a nearby public regional center offered $25.9 million in care of indigents (Downs, 1987:24, 26).

The rise of such chains has troubled many public officials and health care experts, who worry that the United States is headed toward a two-tiered hierarchy of hospitals: private institutions for the affluent and public hospitals for the poor and uninsured. Whereas public hospitals spend an average of 11 percent of their gross patient revenues on "indigent care," private hospitals so allocate only 3 percent of their revenues. Uwe Reinhardt, a health economist, argues that "health care is now a commercial commodity sold in a market in which nice guys [those who render uncompensated care to the indigents] are bound to finish last." Yet an executive for American Medical International—arguing for a free-market view of health care under which government should be responsible for the costs of caring for the indigent—responds that "we don't expect Safeway or A&P to give away free food for people who can't afford it" (P. Taylor, 1985:9; see also Light, 1986).

Viewed from a conflict perspective, the transfer of hospital ownership to large corporations is troubling. David Starkweather (1981) notes that companies may curtail services or even shut down entire health care centers if they do not yield sufficient revenue for the corporation—just as industrial conglomerates sometimes close plants that do not make a "hurdle" (return on investment). Threats of shutdowns can be effective in forcing local communities to make concessions regarding land for hospital expansion, tax breaks, and so forth. From the perspective of conflict theory, the increasing domination of the hospital system by profit-oriented chains such as American Medical International and Humana can only accelerate a trend toward high-quality treatment for the privileged and inferior care—even life-threatening transfers—for the less affluent.

Alternatives to Traditional Health Care

Thus far, we have concentrated exclusively on traditional forms of health care—particularly, reliance on physicians and hospitals for treatment of illness. Yet some Americans attempt to maintain good health or respond to illness through use of alternative health care techniques. For example, in recent decades there has been growing interest in *holistic* (this term is also spelled *wholistic*) medical principles first developed in China. **Holistic medicine** is a means of health maintenance which views the person as an integration of body, mind, and spirit (Sirott and Waitzkin, 1984:246). The individual is regarded as a totality, rather than as a collection of interrelated organ systems. Treatment methodologies include massage, acupuncture (which involves the insertion of fine needles into surface points), respiratory exercises, and the use of herbs as remedies. Nutrition, exercise, and "talking therapy" may also be used to treat ailments generally treated through medication or hospitalization (Chow, 1984; M. Goldstein et al., 1987).

Practitioners of holistic medicine do not necessarily function totally outside the health care system. Some have medical degrees and rely on x-rays and EKG machines for diagnostic assistance. Other holistic clinics, often referred to as *wellness clinics,* reject the use of medical technology. The recent resurgence of holistic medicine comes amidst a widespread recognition of the value of nutrition and the dangers of overreliance on prescription drugs (especially those used to reduce stress, such as valium).

In some cases, movements for political change have generated health care alternatives. For example, as part of the larger feminist movement beginning in the 1960s, women became more vocal in their dissatisfaction with the traditional health care system. Marked by the appearance of the book *Our Bodies, Ourselves* (Boston Women's Health Book Collective, 1969, 1984), the contemporary women's health movement emerged out of the realization that women are by far the most frequent users of health services for themselves, their children, and other dependent family members. Activists agree that women should assume more responsibility for decisions concerning their health. The movement therefore has taken many forms, including organizations working for changes in the health care system, women's clinics, and birth and "self-help" groups.

Although the women's health movement supports greater access to health care for all Americans, it focuses on specific women's health issues such as menstruation, childbirth, abortion rights (see Chapter 11), and menopause. Women's health groups have expressed concern about the hazards of oral contraceptives and the intrauterine device (IUD)—hazards which they feel have been concealed by drug companies and the medical establishment. Activists generally favor a greater voice for women in maternity care, the establishment of midwifery centers, and full representation of female consumers on health policy-making boards. Partly in the name of equal opportunity, but also in the hope of increasing sensitivity to women within the health care establishment, the women's health movement has demanded increased entry of women into medical school and hospital administration positions. Some activists have gone so far as to endorse the exclusion of male medical students from obstetrics and gynecological specialties. Clearly, feminists are resisting the social-control aspects of the male-dominated medical hierarchy (Corea, 1977:252–266; Ruzek, 1978; M. Zimmerman, 1987; Zola, 1983:282).

The goals of the women's health movement are ambitious, but the health care system has proved to be fairly resistant to change. Conflict theorists point out that physicians, medical schools, hospitals, and drug companies all have a vested interest in keeping women in a rather dependent and uninformed position as health care consumers. Although there has been an increase in female doctors, women remain underrepresented in key positions in the American health care system (R. Sidel and Sidel, 1984:268).

MENTAL ILLNESS IN THE UNITED STATES

Terms such as *mental illness* and *insanity* evoke dramatic and often inaccurate images of emotional problems. The media routinely emphasize the most violent behavior of those with disturbances, but mental health and mental illness can more appropriately be viewed as a continuum of behavior that we ourselves move along. Using a less sensational definition, a person can be considered to have a mental disorder "if he or she is so disturbed that coping with routine, everyday life is difficult or impossible" (J. W. Coleman and Cressey, 1980:315).

How prevalent is mental illness in the United States? In the largest study of its kind conducted in this country, Darrell Regier (1988) and his colleagues at the National Institute of Mental Health interviewed 18,571 adults. They found that, in the previous month, 15.4 percent of respondents had suffered from at least one mental disorder. The most common disorders included anxiety disorders (affecting 7 percent of those surveyed) and mood disorders (5 percent). According to Regier, the relative absence of high-quality mental health care is confirmed by the finding that only one-third of the respondents with mental disorders reported receiving treatment during the previous 6 months.

American society has traditionally maintained a negative and suspicious view of those with mental disorders. Holding the status of "mental patient" or even "former mental patient" can have unfortunate and undeserved consequences. For example, during the 1972 election campaign, it was learned that the Democratic vice presidential nominee, Senator Thomas Eagleton of Missouri, had once received treatment for depression. Public reaction was so strong that presidential nominee George McGovern was forced to drop Eagleton from the Democratic ticket.

The media often contribute to the stigma attached to mental illness in American society. Melvin DeFleur and Everette Dennis (1981) conducted a content analysis of the portrayal of mentally ill characters on network television crime and adventure dramas over a 4-month period. Such people were shown as uniformly dangerous and were often designated as "criminally insane." Imprecise, derogatory labels such as "wacko," "psycho," or "sickie" were often applied. These television programs did little to inform the viewing public that mental illness is a complex condition which rarely involves threatening or dangerous behavior toward others. From an interactionist perspective, a key social institution is shaping social behavior by manipulating symbols and thereby intensifying people's fears about the mentally ill (see also Gerbner et al., 1981; Link, 1987).

Theoretical Models of Mental Disorders

In studying mental illness, we can draw on both a medical model and a more sociological approach derived from labeling theory. Each model offers distinctive assumptions regarding treatment of people with mental disorders.

The *medical model* views mental illness as a disease derived from biological causes that can be treated through medical intervention. All mental dysfunctions are attributed to physical causes—whether physiological, biochemical, or genetic. For example, in Chapter 4 we noted that studies among the Amish subculture in Pennsylvania have detected certain genetic factors associated with a predisposition to manic depression. Yet researchers thus far have been able to link conclusively only a few types of mental illness to such physical causes as hormonal imbalances or serious vitamin deficiencies.

In the view of its critics, the medical model relies too heavily on chemical intervention in treating people with mental disorders. Psychologist

BOX 17-3 • *EVERYDAY BEHAVIOR*

ON BEING SANE IN INSANE PLACES

Psychologist David Rosenhan (1973) conducted a series of experiments to assess the admissions process in residential mental institutions. He had eight sane people—ranging from graduate students to a pediatrician—gain admission as patients at 12 different mental hospitals.

All arrived at the hospitals complaining that they had heard voices saying "empty," "hollow," and "third." However, once on the wards, the "patients" behaved normally and told psychiatrists that they felt fine.

Despite their public displays of sanity, Rosenhan's confederates were not quickly discharged. Initially labeled as mentally ill (specifically, schizophrenic), they remained "ill" until they were declared to have recovered. Even normal behavior such as taking notes was redefined as "compulsive writing" to fit the patients' label of "schizophrenic." The lengths of hospitalization for these patients ranged from 7 days to 52 days, and averaged 19 days.

Rosenhan's carefully conceived study demonstrated that a psychiatric label has a life of its own: the perceptions of the staff proved to be more important than the actual behavior of the eight subjects. This finding is especially important given the personal, social, and legal stigmata attached to being an ex-mental patient in the United States.

Albert Bandura (1969:16) argues that this approach has led to the "unremitting search for drugs as quick remedies for interpersonal problems, and long-term neglect of social variables as influential determinants of deviant response patterns." Nonetheless, the medical model continues to be persuasive in treatment of mental illness—in good part because all psychiatrists are first trained as medical doctors (Cockerham, 1989; Conrad, 1975).

In contrast to the medical model, labeling theory suggests that mental illness is not really an "illness," since the individual's problems arise from living in society and not from physical maladies. Psychiatrist Thomas Szasz (1974), in his book *The Myth of Mental Illness,* which first appeared in 1961, advanced the view that numerous personality disorders are not "diseases" but simply patterns of conduct labeled as disorders by significant others. The response to Szasz's challenging thesis was sharp: the commissioner of the New York State Department of Hygiene demanded his dismissal from his university position because Szasz did not "believe" in mental illness. By contrast, many sociologists embraced his model as a logical extension of examining individual behavior in a social context. As we have noted throughout this textbook, a given behavior may be viewed as normal in one society, disapproved of but tolerated in a second, and labeled as "sick" and heavily sanctioned in a third.

Proponents of the labeling model are critical of how such terms as *schizophrenia* are widely and casually used, when there is little evidence of a specific disorder with clearly defined symptoms (much less causes). Labels such as "mentally ill" or "emotionally disturbed" carry a heavy stigma; indeed, studies suggest that college students in the United States, Italy, and Mexico would reduce contacts with other students believed to be former mental patients. Once the label of deviance (in this case, mental illness) is attached, society responds to the person in accordance with that label. Moreover, as is shown in Box 17-3, even staff members in a mental institution can be greatly influenced by the power of an improper psychiatric label.

Although labeling will not typically "make sane people insane," it undoubtedly causes mentally ill patients to feel that they are devalued by the larger society. And the more they believe they are being negatively labeled, the more difficult they will find it to interact with others. Some mentally ill people may keep their problems and treatment a secret and may withdraw from social contacts. Such coping strategies to deal with labeling can lead to negative consequences in terms of employment, social support networks, and self-esteem (Cockerham, 1989:252–256; for a different view, see Gove, 1970, 1975, 1980:103; Link et al., 1989).

In reviewing the medical and labeling models of mental illness, we can conclude that neither model offers a satisfactory overall explanation. Clearly, the medical model is persuasive because it pinpoints causes of mental illness and treatments for disorders. Yet proponents of the labeling perspective maintain that mental illness is a distinctively social process, whatever other processes are involved. From a sociological perspective, the ideal approach to mental illness integrates the insights of labeling theory with those of the medical approach (Scheff, 1975a, 1975b:256–257; see also Meile, 1986; Thoits, 1985).

Patterns of Care

For most of human history, those suffering from mental disorders were deemed the responsibility of their families. Yet mental illness has been a matter of governmental concern much longer than physical illness has. This is because severe emotional disorders threaten stable social relationships and entail prolonged incapacitation (Clausen, 1979:105). As early as the 1600s, European cities began to confine the insane in public facilities along with the poor and criminals. This development brought resistance from prisoners, who were indignant at being forced to live with "lunatics." The isolation of the mentally ill from others in the same facility and from the larger society made physicians the central and ultimate authority for their welfare.

In the United States, the period of the 1840s and 1850s was the "age of the asylum." Before 1810, only a few states had institutions for the mentally ill, but by 1860, 28 of the nation's 33 states had such public facilities. The asylum was put forward as a humanitarian and even utopian institution which would rehabilitate the suffering and serve as a model facility for the rest of society. Its social structure emphasized discipline, neatness, fixed schedules, and work assignments for patients. Existing relationships were deemphasized; families were discouraged from visiting with patients because they would disrupt hospital routines (Perrucci, 1974; D. Rothman, 1971).

As noted in Chapter 4, the residential mental

(Eric A. Roth/The Picture Cube)

Patients in residential mental hospitals undergo "degradation ceremonies" which strip them of identity and destroy personal dignity.

hospital is an example of a total institution in which people are removed from the larger society for an appreciable period of time. Drawing on the work of Erving Goffman, Harold Garfinkel (1956) revealed that people in total institutions undergo "degradation ceremonies" which strip them of their identities, destroy personal dignity, and often lead to confusion and distress. From a functionalist perspective, the crowding and depersonalization inherent in mental hospitals are dysfunctional to society's resolving emotional problems. Moreover, as was shown in Box 17-3, mental patients are often treated in terms of the institutions' own expectations.

A major policy development in caring for those with mental disorders came with the passage of the 1963 Community Mental Health Centers Act. The CMHC program, as it is known, was significant in increasing federal government involvement in the treatment of the mentally ill. It also marked acceptance of the view that community-based mental health centers (which treat clients on an outpatient basis, thereby allowing them to continue working and living at home) provide more effective treatment than the institutionalized programs of state and county mental hospitals do.

The expansion of the federally funded CMHC program decreased inpatient care. Consequently, by the 1980s, community-based mental health care replaced hospitalization as the typical form of treatment. The deinstitutionalization of the mentally ill reached dramatic proportions across the United States. Whereas state mental hospitals had held almost 560,000 long-term patients in 1955, by 1984 they held only 114,000 patients (Hope and Young, 1988).

Deinstitutionalization was often defended as a social reform which would effectively reintegrate the mentally ill into the outside world. However, the authentic humanitarian concern behind deinstitutionalization proved to be convenient for politicians whose goal was simply cost cutting. Sociologist P. R. Dingman (1974:48) has argued that the principal factor in getting rid of state mental hospitals was the rising cost of maintaining such institutions. Moreover, because of severe financial cutbacks fueled by the recessions of the 1970s and 1980s, community care is far from adequate, especially in major cities and rural areas. Although the CMHC program was originally intended to include some 2000 community centers, only 870 are currently in operation (Elshtain, 1981; Hope and Young, 1988; Naparstek and Biegel, 1980; Scull, 1977).

A professor of social work, Mona Wasow (1984:10), argues that for many Americans, deinstitutionalization has become a "nightmare of deprivation and suffering." Without effective community aftercare, released mental patients find it difficult to compete for jobs and housing and experience increasing anxiety. Some join the growing ranks of the nation's homeless population (see Chapter 18). In a comprehensive report in 1984, the American Psychiatric Association concluded that the practice of discharging the mentally ill from state institutions into ill-prepared local communities has been a "major societal tragedy." It defended the basic goals of deinstitutionalization but noted that "implementation was flawed" through failure to provide adequate community care (Boffey, 1984:Al, B12).

A report released in 1990 by the Public Citizen Research Group and the National Alliance for the Mentally Ill reveals that more than 250,000 Americans with serious mental illnesses (schizophrenia or manic-depressive illness) are living untreated in public shelters, on the streets, or in jails. By contrast, only 68,000 people with such illnesses are in mental hospitals. In the view of Dr. E. Fuller Torrey, a psychiatrist who served as lead author of this report, there has been a "near total breakdown in public psychiatric services in the United States" (Hilts, 1990b:A28).

- What are some of the health risks associated with smoking?
- What efforts have been made by various levels of government and by employers to restrict smoking?
- Why is there concern about the efforts of tobacco companies to target racial and ethnic minorities, women, and teenagers as potential customers?

According to former U.S. Surgeon General C. Everett Koop, tobacco users were jailed in sixteenth-century Japan, and anyone possessing tobacco in seventeenth-century China could be beheaded. There are no such penalties for smoking in contemporary American society, but the debate over tobacco has certainly intensified. New York City television reporter David Diaz, who smokes a pack a day, charges: "There's a new tyrannical majority that wants to deprive the rest of us of our rights." By contrast, ABC television Washington correspondent Sam Donaldson, a former smoker, counters: "I don't think smokers have any rights when it comes to a collision of smokers' versus nonsmokers' wishes" (Toufexis, 1986:47).

Advertising by the tobacco industry has conveyed the impression that smoking is an integral aspect of human interaction. Whether or not this is true, cigarette smoking is clearly a popular activity around the world. Over 1 billion people now smoke, consuming almost 5 trillion cigarettes per year. Indeed, global use of tobacco has grown 75 percent during the last 2 decades. Smoking rates are high, especially among males, in societies as diverse as the United States, the Soviet Union, Japan, and Bangladesh. According to a 1990 survey, about 29 percent of the people in the United States are cigarette smokers (Chandler, 1986:9–11; New York Times, 1990c; Rovner, 1986: 3050).

Evidence concerning the health risks associated with smoking first received widespread public attention in 1964, when the U.S. surgeon general issued a report calling cigarettes a "health hazard of sufficient importance . . . to warrant appropriate remedial action." Twenty-five years later, another report by the surgeon general called smoking the "single most important preventable cause of death" in the United States. Smoking was found to be responsible for one of six deaths in the nation (Berke, 1989).

According to the Centers for Disease Control, more than 434,000 Americans died in 1988 from smoking-related ailments—among them, cancer, heart disease, stroke, and respiratory diseases. Currently, one out of three cancer deaths in the United States (and 90 percent of deaths from lung cancer) are due to the use of tobacco—primarily cigarettes. Since 1986, lung cancer has surpassed breast cancer as the leading cause of death from cancer among women. Smoking has also been found to have adverse effects on pregnancy and fetal health, and therefore contributes to infant mortality. Moreover, according to a 1990 report by the Department of Health and Human Services, cigarette smoking costs the United States $52 billion each year in health care expenses or time lost from work (Chandler, 1986:9; Hilts, 1990a; Marmorstein, 1986:27; New York Times, 1991c).

Spurred on by such distressing data, nonsmokers (some of them former smokers) have become politically active in such groups as Action on Smoking and Health (ASH) and Group Against Smoking Pollution (GASP). These organizations have become increasingly vocal in demanding action by government and the private sector to restrict or totally ban smoking in public places and on the job. The anger of antismoking activists has been fueled by recent studies on the impact of "passive smoking."

Only 14 percent of Americans escape being exposed to tobacco smoke in the home or at the workplace. Apparently, such "secondhand smoke" has harmful effects on the health of the nonsmokers. For example, a 1990 report by the Environmental Protection Agency concluded that passive smoking causes 3800 lung cancer deaths each year in the United States. Studies in Germany, Greece, and Japan have established at least a correlation between passive smoking and lung cancer deaths. But fatalities from lung cancer are not the only distressing result of secondhand smoke. In a 1990 review of 11 epidemiological studies, one public health expert estimated that passive smoking kills 50,000 Americans each year, two-thirds of whom die of heart disease (L. Altman, 1990; Byrd et al., 1989; Chandler, 1986:11).

Former Secretary of Health, Education, and Welfare

Joseph Califano (1986:65), a leading advocate of smoking bans, argues: "Smoking is slow-motion suicide. The point . . . is to prevent secondhand smoking from becoming slow-motion murder." Such arguments are bitterly opposed by smokers and by those who defend the rights of smokers. In their view, smokers are being scapegoated, and antismoking regulations are giving "dictatorial power" to nonsmokers. While many voices have been raised on behalf of the nation's smokers, certainly the most powerful is the $55 billion-a-year tobacco industry. According to estimates, cigarette companies are spending at least tens of millions of dollars each year to mobilize opposition to antismoking laws (McGill, 1988).

Despite the imposing power of the tobacco lobby, the federal government has taken action over the last 3 decades to warn Americans of the dangers of smoking and to regulate smoking behavior. In 1970, for example, Congress banned all cigarette advertising on television and radio and strengthened the required warning labels on packages. In 1986, the General Services Administration (GSA) issued regulations to guarantee nonsmoking federal workers a "reasonably smoke-free environment." Then, in 1989, Congress enacted a ban on smoking on all commercial airline flights within the continental United States and on most flights to Alaska and Hawaii.

On the state and local level, as well, there has been increasing regulation of smoking. By 1991, all but five states—Alabama, Missouri, North Carolina, Tennessee, and Wyoming—had enacted statewide laws restricting smoking. Hundreds of municipalities—notably New York, San Francisco, Los Angeles, and Cambridge, Massachusetts—have passed strict regulations concerning smoking. These state and local laws typically restrict smoking in public transportation, elevators, schools, hospitals, nursing homes, and government buildings (Mueller, 1991).

In this climate of growing regulation of smoking, many business firms in the United States have taken similar action. In 1981, only 8 percent of American corporations restricted smoking; by 1990, 68 percent had imposed some formal restrictions. Moreover, disturbed by the number of sick days taken by tobacco users and the impact of their illnesses on insurance premiums, 6 percent of companies have gone even further by refusing to hire smokers. Although presumably beneficial to nonsmokers, such regulation of smoking behavior at the workplace may lead to controversy and to the disruption of informal social networks (Hackett, 1990b).

"I'LL HUFF-COUGH-AND I'LL PUFF-COUGH—AND I'LL BLOW YOUR-WHEEZE-HOUSE DOWN"

(© 1988 by Herblock in the Washington Post)

By 1990, Gallup poll data demonstrated increasing antismoking sentiment in the United States. About 30 percent of respondents supported a complete ban on smoking in restaurants (compared with 17 percent in 1987). The data showed that 25 percent of Americans favored a total prohibition of smoking in workplaces (compared with 17 percent in 1987), while another 69 percent believed companies should set aside designated smoking areas and only 5 percent opposed workplace restrictions on smoking. When asked if smokers should "refrain from smoking in the presence of nonsmokers," 77 percent of respondents agreed and only 18 percent disagreed (Gallup and Newport, 1990).

Antismoking activists have influenced public policy not only in the United States but also in other parts of the world. All countries in the European Economic Community (EEC) ban cigarette advertising on television. Smoking is restricted or forbidden on public

The tobacco industry hopes to offset the decline in cigarette consumption in the United States by increasing sales of American brands in other countries. Shown is a promotion effort in Tokyo for Winston Lights.

transportation in many of the Scandinavian nations. Even in Japan, where three out of five adult males smoke, there has been growing opposition to use of tobacco. For the first time, local governments have banned smoking in their offices (*The Economist,* 1986; Haberman, 1987).

There is little doubt that antismoking campaigns have had an effect on smoking behavior. According to the 1989 report of the U.S. surgeon general, nearly half of all living adults in the nation who ever smoked have quit. Whereas 40 percent of American adults smoked in 1965, by 1990 this figure had fallen to 29

percent. Consequently, the tobacco industry faces the problem of replacing the 2.5 million American smokers it loses each year, almost 435,000 of whom die of tobacco-related illnesses (Berke, 1989; Cotton, 1990b; DeParle, 1989:39).

In response, the tobacco industry has targeted its marketing efforts to racial and ethnic minorities, to women, and, of course, to young people, who are the potential addicted smokers of the future. In 1990, the R. J. Reynolds Tobacco Company canceled its plans to market Uptown, a cigarette aimed primarily at urban Blacks, after a strong denunciation by Secretary of Health and Human Services Louis Sullivan. Unsuccessful efforts were also made to launch Dakota, a new brand that would have aimed at blue-collar women. In devising these marketing strategies, the tobacco industry is well-aware that Blacks are more likely to smoke than Whites or Hispanics are, while young females begin smoking more often than young males and are less likely to quit. Targeting by tobacco firms also has class position in mind: by the year 2000, 30 percent of high school dropouts will smoke, as compared with only 5 percent of college graduates. Viewed from a conflict perspective, the more marginal one's status in society, the more likely one is to smoke cigarettes—and, therefore, to die of smoking-related illnesses (Cotton, 1990b; DeParle, 1988; Mabry, 1990; Woodman, 1990).

Just as antismoking activists and health experts are distressed by the targeting efforts of tobacco companies *within* the United States, so too do they oppose the targeting of Asian markets as a means of counteracting the decline in domestic sales of cigarettes. Already, some 2.5 million people around the world die each year from illnesses linked to smoking. Yet, since 1986, United States trade negotiators have successfully broken down import barriers in Japan, Taiwan, Thailand, and South Korea; as a result, the export of American cigarettes doubled over a 3-year period. These cigarettes are sent abroad without displaying the surgeon general's warning regarding the health hazards of smoking. In the view of Representative Chet Atkins of Massachusetts, this trade policy "is sending Asians a message that their lungs are somehow more expendable than American lungs" (Rudolph, 1989; Schmeisser, 1988:62; World Development Forum, 1989; see also Yu et al., 1990).

SUMMARY

The meanings of **health,** wellness, sickness, and disease are shaped by social definitions of behavior. This chapter considers sociological perspectives on health and illness, the distribution of diseases in a society, the evolution of the American health care system as a social institution, and mental illness in the United States.

1 A relativistic approach to healthy status allows us to view health in a social context and to consider how health varies in different situations or cultures.

2 According to Talcott Parsons, physicians function as "gatekeepers" for the *sick role,* either verifying a person's condition as "ill" or designating the person as "recovered."

3 Conflict theorists use the term *medicalization of society* to refer to medicine's growing role as a major institution of social control.

4 Interactionists emphasize that the patient should not always be viewed as a passive actor within the health care system.

5 Labeling theorists suggest that the designation of a person as "healthy" or "ill" generally involves social definition by significant others.

6 Contemporary *social epidemiology* is concerned not only with epidemics but also with nonepidemic diseases, injuries, drug addiction and alcoholism, suicide, and mental illness.

7 Studies have consistently shown that Americans in the lower classes have higher rates of mortality and disability.

8 The increasing costs of medical care are especially apparent in the event of catastrophic illnesses and nursing home confinement.

9 The preeminent role of physicians within the health care system has given them a position of dominance in their dealings with nurses and patients.

10 Conflict theorists argue that, in the United States, illness may be exploited for profit.

11 The DRG system of reimbursement has contributed to the controversial practice of "dumping," under which patients whose treatment may be unprofitable are transferred by private hospitals to public facilities.

12 The rise of profit-making hospital chains has troubled many public officials and health care experts.

13 American society has traditionally maintained a negative and suspicious view of those with mental disorders.

14 In recent years, there has been growing regulation of smoking by the federal government, by state and local governments, and within the private sector.

KEY TERMS

Culture-bound syndrome A disease or illness that cannot be understood apart from its specific social context. (page 510)

Health As defined by the World Health Organization, a state of complete physical, mental, and social well-being, and not merely the absence of disease and infirmity. (512)

Health maintenance organization (HMO) An organization that provides comprehensive medical services to patients for a preestablished fee. (529)

Holistic medicine A means of health maintenance which views the person as an integration of body, mind, and spirit, rather than as a collection of interrelated organ systems. (531)

Incidence The number of new cases of a specific disorder occurring within a given population during a stated period of time. (518)

Infant mortality rate The number of deaths of infants under 1 year of age per 1000 live births in a given year. (515)

Morbidity rates The incidence of diseases in a given population. (518)

Mortality rate The incidence of death in a given population. (518)

Prevalence The total number of cases of a specific disorder that exist at a given time. (518)

Sick role Societal expectations about the attitudes and behavior of a person viewed as being ill. (512)

Social epidemiology The study of the distribution of disease, impairment, and general health status across a population. (518)

ADDITIONAL READINGS

Cockerham, William C. *Medical Sociology* (4th ed.). Englewood Cliffs, N.J.: Prentice-Hall, 1989. A fine introduction to the sociology of medicine, focusing on both the providers and the recipients of health care.

Grusky, Oscar, and Melvin Pollner (eds.). *The Sociology of Mental Illness: Basic Studies.* New York: Holt, 1981. Along with classic pieces by Freud, Durkeim, and Parsons, the editors include contemporary coverage of the major sociological perspectives and of treatment settings for mental patients.

Hine, Darlene Clark. *Black Women in White: Racial Conflict and Cooperation in the Nursing Profession, 1890–1950*. Bloomington: Indiana University Press, 1990. A historical look at racism that led to the exclusion and ultimately the second-class status of Black women within nursing.

Konner, Melvin. *Becoming a Doctor: A Journey of Initiation in Medical School*. New York: Sifton/Viking, 1987. An anthropological account of the author's years as a student at Harvard Medical School which includes interesting comparisons with healers in other cultures.

Mizrahi, Terry. *Getting Rid of Patients*. New Brunswick, N.J.: Rutgers University Press, 1986. Based on a full year of participant observation at a southern hospital and follow-up interviews 6 years later, Mizrahi's study explores the contradictions in the socialization of physicians.

Payer, Lynn. *Medicine and Culture: Varieties of Treatment in the United States, England, West Germany, and France*. New York: Holt, 1988. A medical journalist examines the ways in which culture contributes to differences in medical care in four industrialized nations.

Salmon, J. Warren (ed.). *Alternative Medicines: Popular and Policy Perspectives*. New York: Tavistock, 1984. A collection of essays analyzing nonconventional forms of medical care, including holistic medicine, folk care, and psychic healing.

Schwartz, Howard D. (ed.). *Dominant Issues in Medical Sociology* (2d ed.). New York: Random House, 1987. A collection of articles which serves as an introduction to medical sociology by examining the clients, the practitioners, and the organizational structures.

Smolan, Rick, Phillip Moffit, and Matthew Naythons (eds.). *The Power to Heal: Ancient Arts and Modern Medicine*. Englewood Cliffs, N.J.: Prentice-Hall, 1990. An illustrated look at medicine as it is practiced throughout the world.

Starr, Paul. *The Social Transformation of American Medicine*. New York: Basic Books, 1982. Starr, a sociologist, traces the progression of health care from a household service to a market commodity and the rise of private medical practice.

Waitzkin, Howard. *The Second Sickness: Contradictions of Capitalist Health Care*. Chicago: University of Chicago Press, 1986. This indictment of medical care delivery in the United States offers interesting comparisons with health care in Cuba and the People's Republic of China.

Zola, Irving Kenneth. *Socio-Medical Inquiries*. Philadelphia: Temple University Press, 1983. A respected medical sociologist integrates his writings, often done from an interactionist perspective, with an autobiographical account of his own medical experiences.

Journals

Among the journals dealing with issues of health, illness, and health care are *Journal of Health and Social Behavior* (founded in 1965), *Milbank Memorial Quarterly* (1923), and *Social Science and Medicine* (1967).

PART FIVE

CHANGING SOCIETY

PART FIVE

CHANGING SOCIETY

Throughout this textbook, we have been reminded that sociologists are vitally concerned with changes in cultures, social institutions, and social behavior. **PART FIVE** will focus more directly on change as a characteristic aspect of human societies.

Chapter 18 describes changes in human communities, with particular emphasis on urban and metropolitan growth. The diversity of suburban and rural communities will also be demonstrated. Chapter 19 considers changing patterns of population growth and their social consequences in the United States and throughout the world. Chapter 20 offers sociological analysis of social change as reflected in collective behavior and social movements. Sources of change and resistance to change will be given special attention.

18

COMMUNITIES

All cities are mad, but the madness is gallant.
All cities are beautiful, but the beauty is grim.
Christopher Morley
"Where the Blue Begins," 1922

LOOKING AHEAD

- How do industrial cities differ from earlier forms of human communities?
- What theories have social scientists proposed to explain the process of urban growth?
- What effect does the size of a community have on people's feelings of identity and belonging?
- How do government subsidies to motorists and highways affect life in American cities?
- What factors have contributed to suburban expansion?
- To what extent are women and Blacks involved in farming in the United States?
- How has the profile of homeless Americans changed in the last decade?

There was widespread celebration in Indianapolis in 1984 when Robert Irsay, owner of football's Baltimore Colts, decided to move the franchise to the midwestern city. More than 20,000 fans appeared at the team's domed stadium at a public ceremony welcoming Irsay. "It's a wonderful thing for our community," noted Mayor William C. Hudnut in an interview. "It's a boost to the city's image nationally and to local morale as a symbol of major league status." Importantly, the arrival of the Colts provided more than an emotional uplift for Indianapolis. The city's new "major league status" is a key asset in its campaign to attract business firms considering relocation, groups of conventiongoers, and other tourists (Malcolm, 1984:22).

Not surprisingly, feelings about the Colts' move were quite different in Baltimore. One longtime fan bitterly noted: "They were a part of us. It's hard to put into words what the Colts meant here. I've got a real bad taste in my mouth for Mr. Irsay." In the late 1950s and 1960s, when the team was led by star quarterback Johnny Unitas and the franchise was at its peak, players often "hung out" at taverns and restaurants near the stadium. "You'd always see them around the neighborhood," remembers the owner of a grocery store in Baltimore's Little Italy district. "Sometimes after the game you'd see the whole team down here." Residents of this neighborhood were particularly distressed by the loss of their favorite athletes (Engelberg, 1984:22).

The impact of the Colts' move on both Indianapolis and Baltimore reminds us that community attachments—including attachments to local institutions such as universities, sports teams, and symphony orchestras—play an important role in people's lives. In sociological terms, a **community** is a spatial or territorial unit of social organization in which people have a sense of identity and a feeling of belonging (Dotson, 1991). Communities influence who our friends will be, since it is difficult to maintain more than a few friendships over long distances. Communities also have an impact on the types of occupations that people seek to enter. A member of an Israeli kibbutz (see Chapter 13), for example, may decide to study irrigation or some other aspect of farming in order to best serve the larger group. Perhaps most important, communities define social standards and exercise formal and informal social control. In 1973, the United States Supreme Court identified "community standards" as appropriate criteria for evaluating whether a book or film is pornographic and can be prohibited from sale.

Anthropologist George Murdock (1949:79) has observed that there are only two truly universal units of human social organization: the family and the community. This chapter will explore the importance of communities from a sociological perspective. It will begin by examining the successive development of early communities, preindustrial cities, and industrial cities. A number of theories used by social scientists to explain urban growth will be presented, including ecological perspectives and conflict theory. Then, the three basic types of communities found in the United States—central cities, suburbs, and rural areas—will be contrasted. Finally, in the social policy section, we will analyze the distressing phenomenon of homelessness in the United States.

HOW DID COMMUNITIES ORIGINATE?

Early Communities

For most of human history, people used *subsistence technology*—the tools, processes, and knowledge that a society requires to meet its basic needs for survival. Thus, the need for an adequate food supply was satisfied through hunting, foraging for fruits or vegetables, fishing, and herding. In comparison with later industrial societies, early civilizations were much more dependent on the physical environment and much less able to alter that environment to their advantage. As we saw in Chapter 15, the emergence of horticultural societies, in which people actually cultivated food rather than merely gathered fruits and vegetables, led to many dramatic changes in human social organization.

Significantly, people no longer had to move from place to place in search of food. In fact, group cultivation required that people remain in specific locations and thereby encouraged the development of more stable and enduring communities. Ultimately, as agricultural techniques became more sophisticated, a cooperative division of labor involving both family members and others developed.

Today, archeologists continue to locate the remains of ancient settlements built by simple horticultural societies. These settlements—actually the first human communities—apparently relied on mixed economies in which horticulture was supplemented with herding, hunting, and gathering. Gradually, it became possible for people to produce more food than they actually needed. Consequently, food could be given, perhaps as part of an exchange, to others who might be involved in nonagricultural labor. This transition from subsistence to surplus represented a critical step in the emergence of cities.

The term *social surplus* refers to the production by a group of people of enough goods to cover their own needs, while at the same time sustaining people who are not engaged in agricultural tasks. Initially, the social surplus of early communities was limited to agricultural products, but it gradually evolved to include all types of goods and services. Residents of a city came to rely on community members who provided crafts products and means of transportation, gathered information, and so forth (Lenski et al., 1991; F. Wilson, 1984:297–298).

With this social surplus came a more elaborate division of labor, as well as a greater opportunity for differential rewards and privileges. So long as everyone was engaged in the same tasks, stratification was limited to such factors as gender, age, and perhaps the ability to perform the task (a skillful hunter could win unusual respect from the community). However, the social surplus allowed for expansion of goods and services, which ironically can lead to greater differentiation, a hierarchy of occupations, and social inequality. Therefore, social surplus was a precondition not only for the establishment of cities but also for the division of members of a community into social classes (see Chapter 8). The emergence of social surplus marked a fundamental shift in human social organization.

Preindustrial Cities

It is difficult to trace the origin of cities. The only tangible evidence available is found in fragmentary archeological materials. Yet we may incor-

The factory system which developed during the industrial revolution led to a much more refined division of labor than had been evident in early preindustrial cities. Shown is a nineteenth-century lithograph of a typical factory town: Pella, Iowa. Workers' homes are shown in the background.

rectly place modern interpretations on ancient artifacts or assume that objects used in an urban settlement for one particular purpose were employed in a similar fashion in every community. In addition, the amount of completed research on the ancient cities of the middle east is much more extensive than, for example, research on the cities of India and China. Further studies of the latter two countries may lead us to modify current thinking concerning the beginnings of urban settlements.

It is estimated that, beginning about 10,000 B.C., permanent settlements free from dependence on crop cultivation emerged. Yet, by today's standards of population, these early communities would barely qualify as cities. The **preindustrial city,** as it is termed, had only a few thousand people living within its borders. These residents relied on perhaps 100,000 farmers and their own part-time farming to provide them with the needed agricultural surplus. The Mesopotamian city of Ur had a population of about 10,000 and was limited to roughly 220 acres of land, including the canals, the temple, and the harbor.

Why were these early cities so small and relatively few in number? Urbanization was restricted by a number of key factors:

1 *Reliance on animal power (both humans and beasts of burden) as a source of energy for economic production.* This limited the ability of humans to make use of and alter the physical environment.
2 *Modest levels of surplus produced by the agricultural sector.* Sociologist Kingsley Davis (1949) has estimated that between 50 and 90 farmers were required to support 1 city resident.
3 *Problems in transportation and storage of food and other goods.* Even an excellent crop could easily be lost as a result of such difficulties.
4 *Hardships of migration to the city.* For many peasants, migration was both physically and economically impossible. A few weeks of travel was out of the question without more sophisticated techniques of food storage.
5 *Dangers of city life.* Concentrating a society's population in a small area left a society open to attack from outsiders, as well as more susceptible to extreme damages from plagues and fires.

Gideon Sjoberg (1960:27–31) examined the available information on early urban settlements of medieval Europe, India, and China. He identified three preconditions of city life: advanced technology in both agricultural and nonagricultural areas (that is, the creation of a social surplus), a favorable physical environment, and a well-developed social organization.

For Sjoberg, the criteria for defining a "favorable" physical environment are variable. Proximity to coal and iron will be helpful only if a society has the technological expertise to use these natural resources. Similarly, proximity to a river will be particularly beneficial if a culture has the means to transport water efficiently to the fields for irrigation and to the cities for consumption.

A sophisticated social organization is also an essential precondition for urban existence. Specialized social roles emerge more fully in industrial societies than in earlier communities. These roles bring people together in new ways through the exchange of goods and services. A well-developed social organization ensures that these relationships are clearly defined and generally acceptable to all parties. This function becomes even more crucial as cities become larger and more industrialized.

Industrial Cities

Advances in agricultural technology led to dramatic changes in community life, but so did the process of industrialization. As was noted in Chapter 15, the *industrial revolution*, which began in the middle of the eighteenth century, focused on the application of nonanimal sources of power to labor tasks. Industrialization had a wide range of effects on people's lifestyles as well as on the structure of communities. Emerging urban settlements became centers not only of industry but also of banking, finance, and industrial management.

The factory system which developed during the industrial revolution led to a much more refined division of labor than was evident in early preindustrial cities. Many new occupations were created, and one by-product was a much more complex set of relationships among workers. Thus, the *industrial city* was not merely more populous than its preindustrial predecessors; it was also based on very different principles of social organization. Contrasts between preindustrial and industrial cities were outlined by Sjoberg (1960: 323–328) and are summarized in Table 18-1.

TABLE 18-1 Comparing Preindustrial and Industrial Cities

PREINDUSTRIAL CITIES	INDUSTRIAL CITIES
Closed class system—pervasive influence of social class at birth	Open class system—mobility based on achieved characteristics
Economic realm controlled by guilds and a few families	Relatively open competition
Beginnings of division of labor in creation of goods	Elaborate specialization in manufacturing of goods
Pervasive influence of religion on social norms	Influence of religion limited to certain areas as society becomes more secularized
Little standardization of prices, weights, and measures	Standardization enforced by custom and law
Population largely illiterate, communication by word of mouth	Emergence of communication through posters, bulletins, and newspapers
Schools limited to elites and designed to perpetuate their privileged status	Formal schooling open to the masses and viewed as a means of advancing the social order

SOURCE: Based on G. Sjoberg, 1960:323–328.

Industrial cities differed from their preindustrial forerunners in many important respects. They not only were larger but also had open class systems, relatively open competition, and elaborate specialization in the manufacturing of goods.

In comparison with industrial cities, preindustrial cities had relatively closed class systems and limited social mobility as well as a much more rigid division of labor by gender. Status in these early cities was based on ascribed characteristics such as family background. Education was limited to members of the elite. However, in industrial cities, formal education gradually became available to many children from poor and working-class families. There was a much greater opportunity for a talented or skilled individual to better his or her social position. In these and other respects, the industrial city is genuinely a "different world" from the preindustrial urban community.

SOCIOLOGICAL APPROACHES TO COMMUNITIES

Ecological Views of Urban Growth

Environmentalist Barry Commoner (1971:39) has stated that "everything is connected to everything else." This simple declaration is the basic principle of ecology, whether applied to the impact of pollution on the fishing industry or to the effects of a new expressway on the established neighborhoods of a city. **Human ecology** is concerned with the interrelationships among people in their spatial setting and physical environment.

Human ecologists have long been interested in

how the physical environment shapes people's lives (rivers can serve as a barrier to residential expansion) and also how people influence the surrounding environment (the advent of air conditioning has played a critical role in the growth of major metropolitan areas in the southwest). Beginning in the 1960s, the misuse of the natural environment became more evident as the result of well-publicized oil spills, radiation leaks, distribution of harmful chemicals in livestock feed, and the worsening problems of air and water pollution. Both scientists and the general public were frequently reminded in disturbing ways that "everything is connected to everything else."

Human ecology is concerned with the interrelationships between people and their environment; **urban ecology** focuses on such relationships as they emerge in urban areas. Early urban ecologists such as Robert Park (1916, 1936) and Ernest Burgess (1925) concentrated on city life but drew upon the approaches used by ecologists in studying plant and animal communities. More recently, the urban ecological perspective has been used to explain why cities in the northeast tend to have more concentrated population distribution than cities of the sun belt. Generally, social scientists have assumed that such differences reflect the *age* of cities; that is, the older cities of the northeast grew in such a manner as to bring about more spatially dense populations. However, sociologist Thomas Guterbock (1987) argues that climate and, specifically, snowfall may be a factor in urban population density.

Guterbock found a strong correlation between the average annual snowfall in over 100 metropolitan areas and these cities' population distribution. But why should snowfall have an impact on population density? Historically, road transportation (automobiles and trucks) has had an important influence on the concentration of population. Yet automobile and truck traffic is especially vulnerable to snowfall accumulation. Since clearing of snow is a costly and time-consuming process, commuters who travel to jobs in urban business centers will certainly be affected by frequent and heavy snowfalls. In terms of population distribution, residents of sun belt cities (where there is little or no measurable annual snowfall) may feel free to live much farther from business districts than residents of Buffalo, New York (which has an annual snowfall of 94 inches), do. Consequently, Guterbock suggests that urban areas adapt to heavy snowfall in part by maintaining greater population density.

Urban ecologists have offered a number of theories to explain the process of urban growth and the interconnection between parts of a city. Each successive theory has expanded on the previous one, as urban ecologists seek to explain a wider variety of settlement patterns. In studying these models of urban expansion, it is important to understand that Ernest Burgess and subsequent theorists were not interested simply in mapping where population groups and institutions were located; they also hoped to discover how the sociological experiences of city life were reflected in spatial relationships (F. Wilson, 1984).

Concentric-Zone Theory With few exceptions, urban ecologists trace their work back to the *concentric-zone theory* devised in the 1920s by Ernest Burgess. Using the city of Chicago as an example, Burgess offered a framework for describing land use in industrial cities. At the center, or nucleus, of such a city is the central business district. Large department stores, hotels, theaters, and financial institutions occupy this highly valued land. Surrounding this urban center are succeeding zones that contain other types of land use and that illustrate the growth of the urban area over time. As presented in Figure 18-1 (page 552), each zone represents a new area of development of the city.

Encircling the central business district is the "zone of transition," which has a temporary character, since its residences are in the immediate path of business and industrial expansion. Homes in this area are generally unpopular; most Americans do not wish to live next to a factory. The zone of transition is populated by those at the bottom of the nation's social hierarchies, including recent immigrants and the poor. When people living in this zone achieve upward mobility, they frequently move to the outer zones of residential housing (zones III, IV, and V in Figure 18-1).

It must be stressed that the creation of zones is a *social* process, not the result of nature alone. Families and business firms compete for the most valuable land; those with the most wealth and power are generally the winners. The concentric-zone theory proposed by Burgess also represented a dynamic model of urban growth. As growth proceeded, each zone would move even further from the central business district.

Sector Theory You may have noted that, in many cases, a city's earliest housing and commercial buildings are found along major railroad lines or roads. In addition, those areas developed last may be found farthest from established lines of transportation. Since the concentric-zone theory did not explicitly consider this phenomenon, Homer Hoyt (1939, 1964) attempted to modify Burgess's work. The focus of *sector theory,* as developed by Hoyt, is the importance of transportation lines in urban growth.

Hoyt examined the changes in "high-rent" districts in 142 American cities over a 36-year period. He found little evidence of circular zones as a consistent pattern. The residences of more affluent Americans were likely to be located on high ground or along rivers and lakes. Hoyt agreed with Burgess that cities tend to develop outward from a central business district and an adjoining zone of transition, but he saw such development occurring in more or less similarly shaped sectors (see Figure 18-2, page 553), rather than in concentric rings of growth. A sector was largely shaped by the presence of railroads, waterways, highways, and other avenues of transportation.

Multiple-Nuclei Theory By the middle of the twentieth century, urban populations had spilled beyond the traditional city limits. No longer could urban ecologists focus exclusively on *growth* in the central city, for large numbers of urban residents were abandoning the cities to live in suburban areas. For example, by 1960 many more people in metropolitan Boston, Philadelphia, Los Angeles, and Washington, D.C., were living outside the city limits than within the cities. This trend has gradually increased over the past 2 decades.

As a response to the emergence of more than one focal point in some metropolitan areas, C. D. Harris and Edward L. Ullman (1945) presented the *multiple-nuclei theory.* In their view, all urban growth does not radiate outward from a central business district. Instead, a metropolitan area may have many centers of development, each of

FIGURE 18-1 Burgess's Concentric-Zone Theory

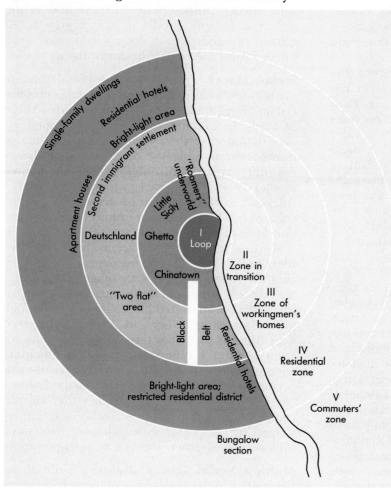

The concentric-zone hypothesis was developed by Ernest Burgess to describe housing and social characteristics of Chicago. However, the model proved to have wider applications.

SOURCE: E. Burgess, 1925:55.

which reflects a particular urban need or activity. Thus, a city may have a financial district, a manufacturing zone, a waterfront area, an entertainment center, and so forth. Certain types of business firms and housing will naturally cluster around each distinctive nucleus.

The rise of suburban shopping malls is a vivid example of the phenomenon of multiple nuclei within metropolitan areas. Initially, all major retailing in American cities was located in the central business district. Each residential neighborhood had its own grocers, bakers, and butchers, but people traveled to the center of the city to make major purchases at department stores.

However, as major metropolitan areas expanded and the suburbs became more populous, an increasing number of Americans began to shop nearer their homes. Today, the suburban mall is a significant retailing and social center for communities across the nation.

Although the three theories of urban growth presented thus far in this section focus on city life in the United States, urbanization is evident throughout the world (see Figure 18-3, page 554). In 1920, only 14 percent of the world's people lived in urban areas, but by 1990 the proportion had risen to 41 percent, and by the year 2025 it is expected to be as high as 62 percent. During the nineteenth and early twentieth centuries, rapid urbanization occurred primarily in European and North American cities; however, since World War II, there has been an urban "explosion" in the world's developing countries. The dramatic growth in urban populations has been fueled by natural increase (excess of births over deaths) and by migration. In Mexico, for example, migration accounts for one-fourth of the expansion of urban areas (Fox, 1987:32–33; Haub et al., 1990; Newland, 1980). Visually, this growth is obvious in the expansion of "squatter settlements" on the edges of Mexico City (see Box 18-1, page 556).

As part of the worldwide urban expansion, some metropolitan areas have spread so far that they have connected with other urban centers. Such a densely populated area, containing two or more cities and their suburbs, has become known as a **megalopolis.** An example is the 500-mile corridor stretching from Boston south to Washington, D.C., and including New York City, Philadelphia, and Baltimore, which accounts for one-sixth of the total population of the United States. Even when it is divided into autonomous political jurisdictions, the megalopolis can be viewed as a single economic entity. The megalopolis is not solely an American phenomenon; such areas are now seen in Great Britain, Germany, Italy, Egypt, India, Japan, and China.

FIGURE 18-2   Comparison of Ecological Theories of Urban Growth

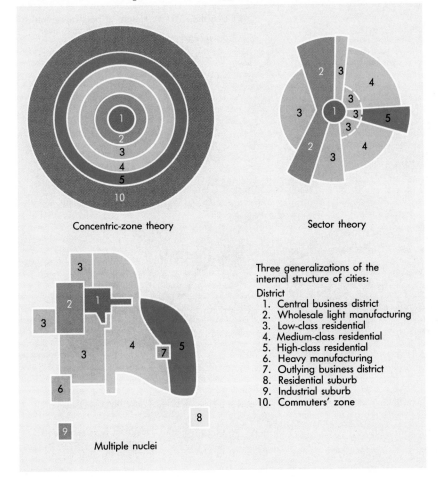

Concentric-zone theory

Sector theory

Three generalizations of the internal structure of cities:

District
1. Central business district
2. Wholesale light manufacturing
3. Low-class residential
4. Medium-class residential
5. High-class residential
6. Heavy manufacturing
7. Outlying business district
8. Residential suburb
9. Industrial suburb
10. Commuters' zone

Multiple nuclei

This figure illustrates similarities and differences among the three ecological theories of urban growth. Only the multiple-nuclei theory does not view growth as radiating from the center of the city.

SOURCE: Harris and Ullman, 1945:13.

FIGURE 18-3   Urban Population Worldwide

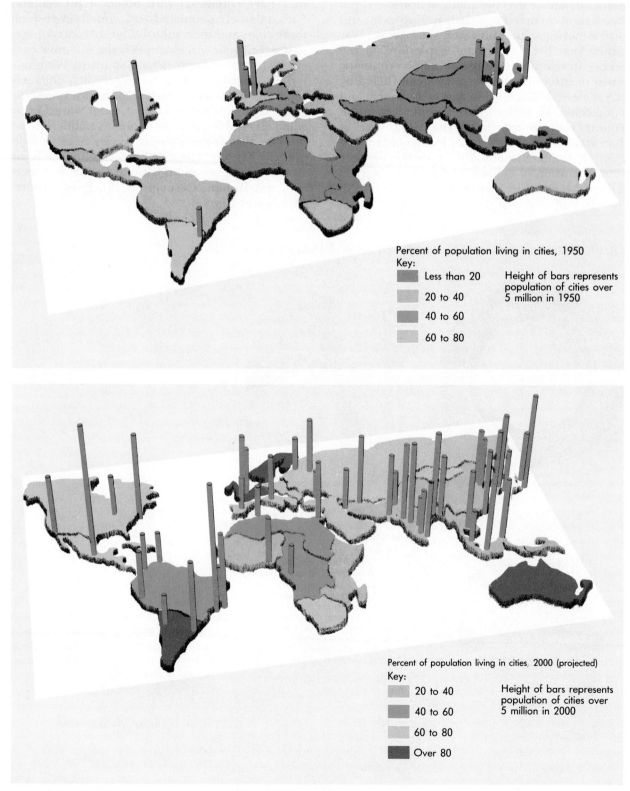

Percent of population living in cities, 1950
Key:

Less than 20   Height of bars represents
                    population of cities over
20 to 40   5 million in 1950

40 to 60

60 to 80

Percent of population living in cities, 2000 (projected)
Key:

20 to 40   Height of bars represents
                    population of cities over
40 to 60   5 million in 2000

60 to 80

Over 80

SOURCE: R. Fox, 1987:10–13.

The figure on the opposite page, based on computer graphics prepared by the Los Alamos Laboratory, shows the astonishing changes that are occurring in major metropolitan areas across the world. In 1950, only 10 cities had 5 million or more inhabitants. However, according to projections made by the United Nations, 48 cities will have 5 million or more people by the year 2000.

Suburban shopping malls like the one shown at the right typify the multiple-nuclei orientation of metropolitan areas. These malls are not limited to retailing but also serve as social, cultural, and recreational centers.

Conflict View of Urban Growth

While acknowledging the descriptive value of urban ecological models, conflict theorists insist that metropolitan growth is not governed by waterways and rail lines, as a purely ecological interpretation might suggest. From a conflict perspective, communities are human creations that reflect people's needs, choices, and decisions—but some people have more influence over these decisions than others.

Conflict theorists argue that ecological approaches typically avoid examining the social forces, largely economic in nature, that guide urban growth. For example, central business districts may be upgraded or abandoned depending on whether urban policymakers grant substantial tax exemptions to developers. The suburban boom was fueled by federal housing policies that channeled investment capital into the construction of single-family homes rather than to afford-able rental housing in the cities. Similarly, while some observers suggest that the growth of sun belt cities is due to a "good business climate," conflict theorists counter that this term is actually a euphemism for hefty government subsidies and antilabor policies (Gottdiener and Feagin, 1988; M. Smith, 1988:183).

Sociologist Joe Feagin has likened urban development to a game in which powerful elites play Monopoly with real money. Feagin (1983:2) notes that class conflict has always been part of the dynamics of urban life:

On the one side we have the progressive city councils and the urban grass-roots people's movements opposing unbridled growth and development. On the other side, we have the class of profit-oriented developers, bankers, landowners, and industrial executives who buy, sell, and develop land and buildings in cities just like they do with other for-profit commodities.

BOX 18-1 • AROUND THE WORLD

SQUATTER SETTLEMENTS

The terms vary depending on the nation and language: *barriadas, favelas, bustees, kampongs,* and *bidonvilles.* But the meaning is the same: "squatter settlements." The term **squatter settlements** refers to areas occupied by the very poor on the fringe of cities. Their housing, which is perhaps more accurately called "shelter," is constructed by the settlers themselves from discarded material, including crates from loading docks and loose lumber from completed building projects.

This type of settlement is not commonly found in the developed nations of North America and Europe but is very typical of cities in the world's developing nations. In such countries, new housing has not kept pace with the combined urban population growth resulting from births and migration from rural areas. In addition, squatter settlements are swelled by city dwellers forced out of housing by astronomical jumps in rent. By definition, squatters living on vacant land are trespassers and can be legally evicted. However, given the large number of poor people who live in such settlements (for example, about half of the 3 million inhabitants of Caracas, Venezuela), governments generally look the other way.

Obviously, squatters live in substandard housing, yet this is only one of the many problems they face. Residents do not receive

(Sebastiao Salgado/Magnum)

People who live in squatter settlements, such as these families in Mexico City, generally have substandard housing and receive few public services.

most public services, since their presence cannot be legally recognized. Thus, police and fire protection, paved streets, and sanitary sewers are virtually nonexistent. Despite such conditions, squatter settlements are not always as bleak as they may appear from the outside. Rather than disorganized collections of people, one often finds a well-developed social organization. A thriving "informal economy" (refer back to Box 9-2 on page 270) typically develops; residents establish small, home-based businesses such as grocery stores, jewelry shops, and the like. Rarely, however, can any but the most ambitious entrepreneurs climb out of poverty through success in this underground economy.

Local churches, men's clubs, and women's clubs are often established in specific neighborhoods within squatter settlements. In addition, areas of a settlement may form governing councils or membership associations. These governing bodies are subject to the usual problems of municipal governments, including charges of corruption and factional splits. Yet, in many cases, they seem to serve their constituents effectively. In Peru, squatters hold annual elections, whereas the rest of the nation has not held local elections for more than 70 years.

Squatter settlements remind us that respected theoretical models of American social science may not be directly applicable to other cultures. The various ecological models of urban growth, for example, would not explain metropolitan expansion that locates the poorest people on the urban fringes. Furthermore, solutions that are logical for a highly industrialized nation may not be relevant in the developing nations. Planners in developing nations, rather than focusing on large-scale solutions to urban problems, must think in terms of basic amenities, such as providing water taps or electrical power lines to the ever-expanding squatter settlements (Castells, 1983:173–212; Patton, 1988).

In the view of conflict theorists, developers, builders, and investment bankers are not especially interested in urban growth when it means providing housing for middle- or low-income Americans. This lack of interest contributes to the problem of homelessness, which will be discussed in the social policy section at the end of the chapter. These urban elites counter that the nation's housing shortage and the plight of the homeless are not their fault—and insist that they do not have the capital needed to construct and support such housing. But affluent Americans *are* interested in growth, and *can* somehow find capital, to build new shopping centers, office towers, and business parks.

Why, then, can't they provide capital for affordable housing, ask conflict theorists? Part of the answer is that developers, bankers, and other powerful real estate interests view housing in quite a different manner from tenants and most homeowners. For a tenant, an apartment is shelter, housing, a home. But for developers and investors—many of them large corporations—an apartment is simply a housing investment. These financiers and owners are primarily concerned with maximizing profit, not with solving social problems (Feagin, 1983:192).

Models of Community Attachment

What effect does the size of a community have on people's feelings of identity and belonging? Do residents of Phoenix feel as deep a sense of community as people who live in the much smaller locality of Tempe, Arizona? What is the impact of one's neighbors' moving in and out on feelings of community attachment?

Two models have been advanced by sociologists to assess the influence of the size of a community's population and its geographical mobility on social behavior: these are the linear-development model and the systemic model. Let's consider each of them in turn.

Linear-Development Model The linear-development model is illustrated by Ferdinand Tönnies's (1988, original edition 1887) use of the concepts of *Gemeinschaft* and *Gesellschaft*. As we saw in Chapter 5, *Gemeinschaft* describes close-knit communities where social interaction among people is intimate and familiar. By contrast, the ideal type of *Gesellschaft* describes modern urban life; there is little sense of commonality, and social relationships often grow out of immediate tasks, such as purchasing a product.

Tönnies and other sociologists contend that as a community grows in size, the nature of relationships between its members changes accordingly. This is termed the **linear-development model,** since a change in one variable (population size) is hypothesized to lead to a direct change in a second variable (feelings of community attachment). Furthermore, it is argued that population size is the primary factor affecting patterns of social behavior in a community. This is somewhat like saying that "people behave differently in cities because they live in cities."

Several decades after Tönnies's work, an American sociologist came to similar conclusions. Louis Wirth (1928), while a graduate student in sociology at the University of Chicago, researched and wrote about a Jewish area in that city. His study was later published as a book entitled *The Ghetto;* it focused attention on the unique lifestyle found among residents of urban areas. Wirth later expanded on this theme in his notable article "Urbanism as a Way of Life" (1938).

Like Tönnies, Wirth argued that a relatively large and permanent settlement leads to distinctive patterns of behavior, which he called **urbanism.** He identified three critical factors contributing to urbanism: the size of the population, population density, and the heterogeneity (variety) of the population. Each of these factors has particular implications for the nature of relations between people within an urban environment. Size prevents residents from getting to know most of the people in the community. It also facilitates spatial (or physical) segregation based on race, ethnicity, social class, and lifestyle ("singles" versus elderly couples).

A frequent result of urbanism, according to Wirth, is that we become insensitive to events around us and restrict our attention to primary groups to which we are emotionally attached.

(Whitney Museum of American Art, New York)

"The Subway" (1950), a painting by George Tooker. According to sociologist Georg Simmel, urban residents (such as these subway passengers) cannot have social relationships with all the people they encounter.

Thus, residents of large cities may walk past alcoholics passed out on the street without offering help.

As early as 1902, German sociologist Georg Simmel (1950:409–424) observed in a lecture that it is impossible to carry on a social relationship with each person one encounters in an urban area. If someone attempted this, he or she might "be completely atomized internally and come to an unimaginable psychic state."

Therefore, the size of an industrial city contributes to a certain distancing in personal relationships outside one's primary groups. On the other hand, there are advantages to living in highly populated areas. C. R. Creekmore (1985) suggests that, in certain respects, city life is healthier than life in rural areas. For example, cities have better medical care, water supplies, sewage systems, and emergency services. Moreover, the greater the number of individuals in a community, the greater the possible range of occupations, ideas, values, and lifestyles. In Wirth's (1938:15) words, the city can become a "mosaic of social worlds."

Systemic Model Some of Wirth's colleagues at the University of Chicago shared his interest in the effects of urbanization on behavior but came to somewhat different conclusions. William I. Thomas (1927), along with Robert Park and Ernest Burgess (1921, 1925), asked if a *Gemeinschaft* was ever truly characteristic of preindustrial societies. They proposed a ***systemic model*** of urbanism as resulting from a variety of factors, of which population size was only one. In their view, in order to understand urbanism fully it is essential to examine the entire social system, including people's interactions, their participation in social institutions, and the influence of societal norms and values. For example, if one is a recent arrival to a city—or if one's neighbors are constantly changing as people move into and out of the city—one's sense of community attachment and belonging will be reduced. The systemic model tends to emphasize geographic mobility, rather than community size, as a crucial determinant of community attachment. Family ties and friendships can overcome the anonymity of densely populated urban areas—but only if people have enough time to get acquainted and to maintain stable and supportive relationships.

The research of sociologists John Kasarda and Morris Janowitz (1974) offers support for the systemic model. Over 2000 adults in England were interviewed and asked if they felt "at home" in their communities, if they would be disappointed if they had to move away, and so forth. The researchers found that length of residence was a better predictor of community attachment than other factors were, including the size of a community's population. Subsequent study of 50 northern California communities by Claude Fischer (1982) also suggested that population size was not the central factor leading to feelings of alienation from friends and neighbors.

We can better understand the evidence for the systemic model if we use the analogy of the classroom. Generally, educators argue that smaller classes promote a more personal relationship among students and faculty—an academic *Gemeinschaft*, in a sense. But suppose that in a 25-member seminar, 4 or 5 new students join the class every week, while a similar number drop the course. It will be difficult to develop any sense of community attachment. On the other hand, if a larger class of 60 students remains together for 2 years, everyone (including the instructor) will get to know each other fairly well. Thus, length of contact, as well as size or density, can be a crucial determinant of social relationships.

The data developed by Kasarda and Janowitz as well as by Fischer appear to lend greater support to the systemic model than to the linear-development model. For both Tönnies and Wirth, large industrial cities are characterized by anonymity and impersonality. However, these researchers may have given insufficient emphasis to the effects of large-scale migration on community attachment within urban centers. Therefore, if we wish to identify key factors which affect urbanism, we need to add mobility to size, density, and heterogeneity of population (Tittle, 1989).

TYPES OF COMMUNITIES

The following sections will examine different types of communities found in the United States, focusing on the distinctive characteristics and problems of central cities, suburbs, and rural communities.

Central Cities

In terms of both land and population, the United States is the fourth-largest nation in the world. Yet three-quarters of the population is concentrated in a mere 1.5 percent of the nation's land area.

In 1988, some 189 million Americans—accounting for 77 percent of the nation's people—lived in metropolitan areas. Of these, about 40 percent lived in central cities, while the balance of metropolitan-area residents were found in the suburbs. Even those people who live outside central cities, such as residents of suburban and rural communities, find that their lifestyles are heavily influenced by urban America (Bureau of the Census, 1990a:27).

Who Are the Urban Americans? Many urban Americans are the descendants of European immigrants—Irish, Italians, Jews, Poles, and others—who came to the United States in the nineteenth and early twentieth centuries. The cities socialized these newcomers to the norms, values, and language of their new homeland and gave them an opportunity to work their way up the economic ladder. In addition, a substantial number of low-income Blacks and Whites came to the cities from rural areas in the period following World War II.

Even today, American cities are the destinations of immigrants from around the world—including Mexico, Ireland, Cuba, Vietnam, and Haiti—as well as migrants from the United States commonwealth of Puerto Rico (refer back to Chapter 10). Yet, unlike those who came to this country 75 or 100 years ago, current immigrants are arriving at a time of growing urban decay. This makes it more difficult for them to find employment and decent housing.

According to sociologist Herbert J. Gans, urban life is noteworthy for its diversity. One category of urban residents, whom Gans calls cosmopolites, *remain in the city to take advantage of its unique cultural and intellectual benefits.*

Urban life is noteworthy for its diversity; it would be a serious mistake to see all city residents as being alike. Sociologist Herbert J. Gans (1991:54–56) has distinguished between five types of people found in American cities:

1 *Cosmopolites.* Such residents remain in cities to take advantage of the unique cultural and intellectual benefits. Writers, artists, and scholars fall into this category.
2 *Unmarried and childless people.* Such people choose to live in cities because of the active nightlife and varied recreational opportunities.
3 *Ethnic villagers.* These Americans prefer to live in their own tight-knit communities. Typically, immigrant groups isolate themselves in such neighborhoods in order to avoid resentment from well-established urban dwellers.
4 *The deprived.* Very poor people and families have little choice but to live in low-rent, and often run-down, neighborhoods.

5 *The trapped.* Some city residents wish to leave urban centers but cannot because of their limited economic resources and prospects. Gans includes the "downward mobiles" in this category—people who once held higher social positions but who are forced to live in less prestigious neighborhoods owing to loss of a job, death of a wage earner, or old age. Both elderly individuals living alone and families may feel "trapped" in part because they resent changes in their communities. Their desire to live elsewhere may reflect their uneasiness with unfamiliar immigrant groups who have become their neighbors.

From the categories first devised by Gans in 1962, we are reminded that the city represents a choice (even a dream) for certain Americans and a nightmare for others. Gans's work underscores the importance of neighborhoods in contemporary urban life. Ernest Burgess, in his study of life in Chicago during the 1920s, had given special attention to the ethnic neighborhoods of that city (refer back to Figure 18-1). Many decades later, residents in such districts as Chinatowns or Greektowns continue to feel attached to their own ethnic communities rather than to the larger unit of a city. Even outside such ethnic enclaves, a special sense of belonging can take hold in a neighborhood.

In a more recent study of Chicago, Gerald Suttles (1972:21–43) coined the term **defended neighborhood** to refer to people's definitions of their community boundaries. Neighborhoods acquire unique identities because they are viewed by residents as geographically separate—and socially different—from adjacent areas. The defended neighborhood, in effect, becomes a sentimental union of similar people. Neighborhood phone directories, community newspapers, school and parish boundaries, and business advertisements all serve to define an area and distinguish it from nearby communities.

In some cases, a neighborhood must literally defend itself. Plans for urban renewal or a super-highway may threaten to destroy an area's unique character and sense of attachment. In resisting such changes, a neighborhood may employ the strategies and tactics of community organization developed by pioneering organizer Saul Alinsky (1909–1972). Like many conflict sociologists, Alinsky was concerned with the ways in which society's most powerful institutions act to maintain the privileges of certain groups (such as real estate developers), while helping to keep other groups (such as slum dwellers) in a subservient position. Alinsky (1946:29) emphasized the need for community residents to fight for power in their localities. In his view, it was "only through the achievement and constructive use of power" that people could better themselves (Horwitt, 1989).

Of course, the possibility exists that a defended neighborhood will acquire its distinctive identity by excluding those who are deemed different or threatening. In 1981 the Supreme Court upheld the right of the city of Memphis, Tennessee, to erect a barrier and close a street connecting an all-White and all-Black neighborhood. White residents requested the closure, claiming that there was too much "undesirable traffic" coming through their own community. In a dissenting opinion, Justice Thurgood Marshall, the first African American to serve on the Supreme Court, called the barrier a "badge of slavery."

In some cases, neighborhoods use more subtle methods to exclude those viewed as "outsiders." Sociologist Judith DeSena (1987) found that White, non-Hispanic residents of the Brooklyn neighborhood of Greenpoint sold or rented apartments and homes only by "word of mouth." Their goal was to keep vacant housing from falling into the hands of minority families. Although Suttles tends to stress that strategies of neighborhood defense are episodic, studies by DeSena and others indicate that such social networks aimed at maintaining housing segregation may be constantly active. Memphis and Greenpoint serve as a reminder that some communities unite to fight off developers and their bulldozers, but others come together to exclude racial and ethnic minorities.

Social Problems of Cities There can be great variance in the types of people and neighborhoods found in an American city. Yet all residents of a central city—regardless of their social class, racial, and ethnic differences—face certain common problems. Crime, air pollution, noise, unemployment, overcrowded schools, inadequate public transportation—these unpleasant realities and many more are an increasing feature of contemporary urban life. They are particularly evident in the nation's older cities, such as New York, Philadelphia, Boston, and Washington, D.C.

Perhaps the most dramatic reflection of the nation's urban ills has been the apparent "death" of entire neighborhoods. In some of America's urban districts, business activity seems virtually nonexistent. One can walk for blocks and find little more than a devastating array of deteriorating, boarded up, abandoned, and burned-out buildings. Observers have gone so far as to compare such neighborhoods to parts of European cities which suffered intense aerial bombing during World War II. Such urban devastation has contributed to the growing problem of homelessness, which will be discussed in the social policy section at the end of the chapter.

Another critical problem for the cities has been mass transportation. Since 1950, the number of cars in the United States has multiplied twice as fast as the number of people. As a result, there has been growing traffic congestion in metropolitan areas, and many cities have recognized a need for safe, efficient, and inexpensive mass transit systems. However, the federal government has traditionally given much more assistance to highway programs than to public transportation (see Box 18-2 on page 562). Proponents of the conflict perspective note that such a bias favors the relatively affluent (automobile owners) as well as corporations such as auto manufacturers, tire makers, and oil companies. Meanwhile, poor residents of metropolitan areas, who are much less likely to own cars than the middle and upper classes, face higher fares on public transit along with deteriorating service.

This disproportionate funding of highways began to be modified only in the 1970s, as Congress passed a number of laws designed to aid the nation's urban mass transportation efforts. Yet federal funding for mass transit has fallen to less than half the 1960 level of spending. Consequently, few new transit systems have been built in the last 2 decades. Some, such as those in Portland and Baltimore, have enjoyed success; others,

BOX 18-2 • SPEAKING OUT

MOTORISTS AS WELFARE RECIPIENTS

Does our government grant undue subsidies to motorists and highways which contribute to the destruction of cities and threaten the long-term well-being of the nation? New York City journalist Daniel Lazare (1990:39–41) argues that such subsidies have had disastrous consequences and have led to our dangerous overdependence on oil:

. . . Americans drive, pollute, and guzzle gasoline as if there were no tomorrow (and thanks to the greenhouse effect there may not be) for the same reason that American corporate farmers fill government silos with excess grain—because the government pays them to. Although most people think of subsidies in terms of public transit, subsidies for private transport in the form of roads, traffic cops, and pollution costs borne by society as a whole, are far larger. By some estimates, the tab comes to an astronomical $400 billion a year, or a subsidy of about $4 per gallon of gas. . . .

The effect of such subsidies on the federal budget, on industrial planning, on the way we live our

Daniel Lazare.

lives, is nearly indescribable. They're the single most important reason why middle-class Americans live in sprawling, auto-dependent suburbs while poor people are condemned to crumbling inner cities; why Americans walk less than Europeans, bike less, and hang out in malls instead of downtown shopping districts; and why mass transit in this country is the worst in the developed

world. . . . And last but not least, they're the chief reason why U.S. troops are currently stationed in and around the Persian Gulf. . . .

The first step toward understanding America's screwed-up auto economics is the problem of quantification, i.e., how much it costs to drive and who pays. The logical place to begin is the $57.5

---

such as Miami's Metrorail, have failed to attract the expected ridership. In fact, the Miami system has been sarcastically labeled "Metrofail" by its critics (Work et al., 1987).

Money—or, more accurately, lack of money—is at the heart of many of our nation's urban problems. It clearly limits each city's ability to rebuild burned-out neighborhoods, to provide housing for homeless individuals and families, and to improve mass transit facilities. Moreover, in the

1970s and early 1980s, certain American cities came near to financial default, while others were forced to close their school systems before the end of the academic year because they could not afford to meet their payrolls. During 1979, Cleveland became the first major city to default since the Depression.

The conventional explanation for the fiscal (in other words, financial) crises of New York and other cities was excessive municipal services. Ad-

BOX 18-2 • SPEAKING OUT

MOTORISTS AS WELFARE RECIPIENTS (Continued)

billion that federal, state, and local governments shelled out for highway construction, maintenance, and related expenses as recently as 1985 versus the $35.6 billion in gas taxes, tolls, and other "user fees" they took in. The difference—$22 billion—works out to . . . about 20 cents per gallon of gasoline. This is money drivers *should* be paying . . . but are not.

But highway expenditures represent only part of the cost of highway maintenance. The other part is the cost of deferred maintenance . . . , which, if addressed immediately, would add another $46 to $53 billion to the nation's annual highway tab, according to conservative estimates. Since the public will undoubtedly be called on one day to make up the difference, the result adds another 40 to 50 cents per gallon to the effective auto subsidy. . . . Finally, there are the various ancillary services needed to make a highway system work—cops, courts, fire and ambulance crews to respond to highway emergencies, and such. . . .

In the early '80s, [Stanley] Hart, [a retired engineer turned graduate student in economics] decided to try to figure out the value of all the highways and mandated parking spaces that society provides motorists nearly for free. . . . He calculated that an average car uses eight parking spaces—one at home, one on the job, and others . . . along the way. . . . Hart also calculated that a typical car needs a roughly equivalent amount of road space, resulting in a grand total of about 4000 square feet of asphalt, or a tenth of an acre, per vehicle. Figuring an average urban land rent of $20,000 an acre . . . , this meant that the average motorist gets $2000 in essentially free rent a year.

Two thousand dollars per vehicle equals approximately $3.30 per gallon. Adding in the cost of highway services and other items brings the total subsidy to more than $4 per gallon. . . . Nationwide, the subsidy comes to around $400 billion a year, or about 8 percent of gross national product, an economic burden that by global standards is unique. America, Stanley Hart discovered, is driving itself to the poorhouse. . . .

Although a typical American motorist . . . regards himself as king of the road and master of the universe, he's, in fact, none of these things, but rather a kind of rolling welfare recipient. Although public outlays for the poor draw all the heat, when tax subsidies such as the income-tax mortgage deduction and other public outlays are taken into account, it's clear that public assistance for the middle class is actually much larger. . . .

In combination with racism and class oppression, American-style auto subsidies have proved more effective as agents of long-term urban destruction than the Luftwaffe, the RAF, or the Enola Gay. Not only a cause, they are a reflection of American capitalism's deep fear of cities and the radical ideas and turbulent political forces they give rise to. . . .

vocates of this view noted that in an era of urban decline, the cities simply could not afford substantial public subsidies for city colleges, municipal hospitals, welfare programs, the arts, and so forth. However, conflict sociologists have rightly questioned this explanation. French urbanologist Manuel Castells (1976, 1977:415–420) argued that New York's "bankruptcy" resulted from the failure of big business to pay additional taxes which would support needed services.

Suburbs

There are various definitions of suburban areas. The term *suburb* derives from the Latin *sub urbe*, meaning "under the city." Until recent times, most suburbs were just that—tiny communities totally dependent on urban centers for jobs, recreation, and even water.

Today, the **suburb** defies any simple definition. The term generally refers to any community near a large city—or, as the Census Bureau would say, any territory within a metropolitan area that is not included in the central city. By that definition, more than 100 million people, or about 45 percent of the American population, lived in the suburbs in 1984. However, as we will see, suburbs often have little in common, apart from their classification as "suburban." For example, the city of Yonkers, New York, borders on parts of New York City. As of 1988, Yonkers had a population of 183,000 and was the eighty-sixth-largest city in the nation. Yet many consider Yonkers to be a suburb of New York City (Bureau of the Census, 1990a:36).

It can also be difficult to distinguish between suburbs and rural areas. Certain criteria are generally used to define suburbs: most people work at urban (as opposed to rural) jobs, and local governments provide services such as water supply, sewage disposal, and fire protection. In rural areas, such services are less common, and a greater proportion of residents are employed in farming and related activities (Gist and Fava, 1974:310–311).

Suburban Expansion Whatever the precise definition of a suburb, it is clear that suburbs have expanded. In fact, suburbanization has been the most dramatic population trend in the United States throughout the twentieth century. Suburban areas grew at first along railroad lines, then at the termini of streetcar tracks, and by the 1950s along the nation's growing systems of freeways and expressways. The suburban boom has been especially evident in the period since World War II.

The suburbs have not simply expanded in size; they have also become more affluent. Data from the 1980 census reveal a widening economic disparity between the nation's central cities and suburbs. In 1970, the median household income in American cities was 80 percent that of the suburbs. However, by 1980 that figure had dropped to 74 percent. Even the city of Dallas—with its sun belt growth—showed a median income of only 76 percent of that of its suburbs. One key point of contrast involves blue-collar job opportunities. Although the number of these jobs declined by 5 percent in the cities from 1970 to 1980,

there was a 20 percent increase in the suburbs during this same period (Herbers, 1983:1, 14).

Suburbanization—or metropolitanization, as the process has also been called—is not necessarily prompted by expansion of transportation services to the fringe of a city. The 1923 earthquake that devastated Tokyo encouraged decentralization of the city. Until the 1970s, dwellings were limited to a height of 102 feet. Initially, the poor were relegated to areas outside municipal boundaries in their search for housing. Many chose to live in squatter-type settlements (refer back to Box 18-1). With the advent of a rail network and rising land costs in the central city, middle-class Japanese began moving to the suburbs after World War II (P. Hall, 1977:225–226).

In the United States, people moved to the suburbs for a variety of reasons. Sociologist Peter Rossi (1955) divided these causes for moving to suburbia into what he called "push" and "pull" factors. People were pushed toward the suburbs by the difficulties associated with life in central cities: crime, pollution, overcrowding, and the like. At the same time, they were pulled toward suburbia by a desire to live in smaller communities, to own their own homes and gardens, to find better schools for their children, or simply to enjoy the status linked to life in an affluent suburb.

In recent decades, large corporations and other businesses are increasingly being pushed away from the cities and pulled toward suburbia. In 1980, less than half of all office construction in the United States was in the suburbs; by 1985, the figure had risen to about two-thirds of all construction. As a result, many suburbs—filled with new skyscrapers, office parks, and high tech industries—have evolved into "outer cities" that rival traditional big-city downtown areas as economic centers. This new development in suburban expansion provides additional support for the multiple-nuclei theory of urban growth (Dentzer, 1986:61; W. Stevens, 1987c).

Diversity in the Suburbs Race and ethnicity remain the most important factors distinguishing American cities from suburbs. After studying 44 central cities and 128 suburbs, Patricia Gober and Michelle Behr (1982) concluded that the size of

(Rob Nelson/Picture Group)

In contrast to prevailing stereotypes, the suburbs include a surprising number of Blacks and Hispanics.

the minority population—more than other variables such as age of population or social class—was the critical distinguishing factor between these two types of communities. Nevertheless, the common assumption that suburbia includes only prosperous White Americans is far from correct.

Between 1977 and 1987, the nation's African American suburban population rose from 4.6 million to 7.1 million, an increase of about 55 percent. Yet the most significant growth in the percentage of suburban Blacks has come from movement into suburbs that are predominantly Black or are adjacent to predominantly Black areas. In many instances, these suburbs are isolated from surrounding White communities and have less satisfactory housing and municipal services (Bureau of the Census, 1979:171; W. Dunn, 1987; Stahura, 1987).

Again in contrast to prevailing stereotypes, the suburbs include a surprising number of low-income Americans from White, Black, and Hispanic backgrounds. In 1982, one out of four people below the poverty line lived in the suburbs; they represented almost 8 percent of all suburban residents. Poverty is not conventionally associated with the suburbs, partly because the suburban poor tend to be scattered amongst more affluent people. As a result, suburban antipoverty agen-

cies may find it difficult to identify and assist prospective clients (P. Berger, 1972; Blumenthal, 1972; Bureau of the Census, 1983a:476).

Surprisingly, the suburbs have also become home to many immigrants from foreign countries. Traditionally, immigrants entering the United States have become entrenched in central-city neighborhoods, many of which have taken on the distinctive culture and ethnic flavor of the newcomers. However, according to population surveys conducted by the Census Bureau between 1975 and 1985, almost half the 4.7 million Asian, Hispanic, and Black immigrants who moved to the United States during that period chose to settle in suburban and nonmetropolitan areas rather than in central cities. Many of these immigrants—especially those from affluent, professional backgrounds—have settled in largely White neighborhoods. For example, Angela and Stephen Yang, a Taiwanese couple with two young sons, live in a suburb of San Antonio that has relatively few Asian immigrants. The Yangs have three prospering stores in the area which sell Asian furniture and jewelry (Herbers, 1986).

Regarding age distribution, the suburbs are "graying" like the rest of the United States (see Chapter 12). For example, Levittown, Long Island— named for its developer, Bill Levitt—had only a three-room country schoolhouse in 1947. The community experienced dramatic growth in the decades after World War II; by 1972, Levittown Memorial High School alone had a senior class of 400 students. Yet, by the early 1980s, the school's graduating class had decreased to 200, and Levittown was attempting to identify locations for indoor pools and community centers that would cater to the growing proportion of elderly residents (Barron, 1983).

Suburban settlements have become so diverse that even the collective term *suburbs* gives undue support to the stereotype of suburban uniformity. Pollster Louis Harris has divided suburbs into four distinct categories based on income level and rate of growth. Higher-income suburbs are categorized as either *affluent bedroom* or *affluent settled*. *Affluent bedroom communities* rank at the highest levels in terms of income, proportion of people employed in professional and managerial occupations, and percentage of homeowners. *Affluent settled communities* tend to be older, and perhaps even declining in population. They are more likely to house business firms and do not serve mainly as a place of residence for commuters.

Harris has recognized that certain suburban areas are composed of individuals and families with low or moderate incomes. *Low-income growing communities* serve as the home of upwardly mobile blue-collar workers who have moved from the central cities. *Low-income stagnant communities* are among the oldest suburbs and are experiencing the full range of social problems characteristic of the central cities. As is true of Gans's model of city residents, Harris emphasizes the diversity found within the general category of *suburbia* (*Time*, 1971).

Clearly, not all suburban residents appreciate the diversity of the suburbs—especially if it means that less affluent families, or members of racial and ethnic minorities, will be moving into their communities. When the Ford Motor Company moved from Richmond, California, to Milpitas, California, the union attempted to build housing for the firm's employees—many of whom were Black. The local government of Milpitas promptly rezoned the area for industrial use (Larson and Nikkel, 1979:235–236).

Zoning laws, in theory, are enacted to ensure that certain standards of housing construction are satisfied. These laws can also separate industrial and commercial enterprises from residential areas. Thus, a suburb might wish to prevent a factory from moving to a quiet residential neighborhood. However, some zoning laws have served as thinly veiled efforts to keep low-income people out of a suburb and have been attacked as "snob statutes." By requiring that a person own a certain number of square feet of land before he or she can build a home—or by prohibiting prefabricated or modular housing—a community can effectively prevent the construction of any homes that lower-class families might be able to afford. The courts have generally let such exclusionary zoning laws stand, even when charges have been made that their enactment was designed to keep out racial minorities (see also Meyer, 1987).

According to a study by researchers at the University of Chicago's Population Research Center, Blacks are more likely than other minority groups to face residential segregation in the suburbs. The study compared suburban settlement patterns for Blacks, Hispanics, and Asians in 59 cities in the United States. Asians were most likely to be accepted in traditionally White suburbs. Hispanics were likely to be accepted if they were perceived as White, but were likely to experience discrimination if they were perceived as Black. The director of the Population Research Center, Douglas S. Massey, concludes that "strong penalties" for being Black were evident in the Center's findings (Hays, 1988:A16; Massey and Denton, 1989b).

Rural Communities

Unlike many peoples of the world, Americans live mainly in urban areas. But, even in the United States, one-fourth of the population lives in towns of 2500 people or less which are not adjacent to a city. As is true of the suburbs, it would be a mistake to view rural communities as fitting into one set image. Turkey farms, coal mining towns, cattle ranches, and gas stations along interstate highways are all part of rural America.

Census data indicate that parts of the country outside metropolitan areas (including suburbs) grew at a rate 62 percent faster than that of metropolitan areas during the 1970s. This was the first time—apart from a brief period during the Depression—that rural areas surpassed urban America in growth. In a 3-year survey of the attitudes of Pennsylvania residents regarding migration, Gordon DeJong (1980) found that people leaving the cities for rural communities were more likely to be married, to have children, to be in white-collar occupations, and to have higher incomes than those moving from rural to urban areas.

DeJong asked people which qualities of their new surroundings were most important in their decisions to migrate. Those who were moving from cities to rural areas frequently mentioned a "healthy environment" and "safety on the streets." By contrast, people who were moving from rural communities to the cities cited job-related factors. On the basis of this study, it appears that the urban resident who moves to the country faces a trade-off. He or she may benefit from a more pleasant home and environment but will have to accept poorer-quality services and more limited job opportunities.

Currently, rural areas are being populated not only by urban residents seeking a change of lifestyle but also by people who want to return to their roots. Geographer Stephen E. White (1983) has pointed out that since 1970 there has been a substantial in-migration to Appalachian Kentucky—reversing the long and historic trend of out-migration. According to White's research, this in-migration has little to do with a revitalized coal economy. Instead, it primarily consists of return migrants who are moving to the most isolated areas of Appalachia. An important factor in this in-migration is the influence of the extended family, which encourages former residents to leave the economic hard times of central cities and return to the "old homestead."

Americans have traditionally maintained a rather idyllic image of life in rural communities. When asked about their living preferences for a 1989 Gallup poll, 56 percent of Americans indicated that they would prefer to live in a small town or a rural farming area. By contrast, only 24 percent chose a suburb, and only 19 percent favored a city—despite the fact that four out of five respondents lived in metropolitan areas (D. Johnson, 1990).

This idyllic image of rural life tends to mask serious problems. In small towns, for example, many retail and service stores are closing—among them, badly needed auto repair outlets. Public services such as fire protection, road maintenance, hospital and medical services, and waste facilities are often inadequate. One study reported that 60 percent of midwestern towns have no public water systems. Although homelessness is not so serious a problem as in central cities, substandard housing conditions are all too common in rural America (J. Reid, 1984).

The recent difficulties of American farmers have been well documented in the mass media (see Box 18-3 on page 568). Although the federal government spends some $8 billion annually to subsidize farm prices, bankruptcies and foreclosures have increased in farming areas across the United States. In 1988, one out of every four farm residents were below the government's poverty line, compared with one out of six nonfarm residents. By the mid-1980s, almost 400,000 people in the United States were leaving farms each year (O'Hare, 1988).

The postindustrial revolution (refer back to Chapter 15) has been far from kind to the rural communities of the United States. Despite the images portrayed in the media, agriculture accounts for only 9 percent of employment in nonurban counties. Yet mining and logging—the two nonagricultural staples of the rural economy—have been in decline along with farming. At the same time, the manufacturing base of such areas has been slow to participate in the growth of high technology industries.

Consequently, with rural economies faltering and poverty on the rise, internal migration data in the 1980s showed a shift away from rural America toward metropolitan areas. Whereas in 1975 rural communities had experienced a net gain of 1.6 million people, in 1988 rural areas suffered a net loss of 150,000 people to metropolitan areas. This decline reduced the number of farmers in the United States below the 5 million mark—the first time this had been true since 1820, when the United States had only 9.6 million inhabitants (Bureau of the Census, 1990g).

One consequence of this rural decline is that policymakers have been confronted with a most

BOX 18-3 • CURRENT RESEARCH

WOMEN, BLACKS, AND FARMING

The problems of Blacks and women—two groups that have traditionally been subordinated in the United States (refer back to Chapters 10 and 11)—have received considerable public attention in recent decades. The apparently unrelated farm crises of the 1980s reminded city dwellers of the vital role that agriculture plays in our economy and our day-to-day lives. Yet rarely are these concerns linked. In contrast to the historic stereotype of the farmer as a White male, African Americans and women continue to play a significant role in agriculture.

Farming women are almost always married and generally have large families. Segregation by gender is typical of farm labor; men are more likely to be engaged in field work, while women serve as their farms' accountants, personnel and equipment managers, and purchasing agents. Increasingly, however, women have had to supplement family incomes by taking on non-farm work (generally jobs in low-skill and low-wage occupations). These duties on and off the farm—coupled with household and child care responsibilities—have taken their toll during the difficult financial times facing farm families. Many studies have documented the high degree of stress experienced by farming women as they attempt to fulfill many demanding roles (Hennon and Marotz-Baden, 1987; Keating

(Alan Carey/The Image Works)

Segregation by gender is typical of farm labor; women often serve as their farms' accountants, personnel and equipment managers, and purchasing agents.

and Munro, 1988; Lofflin, 1988).

Women actively participate in farming across the United States. They are found on large and small farms, in profitable and failing family businesses. By contrast, 90 percent of Black farmers work in the south. Their farms tend to be small—only an average of about 100 acres compared with the national average of 4400 acres. While less than one-fifth of farmers in the United States are age 65 or over, the same is true of almost one-third of Black farmers.

Most Black farmers do not earn enough farm income to support their families; as a result, they must seek other types of jobs as well. However, the average age of these farmers—along with their

health difficulties and lack of training—tends to limit the work they can do and the places where they can hope to find employment. Moreover, Black farmers are concentrated in areas of the country with severe economic difficulties. These areas offer limited job opportunities and supportive services for *any* residents—and even more severely limited opportunities and services for aging African American women and men who work on family farms (Banks, 1987; Hoppe and Bluestone, 1987).

unpleasant responsibility: deciding which ailing towns and counties will be supported with funds for economic development and which will, in effect, be allowed to die. New schools, bridges, and roads can help to save a declining area, but state governments are not in a position to support every area in need. At present, there are no precise data on how many small towns across the United States vanish each decade. Still, Mark Drabensott, an executive with the Federal Reserve Bank in Kansas City, predicts: "There are going to be some rural communities that prosper at the expense of dying neighbors, and I fully expect the trend to continue" (Lapping et al., 1989; Wilkerson, 1990:A16).

SOCIAL POLICIES AND COMMUNITIES
HOMELESSNESS

- Is it correct to assert that the vast majority of homeless Americans are isolated individuals with no sense of community?
- In what ways has gentrification exacerbated the problem of homelessness?
- Are the American people concerned about or indifferent to the plight of the homeless?

John Dore was interviewed in 1986 by sociologist Peter Rossi (1989:5–6) as he huddled over a steam grate in Washington, D.C. Although 45 years old, he appeared to be in his sixties. He was dirty, wore soiled and ragged clothing, and had difficulty answering Rossi's questions. Dore had worked as a warehouse laborer for the General Services Administration (GSA) but lost his job in 1970. Now an alcoholic, he had been homeless in the District of Columbia for more than 4 years at the time of his interview. Dore receives a dollar or two a day from panhandling, his only source of income. Apart from an occasional stay in a detoxification center, he lives on the streets, generally on the steam grate where Rossi found him.

John Dore is but one of many Americans who live on city or suburban streets, in abandoned buildings, in subway stations and train yards, in public parks, or in shelters. According to a 1989 report by the Ford Foundation (1989:19), estimates of the nation's homeless population range from as low as 300,000 to as high as 3 million. Although these estimates of homelessness are widely contested, researchers agree that only 110,000 homeless people across the nation can be sheltered on any given night. Consequently, at a minimum, hundreds of thousands of Americans are homeless and without shelter. With such data in mind, a report to the National Governors Association concluded that "homelessness in the United States has quietly taken on crisis proportions" (Cuomo, 1983:18).

There has been a significant change in the profile of homelessness during the last decade. In the past, homeless Americans were primarily older White males living as alcoholics in skid row areas. However, today's homeless are comparatively younger—with an average age in the low thirties. Overall, an estimated 44 percent of the homeless are from racial and ethnic minority groups (Ford Foundation, 1989:20; R. Rosenthal, 1987; see also Burt and Cohen, 1989).

Although the mass media present the homeless primarily as mentally ill, a study of homeless people in Austin, Texas, concluded that the "linkage between homelessness and mental illness has been overstated." In contrast to the stereotype of homeless people as isolated individuals, recent research suggests that a growing proportion of homeless Americans are *families* without homes (often a woman and her children). Three reports on the homeless—by the U.S. General Accounting Office, the House Committee on Government Operations, and the U.S. Conference of Mayors—estimate that 21 to 27 percent of the homeless are family members (Ford Foundation, 1989:20; Snow et al., 1986:421).

Do homeless people feel any sense of community or neighborhood? Sociologist Barrett Lee (1987) surveyed the homeless in Nashville, Tennessee, and found that most exhibit some type of informal, locally based attachment. Nashville's homeless population was far from transient; their average length of residence in that city was 10 years. Lee found that a siz-

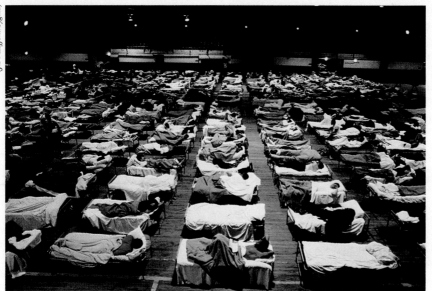

(J.P. Laffont/Sygma)

Policymakers have often been content to steer homeless people toward large, overcrowded, unhealthy shelters.

able portion of homeless people benefit from informal social networks; about one-third stated that they had no trouble finding people to "count on." Nevertheless, although Lee's sample apparently had greater community ties than media stereotypes might suggest, their situation remained far from rosy. Most of the homeless people surveyed perceived themselves as in trouble or in need of assistance.

Studies of homelessness point to a wide variety of causes of this condition, among them unemployment, cutbacks in public assistance, deinstitutionalization of the mentally ill (refer back to Chapter 17), and the decline in affordable housing in metropolitan areas. By the late 1980s, it had become clear that the nation's low-income renters and homeowners were being increasingly priced out of the housing market. Studies show that half of the poorest households (those with incomes below $3000) were paying more than 72 percent of their incomes for rent, leaving them with an average of only $71 per month for all other daily needs. Yet the federal budget for housing had fallen from $30 billion in 1980 to less than $8 billion in 1988. With such data in mind, the National League of Cities issued a 1987 study arguing for a more substantial and effective federal housing program (Kerr, 1986; McBride, 1987; Morganthau, 1988:18).

In recent years, the process of urban renewal has included a noticeable boom in *gentrification* or *neighborhood revitalization.* These terms refer to the resettlement of low-income city neighborhoods by prosperous families and business firms. Conflict theorists note that although the affluent may derive both financial and emotional benefits from gentrification, the impact on the poor is all too familiar. Studies of gentrification in eight cities indicate that about 30 percent of all rental properties typically become owner-occupied, thus narrowing the available housing for those who cannot afford to buy apartments (DeGiovanni, 1984:80).

There has been intense criticism of certain efforts to facilitate the process of gentrification through local legislation. New York City's J-51 tax abatement program, which underwrote conversion of 80 percent of the city's low-rent, single-room occupancy units to upper-income housing, is a prime example. Between 1970 and 1984, partly through the impact of the J-51 program, the city lost 108,500 of its 127,000 single-occupancy rooms. This massive conversion of low-income housing unquestionably contributed to the dramatic increase in homelessness in New York. Opponents of the J-51 program insisted that the city government was granting lucrative tax breaks to developers serving the housing needs of the wealthy, while the poor were being thrown out into the street. Responding to such arguments, the New York State Legislature and the New York City Council took action in 1984 to modify the J-51 program and reduce governmental tax support for such conversions (Bellamy, 1984).

There is an undeniable connection between the nation's growing shortage of affordable housing and the rise in homelessness (Elliott and Krivo, 1991). Yet Peter Rossi (1989, 1990) cautions that it would be incorrect to focus too narrowly on lack of shelter while ignoring the decline in the demand for manual labor in cities, the increasing prevalence of chronically unemployed young men among the homeless, and other structural factors. If these social factors are taken into account, policymakers will need to address the issue of homelessness not only by supporting the creation of more low- and moderate-income housing but also by considering such politically unpopular steps as income maintenance and job- and skills-training programs.

Thus far, however, policymakers have often been content to steer the homeless toward large, overcrowded, unhealthy shelters. Although the federal Emergency Assistance for Families (EAF) program has provided some aid, the 1989 Ford Foundation (1989:20) study of homelessness concluded that the federal role in addressing this serious social problem "remains small." In late 1990, perhaps with such criticisms in mind, Congress passed the McKinney Homeless Assistance Act, which authorizes federal aid for emergency food, shelter, health, mental health care, job training, and education for homeless children and adults (Zuckman, 1990).

Survey data suggest that the American public favors strong action to address the needs of the homeless. A 1990 analysis of both national and local polling data found nearly 60 percent of respondents willing to pay higher taxes to support programs that would attack the root causes of homelessness. This finding runs counter to people's typically negative feeling about taxes and stands in sharp contrast to the public's harsh view of welfare recipients and the poor (Raymond, 1990).

Advocates for the homeless are haunted by the possibility that this moment of public concern may be lost. "I'm worried that if we don't move within the next year or so, we might get used to it," noted Robert Hayes, counsel to the New York–based Coalition for the Homeless. "We'll become the new Calcutta" (Oreskes and Toner, 1989:E5).

SUMMARY

A *community* is a spatial or territorial unit of social organization in which people have a sense of identity and a feeling of belonging. This chapter examines the three basic types of communities that are found in the United States: central cities, suburbs, and rural areas.

1 Anthropologist George Murdock has observed that there are only two truly universal units of human social organization: the family and the community.

2 The single most significant precondition for the emergence of a relatively large and stable community was the creation of a *social surplus* of agricultural production.

3 Gideon Sjoberg identified three preconditions of city life: advanced technology in both agricultural and nonagricultural areas, a favorable physical environment, and a well-developed social organization.

4 An *industrial city* is based on very different principles of social organization than a *preindustrial city* is.

5 Whereas ecological theories of urban growth focus on the impact of waterways, railroads, and the like on settlement patterns, conflict theorists emphasize that urban elites exert significant control over the process of growth.

6 Many urban Americans are recent immigrants from other nations or are the descendants of earlier immigrants.

7 In the last 2 decades, American cities have confronted an overwhelming array of economic and social problems, including the possibility of financial default.

8 Suburbanization has been the most dramatic population trend in the United States throughout the twentieth century.

9 The nation's rural economy is growing more diverse; new industrial, service, and mining jobs are being created in areas previously restricted to farming.

10 In contrast to the stereotype of homeless people as isolated individuals, recent research suggests that a growing proportion of homeless Americans are *families* without homes.

KEY TERMS

Community A spatial or territorial unit of social organization in which people have a sense of identity and a feeling of belonging. (page 546)

Concentric-zone theory A theory of urban growth devised by Ernest Burgess which sees growth in terms of a series of rings radiating from the central business district. (551)

Defended neighborhood Suttles's formulation that area residents identify their neighborhood through defined community borders and through a perception that adjacent areas are geographically separate and socially different. (560)

Gentrification The resettlement of low-income city neighborhoods by prosperous families and business firms. (570)

Human ecology An area of study concerned with the interrelationships among people in their spatial setting and physical environment. (550)

Industrial city A city characterized by relatively large size, open competition, an open class system, and elaborate specialization in the manufacturing of goods. (549)

Industrial revolution A scientific revolution, largely occurring in England between 1760 and 1830, which focused on the application of nonanimal sources of power to labor tasks. (549)

Linear-development model A view of community attachment which points to population size as the primary factor influencing patterns of behavior in a community. (557)

Megalopolis A densely populated area containing two or more cities and their surrounding suburbs. (553)

Multiple-nuclei theory A theory of urban growth developed by Harris and Ullman, which views growth as emerging from many centers of development, each of which may reflect a particular urban need or activity. (551)

Neighborhood revitalization Another term for *gentrification*. (570)

Preindustrial city A city with only a few thousand people living within its borders and characterized by a relatively closed class system and limited mobility. (548)

Sector theory A theory of urban growth developed by Homer Hoyt which focuses on the importance of transportation lines in urban growth. (551)

Social surplus The production by a group of people of enough goods to cover their own needs, while at the same time sustaining people who are not engaged in agricultural tasks. (547)

Squatter settlements Areas occupied by the very poor on the fringes of cities, in which housing is often constructed by the settlers themselves from discarded material. (556)

Subsistence technology The tools, processes, and knowledge that a society requires to meet its basic needs for survival. (547)

Suburb According to the Census Bureau, any territory within a metropolitan area that is not included in the central city. (563)

Systemic model A model of community attachment proposed by Thomas, Park, and Burgess which emphasizes geographical mobility, rather than population size, as a crucial factor in influencing patterns of behavior. (558)

Urban ecology An area of study which focuses on the interrelationships between people and their environment as they emerge in urban areas. (550)

Urbanism A term used by Wirth to describe distinctive patterns of social behavior evident among city residents. (557)

Zoning laws Legal provisions stipulating land use and architectural design of housing and often employed as a means of keeping racial minorities and low-income people out of suburban areas. (566)

ADDITIONAL READINGS

Banfield, Edward C. *The Unheavenly City Revisited.* Boston: Little, Brown, 1974. A critical look at traditional liberal solutions to urban problems such as poverty, crime, and unemployment. For a collection of reactions to the first edition of this book, see the March 1971 issue of *Trans-action.*

Castells, Manuel, *The Urban Question: A Marxist Approach.* Cambridge, Mass.: M.I.T. Press, 1977. A comprehensive view of urban problems from a conflict perspective.

Frey, William H. *Metropolitan America: Beyond the Transition.* Washington, D.C.: Population Reference Bureau, 1990. This concise (52-page) work looks at recent changes in metropolitan areas, including minority population, suburban growth, income distribution, and age of residents.

Glazer, Nathan, and Mark Lilla (eds.). *The Public Face of Architecture: Civic Culture and Public Spaces.* New York: Free Press, 1987. This collection, drawn from a variety of academic disciplines, shows how buildings can shape social life and are, in turn, affected by governmental action.

Hall, Peter. *Great Planning Disasters*. London: Weidenfeld and Nicolson, 1980. This book deals with billion-dollar planning decisions which were later abandoned or widely criticized as disastrous mistakes.

Jackson, Kenneth T. *Crabgrass Frontier: The Suburbanization of the United States*. New York: Oxford University Press, 1986. A historian describes the development of outlying areas from the eighteenth century to the present.

Maldonado, Lionel, and Joan Moore (eds.). *Urban Ethnicity in the United States*. Beverly Hills, Calif.: Sage, 1985. An examination of the changing immigration patterns of the United States and their impact on urban America.

Rossi, Peter H. *Down and Out in America: The Origins of Homelessness*. Chicago: University of Chicago Press, 1989. Rossi analyzes the problems faced both by homeless Americans and by "precariously domiciled" people who are vulnerable to becoming homeless.

Rousseau, Ann Marie. *Shopping Bag Ladies: Homeless Women Speak about Their Lives*. New York: Pilgrim, 1981. Rousseau spent extensive time on city streets observing, photographing, and interviewing homeless women. Her gripping book includes more than 100 photographs, first-person accounts by "bag ladies," and a preface by novelist Alix Kates Shulman.

Suttles, Gerald D. *The Social Order of the Slum*. Chicago: University of Chicago Press, 1968. A major study of a ghetto district in Chicago occupied mainly by Blacks, Italians, Puerto Ricans, and Mexican Americans.

Waterfield, Larry W. *Conflict and Crisis in Rural America*. New York: Praeger, 1986. A journalistic account of the challenges facing rural areas of the United States.

Journals

Among the journals focusing on community issues are the *Journal of Urban Affairs* (founded in 1979), *Rural Sociology* (1936), *Urban Affairs Quarterly* (1965), *Urban Anthropology* (1972), and *Urban Studies* (1964).

19

POPULATION

> *Rich nations have developed an economic system that depends on consuming humanity's stored inheritance, but which provides very unequal access to it, a system that has encouraged humanity to reach an astonishing level of overpopulation.*
>
> Paul Ehrlich and Ann Ehrlich
> The Population Explosion, *1990*

LOOKING AHEAD

- Why is it important to study population issues?
- Why did Karl Marx disagree with Thomas Robert Malthus's view that rising world population was the cause of social ills?
- Is there any danger in the fact that new reproductive technologies open the way for parents to predetermine the gender of their children?
- How does the concept of demographic transition help us to understand world population history?
- If the United States maintains stable population growth, what will be the social implications for our society?
- How does population affect the quality of life?
- Why do critics question the enthusiasm of the United States and other industrial nations for population control in the developing world?

In 1977 the Population Reference Bureau proclaimed the "discovery" of a minicontinent in the Pacific Ocean about the size of California. Since then, the Bureau has used this imaginary land mass, which it named "Populandia," to illustrate the growth of world population. We are to imagine that from January 1, 1978, onward, all the world's natural increase—that is, all people born above the number needed to replace those who die—has been transplanted to Populandia.

According to the Bureau, a jumbo jet arrives at Populandia International Airport every 2 minutes carrying at least 280 more children. By the end of the first day (January 1, 1978), there were already 200,677 people in Populandia—about as many as currently live in Mobile, Alabama. By the beginning of 1991, after only 13 years of "existence," the population of the island was over 1 billion. This made Populandia the world's second-largest nation, and more populous than either the United States or the Soviet Union (Roudi, 1991).

World population growth—as symbolized by the striking growth of Populandia—vitally concerns anyone confronting the social problems of the 1990s. In addition to its size, the composition and distribution of the American population have an important influence on many of the policy issues discussed in this book. For example, the clustering of Americans in metropolitan areas has intensified the nation's housing problems (see Chapter 18). The steep rise in the proportion of citizens over 75 years of age has placed a severe strain on social services available for the elderly (see Chapter 12).

Many natural and social scientists are involved in the study of population-related issues. The biologist explores the nature of reproduction and casts light on factors that affect *fertility* (the amount of reproduction among women of childbearing age). The medical pathologist examines and analyzes trends in the causes of death. Geographers, historians, and psychologists also have distinctive contributions to make to our understanding of population (Wrong, 1977:6). Sociologists, more than these other researchers, focus on the *social* factors that influence population rates and trends.

In their study of population issues, sociologists are keenly aware that various elements of population—such as fertility, *mortality* (the amount of death), and migration—are profoundly affected by the norms, values, and social patterns of a society. Fertility is influenced by people's age of entry into sexual unions and by their use of contraception—both of which, in turn, reflect the social and religious values that guide a particular culture. Mortality is shaped by a nation's level of nutrition, acceptance of immunization, and provisions for sanitation, as well as its general commitment to health care and health education. Migration from one country to another can depend on marital and kinship ties, the relative degree of racial and religious tolerance in various societies, and people's evaluations of employment opportunities (Heer, 1975).

This chapter will consider certain aspects of population as studied by sociologists. It will begin by examining the controversial analysis of population trends presented by Thomas Robert Malthus and the critical response of Karl Marx. The special terminology used in population research will be detailed, and a brief overview of world population history will be offered. Particular attention will be given to the current problem of overpopulation and to the prospects for and potential social consequences of stable population growth in the United States. The impact of population-related factors on the quality of life—and on such social and economic problems as poverty, food shortages, and depletion of natural resources—will be discussed. Finally, the social policy section will consider the United States' policy regarding world population control.

DEMOGRAPHY:
THE STUDY OF POPULATION

Demography is the scientific study of population. It draws upon several components of population, including size, composition, and territorial distribution, in order to understand the social consequences of population. Demographers study geo-

graphical variations and historical trends in their effort to develop population forecasts. In addition, they analyze the structure of a population in terms of such factors as the age, gender, race, and ethnicity of its members.

One of the earliest demographers was Edmond Halley (1656–1742), an English astronomer who became well known through his association with the comet visible most recently during 1985–1986. Halley applied his mathematical skills to outlining the mortality records of the German town of Breslau and eventually developed a table showing death rates by age. Although Halley's statistical techniques have been questioned by later scholars, his analysis does represent the first simulation of the lifetime mortality experiences of a population. Halley was the first scientist to use death statistics in different age groups to determine a person's likelihood of death as he or she passed through each age group (*Population Today*, 1986).

Despite such early contributions, demography has emerged as a science only in the last 200 years. Demographer Judah Matras (1973:10–11) has shown that the scientific study of population could not begin until there were sophisticated systems for reporting vital events (births, deaths, marriages, and divorces) for purposes of taxation and governmental administration. Such systematic compilation of data was first begun on a large scale in nineteenth-century Europe. Moreover, the science of demography required theorists who would offer generalizations concerning the relationship between population factors and social change. A key figure in undertaking this type of analysis was Thomas Malthus.

Malthus's Thesis and Marx's Response

The Reverend Thomas Robert Malthus (1766–1834) was educated at Cambridge University and spent his life teaching history and political economy. His written work contains strong criticisms of two major institutions of his time—the church and slavery—yet, the most significant legacy of Malthus for contemporary scholars is his still-controversial work *Essays on the Principle of Population,* first published in 1798.

Essentially, Malthus suggested that the world's

population was growing more rapidly than the available food supply. Malthus argued that the food supply increases in an arithmetic progression (1, 2, 3, 4, and so on), whereas the population expands by a geometric progression (1, 2, 4, 8, and so on). According to his analysis, the gap between the food supply and the population will continue to grow over time. Even though the food supply will increase, it will not increase nearly enough to meet the needs of an expanding world population.

Malthus saw population control as an answer to the gap between rising population and food supply, yet he explicitly denounced artificial means of birth control because they were not sanctioned by religion. For Malthus, the appropriate way to control population was to postpone marriage. He argued that couples must take responsibility for the number of children they choose to bear; without such restraint, the world would face widespread hunger, poverty, and misery (Malthus et al., 1960, original edition 1824; Petersen, 1979:192–194; Rashid, 1987).

Karl Marx strongly criticized Malthus's views on population. Marx saw the nature of economic relations in Europe's industrial societies as the central problem. He could not accept the Malthusian notion that rising world population, rather than capitalism, was the cause of social ills. In Marx's opinion, there was no special relationship between world population figures and the supply of resources (including food). If society were well-ordered, increases in population should lead to greater wealth, not to hunger and misery.

Of course, Marx did not believe that capitalism operated under these ideal conditions. He maintained that capitalism devoted its resources to the financing of buildings and tools rather than to more equitable distribution of food, housing, and other necessities of life. Marx's work is important to the study of population because he linked overpopulation to the distribution of resources—a topic that will be taken up again later in this chapter. His concern with the writings of Malthus also testifies to the importance of population in political and economic affairs (Hawley, 1950; Meek, 1954; Petersen, 1975:165, 1979:74–77).

The insights of Malthus and Marx regarding population issues have come together in what is termed the *neo-Malthusian* view. Best exemplified by the work of Paul Ehrlich (1968), author of *The Population Bomb,* neo-Malthusians agree with Malthus that world population growth is outstretching natural resources. However, in contrast to the British theorist, they insist that birth control measures are needed to regulate population increases. Neo-Malthusians have a Marxist flavor in their condemnation of developed nations which, despite their low birthrates, consume a disproportionately large share of world resources. While rather pessimistic about the future, these theorists stress that birth control and sensible use of resources are essential responses to rising world population (Tierney, 1990; Weeks, 1989).

Studying Population Today

The relative balance of births and deaths is no less important in the 1990s than it was during the lifetime of Malthus and Marx. The suffering that Malthus spoke of is certainly a reality for many people of the world who are hungry and poor. Malnutrition remains the largest contributing factor to illness and death among children in the developing countries. Almost 15 percent of these children will die before age 5—a rate nearly 14 times higher than in developed nations. Furthermore, warfare and large-scale migration have exacerbated the relationship between population and food supply. In order to combat world hunger, it may be necessary to reduce human births, to dramatically increase the world's food supply, or perhaps to do both at the same time. With this in mind, it seems essential to study population-related issues (World Bank, 1990:240–241).

In the United States and most other countries, the census is the primary mechanism for collecting population information. A *census* is an enumeration or counting of a population. The American Constitution requires that a census be held every 10 years in order to determine congressional representation. This periodic investigation is supplemented by *vital statistics;* these records of births, deaths, marriages, and divorces are gathered through a registration system maintained by government units. In addition, other governmental surveys provide up-to-date information on commercial developments, educational trends, industrial expansion, agricultural practices, and the status of such groups as children, the elderly, racial minorities, and single parents.

In administering a nationwide census and conducting other types of research, demographers employ many of the skills and techniques described in Chapter 2, including questionnaires, interviews, and sampling. Yet, despite its statistical sophistication and reliance on computer analysis, demography is not an exact science. As noted earlier, the processes of birth, death, and migration are each influenced by social factors, among them attitudes toward fertility and acceptance of new medical technology. Researchers are able to advance generalizations about such aspects of human behavior, but they cannot offer definitive forecasts.

The precision of population projections is contingent on the accuracy of a series of estimates that demographers must make. First, they must determine past population trends and establish a base population as of the date for which the forecast began. Next, birth- and death rates must be established, along with estimates of future fluctuations. In making projections for a nation's population trends, demographers must consider migration as well, since a significant number of individuals may enter and leave the country (D. Bogue, 1979:876–877).

Because of the difficulties of estimating future births, deaths, and migration, demographers usually specify a range of projections—from "high" through "medium" to "low." These statistical forecasts are useful to a wide range of concerned parties, including planners, public administrators, economists, and commercial interests.

Elements of Demography

Demographers employ the distinctive terminology of their science in analyzing and projecting population trends. Population facts are communicated with a language derived from the basic elements of human life—birth and death. The **birthrate** (or, more specifically, the *crude birthrate*) is the number of live births per 1000 population in a given year. In 1990, for example, there were 16 live births per 1000 Americans. The birthrate provides information on the actual reproductive

In the United States and most other countries, the census is the primary mechanism for collecting information about the population.

patterns of a society. By contrast, the biological potential of individual women for reproduction in a society is known as **fecundity.** It is very unusual for women—and unknown for any society as a whole—to come even close to this potential.

The concept of fecundity calls our attention to the powerful growth potential in human populations. However, millions of couples around the world cannot conceive as many children as they would like to. Demographers use the term **subfecundity** to refer to a limited or diminished ability to reproduce. Subfecundity may affect one or both members of a couple and may be a temporary or chronic condition. Like many population-related problems, subfecundity is more prevalent in the developing nations than in the developed nations of the world. Disease and malnutrition, two of the primary causes of diminished ability to conceive, are more common in the developing countries.

Even in the world's more developed nations, a significant number of couples are subfecund. The National Center for Health Statistics estimates that 8 percent of American couples are involun-

BOX 19-1 • CURRENT RESEARCH

PRESELECTING A CHILD'S GENDER

N ew advances in reproductive technology have been welcomed because they offer hope to couples having difficulty conceiving and bearing children. However, concern has been raised about the impact of these technologies in light of many couples' desire for male versus female children.

Amniocentesis already allows doctors to learn the gender of a fetus. By utilizing ultrasound "photography" and then abortions, a fertile couple can presumably select a child of the gender they desire. Moreover, in 1987 Japanese newspapers reported that a team of medical researchers had developed a method of sorting sperm cells according to the chromosomes that determine gender. At least one clinic has used this procedure to assist couples who want a child of one gender or the other.

In light of the traditional preference in many cultures for male children, this new medical option could possibly contribute to a further devaluation of females. Japanese philosopher Hisatake Kato, an expert on medical ethics, worries that allowing Japanese couples to select the gender of their children would lead to a predominance of boys, traditionally favored because of the cultural value placed on carrying on the family name. Currently, Japanese physicians refuse to tell prospective parents the gender of a fetus after amniocentesis; they fear that the parents will decide on abortion if the fetus is female. This

(Mousson/Gamma Liaison)

Louise Brown, born in 1978 in England and shown here as a preschooler, was the first child conceived outside her mother's body, in a laboratory. Her birth aroused fears about "test tube babies." Such new reproductive techniques offer hope to millions of subfecund couples but have also raised troubling ethical questions.

issue is also a sensitive one in the United States, where numerous gender preference studies document a preference—especially among fathers—for male children.

In 1988, the western Indian state of Maharashtra, of which Bombay is the capital, passed legislation prohibiting any prenatal testing to determine the gender of a fetus. It had become common in Maharashtra for obstetricians to perform amniocentesis on pregnant women; in many instances, abortions would follow if the fetus was found to be female. Economic pressures contributed to this pattern, especially the increasing size of dowries demanded by families of prospective husbands. While the new law applies only to

Maharashtra, which includes about 10 percent of India's population, some of the nation's cabinet ministers have endorsed a nationwide ban on "prenatal sex-determination tests."

The issue of gender preference is but one aspect of the potentially troubling implications of the new reproductive technologies. Echoing the sentiments of many feminists, Australian educator Robyn Rowland argues that these technologies will reinforce the oppression of women. Some observers suggest that women will be coveted because of their smaller numbers, but Rowland (1985:543) counters that a woman "will be valued for sexual and breeding purposes rather than for her intrinsic worth as a person." Viewed from a conflict perspective, any renewed focus on women's role as potential mothers could signal a return to traditional gender roles and gender stratification (refer back to Chapter 11).

With such concerns in mind, many feminists are cautious, if not suspicious, in assessing reproductive advances developed by a male-dominated medical establishment. Roberta Steinbacher (1981:89) suggests that in evaluating each alleged advance, we should ask: "Who invented it, who manufactures it, who licensed it, who dispenses it? But who dies from it?"

SOURCES: Chira, 1986; R. Collins, 1988:398–399; Dixon and Levy, 1985; Rowland, 1985; Steinbacher, 1981; S. Weisman, 1988.

tarily childless, and the World Health Organization estimates that 10 percent have fewer children than they want. Recent advances in reproductive technology offer hope for couples suffering from subfecundity; yet, as is discussed in Box 19-1, certain scientific advances have provoked controversy. For example, our ability to learn the gender of a fetus has raised fears in light of the traditional preference of many cultures for male babies (McFalls, 1982; Mosher and Pratt, 1990).

One way demography can project future growth in a society is to make use of the *total fertility rate (TFR)*. The TFR is the average number of children born alive to any woman, assuming that she conforms to current fertility rates. The TFR reported for the United States in 1990 was 2.0 births, as compared with over 7.0 births per woman in such developing countries as Uganda, Iraq, and Bangladesh.

Mortality, like fertility, is measured in several different ways. The *death rate* (also known as the *crude death rate*) is the number of deaths per 1000 population in a given year. In 1990 the United States had a death rate of 9.0 per 1000 population. The *infant mortality rate* is the number of deaths of infants under 1 year of age per 1000 live births in a given year. This particular measure serves as an important indicator of a society's level of health care; it reflects prenatal nutrition, delivery procedures, and infant screening measures. The infant mortality rate also functions as a useful indicator of future population growth, since additional infants who survive to adulthood will contribute to further population increases (Chandrasekhar, 1975).

There is a wide disparity among nations in the rate of death of newborn children. In 1990 the infant mortality rate for the United States was 9.7 deaths per 1000 live births, whereas for the world as a whole it was an estimated 73.0 per 1000 live births. At least 21 nations have lower rates of infant mortality than the United States, including Great Britain, Canada, and Sweden (refer back to Figure 17-1 on page 515). In 1990, Japan's infant mortality rate was only 4.8 deaths per 1000 live births—slightly less than half the rate of infant deaths in the United States (Haub et al., 1990).

Another set of health-related measures are *morbidity rates,* which measure the incidence of diseases in a given population. Sociologists are interested in morbidity rates because they reflect the standard of living and availability of medical technology in a society. The fact that morbidity rates are higher among lower-income segments of the American population, as pointed out in Chapter 8, suggests an uneven distribution of medical resources which favors those most able to pay for high-quality health care. In addition, as noted in Chapter 17, less affluent Americans tend to be employed in jobs that leave them more susceptible to occupational hazards.

A general measure of health used by demographers is *life expectancy,* which is the average number of years a person can be expected to live under current mortality conditions. Usually the figure is reported as life expectancy *at birth.* At present, Japan reports a life expectancy at birth of 79 years and Iceland reports 78 years, both slightly higher than the United States' figure of 75 years. By contrast, life expectancy at birth is less than 45 years in many developing nations, including Gambia and Sierra Leone.

The *growth rate* of a society is the difference between births and deaths, plus the difference between *immigrants* (those who enter a country to establish permanent residence) and *emigrants* (those who leave a country permanently) per 1000 population. For the world as a whole, the growth rate is simply the difference between births and deaths per 1000 population, since worldwide immigration and emigration must of necessity be equal. In 1990, the United States had a growth rate of 1.0 percent, compared with an estimated 1.7 percent for the entire world (Bureau of the Census, 1990a:7; Haub et al., 1990).

WORLD POPULATION HISTORY

One important aspect of demographic work involves study of the history of population. However, this is made more difficult by the lack of reliable information for all but the modern era. For example, official national cenuses were relatively rare before 1850. Researchers interested in early population therefore turn to archeological remains of settlements, burial sites, baptismal and tax records, and oral history sources.

TABLE 19-1 For World Population, Estimated Time for Each Successive Increase of 1 Billion People

POPULATION LEVEL	TIME TAKEN TO REACH NEW POPULATION LEVEL	YEAR ATTAINED
First billion	2 to 5 million years	About A.D. 1800
Second billion	Approximately 130 years	1930
Third billion	30 years	1960
Fourth billion	15 years	1975
Fifth billion	12 years	1987
Sixth billion (projected)	11 years	1998

SOURCES: Gupte, 1982; Population Reference Bureau, reported in van der Tak et al., 1979:4.

We think of the world as having a large population—some 5.3 billion in 1990. Yet until modern times, there were relatively few humans living on this planet. One estimate placed the world population of a million years ago at only 125,000 people. As Table 19-1 indicates, the population has exploded in the last 200 years and continues to accelerate rapidly. Merely in the time it has taken you to read this far in this one paragraph, the world population has increased by 97 people!

Patterns of Births and Deaths

The phenomenal growth of world population in recent times can be accounted for by changing patterns of births and deaths. On the basis of historical data from European countries, it appears that preindustrial populations (before 1750) were characterized by both high death rates and high birthrates. Since the world growth rate is the difference between births and deaths, the increase in population was limited. This gradual increase is illustrated in Figure 19-1.

Beginning in the late 1700s—and continuing until the middle 1900s—there was a gradual reduction in death rates in northern and western Europe. People were able to live longer because of advances in food production, sanitation, nutrition, and public health care. While death rates fell, birthrates remained high; as a result, there was unprecedented population growth during this period of European history. However, by the late 1800s, the birthrates of many European countries began to decline, and the rate of population growth also decreased (Matras, 1977:38–44; McKeown, 1976).

During the twentieth century, the world population has expanded at a much faster rate than in earlier periods of history. Whereas it took roughly 130 years to reach the second billion in world population, it took only 30 years to reach the third billion and 12 years to reach the fifth billion.

Demographic Transition

The changes in birth- and death rates in nineteenth-century Europe serve as an example of demographic transition. Demographers use this term to describe an observed pattern in changing vital statistics. Specifically, **demographic transition** is the change from high birthrates and death rates to relatively low birthrates and death rates. This approach, which was first introduced in the 1920s, is now widely used in the study of population trends.

As illustrated in Figure 19-2, demographic transition is typically viewed as a three-stage process:

1 High birth- and death rates with little population growth
2 Declining death rates, primarily the result of reductions in infant deaths, along with high to medium fertility—resulting in significant population growth
3 Low birth- and death rates with little population growth

Demographic transition should be regarded not as a "law of population growth," but rather as

FIGURE 19-1   World Population Growth through History

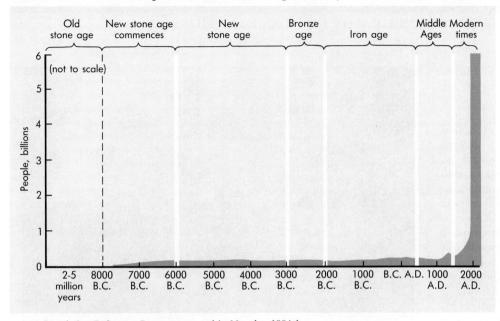

It took several million years before the world population reached its first billion in about A.D. 1800. Rapid population growth during the last 100 years is placing tremendous pressure on the earth's resources and environment.

SOURCE: Population Reference Bureau, reported in Murphy, 1984:1.

a generalization of the population history of industrial nations. Through use of this concept, we can better understand the growth problems faced by the world in the 1990s. About two-thirds of the world's nations have yet to pass fully through the second stage of demographic transition, among

them many countries in which Islam is the dominant religion (see Box 19-2 on page 584). Even if such nations make dramatic advances in fertility control, their populations will nevertheless increase seriously because of the large base of people already at prime childbearing age.

FIGURE 19-2   Demographic Transition

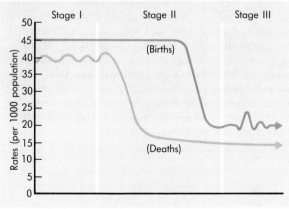

Demographers use the concept of demographic transition *to describe changes in birthrates and death rates during stages of a nation's development. This graph shows the pattern that took place in presently developed nations. In the first stage, both birthrates and death rates were high, so that there was little population growth. In the second stage, the birthrate remained high while the death rate declined sharply, which led to rapid growth. By the last stage, which many developing nations have yet to enter, the birthrate also declined, and there was again little population growth.*

BOX 19-2 • CURRENT RESEARCH

THE DEMOGRAPHY OF ISLAMIC NATIONS

The 47 nations in which Islam is the dominant religion are the fastest-growing group of countries in the world. Currently, nearly one in every five human beings are Moslem. At present rates of growth, the world's Islamic population of about 980 million in 1988 could almost double to 1.9 billion before the year 2020.

Sociologist and demographer John Weeks (1988:5) points out that "although Islam is a proselytizing religion, its proportionate increase in the modern world is much more a result of natural increase (the excess of births over deaths) than it is the conversion of non-Moslems to the Islamic faith." The Islamic nations report higher-than-average fertility, higher-than-average mortality, and rapid rates of population growth. These countries are viewed as being in the early stages of demographic transition from high to low birth- and death rates.

The total fertility rate (TFR) of the Islamic nations is 6.0 projected births per woman, compared with 4.5 births in other developing nations and only 1.7 births per woman in the developed nations. Islamic countries are growing at an average of 2.8 percent per year, or 22 percent faster than the world's other developing nations (Weeks, 1988:12–13).

Weeks (1988:47) reviewed the population policies of these Is-

(Chris K. Walter/The Picture Cube)

lamic countries and found that there was considerable diversity in their positions regarding reproductive behavior and population growth. About half the governments of the Islamic nations reported that they were satisfied with their current rates of population growth; 40 percent stated that their current rates of growth were too high, whereas 10 percent indicated that their growth rates were too low.

Certain Islamic nations have implemented "pronatalist" policies to increase population. For example, Iraq, which has the highest natural increase rate (3.9 percent) of any country in the world, grants allowances and benefits to families. Women receive paid maternity leave at 100 percent of earnings for the first 10

Shown is a family gathering in Turkey. The 47 nations in which Islam is the dominant religion are the fastest-growing group of countries in the world.

weeks of pregnancy. The government's explicit goal is to encourage each woman to have a minimum of four children. By contrast, many Islamic countries either directly implement family planning programs or allow voluntary family planning associations to operate health care facilities and distribute contraceptive methods. Indonesia, Tunisia, Egypt, and Turkey are among the Islamic nations that have made substantial progress in promoting contraceptive use and reducing fertility rates (de Sherbinin, 1990; Weeks, 1988:47).

The pattern of demographic transition varies from nation to nation. One particularly useful distinction is the contrast between the transition now occurring in developing nations—which include about two-thirds of the world's population—and that which occurred over almost a century in more industrialized countries. Demographic transition in developing nations has involved a rapid decline in death rates without adjustments in birthrates. Specifically, until the end of World War II, there was a very gradual decrease in the death rates of developing countries, due primarily to improved water supplies and other public sanitary measures. Yet the birthrates of these countries remained very high—about 30 per 1000 population in the 1940s (as compared with under 19 per 1000 in the United States during the same period).

In the post–World War II period, the death rates of developing nations began a sharp decline. This revolution in "death control" was triggered by antibiotics, immunization, insecticides (such as DDT, used to strike at malaria-bearing mosquitoes), and largely successful campaigns against such fatal diseases as smallpox. Substantial medical and public health technology was imported almost overnight from more developed nations. As a result, the drop in death rates that had taken a century in Europe was telescoped into 2 decades in many developing countries.

Birthrates scarcely had time to adjust. Cultural beliefs about the proper size of families could not possibly change as quickly as the falling death rates. For centuries, couples had given birth to as many as eight or more children with the realization that perhaps two or three would survive to adulthood. Consequently, whereas Europeans had had several generations to restrict their birthrates, peoples of developing nations needed to do the same in less than a lifetime. Many did not, as is evident from the astronomical "population explosion" that was already under way by the middle 1800s (refer back to Figure 19-1). Clearly, families were more willing to accept technological advances that prolonged life than to abandon fertility patterns which reflected centuries of tradition and religious training.

The Population Bomb: Still Ticking

Apart from war, rapid population growth has been perhaps the dominant international social problem of the past 30 years. Often this issue is referred to in emotional terms as the "population bomb" or "population explosion." Such striking language is not surprising, given the staggering increases in world population during the last 2 centuries. As was detailed in Table 19-1, the population of our planet rose from 1 billion around the year 1800 to 5 billion by 1987. The United Nations projects that world population could rise to as high as 6.4 billion by 2000 (Haub et al., 1990; Haupt, 1990).

By the middle 1970s, demographers had observed a slight decline in the growth rate of many developing nations. These countries were still experiencing population increases, yet their rates of increase had declined as death rates could not go much lower and birthrates began to fall. It appears that family planning efforts have been instrumental in this demographic change (see Box 19-3 on page 586). Beginning in the early 1960s, governments in certain developing nations sponsored or supported campaigns to encourage family planning (Tsui and Bogue, 1978; see also Birdsall, 1980). In the social policy section at the end of the chapter, we will examine the United States' policy regarding worldwide family planning.

Through the efforts of many governments (among them the United States and the People's Republic of China) and private agencies (among them Planned Parenthood), the fertility rates of many developing countries have declined. It would be incorrect, however, to suggest that the population bomb is being defused. Even if trends toward lower fertility rates continue, the momentum toward growing world population is well established. Figure 19-3 (p. 587) features a comparison of the population pyramids of rich and poor nations of the world. A *population pyramid* is a special type of bar chart that shows the distribution of population by gender and age; it is generally used to illustrate the population structure of a society. As Figure 19-3 indicates, some 38 percent

BOX 19-3 • AROUND THE WORLD

FAMILY PLANNING IN CHINA

At the end of 1989, the People's Republic of China, by official estimates, had a population of 1.1 billion. Chinese leaders believe that unless the nation's population stabilizes at about 1.2 billion by the year 2000, China's ability to feed itself and progress economically will be in jeopardy. Consequently, the government has set a policy that each couple should have only one child. If this policy is successful over the next 100 years, China's population will fall to 700 million. But if each couple has three children, the population will rise to 4.26 billion over this period.

How can a nation persuade couples to reduce family size? In 1979 China adopted a number of measures to encourage single-child families. Couples who agree to this standard receive more living space, extra ration coupons, free education and health care, and even salary increases. By contrast, if a couple has a second or third child, the family loses all benefits. Moreover, a third child leads to a 10 percent decrease in wages and loss of promotion opportunities.

The ideal of the one-child family was not received with universal enthusiasm by the Chinese people; it clearly conflicted with a traditional cultural emphasis on large extended families. Moreover, as Chinese officials have recognized, the strong preference for male children (refer back to Box 19-1) undermines adherence to the one-child rule in families whose firstborn child is female.

Nevertheless, China's determined efforts to enforce its one-child population policy succeeded in sharply restricting the nation's

(Wally McNamee/Woodfin Camp & Associates)

To combat the traditional preference for male children—which leads some families to have a second child if their first is a girl—Chinese billboards advocating the one-child family invariably show adoring parents with a single, happy daughter.

growth rate. By 1981, almost half of all births in China were the first for the family, whereas this had been true of only 21 percent of births in 1970. Many young people now report that they want only one or two children; the traditional preference for large families has been significantly undermined. Some experts are now predicting that China's population will actually decline after reaching a peak early in the twenty-first century.

By the late 1980s, there were signs that resistance to the one-child norm was increasing, especially in rural areas. The Chinese government responded by relaxing its policies so that a second child was permitted in certain rural districts if the first child was a girl. However, in the aftermath of the crackdown against supporters of democratic reforms following the shootings at Tianamen Square in 1989, the controversy over population planning has become embroiled in the dynamics of post-Tianamen politics. Hardliners have gained ground over defenders of less stringent population policies and have taken steps to reassert a stringent one-child norm. In order to reduce population growth, the government has instituted a new nationwide head tax, has granted new tax exemptions for families with only one child, and has ended supplementary land allotments for peasant households with two or more children.

SOURCES: Brophy, 1989; Kristof, 1990; Tien, 1989, 1990.

of the population of developing nations consists of children under the age of 15 with their child-bearing years still to come, as compared with 23 percent in the developed regions. Thus, the built-in momentum for population growth is much greater in the developing countries.

This is evident in an examination of population data for India, which in 1990 had a population of 853 million. Demographer Leon Bouvier (1984: 25) has projected that, even if India's fertility rates level off to rates near those of North America and Europe, the nation's population will still reach 1.3 billion by the year 2034. That figure is higher than the current combined total for all of North America, South America, Africa, and Europe. Thus, because of the substantial momentum for growth built into India's age structure, the nation will face a staggering increase in population in the coming decades—even if its birthrate declines sharply.

By 1990, population specialists and policymakers, worried about the population bomb, faced the following disturbing facts:

• The world population rose by 93 million between mid-1988 and mid-1989, an all-time record increase.
• Developing nations are not experiencing the declines in fertility that had been predicted earlier by researchers.
• According to projections of the United Nations Food and Agriculture Organization, as many as 64 nations will experience critical food problems in the future. India now produces less food grain per person than it did in 1900 (Haub, 1988).

Later in this chapter, we will see that population growth does not appear to be a problem in certain industrialized nations. Indeed, a handful of nations are adopting policies which *encourage* growth—among them, Japan, which is considering offering benefits to families which have children and upgrading child care services. Nevertheless, a global perspective underscores the dire consequences that could result from continued population growth (T. Reid, 1990).

FIGURE 19-3 **Population Structure of Developing and Developed Regions of the World**

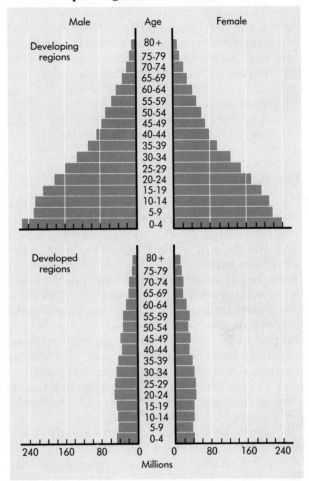

SOURCE: Bouvier, 1984:12.

This population pyramid comprises the population of the world's developed and developing nations. The developing nations face the prospect of continued population growth, since a substantial proportion of their population is approaching childbearing years.

FERTILITY PATTERNS IN THE UNITED STATES

During the last 4 decades, the United States and other industrial nations have passed through two different patterns of population growth—the first marked by high fertility and rapid growth (stage II in the theory of demographic transition), the second marked by decline in fertility and little growth (stage III). Sociologists are keenly aware of the social impact of these fertility patterns.

The Baby Boom

The most recent period of high fertility in the United States has often been referred to as the *baby boom*. After World War II—during which large numbers of military personnel were separated from their spouses—the annual number of births began to rise dramatically. Yet the baby boom was not a return to the large families common in the 1800s. In fact, there was only a slight increase in the proportion of couples having three or more children. The boom resulted from a striking decrease in the number of childless marriages and one-child families. Although a peak was reached in 1957, the nation maintained a relatively high birthrate of over 20 live births per 1000 population until 1964.

It would be a mistake to attribute the baby boom solely to the return home of large numbers of soldiers. High wages and general prosperity during the post–World War II period encouraged many married couples to have children and purchase homes. In addition, several sociologists—as well as feminist author Betty Friedan (1963)—have noted that there were pervasive pressures on women during the 1950s for marriage, homemaking, and motherhood (Bouvier, 1980).

Stable Population Growth

In demographic terms, 1972 was a landmark in American history. In that year, the nation's total fertility rate dropped below replacement-level fertility. The total fertility rate, as was noted earlier, is an estimate of the number of children a woman will bear, assuming that she conforms to current fertility rates. By contrast, *replacement-level fertility* refers to the average number of children women must have in order to replace the adult population. In the United States, the replacement level is 2.12—two for a man and a woman plus an added factor to account for women who fail to reach childbearing age. In 1972 the TFR in the United States was 2.0; it has remained between 1.8 and 2.0 since then. This compares with total fertility rates as high as 3.7 in 1957 (Haub et al., 1990; Haupt and Kane, 1985).

Although the TFR is below replacement-level fertility, the United States continues to grow in size because of two factors: the momentum built into our age structure by the postwar population boom, and the continued high rates of immigration. Because of the upsurge of births in the 1950s, there are now many more Americans in their childbearing years than in older age groups (where most deaths occur). This growth of population represents a "demographic echo" of the baby boom generation, many of whom are now parents. Consequently, the number of people born each year in the United States continues to exceed the number who die. In addition, the nation allows a large number of immigrants to enter each year; these immigrants currently account for between one-fourth and one-third of annual growth. However, assuming relatively low fertility levels and moderate net migration in the coming decades, the United States may reach *zero population growth (ZPG)*.

What Is ZPG? ZPG is the state of a population when the number of births plus immigrants equals deaths plus emigrants (McFalls et al., 1984; Population Reference Bureau, 1978).

A basic shift in American attitudes regarding family size has made it possible for the United States to come closer to zero population growth. In 1945, 49 percent of Americans believed that the ideal family included four or more children. Even in the Depression year of 1936, 30 percent of those surveyed endorsed such a large family. However, in 1986, only 11 percent of Americans agreed with this view of the ideal family size. For 59 percent, the ideal family had two children. A three-child family was preferred by 17 percent of respondents; 5 percent favored one child; and 2

FIGURE 19-4 Countries at or Approaching ZPG through Low Fertility

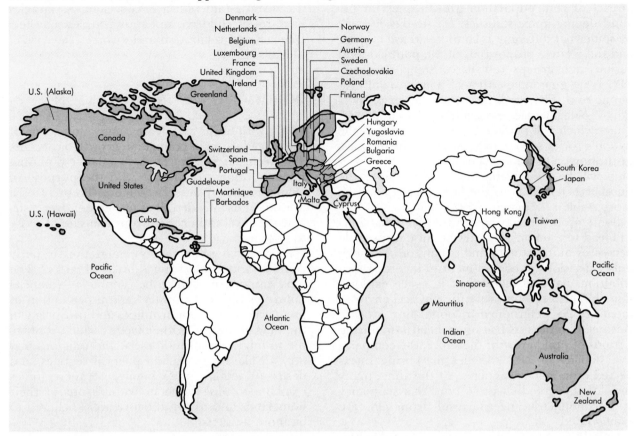

NOTE: The following countries, too small to be identified on the map, are also approaching zero population growth: Aruba, Cayman Islands, Faroes Islands, Liechtenstein, Montserrat, and Netherlands Antilles.
SOURCES: Day, 1978:2; Kent, 1991.

The 45 countries shaded on this map or noted above had fertility patterns approaching zero population growth, according to data available as of 1991.

percent believed that the ideal family has no children (*New York Times*, 1986b:22).

What will a society with stable population growth be like? In demographic terms, it will be quite different from the United States of the 1990s. By the year 2040, there will be relatively equal numbers of people in each age group, and the median age of Americans will be 37 (compared with 32.3 in 1988). As a result, the population pyramid will look more like a rectangle. Yet stable growth does not necessarily mean that people will be nonmobile. Internal migrations—whether "back to the city" or "back to the farm"—are still possible in a ZPG society (Bureau of the Census, 1990a:13; Day, 1978).

The United States is not alone in approaching zero population growth. As is shown in Figure 19-4, 45 nations were at or approaching ZPG in 1991. Collectively, these countries account for about one-fourth of the world's people. In the recent past, although some nations have achieved ZPG, it has been relatively short-lived. However, given the current international concern over world population, more nations may attempt to maintain ZPG in the late twentieth and early twenty-first centuries.

Social and Economic Implications of ZPG The impact of zero population growth goes far beyond demographic statistics. Day-to-day life will be somewhat different as countries cease to grow and the relative proportions of the population in various age groups remain constant. By itself, ZPG is no guarantee either of bounty or of economic ruin. There will be a much larger proportion of older people, especially aged 75 and over, a fact which will place a greater demand on the nation's social service programs and health care institutions. On a more positive note, the economy will be less volatile under ZPG, since the number of entrants to the labor market will be more stable (J. Spengler, 1978:187).

Some observers have expressed fear that ZPG will lead to economic disaster because of possible decreases in investment and expansion. Yet such policy decisions as commitment to income redistribution, national investment in space exploration, and efforts to improve the physical environment are not determined by population growth. Business confidence has often been low during periods of rapid growth; therefore, the comparative stability of ZPG societies may bring unexpected economic advantages. At this time, many sociologists agree that projections that stagnancy and economic decline will result from ZPG are exaggerated.

In industrial societies such as the United States, power and position in the work force have traditionally been determined in part by length of service. With the coming of ZPG, there will be less opportunity for promotion based on time of service, since a large part of the population will be older. For example, in 1988 the United States had 40 percent fewer people aged 50 to 55 than it did aged 20 to 25. By contrast, if the nation reaches ZPG, there will be only 5 to 10 percent fewer Americans of age 50 than of age 20. Consequently, many more people with 20 to 30 years of work experience will be competing for the same desirable positions.

ZPG will also lead to changes in family life. Clearly, as fertility rates continue to decline, women will devote fewer years to childbearing and to the social roles of motherhood. The proportion of married women entering the paid labor force can be expected to rise (see Chapter 11). In addition, there may be further increases in the divorce rate with a ZPG society. As families have fewer children, unhappy couples may feel freer to seek separation and divorce (Day, 1978; McFalls, 1981).

POPULATION AND MIGRATION

Along with births and deaths, migration is one of the three factors in population growth or decline. The term *migration* refers to relatively permanent movement of people with the purpose of changing their place of residence (Prehn, 1991). Migration usually describes movement over a sizable distance, rather than from one side of a city to another.

As a social phenomenon, migration is fairly complex and results from a variety of factors. The most important tend to be economic—financial failure in the "old country" and a perception of greater economic opportunities and prosperity in the new homeland. Other factors which contribute to migration include racial and religious bigotry, dislike for prevailing political regimes, and desire to reunite one's family. All these forces combine to *push* some individuals out of their homelands and to *pull* them to areas believed to be more attractive.

International Migration

International migration—changes of residence across national boundaries—has been a significant force in redistributing the world's population during certain periods of history. For example, the composition of the United States has been significantly altered by immigrants who have come here in the nineteenth and twentieth centuries. Their entry was encouraged or restricted by various immigration policies. The immigration policy of the United States was examined in detail in the social policy section of Chapter 10.

Immigration has been a particularly controversial issue in Great Britain over the past 2 decades. Historically, Britain allowed unlimited entry to immigrants from former colonies; however, this policy changed when hundreds of thousands of non-White immigrants arrived from the West

Indies, India, and Pakistan. In 1962, the British government enacted a transparently racist measure that gave preference to immigrants from the predominantly White, "old Commonwealth" countries of Australia, New Zealand, and Canada over "new Commonwealth" immigrants from Asia, Africa, and the Caribbean. Subsequent legislation removed such distinctions but virtually cut off immigration from any nation. Currently, Blacks and Asians living in Britain face resentment and discrimination from those Whites who cannot accept the idea of a multiracial society (Schaefer, 1976, 1990).

Discussions of international migration frequently overlook the fact that many immigrants eventually return home. Still, immigration is a significant contributor to population growth. For example, the United States is expected to reach a population of 292 million by the year 2080. But if net immigration were reduced to zero, that figure would be only 220 million, or about 25 percent fewer people (Haupt, 1989).

Internal Migration

Migratory movements within societies can vary in important ways. In traditional societies, migration often represents a way of life, as people move to accommodate the changing availability of fertile soil or wild game. In industrial societies, people may relocate as a result of job transfers or because they believe that a particular region has better employment opportunities or a more desirable climate.

Although nations typically have laws and policies governing movement across their borders, the same is not true of internal movement. Generally, residents of a country are legally free to migrate from one locality to another. Of course, this is not the case in all nations; the Republic of South Africa severely restricts the movement of Blacks and other non-Whites through the wide-ranging system of segregation known as *apartheid* (see Chapter 10).

We can identify two distinctive trends of recent internal migration within the United States:

1 *Suburbanization.* During the period 1980–1990, suburban counties grew in population by

Shown are new homes being built in California's Hollywood hills. In the last 20 years, there has been a significant internal migration in the United States—from the "snow belt" of the north central and northeastern states to the "sun belt" in the south and west.

14 percent while the total population of the United States rose by 10 percent. The proportion of the population living in central cities stayed constant at about one-third over the last 40 years. At the same time, the share of the population living in nonmetropolitan areas declined from 44 percent in 1950 to 23 percent in 1986.

2 *"Sunning of America."* In the last 20 years, there has been significant internal migration from the "snow belt" of the north central and northeastern states to the "sun belt" in the south and west. Since 1970, the sun belt has absorbed almost two-thirds of the nation's population growth. Individuals and families move to the sun belt because of its expanding economy and desirable climate. Businesses are attracted by the comparatively inexpensive energy supplies, increased availability of labor, and relative weakness of labor unions (Bureau of the Census, 1989f; Dunn, 1991).

POPULATION AND THE QUALITY OF LIFE

Ultimately, issues such as overpopulation, subfecundity, and immigration are important, because they help to shape the quality of life in our society and on the planet as a whole. "Quality of life" is a difficult concept to measure; at first, researchers regarded it exclusively as an economic standard. However, in the decades after World War II, economic progress in industrialized nations yielded such by-products as ecological pollution and visual decay of the environment. It became apparent that prosperity could bring with it certain negative changes in the quality of life. As a result, in the 1970s researchers adopted a multi-dimensional approach in assessing the quality of life and began to utilize social indicators such as measures of educational achievement, political participation, and leisure-time activity. More recently, discussion of this question has been focused on the *perception* of well-being and therefore on *subjective* evaluations of happiness or satisfaction.

According to sociologist William Catton (1978), all three measurement approaches (economic, social, and subjective) take *quality of life* to mean the degree of *goodness* in life. Catton suggests that the future of the world is not one of continuing growth in a positive sense; the prospect of an overall reduction in the quality of life is quite real. Although Catton could be regarded as a neo-Malthusian, his viewpoint is not quickly dismissed by social scientists, because of increasing concern about world poverty, food shortages, and depletion of natural resources.

Poverty

Central to the concern over quality of life has been the effort to eliminate poverty. While the number of homeless people in the United States has increased in recent years (refer back to Chap-

ter 18), poverty in this country usually means malnutrition and substandard housing, not starvation or total lack of shelter. However, from an international perspective, poverty often *does* mean utter starvation and homelessness.

The World Bank has defined *absolute poverty* as the amount of spending needed to ensure a person a minimum daily diet of 2150 calories. The poverty line corresponds to an annual income per person of about $275 to $370. Using such guidelines, the World Bank estimated in 1990 that at least 1.1 billion people in developing countries—or about one-third of the population of these nations—are extremely poor (Birdsall, 1980:4; World Bank, 1990:27–29).

The effort to combat intense poverty is complicated by the fact that the nations of the world with the highest proportion of poor people lack the resources to undertake massive aid programs. This is not to say that these resources are totally unavailable. The World Bank (1990:28) has estimated that the entire population of developing nations could be lifted above the poverty line simply by transferring the equivalent of 3 percent of the total consumption of industrialized nations to the developing world.

Food Supply

Thomas Malthus argued that population growth would increase more rapidly than the food supply and ultimately would be checked only by starvation and other forms of misery. Contemporary neo-Malthusians agree that there are absolute limits on food, energy, and other resources. Furthermore, they suggest that the problem is intensified by the disproportionate consumption of such resources by industrialized nations. This formulation has been challenged by other researchers, yet none would deny that starvation is a very real fact in the 1990s. Around the world, refugee camps are filled with children whose swollen bellies are a sign of malnutrition. With such images in mind, a representative of the World Bank stated in 1981 that the "ghost of Malthus is not buried yet" (Crittenden, 1981:12; Ehrlich and Ehrlich, 1990).

We often hear of food shortages in specific nations or regions, yet these are not necessarily the result of global shortages. For example, while droughts were slashing crop yields in much of Asia and Africa in the 1980s—leading to famine, malnutrition, and starvation affecting millions of people—American farmers were being encouraged to withhold land from production in order to maintain favorable prices for their crops. The politics of starvation became especially poignant in 1984 when efforts to address suffering in Ethiopia, the Soviet Union's closest ally in Africa, became entangled in the complexities of east-west relations. Despite extensive and tragic famine, relief aid was delayed as western nations and the Soviet Union resolved distribution arrangements. The problem was further complicated by an ongoing civil war centered in those provinces that had been worst hit by famine (Dionne, 1984; Harden, 1984).

Many concerned observers have advocated the establishment of a global reserve of food grains to see the world through shortages, yet no such reserve has been created. A recent study by the World Bank noted that despite repeated international pledges to end hunger, the number of hungry, undernourished people in the world continues to increase. According to World Bank estimates, in 1988 approximately 730 million people around the globe could not afford a minimum dietary standard that would avoid serious health risks and would prevent stunted physical and mental development in children. About 40,000 children are believed to die each day of hunger-related causes. Ironically, while world hunger increases, food is perhaps more abundant and cheaper than ever before, owing to surplus stocks of grains, sugar, and butter (P. Hendry, 1988; P. Lewis, 1987).

With such disturbing ironies in mind, conflict theorists contend that food shortages are actually problems of distribution rather than production. In their view, starvation and malnutrition result from unequal distribution of food as wealthy nations consume disproportionately large shares of the world's food produce. As is shown in Table 19-2 (page 594), there is a consistent difference in health and nutrition between developing and industrial nations. Moreover, in some developing nations the limited supply of subsidized food tends to go to a relatively small group of urban

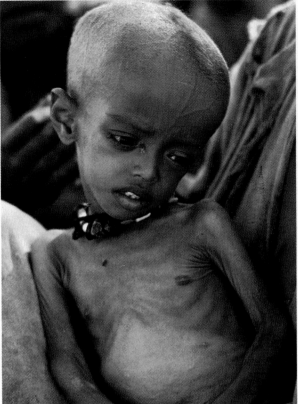

(Anthony Suau/Black Star)

In the 1980s, famine in east Africa and especially Ethiopia attracted international attention to a plight common to most developing nations.

residents. Increasing food yields must be backed by more effective and equitable distribution if the world's poor are to be adequately fed. Even with substantial food aid budgets, nations and international organizations will not resolve this social problem without addressing such basic issues.

Ironically, gains in food supplies do not always lead to progress in the fight against starvation. As people's purchasing power increases, they consume more food. This, in turn, puts pressure on food prices, inflates the cost of eating well-balanced meals, and makes it more difficult for the poor to buy the food they need. In such nations as Mexico, Thailand, and South Korea, rapidly emerging middle classes are eating more meat, thus further straining worldwide food supplies (World Bank, 1990).

TABLE 19-2 Health and Nutrition across the World

	POPULATION PER PHYSICIAN	PERCENT OF BIRTHS WITH LOW BIRTH WEIGHT	DAILY CALORIE SUPPLY PER CAPITA
Developing nations:			
Brazil	1080	8	2656
Haiti	7180	17	1902
Nigeria	7990	25	2146
Industrial nations:			
Japan	660	5	2864
Sweden	390	4	3064
United States	470	7	3645

Quality of life varies sharply around the world. Developing nations experiencing the fastest population growth often lag far behind industrialized nations in various measures of health and nutrition.

SOURCE: World Bank, 1990.

Food experts agree that massive investment in technical assistance, irrigation networks, and agricultural research is necessary if the world is ever to achieve freedom from hunger. Of course, the projected costs of such measures are staggering. The sum of $600 billion—approximately twice the 1989 federal budget for defense—would be needed for irrigation systems to *maintain* (rather than increase) present worldwide levels of food supplies. When one focuses on mineral resources, the outlook is not much better (Crittenden, 1981; for a different view, see Kahn and Simon, 1984).

(Gayle Jann/Care Photo)

Food experts agree that massive investment in technical assistance, irrigation networks, and agricultural research is necessary if the world is ever to achieve freedom from hunger.

Natural Resources

The world's poor are not the only people feeling the effects of increasing population. The rate of which the world is depleting certain natural resources—among them, petroleum, natural gas, uranium, aluminum, copper, and tin—has also concerned many social scientists and government policymakers. As the world population grows, the demand for such resources will certainly intensify. Furthermore, per capita demands for material goods are likely to expand as people's standards of living increase. Thus, the danger of shortages in critical resources may become even more serious in the future.

Beginning with the oil embargo of 1973, again during the prolonged crisis in the Persian Gulf in the late 1980s, and again in the aftermath of Iraq's invasion of Kuwait in 1990, people in the United States became aware of limited oil resources and of the nation's dependence on oil produced outside the United States. Sharp increases in oil prices occurred after each of these crises and have had a number of effects. Per capita consumption immediately falls in the aftermath of initial price hikes but tends to recover and rise again. The higher prices boost the supply of petroleum because the cost of producing synthetic fuels from such abundant sources as oil shale, tar sands, and coal is no longer economically uncompetitive with traditional methods of oil production. Significantly, the price rise in oil hurts developing nations of the world, which find it more costly to purchase oil for energy and for such petroleum-related products as fertilizer and pesticides (Repetto, 1987; Ridker and Cecelski, 1979).

SOCIAL POLICY AND POPULATION
THE UNITED STATES' POPULATION POLICY OVERSEAS

- What are some of the financial and social costs of family planning?
- Why has the United States government reduced its support for international family planning programs?
- How does the American public feel about family planning assistance to developing nations where abortion is legal?

Some people are opposed to birth control on moral and religious grounds, but the government of Thailand has quite a different view. The nation's family planning agency has sponsored birth control carnivals and condom-blowing balloon contests; vasectomy marathons are held on Labor Day and on the birthday of Thailand's king. In 1983, a team of 40 doctors and 80 nurses performed a record-breaking 1190 vasectomies during a 1-day festival. The government's birth control campaign has had dramatic impact: Thailand's total fertility rate fell from 6.1 births per woman in 1970 to only 2.6 in 1990, well below the average of 4.0 births per woman in comparable nations (Haub et al., 1990; World Bank, 1990).

Family planning efforts in developing countries not only reduce unwanted population growth, but also can improve maternal health by assisting women in timing and spacing pregnancies. In many developing nations, pregnancy and childbirth account for more than 25 percent of all deaths of women of childbearing age. Around the world, about half a million women die in childbirth each year, of whom 99 percent are from developing countries (see Figure 19-5, page 596). Because women in these nations—especially women in poorer areas—tend to have many pregnancies, the cumulative risk of dying during pregnancy can be as high as 1 in 20. Yet it is estimated that 25 to 62 percent of maternal deaths in developing countries could be averted by avoiding unwanted pregnancies (Acsadi and Johnson-Acsadi, 1990; World Bank, 1990:83).

Family planning information and services are absolutely essential if such deaths are to be prevented and if population growth is to be contained. Yet the availability of family planning programs varies widely in developing nations. In Indonesia, family planning services reach 44 percent of all women, and the nation's

FIGURE 19-5   Annual Maternal Deaths by Region

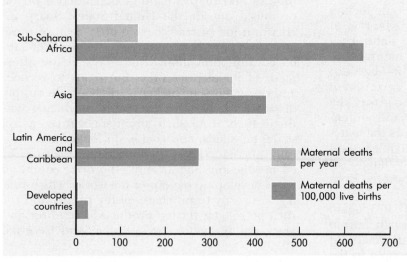

According to data for the early 1980s, about half a million women across the world die in childbirth each year. In developing nations—unlike industrialized nations—childbirth is a major cause of death for women.

SOURCE: World Bank, 1990:83.

total fertility rate has been reduced to 3.3 births per woman. By contrast, family planning services reach less than 7 percent of women in Ghana; that nation's total fertility rate is 6.3 births per woman, almost twice the rate in Indonesia (Donaldson and Tsui, 1990; Haub et al., 1990; World Bank, 1990:82).

Despite its benefits, family planning has both financial and social costs. Modern contraceptives can be an expensive item for families who have little money even for food. Birth control measures may be viewed as unpleasant or cumbersome, and the intention of preventing conception may clash with people's cultural values and religious beliefs. Moreover, children are often seen as an "investment" in societies which offer limited social services. Each child quickly becomes an additional worker in a peasant family, though studies disagree as to whether children are indeed a net financial benefit for parents (Birdsall, 1980; Eberstadt, 1978).

Some critics, reflecting a conflict orientation, have questioned why the United States and other industrialized nations are so enthusiastic about population control in the developing world. In line with Marx's response to Malthus, they argue that large families and even population growth are not the causes of hunger and misery. Rather, the unjust economic domination by the developed states of the world results in an unequal distribution of world resources and in wide-

spread poverty in exploited developing nations (refer back to Chapter 9). For example, one person in the United States consumes as much of the earth's resources as 39 people in a country such as India (Aeppel, 1987; Vobejda, 1990).

From a conflict perspective, there is also criticism regarding efforts by developed nations to impose their values concerning family planning on developing countries. The 1984 World Population Conference—held in Mexico City and attended by delegations from 149 nations—underscored cross-cultural differences in both health care and population policy. The American delegation, while voicing public support for family planning efforts, announced new aid restrictions intended to discourage abortion. The United States indicated that it would cut off its contributions to private agencies that perform or actively promote abortions. Moreover, governmental agencies overseas that receive American aid were required to certify that they were not using such funds to pay for abortions. The overwhelming response from representatives of other nations was that abortion is legal in many countries—among them the United States (see Chapter 11)—and that it plays a major role in controlling population growth.

In countries such as Turkey, Bangladesh, and India, where concern about overpopulation led to the legalization of abortion, local family planning organizations have lost funding because they failed to comply with these United States regulations. In 1990 testimony before a congressional subcommittee, a representative of the Pathfinder Fund, a family planning group based in the United States, attacked American policy for preventing health care providers from even answering a pregnant woman's questions about abortion. "Since abortion is legal in Turkey," testified Turkiz Gokgol, "this puts the health care worker in a position that is unlawful and professionally unethical" (McCulloch, 1990:492).

Despite such criticisms, in 1986 the United States withdrew its contribution of $25 million to the United Nations Fund for Population because some of the funding would have gone to the People's Republic of China. This action came after months of intensive lobbying by antiabortion activists, who assert that China's population program involves widespread use of compulsory abortions. In 1989, the House of Representatives, by a narrow 219–203 vote, allowed President George Bush to continue this policy and revoke $15 million in aid to the U.N. population fund because of its support for family planning programs in China. The Bush administration continued this policy in 1990 despite a nonbinding 57–41 vote in the Senate to remove such aid restrictions (Donaldson and Tsui, 1990; Kalish, 1990; C. Marin, 1989).

For similar reasons, the United States government has attempted to cut off funding for Family Planning International Assistance (FPIA), the international arm of Planned Parenthood. This organization supports 140 family planning programs in 35 Third World countries and provides contraceptive services to 1.4 million people. Planned Parenthood has challenged American policy in federal court, asserting that the First Amendment rights of overseas workers are being curtailed by the prohibition on discussions of abortion. However, in early 1990, a federal judge upheld the president's right to impose such a policy on private organizations. According to a study conducted in 1987, a cutoff of American funding for FPIA would result in 69,000 more abortions, 1200 more pregnancy-related maternal deaths, and an increase of 311,000 births over a 3-year period (McCulloch, 1990).

Overall, there has been a dramatic decline in support by the United States for international family planning efforts. The level of such federal assistance decreased from $298 million in 1985 to $200 million in 1988. Ironically, this reduction in American aid comes just as the need for more funding has become apparent. According to a 1990 report of the Population Cri-

(Bernard Pierre Wolff/Photo Researchers)

Shown is a family planning class in Pakistan. Family planning efforts in developing countries not only reduce unwanted population growth but can improve maternal health by helping women to time and space pregnancies.

sis Committee, a nonprofit organization which advocates family planning, the world population (5.3 billion in 1990) can be stabilized at 9.3 billion by the end of the next century. This goal is feasible if governments and international organizations increase annual support for family planning over the next decade from their current level of $3.2 billion to $10.5 billion. However, according to United Nations projections, if there is no such increase in funding for family planning programs, world population will skyrocket to more than 14 billion by the year 2120. "What we as a society of nations do in this decade will determine population trends for the next century," predicts Sharon Camp, vice president of the Population Crisis Committee (Okie, 1990:37; Population Institute, 1988a).

Survey data suggest that, contrary to recent government policy, the American public is strongly in favor of international family planning assistance—even when directed to countries in which abortion is legal. According to a 1988 national Louis Harris poll, 60 percent of respondents endorsed family planning aid to developing nations. Such funding was approved by 61 percent of American Catholics, 50 percent of evangelical Christians, and 62 percent of Republicans. An overwhelming majority of respondents (89 percent) favored strong and effective family planning programs in the poorer countries of Africa, Asia, and Latin America; only 8 percent were opposed (Population Institute, 1988b:1).

With its annual contribution of $200 million, the United States continues to lead all governments in its financial support for international family planning programs. Nevertheless, when the relative wealth and funding levels of industrialized nations are compared, the United States trails the Netherlands, Denmark, Norway, and Canada in its support for family planning. In its 1990 report, the Population Crisis Committee urged the United States to increase its annual funding for international family planning to $1.2 billion by the year 2000. While not specifically criticizing United States reductions in family planning assistance, Barber Conable, president of the World Bank, called it "alarming that many governments are failing to implement sensible population policies" (Okie, 1990; Population Institute, 1988a:1; Yared, 1989).

SUMMARY

The size, composition, and distribution of the American population have an important influence on many of the policy issues that we have studied in this book. This chapter examines various elements of population, the current problem of overpopulation, the possibility of zero population growth (ZPG), and international and internal migration.

1 Demographers study geographical variations and historical trends which are useful in developing population forecasts.

2 Thomas Robert Malthus suggested that the world's population was growing more rapidly than the available food supply and that this gap would increase over time. However, Karl Marx was critical of Malthus and saw capitalism rather than rising world population as the cause of social ills.

3 The primary mechanism for obtaining population information in the United States and most other countries is the *census.*

4 Until modern times, there were relatively few humans living on this planet.

5 Roughly two-thirds of the world's nations have yet to pass fully through the second stage of *demographic transition,* and thus they continue to experience significant population growth.

6 The United Nations projects that world population will rise to 6.3 billion by the year 2000.

7 By 2040, when most Americans born in the 1970s will be entering retirement age, the United States will be approaching *zero population growth (ZPG).*

8 The most important factors in *migration* tend to be economic—financial failure in the "old country" and a perception of greater economic opportunities elsewhere.

9 Conflict theorists contend that problems of food shortage are actually problems of distribution rather than production.

10 The United States' support for international family planning efforts has dramatically declined in recent years.

KEY TERMS

Birthrate The number of live births per 1000 population in a given year. Also known as the *crude birthrate.* (page 579)

Census An enumeration or counting of a population. (578)

Death rate The number of deaths per 1000 population in a given year. Also known as the *crude death rate.* (581)

Demographic transition A term used to describe the change from high birthrates and death rates to relatively low birthrates and death rates. (582)

Demography The scientific study of population. (577)

Fecundity The biological potential of individual women for reproduction in a society. (579)

Fertility The amount of reproduction among women of childbearing age. (576)

Growth rate The difference between births and deaths, plus the difference between immigrants and emigrants, per 1000 population. (581)

Infant mortality rate The number of deaths of infants under 1 year of age per 1000 live births in a given year. (581)

Life expectancy The average number of years a person can be expected to live under current mortality conditions. (581)

Migration Relatively permanent movement of people with the purpose of changing their place of residence. (590)

Morbidity rates The incidence of diseases in a given population. (581)

Population pyramid A special type of bar chart that shows the distribution of population by gender and age. (585)

Replacement-level fertility The average number of children that women must have in order to replace the adult population. (588)

Subfecundity A limited or diminished ability to reproduce. (579)

Total fertility rate (TFR) The average number of children born alive to a woman, assuming that she conforms to current fertility rates. (581)

Vital statistics Records of births, deaths, marriages, and divorces gathered through a registration system maintained by governmental units. (578)

Zero population growth (ZPG) The state of a population with a growth rate of zero, which is achieved when the number of births plus immigrants is equal to the number of deaths plus emigrants. (588)

ADDITIONAL READINGS

Ehrlich, Paul R., and Anne H. Ehrlich. *The Population Explosion.* New York: Simon and Schuster, 1990. Two biologists advance the neo-Malthusian thesis that unless interventionist policies are adopted to deal with the population bomb, the world will be subjected to natural forces (perhaps massive increases in death rates) that will bring world population back into balance.

Jones, Landon Y. *Great Expectations: America and the Baby Boom Generation.* New York: Ballantine, 1980. This book provides a readable account of the social consequences of the baby boom cohort (1946 to 1964) and the baby bust cohort which followed.

Menard, Scott W., and Elizabeth W. Moen (eds.). *Perspectives on Population: An Introduction to Concepts and Issues.* New York: Oxford University Press, 1987. A collection of classic and contemporary essays covering the scientific study of population.

Menken, Jane (ed.). *World Population and U.S. Policy.* New York: Norton, 1986. A collection of articles dealing with the impact of American policies on other countries' efforts to deal with the problem of population growth.

Russell, Cheryl. "The Business of Demographics." Washington, D.C.: Population Reference Bureau, 1984. Russell, a demographic researcher, describes the applications of the study of population in the marketplace. Published as the June 1984 issue of *Population Bulletin.*

Weeks, John R. *Population: An Introduction to Concepts and Issues* (4th ed.). Belmont, Calif.: Wadsworth, 1989. A sociological treatment of demography with consideration of such social issues as aging, urbanization, economic development, and food supply.

Journals

The Population Reference Bureau (777 14th St., NW, Suite 800, Washington, D.C. 20005) publishes *Population Bulletin* (six times per year), *Population Today* (monthly), *Interchange* (quarterly), and occasionally *Teaching Modules*. These publications provide up-to-date information on population trends. The Bureau of the Census issues *Current Population Reports* which are helpful to researchers. Other journals focusing on demographic issues include *American Demographics* (founded in 1979), *Demography* (1964), and *International Migration Review* (1964).

COLLECTIVE BEHAVIOR AND SOCIAL CHANGE

LOOKING AHEAD

- How do contemporary sociological theorists view collective behavior?
- What functions do rumors perform for a society?
- What impact have social movements had on the course of history and the evolution of social structure?
- How have theorists analyzed the process of social change?
- In the view of sociologists, which sources of change are especially significant in reshaping behavior and social structure?
- Why are efforts to promote social change likely to be met with resistance?
- How has the disability rights movement contributed to societal changes in treatment of Americans with disabilities?

The year 1989 brought tumultuous change in East Germany. That summer, both Hungary and Czechoslovakia began allowing visiting East Germans to continue on to the west. Tens of thousands began to use this escape route; by autumn, as many as 1 million East Germans had applied to emigrate. There were weekly demonstrations against Communist party rule; one demand of protestors was that all restrictions on travel be eliminated.

On October 18, East Germany's ruling Politburo responded to growing pressures for reform by removing Erich Honecker as head of state and replacing him with Egon Krenz. But protests against the Communist regime continued to intensify. Finally, on November 9, a government official announced a new travel decree, under which people who wished to travel to the west could do so if they obtained visas from their local police stations. As word of the new policy spread that evening via radio and television, thousands of East Germans—most of whom had no visas— surged excitedly to the borders by car and by foot. With the approval of Krenz, the gates which had long separated the two Germanys, among them the hated Berlin Wall, were opened. Waves of East Germans were allowed to cross into the west, and West Germans were allowed to cross to the east (Moseley, 1990).

The norms, values, and social structure of Germany were forever altered that November as East and West Germans crossed the borders to see friends and relatives (and, in the case of many East Germans, to begin new lives). Indeed, the entire world was deeply affected by photographs and television coverage of the celebrations at the Berlin Wall. Less than a year later, the world's superpowers consented to the reunification of Germany. The dramatic events of November 9 and 10—the rumors that the borders were open, the gathering of huge crowds, the capitulation of the Communist leadership to social forces they could no longer control—represent an example of both collective behavior and social change, the two focal points of this chapter.

Practically all group activity can be thought of as collective behavior, but sociologists have given distinct meaning to the term. Neil Smelser (1981:431), a sociologist who specializes in this field of study, has defined **collective behavior** as the "relatively spontaneous and unstructured behavior of a group of people who are reacting to a common influence in an ambiguous situation." The crowd behavior evident in the joyous celebrations at the Berlin Wall is but one example of collective behavior.

Social change has been defined by sociologist Wilbert Moore (1967:3) as significant alteration over time in behavior patterns and culture, including norms and values. But what constitutes a "significant" alteration? Certainly the dramatic rise in formal education documented in Chapter 16 represents a change that has had profound social consequences. Other social changes that have had long-term and important consequences include the emergence of slavery as a system of stratification (see Chapter 8), the industrial revolution (Chapters 8 and 15), the greatly increased participation of women in the paid labor force of the United States and Europe (Chapter 11), and the worldwide population explosion (Chapter 19).

This chapter begins with an examination of a number of theories used by sociologists to better understand collective behavior, including the emergent-norm, value-added, and assembling perspectives. Particular attention is given to certain types of collective behavior, among them crowd behavior, disaster behavior, fads and fashions, panics and crazes, rumors, public opinion, and social movements. Contemporary sociology acknowledges the crucial role that social movements can play in mobilizing discontented members of a society and initiating social change.

Efforts to explain long-term social changes have led to the development of theories of change, which will be studied in the second half of the chapter. We will examine some of the sources of change that sociologists see as contributing to significant alterations in behavior and culture, including physical environment, population, science and technology, strains of social inequality, and youth. All theories of social change recognize that there will be resistance to variations in social interaction, norms, and values. This chapter will review the manner in which vested interests can block changes that they perceive as threatening. Finally, in the social policy section, we will focus on changing societal treatment of people with disabilities and on the growing disability rights movement.

(Eric Bouvet/Gamma Liaison)

Jubilant Germans celebrate atop the Berlin Wall, near the Brandenburg Gate, on November 10, 1989. The celebration erupted after East German authorities opened border crossings to West Germany on November 9.

THEORIES OF
COLLECTIVE BEHAVIOR

As Neil Smelser's definition suggests, collective behavior is usually unstructured and spontaneous. This fluidity makes it more difficult for sociologists to generalize about people's behavior in such situations. Nevertheless, sociologists have developed various theoretical perspectives which can help us to study—and deal with in a constructive manner—crowds, riots, fads, and other types of collective behavior.

Emergent-Norm Perspective

The early writings on collective behavior imply that crowds are basically ungovernable. However, this is not always the case. In many situations, crowds are effectively governed by norms and procedures and may even engage in such practices as queuing, or waiting in line. We routinely encounter queues when we await service, as in a fast-food restaurant or bank; or when we wish to enter or exit, as in a movie theater or football stadium. Normally, physical barriers, such as guardrails and checkout counters, help to regulate queuing. When massive crowds are involved, ushers or security personnel may also be present to assist in the orderly movement of the crowd.

In the absence of effective norms, crowds *can* become ungovernable. On December 10, 1979, a large number of fans waited outside Cincinnati's Riverfront Stadium before a concert by the popular rock group The Who. These fans were to be allowed in on a "festival seating" basis, which means "first come, first served." Six hours before the concert—which took place on a cold (40°F) night—a sizable group of fans had already gathered outside the *single* entrance. This crowd subsequently grew at the rate of about 25 people per minute.

Neither the promoters nor the understaffed security forces were able to establish normal procedures for movement and entry that members of a crowd expect. For example, doors were not opened early, and no assurances were given over the public address system that everyone with a proper ticket would be seated. The cold weather and the uncertainty resulting from festival seating made people edge closer and closer to the doors. The crowd's anxiety about being locked out was intensified when The Who began a sound check of equipment 35 minutes before the doors opened.

(East Midlands Pix/Sygma)

In the absence of effective norms, crowds can become ungovernable. When thousands of soccer fans forced their way into a stadium to see the semifinals of the 1989 English Cup, more than 90 people were trampled to death or smothered.

Many fans now suspected that the concert was beginning without them. As the doors finally opened, people in the front were packed so tightly that they fell below an overwhelming crush from the back. Eleven people eventually died from suffocation. Within a few hours, local ordinances had been proposed to ban festival seating and to give Cincinnati police more extensive crowd-control authority (N. Johnson, 1987; D. L. Miller, 1988:46–47).

In 1991, festival seating again led to death—this time *inside* an arena. At a concert in Salt Lake City by the heavy metal group AC/DC, the arena had allowed 4500 fans to roam free on an open floor. As the crowd surged forward, three young people were trampled and died of suffocation (J. Gross, 1991).

Sociologists Ralph Turner and Lewis Killian have offered a view of collective behavior which is helpful in assessing the events in Cincinnati and Salt Lake City. Their emergent-norm perspective begins with the assumption that a large crowd, such as a group of rock fans, is governed by expectations of proper behavior just as much as four people playing doubles tennis. The **emergent-norm perspective** states that a collective definition of appropriate and inappropriate behavior emerges during episodes of collective behavior. Like other social norms, the emergent norm reflects shared convictions held by members of the group and is enforced through sanctions (see Chapter 3). These new norms of proper behavior may arise in what seem at first as ambiguous situations. There is latitude for a wide range of acts, yet within a general framework established by the emergent norms (N. Johnson, 1987; Killian, 1980:284–285; R. Turner, 1964a, 1964b; Turner and Killian, 1987:25–26; for a critique of this perspective, see McPhail, 1991:71–103; K. Tierney, 1980).

Using the emergent-norm perspective, we can see that the fans outside the Who concert found themselves in an ambiguous situation. Normal procedures of crowd control, such as orderly queues, were rapidly dissolving. A new norm was simultaneously emerging: it is acceptable to push forward, even if people in front protest. People began to chant, "One, two, three, push!" Some members of the crowd probably felt that this push forward was justified as a way of ensuring that they would get to hear The Who. Others pushed forward simply to relieve the physical pressure of those pushing behind them. Even individuals who rejected the emergent norm may have felt afraid to oppose it, fearing ridicule or injury. Thus, conforming behavior, which we usually associate with highly structured situations (see Chapter 7), was evident in this rather chaotic crowd, as it was again at the AC/DC concert. It would be misleading to assume that these rock fans acted simply as a united, collective unit in creating a dangerous situation.

Value-Added Perspective

Neil Smelser (1962) continued the sociological effort to analyze collective behavior with his value-added theory. He uses the **value-added model** to explain how broad social conditions are transformed in a definite pattern into some form of collective behavior. This model outlines six important determinants of collective behavior.

Initially, in Smelser's view, certain elements must be present for an incident of collective behavior to take place. He uses the term *structural conduciveness* to indicate that the organization of society can facilitate the emergence of conflicting interests. Structural conduciveness makes collective behavior possible, though not inevitable.

The second determinant of collective behavior, *structural strain,* occurs when the conduciveness of the social structure to potential conflict gives way to a perception that conflicting interests do, in fact, exist. This type of strain was evident in East Germany in 1989: the intense desire of many East Germans to travel to or emigrate to the west placed great strain on the social control exercised by the ruling Communist party. Such structural strain contributes to what Smelser calls a *generalized belief*—a shared view of reality that redefines social action and serves to guide behavior. The overthrow of Communist rule in East Germany and other Soviet-bloc nations occurred in part as a result of a generalized belief that the Communist regimes were oppressive and that popular resistance *could* lead to social change.

Smelser suggests that a specific event or incident, known as a *precipitating factor,* triggers collective behavior. The event may grow out of the social structure, but whatever its origins, it con-

The 1980 Miami riots, during which 18 people were killed, were sparked by the acquittal of five White police officers accused of manslaughter in the death of a Black insurance executive.

tributes to the strains and beliefs shared by a group or community. For example, studies of race riots have found that interracial fights or arrests and searches of minority individuals by police officers often precede disturbances. The 1980 Miami riots, during which 18 people were killed, were sparked by the acquittal of five White police officers accused of manslaughter in the death of a Black insurance executive (M. Dunn and Porter, 1981:19; Lieberson and Silverman, 1965; National Advisory Commission on Civil Disorders, 1968).

According to Smelser, the presence of the four determinants identified above is necessary for collective behavior to occur. Nevertheless, the group must be *mobilized for action*. An extended thundershower or severe snowstorm may preclude such a mobilization. People are more likely to come together on weekends than on weekdays, in the evening rather than during the daytime.

The manner in which *social control is exercised*—both formally and informally—can be significant in determining whether the preceding factors will end in collective behavior. Stated simply, social control may prevent, delay, or interrupt a collective outburst. In some instances, forces of social control may be guilty of misjudgments that intensify the severity of an outbreak. In the view of Dunn and Porter (1981:8–9), local police made a

major strategic miscalculation during the 1980 Miami riots. Their initial response to the outbreak—trying to "cool things off" by pulling patrol cars out of the riot area—created a vacuum that allowed the level of violence to escalate.

The emergent-norm and value-added perspectives have both been questioned because of their imprecise definitions and the difficulty of testing them empirically. For example, the emergent-norm perspective of Turner and Killian has been criticized for being too vague in defining what constitutes a norm; the value-added model has been challenged because of its lack of specificity in defining generalized belief and structural strain. Of these two theories, the emergent-norm perspective appears to offer a more useful explanation of societywide episodes of collective behavior, such as crazes and fashions, than the value-added approach (M. Brown and Goldin, 1973; Quarantelli and Hundley, 1975; Tierney, 1980).

Nevertheless, Smelser's value-added model has been persuasive for many sociologists involved in the study of collective behavior. His perspective represents an advance over earlier theories that treated gatherings as dominated by irrational, extreme impulses. The value-added approach firmly relates episodes of collective behavior to the overall social structure of a society.

Assembling Perspective

As we have seen, one of the key determinants of collective behavior is mobilization for action. Some sociologists have given particular attention to the question of how people come together to undertake collective action. Clark McPhail, perhaps the most prolific researcher of collective behavior in the last 20 years, sees such behavior as involving people and organizations consciously responding to one another's actions. Drawing upon the work of the interactionist approach to sociology, McPhail has observed that organized interactions occur during such diverse events as celebrations and revolutions. People may chant, sing, or gesture with respect to a common object. In the midst of waiting in line outside a rock concert, as we have already seen, they may accept an emergent norm and begin to push forward toward the doors.

Building on the interactionist approach, McPhail and Miller (1973) introduced the concept of the assembling process. Earlier theorists of collective behavior had been content to explain events such as riots without concerning themselves with how gatherings of people actually came together. However, the *assembling perspective* sought for the first time to examine how and why people move from different points in space to a common location.

For example, sociologists David Snow, Louis Zurcher, and Robert Peters (1981) studied a series of football victory celebrations at the University of Texas that spilled over into the main streets of Austin. Some participants actively tried to recruit passersby for the celebrations by thrusting out open palms "to get five" or by yelling at drivers to honk their horns. In fact, encouraging still further assembling became a preoccupation of the celebrators. Whenever spectators were absent, those celebrating were relatively quiet.

A basic distinction has been made between two types of assemblies. *Periodic assemblies* include recurring, relatively routine gatherings of people such as work groups, college classes, and season ticket holders of an athletic series. These assemblies are characterized by advance scheduling and recurring attendance of the majority of participants. Thus, most members of an introductory sociology class may gather together for lectures every Monday, Wednesday, and Friday morning at a regular meeting time. By contrast, *nonperiodic assemblies* include demonstrations, parades, and gatherings at the scene of fires, accidents, and arrests. Such assemblies, for example, the 1989 celebrations at the Berlin Wall after the opening of Germany's borders, often result from word-of-mouth information and are generally less formal than periodic assemblies.

These three approaches to collective behavior give us deeper insight into relatively spontaneous and unstructured situations. Although episodes of collective behavior may seem irrational to outsiders, norms emerge among the participants and organized efforts are made to assemble at a certain time and place.

FORMS OF COLLECTIVE BEHAVIOR

Drawing upon the emergent-norm, value-added, and assembling perspectives—and upon other aspects of sociological examination—sociologists have examined many forms of collective behavior. Among these are crowds, disaster behavior, fads and fashions, panics and crazes, rumors, public opinion, and social movements.

Crowds

Crowds are temporary groupings of people in close proximity who share a common focus or interest. Spectators at a baseball game, participants at a pep rally, and rioters are all examples of crowds. Sociologists have been interested in what characteristics are common to crowds. Of course, it can be difficult to generalize, since the nature of crowds varies dramatically. For example, in terms of the emotions shared by crowds, hostages on a hijacked airplane experience intense fear, whereas participants in a religious revival feel a deep sense of joy.

Like other forms of collective behavior, crowds are not totally lacking in structure. Even during riots, participants are governed by identifiable social norms and exhibit definite patterns of behavior. Sociologists Richard Berk and Howard

Aldrich (1972) examined patterns of vandalism in 15 American cities during the riots of the 1960s. They found that stores of merchants perceived as exploitive were likely to be attacked, while private homes and public agencies with positive reputations were more likely to be spared. Apparently, looters had reached a collective agreement as to what constituted a "proper" or "improper" target for destruction.

If we apply the emergent-norm perspective to urban rioting, we can suggest that a new social norm is accepted (at least temporarily) which basically condones looting. The norms of respect for private property—as well as norms involving obedience to the law—are replaced by a concept of all goods as community property. All desirable items, including those behind locked doors, can be used for the "general welfare." In effect, the emergent norm allows looters to take what they regard as properly theirs (Quarantelli and Dynes, 1970; see also McPhail, 1991).

Disaster Behavior

Newspapers, television reports, and even rumors bring us word of many disasters around the world. The term *disaster* refers to a sudden or disruptive event or set of events that overtaxes a community's resources so that outside aid is necessary (J. Thompson and Hawkes, 1962:268). Traditionally, disasters have been catastrophes related to nature, such as earthquakes, floods, and fires. Yet, in an industrial age, natural disasters have now been joined by such "technological disasters" as airplane crashes, industrial explosions, nuclear meltdowns, and massive chemical poisonings (M. Brown and Goldin, 1973:34; see also Kreps, 1984:311–313).

Sociologists have made enormous strides in disaster research despite the problems inherent in this type of investigation. The work of the Disaster Research Center—established at Ohio State University in 1963 and later relocated to the University of Delaware in 1985—has been especially important. The center has teams of trained researchers prepared to leave for the site of any disaster on 4 hours' notice. Their field kits include material identifying them as center staff members, recording equipment, and general interview guidelines for use in various types of disasters. En route to the scene, these researchers attempt to obtain news information in order to learn about the conditions they may encounter. Upon arrival, the team establishes a communication post to coordinate fieldwork and maintain contact with the center's headquarters.

(Gordon/Reflex/Picture Group)

Workers are shown searching for debris after the 1988 crash of a Pan American Airlines plane in Lockerbie, Scotland. In the wake of many natural and technological disasters, there is increased structure and organization rather than chaos.

Since its founding, the Disaster Research Center has conducted more than 520 field studies of natural and technological disasters in the United States, as well as 24 in other nations. Its research has been used to develop effective planning and programming for dealing with disasters in such areas as delivery of emergency health care, establishment and operation of rumor-control centers, coordination of mental health services after disasters, and implementation of disaster-preparedness and emergency-response programs. In addition, the center has provided extensive training and field research for over 100 graduate students. These students maintain a professional commitment to disaster research and often go on to work for such disaster service organizations as the Red Cross and civil defense agencies (D. L. Miller, 1988:55–56; Quarantelli and Wilson, 1980; see also Cisin and Clark, 1962).

Remarkably, in the wake of many natural and technological disasters, there is increased structure and organization rather than chaos. In the United States, disasters are often followed by the creation of an emergency "operations group" which coordinates public services and even certain services normally carried out by the private sector (such as food distribution). Decision making becomes more centralized than in normal times (Dynes, 1978).

Fads and Fashions

An almost endless list of objects and behavior patterns seems temporarily to catch the fancy of Americans. Examples include silly putty, Davy Crockett coonskin caps, hula hoops, *Star Wars* toys, the Rubik cube, break dancing, Cabbage Patch Kids, *The Simpsons* T shirts, and Nintendo games. Fads and fashions are sudden movements toward the acceptance of some lifestyle or particular taste in clothing, music, or recreation (Aguirre et al., 1988; R. Johnson, 1985).

Fads are temporary patterns of behavior involving large numbers of people; they spring up independently of preceding trends and do not give rise to successors. By contrast, *fashions* are pleasurable mass involvements that feature a certain amount of acceptance by society and have a line of historical continuity (Lofland, 1981:442,

Fads and fashions are sudden movements involving a particular lifestyle or taste in clothing, music, or recreation.

1985). Thus, punk haircuts would be considered a fashion, part of the constantly changing standards of hair length and style, whereas adult roller skating would be considered a fad of the early 1980s.

Typically, when people think of *fashions*, they think of clothing, particularly women's clothing. In reality, fads and fashions enter every aspect of life where choices are not dictated by sheer necessity—vehicles, sports, music, drama, beverages, art, and even selection of pets. Any area of our lives that is subject to continuing change is open to fads and fashions. There is a clear commercial motive behind these forms of collective behavior. For example, in about 7 months of 1955, over $100 million of Davy Crockett items was sold, including coonskin caps, toy rifles, knives, camping gear, cameras, and jigsaw puzzles (Javna, 1986:16; Klapp, 1972:309).

Fads and fashions allow people to identify with something different from the dominant institutions and symbols of a culture. Members of a subculture may break with tradition while remaining "in" with (accepted by) a significant reference group of peers. Fads are generally short-lived and tend to be viewed with amusement or lack of interest by most nonparticipants. Fashions, by contrast, often have wider implications because they can reflect (or falsely give the impression of) wealth and status.

Panics and Crazes

Panics and crazes both represent responses to some generalized belief. A *craze* is an exciting mass involvement which lasts for a relatively long period of time (Lofland, 1981:441, 1985). For example, in late 1973, a press release from a Wisconsin congressman described how the federal bureaucracy had failed to contract for enough toilet paper for government buildings. Then, on December 19, as part of his nightly monologue on the *Tonight Show*, Johnny Carson suggested that it would not be strange if the entire nation experienced a shortage of toilet paper. Millions of Americans took his humorous comment seriously and immediately began stockpiling this item out of fear that it would soon be unavailable. Shortly thereafter, as a consequence of this craze, a shortage of toilet paper actually resulted. Its effects were felt into 1974 (Malcolm, 1974; *Money,* 1987).

By contrast, a *panic* is a fearful arousal or collective flight based on a generalized belief which may or may not be accurate. In a panic, people commonly perceive that there is insufficient time or inadequate means to avoid injury. Panics often occur on battlefields, in overcrowded burning buildings, or during stock market crashes. The key distinction between panics and crazes is that panics are flights *from* something whereas crazes are movements *to* something.

One of the most famous cases of panic in the United States was touched off by a media event: the 1938 Halloween eve radio dramatization of H. G. Wells's science fiction novel *The War of the Worlds*. This CBS broadcast realistically told of an invasion from Mars, with interplanetary visitors landing in New Jersey and taking over New York City 15 minutes later. The announcer indicated at the beginning of the broadcast that the account was fictional, but about 80 percent of the listeners tuned in late.

Clearly, a significant number of listeners became frightened by what they assumed to be a news report. However, some accounts have exaggerated people's reactions to *The War of the Worlds*. One report concluded that "people all over the United States were praying, crying, fleeing frantically to escape death from the Martians" (R. W. Brown, 1954:871). In contrast, a CBS national survey of 460 listeners found that only 91 (or about 20 percent) were genuinely scared by the broadcast (Cantril, 1940:102–107; Houseman, 1972). Although perhaps a million Americans *reacted* to this program, many reacted by switching to other stations to see if the "news" was being carried elsewhere. When viewed properly, this "invasion from outer space" set off a limited panic, rather than mass hysteria.

It is often believed that people engaged in panics or crazes are unaware of their actions, but this is certainly not the case. As the emergent-norm perspective suggests, people take cues from one another as to how to act during such forms of collective behavior. Even in the midst of an escape from a life-threatening situation, such as a fire in a crowded theater, people do not tend to run in a headlong stampede. Rather, they adjust their behavior on the basis of the perceived circumstances and the conduct of others who are assembling in a given location. To outside observers studying the events, people's decisions may seem foolish (pushing against a locked door) or suicidal (jumping from a balcony). Yet, for that individual at that moment, the action may genuinely seem appropriate—or the only desperate choice available (Quarantelli, 1957).

Rumors

A man responding to an advertisement came to the designated address and asked if the ad was correct. "Yes," said the woman at the door, "this almost-new Porsche will be yours for only $50." Hardly believing his good fortune, the man gave the car a test run and presented the woman with a $50 bill. The man finally asked her if she realized that the Porsche she had sold would be a bargain at $5000. Her reply was simple: "My husband ran off with his secretary and left a note instructing me to sell the car and send him the money."

This story has reappeared in newspapers for years, often with such vague introductions as "a doctor at Dallas General said." In 1980, columnist Ann Landers reported the account as fact. However, there is no proof that the incident actually took place. Concerted efforts to investigate its authenticity by the *Chicago Tribune* led to the conclusion that it was a rumor that had spread across the nation. The $50 sports car thus joins such legendary rumors as the alligators in city sewers ("Years ago a boy flushed two pet alligators down the toilet. They were long forgotten until a sewer worker came upon hundreds of giant alligators . . ."). Stories such as these illustrate how people believe, hope, or fear that unlikely events have taken place (Brunvand, 1980, 1981, 1989; see also Allport and Postman, 1947; J. Best and Horiuchi, 1985; Treadway, 1987).

Not all rumors that we hear are so astonishing, but none of us is immune from hearing or starting rumors. A **rumor** is a piece of information gathered informally which is used to interpret an ambiguous situation (R. Berk, 1974:78). As American novelist James Fenimore Cooper noted, it is very tempting to accept a story when one is unable to confirm or deny it—especially if the rumor is entertaining and vaguely plausible.

Rumors about celebrities—whether politicians, movie stars, or members of royal families—have long been a popular pastime around the world. In 1986, for example, Isabelle Adjani, one of the leading actresses in France, had to appear on French television to dispel widespread rumors that (1) she had AIDS and (2) she had died (Blume, 1987). Similarly, a number of American film stars have responded to rumors that they have AIDS by public appearances and denials.

Like celebrities, business firms find that rumors can be damaging. One type of rumor that is particularly worrisome for manufacturers involves ill-founded charges of contamination. In the late 1970s, it was rumored that General Foods' Pop Rocks and Cosmic Candy would explode in children's mouths with tragic results, yet no such explosions took place. Another popular theme of rumors in the marketplace focuses on the charge that a company is using its profits for evil purposes (Koenig, 1985). As is evident in Box 20-1 (page 612), a company engaged in rumor control

may find this process both time-consuming and expensive.

Publics and Public Opinion

The least organized and most individualized form of collective behavior is represented by publics. The term **public** refers to a dispersed group of people, not necessarily in contact with one another, who share interest in an issue. As the term is used in the study of collective behavior, the public does not include everyone. Rather, it is a collective of people who focus on some issue, engage in discussion, agree or disagree, and sometimes dissolve when the issue has been decided (Blumer, 1955:189–191, 1969:195–208; R. Turner and Killian, 1987:158–185).

The term **public opinion** refers to expressions of attitudes on matters of public policy which are communicated to decision makers. The last part of this definition is particularly important. From the point of view of theorists of collective behavior, there can be no public opinion unless there is both a public and a decision maker. We are not concerned here with the formation of an individual's attitudes on social and political issues; this question was explored in Chapter 15. Instead, in studying public opinion, we focus on the ways in which a public's attitudes are communicated to decision makers and on the ultimate outcome of the public's attempts to influence policymaking (R. Turner and Killian, 1987).

Polls and surveys play a major role in the assessment of public opinion. Using the same techniques that are essential in developing reliable questionnaire and interview schedules (see Chapter 2), survey specialists conduct studies of public opinion for business firms (market analyses), the government, the mass media (ratings of programs), and, of course, politicians.

The earliest political polls lacked the scientific rigor that contemporary social scientists require. In a famous example of unscientific and misleading polling, the magazine *Literary Digest* sent over 18 million postcard ballots to Americans to assess voters' opinions on the 1936 presidential election. The 2 million replies indicated that Republican candidate, Alf Landon, would defeat Democratic incumbent Franklin D. Roosevelt. *Literary Digest*

CHAPTER 20 • COLLECTIVE BEHAVIOR AND SOCIAL CHANGE

BOX 20-1 • EVERYDAY BEHAVIOR

PROCTER AND GAMBLE'S FIGHT AGAINST RUMORS OF SATANISM

Procter and Gamble is one of the leading consumer marketers in the United States. Its diverse products include Folger's coffee, Tide detergent, Ivory soap, Head and Shoulders shampoo, Crest toothpaste, Jif peanut butter, and Pampers disposable diapers. Yet, according to persistent rumors, the company that makes Ivory soap is engaged in Satanic activities!

At the center of this sweeping and completely unproven charge is Procter and Gamble's distinctive corporate trademark: the man in the moon and 13 stars. Adapted as the company's trademark in 1850, this presentation was developed by a nineteenth-century art director who drew 13 stars to represent the nation's original colonies. However, beginning in 1978, rumors reported that the trademark was a symbol of Satanism and that Procter and Gamble's profits were channeled into Satanic activities. One fallacious charge was that Procter and Gamble's chairman had appeared on television on *Donahue* and stated that he owed all his success to

(*Procter & Gamble*)

Procter and Gamble's moon and stars trademark was first registered with the U.S. Patent Office in 1882. About 100 years later, it made Procter and Gamble the target of widespread rumors.

Satan. In still another variation of the rumor, Procter and Gamble was alleged to be under the control of the Reverend Sun Myung Moon and his Unification church (refer back to Chapter 14).

As the rumor spread across the United States, Procter and Gamble took action. Press releases were issued denying that any Procter and Gamble executive had ever credited his own or the company's success to Satanism. Religious leaders—among them Billy Graham and Jerry Falwell—were

enlisted to help combat the rumored link between the company and Satanism. At the height of its rumor-control efforts, Procter and Gamble employed 15 staff members to deal with as many as 15,000 monthly inquiries about possible ties to Satan.

By the early 1980s, this rumor seemed to be fading, but it resurfaced again in 1984. Procter and Gamble began a new initiative against these charges, including lawsuits against people who had allegedly spread "false and malicious" statements associating the company with Satanism. But, in the end, the fight against such rumors became so costly that Procter and Gamble regretfully decided upon a symbolic concession. In 1985, it announced that it would gradually remove the moon and stars trademark from Procter and Gamble's product packages. Nevertheless, the trademark still appears on corporate letterheads and publications.

SOURCES: Bacon, 1985; Koenig, 1985:39–54; Madigan, 1982; Procter and Gamble, 1985, 1986.

---

predicted a Landon victory, yet Roosevelt was reelected in a landslide.

Today, this method of polling would be regarded as completely unreliable. The magazine took its original sample from automobile registration lists and telephone books. Yet, in 1936, in the midst of the Depression, those Americans with enough money to own a car or a private telephone were hardly a representative cross section

of the nation's voters. Instead, those polled tended to be prosperous citizens who might be likely to support Republican candidates (Squire, 1988).

Current political polls use more precise and representative sampling techniques. As a result, their projections of presidential elections often fall within a few percentage points of the actual vote. As Table 20-1 indicates, the Gallup poll

TABLE 20-1 Picking Presidential Election Winners: The Gallup Poll's Accuracy, 1956–1988

ELECTION	WINNER	FINAL GALLUP PROJECTION, %	ACTUAL POPULAR VOTE, %
1936	Franklin D. Roosevelt	55.7	60.8
1940	Franklin D. Roosevelt	52.0	54.7
1944	Franklin D. Roosevelt	51.5	53.4
1948	Harry S. Truman	44.5	49.6
1952	Dwight D. Eisenhower	51.0	55.1
1956	Dwight D. Eisenhower	59.5	57.4
1960	John F. Kennedy	51.0	49.7
1964	Lyndon B. Johnson	64.0	61.1
1968	Richard M. Nixon	43.0	43.4
1972	Richard M. Nixon	62.0	60.7
1976	Jimmy Carter	48.0	50.1
1980	Ronald Reagan	47.0	50.7
1984	Ronald Reagan	59.0	58.8
1988	George Bush	53.0	53.4

SOURCES: Bureau of the Census, 1990a:244; R. Cook, 1988; Gallup Opinion Index, 1980; Kenny, 1984.

came within 3.7 percent of Ronald Reagan's vote in 1980, within 0.2 percent of Reagan's vote in 1984, and within 0.4 percent of George Bush's vote in 1988.

While political polling has improved dramatically since the *Literary Digest*'s 1936 fiasco, misleading surveys are still with us. Regrettably, AT&T has marketed call-in "polls" using its 900-area-code numbers. Viewers of television or newspaper readers are asked to call one number to register an opinion on an issue—or a second number to register a different opinion. There are many problems inherent in this type of "polling." The sample that emerges is hardly representative (refer back to Chapter 2) in that it includes only those people who happened to see the commercial or advertisement for the poll and who feel strongly enough about the issue to spend the typical charge of 50 cents per call (Budiansky, 1988).

Social Movements

Social movements are the most all-encompassing type of collective behavior, because they may include aspects of other types such as crowds, rumors, publics, and public opinion. Although such factors as physical environment, population, technology, and social inequality serve as sources of

Techniques of sampling have greatly improved, thereby increasing the accuracy of political polls. The average error in predicting presidential elections from 1936 to 1948 was 3.7 percent. From 1952 to 1964 it was 2.7 percent, whereas from 1968 to 1988 it was only 1.3 percent.

change—as we will discuss more fully later in the chapter—it is the *collective* effort of individuals organized in social movements that ultimately leads to social change. Sociologists use the term **social movements** to refer to organized collective activities to bring about or resist fundamental change in existing society. Herbert Blumer (1955:119), a theorist of collective behavior, recognized the special importance of social movements when he defined them as "collective enterprises to establish a new order of life."

Social movements can be contrasted with the forms of collective behavior described earlier in the chapter. Like publics, social movements tend to focus on issues of public policy. Like crowds and fads, they involve social change—although social movements aim at much more fundamental and long-lasting changes. Social movements persist over longer periods of time than other forms of collective behavior. In part, this is because so-

Social movements try to bring about fundamental changes in society. Shown are a protest by animal rights advocates, Chinese students demonstrating in Tiananmen Square in 1989, and a protest in London against the "poll tax" levied by the British government.

cial movements are more structured; their leadership is frequently well organized and ongoing. Ironically, as Robert Michels (1915) noted (see Chapter 6), political movements fighting for social change eventually take on bureaucratic forms of organization. Leaders dominate the decision-making process without directly consulting their followers.

In many nations, including the United States, social movements have had a dramatic impact on the course of history and the evolution of social structure. It would be naive to ignore the actions of abolitionists, suffragists, civil rights workers, and activists opposed to the war in Vietnam. Members of each social movement stepped outside traditional channels for bringing about social change and yet had a noticeable influence on American public policy (J. Wilson, 1973:5).

Although the importance of change and conflict is implicit in the existence of social movements, their activities can also be analyzed from a functionalist perspective. Even when unsuccessful, social movements contribute to the formation of public opinion. Initially, the ideas of Margaret Sanger and other early advocates of birth control were viewed as "radical," yet contraceptives are now widely available in the United States. Moreover, social movements are viewed by functionalists as providing a training ground for leaders of the political establishment. Such heads of state as Cuba's Fidel Castro and Iran's Ayatollah Khomeini came to power after serving as leaders of revolutionary movements. More recently, Poland's Lech Walesa and Czechoslovakia's Vaclav Havel led protest movements against Communist rule and subsequently became leaders of their countries' governments (Heberle, 1968).

How and why do social movements emerge? Obviously, people are often discontented with the way things are. But what causes them to organize at a particular moment in a collective effort to work for change? Sociologists rely on two explanations for why people mobilize: the relative-deprivation and resource-mobilization approaches.

Relative Deprivation Those members of a society who feel most frustrated and disgruntled by the social and economic conditions of their lives are not necessarily "worst off" in an objective sense. Social scientists have long recognized that what is most significant is how people *perceive* their situation. Karl Marx pointed out that although the misery of the workers was important in reflecting their oppressed state, so was their position relative to the capitalist ruling class. In 1847, Marx noted that

> . . . although the enjoyment of the workers has risen, the social satisfaction that they have has fallen in comparison with the increased enjoyment of the capitalist (Marx and Engels, 1955:94).

The term **relative deprivation** is defined as the conscious feeling of a negative discrepancy between legitimate expectations and present actualities (J. Wilson, 1973:69). It may be characterized by scarcity rather than lack of necessities (refer back to the distinction between absolute and relative poverty in Chapter 8). A relatively deprived person is dissatisfied because he or she feels downtrodden relative to some appropriate reference group. Thus, blue-collar workers who live in two-family houses with little lawn space—though hardly at the bottom of the economic ladder—may nevertheless feel deprived in comparison with corporate managers and professionals who live in lavish and exclusive suburbs.

In addition to the feeling of relative deprivation, two other elements must be present before discontent will be channeled into a social movement. People must feel that they have a right to their goals, that they deserve better than what they have. For example, the struggle against European colonialism in Africa (see Chapter 9) intensified when growing numbers of Africans decided that it was legitimate for them to have political and economic independence. At the same time, the disadvantaged group must perceive that it cannot attain its goals through conventional means. This belief may or may not be correct. Yet, whichever is the case, the group will not mobilize into a social movement unless there is a shared perception that its relative deprivation can be ended only through collective action (Morrison, 1971).

Critics of the relative-deprivation approach have noted that an increase in feelings of deprivation is not always necessary before people are moved to act. In addition, this approach fails to explain why certain feelings of deprivation are transformed into social movements, whereas in other situations there is no collective effort to reshape society. Consequently, in recent years sociologists have given increasing attention to the forces needed to bring about the emergence of social movements (Alain, 1985; Finkel and Rule, 1987; Orum, 1978).

Resource Mobilization Sociologist Anthony Oberschall (1973:199) has argued that in order to sustain social protest or resistance, there must be an "organizational base and continuity of leadership." The term *resource mobilization* is used to refer to the ways in which a social movement utilizes such resources as money, political influence, access to the media, and personnel. The success of a movement for change will depend in good part on how effectively it mobilizes its resources (see also J. Gamson, 1989; Staggenborg, 1989a, 1989b).

As people become part of a social movement, norms develop to guide their behavior. Members of the movement may be expected to attend regular meetings of organizations, pay dues, recruit new adherents, and boycott "enemy" products or speakers. The emergence of a new social movement can be evident from the rise of special language or new words for familiar terms. In recent years, social movements have been responsible for such new terms of self-reference as *Blacks* and *African Americans* (used to replace *Negroes*), the *aged* (used to replace *old folks*), *gays* (used to replace *homosexuals*), and *persons with disabilities* (used to replace *the handicapped*).

Leadership is a central factor in the mobilization of the discontented into social movements. Often a movement will be led by a charismatic figure, such as Dr. Martin Luther King, Jr. As Max Weber described it in 1904, *charisma* is that quality of an individual which sets him or her apart from ordinary people (see Chapter 15). Of course, charisma can fade abruptly; this accounts for the fragility of certain social movements.

Why do certain individuals join a social movement whereas others do not, when all share the same situation of relative deprivation and are sub-

ject to the same opportunities for resource mobilization? Karl Marx recognized the importance of recruitment when he called on workers to become aware of their oppressed status and develop a class consciousness (see Chapter 8). Like the contemporary resource-mobilization approach, Marx held that a social movement (specifically, the revolt of the proletariat) would require leaders to sharpen the awareness of the oppressed. They must help workers to overcome feelings of *false consciousness,* or attitudes that do not reflect workers' objective position, in order to organize a revolutionary movement. Similarly, one of the challenges faced by women's liberation activists of the late 1960s and early 1970s was to convince women that they were being deprived of their rights and of socially valued resources.

Unlike the relative-deprivation approach, the resource-mobilization perspective focuses on strategic difficulties confronted by social movements. Any movement for fundamental change will almost certainly arouse opposition; effective mobilization will depend in part on how the movement deals with resistance to its activities. The reasons people have for resisting social change, and the tactics they employ in resisting, will be discussed later in the chapter. In the following section, we will examine a number of explanations for social change.

THEORIES OF SOCIAL CHANGE

It is clearly a challenge to explain social change in the diverse and complex world of the 1990s. Theorists from several disciplines have sought to analyze social change. In some instances, they have examined historical events in order to arrive at a better understanding of contemporary changes. We will review three theoretical approaches to change: evolutionary theory, functionalist theory, and conflict theory.

Evolutionary Theory

Nineteenth-century theories of social change reflect the influence of Charles Darwin's (1809–1882) pioneering work in biological evolution. According to his approach, there has been a continuing progression of successive life forms. For example, since human beings came at a later stage of evolution than reptiles, we represent a "higher" form of life. Social theorists sought an analogy to this biological model of development and originated *evolutionary theory,* which views society as moving in a definite direction. Early evolutionary theorists generally agreed that society was inevitably progressing to a higher state. As might be expected, they concluded in an ethnocentric fashion that their own behavior and culture were more advanced than those of earlier civilizations.

Auguste Comte (1798–1857), described in Chapter 1 as a founder of sociology, was an evolutionary theorist of change. He saw human societies as moving forward in their thinking from mythology to the scientific method. Similarly, Émile Durkheim (1933, original edition 1893) maintained that society progressed from simple to more complex forms of social organization.

The writings of Comte and Durkheim are examples of *unilinear evolutionary theory.* This approach contends that all societies pass through the same successive stages of evolution and inevitably reach the same end. English sociologist Herbert Spencer (1820–1903), also discussed in Chapter 1, used a similar approach: Spencer likened society to a living body with interrelated parts that were moving toward a common destiny. However, contemporary evolutionary theorists such as Gerhard Lenski, Jr., are more likely to picture social change as multilinear than to rely on the more limited unilinear perspective. *Multilinear evolutionary theory* holds that change can occur in several ways and that it does not inevitably lead in the same direction (Haines, 1988; J. Turner, 1985).

Multilinear theorists recognize that human culture has evolved along a number of lines. For example, the theory of demographic transition graphically demonstrates that population change in developing nations has not necessarily followed the model evident in industrialized nations (see Chapter 19). Medical and public health technology was introduced gradually in the developed nations, which gave them time to adjust to falling death rates and resulting rises in population. However, such technology was imported much more rapidly by developing nations, leading to dramatic population growth and severe pressure on social services and natural resources, including food production (R. Appelbaum, 1970:15–64).

Functionalist Theory

As has been stressed throughout this textbook, functionalist sociologists are concerned with the role of cultural elements in preserving the social order as a whole. They focus on what maintains a system, not on what changes it. This might seem to suggest that functionalists can offer little of value to the study of social change. Yet, as the work of American sociologist Talcott Parsons demonstrates, functionalists have made a distinctive contribution to this area of sociological investigation.

Parsons (1902–1979), a leading proponent of functionalist theory (refer back to Chapter 1), viewed society as naturally being in a state of equilibrium. By "equilibrium," he meant that society tends toward a state of stability or balance. Parsons would view even prolonged labor strikes or civilian riots as temporary disruptions in the status quo rather than as significant alterations in a society's social structure. Therefore, according to his *equilibrium model,* as changes occur in one part of society, there must be adjustments in other parts. If this does not take place, the society's equilibrium will be threatened and strains will occur.

Reflecting an evolutionary approach, Parsons (1966:21–24) maintained that four processes of social change are inevitable. The first, *differentiation,* refers to the increasing complexity of social organization. A change from "medicine man" to physician, nurse, and pharmacist is an illustration of differentiation in the field of health. This process is accompanied by *adaptive upgrading,* whereby social institutions become more specialized in their purposes. The division of labor among physicians into obstetricians, internists, surgeons, and so forth is an example of adaptive upgrading.

The third process identified by Parsons is the *inclusion* of groups into society which were previously excluded by virtue of such factors as gender, race, and social class background. Medical schools have practiced inclusion by opening their doors to increasing numbers of women and Blacks. Finally, Parsons contends that societies experience *value generation,* the development of new values that tolerate and legitimate a greater range of activities. The acceptance of preventive medicine is an example of value generation; American society has broadened its view of desirable health care. All four processes identified by Parsons stress consensus—that is, societal agreement on the nature of social organization and values (B. Johnson, 1975; R. Wallace and Wolf, 1980:50–51).

Parsons's approach explicitly incorporates the evolutionary notion of continuing progress. However, the dominant theme in his model is balance and stability. Society may change, but it remains stable through new forms of integration. In place of the kinship ties that provided social cohesion in the past, there will be laws, judicial processes, and new values and belief systems.

As noted by critics such as sociologist Alvin Gouldner (1960), the functionalist approach virtually disregards the use of coercion by the powerful to maintain the illusion of a stable, well-integrated society. Functionalists assume that social institutions will not persist unless they continue to contribute to the overall society. This leads to an evaluation that altering institutions will threaten societal equilibrium (Abrahamson, 1978:42–50; Colomy, 1986).

Conflict Theory

The functionalist perspective minimizes change. It emphasizes the persistence of social life and views change as necessary in order to maintain the equilibrium (or balance) of a society. By contrast, conflict theorists contend that social institutions and practices continue because powerful groups have the ability to maintain the status quo. Change has crucial significance, since it is needed to correct social injustices and inequalities.

Karl Marx accepted the evolutionary argument that societies develop along a particular path. However, unlike Comte and Spencer, he did not view each successive stage as an inevitable improvement over the previous one. History, according to Marx, proceeds through a series of

stages, each of which has an exploited class of people. Ancient society exploited slaves; the estate system of feudalism exploited serfs; modern capitalist society exploits the working class. Ultimately, through a socialist revolution led by the proletariat, human society will move toward the final stage of development: a classless communist society, or "community of free individuals" as Marx described it in *Das Kapital* (original edition 1867; Bottomore and Rubel, 1956:250).

As was noted earlier in this book, Karl Marx had an important influence on the development of sociology. His thinking offered insights into such institutions as the economy, the family, religion, and government. The Marxist view of social change is appealing because it does not restrict people to a passive role in responding to inevitable cycles or changes in material culture. Rather, Marxist theory offers a tool for those who wish to seize control of the historical process and gain their freedom from injustice. In contrast to functionalists' emphasis on stability, Marx argues that conflict is a normal and desirable aspect of social change. Indeed, change must be encouraged as a means of eliminating social inequality (Lauer, 1982).

One conflict sociologist, Ralf Dahrendorf (1959), has noted that the contrast between the functionalist emphasis on stability and the conflict perspective's focus on change reflects the contradictory nature of society. Human societies are stable and long-lasting, yet they also experience serious conflict. Indeed, Parsons spoke of new functions that result from social change, and Marx recognized the need for change so that societies could function more equitably. In Dahrendorf's view, the functionalist and conflict approaches are ultimately compatible despite their many areas of disagreement.

SOURCES OF SOCIAL CHANGE

The theoretical approaches to social change presented above underscore the multidimensional nature of change as a social phenomenon. This section will examine sources of change identified by sociologists as being particularly significant in reshaping behavior and social structure. Earlier, in Chapter 3, we saw that the general processes of innovation and diffusion contribute to the expansion of human culture. In addition to these processes of change, sociologists have determined that physical environment, population, science and technology, inequality, and youth are key sources of change.

Physical Environment

The dust storms and erosion which became critical in the 1930s helped Americans to realize that soil was not an inexhaustible resource. These "dust bowl" days also precipitated a migration out of farm areas in Nebraska and Oklahoma. Many rural residents moved to the cities in search of better living conditions. The difficulties of life in the "dust bowl" did not dictate *where* migrants went; their choices were determined by the same push and pull factors described in Chapter 19. Nevertheless, the environmental calamities of the region certainly limited the kinds of living patterns that were possible in the area.

Recent assessments of the availability of natural resources have reaffirmed the effects of physical environment in directing change in human behavior. Debates over depletion of fossil fuels such as coal and oil, global warming from the greenhouse effect, the loss of rain forests, and the extinction of animals and plants have all precipitated protests and social movements demanding change.

In 1980, a presidential task force issued its *Global 2000* report, featuring rather discouraging conclusions. While the world's food production will increase 90 percent by the year 2000, most of the increase will benefit nations that currently enjoy relatively high per capita consumption of food. Yet per capita food consumption in the developing nations will barely improve and may even decline. Moreover, though the world's fuel resources of coal, oil, gas, oil shale, and uranium are theoretically sufficient for the coming centuries, these resources are also unevenly distributed. There may need to be significant changes in people's lifestyles—particularly if the developing nations mount a more determined challenge to the unequal distribution of resources (Council on Environmental Quality, 1980; Rifkin, 1980).

Population

Changes in the size, density, and composition of a population have an important impact on social change. This is evident when one studies the problems of our nation's central cities (see Chapter 18). As affluent residents and business firms leave the cities, it becomes much more difficult to support public transportation and social services. Even if the size of a population remains stable, shifts in its composition lead to different demands on government. School buildings may stand empty, while health care facilities become overburdened.

Population changes affect many of the social policy issues that have been considered in this book. An increase in the birthrate of the United States will add to the need for day care facilities (see Chapter 4). High rates of immigration from Mexico and other Latin American countries have contributed to the expansion of bilingual educational programs (see Chapters 3 and 10).

The *Global 2000* report described above emphasizes the potentially damaging impact of overpopulation on the world's limited resources. However, according to critics of the report, population increases throughout history have generally been associated with economic development. A growing population does not necessarily mean that people are getting poorer. Consequently, in the view of critics of the *Global 2000* report, we should adopt a restrained yet optimistic outlook concerning the future (Kahn and Simon, 1984).

Science and Technology

History chronicles the instances in which changes have been set in motion by advances in science and technology. The term **science** refers to the body of knowledge obtained by methods based upon systematic observation. **Technology,** as was noted in Chapter 15, refers to the application of such knowledge to the making of tools and the utilization of natural resources.

Technological developments are closely associated with historical changes; for example, the use of three-masted, seagoing galleons and cannons facilitated European conquest of the world during the sixteenth through nineteenth centuries.

BOX 20-2 • EVERYDAY BEHAVIOR

COMPUTERS AND SOCIAL CHANGE

Computers have "arrived" as a dominant force in American society and a significant contributor to social change. As a technological advance, the development of the computer has facilitated everything from registration for college classes to the maintenance of accounts by credit card companies. Law enforcement officials are increasingly turning to computers for record keeping; writers are using word-processing programs to churn out their latest books. At the same time, personal computers have proved useful in the home for paying bills and doing other financial tasks.

Although computers have undoubtedly been a valuable aid to academic research, sociologists and educators have expressed concern regarding differential access to this form of technology. For example, a 1985 survey found that the wealthiest public school districts in the United States average one computer for every 54 students; by contrast, the poorer

(Harley Schwadron)

"Be reasonable. One can hardly be expected to solve the riddle of existence without a computer."

districts have only one for every 73 students. Fully one-fourth of the schools in the poorest districts have no computers at all, yet the per capita number of computers is rising faster in wealthy districts than in poorer ones (Fiske, 1985).

There is similar concern regard-ing differential use of computers by boys and girls. Computer games, which serve as an important means of early socialization to computers, typically involve sports or skills associated with the male gender role (see Chapters 4 and 11). As a result, computer

---

Advances in agricultural technology, ranging from the iron-tipped plow to the three-crop rotation system, made possible the creation of a social surplus—thereby leading to the emergence of the preindustrial cities described in Chapter 18 (L. White, 1962:78). More recently, as is discussed in Box 20-2 above, computers have become an important factor in social change in the United States.

From a conflict perspective, scientific and technological advances are somewhat like other valued resources in that all nations do not absorb them at the same rate. Less developed countries generally must turn to more industrialized societies for new applications in science. The term *technology transfer* refers to the importation of new applications of knowledge that are available elsewhere, sometimes in a modified form. Unfor-

BOX 20-2 • EVERYDAY BEHAVIOR

COMPUTERS AND SOCIAL CHANGE (Continued)

camps and video arcades have become predominantly male settings. In some instances, institutions explicitly discourage females from seeking computer training. One Wisconsin high school solved the problem of scarce microcomputer equipment by mandating that computers would be reserved for male students, who needed them for "preparation for engineering careers" (Van Gelder, 1985:89).

Survey data clearly reflect differential patterns of computer use by gender. According to one study, first-grade girls and boys display equal interest in learning to program computers. However, by sixth grade the number of boys interested in computers is twice that of girls; by ninth grade, the ratio has risen to four to one (R. Hess and Miura, 1985; Wilder et al., 1985). With such data in mind, social psychologist Sara Kiesler (1983) worries that men's early familiarity with computers will ultimately give them a competitive advantage over women in pursuing careers and professions.

One group of disadvantaged Americans may especially benefit from computer technology: people with disabilities. Terminals lend themselves to ancillary devices that make them adaptable to most types of physical impairments. By 1986, some 30,000 workers were linked full time to their offices, while an additional 100,000 worked at home on a part-time basis using computer linkups. Such home work, known as *telecommuting*, offers an attractive new option for people with limited mobility (Noble, 1986).

The issue of work at home has economic and social implications which go far beyond the special meaning for Americans with disabilities. Sociologist Nathan Keyfitz (1984) notes that since telephones can easily be joined to computers, both the able-bodied and the disabled can perform office work at home. Paradoxically, although the computer stands as the foundation of the postindustrial revolution, it may facilitate a return of the workplace to the

home—a characteristic of horticultural societies. Leaders of labor unions are watching such developments carefully, since they fear that a home-based economy could make it impossible to organize workers and engage in collective bargaining (Leidner, 1988).

Organized labor's fears regarding work at home remind us that, like most forms of social change, computers have spurred resistance. Those people and institutions with a vested interest in the status quo—ranging from manufacturers of slide rules to producers of nondigital watches—fear that they will suffer from the massive entry of silicon chips into the marketplace. Moreover, while use of computers has increased efficiency in both manufacturing and service occupations, many workers have lost their jobs as a result. Middle-aged and elderly workers are especially likely to suffer from such job displacement, since they will have fewer opportunities to redirect their careers (Keyfitz, 1984).

tunately, although the technology sold to developing nations supports the interests of the supplier—whether a government, a multinational corporation, or a smaller firm—it will not necessarily meet the needs of the recipient. For example, a study of 50 industrial plants in Indonesia—plants which produced goods ranging from soft drinks to plastic sandals—revealed that imported technology was often poorly suited to the prevail-

ing conditions of the Indonesian economy and workplace. Furthermore, even when technology transfer is carried out in a manner that is more sensitive to local needs, the low costs and ready availability of imported technology may nevertheless stifle the further development of modern technologies already installed in the developing nation (Sardar and Rosser-Owen, 1977; Wells, 1972).

Social Inequality

As we saw in Chapter 8, people receive unequal amounts of wealth, income, status, and power. This inequality leads those who perceive themselves as deprived to seek a redistribution of valued social rewards. Earlier in the book, we considered movements for social change initiated by racial minorities (Chapter 10), women (Chapter 11), and the elderly (Chapter 12); in the social policy section of this chapter, we will examine the disability rights movement. These movements share a common opposition to social inequality and a desire to transform long-standing patterns of prejudice and discrimination.

Without question, the persistence of social inequality in a society can stimulate efforts toward social change. Sociologist Theda Skocpol (1979) has stressed the role of revolution in rapid yet basic transformation of a society's class structure. Obviously, such revolutions are carried out from below; the powerful have a stake in maintaining the existing stratification systems. Yet, as Karl Marx was well-aware, people may remain oppressed for a long time without calling for change, much less for rebellion and revolution. Like other sources of social change, the strains of inequality do not necessarily lead to actual changes. The discontented must be *mobilized* if change is to occur (W. Moore, 1974:87–90).

Youth

Young people have traditionally been viewed as the vanguard of social change. Even thousands of years ago in Ur, as the opening quotation in this chapter reveals, powerful elders sensed a threat from the actions of the young (A. Roth, 1960:277). In the United States, youth has played a prominent role in many diverse movements fighting for social change. According to historian David Donald (1956:26–27), the median age of abolitionist leaders opposing slavery was 29. Similarly, many young Blacks and Whites joined the civil rights movement of the 1960s. Dr. Martin Luther King, Jr., was only 24 when he began working as an organizer on behalf of civil rights.

It is not simply youth in itself that leads one to become committed to change. The young are less directly involved in established social institutions than their elders and have fewer social and economic ties to the existing social structure. Consequently, they can be mobilized to join movements for change more easily than those who have a greater stake in the status quo.

RESISTANCE TO SOCIAL CHANGE

As has been stressed throughout this chapter, efforts to promote social change are likely to be met with resistance. In the midst of rapid scientific and technological innovations, many people are emotionally frightened by the demands of an ever-changing society. However, certain individuals and groups have a stake in maintaining the existing state of affairs.

Social economist Thorstein Veblen (1857–1929) coined the term *vested interests* to refer to those people or groups who will suffer in the event of social change. For example, the American Medical Association (AMA) has taken strong stands against national health insurance and the professionalization of midwifery (refer back to Chapter 17). National health insurance could lead to limits on the income of physicians, and a rise in the status of midwives could threaten the preeminent position of doctors as the nation's deliverers of babies. In general, those with a disproportionate share of society's wealth, status, and power, such as members of the American Medical Association, have a vested interest in preserving the status quo (Starr, 1982; Veblen, 1919).

Economic factors play an important role in resistance to social change. For example, it can be expensive for manufacturers to meet the highest possible standards for the safety of products and of industrial workers. Conflict theorists argue that, in a capitalist economic system, many firms are not willing to pay the price of meeting strict safety standards. They may resist social change by cutting corners within their plants or by pressuring the government to ease regulations.

Cultural factors also shape resistance to change. As noted in Chapter 3, William F. Ogburn (1922) distinguished between material and nonmaterial aspects of culture. *Material culture* includes inventions, artifacts, and technology; *nonmaterial culture* encompasses ideas, norms, communication, and social organization. Ogburn pointed out that one cannot devise methods for controlling and utilizing new technology before the introduction of a technique. Thus, nonmaterial culture typically must respond to changes in material culture. Ogburn introduced the term *culture lag* to refer to the period of maladjustment during which the nonmaterial culture is still adapting to new material conditions.

In certain cases, changes in material culture can add strain to the relationships between social institutions. For example, new techniques of birth control have been developed in recent decades. Large families are no longer economically necessary, nor are they commonly endorsed by American social norms. But certain religious faiths, among them Roman Catholicism and Mormonism, continue to extol large families and to view methods of limiting family size such as contraception and abortion as undesirable. This represents a lag between aspects of material culture (technology) and nonmaterial culture (religious beliefs). Conflicts may emerge between religion and other social institutions, such as government and the educational system, over the dissemination of

birth control and family planning information (Lauer, 1982:152).

Today, social movements often seem to question the traditional basis for a culture. The feminist and gay liberation movements have challenged cultural beliefs long accepted as "natural"—that the male is the dominant member of the species, that heterosexuality is the only healthy form of sexual orientation, and so forth. Not surprisingly, resistance to such movements is often very strong. The resource-mobilization approach has focused not only on how social movements mobilize but also on how resistance to change is expressed (R. Roberts and Kloss, 1974:153–157; Zald and McCarthy, 1979). Forms of resistance to social movements include:

- *Ridicule.* The women's movement was tagged with the derisive label "women's lib" by its detractors. At the same time, feminists were stereotyped as "bra burners."
- *Cooptation.* One way to pacify members of a social movement is to appear to incorporate, or coopt, its goals or leaders into the political structure. In 1991, while facing strong criticism from Black civil rights groups, President George Bush

(© 1970, Valley Daily News)

When the National Guard shot and killed four students at Kent State University during a 1970 demonstration opposing the American invasion of Cambodia, a generation of youthful protestors learned that participation in a social movement can be extremely risky.

nominated Judge Clarence Thomas to fill a vacancy on the Supreme Court.

- *Formal social control.* During the 1950s, southern communities passed legislation banning civil rights marches. More recently, certain American colleges have denied official recognition of lesbian and gay male student organizations.
- *Violence.* If all other measures used to stop a social movement are unsuccessful, its opponents may resort to violence. When National Guard troops shot and killed four Kent State college students during a 1970 demonstration opposing the American invasion of Cambodia, a generation of young protestors learned that participation in a social movement can be extremely risky.

Social movements face a difficult challenge in their struggle for social change. Almost inevitably, powerful individuals and groups in society have a vested interest in opposing change. While members of a social movement attempt to mobilize their resources, the powerful do the same—and the powerful often have more money, more political influence, and greater access to the media. Nevertheless, human history is a history of change; resistance by those in power has often been overcome. In the social policy section which follows, we will see that disability rights activists have overcome resistance to force important changes in society's treatment of people with disabilities.

SOCIAL POLICY, SOCIAL MOVEMENTS, AND SOCIAL CHANGE
DISABILITY RIGHTS

- How does the medical model of disability compare with the civil rights model?
- In what ways do Americans with disabilities experience prejudice, discrimination, and other forms of social inequality?
- What difficulties does the disability rights movement face in mobilizing as a political bloc?

Throughout history, people with disabilities have often been subjected to cruel and inhuman treatment. For example, in the early twentieth century the disabled were frequently viewed as subhuman creatures who were a menace to society. As one result, many state legislatures passed compulsory sterilization laws aimed at handicapped people. Drawing on similar prejudices against the disabled, Adolf Hitler's Nazi regime persecuted and put to death perhaps as many as 1 million people with disabilities (H. Hahn, 1987:200; M. Rebell, 1986).

Today, such blatantly hostile treatment of disabled people has generally been replaced by a *medical model* which focuses on the functional impairments of the person. Those with disabilities are therefore viewed as chronic patients. In an adaptation of Talcott Parsons's sick role (refer back to Chapter 17), we can say that society assigns the disabled a "handicapped role." They are viewed as helpless, childlike people who are expected to assume a cheerful and continuing dependence on family members, friends, and health care professionals.

Increasingly, however, Americans concerned with the rights of the disabled have criticized this medical model. In the view of these activists, it is the unnecessary and discriminatory barriers present in the environment—both physical and attitudinal—that stand in the way of people with disabilities, more than their biological limitations do. Applying a *civil rights model,* activists emphasize that those with disabilities face widespread prejudice, discrimination, and segregation. For example, most voting places are architecturally inaccessible to wheelchair users and fail to offer ballots that can be used by people unable to read print. Many states continue to deny blind and deaf citizens the right to serve on juries. City and state government hearings, school board meetings, and other important public events are typically held in inaccessible locations and without sign language interpreters. Viewed from a conflict perspective, such public policies reflect unequal treatment that helps to keep people with disabilities in a subservient position (A. Asch, 1986:219; H. Hahn, 1987:194).

Labeling theorists, drawing on the earlier work of Erving Goffman (1963a), have suggested that society attaches a stigma to many forms of disability and that this stigma leads to prejudicial treatment. Indeed, people with disabilities frequently observe that the nondisabled see them only as blind, deaf, wheelchair users, and so forth, rather than as complex human beings with individual strengths and weaknesses whose blindness or deafness is merely one aspect of their lives. In this regard, a review of studies of women with disabilities disclosed that most academic research on the disabled does not differentiate by gender—thereby perpetuating the view that when a disability is present, no other personal characteristic can matter. Consequently, as noted in Chapter 5, disability serves as a master status (M. Fine and Asch, 1981, 1988a, 1988b; Gove, 1980:237; R. T. Smith, 1980).

The mass media have contributed to stereotyping of people with disabilities by treating them with a mixture of pity and fear. Nationwide charity telethons promote negative images of the handicapped by showing them as childlike, incompetent, and nonproductive. By contrast, in literature and film, "evil" characters with disabilities (from Captain Ahab to Dr. Strangelove) reinforce the view that disability is a punishment for evil and that the handicapped, out of a desire for revenge, would destroy the nondisabled if they could. Even ostensibly more favorable treatments of disabled characters tend to focus on unusually courageous and inspirational individuals who achieve striking personal successes against great odds—rather than on the impact of prejudice and discrimination on "ordinary" disabled people (Biklen, 1986; Krossel, 1988; Longmore, 1985; Zola, 1987).

By 1970, a strong social movement for disability rights—drawing on the experiences of the Black civil rights movement, the women's liberation movement, and various self-help movements—had emerged across the United States. This movement now includes organizations of people with a single disability (such as the National Federation of the Blind), organizations of people with different disabilities (such as New York City's Disabled in Action), a cross-disability legal advocacy organization (the Disability Rights Education and Defense Fund), and an activist, cross-disability publication (the Disability Rag). Women and men involved in the disability rights movement are working to challenge negative views of the disabled; to gain a greater voice for the disabled in all agency and public policy decisions that affect them; and to reshape laws, institutions, and environments so that people with disabilities can be fully integrated into mainstream society (Scotch, 1984:33–37).

The movement for disability rights also has a special focus on promoting the independence of people with disabilities. A key role in this effort has been played by the Center for Independent Living in Berkeley, California. The center was founded in 1972 by seven severely disabled people; one of them, Ed Roberts, a quadriplegic, had successfully pressured the University of California to admit him as a student in 1962. The original concept of independent living centers involved people with different disabilities working together, having a major voice in determining policy at the centers, and engaging in activism. Although this vision has not been fully achieved, by 1985 more than 300 independent living programs were assisting people with disabilities (Disability Rag, 1985; Funk, 1987: 14–15; Scotch, 1984:36).

Ironically, the war in Vietnam served as a major factor in advancing the disability rights movement. Because of war-related injuries, a large number of disabled Vietnam veterans joined forces with other Americans with disabilities in demanding full civil rights. Partly through the lobbying of disability rights organizations, a number of federal laws were passed to ensure the rights of people with disabilities. Among these were:

- Architectural Barriers Act of 1968, which provides for the elimination of architectural barriers from new federally funded buildings.
- Education for All Handicapped Children Act of 1975, Public Law 94–142, which promotes maximum integration of handicapped schoolchildren with nonhandicapped children (refer back to Chapter 16).
- Section 504 of the Rehabilitation Act of 1973, which declares that no recipient of federal funds may discriminate against a qualified handicapped person.

Disability rights activists won a dramatic victory in 1988 at Gallaudet University in Washington, D.C., the nation's only liberal arts college for the deaf. Gallaudet had long been governed by a board of trustees composed primarily of people who were not deaf, and the university had never had a deaf person as its president. When the trustees selected a new president who had no hearing impairment and did not know sign language, the campus erupted in protest. Deaf students, supported by many faculty members and alumni, shut down the school and held protest rallies outside the halls of Congress. After a week of demonstrations—which generated support from civic groups, labor unions, and politicians—the students achieved their primary goals. The newly appointed president and the chairwoman of the board of trustees both resigned and were replaced by deaf people. Gary Olson, executive director of the National Association for the Deaf, noted that deaf people "have shown the world that we can win and we're serious about our own human and civil rights" (Ayres, 1988a, 1988b; Reynolds, 1988:11A; see also Treesberg, 1991; L. Walker, 1989).

Despite such successes, by the late 1980s disability rights activists were well-aware that their struggle for equality was far from over. One journalist referred to people with disabilities as "probably the worst educated, most unemployed, most underpaid minority in America." Less than 9 percent of people with handicaps have completed high school. In 1988, only 23.4 percent of disabled men and 13.1 percent of disabled women worked full time. Even when they do find employment, many disabled people are placed in menial, "dead-end" jobs with low wages. While 22 percent of the nation's workers earn less than $15,000 per year, the same is true of 46 percent of workers with disabilities (New York Times, 1989; Virshup, 1990:34).

Architectural barriers and transportation difficulties often add to the problems of disabled people who seek or obtain employment. Simply getting around city streets can be quite difficult; for example, less than 3 percent of the sidewalks in New York City are properly equipped with curb cuts for wheelchair users. A genuinely barrier-free building needs more than a ramp; it should also include automatic doors, raised letters and braille on signs, and toilets that are accessible to the disabled. But even if a disabled person finds a job, and even if the job is in a barrier-free building, he or she still faces the problem of getting to work in a society where most rail stations and buses remain inaccessible to wheelchair users and others with disabilities (T. Cook, 1988; L. Davis, 1987:27; Mazrui, 1987).

With such issues in mind, the disability rights movement won an important victory in 1990 when President Bush signed the Americans with Disabilities Act (ADA). This civil rights law was passed only after a long legislative struggle, behind-the-scenes lobbying to weaken the bill by business groups, and demonstrations at the Capitol Rotunda by disability rights activists. The ADA will affect some 43 million Americans with a disability (defined as a condition that "substantially limits" a "major life activity" such as walking or sight).

This law, which is the most sweeping antidiscrimination law to be approved since the 1964 Civil Rights Act, will prohibit bias in employment, transportation, public accommodations, and telecommunications. Businesses with more than 25 employees will be forbidden to refuse to hire a disabled applicant; these companies will be expected to make a "reasonable

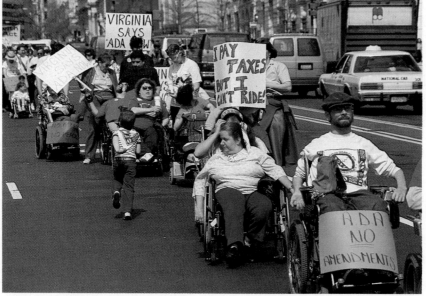

(Johnson/Gamma Liaison)

In early 1990, disability rights activists demonstrated in the streets of Washington, D.C., and outside the Capitol to show their support for the Americans for Disabilities Act (ADA).

accommodation" to permit such a worker to do the job. Commercial establishments such as office buildings, hotels, theaters, supermarkets, and dry cleaners have been barred from denying service to people with disabilities (Garr, 1990; Holmes, 1990e; Wade, 1989).

Opponents of various measures mandating accessibility often insist that these measures will be prohibitively expensive. However, disability rights activists argue that these projected costs are often overstated; backers of the ADA add that the law will benefit society by assisting the disabled to find employment and leave the welfare rolls. The federal government spends about $60 billion each year on people with disabilities, but only $3 billion goes for education, training, and rehabilitation, with the rest for benefits. According to one estimate, if even 10,000 disabled people join the work force each year, the government will save $70 million annually in cash benefits and will, in addition, receive millions in taxes from these new workers (Rasky, 1989b; W. Roth, 1989).

With passage of the ADA, the disability rights movement has begun to emphasize the issue of attendant services. Lack of affordable and reliable home care leaves thousands of severely disabled people powerless to benefit from the ADA—and forces others unnecessarily into nursing homes. Yet state support for home care services varies dramatically: whereas California provides personal assistants for more than 93,000 disabled people, Virginia does so for only 36 people. Disability rights activists view attendant services as a civil rights issue. In their view, advances in employment or accessible transportation are meaningless if a disabled person cannot get needed assistance to get up, get ready for work, and get out of the house (*Disability Rag*, 1990; S. Holmes, 1990g; see also Longmore, 1988).

In order to win future victories, the disability rights movement will need to become stronger as a political bloc. Yet the social movement for disability rights must overcome certain difficulties related to mobilization. Those with disabilities are geographically, socially, and economically dispersed; there is danger of fragmentation because of the diversity evident in the different types and levels of disability. Moreover, many of these individuals—especially those who are successfully employed—may not identify themselves consciously with the movement. Still, activists remain encouraged after passage of the ADA. Mary Johnson (1989:446), editor of the *Disability Rag,* has written: "Discrimination against people with disabilities has now been officially acknowledged. We've got a foot— or a wheel or a cane—in the door" (Bradley, 1990; Scotch, 1988).

SUMMARY

Collective behavior is the relatively spontaneous and unstructured behavior of a group that is reacting to an ambiguous situation. *Social change* is significant alteration over time in behavior patterns and culture, including norms and values. This chapter examines sociological theories used to understand collective behavior, forms of collective behavior, theories of social change, sources of change, and resistance to change.

1 Turner and Killian's *emergent-norm perspective* suggests that new norms of proper behavior may arise in ambiguous situations.

2 Smelser's *value-added model* of collective behavior outlines six important determinants of such behavior: structural conduciveness, structural strain, generalized belief, precipitating factor, mobilization of participants for action, and operation of social control.

3 The *assembling perspective* introduced by McPhail and Miller sought for the first time to examine how and why people move from different points in space to a common location.

4 Unlike certain situations involving collective behavior, *crowds* require people to be in relatively close contact and interaction.

5 The key distinction between a *panic* and a *craze* is that a panic is a flight *from* something whereas a craze is a movement *to* something.

6 A *rumor* serves a social function by providing a group with a shared belief.

7 *Social movements* are more structured than other forms of collective behavior and persist over longer periods of time.

8 Early advocates of *evolutionary theory* of social change believed that society was inevitably progressing to a higher state.

9 Talcott Parsons, a leading advocate of functionalist theory, viewed society as naturally being in a state of equilibrium or balance.

10 Conflict theorists see change as having crucial significance, since it is needed to correct social injustices and inequalities.

11 Important social changes have been set in motion by advances in *science* and *technology.*

12 The persistence of social inequality in a society can stimulate efforts toward social change.

13 In general, those with a disproportionate share of society's wealth, status, and power have a *vested interest* in preserving the status quo.

14 By the 1970s, a strong movement for disability rights had emerged across the United States.

KEY TERMS

Assembling perspective A theory of collective behavior introduced by McPhail and Miller which seeks to examine how and why people move from different points in space to a common location. (page 607)

Collective behavior In the view of sociologist Neil Smelser, the relatively spontaneous and unstructured behavior of a group of people who are reacting to a common influence in an ambiguous situation. (603)

Craze An exciting mass involvement which lasts for a relatively long period of time. (610)

Crowds Temporary gatherings of people in close proximity who share a common focus or interest. (607)

Culture lag Ogburn's term for a period of maladjustment during which the nonmaterial culture is still adapting to new material conditions. (623)

Disaster A sudden or disruptive event or set of events that overtaxes a community's resources so that outside aid is necessary. (608)

Emergent-norm perspective A theory of collective behavior proposed by Turner and Killian which holds that a collective definition of appropriate and inappropriate behavior emerges during episodes of collective behavior. (605)

Equilibrium model Talcott Parsons's functionalist view of society as tending toward a state of stability or balance. (617)

Evolutionary theory A theory of social change which holds that society is moving in a definite direction. (617)

Fads Temporary movements toward the acceptance of some particular taste or lifestyle that involve large numbers of people and are independent of preceding trends. (609)

False consciousness A term used by Karl Marx to describe an attitude held by members of a class that does not accurately reflect its objective position. (616)

Fashions Pleasurable mass involvements in some particular taste or lifestyle that have a line of historical continuity. (609)

Multilinear evolutionary theory A theory of social change which holds that change can occur in several ways and does not inevitably lead in the same direction. (617)

Nonperiodic assemblies Nonrecurring gatherings of people which often result from word-of-mouth information. (607)

Panic A fearful arousal or collective flight based on a generalized belief which may or may not be accurate. (610)

Periodic assemblies Recurring, relatively routine gatherings of people, such as college classes. (607)

Public A dispersed group of people, not necessarily in contact with one another, who share an interest in an issue. (611)

Public opinion Expressions of attitudes on matters of public policy which are communicated to decision makers. (611)

Relative deprivation The conscious feeling of a negative discrepancy between legitimate expectations and present actualities. (615)

Resource mobilization The ways in which a social movement utilizes such resources as money, political influence, access to the media, and personnel. (616)

Rumor A piece of information gathered informally which is used to interpret an ambiguous situation. (610)

Science The body of knowledge obtained by methods based upon systematic observation. (619)

Social change Significant alteration over time in behavior patterns and culture, including norms and values. (603)

Social movements Organized collective activities to bring about or resist fundamental change in existing society. (613)

Technology Application of knowledge to the making of tools and utilization of natural resources. (619)

Technology transfer The importation of new applications of knowledge that are available elsewhere, sometimes in modified form. (620)

Unilinear evolutionary theory A theory of social change which holds that all societies pass through the same successive stages of evolution and inevitably reach the same end. (617)

Value-added model A theory of collective behavior proposed by Neil Smelser to explain how broad social conditions are transformed in a definite pattern into some form of collective behavior. (605)

Vested interests Veblen's term for those people or groups who will suffer in the event of social change and who have a stake in maintaining the status quo. (622)

ADDITIONAL READINGS

Brunvand, Jan Harold. *Curses! Broiled Again!* New York: Norton, 1989. The author, an English professor, has collected another series of rumors which have become such an accepted part of our culture that they can perhaps be considered legends or folklore.

Fine, Michelle, and Adrienne Asch (eds.). *Women with Disabilities: Essays in Psychology, Culture, and Politics.* Philadelphia: Temple University Press, 1988. An anthology exploring scholarly and activist concerns on issues ranging from prejudice to employment policy, from friendship to social justice.

Garson, Barbara. *The Electronic Sweatshop.* New York: Simon and Schuster, 1988. A critical look at the impact of computers on society, arguing that this new technology is transforming the office of the future into the factory of the past.

Gartner, Alan, and Tom Joe (eds.). *Images of the Disabled. Disabling Images.* New York: Praeger, 1987. An anthology of articles by scholars and activists dealing with societal treatment of people with disabilities. Includes articles on images of the disabled in film, in fiction, and in the press.

Johnson, Richard A. *American Fads.* New York: Beech Tree, 1985. A brief presentation of 37 fads, beginning with the swallowing of goldfish in 1939.

Kapferer, Jean-Noel. *Rumors: Uses, Interpretations, and Images.* New Brunswick, N.J.: Transaction, 1990. A comprehensive examination of rumors, gossip, and urban legends drawing upon examples from both Europe and the United States.

Lofland, John. *Protest: Studies of Collective Behavior and Social Movements.* Rutgers, N.J.: Transaction, 1985. A collection of previously published essays dealing with protest actions.

Merton, Robert K. *The Sociology of Science: Theoretical and Empirical Investigations.* Chicago: University of Chicago Press, 1973. A collection of essays by the noted sociologist dealing with the normative structure and reward system of science.

Miller, David L. *Introduction to Collective Behavior.* Prospect Heights, Ill.: Waveland, 1988. The author, associated with the assembling perspective, covers all the major theoretical approaches of the field. He examines rumors, riots, social movements, immigration, and other forms of collective behavior.

Turner, Ralph H., and Lewis M. Killian. *Collective Behavior* (3d ed.). Englewood Cliffs, N.J.: Prentice-Hall, 1987. This textbook incorporates excerpts from theoretical and empirical studies of collective behavior. Turner and Killian advance an emergent-norm thesis that can be used to study collective behavior.

United Way of America. *What Lies Ahead: Countdown to the 21st Century.* Alexandria, Va.: United Way of America, 1989. The social, economic, political, and technological trends of the future are projected through use of a study by volunteer experts representing a variety of disciplines.

Zald, Mayer N., and John D. McCarthy (eds.). *Social Movements in an Organizational Society.* Rutgers, N.J.: Transaction, 1986. A detailed analysis of the processes involved when individuals and groups are mobilized for collective action.

Journals

Among those journals which focus on issues of collective behavior are the *International Journal of Mass Emergencies and Disasters* (founded in 1983), the *Journal of Popular Culture* (1967), and *Public Opinion Quarterly* (1937). *The Futurist* (founded in 1967) is a monthly magazine dedicated to exploring possible social and technological changes and their likely impact on society.

GLOSSARY

Note: Numbers following the definitions indicate pages where terms were identified. Consult the index for further page references.

Absolute poverty A standard of poverty based on a minimum level of subsistence below which families should not be expected to exist. (242)

Achieved status A social position attained by a person largely through his or her own effort. (134, 248)

Activity theory An interactionist theory of aging which argues that elderly people who remain active will be best-adjusted. (361)

Adoption In a legal sense, a process that allows for the transfer of the legal rights, responsibilities, and privileges of parenthood from legal parents to new legal parents. (394)

Affirmative action Positive efforts to recruit minority group members or women for jobs, promotions, and educational opportunities. (471)

Age grades Cultural categories that identify the stages of biological maturation. (360)

Ageism A term coined by Robert N. Butler to refer to prejudice and discrimination against the elderly. (366)

Agrarian society The most technologically advanced form of preindustrial society. Members are primarily engaged in the production of food but increase their crop yield through such innovations as the plow. (449)

Alienation The situation of being estranged or disassociated from the surrounding society. (469)

Altruistic suicide In Durkheim's view, a suicide that results when the individual places the group's welfare above his or her own survival. (11)

Amalgamation The process by which a majority group and a minority group combine through intermarriage to form a new group. (300)

Androgyny A term used to describe a lifestyle in which there is no gender-role differentiation and one can be both "masculine" and "feminine." (330)

Anomic suicide In Durkheim's view, a suicide that results from a society's lack of clear-cut rules of social behavior. (11)

Anomie Durkheim's term for the loss of direction felt in a society when social control of individual behavior has become ineffective. (13, 195)

Anomie theory of deviance A theory developed by Robert Merton which explains deviance as an adaptation either of socially prescribed goals or of the norms governing their attainment. (196)

Anticipatory socialization Processes of socialization in which a person "rehearses" for future positions, occupations, and social relationships. (113)

Anti-Semitism Anti-Jewish prejudice. (312)

Apartheid The policy of the South African government designed to maintain the separation of Blacks, Coloureds, and Asians from the dominant Whites. (301)

Applied sociology The use of the discipline of sociology with the specific intention of yielding practical applications for human behavior and for organizations. (26)

Argot Specialized language used by members of a group or subculture. (83)

Ascribed status A social position "assigned" to a person by society without regard for the person's unique talents or characteristics. (134, 228)

Assembling perspective A theory of collective behavior introduced by McPhail and Miller which seeks to examine how and why people move from different points in space to a common location. (607)

Assimilation The process by which a person forsakes his or her own cultural tradition to become part of a different culture. (300)

Authoritarian personality A psychological construct of a personality type likely to be prejudiced and to use others as scapegoats. (297)

Authority Power that has been institutionalized and is recognized by the people over whom it is exercised. (454)

Basic sociology Sociological inquiry conducted with the objective of gaining a more profound knowledge of the fundamental aspects of social phenomena. Also known as *pure sociology*. (28)

Bilateral descent A kinship system in which both sides of a person's family are regarded as equally important. (384)

Bilingualism The use of two or more languages in places of work or in educational facilities and the treatment of each language as equally legitimate. (90)

Birthrate The number of live births per 1000 population in a given year. Also known as the *crude birthrate*. (579)

Black power A political philosophy promoted by many young Blacks in the 1960s which supported the creation of Black-controlled political and economic institutions. (304)

Bond A term used by Travis Hirschi to refer to the ties of an individual to society and, in particular, to standards of proper behavior. (195)

Bourgeoisie Karl Marx's term for the capitalist class, comprising the owners of the means of production. (231)

Bureaucracy A component of formal organization in which rules and hierarchical ranking are used to achieve efficiency. (166)

Bureaucratization The process by which a group, organization, or social movement becomes increasingly bureaucratic. (170)

Capitalism An economic system in which the means of production are largely in private hands, and the main incentive for economic activity is the accumulation of profits. (231, 449)

Castes Hereditary systems of rank, usually religiously dictated, that are relatively fixed and immobile. (226)

Causal logic The relationship between a condition or variable and a particular consequence with one event leading to the other. (38)

Census An enumeration or counting of a population. (578)

Charismatic authority Max Weber's term for power made legitimate by a leader's exceptional personal or emotional appeal to his or her followers. (457)

Class A term used by Max Weber to refer to people who have a similar level of wealth and income. (232)

Class consciousness In Karl Marx's view, a subjective awareness held by members of a class regarding their common vested interests and need for collective political action to bring about social change. (231)

Classical theory An approach to the study of formal organizations which views workers as being motivated almost entirely by economic rewards. (173)

Class system A social ranking based primarily on economic position in which achieved characteristics can influence mobility. (227)

Clinical sociology The use of the discipline of sociology with the specific intent of altering social relationships and facilitating change. (28)

Closed system A social system in which there is little or no possibility of individual mobility. (248)

Coalition A temporary or permanent alliance toward a common goal. (163)

Code of ethics The standards of acceptable behavior developed by and for members of a profession. (51)

Cognitive theory of development Jean Piaget's theory explaining how children's thought progresses through four stages. (108)

Cohabitation The practice of living together as a male-female couple without marrying. (389)

Collective behavior In the view of sociologist Neil Smelser, the relatively spontaneous and unstructured behavior of a group of people who are reacting to a common influence in an ambiguous situation. (603)

Colonialism The maintenance of political, social, economic, and cultural dominance over a people by a foreign power for an extended period of time. (259)

Color gradient The placement of people on a continuum from light to dark skin color rather than in distinct racial groupings by skin color. (278, 290)

Commune A small, self-supporting community joined voluntarily by people dedicated to cooperative living. (405)

Communism As an ideal type, an economic system under which all property is communally owned and no social distinctions are made on the basis of people's ability to produce. (451)

Community A spatial or territorial unit of social organization in which people have a sense of identity and a feeling of belonging. (546)

Complementary roles Social roles which require that the behavior of two or more people interact in specific ways. (135)

Concentric-zone theory A theory of urban growth devised by Ernest Burgess which sees growth in terms of a series of rings radiating from the central business district. (551)

Conflict perspective A sociological approach which assumes that social behavior is best understood in terms of conflict or tension among competing groups. (20)

Conformity Going along with one's peers, individuals of a person's own status, who have no special right to direct that person's behavior. (188)

Contact hypothesis An interactionist perspective which states that interracial contact of people with equal status in noncompetitive circumstances will reduce prejudice. (295)

Content analysis The systematic coding and objective recording of data, guided by some rationale. (48)

Control group Subjects in an experiment who are not introduced to the independent variable by the researcher. (42)

Control variable A factor that is held constant to test the relative impact of an independent variable. (41)

Correlation A relationship between two variables whereby a change in one coincides with a change in the other. (38)

Correspondence principle A term used by Bowles and Gintis to refer to the tendency of schools to promote the values expected of individuals in each social class and to prepare students for the types of jobs typically held by members of their class. (486)

Cosmology A general theory of the universe advanced by a religion. (423)

Counterculture A subculture that rejects societal norms and values and seeks an alternative lifestyle. (84)

Craze An exciting mass involvement which lasts for a relatively long period of time. (610)

Creationists People who support a literal interpretation of the book of Genesis regarding the origins of the universe and argue that evolution should not be presented as established scientific fact. (423)

Credentialism An increase in the lowest level of education required to enter a field. (484)

Crime A violation of criminal law for which formal penalties are applied by some governmental authority. (204)

Cross-tabulation A table that shows the relationship between two or more variables. (50)

Crowds Temporary gatherings of people in close proximity who share a common focus or interest. (607)

Cult A generally small, secretive religious group that represents either a new religion or a major innovation of an existing faith. (428)

Cultural integration The bringing together of conflicting cultural elements, resulting in a harmonious and cohesive whole. (82)

Cultural relativism The viewing of people's behavior from the perspective of their own culture. (87)

Cultural transmission A school of criminology which argues that criminal behavior is learned through social interactions. (198)

Cultural universals General practices found in every culture. (69, 414)

Culture The totality of learned, socially transmitted behavior. (67)

Culture-bound syndrome A disease or illness that cannot be understood apart from its specific social context. (510)

Culture lag Ogburn's term for a period of maladjustment during which the nonmaterial culture is still adapting to new material conditions. (623)

Culture shock The feeling of surprise and disorientation that is experienced when people witness cultural practices different from their own. (85)

Death rate The number of deaths per 1000 population in a given year. Also known as the *crude death rate*. (581)

Defended neighborhood Suttles's formulation that area residents identify their neighborhood through defined community boundaries and through a perception that adjacent areas are geographically separate and socially different. (560)

Degradation ceremony An aspect of the socialization process within total institutions, in which people are subjected to humiliating rituals. (115)

Demographic transition A term used to describe the change from high birthrates and death rates to relatively low birthrates and death rates. (582)

Demography The scientific study of population. (577)

Denomination A large, organized religion not officially linked with the state or government. (426)

Dependent variable The variable in a causal relationship which is subject to the influence of another variable. (38)

Deviance Behavior that violates the standards of conduct or expectations of a group or society. (193)

Dialectical process A series of clashes between conflicting ideas and forces. (15)

Differential association A theory of deviance proposed by Edwin Sutherland which holds that violation of rules results from exposure to attitudes favorable to criminal acts. (198)

Diffusion The process by which a cultural item is spread from group to group or society to society. (70, 259)

Disaster A sudden or disruptive event or set of events that overtaxes a community's resources so that outside aid is necessary. (608)

Discovery The process of making known or sharing the existence of an aspect of reality. (70)

Discrimination The process of denying opportunities and equal rights to individuals and groups because of prejudice or for other arbitrary reasons. (298)

Disengagement theory A functionalist theory of aging introduced by Cumming and Henry which contends that society and the aging individual mutually sever many of their relationships. (361)

Dominant ideology A set of cultural beliefs and practices that help to maintain powerful social, economic, and political interests. (89)

Dramaturgical approach A view of social interaction, popularized by Erving Goffman, under which people are examined as if they were theatrical performers. (24, 106)

Dyad A two-member group. (161)

Dysfunction An element or a process of society that may disrupt a social system or lead to a decrease in stability. (20, 167)

Ecclesia A religious organization that claims to include most of or all the members of a society and is recognized as the national or official religion. (426)

Economic system The social institution through which goods and services are produced, distributed, and consumed. (447)

Education A formal process of learning in which some people consciously teach while others adopt the social role of learner. (478)

Egalitarian family An authority pattern in which the adult members of the family are regarded as equals. (385)

Egoistic suicide In Durkheim's view, a suicide that occurs when an individual feels little connection to the larger society and an absence of social constraints against self-destructive behavior. (11)

Elite model A view of society as ruled by a small group of individuals who share a common set of political and economic interests. (463)

Emergent-norm perspective A theory of collective behavior proposed by Turner and Killian which holds that a collective definition of appropriate and inappropriate behavior emerges during episodes of collective behavior. (605)

Endogamy The restriction of mate selection to people within the same group. (387)

English immersion An approach to bilingual education under which students are taught primarily in English and their native languages are used only when they do not understand their lessons. (91)

Equilibrium model Talcott Parsons's functionalist view of society as tending toward a state of stability or balance. (617)

Established sect J. Milton Yinger's term for a religious group that is the outgrowth of a sect, yet remains isolated from society. (427)

Estate system A system of stratification under which peasants were required to work land leased to them by nobles in exchange for military protection and other services. Also known as *feudalism*. (227)

Esteem The reputation that a particular individual has within an occupation. (236)

Ethnic group A group which is set apart from others because of its national origin or distinctive cultural patterns. (289)

Ethnocentrism The tendency to assume that one's culture and way of life are superior to all others. (86, 296)

Ethnomethodology A sociological approach which focuses on how people view, describe, and explain shared meanings underlying everyday social life and social routines. (24)

Evangelical faiths Christian faiths which place great emphasis on a personal relationship between the individual and God and believe that each adherent must spread the faith and bear personal witness by openly declaring the religion to nonbelievers. (433)

Evolutionary theory A theory of social change which holds that society is moving in a definite direction. (617)

Exogamy The requirement that individuals select mates outside certain groups. (387)

Experiment An artificially created situation which allows the researcher to manipulate variables and introduce control variables. (42)

Experimental group Subjects in an experiment who are exposed to an independent variable introduced by a researcher. (42)

Exploitation theory A Marxist theory which views racial subordination in the United States as a manifestation of the class system inherent in capitalism. (295)

Expressiveness A term used by Parsons and Bales to refer to concern for maintenance of harmony and the internal emotional affairs of the family. (331)

Extended family A family in which relatives in addition to parents and children—such as grandparents, aunts, or uncles—live in the same home. (382)

Face-work A term used by Erving Goffman to refer to people's efforts to maintain the proper image and avoid embarrassment in public. (106)

Fads Temporary movements toward the acceptance of some particular taste or lifestyle that involve large numbers of people and are independent of preceding trends. (609)

False consciousness A term used by Karl Marx to describe an attitude held by members of a class that does not accurately reflect its objective position. (231, 616)

Familism Pride in the extended family expressed through the maintenance of close ties and strong obligations to kinfolk. (399)

Family A set of people related by blood, marriage (or some other agreed-upon relationship), or adoption who share the responsibility for reproducing and caring for members of society. (381)

Fashions Pleasurable mass involvements in some particular taste or lifestyle that have a line of historical continuity. (609)

Fatalistic suicide In Durkheim's view, a suicide that occurs when the individual feels powerless owing to intolerable amounts of regulation. (11)

Fecundity The biological potential of individual women for reproduction in a society. (579)

Fertility The amount of reproduction among women of childbearing age. (576)

Folkways Norms governing everyday social behavior whose violation raises comparatively little concern. (77)

Force The actual or threatened use of coercion to impose one's will on others. (453)

Formal norms Norms which have generally been written down and which involve strict rules for punishment of violators. (77)

Formal organization A special-purpose group designed and structured in the interests of maximum efficiency. (165)

Formal social control Social control carried out by authorized agents, such as police officers, judges, school administrators, and employers. (191)

Functionalist perspective A sociological approach which emphasizes the way that parts of a society are structured to maintain its stability. (19)

Fundamentalism Adherence to earlier-accepted religious doctrines, often accompanied by a literal application of historical beliefs and scriptures to today's world. (433)

Gemeinschaft A term used by Ferdinand Tönnies for close-knit communities, often found in rural areas, in which strong personal bonds unite members. (146)

Gender identity The self-concept of an individual as being male or female. (325)

Gender roles Expectations regarding the proper behavior, attitudes, and activities of males and females. (116, 326)

Generalized others A term used by George Herbert Mead to refer to the child's awareness of the attitudes, viewpoints, and expectations of society as a whole. (106)

Genocide The deliberate, systematic killing of an entire people or nation. (299)

Gentrification The resettlement of low-income city neighborhoods by prosperous families and business firms. (570)

Gerontocracy Rule by the elderly. (357)

Gerontology The scientific study of the sociological and psychological aspects of aging and the problems of the aged. (360)

Gesellschaft A term used by Ferdinand Tönnies to describe communities, often urban, that are large and impersonal, with little commitment to the group or consensus on values. (146)

Goal displacement Overzealous conformity to official regulations within a bureaucracy. (169)

Goal multiplication The process through which an organization expands its purposes. (178)

Goal succession The process through which an organization identifies an entirely new objective because its traditional goals have been either realized or denied. (179)

Group Any number of people with similar norms, values, and expectations who regularly and consciously interact. (139, 157)

Growth rate The difference between births and deaths, plus the difference between immigrants and emigrants, per 1000 population. (581)

Hawthorne effect The unintended influence that observers or experiments can have on their subjects. (45)

Health As defined by the World Health Organization, a state of complete physical, mental, and social well-being, and not merely the absence of disease and infirmity. (512)

Health maintenance organization (HMO) An organization that provides comprehensive medical services to patients for a preestablished fee. (529)

Holistic medicine A means of health maintenance which views the person as an integration of body, mind, and spirit, rather than as a collection of interrelated organ systems. (531)

Hominids Primates that had characteristics of human beings. (68)

Homophobia Fear of and prejudice against homosexuality. (151)

Horizontal mobility The movement of an individual from one social position to another of the same rank. (248)

Horticultural societies Preindustrial societies in which people plant seeds and crops rather than subsist merely on available foods. (448)

Human ecology An area of study concerned with the interrelationships among people in their spatial setting and physical environment. (550)

Human relations approach An approach to the study of formal organizations which emphasizes the role of people, communication, and participation within a bureaucracy and tends to focus on the informal structure of the organization. (173)

Hunting-and-gathering society A preindustrial society in which people rely on whatever foods and fiber are readily available in order to live. (448)

Hypergamy A woman's marriage to a man of a higher caste. (248)

Hypothesis A speculative statement about the relationship between two or more variables. (38)

Ideal type A construct or model that serves as a measuring rod against which actual cases can be evaluated. (13)

Impression management A term used by Erving Goffman to refer to the altering of the presentation of the self in order to create distinctive appearances and satisfy particular audiences. (106)

Incest taboo The prohibition of sexual relationships between certain culturally specified relatives. (388)

Incidence The number of new cases of a specific disorder occurring within a given population during a stated period of time. (518)

Income Salaries and wages. (225)

Independent variable The variable in a causal relationship which, when altered, causes or influences a change in a second variable. (38)

Index An indicator of attitudes, behavior, or characteristics of people or organizations. (40)

Index crimes The eight types of crime reported annually by the FBI in the *Uniform Crime Reports*. These are murder, rape, robbery, assault, burglary, theft, motor vehicle theft, and arson. (204)

Industrial city A city characterized by relatively large size, open competition, an open class system, and elaborate specialization in the manufacturing of goods. (549)

Industrial revolution A scientific revolution, largely occurring in

England between 1760 and 1830, which focused on the application of nonanimal sources of power to labor tasks. (449, 549)

Industrial society A society which relies chiefly on mechanization for the production of its economic goods and services. (449)

Infant mortality rate The number of deaths of infants under 1 year of age per 1000 live births in a given year. (267, 515, 581)

Influence The exercise of power through a process of persuasion. (455)

Informal economy Transfers of money, goods, or services that are not reported to the government. (270)

Informal norms Norms which are generally understood but which are not precisely recorded. (77)

Informal social control Social control carried out by people casually through such means as laughter, smiles, and ridicule. (190)

In-group Any group or category to which people feel they belong. (158)

Innovation The process of introducing new elements into a culture through either discovery or invention. (70)

Institutional discrimination The denial of opportunities and equal rights to individuals or groups which results from the normal operations of society. (298, 334)

Instrumentality A term used by Parsons and Bales to refer to emphasis on tasks, focus on more distant goals, and a concern for the external relationship between one's family and other social institutions. (331)

Interactionist perspective A sociological approach which generalizes about fundamental or everyday forms of social interaction. (22)

Interaction process analysis (IPA) A technique developed by Robert F. Bales for analyzing a group's structure and processes. (160)

Interest group A voluntary association of citizens who attempt to influence public policy. (462)

Intergenerational mobility Changes in the social position of children relative to their parents. (249)

Interview A face-to-face or telephone questioning of a respondent in order to obtain desired information. (46)

Intragenerational mobility Changes in a person's social position within his or her adult life. (250)

Invention The combination of existing cultural items into a form that did not previously exist. (70)

Iron law of oligarchy A principle of organizational life developed by Robert Michels under which even democratic organizations will become bureaucracies ruled by a few individuals. (172)

Issei The early Japanese immigrants to the United States. (307)

Kibbutz A collective society in Israel in which individuals and groups join together in an economic and social community. (405)

Kinship The state of being related to others. (384)

Labeling theory An approach to deviance popularized by Howard S. Becker which attempts to explain why certain people are *viewed* as deviants while others engaging in the same behavior are not. (200)

Laissez-faire A form of capitalism under which people compete freely, with minimal government intervention in the economy. (450)

Language An abstract system of word meanings and symbols for all aspects of culture. It also includes gestures and other nonverbal communication. (74)

Latent functions Unconscious, covert, or unintended functions; hidden purposes. (20)

Law In a political sense, the body of rules made by government for society, interpreted by the courts, and backed by the power of the state. (77, 191)

Legal-rational authority Max Weber's term for power made legitimate by law. (455)

Liberation theology Use of a church, primarily Roman Catholicism, in a political effort to eliminate poverty, discrimination, and other forms of injustice evident in secular society. (421)

Life chances Max Weber's term for people's opportunities to provide themselves with material goods, positive living conditions, and favorable life experiences. (245)

Life expectancy The average number of years a person can be expected to live under current mortality conditions. (581)

Linear-development model A view of community attachment which points to population size as the primary factor influencing patterns of behavior in a community. (557)

Looking-glass self A phrase used by Charles Horton Cooley to emphasize that the self is the product of our social interactions with others. (105)

Machismo A sense of virility, personal worth, and pride in one's maleness. (399)

Macrosociology Sociological investigation which concentrates on large-scale phenomena or entire civilizations. (17, 145)

Mainstreaming The practice, mandated by Public Law 94-142, of integrating handicapped children into "regular" classrooms whenever possible by placing each child in the "least restrictive environment." (496)

Manifest functions Open, stated, and conscious functions. (20)

Marital power A term used by Blood and Wolfe to describe the manner in which decision making is distributed within families. (386, 453)

Master status A status that dominates others and thereby determines a person's general position within society. (135)

Material culture The physical or technological aspects of our daily lives. (70)

Matriarchy A society in which women dominate in family decision making. (385)

Matrilineal descent A kinship system which favors the relatives of the mother. (384)

Matrilocal A pattern of residence in which a married couple lives with the wife's parents. (384)

Mean The number calculated by adding a series of values and then dividing by the number of values. (36)

Mechanical solidarity A term used by Émile Durkheim to describe a society in which people generally all perform the same tasks and in which relationships are close and intimate. (145)

Median The midpoint or number which divides a series of values into two groups of equal numbers of values. (36)

Megalopolis A densely populated area containing two or more cities and their suburbs. (553)

Microsociology Sociological investigation which stresses study of small groups and often uses laboratory experimental studies. (17, 145)

Midlife crisis A stressful period of self-evaluation, often occurring between the ages of 35 and 50, in which a person realizes that he or she has not achieved certain personal goals and aspirations and that time is running out. (111)

Migration Relatively permanent movement of people with the purpose of changing their place of residence. (590)

Minimum-competency tests (MCTs) Tests which measure a child's knowledge of basic skills, such as reading, writing, and mathematics. (494)

Minority group A subordinate group whose members have significantly less control or power over their own lives than the members of a dominant or majority group have over theirs. (289)

Mode The single most common value in a series of scores. (36)

Modernization The far-reaching process by which a society moves from traditional or less developed institutions to those characteristic of more developed societies. (261)

Monogamy A form of marriage in which one woman and one man are married only to each other. (383)

Monopoly Control of a market by a single business firm. (450)

Morbidity rates The incidence of diseases in a given population. (518, 581)

Mores Norms deemed highly necessary to the welfare of a society. (77)

Mortality rate The incidence of death in a given population. (518)

Multilinear evolutionary theory A theory of social change which holds that change can occur in several ways and does not inevitably lead in the same direction. (617)

Multinational corporations Commercial organizations which, while headquartered in one country, own or control other corporations and subsidiaries throughout the world. (264)

Multiple-nuclei theory A theory of urban growth developed by Harris and Ullman, which views growth as emerging from many centers of development, each of which may reflect a particular urban need or activity. (551)

Natural science The study of the physical features of nature and the ways in which they interact and change. (8)

Negotiated order A social structure that derives its existence from the social interactions through which people define and redefine its character. (133)

Negotiation The attempt to reach agreement with others concerning some objective. (133)

Neighborhood revitalization Another term for *gentrification*. (570)

Neocolonialism Continuing dependence of former colonies on foreign countries. (261)

Neolocal A pattern of residence in which a married couple establishes a separate residence. (384)

Nisei American-born Japanese who were descendants of the Issei. (309)

No-fault divorce A process whereby divorce is granted without proving one of the parties guilty of marital misconduct. (404)

Nonmaterial culture Cultural adjustments to material conditions, such as customs, beliefs, patterns of communication, and ways of using material objects. (70)

Nonperiodic assemblies Nonrecurring gatherings of people which often result from word-of-mouth information. (607)

Nonverbal communication The sending of messages through the use of posture, facial expressions, and gestures. (24)

Norms Established standards of behavior maintained by a society. (76)

Nuclear family A married couple and their unmarried children living together. (382)

Obedience Compliance with higher authorities in a hierarchical structure. (188)

Objective method A technique for measuring social class that assigns individuals to classes on the basis of criteria such as occupation, education, income, and place of residence. (236)

Oligopoly A market with relatively few sellers. (450)

Open system A social system in which the position of each individual is influenced by his or her achieved status. (248)

Operational definition An explanation of an abstract concept that is specific enough to allow a researcher to measure the concept. (37)

Organic solidarity A term used by Émile Durkheim to describe a society in which members are mutually dependent and in which a complex division of labor exists. (145)

Organized crime The work of a group that regulates relations between various criminal enterprises involved in smuggling and sale of drugs, prostitution, gambling, and other activities. (205)

Out-group A group or category to which people feel they do not belong. (159)

Panic A fearful arousal or collective flight based on a generalized belief which may or may not be accurate. (610)

Participant observation A research technique in which an investigator collects information through direct involvement with and observation of a group, tribe, or community. (43)

Patriarchy A society in which men are expected to dominate family decision making. (385)

Patrilineal descent A kinship system which favors the relatives of the father. (384)

Patrilocal A pattern of residence in which a married couple lives with the husband's parents. (384)

Pay equity A policy of equal pay for different types of work judged to be comparable through measurement of such factors as employees' knowledge, skills, effort, responsibility, and working conditions. Also known as *comparable worth*. (340)

Pentecostal faiths Religious groups similar in many respects to evangelical faiths, which in addition believe in the infusion of the Holy Spirit into services and in religious experiences such as faith healing and "speaking in tongues." (433)

Percentage The portion of 100. (36)

Perestroika Soviet leader Mikhail Gorbachev's plan to restructure Soviet society. (169)

Periodic assemblies Recurring, relatively routine gatherings of people, such as college classes. (607)

Personality In everyday speech, a person's typical patterns of attitudes, needs, characteristics, and behavior. (99)

Peter principle A principle of organizational life, originated by Laurence J. Peter, according to which each individual within a hierarchy tends to rise to his or her level of incompetence. (170)

Pluralism Mutual respect between the various groups in a society for one another's cultures, which allows minorities to express their own cultures without experiencing prejudice. (302)

Pluralist model A view of society in which many conflicting groups within a community have access to governmental officials and compete with one another in an attempt to influence policy decisions. (465)

Political action committee (PAC) A political committee established by an interest group—a national bank, corporation, trade association, or cooperative or membership association—to accept voluntary contributions for candidates or political parties. (462)

Political efficacy The feeling that one has the ability to influence politicians and the political order. (460)

Political socialization The process by which individuals acquire political attitudes and develop patterns of political behavior. (458)

Political system The social institution which relies on a recognized set of procedures for implementing and achieving the goals of a group. (447)

Politics In Harold D. Lasswell's words, "who gets what, when, how." (453)

Polyandry A form of polygamy in which a woman can have several husbands at the same time. (383)

Polygamy A form of marriage in which an individual can have several husbands or wives simultaneously. (383)

Polygyny A form of polygamy in which a husband can have several wives at the same time. (383)

Population pyramid A special type of bar chart that shows the distribution of the population by gender and age. (585)

Postindustrial society As defined by Daniel Bell, a society whose economic system is based on the production of information rather than the production of goods. (452)

Power The ability to exercise one's will over others. (232, 453)

Power elite A term used by C. Wright Mills for a small group of military, industrial, and government leaders who control the fate of the United States. (463)

Predestination A Calvinist doctrine which holds that people either will be among the elect, who are rewarded in heaven, or will be condemned to hell and that their futures are not dependent on being righteous or sinful while on earth. (422)

Preindustrial city A city with only a few thousand people living within its borders and characterized by a relatively closed class system and limited mobility. (548)

Prejudice A negative attitude toward an entire category of people, such as a racial or ethnic minority. (296)

Pressure groups A term sometimes used to refer to interest groups. (463)

Prestige The respect and admiration with which an occupation is regarded by society. (236)

Prevalence The total number of cases of a specific disorder that exist at a given time. (518)

Primary group A small group characterized by intimate, face-to-face association and cooperation. (158)

Profane The ordinary and commonplace elements of life, as distinguished from the sacred. (416)

Profession An occupation requiring extensive knowledge and governed by a code of ethics. (467)

Professional criminal A person who pursues crime as a day-to-day occupation, developing skilled techniques and enjoying a certain degree of status among other criminals. (204)

Proletariat Karl Marx's term for the working class in a capitalist society. (231)

Protestant ethic Max Weber's term for the disciplined work ethic, this-worldly concerns, and rational orientation to life emphasized by John Calvin and his followers. (422)

Public A dispersed group of people, not necessarily in contact with one another, who share an interest in an issue. (611)

Public opinion Expressions of attitudes on matters of public policy which are communicated to decision makers. (611)

Quality circles Small groups of about 10 to 15 workers that meet periodically with one or two managers to develop ideas for improving productivity and working conditions. (171)

Questionnaire A printed research instrument employed to obtain desired information from a respondent. (46)

Racial group A group which is set apart from others because of obvious physical differences. (289)

Racism The belief that one race is supreme and all others are innately inferior. (296)

Random sample A sample for which every member of the entire population has the same chance of being selected. (39)

Reference group A term used by Herbert Hyman when speaking of any group that individuals use as a standard in evaluating themselves and their own behavior. (159)

Relative deprivation The conscious feeling of a negative discrepancy between legitimate expectations and present actualities. (615)

Relative poverty A floating standard of deprivation by which people at the bottom of a society, whatever their lifestyles, are judged to be disadvantaged in comparison with the nation as a whole. (242)

Reliability The extent to which a measure provides consistent results. (40)

Religion According to Émile Durkheim, a unified system of beliefs and practices relative to sacred things. (415)

Religious beliefs Statements to which members of a particular religion adhere. (423)

Religious experience The feeling or perception of being in direct contact with the ultimate reality, such as a divine being, or of being overcome with religious emotion. (424)

Religious rituals Practices required or expected of members of a faith. (423)

Replacement-level fertility The average number of children that women must have in order to replace the adult population. (588)

Replication The repetition of a given investigation in substantially the same way as it was originally conducted, either by the original scientist or by other scientists. (49)

Representative sample A selection from a larger population that is statistically found to be typical of that population. (39)

Research design A detailed plan or method for obtaining data scientifically. (42)

Resocialization The process of discarding former behavior patterns and accepting new ones as part of a transition in one's life. (113)

Resource mobilization The ways in which a social movement utilizes such resources as money, political influence, access to the media, and personnel. (616)

Reverse socialization The process whereby people who are normally being socialized are at the same time socializing their socializers. (117)

Rites of passage Rituals marking the symbolic transition from one social position to another. (110)

Role ambiguity Unclear expectations associated with particular social positions. (136)

Role conflict Difficulties that occur when incompatible expectations arise from two or more social positions held by the same person. (137)

Role exit The process of disengagement from a role that is central to one's self-identity, and reestablishment of an identity in a new role. (136)

Role strain Difficulties that result from the differing demands and expectations associated with the same social position. (137)

Role taking The process of mentally assuming the perspective of another, thereby enabling one to respond from that imagined viewpoint. (105)

Routinization of charismatic authority Max Weber's term for the process by which the leadership qualities originally associated with an individual are incorporated into either a traditional or a legal-rational system of authority. (457)

Rumor A piece of information gathered informally which is used to interpret an ambiguous situation. (610)

Sacred Those elements beyond everyday life which inspire awe, respect, and even fear. (416)

Sanctions Penalties and rewards for conduct concerning a social norm. (79, 188)

Sanctuary movement A movement of loosely connected organizations that offers asylum, often in churches, to those who seek refugee status but are regarded by the Immigration and Naturalization Service as illegal aliens. (317)

Sapir-Whorf hypothesis A hypothesis concerning the role of language in shaping cultures. It holds that language is culturally determined and serves to influence our mode of thought. (74)

Scale An indictor of attitudes, behavior, or characteristics of people or organizations. (40)

Scapegoat A person or group that one blames irrationally for one's own problems or difficulties. (297)

Science The body of knowledge obtained by methods based upon systematic observation. (7, 619)

Scientific management approach Another name for the *classical theory* of formal organizations. (173)

Scientific method A systematic, organized series of steps that ensures maximum objectivity and consistency in researching a problem. (35)

Secondary group A formal, impersonal group in which there is little social intimacy or mutual understanding. (158)

Sect A relatively small religious group that has broken away from some other religious organization to renew what it views as the original vision of the faith. (427)

Sector theory A theory of urban growth developed by Homer Hoyt which focuses on the importance of transportation lines in urban growth. (551)

Secularization The process through which religion's influence on other social institutions diminishes. (414)

Segregation The act of physically separating two groups; often imposed on a minority group by a dominant group. (300)

Self According to George Herbert Mead, the sum total of people's conscious perception of their identity as distinct from others. (104)

Self-fulfilling prophecy The tendency of people to respond to and act on the basis of stereotypes, a predisposition which can lead to validation of false definitions. (292)

Self-help group A mutual aid group in which people who face a common concern or condition come together voluntarily for emotional support and practical assistance. (176)

Senilicide The killing of the aged. (357)

Serial monogamy A form of marriage in which a person can have several spouses in her or his lifetime, but can have only one spouse at one time. (383)

Sexism The ideology that one sex is superior to the other. (334)

Sexual harassment The unwanted imposition of sexual requirements in a relationship of unequal power. (179)

Sick role Societal expectations about the attitudes and behavior of a person viewed as being ill. (512)

Significant others A term used by George Herbert Mead to refer to those individuals who are most important in the development of the self, such as parents, friends, and teachers. (106)

Single-parent families Families in which there is only one parent present to care for children. (395)

Slavery A system of enforced servitude in which people are legally owned by others and in which enslaved status is transferred from parents to children. (226)

Small group A group small enough for all members to interact simultaneously, that is, to talk with one another or at least be acquainted. (160)

Social change Significant alteration over time in behavior patterns and culture, including norms and values. (603)

Social control The techniques and strategies for regulating human behavior in any society. (187)

Social epidemiology The study of the distribution of disease, impairment, and general health status across a population. (518)

Social inequality A condition in which members of a society have different amounts of wealth, prestige, or power. (224)

Social institutions Organized patterns of beliefs and behavior centered on basic social needs. (142, 397)

Social interaction The ways in which people respond to one another. (131)

Socialism An economic system under which the means of production and distribution are collectively owned. (450)

Socialization The process whereby people learn the attitudes, values, and actions appropriate to individuals as members of a particular culture. (98)

Social mobility Movement of individuals and groups from one position of a society's stratification system to another. (248)

Social movements Organized collective activities to bring about or resist fundamental change in existing society. (613)

Social network A series of social relationships that link a person directly to others and therefore indirectly to still more people. (141)

Social promotion The practice of passing children from one grade to the next on the basis of age rather than actual educational achievement. (494)

Social role A set of expectations of people who occupy a given social position or status. (135)

Social science The study of various aspects of human society. (8)

Social structure The way in which a society is organized into predictable relationships. (131)

Social surplus The production by a group of people of enough goods to cover their own needs, while at the same time sustaining people who are not engaged in agricultural tasks. (448, 547)

Societal-reaction approach Another name for *labeling theory*. (200)

Society A fairly large number of people who live in the same territory, are relatively independent of people outside their area, and participate in a common culture. (67)

Sociobiology The systematic study of the biological bases of social behavior. (103)

Sociogram A depiction of preferred associations among group members. (160)

Sociological imagination An awareness of the relationship between an individual and the wider society. (6)

Sociology The systematic study of social behavior and human groups. (5)

Squatter settlements Areas occupied by the very poor on the fringes of cities, in which housing is often constructed by the settlers themselves from discarded material. (556)

Status A term used by sociologists to refer to any of the full range of socially defined positions within a large group or society. (134)

Status group A term used by Max Weber to refer to people who have the same prestige or life-style, independent of their class positions. (232)

Stereotypes Unreliable generalizations about all members of a group that do not recognize individual differences within the group. (291)

Stratification A structured ranking of entire groups of people that perpetuates unequal economic rewards and power in a society. (224)

Stratum mobility Another name for *structural mobility*. (250)

Structural mobility The vertical movement of a specific group, class, or occupation relative to others in the stratification system. (250)

Studied nonobservance A term used by Erving Goffman to refer to polite behavior intended to allow saving face. (107)

Subculture A segment of society which shares a distinctive pattern of mores, folkways, and values which differ from the pattern of the larger society. (83)

Subfecundity A limited ability or diminished ability to reproduce. (579)

Subsistence technology The tools, processes, and knowledge that a society requires to meet its basic needs for survival. (547)

Suburb According to the Census Bureau, any territory within a metropolitan area that is not included in the central city. (563)

Survey A study, generally in the form of interviews or questionnaires, which provides sociologists and other researchers with information concerning how people think and act. (46)

Symbols The gestures, objects, and language which form the basis of human communication. (105)

Systemic model A model of community attachment proposed by Thomas, Park, and Burgess which emphasizes geographical mobility, rather than population size, as a crucial factor in influencing patterns of behavior. (558)

Teacher-expectancy effect The impact that a teacher's expectations about a student's performance may have on the student's actual achievements. (489)

Techniques of neutralization Justifications for deviant behavior. (199)

Technology The application of knowledge to the making of tools and the utilization of natural resources. (448, 619)

Technology transfer The importation of new applications of knowledge that are available elsewhere, sometimes in modified form. (620)

Terrorism The use or threat of violence against random or symbolic targets in pursuit of political aims. (454)

Theory In sociology, a set of statements that seeks to explain problems, actions, or behavior. (10)

Total fertility rate (TFR) The average number of children born alive to a woman, assuming that she conforms to current fertility rates. (581)

Total institutions A term coined by Erving Goffman to refer to institutions which regulate all aspects of a person's life under a single authority, such as prisons, the military, mental hospitals, and convents. (113)

Tracking The practice of placing students in specific curriculum groups on the basis of test scores and other criteria. (485)

Traditional authority Legitimate power conferred by custom and accepted practice. (455)

Trained incapacity The tendency of workers in a bureaucracy to become so specialized that they develop blind spots and cannot notice obvious problems. (167)

Triad A three-member group. (161)

Typology A classification scheme containing two or more mutually exclusive categories (types) which is used by sociologists to better understand different forms of behavior. (11)

Underclass Long-term poor people who lack training and skills. (240)

Unilinear evolutionary theory A theory of social change which holds that all societies pass through the same successive stages of evolution and inevitably reach the same end. (617)

Unobtrusive measures Research techniques in which the method of study has no influence on the subjects under investigation. (48)

Urban ecology An area of study which focuses on the interrelationships between people and their environment as they emerge in urban areas. (550)

Urbanism A term used by Wirth to describe distinctive patterns of social behavior evident among city residents. (557)

Validity The degree to which a scale or measure truly reflects the phenomenon under study. (40)

Value-added model A theory of collective behavior proposed by Neil Smelser to explain how broad social conditions are transformed in a definite pattern into some form of collective behavior. (605)

Value neutrality Max Weber's term for objectivity of sociologists in the interpretation of data. (56)

Values Collective conceptions of what is considered good, desirable, and proper—or bad, undesirable, and improper—in a culture. (80)

Variable A measurable trait or characteristic that is subject to change under different conditions. (38)

Verstehen The German word for "understanding" or "insight"; used by Max Weber to stress the need for sociologists to take into account people's emotions, thoughts, beliefs, and attitudes. (13)

Vertical mobility The movement of a person from one social position to another of a different rank. (248)

Vested interests Veblen's term for those people or groups who will suffer in the event of social change and who have a stake in maintaining the status quo. (622)

Veto groups David Riesman's term for interest groups that have the capacity to prevent the exercise of power by others. (465)

Victimization surveys Questionnaires or interviews used to determine whether people have been victims of crime. (211)

Victimless crimes A term used by sociologists to describe the willing exchange among adults of widely desired, but illegal, goods and services. (207)

Vital statistics Records of births, deaths, marriages, and divorces gathered through a registration system maintained by governmental units. (578)

Voluntary associations Organizations established on the basis of common interest whose members volunteer or even pay to participate. (174)

Wealth An inclusive term encompassing all of a person's material assets, including land and other types of property. (225)

White-collar crimes Crimes committed by affluent individuals or corporations in the course of their daily business activities. (206)

World systems theory Immanuel Wallerstein's view of the global economic system as divided between certain industrialized nations who control wealth and developing countries who are controlled and exploited. (261)

Xenocentrism The belief that the products, styles, or ideas of one's society are inferior to those that originate elsewhere. (89)

Zero population growth (ZPG) The state of a population with a growth rate of zero, which is achieved when the number of births plus immigrants is equal to the number of deaths plus emigrants. (588)

Zoning laws Legal provisions stipulating land use and architectural design of housing and often employed as a means of keeping racial minorities and low-income people out of suburban areas. (566)

REFERENCES

Abegglen, James C., and George Stalk, Jr. 1985. *Kaisha: The Japanese Corporation.* New York: Basic Books.

Abelman, Robert, and Kimberly Nevendorf. 1985. "How Religious Is Religious Television Programming," *Journal of Communication,* **35**(Winter): 98–110.

Abercrombie, Nicholas, Stephen Hill, and Bryan S. Turner. 1980. *The Dominant Ideology Thesis.* London: Allen and Unwin.

———, ———, and ——— (eds.). 1990. *Dominant Ideologies.* Cambridge, Mass.: Unwin Hyman.

Aberle, David F., A. K. Cohen, A. K. Davis, M. J. Leng, Jr., and F. N. Sutton. 1950. "The Functional Prerequisites of a Society," *Ethics,* **60**(January):100–111.

Abowitz, Deborah A. 1986. "Data Indicate the Feminization of Poverty in Canada, Too," *Sociology and Social Research,* **70**(April):209–213.

Abrahams, R. G. 1968. "Reaching an Agreement over Bridewealth in Labwor, Northern Uganda: A Case Study," in Audrey Richards and Adam Kuer (eds.), *Councils in Action.* Cambridge, Eng.: Cambridge University Press, pp. 202–215.

Abrahamse, Allan F., Peter A. Morrison, and Linda J. Waite. 1988. *Beyond Stereotypes: Who Becomes a Single Teenage Mother?* Santa Monica, Calif.: Rand Corp.

Abrahamson, Mark. 1978. *Functionalism.* Englewood Cliffs, N.J.: Prentice-Hall.

Acsadi, George T. F., and Gwendolyn Johnson-Acsadi. 1990. "The Role of Family Planning." Background paper for the Safe Motherhood South Asia Conference, Lahore, Pakistan.

Adam, Barry D. 1991. "Culture and Social Relations in the AIDS Crisis," in Joan Huber and Beth S. Schneider (eds.), *The Social Context of AIDS.* Newbury Park, Calif.: Sage, forthcoming.

Adams, Anne L. 1984. "How Caring Is For-Profit Medicine?" *USA Today* (November 28), pp. 1–2.

Adamski-Mietus, Christine. 1983. Growing Old in Polonia: A Symbolic Interactionist Analysis of Aging in a Polish-American Community." Unpublished M.A. thesis, Western Illinois University, Macomb.

Adorno, T. W., Else Frenkel-Brunswik, Daniel J. Levinson, and R. Nevitt Sanford. 1950. *The Authoritarian Personality.* New York: Harper.

Aeppel, Timothy. 1987. "'Birth Death' Effects Begin to Show in Some Developed Nations," *Christian Science Monitor* (March 2), p. 6.

Agger, Ben. "Do Books Write Authors? A Study of Disciplinary Hegemony," *Teaching Sociology,* **17**(July):365–369.

Aguirre, B. E., E. L. Quarantelli, and Jorge L. Mendoza. 1988. "The Collective Behavior of Fads: The Characteristics, Effects, and Career of Streaking," *American Sociological Review,* **53**(August):569–584.

Alain, Michel. 1985. "An Empirical Validation of Relative Deprivation," *Human Relations,* **38**(8):739–749.

Alam, Sultana. 1985. "Women and Poverty in Bangladesh," *Women's Studies International Forum,* **8**(4):361–371.

Alba, Richard D. 1990. *Ethnic Identity: The Transformation of White America.* New Haven, Conn.: Yale University Press.

—— and Gwen Moore. 1982. "Ethnicity in the American Elite," *American Sociological Review,* **47**(June):373–383.

Albas, Daniel, and Cheryl Albas. 1988. "Aces and Bombers: The Post-Exam Impression Management Strategies of Students," *Symbolic Interaction,* **11**(Fall):289–302.

Aldous, Joan. 1987. "New Views on the Family Life of the Elderly and the Near-Elderly," *Journal of Marriage and the Family,* **49**(May):227–234.

Alexander, Ron. 1988. "Aged Homosexuals Celebrate Program," *New York Times* (April 13), p. B3.

Alexander, Vicki, Linda Kahn, Sushaun Robb, and Melanie Tervalon. 1987. "Teenage Mothers: Setting the Record Straight," *AAWO Discussion Paper,* **8**(June):1–8.

Alinsky, Saul. 1946. *Reveille for Radicals.* Chicago: University of Chicago Press.

Allen, Bem P. 1978. *Social Behavior: Fact and Falsehood.* Chicago: Nelson Hall.

Allport, Gordon W. 1962. "Prejudice: Is It Societal or Personal?" *Journal of Social Issues,* **18**(April):120–134.

——. 1979. *The Nature of Prejudice* (25th anniversary ed.). Reading, Mass.: Addison-Wesley.

—— and Louis Postman. 1947. *The Psychology of Rumor.* New York: Holt.

Alonzo, Angelo A. 1989. "Health and Illness and the Definition of the Situation: An Interactionist Perspective." Paper presented at the annual meeting of the Society for the Study of Social Problems, Berkeley, Calif.

Altman, Dennis. 1986. *AIDS in the Mind of America: The Social, Political, and Psychological Impact of a New Epidemic.* Garden City, N.Y.: Anchor/Doubleday.

Altman, Lawrence K. 1989. "Who's Stricken and How: AIDS Pattern Is Shifting," *New York Times* (February 5), pp. 1, 16.

——. 1990. "The Evidence Mounts on Passive Smoking," *New York Times* (May 29), pp. Cl, C8.

—— and Elisabeth Rosenthal. 1990. "Changes in Medicine Bring Pain to Healing Profession," *New York Times* (February 18), pp. 1, 20.

Alvarez, Sonia. 1989. "Contradictions of a 'Women's Space' in a Male-Dominant State: The Political Role of the Commissions on the Status of Women in Pre-Authoritarian Brazil," in Kathleen Staudt (ed.), *The Bureaucratic Mire: Women's Programs in Comparative Perspective.* Philadelphia: Temple University Press, pp. 37–78.

American Association of Retired Persons. 1991. *A Profile of Older Americans: 1990.* Washington, D.C.: A.A.R.P.

American Enterprise. 1990. "Is Abortion a 'Women's Issue'?" **1**(4; July–August):102–104.

American Sociological Association. 1977. *Careers in Sociology.* Washington, D.C.: American Sociological Association.

——. 1984. *Code of Ethics.* Washington, D.C.: American Sociological Association.

Ammerman, Nancy Tatam. 1987. *Bible Believers: Fundamentalists in the Modern World.* New Brunswick, N.J.: Rutgers University Press.

Amoss, Pamela T. 1981. *Other Ways of Growing Old: Anthropological Perspectives.* Palo Alto, Calif.: Stanford University Press.

Anant, Santohk Singh. 1978. "Changing Caste Hindu Attitudes toward Harijans—A Follow-Up after Four Years," in Giri Raj Gupta (ed.), *Cohesion and Conflict in Modern India.* New Delhi: Vikas, pp. 33–45.

Andersen, Margaret L. 1988. "Moving Our Minds: Studying Women of Color and Reconstructing Sociology," *Teaching Sociology,* **16**(April):123–132.

Anderson, Cheryl, and Linda Rouse. 1988. "Intervention in Cases of Woman Battering: An Application of Symbolic Interactionism and Critical Theory," *Clinical Sociological Review,* **6**:134–137.

Andersson-Brolin, Lillemor. 1988. "Ethnic Residential Segregation: The Case of Sweden," *Scandinavian Journal of Development Alternatives,* **7**(March):33–45.

Andrews, L. 1984. "Family Violence in Florida's Panhandle," *Ms.,* **12** (March):23.

Ansell, David A., and Robert L. Schiff. 1987. "Patient Dumping-Status, Implications, and Policy Recommendations," *Journal of the American Medical Association,* **257**(March 20):1500–1502.

Anti-Defamation League of B'nai B'rith. 1991. *1990 Audit of Anti-Semitic Incidents.* New York: ADL.

Antonovsky, Aaron. 1972. "Social Class, Life Expectancy and Overall Mortality," in E. Garty Jaco (ed.), *Patients, Physicians and Illness.* New York: Free Press, pp. 5–30.

Appelbaum, Richard P. 1970. *Theories of Social Change.* Chicago: Markham.

Archer, Dave, and R. M. Akert. 1977. "Words and Everything Else: Verbal and Nonverbal Cues in Social Interpretation," *Journal of Personality and Social Psychology,* **35**(June):443–449.

Archer, Margaret. 1988. *Culture and Agency: The Place of Culture in Social Theory.* Cambridge, Eng.: Cambridge University Press.

Arendell, Terry. 1986. *Mothers and Divorce: Legal, Economic, and Social Problems.* Berkeley: University of California Press.

Arens, W., and Susan P. Montague (eds.). 1976. *The American Dimension: Cultural Myths and Social Realities.* Port Washington, N.Y.: Alfred.

Arensberg, Conrad M., and Arthur H. Niehoff. 1964. *Introducing Social Change.* Chicago: Aldine.

Arias, M. Beatriz (ed.). 1986. "The Education of Hispanic Americans: A Challenge for the Future," special issue of *American Journal of Education,* **95**(November).

Arond, Miriam. 1984. "Women and Doctors," *New York Daily News* (April 16), p. 27.

Aronson, Elliot. 1972. *The Social Animal.* San Francisco: Freeman.

Asch, Adrienne. 1986. "Will Populism Empower Disabled People?" in Harry G. Boyte and Frank Riessman (eds.),

The New Populism: The Politics of Empowerment. Philadelphia: Temple University Press, pp. 213–228.

———. 1989. "Has the Law Made a Difference? What Some Disabled Students Have to Say," in Dorothy Kerzner Lipsky and Alan Gartner (eds.), *Beyond Separate Education: Quality Education for All.* Baltimore: Brookes, pp. 181–205.

Asch, Solomon. 1952. *Social Psychology.* New York: Prentice-Hall.

Astin, Alexander W., Kenneth C. Green, and William S. Korn. 1987. *The American Freshman: Twenty Year Trends.* Los Angeles: Cooperative Institutional Research Program, University of California at Los Angeles.

———, William S. Korn, and Ellyne R. Berz. 1989. *The American Freshman: National Norms Fall 1989.* Los Angeles: Cooperative Institutional Research Program, University of California at Los Angeles.

Astrachan, Anthony. 1986. *How Men Feel: Their Response to Women's Demands for Equality and Power.* New York: Anchor/Doubleday.

Atchley, Robert C. 1967. "Retired Women: A Study of Self and Role." Unpublished doctoral dissertation, University Microfilms, University of Michigan, Ann Arbor.

———. 1985. *The Social Forces in Later Life: An Introduction to Social Gerontology* (4th ed.). Belmont, Calif.: Wadsworth.

Auerbach, Judith D. 1987. "Child Care Responsibility as a Barrier to Women's Achievement of the American Dream: How Employers May Make a Difference." Paper presented at the annual meeting of the Eastern Sociological Society, Boston.

———. 1988. "The Privatization of Child Care: The Limits of Employer Support." Paper presented at the annual meeting of the American Sociological Association, Washington, D.C.

Auster, Carol J. 1985. "Manuals for Socialization: Examples from Girl Scout Handbooks, 1913–1984," *Qualitative Sociology* 8(Winter):359–367.

Aversa, Alfred, Jr. 1987. "When Blue Collars and White Collars Meet at Play: The Case of the Yacht Club."

Paper presented at the annual meeting of the Eastern Sociological Society, Boston.

Axtell, Roger E. 1990. *Do's and Taboos around the World* (2d ed.). New York: Wiley.

Ayres, R. Drummond, Jr. 1988a. "Protest by the Deaf Brings Resignation but Not Yet a Truce," *New York Times* (March 12), pp. 1, 7.

———. 1988b. "Protest That Turned Campus for the Deaf Around," *New York Times* (March 15), p. A16.

Aytac, Isik A. 1987. "Wife's Decision-Making at Work and Contribution to Family Income as Determinate of How Domestic Chores Are Shared." Paper presented at the annual meeting of the Eastern Sociological Society, Boston.

Azumi, Koya, and Jerald Hage. 1972. *Organizational Systems.* Lexington, Mass.: Heath.

Babbie, Earl R. 1980. *Sociology: An Introduction* (2d ed.). Belmont, Calif.: Wadsworth.

Babchuk, Nicholas, and Alan Booth. 1969. "Voluntary Association Membership: A Longitudinal Analysis," *American Sociological Review,* **34**(February):31–45.

Bachrach, Christine A. 1986. "Adoption Plans, Adopted Children, and Adoptive Mothers," *Journal of Marriage and the Family,* **48**(May):243–253.

Bachrach, Peter, and Morton S. Baratz. 1962. "Two Faces of Power," *American Political Science Review,* **56**(December):947–952.

Back, Kurt W. 1981. "Small Groups," in Morris Rosenberg and Ralph H. Turner (eds.), *Social Psychology: Sociological Perspectives.* New York: Basic Books, pp. 320–343.

Backer, Thomas E. 1988. "Managing AIDS at Work," *American Psychologist,* **43**(November):983–987.

Bacon, Phil. 1985. "Facts behind the Trademark," *Moonkeans* (June), pp. 3–5.

Bahr, Howard M., Theodore Caplow, and Bruce A. Chadwick. 1983. "Middletown III: Problems of Replication, Longitudinal Measurement, and Triangulation," in Ralph H. Turner (ed.), *Annual Review of Sociology, 1983.*

Palo Alto, Calif.: Annual Reviews, pp. 243–264.

Bailey, Mike. 1990. "School Choice as 'American as Apple Pie,' Superintendent Says," *Journal Star* (March 16), p. A7

Baldus, David C., Charles A. Pulaski, Jr., and George Woodworth. 1986. "Arbitrariness and Discrimination in the Administration of the Death Penalty: A Challenge to State Supreme Courts," *Stetson Law Review,* **15**(Spring):133–261.

Bales, Robert F. 1950a. "A Set of Categories for the Analysis of Small Group Interaction," *American Sociological Review,* **15**(April):257–263.

———. 1950b. *Interaction Process Analysis: A Method for the Study of Small Groups.* Cambridge, Mass.: Addison-Wesley.

———. 1968. "Interaction Process Analysis," in David L. Sills (ed.), *International Encyclopedia of the Social Sciences,* vol. 7. New York: Macmillan, pp. 465–471.

———. 1970. *Personality and Interpersonal Behavior.* New York: Holt.

——— and Fred L. Strodtbeck. 1951. "Phases in Group Problem Solving," *Journal of Abnormal and Social Psychology,* **46**(October 1):485–495.

Ball, Donald. 1967. "An Abortion Clinic Ethnography," *Social Problems,* **14**(Summer):298–301.

Balswick, Jack, and Charles Peek. 1971. "The Inexpressive Male: A Tragedy of American Society," *Family Coordinator,* **20**(October)363–368.

Baltzell, E. Digby, and Howard G. Schneiderman. 1988. "Social Class in the Oval Office," *Public Opinion,* **25**(September–October):42–49.

Bandura, Albert. 1969. *Principles of Behavior Modification.* New York: Holt, Rinehart and Winston.

Banfield, Edward C. 1974. *The Unheavenly City Revisited.* Boston: Little, Brown.

Banks, Vera J. 1987. *Black Farmers and Their Farms.* Washington, D.C.: U.S. Government Printing Office.

Baran, Paul. 1960. *The Political Economy of Growth.* New York: Monthly Review.

Barden, J. C. 1987. "Marital Rape: Drive for Tougher Laws Is Pressed," *New York Times* (May 13), p. A16.

Barker, Eileen. 1986a. "Religious Movements: Cult and Anticult since Jonestown," in Alex Inkeles (ed.), *Annual Review of Sociology, 1986*. Palo Alto, Calif.: Annual Reviews, pp. 329–346.

———. 1986b. *The Making of a Moonie: Brainwashing or Choice?* New York: Basil Blackwell.

Barmash, Isadore. 1982. "Older Managers Fighting Dismissal," *New York Times* (January 10), p. 52.

Barnet, Richard J. 1990. "But What about Africa?" *Harper's*, **280**(May):43–51.

——— and Ronald E. Müller. 1974. *Global Reach: The Power of the Multinational Corporation*. New York: Simon and Schuster.

Barnouw, Victor. 1978. *An Introduction to Anthropology: Ethnography* (3d ed.). Homewood, Ill.: Dorsey.

Baron, James N., and William T. Bielby. 1986. "The Proliferation of Job Titles in Organizations," *Administrative Science Quarterly*, **31**(December):561–586.

Barringer, Felicity. 1986. "Soviets Cracking Down on Wealthy Cheaters," *New York Times* (June 8), p. L21.

———. 1989. "Minnesota, Scene of Abortion Wars, Watches Supreme Court," *New York Times* (June 25), p. 12.

———. 1990. "Judge Nullifies Law Mandating Use of English," *New York Times* (February 8), pp. Al, B10.

Barron, James. 1983. "A Classic Suburb Feels Graying Pains," *New York Times* (July 13), p. E6.

Bartlett, Kay. 1988. "Sociologist Researches 'Role Exiting' Process," *Galesburg Register-Mail* (August 11), sec. C, p. 1.

Baruch, Grace, Rosalind Barnett, and Caryl Rivers. 1980. "A New Start for Women at Midlife," *New York Times Magazine* (December 7), pp. 196–201.

———, ———, and ———. 1983. *Lifeprints: New Patterns of Love and Work for Today's Women*. New York: McGraw-Hill.

Baskir, Lawrence M., and William A. Strauss. 1978. *Chance and Circumstance: The Draft, the War, and the Vietnam Generation*. New York: Knopf.

Basso, Keith H. 1972. "Ice and Travel among the Fort Norman Slave: Folk Taxonomies and Cultural Rules," *Language in Society*, **1**(March):31–49.

Batra, Ravi. 1987. "An Ominous Trend to Greater Inequality," *New York Times* (May 3), p. F2.

Bauman, David. 1985. "English-Only Drive Gaining Steam," *USA Today* (April 1), p. 3A.

Baxter, Richard L., Cynthia De Riemer, Ann Landini, Larry Leslie, and Michael W. Singletary. 1985. "A Content Analysis of Music Videos," *Journal of Broadcasting and Electronic Media*, **29**(Summer):333–340.

Beck, Kirsten. 1987. "Trouble on TV's Path to Paradise," *TV World* (June–July), pp. 11–12.

Beck, Melinda. 1989. "China: 'Kill the Black Devils,'" *Newsweek*, **103**(January 9):35.

Becker, Howard S. 1952. "Social Class Variations in the Teacher-Pupil Relationship," *Journal of Educational Sociology*, **25**(April):451–465.

———. 1963. *The Outsiders: Studies in the Sociology of Deviance*. New York: Free Press.

——— (ed.). 1964. *The Other Side: Perspectives on Deviance*. New York: Free Press.

———. 1973. *The Outsiders: Studies in the Sociology of Deviance* (rev. ed.). New York: Free Press.

———, Blanche Greer, Everett C. Hughes, and Anselm Strauss. 1961. *Boys in White: Student Culture in Medical School*. Chicago: University of Chicago Press.

Beeghley, Leonard. 1978. *Social Stratification in America: A Critical Analysis of Theory and Research*. Santa Monica, Calif.: Goodyear.

Bell, Daniel. 1953. "Crime as an American Way of Life," *Antioch Review*, **13**(Summer):131–154.

———. 1973. *The Coming of Postindustrial Society*. New York: Basic Books.

Bell, Wendell. 1981a. "Modernization," in *Encyclopedia of Sociology*. Guilford, Conn.: DPG Publishing, pp. 186–187.

———. 1981b. "Neocolonialism," in *Encyclopedia of Sociology*. Guilford, Conn.: DPG Publishing, p. 193.

Bellah, Robert H. 1957. *Tokaguwa Religion. The Values of Pre-Industrial Japan*. Glencoe, Ill.: Free Press.

——— and Frederick E. Greenspan (eds.). 1987. *Uncivil Religion: Interreligious Hostility in America*. New York: Crossroads.

———, Richard Madsen, Anne Swidler, William M. Sullivan, and Steven M. Tipton. 1985. *Habits of the Heart: Individualism and Commitment in American Life*. Berkeley: University of California Press.

Bellamy, Carol. 1984. "Homeless Should Be Rehoused," *New York Times* (May 18), p. A31.

Bem, Sandra Lipsitz. 1978. "Beyond Androgyny," in Julia A. Sherman and Florence L. Dennsk (eds.), *The Psychology of Women: Future Directions of Research*. New York: Psychological Dimensions, pp. 3–23.

Bendix, B. Reinhard. 1968. "Max Weber," in David L. Sills (ed.), *International Encyclopedia of the Social Sciences*. New York: Macmillan, pp. 493–502.

Benner, Richard S., and Susan Tyler Hitchcock. 1986. *Life after Liberal Arts*. Charlottesville: Office of Career Planning and Placement, University of Virginia.

Bennett, Trevor, and Richard Wright. 1984. *Burglars on Burglary*. Brookfield, Vt.: Gover.

Bensman, David, and Roberta Lynch. 1987. *Rusted Dreams: Hard Times in a Steel Community*. New York: McGraw-Hill.

Berg, Bruce L. 1989. *Qualitative Research Methods for the Social Sciences: Sorting the Noodles from the Soup*. Boston: Allyn and Bacon.

Berg, Helen M., and Marianne A. Ferber. 1983. "Men and Women Graduate Students," *Journal of Higher Education*, **54**(November–December):629–648.

Berg, Philip L. 1975. "Racism and the Puritan Mind," *Phylon*, **36**(Spring):1–7.

Berger, Bennett M. 1981. *The Survival of a Counterculture*. Berkeley: University of California Press.

Berger, Peter. 1963. *Invitation to Sociology: A Humanistic Perspective*. New York: Anchor.

———. 1972. "The Myth of Suburbia," in Charles M. Haar (ed.), *The End of*

Innocence: A Suburban Reader. Glenview, Ill.: Scott, Foresman, pp. 36–46.

———. 1973. "Religious Institutions," in Neil J. Smelser (ed.), *Sociology: An Introduction* (2d ed.). New York: Wiley, pp. 303–346.

——— and Thomas Luckmann. 1966. *The Social Construction of Reality.* New York: Doubleday.

Berk, Marc. 1985. "Medical Manpower and the Labeling of Blindness," *Deviant Behavior*, **6**(3):253–265.

Berk, Richard A. 1974. *Collective Behavior.* Dubuque, Iowa: Brown.

——— and Howard E. Aldrich. 1972. "Patterns of Vandalism during Civil Disorders as an Indicator of Selection of Targets," *American Sociological Review*, **37**(October):533–547.

Berke, Richard L. 1989. "U.S. Report Raises Estimate of Smoking Toll," *New York Times* (January 11), p. A20.

Berkeley Wellness Letter. 1990. "The Nest Refilled," **6**(February):1–2.

Berlin, Brent and Paul Kay. 1969. *Basic Color Terms: Their University and Evolution.* Berkeley: University of California Press.

Bernard, Jessie. 1972. "The Paradox of the Happy Marriage," in Vivian Gornick and Barbara K. Moran (eds.), *Woman in Sexist Society: Studies in Power and Powerlessness.* New York: Basic Books, pp. 145–162.

———. 1974. *The Future of Motherhood.* New York: Dial.

———. 1975. *Women, Wives, Mothers: Values and Options.* Chicago: Aldine.

Berney, Barbara. 1990. "In Research, Women Don't Matter," *The Progressive*, **54**(October):24–27.

Bernstein, Richard. 1988. "Asian Newcomers Hurt by Precursors' Success," *New York Times* (July 10), p. 16.

Berreman, Gerald, et al. 1971. *Anthropology Today.* Del Mar, Calif.: CRM Books.

Berryman, Philip. 1987. *Liberation Theology.* Philadelphia: Temple University Press.

Best, Fred, and Ray Eberhard. 1990. "Education for the 'Era of the Adult,'" *The Futurist*, **21**(May–June):23–28.

Best, Joel, and Gerald T. Horiuchi. 1985. "The Razor Blade in the Apple: The Social Construction of Urban Legends," *Social Problems*, **32**(June):488–499.

Bettelheim, Bruno, and Morris Janowitz. 1964. *Social Change and Prejudice.* New York: Free Press.

Biggart, Nicole Woolsey. 1989. *Charismatic Capitalism: Direct Selling Organizations in America.* Chicago: University of Chicago Press.

Biklen, Douglas. 1986. "Framed: Journalism's Treatment of Disability," *Social Policy*, **16**(Winter):45–51.

Birdsall, Nancy. 1980. "Population Growth and Poverty in the Developing World," *Population Bulletin*, **35**(December).

Bishop, Donna M., and Charles E. Frazier. 1988. "The Influence of Race in Juvenile Justice Processing," *Journal of Research in Crime and Delinquency*, **25**(August):242–263.

Bishop, Katherine. 1987. "Getting Permission to Have an Abortion," *New York Times* (November 1), p. E7.

Black, C. E. 1966. *The Dynamics of Modernization: A Study in Comparative History.* New York: Harper and Row.

Blakey, G. Robert, Ronald Goldstock, and Charles H. Rogarin. 1978. *Rackets Bureaus: Investigation and Prosecution of Organized Crime.* Report of National Institute of Law Enforcement and Criminal Justice. Washington, D.C.: U.S. Government Printing Office.

Blanc, Ann Klimas. 1984. "Nonmarital Cohabitation and Fertility in the United States and Western Europe," *Population Research and Policy Review*, **3**:181–193.

Blanck, Peter David, Robert Rosenthal, and La Doris Hazzard Cordell. 1985. "The Appearance of Justice: Judges' Verbal and Nonverbal Behavior in Criminal Jury Trials," *Stanford Law Review*, **38**(November):89–164.

Bland, Dorothy, and Jeanne DeQuinne. 1987. "New Drives Mounted for Official Languages," *USA Today* (August 12), p. 6A.

Blau, Peter M. 1963. *The Dynamics of Bureaucracy: A Study of Interpersonal Relations in Two Government Agencies* (rev. ed.). Chicago: University of Chicago Press.

———. 1964. *Exchange and Power in Social Life.* New York: Wiley.

——— and Otis Dudley Duncan. 1967. *The American Occupational Structure.* New York: Wiley.

——— and Marshall W. Meyer. 1987. *Bureaucracy in Modern Society* (3d ed.). New York: Random House.

Blauner, Robert. 1964. *Alienation and Freedom.* Chicago: University of Chicago Press.

———. 1972. *Racial Oppression in America.* New York: Harper and Row.

Blendon, Robert J. 1986. "The Problems of Cost, Access, and Distribution of Medical Care," *Daedalus*, **115** (Spring):119–135.

——— et al. [4 authors]. 1989. "Access to Medical Care for Black and White Americans," *Journal of the American Medical Association*, **261**(January 13):278–281.

Block, Fred. 1977. "The Ruling Class Does Not Rule: Notes of the Marxist Theory of State," *Socialist Revolution*, **7**(May–June):6–28.

Blodgett, Nancy. 1987. "Death Row Inmates Can't Find Lawyers," *ABA Journal* (January 1), p. 58.

Blood, Robert O., Jr., and Donald M. Wolfe. 1960. *Husbands and Wives: The Dynamics of Married Living.* New York: Free Press.

Bloom, Dave E., and Neil G. Bennett. 1986. "Childless Couples," *American Demographics*, **8**(August):22–25, 54–55.

Bloom, Samuel W., and Robert N. Wilson. 1979. "Patient-Practitioner Relationship," in Howard E. Freeman, Sol Levine, and Leo G. Reider (eds.), *Handbook of Medical Sociology* (3d ed.). Englewood Cliffs, N.J.: Prentice-Hall, pp. 275–296.

Bluestein, Paul. 1989. "Accepting the Reality of Third World Debt," *Washington Post National Weekly Edition*, **6**(March 13):22.

Bluestone, Barry, and Bennett Harrison. 1982. *The Deindustrialization of America.* New York: Basic Books.

——— and ———. 1987. "The Grim Truth about the Job 'Miracle,'" *New York Times* (February 1), p. F3.

Blumberg, Paul. 1980. *Inequality in an Age of Decline.* New York: Oxford University Press.

Blume, Mary. 1987. "The French

Rumor Industry," *International Herald Tribune* (September 7), p. 16.

Blumenthal, Ralph. 1972. "800,000 Suburban Poor Suffer amid Environment of Affluence," in Charles M. Harr (ed.), *The End of Innocence: A Suburban Reader*. Glenview, Ill.: Scott, Foresman, pp. 73–77.

Blumer, Herbert. 1955. "Collective Behavior," in Alfred McClung Lee (ed.), *Principles of Sociology* (2d ed.). New York: Barnes and Noble, pp. 165–198.

———. 1969. *Symbolic Interactionism: Perspective and Method*. Englewood Cliffs, N.J.: Prentice-Hall.

Blumstein, Philip, and Pepper Schwartz. 1983. *American Couples: Money, Work, Sex*. New York: Morrow.

Boff, Leonardo, and Clodovis Boff. 1984. *Salvation and Liberation: In Search of a Balance between Faith and Politics*. Maryknoll, N.Y.: Orbu.

Boffey, Philip M. 1984. "Failure Is Found in the Discharge of Mentally Ill," *New York Times* (September 13), pp. Al, B12.

Bogdan, Robert, and Steven J. Taylor. 1989. "Relationship with Severely Disabled People: The Social Construction of Humanness," *Social Problems*, **36**(April):135–148.

Bogue, Donald. 1979. *Principles of Demography*. New York: Wiley.

Bogue, Grant. 1981. *Basic Sociological Research Design*. Glenview, Ill.: Scott, Foresman.

Bohannan, Paul. 1970. "The Six Stations of Divorce," in Paul Bohannan (ed.), *Divorce and After*. New York: Doubleday, pp. 33–62.

Bohlen, Celestine. 1990. "Ethnic Rivalries Revive in East Europe," *New York Times* (November 12), pp. A1, A12.

Bok, Sissela. 1978. *Lying: Moral Choice in Public and Private Life*. New York: Pantheon.

Bonn, Robert L. 1984. *Criminology*. New York: McGraw-Hill.

Borjas, George. 1990. *Friends or Strangers: The Impact of Immigrants on the U.S. Economy*. New York: Basic Books.

Borman, Kathryn M., and Joel H. Spring. 1984. *Schools in Central Cities: Structure and Process*. New York: Longman.

Bornschier, Volker, and Christopher Chase-Dunn. 1985. *Transnational Corporations and Underdevelopment*. New York: Praeger.

———, ———, and Richard Rubinson. 1978. "Cross-National Evidence of the Effects of Foreign Investment and Aid on Economic Growth and Inequality: A Survey of Findings and A Reanalysis," *American Journal of Sociology*, **84**(November):651–683.

Boserup, Ester. 1977. "Preface," in Wellesley Editorial Committee (ed.), *Women and National Development: The Complexities of Change*. Chicago: University of Chicago Press, pp. xi–xiv.

Boston Women's Health Book Collective. 1969. *Our Bodies, Ourselves*. Boston: New England Free Press.

———. 1984. *The New Our Bodies, Ourselves*. New York: Simon and Schuster.

Bottomore, Tom (ed.). 1983. *A Dictionary of Marxist Thought*. Cambridge, Mass.: Harvard University Press.

——— and Maximilien Rubel (eds.). 1956. *Karl Marx: Selected Writings in Sociology and Social Philosophy*. New York: McGraw-Hill.

Bourne, Patricia Gerald, and Norma Juliet Wikler. 1978. "Commitment and the Cultural Mandate: Women in Medicine," *Social Problems*, **25**(April):430–440.

Bouvier, Leon F. 1980. "America's Baby Boom Generation: The Fateful Bulge," *Population Bulletin*, **35**(April).

———. 1984. "Planet Earth 1984–2034: A Demographic Vision," *Population Bulletin*, **39**(February).

——— and Cary B. Davis. 1982. *The Future Racial Composition of the United States*. Washington, D.C.: Demographic Information Services Center of the Population Reference Bureau.

Bowles, Samuel, and Herbert Gintis. 1976. *Schooling in Capitalist America: Educational Reforms and the Contradictions of Economic Life*. New York: Basic Books.

Boyer, Ernest L. 1983. *High School: A Report on Secondary Education in America*. Carnegie Foundation report. New York: Harper and Row.

Bozzi, Vincent. 1989. "Harassment Charges: Who Wins?" *Psychology Today*, **23**(May):16.

Bradley, Phil. 1990. "The Growing Clout of Voters with Disabilities," *Illinois Issues*, **16**(April):34.

Bradshaw, York W. 1988. "Reassessing Economic Dependency and Uneven Development: The Kenyan Experience," *American Sociological Review*, **53**(October):693–708.

——— and Jie Huang. 1991. "Intensifying Global Dependency: Foreign Debt, Structural Adjustment, and the Third World Underdevelopment," *Sociological Quarterly*, **32**(3) (forthcoming).

Braithwaite, John. 1985. "White Collar Crime," in John Turner (ed.), *Annual Review of Sociology, 1985*. Palo Alto, Calif.: Annual Reviews, pp. 1–25.

Brajuha, Mario, and Lyle Hallowell. 1986. "Legal Intrusion and the Politics of Fieldwork: The Impact of the Brajuha Case," *Urban Life*, **14**(January):454–478.

Braun, Denny. 1991. *The Rich Get Richer*. Chicago: Nelson Hall.

Braverman, Harry. 1974. *Labor and Monopoly Capital: The Degradation of Labor in the Twentieth Century*. New York: Monthly Review.

Brazil. 1981. *Ix Recenseamento Geral do Brasil—1980, 1, Pt. 1*. Rio de Janeiro: Secretaria de Planejamento da Presidência da República, Fundação Instituto Brasilero de Geografia e Estatistica.

Brewer, Rose M. 1989. "Black Women and Feminist Sociology: The Emerging Perspective," *American Sociologist*, **20**(Spring):57–70.

Brinton, Mary C. 1988. "The Social-Institutional Bases of Gender Stratification: Japan as an Illustrative Case," *American Journal of Sociology*, **94**(September):300–334.

———. 1989. "Gender Stratification in Contemporary Urban Japan," *American Sociological Review*, **54**(August):549–564.

Brodkey, Linda, and Michelle Fine. 1988. "Presence of Mind in the Absence of Body," *Journal of Education*, **170**(Fall):84–99.

Bromley, David G., and Anson D. Shupe, Jr. 1980. "Financing the New Religions: A Resource Mobilization Approach," *Journal for the Scientific Study of Religion*, **19**(3):227–239.

Bronfenbrenner, Urie. 1970. *Two Worlds of Childhood: U.S. and U.S.S.R.* New York: Russell Sage.

Brooke, James. 1990a. "Gold's Lure vs. Indian Rights: A Brazilian Conflict Sets the Amazon Aflame," *New York Times* (January 21), p. 3.

———. 1990b. "Brazil's New Chief Gives Radical Plan to Halt Inflation," *New York Times* (March 17), pp. 1, 45.

———. 1990c. "Old Woes Resurge in Brazil," *New York Times* (December 3), pp. D1, D5.

———. 1991a. "Brazil Freezes All Wages and Prices," *New York Times* (February 1), p. A3.

———. 1991b. "'Honor' Killing of Wives Is Outlawed in Brazil," *New York Times* (March 29), p. B16.

Brooks, Andrée. 1981. "Preppies from Abroad," *New York Times Magazine* (November 22), pp. 104–119.

———. 1987. "Women in the Clergy: Struggle to Succeed," *New York Times* (February 16), p. 15.

Brophy, Gwenda. 1989. "China: Part II," *Population Today*, 17(April):17.

Brown, Christopher. 1990. "Discrimination and Immigration Law," *Focus*, 18(August):3–4, 8.

Brown, Lester R. 1986. *State of the World, 1986.* New York: Norton.

Brown, Michael, and Amy Goldin. 1973. *Collective Behavior: A Review and Reinterpretation of the Literature.* Pacific Palisades, Calif.: Goodyear.

Brown, Patricia Leigh. 1987. "Studying Seasons of a Woman's Life," *New York Times* (September 14), p. B17.

———. 1988. "Troubled Millions Heed Call of Self-Help Groups," *New York Times* (July 16), pp. 1, 7.

Brown, Robert McAfee. 1980. *Gustavo Gutiérrez.* Atlanta: John Knox.

Brown, Roger W. 1954. "Mass Phenomena," in Gardner Lindzey (ed.), *Handbook of Social Psychology*, vol. 2. Reading, Mass.: Addison-Wesley, pp. 833–873.

———. 1965. *Social Psychology.* New York: Free Press.

Brownmiller, Susan. 1975. *Against Our Will: Men, Women, and Rape.* New York: Simon and Schuster.

Brozan, Nadine. 1984. "When Children Have 2 Homes," *New York Times* (March 25), p. 59.

———. 1985. "Rate of Pregnancies for U.S. Teenagers Found High in Study," *New York Times* (March 13), pp. Al, C7.

———. 1986. "For Female M.D.'s, Success at a Price," *New York Times* (January 16), pp. C1, C12.

Brunvand, Jan Harold. 1980. "Urban Legends: Folklore for Today," *Psychology Today*, 14(June):50–51, 53, 55, 59–60, 62.

———. 1981. *The Vanishing Hitchhiker.* New Yorker: Norton.

———. 1989. *Curses! Broiled Again!* New York: Norton.

Buckley, Sandra, and Vera Mackie. 1986. "Women in the New Japanese State," in Gavan McCormack and Yoshio Sugimoto (eds.), *Democracy in Contemporary Japan.* New York: Sharpe.

Budiansky, Stephen. 1988. "The Numbers Racket: How Polls and Statistics Lie," *U.S. News and World Report*, 105(July 11):44–47.

Bulle, Wolfgang F. 1987a. *Crossing Cultures? Guidelines for CDC International Travelers.* Atlanta: Centers for Disease Control.

———. 1987b. *Crossing Cultures? Southeast Asian Mainland.* Atlanta: Centers for Disease Control.

Bumpass, Larry L., and James A. Sweet. 1989. "National Estimates of Cohabitation," *Demography*, 26(November): 615–626.

———, ———, and Teresa Castro Martin. 1990. "Changing Patterns of Remarriage," *Journal of Marriage and the Family*, 52(August):747–756.

Burciaga, Cecilia Preciado de, Viola Gonzales, and Ruth A. Hepburn. 1977. "The Chicana as Feminist," in Alice G. Sargent (ed.), *Beyond Sex Roles.* St. Paul, Minn.: West, pp. 266–273.

Bureau of the Census. 1975a. *Historical Statistics of the United States, Colonial Times to 1970.* Washington, D. C.: U.S. Government Printing Office.

———. 1975b. *The Social and Economic Status of the Black Population in the United States: 1974.* Washington, D.C.: U.S. Government Printing Office.

———. 1975c. *Statistical Abstract of the United States: 1975.* Washington,

D.C.: U.S. Government Printing Office.

———. 1976. "A Statistical Portrait of Women in the United States," *Special Studies*, ser. P-23, no. 58. Washington, D.C.: U.S. Government Printing Office.

———. 1979. "The Social and Economic Status of the Black Population in the United States: An Historical View, 1790–1978," *Current Population Reports*, ser. P-23, no. 80. Washington, D.C.: U.S. Government Printing Office.

———. 1981a "Race of the Population by States: 1980," *Current Population Reports*, ser. PC80-S1-3. Washington, D.C.: U.S. Government Printing Office.

———. 1981b. "Population Profile of the United States: 1980," *Current Population Reports*, ser. P-20, no. 363. Washington, D.C.: U.S. Government Printing Office.

———. 1981c. *Statistical Abstract of the United States: 1981.* Washington, D.C.: U.S. Government Printing Office.

———. 1982. "Ancestry and Language in the United States: November 1979," *Current Population Reports*, ser. P-23, no. 116. Washington, D.C.: U.S. Government Printing Office.

———. 1983a. *Statistical Abstract of the United States: 1983.* Washington, D.C.: U.S. Government Printing Office.

———. 1983b. *Monthly Product Announcement: December, 1983.* Washington, D.C.: U.S. Government Printing Office.

———. 1985. *Voting and Registration in the Election of November 1984 (Advance Report)*, ser. P-20, no. 397. Washington, D.C.: U.S. Government Printing Office.

———. 1986a. *Statistical Abstract: 1987.* Washington, D.C.: U.S. Goverment Printing Office.

———. 1986b. "Household Wealth and Asset Ownership: 1984," *Current Population Reports*, ser. P-70, no. 7. Washington, D.C.: U.S. Government Printing Office.

———. 1987. *Statistical Abstract of the United States: 1988.* Washington, D.C.: U.S. Government Printing Office.

———. 1989a. *Poverty in the United States: 1987*, ser. P-60, no. 163. Washington, D.C.: U.S. Government Printing Office.

———. 1989b. "Child Support and Alimony: 1988 (Supplementary Report)," *Current Population Reports,* ser. P-23, no. 154. Washington, D.C.: U.S. Government Printing Office.

———. 1989c. "Changes in American Family Life," *Current Population Reports,* ser. P-23, no. 163. Washington, D.C.: U.S. Government Printing Office.

———. 1989d. "Money Income of Households, Families, and Persons in the United States: 1987," ser P-20, no. 162. Washington, D.C.: U.S. Government Printing Office.

———. 1989e. *Patterns of Metropolitan Area and County Population Growth: 1980 to 1987,* ser. P-20, no. 1039. Washington, D.C.: U.S. Government Printing Office.

———. 1989f. *Money Income and Poverty Status in the United States: 1988,* ser. P-60, no. 166. Washington, D.C.: U.S. Government Printing Office.

———. 1990a. *Statistical Abstract of the United States: 1990.* Washington, D.C.: U.S. Government Printing Office.

———. 1990b. *Money Income and Poverty Status in the United States: 1989,* ser. P-60, no. 168. Washington, D.C.: U.S. Government Printing Office.

———. 1990c. *Measuring the Effect of Benefits and Taxes on Income and Poverty: 1989,* ser. P-60, no. 169-RD. Washington, D.C.: U.S. Government Printing Office.

———. 1990d. *Transitions in Income and Poverty Status: 1985–1986,* ser. P-70, no. 18. Washington, D.C.: U.S. Government Printing Office.

———. 1990e. *Child Support and Alimony, 1987,* ser. P-23, no. 167. Washington, D.C.: U.S. Government Printing Office.

———. 1990f. *Marital Status and Living Arrangements, March 1989,* ser. P-20, no. 445. Washington, D.C.: U.S. Government Printing Office.

———. 1990g. *Residents of Farms and Rural Areas, 1989,* ser. P-20, no. 446. Washington, D.C.: U.S. Government Printing Office.

———. 1991a. *Exports from Manufacturing Establishments,* ser. AR-87, no. 1. Washington, D.C.: U.S. Government Printing Office.

———. 1991b. "Census Bureau Completes Distribution of 1990 Redistricting Tabulations to States." News release. Washington, D.C.: U.S. Government Printing Office.

———. 1991c. "The Hispanic Population in the United States: March 1990," *Current Population Reports,* ser. P-20, no. 449. Washington, D.C.: U.S. Government Printing Office.

Burg, Steven L. 1989. "The Soviet Union's Nationalities Question," *Current History,* **88**(October):341–344, 359–362.

Burgess, Ernest W. 1925. "The Growth of the City," in Robert E. Park, Ernest W. Burgess, and Roderick D. McKenzie (eds.), *The City.* Chicago: University of Chicago Press, pp. 47–62.

Burgess, John. 1989. "Exporting Our Office Work," *Washington Post National Weekly Edition,* **6**(May 1):22.

Burrows, William E. 1982. "Cockpit Encounters," *Psychology Today,* **16**(November):42–47.

Burt, Martha R., and Barbara E. Cohen. 1989. "Differences among Homeless Single Women, Women with Children, and Single Men," *Social Problems,* **36**(December):508–524.

Butler, Robert N. 1975. *Why Survive? Being Old in America.* New York: Harper and Row.

———. 1980. "Ageism: A Forward," *Journal of Social Issues,* **36**(Spring):8–11.

———. 1989. "Dispelling Ageism: The Cross-Cutting Intervention," *Annals* **503**(May):138–147.

Butterfield, Fox. 1984. "Blacks Decrease but Women Increase on University Faculties," *New York Times* (January 28), p. 6.

Byrd, James C., Robyn S. Shapiro, and David L. Schiedermayer. 1989. "Passive Smoking: A Review of Medical and Legal Issues," *American Journal of Public Health,* **79**(February):209–215.

Cabrera, Denise. 1989. "Women on TV: More Than Just a Pretty Sight," *New York Post* (December 15), p. 113.

Cahill, Spencer E. 1986. "Language Practices and Self Definition: The Case of Gender Identity Acquisition," *Sociological Quarterly,* **27**(September):295–312.

Califano, Joseph. 1986. "Restrict Smoking in Public Places: Pro," *U.S. News and World Report,* **101**(July 21):65.

Callen, Michael. 1988. "I Will Survive," *Village Voice,* **33**(May 3):31–35.

Campbell, Colin. 1986. "Anatomy of a Fierce Academic Feud," *The New York Times* (November 9), sec. 12, pp. 58–64.

Camus, Albert. 1948. *The Plague.* New York: Random House.

Cancian, Francesca. 1986. "The Feminization of Love," *Signs,* **11**(Summer): 692–708.

Cantril, Hadley. 1940. *The Invasion from Mars: A Study in the Psychology of Panic.* Princeton, N.J.: Princeton University Press.

Caplan, Arthur L. (ed.). 1978. *The Sociobiology Debate; Reading on Ethical and Scientific Issues.* New York: Harper and Row.

Caplan, Ronald L. 1989. "The Commodification of American Health Care," *Social Science and Medicine,* **28**(11):1139–1148.

Caplow, Theodore. 1956. "A Theory of Coalitions in the Triad," *American Sociological Review,* **20**(August):489–493.

———. 1959. "Further Development of a Theory of Coalitions in Triads," *American Journal of Sociology,* **64**(March):488–493.

———. 1969. *Two against One: Coalitions in Triads.* Englewood Cliffs, N.J.: Prentice-Hall.

Caputi, Jane, and Diana E. H. Russell. 1990. "'Femicide': Speaking the Unspeakable," *Ms.* (September–October), pp. 34–37.

Carmichael, Stokely, and Charles V. Hamilton. 1967. *Black Power: The Politics of Liberation in America.* New York: Random House.

Carmody, Denise Lardner. 1989. *Women and World Religions* (2d ed.). Englewood Cliffs, N.J.: Prentice Hall.

Carroll, John B. 1953. *The Study of Language.* Cambridge, Mass.: Harvard University Press.

———. 1956. *Language, Thought, and Reality: Selected Writings of Benjamin Lee Whorf.* Cambridge, Mass.: M.I.T. Press.

Carson, Rachel. 1962. *The Silent Spring.* Boston: Houghton Mifflin.

Carter, Keith. 1989. "Networking Is the Key to Jobs," *USA Today* (August 7), p. B1.

Cassidy, Claire Monod. 1982. "Protein-Energy Malnutrition as a Culture-Bound Syndrome," *Culture, Medicine and Psychiatry,* **6**:325–345.

Castells, Manuel. 1976. "The Wild City," *Capital and State,* **4,5**(Summer) 2–30.

———. 1977. *The Urban Question: A Marxist Approach.* Cambridge, Mass.: M.I.T. Press.

———. 1983. *The City and the Grass Roots.* Berkeley: University of California Press.

Castro, Janice. 1984. "Earning Profits, Saving Lives," *Time,* **124**(December 10):84–85.

Catton, W. 1978. "Carrying Capacity, Overshoot, and the Quality of Life," in J. Milton Yinger and Stephen J. Cutler (eds.), *Major Social Issues.* New York: Free Press, pp. 231–249.

Center for Educational Statistics. 1987. *Digest of Educational Statistics, 1987.* Washington, D.C.: U.S. Government Printing Office.

Center for the American Woman and Politics. 1987. *Women in Government around the World.* New Brunswick, N.J.: Center for the American Woman and Politics.

———. 1989. *The Gender Gap in Presidential Voting, 1980–1988.* New Brunswick, N.J.: Center for the American Woman in Politics.

———. 1990. *Women in Elective Office, 1990.* New Brunswick, N.J.: Center for the American Woman in Politics.

Cetron, Marvin J. 1989. "The Growing Threat of Terrorism," *Futurist,* **23**(July–August): 20–24.

Chafetz, Janet Saltzman. 1988. *Feminist Sociology: An Overview of Contemporary Theories.* Itasca, Ill.: Peacock.

Chalfant, H. Paul, Robert E. Beckley, and C. Eddie Palmer. 1987. *Religion in Contemporary Society* (2d ed.). Palo Alto, Calif.: Mayfield.

——— et al. [5 others]. 1990. "The Clergy as a Resource for Those Encountering Psychological Distress," *Review of Religious Research,* **31**(March):305–315.

Chambliss, William. 1972. "Introduc-tion," in Harry King, *Box Man.* New York: Harper and Row, pp. ix–xi.

———. 1973. "The Saints and the Roughnecks," *Society,* **11**(November–December):24–31.

——— and Robert B. Seidman. 1971. *Law, Order, and Power.* Reading, Mass.: Addison-Wesley.

Chandler, William U. 1986. "Banishing Tobacco," *The Futurist,* **20**(May–June):9–15.

Chandrasekhar, S. 1975. *Infant Mortality, Population Growth and Family Planning in India* (2d ed.). Chapel Hill: University of North Carolina Press.

Changing Times. 1981. "When Family Anger Turns to Violence," **35**(March):66–70.

Chapman, Fern Schumer. 1987. "Executive Guilt: Who's Taking Care of the Children," *Fortune,* **115**(February 16):30–37.

Chapman, Stephen. 1986. "Off the Respirator," *New Republic,* **197**(June 16): 10–12.

Charon, Joel M. 1985. *Symbolic Interactionsim: An Introduction, an Interpretation, an Integration* (2d ed.). Englewood Cliffs, N.J.: Prentice-Hall.

Cherlin, Andrew S. 1988. *The Changing American Family and Public Policy.* Washington, D.C.: Urban Institute.

Chernin, Kim. 1981. *The Obsession: Reflections on the Tyranny of Slenderness.* New York: Harper and Row.

Chesler, Phyllis. 1986. *Mothers on Trial: The Battle for Children and Custody.* New York: McGraw-Hill.

Chinoy, Ely. 1954. *Sociological Perspectives: Basic Concepts and Their Applications.* New York: Random House.

Chira, Susan. 1986. "Is Any Choice Right in Sex Selection," *New York Times* (October 26), p. E7.

———. 1988. "Many Working Women in Japan Remain Invisible," *New York Times* (December 4), p. 26.

———. 1991. "Bush Presses Bill Allowing Parents to Choose Schools," *New York Times* (April 19), pp. A1, B7.

Chow, Effie Poy Yew. 1984. "Traditional Chinese Medicine: A Holistic System," in J. Warren Salmon (ed.), *Alternative Medicines.* New York: Tavistock, pp. 114–137.

Chronicle of Higher Education. 1982.

"Fact-File: 9-Month Faculty Salaries for 1981–1982," **24**(July 7):10.

Cicone, Michael V., and Diane N. Ruble. 1978. "Beliefs about Males," *Journal of Social Issues,* **34**(Winter):5–16.

Cisin, Ira H., and Walter B. Clark. 1962. "The Methodological Challenge of Disaster Research," in George W. Baker and Dwight W. Chapman (eds.), *Man and Society in Disaster.* New York: Basic Books, pp. 23–40.

Clark, Burton R., and Martin Trow. 1966. "The Organizational Context," in Theodore M. Newcomb and Everett K. Wilson (eds.), *The Study of College Peer Groups.* Chicago: Aldine, pp. 17–70.

Clark, Candace. 1983. "Sickness and Social Control," in Howard Robboy and Candace Clark (eds.), *Social Interaction: Readings in Sociology* (2d ed.). New York: St. Martin's, pp. 346–365.

Clausen, John A. 1979. "Mental Disorder," in Howard E. Freeman, Sol Levine, and Leo G. Reeder (eds.), *Handbook of Medical Sociology* (3d ed.). Englewood Cliffs, N.J.: Prentice-Hall, pp. 97–112.

Clendenin, Dudley. 1986. "Fundamentalists Win a Federal Suit over Schoolbooks," *New York Times* (October 25), pp. 1, 8.

Clift, Eleanor. 1989. "A Victory for the Haves," *Newsweek,* **114**(October 16):38.

Clines, Francis X. 1989. "There's a Crime Wave, or a Perception Wave, in the Soviet Union," *New York Times* (August 17), p. E2.

Cloward, Richard A. 1959. "Illegitimate Means, Anomie, and Deviant Behavior," *American Sociological Review,* **24**(April):164–176.

Coates, James. 1987. *Armed and Dangerous: The Rise of the Survivalist Right.* New York: Hill and Wang.

Cockerham, William C. 1989. *Medical Sociology* (4th ed.). Englewood Cliffs, N.J.: Prentice-Hall.

Cohn, Richard M. 1982. "Economic Development and Status Change of the Aged," *American Journal of Sociology,* **87**(March):1150–1161.

Colasanto, Diane. 1989a. "Homosexuality," *Gallup Report,* **289**(October): 11–16.

———. 1989b. "Public Wants Civil

Rights Widened for Some Groups, Not for Others," *Gallup Poll Monthly*, **291**(December):13–22.

Colclough, Glenna, and E. M. Beck. 1986. "The American Educational Structure and the Reproduction of Social Class," *Sociological Inquiry*, **56**(Fall):456–476.

Cole, Elizabeth S. 1985. "Adoption: History, Policy, and Program," in Joan Laird and Ann Hartman (eds.), *A Handbook of Child Welfare*. New York: Free Press, pp. 638–666.

Cole, Mike. 1988. *Bowles and Gintis Revisited: Correspondence and Contradiction in Educational Theory*. Philadelphia: Falmer.

Coleman, James S., Thomas Hoffer, and Sally Kilgore. 1982. *High School Achievement: Public, Catholic, and Other Private Schools Compared*. New York: Basic Books.

Coleman, James William. 1987. "Toward an Integrated Theory of White-Collar Crime," *American Journal of Sociology*, **93**(September):406–439.

——— and Donald R. Cressey. 1980. *Social Problems*. New York: Harper and Row.

Coleman, Milton. 1984. "18 Words, Seven Weeks Later," *Washington Post* (April 8), p. C8.

Collier, Peter. 1970. "The Red Man's Burden," *Ramparts*, **8**(February 1970):26–38.

Collins, Glenn. 1984. "Experts Debate Impact of Day Care on Children and Society," *New York Times* (September 4), p. B11.

———. 1987. "As Nation Grays, a Mighty Advocate Flexes Its Muscles," *New York Times* (April 2), pp. C1, C8.

Collins, Patricia Hill. 1986. "Learning from the Outsider Within: The Sociological Significance of Black Feminist Thought," *Social Problems*, **33**(October–December):S14–S32.

Collins, Randall. 1975. *Conflict Sociology: Toward an Explanatory Sociology*. New York: Academic.

———. 1979. *The Credential Society: An Historical Sociology of Education and Stratification*. New York: Academic.

———. 1980. "Weber's Last Theory of Capitalism: A Systematization," *American Sociological Review*, **45**(December):925–942.

———. 1982. *Sociological Insight: An Introduction to Non-Obvious Sociology*. New York: Oxford University Press.

———. 1988. *Sociology of Marriage and the Family: Gender, Love, and Property* (2d ed.). Chicago: Nelson Hall.

——— and Michael Makowsky. 1978. *The Discovery of Society*. New York: Random House.

Collins, Sharon M. 1983. "The Making of the Black Middle Class," *Social Problems*, **30**(April):369–382.

———. 1989. "The Marginalization of Black Executives," *Social Problems*, **36**(October):317–331.

Colomy, Paul B. 1986. "Recent Developments in the Functionalist Approach to Change," *Sociological Focus*, **19**(April):139–158.

Commission on Civil Rights. 1974. *Para los Niños—For the Children: Improving Education for Mexican Americans*. Prepared by Frank Sotomayor. Washington, D.C.: U.S. Government Printing Office.

———. 1975. *A Better Chance to Learn: Bilingual, Bicultural Education*. Washington, D.C.: U.S. Government Printing Office.

———. 1976. *A Guide to Federal Laws and Regulations Prohibiting Sex Discrimination*. Washington, D.C.: U.S. Government Printing Office.

———. 1981. *Affirmative Action in the 1980s: Dismantling the Process of Discrimination*. Washington, D.C.: U.S. Government Printing Office.

Commoner, Barry. 1971. *The Closing Circle*. New York: Knopf.

Community Relations Service. 1990. *1989 Annual Report of the Community Relations Service*. Washington, D.C.: Community Relations Service, Department of Justice.

Congressional Digest. 1988. "Family and Medical Leave Policy," **67**(May):129–160.

Conklin, John E. 1981. *Criminology*. New York: Macmillan.

Conly, Catherine H., and J. Thomas McEwen. 1990. "Computer Crime," *NIJ Reports* (January–February), pp. 2–7.

Conover, Pamela J., and Virginia Gray. 1983. *Feminism and the New Right Conflict over the American Family*. New York: Praeger.

Conrad, Peter. 1975. "The Discovery of Hyperkinesis: Notes on the Medicalization of Deviant Behavior," *Social Problems*, **23**(October):12–21.

——— and Rochelle Kern (eds.). 1986. *The Sociology of Health and Illness: Critical Perspectives* (2d ed.). New York: St. Martin's.

——— and Joseph W. Schneider. 1980. *Deviance and Medicalization: From Badness to Sickness*. St. Louis: Mosby.

Cook, Rhodes. 1988. "Bush Victory Fits 20-Year Presidential Pattern," *Congressional Quarterly Weekly Report*, **48**(November 12): 3241–3245.

Cook, Timothy. 1988. "A Ticket to Ride," *The Progressive*, **52**(May):27–28.

Cooley, Charles H. 1902. *Human Nature and the Social Order*. New York: Scribner.

Coppola, Vincent. 1981. "A Vocation Dies in Brooklyn," *Newsweek*, **92**(April 27):81.

Corea, Gena. 1977. *The Hidden Malpractice*. New York: Morrow.

Coser, Lewis A. 1956. *The Functions of Social Conflict*. New York: Free Press.

———. 1977. *Masters of Sociological Thought: Ideas in Historical and Social Context* (2d. ed.). New York: Harcourt Brace Jovanovich.

——— and Rose Laub Coser. 1974. *Greedy Institutions*. New York: Free Press.

Coser, Rose Laub. 1984. "American Medicine's Ambiguous Progress," *Contemporary Sociology*, **13**(January): 9–13.

COSSA (Consortium of Social Science Associations). 1984. "Confidentiality of Research Notes Protected by Law," *COSSA Washington Update*, **3**(March 20):3.

———. 1990a. "Of Budget Battles, Games, and Questions. . . ," *COSSA Washington Update*, **9**(February 23).

———. 1990b. "Senate Debates Social Science, Race, and Death Penalty," *COSSA Washington Update*, **9**(June 1): 1–3.

Cotton, Paul. 1990a. "Is There Still Too

Much Extrapolation from Data on Middle-Aged White Men?" *Journal of the American Medical Association*, **263**(February 23):1049–1050.

———. 1990b. "Tobacco Foes Attack Ads That Target Women, Minorities, Teens, and the Poor," *Journal of the American Medical Association*, **264**(September 26):1505–1506.

Couch, Carl. 1990. "Mass Communication and State Structures," *Social Science Journal*, **27**(2):111–128.

Coughlin, Ellen K. 1983. "Alternative Religions or Dangerous Scams: Scholars Assess the Problems of Cults," *Chronicle of Higher Education*, **26**(March 9):5–7.

———. 1989. "Social Workers' Group Plans No Disciplinary Action against Researcher Who Submitted Bogus Articles," *Chronicle of Higher Education*, **35**(April 5):A40–A41.

Council on Environmental Quality. 1980. *The Global 2000 Report to the President: Entering the Twenty-First Century.* Washington, D.C.: U.S. Government Printing Office.

Council on Scientific Affairs. 1991. "Hispanic Health in the United States," *Journal of the American Medical Association*, **265**(January 9):248–252.

Courtney, Alice E., and Thomas W. Whipple. 1983. *Sex Stereotyping in Advertising.* Lexington, Mass.: Lexington.

Cowell, Alan. 1983. "Political Turmoil Unsettling Kenya," *New York TImes* (May 15), p. 7.

Cowgill, Donald O. 1986. *Aging around the World.* Belmont, Calif.: Wadsworth.

Cox, Harvey. 1965. *The Secular City.* New York: Macmillan.

———. 1984. *Religion in the Secular City.* New York: Simon and Schuster.

Cox, Oliver C. 1948. *Caste, Class, and Race: A Study in Social Dynamics.* Detroit: Wayne State University Press.

———. 1976. *Race Relations: Elements and Social Dynamics.* Detroit: Wayne State University Press.

Creekmore, C. R. 1985. "Cities Won't Drive You Crazy," *Psychology Today*, **19**(January):46–50, 52–53.

Cressey, Donald R. 1960. "Epidemiol-

ogy and Individual Contact: A Case from Criminology," *Pacific Sociological Review*, **3**(Fall):47–58.

Crime and Delinquency. 1980. "Capital Punishment in the United States," **26**(October):441–635.

Crittenden, Ann. 1981. "Demand Outpaces World Food Supply," *New York Times* (August 16), pp. 1, 22.

Crossette, Barbara. 1990. "Campaign to Oust English Is Revived in India," *New York Times* (May 27), p. 4.

Crouse, James, and Dale Trusheim. 1988. *The Case against the S.A.T.* Chicago: University of Chicago Press.

Crow, Ben, and Alan Thomas. 1983. *Third World Atlas.* Milton Keynes, Eng.: Open University Press.

Cruz, Robert. 1989. "Integration Slow on Comic Strip Row," *Chicago Reporter*, **18**(July–August):3–5, 11.

Cuba, Lee J. 1988. *A Short Guide to Writing about Social Science.* Glenview, Ill.: Scott, Foresman.

Cuff, E. C., and G. C. F. Payne. 1979. *Perspectives on Sociology.* Boston: G. Allen.

Cullen, Francis T., Jr., and John B. Cullen. 1977. "The Soviet Model of Soviet Deviance," *Pacific Sociological Review*, **20**(July):389–410.

——— and ———. 1978. *Toward a Paradigm of Labeling Theory*, ser. 58. Lincoln: University of Nebraska Studies.

———, William J. Maakestad, and Gray Cavender. 1987. *Corporate Crime under Attack.* Cincinnati: Anderson.

Cumming, Elaine, and William E. Henry. 1961. *Growing Old: The Process of Disengagement.* New York: Basic Books.

Cummings, Milton C., Jr., and David Wise. 1989. *Democracy under Pressure: An Introduction to the American Political System* (6th ed.). San Diego: Harcourt Brace Jovanovich.

Cuomo, Mario. 1983. *1982/1983—News Again, A Report to the National Governors' Association Task Force on the Homeless.* Albany, N.Y.: Office of the Governor.

Currie, Elliot. 1985. *Confronting Crime: An American Challenge.* New York: Pantheon.

———. 1986. *Confronting Crime: An*

American Challenge. New York: Random House.

Curtiss, Susan. 1977. *Genie: A Psycholinguistic Study of a Modern Day "Wild Child."* New York: Academic.

———. 1981. "Disassociations between Languages and Cognititon: Cases and Implications," *Journal of Autism and Developmental Disabilities*, **11**(March): 15–30.

———. 1982. "Developmental Dissociations of Languages and Cognition," in Loraine Obler and Lise Mann (eds.), *Exceptional Language and Linguistics.* New York: Academic, pp. 285–312.

———. 1985. "The Development of Human Cerebral Lateralization," in D. Frank Benson and Eran Zaidel (eds.), *The Dual Brain.* New York: Guilford, pp. 97–116.

Cusick, Philip A. 1973. *Inside High School: The Student's World.* New York: Holt.

Cutler, Blayne. 1989. "Up the Down Staircase," *American Demographics*, **11**(April):32–36, 41.

Dabrowski, Andrea, Laura López, and Gail Scriven. 1989. "A Chasm of Misery," *Time*, **134**(November 6):64–66.

Dahl, Robert A. 1961. *Who Governs?* New Haven, Conn.: Yale University Press.

Dahrendorf, Ralf. 1958. "Toward a Theory of Social Conflict," *Journal of Conflict Resolution*, **2**(June):170–183.

———. 1959. *Class and Class Conflict in Industrial Sociology.* Stanford, Calif.: Stanford University Press.

———. 1990. *Reflections on the Revolution in Europe.* New York: Random House.

D'Anastasio, Mark. 1987. "Soviet Health System, Despite Early Claims, Is Riddled by Failures," *Wall Street Journal* (August 18), pp. 1, 8.

Daniels, Arlene Kaplan. 1987. "Invisible Work," *Social Problems*, **34**(December):403–415.

———. 1988. *Invisible Careers.* Chicago: University of Chicago Press.

Daniels, Roger, and Harry H. L. Kitano. 1970. *American Racism: Exploration of the Nature of Prejudice.* Englewood Cliffs, N.J.: Prentice-Hall.

Davidson, Miriam. 1990. "The Mexican

Border War," *The Nation,* **251**(November 12):557–560.

Davies, Christie. 1989. "Goffman's Concept of the Total Institution: Criticisms and Revisions," *Human Studies,* **12**(June):77–95.

Davis, James. 1982. "Up and Down Opportunity's Ladder," *Public Opinion,* **5**(June–July):11–15, 48–51.

Davis, Keith, and John W. Newstrom. 1989. *Human Behavior at Work: Organizational Behavior* (8th ed.). New York: McGraw-Hill.

Davis, Kingsley. 1937. "The Sociology of Prostitution," *American Sociological Review,* **2**(October):744–755.

———. 1940. "Extreme Social Isolation of a Child," *American Journal of Sociology,* **45**(January):554–565.

———. 1947. "Final Note on a Case of Extreme Isolation," *American Journal of Sociology,* **52**(March):432–437.

———. 1949. *Human Society.* New York: Macmillan.

——— and Wilbert E. Moore. 1945. "Some Principles of Stratification," *American Sociological Review,* **10**(April):242–249.

Davis, L. J. 1990. "Chronicle of a Debacle Foretold: How Deregulation Begat the S&L Scandal," *Harper's,* **281**(September):50–66.

Davis, Lewis. 1987. "New York City Disables the Disabled," *New York Times* (May 2), p. 27.

Davis, Nancy J., and Robert V. Robinson. 1988. "Class Identification of Men and Women in the 1970s and 1980s," *American Sociological Review,* **53**(February):103–112.

Davis, Nanette J. 1975. *Sociological Constructions of Deviance: Perspectives and Issues in the Field.* Dubuque, Iowa: Brown.

Day, Lincoln H. 1978. "What Will a ZPG Society Be Like?" *Population Bulletin,* **33**(June).

de Beauvoir, Simone. 1953. *The Second Sex.* New York: Knopf.

Deegan, Mary Jo. 1988. "Transcending a Patriarchal Past: Teaching the History of Women in Sociology," *Teaching Sociology,* **16**(April):141–150.

——— and Michael Hill (eds.). 1987. *Women and Symbolic Interaction.* Winchester, Mass.: Allen and Unwin.

DeFleur, Melvin L., and Everette E. Dennis. 1981. *Understanding Mass Communication.* Boston: Houghton Mifflin.

DeGiovanni, Frank F. 1984. "An Examination of the Consequences of Revitalization in Six U.S. Cities," in J. John Palen and Bruce London (eds.), *Gentrification, Displacement and Neighborhood Revitalization.* Albany: State University of New York Press, pp. 67–89.

Degler, Carl N. 1971. *Neither Black nor White: Slavery and Race Relations in Brazil and the United States.* New York: Macmillan.

DeJong, Gordon F. 1980. "Nonmetropolitan Area Migrants: Preference and Satisfaction," *Intercom,* **8**(November–December):8–10.

Deloria, Vine, Jr., and Clifford M. Lytle. 1983. *American Indians, American Justice.* Austin: University of Texas Press.

Demac, Donna A. 1990. *Liberty Denied: The Current Rise of Censorship in America.* New Brunswick, N.J.: Rutgers University Press.

Denisoff, R. Serge. 1988. *Inside MTV.* Rutgers, N.J.: Transaction.

Dentzer, Susan. 1986. "Back to the Suburbs," *Newsweek,* **107**(April 21):60–62.

Denzin, Norman K. 1987. *The Recovering Alcoholic.* Newbury Park, Calif.: Sage.

———. 1990. "The Sociological Imagination Revisited," *Sociological Quarterly,* **31**(1):1–22.

DeParle, Jason. 1989. "Warning: Sports Stars May Be Hazardous to Your Health," *Washington Monthly,* **21**(September):34–49.

———. 1990. "In Rising Debate on Poverty, the Question: Who Is Poor?" *New York Times* (September 3), pp. 1, 10.

Department of Justice. 1987. *White Collar Crime.* Washington, D.C.: U.S. Government Printing Office.

———. 1988. *Report of the Nation on Crime and Justice* (2d ed.). Washington, D.C.: U.S. Government Printing Office.

———. 1989a. *BJS Data Report, 1988.* Washington, D.C.: U.S. Government Printing Office.

———. 1989b. *Capital Punishment, 1988.* Washington, D.C.: U.S. Government Printing Office.

———. 1990a. *Uniform Crime Reports for the United States, 1989.* Washington, D.C.: U.S. Government Printing Office.

———. 1990b. *Criminal Victimization in the United States, 1988.* Washington, D.C.: U.S. Government Printing Office.

Department of Labor. 1980. *Perspectives on Working Women: A Datebook.* Washington, D.C.: U.S. Government Printing Office.

———. 1983. *Handbook of Labor Statistics.* Washington, D.C.: U.S. Government Printing Office.

———. 1986. "Half of Mothers and Children under 3 Now in Labor Force." News release. Washington, D.C.: U.S. Government Printing Office.

———. 1988. *Labor Force Participation Unchanged among Mothers with Young Children.* Washington, D.C.: U.S. Government Printing Office.

DeSena, Judith N. 1987. "The Defended Neighborhood Revisited." Paper presented at the annual meeting of the Eastern Sociological Society, Boston.

de Sherbinin, Alex. 1990. "Iraq," *Population Today,* **18**(October):12.

de Soto, Hernando. 1989. *The Other Path: The Invisible Revolution in the Third World.* New York: Harper and Row.

DeStefano, Linda, and Diane Colasanto. 1990. "Unlike 1975, Today Most Americans Think Men Have It Better," *Gallup Poll Monthly,* **293**(February):25–36.

Deutsch, Morton, and Robert M. Krauss. 1965. *Theories in Social Psychology.* New York: Basic Books.

Devine, Don. 1972. *Political Culture of the United States: The Influence of Member Values on Regime Maintenance.* Boston: Little, Brown.

DeYoung, Karen. 1988. "Condition Critical: Britain's National Health Service Is Fighting for Its Life," *Washington Post National Weekly Edition,* **5**(March 28):6–7.

Diesenhouse, Susan. 1987. "Green-Carpet Treatment for Boston's New Immigrants," *New York Times* (November 8), p. E6.

DiMaggio, Paul. 1990. "Review of *Charismatic Capitalism: Direct Selling Organizations in America*," *Contemporary Sociology,* **19**(March):218–220.

Dingman, P. R. 1974. "The Case for the State Hospital." Mimeograph, Scottsdale, Ariz.: NTIS.

Dionne, E. J., Jr. 1984. "Politics Tangles the Supply Lines to Ethiopia," *New York Times* (November 11), p. E5.

——. 1989. "Struggle for Work and Family Fueling Women's Movement," *New York Times* (August 22), pp. 1, 18.

——. 1990. "The Death Penalty: Getting Mad and Getting Even," *Washington Post National Weekly Edition,* **7**(May 21):37.

Disability Rag. 1985. (Untitled), **6**:33–34.

——. 1990. "The Fight Is On!" (September–October):4–7.

Dittersdorf, Harriet. 1990. "Domestic Partnership: What Used to Define a Traditional Family," *NOW-NYC News,* **14**(July–August):6.

Dixon, Richard D., and Diane E. Levy. 1985. "Sex of Children: A Community Analysis of Preferences and Predetermination Attitudes," *Sociological Quarterly,* **26**(2):251–271.

Domhoff, G. William. 1967. *Who Rules America?* Englewood Cliffs, N.J.: Prentice-Hall.

——. 1970. *The Higher Circles: The Governing Class in America.* New York: Random House.

——. 1978. *Who Really Rules? New Haven and Community Power Reexamined.* New Brunswick, N.J.: Transaction.

——. 1983. *Who Rules America Now? A View for the '80s.* Englewood Cliffs, N.J.: Prentice-Hall.

Donahue, Thomas S. 1985. "U.S. English: Its Life and Works," *International Journal of the Sociology of Language,* **56**:99–112.

Donald, David. 1956. *Lincoln Reconsidered: Essays on the Civil War Era.* New York: Knopf.

Donaldson, Peter J., and Amy Ong Tsui. 1990. "The International Family Planning Movement," *Population Bulletin,* **45**(November).

Dore, Ronald P. 1976. *The Diploma Disease: Education, Qualification and Development.* Berkeley: University of California Press.

Doress, Irwin, and Jack Nusan Porter. 1977. *Kids in Cults: Why They Join, Why They Stay, Why They Leave.* Brookline, Mass.: Reconciliation Associates.

—— and ——. 1981. "Kids in Cults," in Thomas Robbins and Dick Anthony (eds.), *In Gods We Trust.* New Brunswick, N.J.: Transaction, pp. 297–302.

Dotson, Floyd. 1991. "Community," in Dushkin Publishing Group, *Encyclopedic Dictionary of Sociology* (4th ed.). Guilford, Conn.: Dushkin, p. 55.

Dowd, James J. 1980. *Stratification among the Aged.* Monterey, Calif.: Brooks/Cole.

Downs, Peter. 1987. "Your Money or Your Life," *The Progressive,* **51**(January):24–28.

Doyle, James A. 1985. *Sex and Gender: The Human Experience.* Dubuque, Iowa: Brown.

Driscoll, Anne. 1988. "For Salem, a Reminder of a Dark Past," *New York Times* (October 30), p. 51.

Duberman, Lucille. 1976. *Social Inequality: Class and Caste in America.* Philadelphia: Lippincott.

Du Bois, W. E. B. 1909. *The Negro American Family.* Atlanta University. Reprinted 1970, Cambridge, Mass.: M.I.T. Press.

Duff, Robert W., and Lawrence K. Hong. 1986. "Impression Management by Competitive Women Bodybuilders." Paper presented at the annual meeting of the Western Social Science Association, Reno, Nev.

—— and ——. 1988. "Management of Deviant Identity among Competitive Women Bodybuilders," in Pelos H. Kelly (ed.), *Deviant Behavior: Readings in the Sociology of Deviance* (3d ed.). New York: St. Martin's.

Duncan, Greg J. 1984. *Years of Poverty, Years of Plenty.* Ann Arbor: Institute for Social Research, University of Michigan.

——. 1987. "On the Slippery Slope," *American Demographics,* **9**(May):30–35.

—— and Ken R. Smith. 1989. "The Rising Affluence of the Elderly: How Far, How Fair, and How Frail," in W. Richard Scott and Judith Blake (eds.), *Annual Review of Sociology, 1989.* Palo Alto, Calif.: Annual Reviews, pp. 261–289.

Dundes, Alan. 1962. "Earth-Diver: Creation of the Mythopolic Male," *American Anthropologist,* **54**(October):1032–1051.

Dunn, Marvin, and Bruce Porter. 1981. "Miami, 1980: A Different Kind of Riot." Preliminary report to the Ford Foundation, New York.

Dunn, William. 1987. "More Blacks Trade Cities for Suburbs," *USA Today* (June 25), p. A1.

——. 1991. "Suburbs See Census 'Action,'" *USA Today* (January 28), p. 1A.

Durkheim, Émile. 1933. *Division of Labor in Society.* Translated by George Simpson. New York: Free Press (originally published in 1893).

——. 1947. *The Elementary Forms of the Religious Life.* Glencoe, Ill.: Free Press (originally published in 1912).

——. 1951. *Suicide.* Translated by John A. Spaulding and George Simpson. New York: Free Press (originally published in 1897).

——. 1964. *The Rules of Sociological Method.* Translated by Sarah A. Solovay and John H. Mueller. New York: Free Press (originally published in 1895).

Durning, Alan B. 1990. "Life on the Brink," *World Watch,* **3**(March–April):22–30.

Dushkin Publishing Group. 1991. *Encyclopedic Dictionary of Sociology* (4th ed.). Guilford, Conn.: Dushkin.

Dworkin, Rosalind J. 1982. "A Woman's Report: Numbers Are Not Enough," in Anthony Dworkin and Rosalind Dworkin (eds.), *The Minority Report.* New York: Holt, pp. 375–400.

Dychtwald, Ken, with Joe Flower. 1989. *Age Wave: The Challenges and Opportunities of an Aging America.* Los Angeles: Tarcher.

Dynes, Russell R. 1978. "Interorganizational Relations in Communities under Stress," in E. L. Quarantelli (ed.), *Disasters: Theory and Research.* Beverly Hills, Calif.: Sage, pp. 50–64.

Dzidzienyo, Anani. 1987. "Brazil," in Jay A. Sigler (ed.), *International Handbook on Race and Race Relations.* New York: Greenwood, pp. 23–42.

Easterbrook, Gregg. 1987. "The Revolution in Medicine," *Newsweek*, **109**(January 26):40–44, 49–54, 56–59, 61–64, 67–68, 70–74.

Ebaugh, Helen Rose Fuchs. 1988. *Becoming an Ex: The Process of Role Exit*. Chicago: University of Chicago Press.

Eberstadt, Nick. 1978. "World Population Figures Are Misleading," *New York Times* (March 26), p. 18.

Ebron, Betty Lin, and Michael S. Weissberg. 1987. "The Costs of Killer Disease Are Soaring," *New York Daily News* (March 8), bus. sec., pp. 1, 8.

Eckholm, Erik. 1990. "An Aging Nation Grapples with Caring for the Frail," *New York Times* (March 27), pp. A1, A18.

The Economist. 1986. "A Smoke-Free Zone for Europe?" **298**(March 29):40.

Edelhertz, Herbert. 1983. "White-Collar and Professional Crime," *American Behavioral Scientist*, **27**(September–October):109–128.

Eden, Dov, and Abraham B. Shani. 1982. "Pygmalion Goes to Boot Camp: Expectancy, Leadership, and Trainee Performance," *Journal of Applied Psychology*, **67**(April):194–199.

Eder, Donna. 1985. "The Cycle of Popularity: Interpersonal Relations among Female Adolescents," *Sociology of Education*, **58**(July):154–165.

Edwards, Harry. 1973. *Sociology of Sport*. Homewood, Ill.: Dorsey.

———. 1984. "The Black 'Dumb Jock,'" *College Board Review*, **131**(Spring):8–13.

Egeland, Janice A., et al. 1987. "Bipolar Affective Disorders Linked to DNA Markers on Chromosome 11," *Nature*, **325**(February 26):783–787.

Ehrenreich, Barbara. 1989. *Fear of Falling: The Inner Life of the Middle Class*. New York: Pantheon.

——— and Deidre English. 1973. *Witches, Midwives, and Nurses: A History of Women Healers*. Old Westbury, N.Y.: Feminist Press.

——— and Annette Fuentes. 1981. "Life on the Global Assembly," *Ms.*, **9**(January):53–59, 71.

——— and Karin Stallard. 1982. "The Nouveau Poor," *Ms.*, **11**(July–August):217–224.

Ehrlich, Paul R. 1968. *The Population Bomb*. New York: Ballantine.

——— and Anne H. Ehrlich. 1990. *The Population Explosion*. New York: Simon and Schuster.

Eitzen, D. Stanley. 1978. *In Conflict and Order: Understanding Society*. Boston: Allyn and Bacon.

———. 1984a. *Sport in Contemporary Society* (2d ed.). New York: St. Martin's.

———. 1984b. *Conflict Theory and the Sociology of American Sport*. Circulated by the Red Feather Institute.

——— and George H. Sage. 1978. *Sociology of American Sport*. Dubuque, Iowa: Brown.

———, with Maxine Baca Zinn. 1988. *In Conflict and Order: Understanding Society* (4th ed.). Boston: Allyn and Bacon.

Ekman, Paul, Wallace V. Friesen, and John Bear. 1984. "The International Language of Gestures," *Psychology Today*, **18**(May):64–69.

Elaide, Mircea. 1978. *A History of Religious Ideas: From the Stone Age to the Eleusinian Mysteries*. Chicago: University of Chicago Press.

Elam, Stanley M. 1990. "The 22nd Annual Gallup Poll of the Public Schools," *Phi Delta Kappan*, **72**(September):41–55.

——— and Alec M. Gallup. 1989. "The 21st Annual Gallup Poll of the Public's Attitudes toward the Public Schools," *Gallup Report*, **288**(August):31–42.

Elder, Joseph W. 1990. "Religious Fundamentalism in Iran, Sri Lanka, and India." Paper presented at the annual meeting of the American Sociological Association, Washington, D.C.

Elkin, Frederick, and Gerald Handel. 1989. *The Child and Society: The Process of Socialization* (5th ed.). New York: Random House.

Elliott, Marta, and Lauren J. Krivo. 1991. "Structural Determinants of Homelessness in the United States," *Social Problems*, **38**(February):113–131.

Ellis, William N., and Margaret McMahon Ellis. 1989. "Cultures in Transition," *The Futurist*, **23**(March–April):22–26.

Ellison, Ralph. 1952. *Invisible Man*. New York: Random House.

Elsasser, Glen. 1987. "Bias No Bar to Death Penalty," *Chicago Tribune* (April 23), pp. 1, 8.

Elshtain, Jean. 1981. "A Key to Unlock the Asylum?" *The Nation*, **232**(May 16):585, 602–604.

Emerson, Ralph Waldo. 1836. *Nature, Addresses, and Lectures*. Boston: Houghton Mifflin.

Emerson, Rupert. 1968. "Colonialism: Political Aspects," in David L. Sills (ed.), *International Encyclopedia of the Social Sciences*, vol. 3. New York: Macmillan, pp. 1–5.

Empey, La Mar T. 1978. *American Delinquency: Its Meaning and Construction*. Homewood, Ill.: Dorsey.

Engel, Margaret, and Kathy Sawyer. 1985. "AIDS Is Changing the Behavior of Governments and Institutions," *Washington Post National Weekly Edition*, **3**(November 11):31–32.

Engelberg, Stephen. 1984. ". . . but in Baltimore, There's a Void in the Hearts of Fans," *New York Times* (April 8), p. 22.

Engels, Friedrich. 1884. "The Origin of the Family, Private Property, and the State." Excerpted in Lewis Feuer (ed.), *Marx and Engels: Basic Writings on Politics and Philosophy*. Garden City, N.Y.: Anchor, 1959, pp. 392–394.

England, Paula, and George Farkas. 1986. *Households, Employment, and Gender*. New York: Aldine.

——— and Bahar Norris. 1985. "Comparable Worth: A New Doctrine of Sex Discrimination," *Social Science Quarterly*, **66**(September):629–643.

Enloe, Cynthia. 1990. *Bananas, Beaches, and Bases: Making Feminist Sense of International Politics*. Berkeley: University of California Press.

Epstein, Cynthia Fuchs. 1988. *Deceptive Distinctions: Sex, Gender, and the Social Order*. New Haven, Conn.: Yale University Press.

Epstein, William. 1989. Letter to the editor, *Professional Ethics Report*, newsletter of the American Association for the Advancement of Science, Committee on Scientific Freedom and Responsibility, Professional Society Ethics Group, **2**(Summer):3.

———. 1990. "Confirmational Response Bias among Social Work Journals," *Science Technology and Human Values*, **15**(Winter):9–38.

Erickson, J. David, and Tor Bjerkedal. 1982. "Fetal and Infant Mortality in

Norway and the United States," *Journal of the American Medical Association*, **247**(February 19):987–991.

Erikson, Kai. 1966. *Wayward Puritans: A Study in the Sociology of Deviance*. New York: Wiley.

———. 1986. "On Work and Alienation," *American Sociological Review*, **51**(February):1–8.

Eskenazi, Gerald. 1988. "Girls' Participation in Sports Improves," *New York Times* (June 8), pp. A29, A33.

Eskey, Kenneth. 1990. "Survey: Communities Beating Censorship," *Chicago Tribune* (September 9), p. 2.

Espenshade, Thomas J. 1990. "A Short History of U.S. Policy toward Illegal Immigration," *Population Today*, **18**(February):6–9.

Espinosa, Dula. 1987. "The Impact of Affirmative Action Policy on Ethnic and Gender Employment Inequality." Paper presented at the annual meeting of the American Sociological Association, Chicago.

Etzioni, Amitai. 1964. *Modern Organization*. Englewood Cliffs, N.J.: Prentice-Hall.

———. 1985. "Shady Corporate Practices," *New York Times* (November 15), p. A35.

———. 1990. "Going Soft on Corporate Crime," *Washington Post* (April 1), p. C3.

Evans, Daryl Paul. 1985. "Burocrogenesis: The Effects of Medicare's Prospective Reimbursement System (DRGs) on Elderly, Chronically Ill, and Disabled Persons," *Social Science Journal*, **22**(October):59–86.

Evans, Sara. 1980. *Personal Politics: The Roots of Women's Liberation in the Civil Rights Movement and the New Left*. New York: Vintage.

Fager, Marty, Mike Bradley, Lonnie Danchik, and Tom Wodetski. 1971. *Unbecoming Men*. Washington, N.J.: Times Change.

Fallows, Deborah. 1990. "In Japan, Education Isn't a Pastime—It's a Way of Life," *Washington Post National Weekly Edition*, **7**(September 17):25.

Falsey, Barbara, and Barbara Heyns. 1984. "The College Channel: Private and Public Schools Reconsidered," *Sociology of Education*, **57**(April): 111–122.

Fannin, Leon F. 1989. "Thuggee and Professional Criminality," *Michigan Sociological Review*, **3**(Fall):34–44.

Farberman, Harvey A. 1975. "A Criminogenic Market Structure: The Automobile Industry," *Sociological Quarterly*, **16**(Autumn):438–457.

Farnsworth, Clyde H. 1990. "U.S. Falls Short on Its Debt Plan for Third World," *New York Times* (January 9), pp. A1, D3.

Feagin, Joe R. 1983. *The Urban Real Estate Game: Playing Monopoly with Real Money*. Englewood Cliffs, N.J.: Prentice-Hall.

———. 1989. *Minority Group Issues in Higher Education: Learning from Qualitative Research*. Norman: Center for Research on Minority Education, University of Oklahoma.

Featherman, David L., and Robert M. Hauser. 1978. *Opportunity and Change*. New York: Aeodus.

Fein, Esther B. 1989. "Breaking Taboo, Soviets Report Big Jump in Crime," *New York Times* (February 15), p. A9.

Feinglass, Joe. 1987. "Next, the McDRG," *The Progressive*, **51**(January):28.

Fenigstein, Alan. 1984. "Self-Consciousness and the Over-Perception of Self as a Target," *Journal of Personality and Social Psychology*, **47**(4):860–870.

Ferber, Robert, Paul Sheatsley, Anthony Turner, and Joseph Waksberg. 1980. *What is a Survey?* Washington, D.C.: American Statistical Association.

Ferguson, Kathy E. 1983. "Bureaucracy and Public Life: The Feminization of the Polity," *Administration and Society*, **15**(November):295–322.

———. 1984. *The Feminist Case against Bureaucracy*. Philadelphia: Temple University Press.

Ferguson, Philip M., and Adrienne Asch. 1989. "Lessons from Life: Personal and Parental Perspectives on School, Childhood, and Disability," in Douglas Biklen, Dianne Ferguson, and Alison Ford (eds.), *Schooling and Disability: 88th Yearbook of the National Society for the Study of Education, Part II*. Chicago: National Society for the Study of Education.

Fergusson, D. M., L. J. Horwood, and F. T. Shannon. 1984. "A Proportional Hazards Model of Family Breakdown," *Journal of Marriage and the Family*, **46**(August):539–549.

Ferman, Louis A., Stuart Henry, and Michel Hoyman (eds.). 1987. *The Informal Economy*. Newbury Park, Calif.: Sage. Published as September 1987 issue of *The Annals*.

Ferraro, Kathleen J. 1989. "Policing Woman Battering," *Social Problems*, **36**(February):61–74.

——— and John M. Johnson. 1983. "How Women Experience Battering: The Process of Victimization," *Social Problems*, **30**(February):325–339.

Ferrell, Tom. 1979. "More Choose to Live outside Marriage," *New York Times* (July 1), p. E7.

Ferris, Gerald R., and John A. Wagner, III. 1985. "Quality Circles in the United States: A Conceptual Reevaluation," *The Journal of Applied Behavioral Science*, **21**(2):155–167.

Feuer, Lewis S. (ed.). 1959. *Karl Marx and Friederich Engels: Basic Writings on Politics and Philosophy*. Garden City, N.Y.: Doubleday.

Fiechter, Georges-André. 1975. *Brazil since 1964: Modernization under a Military Regime*. New York: Wiley.

Fierman, Jacklyn. 1990a. "Why Women Still Don't Hit the Top," *Fortune*, **122**(July 30):40, 42, 46, 50, 54, 58, 62.

———. 1990b. "Do Women Manage Differently?" *Fortune*, **122**(December 17):115–116, 118.

Fine, Gary Alan. 1984. "Negotiated Orders and Organizational Cultures," in Ralph Turner (ed.), *Annual Review of Sociology, 1984*. Palo Alto, Calif.: Annual Reviews, pp. 239–262.

———. 1987. *With the Boys: Little League Baseball and Preadolescent Culture*. Chicago: University of Chicago Press.

Fine, Michelle, and Adrienne Asch. 1981. "Disabled Women: Sexism without the Pedestal," *Journal of Sociology and Social Welfare*, **8**(July):233–248.

——— and ———. 1988a. *Women with Disabilities: Essays in Psychology, Culture, and Politics*. Philadelphia: Temple University Press.

——— and ———. 1988b. "Disability beyond Stigma: Social Interaction, Discrimination, and Activism," *Journal of Social Issues*, **44**(1):3–21.

Fineberg, Harvey. 1988. "The Social

Dimensions of AIDS," *Scientific American*, **259**(October):128–134.

Fingerhut, Lois A., and Joel C. Kleinman. 1990. "International and Interstate Comparisons of Homicide among Young Males," *Journal of the American Medical Association,* **263**(June 27):3292–3295.

Finkel, Steven E., and James B. Rule. 1987. "Relative Deprivation and Related Psychological Theories of Civil Violence: A Critical Review," *Research in Social Movements,* **9**:47–69.

Fiola, Jan. 1990. "The Informal Economy: Conceptualization, Measurement, Policies." Paper presented at the annual meeting of the Midwest Sociological Society, Chicago.

Firestone, Shulamith. 1970. *The Dialectic of Sex: The Case for Feminist Revolution.* New York: Bantam.

Fischer, Claude S. 1977. *Networks and Places: Social Relations in the Urban Setting.* New York: Free Press.

———. 1982. *To Dwell among Friends: Personal Networks in Town and City.* Chicago: University of Chicago Press.

———. 1988. "Gender and the Residential Telephone, 1890–1940: Technologies of Sociability," *Sociological Forum,* **3**(Spring):211–233.

Fish, Virginia Kemp. 1983. "Feminist Scholarship in Sociology: An Emerging Research Model," *Wisconsin Sociologist,* **20**(Spring–Summer):43–56.

Fisher, B. Aubrey, and Donald G. Ellis. 1990. *Small Group Decision Making: Communication and the Group Process* (3d ed.). New York: McGraw-Hill.

Fishman, Pamela M. 1978. "Interaction: The Work Women Do," *Social Problems,* **25**(April):397–406.

Fiske, Edward B. 1981. "Remarks by Sociologist Stir Debate over Schools," *New York Times* (April 12), p. 11.

———. 1985. "There's a Computer Gap and It's Growing Wider," *New York Times* (August 4), p. E8.

Fitzgerald, Jack D., and Steven Cox. 1984. *Unraveling Social Research* (2d ed.). Dubuque, Iowa: Brown.

Fitzgerald, Louise F., Lauren M. Weitzman, Yael Gold, and Mimi Ormerod. 1988. "Academic Harassment: Sex and Denial in Scholarly Garb," *Psychology of Women Quarterly,* **12**(September):329–340.

Flacks, Richard. 1971. *Youth and Social Change.* Chicago: Markham.

Fletcher, Robert S. 1943. *History of Oberlin College to the Civil War.* Oberlin, Ohio: Oberlin College Press.

Flexner, Eleanor. 1972. *Century of Struggle: The Women's Rights Movement in the United States.* New York: Atheneum.

Foner, Nancy. 1984. *Ages in Conflict.* New York: Columbia University Press.

———. 1985. "Old and Frail and Everywhere Unequal," *Hastings Center Report,* **15**(April):27–31.

Fong-Torres, Ben. 1986. "The China Syndrome," *Moviegoer,* **5**(July):6–7.

Fontaine, Pierre-Michel (ed.). 1986. *Race, Class, and Power in Brazil.* Los Angeles: UCLA Center for Afro-American Studies.

Ford, Clellan, and Frank Beach. 1951. *Patterns of Sexual Behavior.* New York: Harper and Row.

Ford Foundation. 1989. *Affordable Housing: The Years Ahead.* New York: Ford Foundation.

Forer, Lois G. 1984. *Money and Justice: Who Owns the Courts.* New York: Norton.

Form, William H. 1967. "Occupational and Social Integration of Automobile Workers in Four Countries," in William A. Faunce and W. Form (eds.), *Comparative Perspectives on Industrial Society.* Boston: Little, Brown, pp. 222–244.

Forst, Brian. 1983. "Capital Punishment and Deterrence: Conflicting Evidence," *Journal of Criminal Law and Criminology,* **74**(Autumn):927–943.

Fox, Robert. 1987. *Population Images* (2d ed.). New York: United Nations Fund for Population Activities.

France, David. 1988. "ACT-UP Fires Up," Village Voice, **33**(May 3):36.

Frank, Arthur W., III. 1991. "Ethnomethodology," in Dushkin Publishing Group, *The Encyclopedic Dictionary of Sociology* (4th ed.). Guilford, Conn.: Dushkin, pp. 107–108.

Franklin, John Hope, and Alfred A. Moss, Jr. 1988. *From Slavery to Freedom* (6th ed.). New York: Knopf.

Freeman, Howard E., R. R. Dynes, P. H. Rossi, and W. F. Whyte. 1983. *Applied Sociology.* San Francisco: Jossey-Bass.

——— and Peter H. Rossi. 1984. "Furthering the Applied Side of Sociology," *American Sociological Review,* **49**(August):571–580.

Freeman, James M. 1989. *Hearts of Sorrow: Vietnamese-American Lives.* Stanford, Calif.: Stanford University Press.

Freeman, Jo. 1973. "The Origins of the Women's Liberation Movement," *American Journal of Sociology,* **78**(January):792–811.

———. 1975. *The Politics of Women's Liberation.* New York: McKay.

Freeman, Linton C. 1958. "Marriage without Love: Mate Selection in Non-Western Societies," in Robert F. Winch (ed.), *Mate Selection.* New York: Harper and Row, pp. 20–30.

Freidson, Eliot. 1970. *Profession of Medicine.* New York: Dodd, Mead.

Freitag, Peter J. 1975. "The Cabinet and Big Business: A Study of Interlocks," *Social Problems,* **23**(December): 137–152.

Freudenheim, Milt. 1988. "Prepaid Programs for Health Care Encounter Snags," *New York Times* (January 31), pp. 1, 34.

———. 1990. "Employers Balk at High Cost of High-Tech Medical Care," *New York Times* (April 29), pp. 1, 16.

Frey, William H. 1990. *Metropolitan America: Beyond the Transition.* Washington, D.C.: Population Reference Bureau.

Freyre, Gilberto. 1946. *The Masters and the Slaves: A Study in the Development of Brazilian Civilization.* New York: Knopf.

———. 1959. *New World in the Tropics.* New York: Knopf.

———. 1963. *The Mansions and the Shanties: The Making of Modern Brazil.* New York: Knopf.

Friedan, Betty. 1963. *The Feminine Mystique.* New York: Norton.

Friedman, James T. 1984. *The Divorce Handbook, Updated.* New York: Random House.

Friedman, Norman. 1974. "Cookies and Contest: Notes on Ordinary Deviance and Its Neutralization," *Sociological Symposium,* **11**:1–9.

Friedrich, Otto. 1987. "An Rx for Catastrophe," *Time,* **129**(January 5):38–39.

Funk, Robert. 1987. "Disability Rights: From Caste to Class in the Context of

Civil Rights," in Alan Gartner and Tom Joe (eds.), *Images of the Disabled, Disabling Images*. New York: Praeger, pp. 7–30.

Galbraith, John Kenneth. 1978. *The New Industrial State* (3d ed.). Boston: Houghton Mifflin.

Gale Research Company. 1990. *1991 Encyclopedia of Associations*. Detroit: Gale Research Company.

Galinsky, Ellen. 1986. *Investing in Quality Child Care*. Basking Ridge, N.J.: AT&T.

———— and Diane Hughes. 1987. "*Fortune* Magazine Child Care Survey." Unpublished manuscript, Bank Street College, New York.

Gallup, George, Jr., and Frank Newport. 1990. "Many Americans Favor Restrictions on Smoking in Public Places," *Gallup Poll Monthly*, **298**(July):19–27.

Gallup (Opinion Index). 1975. "Vietnamese Refugees," **119**(May):6.

————. 1978. "Religion in America, 1977–1978," **145**(January).

————. 1980. "Presidential Elections," **180**(August):17–19.

————. 1987. "Religion in America, 1987," **259**(April).

Gamson, Josh. 1989. "Silence, Death, and the Invisible Enemy: AIDS Activism and Social Movement 'Newness,'" *Social Problems*, **36**(October): 351–367.

Gamson, William A. 1961a. "An Experimental Test of a Theory of Coalition Formation," *American Sociological Review*, **26**(June):373–382.

————. 1961b. "An Experimental Test of a Theory of Coalition Formation," *American Sociological Review*, **26**(August):565–573.

Gans, Herbert J. 1971. "The Uses of Poverty: The Poor Pay All," *Social Policy*, **2**(July–August):20–24.

————. 1979. *Deciding What's News*. New York: Pantheon.

————. 1991. *People, Plans, and Policies: Essays on Poverty, Racism, and Other National Urban Problems*. New York: Columbia University Press and Russell Sage Foundation.

Ganzeboom, Harry B. G., Ruud Luijkx, and Donald J. Treiman. 1989. "Intergenerational Class Mobility in Comparative Perspective," in Arne L. Kalleberg (ed.), *Research in Social Stratification and Mobility*. Greenwich, Conn.: JAI Press, pp. 3–84.

Garber, H., and F. R. Herber. 1977. "The Milwaukee Project: Indications of the Effectiveness of Early Intervention in Preventing Mental Retardation," in Peter Mittler (ed.), *Research to Practice in Mental Retardation*, vol. 1. Baltimore: University Park Press, pp. 119–127.

Gardner, Carol Brooks. 1989. "Analyzing Gender in Public Places: Rethinking Goffman's Vision of Everyday Life," *American Sociologist*, **20**(Spring): 42–56.

————. 1990. "Safe Conduct: Women, Crime, and Self in Public Places," *Social Problems*, **37**(August):311–328.

Garfinkel, Harold. 1949. "Research Note on Inter- and Intra-Racial Homicides," *Social Forces*, **27**(May): 369–381.

————. 1956. "Conditions of Successful Degradation Ceremonies," *American Journal of Sociology*, **61**(March): 420–424.

————. 1967. *Studies in Ethnomethodology*. Englewood Cliffs, N. J.: Prentice-Hall.

Garner, Joel H., and Christy A. Visher. 1988. "Policy Experiments Come of Age," *NIJ Reports* (September–October), pp. 2–4, 6–8.

Garr, Robin. 1990. "Movement Celebrates Signing of Disabilities Act," *Disability Rag* (September–October): 11–12.

Garson, Barbara. 1988. *The Electronic Sweatshop*. New York: Simon and Schuster.

Gartner, Alan, and Tom Joe (eds.). 1987. *Images of the Disabled, Disabling Images*. New York: Praeger.

———— and Dorothy Kerzner Lipsky. 1987. "Beyond Special Education: Toward a Quality System for All Students," *Harvard Educational Review*, **57**(November):367–395.

Gates, Henry Louis, Jr. 1989. "TV's Black World Turns—But Stays Unreal," *New York Times* (November 12), sec. 2, pp. 1, 40.

Gavzer, Bernard. 1988. "Why Do Some People Survive AIDS?" *Parade* (September 18), pp. 4–7.

————. 1990. "What We Can Learn from Those Who Survive AIDS," *Parade* (June 10), pp. 4–7.

Gaylord, Mark S., and John F. Galliher. 1987. *The Criminology of Edwin Sutherland*. Rutgers, N.J.: Transaction.

Gecas, Viktor. 1981. "Contexts of Socialization," in Morris Rosenberg and Ralph H. Turner (eds.), *Social Psychology: Sociological Perspectives*. New York: Basic Books, pp. 165–199.

————. 1982. "The Self-Concept," in Ralph H. Turner and James F. Short, Jr. (eds.), *Annual Review of Sociology, 1982*. Palo Alto, Calif.: Annual Reviews, pp. 1–33.

Gelles, Richard J., and Claire Pedrick Cornell. 1990. *Intimate Violence in Families* (2d ed.). Newbury Park, Calif.: Sage.

————, Murray A. Straus, and John W. Harrop. 1988. "Has Family Violence Decreased? A Response to J. Timothy Stocks," *Journal of Marriage and Family*, **50**(February):286–291.

Gelman, David. 1985. "Who's Taking Care of Our Parents?" *Newsweek*, **105**(May 6):60–64, 68.

George, Susan. 1988. *A Fate Worse Than Debt*. New York: Grove.

Gerbner, George, et al. 1984. "Summary: Religion and Television." Philadelphia: The Annenberg School of Communications.

————, Larry Gross, Michael Morgan, and Nancy Signorielli. 1981. "Special Report: Health and Medicine on Television," *New England Journal of Medicine*, **305**(October 8):901–904.

Gerson, Judith M. 1985. "Women Returning to School: The Consequences of Multiple Roles," *Sex Roles*, **13**(July):77–92.

Gerstel, Naomi. 1987. "Divorce and Stigma," *Social Problems*, **34**(April): 172–186.

Gerth, H. H., and C. Wright Mills. 1958. *From Max Weber: Essays in Sociology*. New York: Galaxy.

Gesensway, Deborah, and Mindy Roseman. 1987. *Beyond Words: Images from America's Concentration Camps*. Ithaca, N.Y.: Cornell University Press.

Gest, Ted. 1985. "Are White-Collar Crooks Getting Off Too Easy?" *U.S. News and World Report*, **99**(July 1): 43.

Giago, Tim, and Sharon Illoway. 1982. "Dying Too Young," *Civil Rights Quarterly Perspective*, **14**(Fall):29, 31, 33.

Gibbons, Don C. 1981. *Delinquent Behavior* (3d ed.). Englewood Cliffs, N.J.: Prentice-Hall.

Gibbons, Tom. 1985. "Justice Not Equal for Poor Here," *Chicago Sun-Times* (February 24), pp. 1, 18.

Gibbs, Jack P. 1989. "Conceptualization of Terrorism," *American Sociological Review*, **54**(June):329–340.

Gibson, Janice T., and Mika Haritos-Fatouros. 1986. "The Education of a Torturer," *Psychology Today*, **20**(November):50–58.

Giddings, Paula. 1984. *When and Where I Enter*. New York: Morrow.

Gilbert, Dennis, and Joseph A. Kahl. 1987. *The American Class Structure: A New Synthesis* (3d ed.). Chicago: Dorsey.

Gilinsky, Rhoda M. 1983. "Day Care Finds a Home on Campus," *New York Times* (January 9), sec. 12, p. 1.

Gilligan, Carol. 1982. *In a Different Voice*. Cambridge, Mass.: Harvard University Press.

Gilly, M. C. 1988. "Sex Roles in Advertising: A Comparison of Television Advertisements in Australia, Mexico, and the United States," *Journal of Marketing*, **52**(April):75–85.

Gimenez, Martha E. 1987. "Black Family: Vanishing or Unattainable," *Humanity and Society*, **11**(November):420–439.

———. 1990. "The Feminization of Poverty: Myth or Reality?" *Social Justice*, **17**(Fall):43–69.

Gintis, Herbert. 1980. "The American Occupational Structure: Eleven Years Later," *Contemporary Sociology*, **9**(January):12–16.

Gist, Noel P., and Sylvia Fleis Fava. 1974. *Urban Society* (6th ed.). New York: Harper and Row.

Gittelsohn, John. 1987. "An Asian Norma Rae," *U.S. News and World Report*, **103**(September 14):52.

Glaub, Gerald R. 1990. "Gap between State Funding and School Spending Widens," *Illinois School Board Journal*, **58**(July–August):24–26.

Glazer, Nathan, and Mark Lilla (eds.). 1987. *The Public Face of Architecture: Civic Culture and Public Spaces*. New York: Free Press.

Glen, M., and Sipra Bose Johnson. 1978. "Social Mobility among Untouchables," in Giri Raj Gupta (ed.), *Cohesion and Conflict in Modern India*. New Delhi: Vikas, pp. 60–100.

Gober, Patricia, and Michelle Behr. 1982. "Central Cities and Suburbs as Distinct Place Types: Myth or Fact," *Economic Geography*, **58**(October):371–385.

Goduka, Ivy. 1990. "Ethics and Politics of Field Research in South Africa," *Sociological Problems*, **37**(August):329–340.

Godwin, Deborah D., and John Scanzoni. 1989. "Couple Consensus during Marital Joint Decision-Making: A Context, Process, Outcome Model," *Journal of Marriage and the Family*, **31**(November):943–956.

Goffman, Erving. 1959. *The Presentation of Self in Everyday Life*. New York: Doubleday.

———. 1961. *Asylums: Essays on the Social Situation of Mental Patients and Other Inmates*. Garden City, N.Y.: Doubleday.

———. 1963a. *Stigma: Notes on Management of Spoiled Identity*. Englewood Cliffs, N.J.: Prentice-Hall.

———. 1963b. *Behavior in Public Places*. New York: Free Press.

———. 1967. *Interaction Ritual: Essays on Face-to-Face Behavior*. New York: Aldine.

———. 1971. *Relations in Public*. New York: Basic Books.

———. 1977. "The Arrangement between the Sexes," *Theory and Society*, 4:301–331.

Golden, M. Patricia (ed.). 1976. *The Research Experience*. Itasca, Ill.: Peacock.

Goldin, Claudia. 1990. *Understanding the Gender Gap: An Economic History of American Women*. New York: Oxford University Press.

Goldman, Ari L. 1986. "As Call Comes, More Women Answer," *New York Times* (October 19), p. E6.

Goldscheider, Calvin. 1986. *Jewish Continuity and Change: Emerging Patterns in America*. Bloomington: Indiana University Press.

Goldsmith, Jeff C. 1986. "The U.S. Health Care System in the Year 2000," *Journal of the American Medical Association*, **256**(December 26):3371–3376.

Goldstein, Michael S., Dennis T. Joffe, Carol Sutherland, and Josie Wilson. 1987. "Holistic Physicians: Implications for the Study of the Medical Profession," *Journal of Health and Social Behavior*, **28**(June):103–119.

Goleman, Daniel. 1983. "The Electronic Rorschach," *Psychology Today*, **17**(February):36–43.

———. 1986. "Major Personality Study Finds That Traits Are Mostly Inherited," *New York Times* (December 2), p. 417.

———. 1988a. "Researcher Is Criticized for Test of Journal Bias," *New York Times* (September 27), p. C9.

———. 1988b. "Panel Urges Researcher Be Censured over Ethics," *New York Times* (December 20), p. C11.

———. 1990a. "Anger over Racism Is Seen as a Cause of Blacks' High Blood Pressure," *New York Times* (April 24), p. C3.

———. 1990b. "As Bias Crime Seems to Rise, Scientists Study Roots of Racism," *New York Times* (May 29), p. C1.

Goodale, Jane C. 1971. *Tiwi Wives: A Study of Women of Melville Island, North Australia*. Seattle: University of Washington Press.

Goode, William J. 1959. "The Theoretical Importance of Love," *American Sociological Review*, **24**(February):38–47.

———. 1976. "Family Disorganization," in Robert Merton and Robert Nisbet (eds.), *Contemporary Social Problems* (4th ed.). New York: Harcourt Brace Jovanovich, pp. 511–554.

Goodman, Ellen. 1977. "Great (Male) Expectations," *Washington Post* (September 3), p. A11.

Goodman, Norman, and Gary T. Marx. 1978. *Society Today* (3d ed.). New York: CRM/Random House.

Gordon, C. Wayne. 1955. "The Role of the Teacher in the School Structure of the High School," *Journal of Educational Sociology*, **29**(September):21–29.

Gordon, Milton M. 1988. *The Scope of Sociology*. New York: Oxford University Press.

Gordus, Jeanne Prial, and Karen Yamakawa. 1988. "Incomparable Losses: Economic and Labor Market Outcomes for Unemployed Female versus Male Autoworkers," in Patricia Voydanoff and Linda C. Majka (eds.), *Families and Economic Distress*. Newbury Park, Calif.: Sage, pp. 38–54.

Goslin, David A. 1965. *The Schools in Contemporary Society*. Glenview, Ill.: Scott, Foresman.

Gottdiener, Mark. 1985. *The Social Production of Urban Space*. Austin: University of Texas Press.

———— and Joe R. Feagin. 1988. "The Paradigm Shift in Urban Sociology," *Urban Affairs Quarterly*, **24**(December):163–187.

Gough, E. Kathleen. 1974. "Nayar: Central Kerala," in David Schneider and E. Kathleen Gough (eds.), *Matrilineal Kinship*. Berkeley: University of California Press, pp. 298–384.

Gouldner, Alvin. 1950. *Studies in Leadership*. New York: Harper and Row.

————. 1960. "The Storm of Reciprocity," *American Sociological Review*, **25**(April):161–177.

————. 1962. "Anti-Minotaur: The Myth of a Value-Free Sociology," *Social Problems*, **9**(Winter):199–213.

————. 1970. *The Coming Crisis of Western Sociology*. New York: Basic Books.

Gove, Walter R. 1970. "Societal Reaction as an Explanation of Mental Illness: An Evaluation," *American Sociological Review*, **35**(October):873–884.

————. 1975. "The Labelling Theory of Mental Illness: A Reply to Scheff," *American Sociological Review*, **40**(April):242–248.

———— (ed.). 1980. *The Labelling of Deviance* (2d ed.). Beverly Hills, Calif.: Sage.

————. 1987. "Sociobiology Misses the Mark: An Essay on Why Biology but Not Sociobiology Is Very Relevant to Sociology," *American Sociologist*, **18**(Fall):258–277.

———— and Michael Hughes. 1979. "Possible Causes of the Apparent Sex Differences in Physical Health: An Empirical Investigation," *American Sociological Review*, **44**(February):126–146.

Graham, Saxon, and Leo G. Reeder. 1979. "Social Epidemiology of Chronic Diseases," in Howard E. Freeman, Sol Levine, and Leo G. Reeder (eds.), *Handbook in Medical*

Sociology (3d ed.). Englewood Cliffs, N.J.: Prentice-Hall.

Gramsci, Antonio. 1929. *Selections from the Prison Notebooks*. Edited by Quintin Hoare and Geoffrey Nowell Smith. London: Lawrence and Wishort.

Gray, Francine du Plessix. 1990. *Soviet Women: Walking the Tightrope*. New York: Doubleday.

Gray, Jane. 1991. "Tea Room Revisited: A Study of Male Homosexuals in a Public Setting." Paper presented at the annual meeting of the American Criminal Justice Society, Nashville, Tenn.

Greeley, Andrew M. 1972. *The Denominational Society*. Glenview, Ill.: Scott, Foresman.

————. 1989a. "Protestant and Catholic: Is the Analogical Imagination Extinct?" *American Sociological Review*, **54**(August):485–502.

————. 1989b. *Religious Change in America*. Cambridge, Mass.: Harvard University Press.

Greenberg, Joanne. 1970. *In This Sign*. New York: Holt.

Greene, Elizabeth. 1987a. "Jail!" *Chronicle of Higher Education*, **34**(November 4):A42–A44.

————. 1987b. "Asian-Americans Find U.S. Colleges Insensitive, Form Campus Organizations to Fight Bias," *Chronicle of Higher Education*, **34**(November 18):A1, A38–A40.

Greene, Marilyn. 1989. "Seniors Split on Law's Worth," *USA Today* (October 3), p. 2A.

Greenfield, Sheldon, Dolores M. Blanco, Robert M. Elashoff, and Patricia A. Ganz. 1987. "Patterns of Care Related to Age of Breast Cancer Patients," *Journal of the American Medical Association*, **257**(May 22/29):2766–2770.

Greenhouse, Linda. 1989. "Court Bars a Plan Set Up to Provide Jobs to Minorities," *New York Times* (January 24), pp. A1, A19.

————. 1990. "Use of Illegal Drugs as Part of Religion Can Be Prosecuted, High Court Says," *New York Times* (April 18), p. A10.

Greenhouse, Steven. 1990. "In Search of Capitalism with a Human Face," *New York Times* (May 20), p. E3.

Gregory, Paul R. 1988. *Soviet Bureaucratic Behavior: Khoziastvenniks, Apparatchiks, and Technocrats*. Urbana, Ill.: Soviet Interview Project.

Grissmer, David, and Sheila Kirby. 1987. *Teacher Attrition: The Uphill Climb to Staff the Nation's Schools*. Santa Monica, Calif.: Rand Corp.

Gross, Edward, and Gregory P. Stone. 1964. "Embarrassment and the Analysis of Role Requirements," *American Journal of Sociology*, **70**(July):1–15.

Gross, Jane. 1985. "Movies and the Press Are an Enduring Romance," *New York Times* (June 2), pp. H2, H19.

————. 1987. "An Ever-Widening Epidemic Tears at City's Life and Spirit," *New York Times* (March 16), p. 17.

————. 1991. "Surge of Rock Fans, Then Death, Grief, and Anger," *New York Times* (January 25), pp. A1, A16.

Grusky, David B., and Robert M. Hauser. 1984. "Comparative Social Mobility Revisited: Models of Convergence and Divergence in 16 Countries," *American Sociological Review*, **49**(February):19–38.

Grusky, Oscar, and Melvin Pollner (eds.). 1981. *The Sociology of Mental Illness: Basic Studies*. New York: Holt.

Guemple, D. Lee. 1969. "Human Resource Management: The Dilemma of the Aging Eskimo," *Sociological Symposium*, **2**(Spring):59–74.

Gupte, Pranay B. 1982. "U.N. Lowers Estimate of Population in 2000," *New York Times* (June 13), p. 4.

Guterbock, Thomas M. 1987. "The Effect of Snow on Urban Density Patterns in the United States." Paper presented at the annual meeting of the American Sociological Association, Chicago.

Gutiérrez, Gustavo. 1990. "Theology and the Social Sciences," in Paul E. Sigmund, *Liberation Theology at the Crossroads: Democracy or Revolution?* New York: Oxford University Press, pp. 214–225.

Haberman, Clyde. 1987. "U.S. Is Exporting Non-Smoking to Japan," *New York Times* (May 10), p. E6.

Hacker, Andrew. 1964. "Power to Do What?" in Irving Louis Horowitz (ed.), *The New Sociology*. New York: Oxford University Press, pp. 134–146.

Hacker, Helen Mayer. 1951. "Women as a Minority Group," *Social Forces*, **30**(October):60–69.

———. 1973. "Sex Roles in Black Society: Caste versus Caste." Paper presented at the annual meeting of the American Sociological Association, New York City, August 30.

———. 1974. "Women as a Minority Group," Twenty Years Later," in Florence Denmark (ed.), *Who Discriminates against Women*. Beverly Hills, Calif.: Sage, pp. 124–134.

Hackett, Larry. 1990a. "It's About Time," *New York Daily News* (June 3), life sec., pp. 1, 4.

———. 1990b. "Is Big Business Butting In?" *New York Daily News* (June 26), p. 45.

Hagan, John. 1987. "Review Essay: A Great Truth in the Study of Crime," *Criminology*, **25**(2):421–428.

——— and Alberto Palloni. 1986. "Toward a Structural Criminology: Method and Theory in Criminological Research," in Ralph Turner (ed.), *Annual Review of Sociology, 1986*. Palo Alto, Calif.: Annual Reviews, pp. 431–449.

——— and Patricia Parker. 1985. "White-Collar Crime and Punishment: The Class Structure and Legal Sanctioning of Securities Violations," *American Sociological Review*, **50**(June):302–316.

Hahn, Harlan. 1987. "Civil Rights for Disabled Americans: The Foundation of a Political Agenda," in Alan Gartner and Tom Joe (eds.), *Images of the Disabled, Disabling Images*. New York: Praeger, pp. 181–203.

Hahn, Robert A. 1985. "Culture-Bound Syndromes Unbound," *Social Science and Medicine*, **21**(2):165–171.

Haines, Valerie A. 1988. "Is Spencer's Theory an Evolutionary Theory?" *American Journal of Sociology*, **93**(March):1200–1223.

Hakuta, Kenji, and Eugene E. Garcia. 1989. "Bilingualism and Education," *American Psychologist*, **44**(February): 374–379.

Haley, Alex. 1976. *Roots*. New York: Doubleday.

Hall, Edward T. 1959. *The Silent Language*. New York: Doubleday.

Hall, Peter. 1977. *The World Cities*. London: Weidenfeld and Nicolson.

———. 1980. *Great Planning Disasters*. London: Weidenfeld and Nicolson.

Hall, Peter M. 1987. "Interactionism and the Study of Social Organization," *Social Quantity*, **28**(November 1):1–22.

Hall, Richard H. 1963. "The Concept of Bureaucracy: An Empirical Assessment," *American Journal of Sociology*, **69**(July):32–40.

Hall, Robert H. 1982. "The Truth about Brown Lung," *Business and Society Review*, **40**(Winter 1981–82):15–20.

Haller, Max, Wolfgang König, Peter Krause, and Karin Kurtz. 1990. "Patterns of Career Mobility and Structural Positions in Advanced Capitalist Societies: A Comparison of Men in Austria, France, and the United States," *American Sociological Review*, **50**(October):579–603.

Halliday, M. A. K. 1978. *Language as Social Semiotic*. Baltimore: University Park Press.

Hammond, Phillip E. (ed.). 1985. *The Sacred in a Secular Age*. Berkeley: University of California Press.

Hancock, LynNell. 1990. "20 Years of Choice," *Village Voice*, **35**(July 10):11.

Haney, Craig, Curtis Banks, and Philip Zimbardo. 1973. "Interpersonal Dynamics in a Simulated Prison," *International Journal of Criminology and Penology*, **1**(February):69–97.

Hanley, Robert. 1990. "The New Math of Rich and Poor," *New York Times* (June 10), p. E6.

Hanson, Dave. 1990. "Disabled Runner a True Winner," *New York Post* (November 6), p. 60.

Harap, Louis. 1982. "Marxism and Religion: Social Functions of Religious Belief," *Jewish Currents*, **36**(January):12–17, 32–35.

Harden, Blaine. 1984. "The U.S. in Ethiopia: Some Say We're Generous to a Fault," *Washington Post National Weekly Edition*, **2**(December 17):17.

———. 1987. "Charges of Torture and Repression Are Ruining Kenya's Reputation," *Washington Post National Weekly Edition*, **4**(March 30):16–17.

Hardgrave, Robert L., Jr. 1969. *The Nadars of Tamilnad. The Political Culture of a Community of Change*. Berkeley: University of California Press.

Harding, Sue (ed.). 1987. *Feminism and Methodology*. Bloomington: Indiana University Press.

Hare, A. Paul. 1976. *Handbook of Small Group Research* (2d ed.). New York: Free Press.

Harlow, Harry F. 1971. *Learning to Love*. New York: Ballantine.

Harper's. 1984. "Mistakes and the Death Penalty," **269**(July):18–19.

Harrington, Michael. 1963. *The Other America: Poverty in the United States*. Baltimore: Penguin.

———. 1980. "The New Class and the Left," in B. Bruce-Briggs (ed.), *The New Class*. New Brunswick, N.J.: Transaction, pp. 123–138.

Harris, Chauncy D., and Edward Ullman. 1945. "The Nature of Cities," *Annals of the American Academy of Political and Social Sciences*, **242**(November):7–17.

Harris, Diana K., and William E. Cole. 1980. *The Sociology of Aging*. Boston: Houghton Mifflin.

Harris, Lou. 1987. *Inside America*. New York: Vintage.

Harris, Marlys. 1988. "Where Have All the Babies Gone?" *Money*, **17**(December):164–176.

Harris, Marvin. 1958. *Minorities in the New World: Six Case Studies*. New York: Columbia University Press.

———. 1974. *Cows, Pigs, Wars and Witches: The Riddles of Culture*. New York: Random House.

———. 1980. *Culture, People, Nature* (3d ed.). New York: Harper and Row.

Harris, Richard. 1966. *The Sacred Trust*. New York: New American Library.

Harrison, Bennett, and Barry Bluestone. 1988. *The Great U-Turn*. New York: Basic Books.

Hartjen, Clayton A. 1978. *Crime and Criminalization* (2d ed.). New York: Praeger.

Hartmann, Heidi I. 1981. "The Family as the Locus of Gender, Class, and Political Struggle: The Example of Housework," *Signs*, **6**(Spring):366–394.

Hasbrook, Cynthia. 1986. "The Sport Participation–Social Class Relationship: Some Recent Youth Sport Participation Data," *Sociology of Sport Journal*, **3**(June):154–159.

Haub, Carl. 1988. "The World Population Crisis Was Forgotten, but Not Gone," *Washington Post National Weekly Edition,* **5**(September 5):23.

———, Mary Mederios Kent, and Machiko Yanagishita. 1990. *World Population Data Sheet, 1990.* Washington, D.C.: Population Reference Bureau.

Haupt, Arthur. 1979. "World's Refugees Finding No Refuge," *Intercom,* **7**(June–July):1, 15.

———. 1989. "U.S. to Face Population Decline?" *Population Today,* **17**(March):3.

———. 1990. "UN Projections Rise Slightly Higher than 1989," *Population Today,* **18**(November):4.

——— and Thomas T. Kane. 1985. *Population Handbook* (2d ed.). Washington, D.C.: Population Reference Bureau.

Hauser, Robert M., and David B. Grusky. 1988. "Cross-National Variation in Occupational Distributions, Relative Mobility Chances, and Intergenerational Shifts in Occupational Distributions," *American Sociological Review,* **53**(October):723–741.

Havemann, Judith. 1988. "Sexual Harassment: The Personnel Problem That Won't Go Away," *Washington Post National Weekly Edition,* **5**(July 11–17):30–31.

Havighurst, Robert J. 1961. "Successful Aging," *Gerontologist,* **1**(March):8–14.

Haviland, William A. 1985. *Cultural Anthropology* (5th ed.). New York: Holt.

Hawley, Amos H. 1950. *Human Ecology: A Theory of Community Structure.* New York: Ronald.

Hays, Constance L. 1988. "Study Says Blacks Face More Segregation Than Other Groups," *New York Times* (November 23), p. A16.

Hearn, Gordon. 1957. "Leadership and the Spatial Factor in Small Groups," *Journal of Abnormal and Social Psychology,* **54**(March):269–272.

Heaven P. C. and J. M. Niewoudt. 1981. "Authoritarian Attitudes in South Africa," *Journal of Social Psychology,* **115**(December):277–278.

Heberle, Rudolf. 1968. "Social Movements: Types and Functions," in David Sills (ed.), *International Encyclopedia of the Social Sciences,* vol. 14. New York: Macmillan, pp. 438–444.

Hechinger, Fred M. 1986. "Committee Fights Language Pollution," *New York Times* (July 22), p. C12.

———. 1987. "Bilingual Programs," *New York Times* (April 7), p. C10.

Heer, David M. 1975. *Society and Population* (2d ed.). Englewood Cliffs, N.J.: Prentice-Hall.

Heisel, Marsel A. 1985. *Aging in the Context of Population Policies in Developing Countries.* New York: United Nations.

Heller, Celia. 1969. *Socially Structured Social Inequality.* London: Macmillan.

Heller, Scott. 1987. "Research on Coerced Behavior Leads Berkeley Sociologist to Key Role as Expert Witness in Controversial Lawsuits," *Chronicle of Higher Education,* **33**(March 8):1, 13.

Hellmich, Nanci. 1990. "Day-Care Workers' Low Pay 'Horrifying,'" *USA Today* (February 28), p. A1.

Hendricks, Jon. 1982. "The Elderly in Society: Beyond Modernization," *Social Science History,* **6**(Summer): 321–345.

Hendry, Joy. 1981. *Marriage in Changing Japan.* New York: St. Martin's.

———. 1986. *Becoming Japanese: The World of the Pre-School Child.* Honolulu: University of Hawaii Press.

Hendry, Peter. 1988. "Food and Population: Beyond Five Billion," *Population Bulletin,* **43**(April).

Hengstler, Gary. 1987. "Attorneys for the Damned," *ABA Journal* (January 1), pp. 56–60.

Hennon, Charles B., and Ramona Marotz-Baden (eds.). 1987. "Rural Families: Stability and Change," special issue of *Family Relations,* **36**(October):355–460.

Henshaw, Stanley K., and Jennifer Van Vort. 1989. "Teenage Abortion, Birth and Pregnancy Statistics: An Update," *Family Planning Perspective,* **21**(March–April):85–88.

Henslin, James M. (ed.). 1972. *Down to Earth Sociology.* New York: Free Press.

Hentoff, Nat. 1987. "Playing Russian Roulette with AIDS," *Village Voice,* **32**(July 7):37.

Herbers, John. 1983. "Census Data Reveals 70's Legacy," *New York Times* (February 27), pp. 1, 14.

———. 1986. "Suburbs Absorb More Immigrants, Mostly the Affluent and Educated," *New York Times* (December 14), pp. 1, 22.

Herek, Gregory M., and Eric K. Glunt. 1988. "An Epidemic of Stigma," *American Psychologist,* **43**(November): 886–891.

Herman, Edward S., and Gerry O'Sullivan. 1990. *The "Terrorism" Industry: The Experts and Institutions That Shape Our View of Terror.* New York: Pantheon.

Hern, Warren. 1986. "Must Mr. Reagan Tolerate Abortion Clinic Violence," *New York Times* (June 14), p. 27.

Hernández, Beatriz Johnston. 1988. "The Sanctuary Movement: Churches Aid Undocumented Workers," *Village Voice,* **33**(December 6):17–18.

Hershey, Robert D., Jr. 1988. "Underground Economy Is Not Rising to the Bait," *New York Times* (January 24), p. E5.

Herskovits, Melville J. 1930. *The Anthropometry of the American Negro.* New York: Columbia University Press.

———. 1941. *The Myth of the Negro Past.* New York: Harper.

———. 1943. "The Negro in Bahia, Brazil: A Problem in Method," *American Sociological Review,* **8**(August): 394–402.

Hertz, Rosanna. 1986. *More Equal Than Others: Women and Men in Dual-Career Marriages.* Berkeley, Calif.: University of California Press.

Hess, Beth B., and Myra Marx Ferree (eds.). 1987. *Analyzing Gender: A Handbook of Social Science Research.* Newbury Park, Calif.: Sage.

——— and Elizabeth W. Markson. 1980. *Aging and Old Age: An Introduction to Social Gerontology.* New York: Macmillan.

Hess, John L. 1990a. "Confessions of a Greedy Geezer," *The Nation,* **250**(April 2):451–455.

———. 1990b. "The Catastrophic Health Care Fiasco," *The Nation,* **250**(May 21):698–702.

Hess, Robert, and Irene T. Miura. 1985. "Gender Differences in Enrollment in Computer Camps and Classes," *Sex Roles,* **13**(August):193–203.

Heussenstamm, F. K. 1971. "Bumper

Stickers and Cops," *Transaction*, **8**(February):32–33.

Heyward, William L., and James W. Curran. 1988. "The Epidemiology of AIDS in the U.S.," *Scientific American*, **259**(October):72–75, 78–81.

Hiatt, Fred. 1988. "Japanese Kids Are Licking Their Chopsticks," *Washington Post National Weekly Edition*, **5**(March 14–20):19.

———. 1990. "The Stateless Limbo of Koreans in Japan," *Washington Post National Weekly Edition*, **7**(May 28): 17–18.

Hill, Robert B. 1972. *The Strengths of Black Families*. New York: Emerson.

———. 1987. "The Future of Black Families," *Colloqui* (Spring), pp. 22–28.

Hills, Stuart L. (ed.). 1987. *Corporate Violence: Injury and Death for Profit*. Totowa, N.J.: Rowman and Littlefield.

Hilts, Philip J. 1990a. "Smoking's Cost to Society Is $52 Billion a Year, Federal Study Says," *New York Times* (February 21), p. A18.

———. 1990b. "U.S. Returns to 1820's in Care of Mentally Ill, Study Asserts," *New York Times* (September 12), p. A28.

———. 1990c. "Life Expectancy for Blacks in U.S. Shows Sharp Drop," *New York Times* (November 29), p. A1, B27.

———. 1990d. "New Study Challenges Estimates of Adopting a Child," *New York Times* (December 10), p. B10.

Himmelfarb, Milton, and David Singer (eds.). 1981. *American Jewish Year Book, 1982*. New York: American Jewish Committee.

Hinds, Michael deCourcy. 1989. "Better Traps Being Built for Delinquent Parents," *New York Times* (December 9), p. 11.

Hine, Darlene Clark. 1990. *Black Women in White: Racial Conflict and Cooperation in the Nursing Profession, 1890–1950*. Bloomington: Indiana University Press.

Hirschi, Travis. 1969. *Causes of Delinquency*. Berkeley: University of California Press.

——— and Michael Gottfredson. 1987. "Causes of White-Collar Crime," *Criminology*, **25**(November):949–974.

Hirschman, Charles, and Morris G. Wong. 1984. "Socioeconomic Gains of Asian Americans, Blacks, and Hispanics: 1960–1976," *American Journal of Sociology*, **90**(November): 584–607.

Hively, Robert (ed.). 1990. *The Lurking Evil: Racial and Ethnic Conflict on the College Campus*. Washington, D.C.: American Association of State Colleges and Universities.

Hochschild, Arlie Russell. 1973. "A Review of Sex Role Research," *American Journal of Sociology*, **78**(January):1011–1029.

———. 1990. "The Second Shift: Employed Women and Putting in Another Day of Work at Home," *Utne Reader*, **38**(March–April):66–73.

———, with Anne Machung. 1989. *The Second Shift: Working Parents and the Revolution at Home*. New York: Viking.

Hodge, Robert W., and Peter H. Rossi. 1964. "Occupational Prestige in the United States, 1925–1963," *American Journal of Sociology*, **70**(November): 286–302.

Hoebel, E. Adamson. 1949. *Man in the Primitive World: An Introduction to Anthropology*. New York: McGraw-Hill.

———. 1954. *The Law of Primitive Man*. Cambridge, Mass.: Harvard University Press.

Hoffman, Lois Wladis. 1977. "Changes in Family Roles, Socialization, and Sex Differences," *American Psychologist*, **32**(August):644–657.

———. 1985. "The Changing Genetics/Socialization Balance," *Journal of Social Issues*, **41**(Spring):127–148.

——— and F. Ivan Nye. 1975. *Working Mothers*. San Francisco: Jossey-Bass.

Hoffman, Saul, and John Holmes. 1976. "Husbands, Wives, and Divorce," in Greg J. Duncan and James N. Morgan (eds.), *Five Thousand American Families—Patterns of Economic Progress*. Ann Arbor, Mich.: Institute for Social Research, pp. 23–75.

Hoge, Dean R., and David A. Roozen. 1979. *Understanding Church Growth and Decline, 1950–1979*. New York: Pilgrim.

Holcomb, Betty. 1988. "Nurses Fight Back," *Ms.*, **16**(July):72–78.

Holden, Constance. 1987a. "Textbook Controversy Intensifies Nationwide," *Science*, **235**(January 2):19–21.

———. 1987b. "Genes and Behavior: A Twin Legacy," *Psychology Today*, **21**(September):18–19.

———. 1987c. "The Genetics of Personality," *Science*, **237**(August 7): 598–601.

Hollingshead, August B. 1975. *Elmtown's Youth and Elmtown Revisited*. New York: Wiley.

Hollos, Marida, and Philip E. Leis. 1985. "The Hand That Rocks the Cradle Rules the World," *Ethos*, **13**(Winter):340–397.

Holmes, Steven A. 1990a. "House, 265–145, Votes to Widen Day Care Programs in the Nation," *New York Times* (March 30), pp. A1, A14.

———. 1990b. "Day Care Bill Marks a Turn toward Help for the Poor," *New York Times* (April 8), p. E4.

———. 1990c. "House Passes Measure on Family Leave," *New York Times* (May 11), p. B6.

———. 1990d. "Bush Vetoes Bill on Family Leave," *New York Times* (June 30), p. 9.

———. 1990e. "Rights Bill for the Disabled Sent to Bush," *New York Times* (July 14), p. 6.

———. 1990f. "House Backs Bush Veto of Family Leave Bill," *New York Times* (July 26), p. A16.

———. 1990g. "Disabled People Say Home Care Is Needed to Use New Rights," *New York Times* (October 14), p. 22.

Holohan, Ann. 1977. "Diagnosis: The End of Transition," in A. Davis and G. Horobin (eds.), *Medical Encounters: The Experience of Illness and Treatment*. New York: St. Martin's, pp. 87–97.

Homans, George C. 1979. "Nature versus Nurture: A False Dichotomy," *Contemporary Sociology*, **8**(May): 345–348.

Hong, Lawrence K., and Robert W. Duff. 1977. "Becoming a Taxi-Dancer: The Significance of Neutralization in a Semi-Deviant Occupation," *Sociology of Work and Occupations*, **4**(August):327–342.

Hoover, Stewart M. 1988. *Mass Media Religion: The Social Sources of the Elec-*

tronic Church. Newbury Park, Calif.: Sage.

Hope, Marjorie, and James Young. 1988. "Who Cares for the Mentally Ill?" *The Nation,* **245**(January 2): 782–784.

Hoppe, Robert A., and Herman Bluestone. 1987. "Economic and Social Conditions Where Black Farmers Live." Paper presented at the annual meeting of the Eastern Sociological Society, Boston.

Hopper, Pauline, and Edward Zigler. 1988. "The Medical and Social Science Basis for a National Infant Care Leave Policy," *American Journal of Orthopsychiatry,* **58**(July):324–338.

Horn, Jack C., and Jeff Meer. 1987. "The Vintage Years," *Psychology Today,* **21**(May):76–77, 80–84, 88–90.

Hornblower, Margot. 1988. "Gray Power!" *Time,* **131**(January 4):36–37.

Horowitz, Helen Lefkowitz. 1987. *Campus Life.* Chicago: University of Chicago Press.

Horowitz, Irving Louis, and Lee Rainwater. 1970. "Journalistic Moralizers," *Transaction,* **7**(May):5–8.

Horwitt, Sanford D. 1989. *Let Them Call Me Rebel: Saul Alinsky–His Life and Legacy.* New York: Knopf.

Hosier, Richard H. 1987. "The Informal Sector in Kenya: Spatial Variation and Development Alternatives," *Journal of Developing Areas,* **21**(July): 383–402.

Hosokawa, William K. 1969. *Nisei: The Quiet Americans.* New York: Morrow.

Houseman, John. 1972. *Run Through.* New York: Simon and Schuster.

Hout, Michael. 1988. "More Universalism, Less Structural Mobility: The American Occupational Structure in the 1980s," *American Journal of Sociology,* **93**(May):1358–1400.

Hovannisian, Richard G. (ed.). 1986. *The Armenian Genocide in Perspective.* New Brunswick, N.J.: Transaction.

Howard, Michael C. 1989. *Contemporary Cultural Anthropology* (3d ed.). Glenview, Ill.: Scott, Foresman.

Howells, Lloyd T., and Selwyn W. Becker. 1962. "Seating Arrangement and Leadership Emergence," *Journal of Abnormal and Social Psychology,* **64**(February):148–150.

Howlett, Debbie. 1989. "High Court to Rule on Religious Peyote," *USA Today* (November 6), p. 3A.

———, and Judy Keen. 1991. "Role in Military Splits Minorities," *USA Today* (February 18), p. 2A.

Hoyt, Homer. 1939. *The Structure and Growth of Residential Neighborhoods in American Cities.* Washington, D.C.: Federal Housing Authority.

———. 1964. "Recent Distortions of the Classical Models of Urban Structure," *Land Economics,* **40**(May):199–212.

Huang, Gary. 1988. "Daily Addressing Ritual: A Cross-Cultural Study." Paper presented at the annual meeting of the American Sociological Association, Atlanta.

Huber, Bettina J. 1984a. *Career Possibilities for Sociology Graduates.* Washington, D.C.: American Sociological Association.

———. 1984b. "Career Possibilities for Sociology Graduates," *ASA Footnotes,* **12**(December):6–7.

———. 1985. *Employment Patterns in Sociology: Recent Trends and Future Prospects.* Washington, D.C.: American Sociological Association.

———. 1987. "Graduate Education and the Academic Job Market," *American Sociologist,* **18**(Spring):46–52.

Huesmann, L. Rowell, and Neil M. Malamuth (eds.). 1986. "Media Violence and Antisocial Behavior," special issue of the *Journal of Social Issues,* **42**(3).

Huff, Darrell. 1954. *How to Lie with Statistics.* New York: Norton.

Hughes, Everett. 1945. "Dilemmas and Contradictions of Status," *American Journal of Sociology,* **50**(March): 353–359.

Hughes, Langston. 1958. *The Langston Hughes Reader.* New York: Braziller.

Hughes, Susan L. 1988. "Living at Home: A National Evaluation," *Center on Aging,* **4**(Summer):1–2.

Humphreys, Laud. 1970a. "Tearoom Trade," *Transaction,* **7**(January): 10–25.

———. 1970b. *Tearoom Trade: Impersonal Sex in Public Places.* Chicago: Aldine.

———. 1975. *Tearoom Trade: Impersonal Sex in Public Places* (enlarged ed.). Chicago: Aldine.

Hunter, Herbert M., and Sameer Y. Abraham. 1987. *Race, Class, and the World Systems: The Sociology of Oliver C. Cox.* New York: Monthly Review.

Hunter, James D. 1983. *American Evangelicals.* New Brunswick, N.J.: Rutgers University Press.

———. 1985. "Conservative Protestantism," in Phillip E. Hammond (ed.), *The Sacred in a Secular Age.* Berkeley: University of California Press, pp. 150–166.

Hurh, Won Moo, and Kwang Chung Kim. 1986 "The 'Success' Image of Asian Americans: Its Validity, Practical and Theoretical Implications." Paper presented at the annual meeting of the American Sociological Association, New York City.

———. 1989. "The 'Success' Image of Asian Americans: Its Validity, and Its Practical and Theoretical Implications," *Ethnic and Racial Studies,* **12**(October):512–538.

Hurn, Christopher J. 1985. *The Limits and Possibilities of Schooling* (2d ed.). Boston: Allyn and Bacon.

Hyman, Herbert H. 1942. *The Psychology of Status.* Archives of Psychology, no. 269.

Imhoff, Gary (ed.). 1990. *Learning in Two Languages.* New Brunswick, N.J.: Transaction.

Inter-Parliamentary Union. 1990. *Sharp Drop in the Number of Women Holding Seats in Europe's Parliaments.* Geneva: Inter-Parliamentary Union.

Isaacson, Walter. 1989. "Should Gays Have Marriage Rights?" *Time,* **134**(November 20):101–102.

Israel, Glenn D., and Steven Stack. 1987. "Another Look at Celebrities and Suicide." Paper presented at the annual meeting of the American Sociological Association, Chicago.

Jackson, Elton F., Charles R. Tittle, and Mary Jean Burke. 1986. "Offense-Specific Models of the Differential Association Process," *Social Problems,* **33**(April):335–356.

Jackson, Kenneth T. 1986. *Crabgrass Frontier: The Suburbanization of the United States.* New York: Oxford University Press.

Jackson, Philip W. 1968. *Life in Classrooms.* New York: Holt.

Jacobs, Jerry A. 1990. *Revolving Doors: Sex Segregation in Women's Careers.* Palo Alto, Calif.: Stanford University Press.

Jacobs, Paul, and Saul Landau (eds.). 1966. *The New Radicals.* New York: Vintage.

Jacoby, Henry. 1973. *The Bureaucratization of the World.* Berkeley: University of California Press.

Jacquet, Constant H., Jr. 1990. *Yearbook of American and Canadian Churches, 1990.* Nashville: Abingdon.

Jaggar, Alison M. 1983. *Feminist Politics and Human Nature.* Totowa, N.J.: Rowman and Allanheld.

Jamal, Amir. 1983. "Power and the Third World Struggle for Equilibrium," in Jill Torrie (ed.), *Banking on Poverty: The Global Impact of the IMF and World Bank.* Toronto: Between the Lines, pp. 67–78.

Janis, Irving. 1967. *Victims of Groupthink.* Boston: Houghton Mifflin.

Jansen, Anicca C. 1987. "Creating Housing Options for an Aging Population," *Colloqui* (Spring), pp. 42–47.

———. 1991. "Rural Counties Lead Urban in Education Spending, but Is That Enough?" *Rural Development Perspectives,* **7**(October 1990–January 1991):8–14.

Jaschik, Scott. 1990. "U.S. Accuses UCLA of Bias against Asian Americans," *The Chronicle of Higher Education,* **37**(October):A1, A26.

Javna, John. 1986. *Cult TV.* New York: St. Martin's.

Jencks, Christopher, et al. 1979. *Who Gets Ahead? The Determinants of Economic Success in America.* New York: Basic Books.

Jenkins, John G. 1948. "The Nominating Technique as a Method of Evaluating Air Force Group Morale," *Journal of Aviation Medicine,* **19**:12–19.

Jennings, M. Kent, and Richard G. Niemi. 1981. *Generations and Politics.* Princeton, N.J.: Princeton University Press.

John, Kenneth E. 1985. "U.S. Crime vs. Other Nations," *Washington Post National Weekly Edition,* **2**(January 7):38.

Johnson, Benton. 1975. *Functionalism in Modern Sociology: Understanding Talcott Parsons.* Morristown, N.J.: General Learning.

Johnson, Charles S. 1939. "Race Relations and Social Change," in Edgar T. Thompson (ed.), *Race Relations and the Race Problem.* Durham, N.C.: Duke University Press, pp. 217–303.

Johnson, Dirk. 1987. "Fear of AIDS Stirs New Attacks on Homosexuals," *New York Times* (April 24), p. 12.

———. 1990. "Population Decline in Rural America: A Product of Advances in Technology," *New York Times* (September 11), p. A20.

Johnson, Hayes. 1988. "Teachers' Average Salary Hits $28,031," *USA Today* (May 5), p. 1D.

Johnson, Julie. 1989. "Wider Door at Top Colleges Sought by Asian-Americans," *New York Times* (September 9), pp. 1, 8.

Johnson, Mary. 1989. "Enabling Act," *The Nation,* **249**(October 23):446.

Johnson, Norris R. 1987. "Panic at 'The Who Concert Stampede': An Empirical Assessment," *Social Problems,* **34**(October):362–373.

Johnson, Richard A. 1985. *American Fads.* New York: Beech Tree.

Johnson, Sharen Shaw. 1990. "Lawmakers Introduce Bill Making English the Official Language," *USA Today* (October 11), p. 5A.

Johnson, William Weber. 1961. *Mexico.* New York: Time-Life.

Johnston, David. 1990. "Iran-Contra Role Brings Poindexter 6 Months in Prison," *New York Times* (June 12), pp. A1, A16.

Johnstone, Ronald L. 1988. *Religion in Society* (3d ed.). Englewood Cliffs, N.J.: Prentice-Hall.

Joint Center for Political Studies. 1989. *National Roster of Black Elected Officials, 1989.* Washington, D.C.: Joint Center for Political Studies.

Jolidon, Laurence. 1988. "'Man Bites Dog' Not Big News in Seoul," *USA Today* (September 19), p. 7E.

Jones, Elise F., et al. [8 authors]. 1985. "Teenage Pregnancy in Developed Countries: Determinants and Policy Implications," *Family Planning Perspectives,* **17**(March–April):53–63.

——— et al. 1986. *Teenage Pregnancy in Industrialized Countries.* New Haven, Conn., and London: Yale University Press.

Jones, James T., IV. 1988. "Harassment Is Too Often Part of the Job," *USA Today* (August 8), p. 5D.

Jones, Landon Y. 1980. *Great Expectations: America and the Baby Boom Generation.* New York: Ballantine.

Kagay, Michael R. 1988. "Survey Finds Antipathy toward Victims of AIDS," *New York Times* (October 14), p. A12.

Kahn, Herman, and John B. Phelps. 1979. "The Economic Present and Future," *The Futurist,* **13**(June):202–222.

———, and Julian L. Simon. 1984. *The Resourceful Earth.* Oxford, Eng.: Blackwell.

Kalette, Denise, et al. 1987. "The Family Changes Shape," *USA Today* (April 13), p. 4D.

Kalish, Susan. 1990. "Congress Battles over Family Planning Funds," *Population Today,* **18**(December):5.

Kallan, Carla. 1986. "New Leading Ladies," *Emmy Magazine,* **8**(November–December):16.

Kalleberg, Arne L. 1988. "Comparative Perspectives on Work Structures and Inequality," in W. Richard Scott and Judith Blake (eds.), *Review of Sociology, 1988.* Palo Alto, Calif.: Annual Reviews, pp. 203–225.

Kaminer, Wendy. 1984. *Women Volunteering: The Pleasure, Pain, and Politics of Unpaid Work from 1830 to the Present.* Garden City, N.Y.: Anchor/Doubleday.

Kanter, Rosabeth Moss. 1977. *Men and Women of the Corporation.* New York: Basic Books.

———. 1982. "Dilemmas of Managing Participation," *Organizational Dynamics,* **11**:5–27.

Kantrowitz, Barbara. 1988. "And Thousands More," *Newsweek,* **112**(December 12):58–59.

———, with Pat Wingert. 1989. "Parental Leave Cries to Be Born," *Newsweek,* **113**(June 5):65.

———. 1990. "Step by Step," *Newsweek,* **114**(Winter–Spring special issue):24–25, 27, 30, 34.

Kapferer, Jean-Noel. 1990. *Rumors: Uses, Interpretations, and Images.* New Brunswick, N.J.: Transaction.

Karlins, Marvin, Thomas Coffman, and Gary Walters. 1969. "On the Fading of Social Stereotypes: Studies in Three Generations of College Students," *Journal of Personality and Social Psychology,* **13**(September):1–16.

Karp, David A. 1986. "'You Can Take the Boy out of Dorchester, but You Can't Take Dorchester out of the Boy': Toward a Social Psychology of Mobility," *Symbolic Interaction,* **9**(Spring):19–36.

Kasarda, John D., and Morris Janowitz. 1974. "Community Attachment in Mass Society," *American Sociological Review,* **39**(June):328–339.

Kassebaum, Gene G., and Barbara O. Baumann. 1965. "Dimensions of the Sick Role in Chronic Illness," *Journal of Health and Human Behavior,* **6**(Spring):851–872.

Kasza, Gregory J. 1987. "Bureaucratic Politics in Radical Military Regimes," *American Political Science Review,* **81**(September):851–872.

Katovich, Michael A. 1987. Correspondence, June 1.

———— and Ron L. Diamond. 1986. "Selling Time: Situated Transactions in a Noninstitutional Environment," *Sociological Quarterly,* **27**(Summer):253–271.

Katz, Michael. 1971. *Class, Bureaucracy, and the Schools: The Illusion of Educational Change in America.* New York: Praeger.

Katz, Sandor. 1990. "HIV Testing—A Phony Cure," *The Nation,* **250**(May 28):738–742.

Katznelson, Ira, and Mark Kesselman. 1979. *The Politics of Power: A Critical Introduction to American Government* (2d ed.). New York: Harcourt Brace Jovanovich.

Kaufman, Gladis. 1985. "Power Relations in Middle-Class American Families," *Wisconsin Sociology,* **22**(Winter):13–23.

Kay, Paul, and Willett Kempton. 1984. "What Is the Sapir–Whorf Hypothesis?" *American Anthropologist,* **86**(March):65–79.

Keating, Noah, and Brenda Munro. 1988. "Farm Women/Farm Work," *Sex Roles,* **19**(August):155–168.

Kelley, Dean M. 1977. *Why Conservative Churches Are Growing* (rev. ed.). New York: Harper and Row.

————. 1979. "Is Religion a Dependent Variable," in Dean R. Hoge and David A. Roozen (eds.), *Understanding Church Growth and Decline: 1950–1978.* New York: Pilgrim, pp. 334–343.

Kelley, Harold H. 1952. "Two Functions of Reference Groups," in G. F. Swanson, T. M. Newcomb, and E. L. Hartley (eds.), *Readings in Social Psychology* (rev. ed.). New York: Holt, pp. 410–414.

Kelly, Dennis. 1990a. "School Spending Study Is Disputed," *USA Today* (January 16), p. 1D.

————. 1990b. "Tests, Salaries Are Top Concerns," *USA Today* (November 14), p. 5A.

Kenen, Peter B. 1990. "Organizing Debt Relief: The Need for a New Institution," *Journal of Economic Perspectives,* **4**(Winter):7–18.

Kenny, Timothy. 1984. "Pollsters Analyze Their Results," *USA Today* (November 8), p. 5A.

Kent, Mary M. 1991. Correspondence.

Kephart, William M., and William M. Zellner. 1991. *Extraordinary Groups: An Examination of Unconventional Life-Styles* (4th ed.). New York: St. Martin's.

Kerbo, Harold R. 1991. *Social Stratification and Inequality.* New York: McGraw-Hill.

———— and L. Richard Della Fave. 1979. "The Empirical Side of the Power Elite Debate: An Assessment and Critique of Recent Research," *Sociological Quarterly,* **20**(Winter):5–22.

Kerr, Peter. 1986. "The New Homelessness Has Its Roots in Economics," *New York Times* (March 16), p. E5.

Kessler, Ronald C., J. Blake Turner, and James S. House. 1989. "Unemployment, Reemployment, and Emotional Functioning in a Community Sample," *American Sociological Review,* **54**(August):648–657.

Keyfitz, Nathan. 1984. "The Baby Boom Meets the Computer Revolution," *American Demographics,* **6**(May):22–25, 45–46.

Kiesler, Sara. 1983. "Communicating by Computer: The Good News, the Bad News," *U.S. News and World Report,* **95**(July 25):68.

Killian, Lewis M. 1980. "Theory of Collective Behavior: The Mainstream Revisited," in Hubert M. Blalock, Jr. (ed.), *Sociological Theory and Research.* New York: Free Press, pp. 275–289.

Kimlicka, Thomas, Herbert Cross, and John Tarnai. 1983. "A Comparison of Androgynous, Feminine, Masculine, and Undifferentiated Women on Self-Esteem, Body Satisfaction, and Sexual Satisfaction," *Psychology of Women Quarterly,* **7**(Spring):291–294.

Kimmel, Michael S. (ed.). 1987. *Changing Men.* Newbury Park, Calif.: Sage.

King, Harry. 1972. *Box Man: A Professional Thief's Journal.* New York: Harper and Row.

King, Lourdes Miranda. 1974. "Puertorriquenas in the United States: The Impact of Double Discrimination," *Civil Rights Digest,* **6**(Spring):20–37.

King, Martin Luther, Jr. 1968. *Where Do We Go from Here: Chaos or Community?* Boston: Beacon.

King, Stanley H. 1972. "Social-Psychological Factors in Illness," in Howard E. Freeman, Sol Levine, and Leo G. Reeder (eds.), *Handbook of Medical Sociology* (2d ed.). Englewood Cliffs, N.J.: Prentice-Hall, pp. 129–147.

Kinkead, Glen. 1980. "Humana's Hard-Sell Hospitals," *Fortune,* **102**(November 17):68–81.

Kinsella, Kevin. 1988. *Aging in the Third World.* International Population Reports, ser. P-95, no. 79. Washington, D.C.: U.S. Government Printing Office.

Kitagawa, Evelyn. 1972. "Socioeconomic Differences in the United States and Some Implications for Population Policy," in Charles F. Westoff and Robert Parke, Jr. (eds.), *Demographic and Social Aspects of Population Growth.* Washington, D.C.: U.S. Government Printing Office, pp. 87–110.

Kitcher, Philip. 1985. *Vaulting Ambition: Sociobiology and the Quest for Human Nature.* Cambridge, Mass.: M.I.T. Press.

Klapp, Orvin E. 1972. *Currents of Unrest: An Introduction to Collective Behavior.* New York: Holt.

Klausner, Samuel Z. 1988. "Anti-Semitism in the Executive Suite: Yesterday, Today, and Tomorrow," *Moment,* **13**(September):32–39, 55.

Klein, Stephen P., Susan Turner, and Joan Petersilia. 1988. *Racial Equity in Sentencing.* Santa Monica, Calif.: Rand.

Kleinman, Dena. 1983. "Less than 40% of Jews in Survey Observe Sabbath," *New York Times* (February 6), pp. 1, 19.

Kluckhohn, Clyde. 1949. *Mirror for Man*. New York: McGraw-Hill.

Knaus, William A. 1981. *Inside Russian Medicine*. Boston: Beacon.

Knight, Franklin W. 1974. *The African Dimension in Latin American Societies*. New York: Macmillan.

Knight, Jerry. 1990. "Last Rites for S&Ls Past Saving," *Washington Post National Weekly Edition*, **7**(June 18):20.

—— and Susan Schmidt. 1990. "The Bad News Gets Worse," *Washington Post National Weekly Edition*, **7**(October 1):21.

Koenig, Frederick W. 1985. *Rumor in the Marketplace*. Dover, Mass.: Auburn House.

Kohlberg, Lawrence. 1963. "Development of Children's Orientation toward a Moral Order (Part 1): Sequence in the Development of Moral Thought," *Vita Humana*, **6**:11–36.

——. 1981. *The Philosophy of Moral Development: Moral Stages and the Idea of Justice*, vol. 1: *Essays on Moral Development*. San Francisco: Harper and Row.

Kohn, Alfie. 1988. "Girltalk, Guytalk," *Psychology Today*, **22**(February):65–66.

Kohn, Melvin L. 1970. "The Effects of Social Class on Parental Values and Practices," in David Reiss and H. A. Hoffman (eds.), *The American Family: Dying or Developing*. New York: Plenum, pp. 45–68.

——. 1978. "The Benefits of Bureaucracy," *Human Nature* (August), pp. 60–66.

—— (ed.). 1989. *Cross-National Research in Sociology*. Newbury Park, Calif.: Sage.

Kolata, Gina. 1988. "Child Splitting," *Psychology Today*, **22**(November):34, 36.

Konner, Melvin. 1987. *Becoming a Doctor: A Journey of Initiation in Medical School*. New York: Sifton/Viking.

Kornhauser, William. 1961. "'Power Elite' or 'Veto Groups'?" in Seymour Martin Lipset and Leo Lowenthal (eds.), *Culture and Social Character*. New York: Free Press, pp. 252–267.

Kort, Michelle. 1987. "Domestic Terrorism: On the Front Line at an Abortion Clinic," *Ms.*, **15**(May):48–53.

Kotulak, Ronald. 1986. "Youngsters Lose Way in Maze of Family Interstability," *Chicago Tribune* (December 14), sec. 6, pp. 1, 4–5.

Kralewski, John E., Laura Pitt, and Deborah Shatin. 1985. "Structural Characteristics of Medical Group Practices," *Administrative Science Quarterly*, **30**(March):34–45.

Kranichfeld, Marion L. 1987. "Rethinking Family Power," *Journal of Family Issues*, **8**(March):42–56.

Kreps, G. A. 1984. "Sociological Inquiry and Disaster Research," in Ralph Turner (ed.), *Annual Review of Sociology, 1984*. Palo Alto, Calif.: Annual Reviews, pp. 309–330.

Kristof, Nicholas D. 1990. "More in China Willingly Rear Just One Child," *New York Times* (May 9), pp. A1, A8.

Kroeber, Alfred L. 1923. *Anthropology: Culture Patterns and Processes*. New York: Harcourt Brace and World.

Krossel, Martin. 1988. "'Handicapped Heroes' and the Knee-Jerk Press," *Columbia Journalism Review*, **27**(May–June):46–47.

Kudryautsev, Vladimir. 1990. "Reform of the Political System and Social Science," *Social Sciences*, **21**(1):8–21.

Kwong, Peter, and JoAnn Lum. 1988. "Chinese-American Politics: A Silent Minority Tests Its Clout," *The Nation*, **246**(January 16):49–50, 52.

Labaree, David F. 1986. "Curriculum, Credentials, and the Middle Class: A Case Study of a Nineteenth Century High School," *Sociology of Education*, **59**(January):42–57.

Lacayo, Richard. 1986. "Second Thoughts about No-Fault," *Time*, **127**(January 13):55.

Ladner, Joyce. 1986. "Black Women Face the 21st Century: Major Issues and Problems," *Black Scholar*, **17**(September–October):12–19.

La Gory, Mark, Russell Ward, and Thomas Juravich. 1980. "The Age Segregation Process: Explanation for American Cities," *Urban Affairs Quarterly*, **16**(September):79–80.

——, ——, and ——. 1981. "Patterns of Age Segregation," *Sociological Focus*, **14**(January):1–13.

——, ——, and Susan Sherman. 1985. "The Ecology of Aging: Neighborhood Satisfaction in an Older Population," *Sociological Quarterly*, **26**(3):405–418.

Lakoff, Robin. 1976. *Language and Women's Place*. New York: Octagon.

Lambert, Bruce. 1989. "In Shift, Gay Men's Health Group Endorses Testing for HIV Virus," *New York Times* (August 16), pp. A1, B6.

Lamm, Bob. 1977. "Men's Movement Hype," in Jon Snodgrass (ed.), *For Men against Sexism: A Book of Readings*. Albion, Calif.: Times Change, pp. 153–157.

——. 1983. "How Rabbi Faces the Dangers of Deprogramming," *Los Angeles Herald Examiner* (May 7), pp. A2, B8.

Landsberger, Henry A., John R. Carlson, and Richard T. Campbell. 1988. "Education Policy in Comparative Perspective: Similarities in the Underlying Issues in Debate among Educational Elites in the U.S., Britain, and the Federal Republic of Germany." Paper presented at the annual meeting of the American Sociological Association, Atlanta.

Landtman, Gunnar. 1968. *The Origin of Inequality of the Social Class*. New York: Greenwood (original edition 1938, Chicago: University of Chicago Press).

Landy, David. 1985. "Pibloktoq (Hysteria) and Inuit Nutrition: Possible Implication of Hypervitaminosis A," *Social Science and Medicine*, **21**(2):173–185.

Lane, Robert E. 1959. *Political Life*. New York: Free Press.

Langan, Patrick A., and Christopher A. Innes. 1985. *The Risk of Violent Crime*. Washington, D.C.: U.S. Government Printing Office.

Langway, Lynn. 1981. "A New Kind of Life with Father," *Newsweek*, **98**(November 30):93–97.

Lapping, Mark B., Thomas L. Daniels, and John W. Keller. 1989. *Rural Planning and Development*. New York: Guilford.

Larrabee, John. 1990. "Age of Aquarius Lives," *USA Today* (December 7), p. 8A.

Larson, Calvin J., and Stan R. Nikkel. 1979. *Urban Problems: Perspectives on Corporations, Governments, and Cities.* Boston: Allyn and Bacon.

Lasswell, Harold D. 1936. *Politics: Who Gets What, When, How.* New York: McGraw-Hill.

Lauer, Robert H. 1982. *Perspectives on Social Change* (3d ed.). Boston: Allyn and Bacon.

Lavender, Abraham D. 1986. *Ethnic Women and Feminist Values: Toward a "New" Value System.* Lanham, Md.: University Press of America.

Lawson, Carol. 1989. "How France Is Providing Child Care to a Nation," *New York Times* (November 9), pp. C1, C14.

———. 1991. "Getting Congress to Support Adoption," *New York Times* (March 28), pp. C1, C5.

Lazare, Daniel. 1990. "Planes, Trains, and Automobiles," *Village Voice,* **35**(October 23):39–41.

Lazarev, Boris. 1989. "Separation of Powers and the Soviet States' Experience," *Social Sciences,* **20**(4):46–59.

Lazerwitz, Bernard, and Michael Harrison. 1979. "American Jewish Denominations: A Social and Religious Profile," *American Sociological Review,* **44**(August):656–666.

Leacock, Eleanor Burke. 1969. *Teaching and Learning in City Schools.* New York: Basic Books.

Leathers, Charles G. 1984. "Liberation Theology, the New Religious Political Right and Veblen's Ambivalent View of Christianity," *Journal of Economic Issues,* **18**(December):1155–1175.

Leavell, Hugh R., and E. Gurney Clark. 1965. *Preventive Medicine for the Doctor in His Community: An Epidemiologic Approach* (3d ed.). New York: McGraw-Hill.

Lee, Alfred McClung. 1978. *Sociology for Whom?* New York: Oxford University Press.

———. 1983. *Terrorism in North Ireland.* Bayside, N.Y.: General Hall.

Lee, Barrett A. 1987. "Homelessness and Community." Paper presented at the annual meeting of the American Sociological Association, Chicago.

Leerhsen, Charles. 1990. "Unite and Conquer," *Newsweek,* **115**(February 5):50–55.

Leff, Walli, and Marilyn G. Haft. 1984. *Time without Work.* Boston: South End.

Lefkowitz, Monroe, Robert Blake, and Jane Mouton. 1955. "Status Factors in Pedestrian Violation of Traffic Signals," *Journal of Abnormal and Social Psychology,* **51**(November):704–706.

Lehman, Edward C., Jr. 1985. *Women Clergy: Breaking through Gender Barriers.* New Brunswick, N.J.: Transaction.

Leidner, Robin. 1988. "Home Work: A Study in the Interaction of Work and Family Organization," in Ida Harper Simpson and Richard L. Simpson (eds.), *Research in the Sociology of Work,* vol. 4. Greenwich, Conn.: JAI Press, pp. 69–94.

Lemkow, Louis. 1986. "Socio-Economic Status Differences in Health," *Social Science and Medicine,* **22**(11):1257–1262.

———. 1987. "The Employed Unemployed: The Subterranean Economy in Spain," *Social Science and Medicine,* **25**(2):111–113.

Lenski, Gerhard. 1966. *Power and Privilege: A Theory of Social Stratification.* New York: McGraw-Hill.

———, Jean Lenski, and Patrick Nolan. 1991. *Human Societies: An Introduction to Macrosociology.* New York: McGraw-Hill.

Leo, John. 1987. "Exploring the Traits of Twins," *Time,* **129**(January 12):63.

Leslie, Connie. 1988. "Giving Parents a Choice," *Newsweek,* **111**(September 19):77–80.

Leslie, Gerald R., and Sheila K. Korman. 1989. *The Family in Social Context* (7th ed.). New York: Oxford University Press.

Letkemann, Peter. 1973. *Crime as Work.* Englewood Cliffs, N.J.: Prentice-Hall.

Levin, Jack, and William C. Levin. 1980. *Ageism.* Belmont, Calif.: Wadsworth.

Levin, William C. 1988. "Age Stereotyping: College Student Evaluations," *Research on Aging,* **10**(March):134–148.

Levine, Robert. 1987. "Waiting Is a Power Game," *Psychology Today,* **21**(April):24–26, 28, 30–33.

Levinson, Arlene. 1984. "Laws for Live-In Lovers," *Ms.,* **12**(June):101.

Levinson, Daniel. 1978. *The Seasons of a Man's Life.* New York: Knopf.

Levy, Frank. 1987. *Dollars and Dreams: The Changing American Income Distribution.* New York: Russell Sage.

Levy, Judith A. 1988. "Intersections of Gender and Aging," *Sociological Quarterly,* **29**(4):479–486.

Lewandowsky, Stephan, and Ian Spence. 1990. "The Perception of Statistical Graphs," *Sociological Methods and Research,* **18**(February):200–242.

Lewin, Miriam, and Lilli M. Tragos. 1987. "Has the Feminist Movement Influenced Adolescent Sex Role Attitudes? A Reassessment after a Quarter Century," *Sex Roles,* **16**(February):125–137.

Lewin, Tamar. 1987. "Hospitals Pitch Harder for Patients," *New York Times* (May 10), pp. F1, F28.

———. 1989. "Pay Equity for Women's Jobs Finds Success Outside Courts," *New York Times* (October 7), pp. 1, 8.

———. 1990a. "Strategies to Let Elderly Keep Some Control," *New York Times* (March 28), pp. A1, A22.

———. 1990b. "Model Home-Care Program: Savings and Human Dignity," *New York Times* (March 28), p. A22.

———. 1990c. "Too Much Retirement Time? A Move Is Afoot to Change It," *New York Times* (April 22), pp. 1, 26.

———. 1990d. "Abortions Harder to Get in Rural Areas of Nation," *New York Times* (June 28), p. A18.

———. 1990e. "Battle for Family Leave Will Be Fought in States," *New York Times* (July 27), p. A8.

———. 1991. "Nude Pictures Are Ruled Sexual Harassment," *New York Times* (January 23), p. A14.

Lewis, Paul. 1987. "World Hunger Found Still Growing," *New York Times* (April 28), p. 3.

Lewis, Robert. 1973. "A Longitudinal Test of a Developmental Framework for Premarital Dyadic Formation," *Journal of Marriage and the Family,* **35**(February):16–25.

Lieberson, Stanley, and Arnold J. Silverman. 1965. "The Precipitants and Underlying Conditions of Race Riots," *American Sociological Review,* **30**(December):887–898.

Liebman, Charles S. 1973. *The Ambiva-*

lent American Jew. Philadelphia: Jewish Publication Society.

Light, Donald W. 1986. "Corporate Medicine for Profit," *Scientific American,* **255**(December):38–45.

Lin, Nan, and Wen Xie. 1988. "Occupational Prestige in Urban China," *American Journal of Sociology,* **93**(January):793–832.

Linden, Eugene. 1989. "Playing with Fire," *Time,* **136**(September 18):76–80, 82, 85.

Lindsey, Karen. 1977. "Sexual Harassment on the Job," *Ms.,* **6**(November):47–49, 50–51, 74–75, 78.

Lindsey, Robert. 1987a. "Adoption Market: Big Demand, Tight Supply," *New York Times* (April 5), pp. 1, 30.

———. 1987b. "Isolated, Strongly Led Sects Growing in U.S.," *New York Times* (June 22), pp. 1, 22.

Link, Bruce G. 1987. "Understanding Labeling Effects in the Area of Mental Disorders: An Assessment of the Effects of Expectations of Rejection," *American Sociological Review,* **52**(February):96–112.

——— et al. 1989. "A Modified Labeling Theory Approach to Mental Disorders," *American Sociological Review,* **54**(June):400–423.

Linton, Ralph. 1936. *The Study of Man: An Introduction.* New York: Appleton-Century.

Lissakers, Karin. 1983. "Dateline Wall Street: Faustian Finance," *Foreign Policy* (Summer), pp. 160–175.

Little, Kenneth. 1988. "The Role of Voluntary Associations in West African Urbanization," in Johnnetta B. Cole (ed.), *Anthropology for the Nineties: Introductory Readings.* New York: Free Press, pp. 211–230.

Locin, Mitchell. 1990. "Panel Advocates $70 Billion Health Care Plan," *Chicago Tribune* (September 25), p. 4.

Lofflin, John. 1988. "A Burst of Rural Enterprise," *New York Times* (January 3), sec. 3, pp. 1, 23.

Lofland, John. 1977. *Doomsday Cult* (enlarged ed.). New York: Irvington.

———. 1981. "Collective Behavior: The Elementary Forms," in Morris Rosenberg and Ralph Turner (eds.), *Social Psychology: Sociological Perspectives.* New York: Basic Books, pp. 441–446.

———. 1985. *Protest: Studies of Collective Behavior and Social Movements.* Rutgers, N.J.: Transaction.

Lohr, Steve. 1988. "British Health Service Faces a Crisis in Funds and Delays," *New York Times* (August 7), pp. 1, 12.

London, Kathryn A. 1991. *Cohabitation, Marriage, Marital Dissolution, and Remarriage: United States, 1988.* Washington, D.C.: National Center for Health Statistics.

Long, Susan, and Bruce Long. 1982. "Terrible Cancers and Fatal Ulcers: Attitudes toward Cancer in Japan," *Social Science and Medicine,* **16**(24):2101–2108.

Longmore, Paul K. 1985. "Screening Stereotypes: Images of Disabled People," *Social Policy,* **16**(Summer):31–37.

———. 1988. "Crippling the Disabled," *New York Times* (November 26), p. 23.

Lorber, Judith. 1984. *Women Physicians: Careers, Status, and Power.* New York: Tavistock.

Lott, Bernice. 1987. *Women's Lives: Themes and Variations in Gender Learning.* Monterey, Calif.: Brooks/Cole.

Louw-Potgieter, J. 1988. "The Authoritarian Personality: An Inadequate Explanation for Intergroup Conflict in South Africa," *Journal of Social Psychology,* **128**(February):75–88.

Lukacs, Georg. 1923. *History and Class Consciousness.* London: Merlin.

Luker, Kristin. 1984. *Abortion and the Politics of Motherhood.* Berkeley: University of California Press.

Lum, Joanne, and Peter Kwong. 1989. "Surviving in America: The Trials of a Chinese Immigrant Woman," *Village Voice,* **34**(October 31):39–41.

Luster, Tom, Kelly Rhoades, and Bruce Haas. 1989. "The Relation between Parental Values and Parenting Behavior: A Test of the Kohn Hypothesis," *Journal of Marriage and the Family,* **51**(February):139–147.

Luthans, Fred, Richard M. Hodgetts, and Kenneth R. Thompson (eds.). 1987. *Social Issues in Business* (5th ed.). New York: Macmillan.

Luxenburg, Joan, and Thomas E. Guild. 1989. "20 Years after the Stonewall: Legal and Political Move-ment in Gay Rights." Paper presented at the annual meeting of the Society for the Study of Social Problems, Berkeley, Calif.

——— and Lloyd Klein. 1984. "CB Radio Prostitution: Technology and the Displacement of Deviance," *Journal of Offender Counseling, Service, and Rehabilitation,* **9**(Fall–Winter):71–87.

Lynd, Robert S. 1937. *Middletown in Transition: A Study in Cultural Conflicts.* New York: Harcourt, Brace.

——— and Helen M. Lynd. 1929. *Middletown.* New York: Harcourt, Brace.

Mabry, Marcus. 1990. "Fighting Ads in the Inner City," *Newsweek,* **115**(February 5):46.

Maccoby, Eleanor Emmons, and Carol Nagy Jacklin. 1974. *Psychology of Sex Differences.* Stanford, Calif.: Stanford University Press.

Mack, Raymond W., and Calvin P. Bradford. 1979. *Transforming America: Patterns of Social Change* (2d ed.). New York: Random House.

Mackey, Wade C. 1987. "A Cross-Cultural Perspective on Perceptions of Paternalist Deficiencies in the United States: The Myth of the Derelict Daddy," *Sex Roles,* **12**(March):509–534.

MacKinnon, Catharine A. 1979. *Sexual Harassment of Working Women: A Case of Sex Discrimination.* New Haven, Conn.: Yale University Press.

———. 1983. "Feminism, Marxism, Method and State: Toward Feminist Jurisprudence," *Signs,* **8**(Summer):635–658.

MacPherson, Myra. 1984. *Long Time Passing.* Garden City, N.Y.: Doubleday.

Madigan, Charles. 1982. "A Story of Satan That Is Rated P&G," *Chicago Tribune* (July 18), p. 1.

Magnuson, Ed. 1983. "Child Abuse: The Ultimate Betrayal," *Time,* **122**(September 5):20–22.

Maguire, Brendan. 1988. "The Applied Dimension of Radical Criminology: A Survey of Prominent Radical Criminologists," *Sociological Spectrum,* **8**(2):133–151.

Maines, David R. 1977. "Social Organization and Social Structure in Symbolic Interactionist Thought," in Alex

Inkleks (ed.), *Annual Review of Sociology, 1977.* Palo Alto, Calif.: Annual Reviews, pp. 235–259.

———. 1982. "In Search of Mesostructure: Studies in the Negotiated Order," *Urban Life,* **11**(July):267–279.

Makepeace, James M. 1986. "Gender Differences in Courtship Violence Victimization," *Family Relations,* **35**(July):383–388.

———. 1987. "Social Factor and Victim-Offender Differences in Courtship Violence," *Family Relations,* **36**(January):87–91.

Makihara, Kumiko. 1990. "No Longer Willing to Be Invisible," *Time,* **135**(May 28):36.

Makin, John H. 1990. "Runaway Health Costs," *American Enterprise,* **1**(January–February):52–57.

Malcolm, Andrew H. 1974. "The 'Shortage' of Bathroom Tissue: A Classic Study in Rumor," *New York Times* (February 3), p. 29.

———. 1984. "The Colts' Move: For Indianapolis It's a Boom," *New York Times* (April 8), p. 22.

———. 1989. "Capital Punishment Is Popular, but So Are Its Alternatives," *New York Times* (September 10), p. E4.

Malcolm X, with Alex Haley. 1964. *The Autobiography of Malcolm X.* New York: Grove.

Maldonado, Lionel, and Joan Moore (eds.). 1985. *Urban Ethnicity in the United States.* Beverly Hills, Calif.: Sage.

Malthus, Thomas, Julian Huxley, and Frederick Osborn. 1960. *Three Essays on Population.* New York: New American Library (originally published in 1824).

Mann, James. 1983. "One-Parent Family: The Troubles—And the Joys," *U.S. News and World Report,* **95**(November 28):57–58, 62.

Manson, Donald A. 1986. *Tracking Offenders: White-Collar Crime.* Bureau of Justice Statistics Special Report. Washington, D.C.: U.S. Government Printing Office.

Maraniss, David, and Rick Atkinson. 1989. "The Texas S&L Meltdown," *Washington Post National Weekly Edition,* **6**(June 26):6–8.

Marger, Martin. 1981. *Elites and Masses:*

An *Introduction to Political Sociology.* New York: Van Nostrand.

Margolick, David. 1985. "25 Wrongfully Executed in U.S., Study Finds," *New York Times* (November 14), p. A19.

Marin, Catherine. 1989. "The Congressional Checkoff," *Washington Post National Weekly Edition,* **7**(November 20):14.

Markham, James M. 1986. "Bonn Takes Steps against Refugees," *New York Times* (August 28), p. A7.

Marks, Mitchell Lee, et al. 1986. "Employee Participation in a Quality Circle Program: Impact on Quality of Work Life, Productivity, and Absenteeism," *Journal of Applied Psychology,* **71**(February):61–69.

Marks, Stephen R. 1977. "Multiple Roles and Role Strain: Some Notes on Human Energy, Time and Commitment," *American Sociological Review,* **42**(December): 921–936.

Marmorstein, Jerome. 1986. "Tobacco Politics in the American Culture," *The Center Magazine,* **19**(July–August):27–33.

Marshall, Susan E. 1984. "Paradoxes of Change: Culture Crisis, Islamic Revival, and the Reactivation of Patriarchy," *Journal of Asian and African Studies,* **19**(January–April):1–17.

Marshall, Victor (ed.). 1986. *Later Life: The Social Psychology of Aging.* Beverly Hills, Calif.: Sage.

Martin, Douglas. 1987. "Indians Seek a New Life in New York," *New York Times* (March 22), p. 17.

Martin, Linda G. 1989. "The Graying of Japan," *Population Bulletin,* **44**(July):1–43.

Martin, Steven C., Robert M. Arnold, and Ruth M. Parker. 1988. "Gender and Medical Socialization," *Journal of Health and Social Behavior,* **29**(December):333–343.

Martin, Teresa Castro, and Larry L. Bumpass. 1989. "Recent Trends in Marital Disruption," *Demography* **26**(February):37–51.

Martineau, Harriet. 1962. *Society in America.* Edited, abridged, with an introductory essay by Seymour Martin Lipset. Garden City, N.Y.: Doubleday (originally published in 1837).

Marty, Martin E. 1980. "Resurgent Fun-

damentalism," in *Encyclopedia Britannica Book of the Year, 1980.* Chicago: Encyclopedia Britannica, pp. 606–607.

———. 1987. "Religion in a Troubled Land," in *Encyclopedia Britannica Book of the Year, 1987.* Chicago: Encyclopedia Britannica, pp. 330–331.

Martyna, Wendy. 1983. "Beyond the He/Man Approach: The Case for Nonsexist Language," in Barrie Thorne, Cheris Kramorae, and Nancy Henley (eds.), *Language, Gender and Society.* Rowley, Mass.: Newly House, pp. 25–37.

Marx, Karl, and Friedrich Engels. 1955. *Selected Work in Two Volumes.* Moscow: Foreign Languages Publishing House.

Masnick, George, and Mary Jo Bane. 1980. *The Nation's Families: 1960–1990.* Cambridge, Mass.: Joint Center for Urban Studies.

Mason, Marie K. 1942. "Learning to Speak after Six and One-Half Years of Silence," *Journal of Speech Disorders,* **7**(December):295–304.

Massey, Douglas S., and Nancy A. Denton. 1989a. "Residential Segregation of Mexicans, Puerto Ricans, and Cubans in Selected U.S. Metropolitan Areas," *Sociology and Social Research,* **73**(January):73–83.

——— and ———. 1989b. "Hypersegregation in U.S. Metropolitan Areas: Black and Hispanic Segregation along Five Dimensions," *Demography,* **26**(August):373–391.

Matras, Judah. 1973. *Populations and Societies.* Englewood Cliffs, N.J.: Prentice-Hall.

———. 1977. *Introduction to Population: A Sociological Approach.* Englewood Cliffs, N.J.: Prentice-Hall.

Matyko, Alexander J. 1986. *The Self-Defeating Organization: A Critique of Bureaucracy.* New York: Praeger.

Mayer, Egon. 1983. *Children of Intermarriage.* New York: American Jewish Committee.

———. 1985. *Love and Tradition: Marriage between Jews and Christians.* New York: Plenum.

Mayer, Karl Ulrich, and Urs Schoepflin. 1989. "The State and the Life Course," in W. Richard Scott and Judith Blake (eds.), *Annual Review of Sociology, 1989*. Palo Alto, Calif.: Annual Reviews, pp. 187–209.

Mayfield, Mark. 1989. "Kentucky Seeks School Equity," *USA Today* (November 7), p. 8A.

Mazrui, Jamal. 1987. "Architectural vs. Attitudinal Barriers," *Governance* (Summer–Fall), pp. 25–29.

McBride, Nicholas C. 1987. "Urban Officials Launch Bid for Remodeled US Housing Programs," *Christian Science Monitor* (February 23), p. 6.

McCaghy, Charles H. 1980. *Crime in American Society*. New York: Macmillan.

McCord, Colin, and Harold P. Freeman. 1990. "Excess Mortality in Harlem," *New England Journal of Medicine,* **322**(January 18):173–177.

McCrum, Robert, William Oran, and Robert MacNeil. 1986. "Speak English," *Chicago Tribune Magazine* (September 7), pp. 6–8, 10, 12–15, 18–21.

McCulloch, Heather. 1990. "Abortion Cutoff," *The Nation,* **250**(April 9):477, 492.

McFalls, Joseph A., Jr. 1981. "Where Have All the Children Gone?" *USA Today* (March) pp. 30–33.

———. 1982. Correspondence.

———, Brian Jones, and Bernard J. Gallegher, III. 1984. "U.S. Population Growth: Prospects and Policy," *USA Today* (January), pp. 30–34.

McGill, Douglas. 1988. "Cigarette Industry Financing Wide War on Smoking Bans," *New York Times* (December 24), pp. 1, 37.

McGrath, Ellie. 1983. "Schooling for the Common Good," *Time,* **122**(August 1):66–67.

McGuire, Meredith B. 1981. *Religion: The Social Context*. Belmont, Calif.: Wadsworth.

McKeown, Thomas. 1976. *The Role of Medicine: Dream, Mirage, or Nemesis?* London: Nuffield Provincial Hospitals Trust.

McKinlay, John B., and Sonja M. McKinlay. 1977. "The Questionable Contribution of Medical Measures to the Decline of Mortality in the United States in the Twentieth Century," *Milbank Memorial Fund Quarterly,* **55**(Summer):405–428.

McLeod, Beverly. 1986. "The Orien-

tal Express," *Psychology Today,* **20**(July):48–52.

McManus, Ed. 1985. "The Death Penalty and the Race Factor," *Illinois Issues,* **11**(March):47.

McNamara, Patrick H. (ed.). 1984. *Religion: North American Style* (2d ed.). Belmont, Calif.: Wadsworth.

McNulty, Timothy J. 1988. "Child Care: An Issue Comes of Age," *Chicago Tribune* (February 14), pp. 1, 14.

McPhail, Clark. 1991. *The Myth of the Madding Crowd*. New York: de Gruyther.

——— and David Miller. 1973. "The Assembling Process: A Theoretical and Empirical Examination," *American Sociological Review,* **38**(December):721–735.

McPhail, Thomas L. 1981. *Electronic Colonialism: The Future of International Broadcasting and Communication*. Beverly Hills, Calif.: Sage.

McPherson, J. Miller, and Lynn Smith-Lovin. 1982. "Women and Weak Ties: Differences by Sex in the Size of Voluntary Organizations," *American Journal of Sociology,* **87**(January):883–904.

——— and ———. 1986. "Sex Segregation in Voluntary Associations," *American Sociological Review,* **51**(February):61–79.

McWilliams, Carey. 1951. *Brothers under the Skin* (rev. ed.). Boston: Little, Brown.

Mead, George H. 1930. "Cooley's Contribution to American Social Thought," *American Journal of Sociology,* **35**(March):693–706.

———. 1934. In Charles W. Morris (ed.), *Mind, Self and Society*. Chicago: University of Chicago Press.

———. 1964a. In Anselm Strauss (ed.), *On Social Psychology*. Chicago: University of Chicago Press.

———. 1964b. "The Genesis of the Self and Social Control," in Andrew J. Reck (ed.), *Selected Writings: George Herbert Mead*. Indianapolis: Bobbs-Merrill, pp. 267–293.

Mead, Margaret. 1963. *Sex and Temperament in Three Primitive Societies*. New York: Morrow (originally published 1935).

———. 1966. "Marriage in Two Steps," *Redbook,* **127**(July):48–49, 84–85.

———. 1970. *Culture and Commitment: A Study of the Generation Gap*. New York: Doubleday.

———. 1973. "Does the World Belong to Men—Or to Women?" *Redbook,* **141**(October):46–52.

Mechanic, David. 1962. "The Concept of Illness Behavior," *Journal of Chronic Diseases,* **15**(February):189–194.

———. 1978. *Medical Sociology* (2d ed.). New York: Free Press.

———. 1986. *From Advocacy to Allocation: American Health Care*. New York: Free Press.

Meek, Ronald L. (ed.). 1954. *Marx and Engels on Malthus: Selections from the Writings of Marx and Engels Dealing with the Theories of Thomas Robert Malthus*. New York: International Publishers.

Meier, Deborah W. 1991. "Choice Can Save Public Education," *The Nation,* **252**(March 4):253, 266–271.

Meile, Richard C. 1986. "Pathways to Patienthood: Sick Role and Labeling Perspectives," *Social Science and Medicine,* **22**(1):35–40.

Meisenheimer, Joseph R., II. 1989. "Employer Provisions for Parental Leave," *Monthly Labor Review,* **112**(October):20–24.

Melson, Robert. 1986. "Provocation or Nationalism: A Critical Inquiry into the Armenian Genocide of 1915," in Richard G. Hovannisian (ed.), *The Armenian Genocide in Perspective*. New Brunswick, N.J.: Transaction, pp. 61–84.

Memmi, Albert. 1967. *The Colonizer and the Colonized*. Boston: Beacon.

Menard, Scott W., and Elizabeth W. Moen (eds.). 1987. *Perspectives on Population: An Introduction to Concepts and Issues*. New York: Oxford University Press.

Menken, Jane (ed.). 1986. *World Population and U.S. Policy*. New York: Norton.

Merton, Robert K. 1968. *Social Theory and Social Structure*. New York: Free Press.

———. 1973. *The Sociology of Science: Theoretical and Empirical Investigation*. Chicago: University of Chicago Press.

——— and Alice S. Kitt. 1950. "Contributions to the Theory of Reference Group Behavior," in Robert K. Merton and Paul L. Lazarsfeld (eds.), *Continuities in Social Research: Studies in the Scope and Method of the American Soldier*. New York: Free Press, pp. 40–105.

———, G. C. Reader, and P. L. Kendall. 1957. *The Student Physician*. Cambridge, Mass.: Harvard University Press.

Messner, Michael. 1989. "Masculinities and Athletic Careers," *Gender and Society*, **3**(March):71–88.

Meyer, Chuck. 1987. "Zoning and the 'New' Family," *Colloqui* (Spring), pp. 16–20.

Meyrowitz, Joshua. 1985. *No Sense of Place*. New York: Oxford University Press.

Michalowski, Raymond J., and Ronald C. Kramer. 1987. "The Space between Laws: The Problem of Corporate Crime in a Transnational Context," *Social Problems*, **34**(February):34–53.

Michels, Robert. 1915. *Political Parties*. Glencoe, Ill.: Free Press (reprinted 1949).

Middleton, Lorenzo. 1981. "Coleman Study Says Private Schooling Superior to Public; Social Scientists Attack His Findings," *Chronicle of Higher Education*, **22**(April 13):1, 12, 14–15.

——— and Anne C. Roark. 1981. "Living Together Is Widely Accepted among Students Today," *Chronicle of Higher Education*, **22**(July 6):3, 4.

Milbrath, Lester. 1981. "Political Participation," in S. L. Long (ed.), *Handbook of Political Behavior*, vol. 4. New York: Plenum, pp. 197–240.

Milgram, Stanley. 1963. "Behavioral Study of Obedience," *Journal of Abnormal and Social Psychology*, **67**(October):371–378.

———. 1967. "The Small World Problem," *Psychology Today*, **1**(January):61–67.

———. 1975. *Obedience to Authority: An Experimental View*. New York: Harper and Row.

Miller, Annetta. 1989a. "Can You Afford to Get Sick?" *Newsweek*, **113**(January 30):43–51.

———. 1989b. "The Elderly Duke It Out," *Newsweek*, **114**(September 11): 42–43.

Miller, Brent C., and Kristin A. Moore. 1990. "Adolescent Sexual Behavior, Pregnancy, and Parenting: Research through the 1980s," *Journal of Marriage and the Family*, **52**(November):1025–1044.

Miller, David L. 1988. *Introduction to Collective Behavior*. Prospect Heights, Ill.: Waveland.

Miller, Delbert C. 1983. *Handbook of Research Design and Social Measurement* (4th ed.). New York: Longman.

Miller, Reuben. 1988. "The Literature of Terrorism," *Terrorism*, **11**(1):63–87.

Millett, Kate. 1969. *Sexual Politics*. New York: Doubleday.

Millman, Marcia. 1977. *The Unkindest Cut*. New York: Morrow.

Mills, C. Wright. 1956. *The Power Elite*. New York: Oxford University Press.

———. 1959. *The Sociological Imagination*. London: Oxford University Press.

Mindel, Charles H., Robert W. Habenstein, and Roosevelt Wright, Jr. (eds.). 1988. *Ethnic Families in America: Patterns and Variations* (3d ed.). New York: Elsevier.

Mingle, James R. 1987. *Focus on Minorities*. Denver: Education Commission of the States and the State Higher Education Executive Officers.

Minkowitz, Donna. 1989. "Redlining the Arts," *Village Voice*, **34**(August 22):19.

Mintz, Steven, and Susan Kellogg. 1988. *Domestic Revolutions: A Social History of American Family Life*. New York: Free Press.

Minzesheimer, Bob. 1986. "Senate Votes on PAC Limits," *USA Today* (August 12), p. 7A.

Mizrahi, Terry. 1986. *Getting Rid of Patients*. New Brunswick, N.J.: Rutgers University Press.

Molitor, Graham T. T. 1981. "The Information Society: The Path to Post-Industrial Growth," *The Futurist*, **15**(April):23–30.

Molstad, Clark. 1986. "Choosing and Coping with Boring Work," *Urban Life*, **15**(July):215–236.

Money. 1987. "A Short History of Shortages," **16**(Fall; special issue):42.

Montagna, Paul D. 1977. *Occupations and Society: Toward a Sociology of the Labor Market*. New York: Wiley.

Mooney, Linda, and Sarah Brabant. 1986. "Emotionally Measured through Cultural Artifacts: The Expression of Love in Birthday Cards." Paper presented at the annual meeting of the American Sociological Association, New York City.

——— and ———. 1988. "Birthday Cards, Love, and Communication," *Social Science Research*, **72**(January):106–109.

Moore, Joan, and Harry Pachon. 1985. *Hispanics in the United States*. Englewood Cliffs, N.J.: Prentice-Hall.

Moore, Kathryn M. 1982. "The Role of Mentors in Developing Leaders for Academe," *Educational Record*, **63**(Winter):23–28.

Moore, Wilbert E. 1967. *Order and Change: Essays in Comparative Sociology*. New York: Wiley.

———. 1968. "Occupational Socialization," in David A. Goslin (ed.), *Handbook of Socialization Theory and Research*. Chicago: Rand McNally, pp. 861–883.

———. 1974. *Social Change* (2d ed.). Englewood Cliffs, N.J.: Prentice-Hall.

Moran, Theodore. 1978. "Multinational Corporations and Dependency: A Dialogue for Dependentistas and Non-Dependentistas," *International Organization*, **32**(Winter):79–100.

Moreno, Jacob L. 1953. *Who Shall Survive?* (rev. ed.). Beacon, N.Y.: Beacon.

Morganthau, Tom. 1988. "The Housing Crunch," *Newsweek*, **111**(January 4): 18–20.

Morin, Richard. 1989. "Bringing Up Baby the Company Way," *Washington Post National Weekly Edition*, **6**(September 11–17), p. 37.

———. 1990. "Women Asking Women about Men Asking Women about Men," *Washington Post National Weekly Edition*, **7**(January 21):37.

Morrison, Denton E. 1971. "Some Notes toward Theory on Relative Deprivation, Social Movements, and Social Change," *American Behavioral Scientist*, **14**(May–June):675–690.

Morse, Arthur D. 1967. *While Six Million Died: A Chronicle of American Apathy*. New York: Ace.

Mortenson, Thomas G., and Zhijun Wu. 1990. *High School Graduation and College Participation of Young Adults by Family Income Backgrounds 1970 to 1989.* Iowa City, Iowa: American College Testing.

Mortimer, Jeylan E., and Roberta G. Simmons. 1978. "Adult Socialization," in Ralph H. Turner, James Coleman, and Renee C. Fox (eds.), *Annual Review of Sociology, 1978.* Palo Alto, Calif.: Annual Reviews, pp. 421–454.

Mosely, Ray. 1990. "The Night the Wall Fell," *Chicago Tribune* (October 28), pp. 1, 10.

Mosher, William D., and William F. Pratt. 1990. "Fecundity and Infertility in the United States, 1965–88," *Advance Data,* **192**(December 4):1–9.

Mueller, Athena. 1991. *Statewide Laws Restricting Smoking.* Washington, D.C.: Action on Smoking and Health.

Müller, Ronald E., and Arthur L. Domike. 1981. "Cancun's Meaning," *New York Times* (October 18), p. EY23.

Mumford, Emily. 1983. *Medical Sociology: Patients, Providers, and Policies.* New York: Random House.

Murdock, George P. 1945. "The Common Denominator of Cultures," in Ralph Linton (ed.), *The Science of Man in the World Crisis.* New York: Columbia University Press, pp. 123–142.

———. 1949. *Social Structure.* New York: Macmillan.

———. 1957. "World Ethnographic Sample," *American Anthropologist,* **59**(August):664–687.

Murphy, Elaine M. 1984. *Food and Population: A Global Concern.* Washington, D.C.: U.S. Government Printing Office.

Murstein, Bernard. 1976. *Who Will Marry Whom?* New York: Springer.

Muskrat, Joe. 1972. "Assimilate or Starve!" *Civil Rights Digest,* **8**(October):27–34.

Mydans, Seth. 1989. "TV Unites, and Divides, Hispanic Groups," *New York Times* (August 2), p. E4.

Myrdal, Gunnar, with Richard Steiner and Arnold Rose. 1944. *An American Dilemma: The Negro Problem and Modern Democracy.* New York: Harper.

NAACP Legal Defense and Educational Fund. 1989. *The Unfinished Agenda on Race in America.* New York: NAACP Legal Defense and Educational Fund.

Nader, Laura. 1986. "The Subordination of Women in Comparative Perspective," *Urban Anthropology,* **15**(Fall–Winter):377–397.

Nader, Ralph. 1965. *Unsafe at Any Speed.* New York: Grossman.

———. 1985. "America's Crime without Criminals," *New York Times* (May 19), p. F3.

———, Mark Green, and Joel Seligman. 1976. *Taming the Giant Corporation.* New York: Norton.

Nakane, Chie. 1970. *Japanese Society.* Berkeley: University of California Press.

Nakao, Keiko, and Judith Treas. 1990. "Occupational Prestige in the United States Revisited: Twenty-Five Years of Stability and Change." Paper presented at the annual meeting of the American Sociological Association, Washington, D.C.

Naparstek, Arthur J., and David E. Biegel. 1980. "The Care Wasn't There," *New York Times* (January 26), p. 26.

Nash, Manning. 1962. "Race and the Ideology of Race," *Current Anthropology,* **3**(June):285–288.

Natale, Jo Anna. 1990. "Just Deserts," *American School Board Journal* (March):20–25, 42.

National Advisory Commission on Civil Disorders. 1968. *Report.* With introduction by Tom Wicker. New York: Bantam.

National Advisory Commission on Criminal Justice. 1976. *Organized Crime.* Washington, D.C.: U.S. Government Printing Office.

National Aging Resource Center on Elder Abuse. 1990. *Summaries of National Elder Abuse Data: An Exploratory Study.* Washington, D.C.: National Aging Resource Center on Elder Abuse.

National Center for Health Statistics. 1974. *Summary Report: Final Divorce Statistics, 1974.* Washington, D.C.: U.S. Government Printing Office.

———. 1990. *Annual Survey of Births, Marriages, Divorces, and Deaths: United States, 1989.* Washington, D.C.: U.S. Government Printing Office.

———. 1991. "Births, Marriages, Divorces, and Deaths for 1990," *Monthly Vital Statistics Report,* **39**(April 8).

National Commission on Excellence in Education. 1983. *A Nation at Risk: The Imperative for Educational Reform.* Washington, D.C.: U.S. Government Printing Office.

National Council of Teachers of English. 1988. *Quarterly Review of Doublespeak,* **14**(April):1–12.

———. 1989a. *Quarterly Review of Doublespeak,* **15**(January):1–12.

———. 1989b. *Quarterly Review of Doublespeak,* **15**(October):1–12.

Navarro, Vicente. 1976. *Medicine under Capitalism: Crisis, Health, and Medicine.* New York: Prodist.

———. 1984. "Medical History as Justification Rather Than Explanation: A Critique of Starr's 'The Social Transformation of American Medicine,'" *International Journal of Health Services,* **14**(4):511–528.

Nelson, Chris, and Kathleen Short. 1990. *Health Insurance Coverage: 1986 to 1988,* ser. P-70, no. 17. Washington, D.C.: U.S. Government Printing Office.

Nelson, Jill. 1987. "Integration When? A Tale of Three Cities," *Columbia Journalism Review,* **25**(January–February):41–51.

Newland, Kathleen. 1980. *City Limits: Emerging Constraints on Urban Growth.* Washington, D.C.: Worldwatch Institute.

Newman, William M. 1973. *American Pluralism: A Study of Minority Groups and Social Theory.* New York: Harper and Row.

New York Post. 1989. "Girl Makes a Hit, History in LL Series" (August 24), p. 68.

New York Times. 1986a. "9 in 10 Elderly People Found to Maintain Social Contacts" (May 25), p. 32.

———. 1986b. "Poll on Families: Small Is Best" (May 25), p. 22.

———. 1987a. "Amnesty International Assails U.S. on Executions" (February 19), p. A17.

———. 1987b. "Age Bias Found in Breast Cancer Treatment" (May 22), p. A17.

———. 1987c. "Right of School to Demand Use of Texts Upheld" (August 25), pp. A1, A13.

————. 1987d. "Court Reverses a Ban on 'Humanist' Schoolbooks" (August 27), pp. A1, A22.

————. 1989. "Study on Disabled and Jobs Finds Work and Good Pay Are Scarce" (August 16), p. A22.

————. 1990a. "Appeals Court Rules A.M.A. Acted against Chiropractors" (February 9), p. A18.

————. 1990b. "Health Data Show Wide Gap between Whites and Blacks" (March 23), p. A17.

————. 1990c. "U.S. Is in Middle of 33 Nations in Death Rates" (April 7), p. 10.

————. 1990d. "Beware the Little Girl in Red" (May 9), p. A30.

————. 1990e. "Portrait of the Electorate: U.S. House Vote" (November 8), p. B7.

————. 1991a. "Japan Eases Rule on Korean Aliens" (January 11), p. A3.

————. 1991b. "U.S. Reports AIDS Deaths Exceed 100,000" (January 25), p. A18.

————. 1991c. "Death Toll from Smoking Is Worsening" (February 1), p. A14.

Neysmith, Sheila, and Joey Edwardh. 1984. "Economic Dependency in the 1980s: Its Impact on Third World Elderly," *Ageing and Society*, **4**(1): 21–44.

Nixon, Howard L., II. 1979. *The Small Group*. Englewood Cliffs, N.J.: Prentice-Hall.

Noble, Kenneth B. 1984. "Plight of Black Family Is Studied Anew," *New York Times* (January 29), p. E20.

————. 1986. "Commuting by Computer Remains Largely in the Future," *New York Times* (May 11), p. E22.

NORC (National Opinion Research Center). 1990. *General Social Surveys 1972–1990: Cumulative Codebook*. Chicago: National Opinion Research Center.

Northcott, Herbert C. 1983. "Who Stays Home? Working Parents and Sick Children," *International Journal of Women's Studies*, **6**(November–December):387–394.

Novello, Antonia C., Paul H. Wise, and Dushanka V. Kleinman. 1991. "Hispanic Health: Time for Date, Time for Action," *Journal of the American Medical Association*, **265**(January 9):253–255.

Oakes, Jeannie. 1985. *Keeping Track: How Schools Structure Inequality*. New Haven, Conn.: Yale University Press.

————— et al. [4 authors]. 1990. *Multiplying Inequalities: The Effects of Race, Social Class and Tracking on Opportunities to Learn Mathematics and Science*. Santa Monica, Calif.: Rand Corp.

Oberg, Kalervo. 1960. "Culture Shock: Adjustment to Neo-Cultural Environments," *Practical Anthropology*, **12** (July–August):177–182.

Oberschall, Anthony. 1973. *Social Conflict and Social Movements*. Englewood Cliffs, N.J.: Prentice-Hall.

O'Brien, Eileen M. 1990. "States Struggle to Address School Finance Disparities," *Black Issues in Higher Education*, **7**(May 14):1, 10–13.

O'Connell, Martin, and Carolyn C. Rogers. 1983. "Child Care Arrangements of Working Mothers: June 1982," *Current Population Reports*, ser. P-23, no. 129. Washington, D.C.: U.S. Government Printing Office.

O'Driscoll, Patrick. 1985. "But Still Not Moving up the Church Ladder," *USA Today* (April 7), pp. 1A, 2A.

Office of the Federal Register. 1989. *United States Government Manual, 1989–1990*. Washington, D.C.: U.S. Government Printing Office.

Ogbu, John H. 1978. *Minority Education and Caste: The American System in Cross-Cultural Perspective*. New York: Academic.

Ogburn, William F. 1922. *Social Change with Respect to Culture and Original Nature*. New York: Huebsch (reprinted 1966, New York: Dell).

————— and Clark Tibbits. 1934. "The Family and Its Functions," in Research Committee on Social Trends (ed.), *Recent Social Trends in the United States*. New York: McGraw-Hill, pp. 661–708.

O'Hare, William P. 1987. *America's Welfare Population: Who Gets What?* Washington, D.C.: Population Reference Bureau.

————. 1988. *The Rise of Poverty in Rural America*. Washington, D.C.: Population Reference Bureau.

Okie, Susan. 1990. "Billions More for Billions Fewer," *Washington Post National Weekly Edition*, **7**(March 12): 37.

Oliner, Pearl M., and Samuel P. Oliner.

1989. *The Roots of Altruism*. New York: American Jewish Committee.

Oliver, Melvin L. 1988. "The Urban Black Community as Network: Toward a Social Network Perspective," *Sociological Quarterly*, **29**(4):623–645.

Olson, Laura Katz. 1982. *The Political Economy of Aging: The State, Private Power, and Social Welfare*. New York: Columbia University Press.

Olson, Philip. 1987. "A Model of Eldercare in the People's Republic of China," *International Journal of Aging and Human Development*, **24**(4): 279–300.

————. 1988. "Modernization in the People's Republic of China: The Politicization of the Elderly," *Sociological Quarterly*, **29**(2):241–262.

Orcutt, James D., and Lynn Kenneth Harvey. 1985. "Deviance, Rule Breaking, and Male Dominance in Conversation," *Symbolic Interaction*, **8**(Spring): 15–32.

O'Reilly, Jane. 1972. "The Housewife's Moment of Truth," *Ms.*, **1**(Spring):54–55, 57–59.

Oreskes, Michael, and Robin Toner. 1989. "The Homeless at the Heart of Poverty and Policy," *New York Times* (January 29), p. E5.

Orfield, Gary. 1987. *School Segregation in the 1980s*. Chicago: National School Desegregation Report.

Ornstein, Norman J., and Mark Schmitt. 1990. "The New World of Interest Politics," *American Enterprise*, **1**(January–February):46–51.

Orum, Anthony M. 1978. *Introduction to Political Sociology: The Social Anatomy of the Body Politic*. Englewood Cliffs, N.J.: Prentice-Hall.

————. 1989. *Introduction to Political Sociology: The Social Anatomy of the Body Politic* (3d ed.). Englewood Cliffs, N.J.: Prentice Hall.

Orwell, George. 1949. *1984*. New York: Harcourt Brace Jovanovich.

Osborne, Lynn T., Anne H. Rhu, and Ronald W. Smith. 1985. "Labelers in Education: Their Perceptions about Learning Disabilities," *Free Inquiry in Creative Sociology*, **13**:117–122.

Osen, Yaffa. 1987. "Rev. Moon Is Shining Brightly with New Allies," *Morning Freiheit* (March 1), p. 3.

Ostling, Richard N. 1989. "Shootouts in

the Schools," *Time*, **134**(November 20):116.

Oved, Yaacov. 1987. *Two Hundred Years of American Communes*. New Brunswick, N.J.: Transaction.

Oxnam, Robert B. 1986. "Why Asians Succeed Here," *New York Times Magazine* (November 30), pp. 72, 74–75, 88–89, 92.

Page, Charles H. 1946. "Bureaucracy's Other Face," *Social Forces*, **25**(October):89–94.

Pak, Jung Ah, and Sally Solo. 1990. "The Global 500," *Fortune*, **122**(July 30):203–328.

Palazzolo, Charles. 1981. *Small Groups: An Introduction*. New York: Van Nostrand.

Palmer, John L., Timothy Smeeding, and Barbara Boyle Torrey (eds.). 1988. *The Vulnerable*. Washington, D.C.: Urban Institute.

Palmore, Erdman, and Kenneth Manton. 1974. "Modernization and Status of the Aged: International Correlations." *Journal of Gerontology*, **29**(March):205–210.

Pamperin, Bruce F., Willard F. Bailey, and Richard J. Tyson. 1985. *Students and Community Resources: An Attitudinal Study*. Menominee: University of Wisconsin–Stout.

Paneth, Nigel. 1982. "Editorial: Infant Mortality Reexamined," *Journal of the American Medical Association*, **247**(February 19):1027–1028.

Parelius, Ann P., and Robert J. Parelius. 1978. *The Sociology of Education*. Englewood Cliffs, N.J.: Prentice-Hall.

Park, Robert E. 1916. "The City: Suggestions for the Investigation of Human Behavior in the Urban Environment," *American Journal of Sociology*, **20**(March):577–612.

———. 1936. "Succession, an Ecological Concept," *American Sociological Review*, **1**(April):171–179.

——— and Ernest Burgess. 1921. *Introduction to the Science of Sociology*. Chicago: University of Chicago Press.

——— and ———. 1925. *The City*. Chicago: University of Chicago Press.

Parker, Suzy. 1988. "Asian Population," *USA Today* (April 15–17), p. 1.

Parsons, Talcott. 1951. *The Social System*. New York: Free Press.

———. 1966. *Societies: Evolutionary and Comparative Perspectives*. Englewood Cliffs, N.J.: Prentice-Hall.

———. 1972. "Definitions of Health and Illness in the Light of American Values and Social Structure," in E. Gartley Jaco (ed.), *Patients, Physicians and Illness*. New York: Free Press, pp. 166–187.

———. 1975. "The Sick Role and the Role of the Physician Reconsidered," *Milbank Medical Fun Quarterly, Health and Society*, **53**(Summer):257–278.

——— and Robert Bales. 1955. *Family, Socialization, and Interaction Process*. Glencoe, Ill.: Free Press.

——— and Renee Fox. 1952. "Therapy and the Modern Family," *Journal of Social Issues*, **8**(Fall):31–44.

Passuth, Patricia M., David R. Maines, and Bernice Neugarten. 1984. "Age Norms and Age Constraints Twenty Years Later." Paper presented at the annual meeting of the Midwest Sociological Society, Chicago.

Pastor, Manuel. 1986. *The International Monetary Fund and Latin America: Economic Stabilization and Class Conflict*. Boulder, Colo.: Westview.

Patai, Daphne. 1988. *Brazilian Women Speak*. New Brunswick, N.J.: Rutgers University Press.

Patton, Carl V. (ed.). 1988. *Spontaneous Shelter: International Perspectives and Prospects*. Philadelphia: Temple University Press.

Paul, Angus. 1987. "Why Does Terrorism Subside? Researchers Offer Preliminary Theories," *Chronicle of Higher Education*, **34**(September 23):A10.

Paull, Irene, and Bülbül. 1976. *Everybody's Studying Us: The Ironies of Aging in the Pepsi Generation*. San Francisco: Glide.

Pavalko, Ronald M. 1971. *Sociology of Occupations and Professions*. Itasca, Ill.: Peacock.

——— (ed.). 1972. *Sociological Perspectives on Occupations*. Itasca, Ill.: Peacock.

Payer, Lynn. 1988. *Medicine and Culture: Varieties of Treatment in the United States, England, West Germany, and France*. New York: Holt.

Pear, Robert. 1983. "$1.5 Billion Urged for U.S. Japanese Held in War," *New York Times* (June 17), pp. A1, D16.

Pebley, Anne R., and David E. Bloom. 1982. "Childless Americans," *American Demographics*, **4**(January):18–21.

Peirce, Kate. 1989. "Sex-Role Stereotyping of Children on Television: A Content Analysis of the Roles and Attributes of Child Characters," *Sociological Spectrum*, **9**(3):321–328.

Pellegrini, Ann. 1990. "Rape Is a Bias Crime," *New York Times* (May 27), p. E13.

Pelto, Pertti J. 1973. *The Snowmobile Revolution: Technology and Social Change in the Arctic*. Menlo Park, Calif.: Cummings.

Perez, Miguel. 1986. "The Language of Discrimination," *New York Daily News* (November 13), p. 47.

———. 1989. "'English' Racism Is Now Out in the Open," *New York Daily News* (August 10), p. 42.

Perlez, Jane. 1991. "In Kenya, the Lawyers Lead the Call for Freedom," *New York Times* (March 10), p. E2.

Perrow, Charles. 1986. *Complex Organizations* (3d ed.). New York: Random House.

Perrucci, Robert. 1974. *Circle of Madness: On Being Sane and Institutionalized in America*. Englewood Cliffs, N.J.: Prentice-Hall.

Petchesky, Rosalind. 1990. "Giving Women a Real Choice," *The Nation*, **250**(May 28):732–735.

Peter, Laurence J., and Raymond Hull. 1969. *The Peter Principle*. New York: Morrow.

Peterman, Dan J., Carl A. Ridley, and Scott M. Anderson. 1974. "A Comparison of Cohabiting and Noncohabiting College Students," *Journal of Marriage and the Family*, **36**(May):344–354.

Peters, John F. 1985. "Adolescents as Socialization Agents to Parents," *Adolescence*, **2**(Winter):921–933.

Peters, William. 1987. *A Class Divided: Then and Now* (enlarged ed.). New Haven, Conn.: Yale University Press.

Petersen, William. 1975. *Population* (3d ed.). New York: Macmillan

———. 1979. *Malthus*. Cambridge, Mass.: Harvard University Press.

Petersilia, Joan. 1983. *Racial Disparities in the Criminal Justice System*. Santa Monica, Calif.: Rand Corp.

Peterson, Felix. 1987. "Vietnam 'Battle Deaths': Is There a Race or Class Issue," *Focus*, **15**(July):3–4.

Peterson, Richard G. 1984. "Preparing for Apocalypse: Survivalist Strategies," *Free Inquiry in Creative Sociology*, **12**(May):44–46.

Pettigrew, Thomas. 1981. "Race and Class in the 1980s: An Interactive View," *Daedalus*, **110**(Spring): 233–255.

Phi Delta Kappan. 1986. "Civil Liberties Group Reports Increase in Censorship Efforts," **60**(November):254.

Phillips, David P., and Lundie L. Carstensen. 1986. "Clustering of Teenage Suicides after Television News Stories about Suicide," *New England Journal of Medicine*, **315**(September 11):685–689.

Phillips, Leslie. 1990. "Vote Due on Family-Leave Bill," *USA Today* (May 8), p. 4A.

Piaget, Jean. 1954. *The Construction of Reality in the Child*. Translated by Margaret Cook. New York: Basic Books.

Pillemer, Karl A. 1985. "The Dangers of Dependency: New Findings on Domestic Violence against the Elderly," *Social Problems*, **33**(December): 146–158.

——— and Rosalie S. Wolf. 1987. *Elder Abuse: Conflict in the Family*. Dover, Mass.: Auburn House.

Pines, Maya. 1981. "The Civilizing of Genie," *Psychology Today*, **15**(September):28–29, 31–32, 34.

Pleck, Joseph H. 1981. *The Myth of Masculinity*. Cambridge, Mass.: M.I.T. Press.

———. 1985. *Working Wives, Working Husbands*. Beverly Hills, Calif.: Sage.

Plomin, Robert. 1989. "Determinants of Behavior," *American Psychologist*, **44**(February):105–111.

———. 1990. "The Role of Inheritance in Behavior," *Science*, **248**(April 13): 183–187.

Pogrebin, Letty Cottin. 1981. *Growing Up Free: Raising Your Child in the 80's*. New York: McGraw-Hill.

———. 1982. "Are Men Discovering the Joys of Fatherhood?" *Ms.*, **10**(February):41, 43–44, 46.

Polk, Barbara Bovee. 1974. "Male Power and the Women's Movement," *Journal of Applied Behavioral Sciences*, **10**(July):415–431.

Population Crisis Committee. 1988. *Country Rankings of the Status of Women: Poor, Powerless and Pregnant*. Washington, D.C.: Population Crisis Committee.

Population Institute. 1988a. "Population Aid Decline Blasted," *Popline*, **10**(October–November):1.

———. 1988b. "6 of 10 Favor U.S. Family Planning Aid," *Popline*, **10**(October–November):1–2.

Population Reference Bureau. 1978. "World Population: Growth on the Decline," *Interchange*, **7**(May):1–3.

Population Today. 1986. "Halley's Other Comet," **14**(January):3, 10.

Porter, Sylvia. 1985. "Day Care Helps Both Employees and Employers," *New York Daily News* (November 8), p. 52.

Portes, Alejandro, Manuel Castells, and Lauren Benton. 1989. *The Informal Economy: Studies in Advanced and Less Developed Countries*. Baltimore: Johns Hopkins University Press.

Powell, Arthur G., Eleanor Farrar, and David K. Cohen. 1985. *The Shopping Mall High School: Winners and Losers in the Educational Marketplace*. Boston: Houghton Miffin.

Powers, Mary G., and Joan J. Holmberg. 1978. "Occupational Status Scores: Changes Introduced by the Inclusion of Women," *Demography*, **15**(May):183–204.

Pratt, R. Cranford. 1983. "The Global Impact of the World Bank," in Jill Torrie (ed.), *Banking on Poverty: The Global Impact of the IMF and World Bank*. Toronto: Between the Lines, pp. 55–66.

Prehn, John W. 1991. "Migration," in Dushkin Publishing Group, *Encyclopedia of Sociology* (4th ed.). Guilford, Conn.: Dushkin, pp. 190–191.

President's Commission on Law Enforcement and Administration of Justice. 1967. *Task Force Report: Organized Crime*. Washington, D.C.: U.S. Government Printing Office.

Prince, Raymond. 1985. "The Concept of Culture-Bound Syndromes: Anorexia Nervosa and Brain-Fog," *Social Science and Medicine*, **21**(2):197–203.

Princeton Religion Research Center. 1984. "4 in 10 Adults in U.S. Attended Church in Typical Week of 1984," *Emerging Trends*, **6**(December):1.

———. 1986. "Importance of God in Lives," *Emerging Trends*, **8**(November–December):5.

———. 1989a. "Image of TV Evangelists Deteriorates, but Confidence in the Church Unchanged," *Emerging Trends*, **11**(September):3–4.

———. 1989b. "Prejudice against Fundamentalists Seen on Rise in Latest Survey," *Emerging Trends*, **11**(March):1–2.

———. 1990a. *Religion in America, 1990 Report*. Princeton, N.J.: Princeton Religion Research Center.

———. 1990b. "Ranks of the 'Born-Again' Faithful Continue to Grow," *Emerging Trends*, **12**(September):1.

———. 1990c. "Church Attendance Unchanged as We Enter the 1990s," *Emerging Trends*, **12**(June):4.

Procter and Gamble. 1985. "News from Procter & Gamble." News release, May 16.

———. 1986. *Procter & Gamble's Symbol of Quality*. Cincinnati: Procter and Gamble.

Public Opinion. 1979. "Falling Grades for Local Schools," **2**(August–September):36–39.

Purvis, Andrew. 1990. "Research for Men Only," *Time*, **135**(March 5):59–60.

Quadagno, Jill (ed.). 1980. *Aging, the Individual and Society: Readings in Social Gerontology*. New York: St. Martin's.

———. 1984. "Welfare Capitalism and the Social Security Act of 1935," *American Sociological Review*, **49**(October):632–647.

———. 1989a. "Generational Conflict and the Politics of Class," *Politics and Society*, **17** (September):353–376.

———. 1989b. "Foreword," in John F. Myles, *Old Age in the Welfare State: The Political Economy of Public Pensions* (2d ed.). Lawrence: University of Kansas Press, pp. ix–xi.

Quade, Vicki. 1984. "Book Censorship: Whose First Amendment Is It?" *American Bar Association Journal*, **70**(August):32.

Quality Education for Minorities Project. 1990. *Education That Works: An Action Plan for the Education of Minorities*. Cambridge, Mass: Quality Education for Minorities Project.

Quarantelli, E. L. 1957. "The Behavior of Panic Participants," *Sociology and Social Research*, **41**(January):187–194.

——— and Russell R. Dynes. 1970. "Property Norms and Looting: Their Patterns in Community Crises," *Phylon*, **31**(Summer):168–182.

——— and James R. Hundley, Jr. 1975. "A Test of Some Propositions about Crowd Formation and Behavior," in Robert R. Evans (ed.), *Readings in Collective Behavior*. Chicago: Rand McNally, pp. 538–554.

——— and Elizabeth A. Wilson. 1980. "History and Current Activities of the Disaster Research Center." Miscellaneous report no. 26 of Disaster Research Center, Columbus, Ohio.

Quick, Paddy. 1972. "Women's Work," *Review of Radical Political Economics*, **14**(July):2–19.

Quinley, Harold E., and Charles Y. Glock. 1983. *Anti-Semitism in America*. New Brunswick, N.J.: Transaction.

Quinn, Bernard, Herman Anderson, Martin Bradley, Paul Goetting, and Peggy Shriver. 1982. *Churches and Church Membership in the United States 1980*. Atlanta: Glenmary Research Center.

Quinn, Kathleen, Polly Roskin, and Joyce M. Pruitt. 1984. *Cultural Violence: There Are Many Causes*. Springfield, Ill.: Illinois Coalition Against Sexual Assault and the Illinois Coalition Against Domestic Violence.

Quinney, Richard. 1970. *The Social Reality of Crime*. Boston: Little, Brown.

———. 1974. *Criminal Justice in America*. Boston: Little, Brown.

———. 1979. *Criminology* (2d ed.). Boston: Little, Brown.

———. 1980. *Class, State and Crime* (2d ed.). New York: Longman.

Rabben, Linda. 1990a. "Brazil's Military Stakes Its Claim," *The Nation*, **250**(March 12):341–342.

———. 1990b. "Scorched Earth, Barren Lives," *Discovery Channel Magazine* (April), pp. 24–27.

Radcliffe-Brown, Alfred R. 1922. *The Andaman Islanders*. Cambridge, Eng.: Cambridge University Press.

Radelet, Michael L. 1989. "Executions of Whites for Crimes against Blacks: Exceptions to the Rule," *Sociological Quarterly*, **30**(4):529–544.

Radosh, Mary Flanery. 1984. "The Collapse of Midwifery: A Sociological Study of the Decline of a Profession." Unpublished Ph.D. dissertation, Southern Illinois University, Carbondale.

Radosh, Polly F. 1986. "Midwives in the United States: Past and Present," *Population Research and Policy Review*, **5**:129–145.

Ramirez, Anthony. 1986. "America's Super Minority," *Fortune*, **114**(November 24):148–149, 152, 156, 160.

Rand Research Review. 1988. "Research Spotlight on a Health Maintenance Organization," **11**(3):3–5.

Randall, Teri. 1990a. "Domestic Violence Intervention Calls for More Than Treating Injuries," *Journal of the American Medical Association*, **264**(August 22):939–940.

———. 1990b. "Domestic Violence Begets Other Problems of Which Physicians Must Be Aware to Be Effective," *Journal of the American Medical Association*, **264**(August 22):940, 943–944.

Randall, Vicky. 1987. *Women in Politics: An International Perspective* (2d ed.). Chicago: University of Chicago Press.

Rangel, Jesus. 1984. "Survey Finds Hispanic Groups More Unified," *New York Times* (September 8), p. 22.

Rank, Steven G., and Cardell K. Jacobsen. 1977. "Hospital Nurses' Compliance with Medication Overdose Orders: A Failure to Replicate," *Journal of Health and Social Behavior*, **18**(June):188–193.

Rasell, M. Edith, and Lawrence Mishel. 1990. *Shortchanging Education*. Washington, D.C.: Economic Policy Institute.

Rashid, Salim. 1987. "Malthus's *Essay on Population*: The Facts of 'Super-Growth' and the Rhetoric of Scientific Persuasion," *Journal of the History of the Behavioral Sciences*, **23**(January):22–36.

Rasky, Susan F. 1989a. "Study Finds Sex Bias in News Companies," *New York Times* (April 11), p. C22.

———. 1989b. "Bill Barring Bias against Disabled Holds Wide Impact," *New York Times* (August 14), pp. A1, B6.

Rathje, William L. 1974. "The Garbage Project," *Archaeology*, **27**(October): 236–241.

——— and W. W. Hughes. 1975. In W. H. Sinaito and L. A. Broedling (eds.), *Perspectives on Attitude Assessment: Surveys and Their Alternatives*. Washington, D.C.: Smithsonian Institution and Navy Manpower Research and Development, pp. 151–167.

Rawlings, Steve W. 1989. "Single Parents and Their Children," in *Studies in Marriage and the Family. Current Population Reports*, ser. P-23, no. 162, pp. 13–25.

Raymond, Chris. 1990. "Scholarship on Homeless Gets Increased Attention from Many Sociologists and Psychologists," *Chronicle of Higher Education*, **37**(September 5):4, 6.

Reardon, Patrick. 1989. "Study Ties Poor Child Care to Low Wages," *Chicago Tribune* (October 18), p. 5.

Rebell, Michael A. 1986. "Structural Discrimination and the Rights of the Disabled," *Georgetown Law Journal*, **74**(June):1435–1489.

Rebell, Susan. 1987. "National Survey: Americans Call for Child Care," *Ms.*, **15**(March):44.

Rebelsky, Freda, and Cheryl Hanks. 1973. "Fathers' Verbal Interaction with Infants in the First Three Months of Life," in Freda Rebelsky and Lyn Dorman (eds.), *Child Development and Behavior* (2d ed.). New York: Knopf, pp. 145–148.

Reese, William A., II, and Michael A. Katovich. 1989. "Untimely Acts: Extending the Interactionist Conception of Deviance," *Sociological Quarterly*, **30**(2):159–184.

Regier, Darrell, et al. 1988. "One-Month Prevalence of Mental Disorders in the United States," *Archives of General Psychiatry*, **45**(November):977–986.

Reich, Robert B. 1990. "As the World Turns," *The New Republic*, **200**(May 1):23, 26–28.

Reid, J. Norman. 1984. *Availability of Selected Public Facilities in Rural Commu-*

nities. Washington, D.C.: U.S. Department of Agriculture.

Reid, Sue Titus. 1981. *The Correctional System: An Introduction.* New York: Holt.

Reid, T. R. 1990. "Japan Is Making Everything but Babies," *Washington Post National Weekly Edition,* 8(November 5):18.

Reiman, Jeffrey H. 1984. *The Rich Get Richer and the Poor Get Prison* (2d ed.). New York: Wiley.

Reisman, Barbara, Amy J. Moore, and Karen Fitzgerald. 1988. *Child Care, the Bottom Line: An Economic and Child Care Policy Paper.* New York: Child Care Action Campaign.

Repetto, Robert. 1987. "Population, Resources, Environment: An Uncertain Future," *Population Bulletin,* 42(July).

Reskin, Barbara, and Francine Blau. 1990. *Job Queues, Gender Queues: Explaining Women's Inroads into Male Occupations.* Philadelphia: Temple University Press.

Rexroat, Cynthia, and Constance Shehan. 1987. "The Family Life Cycle and Spouses' Time in Housework," *Journal of Marriage and the Family,* 49(November):737–750.

Reynolds, Barbara. 1988. "We've Proved We Are a New Force in Society," *USA Today* (March 15), p. 11A.

Rheingold, Harriet L. 1969. "The Social and Socializing Infant," in David A. Goslin (ed.), *Handbook of Socialization Theory and Research.* Chicago: Rand McNally, pp. 779–790.

Rich, Adrienne. 1979. *On Lies, Secrets, and Silence: Selected Prose 1966–1978.* New York and London: Norton.

Richards, Cara E. 1972. *Man in Perspective: An Introduction to Cultural Anthropology.* New York: Random House.

Richardson, Kenneth, and Robert Caildini. 1981. "Basking and Blasting: Tactics of Indirect Self-Preservation," in James Tedeschi (ed.), *Impression Management: Theory and Research.* New York: Academic, pp. 41–53.

Richardson, Laurel, and Verta Taylor. 1989. *Feminist Frontiers II: Rethinking Sex, Gender, and Society.* New York: Random House.

Richburg, Keith B. 1985. "Learning What Japan Has to Teach," *Washington Post National Weekly Edition,* 3(November 4):9.

Riddle, Lyn. 1988. "Shaker Village Buoyed by New Blood," *New York Times* (August 28), p. 43.

Ridgeway, Cecilia L. 1987. "Nonverbal Behavior, Dominance, and the Basis of Status in Task Groups," *American Sociological Review,* 52(October):683–694.

Ridgeway, James. 1986. "Que Pasa, U.S. English?" *Village Voice,* 31(December 2):32–33.

———. 1987. "Killing Them Softly: Reagan's Real AIDS Policy," *Village Voice,* 32(May 12):31–33.

———. 1988. "Moonrise over Washington," *Village Voice,* 33(January 19):16–17.

Riding, Alan. 1988. "Peruvians Combating Red Tape," *New York Times* (July 24), p. 3.

Ridker, Ronald G., and Elizabeth W. Cecelski. 1979. "Resources, Environment and Population: The Nature of Future Limits," *Population Bulletin,* 34(August).

Riesman, David, with Nathan Glazer and Reuel Denny. 1961. *The Lonely Crowd.* New Haven, Conn.: Yale University Press.

Riessman, Catherine Kohler. 1983. "Women and Medicalization: A New Perspective," *Social Policy,* 14(Summer):3–18.

Rifkin, Jeremy. 1980. *Entropy: A New World View.* New York: Viking.

Riley, Matilda White. 1987. "On the Significance of Age in Sociology," *American Sociological Review,* 52(February):1–14.

Ritzer, George. 1977. *Working: Conflict and Change* (2d ed.). Englewood Cliffs, N.J.: Prentice-Hall.

Rivers, Patrick. 1976. *The Survivalists.* New York: Universe.

———. 1977. "Refugees from the Sick Society," *The Futurist,* 11(April):97–98.

Roberts, D. F. 1975. "The Dynamics of Racial Intermixture in the American Negro—Some Anthropological Considerations," *American Journal of Human Genetics,* 7(December):361–367.

Roberts, Keith A. 1984. *Religion in Sociological Perspective.* Homewood, Ill.: Dorsey.

Roberts, Robert E. Lee. 1987. "Those Who Do Not Watch Television," *Sociology and Social Research,* 71(January):105–107.

Roberts, Ron E. 1991. "Social Control," in Dushkin Publishing Group, *Encyclopedic Dictionary of Sociology* (4th ed.). Guilford, Conn.: Dushkin, p. 274.

——— and Robert March Kloss. 1974. *Social Movements: Between the Balcony and the Barricade.* St. Louis: Mosby.

Robertson, Nan. 1988. "The Changing World of Alcoholics Anonymous," *New York Times Magazine* (February 21), pp. 40, 42–44, 47, 57, 92.

Robertson, Roland. 1988. "The Sociological Significance of Culture: Some General Considerations," *Theory, Culture, and Society,* 5(February):3–23.

Robinson, John P. 1988. "Who's Doing the Housework?" *American Demographics,* 10(December):24–28, 63.

Robinson, Tracey. 1989. "African Heritage Pulses in Brazil's Salvador de Bahia," *Chicago Sun-Times* (April 23), p. D3.

Rock, Andrea. 1990. "Can You Afford Your Kids?" *Money,* 19(July):88–93, 95, 97–99.

Roddick, Jackie. 1988. *The Dance of the Millions: Latin America and the Debt Crisis.* London: Latin America Bureau, Monthly Review Press.

Rodgers, Harrell R., Jr. 1987. *Poor Women, Poor Families.* Armonk, N.Y.: Sharpe.

——— and Michael Harrington. 1981. *Unfinished Democracy: The American Political System.* Glenview, Ill.: Scott, Foresman.

Roethlisberger, Fritz J., and W. J. Dickson. 1939. *Management and the Worker.* Cambridge, Mass.: Harvard University Press.

Rogan, Arleen. 1978. "The Threat of Sociobiology," *Quest,* 4(Summer):85–93.

Rohlen, Thomas P. 1983. *Japan's High Schools.* Berkeley: University of California Press.

Rohter, Larry. 1987. "Women Gain Degrees, but Not Tenure," *New York Times* (January 4), p. E9.

———. 1991. "Are Women Directors

An Endangered Species?" *New York Times* (March 17), pp. H13, H20-H21.

Rokeach, Milton. 1973. *The Nature of Human Values.* New York: Free Press.

Rollins, Judith. 1985. *Between Women: Domestics and Their Employers.* Philadelphia: Temple University Press.

Roman, Monica. 1990. "Women, Beware: An MBA Doesn't Mean Equal Pay," *Business Week* (October 29), p. 57.

Roof, Wade Clark. 1976. "Traditional Religion in Contemporary Society: A Theory of Local-Cosmopolitan Plausibility," *American Sociological Review,* **41**(April):195-208.

———. 1978. *Commitment and Community: Religious Plausibility in a Liberal Protestant Church.* New York: Elsevier.

Rosaldo, Renato. 1985. "Chicano Studies, 1970-1984," in Bernard J. Seigal (ed.), *Annual Review of Anthropology, 1985.* Palo Alto, Calif.: Annual Reviews, pp. 405-427.

Rosario, Ruben, and Tony Marcano. 1989. "A Killer Is Freed," *New York Daily News* (April 1), p. 2.

Rose, Arnold. 1951. *The Roots of Prejudice.* Paris: UNESCO.

Rose, Peter I. (ed.). 1979. *Socialization and the Life Cycle.* New York: St. Martin's.

———, Myron Glazer, and Penina Migcal Glazer. 1979. "In Controlled Environments: Four Cases of Intense Resocialization," in Peter I. Rose (ed.), *Socialization and the Life Cycle.* New York: St. Martin's, pp. 320-338.

Rosecrance, John. 1986. "Why Regular Gamblers Don't Quit: A Sociological Perspective," *Sociological Perspectives,* **29**(July):357-378.

———. 1987. Correspondence, May 1.

Rosenberg, Douglas H. 1991. "Capitalism," in Dushkin Publishing Group, *Encyclopedic Dictionary of Sociology* (4th ed.). Guilford, Conn.: Dushkin, pp. 33-34.

Rosener, Judy. 1990. "Ways Women Lead," *Harvard Business Review,* **60**(November-December):119-125.

Rosenfeld, Anne, and Elizabeth Stark. 1987. "The Prime of Our Lives," *Psychology Today,* **21**(May):62-64, 66, 68-72.

Rosenhan, David L. 1973. "On Being

Sane in Insane Places," *Science,* **179**(January 19):250-258.

Rosenthal, R. 1987. "Homelessness in Paradise: A Map of the Terrain." Unpublished doctoral dissertation, University of California, Santa Barbara.

Rosenthal, Robert, and Elisha Y. Babad. 1985. "Pygmalion in the Gymnasium," *Educational Leadership,* **45**(September):36-39.

——— and Lenore Jacobson. 1968. *Pygmalion in the Classroom.* New York: Holt.

Rossi, Alice S. 1968. "Transition to Parenthood," *Journal of Marriage and the Family,* **30**(February):26-39.

———. 1973. *The Feminist Papers: From Adams to de Beauvoir.* New York: Bantam.

———. 1984. "Gender and Parenthood," *American Sociological Review,* **49**(February):1-19.

Rossi, Peter H. 1955. *Why Families Move.* New York: Free Press.

———. 1987. "No Good Applied Social Research Goes Unpunished," *Society,* **25**(November-December):73-79.

———. 1989. *Down and Out in America: The Origins of Homelessness.* Chicago: University of Chicago Press.

———. 1990. "The Politics of Homelessness." Paper presented at the annual meeting of the American Sociological Association, Washington, D.C.

Rossides, Daniel W. 1990. *Social Stratification: The American Class System in Comparative Perspective.* Englewood Cliffs, N.J.: Prentice-Hall.

Roszak, Theodore. 1969. *The Making of a Counterculture.* Garden City, N.Y.: Doubleday.

Roth, Arthur. 1960. *The Teen-age Years: A Medical Guide for Young People and Their Parents.* Garden City, N.Y.: Doubleday.

Roth, Wendy Carol. 1989. "Let Us Work!" *Parade* (September 17), p. 16.

Rothenberg, Paula S. 1988. *Racism and Sexism: An Integrated Study.* New York: St. Martin's.

Rothman, David. 1971. *The Discovery of the Asylum.* Boston: Little, Brown.

Rothman, Robert. 1986. "Democrats in Congress Open New Push for Child Care Aid," *Congressional Quarterly,* **44**(January 11):63-65, 67.

Rothmyer, Karen. 1984. "Mapping Out Moon's Media Empire," *Columbia Journalism Review,* **23**(November-December):23-31.

Rothschild-Whitt, Joyce. 1979. "The Collectivist Organization: An Alternative to Rational-Bureaucratic Models," *American Sociological Review,* **44**(August):509-527.

Roudi, Nancy. 1991. "Addenda: Populandia Patter," *Population Today,* **19**(January):10.

Rousseau, Ann Marie. 1981. *Shopping Bag Ladies: Homeless Women Speak about Their Lives.* New York: Pilgrim.

Rovner, Julie. 1986. "Anti-Smoking Forces Stoke Legislative Fires," *Congressional Quarterly Weekly,* **44**(December 13):3049-3054.

———. 1990. "Congress Wraps Up Decision on Child-Care Legislation," *Congressional Quarterly Weekly Report,* **48**(October 27):3605-3606.

Rowland, Robyn. 1985. "A Child at Any Price? An Overview of Issues in the Use of the New Reproductive Technologies, and the Threat to Women," *Women's Studies International Forum,* **8**(6):539-546.

Roy, Donald F. 1959. " 'Banana Time': Job Satisfaction and Informal Interaction," *Human Organization,* **18**(Winter, 1959-1960):158-168.

Rubin, Zick. 1970. "Measurement of Romantic Love," *Journal of Personality and Social Psychology,* **16**(February):265-273.

Rudolph, Barbara. 1989. "Fuming over a Hazardous Export," *Time,* **134**(October 2):82.

Rugh, Andrea B. 1984. *Family in Contemporary Egypt.* Syracuse, N.Y.: Syracuse University Press.

Russell, Cheryl. 1984. "The Business of Demographics," *Population Bulletin,* **39**(June).

Ruzek, Sheryl Burt. 1978. *Women's Health Movement: Feminist Alternatives to Medical Control.* New York: Praeger.

Ryan, William. 1976. *Blaming the Victim* (rev. ed.). New York: Random House.

Ryd, Lillian. 1982. "Inequality Reported in Swedish Education." AP wire service report in *Macomb Daily Journal,* February 12.

Saarinen, Thomas F. 1988. "Centering of Mental Maps of the World," *National Geographic Research,* **4**(Winter):112–127.

Sadker, Myra, and David Sadker. 1985. "Sexism in the Schoolroom of the '80s," *Psychology Today,* **19**(March):54–57.

Saetre, Sara. 1989. "Comparable Worth," *Utne Reader,* **31**(January–February):14–15.

Safa, Helen I. 1983. "Women, Production, and Reproduction in Industrial Capitalism: A Comparison of Brazilian and U.S. Factory Workers," in Maria Patricia Fernández-Kelly (ed.), *Women, Men and the International Division of Labor.* Albany: State University of New York Press, pp. 95–116.

Safire, William. 1985. "On Sutton and Hutton," *New York Times* (May 9), p. A31.

Sagarin, Edward, and Jose Sanchez. 1988. "Ideology and Deviance: The Case of the Debate over the Biological Factor," *Deviant Behavior,* **9**(1):87–99.

Salem, Richard, and Stanislaus Grabarek. 1986. "Sociology B.A.s in a Corporate Setting: How Can They Get There and of What Value Are They," *Teaching Sociology,* **14**(October):273–275.

Salholz, Eloise. 1990. "Teenagers and Abortion," *Newsweek,* **115**(January 8):32–33, 36.

Salmon, J. Warren (ed.). 1984. *Alternative Medicines: Popular and Policy Perspectives.* New York: Tavistock.

Saltzman, Amy. 1988. "Hands Off at the Office," *U.S. News and World Report,* **105**(August 1):56–58.

Saluter, Arlene F. 1989. "Singleness in America," in *Current Population Reports,* ser. P-23, no. 162. Washington, D.C.: U.S. Government Printing Office, pp. 1–12.

Salvatore, Diane. 1986. "Babies for Sale," *Ladies Home Journal,* **103**(July):54, 56, 60, 64, 136.

Sampson, Anthony. 1973. *The Sovereign State of ITT.* New York: Stein and Day.

Sampson, Robert J. 1986. "Effects of Socioeconomic Context on Official Reaction to Juvenile Delinquency," *American Sociological Review,* **51**(December):876–885.

Samuelson, Paul A., and William D. Nordhaus. 1989. *Economics* (13th ed.). New York: McGraw-Hill.

Sanders, Clinton R. 1989. *Customizing the Body: The Art and Culture of Tattooing.* Philadelphia: Temple University Press.

Sandler, Bernice R. 1986. *The Campus Climate Revisited: Chilly for Women Faculty, Administrators, and Graduate Students.* Washington, D.C.: Association of American Colleges.

Sapir, Edward. 1929. "The Status of Linguistics as a Science," *Language,* **5**(4):207–214.

Sardar, Ziauddin, and Dawud G. Rosser-Owen. 1977. "Science Policy and Developing Countries," in Ina Spiegel-Rösing and Derek de Solla Price (eds.), *Science, Technology, and Society: A Cross-Disciplinary Perspective.* London: Sage, pp. 535–575.

Sarti, Cynthia. 1989. "The Panorama of Feminism in Brazil," *New Left Review,* **173**(January–February):75–90.

Schaefer, Richard T. 1976. *The Extent and Content of Race Prejudice in Great Britain.* San Francisco: R and E Research Association.

——. 1990. *Racial and Ethnic Groups* (4th ed.). Glenview, Ill.: Scott, Foresman.

—— and Robert P. Lamm (eds.). 1987. *Introducing Sociology.* New York: McGraw-Hill.

—— and Sandra L. Schaefer. 1975. "Reluctant Welcome: U.S. Responses to the South Vietnamese Refugees," *New Community,* **4**(Autumn):366–370.

Scheff, Thomas J. 1975a. *Labeling Madness.* Englewood Cliffs, N.J.: Prentice-Hall.

——. 1975b. "Reply to Chauncey and Gove," *American Sociological Review,* **40**(April):252–257.

Schlenker, Barry R. (ed.). 1985. *The Self and Social Life.* New York: McGraw-Hill.

Schlesinger, Yaffa. 1977. "Sex Roles and Social Change in the Kibbutz," *Journal of Marriage and the Family,* **39**(November):771–779.

Schmeisser, Peter. 1988. "Pushing Cigarettes Overseas," *New York Times Magazine* (July 10), pp. 16, 18–22, 62.

Schmid, Carol. 1980. "Sexual Antagonism: Roots of the Sex-Ordered Division of Labor," *Humanity and Society,* **4**(November):243–261.

Schmidt, William E. 1990. "New Vim and Vigor for the Y.M.C.A.," *New York Times* (July 18), pp. C1, C10.

Schmink, Marianne, and Charles Wood (eds.). 1989. *Frontier Expansion in Amazonia.* Gainesville: University of Florida Press.

Schneider, John J., and D. Stanley Eitzen. 1986. "Racial Segregation by Professional Football Positions: 1960–1985," *Sociology and Social Research,* **70**(July):259–262.

Schopflin, George. 1990. "Eastern European Affairs," in *1990 Britannica Book of the Year.* Chicago: Encyclopaedia Britannica, p. 484.

Schramm, Wilbur, Lyle M. Nelson, and Mere T. Betham. 1981. *Bold Experiment: The Story of Educational Television in American Samoa.* Stanford, Calif.: Stanford University Press.

Schuerman, John R. 1989. "Editorial," *Social Service Review,* **63**(March):1–4.

Schultz, Terri. 1977. "Though Legal, Abortions Are Not Always Available," *New York Times* (January 1), p. E8.

Schur, Edwin M. 1965. *Crimes without Victims: Deviant Behavior and Public Policy.* Englewood Cliffs, N.J.: Prentice-Hall.

——. 1968. *Law and Society: A Sociological View.* New York: Random House.

——. 1983. *Labeling Women Deviant: Gender, Stigma, and Social Control.* Philadelphia: Temple University Press.

——. 1985. "'Crimes without Victims': A 20 Year Reassessment." Paper presented at the annual meeting of the Society for the Study of Social Problems.

Schwartz, Howard D. (ed.). 1987. *Dominant Issues in Medical Sociology* (2d ed.). New York: Random House.

Scimecca, Joseph A. 1980. *Education and Society.* New York: Holt.

Scotch, Richard K. 1984. *From Good Will to Civil Rights: Transforming Federal Disability Policy.* Philadelphia: Temple University Press.

——. 1988. "Disability as the Basis for a Social Movement: Advocacy and the

Politics of Definition," *Journal of Social Issues,* **44**(1):159–172.

Scott, Hilda. 1985. *Working Your Way to the Bottom: The Feminization of Poverty.* London: Routledge.

Scott, Robert A. 1969. *The Making of Blind Men: A Study of Adult Socialization.* New York: Russell Sage.

Scott-Samuel, Alex, and Paul Blackburn. 1988. "Crossing the Health Divide—Mortality Attributable to Social Inequality in Great Britain," *Health Promotion,* **2**(3):243–245.

Scull, Andrew. 1977. *Decarceration, Community Treatment and the Deviant: A Radical View.* Englewood Cliffs, N.J.: Prentice-Hall.

Seckman, Mark A., and Carl J. Couch. 1989. "Jocularity, Sarcasm, and Relationships: An Empirical Study," *Journal of Contemporary Ethnography,* **18**(October):327–344.

Seddon, Terri. 1987. "Politics and Curriculum: A Case Study of the Japanese History Textbook Dispute, 1982," *British Journal of Sociology of Education,* **8**(2):213–226.

Segal, Aaron. 1982. "Kenya," in Carol L. Thompson, Mary M. Anderberg, and Joan B. Antell (eds.), *The Current History of Developing Nations.* New York: McGraw-Hill, pp. 45–49.

Selbyg, Arne. 1984. Correspondence with the author, July 31.

Selowsky, Marcelo, and Herman G. Van Der Tak. 1986. "The Debt Problem and Growth," *World Development,* **14**(9):1107–1124.

Senter, Richard, Terry Miller, Larry T. Reynolds, and Tim Shaffer. 1983. "Bureaucratization and Goal Succession in Alternative Organizations," *Sociological Focus,* **16**(October):239–253.

Shaheen, Jack G. 1984. "Arabs—TV's Villains of Choice," *Channels of Communication,* **3**(March–April):52–53.

———. 1988. "The Media's Image of Arabs," *Newsweek,* **111**(February 29):10.

Shanas, Ethel. 1982. "The Family Relations of Old People," *National Forum,* **4**(Fall):9–11.

Shapiro, Harry L. 1936. *The Heritage of the Bounty.* New York: Simon and Schuster.

Shapiro, Michael. 1986. "A Place in the Sun, on Japanese Terms," *New York Times* (June 18), pp. D27–D28.

———. 1987. "A Japanese Hero Doing Things His Way," *New York Times* (February 11), pp. D27–D29.

Sharpe, Rochelle. 1985. "Anti-Abortionists Go Activist," *USA Today* (December 2), p. 5A.

Shaw, Marvin E. 1981. *Group Dynamics: The Psychology of Small Group Behavior* (3d ed.). New York: McGraw-Hill.

Shaw, Susan. 1988. "Gender Differences in the Definition and Perception of Household Labor," *Family Relations,* **37**(July):333–337.

Sheehy, Gail. 1976. *Passages: Predictable Crises of Adult Life.* New York: Dutton.

———. 1981. *Pathfinders.* Toronto: Bantam.

Shell, Ellen Rippel. 1988. "Babies in Day Care," *Atlantic,* **262**(August):73–74.

Shelley, Louise I. 1980. "The Geography of Soviet Criminality," *American Sociological Review,* **45**(February):111–122.

———. 1985. "Soviet Justice," *Problems of Communism,* **34**(July–August):69–73.

———. 1987. "Inter-Personal Violence in the U.S.S.R.," *Violence, Aggression and Terrorism,* **1**(2):41–67.

Sherman, Arnold K., and Aliza Kolker. 1987. *The Social Bases of Politics.* Belmont, Calif.: Wadsworth.

Sherman, Lawrence W., and Richard A. Berk. 1984. "The Specific Deterrent Effects of Arrest for Domestic Assault," *American Sociological Review,* **49**(April):261–272.

Shilts, Randy. 1987. *And the Band Played On: Politics, People, and the AIDS Epidemic.* New York: St. Martin's.

———. 1989. "The Era of Bad Feelings," *Mother Jones,* **14**(November):32–36, 58–60.

Shipler, David K. 1983. *Russia: Broken Idols, Solemn Dreams.* New York: Times Books.

Shipp, E. R. 1991. "Scandals Emptied Pews of Electronic Churches," *New York Times* (March 3), p. 24.

Shover, Neal. 1971. "Burglary as an Occupation." Ph.D. dissertation, University of Illinois at Urbana-Champaign.

———. 1973. "The Social Organization of Burglary," *Social Problems,* **20**(Spring):499–514.

Shupe, Anson D., and David G. Bromley. 1980. "Walking a Tightrope," *Qualitative Sociology,* **2**:8–21.

——— and ———. 1985. "Social Response to Cults," in Phillip E. Hammond (ed.), *The Sacred in a Secular Age.* Berkeley: University of California Press, pp. 58–72.

——— and Jeffrey K. Hadden (eds.). 1988. *The Politics of Religion and Social Change.* New York: Paragon.

Sidel, Ruth, and Victor Sidel. 1984. "Toward the Twenty-First Century," in V. Sidel and R. Sidel (eds.), *Reforming Medicine.* New York: Pantheon, pp. 267–284.

Sidel, Victor, and Ruth Sidel (eds.). 1984. *Reforming Medicine.* New York: Pantheon.

Sigmund, Paul E. 1990. *Liberation Theology at the Crossroads: Democracy or Revolution?* New York: Oxford University Press.

Silberman, Charles E. 1978. *Criminal Violence, Criminal Justice.* New York: Random House.

Sills, David L. 1957. *The Volunteers: Means and Ends in a National Organization.* Glencoe, Ill.: Free Press.

———. 1968a. "Voluntary Associations: Sociological Aspects," in D. L. Sills (ed.), *International Encyclopedia of the Social Sciences,* vol. 16. New York: Macmillan, pp. 362–379.

——— (ed.). 1968b. *International Encyclopedia of the Social Sciences.* New York: Macmillan.

Silva, Nelson De Valle. 1985. "Updating the Cost of Not Being White in Brazil," in Pierre-Michel Fontaine (ed.), *Race, Class, and Power in Brazil.* Los Angeles: Center for Afro-American Studies, University of California at Los Angeles, pp. 42–55.

Silverstein, Ken. 1990. "Shock Treatment for the Poor," *The Nation,* **251**(November 12):554–557.

Simmel, Georg. 1950. *Sociology of Georg Simmel.* Translated by K. Wolff. Glencoe, Ill.: Free Press (originally written in 1902–1917).

Simon, Carl P., and Ann P. Witte. 1982. *Beating the System: The Undergrad Economy.* Boston, Mass.: Auburn House.

Simon, Julian, and Paul Burstein. 1985. *Basic Research Methods in Social Sciences* (3d ed.). New York: Random House.

Simons, Marlise. 1988. "Brazil's Blacks Feel Prejudice 100 Years after Slavery's End," *New York Times* (May 14), pp. 1, 6.

———. 1989. "Abortion Fight Has New Front in Western Europe," *New York Times* (June 28), pp. A1, A9.

Simpson, George Eaton, and J. Milton Yinger. 1985. *Racial and Cultural Minorities: An Analysis of Prejudice and Discrimination* (5th ed.). New York: Plenum.

Sirott, Larry, and Howard Waitzkin. 1984. "Holism and Self-Care: Can the Individual Succeed Where Society Fails?" in V. Sidel and R. Sidel (eds.), *Reforming Medicine*. New York: Pantheon, pp. 245–264.

Sizer, Theodore R. 1984. *Horace's Compromise: The Dilemma of the American High School*. Boston: Houghton Mifflin.

Sjoberg, Gideon. 1960. *The Preindustrial City: Past and Present*. Glencoe, Ill.: Free Press.

Skafte, Peter. 1979. "Smoking Out Secrets of the Mysterious 'Snakers' of India," *Smithsonian*, 10(October):121–126.

Skocpol, Theda. 1979. *States and Social Revolutions*. Cambridge, Eng.: Cambridge University Press.

Skogan, Wesley G. 1981. *Issues in the Measurement of Victimization*. U.S. Department of Justice. Washington, D.C.: U.S. Government Printing Office.

Skolnick, Jerome H., and Elliott Currie (eds.). 1988. *Crisis in American Institutions* (7th ed.). Glenview, Ill.: Scott, Foresman.

Slater, Philip E. 1958. "Contrasting Correlates of Group Size," *Sociometry*, 21(June): 29–139.

Smelser, Neil. 1962. *Theory of Collective Behavior*. New York: Free Press.

———. 1963. *The Sociology of Economic Life*. Englewood Cliffs, N.J.: Prentice-Hall.

———. 1981. *Sociology*. Englewood Cliffs, N.J.: Prentice-Hall.

——— (ed.). 1988. *Handbook of Sociology*. Newbury Park, Calif.: Sage.

Smith, Donald H. 1980. *Admission and Retention Problems of Black Students at Seven Predominantly White Universities*. Washington, D.C.: U.S. Government Printing Office.

———. 1981. "Social and Academic Environments of Black Students on White Campuses," *Journal of Negro Education*, 50(Summer):299–306.

Smith, James P. 1986. *The Distribution of Wealth*. Ann Arbor, Mich.: Survey Research Center.

Smith, Michael Peter. 1988. *City, State, and Market*. New York: Basil Blackwell.

Smith Richard T. 1980. "Societal Reaction and Physical Disability: Contrasting Perspectives," in Walter R. Gove (ed.), *The Labelling of Deviance*. Beverly Hills, Calif.: Sage, pp. 227–236.

Smith, Wes. 1989. "Sushi Meets Steak," *Chicago Tribune* (January 18), sec. 2, pp. 1–2.

Smolan, Rick, Phillip Moffitt, and Matthew Naythons (eds.). 1990. *The Power to Heal: Ancient Arts and Modern Medicine*. New York: Prentice-Hall.

Snarey, John. 1985. "Cross-Cultural University of Social-Moral Development: A Critical Review of Kohlbergian Research," *Psychological Bulletin*, 97(March):202–232.

———. 1987. "A Question of Morality," *Psychology Today*, 21(June):6, 8.

Snow, David A., Susan G. Baker, Leon Anderson, and Michael Martin. 1986. "The Myth of Pervasive Mental Illness among the Homeless," *Social Problems*, 33(June):407–423.

———, Louis A. Zurcher, Jr., and Robert Peters. 1981. "Victory Celebrations as Theater: A Dramaturgical Approach to Crowd Behavior," *Symbolic Interaction*, 4:21–42.

Snyder, Eldon E., and Elmer A. Spreitzer. 1983. *Social Aspects of Sport* (2d ed.). Englewood Cliffs, N.J.: Prentice-Hall.

Soldo, Beth J., and Emily M. Agree. 1988. *America's Elderly*. Washington, D.C.: Population Reference Bureau.

Solomon, Peter H., Jr. 1987a. "The Case of the Vanishing Acquittal: Informal Norms and the Practice of Soviet Criminal Justice," *Working Paper No. 28*. Champaign, Ill.: Soviet Interview Project.

———. 1987b. "Soviet Politicians and Criminal Prosecutions: The Logic of Party Intervention," *Working Paper No. 33*. Champaign, Ill.: Soviet Interview Project.

Solórzano, Lucia. 1986. "Teaching in Trouble," *U.S. News and World Report*, 100(May 26):52–57.

Son, In Soo, Suzanne W. Model, and Gene A. Fisher. 1989. "Polarization and Progress in the Black Community: Earnings and Status Gains for Young Black Males in the Era of Affirmative Action," *Sociological Forum*, 4(September):309–327.

Sorokin, Pitirim A. 1959. *Social and Cultural Mobility*. New York: Free Press (original edition 1927, New York: Harper and Brothers).

Sorrel, Lorraine, and Susan Sojourner. 1982. "With the Wisdom of the Owl: An Interview with Tish Sommers," *Off Our Backs*, 12(January):6–7.

Sorrentino, Constance. 1990. "The Changing Family in International Perspective," *Monthly Labor Review*, 113(March):41–56.

Spain, Daphne, and Steven Nock. 1984. "Two-Career Couples, a Portrait," *American Demographics*, 6(August):25–27, 45.

Spanier, Graham B. 1983. "Married and Unmarried Cohabitation in the United States 1980," *Journal of Marriage and the Family*, 45(May):277–288.

——— and Elaine A. Anderson. 1979. "The Impact of the Legal System on Adjustment to Marital Separation," *Journal of Marriage and the Family*, 41(August):605–613.

——— and Frank F. Furstenberg, Jr. 1987. "Remarriage and Reconstituted Families," in Marvin B. Sussman and Suzanne K. Steinmetz (eds.), *Handbook of Marriage and Family*. New York: Plenum, pp. 419–434.

Spector, Michael. 1989. "Searching for the Best Medical Care Money Can't Buy," *Washington Post National Weekly Edition*, 7(December 25):31–32.

———. 1990. "The National Health Care Crisis," *Washington Post National Weekly Edition*, 7(June 18–24), p. 6.

Spence, J. T., and R. L. Helmrich. 1978. *The Psychological Dimensions of Masculinity and Femininity: Their Correlates and Antecedents.* Austin: University of Texas Press.

Spencer, Gregory. 1989. *Projections of the Population of the United States, by Age, Sex, and Race: 1988 to 2080.* Current Population Reports, ser. P-25, no. 1018. Washington, D.C.: U.S. Government Printing Office.

Spengler, Joseph J. 1978. *Facing Zero Population Growth: Reactions and Interpretations, Past and Present.* Durham, N.C.: Duke University Press.

Spiro, Melford, 1954. "Is the Family Universal?" *American Anthropologist,* **56**(October):839–846. Reprinted with addendum in Normal W. Bell and Ezra F. Vogel (eds.), *A Modern Introduction to the Family* (2d ed.). New York: Free Press, 1968, pp. 68–79.

Spradley, James P. 1970. *You Owe Yourself a Drunk: An Ethnography of Urban Nomads.* Boston: Little, Brown.

———— and David W. McCurdy. 1980. *Anthropology: The Cultural Perspective* (2d ed.). New York: Wiley.

Squire, Peverill. 1988. "Why the 1936 *Literary Digest* Poll Failed," *Public Opinion Quarterly,* **52**(Spring):125–133.

Stacey, Julie. 1987. "Who Pays Health-Care Costs," *USA Today* (July 1), p. 1B.

Stack, Steven. 1987. "Celebrities and Suicide: A Taxonomy and Analysis, 1948–1983," *American Sociological Review,* **52**(June):401–412.

Staggenborg, Suzanne. 1986. "Coalition Work in the Pro-Choice Movement: Organizational and Environmental Opportunities and Obstacles," *Social Problems,* **33**(June):374–390.

————. 1988. "Consequences of Professionalization and Formalization," *American Sociological Review,* **53**(August):585–606.

————. 1989a. "Stability and Innovation in the Women's Movement: A Comparison of Two Movement Organizations," *Social Problems,* **36**(February):75–92.

————. 1989b. "Organizational and Environmental Influences on the Development of the Pro-Choice

Movement," *Social Forces,* **68**(September):204–240.

Stahura, John M. 1986. "Suburban Development, Black Suburbanization and the Civil Rights Movement since World War II," *American Sociological Review,* **51**(February):131–144.

————. 1987. "Characteristics of Black Suburbs, 1950–1980," *Sociology and Social Research,* **71**(January):135–138.

Staples, Robert E. 1976. *Introduction to Black Sociology.* New York: McGraw-Hill.

Stark, Rodney, et al. 1973. *Society Today* (2d ed.). Del Mar, Calif.: CRM Books.

———— and William Sims Bainbridge. 1979. "Of Churches, Sects, and Cults: Preliminary Concepts for a Theory of Religious Movements," *Journal for the Scientific Study of Religion,* **18**(June):117–131.

————. 1985. *The Future of Religion.* Berkeley: University of California Press.

Starkweather, David B. 1981. "U.S. Hospitals: Corporate Concentration vs. Local Community Control," *Public Affairs Report,* **22**(April):1–8.

Starr, Paul. 1982. *The Social Transformation of American Medicine.* New York: Basic Books.

Statham, Ann. 1987. "The Gender Model Revisited: Differences in the Management Styles of Men and Women," *Sex Roles,* **16**(April):409–429.

————, Eleanor M. Miller, and Hans O. Mauksch (eds.). 1988. *The Worth of Women's Work.* Albany: State University of New York Press.

Steiber, Steven R. 1979. "The World System and World Trade: An Empirical Exploration of Conceptual Conflicts," *Sociological Quarterly,* **20**(Winter):23–36.

Stein, Leonard. 1967. "The Doctor-Nurse Game," *Archives of General Psychiatry,* **16**:699–703.

Stein, Peter J. 1975. "Singlehood: An Alternative to Marriage," *Family Coordinator,* **24**(October):489–503.

———— (ed.). 1981. *Single Life: Unmarried Adults in Social Context.* New York: St. Martin's.

————. 1984. "Men in Families," *Marriage and Family Review,* **7**(Fall–Winter):143–168.

Steinbacher, Roberta. 1981. "Futuristic Implications of Sex Preselection," in H. Holmes, B. Hoskins, and M. Gross (eds.), *The Custom-Made Child? Woman-Centered Perspectives.* Clifton, N.J.: Humana Press, pp. 187–191.

Steinberg, Stephen. 1989. *The Ethnic Myth: Race, Ethnicity, and Class in America* (new ed.). Boston: Beacon.

Steinzor, Bernard. 1950. "The Spatial Factor in Face-to-Face Discussion Groups," *Journal of Abnormal and Social Psychology,* **45**(July):552–555.

Stellman, Jeanne Mager, and Joan E. Berten. 1990. "Science's Anti-Female Bias," *New York Times* (June 4), p. A23.

Stenning, Derrick J. 1958. "Household Viability among the Pastoral Fulani," in John R. Goody (ed.), *The Developmental Cycle in Domestic Groups.* Cambridge, Eng.: Cambridge University Press, pp. 92–119.

Stets, Jan E., and Maureen A. Pirog-Good. 1987. "Violence in Dating Relationships," *Social Psychology Quarterly,* **50**(September):237–246.

Stevens, Evelyn P. 1973. "Machismo and Marianismo," *Society,* **10**(September–October):57–63.

Stevens, William K. 1987a. "Reagan Insurance Plan Appears Helpful to Few," *New York Times* (March 8), p. 24.

————. 1987b. "Despite Defeats, Fundamentalists Vow to Press Efforts to Reshape Schools," *New York Times* (August 29), p. 6.

————. 1987c. "Beyond the Mall: Suburbs Evolving into 'Outer Cities,'" *New York Times* (November 8), p. E5.

Stimpson, Catharine. 1971. "Thy Neighbor's Wife, Thy Neighbor's Servants; Women's Liberation and Black Civil Rights," in Vivian Gornick and Barbara K. Moran (eds.), *Woman in Sexist Society.* New York: Basic Books, pp. 622–657.

Stocks, J. Timothy. 1988. "Has Family Violence Decreased? A Reassessment of the Straus and Gelles Data," *Journal of Marriage and the Family,* **50**(February):281–285.

Stoeckel, John, and N. L. Sirisena. 1988. "Gender-Specific Socioeconomic Impacts of Development Programs in Sri

Lanka," *Journal of Developing Areas*, **23**(October):31–42.

Stoltz, Barbara Ann. 1984. "Interest Groups and Criminal Law: The Case of Federal Criminal Code Revision," *Crime and Delinquency*, **30**(January):91–106.

Stone, Gregory P. 1977. "Personal Acts," *Symbolic Interaction*, **1**(Fall):1–21.

Strasser, Steven, et al. 1981. "A Survival Summit," *Newsweek*, **98**(October 26):36–44.

Straus, Murray, A., and Richard J. Gelles (eds.). 1990. *Physical Violence in American Families*. New Brunswick, N.J.: Transaction.

Straus, Roger (ed.). 1985. *Using Sociology*. Bayside, N.Y.: General Hall.

Strauss, Anselm. 1977. *Negotiations: Varieties, Contexts, Processes, and Social Order*. San Francisco: Jossey-Bass.

———. 1985. "Work and the Division of Labor," *Sociological Quarterly*, **26**(Spring):1–19.

———. 1987. "Health Policy and Chronic Illness," *Society*, **25**(November–December):33–39.

Strodtbeck, Fred L., and H. L. Hook. 1961. "The Social Dimensions of a Twelve Man Jury Table," *Sociometry*, **24**(December):397–415.

Stuart, Reginald. 1982. "Judge Overturns Arkansas Law on Creationism," *New York Times* (January 6), pp. A1, B7, B8.

Stump, Roger W. 1986. "Women Clergy in the United States: A Geographical Analysis of Religious Change," *Social Science Quarterly*, **67**(June):337–352.

Sudnow, David. 1967. *Passing On: The Social Organization of Dying*. Englewood Cliffs, N.J.: Prentice-Hall.

Sullivan, Joseph F. 1990. "New Jersey Ruling to Lift School Aid for Poor Districts," *New York Times* (June 6), pp. A1, B4.

Sumner, William G. 1906. *Folkways*. New York: Ginn.

Suro, Roberto. 1989. "1986 Amnesty Law Is Seen as Failing to Slow Alien Tide," *New York Times* (June 18), pp. 1, 16.

———. 1990a. "Courts Ordering Financing Changes in Public Schools," *New York Times* (March 11), pp. 1, 28.

———. 1990b. "Traffic in Fake Documents Is Blamed as Illegal Immigration Rises Anew," *New York Times* (November 26), p. A14.

Sussman, Marvin B., and Suzanne K. Steinmetz (eds.). 1982. *Handbook of Marriage and Family*. New York: Plenum.

Sutherland, Edwin H. 1937. *The Professional Thief*. Chicago: University of Chicago Press.

———. 1940. "White-Collar Criminality," *American Sociological Review*, **5**(February):1–11.

———. 1949. *White Collar Crime*. New York: Dryden.

———. 1983. *White Collar Crime: The Uncut Version*. New Haven, Conn.: Yale University Press.

——— and Donald R. Cressey. 1978. *Principles of Criminology* (10th ed.). Philadelphia: Lippincott.

Suttles, Gerald D. 1968. *The Social Order of the Slum*. Chicago: University of Chicago Press.

———. 1972. *The Social Construction of Communities*. Chicago: University of Chicago Press.

Swartz, Leslie. 1985. "Anorexia Nervosa as a Culture-Bound Syndrome," *Social Science and Medicine*, **20**(7):275–730.

Sweeney, Joan. 1983. "Divorce—New Family Form Grows," *Los Angeles Times* (February 27), pp. 1, 3, 22–23.

Sweet, Ellen. 1982. "Tish Sommers: Organize—Don't Agonize," *Ms.*, **10**(January):61, 80.

Sweet, James A., and Larry L. Bumpass. 1987. *American Families and Households*. New York: Russell Sage.

Swinton, David. 1987. "Economic Status of Blacks, 1986," in Janet Dewart (ed.), *The State of Black America*. New York: National Urban League, pp. 49–73.

Sykes, Gresham, and David Matza. 1957. "Techniques of Neutralization: A Theory of Delinquency," *American Sociological Review*, **22**(December):664–670.

Szasz, Thomas. 1974. *The Myth of Mental Illness* (rev. ed.). New York: Harper and Row.

Szelenyi, I. 1983. *Urban Inequalities under State Socialism*. London: Oxford University Press.

Szulc, Tad. 1988. "How Can We Help Ourselves Age with Dignity?" *Parade* (May 29), pp. 4–7.

Szymanski, Albert. 1983. *Class Structure: A Critical Perspective*. New York: Praeger.

Tachibana, Judy. 1990. "Model Minority Myth Presents Unrepresentative Portrait of Asian Americans, Many Educators Say," *Black Issues in Higher Education*, **6**(March 1):1, 11.

Takaki, Ronald. 1989. *Strangers from a Different Shore: A History of Asian Americans*. Boston: Little, Brown.

———. 1990. "The Harmful Myth of Asian Superiority," *New York Times* (June 16), p. 21.

Taylor, Paul. 1985. "Uninsured? Find Another Hospital," *Washington Post National Weekly Edition*, **2**(July 22): 8–9.

———. 1990. "The Democrats Discover the Savings and Loan Scandal," *Washington Post National Weekly Edition*, **7**(June 4):13.

Taylor, Stuart, Jr. 1987a. "Court, 5-4, Rejects Racial Challenge to Death Penalty," *New York Times* (April 23), pp. A1, B13.

———. 1987b. "Ruling Foils Latest Strategy in Fighting Idea of Evolution," *New York Times* (June 20), pp. 1, 6.

———. 1987c. "High Court Voids Curb on Teaching Evolution Theory," *New York Times* (June 20), pp. 1, 7.

Tellegen, Auke, et al. [5 others]. 1988. "Personality Similarity in Twins Reared Apart and Together," *Journal of Personality and Social Psychology*, **54**(June):1031–1039.

Terkel, Studs. 1974. *Working*. New York: Random House.

Theroux, Paul. 1982. "Subway Odyssey," *New York Times Magazine* (January 31), pp. 20–23, 71, 74–76.

Thirlwall, A. P. 1989. *Growth and Development* (4th ed.). London: Macmillan.

Thoits, Peggy A. 1985. "Self-Labeling Processes in Mental Illness: The Role of Emotional Deviance," *American Journal of Sociology*, **91**(September):221–249.

Thomas, Gordon, and Max Morgan Witts. 1974. *Voyage of the Damned*. Greenwich, Conn.: Fawcett Crest.

Thomas, Jim. 1984. "Some Aspects of

REFERENCES

Negotiating Order: Loose Coupling and Mesostructure in Maximum Security Prisons," *Symbolic Interaction*, **7**(Fall):213–231.

Thomas, William I. 1923. *The Unadjusted Girl*. Boston: Little, Brown.

———. 1927. *The Polish Peasant in Europe and America*. New York: Knopf.

Thompson, Carol L., Mary M. Anderburg, and Joan B. Antell (eds.). 1982. *The Current History Encyclopedia of Developing Nations*. New York: McGraw-Hill.

Thompson, James D., and Robert W. Hawkes. 1962. "Disaster, Community Organization, and Administrative Process," in G. W. Baker and D. W. Chapman (eds.), *Man and Society in Disaster*. New York: Basic Books, pp. 268–300.

Thompson, Linda, and Alexis J. Walker. 1989. "Gender in Families: Women and Men in Marriage, Work, and Parenthood," *Journal of Marriage and the Family*, **51**(November):845–871.

Thornburgh, Richard. 1990. "The Soviet Union and the Rule of Law," *Foreign Affairs*, **69**(Spring):13–27.

Thorne, Barrie. 1987. "Re-Visioning Women and Social Change: Where Are the Children?" *Gender and Society*, **1**(March):85–109.

Thornton, Arland. 1985. "Changing Attitudes toward Separation and Divorce: Causes and Consequences," *American Journal of Sociology*, **90**(January):856–872.

———, Duane F. Alwin, and Donald Camburn. 1983. "Causes and Consequences of Sex-Role Attitudes and Attitude Change," *American Sociological Review*, **48**(April):211–227.

Thurow, Lester. 1984. "It's Not Just Demographics: The Disappearance of the Middle Class," *New York Times* (February 5), p. F3.

Tiano, Susan. 1987. "Gender, Work, and World Capitalism: Third World Women's Role in Development," in Beth B. Hess and Myra Marx Ferree (eds.), *Analyzing Gender: A Handbook of Social Science Research*. Newbury Park, Calif.: Sage, pp. 216–243.

Tiefer, Lenore. 1978. "The Kiss," *Human Nature*, **1**(July):28, 30–37.

Tien, H. Yuan. 1989. "Second Thoughts on the Second Child: A Talk with Peng Peryun," *Population Today*, **17**(April):6–8.

———. 1990. "China's Population Planning after Tiananmen," *Population Today*, **18**(September):6–8.

Tierney, John. 1990. "Betting the Planet," *New York Times Magazine* (December 2), pp. 52–53, 71, 74, 76, 78, 80–81.

Tierney, Kathleen. 1980. "Emergent Norm Theory as 'Theory': An Analysis and Critique of Turner's Formulation," in Meredith David Pugh (ed.), *Collective Behavior: A Source Book*. St. Paul, Minn.: West, pp. 42–53.

Tietjen, A., and L. Walker. 1984. "Moral Reasoning and Leadership among Men in a Papua, New Guinea Village." Unpublished manuscript, University of British Columbia, Vancouver, Can.

Tiger, Lionel, and Joseph Shepher. 1975. *Women in the Kibbutz*. New York: Harcourt Brace Jovanovich.

Time. 1971. "Suburbia: The New American Plurality," **97**(March 15):14–20.

Tinker, Irene (ed.). 1990. *Persistent Inequalities: Women and World Development*. New York: Oxford University Press.

Tipps, Havens C., and Henry A. Gordon. 1983. "Inequality at Work: Race, Sex, and Underemployment." Paper presented at the annual meeting of the American Sociological Association, Detroit.

Tittle, Charles R. 1989. "Influences on Urbanism: A Test of Predictions from Three Perspectives," *Social Problems*, **36**(June):270–288.

Tobin, Joseph J., David Y. H. Wu, and Dana H. Davidson. 1989. *Preschool in Three Cultures: Japan, China, and the United States*. New Haven, Conn.: Yale University Press.

Tocqueville, Alexis de. 1835. *Democracy in America*. New edition 1966, by J. P. Mayer and Max Lerner (eds.), New York: Harper and Row.

Tolchin, Martin. 1989. "Richest Got Richer and Poorest Poorer in 1979–87," *New York Times* (March 23), pp. A1, A24.

———. 1990a. "Paying for Long-Term Care: The Struggle for Lawmakers," *New York Times* (March 29), pp. A1, A20.

———. 1990b. "Other Countries Do Much More for Disabled," *New York Times* (March 29), p. A20.

Toner, Robin. 1987. "Schoolbooks Ruled Biased on Religion," *New York Times* (March 5), p. A12.

Tonkinson, Robert. 1978. *The Mardudjara Aborigines*. New York: Holt.

Tönnies, Ferdinand. 1988. *Community and Society*. Rutgers, N.J.: Transaction (originally published in 1887).

Torres-Gil, Fernando. 1990. "Seniors React to the Medicare Catastrophic Bill: Equity or Selfishness?" *Journal of Aging and Social Policy*, **2**(1):1–8.

Toufexis, Anastasia. 1986. "A Cloudy Forecast for Smokers," *Time*, **127**(April 7):47.

———. 1989. "Now for a Woman's Point of View," *Time*, **133**(April 17):51–52.

Touraine, Alain. 1971. *The Postindustrial Society: Tomorrow's Social History: Classes, Conflicts and Culture in the Programmed Society*. New York: Random House.

———. 1974. *The Academic System in American Society*. New York: McGraw-Hill.

Treadway, Molly. 1987. "Cite Unseen: Distortions of the Allport and Postman Rumor Study in the Eyewitness Testimony Literature," *Law and Human Behavior*, **11**(March):19–25.

Treesberg, Judith. 1991. "The Death of a 'Strong Deaf,'" *The Nation*, **252**(February 11):154, 156–158.

Treiman, Donald J. 1977. *Occupational Prestige in Comparative Perspective*. New York: Academic.

Treviño, Fernando M., et al. [5 authors]. 1991. "Health Insurance Coverage and Utilization of Health Services by Mexican Americans, Mainland Puerto Ricans, and Cuban Americans," *Journal of the American Medical Association*, **265**(January 9):233–237.

Trujillo, Nick. 1986. "Toward a Taxonomy of Small Group Interaction-Coding Systems," *Small Group Behavior*, **17**(November):371–394.

Tsui, Amy Ong, and Donald J. Bogue. 1978. "Declining World Fertility: Trends, Causes, Implications," *Population Bulletin*, **33**(October).

Tucker, Sharon. 1985. "Careers of Men and Women MBAs," *Work and Occupations,* **12**(May):166–185.

Tumin, Melvin M. 1953. "Some Principles of Stratification: A Critical Analysis," *American Sociological Review,* **18**(August):387–394.

———. 1985. *Social Stratification* (2d ed.). Englewood Cliffs, N.J.: Prentice-Hall.

Turk, Austin T. 1969. *Criminality and Legal Order.* Chicago: Rand McNally.

Turnbull, Colin. 1982. "Bali's New Gods," *Natural History,* **91**(January):26, 30, 32.

Turner, J. H. 1985. *Herbert Spencer: A Renewed Application.* Beverly Hills, Calif.: Sage.

Turner, Ralph H. 1962. "Role Taking: Process vs. Conformity," in Arnold Rose (ed.), *Human Behavior and Social Processes.* Boston: Houghton Mifflin, pp. 20–40.

———. 1964a. "Collective Behavior," in Robert E. L. Faris (ed.), *Handbook of Modern Sociology.* Chicago: Rand McNally, pp. 382–425.

———. 1964b. "New Theoretical Frameworks," *Sociological Quarterly,* **5**(Spring):122–132.

——— and Lewis M. Killian. 1987. *Collective Behavior* (3d ed.). Englewood Cliffs, N.J.: Prentice-Hall.

Turner, Wallace. 1987. "An Anti-Abortion PAC Falls on Difficult Times," *New York Times* (August 9), p. 25.

Twaddle, Andrew. 1974. "The Concept of Health Status," *Social Science and Medicine,* **8**(January):29–38.

——— and Richard M. Hessler. 1987. *A Sociology of Health* (2d ed.). New York: Macmillan.

Tyler, William B. 1985. "The Organizational Structure of the School," in Ralph H. Turner (ed.), *Annual Review of Sociology, 1985.* Palo Alto, Calif.: Annual Reviews, pp. 49–73.

Tyree, Andrea, Moshe Semyonov, and Robert W. Hodge. 1979. "Gaps and Glisandos: Inequality, Economic Development, and Social Mobility in 24 Countries," *American Sociological Review,* **44**(June):410–424.

Udy, Stanley H., Jr. 1959. "Bureaucracy and Rationality in Weber's Organizational Theory: An Empirical Study," *American Sociological Review,* **24**(December):791–795.

United Way of America. 1989. *What Lies Ahead: Countdown to the 21st Century.* Alexandria, Va.: United Way of America.

USA Today. 1991. "Business PACs Kept Dems in the Money" (May 3), p. 11A.

Vail, Elaine. 1982. *A Personal Guide to Living with Loss.* New York: Wiley.

Van den Berg, Ger P. 1985. *The Soviet System of Justice: Figures and Policy.* Dordrecht, Neth.: Martinus Nijhoff.

van den Berghe, Pierre. 1978. *Race and Racism: A Comparative Perspective* (2d ed.). New York: Wiley.

van der Tak, Jean, Carl Haub, and Elaine Murphy. 1979. "Our Population Predicament: A New Look," *Population Bulletin,* **34**(December).

Vander Zanden, James W. 1983. *American Minority Relations* (4th ed.). New York: Knopf.

Vanfossen, Beth E., James D. Jones, and Joan Z. Spade. 1987. "Curriculum Tracking and Status Maintenance," *Sociology of Education,* **60**(April):104–122.

Van Gelder, Lindsey. 1985. "Help for Technophobes," *Ms.,* **13**(January):89–91.

Van Maanen, John. 1982. *Varieties of Qualitative Research.* Beverly Hills, Calif.: Sage.

Vanneman, Reeve, and Lynn Weber Cannon. 1987. *The American Perception of Class.* Philadelphia: Temple University Press.

Vasquez, Enriqueta Longauex y. 1970. "The Mexican-American Woman," in Robin Morgan (ed.), *Sisterhood Is Powerful.* New York: Random House, pp. 379–384.

Vayda, Eugene, and Ralsa B. Deber. 1984. "The Canadian Health Care System: An Overview," *Social Science and Medicine,* **18**:191–197.

Veatch, Robert M. 1986. "DRGs and the Ethical Reallocation of Resources," *Hastings Center Report,* **16**(June):32–40.

Veblen, Thorstein. 1919. *The Vested Interests and the State of the Industrial Arts.* New York: Huebsch.

Vecsey, George. 1989. "Postema Blazed Trail for Somebody Else," *New York Times* (December 17), p. S3.

Verbrugge, Lois M. 1985. "Gender and Health: An Update on Hypotheses and Evidence," *Journal of Health and Social Behavior,* **26**(September):156–182.

Vernon, Glenn. 1962. *Sociology and Religion.* New York: McGraw-Hill.

Vernon, Raymond. 1977. *Storm over the Multinationals: The Real Issues.* Cambridge, Mass.: Harvard University Press.

Vinokur, Aaron, and Gur Ofer. 1986. *Inequality of Earnings, Household Income, and Wealth in the Soviet Union in the '70s.* Champaign, Ill.: Soviet Interview Project.

Virshup, Amy. 1990. "The Endless Trial of Joe Gibney," *Village Voice,* **35**(August 7):33–37.

Vobejda, Barbara. 1990. "The Overpopulation Scare Has Gotten Lost in the Crowd," *Washington Post National Weekly Edition,* **7**(July 9):31.

Vold, George B. 1979. *Theoretical Criminology* (2d ed., prepared by Thomas Al Bernard). New York: Oxford University Press.

Von Hoffman, Nicholas. 1970. "Sociological Snoopers," *Transaction,* **7**(May):4, 6.

Voydanoff, Patricia, and Linda C. Majka (eds.). 1988. *Families and Economic Distress.* Newbury Park, Calif.: Sage.

Wade, Betsy. 1989. "A Bill of Rights for the Disabled Nears Passage," *New York Times* (December 17), sec. xx, p. 3.

Waitzkin, Howard. 1986. *The Second Sickness: Contradictions of Capitalist Health Care.* Chicago: University of Chicago Press.

———. 1989. "Marxist Perspectives in Social Medicine," *Social Science and Medicine,* **28**(11):1099–1101.

——— and Barbara Waterman. 1974. *The Exploitation of Illness in Capitalist Society.* Indianapolis: Bobbs-Merrill.

Walker, Billy D. 1990. "The Texas Experience with School Finance Reform and Litigation." Paper presented at the annual meeting of the Illinois Association of School Boards, Chicago.

Walker, Gillian A. 1986. "Burnout: From Metaphor to Ideology," *Canadian Journal of Sociology,* **11**(Spring):35–55.

Walker, Lawrence J. 1984. "Sex Differences in the Development of Moral Reasoning: A Critical Review," *Child Development,* **55**(June):677–691.

Walker, Lou Ann. 1989. "I Know How to Ask for What I Want," *Parade* (April 23), pp. 4–6.

Wallace, Anthony. 1966. *Religion: An Anthropological View*. New York: Random House.

Wallace, Ruth A., and Alison Wolf. 1980. *Contemporary Sociological Theory*. Englewood Cliffs, N.J.: Prentice-Hall.

Wallace, Stephen. 1984. "Macro and Micro Issues in Intergenerational Relationships within the Latino Family and Community." Paper presented at the annual meeting of the Society for the Study of Social Problems, San Antonio, Tex.

Wallerstein, Immanuel. 1974. *The Modern World System*. New York: Academic.

———. 1979. *Capitalist World Economy*. Cambridge, Eng.: Cambridge University Press.

Wallerstein, Judith, and Sandra Blakeslee. 1989. *Second Chances: Men, Women, and Children a Decade after Divorce*. New York: Ticknor and Fields.

Wallis, Claudia. 1981. "Southward Ho for Jobs," *Time*, **117**(May 11):23.

———. 1987. "Is Mental Illness Inherited?" *Time*, **129**(March 9):67.

Walsh, D. 1986. *Heavy Business: Commercial Burglary and Robbery*. London: Routledge.

Walton, John, and Charles Ragin. 1988. "Global and National Sources of Political Protest: Third World Response to the Debt Crisis." Paper presented at the annual meeting of the American Sociological Association, Atlanta.

——— and ———. 1989. "Austerity and Dissent: Social Basis of Popular Struggle in Latin America," in William L. Canak (ed.), *Lost Promises, Debt, Austerity, and Development in Latin America*. Boulder, Colo.: Westview, pp. 216–232.

Waring, Marilyn. 1988. *If Women Counted: A New Feminist Economics*. San Francisco: Harper and Row.

Washington Post. 1984. "The Congressional Checkoff," *Washington Post National Weekly Edition*, **1**(October 15):14–15.

Wasielewski, Patricia. 1985. "The Emotional Basis of Charisma," *Symbolic Interaction*, **8**(2):207–222.

Wasow, Mona. 1984. "Deinstitutionalization," *Practice Digest*, **6**(Spring):10–12.

Wasserman, Ira. 1984. "Imitation and Suicide: A Re-Examination of the Weorther Effect," *American Sociological Review*, **49**(June):427–436.

Waterfield, Larry W. 1986. *Conflict and Crisis in Rural America*. New York: Praeger.

Waters, Harry F., and Janet Huck. 1989. "Networking Women," *Newsweek*, **103**(March 13):48–54.

Watson, Kenneth M. 1986. "Birth Families: Living with the Adoption Decision," *Public Welfare*, **44**(Spring):5–10.

Watson, Russell. 1984. "A Hidden Epidemic," *Newsweek*, **103**(May 14):30–36.

Watson, Tracey. 1987. "Women Athletes and Athletic Women: The Dilemmas and Contradictions of Managing Incongruent Identities," *Sociological Inquiry*, **57**(Fall):431–446.

Watts, W. David, and Ann Marie Ellis. 1989. "Assessing Sociology Educational Outcomes: Occupational Status and Mobility of Graduates," *Teaching Sociology*, **17**(July):297–306.

Weaver, Warren, Jr. 1982. "Age Discrimination Charges Found in Sharp Rise in U.S.," *New York Times* (February 22), p. A12.

Webb, Eugene J., Donald T. Campbell, Richard D. Schwartz, Lee Sechrist, and Janet Belew Grove. 1981. *Nonreactive Measures in the Social Sciences* (2d ed.). Boston: Houghton Mifflin.

Weber, Max. 1947. *The Theory of Social and Economic Organization*. Translated by A. Henderson and T. Parsons. New York: Free Press (originally published during the period 1913–1922).

———. 1949. *Methodology of the Social Sciences*. Translated by Edward A. Shills and Henry A. Finch. Glencoe, Ill.: Free Press (originally published in 1904).

———. 1958a. *The Protestant Ethic and the Spirit of Capitalism*. Translated by Talcott Parsons. New York: Scribner (originally published in 1904).

———. 1958b. *The Religion of India: The Sociology of Hinduism and Buddhism*. New York: Free Press (originally published in 1916).

Webster, Peggy Lovell, and Jeffrey W. Dwyer. 1988. "The Cost of Being Nonwhite in Brazil," *Social Science Research*, **72**(January):136–142.

Weeks, John R. 1988. "The Demography of Islamic Nations," *Population Bulletin*, **43**(December).

———. 1989. *Population: An Introduction to Concepts and Issues* (4th ed.). Belmont, Calif.: Wadsworth.

Weigart, Andrew J., and Derwin L. Thomas. 1971. "Family as a Conditional Universal," *Journal of Marriage and the Family*, **33**(February):188–194.

Weinberg, Martin S., and Colin J. Williams. 1980. "Sexual Embourgeoisement? Social Class and Sexual Activity: 1938–1970," *American Sociological Review*, **45**(February):33–48.

Weisman, Carol S., and Martha Ann Teitelbaum. 1985. "Physician Gender and the Physician-Patient Relationship: Recent Evidence and Relevant Questions," *Social Science and Medicine*, **20**(July):1119–1127.

Weisman, Steven R. 1988. "No More Guarantees of a Son's Birth," *New York Times* (July 20), pp. A1, A9.

Weiss, Samuel. 1984. "Curriculum Competition Blossoms in High Schools," *New York Times* (September 9), p. E6.

Weitz, Shirley. 1977. *Sex Roles: Biological, Psychological, and Social Foundations*, New York: Oxford University Press.

Weitzman, Lenore J. 1985. *The Divorce Revolution: The Unexpected Social and Economic Consequences for Women and Children in America*. New York: Free Press.

——— and Ruth B. Dixon. 1983. "The Transformation of Legal Marriage through No-Fault Divorce," in Arlene S. Skolnick and Jerome A. Skolnick (eds.), *Family in Transition* (4th ed.). Boston: Little, Brown, pp. 353–366.

Wellborn, Stanley N. 1987. "How Genes Shape Personality," *U.S. News and World Report*, **102**(April 13):58–59, 61–62.

Wells, L. T. 1972. "Economic Man and Engineering Man: Choice of Technology in Low Wage Country," *Economic Development Report* (Autumn).

Wenneker, Mark B., and Arnold M.

Epstein. 1989. "Racial Inequalities in the Use of Procedures for Patients with Ischemic Heart Disease in Massachusetts," *Journal of the American Medical Association*, **261**(January 13):253–257.

———, Joel S. Weissman, and Arnold M. Epstein. 1990. "The Association of Payer with Utilization of Cardiac Procedures in Massachusetts," *Journal of the American Medical Association*, **264**(September 12):1255–1260.

West, Candace. 1984. "When the Doctor Is a 'Lady': Power, Status, and Gender in Physician-Patient Encounters," *Symbolic Interaction*, **7**(Spring):87–106.

——— and Don H. Zimmerman. 1983. "Small Insults: A Study of Interruptions in Cross Sex Conversations between Unacquainted Persons," in Barrie Thorne, Cheris Kramarae, and Nancy Henley (eds.), *Language, Gender, and Society*. Rowley, Mass.: Newbury House, pp. 86–111.

——— and ———. 1987. "Doing Gender," *Gender and Society*, **1**(June):125–151.

West, Edwin G. 1984. "Are American Schools Working? Disturbing Cost and Quality Trends," *American Education*, **20**(January–February):11–21.

Westrum, Ron, and Khalil Samaha. 1984. *Complex Organizations: Growth, Struggle, and Change*. Englewood Cliffs, N.J.: Prentice-Hall.

White, Lynn, Jr. 1962. *Medieval Technology and Social Change*. New York: Oxford University Press.

White, Merry. 1987. *The Japanese Educational Challenge: A Commitment to Children*. New York: Free Press.

White, Stephen E. 1983. "Return Migration to Appalachian Kentucky: An Atypical Case of Nonmetropolitan Migration Reversal," *Rural Sociology*, **48**(3):471–491.

Whiting, Robert. 1986. "East Meets West in the Japanese Game of Besuboru," *Smithsonian*, **17**(September):108–119.

Whyte, William Foote. 1981. *Street Corner Society: Social Structure of an Italian Slum* (3d ed.). Chicago: University of Chicago Press.

———. 1989. "Advancing Scientific Knowledge through Participatory Action Research," *Sociological Forum*, **4**(September):367–385.

Wickenhaver, Janet. 1988. "Racial Terror on the Gold Coast: New Jersey Indians Confront 'Dotbusters,'" *Village Voice*, **33**(January 26):10, 12.

Wickman, Peter M. 1991. "Deviance," in Dushkin Publishing Group, *Encyclopedic Dictionary of Sociology* (4th ed.). Guilford, Conn.: Dushkin, pp. 85–87.

Wiener, Jon. 1990. "Frosh Activists," *The Nation*, **250**(April 16):513.

Wilder, Gita, Diane Mackie, and Joel Cooper. 1985. "Gender and Computers: Two Surveys of Computer-Related Attitudes," *Sex Roles*, **13**(August):215–228.

Wilhite, Allen, and Theilmann, John. 1986. "Women, Blacks, and PAC Discrimination," *Social Science Quarterly*, **67**(July):283–298.

Wilkerson, Isabel. 1987. "Growth of the Very Poor Is Focus of New Studies," *New York Times* (December 20), p. 15.

———. 1990. "With Rural Towns Vanishing, States Choose Which to Save," *New York Times* (January 3), pp. A1, A16.

Wilkinson, Doris K. 1980. "A Synopsis: Projections for the Profession in the 1980's," *ASA Footnotes*, **8**(April 1):6–7.

Will, J. A., P. A. Self, and N. Datan. 1976. "Maternal Behavior and Perceived Sex of Infant," *American Journal of Orthopsychiatry*, **46**:135–139.

Williams, J. Allen, Jr., Nicholas Batchuk, and David R. Johnson. 1973. "Voluntary Associations and Minority Status: A Comparative Analysis of Anglo, Black and Mexican Americans," *American Sociological Review*, **38**(October):637–646.

Williams, Lena. 1986. "Older Women Are Found Struggling," *New York Times* (May 8), p. A21.

———. 1987. "Women's Caucus Pushes for Benefits," *New York Times* (June 3), p. B9.

Williams, Robin M., Jr. 1970. *American Society* (3d ed.). New York: Knopf.

———, in collaboration with John P. Dean and Edward A. Suchman. 1964. *Strangers Next Door: Ethnic Relations in American Communities*. Englewood Cliffs, N.J.: Prentice-Hall.

Williams, Simon Johnson. 1986. "Appraising Goffman," *British Journal of Sociology*, **37**(September):348–369.

Willig, Ann C. 1985. "A Meta-Analysis of Selected Studies on the Effectiveness of Bilingual Education," *Review of Educational Research*, **55**(Fall):269–317.

Willis, David K. 1986. *Klass: How Russians Really Live*. New York: St. Martin's.

Willis, Ellen. 1980. (Untitled column), *Village Voice*, **25**(March 3):8.

Willis, John. 1975. "Variations in State Casualty Rates in World War II and the Vietnam War," *Social Problems*, **22**(April):558–568.

Willwerth, James. 1989. "Facts of Life: California Sides with Darwin," *Time*, **134**(November 20):118.

Wilson, Edward O. 1975. *Sociobiology: The New Synthesis*. Cambridge, Mass.: Harvard University Press.

———. 1977. "Biology and the Social Sciences," *Daedalus*, **106**(Spring):127–140.

———. 1978. *On Human Nature*. Cambridge, Mass.: Harvard University Press.

Wilson, Franklin D. 1984. "Urban Ecology: Urbanization and Systems of Cities," in Ralph Turner (ed.), *Annual Review of Sociology, 1984*. Palo Alto, Calif.: Annual Reviews, pp. 283–307.

Wilson, James Q., and Richard J. Hernstein. 1986. *Crime and Human Nature*. New York: Simon and Schuster.

Wilson, John. 1973. *Introduction to Social Movements*. New York: Basic Books.

———. 1978. *Religion in American Society: The Effective Presence*. Englewood Cliffs, N.J.: Prentice-Hall.

Wilson, Michele, and John Lynxwiler. 1988. "Abortion Clinic Violence as Terrorism," *Terrorism*, **11**(4):263–273.

Wilson, Robin. 1990. "Foreign Students in U.S. Reach a Record 386,000," *Chronicle of Higher Education*, **37**(November 28):A1, A36.

Wilson, Thomas C. 1986. "Community Population Size and Social Heterogeneity: An Empirical Test," *American Journal of Sociology*, **91**(March):1154–1169.

Wilson, Warner, Larry Dennis, and Allen P. Wadsworth, Jr. 1976. "Authoritarianism Left and Right," *Bulletin of the Psychonomic Society*, **7**(March): 271–274.

Wilson, William Julius. 1980. *The Declining Significance of Race: Blacks and Changing American Institutions* (2d ed.). Chicago: University of Chicago Press.

———. 1987. *The Truly Disadvantaged: The Inner City, the Underclass and Public Policy*. Chicago: University of Chicago Press.

———. 1988. "The Ghetto Underclass and the Social Transformation of the Inner City," *The Black Scholar*, **19**(May–June):10–17.

——— (ed.). 1989. *The Ghetto Underclass: Social Science Perspectives*. Newbury Park, Calif.: Sage.

Wimberley, Dale W. 1990. "Investment Dependence and Alternative Explanations of Third World Mortality: A Cross-National Study," *American Sociological Review*, **55**(February):75–91.

Wines, Michael. 1986. "Rich in U.S. Get Richer, Study Finds," *International Herald Tribune* (July 28), p. 3.

Winter, J. Alan. 1977. *Continuities in the Sociology of Religion*. New York: Harper and Row.

Wirth, Louis. 1928. *The Ghetto*. Chicago: University of Chicago Press.

———. 1931. "Clinical Sociology," *American Journal of Sociology*, **37**(July):49–66.

———. 1938. "Urbanism as a Way of Life," *American Journal of Sociology*, **44**(July):1–24.

Wisendale, Steven K., and Michael D. Allison. 1989. "Family Leave Legislation: State and Federal Initiatives," *Family Relations*, **38**(April):182–189.

Withers, Claudia, and Anne Benaroya. 1989. *Sexual Harassment Update 1989: Selected Issues*. Washington, D.C.: Women's Legal Defense Fund.

Wohl, Stanley. 1984. *Medical Industrial Complex*. New York: Harmony.

Wolf, Eric. 1979. "The Virgin of Guadalupe: A Mexican National Symbol," in William A. Lessa and Evon Z. Vogt (eds.), *Reader in Comparative Religion: An Anthropological Approach* (4th ed.). New York: Harper and Row, pp. 112–115.

Wolfe, Tom. 1980. *The Right Stuff*. New York: Bantam.

Wolinsky, Frederic P. 1980. *The Sociology of Health*. Boston: Little, Brown.

Woller, Barbara. 1987. "Study Shows Mental Illness Can Be Inherited," *USA Today* (February 26), p. 1D.

Wong, Raymond Sin-Kwok. 1990. "Understanding Cross-National Variation in Occupational Mobility," *American Sociological Review*, **55**(August):560–573.

Wood, Charles, and José de Carvalho. 1988. *The Demography of Inequality in Brazil*. Cambridge, Eng.: Cambridge University Press.

Woodman, Sue. 1990. "Target," *Mirabella*, **1**(April):81–84.

Work, Clemens P., et al. 1987. "Jam Sessions," *U.S. News and World Report*, **103**(September 7):20–27.

The World Bank. 1987. *World Development Report 1987*. New York: Oxford University Press.

———. 1989. *World Development Report 1989*. New York: Oxford University Press.

———. 1990. *World Development Report 1990: Poverty*. New York: Oxford University Press.

World Development Forum. 1988. "Women—An Endangered Species," **5**(November 30):1–2.

———. 1989. "War on Drugs—Tobacco Connection," **7**(September 30):1–2.

———. 1990. "The Danger of Television," **8**(July 15):4.

Woronoff, John. 1986. *"The Japan Syndrome: Symptoms, Ailments and Remedies*. New Brunswick, N.J.: Transaction.

Wouk, Herman. 1951. *The Caine Mutiny*. Garden City, N.Y.: Doubleday.

Wright, Erik Olin, David Hachen, Cynthia Costello, and Joy Sprague. 1982. "The American Class Structure," *American Sociological Review*, **47**(December):709–726.

Wright, Robin. 1987. "Liberation Theology," *Christian Science Monitor* (June 5), pp. B1–B2.

Wrong, Dennis H. 1977. *Population and Society* (4th ed.). New York: Random House.

Wuthnow, Robert, and Marsha Witten. 1988. "New Directions in the Study of Culture," in W. Richard Scott and Judith Blake (eds.), *Annual Review of Sociology, 1988*. Palo Alto, Calif.: Annual Reviews, pp. 49–67.

Yared, Roberta. 1989. "Aid to Population Programs," *Population Today*, **17**(March):5.

Yates, Ronald E. 1985. "Japanese Merrily Leave the Christ out of 'Kurisumasu,'" *Chicago Tribune* (December 22), p. 13.

Yinger, J. Milton. 1960. "Countraculture and Subculture," *American Sociological Review*, **25**(October):625–635.

———. 1970. *The Scientific Study of Religion*. New York: Macmillan.

———. 1974. "Religion, Sociology of," in *Encyclopaedia Britannica*, vol. 15. Chicago: Encyclopedia Britannica, pp. 604–613.

———. 1982. *Countercultures*. New York: Free Press.

Young, T. R. 1981. "The Typification of Christ at Christmas and Easter: Political and Social Uses of the Jesus Symbol." Paper presented at the annual meeting of the Association of Humanist Sociologists, Cincinnati.

Yu, Jing Jie, et al. [7 authors]. 1990. "A Comparison of Smoking Patterns in the People's Republic of China with the United States: An Impending Health Catastrophe in the Middle Kingdom," *Journal of the American Medical Association*, **264**(September 26):1575–1579.

Zablocki, Benjamin. 1980. *Alienation and Charisma: A Study of Contemporary American Communes*. New York: Free Press.

Zald, Mayer N. 1970. *Organizational Change: The Political Economy of the YMCA*. Chicago: University of Chicago Press.

——— and John D McCarthy (eds.). 1979. *The Dynamics of Social Movements*. Cambridge, Mass.: Winthrop.

——— and ———. 1986. *Social Movements in an Organizational Society*. Rutgers, N.J.: Transaction.

Zeitlin, Maurice, Kenneth G. Lutterman, and James W. Russell. 1973. "Death in Vietnam: Class, Poverty and the Risks of War," *Politics and Society*, **3**(Spring):313–328.

Zellner, William M. 1978. "Vehicular Suicide: In Search of Incidence." Unpublished M.A. thesis, Western Illinois University, Macomb.

Zelnick, Melvin, and J. Kim Young. 1982. "Sex Education and Its Association with Teenage Sexual Activity, Pregnancy, and Contraceptive Use," *Family Planning Perspectives,* **14**:117–26.

Zia, Helen. 1990. "Midwives: Talking about a Revolution," *Ms.,* **1**(November–December):91.

Zimbardo, Philip C. 1972. "Pathology of Imprisonment," *Society,* **9**(April):4,6,8.

———. 1974. "On the Ethics of Intervention in Human Psychological Research: With Special Reference to the Stanford Prison Experiment," *Cognition,* **2**(2):243–256.

Zimmerman, Don H., and Candace West. 1975. "Sex Roles, Interruptions, and Silences in Conversation," in Barrie Thorne and Nancy Henley (eds.), *Language and Sex: Difference and Dominance.* Rowley Mass.: Newbury House, pp. 105–129.

Zimmerman, Mary K. 1981. "The Abortion Clinic: Another Look at the Management of Stigma," in Gregory Stone and Harvey Faberman (eds.), *Social Psychology through Symbolic Interaction* (2d ed.). Lexington, Mass.: Ginn, pp. 43–52.

———. 1987. "The Women's Health Movement: A Critique of Medical Enterprise, and the Position of Women," in Beth Hess and Myra Marx Ferree (eds.), *Analyzing Gender: A Handbook of Social Science Research.* Newbury Park, Calif.: Sage, pp. 442–472.

Zola, Irving K. 1966. "Culture and Symptoms: An Analysis of Patients Presenting Complaints," *American Sociological Review,* **31**(October):615–630.

———. 1972. "Medicine as an Institution of Social Control," *Sociological Review,* **20**(November):487–504.

———. 1983. *Socio-Medical Inquiries.* Philadelphia: Temple University Press.

———. 1987. "The Portrayal of Disability in the Crime Mystery Genre," *Social Policy,* **17**(Spring):34–39.

Zorn, Eric. 1988. "Archeologist Digs in Garbage Dumps to Get the Dirt on Us," *Chicago Tribune* (February 21), sec. 1, p. 19.

Zuckman, Jill. 1990. "Conferees Trying to Blend Shelter, Social Services," *Congressional Quarterly,* **48**(September 29):3122–3123.

Zwerdling, Daniel. 1980. *Workplace Democracy.* New York: Harper and Row.

ACKNOWLEDGMENTS

PART-OPENING PHOTOGRAPHS

Part One: Jonathan Blair/Woodfin Camp & Associates.

Part Two: Bob Daemmrich/Stock, Boston.

Part Three: Eric Carle/Stock, Boston.

Part Four: Wally McNamee/Woodfin Camp & Associates.

Part Five: Pascal Maitre/Gamma Liaison.

CHAPTER 1

Chapter-opening photograph: Frederica Georgia/Photo Researchers.

Box 1-3: Quoted material from Carol Brooks Gardner. 1989. "Analyzing Gender in Public Places: Rethinking Goffman's Vision of Everyday Life," *American Sociologist,* **20**(Spring):42–56. Reprinted by permission of the American Sociological Association.

Box 1-4: Figure from W. David Watts and Ann Marie Ellis. 1989. "Assessing Sociology Educational Outcomes: Occupational Status and Mobility of Graduates," *Teaching Sociology,* **17**(July):301. Reprinted by permission of the American Sociological Association and the authors.

CHAPTER 2

Chapter-opening photograph: J. P. Laffont/Sygma.

Figure 2-3: Sharon M. Collins. 1989. "The Marginalization of Black Executives," *Social Problems,* **36**(4; October): 317–331. © 1989 by the Society for the Study of Social Problems. Adapted by permission of the publisher and author.

Box 2-2: Quoted material from David Sudnow. 1967. *Passing On: The Social Organization of Dying,* pp. 101, 104. Reprinted by permission of Prentice Hall, Inc.

Box 2-3: Table from Diane Colasanto. 1989. "Homosexuality," *Gallup Report* (**289;** October):11–16. Reprinted by permission.

Box 2-4: Quoted material from John Lofland, 1977. *Doomsday Cult,* pp. xi and 345–346. Reprinted by permission of Irvington Publishers, Inc.

Excerpt on pages 56–57: Peter Rossi, 1987. "No Good Applied Social Research Goes Unpunished," *Society,* **25**(November-December):73, 79. Reprinted by permission.

694

CHAPTER 3

Chapter-opening photograph: Anderson/Gamma Liaison.

Figure 3-1: Data from Higher Education Research Institute, UCLA. Adapted by permission.

Figure 3-2: Thomas F. Saarinen. 1988. "Centering the Mental Maps of the World," *National Geographic Research*, **4**(Winter):124. Reprinted by permission of the author.

Box 3-1: Quoted material from Robert Whiting. 1986. "East Meets West in the Japanese Game of Besuboru," *Smithsonian*, **17**(September):109–110, 118. Reprinted by permission.

Box 3-2: Quoted material from Joanne Greenberg. 1970. *In This Sign*. Copyright © 1970 by Joanne Greenberg. Reprinted by permission of Henry Holt & Co., Inc.

Box 3-3: Quoted material from Leon F. Fannin. 1989. "Thuggee and Professional Criminality," *Michigan Sociological Review*, **3**(Fall):35, 37. Reprinted by permission.

Excerpt on page 69: George P. Murdock. 1945. "The Common Denominator of Cultures," in Ralph Linton (ed.), *The Science of Man in the World Crisis*, p. 124. Reprinted by permission of Columbia University Press.

CHAPTER 4

Chapter-opening photograph: Stephanie Maze/Woodfin Camp & Associates.

Figure 4-1: Susan Curtiss. 1977. *Genie: A Psycholinguistic Study of a Modern Day "Wild Child"*, p. 274. Copyright © 1977 by Academic Press, Inc. Reprinted by permission.

Figure 4-2: Daniel Levinson. 1978. *The Seasons of a Man's Life*, p. 57. Copyright © 1978 by Daniel J. Levinson. Reprinted by permission of Alfred A. Knopf, Inc.

Table 4-1: Patricia M. Passuth, David R. Maines, and Bernice Neugarten. 1984. "Age Norms and Age Constraints Twenty Years Later," paper presented at the annual meeting of the Midwest Sociological Society, Chicago. Reprinted by permission of the authors.

Box 4-2: Quoted material from John Snarey. 1985. "Cross-Cultural University of Social-Moral Development: A Critical Review of Kohlbergian Research," *Psychological Bulletin*, **97**(March):218–219. Reprinted by permission.

Excerpt on page 99: Marie K. Mason, 1942. "Learning to Speak After Six and One-Half Years of Silence," *Journal of Speech Disorders*, **7**(December):299. Reprinted by permission of the American Speech-Language-Hearing Association.

CHAPTER 5

Chapter-opening photograph: M. Dwyer/Stock, Boston.

Box 5-1: Quoted material from Kay Bartlett. 1988. "Sociologist Researches 'Role Exiting' Process," Galesburg [IL] *Register-Mail* (August 11), p. C1. Reprinted by permission.

Excerpt on page 132: Malcolm X (with Alex Haley). 1964. *The Autobiography of Malcolm X*, p. 37. Reprinted by permission of Ballantine Books, a Division of Random House, Inc.

Excerpt on page 139: Jane Gross. 1985. "Movies and the Press Are an Enduring Romance," *New York Times* (June 2), pp. H2, H19. Copyright © 1985 by The New York Times Company. Reprinted by permission.

CHAPTER 6

Chapter-opening photograph: Bob Daemmrich/Stock, Boston.

Table 6-2: National Council of Teachers of English. 1988, 1989. "Bureaucratic Doublespeak," *Quarterly Review of Doublespeak*, **14**(April 1988), **15**(January 1989), and **16**(October 1989). Adapted by permission.

Box 6-1: Figures from Gary Alan Fine. 1987. *With the Boys: Little League Baseball and Preadolescent Culture*, pp. 144 and 141. © 1987 by The University of Chicago. All rights reserved. Reprinted by permission of The University of Chicago Press.

Excerpt on page 156: Nicole Woolsey Biggart. 1989. *Charismatic Capitalism: Direct Selling Organizations in America*, p. 143. © 1989 by The University of Chicago. All rights reserved. Reprinted by permission of The University of Chicago Press.

Box 6-3: Quoted material from Norman K. Denzin. 1987. *The Recovering Alcoholic*, p. 145. Copyright © 1987 by Sage Publications, Inc. Reprinted by permission.

Excerpt on page 179: Karen Lindsey. 1977. "Sexual Harassment on the Job," *Ms. Magazine*, **6**(November), p. 47. Reprinted by permission of the author.

Excerpt on page 181: Claudia Withers and Anne Benaroya. 1989. *Sexual Harassment Update 1989: Selected Issues*, pp. 22–23. Copyright 1989 Women's Legal Defense Fund. Reprinted by permission of the authors.

CHAPTER 7

Chapter-opening photograph: Frederica Georgia/Photo Researchers.

Table 7-1: William A. Reese and Michael A. Katovich. 1989. "Untimely Acts: Extending the Interactionist Conception of Deviance," *The Sociological Quarterly*, **30**(2):159–184. Reprinted by permission of JAI Press, Inc.

Table 7-2: Robert Merton. 1968. *Social Theory and Social Structure*, p. 194. Copyright © 1967, 1968 by Robert K. Merton. Adapted by permission of The Free Press, a Division of Macmillan, Inc.

Box 7-3: Quoted material from Ann Pellegrini. 1990. "Rape Is a Bias Crime," *New York Times* (May 27), p. E13. Copyright © 1990 by The New York Times Company. Reprinted by permission.

Excerpt on page 186: Clinton Sanders. 1989. *Customizing the Body: The Art and Culture of Tattooing*, p. 42. © 1989 by Temple University. Reprinted by permission of Temple University Press.

Excerpt on page 196: William Chambliss. 1972. Introduction to Harry King, *Box Man: A Professional Thief's Journey*, p. x. Published by Harper & Row. Copyright 1972 by William Chambliss. Reprinted by permission.

CHAPTER 8

Chapter-opening photograph: Corrodi/ Black Star.

Figure 8-3: Thomas G. Mortenson and Zhijun Wu. 1990. *ACT Student Financial Aid Research Report*, series 90-3, p. 42 and table 19. Copyright 1990 by The American College Testing Program. Reprinted by permission.

Figure 8-4: Maurice Zeitlin, Kenneth G. Lutterman, and James W. Russell. 1973. "Death in Vietnam: Class, Poverty and the Risks of War," *Politics and Society*, **3**(Spring):328. Copyright 1973 by Butterworth-Heinemann. Reprinted by permission.

Table 8-2: Gerhard Lenski, Jr. 1966. *Power and Privilege: A Theory of Social Stratification*. Published by McGraw-Hill Book Company. Copyright 1966 by Gerhard Lenski, Jr. Adapted by permission.

Box 8-2: Quoted material from William Ryan. 1971 (revised edition 1976). *Blaming the Victim*. Copyright © 1971, 1976 by William Ryan. Reprinted by permission of Pantheon Books, a division of Random House, Inc.

Box 8-3: Quoted material from David Karp. 1986. " 'You Can Take the Boy Out of Dorchester, but You Can't Take Dorchester Out of the Boy': Toward a Social Psychology of Mobility," *Symbolic Interaction*, **9**(Spring):24, 25, 31. Reprinted by permission.

CHAPTER 9

Chapter-opening photograph: Ilene Perlman/Stock, Boston.

Figure 9-2: C. E. Black. 1966. *Dynamics of Modernization: A Study in Comparative History*. Copyright © 1966 by C.E. Black. Adapted by permission of HarperCollins Publishers.

Figure 9-3: World Bank. 1989 and 1990. *World Development Report 1989*, pp. 222–223 and 245–246; and *World Development Report 1990: Poverty*, pp. 236–237. Copyright © 1989 and 1990 by The International Bank for Reconstruction and Development/The World Bank. Reprinted by permission of Oxford University Press, Inc.

Table 9-1: Jung Ah Pak and Sally Solo. 1990. "The Global 500," *Fortune*, **122** (July 30), p. 269. FORTUNE, © 1990 The Time Inc. Magazine Company. All rights reserved. Adapted by permission.

Table 9-2: Donald J. Treiman. 1977. *Occupational Prestige in Comparative Perspective*, pp. 318–405. Copyright © 1977 by Academic Press, Inc. Adapted by permission.

Box 9-1: Quoted material from Colin Turnbull. 1982. "Bali's New Gods," *Natural History*, **91**(January):26. Reprinted by permission of the author and the author's agents, Scott Meredith Literary Agency, Inc.

Excerpt on page 258: Alan B. Durning. 1990. "Life on the Brink," *World Watch*, **3**(March-April):22–30. Reprinted by permission of Worldwatch Institute.

Excerpt on page 259: Albert Memmi. 1967. *The Colonizer and the Colonized*, p. 8. Copyright © 1965 by Albert Memmi. All rights reserved. Reprinted by permission of Viking Penguin, Inc.

Excerpt on page 284: Amir Jamal. 1983. "Power and the Third World Struggle for Equilibrium" in Jill Torrie (ed.), *Banking on Poverty: The Global Impact of the IMF and the World Bank*, pp. 73, 75–76. Reprinted by permission of Between the Lines, Toronto.

CHAPTER 10

Chapter-opening photograph: Peter B. Kaplan/Photo Researchers.

Figure 10-1: Richard T. Schaefer. 1990. *Racial and Ethnic Groups*, 4th edition, p. 24. Copyright © 1990 by Richard T. Schaefer. Reprinted by permission of HarperCollins Publishers.

Table 10-3: Richard D. Alba and Gwen Moore. 1982. "Ethnicity in the American Elite," *American Sociological Review*, **47**(June). Adapted by permission of the American Sociological Association.

Box 10-3: Figure from Leon F. Bouvier and Cary B. Davis. 1982. *The Future Racial Composition of the United States*, p. 40. Adapted by permission of the Population Reference Bureau, Inc., Washington, DC.

Excerpt on page 288: Langston Hughes. 1951. "Harlem," *Selected Poems of Langston Hughes*. Copyright 1951 by Langston Hughes. Reprinted by permission of Alfred A. Knopf, Inc.

Excerpt on page 309: Richard Bernstein. 1988. "Asian Newcomers Hurt by Precursors' Success," *New York Times* (July 10), p. 16. Copyright © 1988 by The New York Times Company. Reprinted by permission.

CHAPTER 11

Chapter-opening photograph: Michal Heron/Woodfin Camp & Associates.

Figure 11-2: Linda DeStefano and Diane Colasanto. 1990. "Unlike 1975, Today Most Americans Think Men Have It Better," *Gallup Poll Monthly*, 293(February):31. Reprinted by permission of the Gallup Organization, Princeton, NJ.

Table 11-2: Kristin Luker. 1984. *Abortion and the Politics of Motherhood*, pp. 195–197. Copyright © 1984 The Regents of the University of California. Adapted by permission of University of California Press.

Box 11-1: National Organization for Men Against Sexism. Statement of Principles. Reprinted by permission of the National Organization for Men Against Sexism.

Box 11-2: Quoted material from Letty Cottin Pogrebin. 1982. "Big Changes in Parenting," *Ms. Magazine* (February); reprinted in Letty Cottin Pogrebin, 1982, *Growing Up Free: Raising Your Child in the 80's* (McGraw-Hill Book Company). Copyright 1982 by Letty Cottin Pogrebin. Reprinted by permission.

Excerpt on page 327: Marty Fager, Mike Bradley, Lonnie Danchik, and Tom Wodetski. 1971. *Unbecoming Men*, p. 36. © 1971 by Times Change Press, Ojai, CA. Reprinted by permission.

Excerpt on page 328: Anthony Astrachan, 1986. *How Men Feel: Their Responses to Women's Demands for Equality and Power*, p. 403. © 1986 by Anthony Astrachan. Reprinted by permission of Anthony Astrachan and Georges Borchardt, Inc.

Excerpt on page 329: Margaret Mead, 1963 (original edition 1935). *Sex and Temperament in Three Primitive Societies*, preface to 1950 edition and p. 260 of 1963 edition. Copyright 1935, 1950, 1963 by Margaret Mead. Reprinted by permission of William Morrow & Company.

Excerpt on page 330: Sandra Lipsitz Bem. 1978. "Beyond Androgyny," in Julia A. Sherman and Florence Dennsk (eds.), *The Psychology of Women: Future Directions of Research*, p. 6. Reprinted by permission of Sandra Lipsitz Bem.

Excerpt on page 332: Barbara Bovee Polk, "Male Power and the Women's Movement," *Journal of Applied Behavioral Science*, **10**(July):419. Reprinted by permission of JAI Press, Inc.

Excerpt on page 344: Arlie Russell Hochschild. 1989 and 1990. *The Second Shift*, excerpted in *Utne Reader*, **38**(March/April 1990):66–73. Reprinted by permission of Penguin USA.

Excerpt on pages 344–345: Jane O'Reilly. 1972. "The Housewife's Moment of Truth," *Ms. Magazine*, **1**(Spring). Reprinted by permission of *Ms. Magazine* and the author.

CHAPTER 12

Chapter-opening photograph: Mark Antman/The Image Works.

Box 12-2: Quoted material from Irene Paull and Bülbül. 1976. *Everybody's Studying Us*, p. 79. Reprinted by permission of Volcano Press on behalf of California Association of Older Americans.

Excerpt on page 356: "When I'm Sixty-Four." Words and music by John Lennon and Paul McCartney. Copyright © 1967 by Northern Songs. All rights controlled and administered by MCA Music Publishing, a division of MCA Inc. under license from Northern Songs. All rights reserved. International copyright secured. Used by permission.

Excerpt on page 356: Tad Szulc. 1988. "How Can We Help Ourselves Age with Dignity?" *Parade* (May 29), p. 5. Copyright © 1988. Reprinted by permission of Parade Publications and Janklow & Nesbit Associates.

Excerpt on page 374: Michael Spector. 1990. "The National Health Care Crisis," *Washington Post National Weekly Edition*, **7**(June 18–24), p. 6. © 1990 The Washington Post. Reprinted by permission.

CHAPTER 13

Chapter-opening photograph: Charles Gupton/Stock, Barton.

Figure 13-1: George Masnick and Mary Jo Bane. 1980. *The Nation's Families: 1960–1990*, p. 56. Copyright © 1980 by the Joint Center for Urban Studies of MIT and Harvard University. Reprinted by permission of Greenwood Publishing Group, Inc., Westport, CT.

Table 13-1: Peter J. Stein. 1975 and 1981. "Singlehood: An Alternative to Marriage," *Family Coordinator*, **24**(October 1975), reprinted in *Single Life* (St. Martin's Press, 1981), p. 18. © 1975 by The National Council on Family Relations, St. Paul, MN. Reprinted by permission of the author.

Table 13-3: William J. Goode. 1976. "Likelihood of Divorce," in Robert Merton and Robert Nisbet (eds.), *Contemporary Social Problems*, 4th ed., pp. 537–538. Adapted table, "Background Characteristics Associated with Greater to Lesser Proneness to Divorce." Copyright © 1976 by Harcourt Brace Jovanovich, Inc. Adapted by permission of the publisher.

Box 13-2: Quoted material from Philip Blumstein and Pepper Schwartz. 1983. *American Couples: Money, Work, Sex*. Reprinted by permission of William Morrow & Company.

Excerpt on page 380: Barbara Kantrowitz and Pat Wingert. 1990. "Step by Step," *Newsweek*, **114**(Winter/Spring Special Issue), pp. 24, 99. © 1990, Newsweek, Inc. All rights reserved. Reprinted by permission.

Excerpt on page 387: Andrea B. Rugh. 1984. *Family Planning in Contemporary Egypt*, p. 137. Reprinted by permission of Syracuse University Press.

CHAPTER 14

Chapter-opening photograph: D. Goldberg/Sygma.

Figure 14-1: Based on data from *Britannica Book of the Year*. 1990. © 1991 by Encyclopaedia Britannica, Inc. Adapted by permission.

Figure 14-2: Bernard Quinn, Herman Anderson, Martin Bradley, Paul Goetting, and Peggy Shriver. 1982. *Churches and Church Membership in the United States, 1980*. Reprinted by permission of Glenmary Research Center, Atlanta, GA.

Figure 14-3: Based on data from *Gallup Opinion Index*, 1987, pp. 20–27, 29. Adapted by permission of The Gallup Report, Princeton, NJ.

Figure 14-4: Based on data from Princeton Religion Research Center. 1984 and 1990. "Four in 10 Adults in U.S. Attended Church in Typical Week of 1984," *Emerging Trends*, **6**(December):1; and "Church Attendance Unchanged as We Enter the 1990s," *Emerging Trends*, **12**(June):4. Adapted by permission.

Table 14-1: Glenn Vernon. 1962. *Sociology and Religion*. Adapted by permission of McGraw-Hill Book Company.

Table 14-2: Constant H. Jacquet, Jr. 1990. *Yearbook of American and Canadian Churches, 1990*. Copyright © 1990 The National Council of The Churches of Christ in the USA. Used by permission of the publisher, Abingdon Press.

CHAPTER 15

Chapter-opening photograph: Thomas Porett/Photo Researchers.

Figure 15-1: Center for the American Woman and Politics. 1987. *Women in Government around the World*. Reprinted by permission of Center for the American Woman and Politics, Eagleton Institute of Politics, Rutgers University, New Brunswick, NJ.

Table 15-3: William Kornhauser. 1961. "'Power Elite' or 'Veto Group'?" in Seymour Lipset and Leo Lowenthal (eds.), *Culture and Social Character*. Copyright © 1961 by The Free Press. Reprinted by permission of The Free Press, a Division of Macmillan, Inc.

Box 15-2: Quoted material from Martin Luther King, Jr. 1968. *Where Do We Go from Here: Chaos or Community?*, pp. 181, 185–186, 191. Copyright © 1967 by Martin Luther King, Jr. Reprinted by permission of Harper & Row, Publishers, Inc.

Excerpt on page 469: Studs Terkel. 1974. *Working*, p. 159. Reprinted by permission of Pantheon Books, a Division of Random House, Inc.

CHAPTER 16

Chapter-opening photograph: Charles Gupton/Stock, Boston.

Box 16-2: Quoted material from Philip Ferguson and Adrienne Asch. 1989. "Lessons from Life: Personal and Parental Perspectives on School, Childhood, and Disability," in National Society for the Study of Education, *Schooling and Disability: 88th Yearbook of the National Society for the Study of Education, Part II*, pp. 120, 122–124. Copyright © 1989 by the National Society for the Study of Education. Reprinted by permission.

CHAPTER 17

Chapter-opening photograph: Bob Daemmrich/Stock, Boston.

Figure 17-1: Population Reference Bureau. 1990. *World Population Data Sheet, 1990*. Reprinted by permission.

Excerpt on pages 516–517: Ann Holohan. 1977. "Diagnosis: The End of Transition," in A. Davis and G. Horobin (eds.), *Medical Encounters: The Experiences of Illness and Treatment*, p. 88. Copyright © 1977 Alan Davis and Gordon Horobin. All rights reserved. Reprinted by permission of St. Martin's Press.

Excerpt on page 518: Lois M. Verbrugge. 1985. "Gender and Health: An Update on Hypotheses and Evidence," *Journal of Health and Social Behavior*, **26**(September):162–163. Reprinted by permission of the publisher and author.

Excerpt on page 528: Joe Feinglass, 1987. "Next, the McDRG," *The Progressive*, **51**(January):28. Reprinted by permission of The Progressive, Inc.

CHAPTER 18

Chapter-opening photograph: Craig Aurness/Woodfin Camp & Associates.

Figure 18-1: Ernest W. Burgess. 1925. "The Growth of the City," in Robert E. Park, Ernest W. Burgess, and Roderick D. McKenzie (eds.), *The City*, p. 55. Copyright © 1925 by The University of Chicago Press. All rights reserved. Reprinted by permission.

Figure 18-2: Chauncy D. Harris and Edward L. Ullman. 1945. "The Nature of Cities: Comparison Theories of Urban Growth," *Annals of the American Academy of Political and Social Sciences*, **242**(November):13. Reprinted by permission of Sage Publications and the authors.

Figure 18-3: Robert Fox. 1987. *Population Images*, 2d edition, pp. 10–13. Reprinted by permission of the United Nations Fund for Population Activities.

Table 18-1: Gideon Sjoberg. 1960. *The Preindustrial City: Past and Present*, pp. 323–328. Copyright © 1960 by The Free Press; copyright renewed 1988. Adapted by permission of The Free Press, a Division of Macmillan, Inc.

Box 18-2: Quoted material from Daniel Lazare. 1990. "Planes, Trains and Automobiles," *The Village Voice* (October 23), pp. 39–41. Reprinted by permission of *The Village Voice* and the author.

Excerpt on page 546: Christopher Morley. 1922. "Where the Blue Begins," *Poems* by Christopher Morley. Reprinted by permission of Harper & Row, Publishers, Inc.

Excerpt on page 555: Joe R. Feagin, 1983. *The Urban Real Estate Game: Playing Monopoly with Real Money*, p. 2. © 1983. Reprinted by permission of Prentice Hall, a Division of Simon & Schuster, Inc.

Excerpt on page 560: Herbert J. Gans. 1991. *People, Plans and Policies: Essays on Poverty, Racism and Other National Urban Problems*, pp. 54–56. Published by Columbia University Press and Russell Sage Foundation. Adapted by permission of the author.

CHAPTER 19

Chapter-opening photograph: J.P. Laffont/Sygma.

Figure 19-3: Leon F. Bouvier, 1984. "Planet Earth 1984–2034," *Population Bulletin*, **39**(February):12. Reprinted by permission of the Population Reference Bureau.

Figure 19-5: World Bank. 1990. *World Development Report 1990: Poverty*, p. 83. Copyright © 1991 by The International Bank for Reconstruction and Development/The World Bank. Reprinted by permission of Oxford University Press, Inc.

Table 19-2: World Bank. 1990. *World Development Report 1990: Poverty*, pp. 232–233. Copyright © 1990 by The International Bank for Reconstruction and Development/The World Bank. Reprinted by permission of Oxford University Press, Inc.

CHAPTER 20

Chapter-opening photograph: J.L. Atlan/Sygma.

INDEXES

NAME INDEX

SUBJECT INDEX

Multilinear evolutionary theory, 617, 628, 638
Multinational corporations, 264–268, 284–285, 638
Multiple-nuclei theory, 551, 572, 638
Mundugumor, 329
Muslims, 584

Nadars, 250
National Association for the Advancement of Colored People (NAACP), 217, 304
National Opinion Research Center (NORC), 177, 236–237, 459
National Organization for Men against Sexism, 328
National Organization for Women (NOW), 370, 462
National Rifle Association (NRA), 462
Natural science, 8, 30, 638
Nature versus nurture, 99, 329
Negotiated order, 133, 152, 638
Negotiation, 133, 152, 638
Neighborhood, defended, 560, 572, 634
Neighborhood revitalization, 570, 572, 638
Neocolonialism, 261, 268, 284–285, 638
Neolocal pattern of residence, 384, 409, 638
Neo-Malthusians, 578
Networks, social, 9, 141–142, 152, 363, 642
Neutralization, techniques of, 198–199, 218, 643
Nisei, 309, 319, 638
No-fault divorce, 403–405, 409, 638
Nonmaterial culture, 70–71, 93, 622–623, 638
Nonperiodic assemblies, 607, 628, 638
Nonverbal communication, 24, 29–30, 639
NORC (National Opinion Research Center), 177, 236–337, 459
Norms, 76–80, 92–93, 173, 417, 639
    formal, 76–77, 80, 92–93, 635
    informal, 76–77, 80, 92–93, 173, 637
Nuclear family, 382, 408–409, 639

Obedience, 217–218, 639
Objective method, 236, 255, 639
Observation, 52
Occupations, 466–467
Oligarchy, 172
    iron law of, 172
Oligopoly, 450, 474, 639
Open class system, 248, 254–255, 639
Operational definition, 37, 59, 639
Organic solidarity, 145, 152, 639
Organized crime, 217–218, 639
Out-group, 158–159, 181–182, 289, 639

PAC (political action committee), 462–463, 474, 639
Panic, 610, 628, 639
Parental marriage, 389
Parenthood, 392–394
Participant observation, 43–46, 52, 59–60, 639
Patriarchy, 385, 408–409, 639
Patrilineal descent, 384, 409, 639
Patrilocal pattern of residence, 384, 409, 639
Pay equity, 340, 351, 639
Peer groups, 119
Pentecostal faiths, 433, 442, 639
Percentage, 36, 59–60, 639
Perestroika, 169, 182, 639
Periodic assemblies, 607, 627–628, 639
Periphery nations, 261, 264, 282, 284
Personality, 99, 126, 639
Peter principle, 167, 170, 182, 639
Play stage, 105
Pluralism, 301–302, 318–319, 639
Pluralist model, 465–466, 473–474, 639
Polish Americans, 289, 291, 294

Political action committee (PAC), 462, 639
Political efficacy, 460, 474, 639
Political socialization, 458, 473–474, 639
Political system, 447–466, 473–474, 639
Politics, 453, 474, 639
Polyandry, 383, 409, 639
Polygamy, 383, 409, 639
Polygyny, 383, 409, 639
Population, 575–599
Population pyramid, 585, 599, 640
Postindustrial society, 452–453, 473–474, 567, 640
Poverty, 239–243, 304–305, 396–397, 592
    absolute, 242, 254, 592, 631
    feminization of, 240, 252–254, 528
    relative, 242–243, 255, 640
Poverty line, 242
Power, 232–233, 255, 453, 473–474, 640
Power elite, 463–466, 474, 640
Precipitating factor, 605
Predestination, 422, 442, 640
Preindustrial city, 547–549, 571–572, 640
Preindustrial societies, 447–449
Prejudice, 296–299, 301, 307, 318–319, 363, 624, 640
Preparatory stage, 105
Pressure group, 463, 474, 640
Prestige, 236–237, 255, 640
Prevalence, 518, 539, 640
Primary group, 158, 181–182, 640
Profane, the, 416, 442, 640
Profession, 466, 473–474, 640
Professional criminals, 204, 217, 640
Project Head Start, 483
Proletariat, 231, 255, 640
Protestant ethic, 422, 442, 640
Public, 611, 627–628, 640
Public opinion, 611, 628, 640
Puerto Ricans, 289, 291–292, 294, 298, 310–312
Pure sociology, 28
Pygmalion effect, 489

Quality circles, 171, 182, 640
Questionnaire, 46, 59–60, 640

Race, 213–214
Racial group, 289–291, 302–310, 313, 318–319, 640
Racism, 296, 319, 640
Random sample, 39, 60, 640
Rape, 211–213, 400
Rebellion, 196–197
Reconstituted families, 380
Reference group, 159–160, 181–182, 640
Refugees, 310, 317
Relative deprivation, 615–616, 628, 640
Relative poverty, 242–243, 255, 640
Reliability, 40, 59–60, 640
Religion, 415–442, 640
Religious beliefs, 423, 429, 441–442, 640
Religious experience, 424–425, 441–442, 640
Religious rituals, 423–425, 429, 441, 640
Religious values, 423
Replacement-level fertility, 588, 599, 640
Replication, 49, 51, 60, 640
Representative sample, 39, 60, 640
Research, ethics of, 51
Research design, 40, 42–49, 60, 640
Residence, patterns of:
    matrilocal, 384, 409, 638
    neolocal, 384, 409, 638
    patrilocal, 384, 409, 639
Resocialization, 113–114, 126, 641
Resource mobilization, 616, 628, 641
Resurgent fundamentalism, 433
Retreatism, 196–197
Reverse discrimination, 472

Reverse socialization, 117, 126, 641
Rites of passage, 110, 126, 641
Ritualism, 196–197
Roe v. Wade, 348–349
Role ambiguity, 135–137, 152, 641
Role conflict, 137–138, 152, 641
Role exit, 136, 152, 361, 641
Role strain, 135, 137, 152, 490, 641
Role taking, 105, 126, 641
Roman Catholics, 346
Routinization of charismatic authority, 457, 474, 641
Rules and regulations, 168–169
Rumors, 610, 627–628, 641
Rural areas, 565–568

Sacred, the, 415–416, 442, 641
Sample, 39
San Antonio v. Rodriguez, 504
Sanctions, 79–80, 92–93, 188, 218, 641
Sanctuary movement, 317–319, 641
Sapir-Whorf hypothesis, 75, 93, 641
Savings and loan industry, 446–447
Scale, 40, 60, 641
Scapegoat, 297, 319, 641
School choice programs, 494–495
Science, 7, 10, 30, 619, 628, 641
Scientific management approach, 173, 182, 641
Scientific method, 35, 40, 42, 60, 483, 641
Secondary group, 158, 182, 641
Sector theory, 551, 572, 641
Sects, 427–428, 438–439, 442, 641
Secular humanism, 439
Secularization, 414, 421, 442, 641
Segregation, 300–301, 319, 641
Self, 104–107, 126, 641
Self-fulfilling prophecy, 292–294, 319, 641
Self-help groups, 176, 182, 641
Semiperiphery nations, 261
Senilicide, 357, 374, 641
Senior Action in a Gay Environment (SAGE), 371
Serial monogamy, 383, 409, 641
Settlement houses, 16
Sex roles (*see* Gender roles)
Sexism, 48, 334–335, 351, 641
Sexual behavior, 230
Sexual harassment, 179–182, 641
Sexual relations, 88
Shakers, 142
Sick role, 512–513, 524, 539, 624, 641
Sign language, 74
Significant others, 106, 126, 387, 641
Single-parent families, 395–397, 409, 641
Slavery, 226, 255, 642
Small group, 160, 181–182, 642
Smoking, 536–538
Social change, 603, 616–628, 642
Social class (*see* Class)
Social control, 187, 217, 513, 606, 642
    formal, 191, 218
    informal, 190, 217–218
Social epidemiology, 518–522, 539, 642
Social inequality, 221–256, 642
Social institutions, 142, 151–152, 377, 409, 479, 642
Social interaction, 131, 152, 642
Social mobility, 248–252, 254–255, 275–277, 642
Social movements, 613–616, 627–628, 642
Social network, 9, 141–142, 152, 363, 642
Social norm (*see* Norm)
Social promotion, 494, 505, 642
Social role, 135, 151–152, 642
Social science, 8, 29–30, 642
Social Security, 372–373
Social structure, 131, 151–152, 642